AF660003

Fully Revised **Edition**

Understanding Physics

JEE Main & Advanced

Optics and Modern Physics

DC Pandey
[B.Tech, M.Tech, Pantnagar, ID 15722]

arihant
SUCCESS AND NOTHING LESS

arihant
SUCCESS AND NOTHING LESS

ARIHANT PRAKASHAN (Series), MEERUT

- **Administrative & Production Offices**

Regd. Office
'Ramchhaya' 4577/15, Agarwal Road, Darya Ganj, New Delhi -110002
Tele: 011- 47630600, 43518550

Head Office
Kalindi, TP Nagar, Meerut (UP) - 250002
Tel: 0121-7156203, 7156204

- **Sales & Support Offices**

Agra, Ahmedabad, Bengaluru, Bareilly, Chennai, Delhi, Guwahati, Hyderabad, Jaipur, Jhansi, Kolkata, Lucknow, Nagpur & Pune.

- **PRICE** ₹460.00

- **PO No :** TXT-59-T063295-02-25

Published by Arihant Publications (India) Ltd.

For further information about the books published by Arihant, log on to www.arihantbooks.com or e-mail at info@arihantbooks.com

Follow us on

Preface

"The overwhelming response to the previous editions of this book gives me an immense feeling of satisfaction, and I take this as an opportunity to introduce you to the new version of the book, "Optics and Modern Physics".

"Optics and Modern Physics" has undergone meticulous revision to ensure accuracy and relevance. We take pride in affirming that this book serves as a standalone resource, encompassing all essential topics without any extraneous content.

This book is designed with a singular focus on providing concise yet complete theory, coupled with an ample number of practice questions covering all pertinent concepts essential for success in JEE Mains & Advanced.

With each chapter, or as we call them, units, subdivided into modular formats, "Optics and Modern Physics" ensures an organized and structured approach to learning. Each module within a unit is self-contained, comprising theory, illustrative examples, and exercises aimed at reinforcing understanding.

At the end of every unit, readers will find unit exercises presented in two levels, offering ample opportunities for practice and self-assessment. Furthermore, to aid in problem-solving, most exercises are accompanied by helpful hints.

Our commitment to excellence extends to the inclusion of logical problems sourced from reputable resources like **Irodov** and **previous years' question papers.** The level of questions spans from foundational to 1.25 times the highest difficulty level of the JEE Advanced examination, ensuring comprehensive preparation.

In conclusion, I am confident that "Optics and Modern Physics" will prove to be an indispensable companion for aspirants aiming for success in JEE. It is my belief that with dedication and diligent practice using this book, students will be well-equipped to excel in both JEE Mains and Advanced examinations.

I take this opportunity to express my gratitude to **Prof. Lalit Kumar,** who gave me valuable advice and was kind enough to find time for fruitful discussions. I would also like to thank my student Dheeraj Yadav for managing this project as per my expectations. I am also thankful to Mr. Anoop Dhyani and Mr. Ashish, due to their tireless efforts this book could be transformed into the present form.

To err is human, hence despite such tireless efforts, there may still be scope for improvement in this book. So, comments and criticism from readers will be highly appreciated and incorporated in subsequent editions." I also request the readers to drop me a mail at **arihantcorrections@gmail.com,** if you find any corrections in the book. Your feedback is greatly appreciated and will help to improve the quality of the book.

Thankyou for your support and contribution in making this book the **Best it can be.**

DC Pandey
[B.Tech, M.Tech, Pantnagar, ID 15722]

Contents

This book

is dedicated to

my Honourable Grandfather

(Late) Sh. Pitamber Pandey

a Kumaoni poet and a resident of Village
Dhaura (Almora), Uttarakhand

UNIT-7

ELECTROMAGNETIC WAVES

Learning Modules

1. Introduction
2. Propagation of Electromagnetic Waves
3. Electromagnetic Spectrum

MODULE 1

Introduction

Dual Nature of Electromagnetic Waves

We regard electromagnetic waves as waves because under suitable circumstances they exhibit diffraction, interference and polarization. Similarly, we shall see that under other circumstances they behave as a stream of particles. Rather we can say that they have the **dual nature.**

The wave nature of light (a part of electromagnetic waves) was first demonstrated by Thomas Young, who observed the interference pattern of two coherent sources. The particle nature of light was first proposed by Albert Einstein in 1905 in his explanation of the photoelectric effect. A particle of light called a **photon** has energy E that is related to the frequency f and wavelength λ of light wave by the Einstein equation,

$$\boxed{E = hf = \frac{hc}{\lambda}} \qquad \text{...(i)}$$

where, c is the speed of light (in vacuum) and h is Planck's constant.

$$h = 6.626 \times 10^{-34} \text{ J-s}$$
$$= 4.136 \times 10^{-15} \text{ eV-s}$$

Since, energies are often given in electron volt ($1 \text{ eV} = 1.6 \times 10^{-19}$ J) and wavelengths are in Å, it is convenient to the combination hc in eV-Å. We have,

$$\boxed{hc = 12375 \text{ eV-Å}}$$

Hence, Eq. (i) in simpler form can be written as

$$\boxed{E \text{ (in eV)} = \frac{12375}{\lambda \text{ (in Å)}}} \qquad \text{...(ii)}$$

The propagation of light is governed by its wave properties, whereas the exchange of energy between light with matter is governed by its particle properties. The wave particle duality is a general property of nature. For example, electrons (and other particles) also propagate as waves and exchange energy as particles.

Momentum and Radiation Pressure

An electromagnetic wave transports linear momentum. We state, without proof that the linear momentum carried by an electromagnetic wave is related to the energy it transports according to

$$\boxed{p = \frac{E}{c}} \qquad \text{...(iii)}$$

If the wave is incident in the direction perpendicular to a surface and is completely absorbed, then Eq. (i) tells us the linear momentum imparted to the surface. If surface is perfectly reflecting, the momentum change of the wave is doubled. Consequently, the momentum imparted to the surface is also doubled.

According to Newton's second law, the force exerted by an electromagnetic wave on a surface may be related by the equation

$$F = \frac{\Delta p}{\Delta t}$$

From Eq. (iii), $\dfrac{\Delta p}{\Delta t} = \dfrac{1}{c}\left(\dfrac{\Delta E}{\Delta t}\right)$

$$\therefore \qquad F = \frac{1}{c}\left(\frac{\Delta E}{\Delta t}\right) \qquad \text{...(iv)}$$

Intensity (I) of a wave is the energy transported per unit area per unit time.

or $$I = \left(\frac{1}{S}\right)\frac{\Delta E}{\Delta t}$$

$$\therefore \qquad \frac{\Delta E}{\Delta t} = IS$$

Substituting in Eq. (iv), $F = \dfrac{IS}{c}$

or $$\frac{F}{S} = \text{pressure} = \frac{I}{c}$$

or $$\boxed{p_{rad} = \frac{I}{c}}$$

$\dfrac{I}{c}$ is also equal to the energy density (energy per unit volume) u.

Hence, $$\boxed{p_{rad} = u} \qquad \text{...(v)}$$

The radiation pressure is thus equal to the energy density ($\text{N/m}^2 = \text{J/m}^3$). At a perfectly reflecting surface, the pressure on the surface is doubled. Thus, we can write

$$p_{rad} = \frac{I}{c} = u \qquad \text{(wave totally absorbed)}$$

and $$p_{rad} = \frac{2I}{c} = 2u \qquad \text{(wave totally reflected)}$$

Miscellaneous Examples

Ex. 1 The intensity of direct sunlight before it passes through the earth's atmosphere is 1.4 kW/m^2. If it is completely absorbed, find the corresponding radiation pressure.

Sol. For completely absorbing surface,

$$p_{rad} = \frac{I}{c} = \frac{1.4 \times 10^3}{3.0 \times 10^8} = 4.7 \times 10^{-6}\ \text{Nm}^{-2} \quad \textbf{Ans.}$$

Ex. 2 Light with an energy flux of 18 W/cm^2 falls on a non-reflecting surface at normal incidence. If the surface has an area of 20 cm^2, find the average force exerted on the surface during a 30 minute time span.

Sol. Pressure $= \dfrac{I}{c}$

$\therefore$ Force = Pressure × Area

$$= \frac{IA}{c} = \frac{(18 \times 10^4)(20 \times 10^{-4})}{3 \times 10^8}$$

$$= 1.2 \times 10^{-6}\ \text{N} \quad \textbf{Ans.}$$

Ex. 3 In the above example what is the average force if surface is perfectly reflecting?

Sol. If the surface is perfectly reflecting, then

$$\text{Pressure} = \frac{2I}{c}$$

Therefore, average force is doubled or

$$F_{av} = 2.4 \times 10^{-6}\ \text{N} \quad \textbf{Ans.}$$

Ex. 4 About 5% of the power of a 100 W light bulb is converted to visible radiation. What is the average intensity of visible radiation

(a) at a distance of 1 m from the bulb?

(b) at a distance of 10 m?

Sol. Effective power (energy radiated per second)

$$= 5\% \text{ of } 100 \text{ W}$$

$$P = 5 \text{ W}$$

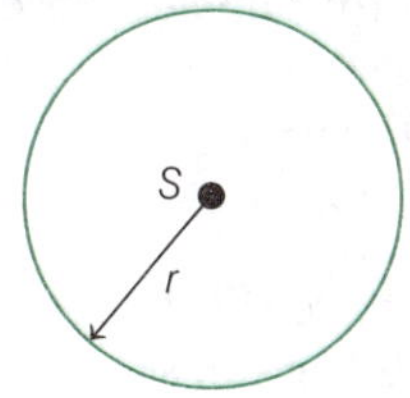

This energy will distribute on a sphere. At a distance r from the point source, area on which light is incident is

$$S = 4\pi r^2$$

$\therefore$ Intensity at distance r from the point source,

$$I = \frac{P}{S} = \frac{5}{4\pi r^2}$$

= Energy incident per unit area per unit time

(a) At $r = 1$ m,

$$I = \frac{5}{4\pi (1)^2}$$

$$= 0.4\ \text{W/m}^2 \quad \textbf{Ans.}$$

(b) At $r = 10$ m,

$$I = \frac{5}{4\pi (10)^2}$$

$$= 0.004\ \text{W/m}^2 \quad \textbf{Ans.}$$

MODULE 1 Exercise

Single Correct Option

1. Light with an energy flux of 20 W/cm^2 falls on a non-reflecting surface at normal incidence. If the surface has an area of 30 cm^2. The total momentum delivered (for complete absorption) during 30 minutes is
   (a) 36×10^{-5} kg - m/s
   (b) 36×10^{-4} kg - m/s
   (c) 1.08×10^{4} kg - m/s
   (d) 1.08×10^{7} kg - m/s

2. Light is incident normally on a completely absorbing surface with an energy flux of 25 W cm^{-2}. If the surface has an area of 25 cm^2, the momentum transferred to the surface in 40 min time duration will be **(2019 Main)**
   (a) 6.3×10^{-4} N-s (b) 1.4×10^{-6} N-s
   (c) 5.0×10^{-3} N-s (d) 3.5×10^{-6} N-s

3. 50 W/m^2 energy density of sunlight is normally incident on the surface of a solar panel. Some part of incident energy (25%) is reflected from the surface and the rest is absorbed. The force exerted on 1 m^2 surface area will be close to ($c = 3 \times 10^8$ m/s) **(2019 Main)**
   (a) 15×10^{-8} N
   (b) 20×10^{-8} N
   (c) 10×10^{-8} N
   (d) 35×10^{-8} N

Multiple Correct Options

4. An electromagnetic wave of intensity I falls on a surface kept in vacuum and exerts radiation pressure p on it. Which of the following are true?
   (a) Radiation pressure is I/c if the wave is totally absorbed
   (b) Radiation pressure is I/c if the wave is totally reflected
   (c) Radiation pressure is $2I/c$ if the wave is totally reflected
   (d) Radiation pressure is in the range $I/c < p < 2I/c$ for real surfaces

Subjective Question

5. An isotropic point source emits light with wavelength $\lambda = 589$ nm. The radiation power of the source is $P = 10$ W. Find the mean density of the flow of photons at a distance $r = 2.0$ m from the source. **(Irodov 5.260)**

Answers

1. (b) **2.** (c) **3.** (b) **4.** (a,c,d) **5.** 6×10^{13} cm^{-2}s^{-1}

See hints on page 16.

MODULE 2

Propagation of Electromagnetic Waves

(i) When electromagnetic waves propagate in space then electric and magnetic fields oscillate in mutually perpendicular directions. Further, they are perpendicular to the direction of propagation of electromagnetic wave also.

(ii) Consider a plane electromagnetic wave propagating along the z-direction. The electric field E_x is along the x-axis and varies sinusoidally. The magnetic field B_y is along the y-axis and again varies sinusoidally. We can write E_x and B_y as

$$E_x = E_0 \sin(\omega t - kz)$$

and

$$B_y = B_0 \sin(\omega t - kz)$$

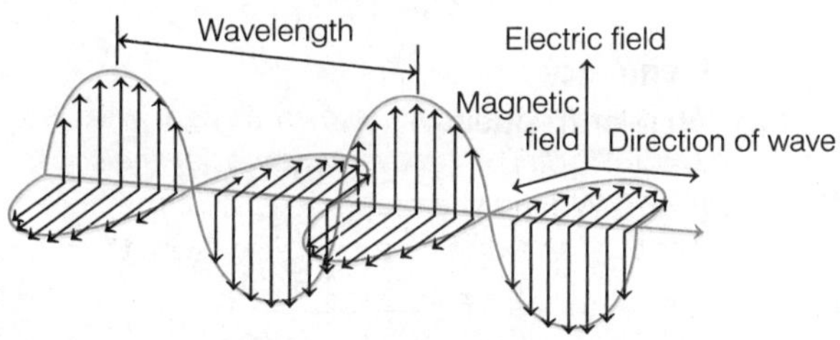

Thus, electromagnetic wave travels in the direction of **E × B.**

(iii) From Maxwell's equations and the knowledge of waves we can write the following expressions,

$$k = 2\pi/\lambda$$
$$\omega = 2\pi f$$
$$\text{Speed of light in vacuum} = c = \frac{\omega}{k} = f\lambda = \frac{E_0}{B_0} = \frac{1}{\sqrt{\varepsilon_0 \mu_0}}$$

where, f is the frequency of electromagnetic wave and λ its wavelength.

(iv) Unlike a mechanical wave (like sound wave) an electromagnetic wave does not require any material medium for the oscillations of electric and magnetic fields. They can travel in vacuum also. Oscillations of electric and magnetic fields are self sustaining in free space or vacuum.

(v) In a material medium (like glass, water etc.), electric and magnetic fields are different from the external fields. They are described in terms of permittivity ε and magnetic permeability μ. In Maxwell's equations, ε_0 and μ_0 are thus replaced by ε and μ and the velocity of light becomes,

$$v = \frac{1}{\sqrt{\varepsilon\mu}}$$

Thus, the velocity of light depends on electric and magnetic properties of the medium.

(vi) Like other waves, electromagnetic waves also carry energy and momentum. We have studied that, energy density (or average energy density) in electric field $= \frac{1}{2}\varepsilon_0 E^2$ and energy density in magnetic field $= \frac{B^2}{2\mu_0}$.

Here E and B are their rms values.

An electromagnetic wave contains both electric and magnetic field. Therefore, total average energy density is equal to $u = \frac{1}{2}\varepsilon_0 E^2 + \frac{B^2}{2\mu_0} = \frac{1}{2}\varepsilon_0 E_0^2 = \frac{B_0^2}{2\mu_0}$

Note *Here E_0 and B_0 are the peak values.*

(vii) The energy transferred per unit area per unit time perpendicular to the direction of propagation of electromagnetic wave is called the intensity of wave. It is given by

$$I = u \times c = \frac{1}{2}\varepsilon_0 E_0^2 c$$

Note *Contribution due to electric and magnetic fields will be equal and half of the above value. Thus,*

$$I_E = \frac{1}{2}\varepsilon_0 E^2 c = \frac{1}{4}\varepsilon_0 E_0^2 c \quad \text{and} \quad I_B = \frac{B^2}{2\mu_0}c = \frac{B_0^2}{\mu_0}c$$

Miscellaneous Examples

Ex. 1 Calculate the electric and magnetic fields produced by the radiation coming from a 100 W bulb at a distance of 3 m. Assume that the efficiency of the bulb is 2.5 % and it is a point source.

Sol. Intensity at a distance r from a point source of power P is given by

$$I = \frac{P}{4\pi r^2}$$

So, intensity at a distance of 3 m from the bulb with 2.5% efficiency will be

$$I = \frac{100}{4\pi (3)^2} \times \frac{2.5}{100} = 0.022 \text{ W/m}^2$$

Half of the intensity is provided by electric field and half by magnetic field.

$$\therefore \quad I_E = \frac{I}{2} = 0.011 \text{ W/m}^2$$

But, $\quad I_E$ is given by $\frac{1}{2}\varepsilon_0 E^2 c$

$$\therefore \quad I_E = \frac{1}{2}\varepsilon_0 E^2 c \quad \text{or} \quad E = \sqrt{\frac{2 I_E}{\varepsilon_0 c}}$$

Substituting the values, we have

$$E = \sqrt{\frac{2 \times 0.011}{(8.85 \times 10^{-12})(3 \times 10^8)}}$$

$$= 2.9 \text{ V/m}$$ **Ans.**

Note *that this is actually the rms value of electric field.*

From the equation, $c = E/B$

$$B = \frac{E}{c} = \frac{2.9}{3.0 \times 10^8}$$

$$= 9.6 \times 10^{-9} \text{ T}$$ **Ans.**

This is again the rms value of magnetic field.

Ex. 2 A plane electromagnetic wave of frequency 25 MHz travels in free space along the x-direction. At a particular point in space and time, $\mathbf{E} = (6.3\,\hat{\mathbf{j}})$ V/m. What is $\mathbf{B}$ at this point?

Sol. $c = \frac{E_0}{B_0}$

$$\therefore \quad B_0 = \frac{E_0}{c}$$

Substituting the values in SI units,

$$B_0 = \frac{6.3}{3 \times 10^8} = 2.1 \times 10^{-8} \text{ T}$$

$\mathbf{c}$ is in the direction of $\mathbf{E} \times \mathbf{B}$.

Therefore we can see that $\mathbf{B}$ is along positive z-direction. Because, $\mathbf{E}$ is along $\hat{\mathbf{j}}$ direction and $\mathbf{c}$ along $\hat{\mathbf{i}}$ direction.

$$\therefore \quad \mathbf{B} = (2.1 \times 10^{-8} \text{ T})\,\hat{\mathbf{k}}$$ **Ans.**

Ex. 3 The magnetic field in a plane electromagnetic wave is given by $B_y = (2 \times 10^{-7} \text{ T}) \sin (0.5 \times 10^3 x + 1.5 \times 10^{11} t)$ T

(a) What is the wavelength and frequency of the wave?

(b) Write an expression for the electric field.

Sol. (a) **Wavelength**

From the given equation, we can see that

$$k = 0.5 \times 10^3 \text{ m}^{-1}$$

But, $\quad k = \frac{2\pi}{\lambda}$

$$\therefore \quad \lambda = \frac{2\pi}{k} = \frac{2\pi}{0.5 \times 10^3}$$

$$= 1.25 \times 10^{-2} \text{ m}$$ **Ans.**

Frequency

Angular frequency,

$$\omega = 1.5 \times 10^{11} \text{ rad/s}$$

But, $\quad \omega = 2\pi f$

$$\therefore \quad f = \frac{\omega}{2\pi} = \frac{1.5 \times 10^{11}}{2\pi}$$

$$= 2.39 \times 10^{10} \text{ Hz}$$ **Ans.**

(b) $c = \frac{E_0}{B_0}$

$$\therefore \quad E_0 = cB_0$$

$$= (3.0 \times 10^8)(2 \times 10^{-7}) = 60 \text{ V/m}$$

$\mathbf{c}$ is in the direction of $\mathbf{E} \times \mathbf{B}$.

Therefore we can see that $\mathbf{E}$ is along z-direction.

$$\therefore \quad E_z = (60 \text{ V/m}) \sin (0.5 \times 10^3 x + 1.5 \times 10^{11} t) \text{ V/m}$$ **Ans.**

Ex. 4 A plane electromagnetic wave propagating in the x-direction has a wavelength of 5.0 mm. The electric field is in the y-direction and its maximum magnitude is 30 Vm^{-1}. Write suitable equations for the electric and magnetic fields as a function of x and t.

Sol. Given, $\lambda = 5 \text{ mm} = 5 \times 10^{-3}$ m

$$k = \frac{2\pi}{\lambda} = \frac{2\pi}{5 \times 10^{-3}} \text{ m}^{-1} = 1257 \text{ m}^{-1}$$

From the equation, $c = \frac{\omega}{k}$

$$\omega = c\,k = (3 \times 10^8)(1257)$$

$$= 3.77 \times 10^{11} \text{ rad/s}$$

$$E_0 = 30 \text{ V/m}$$

$$c = \frac{E_0}{B_0}$$

$$\therefore \quad B_0 = \frac{E_0}{c} = \frac{30}{3 \times 10^8} = 10^{-7} \text{ T}$$

Now, $E_y = E_0 \sin(\omega t - kx)$

$$= (30 \text{V/m}) \sin[(3.77 \times 10^{11} \text{ s}^{-1})t - (1257 \text{ m}^{-1})x]$$

and

$$B_z = (10^{-7} \text{ T}) \sin[(3.77 \times 10^{11} \text{ s}^{-1})t - (1257 \text{ m}^{-1})x]$$ **Ans.**

Ex. 5 A light beam travelling in the x-direction is described by the electric field $E_y = (300 \text{ Vm}^{-1}) \sin \omega(t - x/c)$. An electron is constrained to move along the y-direction with a speed of $2.0 \times 10^7 \text{ ms}^{-1}$. Find the maximum electric force and the maximum magnetic force on the electron.

Sol. Maximum Electric Force

Maximum electric field, $E_0 = 300$ V/m

$\therefore$ Maximum electric force $F = qE_0$

$$= (1.6 \times 10^{-19})(300)$$

$$= 4.8 \times 10^{-17} \text{ N}$$ **Ans.**

Maximum Magnetic Force

From the equation, $c = \dfrac{E_0}{B_0}$

Maximum magnetic field, $B_0 = \dfrac{E_0}{c}$

or $$B_0 = \frac{300}{3.0 \times 10^8}$$

$$= 10^{-6} \text{ T}$$

$\therefore$ Maximum magnetic force $= B_0 qv \sin 90^\circ = B_0 qv$

Substituting the values, we have

Maximum magnetic force

$$= (10^{-6})(1.6 \times 10^{-19})(2.0 \times 10^7)$$

$$= 3.2 \times 10^{-18} \text{ N}$$ **Ans.**

Ex. 6 Suppose that the electric field of an electromagnetic wave in vacuum is $\mathbf{E} = \{(3.0 \text{ N/C}) \cos[(1.8 \text{ rad/m})y + (5.4 \times 10^6 \text{rad/s})t]\}\hat{\mathbf{i}}$.

(a) What is the direction of propagation of wave?

(b) What is the wavelength λ?

(c) What is the frequency f?

(d) What is the amplitude of the magnetic field of the wave?

(e) Write an expression for the magnetic field of the wave.

Sol. (a) From the knowledge of wave we can see that electromagnetic wave is travelling along negative y-direction, as ωt and ky both are positive.

(b) $k = 1.8$ rad/m

$$k = \frac{2\pi}{\lambda}$$

$$\therefore \quad \lambda = \frac{2\pi}{k} = \frac{2\pi}{1.8} = 3.5 \text{ m}$$ **Ans.**

(c) $\omega = 5.4 \times 10^6$ rad/s

$$\omega = 2\pi f$$

$$\therefore \quad f = \frac{\omega}{2\pi} = \frac{5.4 \times 10^6}{2\pi}$$

$$= 8.6 \times 10^5 \text{ Hz}$$ **Ans.**

(d) $E_0 = 3.0$ N/C

From the relation, $c = \dfrac{E_0}{B_0}$

We have, $$B_0 = \frac{E_0}{c} = \frac{3.0}{3.0 \times 10^8} = 10^{-8} \text{ T}$$ **Ans.**

(e) **E** is along $\hat{\mathbf{i}}$ direction, wave is travelling along negative y-direction. Therefore, oscillations of **B** are along z-direction or

$$\mathbf{B} = (10^{-8} \text{ T}) \cos[(1.8 \text{ rad/m})y + (5.4 \times 10^6 \text{rad/s})t]\hat{\mathbf{k}}$$ **Ans.**

Ex. 7 The magnetic field of an electromagnetic wave is given by,

$$\mathbf{B} = 1.6 \times 10^{-6} \cos(2 \times 10^7 z + 6 \times 10^{15} t)(2\hat{\mathbf{i}} + \hat{\mathbf{j}}) \frac{\text{Wb}}{\text{m}^2}$$

The associated electric field will be,

(a) $\mathbf{E} = 4.8 \times 10^2 \cos(2 \times 10^7 z + 6 \times 10^{15} t)(-\hat{\mathbf{i}} + 2\hat{\mathbf{j}}) \dfrac{\text{V}}{\text{m}}$

(b) $\mathbf{E} = 4.8 \times 10^2 \cos(2 \times 10^7 z + 6 \times 10^{15} t)(-2\hat{\mathbf{j}} + 2\hat{\mathbf{j}}) \dfrac{\text{V}}{\text{m}}$

(c) $\mathbf{E} = 4.8 \times 10^2 \cos(2 \times 10^7 z + 6 \times 10^{15} t)(\hat{\mathbf{i}} + 2\hat{\mathbf{j}}) \dfrac{\text{V}}{\text{m}}$

(d) $\mathbf{E} = 4.8 \times 10^2 \cos(2 \times 10^7 z + 6 \times 10^{15} t)(2\hat{\mathbf{i}} + \hat{\mathbf{j}}) \dfrac{\text{V}}{\text{m}}$

Sol. (i) **E** and **B** are in same phase. Therefore phase angle will be same.

(ii) $\mathbf{E} \perp \mathbf{B} \quad \therefore \mathbf{E} \cdot \mathbf{B} = 0$

(iii) Wave it travelling along $-z$-direction.

$\therefore$ **c** should be in the direction of $\mathbf{E} \times \mathbf{B}$.

In option (a)

$$(-\hat{\mathbf{i}} + 2\hat{\mathbf{j}}) \cdot (2\hat{\mathbf{i}} + \hat{\mathbf{j}}) = 0$$

and $$(-\hat{\mathbf{i}} + 2\hat{\mathbf{j}}) \times (2\hat{\mathbf{i}} + \hat{\mathbf{j}}) = -5\hat{\mathbf{k}}$$

$\therefore$ The correct option is (a).

MODULE 2 Exercise

Single Correct Option

1. Select the correct statement from the following **(2013 Main)**
   (a) Electromagnetic waves cannot travel in vacuum.
   (b) Electromagnetic waves are longitudinal waves.
   (c) Electromagnetic waves are produced by charges moving with uniform velocity.
   (d) Electromagnetic waves carry both energy and momentum as they propagate through space.

2. In an electromagnetic wave, electric field oscillates as $E_y = E_0 \sin(\omega t - kx)$ V/m, then magnetic field is given by
   (a) $B_x = \frac{E_0}{c} \sin(\omega t - kx)$
   (b) $B_z = \frac{E_0}{c} \sin(\omega t - kx)$
   (c) $B_z = \frac{E_0}{c} \sin(\omega t + kx)$
   (d) $B_x = \frac{E_0}{c} \cos(\omega t + kx)$

3. A plane electromagnetic wave travelling along the x-direction has a wavelength of 3 mm. The variation in the electric field occurs in the y-direction with an amplitude 66 Vm^{-1}. The equations for the electric and magnetic fields as a function of x and t are respectively
   (a) $E_y = 66 \cos \pi \times 10^{11}\left(t - \frac{x}{c}\right)$,
   $B_z = 2.2 \times 10^{-7} \cos \pi \times 10^{11}\left(t - \frac{x}{c}\right)$
   (b) $E_y = 11 \cos 2\pi \times 10^{11}\left(t - \frac{x}{c}\right)$,
   $B_z = 11 \times 10^{-7} \cos 2\pi \times 10^{11}\left(t - \frac{x}{c}\right)$
   (c) $E_y = 33 \cos \pi \times 10^{11}\left(t - \frac{x}{c}\right)$,
   $B_z = 11 \times 10^{-7} \cos \pi \times 10^{11}\left(t - \frac{x}{c}\right)$
   (d) $E_y = 66 \cos 2\pi \times 10^{11}\left(t - \frac{x}{c}\right)$,
   $B_z = 2.2 \times 10^{-7} \cos 2\pi \times 10^{11}\left(t - \frac{x}{c}\right)$

4. The electromagnetic waves travel in a medium at a speed of 2.0×10^8 m/s. The relative permeability of the medium is 1.0. The relative permittivity of the medium will be **(2022 Main)**
   (a) 2.25 (b) 4.25
   (c) 6.25 (d) 8.25

5. Electric field in a plane electromagnetic wave is given by $E = 50 \sin(500x - 10 \times 10^{10} t)$ V/m. The velocity of electromagnetic wave in this medium is
   (Given, c = speed of light in vacuum) **(2021 Main)**
   (a) $\frac{3}{2}c$ (b) c
   (c) $\frac{2}{3}c$ (d) $\frac{c}{2}$

6. The electric field in an electromagnetic wave is given by $\mathbf{E} = \hat{\mathbf{i}}\, 40 \cos \omega\left(t - \frac{z}{c}\right) \text{NC}^{-1}$. The magnetic field induction of this wave is (in SI unit) **(2024 Main)**
   (a) $\mathbf{B} = \hat{\mathbf{i}}\, \frac{40}{c} \cos \omega\left(t - \frac{z}{c}\right)$
   (b) $\mathbf{B} = \hat{\mathbf{k}}\, \frac{40}{c} \cos \omega\left(t - \frac{z}{c}\right)$
   (c) $\mathbf{B} = \hat{\mathbf{j}}\, \frac{40}{c} \cos \omega\left(t - \frac{z}{c}\right)$
   (d) $\mathbf{B} = \hat{\mathbf{j}}\, 40 \cos \omega\left(t - \frac{z}{c}\right)$

7. The electric field and magnetic field components of an electromagnetic wave going through vacuum is described by
   $$E_x = E_0 \sin(kz - \omega t);\ B_y = B_0 \sin(kz - \omega t)$$
   Then the correct relation between E_0 and B_0 is given by **(2023 Main)**
   (a) $kE_0 = \omega B_0$ (b) $E_0 B_0 = \omega k$
   (c) $\omega E_0 = k B_0$ (d) $E_0 = k B_0$

8. If the magnetic field in a plane electromagnetic wave is given by $\mathbf{B} = 3 \times 10^{-8} \sin(1.6 \times 10^3 x + 48 \times 10^{10} t)\,\hat{\mathbf{j}}$ T, then what will be expression for electric field? **(2020 Main)**
   (a) $\mathbf{E} = 60 \sin(1.6 \times 10^3 x + 48 \times 10^{10} t)\,\hat{\mathbf{k}}$ V/m
   (b) $\mathbf{E} = 9 \sin(1.6 \times 10^3 x + 48 \times 10^{10} t)\,\hat{\mathbf{k}}$ V/m
   (c) $\mathbf{E} = 3 \times 10^{-8} \sin(1.6 \times 10^3 x + 48 \times 10^{10} t)\,\hat{\mathbf{k}}$ V/m
   (d) $\mathbf{E} = 3 \times 10^{-8} \sin(1.6 \times 10^3 x + 48 \times 10^{10} t)\,\hat{\mathbf{k}}$ V/m

9. Magnetic field in a plane electromagnetic wave is given by $\mathbf{B} = B_0 \sin(kx + \omega t)\,\hat{\mathbf{j}}$ T.
   Expression for corresponding electric field will be (where, c is speed of light). **(2017 Main)**
   (a) $\mathbf{E} = B_0 c \sin(kx + \omega t)\,\hat{\mathbf{k}}$ V/m
   (b) $\mathbf{E} = \frac{B_0}{c} \sin(kx + \omega t)\,\hat{\mathbf{k}}$ V/m
   (c) $\mathbf{E} = -B_0 c \sin(kx + \omega t)\,\hat{\mathbf{k}}$ V/m
   (d) $\mathbf{E} = B_0 c \sin(kx - \omega t)\,\hat{\mathbf{k}}$ V/m

Multiple Correct Options

10. A plane electromagnetic wave propagating along x-direction can have the following pairs of **E** and **B**
    (a) E_x, B_y
    (b) E_y, B_z
    (c) B_x, E_y
    (d) E_z, B_y

Subjective Questions

11. A radio can tune into any station in the 7.5 MHz to 12 MHz band. What is the corresponding wavelength of band?
12. Suppose that the electric field amplitude of an electromagnetic wave is $E_0 = 120$ N/C and that its frequency is 50.0 MHz. (a) Determine B_0, ω, k and λ,
    (b) Find expressions for **E** and **B**. Electro magnetic wave is travelling along x-direction.

Answers

1. (d) **2.** (b) **3.** (d) **4.** (a) **5.** (c) **6.** (c) **7.** (a) **8.** (b) **9.** (a) **10.** (b)

11. (Wavelength band from 40m to 25m)

12. (a) 400 nT, 3.14×10^8 rad/s, 1.05 rad/m, 6.00 m (b) $\mathbf{E} = (120\ \text{N/C})\ \sin\ [(1.05\ \text{rad/m})]\ x - (3.14 \times 10^8\ \text{rad/s})t]\ \hat{\mathbf{j}}$

$\mathbf{B} = (400\ \text{nT})\ \sin\ [(1.05\ \text{rad/m})]\ x - (3.14 \times 10^8\ \text{rad/s})\ t]\ \hat{\mathbf{k}}$

See hints on pages 16-17.

MODULE 3

Electromagnetic Spectrum

The classification of electromagnetic waves according to frequency or wavelength is called electromagnetic spectrum. Table below gives range of wavelengths and frequencies for different waves.

Table

S.No.	Type	Wavelength range	Frequency range
1.	Radio waves	>0.1 m	$<3\times10^{9}$ Hz
2.	Micro waves	0.1 m to 1 mm	3×10^{9} Hz to 3×10^{11} Hz
3.	Infrared	1 mm to 7000 Å	3×10^{11} Hz to 4.3×10^{14} Hz
4.	Visible light	7000 Å to 4000 Å	4.3×10^{14} Hz to 7.5×10^{14} Hz
5.	Ultraviolet	4000 Å to 100 Å	7.5×10^{14} Hz to 3×10^{16} Hz
6.	X-rays	100 Å to 0.1 Å	3×10^{16} Hz to 3×10^{19} Hz
7.	Gamma rays	< 0.1 Å	$>3\times10^{19}$ Hz

Now, let us discuss them in brief in the order of increasing wavelength.

γ-Rays

These were identified by P. Villiard in 1900. These are usually produced within the nucleus of an atom and extremely energetic. They cover the range from 0.1 Å down or equivalently from 10^{19} Hz up.

X-Rays

X-rays, discovered in 1895 by W. Roentgen extend from 100 Å to 0.1 Å. These are produced by the rapid deceleration of electrons that bombard a heavy metal target. These are also produced by electronic transitions between the energy levels in an atom. X-rays are used to study the atomic structure of crystals or molecules such as DNA. Besides their diagnostic and therapeutic use in medicine they have become an important tool in studying the universe.

Ultraviolet Radiation

Ultraviolet (UV) rays were first discovered by J.W. Ritter in 1801. The ultraviolet region extends from 4000 Å to 100 Å. It plays a role in the production of vitamin D in our skins. But prolonged doses of UV radiation can induce cancers in humans. Glass absorbs UV radiation and hence, can provide some protection against the sun's rays. If the ozone in our atmosphere did not absorb the UV below 3000 Å, there would be a large number of cell mutations, especially cancerous ones, in humans. For this reason, the depletion of the ozone in our atmosphere by chlorofluorocarbons (CFCs) is now a matter of international concern.

Visible Light

A lot of discussion has already been done on visible light in previous chapters. As electrons undergo transitions between energy levels in an atom, light is produced at well defined wavelengths. Light covering a continuous range of wavelengths is produced by the random acceleration of electrons in hot bodies. Our sense of vision and the process of photosynthesis in plants have evolved within the range of those wavelengths of sunlight that our atmosphere does not absorb.

Infrared Radiation

The infrared region (IR) starts at 7000 Å and extends to about 1 mm. It was discovered in 1800 by M. Herchel. It is associated with the vibration and rotation of molecules and is perceived by us as heat. IR is used in the early detection of tumours.

Microwaves

Microwaves cover wavelengths from 1 mm to about 10 cm. Microwaves upto about 30 GHz may be generated by the oscillations of electrons in a device called klystron. Microwave ovens are used in kitchens. Modern intercity communications such as phone conversations and TV programs are often carried *via* a cross country network of microwave antennas.

Radio and TV Signals

Radio waves are generated when charges are accelerating through conducting wires. Their wavelengths lie in the range 10^{14} m to 10 cm. They are generated by *LC* oscillators and are used in radio and television communication systems.

Important POINTS

Our eyes are sensitive to visible light (λ between 4000 Å to 7000 Å). Similarly, different animals are sensitive to different ranges of wavelengths. For example, snakes can detect infrared waves.

The basic difference between different types of electromagnetic waves lies in their frequencies and wavelengths. All of them travel with same speed in vacuum. Further they differ in their mode of interaction with matter.

For example infrared waves vibrate the electrons, atoms and molecules of a substance. These vibrations increase the internal energy and temperature of the substance. This is why infrared waves are also called heat waves.

Electromagnetic waves interact with matter *via* their electric and magnetic fields, which set in oscillation with the charges present in all matter. This interaction depends on the wavelength of the electromagnetic wave and the nature of atoms or molecules in the medium.

- **Microwave Oven** In electromagnetic spectrum frequency and energy of microwaves is smaller than the visible light. Water content is required for cooking food in microwave oven. Almost all food items contain some water content. Microwaves interact with water molecules and atoms *via* their electric and magnetic fields. Temperature of water molecules increases by this. These water molecules share this energy with neighboring food molecules, heating up the food.

  Porcelain vessels are used for cooking food in microwave oven. Because its large molecules vibrate and rotate with much smaller frequencies and do not get heated up. We cannot use metal vessels. Metal vessels interact with microwaves. These vessels may melt due to heating.

MODULE 3 Exercise

Assertion and Reason

Directions : Choose the correct option

*(a) If both **Assertion** and **Reason** are true and the **Reason** is correct explanation of the **Assertion**.*

*(b) If both **Assertion** and **Reason** are true but **Reason** is not the correct explanation of **Assertion**.*

*(c) If **Assertion** is true, but the **Reason** is false.*

*(d) If **Assertion** is false but the **Reason** is true.*

*(e) If both **Assertion** and **Reason** are false.*

1. **Assertion :** EM waves used for optical communication have longer wavelengths than that of microwave, employed in Radar technology.

   Reason : Infrared EM waves are more energetic than microwaves (used in Radar). **(2023 Main)**

Single Correct Option

2. Which of the following are not electromagnetic waves?

   (a) Cosmic rays (b) γ-rays
   (c) Radio waves (d) X-rays

3. Which is the correct ascending order of wavelengths? **(2022 Main)**

   (a) $\lambda_{\text{visible}} < \lambda_{\text{X-rays}} < \lambda_{\text{gamma-rays}} < \lambda_{\text{microwaves}}$
   (b) $\lambda_{\text{gamma-rays}} < \lambda_{\text{X-rays}} < \lambda_{\text{visible}} < \lambda_{\text{microwaves}}$
   (c) $\lambda_{\text{X-rays}} < \lambda_{\text{gamma-rays}} < \lambda_{\text{visible}} < \lambda_{\text{microwaves}}$
   (d) $\lambda_{\text{microwaves}} < \lambda_{\text{visible}} < \lambda_{\text{gamma-rays}} < \lambda_{\text{X-rays}}$

4. Choose the correct option relating wavelengths of different parts of electromagnetic wave spectrum.

   (a) $\lambda_{\text{visible}} < \lambda_{\text{microwaves}} < \lambda_{\text{radiowaves}} < \lambda_{\text{X-rays}}$ **(2020 Main)**
   (b) $\lambda_{\text{radiowaves}} > \lambda_{\text{microwaves}} > \lambda_{\text{visible}} > \lambda_{\text{X-rays}}$
   (c) $\lambda_{\text{X-rays}} < \lambda_{\text{microwaves}} < \lambda_{\text{radiowaves}} < \lambda_{\text{visible}}$
   (d) $\lambda_{\text{visible}} > \lambda_{\text{X-rays}} > \lambda_{\text{radiowaves}} > \lambda_{\text{microwaves}}$

5. Arrange the following electromagnetic radiation in the order of increasing energy **(2016 Main)**

   A : Blue light B : Yellow light
   C : X-ray D : Radiowave
   (a) C, A, B, D (b) B, A, D, C
   (c) D, B, A, C (d) A, B, D, C

6. Microwave oven acts on the principle of **(2016 Main)**

   (a) giving rotational energy to water molecules
   (b) giving translational energy to water molecules
   (c) giving vibrational energy to water molecules
   (d) transferring electrons from lower to higher energy levels in water molecules

7. If microwaves, X-rays, infrared, gamma rays, ultra-violet, radio waves and visible parts of the electromagnetic spectrum are denoted by M, X, I, G, U, R and V, then which of the following is the arrangement is ascending order of wavelength? **(2014 Main)**

   (a) R, M, I, V, U, X and G (b) M, R, V, X, U, G and I
   (c) G, X, U, V, I, M and R (d) I, M, R, U, V, X and G

8. Photons of an electromagnetic radiation has an energy 11 keV each. To which region of electromagnetic spectrum does it belong? **(2023 Main)**

(a) X-ray region (b) Ultra violet region
(c) Infrared region (d) Visible region

Match the Columns

9. Match List-I with List-II.

	List-I		List-II
A.	Microwave	I.	400 nm to 1 nm
B.	Ultraviolet	II.	1 nm to 10^{-3} nm
C.	X-ray	III.	1 mm to 700 nm
D.	Infrared	IV.	0.1 m to 1 mm

Choose the correct answer from the options given below. **(2023 Main)**

(a) A-IV, B-I, C-II, D-III (b) A-I, B-IV, C-II, D-III
(c) A-IV, B-II, C-I, D-III (d) A-IV, B-I, C-III, D-II

10. Match List-I with List-II.

	List-I		List-II
(a)	UV-rays	(i)	Diagnostic tool in medicine
(b)	X-rays	(ii)	Water purification
(c)	Microwave	(iii)	Communication, radar
(d)	Infrared wave	(iv)	Improving visibility in foggy days

Choose the correct answer from the options given below : **(2022 Main)**

(a) (a)-(iii), (b)-(ii), (c)-(i), (d)-(iv)
(b) (a)-(ii), (b)-(i), (c)-(iii), (d)-(iv)
(c) (a)-(ii), (b)-(iv), (c)-(iii), (d)-(i)
(d) (a)-(iii), (b)-(i), (c)-(ii), (d)-(iv)

11. Match List-I with List-II.

	List-I		List-II
A.	Source of microwave frequency	1.	Radioactive decay of nucleus
B.	Source of infrared frequency	2.	Magnetron
C.	Source of gamma rays	3.	Inner shell electrons
D.	Source of X-rays	4.	Vibration of atoms and molecules
		5.	LASER
		6.	R - C circuit

Choose the correct answer from the options given below. **(2021 Main)**

	A	B	C	D		A	B	C	D
(a)	6	4	1	5	(b)	6	5	1	4
(c)	2	4	6	3	(d)	2	4	1	3

12. Match Column I (Electromagnetic wave type) with Column II (Its association/application) and select the correct option from the choices given below the lists. **(2014 Main)**

	Column I		Column II
A.	Infrared waves	1.	To treat muscular strain
B.	Radio waves	2.	For broadcasting
C.	X-rays	3.	To detect fracture of bones
D.	Ultraviolet	4.	Absorbed by the ozone layer of the atmosphere

Codes

	A	B	C	D		A	B	C	D
(a)	4	3	2	1	(b)	1	2	4	3
(c)	3	2	1	4	(d)	1	2	3	4

Answers

1. (d) **2.** (a) **3.** (b) **4.** (b) **5.** (c) **6.** (c) **7.** (c) **8.** (a) **9.** (a) **10.** (b)
11. (d) **12.** (d)

See hints on pages 17-18.

Unit Exercise (Cumulative)

Statement Type Question

1. Given below are two statements.

Statement I : Electromagnetic waves are not deflected by electric and magnetic field.

Statement II : The amplitude of electric field and the magnetic field in electromagnetic waves are related to each other as $E_0 = \sqrt{\frac{\mu_0}{\varepsilon_0}} B_0$.

In the light of the above statements, choose the correct answer from the options given below **(2023 Main)**

(a) Statement I is false but Statement II is true
(b) Statement I is true but Statement II is false
(c) Both Statement I and Statement II are true
(d) Both Statement I and Statement II are false

Single Correct Option

2. One requires 11eV of energy to dissociate a carbon monoxide molecule into carbon and oxygen atoms. The minimum frequency of the appropriate electromagnetic radiation to achieve the dissociation lies in
(a) visible region (b) infrared region
(c) ultraviolet region (d) microwave region

3. Total average energy density of an electromagnetic wave in free space is given by
(a) $\frac{1}{2}\varepsilon_0 E_{rms}^2 + \frac{B_{rms}^2}{2\mu_0}$ (b) $\frac{1}{2}\mu_0 E_0^2 + \frac{1}{2}\varepsilon_0 B_0^2$
(c) $\frac{1}{2}\varepsilon_0 E_0^2$ (d) $\frac{E_0^2 + B_0^2}{2c}$

4. In a uniform magnetic field of 10^{-5} T in free space, the energy density is u. The electric field which will produce the same energy density in free space is
(a) 10^5 V/m (b) 3×10^3 V/m
(c) 10 V/m (d) 9×10^{-3} V/m

5. A point source of electromagnetic radiation has an average power output of 800 W. The maximum value of electric field at a distance 4.0 m from the source is
(a) 68.20 V/m (b) 54.77 V/m
(c) 50.32 V/m (d) 48.10 V/m

6. The rms value of the electric field of the light coming from the sun is 720 N/C. The average total energy density of the electromagnetic wave is
(a) 81.35×10^{-12} J/m^3 (b) 3.3×10^{-3} J/m^3
(c) 4.58×10^{-6} J/m^3 (d) 6.37×10^{-9} J/m^3

7. A plane electromagnetic wave propagating in x-direction is described by $E_y = (200 \text{ Vm}^{-1}) \sin[1.5 \times 10^7 t - 0.05x]$. The intensity of the wave is (Use $\varepsilon_0 = 8.85 \times 10^{-12}$ C^2 N^{-1} m^{-2}) **(2024 Main)**
(a) 53.1 Wm^{-2}
(b) 106.2 Wm^{-2}
(c) 26.6 Wm^{-2}
(d) 35.4 Wm^{-2}

8. For the plane electromagnetic wave given by $E = E_0 \sin(\omega t - kx)$ and $B = B_0 \sin(\omega t - kx)$, the ratio of average electric energy density to average magnetic energy density is **(2023 Main)**
(a) 2 (b) 1/2 (c) 1 (d) 4

9. The energy of an electromagnetic wave contained in a small volume oscillates with **(2023 Main)**
(a) zero frequency
(b) double the frequency of the wave
(c) half the frequency of the wave
(d) the frequency of the wave

10. The electric field in an electromagnetic wave is given as $\mathbf{E} = 20 \sin\omega\left(t - \frac{x}{c}\right)\hat{\mathbf{j}}$ NC^{-1}, where ω and c are angular frequency and velocity of electromagnetic wave respectively. The energy contained in a volume of 5×10^{-4} m^3 will be (Given, $\varepsilon_0 = 8.85 \times 10^{-12}$ C^2/Nm^2) **(2023 Main)**
(a) 28.5×10^{-13} J (b) 17.7×10^{-13} J
(c) 8.85×10^{-13} J (d) 88.5×10^{-13} J

11. The relative permittivity of distilled water is 81. The velocity of light in it will be (Given, $\mu_r = 1$) **(2021 Main)**
(a) 4.33×10^7 m/s
(b) 2.33×10^7 m/s
(c) 3.33×10^7 m/s
(d) 5.33×10^7 m/s

12. A 27 m W laser beam has a cross-sectional area of 10 mm^2. The magnitude of the maximum electric field in this electromagnetic wave is given by (Given, permittivity of space $\varepsilon_0 = 9 \times 10^{-12}$ SI units, speed of light $c = 3 \times 10^8$ m/s) **(2019 Main)**
(a) 2 kV/m
(b) 0.7 kV/m
(c) 1 kV/m
(d) 1.4 kV/m

13. For plane electromagnetic waves propagating in the z-direction, which one of the following combination gives the correct possible directions for **E** and **B** field, respectively? **(2015 Main)**
(a) $(2\hat{i}+3\hat{j})$ and $(\hat{i}+2\hat{j})$
(b) $(-2\hat{i}-3\hat{j})$ and $(3\hat{i}-2\hat{j})$
(c) $(3\hat{i}+4\hat{j})$ and $(4\hat{i}-3\hat{j})$
(d) $(\hat{i}+2\hat{j})$ and $(2\hat{i}-\hat{j})$

14. A radar sends an electromagnetic signal of electric field $E_0 = 2.25$ V/m and magnetic field $B_0 = 1.5 \times 10^{-8}$ T which strikes a target on line of sight at a distance of 3 km in a medium. After that, a pail of signal (echo) reflects back towards the radar with same velocity and by same path. If the signal was transmitted at time t_0 from radar, then after how much time echo will reach to the radar? **(2022 Main)**
(a) 2.0×10^{-5} s
(b) 4.0×10^{-5} s
(c) 1.0×10^{-5} s
(d) 8.0×10^{-5} s

Multiple Correct Options

15. The source of electromagnetic waves can be a charge
(a) moving with a constant velocity
(b) moving in a circular orbit
(c) at rest
(d) falling in an electric field

16. A charged particle oscillates about its mean equilibrium position with a frequency of 10^9 Hz. The electromagnetic waves produced
(a) will have frequency of 10^9 Hz
(b) will have frequency of 2×10^9 Hz
(c) will have a wavelength of 0.3 m
(d) fall in the region of radio waves

17. The electric field associated with an electromagnetic wave propagating in a dielectric medium is given by $\mathbf{E} = 30(2\hat{x}+\hat{y}) \sin\left[2\pi\left(5\times 10^{14}t - \frac{10^7}{3}z\right)\right]$ Vm^{-1}. Which of the following option(s) is (are) correct?
[Given : The speed of light in vacuum, $c = 3 \times 10^8 \text{ms}^{-1}$] **(2023 Adv.)**
(a) $B_x = -2 \times 10^{-7} \sin\left[2\pi\left(5\times 10^{14}t - \frac{10^7}{3}z\right)\right]$ Wb m^{-2}
(b) $B_y = 2 \times 10^{-7} \sin\left[2\pi\left(5\times 10^{14}t = \frac{10^7}{3}z\right)\right]$ Wb m^{-2}
(c) The wave is polarized in the xy-plane with polarization angle 30° with respect to the x-axis
(d) The refractive index of the medium is 2.

Subjective Questions

18. Can an electromagnetic wave be deflected by an electric field? By a magnetic field?

19. What physical quantity is the same for X-rays of wavelength 10^{-10}m, red light of wavelength 6800 Å and radio waves of wavelength 500 m?

20. A laser beam has intensity 2.5×10^{14} Wm^{-2}. Find the amplitudes of electric and magnetic fields in the beam.

21. In a plane electromagnetic wave, the electric field oscillates sinusoidally at a frequency of 2.0×10^{10} Hz and amplitude 48 Vm^{-1}.
(a) What is the wavelength of the wave?
(b) What is the amplitude of the oscillating magnetic field?
(c) Show that the average energy density of the field **E** equals the average energy density of the field **B**. [$c = 3 \times 10^8$ ms^{-1}].

Integer Type Questions

22. In a medium, the speed of light wave decreases to 0.2 times to its speed in free space. The ratio of relative permittivity to the refractive index of the medium is x : 1. The value of x is ....
(Given, speed of light in free space $= 3 \times 10^8$ m s^{-1} and for the given medium $\mu_r = 1$) **(2023 Main)**

23. The intensity of the light from a bulb incident on a surface is 0.22 W/m^2. The amplitude of the magnetic field in this light-wave is ______ $\times 10^{-9}$ T.
(Given, permittivity of vacuum $\varepsilon_0 = 8.85 \times 10^{-12}$ C^2 N^{-1} m^{-2}, speed of light in vacuum $c = 3 \times 10^8$ m/s) **(2022 Main)**

24. An electromagnetic wave of frequency 5 GHz, is travelling in a medium whose relative electric permittivity and relative magnetic permeability both are 2. Its velocity in this medium is .... $\times 10^7$ m/s. **(2022 Main)**

25. The electric field in an electromagnetic wave is given by $E = (50 \text{ NC}^{-1}) \sin\omega(t - x/c)$.
The energy contained in a cylinder of volume V is 5.5×10^{-12} J. The value of V is .... cm^3.
(Given, $\varepsilon_0 = 8.8 \times 10^{-12}$ C^2 N^{-1} m^{-2}) **(2021 Main)**

26. The electric field in a plane electromagnetic wave is given by

$$E = 200 \cos\left[\left(\frac{0.5 \times 10^3}{m}\right)x - \left(1.5 \times 10^{11} \frac{rad}{s} \times t\right)\right]\frac{V}{m}\hat{j}$$

If this wave falls normally on a perfectly reflecting surface having an area of 100 cm^2. If the radiation pressure exerted by the EM wave on the surface during a 10 min exposure is $\frac{x}{10^9} \frac{N}{m^2}$.

Find the value of x. **(2021 Main)**

27. A point source of light is placed at the centre of curvature of a hemispherical surface. The source emits a power of 24 W. The radius of curvature of hemisphere is 10 cm and the inner surface is completely reflecting. The force on the hemisphere due to the light falling on it is .... $\times 10^{-8}$ N. **(2023 Main)**

28. If 2.5×10^{-6} N average force is exerted by a light wave on a non-reflecting surface of 30 cm^2 area during 40 min of time span, the energy flux of light just before it falls on the surface is .... W/cm^2.

(Round off to the nearest integer)

(Assume complete adsorption and normal incidence conditions are there)

(2021 Main)

29. A radiation is emitted by 1000 W bulb and it generates an electric field and magnetic field at P, placed at a distance of 2 m. The efficiency of the bulb is 1.25%. The value of peak, electric field at P is $x \times 10^{-1}$ V/m. Value of x is ....

(Rounded-off to the nearest integers)

(2021 Main)

[Take, $\varepsilon_0 = 8.85 \times 10^{-12} C^2 N^{-1} m^{-2}, c = 3 \times 10^8 ms^{-1}$]

Answers

1. (b) **2.** (c) **3.** (a) **4.** (b) **5.** (b) **6.** (c) **7.** (a) **8.** (c) **9.** (b) **10.** (c)
11. (c) **12.** (d) **13.** (b) **14.** (b) **15.** (b, d) **16.** (a, c, d) **17.** (a, d) **18.** No, No
19. The speed in vacuum is the same for all **20.** 4.3×10^8 N/C, 1.43 T **21.** (a) 1.5×10^{-2} m (b) 1.6×10^{-7} T
22. (5) **23.** (43) **24.** (15) **25.** (500) **26.** (354) **27.** (4) **28.** (25) **29.** (137)

See hints on pages 18-20.

Hints & SOLUTIONS

Module 1.

1. In case of perfectly non-reflecting surface,

$$\Delta p = \frac{E}{c}$$

where, $E = 20 \times 30 \times 30 \times 60$

$$= 1.08 \times 10^6 \text{ J}$$

$$\therefore \quad \Delta p = \frac{1.08 \times 10^6}{3 \times 10^8} = 36 \times 10^{-4} \text{ kg-m/s}$$

2. We know that radiation pressure,

$$p = \frac{I}{c}$$

$$\Rightarrow \quad \frac{F}{A} = \frac{I}{c}$$

$$\Rightarrow \quad F = \frac{IA}{c} = \frac{\Delta p}{\Delta t}$$

$$\Rightarrow \quad \Delta p = \frac{I}{c} A \Delta t$$

$$= \frac{(25 \times 25) \times 10^4 \times 10^{-4} \times 40 \times 60}{3 \times 10^8} \text{ N-s}$$

$$= 5 \times 10^{-3} \text{ N-s}$$

3. We know that force exerted,

$$F = (1 + r)\frac{IA}{c}$$

$$= \frac{(1 + 0.25) \times 50 \times 1}{3 \times 10^8}$$

$$\simeq 20 \times 10^{-8} \text{ N}$$

4. Theory based question.

5. Energy of one photon $= \frac{hc}{\lambda}$

Energy radiated per second $= P$

$\therefore$ Number of photons radiated per second,

$$N = \frac{\text{Energy radiated per second}}{\text{Energy of one photon}}$$

or $$N = \frac{P}{hc/\lambda} = \frac{P\lambda}{hc}$$

At a distance r, these photons are falling on an area $4\pi r^2$. Therefore density of photons = number of photons per unit area per unit time

$$= \frac{N}{4\pi r^2} = \frac{P\lambda}{(4\pi r^2)(hc)}$$

Substituting the proper values this comes out to be,

$6 \times 10^{13} \text{ cm}^{-2} \text{ s}^{-1}$

Module 2.

1. Electromagnetic waves do not require any material medium for their propagation. They are transverse in nature like light. They carry both energy and momentum.

A changing electric field produces a changing magnetic field and *vice-versa*. which gives rise to a transverse wave known as electromagnetic wave.

2. In option (b), electromagnetic wave is travelling towards positive x-direction, as ωt and kx have opposite signs. Oscillations of y are taking place along y- direction as the expression starts from E_y.

c should be along $\mathbf{E} \times \mathbf{B}$. So, oscillations of $\mathbf{B}$ must be along z-direction.

3. $\lambda = 3 \text{ mm}$, $E_0 = 66 \text{ V/m}$

$$c = \frac{E_0}{B_0}$$

$$B_0 = \frac{E_0}{c} = \frac{66}{3 \times 10^8} = 2.2 \times 10^{-7} \text{ T}$$

$$\omega = 2\pi f = \frac{2\pi c}{\lambda} = \frac{2\pi \times 3 \times 10^8}{3 \times 10^{-3}}$$

$$= 2\pi \times 10^{11} \text{ rad/s}$$

$$c = \frac{\omega}{k}$$

$$\therefore \quad k = \frac{\omega}{c}$$

Therefore, the correct option is (d).

4. Speed of EM wave in medium,

$$v = \frac{c}{\sqrt{\mu_r \varepsilon_r}}$$

$$\Rightarrow \quad 2 \times 10^8 = \frac{3 \times 10^8}{\sqrt{1 \times \varepsilon_r}}$$

$$\Rightarrow \quad \sqrt{\varepsilon_r} = 1.5$$

$$\Rightarrow \quad \varepsilon_r = 1.5^2$$

$$= 2.25$$

5. Given, $E = 50 \sin(500x - 10 \times 10^{10} t)$

$$v = \frac{\omega}{K} = \frac{10 \times 10^{10}}{500}$$

$$= 2 \times 10^8 \text{ m/s}$$

$$\Rightarrow \quad v = \frac{2}{3} \times 3 \times 10^8 \text{ m/s}$$

$$= \frac{2c}{3}$$

6. Given,

$$\mathbf{E} = \hat{\mathbf{i}}\, 40 \cos \omega \left(t - \frac{z}{c}\right) \frac{\text{N}}{\text{C}}$$

Compare it with standard equation,

$$\mathbf{E} = \mathbf{E}_0 \cos \omega t$$

$$\mathbf{E}_0 = 40\hat{\mathbf{i}}$$

Using the relation for magnitude,

$$B_0 = \frac{E_0}{c}$$

and as $c = \mathbf{E} \times \mathbf{B}$, B should be along y-axis.

$$\therefore \quad \mathbf{B} = \hat{\mathbf{j}} \frac{40}{c} \cos \omega \left(t - \frac{z}{c}\right)$$

Hence, correct option is (c).

7. As, $\frac{E_0}{B_0} = c = \frac{\omega}{k}$

$$\Rightarrow \quad kE_0 = \omega B_0$$

8. Given,

$$\mathbf{B} = 3 \times 10^{-8} \sin (1.6 \times 10^3 x + 48 \times 10^{10} t)$$

We know that,

$$E_0 = B_0 \times c$$
$$= 3 \times 10^{-8} \times 3 \times 10^8 = 9 \text{ V/m}$$

$\therefore$ Expression for electric field,

$$\mathbf{E} = 9 \sin(1.6 \times 10^3 x + 48 \times 10^{10} t)\, \hat{\mathbf{k}} \text{ V/m}$$

9. We know that, $c = \frac{E_0}{B_0}$

$$\Rightarrow \quad \mathbf{E} = cB_0 \sin(kx + \omega t)\, \hat{\mathbf{k}} \text{ V/m}$$

Further **c** is along $\mathbf{E} \times \mathbf{B}$.

10. **E**, **B** and velocity of electromagnetic waves are mutually perpendicular.

c is along $\mathbf{E} \times \mathbf{B}$.

11. $\lambda = \frac{c}{f}$

$$\lambda_1 = \frac{3 \times 10^8}{7.5 \times 10^6} = 40 \text{ m}$$

$$\lambda_2 = \frac{3 \times 10^8}{12 \times 10^6} = 25 \text{ m}$$

12. (a) $c = \frac{E_0}{B_0}$

$$\therefore \quad B_0 = \frac{E_0}{c}$$

$$\omega = 2\pi f$$

$$c = v = \frac{\omega}{k}$$

$$\therefore \quad k = \frac{\omega}{c}$$

$$\lambda = \frac{2\pi}{k}$$

c is along $\mathbf{E} \times \mathbf{B}$.

Module 3.

1. Optical communication is performed in the frequency range of 1 THz to 1000 THz.

From microwave to UV range.

So, EM wave used for optical communication have shorter wavelength than that of microwaves used in RADAR.

Also, $\quad \nu_{\text{infrared}} > \nu_{\text{microwaves}}$

$\therefore$ Infrared EM waves are more energetic than microwave.

Hence, Assertion is false and Reason is true.

2. Cosmic rays are showers of subatomic particles coming from beyond our solar system or from distant galaxies and super nova. They mainly contain protons, nucleus of atoms and other subatomic particles.

3. The correct order of waves in ascending order of wavelength is as

$$\lambda_{\gamma\text{-rays}} < \lambda_{\text{X-rays}} < \lambda_{\text{visible}} < \lambda_{\text{microwaves}}$$

4. The order of differents EM wave in decreasing order of wavelength is as $\lambda_{\text{radiowaves}} > \lambda_{\text{microwaves}} > \lambda_{\text{visible}} > \lambda_{\text{X-rays}}$

5. Radiowave < yellow light < blue light < X-rays (Increasing order of energy)

$$\because \quad E = h\nu$$

ν is frequency and is minimum for radio wave.

6. As microwave oven heats food by passing microwave radiation through food. It acts on the principle of giving vibrational energy to water molecules.

7. The arrangement in ascending order of wavelength is as follow Gamma rays < X-rays < Ultra violet < Visible rays < Infrared rays < Microwaves < Radiowaves.

8. As we know that,

$$E = \frac{hc}{\lambda} \Rightarrow \lambda = \frac{hc}{E}$$

$$\Rightarrow \quad \lambda = \frac{6.6 \times 10^{-34} \times 3 \times 10^8}{11 \times 1000 \times 1.6 \times 10^{-19}}$$

$$= 12.4 \text{ Å}$$

Which belongs to X-ray region.

9.

EM Wave	Wavelength range
Microwave	0.1 m to 1 mm
Ultraviolet	400 nm to 1 nm
X-rays	1 nm to 10^{-3} nm
Infrared	1 mm to 700 nm

Hence, A $\rightarrow$ IV, B $\rightarrow$ I, C $\rightarrow$ II, D $\rightarrow$ III

10. UV-rays are used in water purification.

X-rays are used for diagnosing fracture.

Microwave are used for mobile and radar communication. Infrared waves show less scattering effect, therefore these waves are used in foggy days.

Hence, option (b) is correct.

11. As we know that;
   A. Source of microwave frequency is magnetron.
   B. Source of infrared frequency is vibration of atoms and molecules.
   C. Source of gamma ray is radioactive decay of nucleus.
   D. Source of X-ray is transition of electron in inner shells.

   ∴ The correct match is

   $$A \to (2),\ B \to (4),\ C \to (1),\ D \to (3).$$

12. A-1
   Infrared waves are used to treat muscular pain due to its heating nature.
   B-2
   Radiowaves are used in broadcasting due to its large wavelength.
   C-3
   X-rays are used in medicine to detect the fracture of bones.
   D-4
   Ultraviolet rays are absorbed by ozone layer in atmosphere.

Unit Exercise (Cumulative)

1. Electromagnetic waves are photon stream and they are not deflected by electric or magnetic fields.
   Also, $\frac{E_0}{B_0} = c = \frac{1}{\sqrt{\varepsilon_0 \mu_0}}$

2. 11 eV energy radiation lies in UV range.

3. Total average energy density is the sum of the electric field energy density and magnetic field energy density.

4. $\frac{B^2}{2\mu_0} = \frac{1}{2}\varepsilon_0 E^2$

   $$\therefore \quad E = \frac{B}{\sqrt{\varepsilon_0 \mu_0}} = cB$$
   $$= (3 \times 10^8)(10^{-5})$$
   $$= 3 \times 10^3 \text{ V/m}$$

5. Intensity $I = \frac{P}{4\pi R^2} = \left(\frac{1}{2}\varepsilon_0 E_0^2\right) \times (c)$

   or $$\frac{P}{4\pi R^2} = \frac{1}{2}\varepsilon_0 E_0^2 \times c$$

   $$\therefore \quad E_0 = \sqrt{\frac{P}{2\pi R^2 \varepsilon_0 c}}$$

   Substituting the values, we get
   $$E_0 = 54.77 \text{ V/m}$$

6. Average total energy density
   $$= 2\left[\frac{1}{2}\varepsilon_0 E_{rms}^2\right] = \varepsilon_0 E_{rms}^2$$
   $$= 8.86 \times 10^{-12} \times (720)^2$$
   $$= 4.58 \times 10^{-6} \text{ J/m}^3$$

7. EM wave
   $$E = 200 \sin[1.5 \times 10^7 t - 0.05x] \frac{\text{N}}{\text{C}}$$
   $$I = \frac{1}{2}\varepsilon_0 E_0^2 \cdot c = \frac{1}{2}\varepsilon_0 E_0^2 \cdot \left(\frac{\omega}{k}\right)$$
   $$= \frac{1}{2} \times 8.85 \times 10^{-12} \times [200]^2 \times \frac{1.5 \times 10^7}{0.05}$$
   $$I = 53.1 \text{ W/m}^2$$

8. Given, $E = E_0 \sin(\omega t - kx)$
   $$B = B_0 \sin(\omega t - kx)$$
   In EM waves, average electric energy density is equal to average magnetic energy density.
   $$\frac{1}{4}\varepsilon_0 E_0^2 = \frac{1}{4\mu_0} B_0^2$$
   Hence, the ratio is 1.

9. Energy of electromagnetic wave remains constant with time. But frequency of change of magnetic energy into electric and electric into magnetic occurs at frequency double the frequency of wave.

10. Given,
   $$\mathbf{E} = 20 \sin \omega\left(t - \frac{x}{c}\right) \quad \text{[Given] ...(i)}$$
   $$\mathbf{E} = E_0 \sin \omega\left(t - \frac{x}{c}\right) \quad \text{...(ii)}$$
   On comparing Eqs. (i) and (ii), we get
   $$E_0 = 20$$
   $$\text{Energy density} = \frac{1}{2}\varepsilon_0 E_0^2$$
   $$= \frac{1}{2} \times 8.85 \times 10^{-12} \times 400 \text{ J/m}^3$$
   Energy contained in the given volumes
   $$= 200 \times 8.85 \times 10^{-12} \times 5 \times 10^{-4}$$
   $$= 8.85 \times 10^{-12} \times 10^{-4} \times 1000 = 8.85 \times 10^{-13} \text{ J}$$

11. Given, $\varepsilon_r = 81$
   $$c = 3 \times 10^8 \text{ m/s}$$
   Velocity of light in distilled water is
   $$v = \frac{c}{\sqrt{\mu_r \varepsilon_r}}$$
   $$\Rightarrow \quad v = \frac{3 \times 10^8}{\sqrt{1 \times 81}} = 3.33 \times 10^7 \text{ m/s}$$

12. Intensity of EM wave is given by
   $$\Rightarrow \quad I = \frac{\text{Power}}{\text{Area}} = \frac{1}{2}\varepsilon_0 E_0^2 c$$
   $$\Rightarrow \quad \frac{27 \times 10^{-3}}{10 \times 10^{-6}} = \frac{1}{2} \times 9 \times 10^{-12} \times E_0^2 \times 3 \times 10^8$$
   $$\Rightarrow \quad E_0 = \sqrt{2} \times 10^3 \text{ kV/m}$$
   $$E_0 = 1.4 \text{ kV/m}$$

13. As we know, $\mathbf{E}\cdot\mathbf{B}=0 \because [\mathbf{E}\perp\mathbf{B}]$

and $\mathbf{E}\times\mathbf{B}$ should be along z-direction

Thus, $(-2\hat{\mathbf{i}}-3\hat{\mathbf{j}})\times(3\hat{\mathbf{i}}-2\hat{\mathbf{j}})=13\hat{\mathbf{k}}$

14. We know that velocity of electromagnetic signal,

$$v=\frac{E_0}{B_0}=\frac{2.25}{1.5\times10^{-8}}=\frac{2.25\times10^{8}}{1.5}=1.5\times10^{8}\text{ m/s}$$

$$t=\frac{\text{Total distance}}{\text{velocity of work}}=\frac{6\times10^{3}}{1.5\times10^{8}}=4\times10^{-5}\text{ s}$$

15. Every accelerated charged particle produces electromagnetic waves.

16. $\lambda=\frac{c}{f}=\frac{3\times10^{8}}{10^{9}}=0.3\text{ m}$

This wavelength lies in radio waves region.

17. (i) $\mu=\frac{c}{v}=\frac{c}{\omega/k}=\frac{kc}{\omega}$

$$=\frac{\left(\frac{2\pi\times10^{7}}{3}\right)(3\times10^{8})}{2\pi\times5\times10^{14}}=2$$

(ii) $v=\frac{c}{\mu}=\frac{3\times10^{8}}{2}$

$$=1.5\times10^{8}\text{ m/s}$$

(iii) Wave is travelling along +ve z direction, because ωt and kz are of opposite signs.

(iv) Unit vector along **E** is

$$\hat{\mathbf{E}}=\frac{2\hat{\mathbf{i}}+\hat{\mathbf{j}}}{|2\hat{\mathbf{i}}+\hat{\mathbf{j}}|}=\frac{2\hat{\mathbf{i}}+\hat{\mathbf{j}}}{\sqrt{5}}$$

So, **E** can also be written as,

$$\mathbf{E}=30\sqrt{5}\,\hat{\mathbf{E}}\sin\left[2\pi\left(5\times10^{14}t-\frac{10^{7}}{3}z\right)\right]\frac{\text{V}}{\text{m}}$$

(v) **v** is along $\hat{\mathbf{E}}$ and $\hat{\mathbf{B}}$ and all three are mutually perpendicular.

So, we can see that,

$$\hat{\mathbf{B}}=\hat{\mathbf{v}}\times\hat{\mathbf{E}} \quad (\hat{\mathbf{v}}\text{ is along }\hat{\mathbf{k}}\text{ direction})$$

$$=(\hat{\mathbf{k}})\times\left(\frac{2\hat{\mathbf{i}}+\hat{\mathbf{j}}}{\sqrt{5}}\right)$$

$$=\frac{1}{\sqrt{5}}(2\hat{\mathbf{j}}-\hat{\mathbf{i}})$$

Further, $v=\frac{E_0}{B_0}$

$$\therefore\quad B_0=\frac{E_0}{v}=\frac{30\sqrt{5}}{1.5\times10^{8}}=2\sqrt{5}\times10^{-7}\text{T}$$

Now, $\mathbf{B}=(B_0)\hat{\mathbf{B}}\sin\left[2\pi\left(5\times10^{14}t-\frac{10^{7}}{3}\right)z\right]\text{T}$

$$=(2\sqrt{5}\times10^{-7})\left(\frac{1}{\sqrt{5}}\right)(2\hat{\mathbf{j}}-\hat{\mathbf{i}})\sin\left[2\pi\left(5\times10^{14}t-\frac{10^{7}}{3}z\right)\right]\text{T}$$

$$=(2\times10^{-7})(2\hat{\mathbf{j}}-\hat{\mathbf{i}})\sin\left[2\pi\left(5\times10^{14}t-\frac{10^{7}}{3}z\right)\right]\text{T}$$

$$\therefore\quad B_x=-2\times10^{7}\sin\left[2\pi\left(5\times10^{14}t-\frac{10^{7}}{3}z\right)\right]\text{T}$$

and $B_y=4\times10^{7}\sin\left[2\pi\left(5\times10^{14}t-\frac{10^{7}}{3}z\right)\right]\text{T}$

(vi) Polarization angle $\theta=\tan^{-1}\left(\frac{E_y}{E_x}\right)=\tan^{-1}\left(\frac{1}{2}\right)$

18. Theory based question.

19. Theory based question.

20. $I_E=\frac{I}{2}=\frac{1}{2}\varepsilon_0E^2c$

$$=\frac{1}{2}\varepsilon_0\left(\frac{E_0}{\sqrt{2}}\right)^2c$$

$$\therefore\quad E_0=\sqrt{\frac{2I}{\varepsilon_0c}}=\sqrt{\frac{2\times2.5\times10^{14}}{8.86\times10^{-12}\times3\times10^{8}}}=4.3\times10^{8}\text{ N/C}$$

Now, $c=\frac{E_0}{B_0}$

or $B_0=\frac{E_0}{c}$

21. (a) $\lambda=\frac{c}{f}$

(b) $c=\frac{E_0}{B_0}$ or $B_0=\frac{E_0}{c}$

(c) $u_E=\frac{1}{2}\varepsilon_0E^2=\frac{1}{2}\varepsilon_0\left(\frac{E_0}{\sqrt{2}}\right)^2=\frac{1}{4}\varepsilon_0E_0^2$

Similarly, $u_B=\frac{B_0^2}{4\mu_0}$

After substituting the values we get,

$$u_E=u_B$$

22. Given that speed in medium,

$$v = 0.2\,c$$

Refractive index, $n = \frac{c}{v}$

$$n = \frac{c}{0.2\,c} = 5$$

$$\therefore \quad n = \sqrt{\mu_r \varepsilon_r}$$

$$\text{or} \quad n^2 = \mu_r \varepsilon_r$$

$$\text{or} \quad \frac{\varepsilon_r}{n} = \frac{n}{\mu_r} = \frac{5}{1}$$

On comparing with $\frac{\varepsilon_r}{n} = \frac{x}{1}$, we get

$$x = 5$$

23. As we know that,

$$I = \frac{B^2 c}{2\mu_0}$$

$$\Rightarrow \quad B = \sqrt{\frac{2\mu_0 I}{c}} = \sqrt{\frac{2 \times 4\pi \times 10^{-7} \times 0.22}{3 \times 10^8}}$$

$$= 4.29 \times 10^{-8}\ \text{T}$$

$$\simeq 43 \times 10^{-9}\ \text{T}$$

24. Given, $\nu = 5\ \text{GHz} = 5 \times 10^9\ \text{Hz}$

$$\varepsilon_r = 2$$

$$\mu_r = 2$$

Since speed of light in a medium,

$$v = \frac{1}{\sqrt{\mu\varepsilon}}$$

$$= \frac{1}{\sqrt{\mu_r \mu_0 \varepsilon_r \varepsilon_0}} = \frac{c}{\sqrt{\mu_r \varepsilon_r}}$$

$$\therefore \quad v = \frac{3 \times 10^8}{\sqrt{4}} = \frac{30 \times 10^7}{2}\ \text{m/s}$$

$$= 15 \times 10^7\ \text{m/s}$$

25. Expression of EM wave is given as $E = 50 \sin\left(\omega t - \frac{\omega}{c} x\right)$

$$[\because E_0 = 50\ \text{NC}^{-1}]$$

Thus, energy density $= \frac{1}{2} \varepsilon_0 E_0^2$

$\Rightarrow$ Energy = energy density × volume

$$\Rightarrow \quad \frac{1}{2} \varepsilon_0 E_0^2 \cdot V = 5.5 \times 10^{-12}$$

$$\Rightarrow \quad \frac{1}{2} 8.8 \times 10^{-12} \times (50)^2 \times V = 5.5 \times 10^{-12}$$

$$\Rightarrow \quad V = \frac{5.5 \times 2}{2500 \times 8.8} = 500\ \text{cm}^3$$

26. We know that, intensity of EM wave

$$I = \frac{1}{2} \varepsilon_0 E_0^2 c$$

$\therefore$ Radiation pressure reflecting surface

$$p = \frac{2I}{c} = \frac{2}{c} \times \frac{1}{2} \varepsilon_0 E_0^2 c = \varepsilon_0 E_0^2$$

$$= 8.85 \times 10^{-12} \times 200^2$$

$$= 8.85 \times 10^{-8} \times 4 = \frac{354}{10^9}\ \text{N/m}^2$$

Hence, $x = 354$

27. Radiation pressure over a perfectly reflecting surface is given by $p = \frac{2I}{c}$

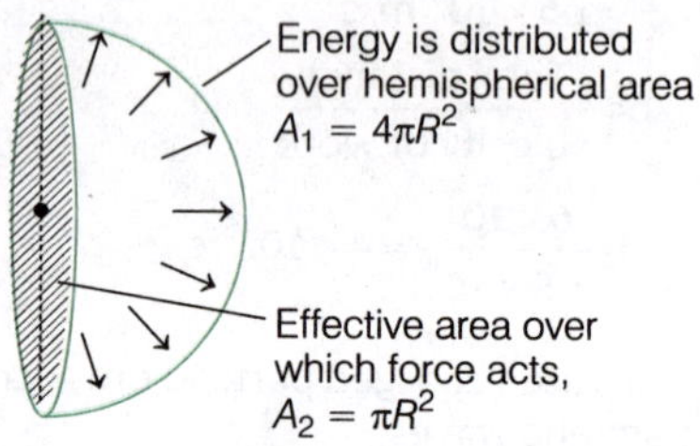

Now, Intensity $I = \frac{\text{Energy}}{\text{Area} \times \text{time}} = \frac{\text{Power}}{\text{Area}}$

So, force on hemispherical surface,

$$F = p \times A_2 = \frac{2I}{c} \times A_2$$

$$= \frac{2(P / A_1) \times A_2}{c}$$

$$= \frac{2 \times 24 \times \pi R^2}{4\pi R^2 \times 3 \times 10^8}$$

$$= 4 \times 10^{-8}\ \text{N}$$

28. Given,

$$F = 2.5 \times 10^{-6}\ \text{N},$$

$$A = 30\ \text{cm}^2, I = ?$$

Radiation pressure for absorbing surface,

$$p = \frac{I}{c} \quad \text{or} \quad \frac{F}{A} = \frac{I}{c}$$

$$\Rightarrow \quad I = \frac{F \times c}{A}$$

$$\Rightarrow \quad I = \frac{2.5 \times 10^{-6} \times 3 \times 10^8}{30}$$

$$= 25\ \text{W cm}^{-2}$$

29. As we know that,

$$I = \frac{\eta P}{4\pi r^2} = \frac{1}{2} \varepsilon_0 E_0^2 c$$

$$\Rightarrow \quad \frac{0.0125 \times 1000}{4 \times 3.14 \times 2^2}$$

$$= \frac{1}{2} \times 8.85 \times 10^{-12} \times 3 \times 10^8 E_0^2$$

$$\Rightarrow \quad E_0 = 13.69\ \text{V/m}$$

$$= 136.89 \times 10^{-1}\ \text{V/m}$$

$$\therefore \quad x = 137 \quad \text{(Rounding off to nearest integer)}$$

UNIT-8

REFLECTION OF LIGHT

Learning Modules

1. General Concepts used in Geometrical Optics
2. Reflection from a Plane Mirror
3. Reflection from a Spherical Mirror

MODULE 1

General Concepts used in Geometrical Optics

Introduction

The branch of physics called **optics** deals with the behaviour of light and other electromagnetic waves. Light is the principal means by which we gain knowledge of the world.

Consequently, the nature of light has been the source of one of the longest debates in the history of science.

Electromagnetic radiation with wavelengths in the range of about 4000 Å to 7000 Å, to which eye is sensitive is called light.

In the present and next two units we will investigate the behaviour of a beam of light when it encounters simple optical devices like mirrors, lenses and apertures. Under many circumstances, the wavelength of light is negligible compared with the dimensions of the device as in the case of ordinary mirrors and lenses.

A light beam can then be treated as a ray whose propagation is governed by simple geometric rules. The part of optics that deals with such phenomena is known as **geometric optics.**

However, if the wavelength is not negligible compared with the dimensions of the device (for example a very narrow slit), the ray approximation becomes invalid and we have to examine the behaviour of light in terms of its wave properties. This study is known as **physical optics.**

General Concepts used in Geometrical Optics

Some general concepts which are used in whole geometrical optics are given below.

1. Normal incidence means angle of incidence (with normal) is 0°. If angle of incidence is 90°, it is called grazing incidence.

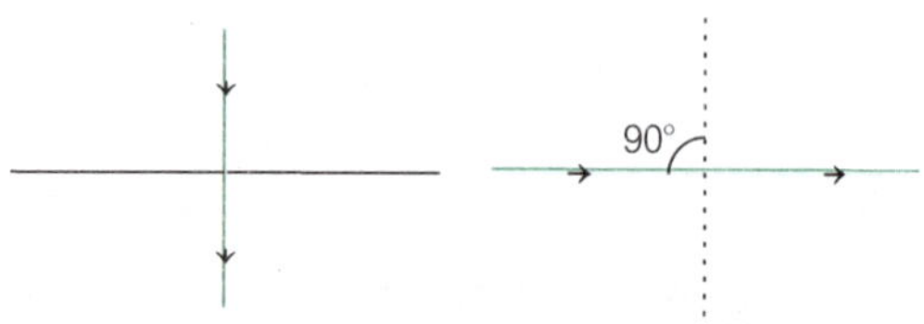

Normal incidence $\angle i = 0°$ Grazing incidence $\angle i = 90°$

2. An image is formed either by reflection or refraction. Minimum two (reflected or refracted) rays are required for image formation. More the number of rays, more will be the intensity of image.

3. A light is reflected only from a silvered surface. Without any reflecting surface on the path of ray of light it keeps on moving ahead.

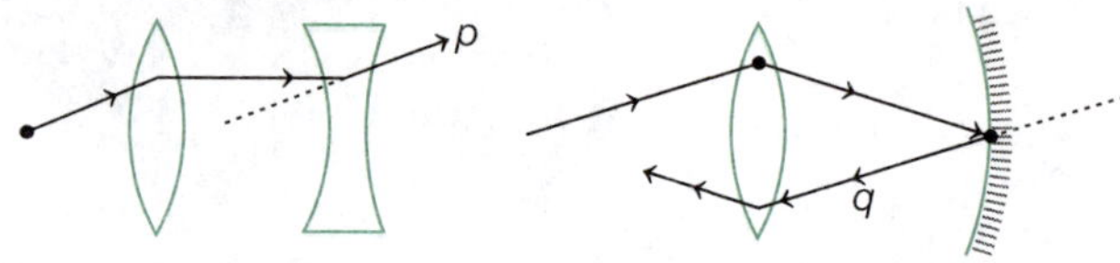

(i)   (ii)

In figure (i) For image formation, if refracted ray-p is required to the left of concave lens, then we will take it as dotted line.

In figure (ii) For image formation, if reflected ray-q is required to the right of concave mirror, then we will take it as dotted line.

4. **Real object, virtual object, real image, virtual image**

The point where the rays meet (or appear to meet) before refraction or reflection is called object and the point where the rays meet (or appear to meet) after refraction or reflection is called image. Further, object (or image) is real if dark lines meet and virtual if dotted lines meet.

In figure (a), object is real, while image is virtual.

In figure (b), object is virtual while its image is real.

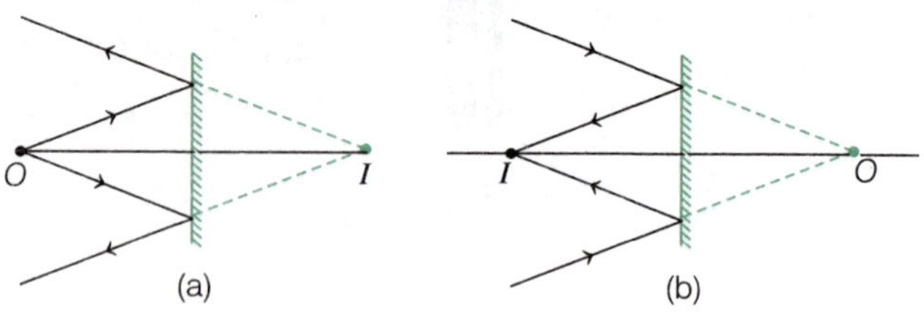

(a)   (b)

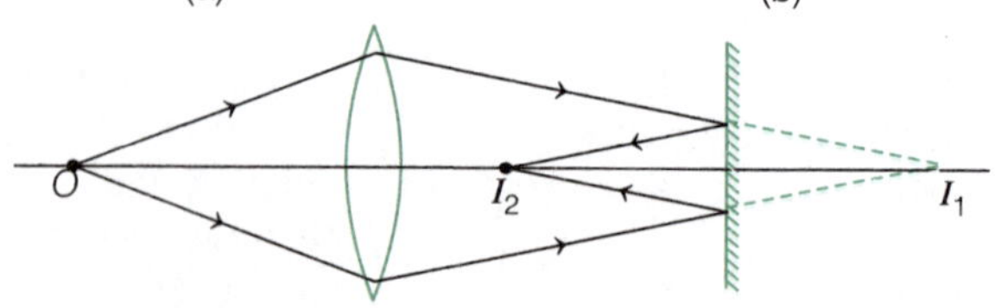

(c)

In figure (c), the object O is real. Its image formed by the lens (i.e. I_1) is real. But, it acts as a virtual object for mirror which forms its real image I_2.

5. The virtual images cannot be taken on screen. But, they can be seen by our eye. Because our eye lens forms their real image on our retina. Thus, if we put a screen at I in the above figure (a) no image will be formed on it. At the same time if we put the screen at I in figure (b), image will be formed.
6. Normally, the object is kept on the left hand side of the optical instrument (mirror, lens etc.), i.e. the ray of light travels from left to right. Sometimes, it may happen that the light is travelling in opposite direction. See the figure.

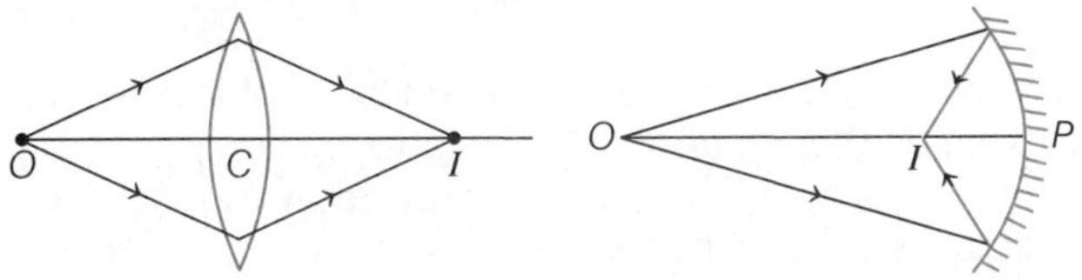

(a) $O \rightarrow$ Object $I \rightarrow$ Image (b)

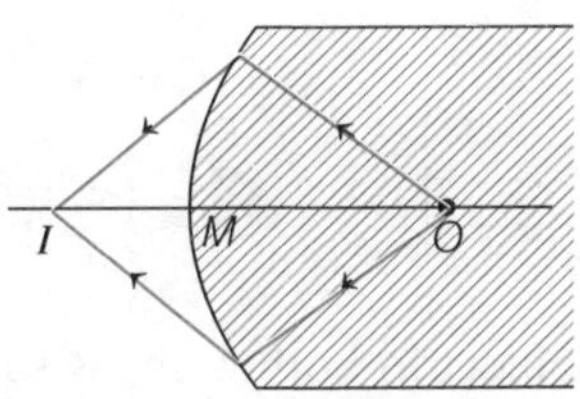

(c)

In figures (a) and (b), light is travelling from left to right and in figure (c) it is travelling from right to left.

7. **Sign convention** The distances measured along the incident light are taken as positive while the distances against incident light are taken as negative. For example, in figures (a) and (b) the incident light travels from left to right. So, the distances measured in this direction are positive. While in figure (c) the incident light travels from right to left. So, in this case right to left direction will be positive. Distances are measured from pole of the mirror [point P in figure (b)], optical centre of the lens [point C in figure (a)] and the centre of the refracting surface [point M in figure (c)].

It may happen in some problem that sign convention does not remain same for the whole problem.

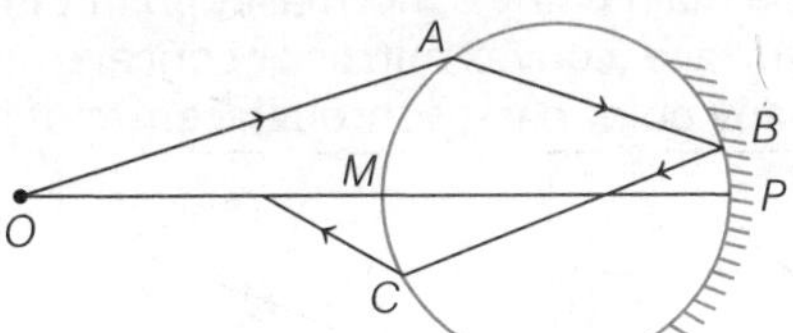

For example, in the figure shown, the ray of light starting from O first undergoes refraction at A, then reflection at B and then finally refraction at C. For refraction and reflection at A and B the incident light is travelling from left to right, so distances measured along this direction are positive. For final refraction at C the incident light travels from right to left, so now the sign convention will change or right to left is positive.

8. Object distance (from P, C or M along the optic axis) in above figure (in Point 6) is shown by u and image distance by v.
9. In front of mirror, object (or image) is always real, lines are always dark and u (or v) are always negative.

Behind the mirror, object (or image) is always virtual, lines are always dotted and u (or v) are always positive.

This is because light always falls from front side of the mirror.

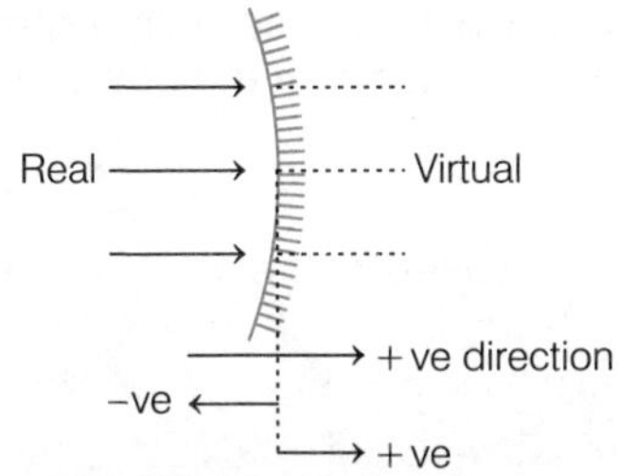

10. In most of the cases, objects are real (whether refraction or reflection) and u for them is negative.

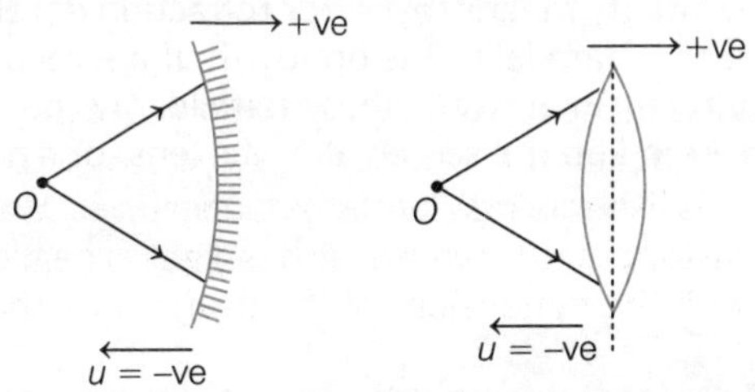

11. In case of mirror light always falls from front of the mirror. But in a lens (or some other refracting surface like slab) light can fall from both sides.

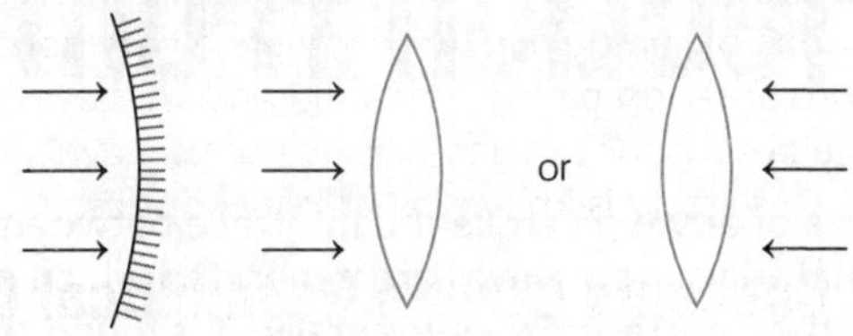

12. **Total steps and reduced steps**

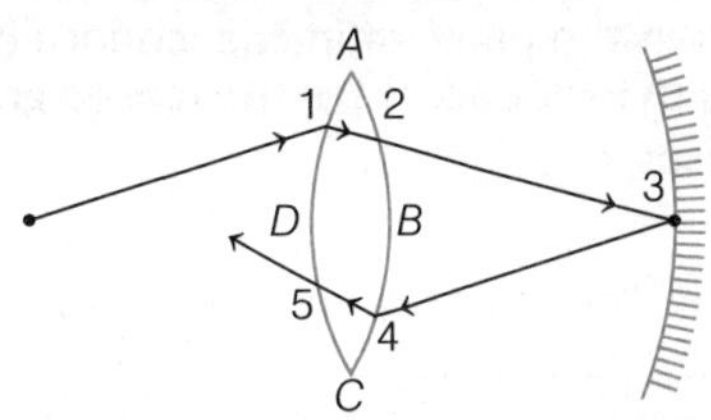

In the figure shown above total steps are five. Four of them are refraction. Only third is reflection. But we have made a lens formula for steps 1 and 2 or 4 and 5. So, the reduced steps are three,

lens $\rightarrow$ mirror $\rightarrow$ lens.

13. **Image real or virtual** In above figure, if we wish to find the nature of I_2 (after 2nd refraction), then it is real if it is formed to the right of *ABC* because ray of light has moved to this side and it is virtual to the left of *ABC*. Similarly, I_5 is real to the left of *ADC* and virtual to the right of *ADC*.
14. **Final image coincides with the object** In most of these cases there will be one mirror, plane or spherical (convex or concave) and light will be falling normal ($\angle i = 0°$) to this mirror. In case of spherical mirror it is normal if ray of light passes through centre of curvature.
In case of normal incidence, ray of light retraces its path and final image coincides with the object.

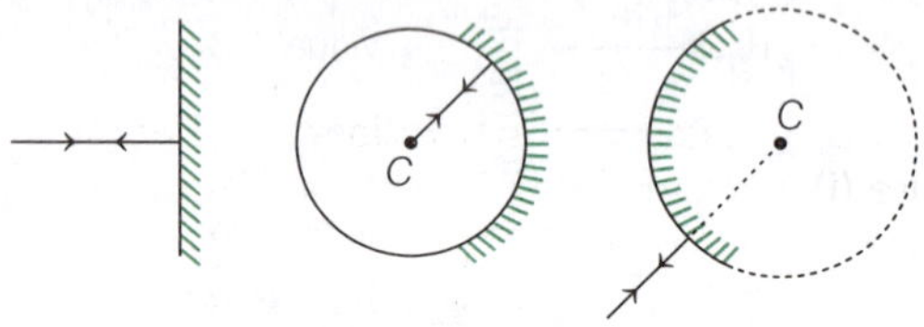

In all above figures, $\angle i = 0°$ (normal incidence). Ray of light retraces its path.

15. Image at infinity means rays after refraction or reflection have become parallel to the optic axis. If a screen is placed directly in between these parallel rays no image will be formed on the screen. But, if a lens (or a mirror) is placed on the path of these parallel rays, then image is formed at focus. Sometimes, our eye plays the role of this lens and the image is formed on our retina.

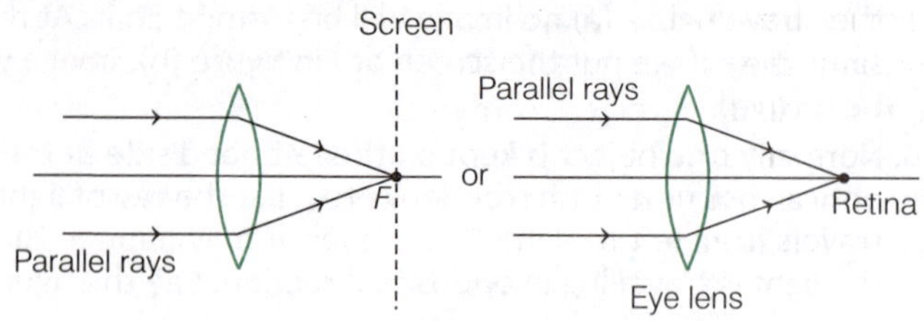

16. **Visual angle θ** Angle subtended by an object on our eye is called the visual angle. The apparent size depends on the visual angle. As the object moves away from the eye, actual size remains the same but visual angle decreases. Therefore, apparent size decreases.

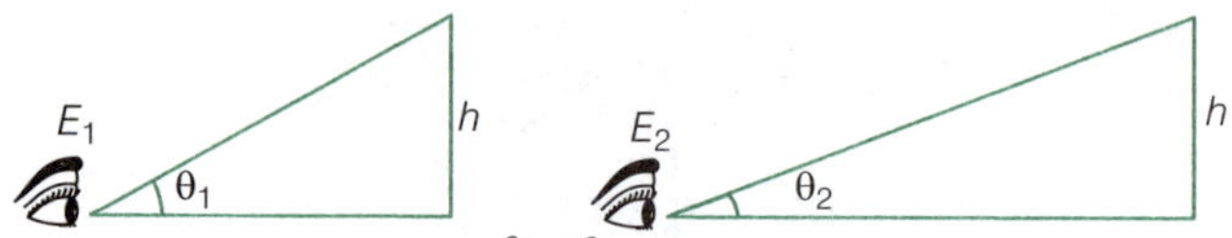

$\theta_2 < \theta_1$

Actual size of object in both cases is same (= *h*). But the apparent size to E_2 is less because the visual angle $\theta_2 < \theta_1$.

MODULE 2

Reflection from a Plane Mirror

When waves of any type strike the interface between two different materials, new waves are generated which move away from the interface. Experimentally, it is found that the rays corresponding to the incident and reflected waves make equal angles with the normal to the interface and that the reflected ray lies in the plane of incidence formed by the incident ray and the normal. Thus, the two laws of reflection can be summarised as under:

(i) $\angle i = \angle r$

(ii) Incident ray, reflected ray and normal lie on the same plane.

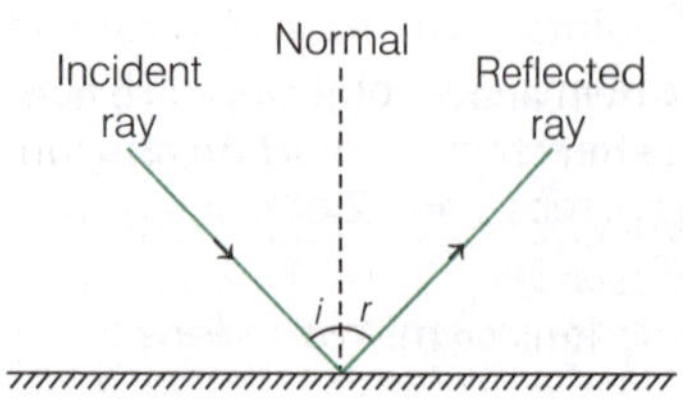

Two Important Points in Reflection Laws

1. The first law $\angle i = \angle r$ can be applied for any type of surface. The main point is, normal at point of incidence. In spherical surface (convex mirror or concave mirror) normal at any point passes through centre of curvature.

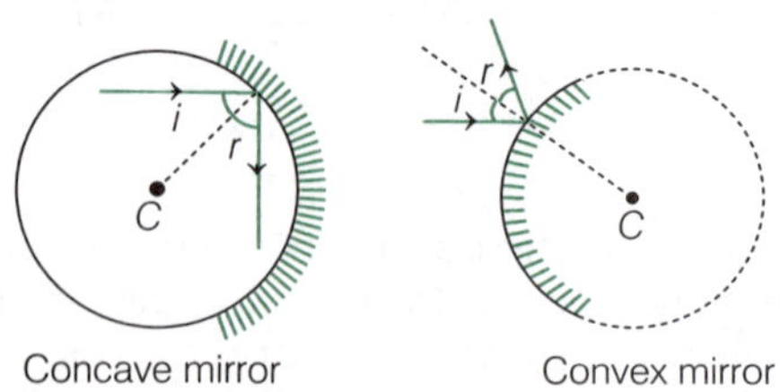

$\angle i = \angle r$

2. Incident ray, reflected ray and normal are sometimes represented in the form of three vectors. Then, these three vectors should be coplanar.

Reflection from a Plane Surface
(or Plane Mirror)

All of us are familiar with the image formed by a plane mirror. If the object is real, the image formed by a plane mirror is virtual, erect, of same size and at the same distance from the mirror. The ray diagram of the image of a point object and of an extended object is as shown below.

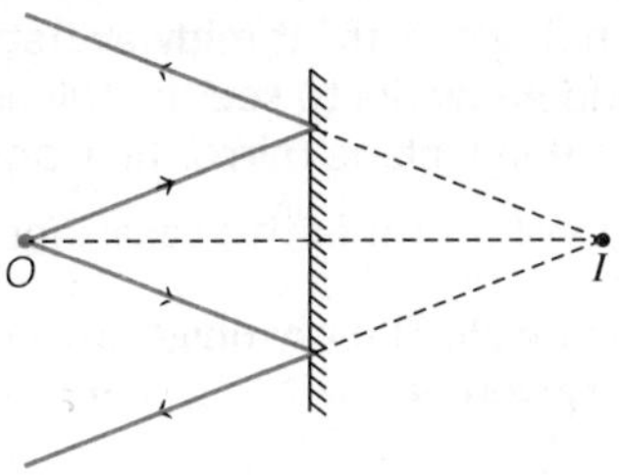

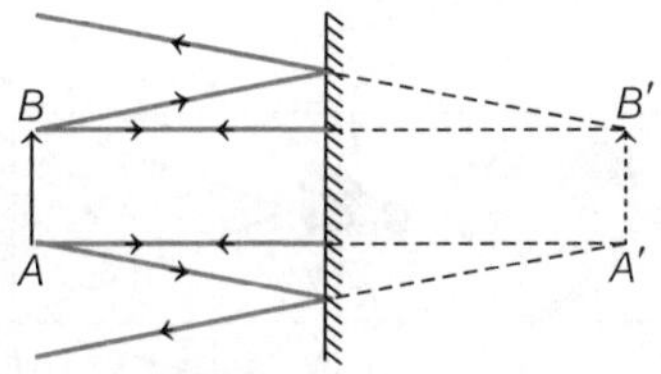

Important Points in Reflection from Plane Mirror

1. Relation between object distance (u) and the image distance (v) in case of plane mirror is

$$\boxed{v = -u}$$

Here, v and u are measured from the plane surface. Two conclusions can be drawn from this equation.

(i) Negative sign implies that object and image are on opposite sides of the mirror. So, if object is real then image is virtual and *vice-versa*.

(ii) $|v| = |u|$

This implies that perpendicular distance of the object from the mirror is equal to the perpendicular distance of image from the mirror.

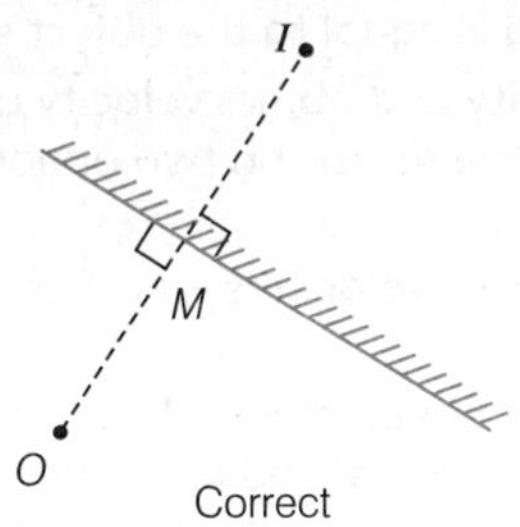

Correct
$OM = MI$

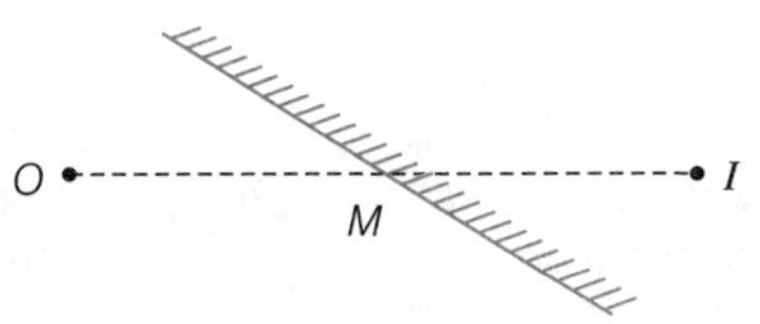

Wrong
$OM = MI$

2. **Ray Diagram** Let us draw the ray diagram of a point object and an extended object.

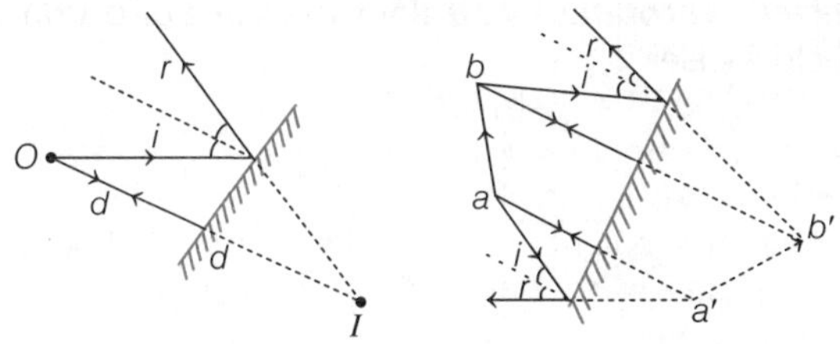

(i) $O \rightarrow$ Real, $I \rightarrow$ Virtual

(ii) $ab \rightarrow$ Real, $a'b' \rightarrow$ Virtual

$$\angle i = \angle r$$

Just as we have drawn the ray diagram of point object O in figure (i), we can also draw the ray diagrams of points a and b as in figure (ii).

3. **Field of view of an object for a given mirror**

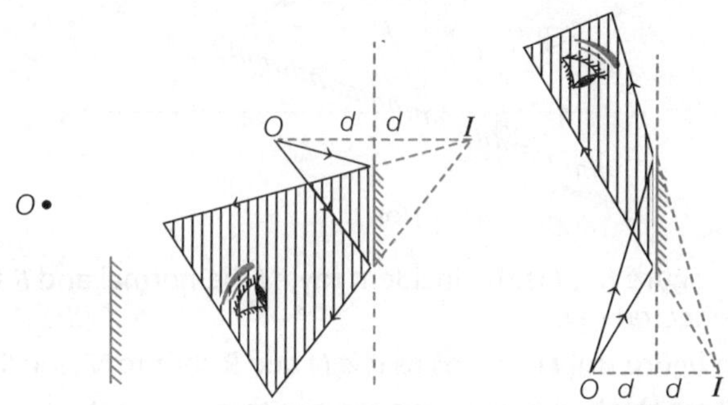

(a) (b) (c)

Suppose a point object O is placed in front of a small mirror as shown in figure (a), then a question arises in mind whether this mirror will make the image of this object or not. Or suppose an elephant is standing in front of a small mirror, will the mirror form the image of the elephant or not. The answer is yes, it will form.

A mirror whatever may be the size of it forms the images of all objects lying in front of it. But every object has its own field of view for the given mirror. The field of view is the region between the extreme reflected rays and depends on the location of the object in front of the mirror.

If our eye lies in the field of view then only we can see the image of the object otherwise not. The field of view of an object placed at different locations in front of a plane mirror are shown in figures (b) and (c).

The region between extreme reflected rays (reflected from the end points of the mirror) is called the field of view. To see the image of object eye should lie in this region, as all reflected rays lie in this region.

Note *Convex mirror gives a wider field of view than a plane mirror. This is the reason why convex mirrors as rear view mirrors in cars or scooters. Although, they make the estimation of distances more difficult but still they are preferred because there is only a small movement of the image for a large movement of the object.*

4. Suppose a mirror is rotated by an angle θ (say anti-clockwise), keeping the incident ray fixed then the reflected ray rotates by 2θ along the same direction, i.e. anti-clockwise.

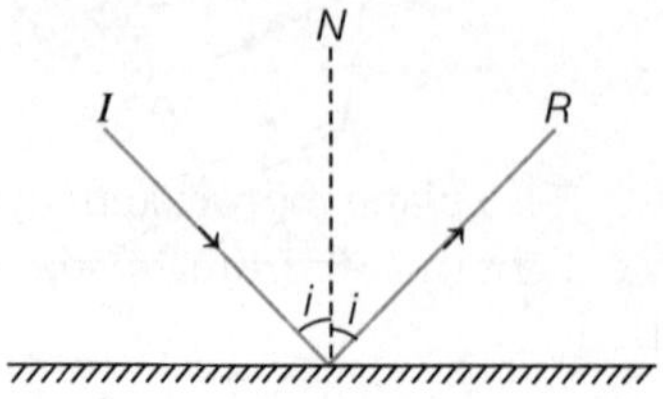

(a)

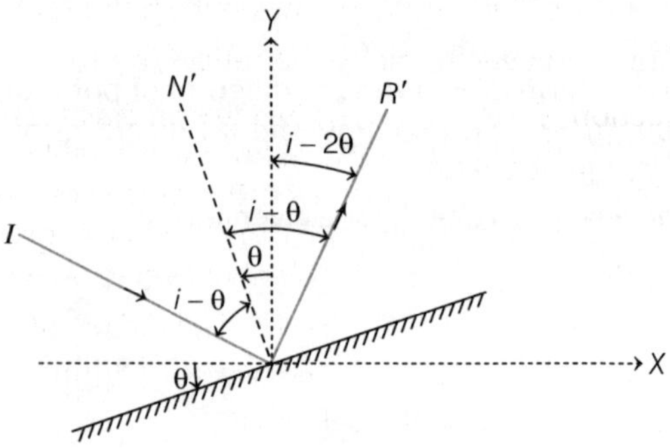

(b)

In figure (a), I is the incident ray, N the normal and R the reflected ray.

In figure (b), I remains as it is N and R shift to N' and R'.

From the two figures, we can see that earlier the reflected ray makes an angle i with y-axis while after rotating the mirror it makes an angle $i - 2\theta$. Thus, we may conclude that the reflected ray has been rotated by an angle 2θ.

5. The minimum length of a plane mirror to see one's full height is $\frac{H}{2}$, where H is the height of person. But, the mirror should be placed in a fixed position which is shown in the figure given below.

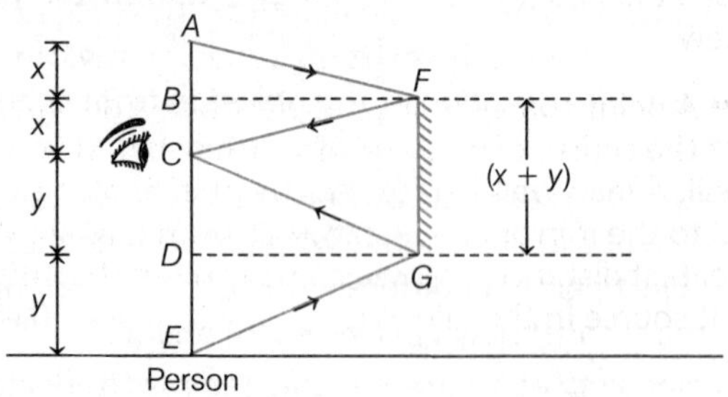

A ray starting from head (A) after reflecting from upper end of the mirror (F) reaches the eye at C. Similarly, the ray starting from the foot (E) after reflecting from the lower end (G) also reaches the eye at C. In the two similar triangles ABF and BFC, $AB = BC = x$ (say), Similarly in triangles CDG and DGE,

$$CD = DE = y \text{ (say)}$$

Now, we can see that height of the person is $2(x + y)$ and that of mirror is $(x + y)$, i.e. height of the mirror is half the height of the person.

Note *The mirror can be placed anywhere between the centre lines BF (of AC) and DG (of CE). As the mirror is moved away on this line, image also moves away from the person. So, apparent size keeps on decreasing.*

6. A person is standing exactly at midway between a wall and a mirror and he wants to see the full height of the wall (behind him) in a plane mirror (in front of him). The minimum length of mirror in this case should be $\frac{H}{3}$, where H is the height of wall. The ray diagram in this case is shown in figure given below.

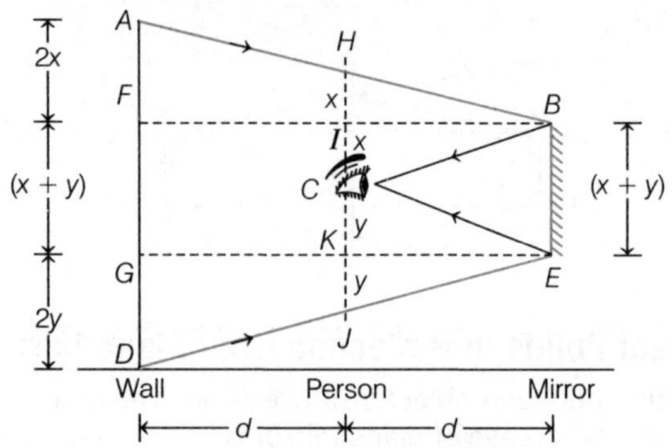

In triangles HBI and IBC, $HI = IC = x$ (say). Now, in triangles HBI and ABF,

$$\frac{AF}{HI} = \frac{FB}{BI} \quad \text{or} \quad \frac{AF}{x} = \frac{2d}{d}$$

or

$$AF = 2x$$

Similarly, we can prove that $DG = 2y$ if, $CK = KJ = y$

Now, we can see that height of the wall is $3(x + y)$ while that of the mirror is $(x + y)$.

7. **Object and image velocity** There are four important points related to object and image velocity.
   (i) Image speed is equal to the object speed.
   (ii) Image velocity and object velocity make same angles from the plane mirror on two opposite sides of the mirror.
   (iii) Components of velocities which are along the mirror are equal.
   (iv) Components of velocities which are perpendicular to the mirror are equal and opposite.

   The following four figures demonstrate the above four points.

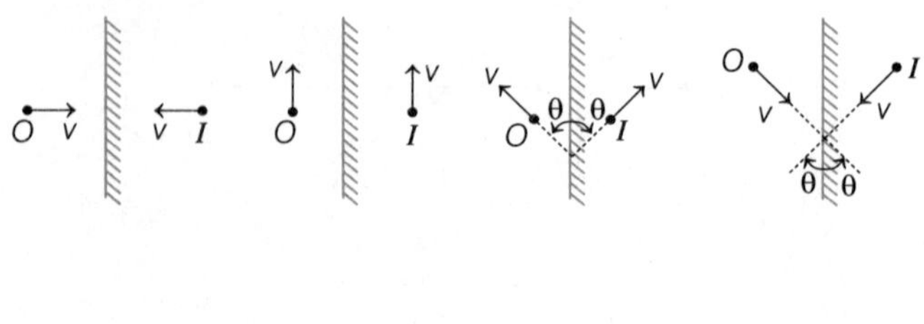

Typed Problems

Type 1. *Based on law of reflection* $\angle i = \angle r$

Concept

These problems are purely based on geometry. Proper normal at point of incidence is very important.

Ex. 1 Two plane mirrors M_1 and M_2 are inclined at angle θ as shown. A ray of light 1, which is parallel to M_1 strikes M_2 and after two reflections, the ray 2 becomes parallel to M_2. Find the angle θ. **(2019 Main)**

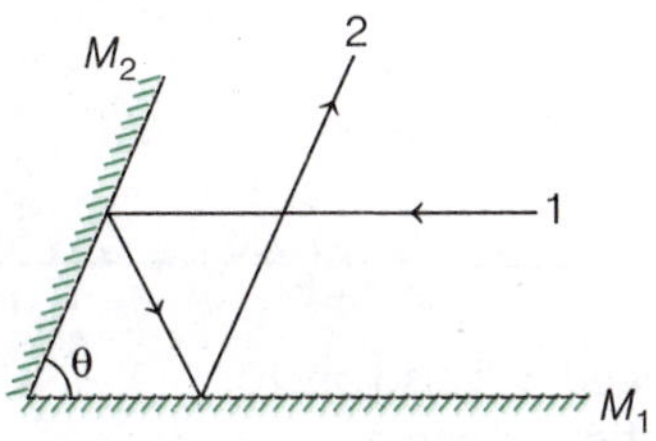

Sol. Different angles are as shown in figure. In triangle *ABC*,

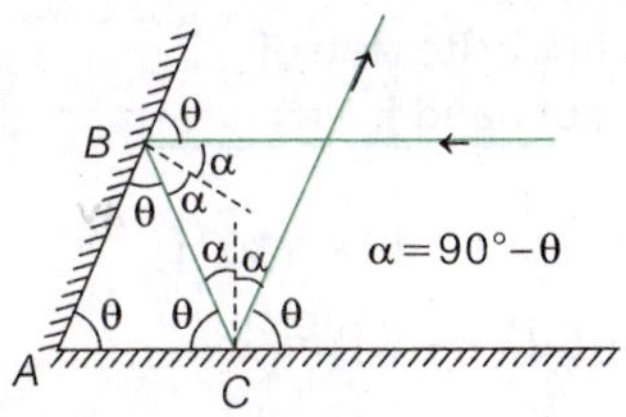

$$\theta + \theta + \theta = 180^\circ$$

$$\therefore \qquad \theta = 60^\circ \qquad \textbf{Ans.}$$

Ex. 2 Prove that for any value of angle *i*, rays 1 and 2 are parallel.

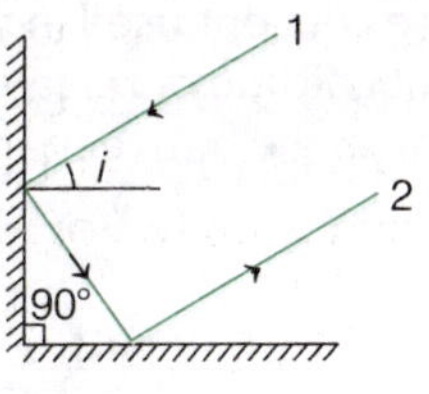

Sol. *PQ* and *MN* are mutually parallel. Rays 1 and 2 are making equal angles ($= \angle i$) from *PQ* and *MN*. So, they are mutually parallel.

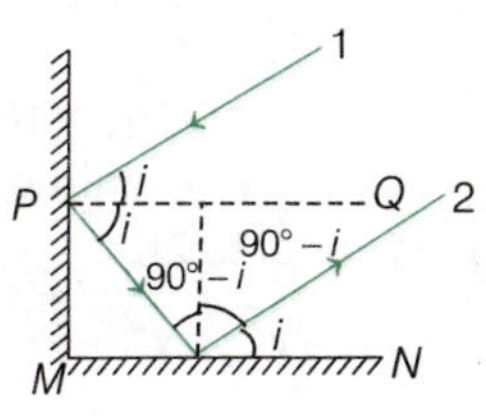

Important Result Two plane mirrors kept at 90° deviate each ray of light by 180° from its original path after two reflections.

Ex. 3 A ray of light is incident on a plane mirror along a vector $\hat{i} + \hat{j} - \hat{k}$. The normal on incidence point is along $\hat{i} + \hat{j}$. Find a unit vector along the reflected ray.

Sol. Reflection of a ray of light is just like an elastic collision of a ball with a horizontal ground. Component of incident ray along the inside normal gets reversed while the component perpendicular to it remains unchanged. Thus, the component of incident ray vector $\mathbf{A} = \hat{i} + \hat{j} - \hat{k}$ parallel to normal, i.e. $\hat{i} + \hat{j}$ gets reversed while perpendicular to it, i.e. $-\hat{k}$ remains unchanged. Thus, the reflected ray can be written as

$$\mathbf{R} = -\hat{i} - \hat{j} - \hat{k}$$

$\therefore$ A unit vector along the reflected ray will be

$$\hat{r} = \frac{\mathbf{R}}{R} = \frac{-\hat{i} - \hat{j} - \hat{k}}{\sqrt{3}}$$

or $$\hat{r} = -\frac{1}{\sqrt{3}}(\hat{i} + \hat{j} + \hat{k}) \qquad \textbf{Ans.}$$

Note *In this problem, given normal is inside the mirror surface. Think why?*

Type 2. *Based on field of view.*

Concept

The region between extreme reflected rays is called field of view. To see the image of object our eye should lie in the field of view.

Ex. 4 A point source of light *S*, placed at a distance *L* in front of the centre of a mirror of width *d*, hangs vertically on a wall. A man walks in front of the mirror along a line parallel to the mirror at a distance 2*L* from it as shown. The greatest distance over which he can see the image of the light source in the mirror is **(2000 JEE)**

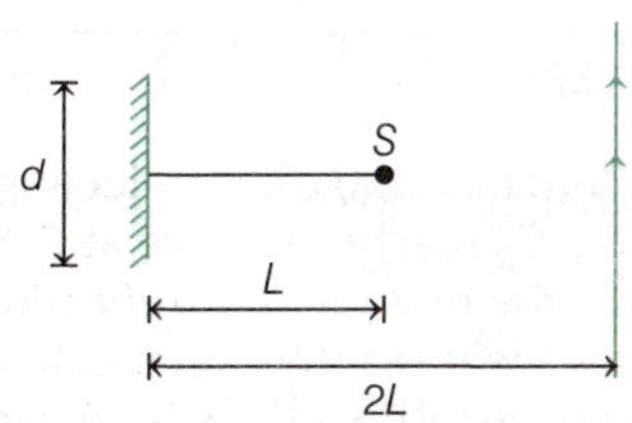

(a) *d*/2 (b) *d* (c) 2 *d* (d) 3 *d*

Sol. (d) $\frac{AB}{MB} = \frac{MO}{PO}$

Substituting $AB = y, MB = 2L, MO = \frac{d}{2}$

and $PO = L$ in the above equation, we get

$$\frac{y}{2L} = \frac{d/2}{L}$$

$\Rightarrow \quad y = d$

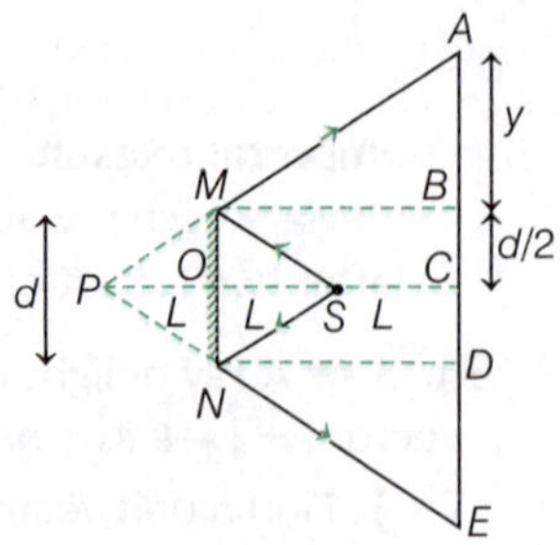

By the symmetry of the above figure, we can see the width of the image is,

$$AE = y + \frac{d}{2} + \frac{d}{2} + y$$

Substituting $y = d$ in the above equation, we get

$$AE = d + \frac{d}{2} + \frac{d}{2} + d$$

$$\therefore \quad AE = 3d$$

Ex. 5 A pole of height 4 m is kept in front of a vertical plane mirror of length 2 m. The lower end of the mirror is at a height of 6 m from the ground. The horizontal distance between the mirror and the pole is 2 m. Upto what minimum and maximum heights a man can see the image of top of the pole at a horizontal distance of 4 m (from the mirror) standing on the same horizontal line which is passing through the pole and the horizontal point below the mirror?

Sol. PQ = Pole, MN = Image of pole

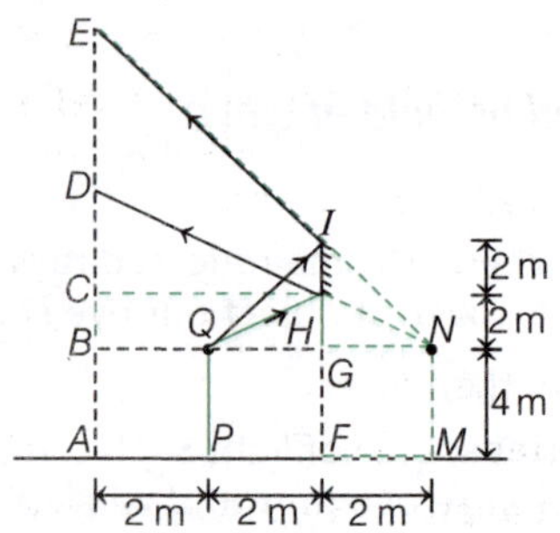

HD and IE are two extreme reflected rays

$$\frac{HG}{GN} = \frac{BD}{BN}$$

$$\therefore \quad BD = \frac{(HG)(BN)}{GN} = \frac{(2)(6)}{2} = 6 \text{ m}$$

Minimum height required $= AD = BD + AB = 10$ m

Further, $\frac{IG}{GN} = \frac{BE}{BN}$

$$\therefore \quad BE = \frac{(IG)(BN)}{GN} = \frac{(4)(6)}{2} = 12 \text{ m}$$

$\therefore$ Maximum height required $= AE$

$$= BE + AB = 16 \text{ m}$$

Type 3. *Based on object and image velocity.*

Ex. 6 A plane mirror is lying in x-y plane. Object velocity is $\mathbf{v}_O = (2\hat{\mathbf{i}} - 3\hat{\mathbf{j}} + 4\hat{\mathbf{k}})$ m/s. Find the image velocity.

Sol. Components of object velocity parallel to plane mirror (or lying in x-y plane) remain unchanged. But, component perpendicular to plane mirror changes its direction but magnitude remains the same. Hence, the image velocity is

$$\mathbf{v}_I = (2\hat{\mathbf{i}} - 3\hat{\mathbf{j}} - 4\hat{\mathbf{k}}) \text{ m/s}$$ **Ans.**

Ex. 7 An object is falling vertically downwards with velocity 10 m/s. In terms of $\hat{\mathbf{i}}$ and $\hat{\mathbf{j}}$, find the image velocity.

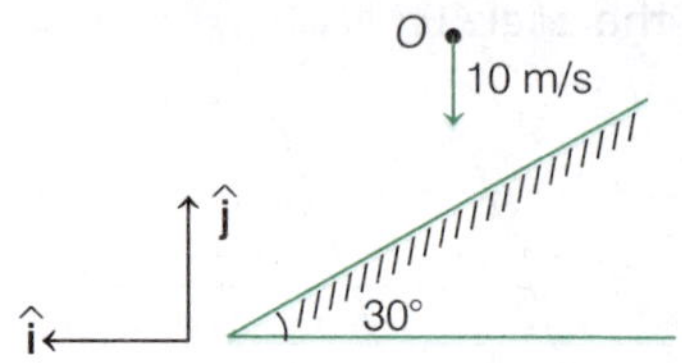

Sol. Image speed will also be 10 m/s. Further, image velocity will make same angle (= 60°) from the mirror on opposite side of it. In terms of $\hat{\mathbf{i}}$ and $\hat{\mathbf{j}}$,

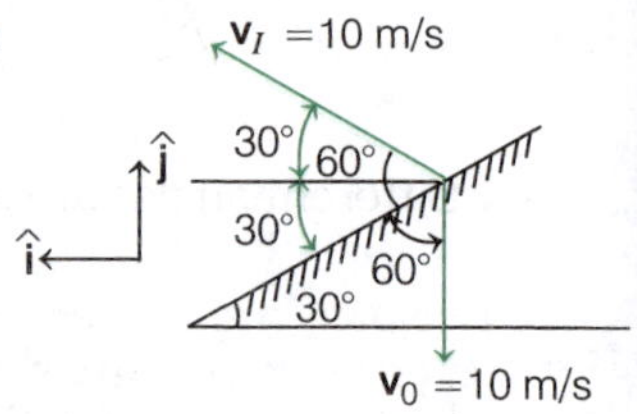

$$\mathbf{v}_I = 10 \cos 30° \,\hat{\mathbf{i}} + 10 \sin 30° \,\hat{\mathbf{j}}$$

or $\quad \mathbf{v}_I = (5\sqrt{3}\,\hat{\mathbf{i}} + 5\,\hat{\mathbf{j}})$ m/s **Ans.**

Ex. 8 A point object is moving with a speed v before an arrangement of two mirrors as shown in figure. Find the magnitude of velocity of image in mirror M_1 with respect to image in mirror M_2.

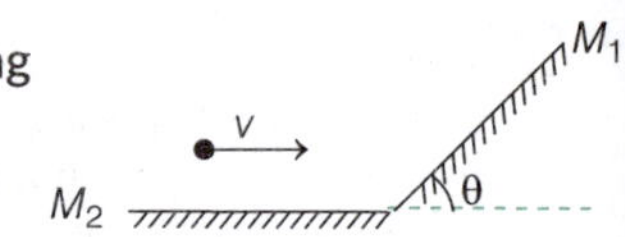

Sol. Using the same concept used in above problem, we have to find magnitude of relative velocity between $\mathbf{v}_{I_1}$ and $\mathbf{v}_{I_2}$. The angle between these two vectors is 2θ.

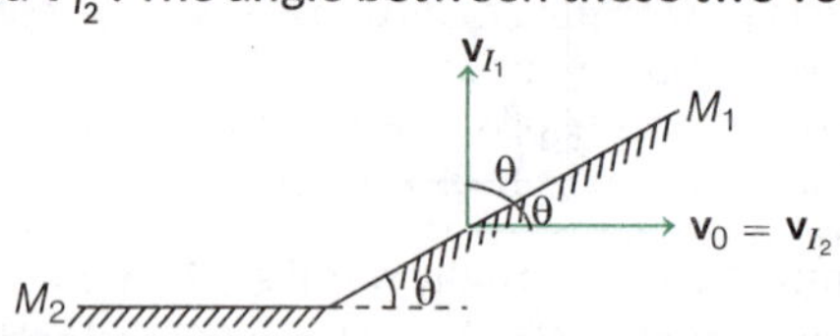

Hence, $\quad \mathbf{v}_r = \mathbf{v}_{I_1} - \mathbf{v}_{I_2}$

$$\therefore \quad |\mathbf{v}_r| = |\mathbf{v}_{I_1} - \mathbf{v}_{I_2}|$$

This is nothing but magnitude of subtraction of two velocity vectors of equal magnitudes v each and angle between them is equal to 2θ.

Hence, $\quad |\mathbf{v}_r| = \sqrt{v^2 + v^2 - 2(v)(v)\cos 2\theta}$

Solving these two equations, we get

$$|\mathbf{v}_2| = 2v \sin\theta$$ **Ans.**

MODULE 2 Exercise

Assertion and Reason

See directions on page 11.

1. **Assertion :** Any ray of light suffers a deviation of $(180° - 2i)$ after one reflection.

   Reason : For normal incidence of light deviation is zero in reflection.

2. **Assertion :** Light converges on a virtual object.

   Reason : Virtual object is always behind a mirror.

Single Correct Options

3. A plane mirror reflects a beam of light to form a real image. The incident beam should be
   (a) parallel (b) convergent
   (c) divergent (d) not possible

4. A watch shows the time as 3 : 25. What will be the time that appears when seen through a plane mirror?
   (a) 8 : 35 (b) 9 : 35
   (c) 7 : 35 (d) 8 : 25

5. Two plane mirrors are inclined at 70°. A ray incident on one mirror at incidence angle θ, after reflection falls on the second mirror and is reflected from there parallel to the first mirror. The value of θ is
   (a) 50° (b) 45°
   (c) 30° (d) 25°

6. A boy of height 1.5 m with his eye level at 1.4 m stands before a plane mirror of length 0.75 m fixed on the wall. The height of the lower edge of the mirror above the floor is 0.8 m. Then,
   (a) the boy will see his full image
   (b) the boy cannot see his hair
   (c) the boy cannot see his feet
   (d) the boy can see neither his hair nor his feet

7. A particle moves perpendicularly towards a plane mirror with a constant speed of 4 cm/s. What is the speed of the image observed by an observer moving with 2 cm/s along the same direction? Mirror is also moving with a speed of 10 cm/s in the opposite direction.
   (All speeds are with respect to ground frame of reference)
   (a) 4 cm/s (b) 12 cm/s
   (c) 14 cm/s (d) 26 cm/s

8. A man is 180 cm tall and his eyes are 10 cm below the top of his head. In order to see his entire height from top to head, he uses a plane mirror kept at a distance of 1m from him. The minimum length of the plane mirror is
   (a) 180 cm (b) 90 cm
   (c) 85 cm (d) 170 cm

9. Figure below shows two plane mirrors and an object O placed between them. What will be distance of the first three images from the mirror M_2?

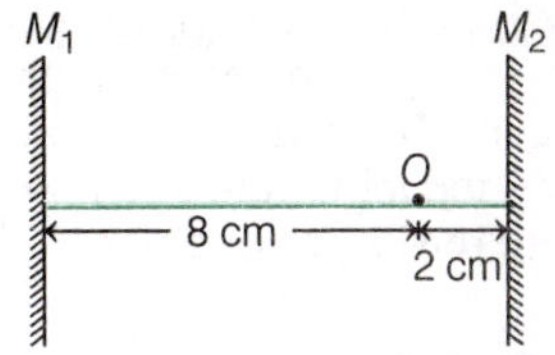

   (a) 2 cm, 8 cm, 14 cm (b) 2 cm, 12 cm, 18 cm
   (c) 2 cm, 18 cm, 22 cm (d) 2 cm, 24 cm, 38 cm

10. When a plane mirror is placed horizontally on level ground at a distance of 60 m from the foot of a tower, the top of the tower and its image in the mirror subtend an angle of 90° at the corner of the mirror nearer to the foot of tower. The height of the tower is
   (a) 30 m (b) 60 m
   (c) 90 m (d) 120 m

11. An object is placed at a distance of 12 cm infront of a plane mirror. A virtual and erect image is formed by the mirror. Now, the mirror is moved by 4 cm towards the stationary object. The distance by which the position of image would be shifted, will be **(2023 Main)**
   (a) 4 cm towards mirror (b) 8 cm away from mirror
   (c) 2 cm towards mirror (d) 8 cm towards mirror

12. The light rays from an object have been reflected towards an observer from a standard flat mirror, the image observed by the observer are
   A. real
   B. erect
   C. smaller in size then object
   D. laterally inverted
   Choose the most appropriate answer from the options given below. **(2023 Main)**
   (a) B and C Only (b) B and D Only
   (c) A, C and D Only (d) A and D Only

Multiple Correct Options

13. A point object is moving towards a plane mirror as shown in figure. Choose the correct options.

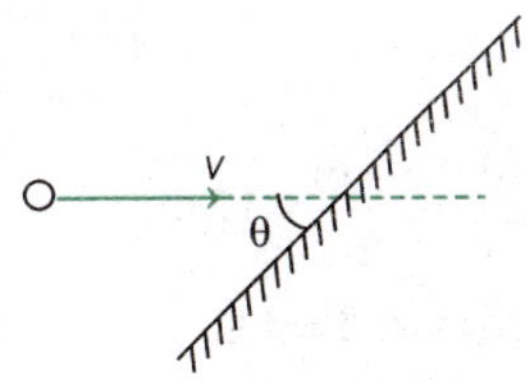

(a) Speed of image is also v
(b) Image velocity will also make an angle θ with mirror
(c) Relative velocity between object and image is $2v$
(d) Relative velocity between object and image is $2v \sin \theta$

Subjective Questions

14. An object M is placed at a distance of 3 m from a mirror with its lower end at 2 m from ground as shown in figure. There is a person at a distance of 4 m from object. Find minimum and maximum height of person to see the image of object.

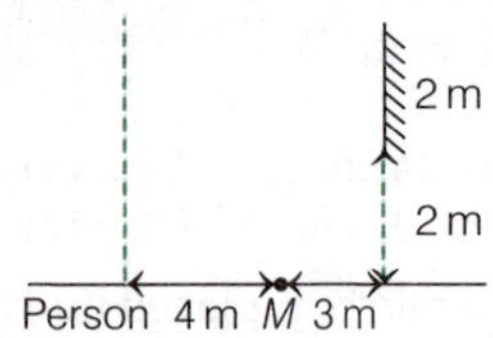

15. In terms of θ find the value of i, so that ray of light retraces its path after third reflection.

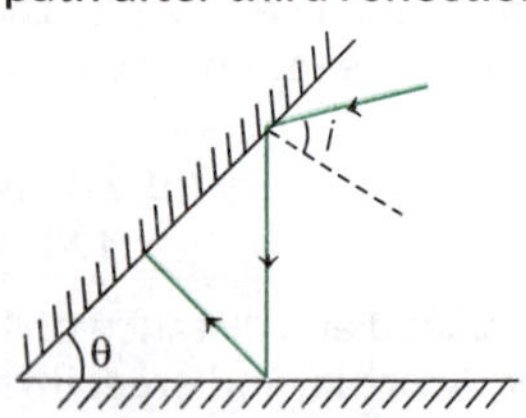

16. A plane mirror lies face up, making an angle of 15° with the horizontal. A ray of light shines down vertically on the mirror. What is the angle of incidence? What will be the angle between the reflected ray and the horizontal?

17. Two plane mirrors each 1.6 m long, are facing each other. The distance between the mirrors is 20 cm. A light incident on one end of one of the mirrors at an angle of incidence of 30°. How many times is the ray reflected before it reaches the other end?

18. Two plane mirrors are inclined to each other at an angle θ. A ray of light is reflected first at one mirror and then at the other. Find the total deviation of the ray.

Integer Type Questions

19. Two vertical parallel mirrors A and B are separated by 10 cm. A point object O is placed at a distance of 2 cm from mirror A. The distance of the second nearest image behind mirror A from the mirror A is ……… cm. **(2023 Main)**

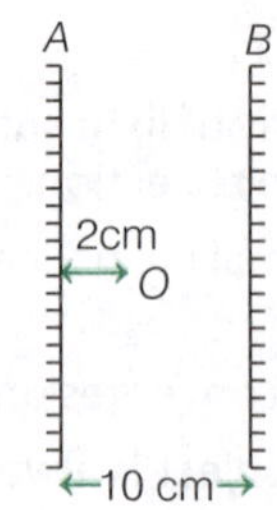

20. A light ray is incident, at an incident angle θ_1, on the system of two plane mirrors M_1 and M_2 having an inclination angle 75° between them (as shown in figure). After reflecting from mirror M_1 it gets reflected back by the mirror M_2 with an angle of reflection 30°. The total deviation of the ray will be ……… degree. **(2022 Main)**

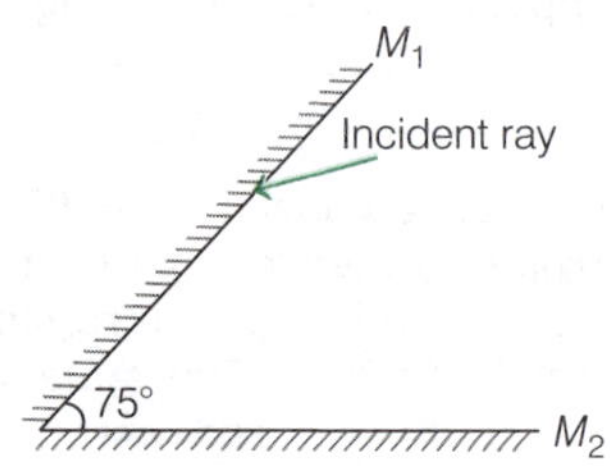

Answers

1. (c)	**2.** (b)	**3.** (b)	**4.** (a)	**5.** (a)
6. (c)	**7.** (d)	**8.** (b)	**9.** (c)	**10.** (b)
11. (d)	**12.** (b)	**13.** (a,b,d)	**14.** $\frac{20}{3}$ m, $\frac{40}{3}$ m	
15. 2θ	**16.** 15°, 60°	**17.** 14	**18.** $360° - 2\theta$	
19. (18)	**20.** (210)			

See hints on pages 51-53.

MODULE 3

Reflection from a Spherical Mirror

Terms and Definitions

There are two types of spherical mirrors, concave and convex.

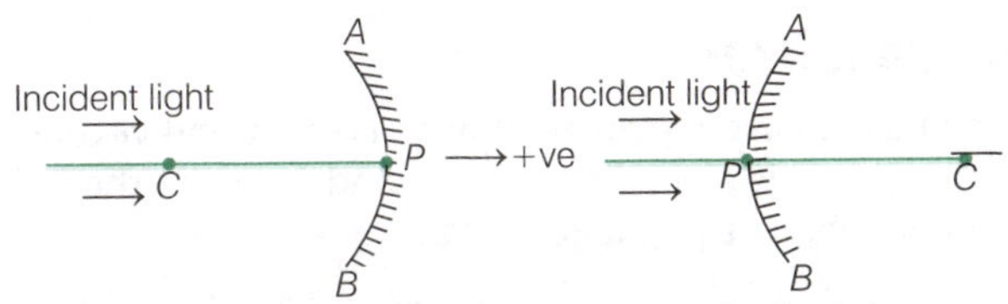

(a) Concave mirror (b) Convex mirror

Centre C of the sphere of which the mirror is a part is called the **centre of curvature** of the mirror and P the centre of the mirror surface, is called the **pole.** The line CP produced is the **principal axis** and AB is the **aperture** of the mirror. The distance CP is called the **radius of curvature (*R*).** All distances are measured from point P. We can see from the two figures that R is positive for convex mirror and negative for concave mirror.

Principal Focus

Observation shows that a narrow beam of rays, parallel and near to the principal axis, is reflected from a concave mirror so that all rays converge to a point F on the principal axis. F is called the **principal focus** of the mirror and it is a **real** focus, since, light actually passes through it.

Concave mirrors are also known as converging mirrors because of their action on a parallel beam of light. They are used in car head-lights, search-lights and telescopes.

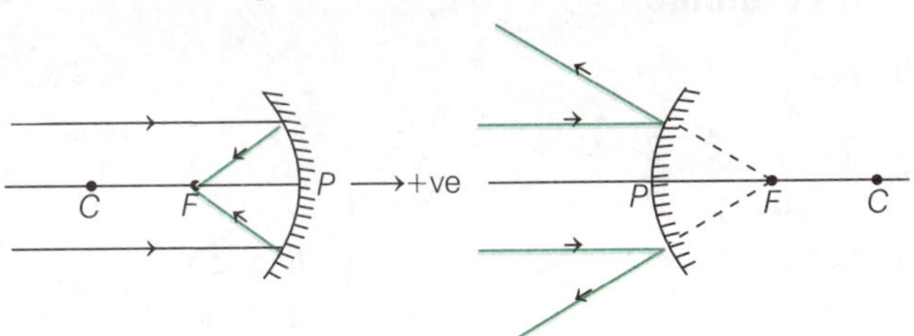

(a) A converging mirror (b) A diverging mirror

A narrow beam of rays, parallel and near to the principal axis, falling on a convex mirror is reflected to form a divergent beam which appears to come from a point F behind the mirror. A convex mirror thus has a virtual principal focus. It is also called a diverging mirror. The distance FP is called the **focal length (*f*)** of the mirror.

Further, we can see that f is negative for a concave mirror and positive for convex mirror. Later, we will see that $f = R/2$.

Paraxial rays Rays which are close to the principal axis and make small angles with it, i.e. they are nearly parallel to the axis, are called paraxial rays.

Our treatment of spherical mirrors will be restricted to such rays which means we shall consider only mirrors of small aperture. In diagrams, however, they will be made larger for clarity.

Images formed by Spherical Mirrors

In general position of image and its nature (i.e. whether it is real or virtual, erect or inverted, magnified or diminished) depend on the distance of object from the mirror.

Case 1 **Concave mirror**

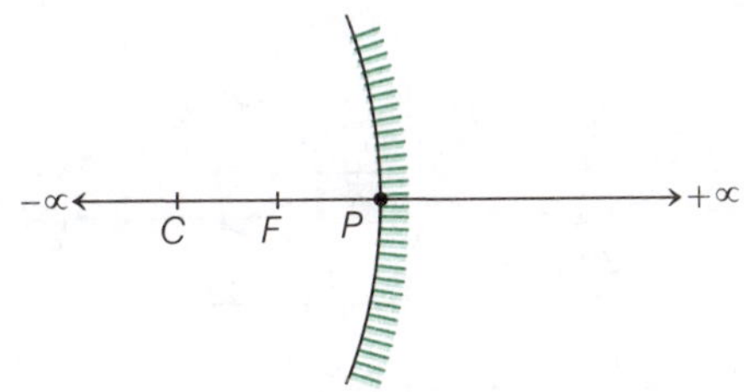

Table 1.

Object position	Image position	Image nature	Object speed and image speed
P	P	–	–
F	$\pm\infty$	–	–
C	C	Real, inverted and same size	$v_I = v_O$
Between P and F	Between P and $+\infty$	Virtual, erect and magnified	$v_I > v_O$
Between F and C	Between $-\infty$ and C	Real, inverted and magnified	$v_I > v_O$
Between C and $-\infty$	Between C and F	Real, inverted and diminished	$v_O > v_I$

Note *(i) The above table is only for real objects lying in front of the mirror for which u is negative.*

(ii) v_I and v_O are image and object speeds.

(iii) From the above table we can see that image and object always travel in opposite directions as long as they move along the principal axis.

Case 2 Convex mirror For real objects there is only one case

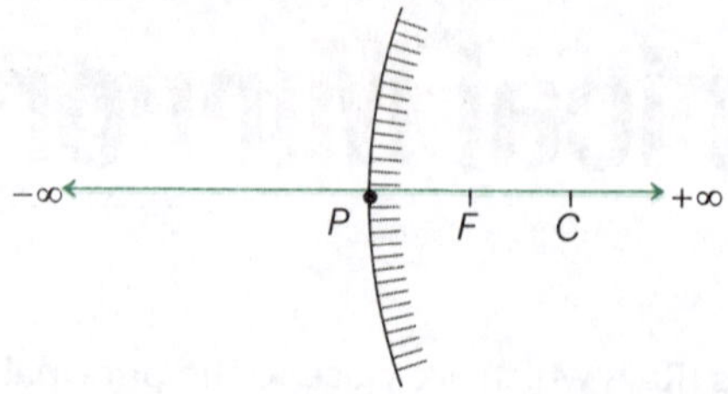

Object lies between P and $-\infty$, then image lies between P and F. Image is virtual, erect and diminished. Object speed is greater than the image speed and they travel in opposite directions (along the principal axis).

Ray diagrams We shall consider the small objects and mirrors of small aperture so that all rays are paraxial. To construct the image of a point object two of the following four rays are drawn passing through the object. To construct the image of an extended object, the image of two end points is only drawn. The image of a point object lying on principal axis is formed on the principal axis itself. The four rays are as under:

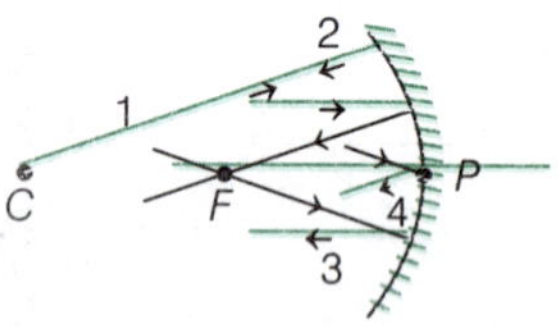

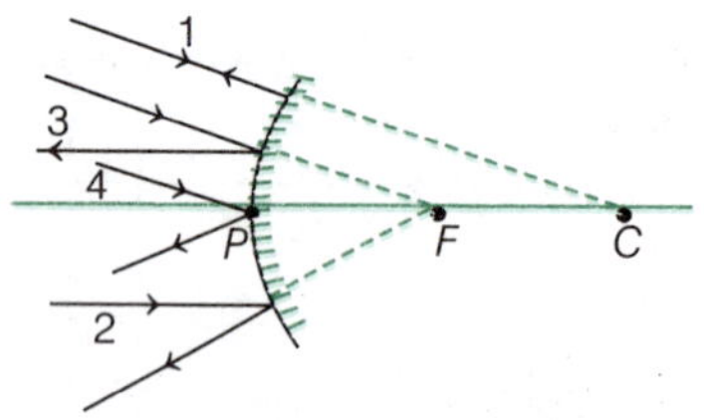

Ray 1. A ray through the centre of curvature which strikes the mirror normally and is reflected back along the same path.

Ray 2. A ray parallel to principal axis after reflection either actually passes through the principal focus F or appears to diverge from it.

Ray 3. A ray passing through the principal focus F or a ray which appears to converge at F is reflected parallel to the principal axis.

Ray 4. A ray striking at pole P is reflected symmetrically back in the opposite side.

Note *$\angle i = \angle r$ is obeyed in all the four rays discussed above. We can also take any general ray of light for making the ray diagram. The normal at any point will pass through the centre of curvature C. The following two figures will inustrate the concept.*

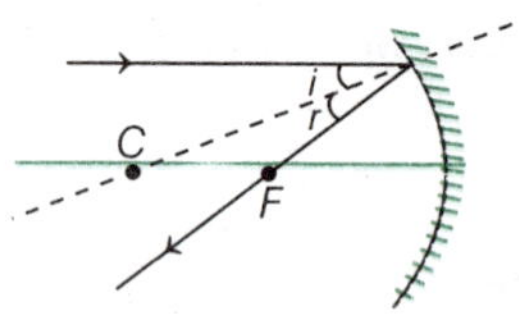

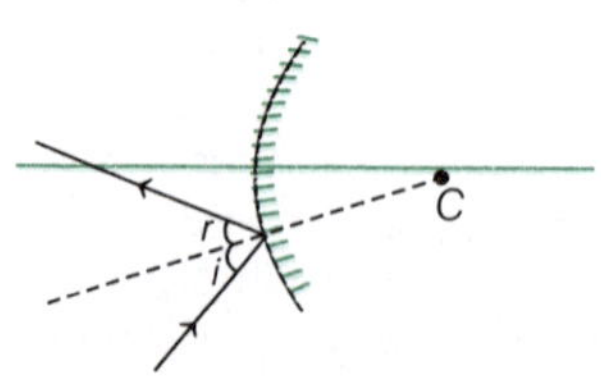

Convex Mirror

Image formed by convex mirror is always virtual, erect and diminished, no matter where the object is.

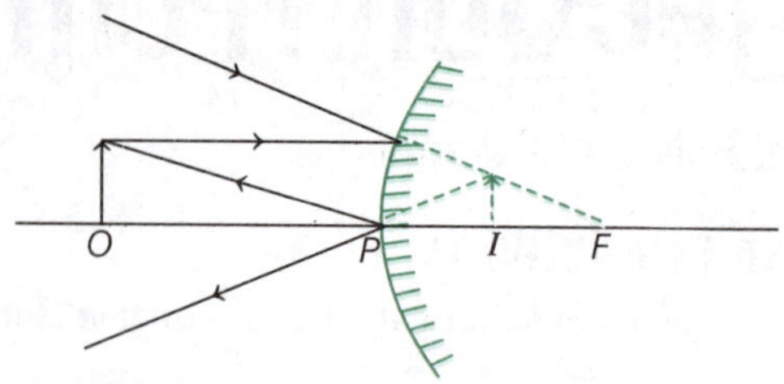

Concave Mirror

In case of a concave mirror the image is erect and virtual when the object is placed between F and P. In all other positions of object the image is real.

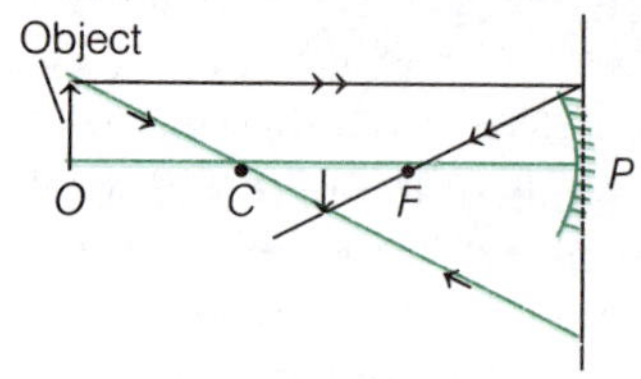

(a) Object beyond C
Image between C and F, real, inverted, diminished

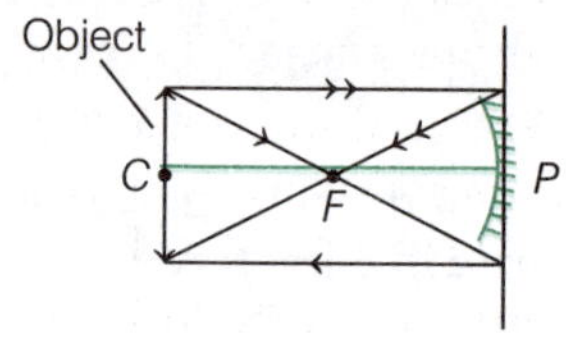

(b) Object at C
Image at C, real, inverted, same size

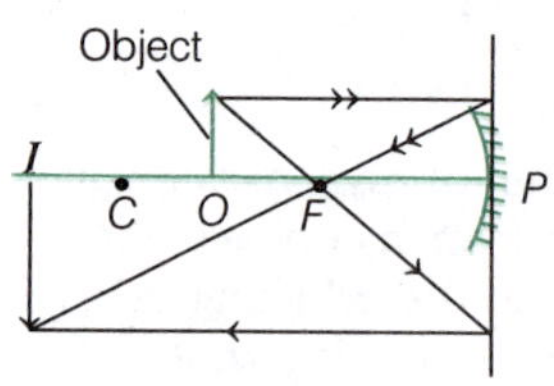

(c) Object between C and F
Image beyond C, real inverted, magnified

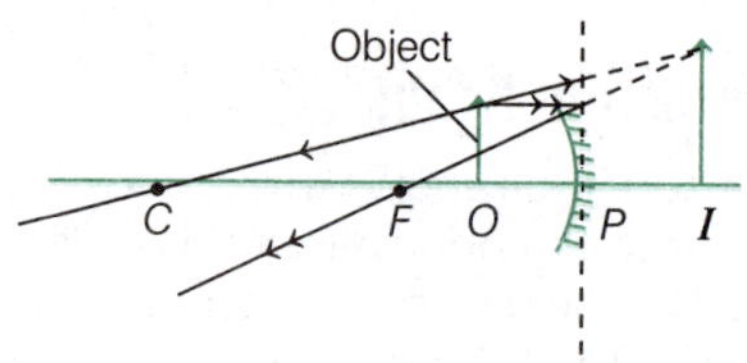

(d) Object between F and P
Image behind mirror, virtual upright, magnified

List of Formulae

(i) $f = \dfrac{R}{2}$

(ii) $\dfrac{1}{v} + \dfrac{1}{u} = \dfrac{1}{f} = \dfrac{2}{R}$

(iii) Lateral, transverse or linear magnification,

$$m = \frac{\text{Image height}}{\text{Object height}} = \frac{I}{O} = \frac{-v}{u}$$

(iv) Power of a mirror (in dioptre) $= -\dfrac{1}{\text{Focal length (in metre)}}$

(v) Image velocity

Case 1 Along the principal axis, $\mathbf{v}_I = -m^2 \mathbf{v}_O$

Here, negative sign implies that object and image always travel in opposite directions.

Case 2 Perpendicular to principal axis,

$$\mathbf{v}_I = m\mathbf{v}_O$$

Here, m has to be substituted with sign. If m is positive, then $\mathbf{v}_I$ and $\mathbf{v}_O$ travel in same direction. If m is negative, then they travel in opposite directions.

Important Points in Formulae

(i) For plane mirror, $R = \infty$

$$\therefore \quad f = \frac{R}{2} \quad \text{or} \quad f = \infty$$

$$\text{and} \quad \frac{1}{v} + \frac{1}{u} = \frac{2}{R} = \frac{2}{\infty} = 0 \quad \text{or} \quad v = -u$$

(ii) From the value of m, we can know nature of image, type of mirror and an approximate location of object. But, always remind that real (and inverted) image is formed only by a concave mirror (for real objects) but virtual image is formed by all three mirrors.

The only difference is, in their sizes. Magnified virtual image is obtained from concave mirror, same size from plane mirror and diminished size from convex mirror. Following table will explain the concept in detail.

Table 2.

Value of m	Nature of image	Type of mirror	Object position
-4	Inverted, real and magnified	Concave	Between F and C
-1	Inverted, real and same size	Concave	At C
$-\frac{1}{2}$	Inverted, real and diminished	Concave	Between C and $-\infty$
$+3$	Erect, virtual and magnified	Concave	Between P and F
$+1$	Erect, virtual and same size	Plane	For all positions
$+\frac{1}{2}$	Erect, virtual and diminished	Convex	Between P and $-\infty$

(iii) **Power** Optical power means power of bending of light. By convention, converging nature is taken as the positive power and diverging nature as negative power.

$$\text{Power of a lens (in dioptre)} = +\frac{1}{f\,(\text{in metre})}$$

$$\text{Power of a mirror (in dioptre)} = -\frac{1}{f\,(\text{in metre})}$$

Different cases are given in the following table.

Table 3.

Lens/Mirror	f	P	Converging/ Diverging	Diagram
Convex lens	+ ve	− ve	Converging	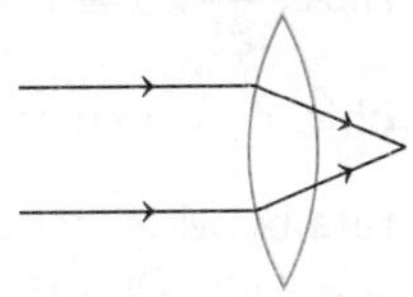
Concave lens	− ve	− ve	Diverging	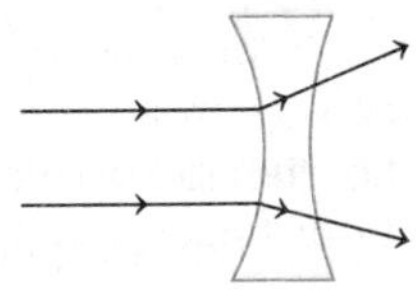
Convex mirror	+ ve	− ve	Diverging	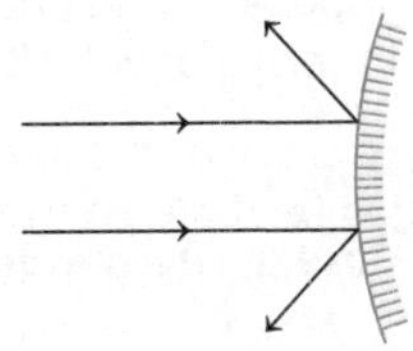
Concave mirror	− ve	+ ve	Converging	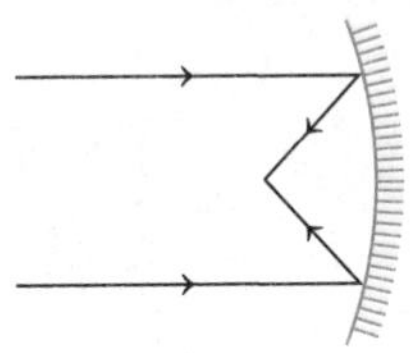

(iv) **Image velocity**

Case 1 **Along the principal axis**

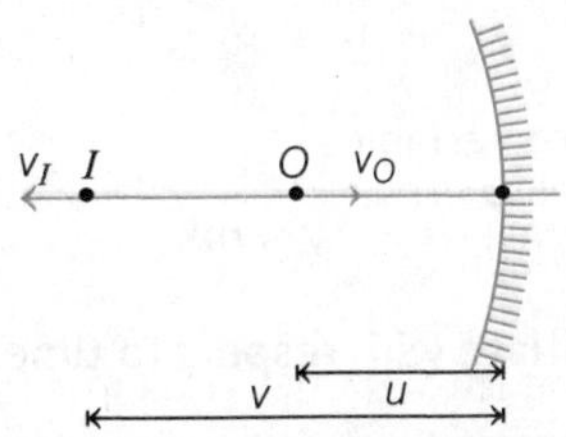

By the motion of object and image v and u will change but focal length will remain unchanged.

If we differentiate the mirror formula

$$\frac{1}{v} + \frac{1}{u} = \frac{1}{f}$$

with respect to time, we get

$$-v^{-2}.\frac{dv}{dt} - u^{-2}\frac{du}{dt} = 0 \qquad (\text{as } f = \text{constant})$$

or $$\boxed{\frac{dv}{dt} = -\left(\frac{v^2}{u^2}\right)\frac{du}{dt}}$$

Here, $\frac{du}{dt}$ is the rate by which u is changing. Or it is the object speed if mirror is stationary. Similarly, $\frac{dv}{dt}$ is the rate by which v (distance between image and mirror) is changing. Or it is image speed if mirror is stationary.

$$\frac{v^2}{u^2} = m^2$$

So, the above relation becomes :

$$\text{image speed} = m^2 \times \text{object speed}$$

As, object and image travel in opposite directions. So, in terms of velocity, the correct relation is

$$\boxed{\mathbf{v}_I = -m^2 \mathbf{v}_O}$$

Case 2 **Perpendicular to axis**

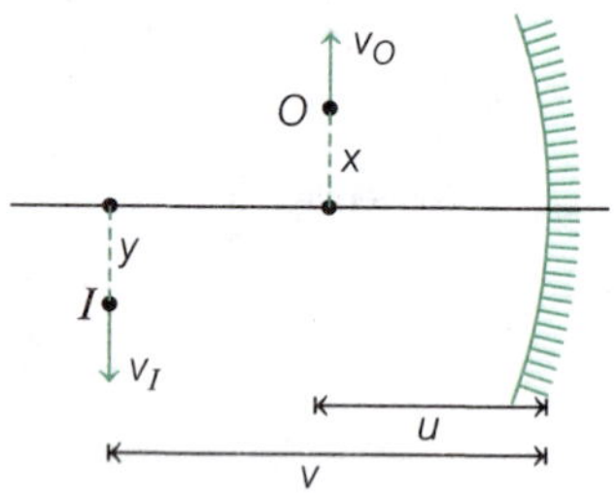

This time v and u are constants. Therefore, $m = -\frac{v}{u}$ is also constant.

But, x and y are variables

$$m = \frac{I}{O} = \frac{y}{x} \Rightarrow y = mx$$

If we differentiate with respect to time, we get,

$$\frac{dy}{dt} = m\frac{dx}{dt} \Rightarrow \boxed{\mathbf{v}_I = m\mathbf{v}_O}$$

Proofs of Different Formulae Discussed in Theory

(i) **Relation between f and R** A ray AM parallel to the principal axis of a concave mirror of small aperture is reflected through the principal focus F. If C is the centre of curvature, CM is the normal to the mirror at M.

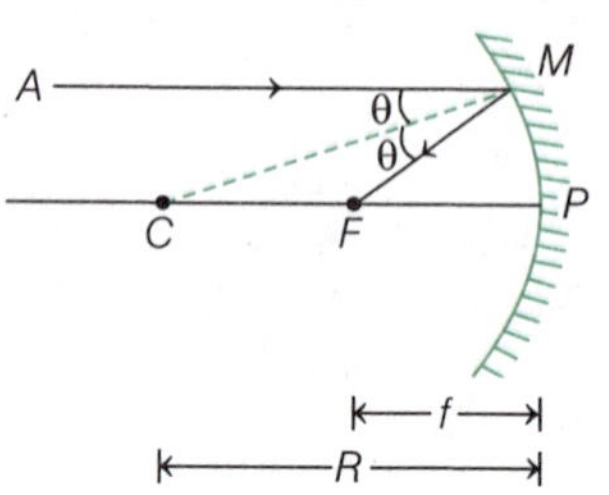

$$\angle i = \angle r$$

or $\angle AMC = \angle CMF = \theta$ (say)

But, $\angle AMC = \angle MCF$ (alternate angles)

$\therefore$ $\angle CMF = \angle MCF$

Therefore, ΔFCM is thus isosceles with $FC = FM$.

The rays are paraxial and so M is very close to P. Therefore,

$$FM \approx FP$$

$\therefore$ $FC = FP$

or $FP = \frac{1}{2}CP$

or $$\boxed{f = \frac{R}{2}}$$

EXERCISE Prove the above relation for convex mirror.

(ii) **The mirror formula** In figure (a) and (b), a ray OM from a point object O on the principal axis is reflected at M so that the angle θ, made by the incident and reflected rays with the normal CM are equal. A ray OP strikes the mirror normally and is reflected back along PO.

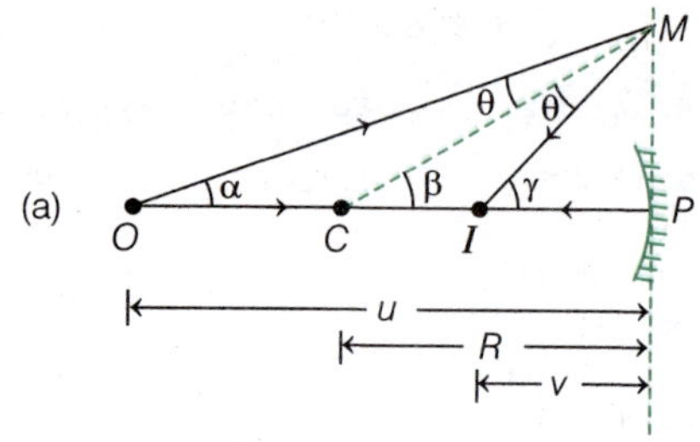

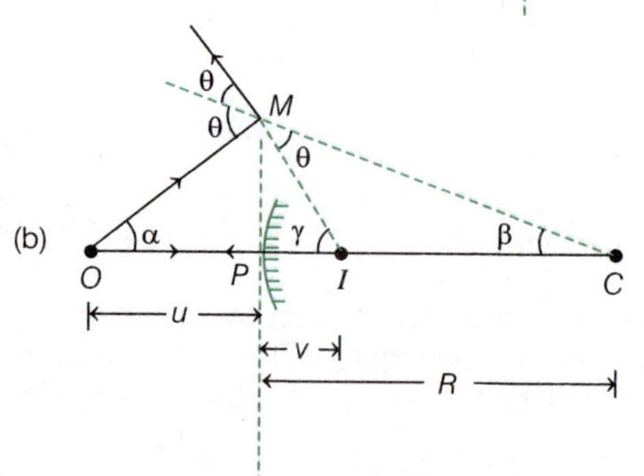

The intersection I of the reflected rays MI and PO in figure (a) gives a **real** point image of O and in figure (b) gives a **virtual** point image of O. Let α, β and γ be the angles as shown. As the rays are paraxial, these angles are small, we can take

$$\alpha \approx \tan\alpha = \frac{MP}{OP},$$

$$\beta = \frac{MP}{CP}$$

and $$\gamma = \frac{MP}{IP}$$

Now, let us take the two figures simultaneously.

Table 4.

Concave	Convex
In triangle CMO, $\beta = \alpha + \theta$ (the exterior angle)	In triangle CMO, $\theta = \alpha + \beta$ ...(iv) (the exterior angle)
or $\theta = \beta - \alpha$ ...(i)	
In Δ CMI, $\gamma = \beta + \theta$	In ΔCMI $\gamma = \theta + \beta$
$\therefore$ $\theta = \gamma - \beta$ ...(ii)	or $\theta = \gamma - \beta$ ...(v)
From Eqs. (i) and (ii), we get $2\beta = \gamma + \alpha$ ...(iii)	From Eqs. (iv) and (v), we get $2\beta = \gamma - \alpha$ ...(vi)
Substituting the values of α, β and γ, we get $\frac{2}{CP} = \frac{1}{IP} + \frac{1}{OP}$ ...(A)	Substituting the values of α, β and γ, we get $\frac{2}{CP} = \frac{1}{IP} - \frac{1}{OP}$ ...(B)
If we now substitute the values with sign, i.e. $CP = -R, IP = -v$ and $OP = -u$	If we now substitute the values with sign, i.e. $CP = +R, IP = +v$ and $OP = -u$,
we get, $\frac{2}{R} = \frac{1}{v} + \frac{1}{u}$	we get $\frac{2}{R} = \frac{1}{v} + \frac{1}{u}$
or $\boxed{\frac{1}{v} + \frac{1}{u} = \frac{1}{f}}$ $\left(\text{as } f = \frac{R}{2}\right)$	or $\boxed{\frac{1}{v} + \frac{1}{u} = \frac{1}{f}}$ $\left(\text{as } f = \frac{R}{2}\right)$

(iii) Magnification The lateral, transverse or linear magnification m is defined as

$$m = \frac{\text{Height of image}}{\text{Height of object}} = \frac{I'I}{O'O} = \frac{IP}{OP} \quad \text{...(i)}$$

(From similar triangles)

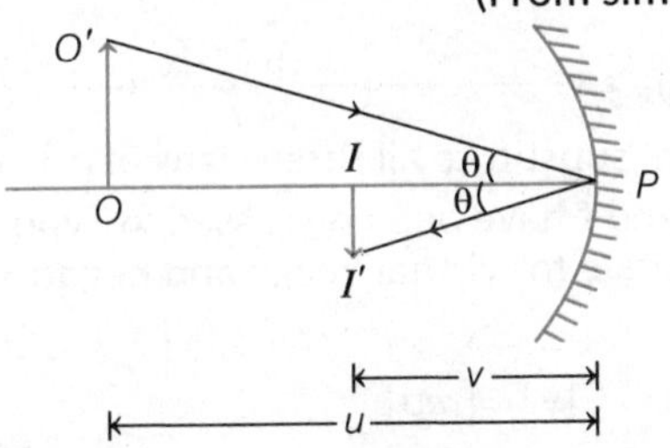

Here, $IP = -v$ and $OP = -u$, further object is erect and image is inverted so we can take $I'I$ as negative and $O'O$ as positive and Eq. (i) will then become

$$\frac{I'I}{O'O} = -\frac{v}{u}$$

or $\boxed{m = -\frac{v}{u}}$

EXERCISE Why do we use sign convention twice in mirror formula. Once at the time of derivation the formula and second time at the time of using this formula.

Explanation This is done to generalise the formula which is applicable under all conditions.

Let us take an example : Suppose we want to derive a formula of magnitude of distance between two points at co-ordinates x_1 and x_2. We are taking here two situations and at the time of deriving the formula we will put x_1 and x_2 with sign. We will see that in both situations formula comes out to be same. But we will have to substitute x_1 and x_2 again with sign while using that common formula.

Situation-I

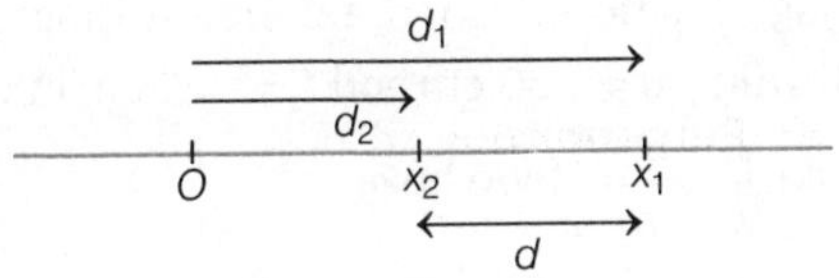

$$|d| = |d_1 - d_2|$$

$\therefore$ $$|d| = |(+x_1) - (+x_2)|$$

or $$|d| = |x_1 - x_2|$$

Situation-2

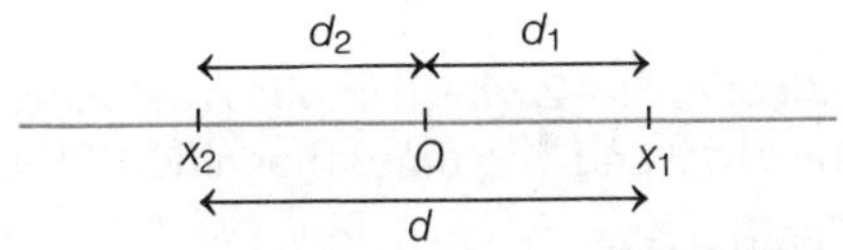

$$|d| = |d_1 + d_2|$$

or $$|d| = |(+x_1) + (-x_2)|$$

or $$|d| = |x_1 - x_2|$$

In both the cases we can see that formula is same,

$$|d| = |x_1 - x_2|$$

Typed Problems

Types of Problems in Spherical Mirror

Type 1. *To find image distance and its magnification corresponding to given object distance and focal length of mirror.*

How to Solve?

- In the mirror formula substitute signs of only u and f. Sign of v automatically appears after calculations. For real objects sign of u is always negative, sign of f is positive for convex mirror and negative for concave mirror.

Ex. 1 An object is placed at a distance of 30 cm from a concave mirror of focal length 20 cm. Find image distance and its magnification. Also, draw the ray diagram.

Sol. Substituting $u = -30$ cm and $f = -20$ cm in the mirror formula $\frac{1}{v} + \frac{1}{u} = \frac{1}{f}$, we have

$$\frac{1}{v} + \frac{1}{-30} = \frac{1}{-20}$$

Solving, we get $\quad v = -60$ cm **Ans.**

Magnification, $\quad m = \frac{-v}{u} = -\frac{(-60)}{(-30)}$

or $\quad m = -2$ **Ans.**

Magnification is -2, which implies that image is inverted, real and two times magnified.

Ray diagram is as shown below.

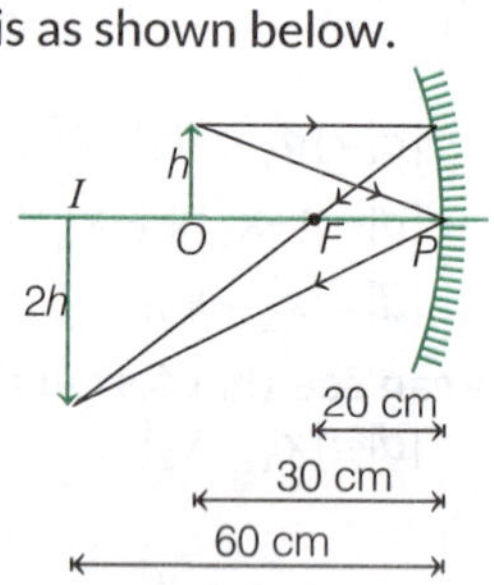

Ex. 2 An object is placed at a distance of 40 cm from a convex mirror of focal length 40 cm. Find image position and its magnification. Also, draw its ray diagram.

Sol. Substituting, $u = -40$ cm and $f = +40$ cm in the mirror formula

$$\frac{1}{v} + \frac{1}{u} = \frac{1}{f}, \text{ we have}$$

$$\frac{1}{v} + \frac{1}{-40} = \frac{1}{+40}$$

We get, $\quad v = +20$ cm **Ans.**

Magnification, $m = -\frac{v}{u} = -\frac{(+20)}{(-40)} = +\frac{1}{2}$

Magnification is $+\frac{1}{2}$, which implies that image is erect, virtual and half in size.

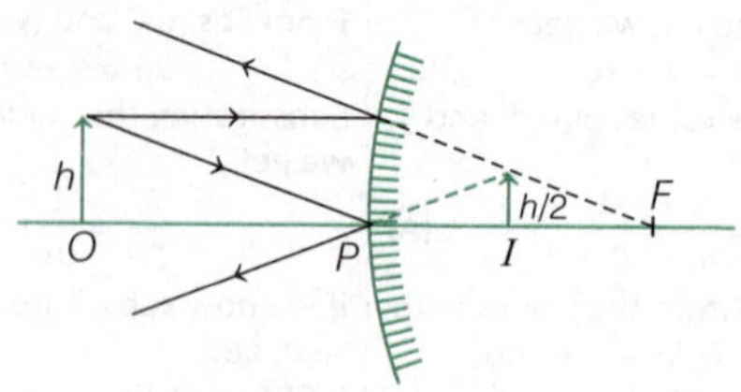

Ray diagram is as shown.

$$PO = PF = 40 \text{ cm}$$

$$PI = 20 \text{ cm}$$

Note *Here, PO = PF = 40 cm or object is placed at a distance of its focal length, but object is not actually kept at F. Otherwise, image would be formed at infinity.*

Type 2. *To find object/image distance corresponding to given magnification of image if focal length of mirror is also given.*

How to Solve?

- In this type, substitute all three signs of u, v and f.
- Signs of u and f have been discussed in Type 1. Sign of v will be positive for virtual image and negative for real image.
- $m = -\frac{v}{u} \Rightarrow |v| = |mu|$

Ex. 3 Find the distance of object from a concave mirror of focal length 10 cm so that image size is four times the size of the object.

Sol. Concave mirror can form real as well as virtual image. Here, nature of image is not given in the question. So, we will consider two possible cases.

***Case* 1 (When image is real)** Real image is formed on the same side of the object, i.e. u, v and f all are negative. So let,

$$u = -x$$

then $\quad v = -4x \quad$ as $\quad \left|\frac{v}{u}\right| = |m| = 4$

and $\quad f = -10$ cm

Substituting in $\quad \frac{1}{v} + \frac{1}{u} = \frac{1}{f}$

We have $\quad \frac{1}{-4x} - \frac{1}{x} = \frac{1}{-10} \quad$ or $\quad \frac{5}{4x} = \frac{1}{10}$

$\therefore \quad x = 12.5$ cm **Ans.**

Note *$|f|<|x|<|2f|$ and we know that in case of a concave mirror, image is real, inverted and magnified when object lies between F and C.*

Case 2 (When image is virtual) In case of a mirror, image is virtual, when it is formed behind the mirror, i.e. u and f are negative, while v is positive. So let,

$$u = -y$$

then $v = +4y$

and $f = -10$ cm

Substituting in $\frac{1}{v} + \frac{1}{u} = \frac{1}{f}$

We have $\frac{1}{4y} - \frac{1}{y} = \frac{1}{-10}$ or $\frac{3}{4y} = \frac{1}{10}$

or $y = 7.5$ cm **Ans.**

Note *Here, $|y|<|f|$. We know that image is virtual erect and magnified when the object lies between F and P.*

Type 3. *Based on making some condition.*

How to Solve?

- Initially, substitute sign of f only.
- Make an equation of v.
- Now, for real image v should be negative and for virtual image v should be positive. With these concepts we can make the necessary condition.

Ex. 4 Find the condition under which a convex mirror can make a real image.

Sol. Substituting the sign of f only in the mirror formula, we have

$$\frac{1}{v} + \frac{1}{u} = \frac{1}{+f}$$

$$\Rightarrow \quad \frac{1}{v} = \frac{1}{f} - \frac{1}{u}$$

For real image v should be negative and for this u should be positive and less than f. Object distance u is positive means object should be virtual and lying between P and F.

The ray diagram is as shown below.

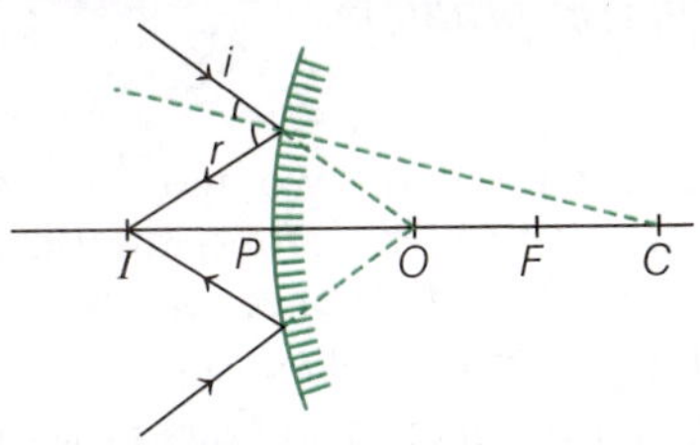

Here, O is virtual lying between P and F, I is real.

Note *Under normal conditions a concave mirror makes a real image. But, it makes a virtual image if a real object is kept between P and F. On the other hand a convex mirror makes a virtual image. But it makes a real image if a virtual object is kept between P and F.*

Type 4. *To find nature of image and type of mirror corresponding to given optic axis of mirror a point object and a point image. With the help of ray diagram we have to find focus and pole of the mirror also.*

Ex. 5 An image I is formed of a point object O by a mirror whose principal axis is AB as shown in figure.

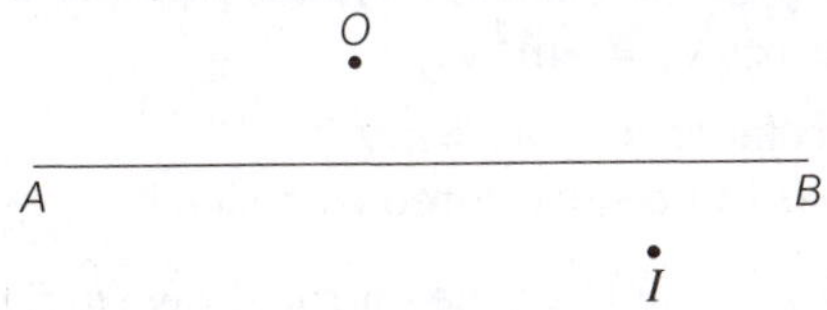

(a) State whether it is a convex mirror or a concave mirror.

(b) Draw a ray diagram to locate the mirror and its focus. Write down the steps of construction of the ray diagram. Consider the possible two cases:
  (1) When distance of I from AB is more than the distance of O from AB and
  (2) When distance of O from AB is more than the distance of I from AB

Sol.

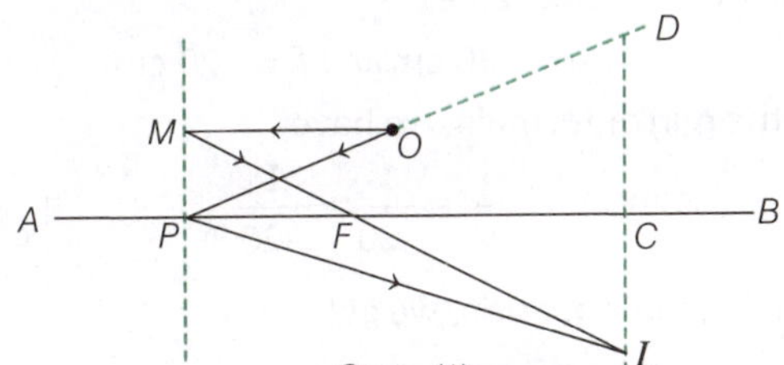

Case (1)

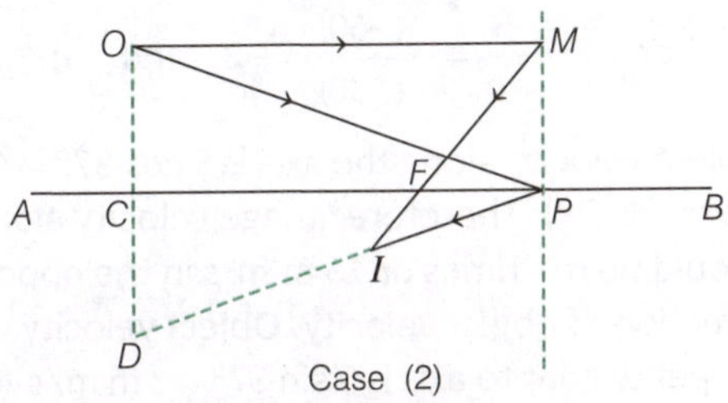

Case (2)

(a) As the image is on the opposite side of the principal axis, the mirror is concave. Because convex mirror always forms an erect image.

(b) Two different cases are shown in figure. Steps are as under :
  (i) From I or O drop a perpendicular on principal axis, such that $CI = CD$ or $OC = CD$.
  (ii) Draw a line joining D and O or D and I so that it meets the principal axis at P. The point P will be the pole of the mirror as a ray reflected from the pole is always symmetrical about principal axis.
  (iii) From O draw a line parallel to principal axis towards the mirror so that it meets the mirror at M. Join M to I, so that it intersects the principal axis at F.
  F is the focus of the mirror as any ray parallel to principal axis after reflection from the mirror intersects the principal axis at the focus.

Note *In both figures, mirror should face towards the object.*

Exercise In the above problem, find centre of curvature of the mirror with the help of only ray diagram.

Type 5. *Based on velocity of image.*

How to Solve?

- Using the steps discussed in Type 1, find v and then m
- Along the axis $v_I = -m^2 v_O$
- Perpendicular to axis $v_I = m v_O$

Here, m has to be substituted with sign.

Ex. 6 Focal length of the mirror shown in figure is 20 cm. Find the image position and its velocity.

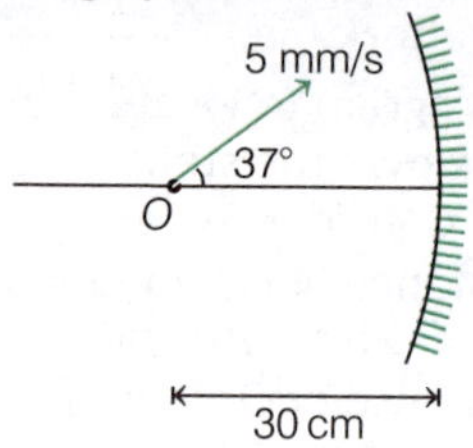

Sol. Substituting the values,

$$u = -30 \text{ cm and } f = -20 \text{ cm}$$

in the mirror formula, we have

$$\frac{1}{v} + \frac{1}{-30} = \frac{1}{-20}$$

Solving this equation, we get

$$v = -60 \text{ cm}$$

Further, $m = -\frac{v}{u} = -\frac{(-60)}{(-30)} = -2$ and $m^2 = 4$

Object velocity along the axis is $5 \cos 37° = 4$ mm/s (towards OP). Therefore, image velocity along the axis should be m^2 times or 16 m m/s in the opposite direction of object velocity. Object velocity perpendicular to axis is $5 \sin 37° = 3$ m m/s (upwards). Therefore, image velocity will be m times or -6 m m/s or 6mm/s downwards. The position and velocity of image is shown below.

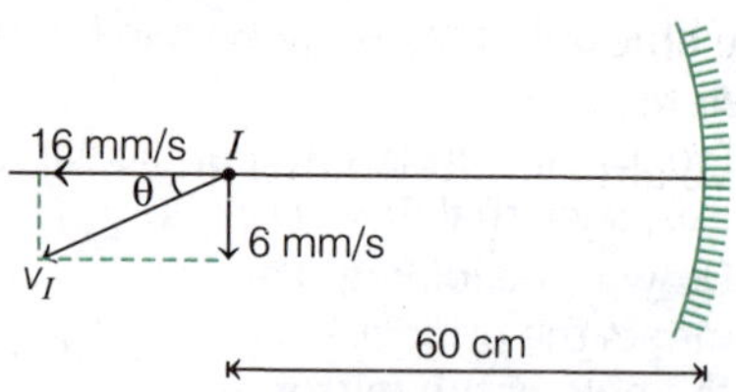

$$v_I = \sqrt{(16)^2 + (6)^2} = \sqrt{292} \text{ m m/s}$$

$$\tan \theta = \frac{6}{16} = \frac{3}{8} \text{ or } \theta = \tan^{-1}\left(\frac{3}{8}\right)$$

Type 6. *To find a rough image of a square or rectangular type of object kept along the axis.*

Concept

(i) If object is towards P or C, then its image is also towards P or C.

(ii) If object is towards F, then its image is towards infinity and it is more magnified.

Ex. 7 A square $mnqp$ is kept between F and C on the principal axis of a concave mirror as shown in figure. Find a rough image of this object.

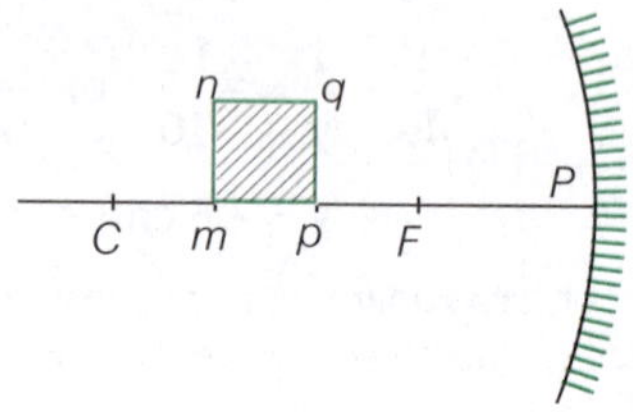

Sol. Object is placed between F and C, therefore, image is real, inverted magnified and beyond C. Further pq is towards F. Therefore, its image $p'q'$ is towards infinity and it is more magnified. A rough image is as shown alongside.

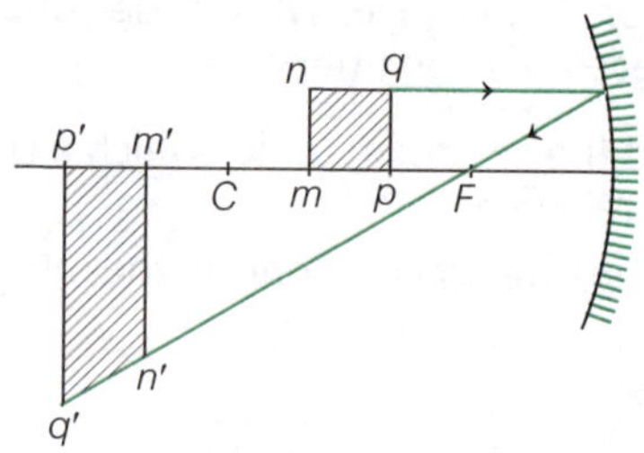

From the ray shown in figure, we can see that $n'q'$ will be a straight line.

Exercise In the given problem, focal length of mirror is 30 cm and side of square is 10 cm with $pP = 40$ cm. Find perimeter of the image

Ans $(90 + 15\sqrt{10})$ cm

Type 7. *Two mirror problems.*

Concept

If an object is placed between two mirrors, then infinite reflections will take place. Therefore, infinite images are formed. But normally position of second image is asked. So, we have to apply mirror formula two times.

Image from first mirror acts as an object for the second mirror. Sign convention for second reflection will change but sign of focal length will not change.

Ex. 8 Focal length of convex mirror M_1 is 20 cm and that of concave mirror M_2 is 30 cm. Find position of second image I_2. Take first reflection *from* M_1.

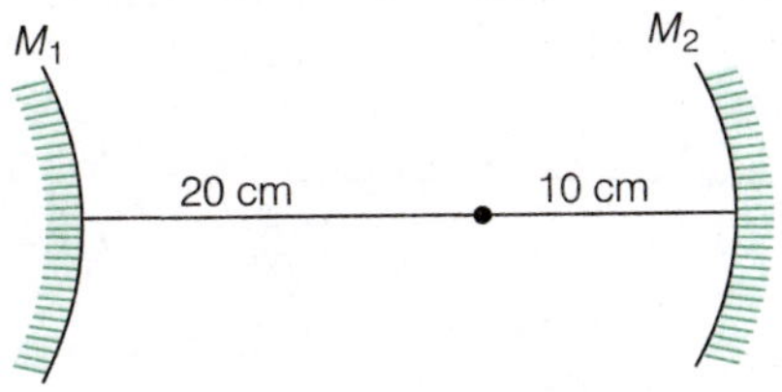

Sol.

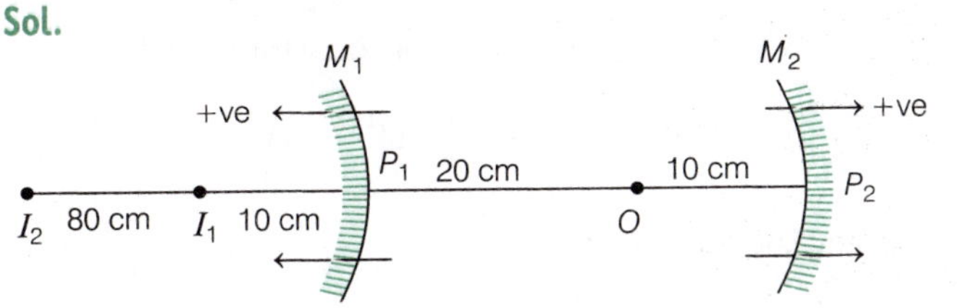

For M_1 $u_1 = -20$ cm

$f_1 = +20$ cm

Using the mirror formula,

$$\frac{1}{v} + \frac{1}{u} = \frac{1}{f}, \text{ we have}$$

$$\frac{1}{v_1} + \frac{1}{-20} = \frac{1}{+20}$$

Solving, we get

$$v_1 = +10 \text{ cm}$$

For M_2 $u_2 = -40$ cm ($PI_1 = 40$ cm)

$f_2 = -30$ cm

Using the mirror formula,

$$\frac{1}{v} + \frac{1}{u} = \frac{1}{f}$$

We have,

$$\frac{1}{v_2} + \frac{1}{-40} = \frac{1}{-30}$$

$$\therefore \quad v_2 = P_2 I_2$$

$$= -120 \text{ cm}$$

Note *I_1 is virtual from M_1 point of view (behind M_1). But it behaves like a real object for M_2 (in front of M_2).*

Type 8. *An extended object is kept perpendicular to principal axis and we have to make its image.*

How to Solve?

With the help of Type 1 first find v and then m. Now, suppose $m = -2$ and object is 2 mm above the principal axis, then its image will be formed 4 mm below its principal axis.

Ex. 9

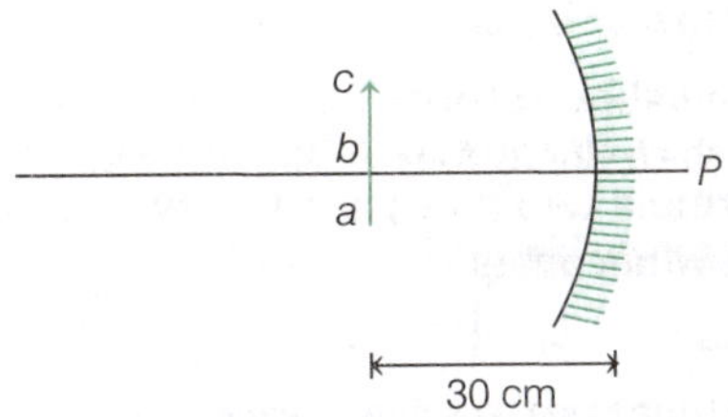

Focal length of the concave mirror shown in figure is 20 cm.

$$ab = 1 \text{ mm and } bc = 2 \text{ mm}$$

For the given situation, make its image

Sol. $u = -30$ cm and $f = -20$ cm

Using the mirror formula, $\frac{1}{v} + \frac{1}{u} = \frac{1}{f}$, we have

$$\frac{1}{v} + \frac{1}{-30} = \frac{1}{-20}$$

Solving this equation, we get $v = -60$ cm

Now, $$m = -\frac{v}{u} = -\frac{(-60)}{(-30)} = -2$$

Now c point is 2 mm above the principal axis and magnification is −2. Hence, image c' will be formed 4 mm below the principal axis. Similarly a point is 1 mm below the principal axis and value of m is −2. Hence, image a' is formed 2 mm above the principal axis. Image with ray diagram of c is as shown below.

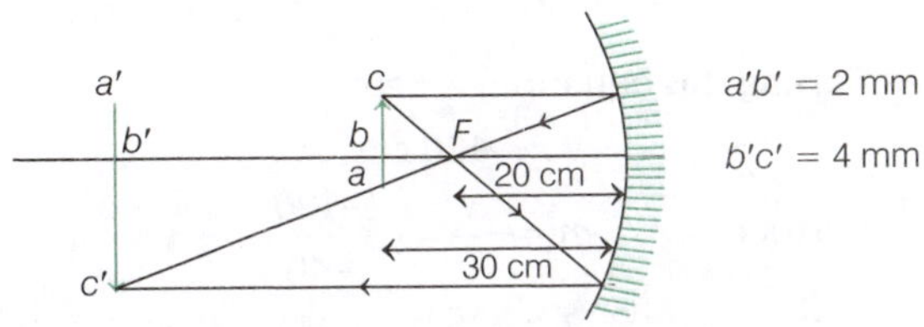

Type 9. *An extended object is kept along the principal axis and we have to find the image length. In this type further two cases are possible.*

Case 1 **When object size is very small.**

In this case image length,

$$L_I = m^2 (L_o)$$

Here, L_o is the object length. So, using Type 1, we have to find v and then m.

Proof We have already proved that image speed.

$$v_I = m^2 v_O \quad \text{(Along the axis)}$$

or

$$\frac{dv}{dt} = m^2 \left(\frac{du}{dt}\right)$$

For small change in the values of v and u, we can write

$$|\Delta v| = |m^2 \times \Delta u|$$

Δv is nothing but difference in two values of v or image length L_I. Similarly, Δu is object length L_o.

Case 2 When object size is large.

If an extended object is lying along the principal axis, then we will get two values of u corresponding to its two ends. Now, apply mirror formula two times and find two values of v. The image length now becomes,

$$L_I = |v_1 \sim v_2|$$

Note *If one end of the object is placed either at C or P, then its image will also be formed at C or P. So, we will have to apply the mirror formula only for the other end.*

Ex. 10

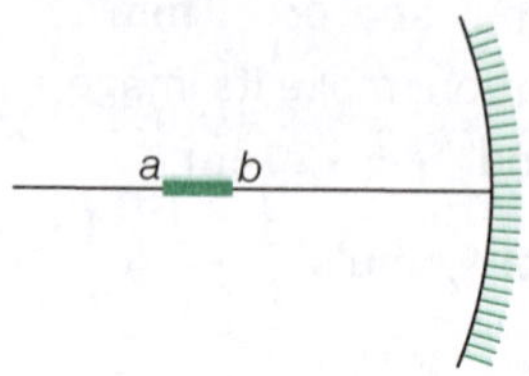

A small object ab of size 1 mm is kept at a distance of 40 cm from a concave mirror of focal length 30 cm. Make image of this object.

Sol. Here, object size is very small. So, this is case 1.

$$u = -40 \text{ cm} \quad \text{and} \quad f = -30 \text{ cm}$$

Applying the mirror formula

$$\frac{1}{v} + \frac{1}{u} = \frac{1}{f}, \text{ we have}$$

$$\frac{1}{v} + \frac{1}{-40} = \frac{1}{-30}$$

Solving this equation, we get

$$v = -120 \text{ cm}$$

Further, $$m = -\frac{v}{u} = -\frac{(-120)}{(-40)} = -3$$

$$m^2 = 9$$

Now, $$L_I = m^2 L_o = (9)(1 \text{ mm})$$

$$= 9 \text{ mm}$$

Image diagram is as shown below.

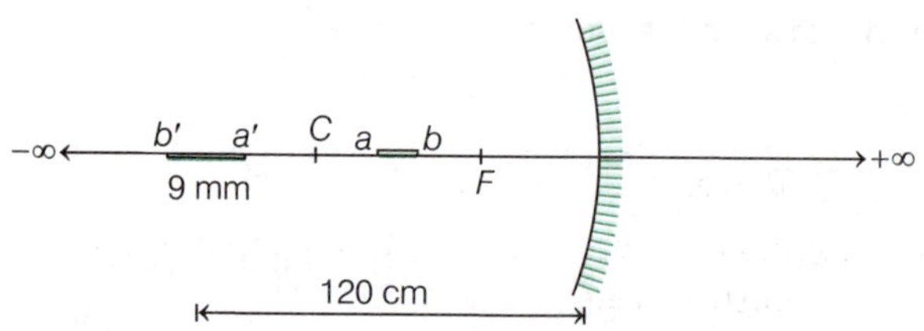

Note *Point b is towards F, therefore its image b′ should be towards −∞.*

Ex. 11 A thin rod of length $\frac{f}{3}$ is lying along the principal axis of a concave mirror of focal length f. Image is real, magnified and inverted and one of the end of rod coincides with its image itself. Find length of the image.

(1991 JEE)

Sol. Image is real, magnified and inverted. So, the given rod lies between F and C. Further, one end of the rod is coinciding with its image itself. Therefore, it is lying at C. So, the thin rod CR is kept as shown below.

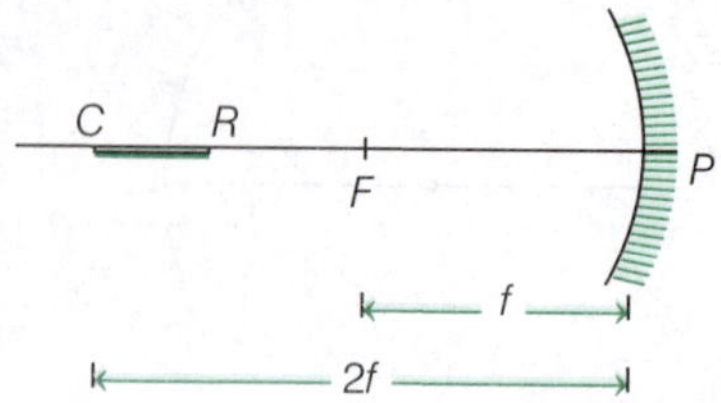

$$CR = \frac{f}{3}$$

$$PR = 2f - \frac{f}{3} = \frac{5f}{3}$$

We have to apply mirror formula only for point R.

$$u = -\frac{5f}{3}, \text{ focal length} = -f$$

Using the mirror formula $\frac{1}{v} + \frac{1}{u} = \frac{1}{f}$

We have, $$\frac{1}{v} + \frac{1}{-\frac{5f}{3}} = \frac{1}{-f}$$

Solving this equation, we get

$$v = \frac{-5f}{2} \quad \text{or} \quad -2.5f$$

So, the image of rod CR is $C'R'$ as shown below.

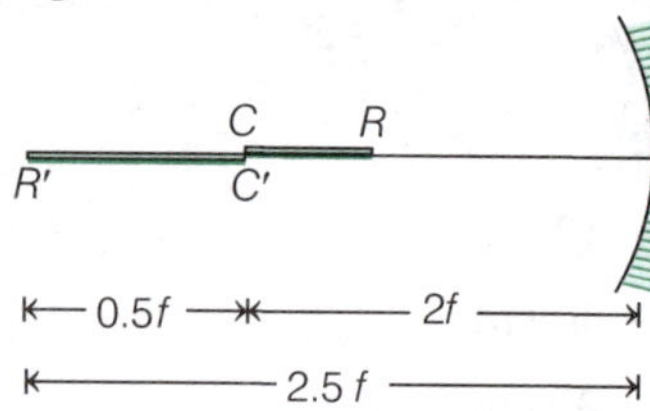

So, image length $= C'R' = 0.5 f$ or $\frac{f}{2}$.

Note *In this problem if magnification of rod is asked then we can write*

$$m = -\frac{L_I}{L_O} = -\frac{f/2}{f/3} = -\frac{3}{2}$$

Negative sign has been used for inverted image.

Type 10. *Based on u versus v graph or 1/u versus 1/v graph (only for real objects).*

Ex. 12 Draw u versus v graph or $\frac{1}{u}$ versus $\frac{1}{v}$ graph for a concave mirror of focal length f.

Sol. The mirror formula is

$$\frac{1}{v} + \frac{1}{u} = \frac{1}{f}$$

If we take $\frac{1}{v}$ along y-axis and $\frac{1}{u}$ along x-axis, then the above equation becomes

$$y + x = c \qquad \left(\text{as } \frac{1}{f} = \text{constant}\right)$$

Therefore, $\frac{1}{v}$ *versus* $\frac{1}{u}$ graph will be a straight line. Let us take origin at pole.

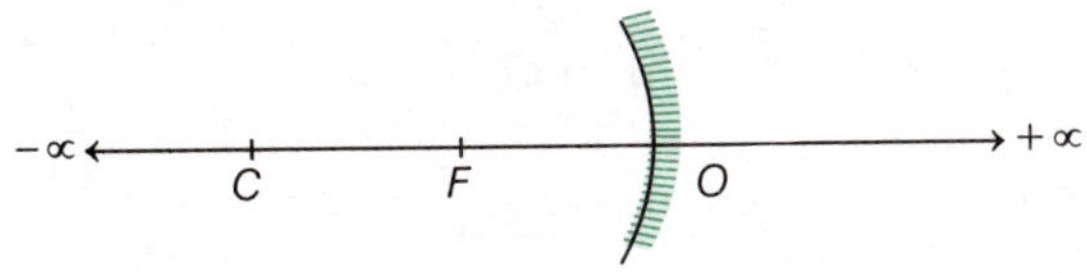

Table 5.

S.No.	u	v	$\frac{1}{u}$	$\frac{1}{v}$
1.	0 to $-f$	0 to $+\infty$	$-\infty$ to $-\frac{1}{f}$	$+\infty$ to 0
2.	$-f$ to $-2f$	$-\infty$ to $-2f$	$-\frac{1}{f}$ to $-\frac{1}{2f}$	0 to $-\frac{1}{2f}$
3.	$-2f$ to $-\infty$	$-2f$ to $-f$	$-\frac{1}{2f}$ to 0	$-\frac{1}{2f}$ to $-\frac{1}{f}$

u versus v and $\frac{1}{u}$ *versus* $\frac{1}{v}$ graphs are as shown below.

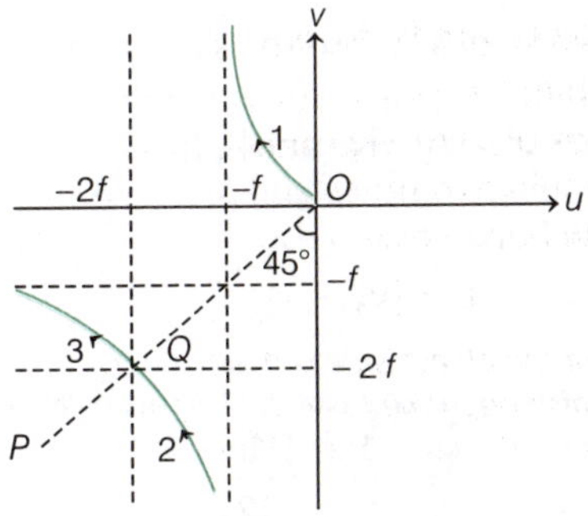

Note *OP line cuts the u - v graph at Q $(-2f, -2f)$*

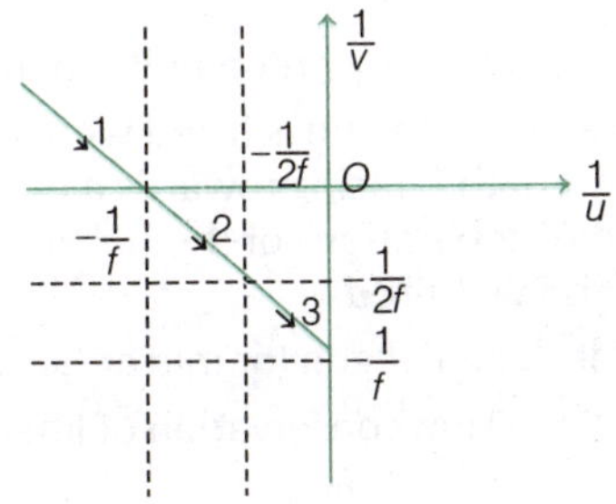

Exercise Draw above two graphs for convex mirror.

Miscellaneous Examples

Ex. 13 An object is 30.0 cm from a spherical mirror, along the central axis. The absolute value of lateral magnification is $\frac{1}{2}$. The image produced is inverted. What is the focal length of the mirror?

Sol. Image is inverted, so it is real. u and v both are negative. Magnification is $\frac{1}{2}$, therefore, $v = \frac{u}{2}$.

Given, $u = -30$ cm, $v = -15$ cm

Using the mirror formula,

$$\frac{1}{v} + \frac{1}{u} = \frac{1}{f}$$

We have, $$\frac{1}{f} = \frac{1}{-15} - \frac{1}{30} = -\frac{1}{10}$$

$\therefore$ $$f = -10 \text{ cm}$$ **Ans.**

Ex. 14 A concave mirror has a radius of curvature of 24 cm. How far is an object from the mirror if an image is formed that is :

(a) virtual and 3.0 times the size of the object,

(b) real and 3.0 times the size of the object and

(c) real and 1/3 the size of the object?

Sol. Given, $R = -24$ cm (concave mirror)

Hence, $$f = \frac{R}{2} = -12 \text{ cm}$$

(a) Image is virtual and 3 times larger. Hence, u is negative and v is positive.

Simultaneously, $|v| = 3|u|$. So let,

$$u = -x$$

then $$v = +3x$$

Substituting in the mirror formula,

$$\frac{1}{v} + \frac{1}{u} = \frac{1}{f}$$

We have,

$$\frac{1}{3x} - \frac{1}{x} = \frac{1}{-12}$$

$\therefore$ $$x = 8 \text{ cm}$$

Therefore, object distance is 8 cm. **Ans.**

(b) Image is real and three times larger. Hence, u and v both are negative and $|v| = 3|u|$.

So let,

$$u = -x$$

then $$v = -3x$$

Substituting in mirror formula, we have

$$\frac{1}{-3x} - \frac{1}{x} = -\frac{1}{12}$$

or $$x = 16 \text{ cm}$$

$\therefore$ Object distance should be 16 cm. **Ans.**

(c) Image is real and $\frac{1}{3}$ rd the size of object. Hence, both u and v are negative and $|v| = \frac{|u|}{3}$.

So let, $u = -x$

then $v = -\frac{x}{3}$

Substituting in the mirror formula, we have

$$-\frac{3}{x} - \frac{1}{x} = -\frac{1}{12}$$

$\therefore$ $x = 48$ cm

$\therefore$ Object distance should be 48 cm. **Ans.**

Ex. 15 A gun of mass m_1 fires a bullet of mass m_2 with a horizontal speed v_0. The gun is fitted with a concave mirror of focal length f facing towards a receding bullet. Find the speed of separations of the bullet and the image just after the gun was fired.

Sol. Let v_1 be the speed of gun (or mirror) just after the firing of bullet. From conservation of linear momentum,

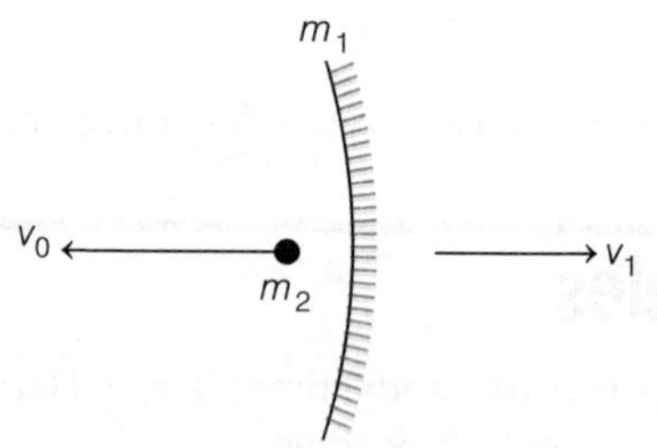

$$m_2 v_0 = m_1 v_1$$

or $$v_1 = \frac{m_2 v_0}{m_1} \qquad \text{...(i)}$$

Now, $\frac{du}{dt}$ is the rate at which distance between mirror and bullet is increasing $= v_1 + v_0$ ...(ii)

We have already read that :

$$\therefore \quad \frac{dv}{dt} = \left(\frac{v^2}{u^2}\right)\frac{du}{dt} \qquad \text{(magnitudewise)}$$

Here, $\frac{v^2}{u^2} = m^2 = 1$

(as at the time of firing, bullet is at pole).

$$\therefore \quad \frac{dv}{dt} = \frac{du}{dt} = v_1 + v_0 \qquad \text{...(iii)}$$

Here, $\frac{dv}{dt}$ is the rate at which distance between image (of bullet) and mirror is increasing. So, if v_2 is the absolute velocity of image (towards right), then

$$v_2 - v_1 = \frac{dv}{dt}$$

$$= v_1 + v_0$$

or $$v_2 = 2v_1 + v_0 \qquad \text{...(iv)}$$

Therefore, speed of separation of bullet and image will be

$$v_r = v_2 + v_0$$

$$= 2v_1 + v_0 + v_0$$

or $$v_r = 2(v_1 + v_0)$$

Substituting value of v_1 from Eq. (i), we have

$$v_r = 2\left(1 + \frac{m_2}{m_1}\right)v_0$$ **Ans.**

MODULE 3 Exercise

Assertion and Reason

See directions on page 11.

1. **Assertion :** Focal length of a convex mirror is 20 cm. If a real object is placed at distance 20 cm from the mirror, its virtual erect and diminished image will be formed.

   Reason : If a virtual object is placed at 20 cm distance, its image is formed at infinity.

2. **Assertion :** Rear view mirror of vehicles is a convex mirror.

   Reason : It never makes real image of real objects.

3. **Assertion :** If magnification of a real object is −2. Then, it is definitely a concave mirror.

   Reason : Only concave mirror can make real images of real objects.

4. **Assertion :** For real objects, image formed by a convex mirror always lies between pole and focus.

   Reason : When object moves from pole to infinity, its image will move from pole to focus.

5. **Assertion :** The formula connecting u, v and f for a spherical mirror is valid only for mirrors whose sizes are very small compared to their radii of curvature.

   Reason : Laws of reflection are strictly valid for plane surfaces, but not for large spherical surfaces. **(2007 JEE)**

Single Correct Option

6. When an object lies at the focus of a concave mirror, then the position of the image formed and its magnification are
   (a) pole and unity
   (b) infinity and unity
   (c) infinity and infinity
   (d) centre of curvature and unity

7. A concave mirror cannot form
   (a) virtual image of virtual object
   (b) virtual image of real object
   (c) real image of real object
   (d) real image of virtual object

8. All the following statements are correct except (for real objects)
   (a) the magnification produced by a convex mirror is always less than one
   (b) a virtual, erect and same sized image is obtained using a plane mirror
   (c) a virtual, erect, magnified image can be formed using a concave mirror
   (d) a real, inverted same sized image can be formed using a convex mirror

9. The minimum distance between the object and its real image for concave mirror is
   (a) f (b) $2f$ (c) $4f$ (d) Zero

10. The radius of curvature of a convex mirror is 60 cm. When an object is placed at A, its image is formed at B. If the size of image is half that of the object, then the distance between A and B is
    (a) 30 cm (b) 60 cm (c) 45 cm (d) 90 cm

11. A spherical mirror forms an erect image three times the size of the object. If the distance between the object and the image is 80 cm, the nature and the focal length of the mirror are
    (a) concave, 30 cm (b) convex, 30 cm
    (c) concave, 15 cm (d) convex, 15 cm

12. A convex mirror of focal length f produces an image $(1/n)^{\text{th}}$ of the size of the object. The distance of the object from the mirror is
    (a) nf (b) f/n (c) $(n+1)f$ (d) $(n-1)f$

13. An object is moving towards a concave mirror of focal length 24 cm. When it is at a distance of 60 cm from the mirror, its speed is 9 cm/s. The speed of its image at that instant, is
    (a) 4 cm/s towards the mirror
    (b) 6 cm/s towards the mirror
    (c) 4 cm/s away from the mirror
    (d) 6 cm/s away from the mirror

14. The focal length of a concave mirror is 50 cm. At what distance from the mirror an object be placed, so that its image is two times and inverted
    (a) 75 cm (b) 60 cm
    (c) 125 cm (d) 50 cm

15. Two objects A and B are placed at 15 cm and 25 cm from the pole in front of a concave mirror having radius of curvature 40 cm. The distance between images formed by the mirror is .... **(2023 Main)**
    (a) 60 cm (b) 40 cm
    (c) 160 cm (d) 100 cm

16. Car B overtakes another car A at a relative speed of 40 ms^{-1}. How fast will the image of car B appear to move in the mirror of focal length 10 cm fitted in car A, when the car B is 1.9 m away from the car A? **(2021 Main)**
    (a) 4 ms^{-1} (b) 0.2 ms^{-1}
    (c) 40 ms^{-1} (d) 0.1 ms^{-1}

17. A concave mirror for face viewing has focal length of 0.4 m. The distance at which you hold the mirror from your face in order to see your image upright with a magnification of 5 is **(2019 Main)**
    (a) 0.16 m (b) 1.60 m
    (c) 0.32 m (d) 0.24 m

Multiple Correct Options

18. The image formed by a concave mirror is twice the size of the object. The focal length of the mirror is 20 cm. The distance of the object from the mirror is/are
(a) 10 cm (b) 30 cm (c) 25 cm (d) 15 cm

19. Magnitude of focal length of a spherical mirror is f and magnitude of linear magnification is $\frac{1}{2}$.
(a) If image is inverted, it is a concave mirror
(b) If image is erect, it is a convex mirror
(c) Object distance from the mirror may be $3f$
(d) Object distance from the mirror may be f

Subjective Questions

20. Assume that a certain spherical mirror has a focal length of – 10.0 cm. Locate and describe the image for object distances of (a) 25.0 cm (b) 10.0 cm (c) 5.0 cm.

21. A ball is dropped from rest 3.0 m directly above the vertex of a concave mirror that has a radius of 1.0 m and lies in a horizontal plane.
(a) Describe the motion of ball's image in the mirror.
(b) At what time do the ball and its image coincide?

22. An object 6.0 mm is placed 16.5 cm to the left of the vertex of a concave spherical mirror having a radius of curvature of 22.0 cm.
(a) Draw principal ray diagram showing formation of the image.
(b) Determine the position, size, orientation, and nature (real or virtual) of the image.

23. By means of ray diagram find:
(a) the path of a light ray after reflection from a concave and convex spherical mirrors see figure, where F is the focal point, OO' is the optical axis)

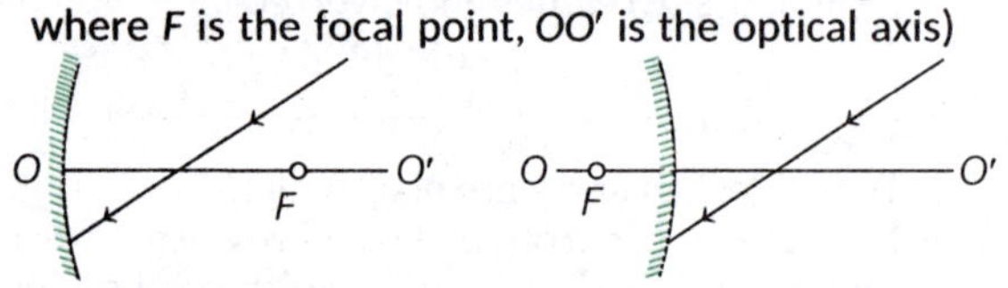

(i) (ii)

(b) the positions of the mirror and its focal point in the cases illustrated in figure, where P and P' are the object and image points. **(Irodov 5.26)**

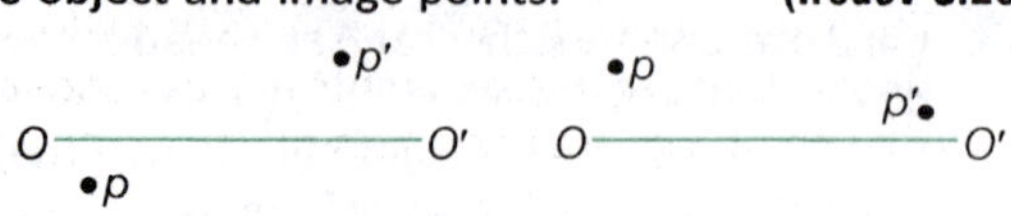

(i) (ii)

24. Determine the focal length of a concave mirror if:
(a) with the distance between an object and its image being equal to $l = 15$ cm, the transverse magnification $m = -2.0$
(b) in a certain position of the object the transverse magnification is $m_1 = -0.50$ and in another position displaced with respect to the former by a distance $l = 5.0$ cm the transverse magnification $m_2 = -0.25$. **(Irodov 5.27)**

Integer Type Questions

25. A thin cylindrical rod of length 10 cm is placed horizontally on the principle axis of a concave mirror of focal length 20 cm. The rod is placed in such a way that mid-point of the rod is at 40 cm from the pole of mirror. The length of the image formed by the mirror will be $x/3$ cm. The value of x is .... **(2023 Main)**

26. An object O is placed at a distance of 100 cm in front of a concave mirror of radius of curvature 200 cm as shown in the figure. The object starts moving towards the mirror at a speed 2 cm/s. The position of the image from the mirror after 10 s will be at .... cm. **(2022 Main)**

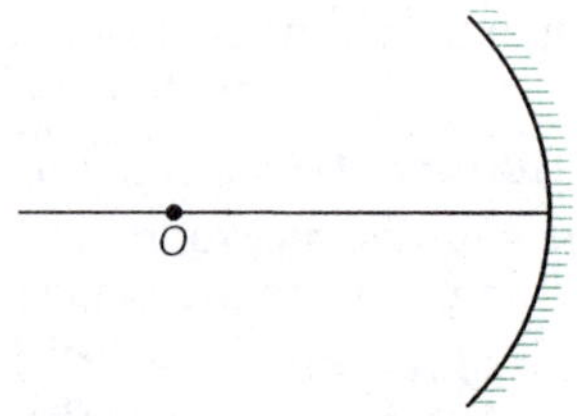

Answers

1. (b)	**2.** (b)	**3.** (a)	**4.** (a)	**5.** (c)
6. (c)	**7.** (a)	**8.** (d)	**9.** (d)	**10.** (c)
11. (a)	**12.** (d)	**13.** (c)	**14.** (a)	**15.** (c)
16. (d)	**17.** (c)	**18.** (a,b)	**19.** (a,b,c,d)	

20. (a) – 16.7 cm, real (b) ∞ (c) + 10.0 cm, virtual

21. (a) A real image moves from – 0.6 m to $-\infty$, then a virtual image moves from $+\infty$ to 0 (b) 0.639 s and 0.782 s.

22. (b) 33.0 cm to the left of vertex 1.20 cm tall, inverted, real

24. (a) $f = -10$ cm, (b) $f = -2.5$ cm

25. (32) **26.** (400)

See hints on pages 53-56.

Unit Exercise (Cumulative)

Level 1

Single Correct Option

1. A point object is placed at a distance of 10 cm and its real image is formed at a distance of 20 cm from a concave mirror. If the object is moved by 0.1 cm towards the mirror, the image will shift by about
(a) 0.4 cm away from the mirror
(b) 0.8 cm away from the mirror
(c) 0.4 cm towards the mirror
(d) 0.8 cm towards the mirror

2. A convex and a concave mirror of radii 10 cm each are placed facing each other and 15 cm apart. An object is placed exactly between them. If the reflection first takes place in concave and then in convex mirror, the position of the final image will be
(a) 10 cm behind concave mirror
(b) at the pole of the concave mirror
(c) at the pole of the convex mirror
(d) 5 cm in front of concave mirror

3. A spherical mirror forms an erect image three times the size of the object. If the distance between the object and the image is 80 cm, the nature and the focal length of the mirror are
(a) concave, 15 cm (b) convex, 30 cm
(c) concave, 30 cm (d) convex, 15 cm

4. In a concave mirror an object is placed at a distance x from the focus and the real image is formed at a distance y from the focus. The focal length of the mirror is
(a) $x \sim y$ (b) $\sqrt{xy}$
(c) $x + y$ (d) None of these

5. Two plane mirrors L_1 and L_2 are parallel to each other and 3 m apart. A person standing x m from the right mirror L_2 looks into this mirror and sees a series of images. The distance between the first and second image is 4 m. Then, the value of x is

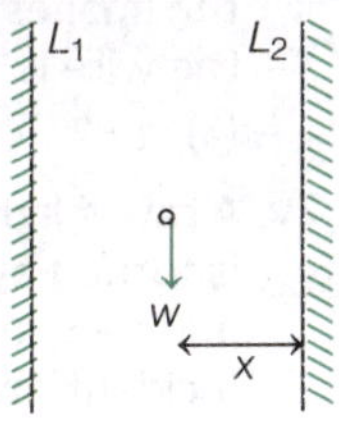

(a) 2 m (b) 1.5 m (c) 1 m (d) 2.5 m

6. A point object at 15 cm from a concave mirror of radius of curvature 20 cm is made to oscillate along the principal axis with amplitude 2 mm. The amplitude of its image will be
(a) 2 mm (b) 4 mm
(c) 8 mm (d) None of these

7. A person AB of height 170 cm is standing in front of a plane mirror. His eyes are at height 164 cm. At what distance from P should a hole be made in mirror so that he cannot see his hair?

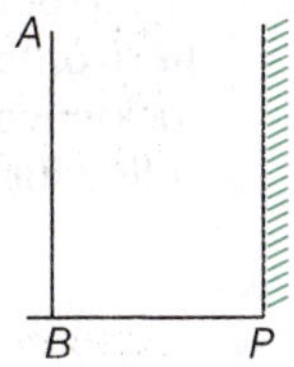

(a) 167 cm (b) 161 cm
(c) 163 cm (d) 165 cm

8. A plane mirror is moving with velocity $4\hat{\mathbf{i}} + 4\hat{\mathbf{j}} + 8\hat{\mathbf{k}}$. A point object in front of the mirror moves with a velocity $3\hat{\mathbf{i}} + 4\hat{\mathbf{j}} + 5\hat{\mathbf{k}}$. Here, $\hat{\mathbf{k}}$ is along the normal to the plane mirror and facing towards the object. The velocity of the image is
(a) $-3\hat{\mathbf{i}} - 4\hat{\mathbf{j}} + 5\hat{\mathbf{k}}$
(b) $3\hat{\mathbf{i}} + 4\hat{\mathbf{j}} + 11\hat{\mathbf{k}}$
(c) $-4\hat{\mathbf{i}} + 5\hat{\mathbf{j}} + 11\hat{\mathbf{k}}$
(d) $7\hat{\mathbf{i}} + 9\hat{\mathbf{j}} + 3\hat{\mathbf{k}}$

9. A convex mirror of radius of curvature 20 cm is shown in figure. An object O is placed in front of this mirror. Its ray diagram is shown. How many mistakes are there in the ray diagram (AB is principal axis)

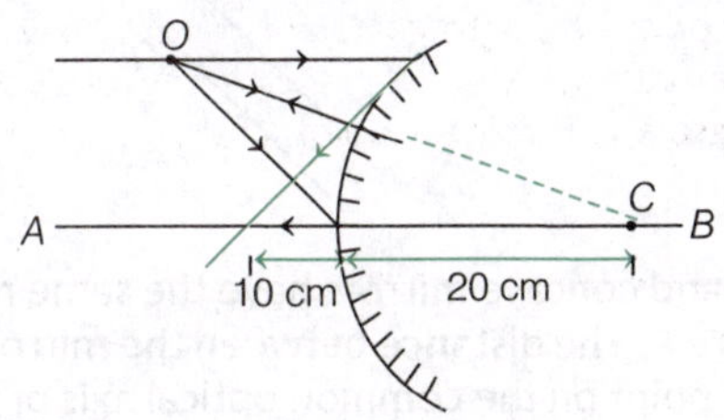

(a) 3 (b) 2
(c) 1 (d) 0

10. The graph shows part of variation of v with change in u for a concave mirror. Points plotted above the point P on the curve are for values of v :

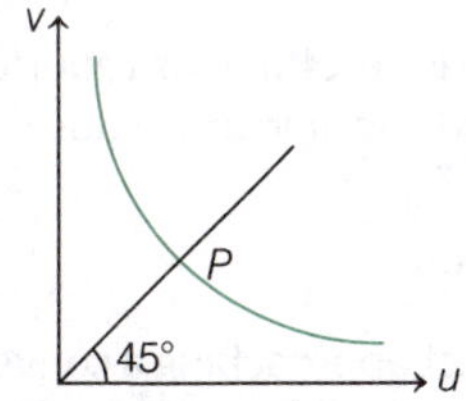

(a) smaller than f
(b) smaller than $2f$
(c) larger than $2f$
(d) larger than f but less than $2f$

11. A plane mirror is placed along the y-axis such that x-axis is normal to the plane of the mirror. The reflecting surface of the mirror is towards negative x-axis. The mirror moves in positive x-direction with uniform speed of 5 m/s and a point object P is moving with constant speed 3 m/s in negative x-direction. The speed of image with respect to mirror is
(a) 8 m/s (b) 2 m/s (c) 4 m/s (d) 16 m/s

12. A mirror is inclined at an angle of θ with the horizontal. If a ray of light is incident at an angle of incidence θ, then the reflected ray makes the following angle with horizontal.

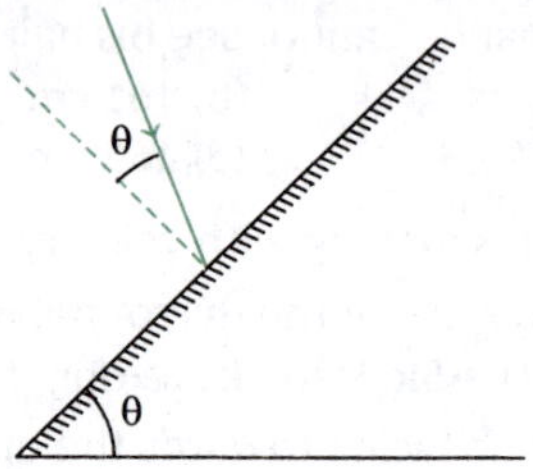

(a) θ (b) 2θ
(c) $\frac{\theta}{2}$ (d) None of these

Subjective Questions

13. Figure shows two rays P and Q being reflected by a mirror and going as P' and Q'. State which type of mirror is this?

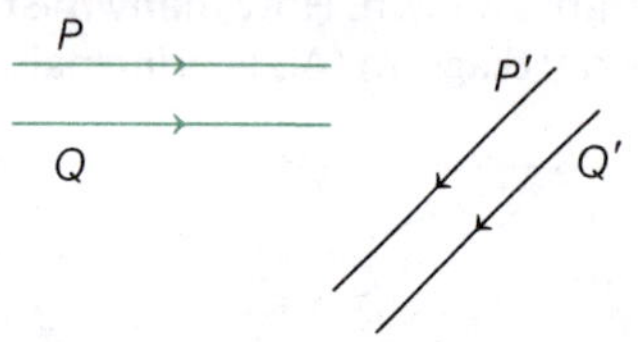

14. Convex and concave mirrors have the same radii of curvature R. The distance between the mirrors is $2R$. At what point on the common optical axis of the mirrors should a point source of light A be placed for the rays to coverage at the point A after being reflected first on the convex and then on the concave mirror?

15. A spherical mirror is to be used to form on a screen 5.0 m from the object an image five times the size of the object.
(a) Describe the type of mirror required.
(b) Where should the mirror be positioned relative to the object?

Integer Type Question

16. Image of an object approaching a convex mirror of radius of curvature 20 m along its optical axis is observed to move from $\frac{25}{3}$ m to $\frac{50}{7}$ m in 30 s. What is the speed of the object in km h^{-1}? **(2010 JEE)**

Level 2

Single Correct Option

17. An insect of negligible mass is sitting on a block of mass M, tied with a spring of force constant k. The block performs simple harmonic motion with amplitude A in front of a plane mirror as shown. The maximum speed of insect relative to its image will be

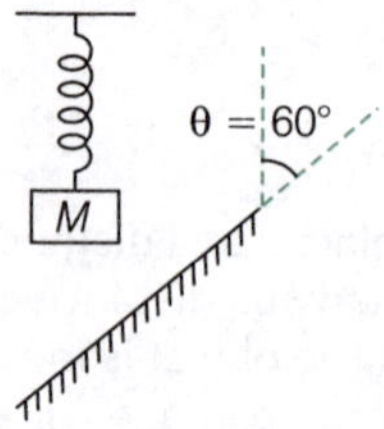

(a) $A\sqrt{\frac{k}{M}}$ (b) $\frac{A\sqrt{3}}{2}\sqrt{\frac{k}{M}}$
(c) $A\sqrt{3}\sqrt{\frac{k}{M}}$ (d) $2A\sqrt{\frac{M}{k}}$

18. A plane mirror is falling vertically as shown in the figure. If S is a point source of light, the rate of increase of the length AB is

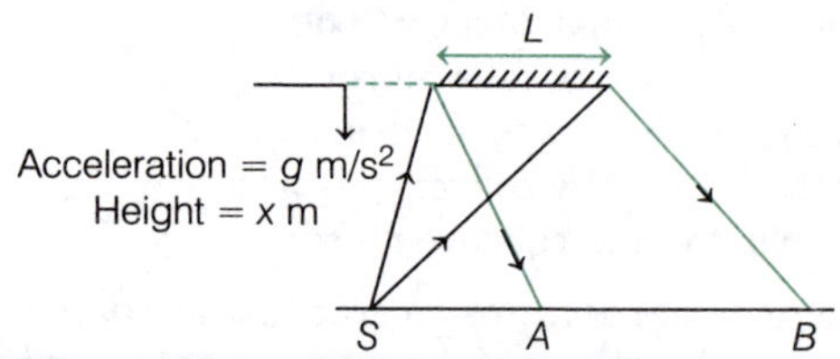

(a) directly proportional to x
(b) constant but not zero
(c) inversely proportional to x
(d) zero

19. A piece of wire bent into an L shape with upright and horizontal portion of equal lengths 10 cm each is placed with the horizontal portion along the axis of the concave mirror towards pole of mirror whose radius of curvature is 10 cm. If the bend is 20 cm from the pole of the mirror, then the ratio of the lengths of the images of the upright and horizontal portion of the wire is
(a) 1 : 2 (b) 1 : 3 (c) 1 : 1 (d) 2 : 1

20. A ray of light falls on a plane mirror. When the mirror is turned by 20° the angle between the incident ray and new reflected ray is 45°. The angle between the incident ray and original reflected ray was therefore
(a) 35° or 50° (b) 25° or 65°
(c) 45° or 5° (d) None of these

21. Two blocks each of masses m lie on a smooth table. They are attached to two other masses as shown in figure. The pulleys and strings are light. An object O is kept at rest on the table. The sides AB and CD of the two blocks are made reflecting. The acceleration of

two images formed in those two reflecting surfaces with respect to each other is

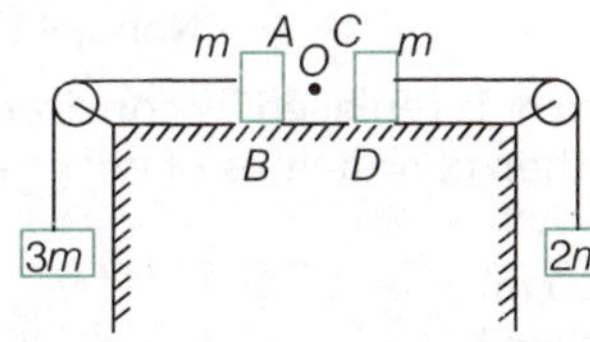

(a) $\frac{5g}{6}$ (b) $\frac{5g}{3}$ (c) $\frac{17g}{12}$ (d) $\frac{17g}{6}$

22. An elevator at rest which is at 10th floor of a building is having a plane mirror fixed to its floor. A particle is projected with a speed $\sqrt{2}$ m/s and at 45° with the horizontal as shown in the figure. At the same instant of projection, the cable of the elevator breaks and the elevator starts falling freely. What will be the separation between the particle and is image 0.5 s after the instant of projection?

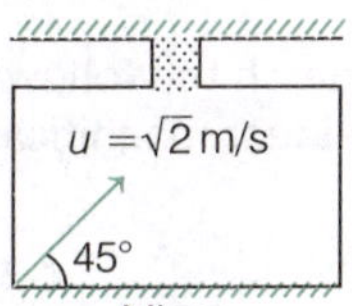

(a) 0.5 m (b) 1 m (c) 2 m (d) 1.5 m

23. Point A (0, 1 cm) and B (12 cm, 5 cm) are the coordinates of object and image. x-axis is the principal axis of the mirror. Then, this object-image pair is
(a) due to a convex mirror of focal length 2.5 cm
(b) due to a concave mirror having its pole at (2 cm, 0)
(c) due to a concave mirror having its pole at (−2 cm, 0)
(d) Data is insufficient

24. Two plane mirrors AB and AC are inclined at an angle $\theta = 20°$. A ray of light starting from point P is incident at point Q on the mirror AB, then at R on mirror AC and again on S on AB. Finally, the ray ST goes parallel to mirror AC. The angle which the ray makes with the normal at point Q on mirror AB is

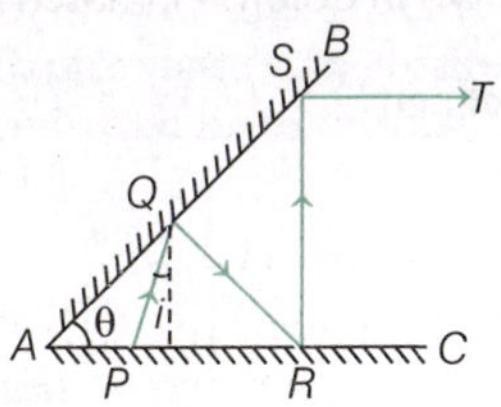

(a) 20° (b) 30° (c) 40° (d) 60°

25. A ray of light makes an angle of 10° with the horizontal and strikes a plane mirror which is inclined at an angle θ to the horizontal. The angle θ for which the reflected ray becomes vertical, is
(a) 40° (b) 50°
(c) both are correct (d) both are wrong

26. A ball is projected from top of the table with initial speed u at an angle of inclination θ, motion of image of ball w.r.t ball is

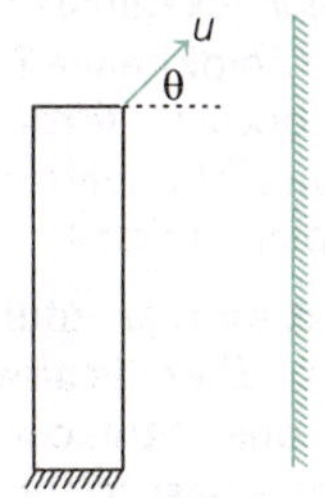

(a) a parabola
(b) a straight line and vertical
(c) a straight line and horizontal
(d) None of the above

27. A ray of light travelling in the direction $\frac{1}{2}(\hat{i} + \sqrt{3}\,\hat{j})$ is incident on a plane mirror. After reflection, it travels along the direction $\frac{1}{2}(\hat{i} - \sqrt{3}\,\hat{j})$. The angle of incidence is
(a) 30° (b) 45°
(c) 60° (d) 75°

28. A wire is bent in the shape of a right angled triangle and is placed in front of a concave mirror of focal length f as shown in the figure. Which of the figures shown in the four options qualitatively represent(s) the shape of the image of the bent wire? (These figures are not to scale.) **(2018 Adv.)**

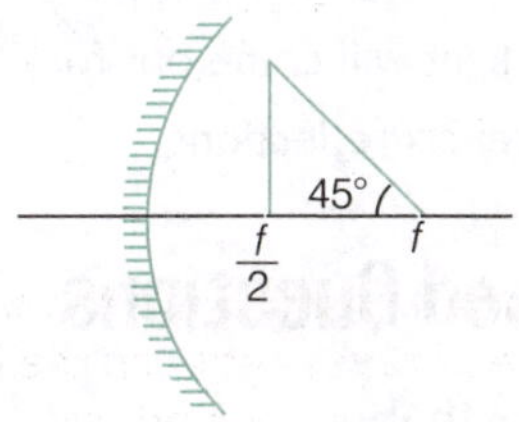

(a) 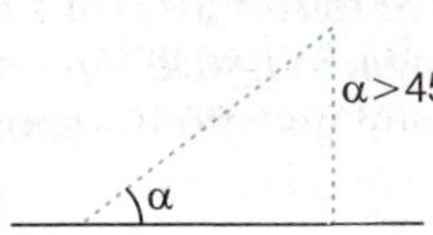

(b) 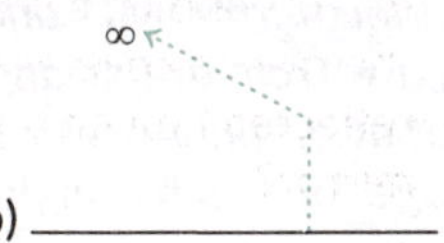

(c) 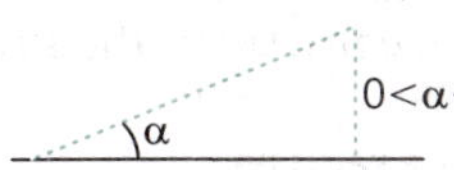

(d) 

Multiple Correct Options

29. A point object is placed at equal distance $3f$ in front of a concave mirror, a convex mirror and a plane mirror separately (event-1). Now, the distance is decreased to $1.5f$ from all the three mirrors (event-2). Magnitude of focal length of convex mirror and concave mirror is f. Then, choose the correct options.

(a) Maximum distance of image in event-1 from the mirror is from plane mirror
(b) Minimum distance of image in event-1 from the mirror is from convex mirror
(c) Maximum distance of image in event-2 from the mirror is from concave mirror
(d) Minimum distance of image in event-2 from the mirror is from plane mirror

30. Three plane mirrors form an equilateral triangle with each side of length L. There is a small hole at a distance $l > 0$ from one of the corners as shown in the figure. A ray of light is passed through the hole at an angle θ and can only come out through the same hole. The cross-section of the mirror configuration and the ray of light lie on the same plane. **(2022 Adv.)**

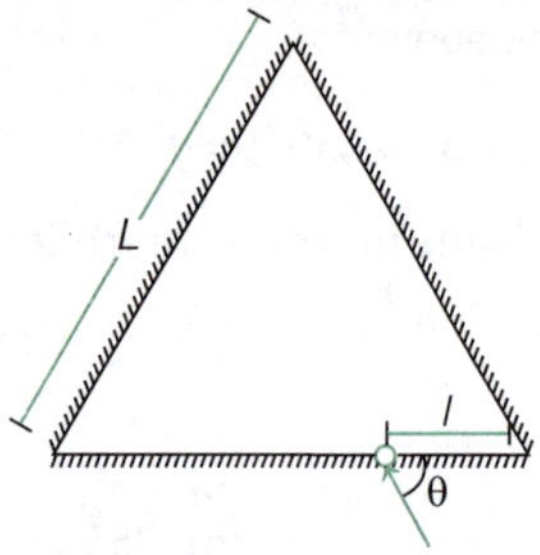

Which of the following statement(s) is(are) correct?
(a) The ray of light will come out for $\theta = 30°$, for $0 < l < L$.
(b) There is an angle for $l = L/2$ at which the ray of light will come out after two reflections.
(c) The ray of light will never come out for $\theta = 60°$, and $l = L/3$.
(d) The ray of light will come out for $\theta = 60°$, and $0 < l < \frac{L}{2}$ after six reflections.

Passage Based Questions

Passage (Q.No. 31 to 34)

A plane mirror (M_1) and a concave mirror (M_2) of focal length 10 cm are arranged as shown in figure. An object is kept at origin. Answer the following questions. (consider image formed by single reflection in all cases)

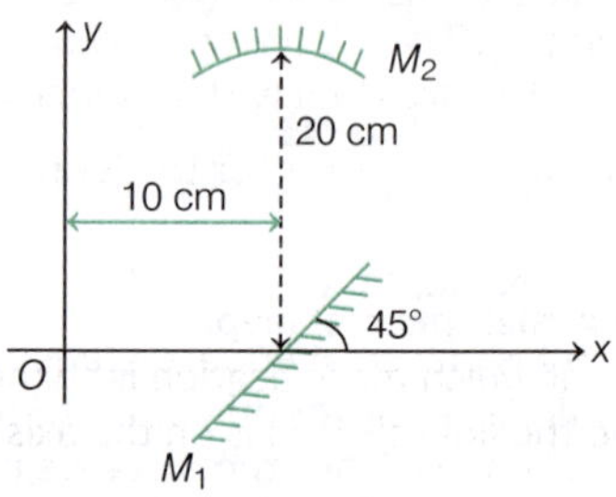

31. The coordinates of image formed by plane mirror are
(a) (−20 cm, 0) (b) (10 cm, −60 cm)
(c) (10 cm, −10 cm) (d) (10 cm, 10 cm)

32. The coordinates of image formed by concave mirror are
(a) (10 cm, −40 cm) (b) (10 cm, −60 cm)
(c) (10 cm, 8 cm) (d) None of these

33. If concave mirror is replaced by convex mirror of same focal length, then coordinates of image formed by M_2 will be
(a) (10 cm, 12 cm)
(b) (10 cm, 22 cm)
(c) (10 cm, 8 cm)
(d) None of the above

34. If concave mirror is replaced by another plane mirror parallel to x-axis, then coordinates of image formed by M_2 are
(a) (40 cm, 20 cm)
(b) (20 cm, 40 cm)
(c) (−20 cm, 20 cm)
(d) None of the above

Match the Columns

35. For real objects, match the following two columns corresponding to linear magnification m given in Column I.

	Column I		Column II
(a)	$m = -2$	(p)	convex mirror
(b)	$m = -\frac{1}{2}$	(q)	concave mirror
(c)	$m = +2$	(r)	real image
(d)	$m = +\frac{1}{2}$	(s)	virtual image

36. For virtual objects, match the following two columns.

	Column I		Column II
(a)	Plane mirror	(p)	only real image
(b)	Convex mirror	(q)	only virtual image
(c)	Concave mirror	(r)	may be real or virtual image

37. Principal axis of a mirror (AB), a point object O and its image I are shown in Column I, match it with Column II.

	Column I		Column II
(a)		(p)	plane mirror
(b)	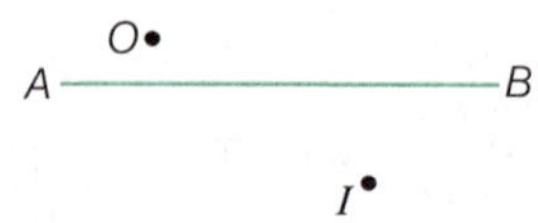	(q)	convex mirror
(c)		(r)	concave mirror
(d)		(s)	not possible

38. Focal length of a concave mirror M_1 is -20 cm and focal length of a convex mirror M_2 is $+20$ cm. A point object is placed at a distance X in front of M_1 or M_2. Match the following two columns.

	Column I		Column II
(a)	$X = 20$, mirror is M_1	(p)	image is at infinity
(b)	$X = 20$, mirror is M_2	(q)	image is real
(c)	$X = 30$, mirror is M_1	(r)	image is virtual
(d)	$X = 30$, mirror is M_2	(s)	image is magnified

39. Focal length of a concave mirror is -20 cm. Match the object distance given in Column II corresponding to magnification (only magnitude) given is Column I.

	Column I		Column II
(a)	2	(p)	10 cm
(b)	1/2	(q)	30 cm
(c)	1	(r)	20 cm
(d)	1/4	(s)	None of these

Subjective Questions

40. A concave mirror forms the real image of a point source lying on the optical axis at a distance of 50 cm from the mirror. The focal length of the mirror is 25 cm. The mirror is cut into two halves and its halves are pulled a distance of 1 cm apart in a direction perpendicular to the optical axis. How will the image formed by the halves of the mirror be arranged?

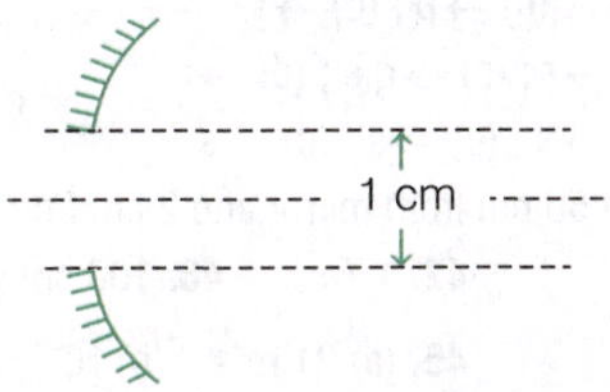

41. A point source of light S is placed on the major optical axis of the concave mirror at a distance of 60 cm. At what distance from the concave mirror should a flat mirror be placed for the rays to converge again at the point S having been reflected from the concave mirror and then from the flat one? Will the position of the point where the rays meet change if they are first reflected from the flat mirror? The radius of the concave mirror is 80 cm.

42. A balloon is moving upwards with a speed of 20 m/s. When it is at a height of 14 m from ground in front of a plane mirror in the situation as shown in figure, a boy drops himself from the balloon. Find the time duration for which he will see the image of source S placed symmetrically before plane mirror during free fall.

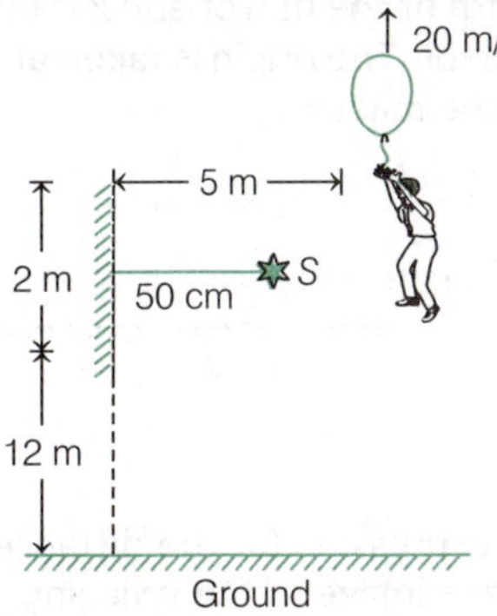

43. A plane mirror and a concave mirror are arranged as shown in figure and O is a point object. Find the position of image formed by two reflections, first one taking place at concave mirror.

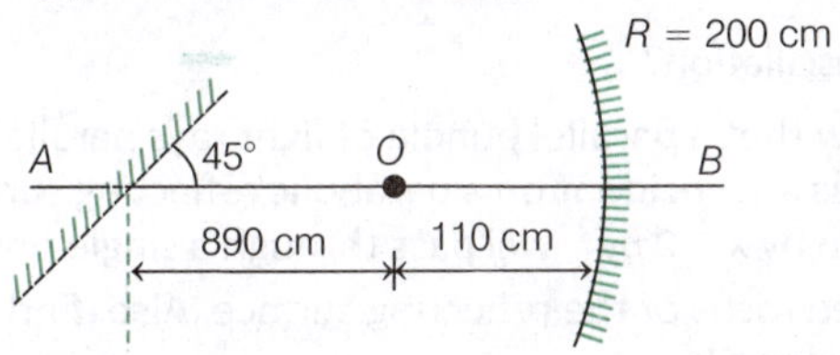

44. Figure shows a torch producing a straight light beam falling on a plane mirror at an angle 60°. The reflected beam makes a spot P on the screen along y-axis. If at $t = 0$, mirror starts rotating about the hinge A with an angular velocity $\omega = 1°$ per second clockwise. Find the speed of the spot on screen after time $t = 15$ s.

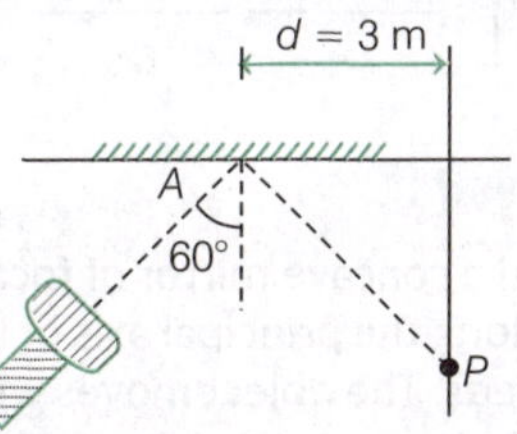

45. A thief is running away in a car with velocity of 20 m/s. A police jeep is following him, which is sighted by thief in his rear view mirror, which is a convex mirror of focal length 10 m. He observes that the image of jeep is moving towards him with a velocity of 1 cm/s. If the magnification of mirror for the jeep at that time is $\frac{1}{10}$.

Find

(a) the actual speed of jeep,

(b) rate at which magnification is changing.

Assume the police's jeep is on the axis of the mirror.

46. A ball swings back and forth in front of a concave mirror. The motion of the ball is described approximately by the equation $x = f \cos \omega t$, where f is the focal length of the mirror and x is measured along the axis of mirror. The origin is taken at the centre of curvature of the mirror.

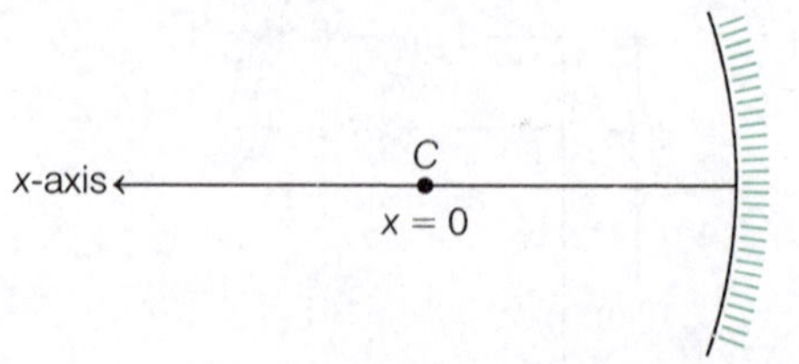

(a) Derive an expression for the distance from the mirror of the image of the swinging ball.
(b) At what point does the ball appear to coincide with its image?
(c) What will be the lateral magnification of the image of the ball at time $t = \frac{T}{2}$, where T is time period of oscillation?

47. Show that a parallel bundle of light rays parallel to the x-axis and incident on a parabolic reflecting surface given by $x = 2by^2$, will pass through a single point called focus of the reflecting surface. Also, find the focal length.

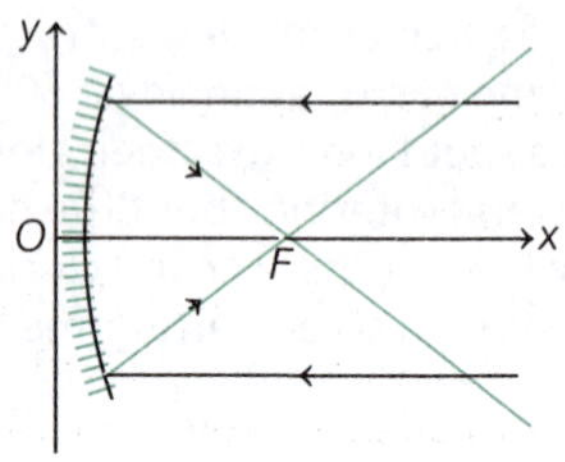

Integer Type Question

48. An object and a concave mirror of focal length $f = 10$ cm both move along the principal axis of the mirror with constant speeds. The object moves with speed $v_0 = 15 \text{ cm s}^{-1}$ towards the mirror with respect to a laboratory frame. The distance between the object and the mirror at a given moment is denoted by u. When $u = 30$ cm, the speed of the mirror v_m is such that the image is instantaneously at rest with respect to the laboratory frame and the object forms a real image. The magnitude of v_m is .... cm s^{-1}. **(2022 Adv.)**

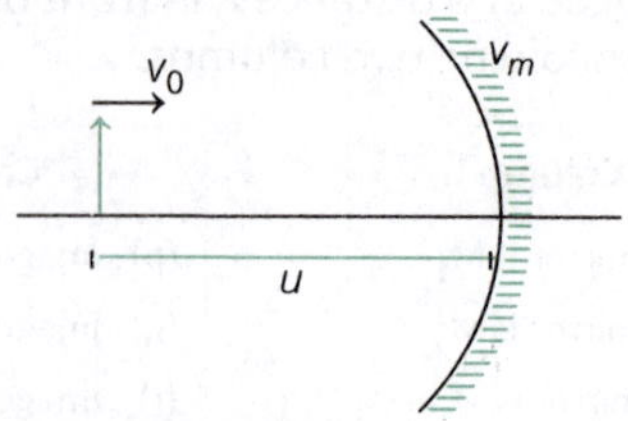

Answers

Level 1

1. (a)	**2.** (c)	**3.** (c)	**4.** (b)	**5.** (c)
6. (c)	**7.** (a)	**8.** (b)	**9.** (b)	**10.** (c)
11. (a)	**12.** (d)	**13.** Plane mirror		

14. At a distance $\left(\frac{\sqrt{3}+1}{2}\right) R$ from convex mirror

15. (a) A concave mirror with radius of curvature 2.08 m
(b) 1.25 m from the object **16.** (3)

Level 2

17. (c)	**18.** (d)	**19.** (c)	**20.** (d)	**21.** (d)
22. (b)	**23.** (b)	**24.** (b)	**25.** (c)	**26.** (c)
27. (a)	**28.** (d)	**29.** (a,b,c)	**30.** (a,b)	**31.** (c)
32. (d)	**33.** (d)	**34.** (d)		

35. (a) $\to$ q,r ; (b) $\to$ q,r ; (c) $\to$ q,s ; (d) $\to$ p,s
36. (a) $\to$ p ; (b) $\to$ r ; (c) $\to$ p
37. (a) $\to$ r ; (b) $\to$ r ; (c) $\to$ p ; (d) $\to$ r
38. (a) $\to$ p,s ; (b) $\to$ r ; (c) $\to$ q,s ; (d) $\to$ r
39. (a) $\to$ p,q ; (b) $\to$ s ; (c) $\to$ s ; (d) $\to$ s
40. At a distance of 50 cm from mirror and 2 cm from each other
41. 90 cm, Yes **42.** 1.7 s **43.** 100 cm vertically below A
44. $\frac{2\pi}{15}$ m/s **45.** (a) 21 m/s (b) 10^{-3}/s
46. (a) Distance $= \left(\frac{2+\cos \omega t}{1+\cos \omega t}\right) f$ (b) At $x = 0$ (c) $m = \infty$
47. $f = \frac{1}{8b}$ **48.** (3)

See hints on pages 56-63.

Hints & SOLUTIONS

Module 2.

1.

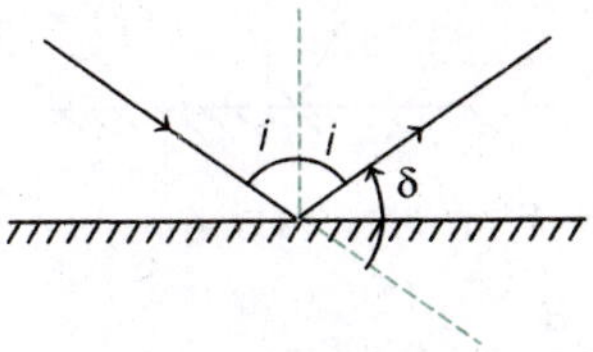

$$\delta = 180° - 2i$$

For normal incidence, $i = 0°$

$\therefore \quad \delta = 180°$

3. Image is real and incident beam is convergent.

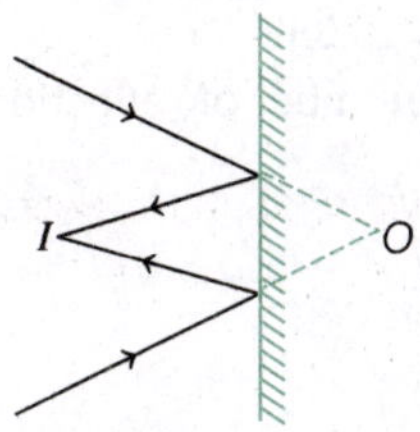

4. The hour hand is lying between 3 and 4. So, on the mirror it will appear between 8 and 9.
The minute hand is lying at 25. So, on mirror it will appear at 35.

5.

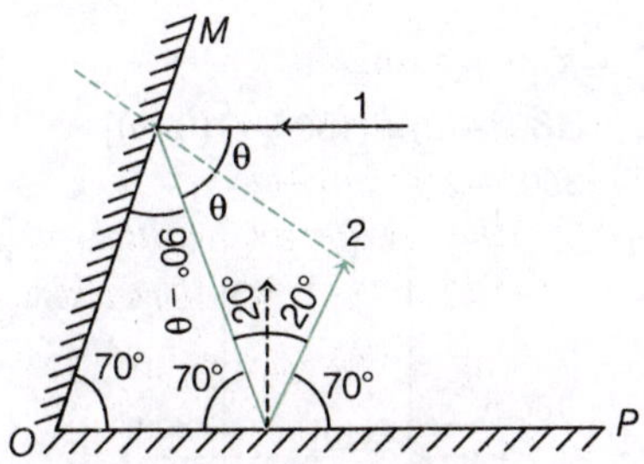

$$90° - \theta + 70° + 70° = 180°$$

$\therefore \quad \theta = 50°$

6.

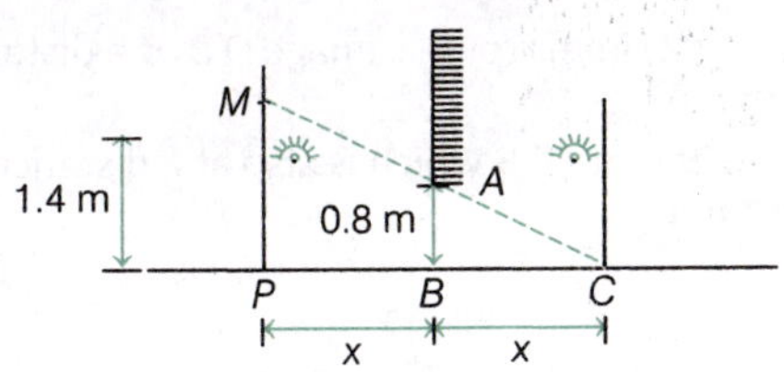

$$\frac{MP}{PC} = \frac{AB}{BC}$$

$\therefore \quad \frac{MP}{2x} = \frac{0.8}{x}$

or $\quad MP = 1.6 \text{ m} > 1.4 \text{ m}$

Hence, the boy cannot see his feet.

7.

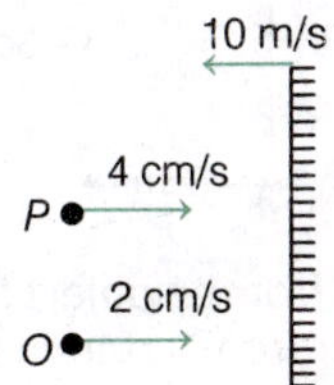

$$v_{PM} = 14 \text{ cm/s towards right}$$
$$v_{IM} = 14 \text{ cm/s towards left}$$

So, actual speed of image = 24 cm/s towards left

$\therefore \quad v_{IO} = 26 \text{ cm/s towards left.}$

8. According to ray diagram as shown in figure

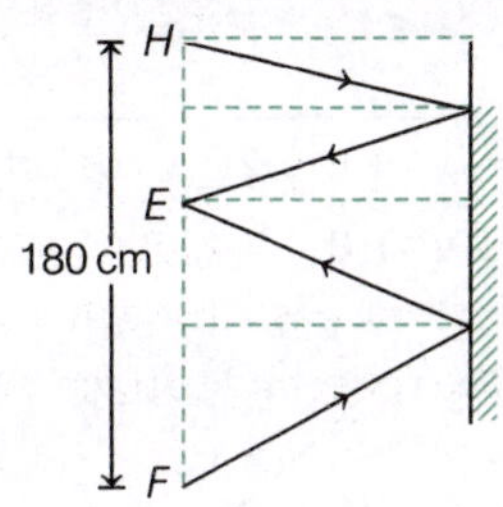

$$\text{Length of mirror} = \frac{1}{2}(10 + 170)$$
$$= 90 \text{ cm}$$

9. Image of O from M_1 is at a distance of 8 cm to the left of M_1. This image is at a distance of 18 cm in front of M_2. So, its image is formed at a distance of 18 cm to the right of M_2.
First image of O from M_2 is at 2 cm behind M_2. So, it is at a distance of 12 cm from M_1. Hence, M_1 will make its image at a distance of 12 cm from M_1 towards left. This image is at a distance of 22 cm from M_2.

10. Given, $AC = 60 \text{ m}$ and $\angle BCB' = 90°$

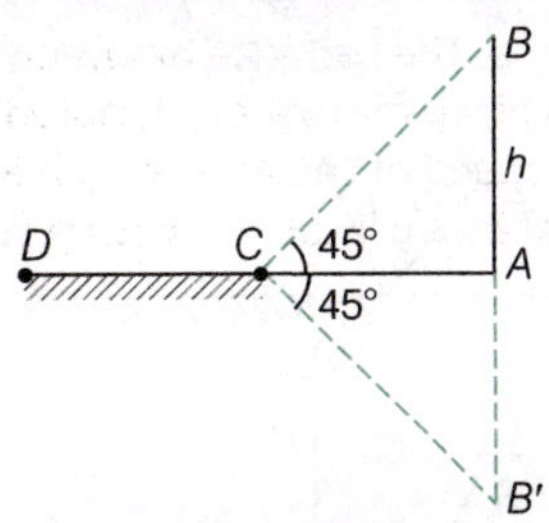

$\therefore \quad \angle BCA = \frac{\angle BCB'}{2} = 45°$

$$AB = AC = 60 \text{ m}$$

11. In a plane mirror, image is always at same distance from object.
From below diagrams, distance by which image moved is 8 cm towards mirror (from it's previous position).

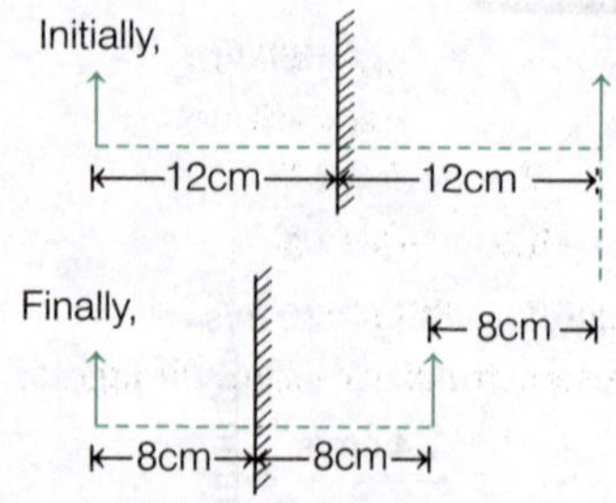

12. When the light rays from an object have been reflected towards an observer from a standard flat mirror is the image observed by the observer is virtual, **erect**, same size as the object and **laterally inverted.**

13.

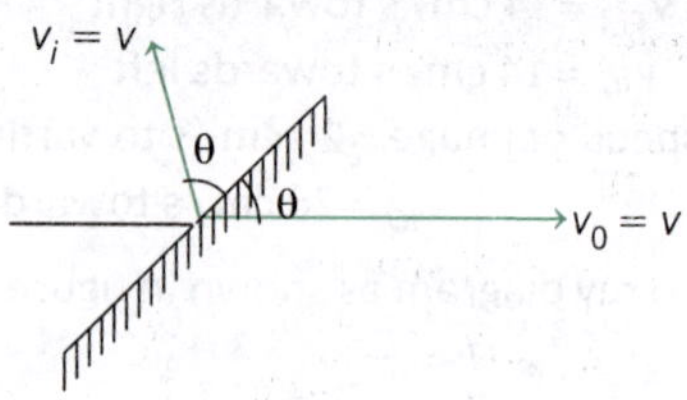

$$v_r = \sqrt{v^2 + v^2 - 2v \cdot v \cos 2\theta}$$
$$= 2\,v \sin\theta$$

14.

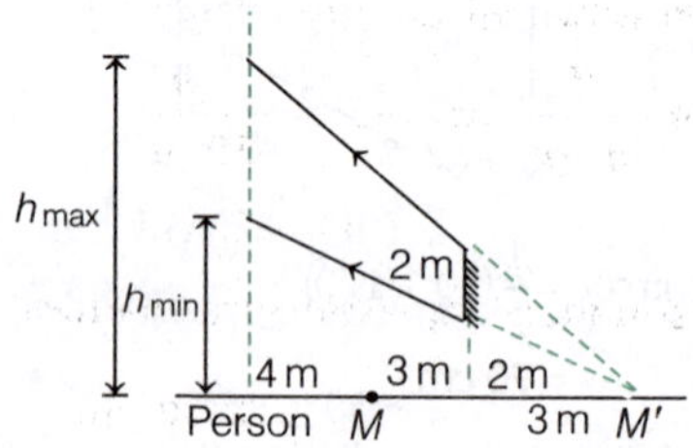

$$\therefore \quad h_{min} = \frac{20}{3}\text{ m}$$
$$\frac{h_{max}}{10} = \frac{4}{3}$$
$$\therefore \quad h_{max} = \frac{40}{3}\text{ m}$$

15.

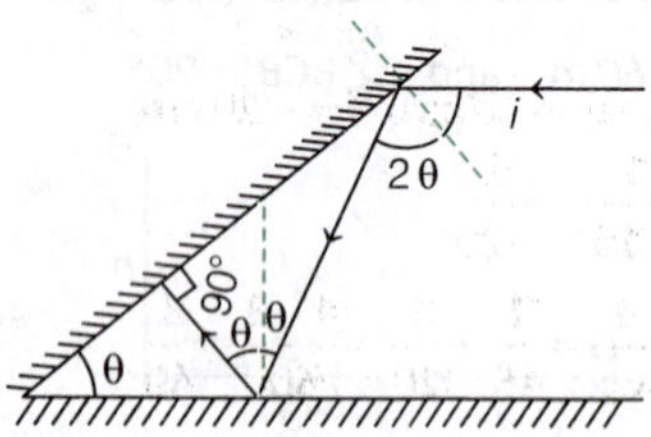

$i = 2\theta$

16.

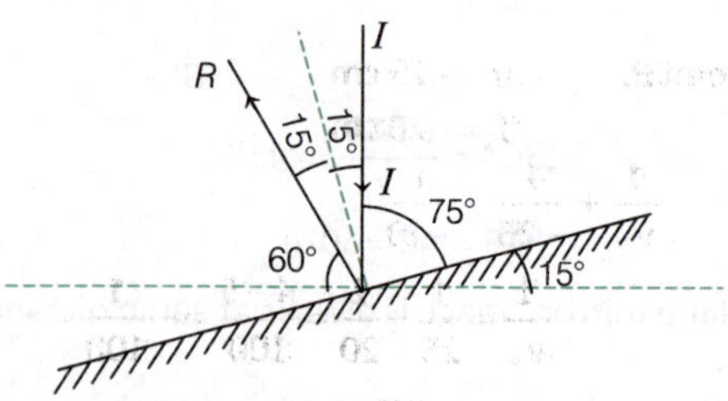

where, I = incident ray

R = reflected ray

Angle of incidence = 15°

Angle between reflected ray and horizontal = 60°

17.

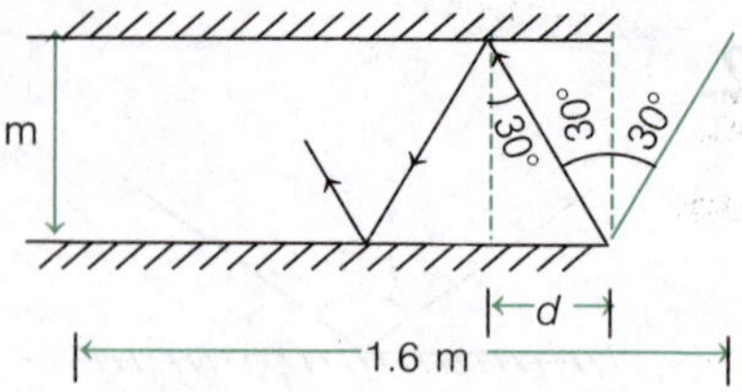

$$\frac{d}{0.2} = \tan 30° = \frac{1}{\sqrt{3}}$$
$$\therefore \quad d = \frac{0.2}{\sqrt{3}}$$
$$N = \frac{1.6}{d} = 8\sqrt{3}$$
$$= 13.85$$

Therefore, actual number of reflections required are 14.

18.

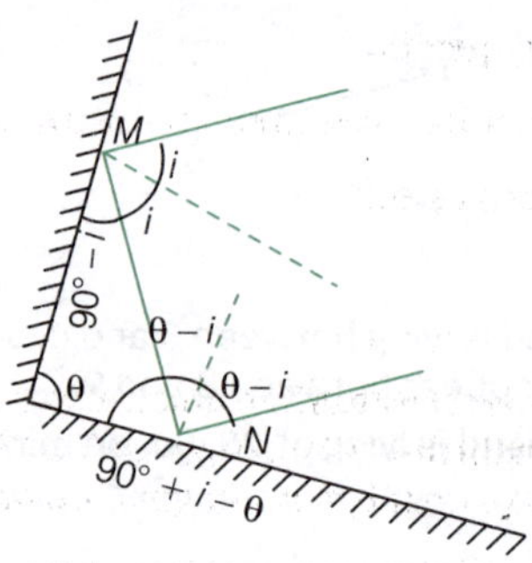

$$\delta_{Total} = \delta_M + \delta_N$$
$$= (180° - 2i) + [180° - 2(\theta - i)]$$
$$= 360° - 2\theta$$

19.

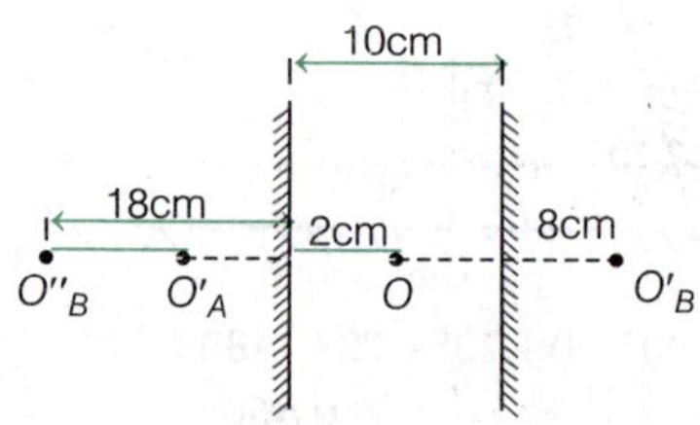

Reflection of O in mirror B is image $O'B$ at a distance of 18 cm from A.

Image of $O'B$ is at $O''B$ which is also at a distance of 18 cm from A.

20.

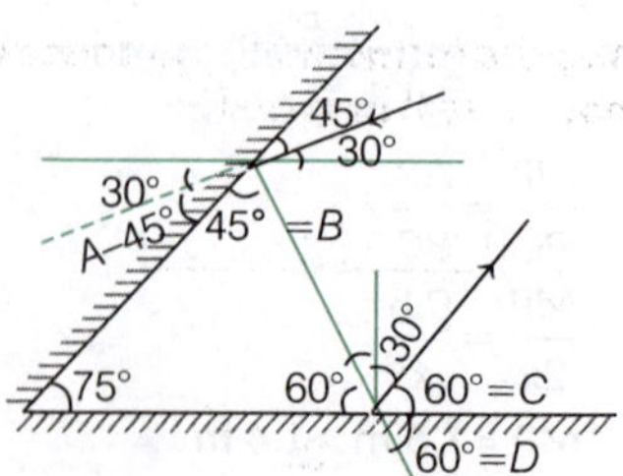

We have,

$$\delta = \delta_1 + \delta_2$$
$$= (A+B) + (C+D)$$
$$= 45° + 45° + 60° + 60°$$
$$= 210°$$

Module 3.

1. **Assertion**

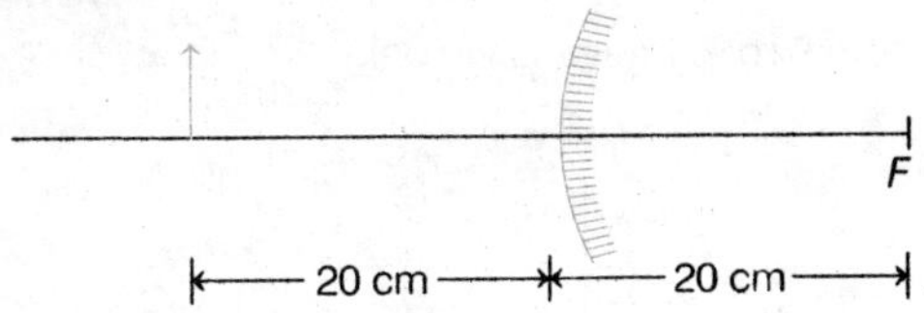

Real object is in front of mirror, not at F. So, image is not at infinity.

2. Field of view of convex mirror is large.
3. $m = -2$, means image is real, inverted an 2-times magnified.
4. Theory based question.
5. Laws of reflection can be applied to any type of surface.
6. Theory based question.
7. $$\frac{1}{v} + \frac{1}{u} = \frac{1}{f} \quad \text{...(i)}$$

For virtual object u is positive and for concave mirror f is negative. Substituting these signs in Eq. (i), we can see that v is always negative or image is always real.

8. For real objects image formed by a convex mirror is always virtual, erect and diminished.
9. If object is placed at centre of curvature its image is also formed at centre of curvature.
10.

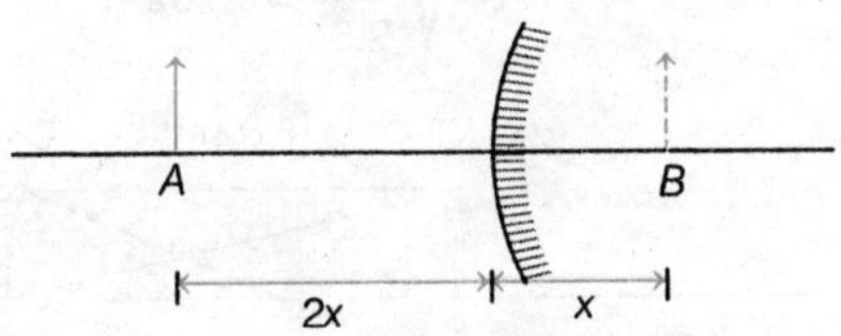

$$f = \frac{R}{2} = 30 \text{ cm}$$

$$\frac{1}{+x} + \frac{1}{-2x} = \frac{1}{+30}$$

$\therefore \quad x = 15$ cm

Hence, $\quad AB = 3x = 45$ cm

11. Magnified image is formed only by concave mirror. But this image may be real or virtual.

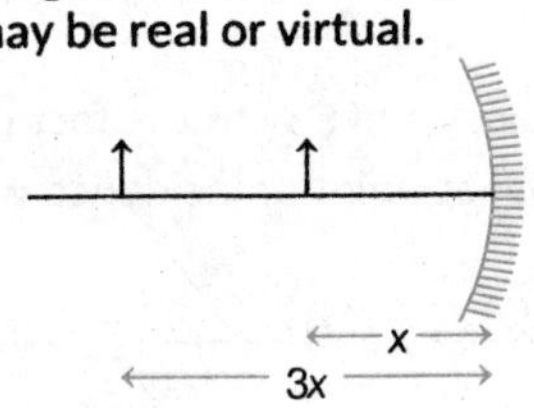

For real image,

$$2x = 80 \text{ cm}$$

$$\therefore \quad x = 40 \text{ cm}$$

$$\frac{1}{-120} + \frac{1}{-40} = \frac{1}{f}$$

Solving, we get $f = -30$ cm

Similarly, we can check for virtual image.

12. Let, $u = -x$

Then, $\quad v = +\frac{x}{n}$

$$\frac{1}{(+x/n)} + \frac{1}{-x} = \frac{1}{+f}$$

Solving, we get $x = (n-1)f$

13. $$\frac{1}{v} + \frac{1}{-60} = \frac{1}{-24}$$

$\therefore \quad v = -40$ cm

$$m = -\frac{v}{u} = -\frac{(40)}{(-60)} = \frac{-2}{3}$$

Image speed is m^2-times the object speed and opposite to the direction of object velocity.

14. In case of concave mirror, $m = -2$

Also, $\quad m = \frac{f}{f-u} \Rightarrow -2 = \frac{-50}{-50-u}$

$\therefore \quad u = -75$ cm

15. The given situation in question is as follows.

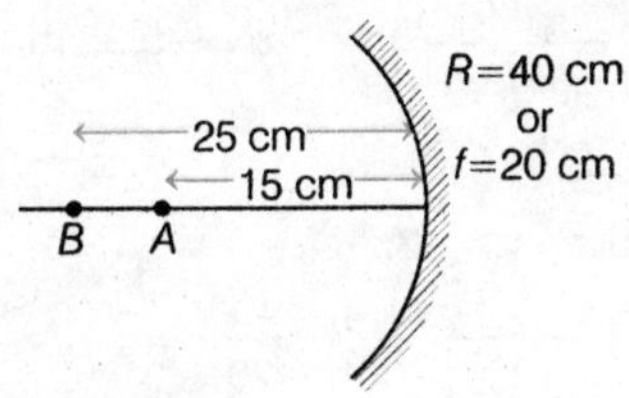

Using mirror formula,

$$\frac{1}{v} + \frac{1}{u} = \frac{1}{f}$$

For point A, $u = -15$ cm, $f = -20$ cm

$$\frac{1}{v_A} + \frac{1}{-15} = \frac{1}{-20}$$

$$\frac{1}{v_A} = \frac{1}{15} - \frac{1}{20} = \frac{4-3}{60} = \frac{1}{60}$$

$$v_A = +60 \text{ cm}$$

For point B, $\quad u = -25$ cm

$f = -20$ cm

$$\frac{1}{v_B} + \frac{1}{-25} = \frac{1}{-20}$$

$$\Rightarrow \quad \frac{1}{v_B} = \frac{1}{25} - \frac{1}{20} = \frac{4-5}{100} = -\frac{1}{100}$$

$$\Rightarrow \quad v_B = -100 \text{ cm}$$

Since, the sign of image formed by concave mirror is opposite i.e., both images lie opposite to pole.

Hence, the distance between images formed by the mirror is

$$d = |v_A - v_B| = |60 - (-100)|$$

$$\Rightarrow \quad d = 160 \text{ cm}$$

16. 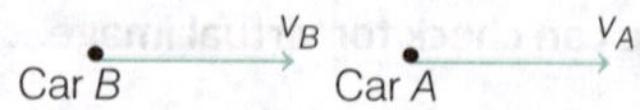

For convex mirror

$$v_i = -m^2 v_o \quad \text{...(i)}$$

v_i is velocity of image w.r.t. convex mirror

v_o is velocity of object w.r.t. convex mirror

$$v_o = 40 \text{ m/s}$$

Magnification

$$m = \frac{f}{f-u} = \frac{10}{10+190} = \frac{1}{20}$$

From Eq. (i)

$$v_i = -\frac{1}{20^2} \times 40 = -0.1 \text{ m/s}$$

17. Magnification, $m = -\frac{v}{u}$

Using mirror formula,

$$\frac{1}{v} + \frac{1}{u} = \frac{1}{f} \quad \Rightarrow \quad \frac{1}{v} = \frac{u-f}{uf}$$

$$\Rightarrow \quad v = \frac{uf}{u-f} \quad \Rightarrow \quad m = \frac{f}{f-u}$$

$$\Rightarrow \quad 5 = \frac{-0.4}{-0.4-u} \quad \Rightarrow \quad u = -0.32 \text{ m}$$

18. For real image,

Let $u = -x$, then $v = -2x$

$$\therefore \quad \frac{1}{-2x} + \frac{1}{-x} = \frac{1}{-20}$$

Solving, we get $x = 30$ cm.

For virtual image,

Let $u = -x$, then $v = +2x$

$$\therefore \quad \frac{1}{2x} + \frac{1}{-x} = \frac{1}{-20} \quad \text{or} \quad x = 10 \text{ cm}$$

19. Inverted and real image is formed by concave mirror.

Let $u = -x$, then $v = +x/2$

$$\therefore \quad \frac{1}{+x/2} + \frac{1}{-x} = \frac{1}{+f}$$

$$\therefore \quad x = 3f$$

Erect and virtual image is formed by convex mirror.

Let $u = -x$, then $v = +\frac{x}{2}$

$$\frac{1}{-x/2} + \frac{1}{-x} = \frac{1}{+f}$$

$$\Rightarrow \quad x = +f$$

20. Apply $\frac{1}{v} + \frac{1}{u} = \frac{1}{f}$

(a) $f = -10$ cm, $u = -25$ cm

Solving, we get

$$v = -16.7 \text{ cm}$$

Since, v is negative, image is in front of mirror. So, it is real. Similarly, we can solve for other parts.

21. (a) From O to F, image is real.

From F to P, image is virtual.

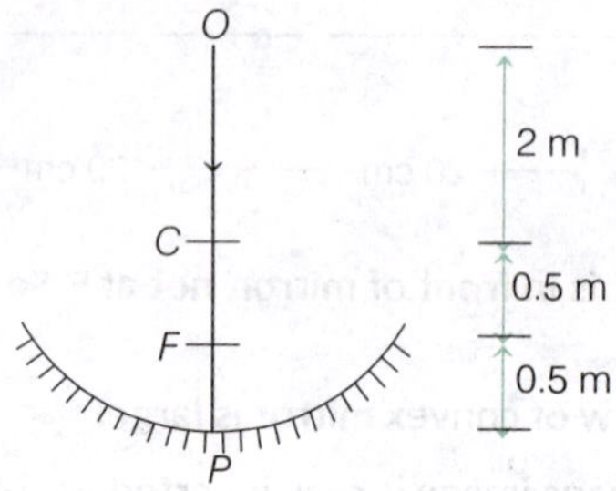

At O $$\frac{1}{v} + \frac{1}{u} = \frac{1}{f}$$

$$\therefore \quad \frac{1}{v} + \frac{1}{-3.0} = \frac{1}{-0.5}$$

$$v = -0.6 \text{ m}$$

(b) When object is at C and P, image coincides with object.

Using $$s = \frac{1}{2} g t^2$$

or $$t = \sqrt{\frac{2s}{g}}$$

At C $$t = \sqrt{\frac{2 \times 2}{9.8}} = 0.639 \text{ s}$$

At P $$t = \sqrt{\frac{2 \times 3}{9.8}} = 0.782 \text{ s}$$

22. (a)

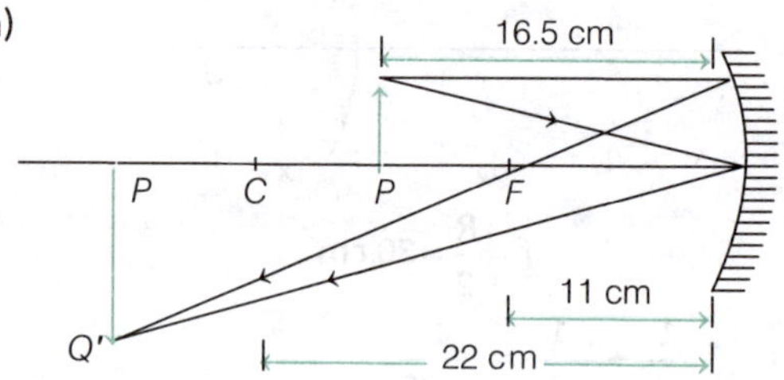

(b) Apply $\frac{1}{v} + \frac{1}{u} = \frac{1}{f}$

and $$m = -\frac{v}{u}$$

23. (a) Find the position of C with the fact that, $OF = OC$. Then normal at point of incidence will pass through C.

Finally apply $\angle i = \angle r$

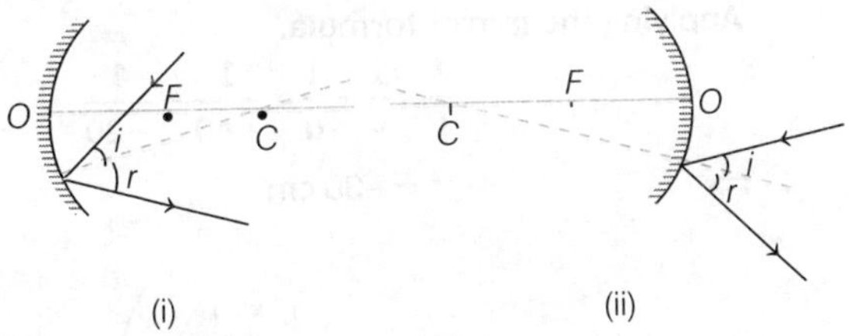

(b) (i)

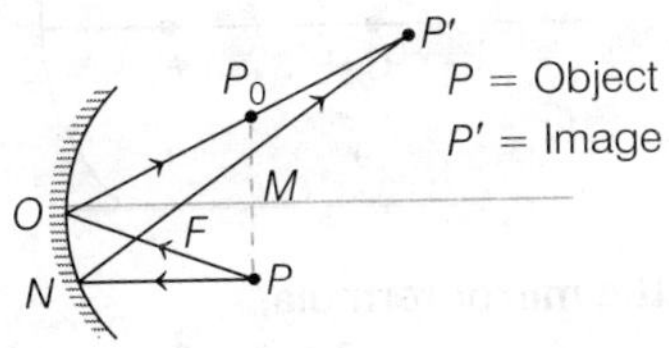

- Image is inverted, real and magnified. Hence mirror is concave and object lies between F and C.
- Take a point P_0 above the principal axis such that $PM = P_0M$.
- Draw a straight line joining P_0 and P'. The point where it cuts the principal axis becomes the pole O of concave mirror.
- Mirror should face towards the object P.
- Draw a line parallel to principal axis passing through P. Suppose it meets the mirror at point N. Now join N with P'. The point where it intersects the principal axis becomes the focus F.
- $\angle P'OM = \angle i, \angle MOP = \angle r, \angle i = \angle r$

(ii) Image P' is erect, virtual and smaller in size. Hence mirror is convex. Following the same points discussed above we can find pole O and focus F of mirror.

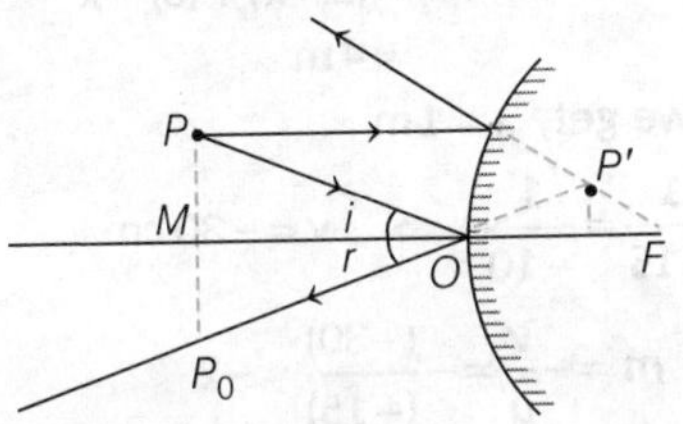

24. (a) $m = -2$, means image is inverted, real and magnified. Further if $u = -x$ then v should be $-2x$ so that magnification becomes -2.

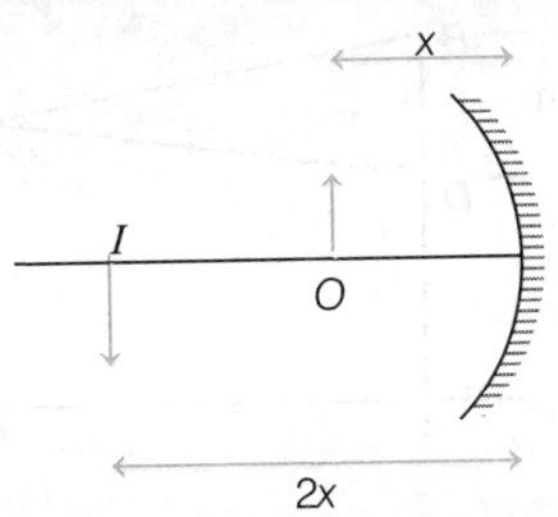

Given, $2x - x = 15$ cm

$\therefore$ $x = 15$ cm

and $2x = 30$ cm

Using the mirror formula,

$$\frac{1}{f} = \frac{1}{v} + \frac{1}{u} = \frac{1}{-30} + \frac{1}{-15}$$

$$\therefore \quad f = -10 \text{ cm}$$

(b) $m_1 = -\dfrac{1}{2}$

Let $u = -x$, then $v = -\dfrac{x}{2}$

Applying mirror formula, we have

$$\frac{1}{f} = \frac{1}{(-x/2)} + \frac{1}{(-x)} = -\frac{3}{x}$$

or $x = -3f$

Now, $m_2 = -\dfrac{1}{4}$

To decrease magnitude of magnification v should decrease and u should increase.

So, $u = -(x+5)$

and $v = -\left(\dfrac{x+5}{4}\right)$

Again using the mirror formula, we have

$$\frac{1}{f} = \frac{1}{-\left(\dfrac{x+5}{4}\right)} + \frac{1}{[-(x+5)]}$$

Putting $x = -3f$, we get

$$f = -2.5 \text{ cm}$$

25.

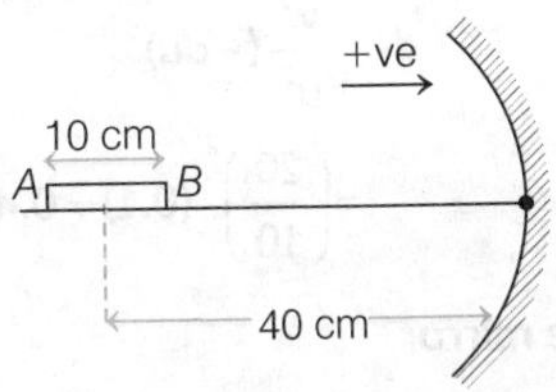

$$u_A = -45 \text{ cm}, f = -20 \text{ cm}$$

$$\therefore \quad v = \frac{uf}{u-f}$$

$$v_A = \frac{-45 \times (-20)}{-45-(-20)} = \frac{-900}{25} = -36 \text{ cm}$$

and $u_B = -35$ cm

$$\therefore \quad v_B = \frac{-35 \times (-20)}{-35-(-20)} = \frac{700}{-15}$$

$$\therefore \quad v_A - v_B = \text{length of image}$$

$$= -36 + \frac{140}{3}$$

$$= \frac{-108+140}{3} = \frac{32}{3} \text{ cm}$$

$$\therefore \quad x = 32$$

26. Given, initial object distance,

$$u_i = -100 \text{ cm}$$

Radius of curvature of mirror,

$$R = -200 \text{ cm}$$

Speed of object, $v_o = 2$ cm/s

Time, $t = 10$ s

Focal length of mirror,

$$f=\frac{R}{2}=\frac{-200}{2}=-100 \text{ cm}$$

After 10 s, the distance moved by the object,

$$d=v_o \times t=2\times 10=20 \text{ cm}$$

So, distance of object from mirror after 10 s,

$$u_f=-100-(-20)=-80 \text{ cm}$$

Using mirror formula,

$$\frac{1}{v}+\frac{1}{u_f}=\frac{1}{f}$$

$$\Rightarrow \quad \frac{1}{v}=\frac{1}{f}-\frac{1}{u_f}=-\frac{1}{100}+\frac{1}{80}$$

$$=\frac{-4+5}{400}=\frac{1}{400}$$

or $\quad v=400 \text{ cm}$

Unit Exercise (Cumulative)

Level 1

1. From the relation,

$$\frac{1}{v}+\frac{1}{u}=\frac{1}{f}$$

We have, $\frac{-dv}{v^2}-\frac{du}{u^2}=0$

$$\therefore \quad dv=\frac{v^2}{u^2}(-du)$$

$$=\left(\frac{20}{10}\right)^2 (0.1)=0.4 \text{ cm}$$

2. For concave mirror,

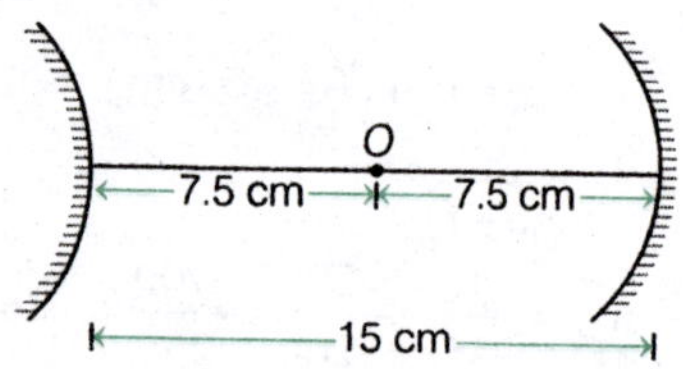

$$\frac{1}{v}-\frac{1}{7.5}=-\frac{1}{5}$$

$$\therefore \quad v=-15 \text{ cm}$$

3. Image is magnified, so mirror is concave because convex mirror always makes diminished image. Further, image is erect and magnified. So, the object lies between P and F and its image is virtual.

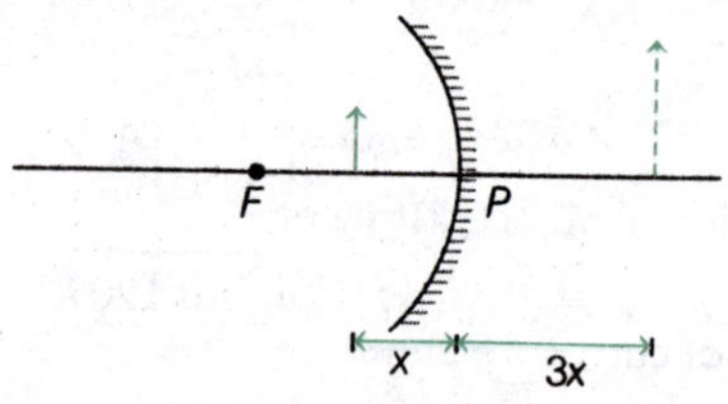

$$4x=80 \text{ cm}$$

$$\Rightarrow \quad x=20 \text{ cm}$$

and $\quad 3x=60 \text{ cm}$

Applying the mirror formula,

$$\frac{1}{f}=\frac{1}{v}+\frac{1}{u}=\frac{1}{+60}+\frac{1}{-20}$$

$$\Rightarrow \quad f=-30 \text{ cm}$$

4.

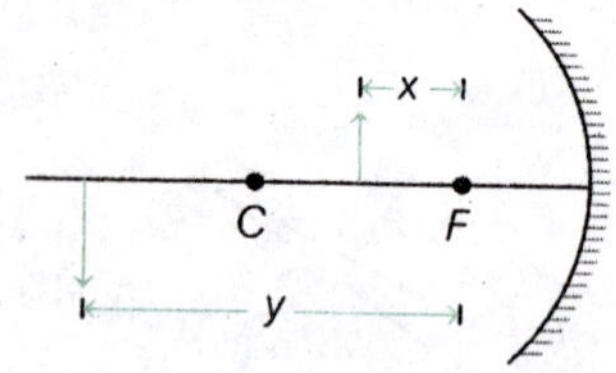

Applying the mirror formula,

$$\frac{1}{v}+\frac{1}{u}=\frac{1}{f}$$

or $$\frac{1}{-(f+y)}+\frac{1}{-(f+x)}=\frac{1}{-f}$$

$$\Rightarrow \quad \frac{f+x+f+y}{(f+x)(f+y)}=\frac{1}{f}$$

$$\Rightarrow \quad 2f^2+f(x+y)=f^2+xy+f(x+y)$$

$$\Rightarrow \quad f=\sqrt{xy}$$

5.

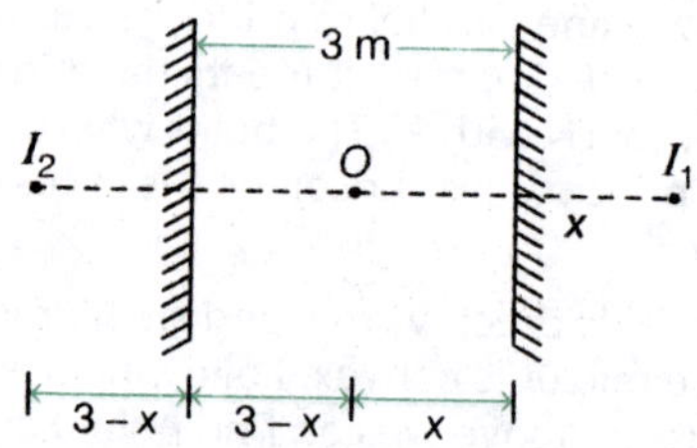

$$I_1I_2=(3-x)+(3)+x$$

$$=4 \text{ m}$$

Solving we get, $x=1 \text{ m}$

6 $\frac{1}{v}+\frac{1}{-15}=\frac{1}{-10} \Rightarrow v=-30 \text{ cm}$

$$m=-\frac{v}{u}=-\frac{(-30)}{(-15)}=-2$$

$$|\Delta v|=m^2|\Delta u|=(-2)^2(2 \text{ mm})$$

$$=8 \text{ mm}$$

7.

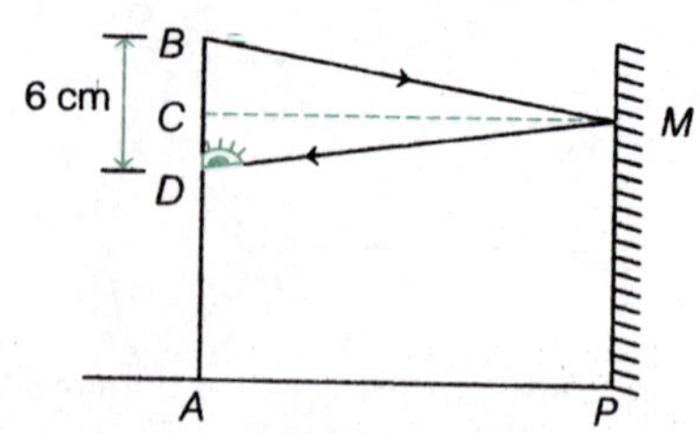

$$PM=AC=AD+DC$$

$$=AD+\frac{DB}{2}=164+\frac{6}{2}=167 \text{ cm}$$

8. $\mathbf{v}_{OM}=\mathbf{v}_O-\mathbf{v}_M=(-\hat{\mathbf{i}}-3\hat{\mathbf{k}})$

$$\therefore \quad \mathbf{v}_{IM}=(-\hat{\mathbf{i}}+3\hat{\mathbf{k}})=\mathbf{v}_I-\mathbf{v}_M$$

or $\quad \mathbf{v}_I = (-\hat{\mathbf{i}} + 3\hat{\mathbf{k}}) + \mathbf{v}_M$

$\quad = (3\hat{\mathbf{i}} + 4\hat{\mathbf{j}} + 11\hat{\mathbf{k}})$

9. Ray passing through c is only correct.

10. At P, $u = v$ which is possible only when $u = 2f$

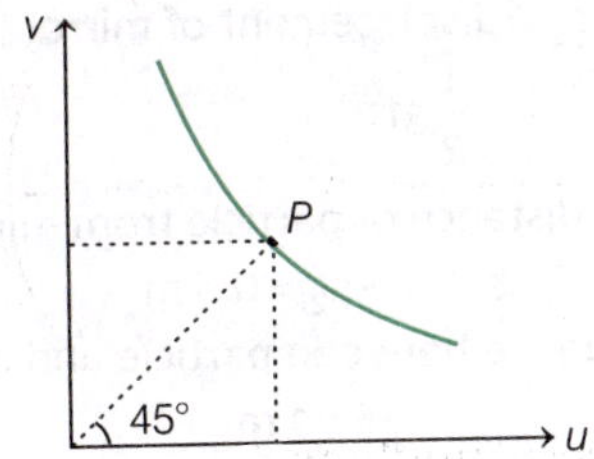

11. $\because\ v_{CM} = 8$ m/s

$\Rightarrow \quad v_{IM} = 8$ m/s

12. $90° - \theta + 2\theta = 90°$

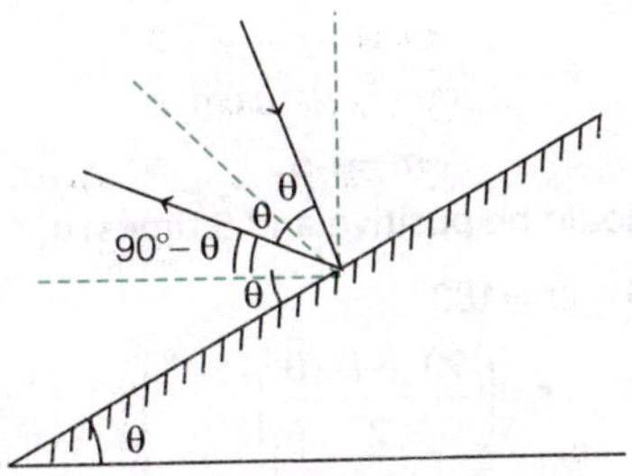

$\therefore \quad \theta = 0°$

Angle of reflected ray with horizontal

$= 90° - \theta = 90°$

13. Reflected rays are neither converging nor diverging. Hence, mirror is a plane.

14.

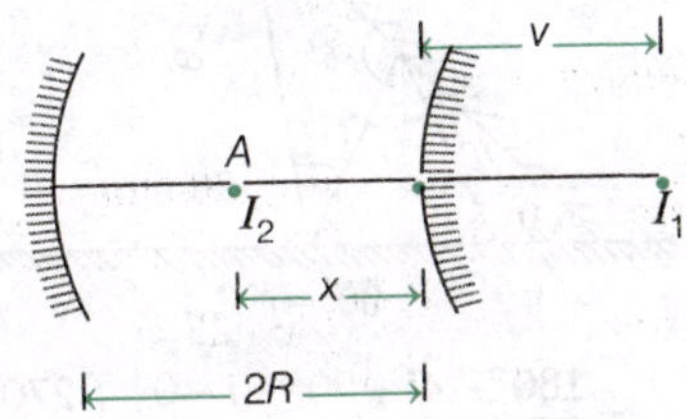

For convex mirror

$$\frac{1}{v} + \frac{1}{-x} = \frac{1}{+R/2}$$

$$\therefore \quad \frac{1}{v} = \frac{2}{R} + \frac{1}{x}$$

or $$v = \frac{Rx}{R + 2x}$$

Now, applying mirror formula for concave mirror we have

$$\frac{1}{-(2R - x)} + \frac{1}{-(2R + v)} = \frac{1}{-R/2}$$

Solving this equation, we can find value of x.

15. (a) Image has to be taken on a screen. So, it should be real. Hence, mirror should be concave.

(b)

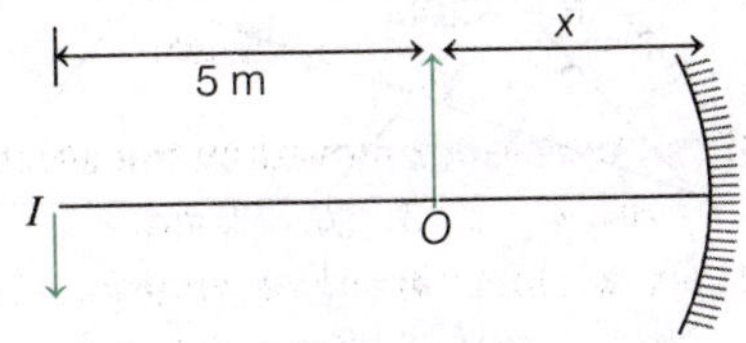

Image is 5 times magnified.

Hence, $\quad |v| = 5|u|$

or $\quad (5 + x) = 5x$

Solving we get,

$$x = 1.25 \text{ m}$$

Now using,

$$\frac{1}{v} + \frac{1}{u} = \frac{1}{f} = \frac{2}{R}$$

We have,

$$\frac{1}{-6.25} - \frac{1}{1.25} = \frac{2}{R}$$

Solving we get,

$$R = -2.08 \text{ m}$$

16. Using mirror formula twice,

$$\frac{1}{+25/3} + \frac{1}{-u_1} = \frac{1}{+10}$$

or $$\frac{1}{u_1} = \frac{3}{25} - \frac{1}{10}$$

or $$u_1 = 50 \text{ m}$$

and $$\frac{1}{(+50/7)} + \frac{1}{-u_2} = \frac{1}{+10}$$

$$\therefore \quad \frac{1}{u_2} = \frac{7}{50} - \frac{1}{10}$$

or $$u_2 = 25 \text{ m}$$

Speed of object $= \dfrac{u_1 - u_2}{\text{time}} = \dfrac{25}{30} \text{ ms}^{-1}$

$= 3 \text{ kmh}^{-1}$

Level 2

17.

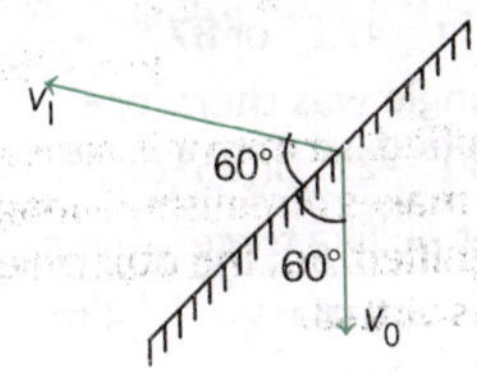

$$v_0 = v_I = \omega A = \left(\sqrt{\frac{k}{M}}\right) A$$

$$v_r = \sqrt{v_0^2 + v_I^2 - 2v_0 \cos 120°}$$

$$= \sqrt{3}\, A \sqrt{\frac{k}{M}}$$

18.

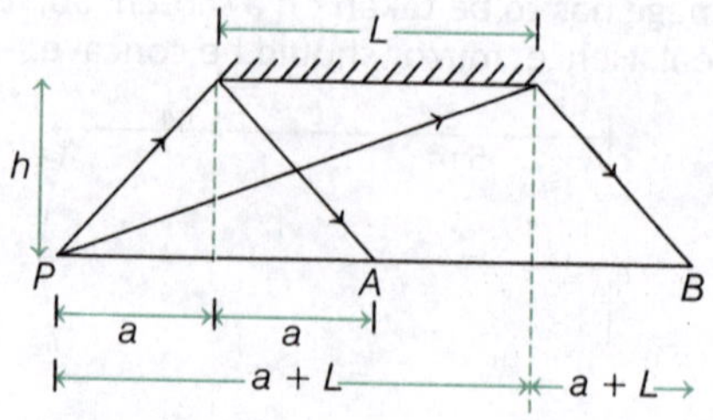

$$AB = PB - PA = 2(a+L) - 2a$$
$$= 2L = \text{constant}$$

19. Image of c will coincide with this.

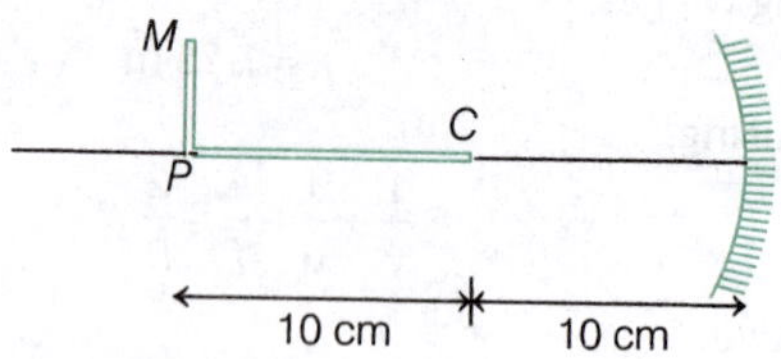

For P :

$$\frac{1}{v} + \frac{1}{-20} = \frac{1}{-5}$$

$\therefore$ $$v = -\frac{20}{3}\text{ cm}$$

$$m = -\frac{v}{u} = -\frac{(-20/3)}{(-20)} = -\frac{1}{3}$$

Length of image of PM :

$$l_1 = 10 \times \frac{1}{3} = \frac{10}{3}\text{ cm}$$

Length of image of PC :

$$l_2 = 10 - \frac{20}{3} = \frac{10}{3}\text{ cm}$$

$\therefore$ $$\frac{l_1}{l_2} = 1$$

20. Let i is the angle of incidence. Then, initial angle between incident ray and reflected ray will be $180° - 2i$. When mirror is rotated by $20°$, then reflected ray will rotate by $40°$.

$\therefore$ $$180° - 2i \pm 40° = 45°$$

Solving we get,

$$i = 47.5° \text{ or } 87.5°$$

The original angle was therefore

$$180° - 21° \text{ or } 85° \text{ or } 5°.$$

21. $$a_{LHS} = a_1 = \frac{\text{Net pulling force}}{\text{Total mass}} = \frac{3\,mg}{4\,m} = \frac{3}{4}g$$

$$a_{l_1} = 2a_1 = \frac{3}{2}g$$

$$a_{RHS} = a_2 = \frac{\text{Net pulling force}}{\text{Total mass}} = \frac{2\,mg}{3\,m}$$

$$= \frac{2}{3}g \Rightarrow a_{l_2} = 2a_2 = \frac{4}{3}g$$

The relative acceleration is therefore :

$$\frac{3}{2}g + \frac{4}{3}g = \frac{17}{6}g$$

22. $u_y = \sqrt{2}\sin 45° = 1\text{ m/s}$

In vertical direction,

s_1 = displacement of particle

$$= (1)(0.5) - \frac{1}{2}gt^2 = 0.5 - \frac{1}{2}gt^2$$

s_2 = displacement of mirror

$$= -\frac{1}{2}gt^2$$

$\therefore$ Vertical distance of particle from mirror,

$$s = s_1 - s_2 = 0.5\text{ m}$$

Hence, distance between particle and its image

$$= 2s = 1\text{ m}$$

23.

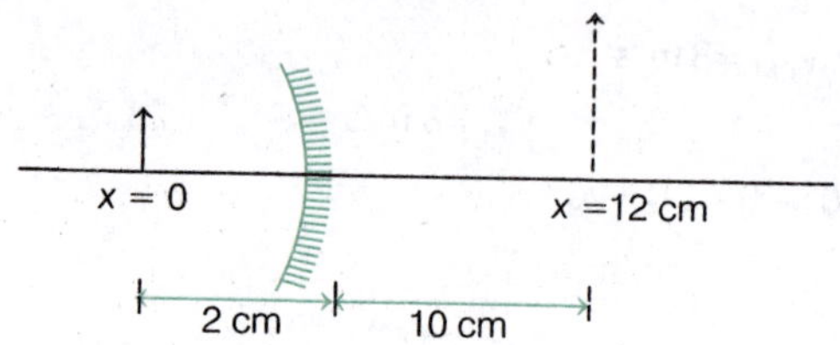

$$m = +5$$

$\therefore$ v should be positive and 5 times $|u|$.

24. $90° - i\theta + 2r = 180°$

$\therefore$ $$r = \left(\frac{90° + i - \theta}{2}\right)$$

$$p = 180° - (90° - r) - 2i$$
$$= 180° - 90° + \left(\frac{90° + i - \theta}{2}\right) - 2i$$

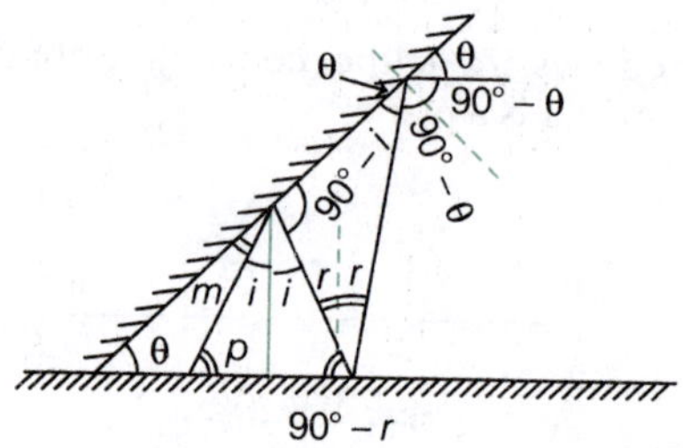

$$= \frac{180° - 4i + 90° + i - \theta}{2} = \left(\frac{270° - 3i - \theta}{2}\right)$$

$$m = p - \theta = 180° - (90° - i) - 2i$$

$\therefore$ $$\left(\frac{270° - 3i - \theta}{2}\right) - \theta = 90° - i$$

Substituting $\theta = 20°$, we get

$$i = 30°$$

25.

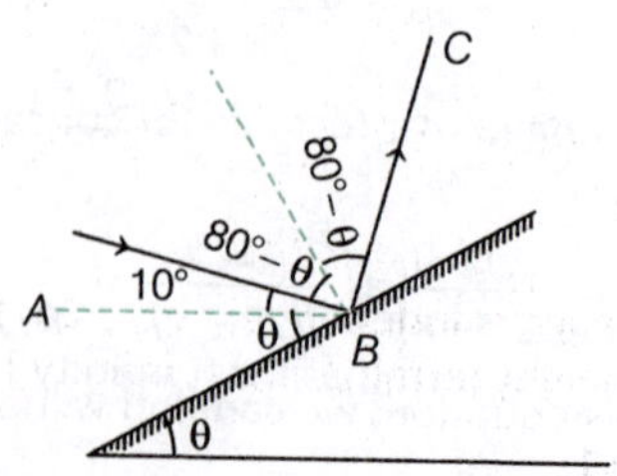

$$\angle ABC = 90°$$

$$\Rightarrow \quad 10° + (80° - \theta) + (80° - \theta) = 90°$$
$$\Rightarrow \quad \theta = 40°$$

Note *If we take 10° downwards from horizontal then* $\theta = 50°$

26. Relative acceleration $= 0$

Relative velocity $= 2u\cos\theta$ in horizontal direction. Hence, motion of image of ball with respect to ball is a straight line and horizontal.

27.

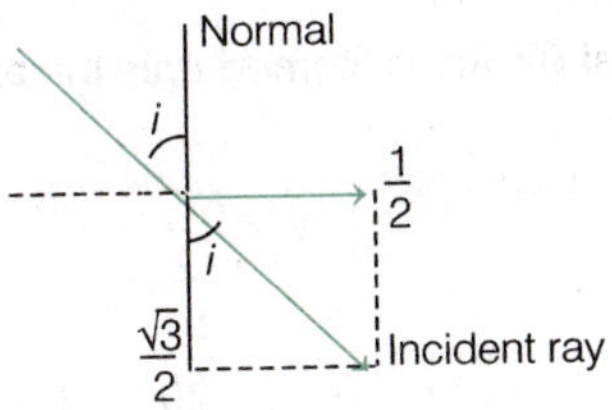

$$\tan i = \frac{1/2}{\sqrt{3}/2} = \frac{1}{\sqrt{3}} \Rightarrow i = 30°$$

28. Image of point A

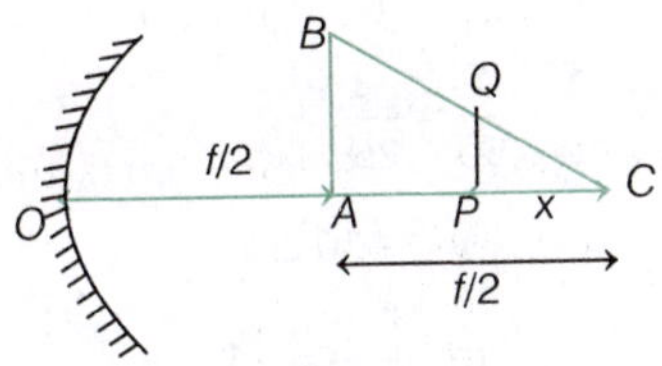

$$\frac{PQ}{x} = \frac{AB}{f/2}$$
$$\Rightarrow \quad PQ = \frac{2(AB)x}{f}$$

For A : $\frac{1}{v} + \frac{1}{[-(f/2)]} = \frac{1}{-f}$

$$\Rightarrow \quad v = f$$
$$\Rightarrow \quad \frac{I_{AB}}{AB} = -\frac{v}{u} = -\frac{f}{\left(-\frac{f}{2}\right)}$$
$$\Rightarrow \quad I_{AB} = 2\,AB$$

For height of PQ,

$$\frac{1}{v} + \frac{1}{-[(f-x)]} = \frac{1}{-f}$$
$$\Rightarrow \quad \frac{1}{v} = \frac{1}{(f-x)} - \frac{1}{f}$$
$$\Rightarrow \quad v = \frac{f(f-x)}{x}$$
$$\Rightarrow \quad \frac{I_{PQ}}{PQ} = -\frac{v}{u} = \frac{f(f-x)}{x[(f-x)]} = \left(\frac{f}{x}\right)$$
$$\Rightarrow \quad I_{PQ} = \frac{f}{x}PQ = \left(\frac{f}{x}\right)\left(\frac{2(AB)x}{f}\right) \quad \left[\because PQ = \frac{2(AB)x}{f}\right]$$
$$I_{PQ} = 2AB$$

(Size of image is independent of x. So, final image will be of same height terminating at infinity.)

29. **In event -1**

For concave mirror,

$$\frac{1}{v} + \frac{1}{-3f} = \frac{1}{-f}$$
$$\Rightarrow \quad v = -1.5f$$

For convex mirror,

$$\frac{1}{v} + \frac{1}{-3f} = \frac{1}{+f} \Rightarrow v = \frac{3}{4}f = 0.75f$$

For plane mirror,

$$v = +3f$$

In event-2

For concave mirror,

$$\frac{1}{v} + \frac{1}{-1.5f} = \frac{1}{-f}$$
$$\therefore \quad v = -3f$$

For convex mirror,

$$\frac{1}{v} + \frac{1}{-1.5f} = \frac{1}{+f}$$
$$\therefore \quad v = \frac{3f}{5} = 0.6f$$

For plane mirror,

$$v = +1.5f$$

30.

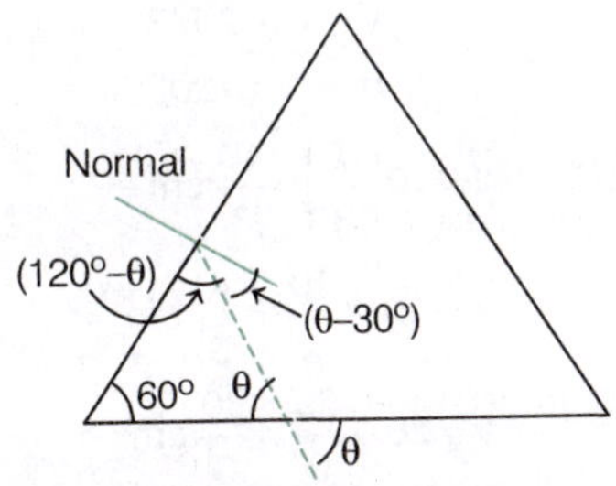

As we can see, for $\theta = 30°$, the ray will incident normally and hence, will retrace its path.

$\Rightarrow$ Option (a) is correct.

Considering the symmetry of the situation, we can have

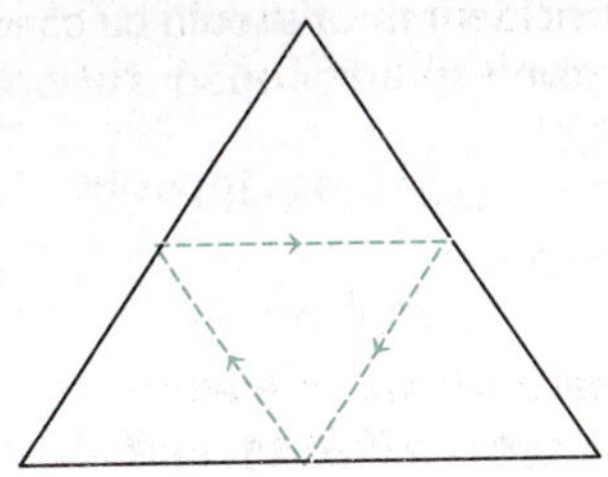

$\Rightarrow$ Option (b) is correct.

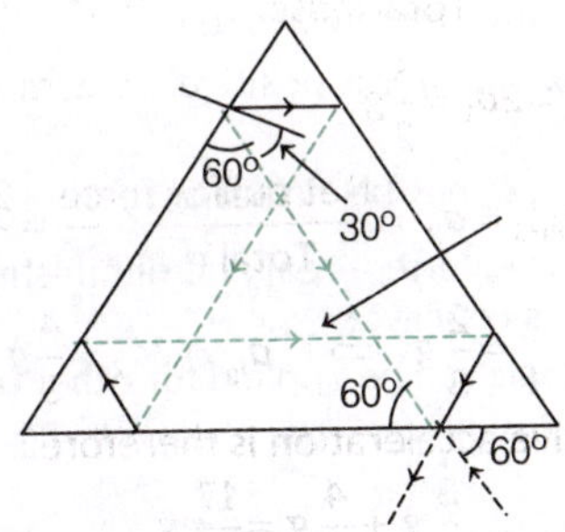

As it clear from the above diagram, ray comes out.

$\Rightarrow$ Option(c) is not correct.

Also, as is clear from the above diagram, total number of reflections $=5$

$\Rightarrow$ Option (d) is not correct.

31. 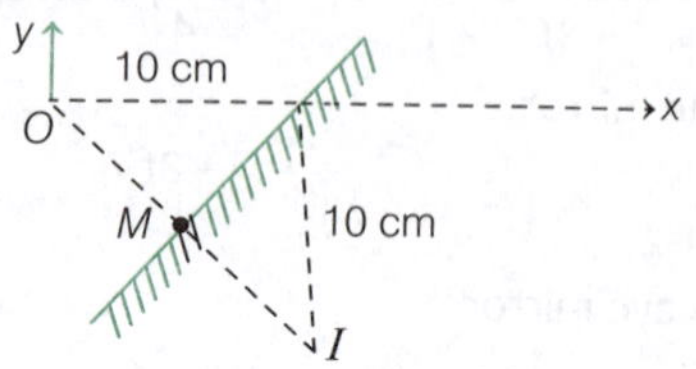

$$OM = MI$$

Coordinates of I are (10 cm, -10 cm).

32. Object is placed at centre at curvature of mirror. Hence, image is at the same point, real, inverted and of same size. Hence, coordinates are (20 cm, 0).

33. $\frac{1}{v} + \frac{1}{-20} = \frac{1}{+10}$

$\therefore \quad v = +\frac{20}{3}$ cm

$$m = -\frac{v}{u} = -\frac{(+20/3)}{(-20)} = +\frac{1}{3}$$

$\therefore \quad I = 10\left(\frac{1}{3}\right) = \frac{10}{3}$ cm

$$x = 10 - \frac{10}{3} = \frac{20}{3} \text{ cm}$$

and $\quad y = 20 + \frac{20}{3} = \frac{80}{3}$ cm

34. Plane mirror forms image at equal distance on opposite sides.

Hence, $\quad x = 0, y = 40$ cm

35. (a) $m = -2$ means image is real, inverted and 2-times magnified. So, mirror should be concave. Same logic can be given for other options also.

36. $\frac{1}{v} + \frac{1}{+u} = \frac{1}{f}$ $\quad$ (as u is positive for virtual objects)

$\therefore \quad \frac{1}{v} = \frac{1}{f} - \frac{1}{u}$

For plane mirror, $f = \infty$. So, v is always negative. Hence, image is always real.

For concave mirror, f is negative. So, v is again negative. Therefore, image is always real.

For convex mirror, f is positive. So, v may be positive or negative.

Hence, image may be virtual or real.

37. (a) Image is inverted, real and diminished. Hence, mirror is concave.

Same logic can be applied for other options too.

38. (a) $\frac{1}{v} + \frac{1}{-20} = \frac{1}{-20}$

$\therefore \quad v = \infty$

$$m = -\frac{v}{u} = \infty$$

Same formulae can be applied for other options too.

39. (a) Magnified image from concave mirror may be real or virtual.

(b) Half size image is formed only in case of real image.

Let $u = -x$,

then $\quad v = -\frac{x}{2}$

Now, $\quad \frac{1}{-x/2} + \frac{1}{-x} = \frac{1}{-20}$

$\therefore \quad x = 60$ cm

In the similar manner, other options can be solved.

40. Using mirror formula, $\left(\frac{1}{v} + \frac{1}{u} = \frac{1}{f}\right)$

$$\frac{1}{v} - \frac{1}{50} = \frac{-1}{25}$$

$\therefore \quad v = -50$ cm

$$m = -\frac{v}{u} = -1 \qquad \textbf{Ans.}$$

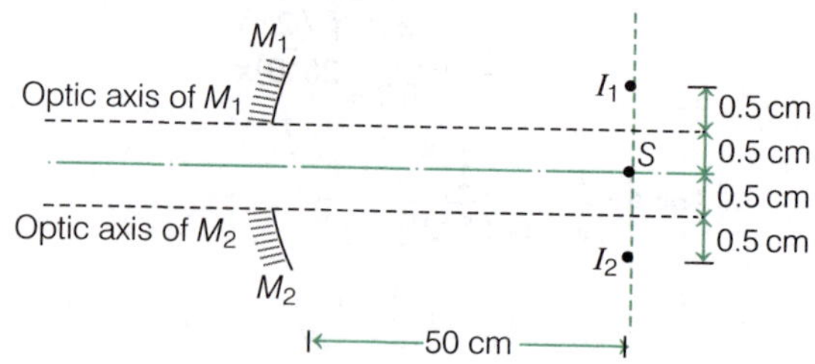

41. Using mirror formula $\frac{1}{v} + \frac{1}{u} = \frac{1}{f}$ for concave mirror first, we have

$$\frac{1}{v} - \frac{1}{60} = \frac{1}{-40} \qquad \left(\because f = \frac{R}{2}\right)$$

or $\quad v = -120$ cm

First image I_1 at 120 cm from concave mirror will act as virtual object for plane mirror. Plane mirror will form real image of I_1 at S.

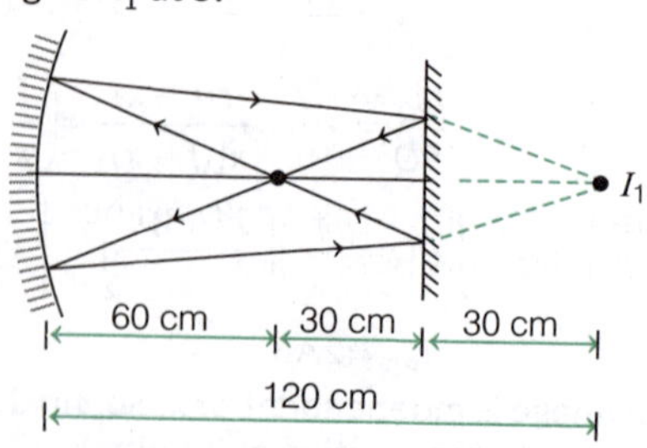

Ray diagram is shown in figure.
Distance between two mirrors is 90 cm. **Ans.**

42.

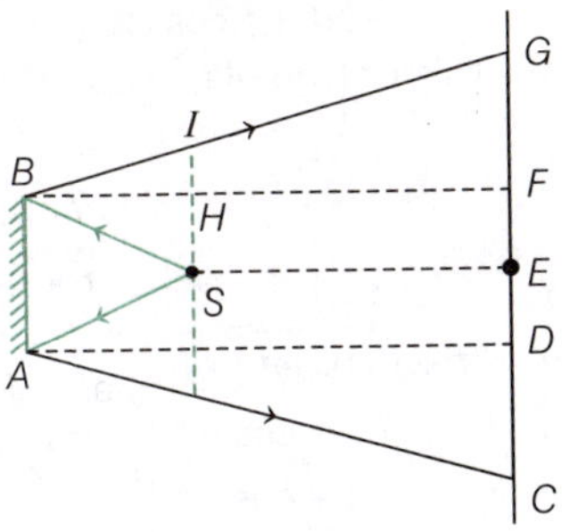

$$\frac{FG}{BF} = \frac{IH}{BH} = \frac{HS}{BH}$$

$$\therefore \quad FG = (BF)\left(\frac{HS}{BH}\right)$$

$$= (5)\left(\frac{1.0}{0.5}\right) = 10\,\text{m}$$

$$FC = 2 + 10 = 12\,\text{m}$$

The boy has dropped himself at point F. So, his velocity is 20 m/s in upward direction.
Let us first find the time to move from F to topmost point and then from topmost point to point C. From $s = ut + \frac{1}{2}at^2$, we have

$$-12 = (20t) + \frac{1}{2}(-10)\,t^2$$

Solving this equation we get, $t_1 = 4.53$ s.
Velocity of boy at point G,

$$v = \sqrt{(20)^2 - 2 \times 10 \times 10}$$

$$= 14.14\,\text{m/s} \qquad (\because\ v^2 = u^2 - 2gh)$$

Time taken to move the boy from G to topmost point and then from topmost point to G will be

$$t_2 = \frac{2v}{g} = 2.83\,\text{s}$$

$\therefore$ The required time is

$$t = t_1 - t_2 = 1.7\,\text{s}$$ **Ans.**

43. Applying mirror formula for concave mirror first $\left(\frac{1}{v} + \frac{1}{u} = \frac{1}{f}\right)$ we have,

$$\frac{1}{v} - \frac{1}{110} = \frac{1}{-100}$$

$$v = -1100\,\text{cm}$$

$AI_1 = 100$ cm. Therefore, final image will be real and at distance 100 cm below point A at I_2.

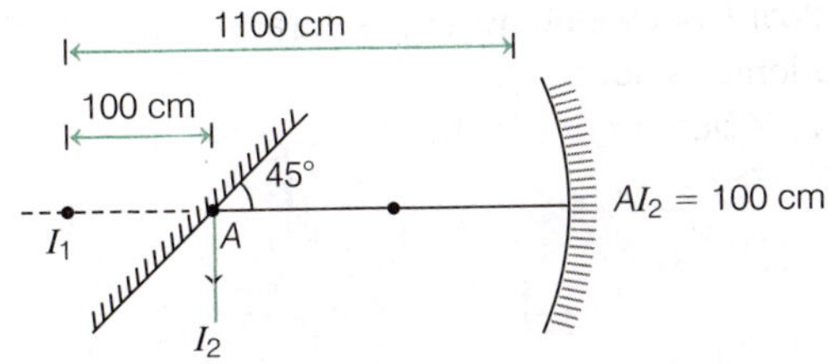

44. In 15 seconds, mirror will rotate 15° in clockwise direction.

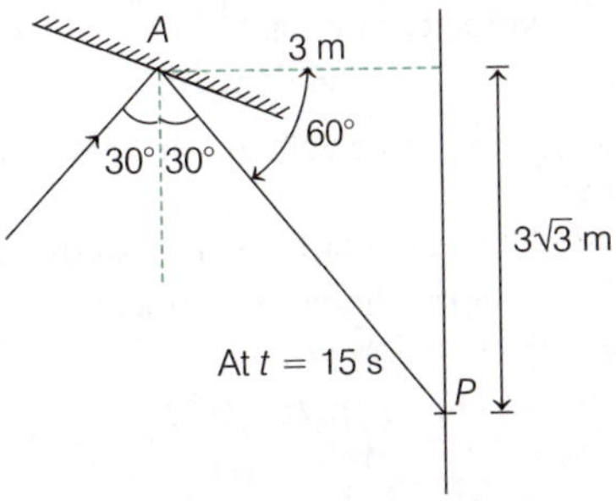

Hence, the reflected ray will rotate 30° in clockwise direction.

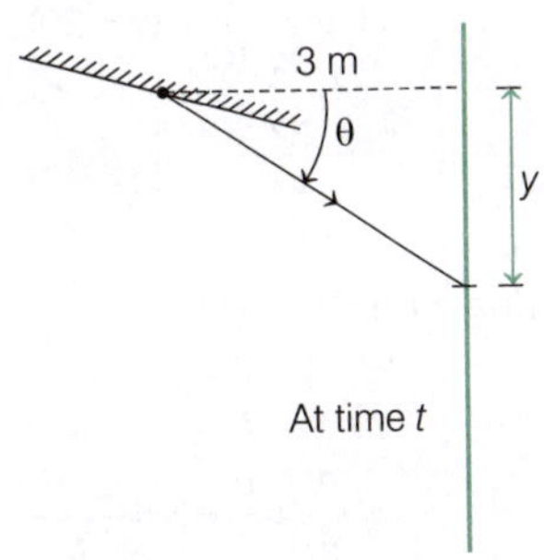

$$y = 3\tan\theta$$

$$\therefore \quad \frac{dy}{dt} = (3\sec^2\theta)\cdot\frac{d\theta}{dt} \qquad \text{...(i)}$$

Here, $\frac{dy}{dt} = v_P,\ \frac{d\theta}{dt} = 2°$ per second

$$= \frac{2 \times \pi}{180} = \frac{\pi}{90} \text{ rad per second}$$

At $t = 15$ s and $\theta = 60°$
Substituting the values in Eq. (i), we have

$$v_P = \{3\sec^2 60°\}\left\{\frac{\pi}{90}\right\}$$

$$= 3 \times 4 \times \frac{\pi}{90}$$

$$= \frac{2\pi}{15}\,\text{m/s}$$ **Ans.**

45. (a) Differentiating the mirror formula, (w.r.t to time)

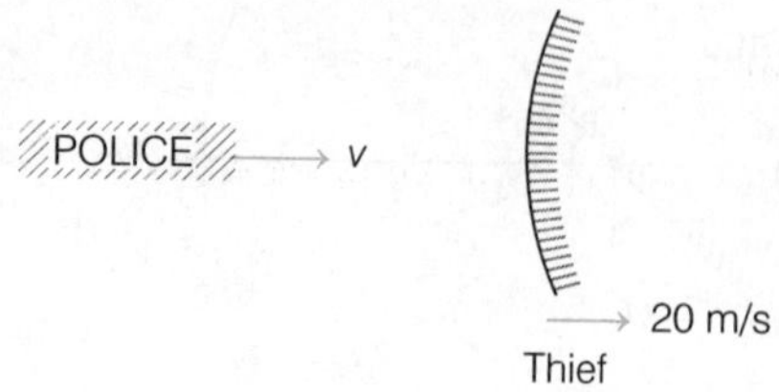

$$\frac{1}{v}+\frac{1}{u}=\frac{1}{f}$$

We get velocity of image,

$$v_I=(m)^2v_O \quad ...(i)$$

Here, v_O = relative velocity of object with respect to mirror

v_I = relative velocity of image

m = linear magnification

Here, $v_O=(v-20)$ m/s

$v_I=1$ cm/s $=0.01$ m/s

$$m=\frac{1}{10}$$

Substituting in Eq. (i) we have,

$$0.01=\left(\frac{1}{10}\right)^2(v-20)$$

$\therefore \quad v=21$ m/s

(b) $\frac{1}{v}+\frac{1}{u}=\frac{1}{f}$

Multiplying with u we get,

$$\frac{u}{v}+1=\frac{u}{f}$$

or $$\frac{1}{m}=\frac{u}{f}-1=\frac{u-f}{f}$$

$\therefore$ $$m=\frac{f}{u-f}$$

Differentiating we have,

$$\left(\frac{dm}{dt}\right)=-\frac{f}{(u-f)^2}\cdot\frac{du}{dt} \quad ...(ii)$$

Using mirror formula to find u with magnification $m=\frac{1}{10}$ we get,

$$\frac{1}{u/10}-\frac{1}{u}=\frac{1}{10}$$

or $u=90$ m (with sign $u=-90$ m)

Substituting in Eq. (ii) we have,

$$\frac{dm}{dt}=-\frac{(10)}{(-90-10)^2}(-1)$$

$$=10^{-3} \text{ per second}$$ **Ans.**

Note *u is decreasing at a rate of v – 20 or (21 – 20) or 1 m/s*

$\therefore$ $$\frac{du}{dt}=-1\text{ m/s}$$

46. (a) At $t=t$,

$$u=-(2f+x)$$
$$=-(2f+f\cos\omega t)$$

Using the mirror formula,

$$\frac{1}{v}+\frac{1}{u}=\frac{1}{f}$$

We have,

$$\frac{1}{v}-\frac{1}{2f+f\cos\omega t}=\frac{-1}{f}$$

$\therefore$ $$v=-\left(\frac{2+\cos\omega t}{1+\cos\omega t}\right)f$$

i.e. distance of image from mirror at time t is

$$\left(\frac{2+\cos\omega t}{1+\cos\omega t}\right)f$$ **Ans.**

(b) Ball coincides with its image at centre of curvature, i.e. at $x=0$.

(c) At $t=T/2$

or $\omega t=\pi$, $x=-f$

i.e. $u=-f$ or ball is at focus. So, its image is at ∞.

$$m=\infty$$

47. Let the ray is incident at a point $P=(x_1, y_1)$ on the mirror. Then, slope at P,

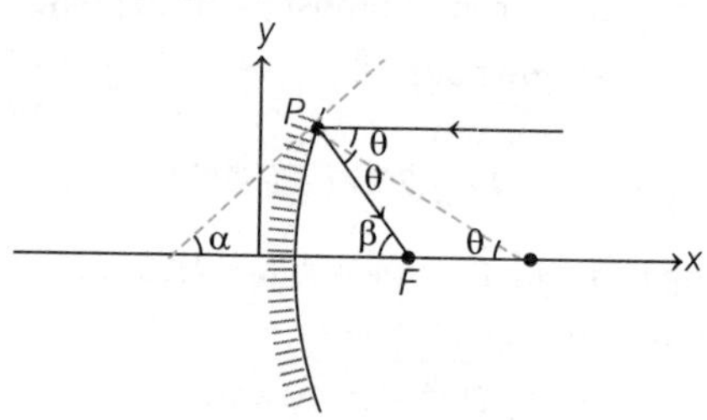

$$\tan\alpha=\left(\frac{dy}{dx}\right)_{(x_1y_1)}=\frac{1}{4by_1} \quad ...(i)$$

$$\alpha=90°-\theta$$

and $$\beta=2\theta$$

Now, the reflected ray is passing through $P(x_1y_1)$ and has a slope $-\tan\beta$. Hence, the equation will be

$$\left(\frac{y-y_1}{x-x_1}\right)=-\tan\beta$$

$$=-\tan 2\theta=\frac{-2\tan\theta}{1-\tan^2\theta}$$

$\therefore$ $$y-y_1=\frac{2\cot\alpha}{1+\cot^2\alpha}(x_1-x) \quad ...(ii)$$

Further, $$x_1=4by_1^2 \quad ...(iii)$$

At F, $$x=0 \quad ...(iv)$$

From Eq. (i) to Eq. (iv),

we get $$x=\frac{1}{8b}$$

It shows that the coordinates of F are unique $\left(\dfrac{1}{8b}, 0\right)$.

Hence, the reflected ray passing through one focus and the focal length is $\dfrac{1}{8b}$. **Hence proved.**

48. 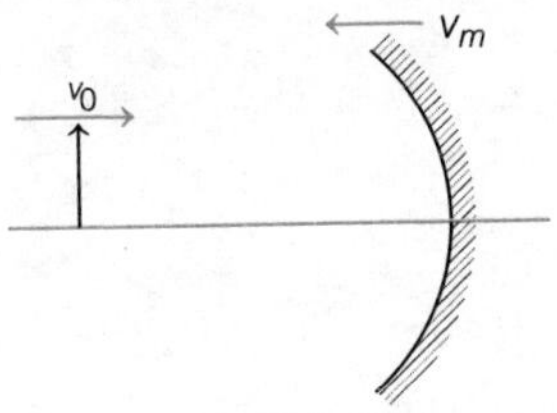

$f = 10$ cm

Let 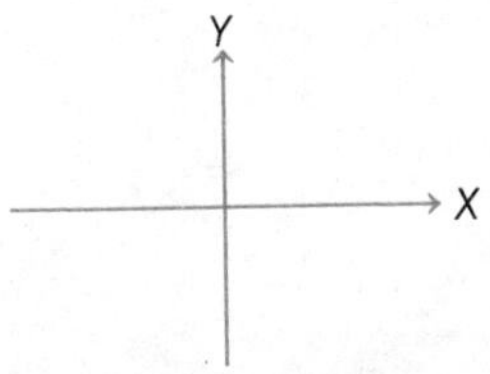

$$u = -30 \text{ cm}; f = -10 \text{ cm}$$

$$\therefore \quad \frac{1}{v} + \frac{1}{u} = \frac{1}{f}$$

$$\Rightarrow \quad \frac{1}{v} - \frac{1}{30} = \frac{1}{-10}$$

or $\quad v = -15$ cm

Further, $\quad \dfrac{1}{v} + \dfrac{1}{u} = \dfrac{1}{f}$

Differentiating w.r.t. time, we get

$$\frac{du}{dt} = -\frac{v^2}{u^2}\frac{du}{dt}$$

$$\mathbf{v}_{IM} = -\left(\frac{v}{u}\right)^2 \mathbf{v}_{OM}$$

Given, $\quad \mathbf{v}_I = 0$

$$\mathbf{v}_I - \mathbf{v}_M = -\left(\frac{-15}{-30}\right)^2 (\mathbf{v}_{OM})$$

$$\Rightarrow \quad \mathbf{v}_I - \mathbf{v}_M = -\frac{1}{4}\mathbf{v}_O + \frac{1}{4}\mathbf{v}_M$$

Since, $\quad \mathbf{v}_O = 15 \text{ cm/s } \hat{\mathbf{i}}$

and $\quad \mathbf{v}_I = 0$

$$\therefore \quad \frac{5}{4}\mathbf{v}_M = \frac{\mathbf{v}_O}{4}$$

$$\Rightarrow \quad \mathbf{v}_M = \frac{\mathbf{v}_O}{4} = \frac{15 \text{ cm/s}\hat{\mathbf{i}}}{5}$$

$$= 3 \text{ cm/s } \hat{\mathbf{i}}$$

$$\Rightarrow \quad |\mathbf{v}_M| = 3$$

UNIT-9

REFRACTION OF LIGHT

Learning Modules

1. Refraction of Light and Refractive Index
2. Law of Refraction (Snell's Law)
3. Single Refraction from Plane Surface
4. Shift Due to a Glass Slab
5. Refraction from Spherical Surface
6. Lens Theory
7. Total Internal Reflection
8. Refraction through Prism
9. Optical Instrument

MODULE 1

Refraction of Light and Refractive Index

When a ray of light travels from one medium to other medium with or without bending, the phenomenon is called refraction of light. Under following two conditions the ray of light does not bend in refraction.

(i) For normal incidence ($\angle i = 0$)

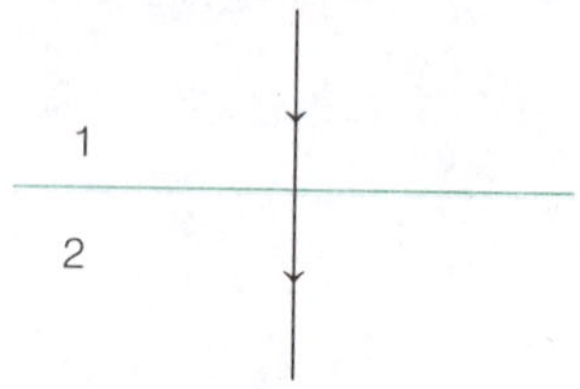

(ii) If refractive index of both media is same, angle of incidence does not matter in this case.

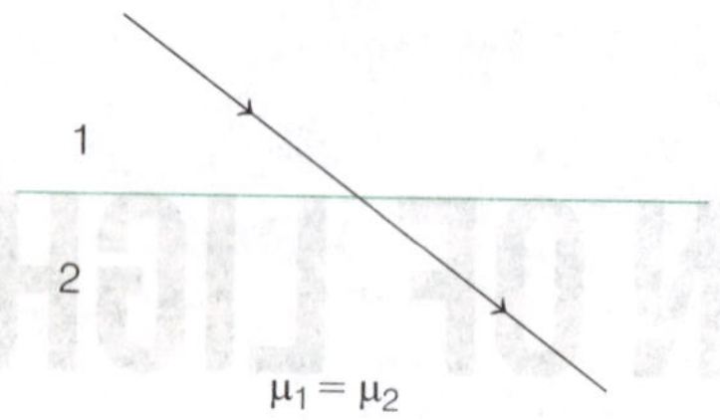

Here, μ = refractive index of medium

Refractive Index

(i) In general speed of light in any medium is less than its speed in vacuum. It is convenient to define refractive index μ of a medium as,

$$\mu = \frac{\text{Speed of light in vacuum}}{\text{Speed of light in medium}} = \frac{c}{v}$$

(ii) When a ray of light travels from medium 1 to medium 2, its wavelength changes but its frequency remains unchanged.

$$\mu_2 > \mu_1, v_1 > v_2, \lambda_1 > \lambda_2$$

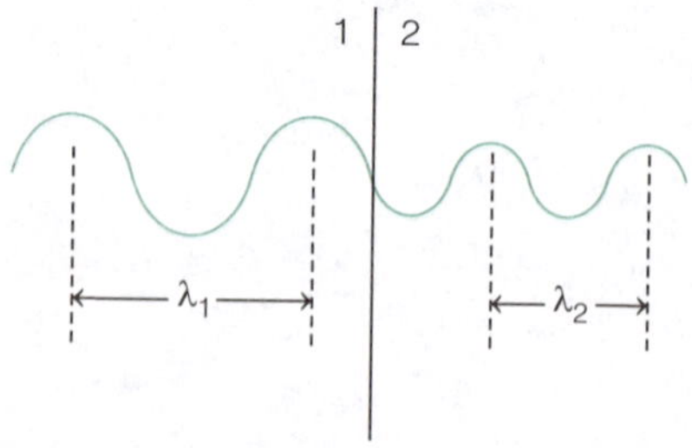

(iii) $_1\mu_2 = \frac{\mu_2}{\mu_1}$ = Refractive index of 2 w.r.t. 1

and $_2\mu_1 = \frac{\mu_1}{\mu_2}$ = Refractive index of 1 w.r.t. 2

$$\therefore \quad \boxed{_1\mu_2 = \frac{1}{_2\mu_1}}$$

(iv) $_1\mu_2 = \frac{\mu_2}{\mu_1}$, $_2\mu_3 = \frac{\mu_3}{\mu_2}$ and $_3\mu_1 = \frac{\mu_1}{\mu_3}$

$$\therefore \quad \boxed{_1\mu_2 \times {_2\mu_3} \times {_3\mu_1} = 1}$$

(v) $v = \frac{c}{\mu}$ and $\lambda = \frac{\lambda_0}{\mu}$

Here, λ is the wavelength in a medium and λ_0 the wavelength in vacuum. Thus, in travelling from vacuum to a medium speed and wavelength decrease μ times but frequency remains unchanged.

(vi) $_1\mu_2 = \frac{\mu_2}{\mu_1} = \frac{c/v_2}{c/v_1} = \frac{v_1}{v_2} = \frac{f\lambda_1}{f\lambda_2} = \frac{\lambda_1}{\lambda_2}$

Here, f = frequency of light which remains same in both media.

Thus, $$\boxed{_1\mu_2 = \frac{\mu_2}{\mu_1} = \frac{v_1}{v_2} = \frac{\lambda_1}{\lambda_2}}$$

Example 1 (a) Find the speed of light of wavelength $\lambda = 780\text{nm}$ (in air) in a medium of refractive index $\mu = 1.55$.

(b) What is the wavelength of this light in the given medium?

Sol. (a) $v = \frac{c}{\mu} = \frac{3.0 \times 10^8}{1.55} = 1.94 \times 10^8$ m/s **Ans.**

(b) $\lambda_{\text{medium}} = \frac{\lambda_{\text{air}}}{\mu} = \frac{780}{1.55} = 503\text{ nm}$ **Ans.**

Example 2 Refractive index of glass with respect to water is (9/8). Refractive index of glass with respect to air is (3/2). Find the refractive index of water with respect to air.

Sol. Given, $_w\mu_g = 9/8$ and $_a\mu_g = 3/2$

As, $$_a\mu_g \times {_g\mu_w} \times {_w\mu_a} = 1$$

$$\therefore \quad \frac{1}{_w\mu_a} = {_a\mu_w} = {_a\mu_g} \times {_g\mu_w} = \frac{_a\mu_g}{_w\mu_g}$$

$$\therefore \quad {}_a\mu_w = \frac{3/2}{9/8} = \frac{4}{3} \quad \textbf{Ans.}$$

Example 3 A ray of light passes through two slabs of same thickness. In the first slab n_1 waves are formed and in the second slab n_2. Find refractive index of second medium with respect to first.

Sol. One wave means one wavelength. So, if t is the thickness of slab, λ the wavelength and n the number of waves, then

$$n\lambda = t$$

$$\Rightarrow \quad \lambda = \frac{t}{n}$$

or $\quad \lambda \propto \frac{1}{n}$ (as t is same)

or $\quad \frac{\lambda_1}{\lambda_2} = \frac{n_2}{n_1}$

Now, refractive index of second medium w.r.t. first medium is

$${}_1\mu_2 = \frac{\lambda_1}{\lambda_2} = \frac{n_2}{n_1} \quad \textbf{Ans.}$$

MODULE 1 Exercise

Single Correct Option

1. The refractive index of water is 4/3. The speed of light in water is
   (a) 1.50×10^8 m/s
   (b) 1.78×10^8 m/s
   (c) 2.25×10^8 m/s
   (d) 2.67×10^8 m/s

2. Time taken by light to travel in two different materials A and B of refractive indices μ_A and μ_B of same thickness is t_1 and t_2, respectively. If $t_2 - t_1 = 5 \times 10^{-10}$ s and the ratio of μ_A to μ_B is 1 : 2. Then, the thickness of material in metre is (Given, v_A and v_B are velocities of light in A and B materials, respectively.) **(2022 Main)**
   (a) $5 \times 10^{-10} \times v_A$ m
   (b) 5×10^{-10} m
   (c) 1.5×10^{-10} m
   (d) $5 \times 10^{-10} \times v_B$ m

Subjective Questions

3. Given that ${}_1\mu_2 = 4/3$, ${}_2\mu_3 = 3/2$. Find ${}_1\mu_3$.

4. A monochromatic light beam of frequency 6.0×10^{14} Hz crosses from air into a transparent material where its wavelength is measured to be 300 nm. What is the index of refraction of the material?

5. Light from a sodium lamp ($\lambda_0 = 589$ nm) passes through a tank of glycerin (refractive index $= 1.47$) 20 m long in a time t_1. If it takes a time t_2 to pass the same tank when filled with carbon disulfide (index $= 1.63$), determine the difference $t_2 - t_1$.

6. A light beam of wavelength 600 nm in air passes through film 1 ($n_1 = 1.2$) of thickness 1.0 μm, then through film 2 (air) of thickness 1.5 μm, and finally through film 3 ($n_3 = 1.8$) of thickness 1.0 μm
   (a) Which film does the light cross in the least time, and what is that least time?
   (b) What are the total number of wavelengths (at any instant) across all three films together?

Answers

1. (c) **2.** (a) **3.** (2) **4.** (1.67) **5.** 1.07×10^{-8} s **6.** (a) First film, $t_{min} = 4 \times 10^{-15}$ s (b) 7.5

See hints on page 148.

MODULE 2

Law of Refraction (Snell's Law)

If a ray of light passes through one medium to other medium, then according to Snell's law,

$$\mu \sin i = \text{constant} \qquad \text{...(i)}$$

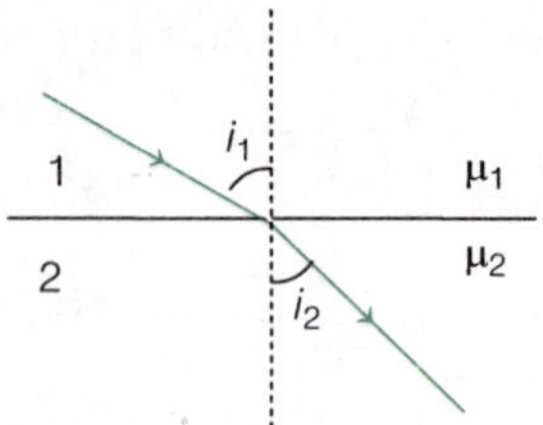

For two media, $\mu_1 \sin i_1 = \mu_2 \sin i_2$

or

$$\frac{\mu_2}{\mu_1} = \frac{\sin i_1}{\sin i_2} = {}_1\mu_2 \qquad \text{...(ii)}$$

From Eq. (i) we can see that $i_1 > i_2$ if $\mu_2 > \mu_1$, i.e. if a ray of light passes from a rarer to a denser medium, it bends towards normal.

Eq. (ii) can be written as,

$${}_1\mu_2 = \frac{\sin i_1}{\sin i_2} = \frac{v_1}{v_2} = \frac{\lambda_1}{\lambda_2} = \frac{\mu_2}{\mu_1} \qquad \text{...(iii)}$$

Here, v_1 is the speed of light in medium 1 and v_2 in medium 2. Similarly, λ_1 and λ_2 are the corresponding wavelengths.

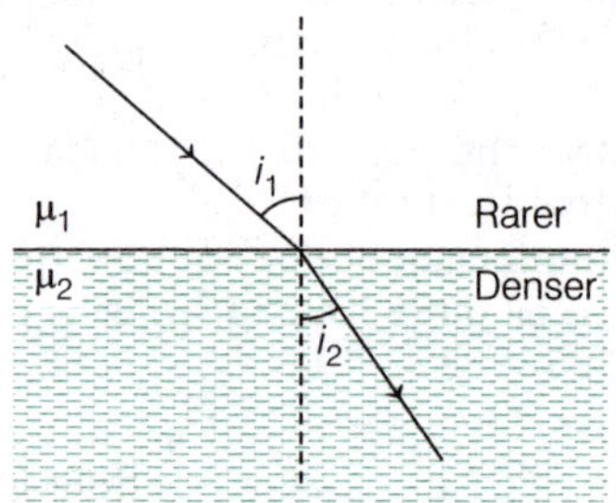

If $\mu_2 > \mu_1$ then $v_1 > v_2$ and $\lambda_1 > \lambda_2$, i.e. in a rarer medium speed and hence, wavelength of light is more.

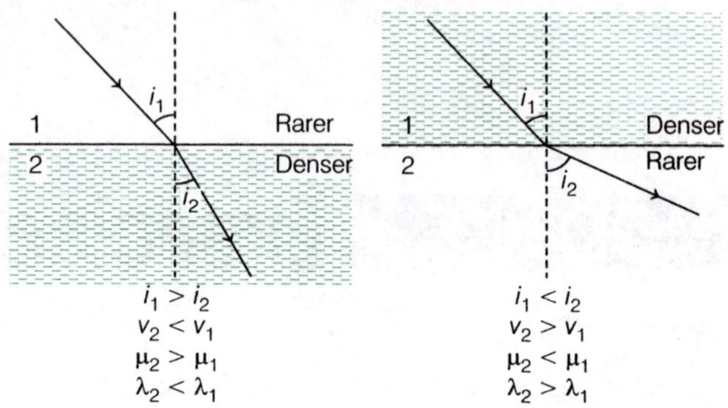

If the boundaries of the media are parallel, the emergent ray *CD* although laterally displaced, is parallel to the incident ray *AB* if $\mu_1 = \mu_5$. We can also directly apply the Snell's law ($\mu \sin i = \text{constant}$) in medium 1 and 5, i.e.

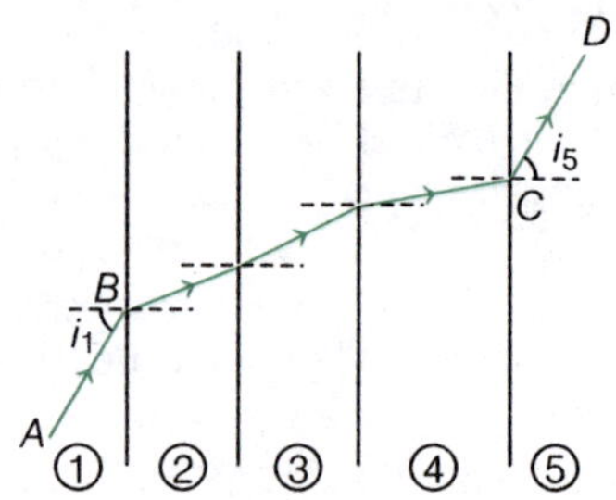

$$\mu_1 \sin i_1 = \mu_5 \sin i_5$$

So, $i_1 = i_5$

if $\mu_1 = \mu_5$

If any of the boundary is not parallel we cannot use this law directly by jumping the intervening media.

Important POINTS

- $\mu = \dfrac{\sin i}{\sin r}$ is a special case of Snell's law when one medium is air.

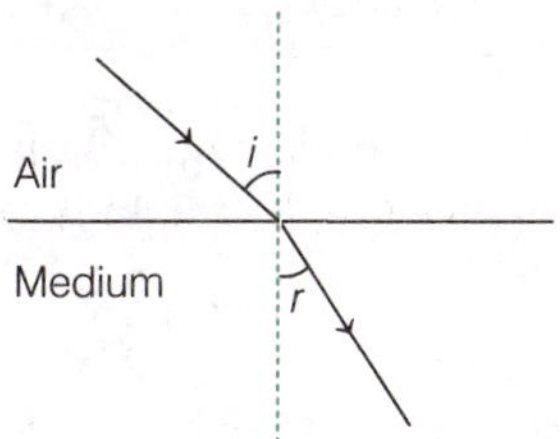

In figure, if we apply the Snell's law in original form then it is

$$\mu_{air} \sin i_{air} = \mu_{medium} \sin i_{medium}$$

or $$(1) \sin i = (\mu) \sin r$$

$\therefore$ $$\mu = \frac{\sin i}{\sin r}$$

- In $\mu = \dfrac{\sin i}{\sin r}$, angle i is not always the angle of incidence but it is the angle of ray of light in air (with normal).

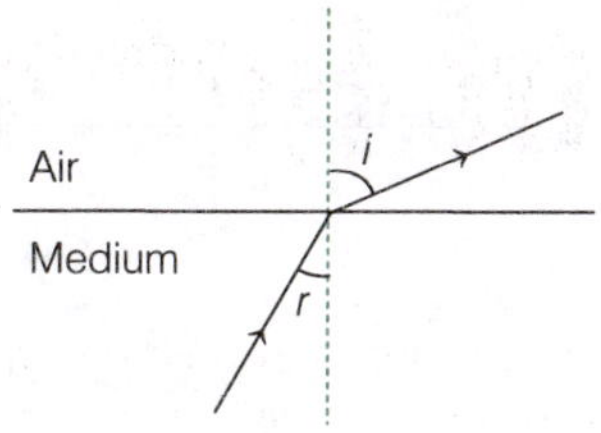

In the above figure, ray of light is travelling from some medium to air. So, angle of incidence is actually r. But we have to take $\angle i$ in air and now we can apply $\mu = \dfrac{\sin i}{\sin r}$.

- In $\mu = \dfrac{\sin i}{\sin r}$, if i is changed, then r angle also changes. But $\dfrac{\sin i}{\sin r}$ remains constant and this constant is called refractive index of that medium.
- $\mu = \dfrac{\sin i}{\sin r}$ can be applied for any pair of angles i and r except the normal incidence for which $\angle i = \angle r = 0°$ and $\mu = \dfrac{\sin i}{\sin r}$ is an indeterminant form.

Example 1 A light beam passes from medium 1 to medium 2. Show that the emerging beam is parallel to the incident beam.

Sol. Applying Snell's law at A,

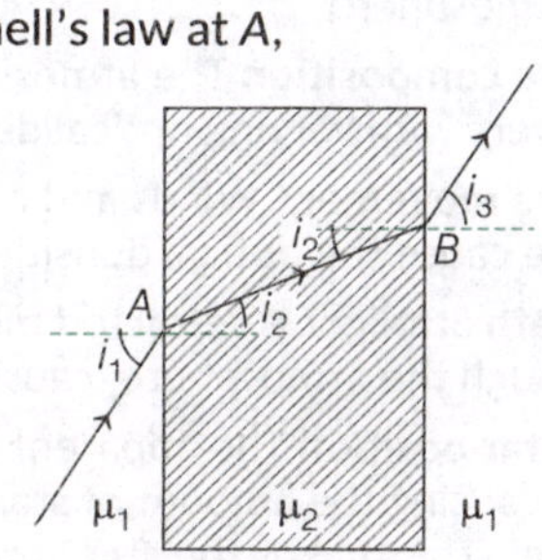

$$\mu_1 \sin i_1 = \mu_2 \sin i_2$$

or $$\frac{\mu_1}{\mu_2} = \frac{\sin i_2}{\sin i_1} \quad \text{...(i)}$$

Similarly at B,

$$\mu_2 \sin i_2 = \mu_1 \sin i_3$$

$\therefore$ $$\frac{\mu_1}{\mu_2} = \frac{\sin i_2}{\sin i_3} \quad \text{...(ii)}$$

From Eqs. (i) and (ii), we have

$$i_3 = i_1$$

i.e. the emergent ray is parallel to incident ray. **Proved.**

Problems Based on $\mu = \dfrac{\sin i}{\sin r}$

Example 2 A ray of light falls on a glass plate of refractive index $\mu = 1.5$. What is the angle of incidence of the ray if the angle between the reflected and refracted rays is 90°?

Sol. In the figure, $r = 90° - i$

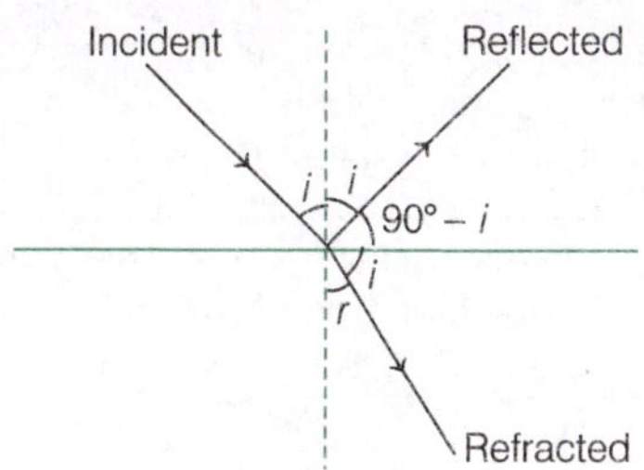

From Snell's law, $1.5 = \dfrac{\sin i}{\sin r} = \dfrac{\sin i}{\sin (90° - i)} = \tan i$

$\therefore$ $$i = \tan^{-1}(1.5) = 56.3°$$ **Ans.**

Example 3 A pile 4 m high driven into the bottom of a lake is 1 m above the water. Determine the length of the shadow of the pile on the bottom of the lake if the sun rays make an angle of 45° with the water surface. The refractive index of water is 4/3.

Sol. From Snell's law, $\frac{4}{3} = \frac{\sin 45^\circ}{\sin r}$

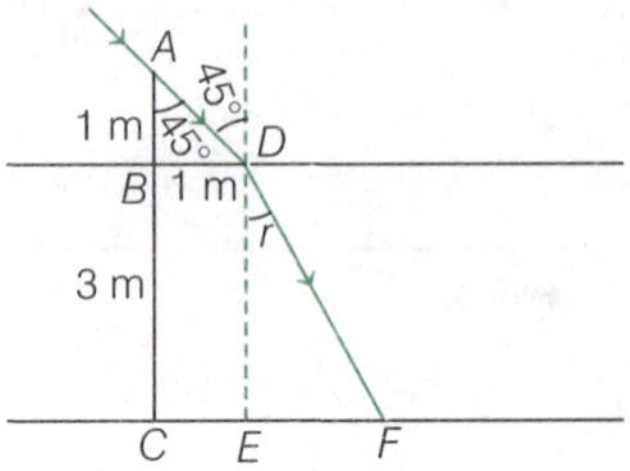

Solving this equation, we get

$$r = 32^\circ$$

Further, $EF = (DE) \tan r = (3) \tan 32^\circ$
$= 1.88$ m

$\therefore$ Total length of shadow, $L = CF$

or $L = (1 + 1.88)$ m
$= 2.88$ m **Ans.**

Example 4 An observer can see through a pin-hole the top end of a thin rod of height h, placed as shown in the figure. The beaker height is $3h$ and its radius h. When the beaker is filled with a liquid up to a height $2h$, he can see the lower end of the rod. Then, the refractive index of the liquid is **(2002 JEE)**

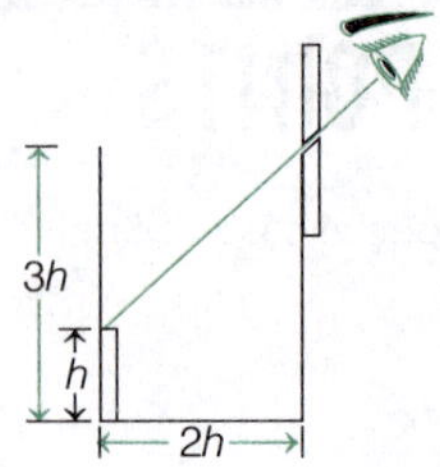

(a) $\frac{5}{2}$ (b) $\sqrt{\frac{5}{2}}$

(c) $\sqrt{\frac{3}{2}}$ (d) $\frac{3}{2}$

Sol. $PQ = QR = 2h$

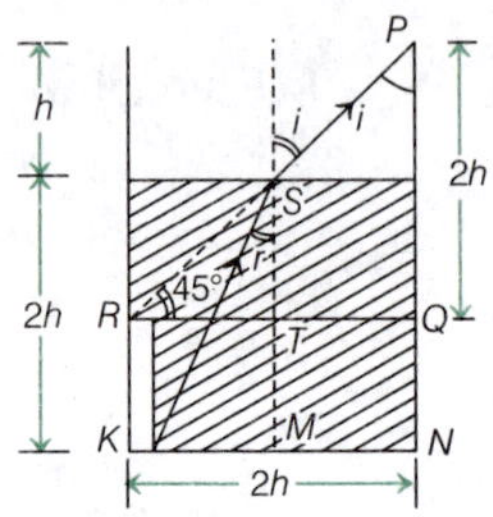

$\therefore \angle i = 45^\circ$

$\therefore ST = RT = h = KM = MN$

So, $KS = \sqrt{h^2 + (2h)^2} = h\sqrt{5}$

$\therefore \sin r = \frac{h}{h\sqrt{5}} = \frac{1}{\sqrt{5}}$

$\therefore \mu = \frac{\sin i}{\sin r} = \frac{\sin 45^\circ}{1/\sqrt{5}} = \sqrt{\frac{5}{2}}$

$\therefore$ The correct answer is (b).

Important POINTS

Fermat's principle :

1. A ray of light follows that path in reaching from one point to another point along which it takes the shortest time. Let us take an example.

   In figure, P is a point in air and Q a point in a medium of refractive index μ.

   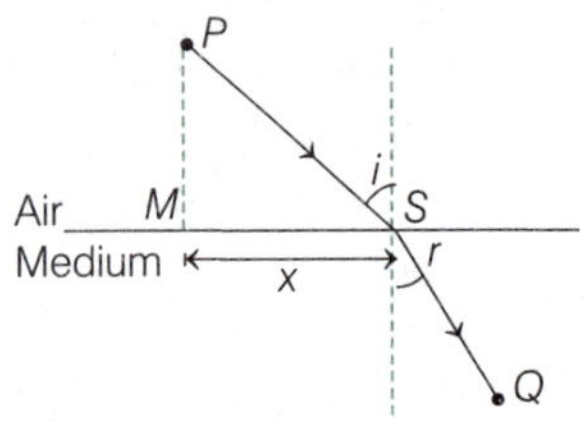

   In air, speed of light is c and in the medium speed of light is $v = c/\mu$. Suppose that, the ray of light follows a path PSQ where S is at a distance x from M. Then, time taken by the ray of light in reaching from P to Q is

   $$t = \frac{PS}{c} + \frac{SQ}{v} = \frac{PS}{c} + \frac{SQ}{(c/\mu)} \quad \text{or} \quad t = \frac{PS}{c} + \frac{\mu SQ}{c}$$

   To make the time minimum one has to differentiate it with respect to x and find the point S when t is a minimum. From differentiation (we are skipping here) we find that t is minimum when,

   $$\frac{\sin i}{\sin r} = \mu$$

   This is nothing but the Snell's law.

2. Eye is most sensitive to yellow-green light ($\lambda = 5550$ Å).
3. Frequency of visible light is of the order of 10^{15} Hz.
4. Colour of light is determined by its frequency and not the wavelength. During refraction of light frequency and colour of light do not change.
5. **Twinkling of stars** Stars twinkle because of atmospheric refraction, which is when starlight is bent and distorted by the earth's atmosphere:
   - **Atmosphere composition** The atmosphere is made up of multiple layers with varying optical densities.
   - **Atmosphere movement** Winds and air currents in the atmosphere cause the optical densities to change.
   - **Starlight path** Starlight is refracted multiple times as it passes through the atmosphere, causing its path to vary.
   - **Apparent star position** The apparent position of the star fluctuates, causing the amount of starlight entering the eye to flicker. This makes the star appear to twinkle, sometimes brighter and sometimes fainter.
6. **Oval shape of sun in the morning and evening** The sun appears oval in the morning and evening because of atmospheric refraction, which is the bending of light as it passes through different densities of materials.

   Here's why the sun appears oval at sunrise and sunset:
   - **Sun's position** The sun is near the horizon during sunrise and sunset.
   - **Atmospheric density** The atmosphere closer to the horizon is denser.
   - **Light refraction** The rays of light from the sun's upper and lower edges bend unequally as they pass through the atmosphere. The rays from the lower edges are refracted more, while the rays from the upper edges have to pass through at thicker part of the atmosphere.

- **Apparent flattening** The lower limbs of the sun appear closer to the horizon, while the upper limbs appear farther away. This makes the lower limb of the sun appear oval.

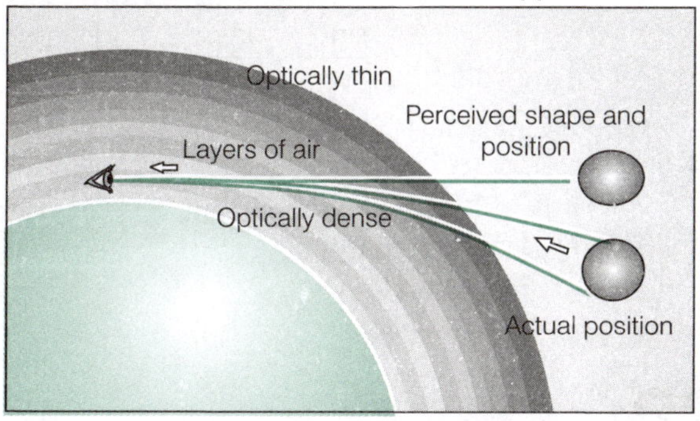

7. **Advance sunrise and delayed sunset** Refraction in the air causes the phenomenon of early sunrise and late dusk. In this scenario, the sun appears to rise 2 minutes earlier and set 2 minutes later. The sun's rays are refracted when they hit the atmosphere. As a result, the sun appears to be in an elevated position, indicating that it has already risen.

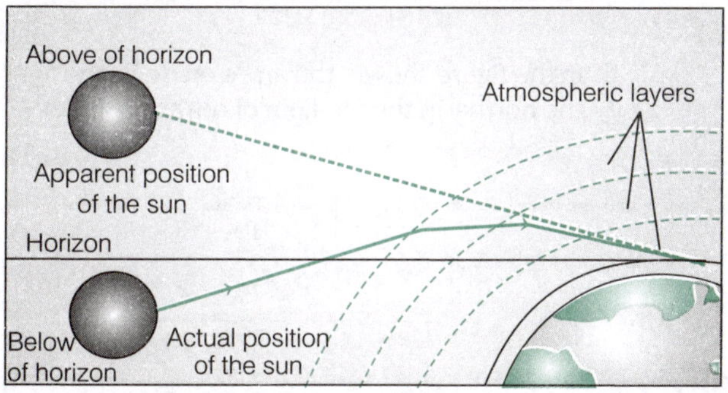

8. **Scattering of light** The molecules of a medium after absorbing incoming radiations (light) emit them in all possible directions. This process is called scattering. In scattering if the wavelength of radiation remains unchanged the scattering is called elastic otherwise inelastic.

Rayleigh has shown, theoretically that in case of elastic scattering of light by molecules, the intensity of scattered light depends on both nature of molecules and wavelength of light. According to him, intensity of scattered light $\propto \frac{1}{\lambda^4}$.

Raman effect was based on inelastic scattering. For this **C.V. Raman** was awarded the Nobel Prize in 1930.

Scattering helps us in understanding the following:

Why sky is Blue When white light from the sun enters the earth's atmosphere, scattering takes place. As scattering is proportional to $\frac{1}{\lambda^4}$, blue is scattered most. When we look at the sky we receive scattered light which is rich in blue and hence, the sky appears blue.

Why sun appears red during sunset and sunrise In the morning and evening when sun is at the horizon, due to oblique incidence, light reaches earth after traversing maximum path in the atmosphere and so suffers maximum scattering.

Now, as scattering $\propto \frac{1}{\lambda^4}$, shorter wavelengths are scattered most leaving the longer one. As red light has longest wavelength in the visible region, it is scattered least. This is why sun appears red in the morning and evening. The same reason is why red light is used for danger signals.

Example 5 Using Fermat's principle derive the laws of reflection and refraction of light on the plane interface between two media. **(Irodov 5.25)**

Sol.

Principle According to this principle time taken by a ray of light follows that path in reaching from one point to another point (in reflection or refraction) where it is minimum.

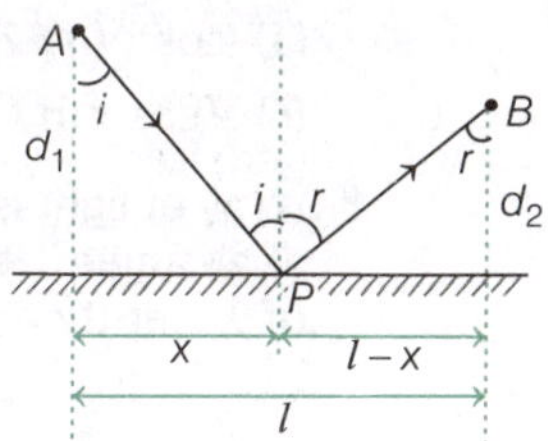

Proof of law of reflection

Let v be the speed of light in the given medium.

In the figure l, d_1 and d_2 are constants and x is variable. Time taken by the light in travelling from A to B will be,

$$t = \frac{AP + BP}{v}$$

$$= \frac{\sqrt{x^2 + d_1^2} + \sqrt{(l-x)^2 + d_2^2}}{v}$$

For t to be minimum,

$$\frac{dt}{dx} = 0$$

$$\Rightarrow \quad \frac{1}{v}\left[\frac{x}{\sqrt{x^2 + d_1^2}} - \frac{(l-x)}{\sqrt{(l-x)^2 + d_2^2}}\right] = 0$$

$$\Rightarrow \quad \frac{1}{v}\left[\frac{x}{AP} - \frac{(l-x)}{BP}\right] = 0$$

$$\Rightarrow \quad \frac{1}{v}(\sin i - \sin r) = 0$$

or $\quad \angle i = \angle r$ **Hence proved.**

Proof of law of refraction

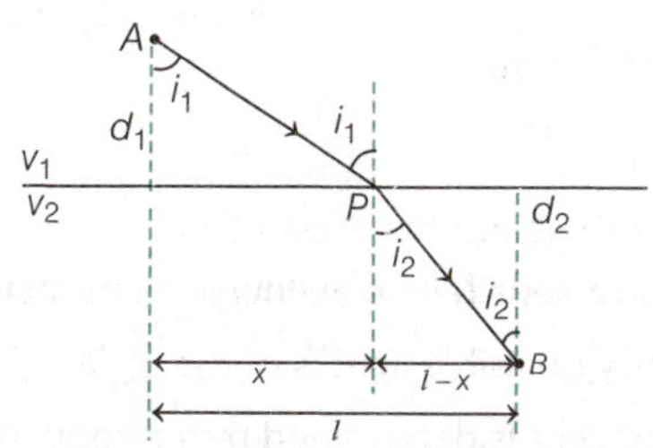

$$t = \frac{AP}{v_1} + \frac{PB}{v_2}$$

$$= \frac{\sqrt{x^2 + d_1^2}}{v_1} + \frac{\sqrt{(l - x)^2 + d_2^2}}{v_2}$$

For t to be minimum,

$$\frac{dt}{dx} = 0$$

$$\therefore \left(\frac{1}{v_1}\right)\left(\frac{x}{\sqrt{x^2 + d_1^2}}\right) - \left(\frac{1}{v_2}\right)\left(\frac{l - x}{\sqrt{(l - x)^2 + d_2^2}}\right) = 0$$

$$\frac{\sin i_1}{v_1} - \frac{\sin i_2}{v_2} = 0$$

But $v = \dfrac{c}{\mu}$ or $\mu_1 \sin i_1 = \mu_2 \sin i_2$

$\mu \sin i = \text{constant}$ **Hence proved.**

MODULE 2 Exercise

Fill in the Blank

1. A monochromatic beam of light of wavelength 6000Å in vacuum enters a medium of refractive index 1.5. In the medium its wavelength is ......, and its frequency is ...... **(1985 JEE)**

2. A light wave of frequency 5×10^{14} Hz enters a medium of refractive index 1.5. In the medium the velocity of the light wave is ...... and its wavelength is .... **(1983 JEE)**

Single Correct Option

3. When light enters from air to water, then its
   (a) frequency increases and speed decreases
   (b) frequency is same, but the wavelength is smaller in water than in air
   (c) frequency is same but the wavelength in water is greater than in air
   (d) frequency decreases and wavelength is smaller in water than in air

4. In the figure shown $\dfrac{\sin i}{\sin r}$ is equal to

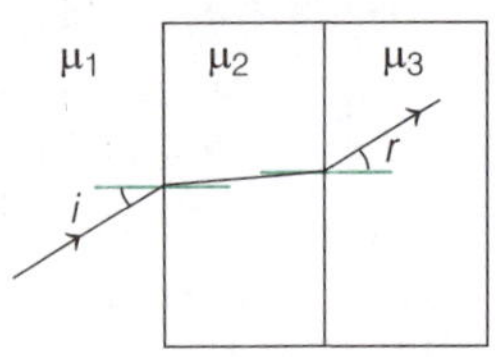

   (a) $\dfrac{\mu_2^2}{\mu_3 \mu_1}$ (b) $\dfrac{\mu_3}{\mu_1}$
   (c) $\dfrac{\mu_3 \mu_1}{\mu_2^2}$ (d) $\dfrac{\mu_1}{\mu_3}$

5. A ray of light, travelling in a medium of refractive index μ, is incident at an angle i on a composite transparent plate consisting of three plates of refractive indices μ_1, μ_2 and μ_3. The ray emerges from the composite plate into a medium of refractive index μ_4, at angle x. Then,
   (a) $\sin x = \sin i$ (b) $\sin x = \dfrac{\mu}{\mu_4} \sin i$
   (c) $\sin x = \dfrac{\mu_4}{\mu} \sin i$ (d) $\sin x = \dfrac{\mu_1 \mu_3 \mu}{\mu_2 \mu_2 \mu_4} \sin i$

6. In the figure shown, the angle made by the light ray with the normal in the medium of refractive index $\sqrt{2}$ is

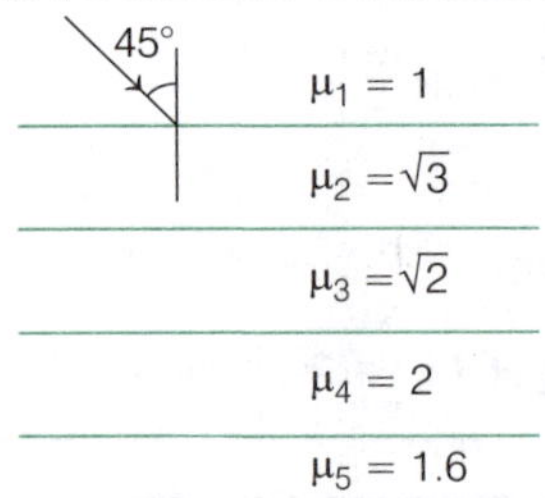

   (a) 30° (b) 60°
   (c) 90° (d) None of these

7. A ray of light passes from vacuum into a medium of refractive index n. If the angle of incidence is twice the angle of refraction, then the angle of incidence is
   (a) $\cos^{-1}(n/2)$ (b) $\sin^{-1}(n/2)$
   (c) $2\cos^{-1}(n/2)$ (d) $2\sin^{-1}(n/2)$

8. A ray of light is incident at the glass-water interface at an angle i, it emerges finally parallel to the surface of water then the value of μ_g would be **(2003 JEE)**

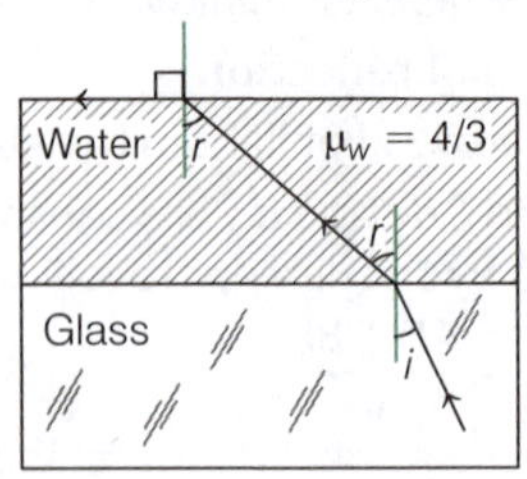

   (a) (4/3) $\sin i$ (b) $1/\sin i$ (c) 4/3 (d) 1

9. The xz-plane separates two media A and B with refractive indices μ_1 and μ_2, respectively. A ray of light travels from A and B. Its directions in the two

media are given by the unit vectors $\hat{\mathbf{r}}_A = a\hat{\mathbf{i}} + b\hat{\mathbf{j}}$ and $\hat{\mathbf{r}}_B = \alpha\hat{\mathbf{i}} + \beta\hat{\mathbf{j}}$ respectively, where $\hat{\mathbf{i}}$ and $\hat{\mathbf{j}}$ are unit vectors in the x and y-directions. Then,

(a) $\mu_1 a = \mu_2 \alpha$
(b) $\mu_1 \alpha = \mu_2 a$
(c) $\mu_1 b = \mu_2 \beta$
(d) None of the above

10. Consider a light ray travelling in air is incident into a medium of refractive index $\sqrt{2n}$. The incident angle is twice that of refracting angle, the angle of incidence will be **(2022 Main)**

(a) $\sin^{-1}(\sqrt{n})$ (b) $\cos^{-1}\left(\sqrt{\frac{n}{2}}\right)$
(c) $\sin^{-1}(\sqrt{2n})$ (d) $2\cos^{-1}\left(\sqrt{\frac{n}{2}}\right)$

11. If a wave gets refraction into a denser medium, then which of the following is true? **(2022 Main)**

(a) wavelength, speed and frequency decrease.
(b) wavelength increases, speed decreases and frequency remains constant.
(c) wavelength and speed decrease but frequency remains constant.
(d) wavelength, speed and frequency increase

12. A ray of light passes through four transparent media with refractive indices μ_1, μ_2, μ_3 and μ_4 as shown in the figure. The surfaces of all media are parallel. If the emergent ray CD is parallel to the incident ray AB, we must have **(2001 JEE)**

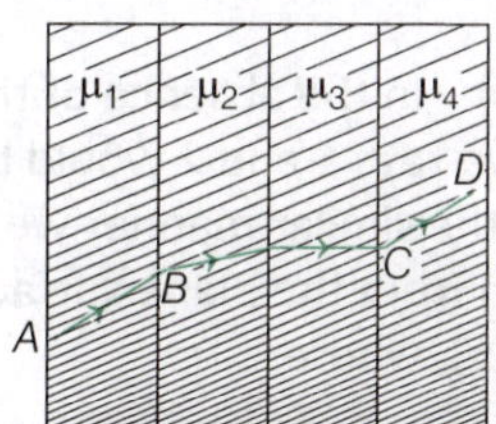

(a) $\mu_1 = \mu_2$
(b) $\mu_2 = \mu_3$
(c) $\mu_3 = \mu_4$
(d) $\mu_4 = \mu_1$

Subjective Questions

13. In the figure shown, find ${}_1\mu_2$.

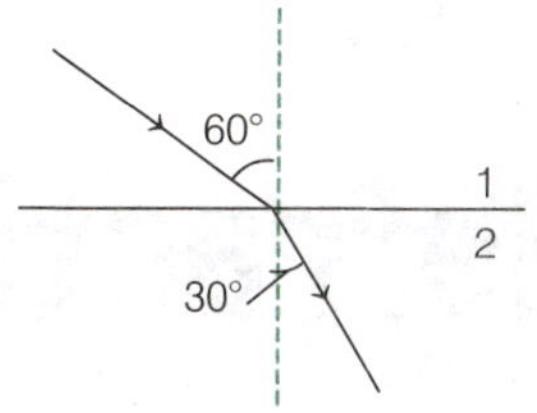

14. If ${}_1\mu_2$ is 1.5, then find the value of $\frac{\lambda_1}{\lambda_2}$.

15. A shallow glass dish is 4.00 cm wide at the bottom as shown in figure. When an observer's eye is positioned as shown, the observer sees the edge of the bottom of the empty dish. When this dish is filled with water, the observer sees the centre of the bottom of the dish. Find the height of the dish $\mu_w = 4/3$.

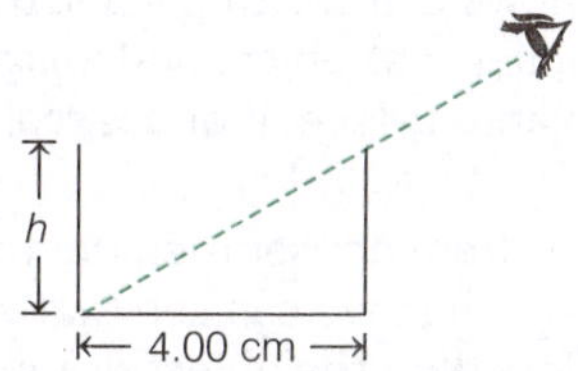

16. At what value of the angle of incidence θ_1 light reflected from the surface of water is perpendicular to the refracted light? **(Irodov 5.15)**

Note *Take refractive index of glass,* $\mu_g = \frac{3}{2}$ *and refractive index of water* $\mu_w = \frac{4}{3}$.

Integer Type Question

17. A pole is vertically submerged in a swimming pool, such that it gives a length of shadow 2.15 m within water when sunlight is incident at an angle of 30° with the surface of water. If swimming pool is filled to a height of 1.5 m, then the height of the pole above the water surface in centimeters is ($n_w = 4/3$) .... **(2023 Main)**

Answers

1. 400 Å, 5×10^{14} Hz **2.** 2×10^8 m/s, 4×10^{-7}m **3.** (b)
4. (b) **5.** (b) **6.** (a) **7.** (c) **8.** (b)
9. (a) **10.** (d) **11.** (c) **12.** (d) **13.** $\sqrt{3}$
14. 3/2 **15.** 2.4 cm **16.** $\theta_1 = 53°$
17. (50)

See hints on pages 148-150.

MODULE 3

Single Refraction from Plane Surface

(i) If ray of light travels from first medium (refractive index μ_1) to second medium (refractive index μ_2), then image distance (or v) from the plane surface is given by

$$\boxed{v = \frac{\mu_2}{\mu_1} u}$$

(ii) From this equation, we can see that v and u are of same sign. This implies that object and image lie on same side of the plane surface. If one is real, then the other is virtual.

(iii) If ray of light travels from denser medium to rarer medium (or $\mu_1 > \mu_2$), then we can see that $v < u$) or the image distance is less than the object distance. If the light travels from rarer to denser medium ($\mu_1 < \mu_2$), then $v > u$ or the image distance is greater than the object distance.

Further, if rarer medium is air (or vacuum), then this decrease or increase in image distance will be μ times.

(iv) In all the four figures shown below, single refraction is taking place through a plane surface. Refractive index of medium is μ. In figures (a) and (d), the ray of light is travelling from denser to rarer medium and hence, it bends away from the normal. In figures (b) and (c), the ray of light is travelling from a rarer to a denser medium and hence, it bends towards the normal.

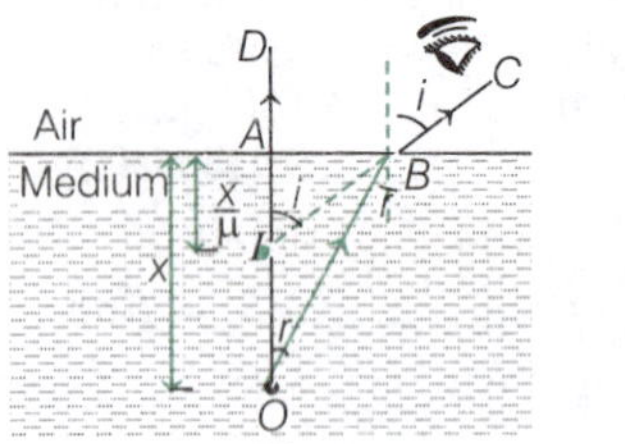

(a)

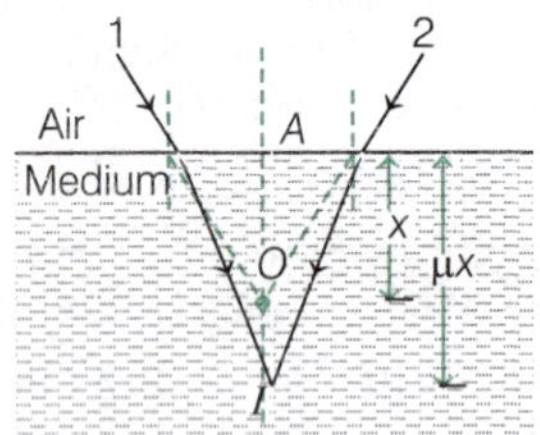

(b)

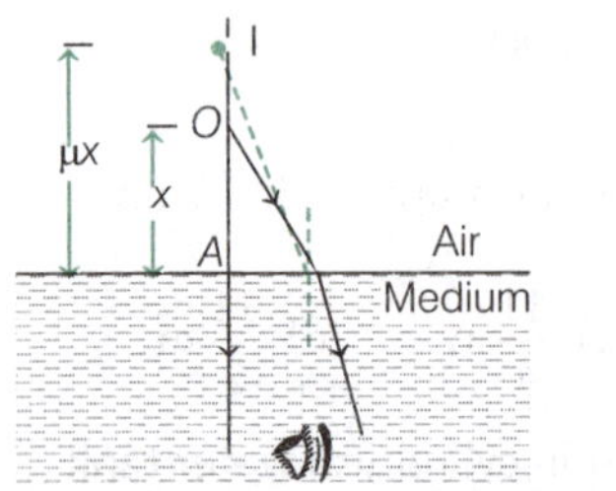

(c)

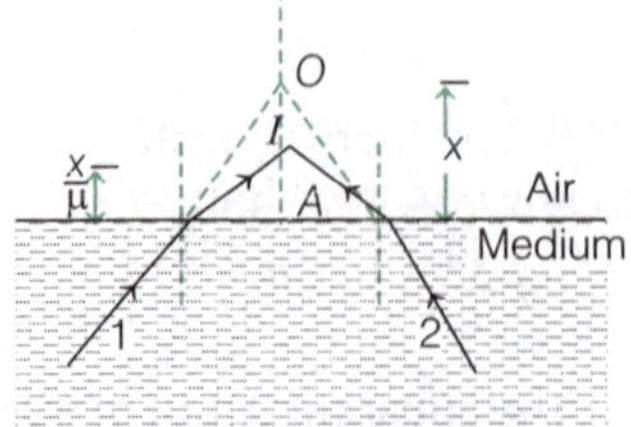

(d)

Refer figure (a) Object O is placed at a distance x from A. Ray OA, which falls normally on the plane surface, passes undeviated as AD. Ray OB, which falls at angle r (with the normal) on the plane surface, bends away from the normal and passes as BC in air. Rays AD and BC meet at I after extending these two rays backwards. Let BC makes an angle i (> r) with normal.

In the figure, $\angle AOB$ will be r and $\angle AIB$ is i. For normal incidence (i.e. small angles of i and r)

$$\sin i \approx \tan i = \frac{AB}{AI} \quad \text{...(i)}$$

and

$$\sin r \approx \tan r = \frac{AB}{AO} \quad \text{...(ii)}$$

Dividing Eq. (i) by Eq. (ii), we have

$$\frac{\sin i}{\sin r} = \frac{AO}{AI} \quad \text{or} \quad \mu = \frac{AO}{AI} \qquad \left(\text{as } \frac{\sin i}{\sin r} = \mu\right)$$

$$\therefore \quad AI = \frac{AO}{\mu} = \frac{x}{\mu}$$

If point O is at a depth of d from the water surface, then the above result is also written as,

$$\boxed{d_{\text{apparent}} = \frac{d_{\text{actual}}}{\mu}}$$

or the apparent depth is μ times less than the actual depth.

Refer figure (b) In the absence of the plane refracting surface, the two rays 1 and 2 would have met at O. Proceeding in the similar manner we can prove that after refraction from the plane surface, they will now meet at a point I, where

$$AI = \mu x \qquad \text{(if } AO = x\text{)}$$

Refer figure (c) In this case object is at O, a distance $AO = x$ from the plane surface. When seen from inside the medium, it will appear at I, where

$$AI = \mu x$$

If point O is at a height of h from the water surface, then the above relation can be written as

$$\boxed{h_{\text{app}} = \mu h}$$

Refer figure (d) The two rays 1 and 2 meeting at O will now meet at I after refraction from the plane surface, where $AI = \frac{AO}{\mu} = \frac{x}{\mu}$.

Note *In all the four cases, the change in the value of x is μ times whether it is increasing or decreasing. All the relations can be derived for small angles of incidence as done in part (a).*

Exercise Three immiscible liquids of refractive indices μ_1, μ_2 and μ_3 (with $\mu_3 > \mu_2 > \mu_1$) are filled in a vessel.

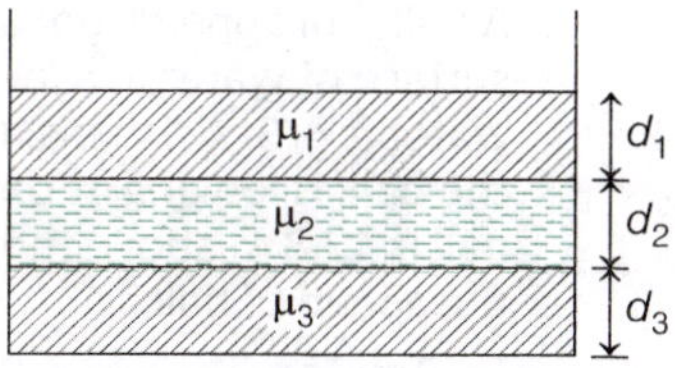

Their depths are d_1, d_2 and d_3 respectively. Prove that the apparent depth (for almost normal incidence) when seen from top of the first liquid will be

$$d_{app} = \frac{d_1}{\mu_1} + \frac{d_2}{\mu_2} + \frac{d_3}{\mu_3}$$

Example 1 In figure, find position of second image I_2 formed after two times refraction from two plane surfaces AB and CD.

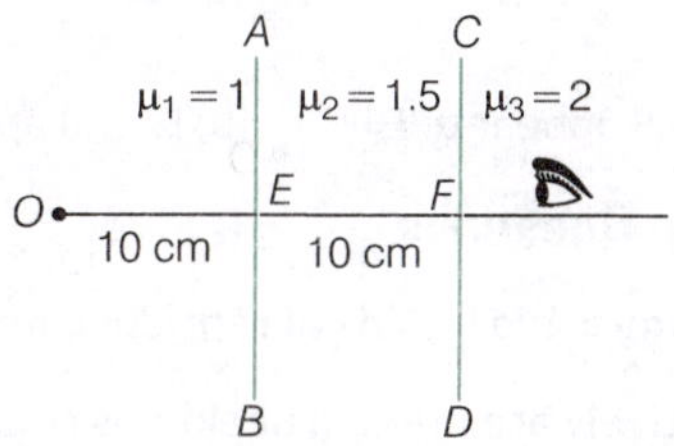

Sol. We will apply $v = \frac{\mu_2}{\mu_1} u$, and the fact that object and image are on the same side of the plane surface.

Refraction from *AB*

$$\mu_1 = 1 \Rightarrow \mu_2 = 1.5$$

$$u = EO = 10 \text{ cm}$$

(towards left of AB)

$$\therefore \quad v = \left(\frac{\mu_2}{\mu_1}\right) u = \frac{1.5}{1}(10)$$

or $\quad v = EI_1 = 15$ cm

(towards left of AB)

Refraction from *CD* I_1 will act as an object for refraction from CD

$$\mu_1 = 1.5 \text{ and } \mu_2 = 2$$

$$u = FI_1 = FE + EI_1 = (10 + 15) \text{ cm}$$

$$= 25 \text{ cm} \quad \text{(towards left of } CD\text{)}$$

$$\therefore \quad v = \left(\frac{\mu_2}{\mu_1}\right)(u) = \left(\frac{2}{1.5}\right)(25) = \frac{100}{3} \text{ cm}$$

(towards left of CD)

$$= FI_2$$

The correct figure is as shown below

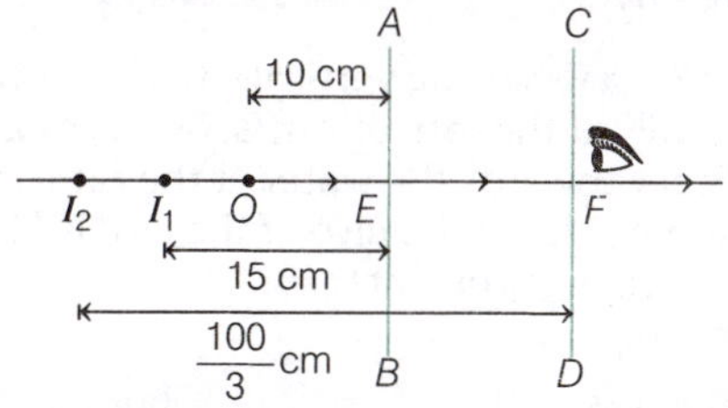

Note I_1 *and* I_2 *both are virtual as the light has moved towards right of AB and CD (because it is a refraction) but* I_1 *and* I_2 *are towards left of AB or CD.*

Example 2 Refractive index of the glass slab is 1.5. There is a point object O inside the slab as shown. To eye E_1 object appears at a distance of 6 cm (from the top surface) and to eye E_2 it appears at a distance of 8 cm (from the bottom surface). Find actual thickness of the glass slab.

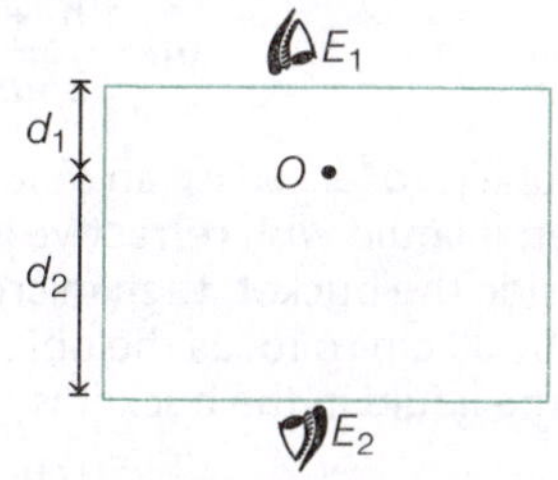

Sol. Applying $d_{app} = \frac{d}{\mu} \Rightarrow d = (\mu)\, d_{app}$

$$\therefore \quad d_1 = (1.5)(6) = 9 \text{ cm}$$

$$d_2 = (1.5)(8) = 12 \text{ cm}$$

Therefore, actual thickness of the glass slab is

$$d_1 + d_2 = 21 \text{ cm}$$ **Ans.**

MODULE 3 Exercise

Single Correct Option

1. An under water swimmer is at a depth of 12 m below the surface of water. A bird is at a height of 18 m from the surface of water, directly above his eyes. For the swimmer, the bird appears to be at a distance from the surface of water equal to (Refractive index of water is 4/3)

   (a) 24 m (b) 12 m (c) 18 m (d) 9 m

2. A bird is flying over a swimming pool at a height of 2 m from the water surface. If the bottom is perfectly plane reflecting surface and depth of swimming pool is 1 m, then the distance of final image of bird from the bird itself is $\mu_w = 4/3$

   (a) $\frac{11}{3}$ m (b) $\frac{23}{3}$ m (c) $\frac{11}{4}$ m (d) $\frac{11}{2}$ m

3. The apparent depth of water in cylindrical water tank of diameter $2R$ cm is reducing at the rate of x cm/min when water is being drained out at a constant rate. The amount of water drained in cc/min is (n_1 = refractive index of air, n_2 = refractive index of water)

   (a) $\frac{x\pi R^2 n_1}{n_2}$ (b) $\frac{x\pi R^2 n_2}{n_1}$ (c) $\frac{2\pi R n_1}{n_2}$ (d) $\pi R^2 x$

4. A bird in air looks at a fish directly below it inside in a transparent liquid in a tank. If the distance of the fish as estimated by the bird is h_1 and that of the bird as estimated by the fish is h_2, then the refractive index of the liquid is

(a) $\frac{h_2}{h_1}$ (b) $\frac{h_1}{h_2}$

(c) $\frac{h_1+h_2}{h_1-h_2}$ (d) $\frac{h_1-h_2}{h_1+h_2}$

5. In a lake, a fish rising vertically to the surface of water uniformly at the rate of 3 m/s, observes a bird diving vertically towards the water at the rate of 9 m/s. The actual velocity of the dive of the bird is (Given, refractive index of water = 4/3)

(a) 3.6 m/s
(b) 4.5 m/s
(c) 6.0 m/s
(d) 12.0 m/s

6. A vessel of depth 'd' is half filled with oil of refractive index n_1 and the other half is filled with water of refractive index n_2. The apparent depth of this vessel when viewed from above will be **(2023 Main)**

(a) $\frac{2d(n_1+n_2)}{n_1n_2}$ (b) $\frac{dn_1n_2}{2(n_1+n_2)}$

(c) $\frac{dn_1n_2}{(n_1+n_2)}$ (d) $\frac{d(n_1+n_2)}{2n_1n_2}$

7. A microscope is focussed on an object at the bottom of a bucket. If liquid with refractive index $5/3$ is poured inside the bucket, then microscope have to be raised by 30 cm to focus the object again. The height of the liquid in the bucket is **(2023 Main)**

(a) 75 cm (b) 50 cm
(c) 12 cm (d) 18 cm

8. A glass tumbler having inner depth of 17.5 cm is kept on a table. A student starts pouring water ($\mu = 4/3$) into it while looking at the surface of water from the above. When he feels that the tumbler is half filled, he stops pouring water. Up to what height the tumbler is actually filled? **(2021 Main)**

(a) 11.7 cm (b) 10 cm
(c) 7.5 cm (d) 8.75 cm

9. A ball is dropped from a height of 20 m above the surface of water in a lake. The refractive index of water is 4/3. A fish inside the lake, in the line of fall of the ball, is looking at the ball. At an instant, when the ball is 12.8 m above the water surface, the fish sees the speed of ball as **(2009 JEE)**

(a) 9 ms^{-1} (b) 12 ms^{-1}
(c) 16 ms^{-1} (d) 21.33 ms^{-1}

Subjective Question

10. In the figure shown, at what distance

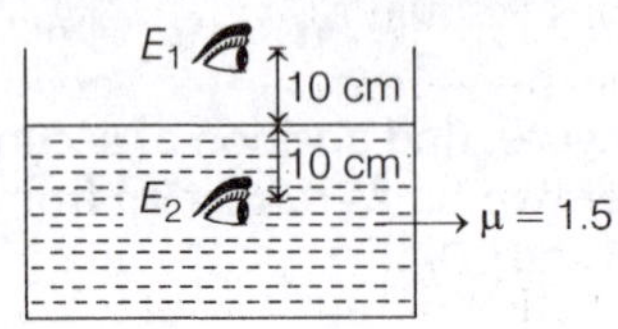

(a) E_2 will appear to E_1 (b) E_1 will appear to E_2

Integer Type Questions

11. Two immiscible liquids of refractive indices $\frac{8}{5}$ and $\frac{3}{2}$ respectively are put in a beaker as shown in the figure. The height of each column is 6 cm. A coin is placed at the bottom of the beaker. For near normal vision, the apparent depth of the coin is $\frac{\alpha}{4}$ cm. The value of α is .... **(2024 Main)**

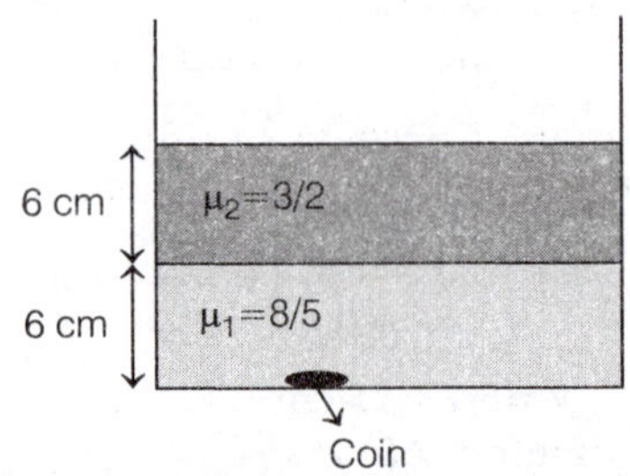

12. A fish rising vertically upward with a uniform velocity of 8 ms^{-1}, observes that a bird is diving vertically downward towards the fish with the velocity of 12 ms^{-1}. If the refractive index of water is 4/3, then the actual velocity of the diving bird to pick the fish, will be .... ms^{-1}. **(2023 Main)**

Answers

1. (a) **2.** (d) **3.** (b) **4.** (a) **5.** (b) **6.** (d) **7.** (a) **8.** (a) **9.** (c)
10. (a) $\frac{50}{3}$ cm (b) 25 cm **11.** (31) **12.** (3)

See hints on pages 150-151.

MODULE 4

Shift Due to a Glass Slab

(i) Refraction from a glass slab is a case of double refraction from two plane surfaces. So, we are talking about the second (or final) image. Let us call it *I*.

(ii) If *O* is real then second image *I* is virtual and *vice-versa*.

(iii) *I* is shifted (w.r.t.) *O* by a distance $OI = \text{shift} = \left(1 - \frac{1}{\mu}\right)t$ in the direction of ray of light.

(iv) If E_1 observes E_2, then E_2 is object. So, light travels from E_2 towards E_1. So, shift is also in the same direction or E_1 will observe second image of E_2 at a distance

$$d_1 = d - \text{shift}$$

Same is the case when E_2 observes E_1.

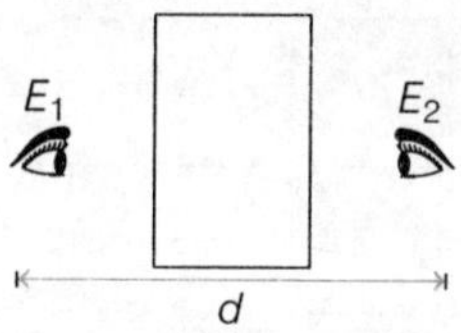

(v) If two or more than two slabs are kept jointly or separately, then total shift is added.

$$\therefore\ S_{\text{Total}} = S_1 + S_2 = \left(1 - \frac{1}{\mu_1}\right)t_1 + \left(1 - \frac{1}{\mu_2}\right)t_2$$

(vi)

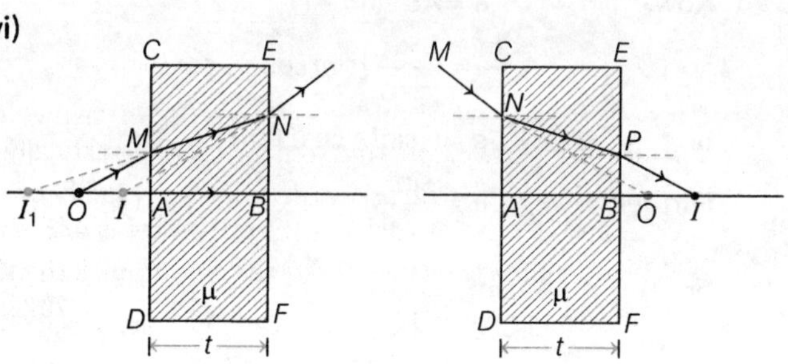

(a) (b)

Refer figure (a) An object is placed at *O*. Plane surface *CD* forms its image (virtual) at I_1. This image acts as an object for *EF* which finally forms the image (virtual) at *I*. Distance *OI* is called the normal shift and its value is

$$OI = \left(1 - \frac{1}{\mu}\right)t$$

This can be proved as under:

Let $\quad OA = x$

then $\quad AI_1 = \mu x \quad$ (Refraction from *CD*)

$$BI_1 = \mu x + t$$

$$BI = \frac{BI_1}{\mu} = x + \frac{t}{\mu} \quad \text{(Refraction from } EF\text{)}$$

$$\therefore \quad OI = (AB + OA) - BI$$

$$= (t + x) - \left(x + \frac{t}{\mu}\right)$$

$$= \left(1 - \frac{1}{\mu}\right)t$$

Hence Proved.

Note *For two refractions (at CD and EF) we have used,*

$$v = \left(\frac{\mu_2}{\mu_1}\right)\mu$$

Refer figure (b) The ray of light which would have met line *AB* at *O* will now meet this line at *I* after two times refraction from the slab. Here,

$$OI = \left(1 - \frac{1}{\mu}\right)t$$

Example 1 Refractive index of glass slab shown in figure is 1.5. Focal length of mirror is 20 cm. Find

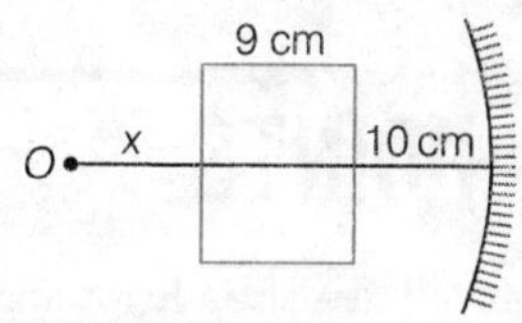

(a) total number of refractions and reflections before final image is formed.

(b) reduced steps.

(c) value of x, so that final image coincides with the object.

Sol. (a) There are total four refractions and one reflection.

(b) Reduced steps are three: slab, then mirror and then again slab.

(c) Shift due to the slab,

$$s = \left(1 - \frac{1}{\mu}\right)t = \left(1 - \frac{2}{3}\right)(9) = 3\ \text{cm}$$

Actual distance from mirror to object is $(19 + x)$ cm. Slab will reduce this distance by 3 cm. So, apparent distance will become $(16 + x)$ cm.

Now, if $16 + x = R = 2f = 40$ cm

or $\quad x = 24$ cm

then ray of light will fall normal to the concave mirror. It will retrace its path and final image will coincide with the object

$\therefore \quad x = 24$ cm **Ans.**

Note *If ray of light falls normal to a mirror, then there is no need of applying the slab formula in return journey of ray of light. Path is retracing, means slab formula is automatically applied in return journey. But if it is not normal, then we will have to apply the slab formula in return journey too.*

Example 2 A point object O is placed in front of a concave mirror of focal length 10 cm. A glass slab of refractive index $\mu = 3/2$ and thickness 6 cm is inserted between object and mirror. Find the position of final image when the distance x shown in figure is

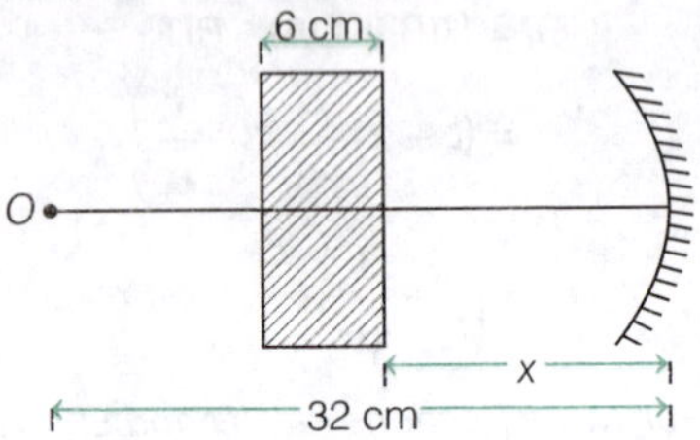

(a) 5 cm (b) 20 cm

Sol. The normal shift produced by the glass slab :

$$s = \left(1 - \frac{1}{\mu}\right) t = \left(1 - \frac{2}{3}\right)(6)$$

$$= 2 \text{ cm}$$

i.e. for the mirror the object is placed at a distance $(32 - s) = 30$ cm from it. Applying mirror formula

$$\frac{1}{v} + \frac{1}{u} = \frac{1}{f}$$

or $$\frac{1}{v} - \frac{1}{30} = -\frac{1}{10}$$

or $$v = -15 \text{ cm}$$

(a) **When x = 5 cm**

The light falls on the slab on its return journey as shown. But the slab will again shift it by a distance $s = 2$ cm. Hence, the final **real** image is formed at a distance $(15 + 2) = 17$ cm from the mirror.

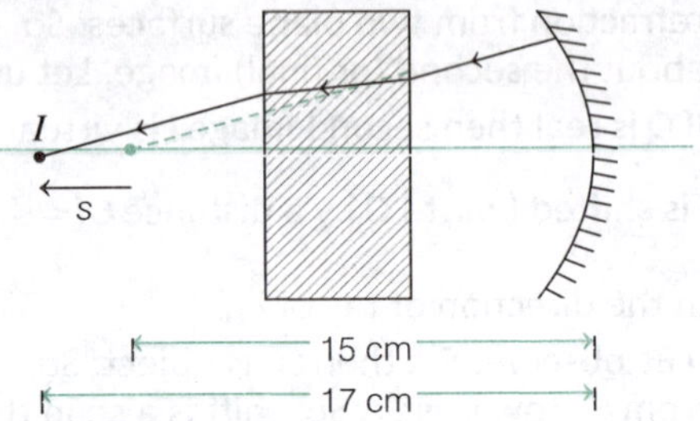

(b) **When x = 20 cm**

This time also the final image is at a distance 17 cm from the mirror but it is **virtual** as shown.

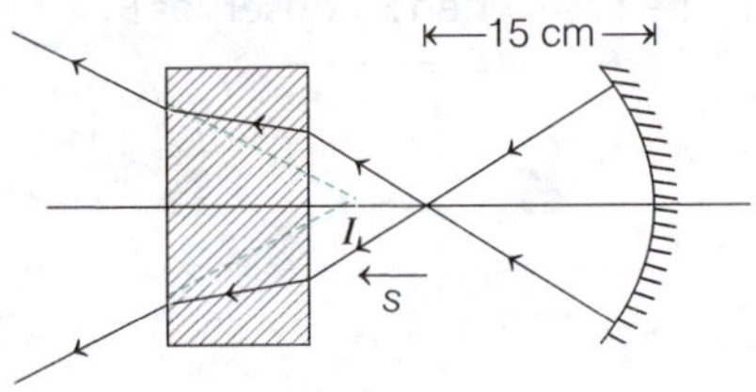

Important POINTS

Lateral shift We have already discussed that ray *MA* is parallel to ray *BN*. But the emergent ray is displaced laterally by a distance *d*, which depends on μ, *t* and *i* and its value is given by the relation,

$$d = t\left(1 - \frac{\cos i}{\sqrt{\mu^2 - \sin^2 i}}\right)\sin i$$

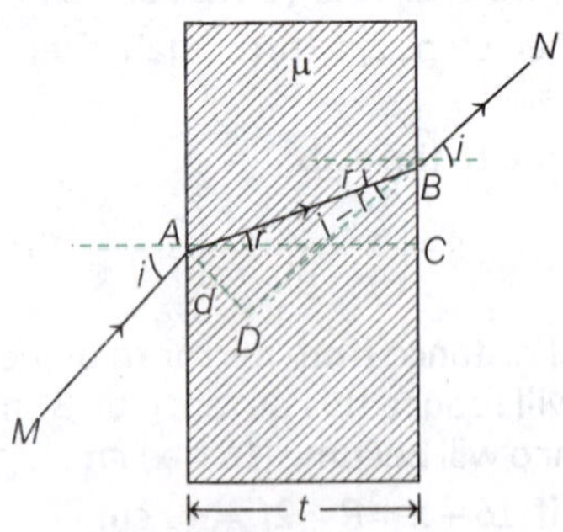

Proof $$AB = \frac{AC}{\cos r} = \frac{t}{\cos r} \quad (\text{as } AC = t)$$

Now, $$d = AB \sin(i - r)$$

$$= \frac{t}{\cos r}[\sin i \cos r - \cos i \sin r]$$

or $$d = t[\sin i - \cos i \tan r] \quad \text{...(i)}$$

Further, $$\mu = \frac{\sin i}{\sin r}$$

or $$\sin r = \frac{\sin i}{\mu}$$

$\therefore$ $$\tan r = \frac{\sin i}{\sqrt{\mu^2 - \sin^2 i}}$$

Substituting in Eq. (i), we get

$$d = \left[1 - \frac{\cos i}{\sqrt{\mu^2 - \sin^2 i}}\right] t \sin i$$ **Hence Proved.**

Exercise Show that for small angles of incidence,

$$d = ti\left(\frac{\mu - 1}{\mu}\right)$$

MODULE 4 Exercise

Assertion and Reason

See directions on page 11.

1. **Assertion :** There is a glass slab between Ram and Anoop. Then, Ram appears nearer to Anoop as compared to the actual distance between them.

   Reason : Ray of light starting from Ram will undergo two times refraction before reaching Anoop.

Single Correct Option

2. A plane glass slab is placed over various coloured letters. The letter which appears to be raised the least is

   (a) violet (b) yellow
   (c) red (d) green

3. P is a point on the axis of a concave mirror. The image of P, formed by the mirror, coincides with P. A rectangular glass slab of thickness t and refractive index μ is now introduced between P and the mirror. For the image of P to coincide with P again, the mirror must be moved.

   (a) towards P by $(\mu - 1)t$
   (b) away from P by $(\mu - 1)t$
   (c) away from P by $t\left(1 - \frac{1}{\mu}\right)$
   (d) towards P by $t\left(1 - \frac{1}{\mu}\right)$

4. An object is seen through a glass slab of thickness 36 cm and refractive index 3/2. The observer, and the slab are dipped in water ($\mu = 4/3$). The shift produced in the position of the object is

   (a) 12 cm (b) 4 cm
   (c) 6 cm (d) 8 cm

5. A flat glass slab of thickness 6 cm and index 1.5 is placed in front of a plane mirror. An observer is standing behind the glass slab and looking at the mirror. The actual distance of the observer from the mirror is 50 cm. The distance of his image from himself, as seen by the observer is

   (a) 94 cm (b) 96 cm
   (c) 98 cm (d) 100 cm

Subjective Question

6. At what distance eye E will observe the fourth image (after four refractions from plane surfaces) of object O from itself.

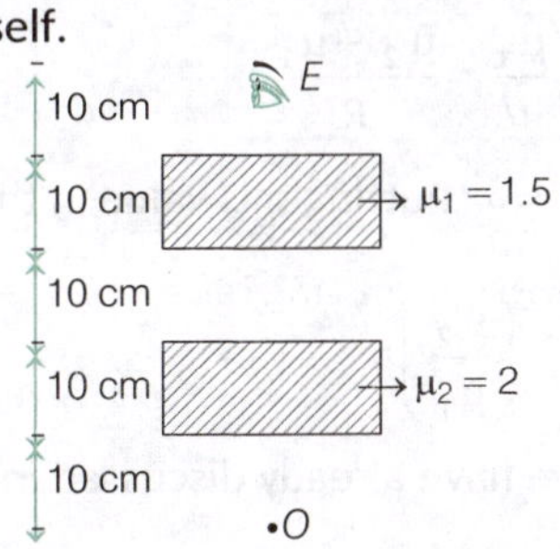

Answers

1. (b) 2. (c) 3. (c) 4. (b) 5. (b) 6. $\frac{125}{3}$ cm

See hints on page 151.

MODULE 5

Refraction from Spherical Surface

(i) There are two types of spherical surfaces, concave and convex.

(ii)

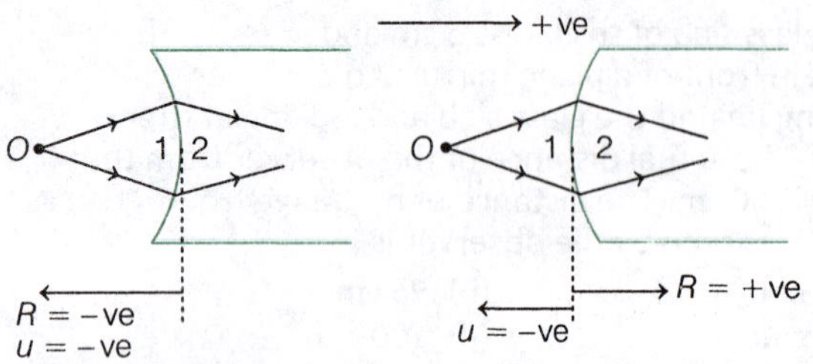

If the ray of light is travelling from first medium to second medium, then for image distance v, we have the formula

$$\boxed{\frac{\mu_2}{v} - \frac{\mu_1}{u} = \frac{\mu_2 - \mu_1}{R}}$$

(iii) For plane surface $R = \infty$. Putting this value in the above formula, we get

$$v = \left(\frac{\mu_2}{\mu_1}\right)u$$

and this formula, we have already discussed in Module-3.

(iv) Ray of light has moved in medium-2, so image formed in medium-2 will be real and v in this medium will be positive.

Proof

Consider two transparent media having indices of refraction μ_1 and μ_2, where the boundary between the two media is a spherical surface of radius R. We assume that $\mu_1 < \mu_2$. Let us consider a single ray leaving point O and focusing at point I. Snell's law applied to this refracted ray gives,

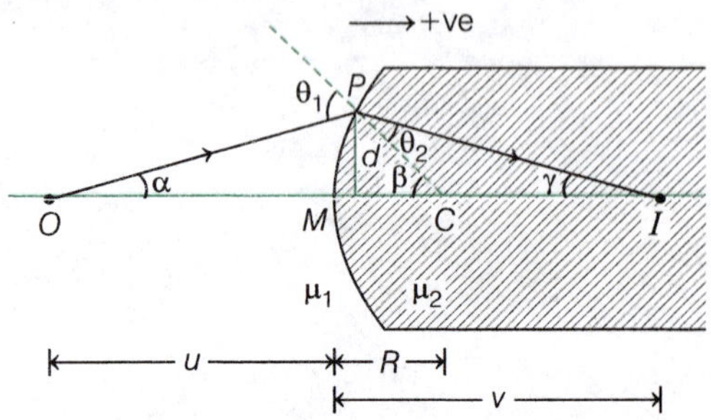

$$\mu_1 \sin\theta_1 = \mu_2 \sin\theta_2$$

Because θ_1 and θ_2 are assumed to be small, we can use the small angle approximation

$$\sin\theta \approx \theta \quad \text{(angles in radians)}$$

and say that

$$\mu_1\theta_1 = \mu_2\theta_2 \quad \text{...(i)}$$

From the geometry shown in the figure,

$$\theta_1 = \alpha + \beta \quad \text{...(ii)}$$

and

$$\beta = \theta_2 + \gamma \quad \text{...(iii)}$$

The above three equations can be rearranged as,

$$\beta = \frac{\mu_1}{\mu_2}(\alpha + \beta) + \gamma$$

So,

$$\mu_1\alpha + \mu_2\gamma = (\mu_2 - \mu_1)\beta \quad \text{...(iv)}$$

Since, the arc PM (of length s) subtends an angle β at the centre of curvature,

$$\beta = \frac{s}{R}$$

Also in the paraxial approximation, $\alpha = \frac{s}{u}$ and $\gamma = \frac{s}{v}$

Using these expressions in Eq. (iv) with proper signs, we are left with,

$$\frac{\mu_1}{-u} + \frac{\mu_2}{v} = \frac{\mu_2 - \mu_1}{R}$$

or

$$\boxed{\frac{\mu_2}{v} - \frac{\mu_1}{u} = \frac{\mu_2 - \mu_1}{R}} \quad \text{...(v)}$$

Although the formula (v) is derived for a particular situation, it is valid for all other situations of refraction at a single spherical surface.

Example 1 A glass sphere of radius $R = 10$ cm is kept inside water. A point object O is placed at 20 cm from A as shown in figure. Find the position and nature of the image when seen from other side of the sphere. Also draw the ray diagram. Given, $\mu_g = 3/2$ and $\mu_w = 4/3$.

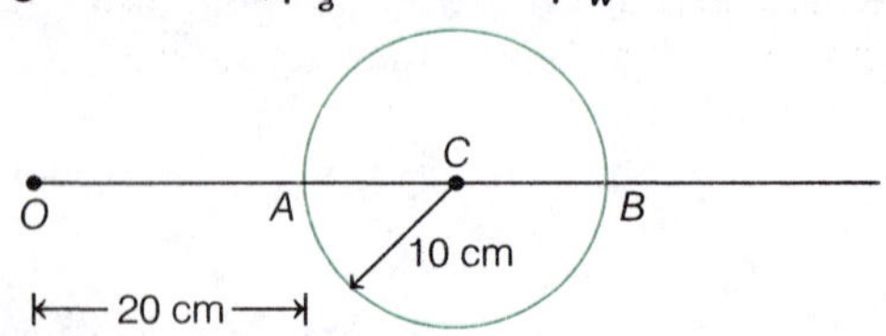

Sol. A ray of light starting from O gets refracted twice. The ray of light is travelling in a direction from left to right. Hence, the distances measured in this direction are taken positive.

Applying $\frac{\mu_2}{v} - \frac{\mu_1}{u} = \frac{\mu_2 - \mu_1}{R}$, twice with proper signs.

We have,

$$\frac{3/2}{AI_1} - \frac{4/3}{-20} = \frac{3/2 - 4/3}{10}$$

or $$AI_1 = -30 \text{ cm}$$

Now, the first image I_1 acts as an object for the second surface, where

$$BI_1 = u = -(30 + 20) = -50 \text{ cm}$$

$$\therefore \quad \frac{4/3}{BI_2} - \frac{3/2}{-50} = \frac{4/3 - 3/2}{-10}$$

$$\therefore \quad BI_2 = -100 \text{ cm},$$

i.e. the final image I_2 is **virtual** and is formed at a distance 100 cm (towards left) from B.

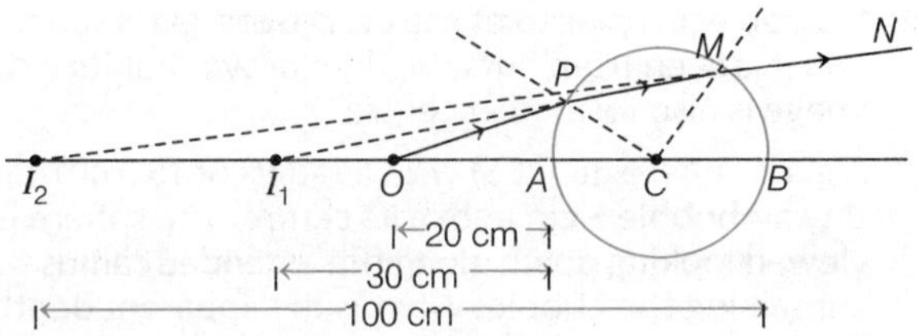

The ray diagram is as shown in figure.

Following points should be noted while drawing the ray diagram.

(i) At P the ray of light travels from rarer to a denser medium. Hence, it will bend towards normal PC. At M, it travels from a denser to a rarer medium, hence, it moves away from the normal MC.

(ii) PM ray when extended backwards meets at I_1 and MN ray when extended meets at I_2.

Example 2 A solid glass sphere with radius R and an index of refraction 1.5 is silvered over one hemisphere. A small object is located on the axis of the sphere at a distance $2R$ to the left of the vertex of the unsilvered hemisphere. Find the position of final image after all refractions and reflections have taken place.

Sol. The ray of light first gets refracted then reflected and then again refracted. For first refraction and then reflection the ray of light travels from left to right while for the last refraction it travels from right to left. Hence, the sign convention will change accordingly.

First refraction Using $\frac{\mu_2}{v} - \frac{\mu_1}{u} = \frac{\mu_2 - \mu_1}{R}$ with proper sign conventions, we have

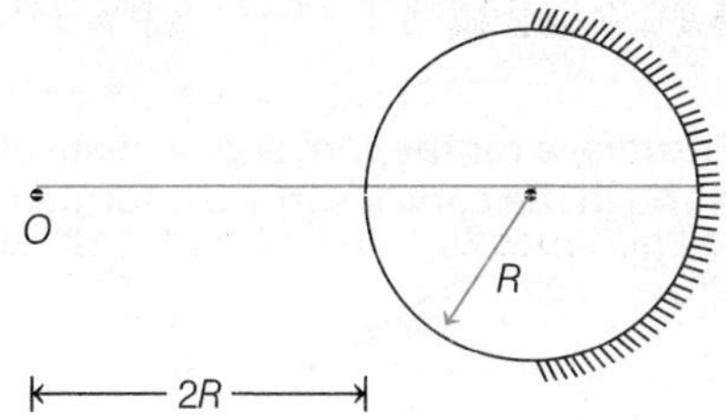

$$\frac{1.5}{v_1} - \frac{1.0}{-2R} = \frac{1.5 - 1.0}{+R}$$

$$\therefore \quad v_1 = \infty$$

Second reflection Using $\frac{1}{v} + \frac{1}{u} = \frac{1}{f} = \frac{2}{R}$ with proper sign conventions, we have

$$\frac{1}{v_2} + \frac{1}{\infty} = -\frac{2}{R}$$

$$\therefore \quad v_2 = -\frac{R}{2}$$

Third refraction Again using $\frac{\mu_2}{v} - \frac{\mu_1}{u} = \frac{\mu_2 - \mu_1}{R}$ with reversed sign convention, we have

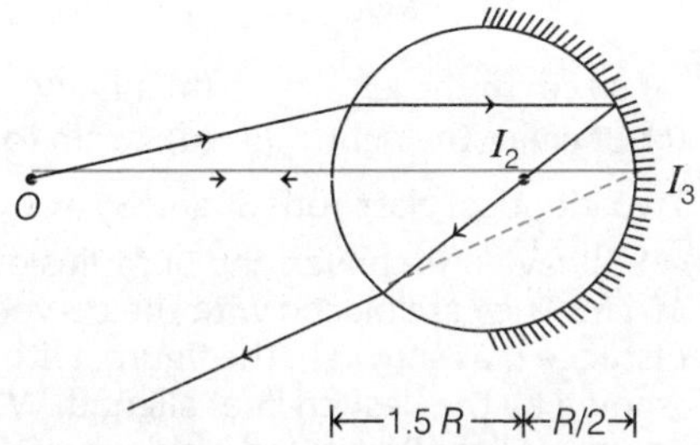

$$\frac{1.0}{v_3} - \frac{1.5}{-1.5R} = \frac{1.0 - 1.5}{-R}$$

or $$v_3 = -2R$$

i.e. final image is formed on the vertex of the silvered face.

MODULE 5 Exercise

Single Correct Option

1. The image for the converging beam after refraction through the curved surface is formed at

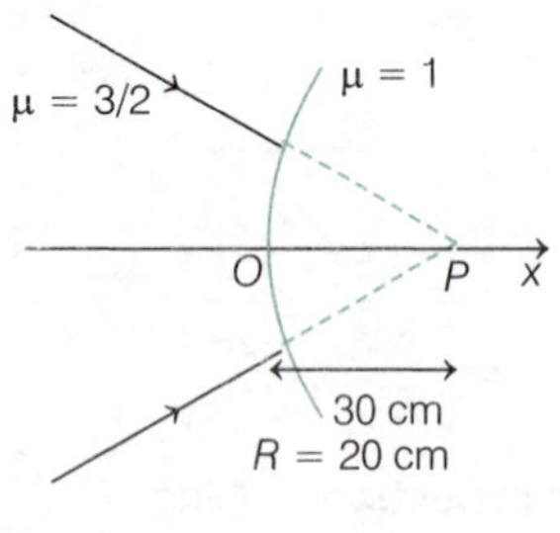

(a) $x = 40$ cm (b) $x = 40/3$ cm
(c) $x = -40/3$ cm (d) $x = 20$ cm

2. A point object O is placed in front of a glass rod having spherical end of radius of curvature 30 cm. The image would be formed at ($\mu_g = 3/2$)

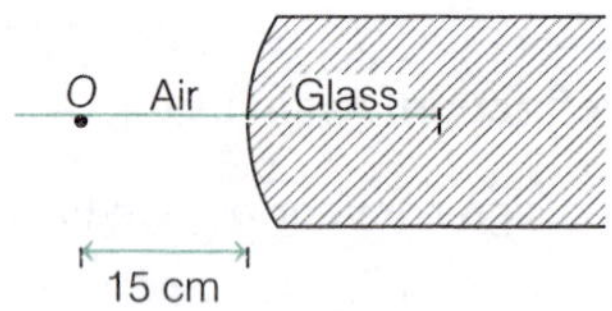

(a) 30 cm to the left (b) infinity
(c) 10 cm to the right (d) 18 cm to the left

3. Two identical glass rods S_1 and S_2 (refractive index $= 1.5$) have one convex end of radius of curvature 10 cm. They are placed with the curved surfaces at a distance d as shown in the figure, with their axes (shown by the dashed line) aligned. When a point source of light P is placed inside rod S_1 on its axis at a distance of 50 cm from the curved face, the light rays emanating from it are found to be parallel to the axis inside S_2. The distance d is **(2015 Adv.)**

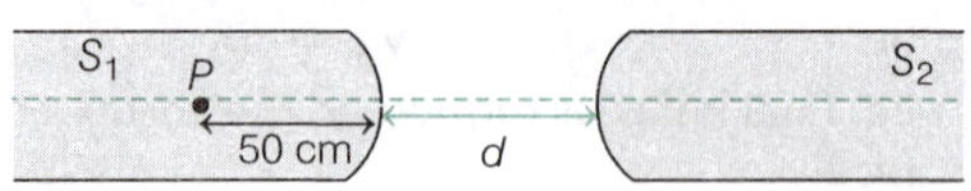

(a) 60 cm (b) 70 cm
(c) 80 cm (d) 90 cm

4. The eye can be regarded as a single refracting surface. The radius of curvature of this surface is equal to that of cornea (7.8 mm). This surface separates two media of refractive indices 1 and 1.34. Calculate the distance from the refracting surface at which a parallel beam of light will come to focus. **(2019 Main)**

(a) 4.0 cm (b) 2 cm
(c) 3.1 cm (d) 1 cm

5. A ray incident at a point at an angle of incidence of 60° enters a glass sphere of refractive index $n = \sqrt{3}$ and is reflected and refracted at the other surface of the sphere. The angle between the reflected and refracted rays at this surface is

(a) 50° (b) 60°
(c) 90° (d) 40°

Subjective Questions

6. If an object is placed at the centre of a glass sphere and it is seen from outside, then prove that its virtual image is also formed at centre.

7. A glass sphere ($\mu = 1.5$) with a radius of 15.0 cm has a tiny air bubble 5 cm above its centre. The sphere is viewed looking down along the extended radius containing the bubble. What is the apparent depth of the bubble below the surface of the sphere?

8. One end of a long glass rod ($\mu = 1.5$) is formed into a convex surface of radius 6.0 cm. An object is positioned in air along the axis of the rod. Find the image positions corresponding to object distances of (a) 20.0 cm, (b) 10.0 cm, (c) 3.0 cm from the end of the rod.

9. A parallel beam of light enters a clear plastic bead 2.50 cm in diameter and index 1.44. At what point beyond the bead are these rays brought to a focus?

10. A glass prism in the shape of a quarter cylinder lies on a horizontal table. A uniform, horizontal light beam falls on its vertical plane surface as shown in the figure. If the radius of the cylinder is $R = 5$ cm and the refractive index of the glass is $n = 1.5$, where on the table beyond the cylinder, will the light converge ?

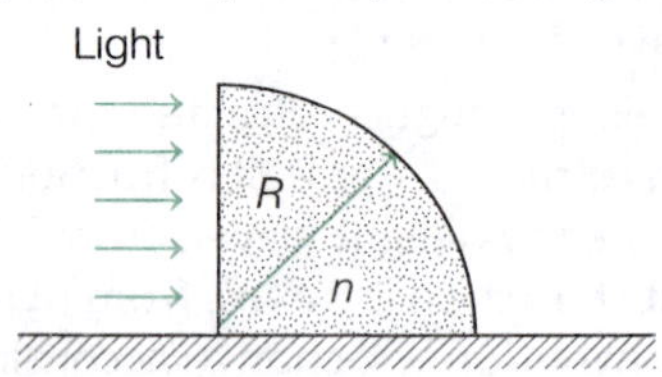

11. A glass sphere with 10 cm radius has a 5 cm radius spherical hole at its centre. A narrow beam of parallel light is directed into the sphere from the left. Where, if anywhere, will the sphere produce an image? The index of refraction of the glass is 1.50.

12. A glass sphere has a radius of 5.0 cm and a refractive index of 1.6. A paperweight is constructed by slicing through the sphere on a plate that is 2.0 cm from the centre of the sphere and perpendicular to a radius of the sphere that passes through the centre of the circle formed by the intersection of the plane and the sphere. The paperweight is placed on a table and

viewed from directly above by an observer who is 8.0 cm from the table top, as shown in figure. When viewed through the paperweight, how far away does the table top appear to the observer?

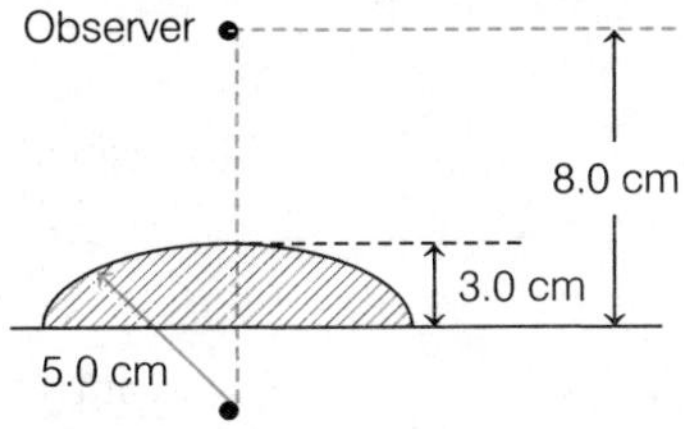

13. A quarter cylinder of radius R and refractive index 1.5 is placed on a table. A point object P is kept at a distance of mR from it. Find the value of m for which a ray from P will emerge parallel to the table as shown in figure. **(1999 JEE)**

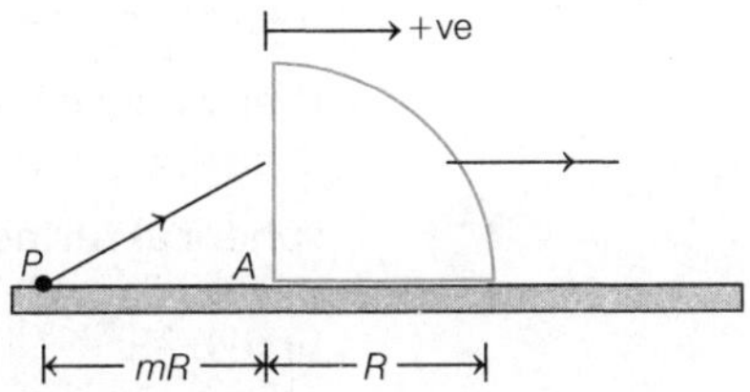

14. Two transparent media having refractive indices 1.0 and 1.5 are separated by a spherical refracting surface of radius of curvature 30 cm., The centre of curvature of surface is towards denser medium and a point object is placed on the principle axis in rarer medium at a distance of 15 cm from the pole of the surface. The distance of image from the pole of the surface is .... cm. **(2023 Main)**

Answers

1. (a) **2.** (a) **3.** (b) **4.** (c) **5.** (c) **7.** 8.57 cm **8.** (a) 45.0 cm (b) –90.0 cm (c) –6.0 cm
9. 4.0 cm **10.** 1.7 cm **11.** 4.67 cm to the left of extreme right edge
12. 7.42 cm **13.** (4/3) **14.** (30)

See hints on pages 151-153.

MODULE 6

Lens Theory

(i) A lens is one of the most familiar optical devices for a human being. A lens is an optical system with two refracting surfaces. The simplest lens has two spherical surfaces close enough together that we can neglect the distance between them (the thickness of the lens). We call this a **thin lens.**

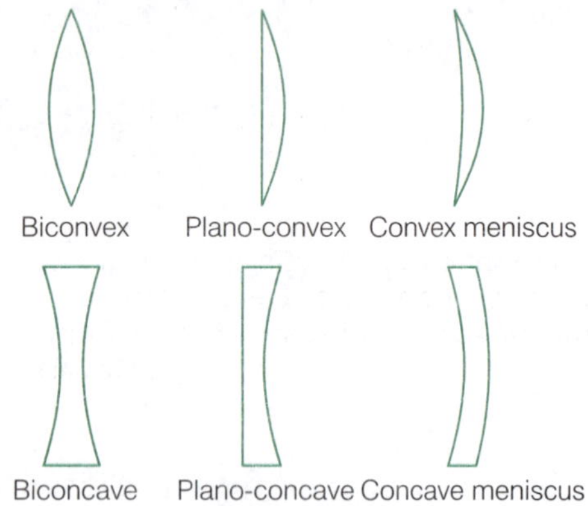

Types of lens

Lenses are of two basic types **convex** (converging) which are thicker in the middle than at the edges and **concave** (diverging) for which the reverse holds.

As there are two spherical surfaces, there are two centres of curvature C_1 and C_2 correspondingly two radii of curvature R_1 and R_2.

The line joining C_1 and C_2 is called the **principal axis** of the lens. The centre P of the thin lens which lies on the principal axis, is called the **optical centre.**

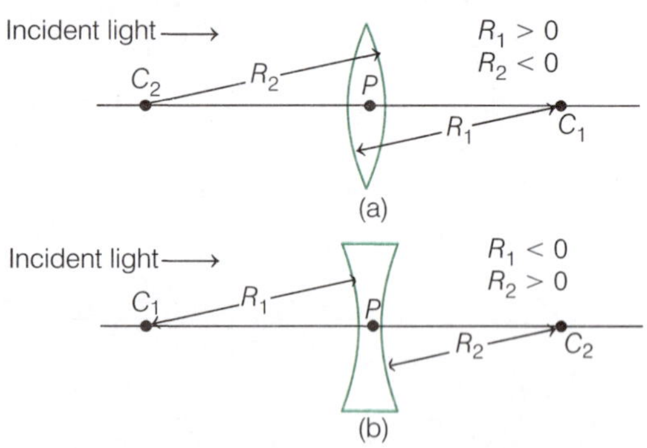

(a) A converging thin lens and

(b) a diverging thin lens

(ii) All lens formulae (which we will use in this chapter) can be applied directly under following two conditions.

Condition 1 Lens should be thin or its thickness should be negligible.

Condition 2 On both sides of the lens, medium should be same (not necessarily air)

(iii) If either of the above two conditions are not satisfied, then apply refraction formulae $\left(\frac{\mu_2}{v} - \frac{\mu_1}{u} = \frac{\mu_2 - \mu_1}{R}\right.$ for spherical surface or $v = \frac{\mu_2}{\mu_1} u$ for plane surface) two times.

(iv) In a biconvex (or equiconvex) or biconcave (or equiconcave) lens,

$$|R_1| = |R_2|$$

(v) **Use of thin lens** If the lens is thin, then the first image distance v_1 is exactly equal to the second object distance u_2.

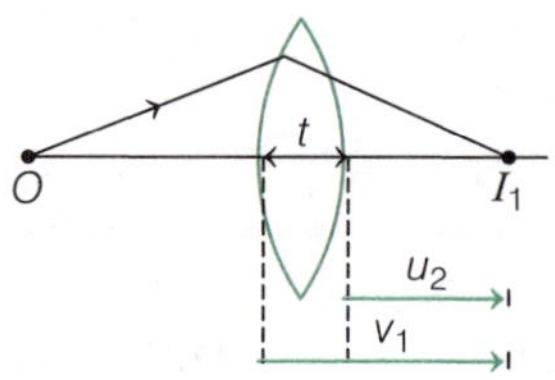

In the figure, we can see that $u_2 = v_1 - t$

But, $u_2 = v_1$ if $t = 0$

(vi) Unlike a mirror, a lens has two foci :

First focus (F_1)

It is defined as a point at which if an object (real in case of a convex lens and virtual for concave) is placed, the image of this object is formed at infinity. Or we can say that rays passing through F_1 become parallel to the principal axis after refraction from the lens. The distance PF_1 is the first focal length f_1.

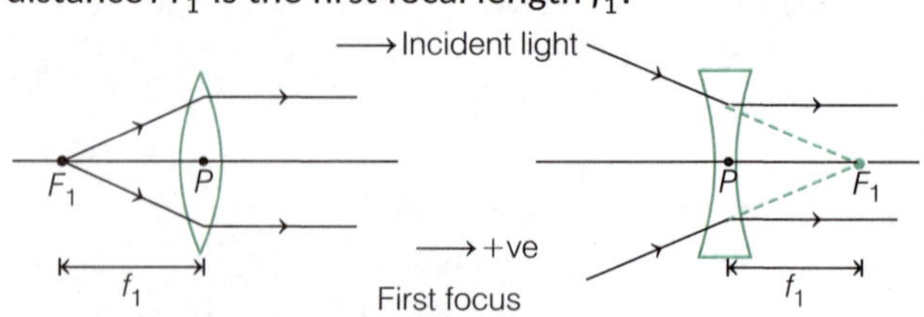

Second focus or principal focus (F_2)

A narrow beam of light travelling parallel to the principal axis either converge (in case of a convex lens) or diverge (in case of a concave lens) at a point F_2 after refraction from the lens.

This point F_2 is called the second or principal focus. If the rays converge at F_2, the lens is said a converging lens and if they diverge, they are called diverging lens. Distance PF_2 is the second focal length f_2.

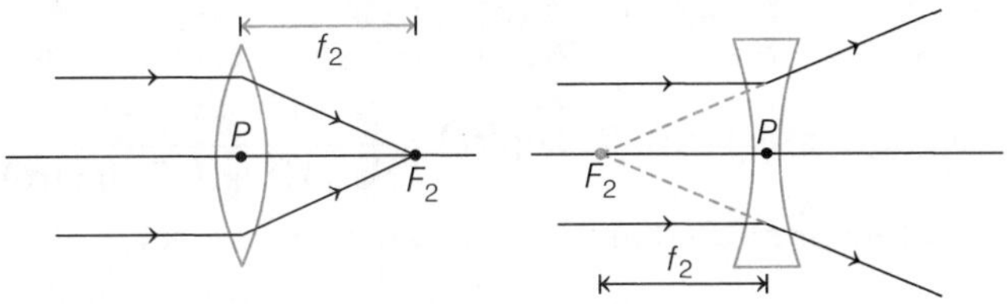

From the figures, we can see that f_1 is negative for a convex lens and positive for a concave lens. But, f_2 is positive for convex lens and negative for concave lens.

(vii) We are mainly concerned with the second focus f_2. Thus, wherever we write the focal length f, it means the second or principal focal length. Thus, $f = f_2$ and hence, f is positive for a convex lens and negative for a concave lens.

(viii) If the two conditions mentioned in point number (ii) are satisfied, then

$$|f_1| = |f_2|$$

although their signs are different.

(ix) If those two conditions are satisfied, then object can be placed on either side of the lens or light can fall from both sides of the lens. Image distance v will remain same for given object distance v. Following figures will help you to clear this concept.

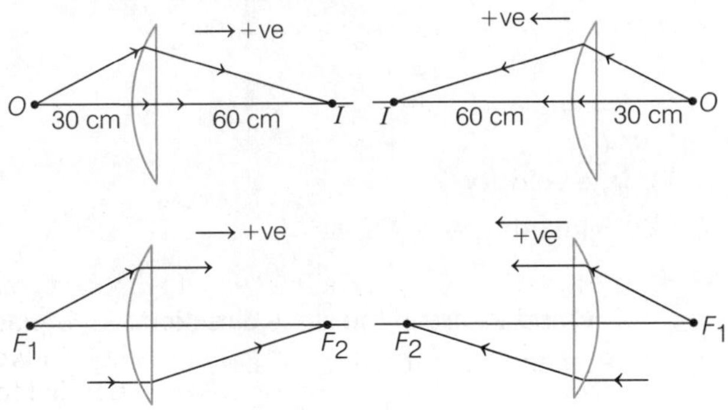

Image Position, its Nature and Speed

Case 1 **Convex lens**

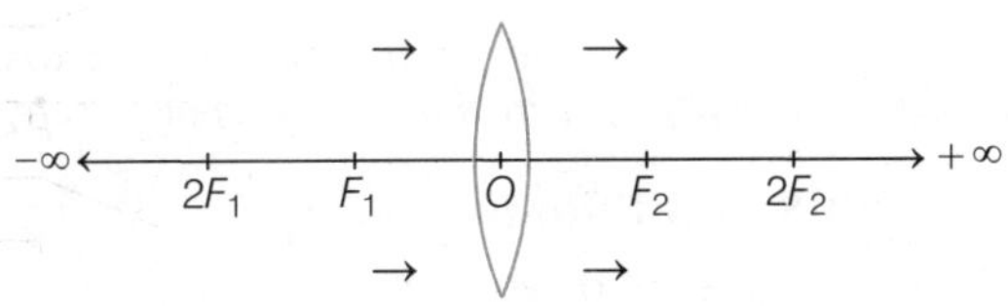

Table 1.

Object	Image	Nature of image	Speed
At F_1	$\pm \infty$	–	–
At $2F_1$	At $2F_2$	Real, Inverted and same size	$v_I = v_O$
At $-\infty$	At F_2	–	–
Between O and F_1	Between O and $-\infty$	Virtual, Erect and magnified	$v_I > v_O$
Between F_1 and $2F_1$	Between $+\infty$ and $2F_2$	Real, Inverted and magnified	$v_I > v_O$
Between $2F_1$ and $-\infty$	Between $2F_2$ and F_2	Real, Inverted and diminished	$v_O > v_I$

Note *(i) The above table has been made only for real objects (lying between O and $-\infty$), object distance u for them is negative.*

(ii) Since $|f_1| = |f_2|$ (when two conditions discussed earlier are satisfied). Therefore, F_1 and F_2 are sometimes denoted by F and $2F_1$ or $2F_2$ by 2F.

(iii) If object is travelling along the principal axis, then image also travels along the principal axis in the same direction.

Case 2 **Concave lens** In case of concave lens, there is only one case for real objects.

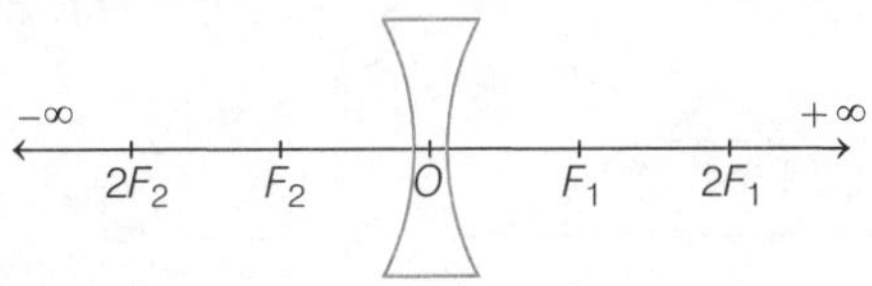

Object lies between O and $-\infty$, then image lies between O and F_2. Nature of image is virtual, erect and diminished. Object speed is always greater than image speed ($v_O > v_I$). Both travel in the same direction.

Three Standard Rays for making Ray Diagrams

1. A ray parallel to the principal axis after refraction passes through the principal focus or appears to diverge from it.

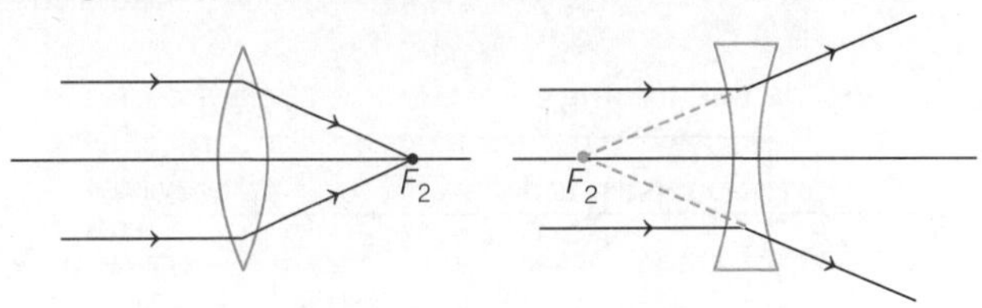

2. A ray passing through the optical centre P passes undeviated because the middle of the lens acts like a thin parallel-sided slab.

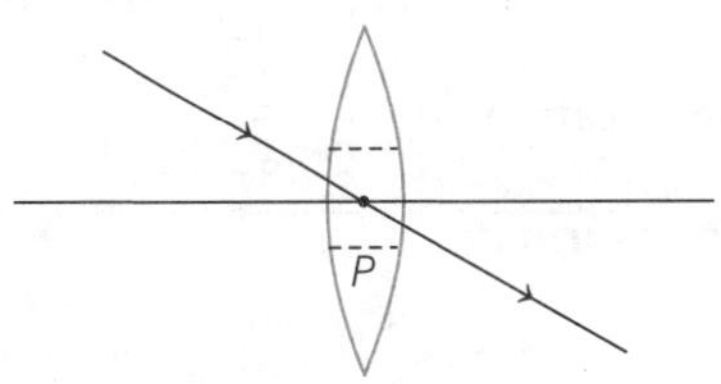

3. A ray passing through the first focus F_1 becomes parallel to the principal axis after refraction.

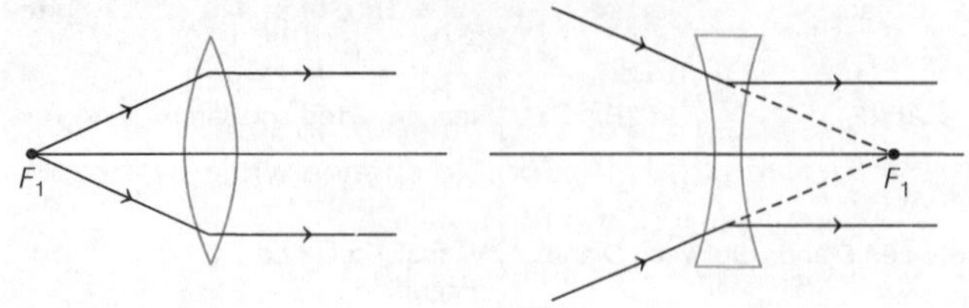

Ray Diagrams

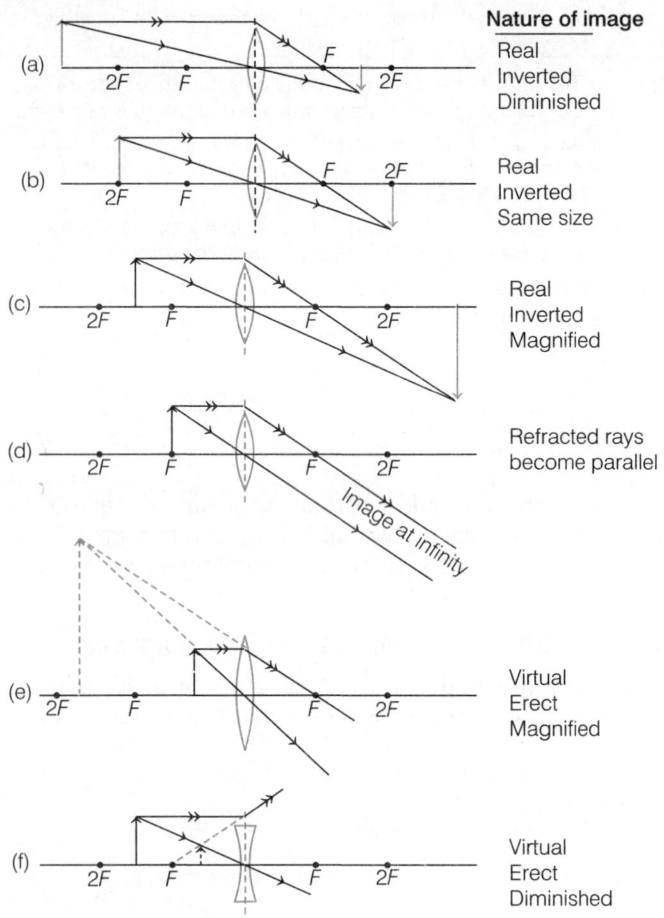

List of Formulae

(i) $\dfrac{1}{v} - \dfrac{1}{u} = \dfrac{1}{f}$

(ii) Linear magnification, $m = \dfrac{\text{Image height}}{\text{Object height}} = \dfrac{I}{O} = \dfrac{v}{u}$

(iiii) **Lens maker's formula**

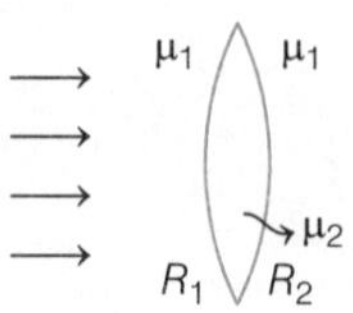

$$\frac{1}{f} = \left(\frac{\mu_2}{\mu_1} - 1\right)\left(\frac{1}{R_1} - \frac{1}{R_2}\right)$$

In air, $\mu_1 = 1$ and $\mu_2 = \mu$. Therefore,

$$\frac{1}{f} = (\mu - 1)\left(\frac{1}{R_1} - \frac{1}{R_2}\right)$$

(iv) Power of a lens (in dioptre) $= \dfrac{1}{\text{Focal length (in metre)}}$

(v) Two or more than two thin lenses in contact.

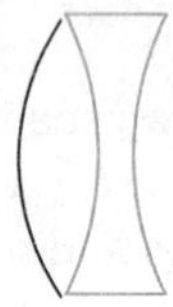

$$\frac{1}{F} = \frac{1}{f_1} + \frac{1}{f_2} \quad \text{or} \quad P = P_1 + P_2$$

(vi) Two or more than two thin lenses at some distance

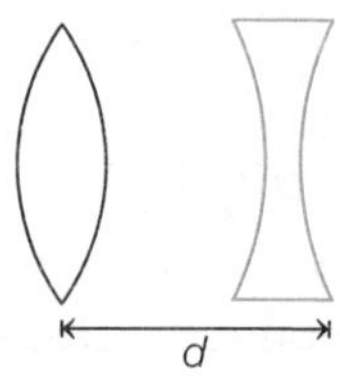

$$\frac{1}{F} = \frac{1}{f_1} + \frac{1}{f_2} - \frac{d}{f_1 f_2}$$

or $\quad P = P_1 + P_2 - dP_1P_2$

Note *In the above two equations if $d = 0$, then*

$$\frac{1}{F} = \frac{1}{f_1} + \frac{1}{f_2}$$

and $\quad P = P_1 + P_2$

(vii) **Image velocity**

(a) Along the principal axis,

$$\mathbf{v}_I = m^2 \mathbf{v}_O$$

$\therefore \mathbf{v}_I$ and $\mathbf{v}_O$ are in the same direction.

(b) Perpendicular to principal axis,

$$\mathbf{v}_I = m\mathbf{v}_O$$

If m is positive then $\mathbf{v}_I$ and $\mathbf{v}_O$ are in the same direction and if m is negative, then $\mathbf{v}_I$ and $\mathbf{v}_O$ are in opposite directions.

Note *The above two formulae have been derived in the previous unit of reflection. So, same method can be applied here.*

Important points in formulae

(i) **On linear magnification m**

From the value of m, we can determine nature of image, type of lens and an approximate position of object. Following table illustrates this point.

Table 2.

Value of m	Nature of image	Type of lens	Object position
-3	Inverted, real and magnified	convex	Between F_1 and $2F_1$
-1	Inverted, real and same size	convex	at $2F_1$
$-\frac{1}{2}$	Inverted, real and diminished	convex	Between $2F_1$ and $-\infty$
$+2$	Erect, virtual and magnified	convex	Between O and F_1
$+\frac{1}{4}$	Erect, virtual and diminished	convex	Between O and $-\infty$

Note *For real objects, real image is formed only by convex lens. But virtual image is formed by both types of lenses. Their sizes are different. Magnified virtual image is formed by convex lens. Diminished virtual image is formed by concave lens.*

(ii) **On lens maker's formula**

(a) $$\frac{1}{f}=\left(\frac{\mu_2}{\mu_1}-1\right)\left(\frac{1}{R_1}-\frac{1}{R_2}\right) \qquad \ldots\text{(i)}$$

$$=(\mu-1)\left(\frac{1}{R_1}-\frac{1}{R_2}\right) \text{ in air} \qquad \ldots\text{(ii)}$$

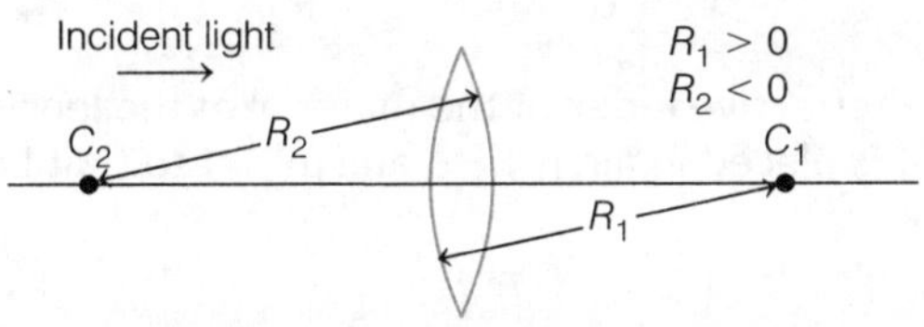

(a)

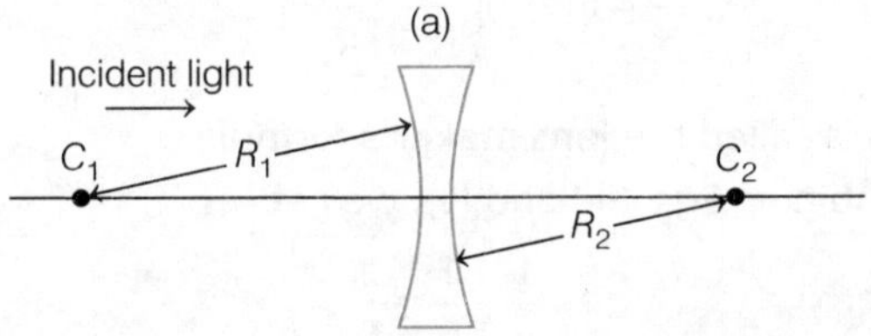

(b)

For a converging lens, R_1 is positive and R_2 is negative. Therefore, $\left(\frac{1}{R_1}-\frac{1}{R_2}\right)$ in Eq. (ii) comes out a positive quantity and if the lens is placed in air, $(\mu-1)$ is also a positive quantity. Hence, the focal length f of a converging lens turns out to be positive. For a diverging lens however, R_1 is negative and R_2 is positive and the focal length f becomes negative.

(b) Focal length of a mirror $\left(f_M=\frac{R}{2}\right)$ depends only upon the radius of curvature R while that of a lens [Eq. (i)] it depends upon μ_1, μ_2, R_1 and R_2. Thus, if a lens and a mirror are immersed in some liquid, the focal length of lens would change while that of the mirror will remain unchanged.

Suppose $\mu_2 < \mu_1$ in Eq. (i), i.e. refractive index of the medium (in which lens is placed) is more than the refractive index of the material of the lens, then $\left(\frac{\mu_2}{\mu_1}-1\right)$ becomes a negative quantity, i.e. the lens changes its behaviour. A converging lens behaves as a diverging lens and *vice-versa*. An air bubble in water seems as a convex lens but behaves as a concave (diverging) lens.

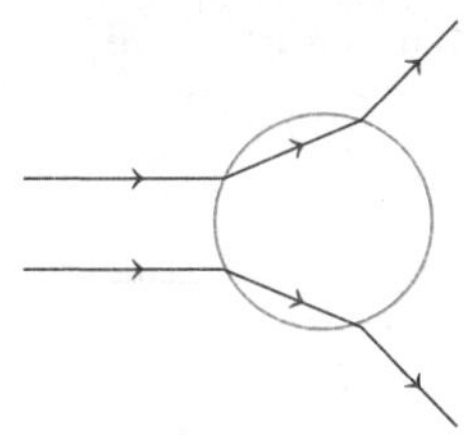

(iii) **Power of lens**

By optical power of an instrument (whether it is a lens, mirror or a refractive surface) we mean the ability of the instrument to bend the path of rays passing through it. If the instrument converges the rays parallel to the principal axis its power is said to be positive and if it diverges the rays, it is said a negative power.

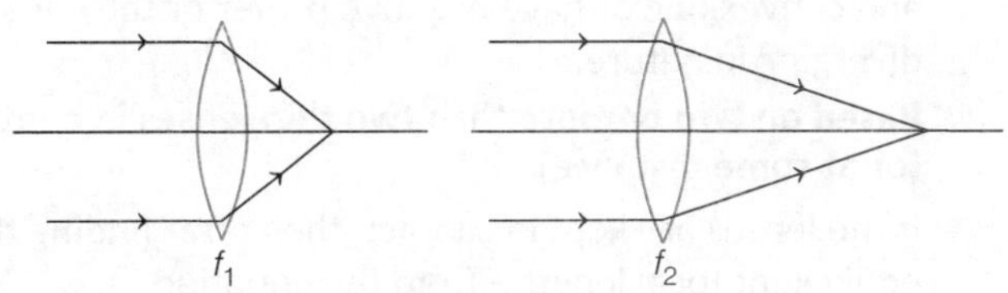

The shorter the focal length of a lens (or a mirror) the more it converges or diverges the light. As shown in the figure,

$$f_1 < f_2$$

and hence the power $P_1 > P_2$, as bending of light in case 1 is more than that of case 2. For a lens,

$$P\text{ (in dioptre)}=\frac{1}{f\text{ (in metre)}}$$

and for a mirror, $$P\text{ (in dioptre)}=\frac{-1}{f\text{ (in metre)}}$$

Following table gives the sign of P and f for different types of lens and mirror.

Table 3.

Nature of lens/mirror	Focal length (f)	Power $P_L = \frac{1}{f}$, $P_M = -\frac{1}{f}$	Converging/diverging	Ray diagram
Convex lens	+ ve	+ ve	converging	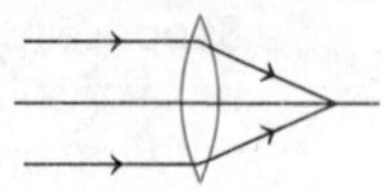
Concave mirror	- ve	+ ve	converging	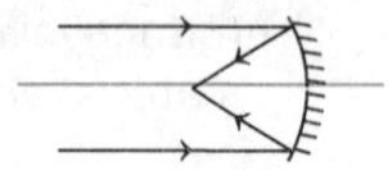
Concave lens	- ve	- ve	diverging	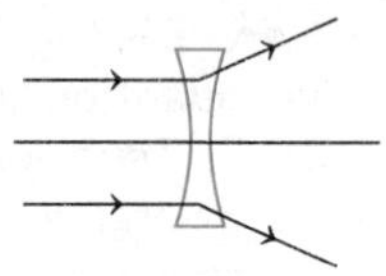
Convex mirror	+ ve	- ve	diverging	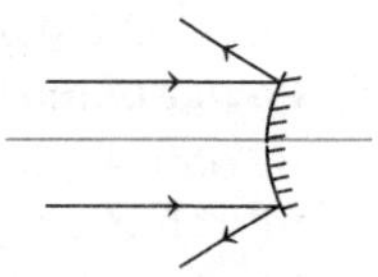

Thus, convex lens and concave mirror have positive power or they are converging in nature. Concave lens and convex mirror have negative power or they are diverging in nature.

(iv) **Based on two or more than two thin lenses in contact (or at some distance)**

If the lenses are kept in contact, then after finding the equivalent focal length F from the equation

$$\frac{1}{F} = \frac{1}{f_1} + \frac{1}{f_2}$$

We can directly apply the formula

$$\frac{1}{v} - \frac{1}{u} = \frac{1}{F}$$

for finding the image distance v, but we will have to apply lens formula, $\frac{1}{v} - \frac{1}{u} = \frac{1}{f}$ two times if the lenses are kept at some distance.

Proofs of Different Formulae

(i) Consider an object O placed at a distance u from a convex lens as shown in figure. Let its image I after two refractions from spherical surfaces of radii R_1 (positive) and R_2 (negative) be formed at a distance v from the lens. Let v_1 be the distance of image formed by refraction from the refracting surface of radius R_1. This image acts as an object for the second surface.

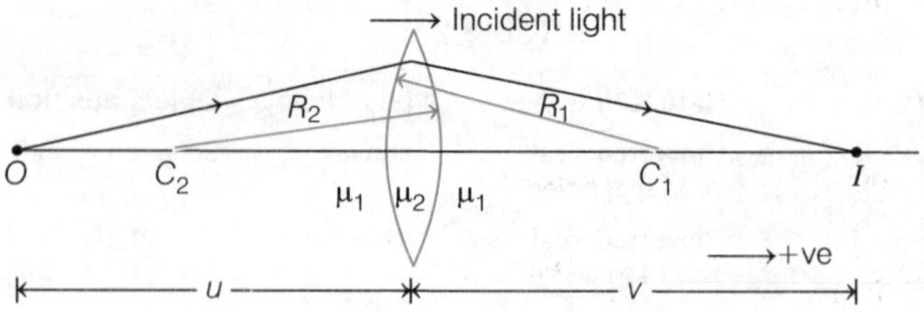

Using, $$\frac{\mu_2}{v} - \frac{\mu_1}{u} = \frac{\mu_2 - \mu_1}{R}$$

For first surface, $$\frac{\mu_2}{v_1} - \frac{\mu_1}{u} = \frac{\mu_2 - \mu_1}{R_1} \quad \text{...(i)}$$

and for second surface, $$\frac{\mu_1}{v} - \frac{\mu_2}{v_1} = \frac{\mu_1 - \mu_2}{-R_2} \quad \text{...(ii)}$$

Adding Eqs. (i) and (ii) and then simplifying, we get

$$\frac{1}{v} - \frac{1}{u} = \left(\frac{\mu_2}{\mu_1} - 1\right)\left(\frac{1}{R_1} - \frac{1}{R_2}\right) \quad \text{...(iii)}$$

The **focal length** f of a thin lens is the image distance that corresponds to an object at infinity. So, putting $u = \infty$ and $v = f$ in the above equation, we have

$$\boxed{\frac{1}{f} = \left(\frac{\mu_2}{\mu_1} - 1\right)\left(\frac{1}{R_1} - \frac{1}{R_2}\right)} \quad \text{...(iv)}$$

If the refractive index of the material of the lens is μ and it is placed in air, $\mu_2 = \mu$ and $\mu_1 = 1$ so that Eq. (iv) becomes

$$\boxed{\frac{1}{f} = (\mu - 1)\left(\frac{1}{R_1} - \frac{1}{R_2}\right)} \quad \text{...(v)}$$

This is called the **lens maker's formula**.

Combining Eqs. (iii) and (v), we get

$$\boxed{\frac{1}{v} - \frac{1}{u} = \frac{1}{f}} \quad \text{...(vi)}$$

Which is known as the **lens formula.**

(ii) **Magnification** The lateral, transverse or linear magnification m produced by a lens is defined by

$$\boxed{m = \frac{\text{Height of image}}{\text{Height of object}} = \frac{I}{O}}$$

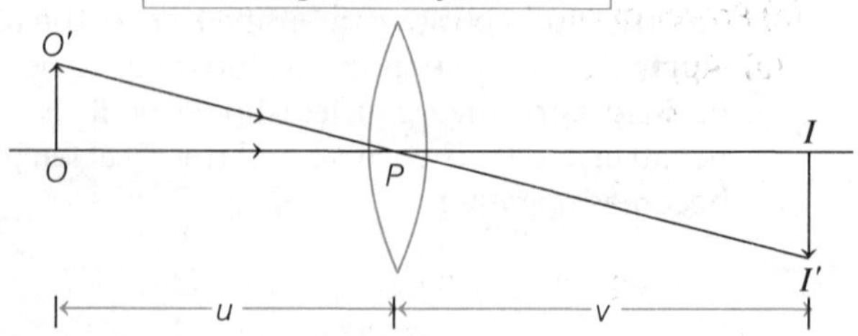

A real image II' of an object OO' formed by a convex lens is shown in figure.

$$\frac{\text{Height of image}}{\text{Height of object}} = \frac{II'}{OO'} = \frac{v}{u}$$

Substituting v and u with proper sign,

$$\frac{II'}{OO'} = \frac{-I}{O} = \frac{v}{-u}$$

or $$\frac{I}{O} = m = \frac{v}{u}$$

Thus, $$m = \frac{v}{u}$$

(iii) Focal length of two or more than two thin lenses in contact

Combinations of lenses in contact are used in many optical instruments to improve their performance.

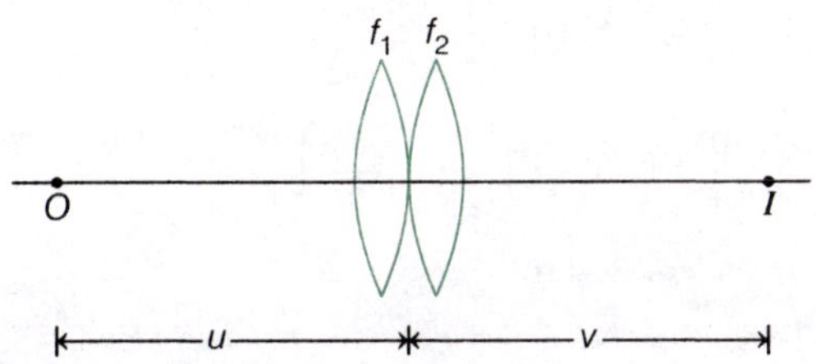

Suppose two lenses of focal lengths f_1 and f_2 are kept in contact and a point object O is placed at a distance u from the combination. The first image (say I_1) after refraction from the first lens is formed at a distance v_1 (whatever may be the sign of v_1) from the combination. This image I_1 acts as an object for the second lens and let v be the distance of the final image from the combination.

Applying the lens formula,

$$\frac{1}{v} - \frac{1}{u} = \frac{1}{f}$$

For the two lenses, we have

$$\frac{1}{v_1} - \frac{1}{u} = \frac{1}{f_1} \quad \text{...(i)}$$

and $$\frac{1}{v} - \frac{1}{v_1} = \frac{1}{f_2} \quad \text{...(ii)}$$

Adding Eqs. (i) and (ii), we have

$$\frac{1}{v} - \frac{1}{u} = \frac{1}{f_1} + \frac{1}{f_2} = \frac{1}{F} \quad \text{(say)}$$

Here, F is the equivalent focal length of the combination. Thus,

$$\frac{1}{F} = \frac{1}{f_1} + \frac{1}{f_2}$$

Similarly for more than two thin lenses in contact, the equivalent focal length is given by the formula,

$$\frac{1}{F} = \sum_{i=1}^{n} \frac{1}{f_i}$$

Note *Here, f_1, f_2 etc., are to be substituted with sign.*

Typed Problems

Problems in Lens

Type 1. *Based on two or more than two thin lenses in contact.*

How to Solve ?

Apply, $$\frac{1}{F} = \frac{1}{f_1} + \frac{1}{f_2}$$

and $$P = P_1 + P_2$$

Ex. 1 A convex lens of power 2D and a concave lens of focal length 40 cm are kept in contact, find

(a) Power of combination (b) Equivalent focal length

Sol. (a) Applying

$$P = P_1 + P_2 = P_{convex} + P_{concave}$$

$$= 2 + \frac{1}{(-0.4)} \qquad \left[P \text{ (in D)} = \frac{1}{f \text{ (in m)}}\right]$$

$$= 2 - 2.5 = -0.5 \text{ D}$$ **Ans.**

(b) $$F = \frac{1}{P} = \frac{1}{-0.5} = -2 \text{ m}$$

$$= -200 \text{ cm}$$ **Ans.**

Note *F and P are negative so, the system behaves like a concave lens.*

Ex. 2 A converging lens of focal length 5.0 cm is placed in contact with a diverging lens of focal length 10.0 cm. Find the combined focal length of the system.

Sol. Here, $f_1 = +5.0$ cm and $f_2 = -10.0$ cm

Therefore, the combined focal length F is given by

$$\frac{1}{F} = \frac{1}{f_1} + \frac{1}{f_2} = \frac{1}{5.0} - \frac{1}{10.0} = +\frac{1}{10.0}$$

$\therefore$ $$F = +10.0 \text{ cm}$$ **Ans.**

i.e. the combination behaves as a converging lens of focal length 10.0 cm.

Type 2. *Based on lens maker's formula.*

How to Solve ?

Apply, $$\frac{1}{f} = \left(\frac{\mu_2}{\mu_1} - 1\right)\left(\frac{1}{R_1} - \frac{1}{R_2}\right)$$

or $$\frac{1}{f} = (\mu - 1)\left(\frac{1}{R_1} - \frac{1}{R_2}\right)$$

Note *If initial two conditions are satisfied (thin lens and same medium on both sides,) then we can find focal length of the lens (f or f_2) from either side of the lens. Result comes out to be same.*

Ex. 3 Find focal length of the system shown in below figure from left hand side.

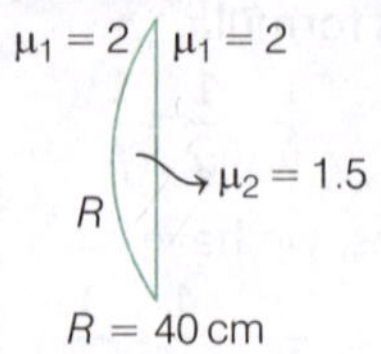

Sol. $\mu_1 = 2, \mu_2 = 1.5, R_1 = +40$ and $R_2 = \infty$

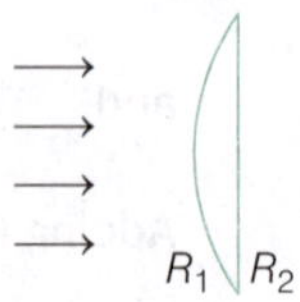

Using the equation

$$\frac{1}{f} = \left(\frac{\mu_2}{\mu_1} - 1\right)\left(\frac{1}{R_1} - \frac{1}{R_2}\right),$$

we have

$$\frac{1}{f} = \left(\frac{1.5}{2} - 1\right)\left(\frac{1}{+40} - \frac{1}{\infty}\right)$$

$\Rightarrow \quad f = -160$ cm

Therefore, from left hand side it behaves like a concave lens of focal length 160 cm.

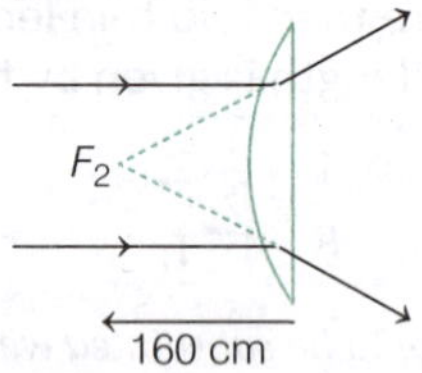

Exercise Find focal length of the above system from right hand side and prove that it is also −160 cm.

Ex. 4 Focal length of a convex lens in air is 10 cm. Find its focal length in water. Given that $\mu_g = 3/2$ and $\mu_w = 4/3$.

Sol.
$$\frac{1}{f_{air}} = (\mu_g - 1)\left(\frac{1}{R_1} - \frac{1}{R_2}\right) \quad \text{...(i)}$$

and
$$\frac{1}{f_{water}} = \left(\frac{\mu_g}{\mu_w} - 1\right)\left(\frac{1}{R_1} - \frac{1}{R_2}\right) \quad \text{...(ii)}$$

Dividing Eq. (i) by Eq. (ii), we get

$$\frac{f_{water}}{f_{air}} = \frac{(\mu_g - 1)}{(\mu_g/\mu_w - 1)}$$

Substituting the values, we have

$$f_{water} = \frac{(3/2 - 1)}{\left(\frac{3/2}{4/3} - 1\right)} f_{air}$$

$$= 4 f_{air} = 4 \times 10 = 40 \text{ cm}$$ **Ans.**

Note *(i) Students can remember the result $f_{water} = 4 f_{air}$, if $\mu_g = 3/2$ and $\mu_w = 4/3$.*

(ii) In water focal length has become four times and power (power of bending of light) remains $\frac{1}{4}$th. This is because, difference in refractive index between glass and water has been decreased (compared to glass and air). So, there will be less bending of light.

Ex. 5 A biconvex lens ($\mu = 1.5$) has radius of curvature 20 cm (both). Find its focal length in air.

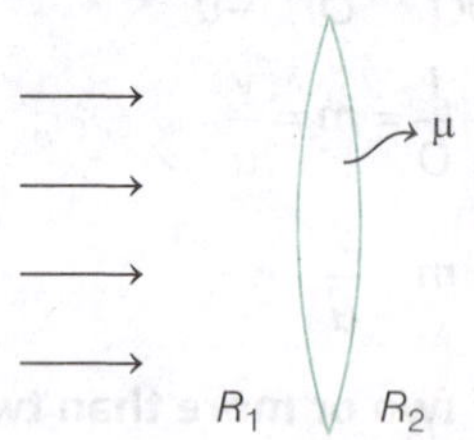

Sol. $R_1 = +20$ cm, $R_2 = -20$ cm, $\mu = 1.5$

Substituting the values in the equation

$$\frac{1}{f} = (\mu - 1)\left(\frac{1}{R_1} - \frac{1}{R_2}\right), \text{ we have}$$

$$\frac{1}{f} = (1.5 - 1)\left(\frac{1}{20} - \frac{1}{-20}\right)$$

or $\quad f = +20$ cm **Ans.**

Note *If a biconvex or biconcave lens has refractive index $\mu = 1.5$, then $|R_1| = |R_2| = |f|$*

Type 3. *To find image distance and its magnification corresponding to given object distance.*

How to Solve?

- Substitute signs of u and f. Sign of v automatically appears after applying the lens formula. Sign of u is negative for real objects. Sign of f is positive for convex lens and negative for concave lens.

Ex. 6 Find distance of image from a convex lens of focal length 20 cm if object is placed at a distance of 30 cm from the lens. Also find its magnification.

Sol. $u = -30$ cm, $f = +20$ cm

Applying the lens formula

$$\frac{1}{v} - \frac{1}{u} = \frac{1}{f}$$

We have,

$$\frac{1}{v} - \frac{1}{-30} = \frac{1}{+20}$$

Solving, we get

$v = +60$ cm **Ans.**

$$m = \frac{v}{u} = \frac{+60}{-30} = -2$$ **Ans.**

m is −2, it implies that image is real, inverted and two times magnified. The ray diagram is as shown below.

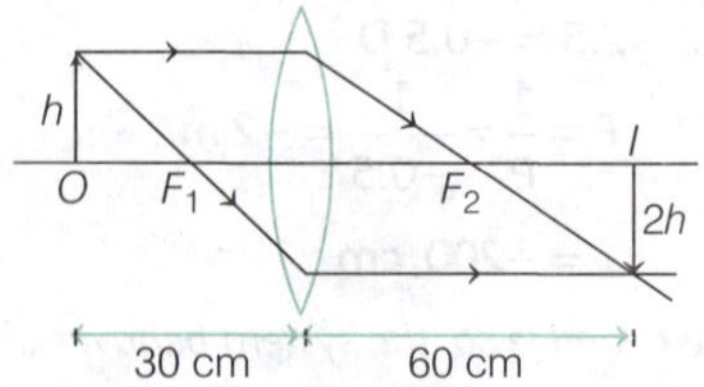

Type 4. *To find object/image distance corresponding to given magnification of image and focal length of lens.*

How to Solve?

- Substitute all three signs of u, v and f. Signs of u and f have been discussed in the above type. Sign of v is positive for real image (see the above example) and it is negative for virtual image.
- $m = \frac{v}{u} \Rightarrow |v| = |m \times u|$

Ex. 7 Find the distance of an object from a convex lens if image is two times magnified. Focal length of the lens is 10 cm.

Sol. Convex lens forms both types of images, real as well as virtual. Since, nature of the image is not mentioned in the question, we will have to consider both the cases.

When image is real Means v is positive and u is negative with $|v| = 2|u|$. Thus, if

$$u = -x, \quad \text{then } v = 2x \quad \text{and } f = 10 \text{ cm}$$

Substituting in $\frac{1}{v} - \frac{1}{u} = \frac{1}{f}$

We have $\frac{1}{2x} + \frac{1}{x} = \frac{1}{10}$

or $\frac{3}{2x} = \frac{1}{10}$

$\therefore$ $x = 15$ cm **Ans.**

$x = 15$ cm, means object lies between F and $2F$.

When image is virtual Means v and u both are negative. So let,

$$u = -y, \quad \text{then } v = -2y \quad \text{and } f = 10 \text{ cm}$$

Substituting in, $\frac{1}{v} - \frac{1}{u} = \frac{1}{f}$

We have, $\frac{1}{-2y} + \frac{1}{y} = \frac{1}{10}$ or $\frac{1}{2y} = \frac{1}{10}$

$\therefore$ $y = 5$ cm **Ans.**

$y = 5$ cm, means object lies between F and O.

Type 5. *To make some conditions.*

How to Solve?

- Initially, substitute sign of only f, then make equation of v. From this equation of v, make the asked condition.

Ex. 8 Under what condition, a concave lens can make a real image.

Sol. Substituting sign of f in the lens formula, we have

$$\frac{1}{v} - \frac{1}{u} = \frac{1}{-f} \text{ or } \frac{1}{v} = \frac{1}{u} - \frac{1}{f} \quad \dots\text{(i)}$$

For real image v should be positive. Therefore, from Eq. (i) we can see that u should be positive and less than f. Further, u is positive and less than f means a virtual object should lie between O and F_1.

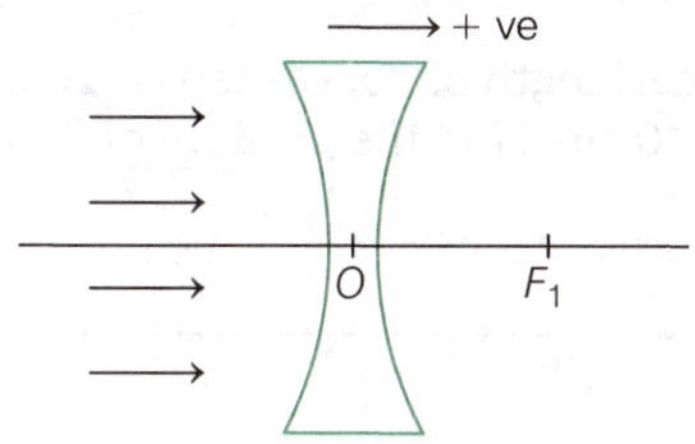

Important Result

Under normal conditions, a convex lens makes a real image. But the image is virtual (and magnified) if a real object is placed between O and F_1.

Opposite is the case with concave lens. Under normal conditions it makes a virtual image (for all real objects). But the image is real if a virtual object is placed between O and F_1.

Type 6. *To find image nature, type of lens, its optical centre and focus for given principal axis, point object and its point image.*

Ex. 9 An image I is formed of point object O by a lens whose optic axis is AB as shown in figure.

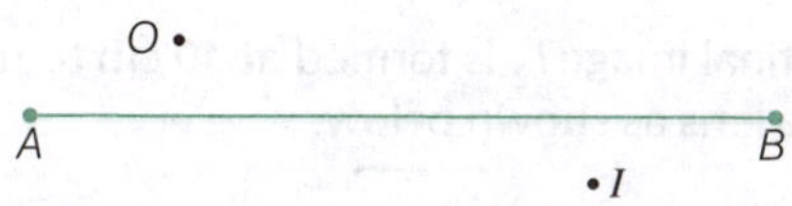

(a) State whether it is a convex lens or concave?

(b) Draw a ray diagram to locate the lens and its focus.

Sol. (a) (i) Concave lens always makes an erect image. The given image I is on the other side of the optic axis. So, it is inverted. Hence, the lens is **convex**.

(ii) Join O with I. Line OI cuts the optic axis AB at optical centre (P) of the lens. The dotted line shows the position of lens.

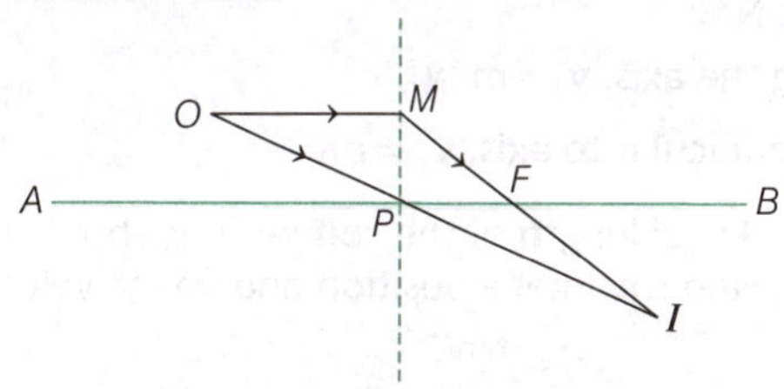

From point O, draw a line parallel to AB. Let it cuts the dotted line at M. Join M with I. Line MI cuts the optic axis at focus (F) of the lens.

Type 7. *Two lens problems.*

How to Solve?

- We have to apply lens formula two times. The first image behaves like an object for the second lens.

Ex. 10 Focal length of convex lens is 20 cm and of concave lens 40 cm. Find the position of final image.

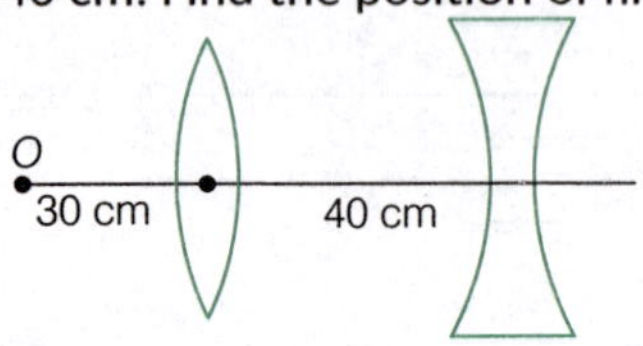

Sol. Using the lens formula for convex lens,

$$u = -30 \text{ cm}, f = +20 \text{ cm}$$

$$\therefore \quad \frac{1}{v} - \frac{1}{-30} = \frac{1}{+20}$$

Solving this equation, we get $v = +60$ cm. Therefore, the first image is 60 cm to the right of convex lens or 20 cm to the right of concave lens. Again applying lens formula for concave lens,

$$u = +20 \text{ cm}$$

$$f = -40 \text{ cm, we have}$$

$$\frac{1}{v} - \frac{1}{+20} = \frac{1}{-40}$$

$$v = +40 \text{ cm}$$

So, the final image I_2 is formed at 40 cm to the right of concave lens as shown below.

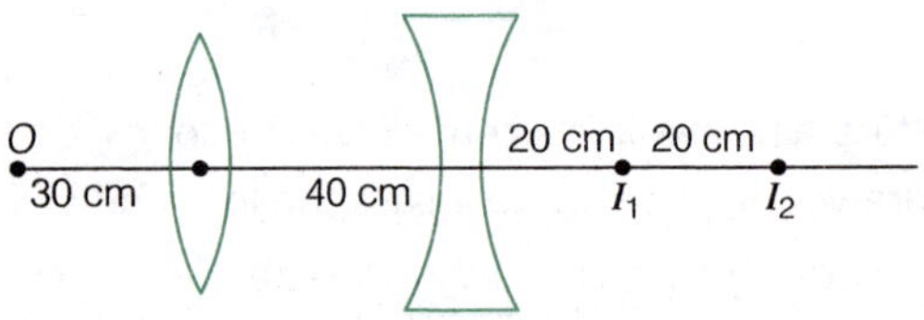

Type 8. *Based on image velocity.*

How to Solve?

- Using the methods discussed in Type 3, first find v and then m. Now,

  (i) Along the axis, $\mathbf{v}_I = m^2 \mathbf{v}_O$

  (ii) Perpendicular to axis, $\mathbf{v}_I = m\mathbf{v}_O$

Ex. 11 Focal length of the convex lens shown in figure is 20 cm. Find the image position and image velocity.

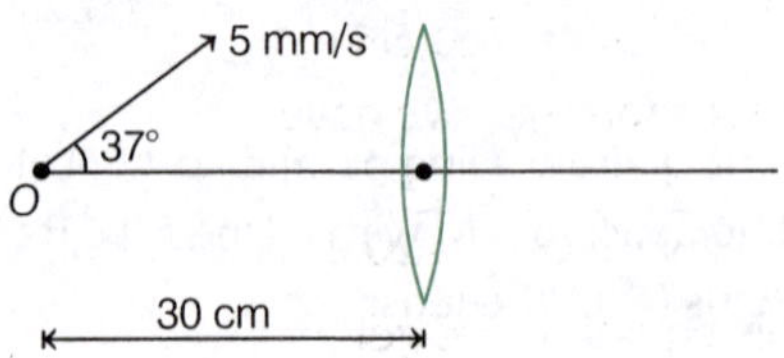

Sol. For the given condition,

$$u = -30 \text{ cm}, f = +20 \text{ cm}$$

Using the lens formula, we have

$$\frac{1}{v} - \frac{1}{-30} = \frac{1}{+20}$$

Solving this equation, we get

$$v = +60 \text{ cm and}$$

$$m = \frac{v}{u} = \frac{+60}{-30} = -2$$

$$m^2 = 4$$

Component of velocity of object along the axis $= 5 \cos 37° = 4$ mm/s (towards the lens).

$\therefore$Component of velocity of image along the axis $= m^2 (4 \text{ mm/s}) = 4 \times 4 = 16$ mm/s. This component is away from the lens (in the same direction of component of object velocity).

Component of velocity of object perpendicular to the axis $= 5 \sin 37° = 3$ mm/s (upwards).

$\therefore$ Component of velocity of image perpendicular to axis $= m(3 \text{ mm/s})$ or $(-2)(3 \text{ mm/s}) = -6$ mm/s or this component is 6 mm/s downwards. These all points are shown in the figure given below.

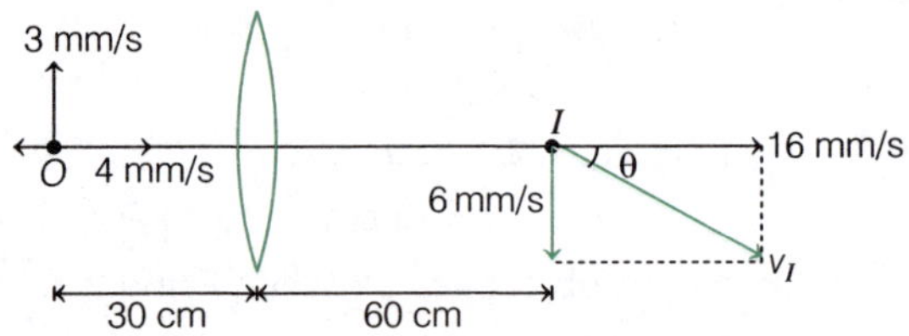

$$v_I = \sqrt{(16)^2 + (6)^2} = \sqrt{292} \text{ mm/s}$$

$$\tan \theta = \frac{6}{16} = \frac{3}{8}$$

or $$\theta = \tan^{-1}(3/8)$$

Type 9. *An extended object kept perpendicular to principal axis.*

How to Solve?

- Using the methods discussed in Type 3, first find v and then m. Now, suppose m is -2 and object is 1 mm above the principal axis, then image will be 2 mm below the principal axis.

Ex. 12 Focal length of concave lens shown in figure is 60 cm. Find image position and its magnification.

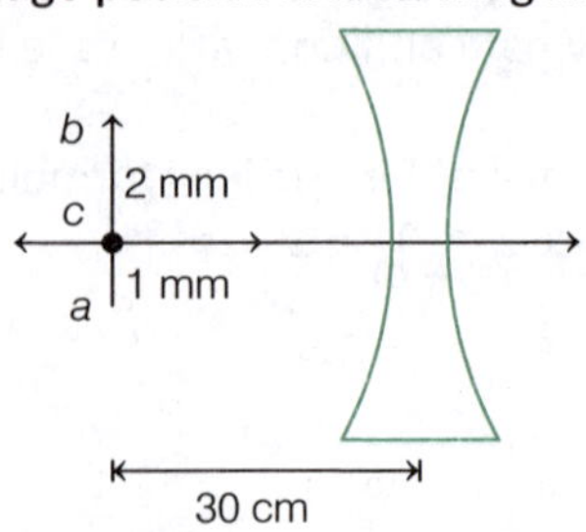

Sol. For the given situation,

$$u = -30 \text{ cm}, f = -60 \text{ cm}$$

Using the lens formula, we have

$$\frac{1}{v} - \frac{1}{-30} = \frac{1}{-60}$$

Solving this equation, we get

$$v = -20 \text{ cm}$$

Further, $m = \frac{v}{u} = \frac{-20}{-30} = +\frac{2}{3}$.

Point b is 2 mm above the principal axis. Therefore, its image b' will be $(2)\left(\frac{2}{3}\right)$ or $\frac{4}{3}$ mm, above the principal axis.

Similarly, point a is 1 mm below the principal axis. Therefore, its image a' will be $(1)\left(\frac{2}{3}\right)$ or $\frac{2}{3}$ mm below the principal axis. The final image is as shown in figure.

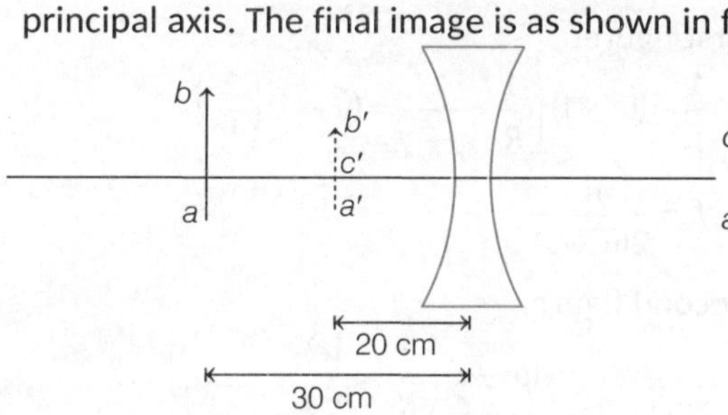

Type 10. *To plot u versus v or $\frac{1}{u}$ versus $\frac{1}{v}$ graph.*

Concept

- In the previous unit, we have seen that $\frac{1}{v}$ *versus* $\frac{1}{u}$ graph will be a straight line. Further for real objects, u is always negative. So, u varies from 0 to $-\infty$. Therefore, $\frac{1}{u}$ will vary from $-\infty$ to 0.

Ex. 13 Plot u *versus* v and $\frac{1}{u}$ *versus* $\frac{1}{v}$ graph for convex lens (only for real objects)

Sol.

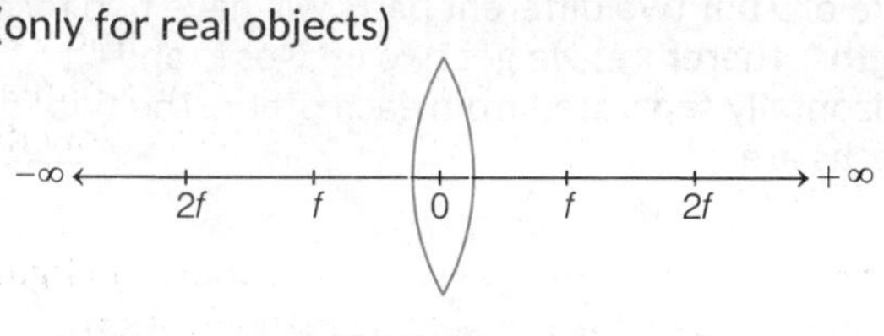

Table 4.

S.No.	u	v	$\frac{1}{u}$	$\frac{1}{v}$
1	0 to $-f$	0 to $-\infty$	$-\infty$ to $-\frac{1}{f}$	$-\infty$ to 0
2	$-f$ to $-2f$	$+\infty$ to $+2f$	$-\frac{1}{f}$ to $-\frac{1}{2f}$	0 to $+\frac{1}{2f}$
3	$-2f$ to $-\infty$	$+2f$ to $+f$	$-\frac{1}{2f}$ to 0	$+\frac{1}{2f}$ to $+\frac{1}{f}$

***u versus* graph**

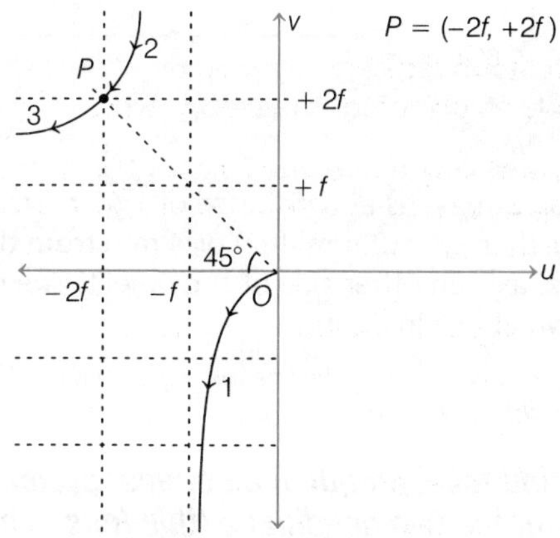

$\frac{1}{u}$ *versus* $\frac{1}{v}$ graph

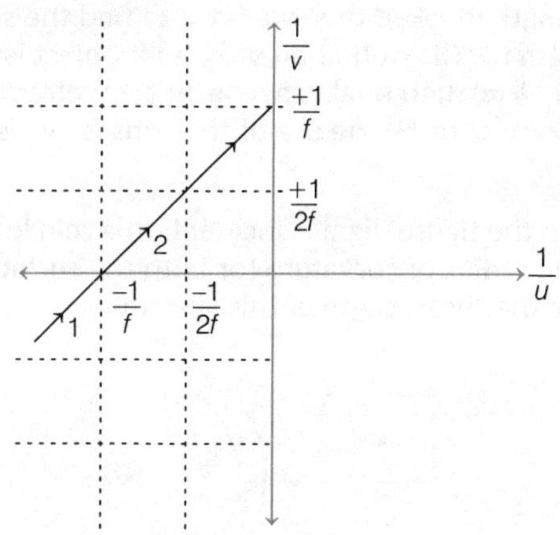

Type 11. *Problems of inclined lenses.*

Ex. 14 O_1P is the principal axis and O is the point object. Given, $O_1P = 30$ cm, $f = 20$ cm and $OP = 2$ mm. Find the image distance and its position.

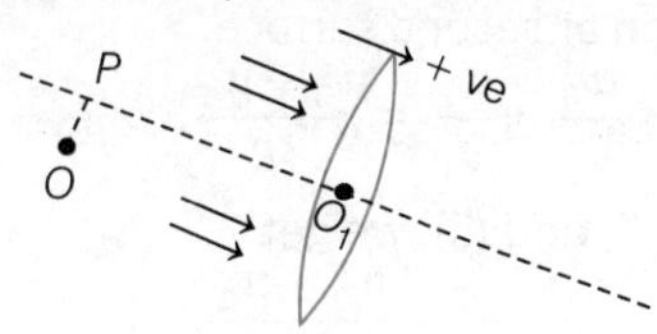

Sol. For the given situation,

$$u = -30 \text{ cm}$$

and

$$f = +20 \text{ cm}$$

Using the lens formula, we have

$$\frac{1}{v} - \frac{1}{-30} = \frac{1}{+20}$$

Solving this equation, we get

$$v = +60 \text{ cm}$$

Further, $$m = \frac{v}{u} = \frac{+60}{-30} = -2$$

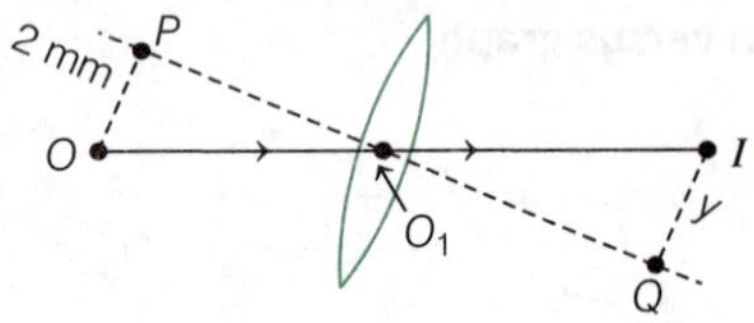

$O_1Q = 60$ cm

$QI = 4$ mm

Therefore, image is at a distance of + 60 cm from the lens. Further, $QI = (2 \text{ mm}) (-2)$ or 4 mm from the principal axis on other side of the object. The image is as shown above in figure.

Note *Image will always lie on the line joining O and O_1. This is because the ray OO_1 passes undeviated.*

Type 12. *To find focal length of an optical system for which either of the two conditions (thin lens and same medium on both sides) is not satisfied.*

Concept

- If focal length is asked then we have to find the second focal length f_2. The definition of F_2 is : if object is at infinity ($u_1 = \infty$) then final image after two refractions will be at $F_2 (v_2 = f_2$ or $f)$. The use of thin lens is : v_1 is exactly equal to u_2.

Ex. 15 In the figure, light is incident on a thin lens as shown. The radius of curvature for both the surfaces is R. Determine the focal length of this system. **(2003 JEE)**

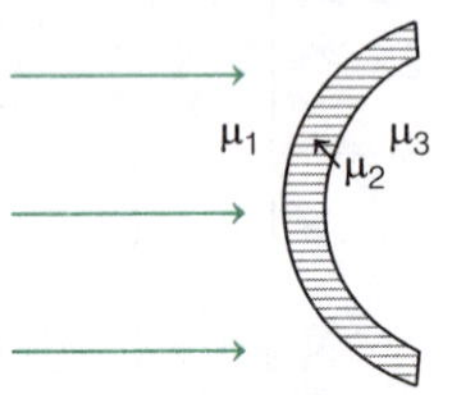

Sol. For refraction at first surface,

$$\frac{\mu_2}{v_1} - \frac{\mu_1}{-\infty} = \frac{\mu_2 - \mu_1}{+R} \quad \text{...(i)}$$

For refraction at second surface,

$$\frac{\mu_3}{v_2} - \frac{\mu_2}{v_1} = \frac{\mu_3 - \mu_2}{+R} \quad \text{... (ii)}$$

Adding Eqs. (i) and (ii), we get

$$\frac{\mu_3}{v_2} = \frac{\mu_3 - \mu_1}{R}$$

or

$$v_2 = \frac{\mu_3 R}{\mu_3 - \mu_1}$$

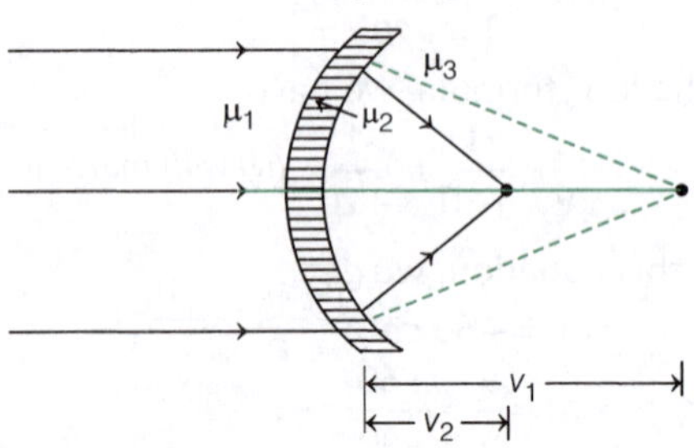

Therefore, focal length of the given lens system is

$$f = v_2 = \frac{\mu_3 R}{\mu_3 - \mu_1}$$

Note *If we find the focal length of the above system from right hand side, then it will be different because medium on both sides is not same.*

Important Points in Lens Theory

1.

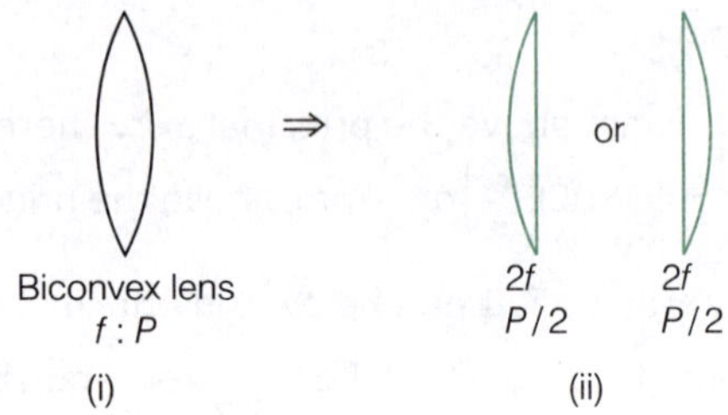

In the first figure,

$$\frac{1}{f} = (\mu - 1)\left(\frac{1}{R} - \frac{1}{-R}\right) = (\mu - 1)\left(\frac{2}{R}\right)$$

$$\therefore \quad f = \frac{R}{2(\mu - 1)}$$

In the second figure,

$$\frac{1}{f'} = (\mu - 1)\left(\frac{1}{R} - \frac{1}{\infty}\right)$$

$$\therefore \quad f' = \frac{R}{\mu - 1}$$

or $\quad f' = 2f$

2.

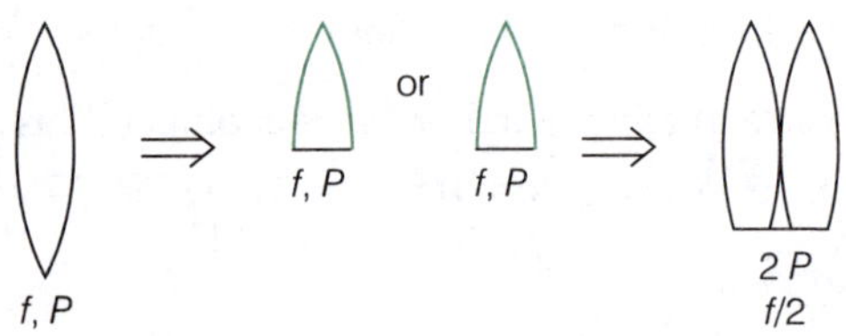

3. The system shown in the figure given below has single value of u but two different parts will have two focal lengths. Therefore, we get two images I_1 and I_2, horizontally separated from each other. The two focal lengths are

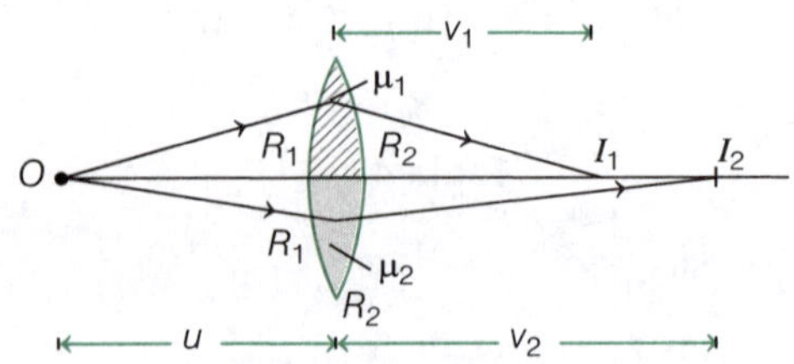

$$\frac{1}{f_1} = (\mu_1 - 1)\left(\frac{1}{R_1} - \frac{1}{R_2}\right)$$

and

$$\frac{1}{f_2} = (\mu_2 - 1)\left(\frac{1}{R_1} - \frac{1}{R_2}\right)$$

4. The system shown in the figure given below has single values of u and f. Therefore, we will get single value of v. Still, we will get two images, vertically separated from each other. Let us take an example in support of this.

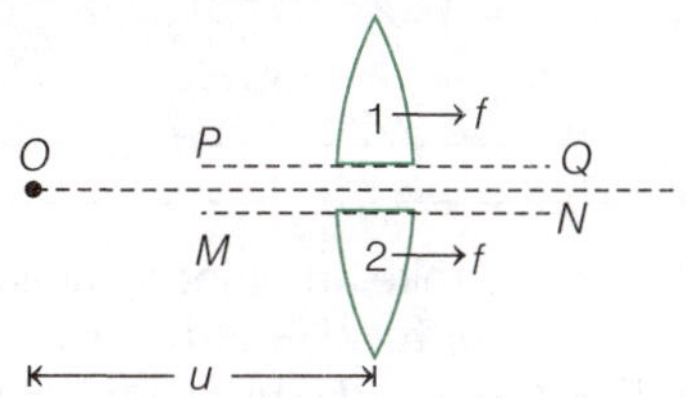

If $u = 30$ cm, f is 20 cm, principal axis PQ of upper part 1 is 1 mm above the object and principal axis MN of lower part 2 is 1 mm below the object O. Then, after applying lens formula, we get

$$v = +60 \text{ cm and } m = -2$$

Now, O is 1 mm below PQ and $m = -2$. Therefore, upper part will make I_1, 2 mm above PQ. Similarly, O is 1 mm above MN, therefore lower part will make I_2, 2 mm below MN. Ray diagram from the two parts is as shown in figure given below

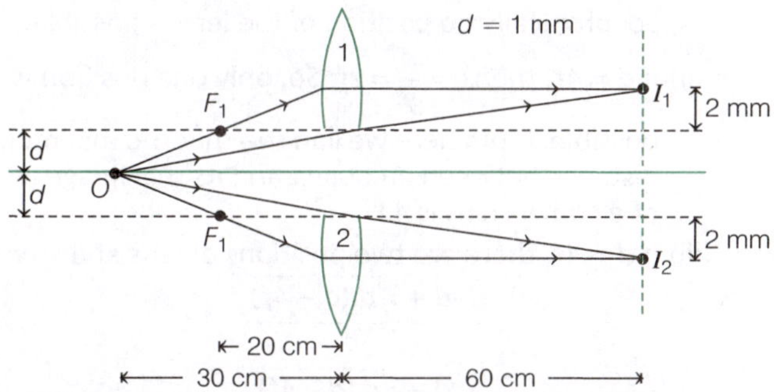

5. If a liquid is filled between two thin convex glass lenses, then it is a group of three lenses as shown in figure.

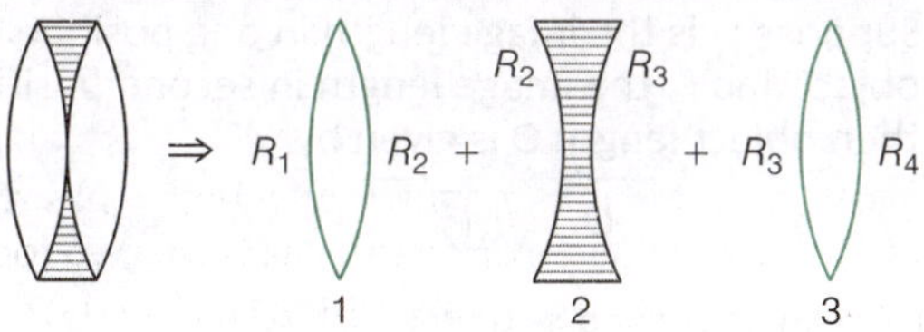

$$\therefore \qquad \frac{1}{F} = \frac{1}{f_1} + \frac{1}{f_2} + \frac{1}{f_3}$$

where, $$\frac{1}{f_1} = (\mu_g - 1)\left(\frac{1}{R_1} - \frac{1}{R_2}\right)$$

$$\frac{1}{f_2} = (\mu_l - 1)\left(\frac{1}{R_2} - \frac{1}{R_3}\right) \text{ and}$$

$$\frac{1}{f_3} = (\mu_g - 1)\left(\frac{1}{R_3} - \frac{1}{R_4}\right)$$

6. The system shown in figure behaves like a lens of zero power (or $f = \infty$). This is because

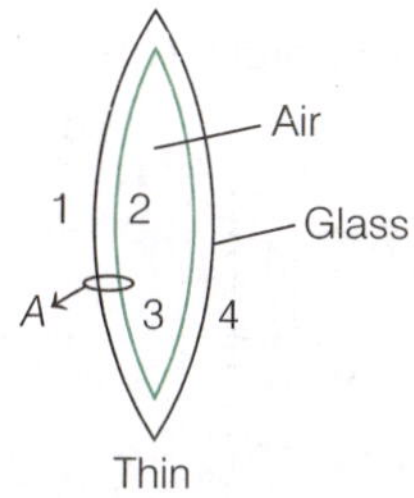

$$R_1 \approx R_2 \quad \text{and} \quad R_3 \approx R_4$$

Now if we find focal length or power of part A, then

$$\frac{1}{f} \text{ or } P = (\mu_g - 1)\left(\frac{1}{R_1} - \frac{1}{R_2}\right) = 0 \quad \text{as} \quad R_1 \approx R_2$$

Similarly, we can prove that power of other part is also zero.

7. Minimum distance between real object and its real image from a convex lens is $4f$.

Exercise Prove the above result.

8. Silvered lens A point object O is placed in front of a silvered lens as shown in figure.

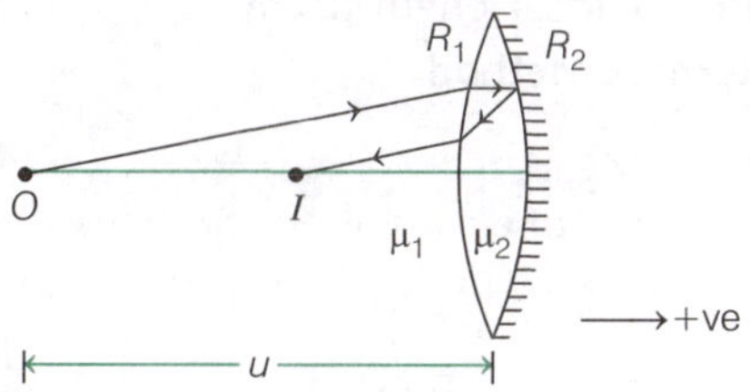

Ray of light is first refracted, then reflected and then again refracted. In first two steps, light is travelling from left to right and in the last one, direction of light is reversed. But we will take one sign convention, i.e. left to right as positive and in the last step will take v, u and R as negative.

$$\frac{\mu_2}{v_1} - \frac{\mu_1}{u} = \frac{\mu_2 - \mu_1}{R_1} \qquad \text{...(i)}$$

$$\frac{1}{v_2} + \frac{1}{v_1} = \frac{1}{f_{\text{mirror}}} = \frac{2}{R_2} \qquad \text{...(ii)}$$

$$\frac{\mu_1}{-v} - \frac{\mu_2}{-v_2} = \frac{\mu_1 - \mu_2}{-R_1} \qquad \text{...(iii)}$$

Solving Eqs. (i), (ii) and (iii), we get

$$\frac{1}{v} + \frac{1}{u} = \frac{2(\mu_2/\mu_1)}{R_2} - \frac{2(\mu_2/\mu_1 - 1)}{R_1} \qquad \text{...(iv)}$$

This is the desired formula for finding position of image for the given situation.

Note *The given system behaves as a mirror because the ray of light finally reflects in the same medium. Whose focal length can be found by comparing Eq. (iv) with mirror formula* $1/v + 1/u = 1/f$.

$$\boxed{\frac{1}{f} = \frac{2(\mu_2/\mu_1)}{R_2} - \frac{2(\mu_2/\mu_1 - 1)}{R_1}} \qquad \text{...(v)}$$

Let us take one example in support of this.

Ex. 16

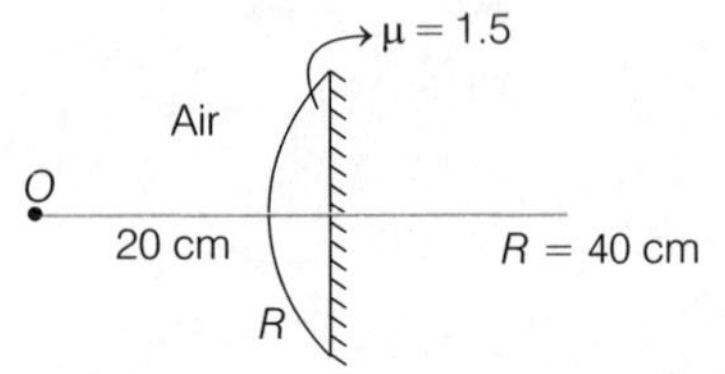

(a) Find focal length of the system as shown in figure.

(b) Find image position.

Sol. (a) $\mu_1 = 1, \mu_2 = 1.5, R_1 = R = +40$ cm and $R_2 = \infty$

Using the formula,

$$\frac{1}{f} = \frac{2(\mu_2/\mu_1)}{R_2} - \frac{2(\mu_2/\mu_1 - 1)}{R_1}$$

$$= \frac{2(1.5)}{\infty} - \frac{2(1.5-1)}{40}$$

or $f = -40$ cm

Thus, the given system behaves like a concave mirror of focal length 40 cm.

Alternate Method

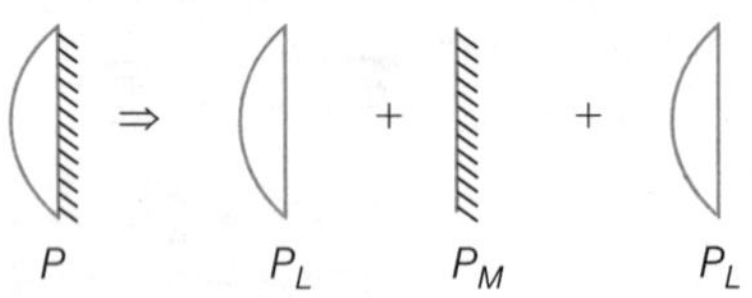

$$P = 2P_L + P_M$$

$$= \text{Power of equivalent mirror} \left(= -\frac{1}{f} \right)$$

$$\therefore \quad \frac{1}{-f} = 2(1.5-1)\left(\frac{1}{+0.4} - \frac{1}{\infty}\right) + \frac{1}{\infty}$$

$\Rightarrow \quad f = -0.4$ m or -40 cm

(b) Using the mirror formula, we have

$$\frac{1}{v} + \frac{1}{u} = \frac{1}{f}$$

$$\therefore \quad \frac{1}{v} + \frac{1}{-20} = \frac{1}{-40}$$

$$\therefore \quad v = +40 \text{ cm}$$

Therefore, image will be formed at a distance of 40 cm to the right hand side of the given system.

9. Displacement method of finding focal length of a convex lens

If the distance d between an object and screen is greater than 4 times the focal length of a convex lens, then there are two positions of the lens between the object and the screen at which a sharp image of the object is formed on the screen. This method is called **displacement method** and is used in laboratory to determine the focal length of convex lens.

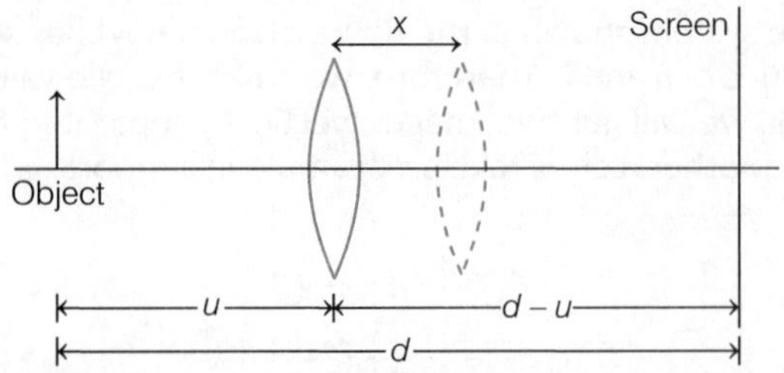

To prove this, let us take an object placed at a distance u from a convex lens of focal length f. The distance of image from the lens $v = (d - u)$. From the lens formula,

$$\frac{1}{v} - \frac{1}{u} = \frac{1}{f}$$

We have, $$\frac{1}{d-u} - \frac{1}{-u} = \frac{1}{f}$$

or $$u^2 - du + df = 0$$

$$\therefore \quad u = \frac{d \pm \sqrt{d(d-4f)}}{2}$$

Now, there are following possibilities:

(i) If $d < 4f$, then u is imaginary.

So, physically no position of the lens is possible.

(ii) If $d = 4f$, then $u = \frac{d}{2} = 2f$. So, only one position is possible. From here we can see that the minimum distance between an object and its real image in case of a convex lens is $4f$.

(iii) If $d > 4f$, there are two positions of lens at distances

$$\frac{d + \sqrt{d(d-4f)}}{2}$$

and $$\frac{d - \sqrt{d(d-4f)}}{2}$$

for which real image is formed on the screen.

(iv) Suppose I_1 is the image length in one position of the object and I_2 the image length in second position, then object length O is given by

$$\boxed{O = \sqrt{I_1 I_2}}$$

This can be proved as under

$$|u_1| = \frac{d + \sqrt{d(d-4f)}}{2}$$

$$\therefore \quad |v_1| = d - |u_1| = \frac{d - \sqrt{d(d-4f)}}{2}$$

$$|u_2| = \frac{d - \sqrt{d(d-4f)}}{2}$$

$$\therefore \quad |v_2| = d - |u_2| = \frac{d + \sqrt{d(d-4f)}}{2}$$

Now, $|m_1 m_2| = \frac{I_1}{O} \times \frac{I_2}{O} = \frac{|v_1|}{|u_1|} \times \frac{|v_2|}{|u_2|}$

Substituting the values, we get $\frac{I_1 I_2}{O^2} = 1$

or $O = \sqrt{I_1 I_2}$ **Hence Proved.**

(v) $m_1 m_2 = 1$

So, if $m_1 = -\frac{1}{2}$, then $m_2 = -2$.

Or, if one image is half in size, then the other image will be twice in size.

(vi) Focal length of the lens is given by

$$\boxed{f = \frac{d^2 - x^2}{4d}}$$

Proof In the figure, we can see that difference of two values of u is x. Thus,

$$|u_1| - |u_2| = x$$

or $$\left[\frac{d + \sqrt{d(d - 4f)}}{2}\right] - \left[\frac{d - \sqrt{d(d - 4f)}}{2}\right] = x$$

Solving this equation, we can find that

$$f = \frac{d^2 - x^2}{4d}$$

Ex. 17 A thin plano-convex lens of focal length f is split into two halves. One of the halves is shifted along the optical axis as shown in figure. The separation between object and image planes is 1.8 m. The magnification of the image formed by one of the half lens is 2. Find the focal length of the lens and separation between the two halves. Draw the ray diagram for image formation. **(1996 JEE)**

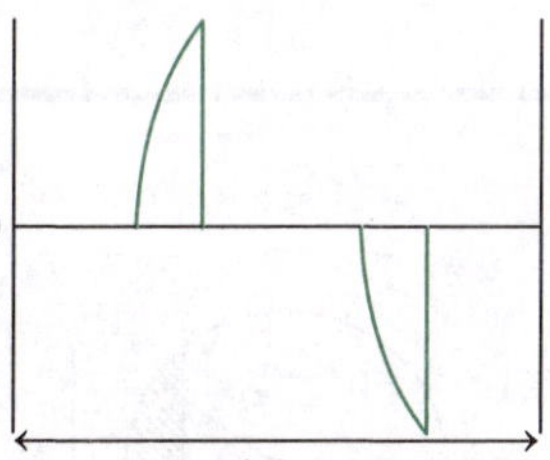

Sol. For both the halves, position of object and image is same. Only difference is of magnification. Magnification for one of the halves is given as 2 (> 1). This can be for the first half on left hand side, because for this, $|v| > |u|$. Therefore, magnification, $|m| = |v/u| > 1$.

So, for the first half

$$|v/u| = 2$$

or $|v| = 2|u|$

Let $u = -x$,

then $v = +2x$

and $|u| + |v| = 1.8$ m

i.e. $3x = 1.8$ m

or $x = 0.6$ m

Hence, $u = -0.6$ m

and $v = +1.2$ m

Using $\frac{1}{f} = \frac{1}{v} - \frac{1}{u}$

$$= \frac{1}{1.2} - \frac{1}{-0.6} = \frac{1}{0.4}$$

$\therefore$ $f = 0.4$ m **Ans.**

For the second half,

$$\frac{1}{f} = \frac{1}{1.2 - d} - \frac{1}{-(0.6 + d)}$$

or $$\frac{1}{0.4} = \frac{1}{1.2 - d} + \frac{1}{(0.6 + d)}$$

Solving this, we get $d = 0.6$ m **Ans.**

Magnification for the second half will be

$$m_2 = \frac{v}{u} = \frac{0.6}{-(1.2)} = -\frac{1}{2}$$

and magnification for the first half is

$$m_1 = \frac{v}{u} = \frac{1.2}{-(0.6)} = -2$$

The ray diagram is as follows:

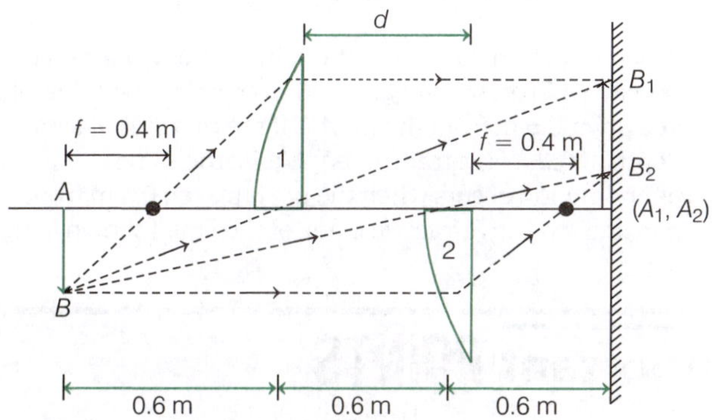

INTRODUCTORY Exercise

1. When an object is placed 60 cm in front of a diverging lens, a virtual image is formed 20 cm from the lens. The lens is made of a material of refractive index $\mu = 1.65$ and its two spherical surfaces have the same radius of curvature. What is the value of this radius?
2. A converging lens has a focal length of 30 cm. Rays from a 2.0 cm high filament that pass through the lens form a virtual image at a distance of 50 cm from the lens. Where is the filament located? What is the height of the image?
3. Show that the focal length of a thin lens is not changed when the lens is rotated so that the left and the right surfaces are interchanged.
4. As an object is moved from the surface of a thin converging lens to a focal point, over what range does the image distance vary?

5. A diverging lens is made of material with refractive index 1.3 and has identical concave surfaces of radius 20 cm. The lens is immersed in a transparent medium with refractive index 1.8.
   (a) What is now the focal length of the lens?
   (b) What is the minimum distance that an immersed object must be from the lens so that a real image is formed?
6. An object is located 20 cm to the left of a converging lens with $f = 10$ cm. A second identical lens is placed to the right of the first lens and then moved until the image it produces is identical in size and orientation to the object. What is the separation between the lenses?
7. Suppose an object has thickness du so that it extends from object distance u to $u + du$. Prove that the thickness dv of its image is given by $\left(-\frac{v^2}{u^2}\right)du$, so the longitudinal magnification $\frac{dv}{du} = -m^2$, where m is the lateral magnification.
8. Two thin similar convex glass pieces are joined together front to front, with its rear portion silvered such that a sharp image is formed 0.2 m for an object at infinity. When the air between the glass pieces is replaced by water $\left(\mu = \frac{4}{3}\right)$, find the position of image.
9. When a pin is moved along the principal axis of a small concave mirror, the image position coincides with the object at a point 0.5 m from the mirror. If the mirror is placed at a depth of 0.2 m in a transparent liquid, the same phenomenon occurs when the pin is placed 0.4 m from the mirror. Find the refractive index of the liquid shown in figure.

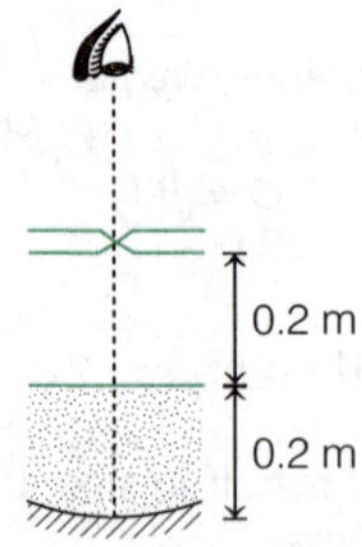

10. When a lens is inserted between an object and a screen which are a fixed distance apart, the size of the image is either 6 cm or $\frac{2}{3}$ cm. Find size of the object.
11. A lens of focal length 12 cm forms an upright image three times the size of a real object. Find the distance in cm between the object and image.
12. The distance between an object and its upright image is 20 cm. If the magnification is 0.5, what is the focal length of the lens that is being used to form the image?
13. A thin lens of focal length + 10.0 cm lies on a horizontal plane mirror. How far above the lens should an object be held if its image is to coincide with the object?

Answers

1. $R = 39$ cm **2.** $v = -18.75$ cm, $h = 5.33$ cm
4. From the surface to infinity on object side
5. (a) + 36 cm (b) 36 cm **6.** 40 cm **8.** 12 cm
9. 1.5 **10.** 2 cm **11.** 16 cm **12.** $f = -40$ cm
13. At 10 cm

See hints on pages 153-154.

Important POINTS

1. In case of spherical mirrors if object distance x_1 and image distance x_2 are measured from focus instead of pole, then :

$$x_1 x_2 = f^2$$

This formula is called **Newton's formula.**

This formula applies to a lens also, but in that case x_1 is the object distance from first focus and x_2 the image distance from second focus.

Exercise: Derive the above relation.

2. **Diameter of a lens**

We know that spherical surface of a lens is a part of sphere. But the diameter of a lens (say d) is different from diameter D of sphere from which lens is made.

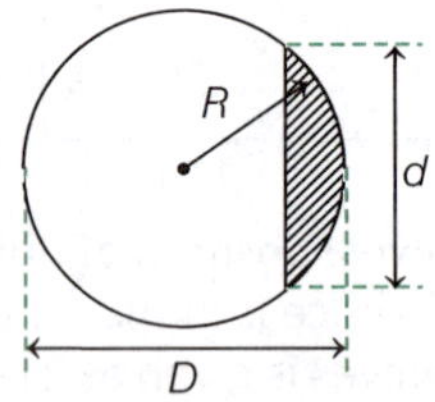

Following figure will illustrate this point for a plano convex lens.

$$d \neq D \Rightarrow R = \frac{D}{2}$$

$$R \neq \frac{d}{2} \text{ and } \frac{1}{f} = (\mu - 1)\left(\frac{1}{\infty} - \frac{1}{-R}\right)$$

Ex. 18 A spherical convex surface separates two media of refractive indices 1.0 and $\frac{4}{3}$. If radius of curvature of the surface is 10 cm, find its power.

Sol. Let us see where does the parallel rays converge (or diverge) on the principal axis. Let us call it the focus and the corresponding length the focal length f. Using $\frac{\mu_2}{v} - \frac{\mu_1}{u} = \frac{\mu_2 - \mu_1}{R}$ with proper values and signs, we have

$$\frac{4/3}{f} - \frac{1.0}{\infty} = \frac{4/3 - 1.0}{+10}$$

or $$f = 40 \text{ cm} = 0.4 \text{ m}$$

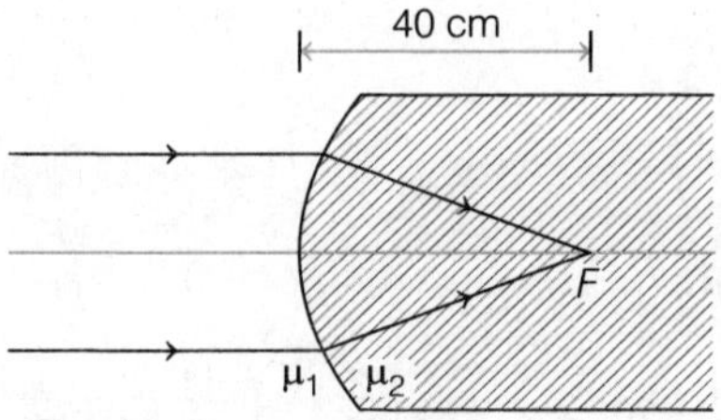

Since, the rays are converging, its power should be positive. Hence,

$$P \text{ (in dioptre)} = \frac{+1}{f \text{ (metre)}} = \frac{1}{0.4}$$

or $$P = 2.5 \text{ dioptre}$$ **Ans.**

Ex. 19 The distance between two point sources of light is 24 cm. Find out where would you place a converging lens of focal length 9 cm, so that the images of both the sources are formed at the same point.

Sol. For S_1 : $\frac{1}{v_1} - \frac{1}{-x} = \frac{1}{9}$

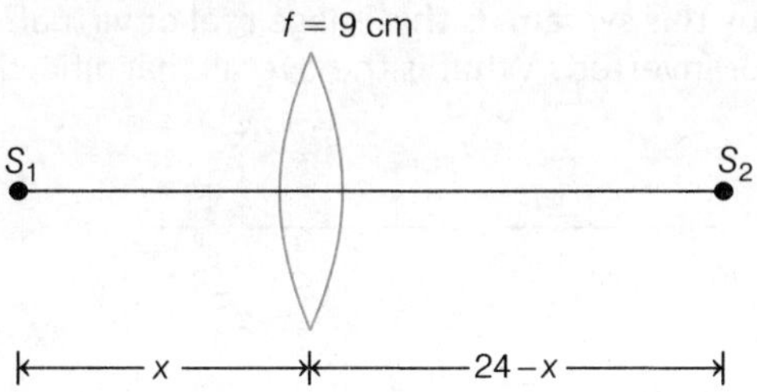

$$\therefore \quad \frac{1}{v_1} = \frac{1}{9} - \frac{1}{x} \quad \text{...(i)}$$

For S_2 : $\frac{1}{v_2} - \frac{1}{-(24-x)} = \frac{1}{9}$

$$\therefore \quad \frac{1}{v_2} = \frac{1}{9} - \frac{1}{24-x} \quad \text{...(ii)}$$

Since, sign convention for S_1 and S_2 are just opposite. Hence,

$$v_1 = -v_2$$

or $$\frac{1}{v_1} = -\frac{1}{v_2}$$

$$\therefore \quad \frac{1}{9} - \frac{1}{x} = \frac{1}{24-x} - \frac{1}{9}$$

Solving this equation we get, $x = 6$ cm. Therefore, the lens should be kept at a distance of 6 cm from either of the object. **Ans.**

Ex. 20 A source of light is located at a distance $2f$ from a convergent lens. The focal length of the lens is $f = 30$ cm. At what distance from the lens should a flat mirror be placed, so that the rays reflected from the mirror are parallel after passing through the lens for the second time?

Sol. Object is at a distance of $2f = 60$ cm from the lens. Image I_1 formed by lens, should be at a distance 60 cm from the lens. Now I_2, the image formed by plane mirror should lie at focus or at a distance of 30 cm from the lens. Hence, the mirror should be placed at distance 45 cm from the lens as shown in figure.

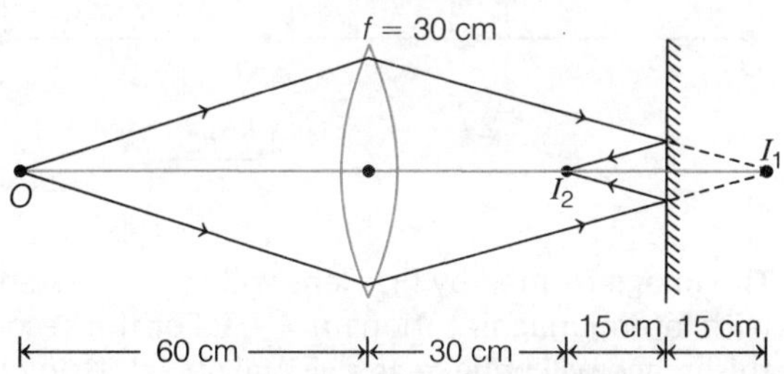

Ex. 21 Two equi-convex lenses of focal lengths 30 cm and 70 cm, made of material of refractive index = 1.5, are held in contact coaxially by a rubber band round their edges. A liquid of refractive index 1.3 is introduced in the space between the lenses filling it completely. Find the position of the image of a luminous point object placed on the axis of the combination lens at a distance of 90 cm from it.

Sol. $|R_1| = |R_2| = f_1 = 30$ cm (as $\mu = 1.5$)

Similarly, $|R_3| = |R_4| = f_2 = 70$ cm

The focal length of the liquid lens (in air).

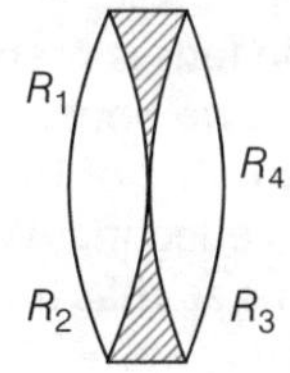

$$\frac{1}{f_3} = (\mu - 1)\left(\frac{1}{R_2} - \frac{1}{R_3}\right)$$

$$= (1.3 - 1)\left(\frac{1}{-30} - \frac{1}{+70}\right) = -\frac{1}{70}$$

Further, equivalent focal length of the combination,

$$\frac{1}{F}=\frac{1}{f_1}+\frac{1}{f_2}+\frac{1}{f_3}=\frac{1}{30}+\frac{1}{70}-\frac{1}{70}=\frac{1}{30}$$

Using the lens formula $\frac{1}{v}-\frac{1}{u}=\frac{1}{F}$, we have

$$\frac{1}{v}-\frac{1}{-90}=\frac{1}{30}$$

$$\therefore \qquad v=+45 \text{ cm}$$

Thus, image will be formed at a distance of 45 cm from the combination.

Ex. 22 Two thin converging lenses are placed on a common axis, so that the centre of one of them coincides with the focus of the other. An object is placed at a distance twice the focal length from the left hand lens. Where will its image be? What is the lateral magnification? The focal of each lens is f.

Sol.

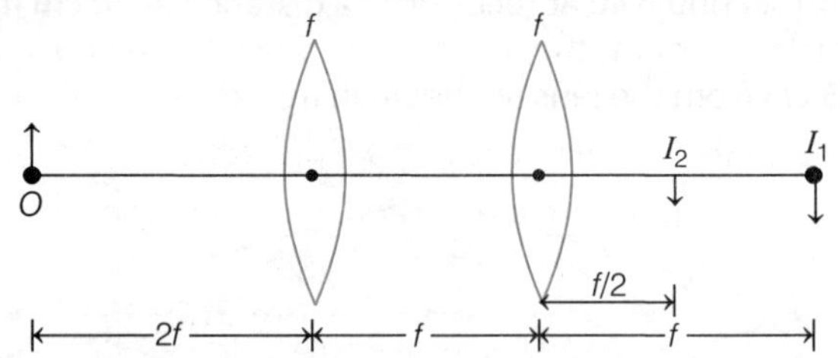

The image formed by first lens will be at a distance $2f$ with lateral magnification $m_1=-1$. For the second lens this image will behave as a virtual object. Using the lens formula, $\frac{1}{v}-\frac{1}{u}=\frac{1}{f}$ we have,

$$\frac{1}{v}-\frac{1}{f}=\frac{1}{f} \Rightarrow v=\frac{f}{2}$$

$$m_2=\frac{v_2}{u_2}=\frac{(f/2)}{f}=\frac{1}{2}$$

Therefore, final image is formed at a distance $\frac{f}{2}$ from the second lens with total lateral magnification,

$$m=m_1\times m_2=(-1)\times\left(\frac{1}{2}\right)=-\frac{1}{2}$$ **Ans.**

Ex. 23 A biconvex thin lens is prepared from glass of refractive index 3/2. The two bounding surfaces have equal radii of 25 cm each. One of the surfaces is silvered from outside to make it reflecting. Where should an object be placed before this lens so that the image coincides with the object.

Sol. Equivalent focal length of this system which behaves like a mirror is given by

$$\frac{1}{f}=\frac{2(\mu_2/\mu_1)}{R_2}-\frac{2(\mu_2/\mu_1-1)}{R_1}$$

Here, $R_1=+25$ cm, $R_2=-25$ cm, $\mu_1=1$ and $\mu_2=3/2$

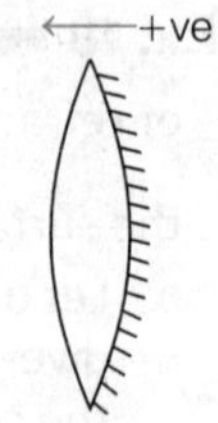

Image coincides with object, hence,

$u=v=-x$ (say)

Substituting in mirror formula, we have

$$\frac{1}{-x}-\frac{1}{x}=\frac{2(3/2)}{-25}-\frac{2(3/2-1)}{25}$$

or

$$\frac{2}{x}=\frac{3}{25}+\frac{1}{25}=\frac{4}{25}$$

$$\therefore \qquad x=12.5 \text{ cm}$$ **Ans.**

Hence, the object should be placed at a distance 12.5 cm in front of the silvered lens.

Alternate solution

$$P_M=-\frac{1}{f}=-\frac{2}{R}$$

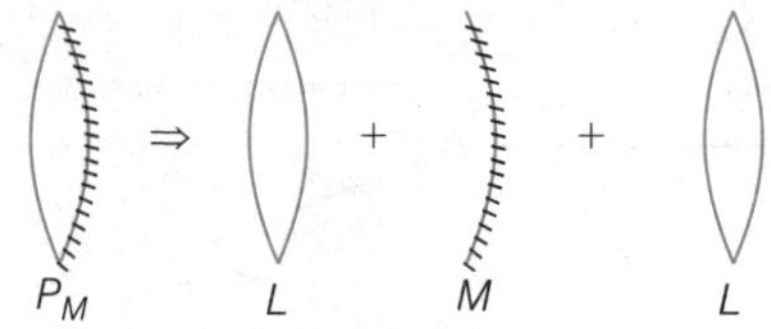

$$P_M=\frac{1}{-f_M}=2P_L+P_M=2\left(\frac{3}{2}-1\right)\left(\frac{1}{0.25}-\frac{1}{-0.25}\right)+\frac{2}{0.25}$$

$$\therefore \qquad f_M=-\frac{0.25}{4}\text{ m}=-6.25 \text{ cm}$$

So the combination behaves like a concave mirror of focal length 6.25 cm.

Object will coincide the object if kept at a distance $2f_M$ or 12.5 cm.

Ex. 24 An object is midway between the lens and the mirror as shown. The mirror's radius of curvature is 20.0 cm and the lens has a focal length of – 16.7 cm. Considering only the rays that leaves the object and travels first toward the mirror, locate the final image formed by this system. Is this image real or virtual? Is it upright or inverted? What is the overall magnification?

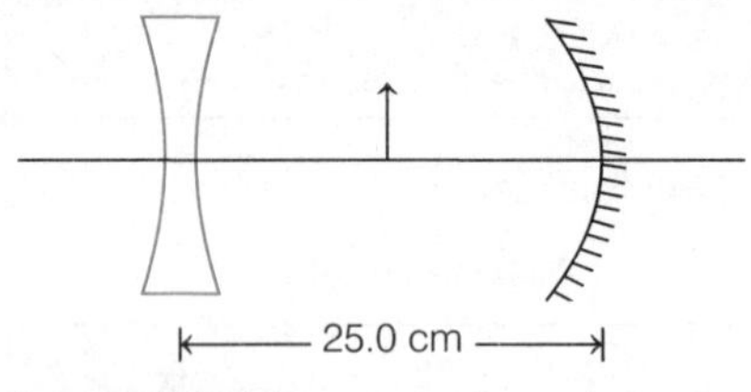

Sol. Image formed by mirror Using mirror formula

$$\frac{1}{v}+\frac{1}{u}=\frac{1}{f}=\frac{2}{R} \qquad \left(\text{as } f=\frac{R}{2}\right)$$

We have, $$\frac{1}{v_1}+\frac{1}{-12.5}=\frac{2}{-20}$$

$$\therefore \qquad v_1=-50 \text{ cm}$$

$$m_1=-\frac{v}{u}=-\frac{(-50)}{(-12.5)}=-4$$

i.e. image formed by the mirror is at a distance of 50 cm from the mirror to the left of it. It is inverted and four times larger.

Image formed by lens Image formed by mirror acts as an object for lens. It is at a distance of 25.0 cm to the left of lens. Using the lens formula,

$$\frac{1}{v}-\frac{1}{u}=\frac{1}{f}$$

We have, $\frac{1}{v_2}-\frac{1}{25}=\frac{1}{-16.7}$

$\therefore \quad v_2=-50.3$ cm

and $\quad m_2=\frac{v}{u}=\frac{-50.3}{25}=-2.012$

Overall magnification is

$$m=m_1\times m_2=8.048$$

Thus, the final image is at a distance 25.3 cm to the right of the mirror, virtual, upright enlarged and 8.048 times. Positions of the two images are shown in figure.

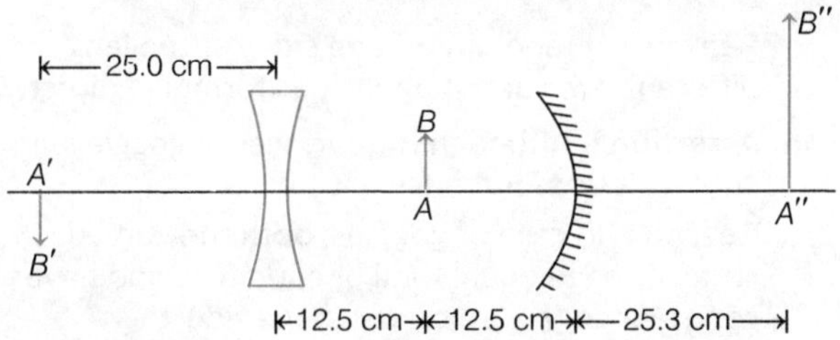

Ex. 25 An object is placed 12 cm to the left of a diverging lens of focal length – 6.0 cm. A converging lens with a focal length of 12.0 cm is placed at a distance *d* to the right of the diverging lens. Find the distance *d* that corresponds to a final image at infinity.

Sol.

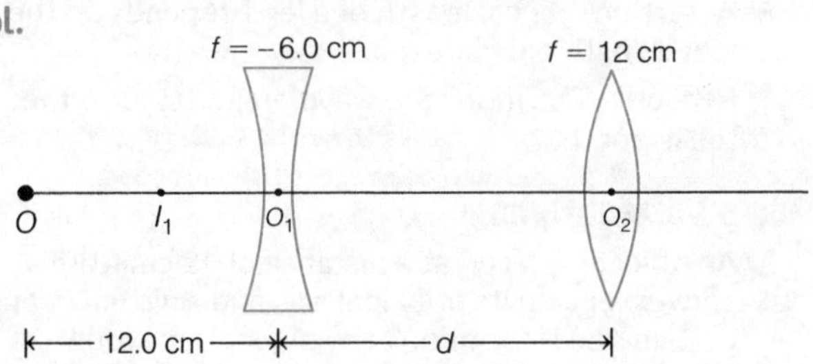

Applying lens formula $\frac{1}{v}-\frac{1}{u}=\frac{1}{f}$ twice we have,

$$\frac{1}{v_1}-\frac{1}{-12}=\frac{1}{-6}$$

$$v_1=-4 \text{ cm or } O_1I_1=4 \text{ cm}$$

$$O_2I_1=f_L=12 \text{ cm}$$

or $\quad d+4=12$ cm

$\therefore \quad d=8$ cm **Ans.**

Ex. 26 A converging lens forms a five fold magnified image of an object. The screen is moved towards the object by a distance $d=0.5$ m, and the lens is shifted so that the image has the same size as the object. Find the power of lens and the initial distance between the object and the screen.

Sol. In the first case image is five times magnified. Hence, $|v|=5|u|$. In the second case, image and object are of equal size. Hence, $|v|=|u|$. From the two figures,

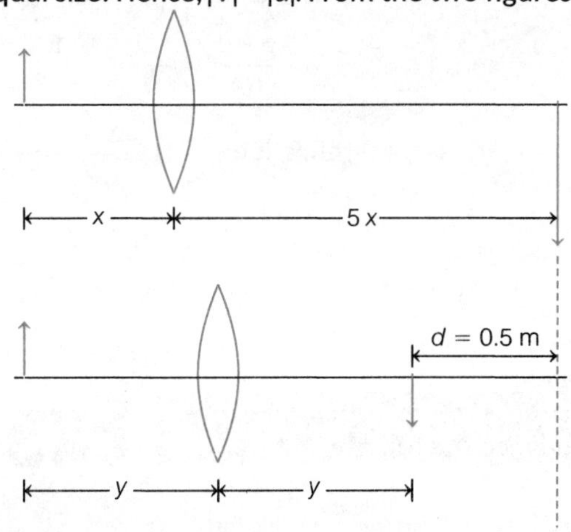

$$6x=2y+d$$

or $\quad 6x-2y=0.5$ ...(i)

Using the lens formula for both the cases,

$$\frac{1}{5x}-\frac{1}{-x}=\frac{1}{f} \text{ or } \frac{6}{5x}=\frac{1}{f} \quad \text{...(ii)}$$

$$\frac{1}{y}-\frac{1}{-y}=\frac{1}{f} \text{ or } \frac{2}{y}=\frac{1}{f} \quad \text{...(iii)}$$

Solving these three equations, we get

$$x=0.1875 \text{ m}$$

and $\quad f=0.15625$ m

Therefore, initial distance between the object and the screen $=6x=1.125$ m **Ans.**

Power of the lens, $P=\frac{1}{f}=\frac{1}{0.15625}=6.4$ D **Ans.**

Ex. 27 Surfaces of a thin equi-convex glass lens have radius of curvature *R*. Paraxial rays are incident on it. If the final image is formed after *n* internal reflections, calculate distance of this image from pole of the lens. Refractive index of glass is μ.

Sol. The rays will first get refracted, then *n*-times reflected and finally again refracted.

So, using $\frac{\mu_2}{v}-\frac{\mu_1}{u}=\frac{\mu_2-\mu_1}{R}$ for first refraction, we have

$$\frac{\mu}{v_i}-\frac{1}{\infty}=\frac{\mu-1}{R} \Rightarrow v_i=\left(\frac{\mu}{\mu-1}\right)R$$

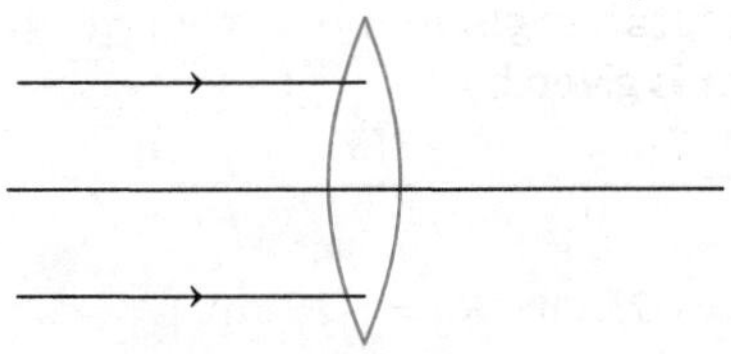

For first reflection, let us use

$$\frac{1}{v}+\frac{1}{u}=\frac{1}{f}=\frac{2}{R}$$

$$\therefore \quad \frac{1}{v_1}+\left(\frac{\mu-1}{\mu R}\right)=\frac{-2}{R} \text{ or } \frac{1}{v_1}=-\left(\frac{3\mu-1}{\mu R}\right)$$

For second reflection, $\frac{1}{v_2}+\frac{3\mu-1}{\mu R}=\frac{-2}{R}$

or $$\frac{1}{v_2}=-\left(\frac{5\mu-1}{\mu R}\right)$$

Similarly, after n^{th} reflection,

$$\frac{1}{v_n}=-\left[\frac{(2n+1)\mu-1}{\mu R}\right]$$

Finally, using $\frac{\mu_2}{v}-\frac{\mu_1}{u}=\frac{\mu_2-\mu_1}{R}$, we have

$$\frac{1}{v_f}-\left\{\frac{(2n+1)\mu-1}{R}\right\}=\frac{1-\mu}{-R}$$

or $$v_f=\frac{R}{2(\mu n+\mu-1)}$$ **Ans.**

MODULE 6 Exercise

True/False

1. A convex lens of focal length 1 m and a concave lens of focal length 0.25 m are kept 0.75 m apart. A parallel beam of light first passes through the convex lens, then through the concave lens and comes to a focus 0.5 m away from the concave lens. **(1983 JEE)**

Assertion and Reason

See directions on page 11.

2. **Assertion :** Minimum distance between object and its real image by a convex lens is $4f$.

   Reason : If object distance from a convex lens is $2f$, then its image distance is also $2f$.

3. **Assertion :** If object is placed at infinity, then a virtual image will be formed at first focus of a concave lens.

   Reason : First focal length of a concave lens is positive.

4. **Assertion :** A convex lens and a concave lens are kept in contact. They will behave as a diverging lens if focal length of convex lens is more.

   Reason : Power of a concave lens is always less than the power of a convex lens, as power of concave lens is negative whereas power of convex lens is positive.

5. **Assertion :** In the figure shown $|R_1|>|R_2|$. Two point objects O_1 and O_2 are kept at same distance from the lens. Image distance of O_1 from the lens will be more compared to the image distance of O_2.

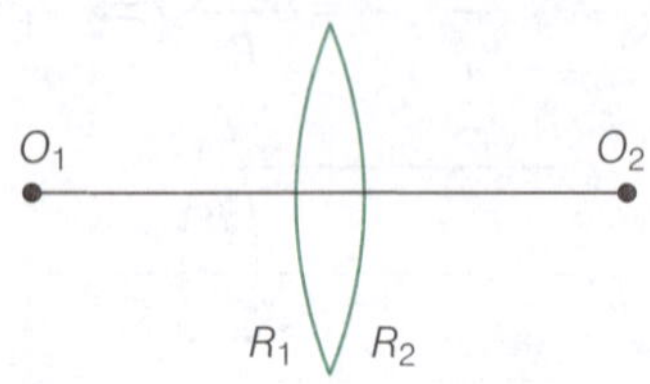

   Reason : If medium on two sides of the lens is different, we cannot apply lens formulae directly.

6. **Assertion :** Although the surfaces of goggle lens are curved, it does not have any power.

   Reason : In case of goggles, both the curved surfaces have equal radii of curvature and have centre of curvature on the same side.

7. **Assertion :** A diverging lens (in air) cannot be made more diverging whatever be the medium we choose to completely cover the lens.

   Reason : The minimum refractive index of any medium is 1.

8. **Assertion :** Focal length of a lens depends on the wavelength of light used.

   Reason : The more the wavelength lesser is the focal length.

Single Correct Option

9. An object is placed at a distance of 12 cm from a convex lens on its principal axis and a virtual image of certain size is formed. If the object is moved 8 cm away from the lens, a real image of the same size as that of the virtual image is formed. The focal length of the lens in cm is

   (a) 15 (b) 16 (c) 18 (d) 20

10. The power in dioptre of an equi-convex lens with radii of curvature of 10 cm and refractive index 1.6 is

   (a) +12 (b) +18 (c) +1.2 (d) +1.8

11. A thin equi-convex lens is made of glass of refractive index 1.5 and its focal length is 0.2 m. If it acts as a concave lens of 0.5 m focal length when dipped in a liquid, the refractive index of the liquid is

   (a) $\frac{17}{8}$ (b) $\frac{15}{8}$

   (c) $\frac{13}{8}$ (d) $\frac{9}{8}$

12. The given equi-convex lens is broken into four parts and rearranged as shown. If the initial focal length is f, then after rearrangement the equivalent focal length is

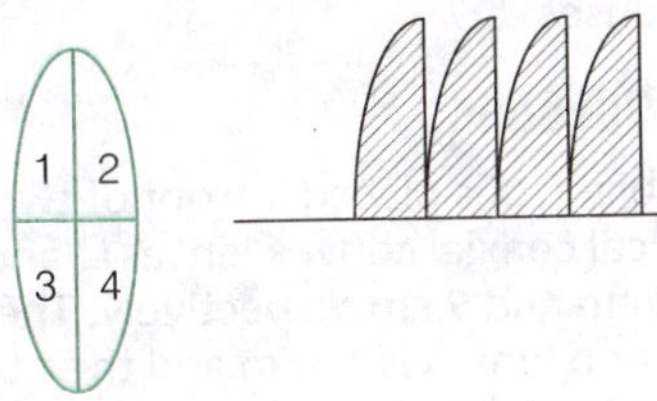

(a) f (b) $f/2$ (c) $f/4$ (d) $4f$

13. Two convex lenses of focal length 10 cm and 20 cm respectively placed coaxially and are separated by some distance d. The whole system behaves like a concave lens . One of the possible value of d is

(a) 15 cm (b) 20 cm (c) 25 cm (d) 40 cm

14. The focal length of a convex lens is f and the distance of an object from the first focus is x. The ratio of the size of the real image to the size of the object is

(a) $\frac{f}{x}$ (b) $\frac{x}{f}$ (c) $\frac{f+x}{f}$ (d) $\frac{f}{f+x}$

15. The focal length of a combination of two lenses is doubled if the separation between them is doubled. If the separation is increased to 4 times, the magnitude of focal length is (as compared to original)

(a) doubled (b) quadrupled
(c) halved (d) same

16. A convexo-concave convergent lens is made of glass of refractive index 1.5 and focal length 24 cm. Radius of curvature for one surface is double than that of the other. Then, radii of curvature for the two surfaces are (in cm)

(a) 6, 12 (b) 12, 24 (c) 3, 6 (d) 18, 36

17. A point object is placed at a distance of 12 cm from a convex lens of focal length 10 cm. On the other side of the lens, a convex mirror is placed at a distance of 10 cm from the lens such that the image formed by the combination coincides with the object itself. The focal length of the convex mirror is

(a) 20 cm (b) 25 cm (c) 15 cm (d) 30 cm

18. An object, a convex lens of focal length 20 cm and a plane mirror are arranged as shown in the figure. How far behind the mirror is the second image formed?

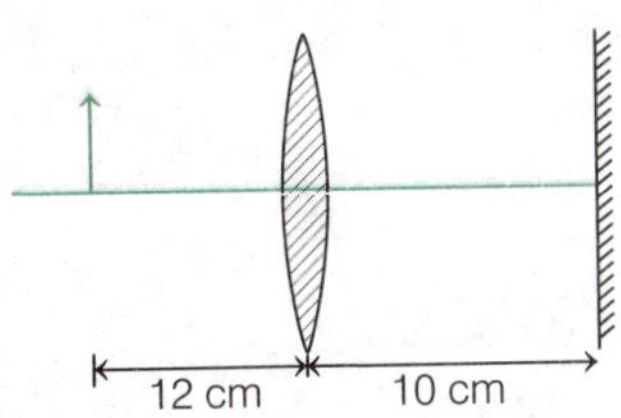

(a) 30 cm (b) 20 cm (c) 40 cm (d) 50 cm

19. An effective power of a combination of 5 identical convex lenses which are kept in contact along the principal axis is 25 D. Focal length of each of the convex lens is **(2024 Main)**

(a) 25 cm (b) 500 cm (c) 50 cm (d) 20 cm

20. For an object placed at a distance 2.4 m from a lens, a sharp focused image is observed on a screen placed at a distance 12 cm from the lens. A glass plate of refractive index 1.5 and thickness 1 cm is introduced between lens and screen. By what distance should the object be shifted so that a sharp focused image is observed again on the screen? **(2022 Main)**

(a) 0.8 m (b) 3.2 m (c) 1.2 m (d) 5.6 m

21. A convex lens has power P. It is cut into two halves along its principal axis. Further one piece (out of the two halves) is cut into two halves perpendicular to the principal axis (as shown in figures). Choose the **incorrect** option for the reported pieces. **(2022 Main)**

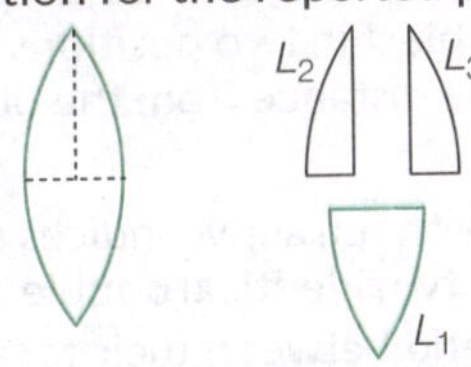

(a) Power of $L_1 = \frac{P}{2}$ (b) Power of $L_2 = \frac{P}{2}$

(c) Power of $L_3 = \frac{P}{2}$ (d) Power of $L_1 = P$

22. An extended object is placed at point O, 10 cm in front of a convex lens L_1 and a concave lens L_2 is placed 10 cm behind it, as shown in the figure. The radii of curvature of all the curved surfaces in both the lenses are 20 cm. The refractive index of both the lenses is 1.5. The total magnification of this lens system is **(2021 Adv.)**

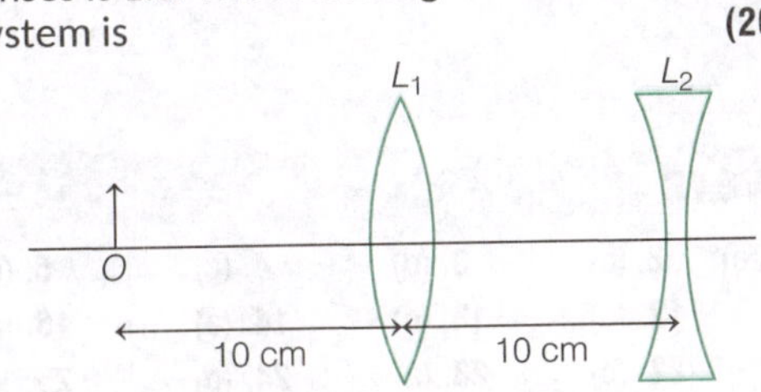

(a) 0.4 (b) 0.8 (c) 1.3 (d) 1.6

23. Find the distance of the image from object O, formed by the combination of lenses in the figure. **(2021 Main)**

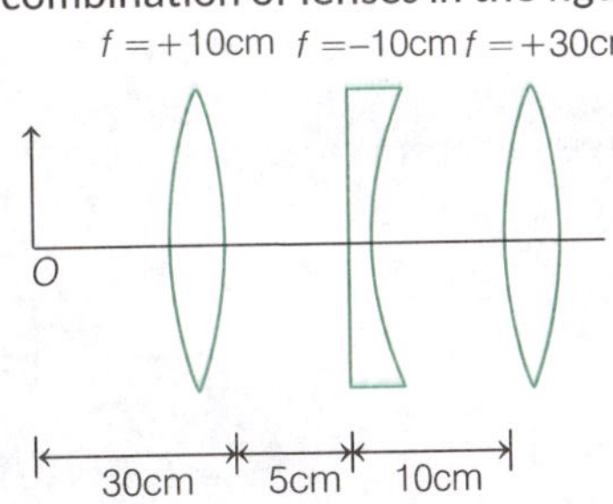

(a) 75 cm (b) 10 cm (c) 20 cm (d) infinity

24. What is the position and nature of image formed by lens combination shown in figure? (where, f_1 and f_2 are focal lengths) **(2019 Main)**

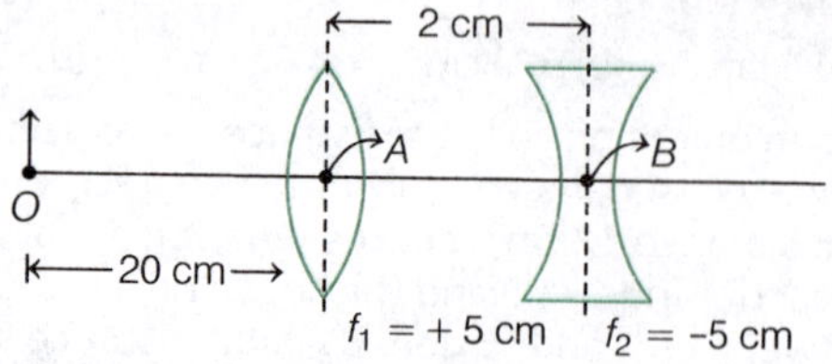

(a) 20/3 cm from point B at right, real
(b) 70 cm from point B at right, real
(c) 40 cm from point B at right, real
(d) 70 cm from point B at left, virtual

Subjective Questions

25. A lens with a focal length of 16 cm produces a sharp image of an object in two positions, which are 60 cm apart. Find the distance from the object to the screen.

26. Two glasses with refractive indices of 1.5 and 1.7 are used to make two identical double convex lenses.
(a) Find the ratio between their focal lengths.
(b) How will each of these lenses act on a ray parallel to its optical axis if the lenses are submerged into a transparent liquid with a refractive index of 1.6?

27. A converging beam of rays is incident on a diverging lens. Having passed through the lens the rays intersect at a point 15 cm from the lens. If the lens is removed, the point where the rays meet, move 5 cm closer to the mounting that holds the lens. Find the focal length of the lens.

28. A parallel beam of rays is incident on a convergent lens with a focal length of 40 cm. Where a divergent lens with a focal length of 15 cm be placed for the beam of rays to remain parallel after passing through the two lenses.

Integer Type Questions

29. A point object, O is placed infront of two thin symmetrical coaxial convex lenses L_1 and L_2 with focal length 24 cm and 9 cm respectively. The distance between two lenses is 10 cm and the object is placed 6 cm away from lens L_1 as shown in the figure. The distance between the object and the image formed by the system of two lenses is .... cm. **(2023 Main)**

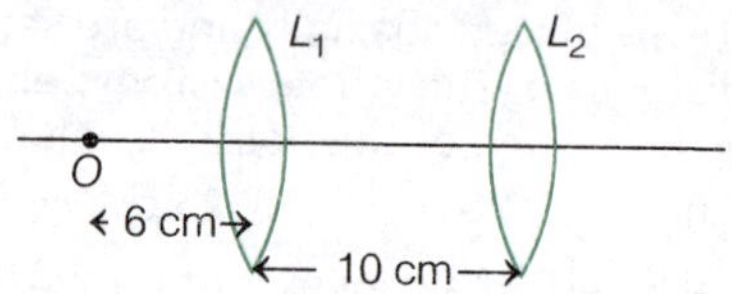

30. The radius of curvature of each surface of a convex lens having refractive index 1.8 is 20 cm. The lens is now immersed in a liquid of refractive index 1.5. The ratio of power of lens in air to its power in the liquid will be $x : 1$. The value of x is .... **(2023 Main)**

31. Two convex lenses of focal length 20 cm each are placed coaxially with a separation of 60 cm between them. The image of distant object formed by the combination is at .... cm from the first lens. **(2023 Main)**

32. A biconvex lens of focal length 10 cm is cut in two identical parts along a plane perpendicular to the principal axis. The power of each lens after cut is .... D. **(2023 Main)**

Answers

1. (False) **2.** (b) **3.** (d) **4.** (c) **5.** (d) **6.** (a) **7.** (a) **8.** (c) **9.** (b) **10.** (a)
11. (b) **12.** (b) **13.** (d) **14.** (a) **15.** (a) **16.** (a) **17.** (b) **18.** (c) **19.** (d) **20.** (b)
21. (a) **22.** (b) **23.** (a) **24.** (b) **25.** 100 cm
26. (a) 1.4 (b) The first lens will be a diverging and the second a converging one **27.** $f = -30$ cm **28.** 25 cm **29.** (34)
30. (4) **31.** (100) **32.** (5)

See hints on pages 154-158.

MODULE 7

Total Internal Reflection

(i) When a ray of light strikes the boundary separating two different media, then part of it is refracted and part is reflected.

(ii) If a ray of light is travelling from a denser to a rarer medium with angle of incidence greater than a critical angle ($i > \theta_C$), then no refraction takes place but ray of light is 100% reflected in the same medium. This phenomenon is called TIR.

(iii) $\sin\theta_C = \dfrac{\mu_R}{\mu_D}$

Here, R stands for rarer medium and D for denser medium. If rarer medium is air, then

$$\sin\theta_C = \frac{1}{\mu}$$

$$\therefore \quad \boxed{\theta_C = \sin^{-1}\left(\frac{\mu_R}{\mu_D}\right) \quad \text{or} \quad \sin^{-1}\left(\frac{1}{\mu}\right)}$$

(iv) If value of μ increases, then critical angle θ_C decreases. Therefore, chances of TIR increase in travelling from denser to rarer medium.

(v)

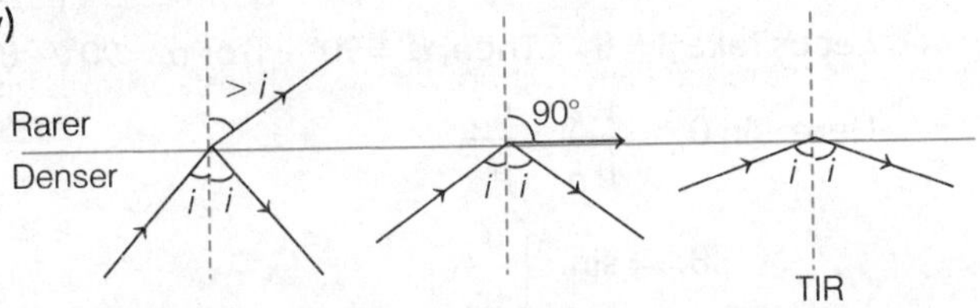

$i < \theta_C$ (a) $i = \theta_C$ (b) $i > \theta_C$ (c)

Applying Snell's law of refraction in Fig. (b), we have

$$\mu_R \sin 90° = \mu_D \sin\theta_C$$

or
$$\sin\theta_C = \frac{\mu_R}{\mu_D}$$

or
$$\theta_C = \sin^{-1}\left(\frac{\mu_R}{\mu_D}\right)$$

(vi) In critical case (Fig. b), angle in denser medium is θ_C and angle in rarer medium is 90°.

TIR has following applications

(i) **Totally reflecting prisms**

Refractive index of crown glass is 3/2. Hence,

$$\theta_C = \sin^{-1}\left(\frac{1}{\mu}\right) = \sin^{-1}\left(\frac{2}{3}\right) \approx 42°$$

A ray OA incident normally on face PQ of a crown glass prism suffers TIR at face PR since, the angle of incidence in the optically denser medium is 45°. A bright ray AB emerges at right angles from face QR. The prism thus, reflects the ray through 90°. Light can be reflected through 180° and an erect image can be obtained of an inverted one if the prism is arranged as shown in figure (b).

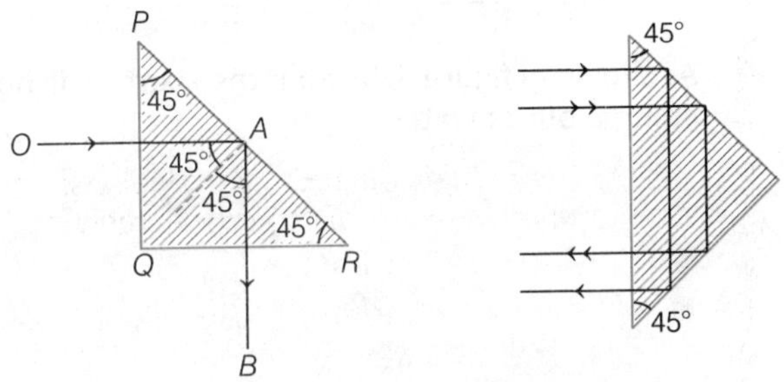

(a) (b)

(ii) **Optical fibres** Light can be confined within a bent glass rod by TIR and so 'piped' along a twisted path as in figure. The beam is reflected from side to side practically without loss (except for that due to absorption in the glass) and emerges only at the end of the rod where it strikes the surface almost normally, i.e. at an angle less than the critical angle.

A single, very thin, solid glass fibre behaves in the same way and if several thousands are taped together a flexible light pipe is obtained that can be used. For example in medicine and engineering to illuminate an inaccessible spot. Optical fibres are now a days used to carry telephone, television and computer signals from one place to the other.

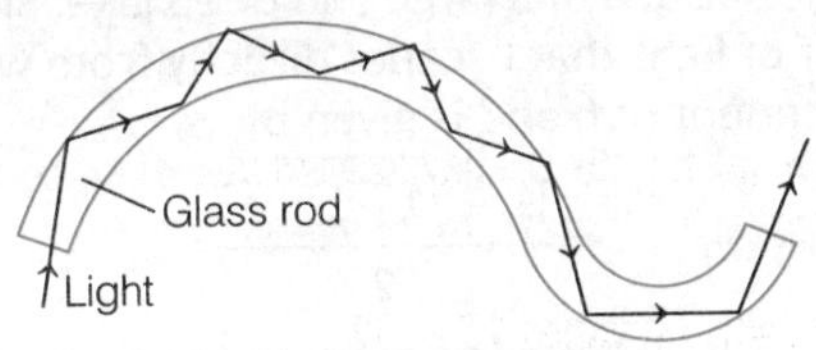

Principle of an optical fibre

Note *As we have seen* $\theta_C = \sin^{-1}\left(\dfrac{\mu_R}{\mu_D}\right)$

Suppose we have two sets of media 1 and 2 and

$$\left(\frac{\mu_R}{\mu_D}\right)_1 < \left(\frac{\mu_R}{\mu_D}\right)_2$$

then $(\theta_C)_1 < (\theta_C)_2$

So, a ray of light has more chances to have TIR in case 1.

Examples of TIR

Example 1 An isotropic point source is placed at a depth h below the water surface. A floating opaque disc is placed on the surface of water so that the source is not visible from the surface. What is the minimum radius of the disc? Take refractive index of water $= \mu$.

Sol.

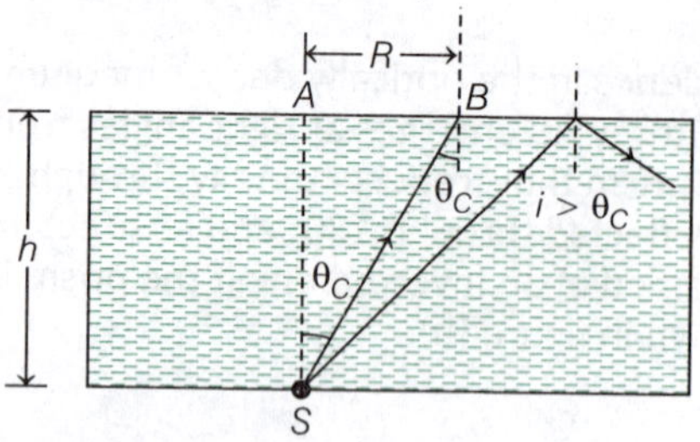

As shown in figure light from the source will not emerge out of water if $i > \theta_C$.

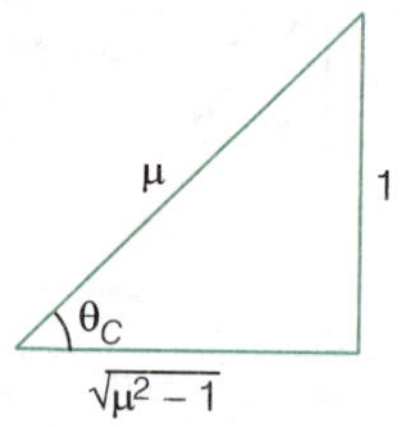

$$\sin \theta_c = \frac{1}{\mu}$$

Therefore, minimum radius R corresponds to $i = \theta_C$

In ΔSAB,

$$\frac{R}{h} = \tan\theta_C$$

$$\therefore \quad R = h\tan\theta_C$$

or $$R = \frac{h}{\sqrt{\mu^2 - 1}}$$ **Ans.**

Note *Only that portion of light refracts in air which falls on the circle (on the surface of water) with A as centre and AB as radius.*

Example 2 A point source of light is placed at a distance h below the surface of a large and deep lake. Show that the fraction f of light that escapes directly from water surface is independent of h and is given by

$$f = \frac{[1 - \sqrt{1 - 1/\mu^2}]}{2}$$

Sol. Due to TIR, light will be reflected back into the water if $i > \theta_C$. So, only that portion of incident light will escape which passes through the cone of angle $\theta = 2\theta_C$.

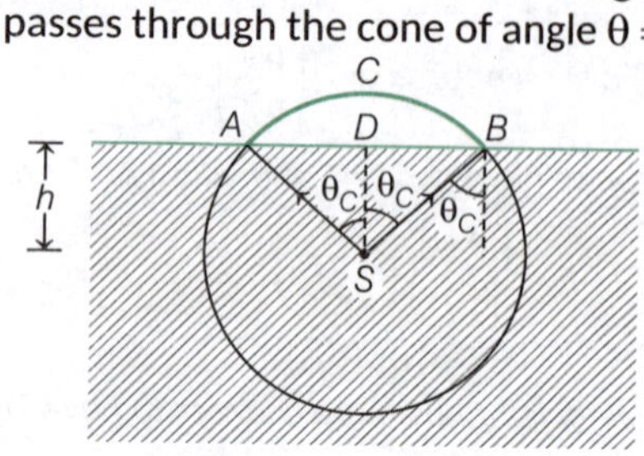

So, the fraction of light escaping

$$f = \frac{\text{Area } ACB}{\text{Total area of sphere}}$$

$$= \frac{2\pi R^2(1 - \cos\theta_C)}{4\pi R^2}$$

$$= \frac{1 - \cos\theta_C}{2}$$

Now, as f depends on θ_C and which depends only on μ, it is independent of h. **Proved.**

Further $$\cos\theta_C = \frac{\sqrt{\mu^2 - 1}}{\mu} = \sqrt{1 - 1/\mu^2}$$

$$\Rightarrow \quad f = \frac{1 - \sqrt{1 - 1/\mu^2}}{2}$$ **Ans.**

Note *Area of ACB $= 2\pi R^2(1 - \cos\theta_C)$ can be obtained by integration. In the above example, we have seen that light falling on the circle with centre at D and radius DB will only refract in air and in the absence of water surface only that light would fall on surface ACB of sphere.*

Example 3 In the figure shown, $\mu_1 > \mu_2$. Find minimum value of i so that TIR never takes place at P.

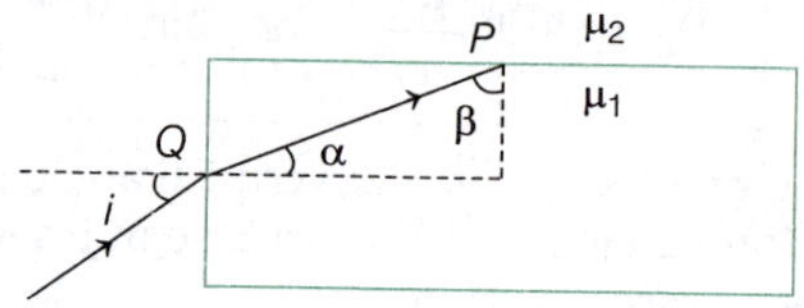

Sol. Let us take $\beta = \theta_C$. Then, $\alpha = 90° - \beta$ or $\alpha = 90° - \theta_C$

Here, $$\sin\theta_C = \frac{\mu_R}{\mu_D} = \frac{\mu_2}{\mu_1}$$

$$\therefore \quad \theta_C = \sin^{-1}\left(\frac{\mu_2}{\mu_1}\right)$$

Applying Snell's law at point Q,

$$\mu_2 \sin i = \mu_1 \sin\alpha = \mu_1 \sin(90° - \theta_C)$$

$$= \mu_1 \cos\theta_C = \mu_1 \cos\sin^{-1}\left(\frac{\mu_2}{\mu_1}\right)$$

$$\therefore \quad i = \sin^{-1}\left[\frac{\mu_1}{\mu_2}\cos\sin^{-1}\left(\frac{\mu_2}{\mu_1}\right)\right]$$ **Ans.**

Now, we can see that starting from this value of i, we get $\beta = \theta_C$.

If i is increased from this value, then α will also increase (becomes $> 90° - \theta_C$) and β decreases from the value θ_C (becomes $< \theta_C$) and no TIR takes place at P.

So far no TIR condition i has to be increased from the above value. Or this is the minimum value of i.

Example 4 Monochromatic light is incident on a plane interface AB between two media of refractive indices μ_1 and μ_2 $(\mu_2 > \mu_1)$ at an angle of incidence θ as shown in the figure.

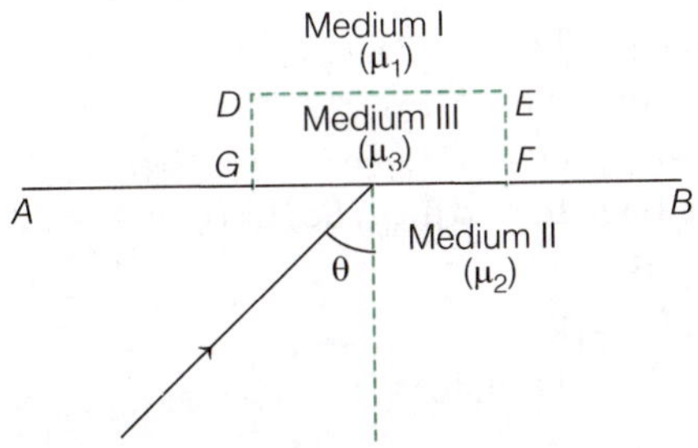

The angle θ is infinitesimally greater than the critical angle for the two media so that total internal reflection takes place. Now if a transparent slab *DEFG* of uniform thickness and of refractive index μ_3 is introduced on the interface (as shown in the figure), show that for any value of μ_3 all light will ultimately be reflected back again into medium II.

Consider separately the cases. **(1986 JEE)**

(a) $\mu_3 < \mu_1$ (b) $\mu_3 > \mu_1$

Sol. Given, θ is slightly greater than $\sin^{-1}\left(\frac{\mu_1}{\mu_2}\right)$.

(a) **When** $\mu_3 < \mu_1$

i.e. $\mu_3 < \mu_1 < \mu_2$

or $\frac{\mu_3}{\mu_2} < \frac{\mu_1}{\mu_2}$ or $\sin^{-1}\left(\frac{\mu_3}{\mu_2}\right) < \sin^{-1}\left(\frac{\mu_1}{\mu_2}\right)$

Hence, critical angle for III and II will be less than the critical angle for II and I. So, if TIR is taking place between I and II, then TIR will definitely take place between II and III.

(b) **When** $\mu_3 > \mu_1$ Two cases may arise :

Case 1 $\mu_1 < \mu_3 < \mu_2$

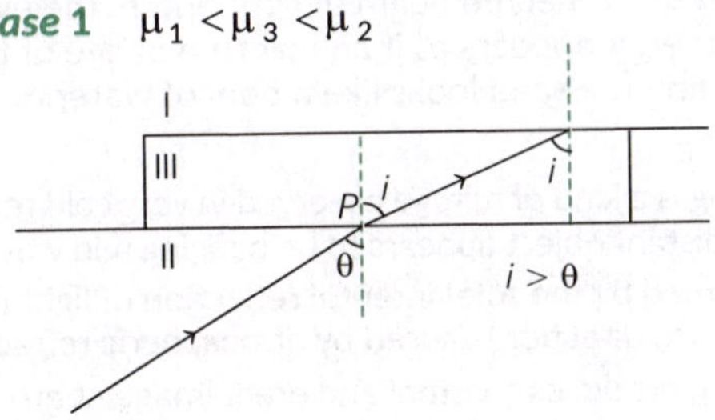

$$\frac{\mu_3}{\mu_2} > \frac{\mu_1}{\mu_2}$$

$\therefore \quad (\theta_c)_{III,II} > (\theta_c)_{I,II}$

$\therefore$ In this case, there will be no TIR between II and III. Because TIR was just taking place between I and II. But TIR will take place between III and I. This is because:

ray of light first enters from II to III. i.e. from denser to rarer.

$\therefore \quad i > \theta$

Applying Snell's law at *P*,

$$\mu_2 \sin\theta = \mu_3 \sin i$$

or $$\sin i = \left(\frac{\mu_2}{\mu_3}\right)\sin\theta$$

Since, $\sin\theta$ is slightly greater than $\frac{\mu_1}{\mu_2}$.

$\therefore$ $\sin i$ is slightly greater than $\frac{\mu_2}{\mu_3} \times \frac{\mu_1}{\mu_2}$ or $\frac{\mu_1}{\mu_3}$

but $\frac{\mu_1}{\mu_3}$ is nothing but $\sin(\theta_C)_{I,III}$

$\therefore$ $\sin(i)$ is slightly greater than $\sin(\theta_C)_{I,III}$

or TIR will now take place on I and III and the ray of light will be reflected back.

Case 2 $\mu_1 < \mu_2 < \mu_3$

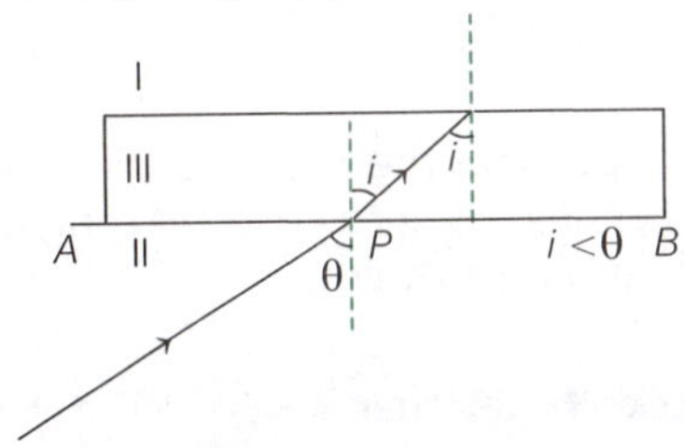

This time while moving from II to III, ray of light will bend towards normal. Again applying Snell's law at *P*,

$$\mu_2 \sin\theta = \mu_3 \sin i$$

$$\sin i = \frac{\mu_2}{\mu_3}\sin\theta$$

Since, $\sin\theta$ is slightly greater than $\frac{\mu_1}{\mu_2}$.

Therefore, $\sin i$ will be slightly greater than

$$\frac{\mu_2}{\mu_3} \times \frac{\mu_1}{\mu_2} \text{ or } \frac{\mu_1}{\mu_3}$$

But, $\frac{\mu_1}{\mu_3}$ is $\sin(\theta_C)_{I,III}$

i.e. $\sin i > \sin(\theta_C)_{I,III}$

or $i > (\theta_C)_{I,III}$

Therefore, TIR will again take place between I and III and the ray of light will be reflected back.

Note *Two cases of $\mu_3 > \mu_1$ can be explained by one single equation. But two cases are deliberately taken for better understanding of refraction, Snell's law and total internal reflection (TIR).*

Example 5 A right angled prism is to be made by selecting a proper material and the angles *A* and *B* ($B \le A$), as shown in figure. It is desired that a ray of light incident on the face *AB* emerges parallel to the incident direction after two internal reflections.

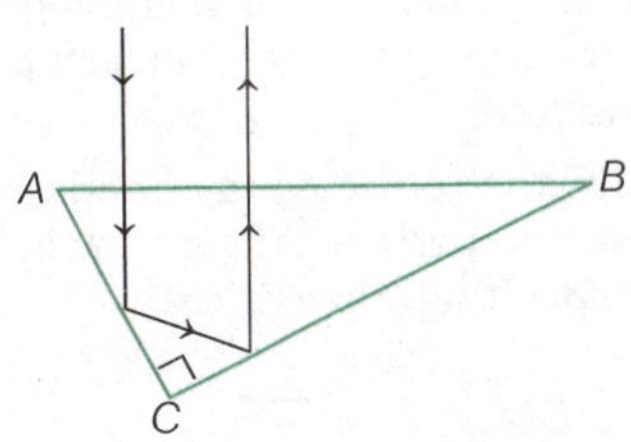

(a) What should be the minimum refractive index n for this to be possible? **(1987 JEE)**

(b) For $n = 5/3$ is it possible to achieve this with the angle B equal to 30 degrees?

Sol. (a) Using geometry we can see that at P, angle of incidence $i_A = A$ and at Q, angle of incidence $i_B = B$

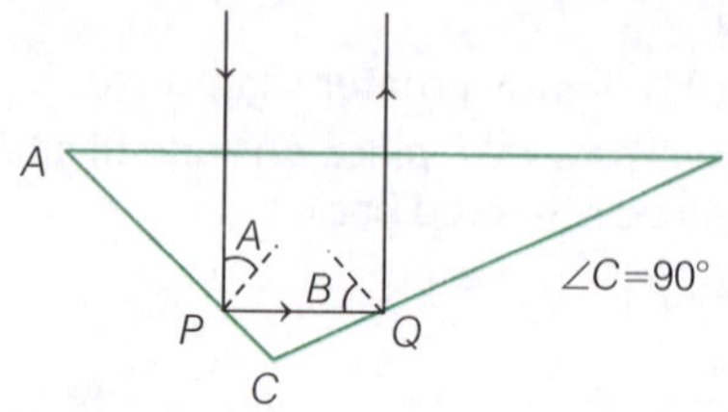

If TIR satisfies for the smaller angle of incidence than for larger angle of incidence TIR condition is automatically satisfied.

$$B \le A$$

If we take $B = 30°$ then $A = 60°$

So, $\theta_c \le 30° (i_A = 60°, i_B = 30°)$

For this let

RI is μ_1.

Now let i_B or $B = 40°$ then i_A or $A = 50°$

So, $\theta_c \le 40°$

For this let $R.I$ is μ_2.

Now $\mu_2 < \mu_1$

We have to find μ_{min}. So, fix i_A or $A = 45°$ and i_B or $B = 45°$.

So, $\theta_c = 45°$

In critical case, $\theta_c = 45°$

$\therefore \sin\theta_c = \dfrac{1}{\mu}$ or $\mu = \sqrt{2}$

Now keep μ slightly greater than $\sqrt{2}$. So that θ_c is slightly less than 45°. We have taken $A = B = 45°$ or $i_A = i_B = 45°$

Both i_A and $i_B > \theta_c$

So, TIR takes place at both points P and Q.

$\therefore$ Minimum value of μ is $\sqrt{2}$.

(b) For $\mu = \dfrac{5}{3}$, $\sin\theta_C = \dfrac{1}{\mu} = \sin^{-1}\left(\dfrac{3}{5}\right) \approx 37°$

If $B = 30°$, then $i_B = 30°$ and $A = 60°$

or $i_A = 60°$,

$i_A > \theta_C$ but $i_B < \theta_C$

i.e. TIR will take place at A but not at B.

Important POINTS

1. The sparkling of diamond is due to total internal reflection inside it.
2. **Mirage**
   - The mirage is caused by the **total internal reflection** of light at layers of air of different densities.
   - In a desert, the sand is very hot during day time and a result the layer of air in contact with it gets heated up and becomes lighter. The lighter air rises up and the denser air from above comes down.

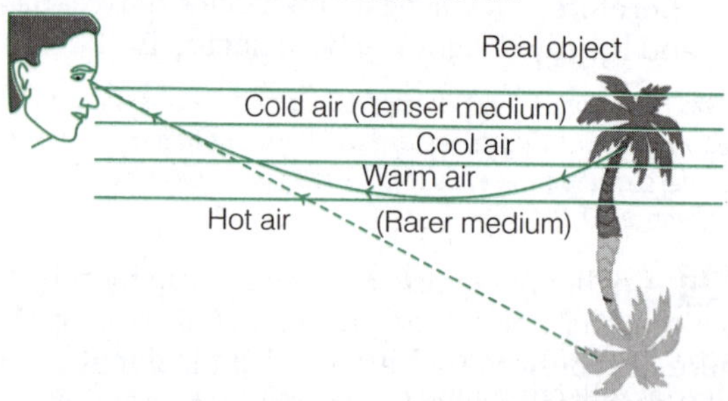

   - As a result, the successive upper layers are denser than those below them. A ray of light coming from a distant object, like the top a tree, gets **refracted** from a **denser to a rarer medium.**
   - Consequently, the **refracted ray bends away** from the **normal until**, at a particular layer, the light is incident at an **angle greater than the critical.**
   - At this stage, the incident ray suffers total internal reflection and is reflected upwards.
   - When this reflected beam of light enters the eyes of the observer, it appears as if an inverted image of the tree is seen and the sand looks like a pool of water.
3. **Looming**

   Looming is a kind of mirage observed in very cold regions in which distant object appears to be hanging mid way in the air. It is formed by the total internal reflection of light (in downward direction) caused by atmospheric refraction.

   Looming produces a virtual and erect image of an object above horizon where the warmer (optically rarer) air remains above the colder (optically denser) air in the atmosphere.

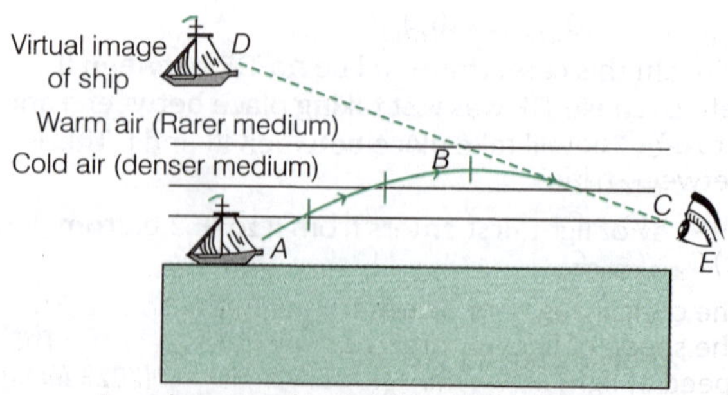

Looming caused by total internal reflection

MODULE 7 Exercise

Single Correct Option

1. An endoscope is employed by a physician to view the internal parts of body organ. It is based on the principle of
   (a) refraction
   (b) reflection
   (c) total internal reflection
   (d) dispersion

2. White light is incident on the interface of glass and air as shown in the figure. If green light is just totally internally reflected, then the emerging ray in air contains

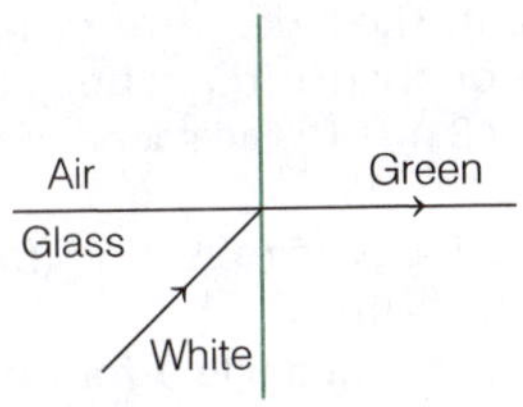

   (a) yellow, orange, red
   (b) violet, indigo, blue
   (c) all colours
   (d) all colours except green

3. In figure, the reflected ray B makes an angle 90° with the ray C. If i, r_1 and r_2 are the angles of incidence, reflection and refraction, respectively. Then, the critical angle of the medium is

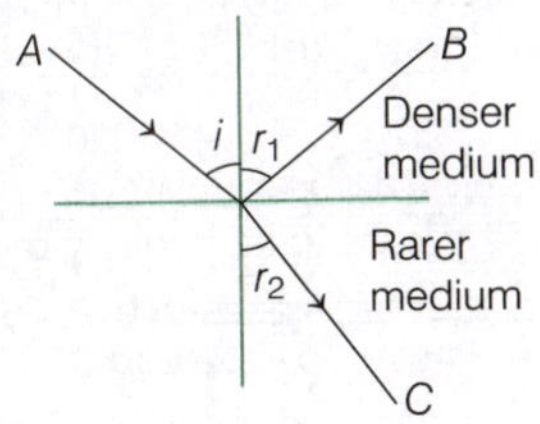

   (a) $\sin^{-1}(\tan i)$ (b) $\sin^{-1}(\cot i)$
   (c) r_1 (d) r_2

4. A, B and C are three optical media of respective critical angles C_1, C_2 and C_3 w.r.t. air. Total internal reflection of light can occur from A to B and also from B to C but not from C to A. Then, the correct relation between critical angles is
   (a) $C_1 > C_2 > C_3$ (b) $C_1 = C_2 = C_3$
   (c) $C_3 > C_1 > C_2$ (d) $C_1 < C_2 < C_3$

5. The critical angle for a denser-rarer interface is 45°. The speed of light in rarer medium is 3×10^8 m/s. The speed of light in the denser medium is **(2023 Main)**
   (a) 5×10^7 m/s (b) 2.12×10^8 m/s
   (c) $\sqrt{2} \times 10^8$ m/s (d) 3.12×10^7 m/s

6. Light travels in two media M_1 and M_2 with speeds 1.5×10^8 ms^{-1} and 2.0×10^8 ms^{-1} respectively. The critical angle between them is **(2022 Main)**
   (a) $\tan^{-1}\left(\frac{3}{\sqrt{7}}\right)$ (b) $\tan^{-1}\left(\frac{2}{3}\right)$
   (c) $\cos^{-1}\left(\frac{3}{4}\right)$ (d) $\sin^{-1}\left(\frac{2}{3}\right)$

7. The speed of light in media A and B are 2.0×10^{10} cm/s and 1.5×10^{10} cm/s respectively. A ray of light enters from the medium B to A at an incident angle θ. If the ray surffers total internal reflection, then **(2022 Main)**
   (a) $\theta = \sin^{-1}\left(\frac{3}{4}\right)$ (b) $\theta > \sin^{-1}\left(\frac{2}{3}\right)$
   (c) $\theta < \sin^{-1}\left(\frac{3}{4}\right)$ (d) $\theta > \sin^{-1}\left(\frac{3}{4}\right)$

8. A ray of light entering from air into a denser medium of refractive index 4/3, as shown in figure. The light ray suffers total internal reflection at the adjacent surface as shown. The maximum value of angle θ should be equal to **(2021 Main)**

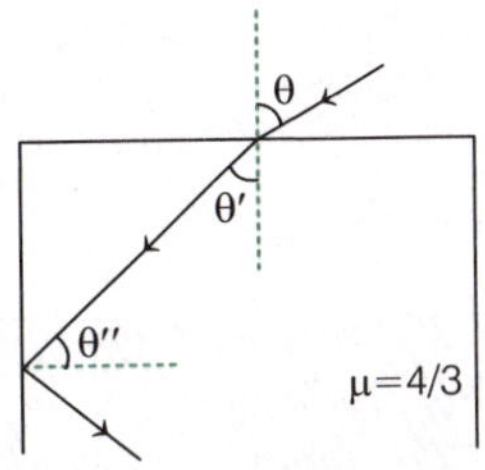

   (a) $\sin^{-1}\frac{\sqrt{7}}{3}$ (b) $\sin^{-1}\frac{\sqrt{5}}{4}$
   (c) $\sin^{-1}\frac{\sqrt{7}}{4}$ (d) $\sin^{-1}\frac{\sqrt{5}}{3}$

9. A transparent cube of side d, made of a material of refractive index μ_2, is immersed in a liquid of refractive index $\mu_1 (\mu_1 < \mu_2)$. A ray is incident on the face AB at an angle θ (shown in the figure). Total internal reflection takes place at point E on the face BC. Then, θ must satisfy **(2019 Main)**

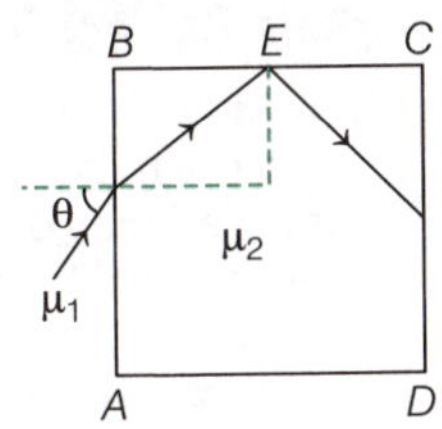

   (a) $\theta < \sin^{-1}\frac{\mu_1}{\mu_2}$ (b) $\theta > \sin^{-1}\sqrt{\frac{\mu_2^2}{\mu_1^2} - 1}$
   (c) $\theta < \sin^{-1}\sqrt{\frac{\mu_2^2}{\mu_1^2} - 1}$ (d) $\theta > \sin^{-1}\frac{\mu_1}{\mu_2}$

10. A light beam is travelling from Region I to Region IV (Refer Figure). The refractive index in Regions I, II, III and IV are $n_0, \frac{n_0}{2}, \frac{n_0}{6}$ and $\frac{n_0}{8}$, respectively. The angle of incidence θ for which the beam just misses entering Region IV is **(2008 JEE)**

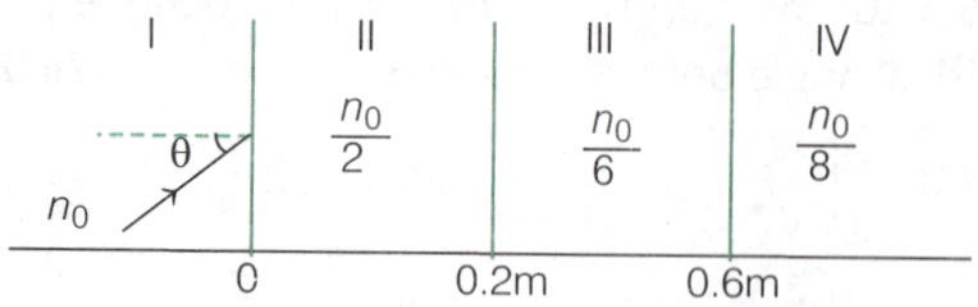

(a) $\sin^{-1}\left(\frac{3}{4}\right)$ (b) $\sin^{-1}\left(\frac{1}{8}\right)$

(c) $\sin^{-1}\left(\frac{1}{4}\right)$ (d) $\sin^{-1}\left(\frac{1}{3}\right)$

11. A ray of light travelling in water is incident on its surface open to air. The angle of incidence is θ, which is less than the critical angle. Then there will be **(2007 JEE)**

(a) only a reflected ray and no refracted ray
(b) only a refracted ray and no reflected ray
(c) a reflected ray and a refracted ray and the angle between them would be less than $180° - 2\theta$
(d) a reflected ray and a refracted ray and the angle between them would be greater than $180° - 2\theta$

12. White light is incident on the interface of glass and air as shown in the figure. If green light is just totally internally reflected then the emerging ray in air contains. **(2004 JEE)**

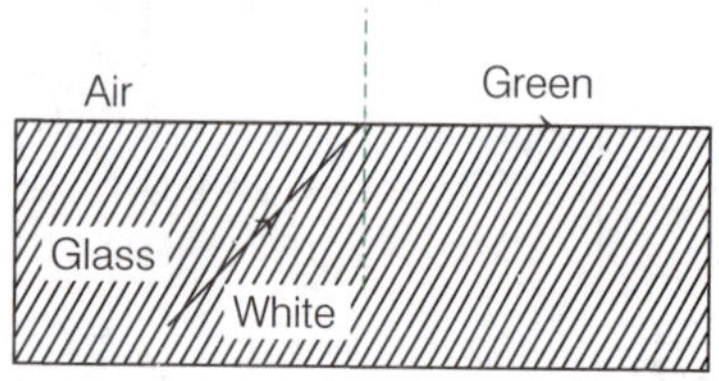

(a) yellow, orange, red (b) violet, indigo, blue
(c) all colours (d) all colours except green

Multiple Correct Options

13. A wide slab consisting of two media of refractive indices n_1 and n_2 is placed in air as shown in the figure. A ray of light is incident from medium n_1 to n_2 at an angle θ, where $\sin\theta$ is slightly larger than $1/n_1$. Take, refractive index of air as 1. Which of the following statement(s) is(are) correct? **(2021 Adv.)**

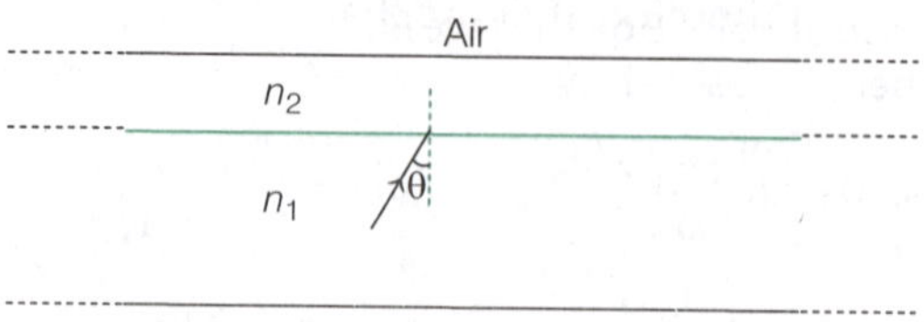

(a) The light ray enters air if $n_2 = n_1$
(b) The light ray is finally reflected back into the medium of refractive index n_1 if $n_2 < n_1$
(c) The light ray is finally reflected back into the medium of refractive index n_1 if $n_2 > n_1$
(d) The light ray is reflected back into the medium of refractive index n_1 if $n_2 = 1$

14. A ray of light travelling in a transparent medium falls on a surface separating the medium from air at an angle of incidence 45°. The ray undergoes total internal reflection. If n is the refractive index of the medium with respect to air, select the possible value (s) of n from the following **(1998 JEE)**

(a) 1.3 (b) 1.4
(c) 1.5 (d) 1.6

Subjective Questions

15. The laws of reflection or refraction are the same for sound and light. The index of refraction of a medium (for sound) is defined as the ratio of the speed of sound in air 343 m/s to the speed of sound in the medium.
(a) What is the index of refraction (for sound) of water ($v = 1498$ m/s)?
(b) What is the critical angle θ, for total reflection of sound from water?

16. Light is incident normally on the short face of a 30° - 60° - 90° prism. A liquid is poured on the hypotenuse of the prism. If the refractive index of the prism is $\sqrt{3}$, find the maximum refractive index of the liquid so that light is totally reflected.

17. In figure, light refracts from material 1 into a thin layer of material 2, crosses that layer, and then is incident at the critical angle on the interface between materials 2 and 3.

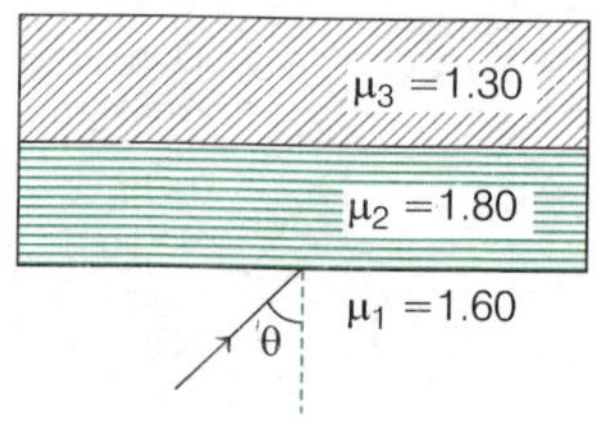

(a) What is the angle θ?
(b) If θ is decreased, is there refraction of light into material 3?

Answers

1. (c) **2.** (a) **3.** (a) **4.** (d) **5.** (b)
6. (a) **7.** (d) **8.** (a) **9.** (c) **10.** (b)
11. (c) **12.** (a) **13.** (b,c,d) **14.** (c,d)
15. (a) 0.229 (b) 13.2° **16.** 1.5
17. (a) $\theta = \sin^{-1}\left(\frac{13}{16}\right)$ (b) Yes

See hints on pages 158-161.

MODULE 8

Refraction Through Prism

A prism has two plane surfaces AB and AC inclined to each other as shown in figure. $\angle A$ is called the **angle of prism** or **refracting angle of prism.**

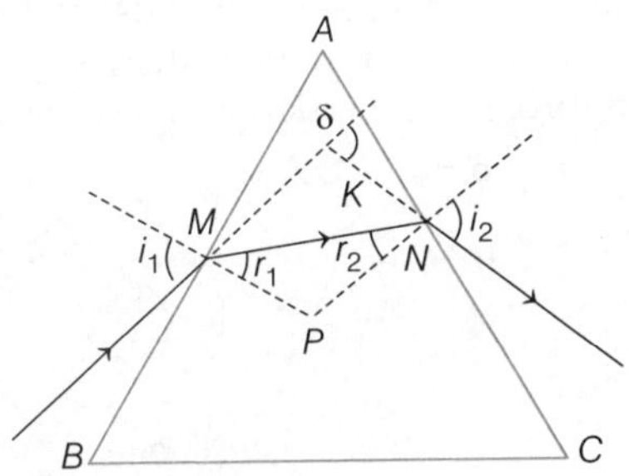

General Formulae

(i) In quadrilateral $AMPN$, $\angle AMP + \angle ANP = 180°$

$$\therefore \quad A + \angle MPN = 180° \qquad \text{...(i)}$$

In triangle MNP, $r_1 + r_2 + \angle MPN = 180°$ ...(ii)

From Eqs. (ii) and (iii), we have

$$\boxed{r_1 + r_2 = A} \qquad \text{...(iii)}$$

(ii) **Deviation** Deviation δ means angle between incident ray and emergent ray.

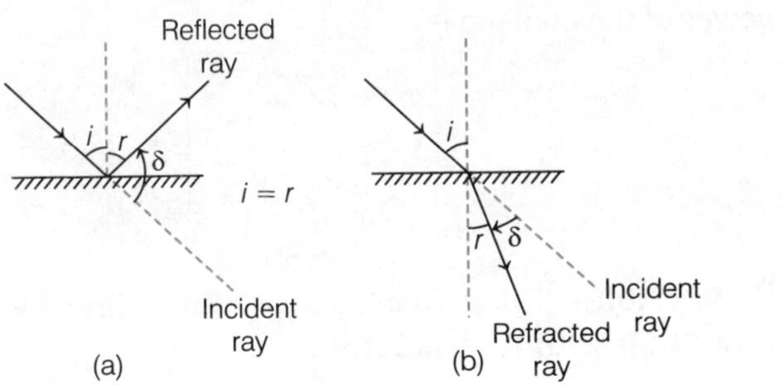

In reflection,

$$\delta = 180° - 2i = 180° - 2r$$

In refraction,

$$\delta = |i - r|$$

In prism, a ray of light gets refracted twice one at M and other at N. At M its deviation is $i_1 - r_1$ and at N it is $i_2 - r_2$. These two deviations are added as both are clockwise. So, the net deviation is

$$\delta = (i_1 - r_1) + (i_2 - r_2) = (i_1 + i_2) - (r_1 + r_2) = (i_1 + i_2) - A$$

Thus, $$\boxed{\delta = (i_1 + i_2) - A} \qquad \text{...(iv)}$$

(iii) **If A and i_1 are small** $\mu = \dfrac{\sin i_1}{\sin r_1}$.

Since i_1 is small, so r_1 is also small.

$\therefore \mu \approx \dfrac{i_1}{r_1}$ or $i_1 = \mu r_1$

Also, $A = r_1 + r_2$ and so if A and r_1 are small then r_2 and i_2 will also be small. From $\mu = \dfrac{\sin i_2}{\sin r_2}$, we can say $i_2 \approx \mu r_2$

Substituting these values in Eq. (iv), we have

$$\delta = (\mu r_1 + \mu r_2) - A$$
$$= \mu (r_1 + r_2) - A = \mu A - A$$

or $$\boxed{\delta = (\mu - 1)A} \qquad \text{...(v)}$$

This expression shows that all rays entering a small angle prism at small angles of incidence suffer the same deviation.

(iv) **Minimum deviation** It is found that the angle of deviation δ varies with the angle of incidence i_1 of the ray incident on the first refracting face of the prism. The variation is shown in figure and for one angle of incidence it has a minimum value δ_{min}. At this value, the ray passes symmetrically through the prism, i.e. the angle of emergence of the ray from the second face equals the angle of incidence of the ray on the first face.

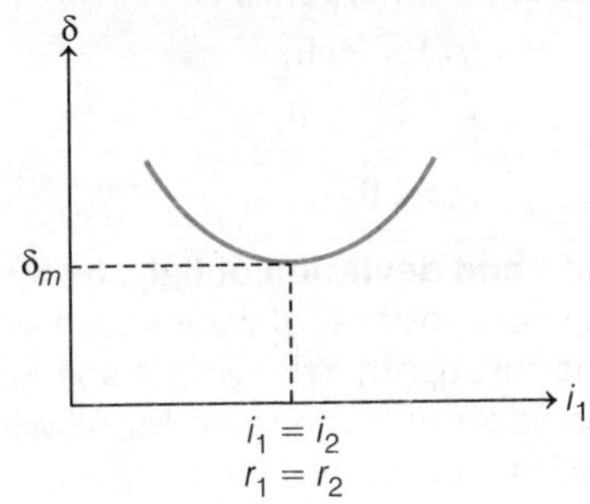

$$i_2 = i_1 = i \qquad \text{...(vi)}$$

It therefore, follows that

$$r_1 = r_2 = r \qquad \text{...(vii)}$$

From Eqs. (iii) and (vii), we get

$$r = \frac{A}{2}$$

and $$\delta = \delta_m = (i + i) - A$$

or $$i = \frac{A + \delta_m}{2} \qquad \text{...(viii)}$$

$$\therefore \quad \mu = \frac{\sin i}{\sin r} \quad \text{or} \quad \boxed{\mu = \frac{\sin\left(\frac{A+\delta_m}{2}\right)}{\sin\frac{A}{2}}} \quad \ldots(\text{ix})$$

Note *If a prism of refractive index* μ_P *is immersed in a liquid of refractive index* μ_L, *then:*

$$\boxed{{}_L\mu_P = \frac{\mu_P}{\mu_L} = \frac{\sin\left(\frac{A+\delta_m}{2}\right)}{\sin\left(\frac{A}{2}\right)}}$$

(v) **Condition of no emergence** In this section, we want to find the condition such that a ray of light entering the face AB does not come out of the face AC for any value of angle i_1, i.e. TIR takes place on AC

$$r_1 + r_2 = A$$

$$\therefore \quad r_2 = A - r_1$$

or $$(r_2)_{\min} = A - (r_1)_{\max} \quad \ldots(\text{x})$$

Now, r_1 will be maximum when i_1 is maximum and maximum value of i_1 can be 90°.

Hence, $$\mu = \frac{\sin(i_1)_{\max}}{\sin(r_1)_{\max}} = \frac{\sin 90^\circ}{\sin(r_1)_{\max}}$$

$$\therefore \quad \sin(r_1)_{\max} = \frac{1}{\mu} = \sin\theta_C$$

$$\therefore \quad (r_1)_{\max} = \theta_C$$

$\therefore$ From Eq. (x),

$$(r_2)_{\min} = A - \theta_C \quad \ldots(\text{xi})$$

Now, if minimum value of r_2 is greater than θ_C then obviously all values of r_2 will be greater than θ_C and TIR will take place under all conditions. Thus, the condition of no emergence is

$$(r_2)_{\min} > \theta_C$$

or $$A - \theta_C > \theta_C$$

or $$\boxed{A > 2\theta_C} \quad \ldots(\text{xii})$$

(vi) **Dispersion and deviation of light by a prism** White light is a superposition of waves with wavelengths extending throughout the visible spectrum. The speed of light in vacuum is the same for all wavelengths, but the speed in a material substance is different for different wavelengths. Therefore, the index of refraction of a material depends on wavelength. In most materials, the value of refractive index μ decreases with increasing wavelength.

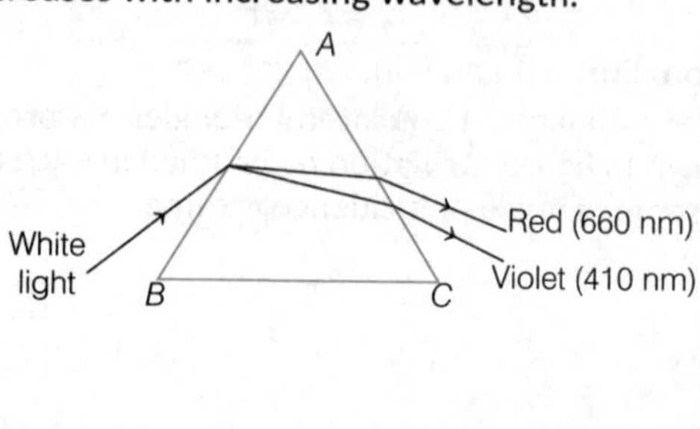

If a beam of white light, which contains all colours, is sent through the prism, it is separated into a spectrum of colours. The spreading of light into its colour components is called **dispersion.**

Dispersive Power

When a beam of white light is passed through a prism of transparent material, light of different wavelengths are deviated by different amounts. If δ_r, δ_y and δ_v are the deviations for red, yellow and violet components then average deviation is measured by δ_y as yellow light falls in between red and violet. $\delta_v - \delta_r$ is called **angular dispersion.** The **dispersive power** of a material is defined as the ratio of angular dispersion to the average deviation when a white beam of light is passed through it. It is denoted by ω As we know

$$\delta = (\mu - 1)A$$

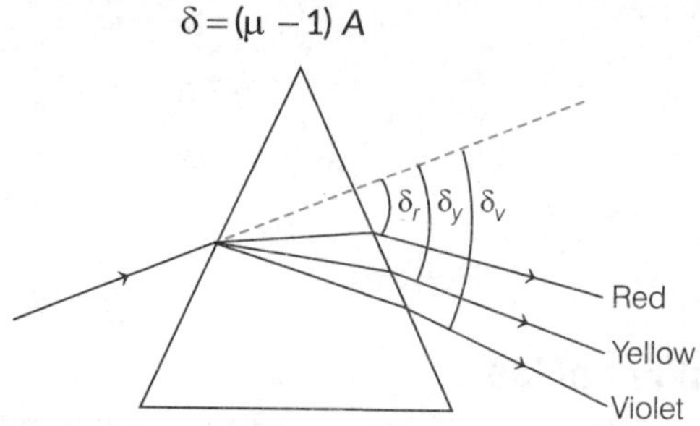

This equation is valid when A and i are small. Suppose, a beam of white light is passed through such a prism, the deviation of red, yellow and violet light are

$$\delta_r = (\mu_r - 1)A, \quad \delta_y = (\mu_y - 1)A$$

and $$\delta_v = (\mu_v - 1)A$$

The angular dispersion is $\delta_v - \delta_r = (\mu_v - \mu_r)A$ and the average deviation is $\delta_y = (\mu_y - 1)A$. Thus, the dispersive power of the medium is

$$\boxed{\omega = \frac{\delta_v - \delta_r}{\delta_y} = \frac{\mu_v - \mu_r}{\mu_y - 1}} \quad \ldots(\text{i})$$

Dispersion without Average Deviation and Average Deviation without Dispersion

Figure shows two prisms of refracting angles A and A' and dispersive powers ω and ω' respectively. They are placed in contact in such a way that the two refracting angles are reversed with respect to each other. A ray of light passes through the combination as shown. The deviations produced by the two prisms are

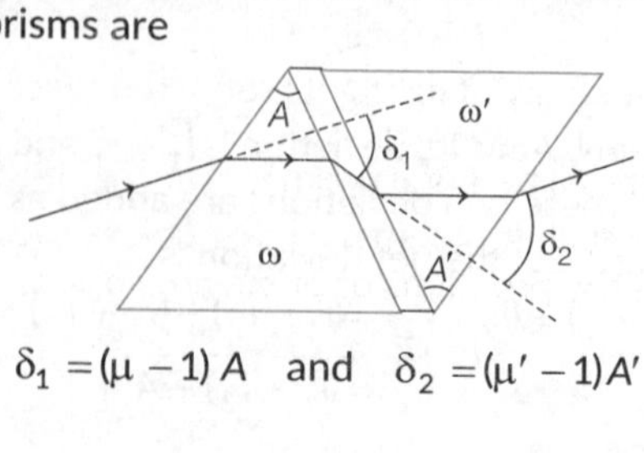

$$\delta_1 = (\mu - 1)A \quad \text{and} \quad \delta_2 = (\mu' - 1)A'$$

As the two deviations are opposite to each other, the net deviation is

$$\delta = \delta_1 - \delta_2 = (\mu - 1)A - (\mu' - 1)A' \quad ...(ii)$$

Using this equation, the average deviation produced by the combination if white light is passed is

$$\delta_y = (\mu_y - 1)A - (\mu'_y - 1)A' \quad ...(iii)$$

and the net angular dispersion is

$$\delta_v - \delta_r = (\mu_v - \mu_r)A - (\mu'_v - \mu'_r)A'$$

But, as $\mu_v - \mu_r = \omega(\mu_y - 1)$ from Eq. (i), we have

$$\delta_v - \delta_r = (\mu_y - 1)\,\omega A - (\mu'_y - 1)\,\omega' A' \quad ...(iv)$$

Dispersion without average deviation

From Eq. (iii),

$$\delta_y = 0 \text{ if}$$

$$\boxed{\frac{A}{A'} = \frac{\mu'_y - 1}{\mu_y - 1}} \quad ...(v)$$

This is the required condition of dispersion without average deviation. Using this in Eq. (iv), the net angular dispersion produced is

$$\delta_v - \delta_r = (\mu_y - 1)A\,(\omega - \omega')$$

Average deviation without dispersion

From Eq. (iv),

$$\delta_v - \delta_r = 0 \text{ if}$$

$$\boxed{\frac{A}{A'} = \frac{(\mu'_y - 1)\,\omega'}{(\mu_y - 1)\,\omega} = \frac{\mu'_v - \mu'_r}{\mu_v - \mu_r}} \quad ...(vi)$$

This is the required condition of average deviation without dispersion. Using the above condition in Eq. (iii), the net average deviation is

$$\delta_y = (\mu_y - 1)A\left(1 - \frac{\omega}{\omega'}\right)$$

Important Points in Prism

1. Equation $r_1 + r_2 = A$ can be applied at any of the three vertices. For example in the figure shown, $r_1 + r_2 = B$.

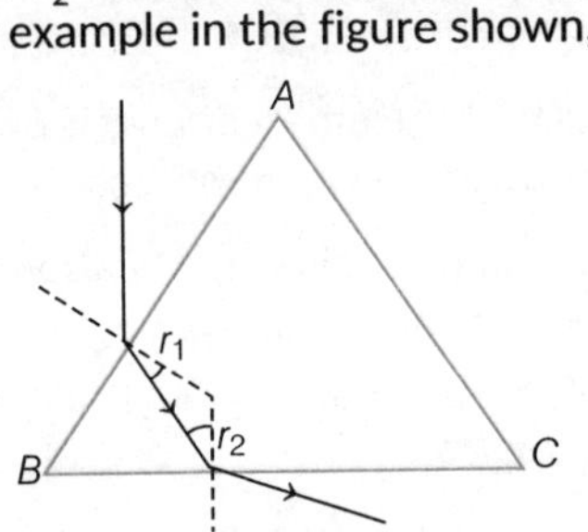

2. Sometimes a part of a prism is given as shown in figure (a). To solve such problems, first complete the prism then solve as the problems of prism are solved.

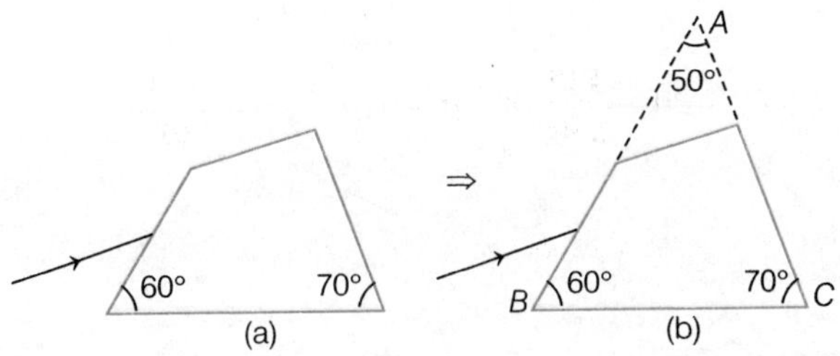

3. For isosceles or equilateral triangle ($\angle B = \angle C$), ray of light is parallel to base of the prism at minimum deviation condition.

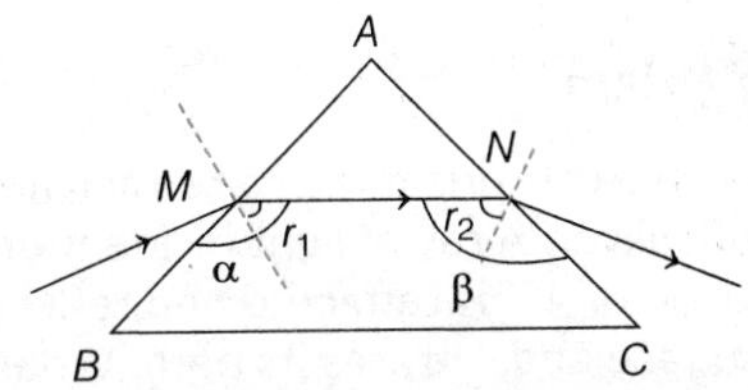

Under minimum deviation condition, we know that $r_1 = r_2 \Rightarrow \alpha = \beta$. Because, $\alpha = 90° + r_1$ and $\beta = 90° + r_2$. Further, it is given that $\angle B = \angle C$. Therefore, MN is parallel to BC.

4. In some cases, when deviation at M is clockwise and deviation at N is anti-clockwise, then

$$r_1 - r_2 = A$$

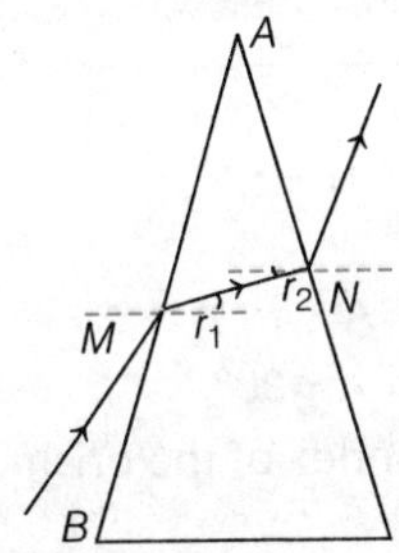

This condition is normally obtained with thin angle prisms as shown above.

At M, deviation is clockwise and at N deviation is anti-clockwise. In triangle AMN,

$$A + (90° - r_1) + (90° + r_2) = 180°$$

$$\therefore \quad r_1 - r_2 = A$$

5. In the ray diagram shown in figure, we can treat it like a prism ABC of $\angle A = 90°$

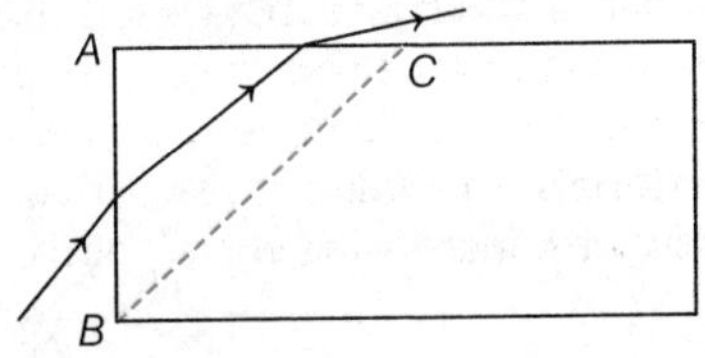

6. Different identical equilateral triangles are arranged as shown in figure. Deviation by prism(s) in each case will be same, if angle of incidence is same.

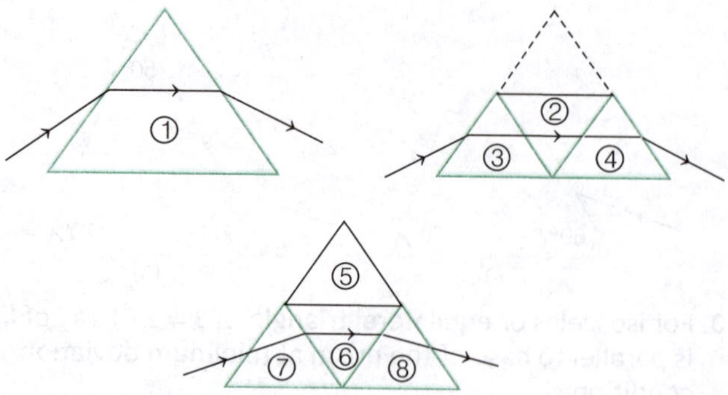

Examples of Prism

Example 1 One face of a prism with a refractive angle of 30° is coated with silver. A ray of light incident on another face at an angle of 45° is refracted and reflected from the silver coated face and retraces its path. What is the refractive index of the prism?

Sol.

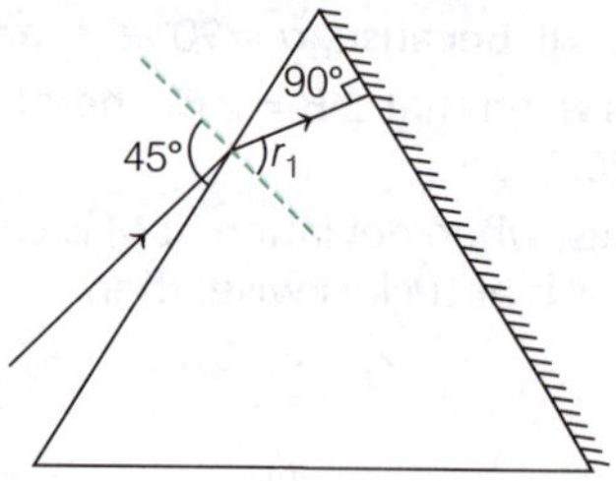

Given, $A = 30°$, $i_1 = 45°$

and $r_2 = 0$ (normal incidence)

Since, $r_1 + r_2 = A$

$\therefore$ $r_1 = A = 30°$

Now, refractive index of the prism,

$$\mu = \frac{\sin i_1}{\sin r_1} = \frac{\sin 45°}{\sin 30°} = \frac{\frac{1}{\sqrt{2}}}{\frac{1}{2}} = \sqrt{2}$$ **Ans.**

Example 2 In the shown figure, mirror is rotated by an angle θ. Find θ if

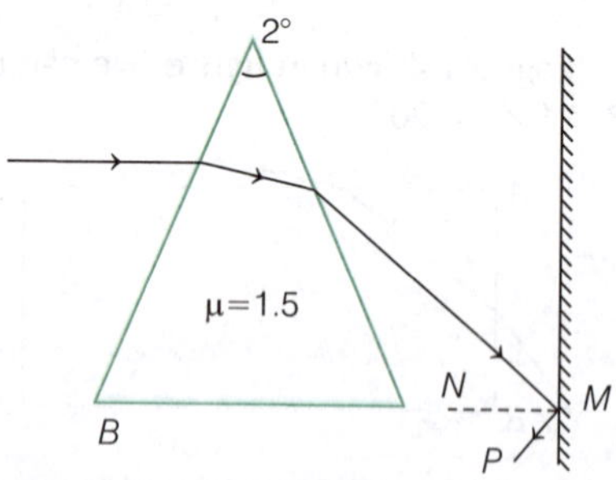

(a) ray of light retraces its path after reflection from M

(b) ray of light MP turns in the direction of MN.

Sol. In this case, A and i_1 are small. Therefore, deviation by prism can be obtained by

$$\delta = (\mu - 1)A = (1.5 - 1)(2°) = 1°$$

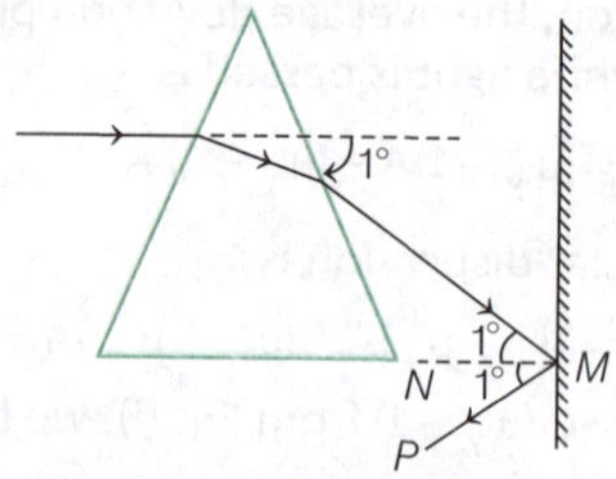

Hence, the prism will deviate the ray of light by 1° from its original path as shown in figure.

(a) In the absence of prism, ray of light was falling normal to the mirror. So, ray of light was already retracing its path. Prism has rotated the ray by 1° in clockwise direction. So if we rotate the mirror also by 1° in clockwise direction, then ray of light will further fall normal to the mirror and it again retraces its path. Therefore, the correct answer is

$$\theta = 1°, \text{ clockwise}$$ **Ans.**

(b) If we rotate a plane mirror by θ in clockwise direction, then reflected ray also rotates in clockwise direction by an angle 2θ.

Here, we have to rotate reflected ray MP by 1° in clockwise direction to make it in the direction of MN. Therefore, we will have to rotate the mirror by 0.5° in clockwise direction. Therefore, the correct answer is

$$\theta = 0.5°, \text{ clockwise}$$ **Ans.**

Example 3 A ray of light is incident at an angle of 60° on the face of a prism having refracting angle 30°. The ray emerging out of the prism makes an angle 30° with the incident ray. Show that the emergent ray is perpendicular to the face through which it emerges.

Sol. Given, $i_1 = 60°$, $A = 30°$ and $\delta = 30°$.

From the relation, $\delta = (i_1 + i_2) - A$

we have, $i_2 = 0$

This means that the emergent ray is perpendicular to the face through which it emerges. **Ans.**

Example 4 The angle of minimum deviation for a glass prism with $\mu = \sqrt{3}$ equals the refracting angle of the prism. What is the angle of the prism?

Sol. Given, $A = \delta_m$

Using, $$\mu = \frac{\sin\left(\frac{A + \delta_m}{2}\right)}{\sin\left(\frac{A}{2}\right)}$$

We have, $\sqrt{3} = \dfrac{\sin\left(\dfrac{A+A}{2}\right)}{\sin\left(\dfrac{A}{2}\right)}$

or $\sqrt{3} = \dfrac{\sin A}{\sin\left(\dfrac{A}{2}\right)} = \dfrac{2\sin\dfrac{A}{2}\cdot\cos\dfrac{A}{2}}{\sin\left(\dfrac{A}{2}\right)}$

$\therefore \cos\dfrac{A}{2} = \dfrac{\sqrt{3}}{2}$

$\therefore \dfrac{A}{2} = 30°$

or $A = 60°$ **Ans.**

Example 5 The refracting angle of a glass prism is 30°. A ray is incident onto one of the faces perpendicular to it. Find the angle δ between the incident ray and the ray that leaves the prism. The refractive index of glass is $\mu = 1.5$.

Sol. Given, $A = 30°, \mu = 1.5$ and $i_1 = 0°$

Since, $i_1 = 0°$, therefore, r_1 is also equal to 0°.

Further, since, $r_1 + r_2 = A$

$\therefore r_2 = A = 30°$

Using, $\mu = \dfrac{\sin i_2}{\sin r_2}$

We have, $1.5 = \dfrac{\sin i_2}{\sin 30°}$

or $\sin i_2 = 1.5 \sin 30°$

$= 1.5 \times \dfrac{1}{2} = 0.75$

$\therefore i_2 = \sin^{-1}(0.75) = 48.6°$

Now, the deviation, $\delta = (i_1 + i_2) - A$

$= (0 + 48.6) - 30$

or $\delta = 18.6°$ **Ans.**

Example 6 **General method of finding deviation by prism.**

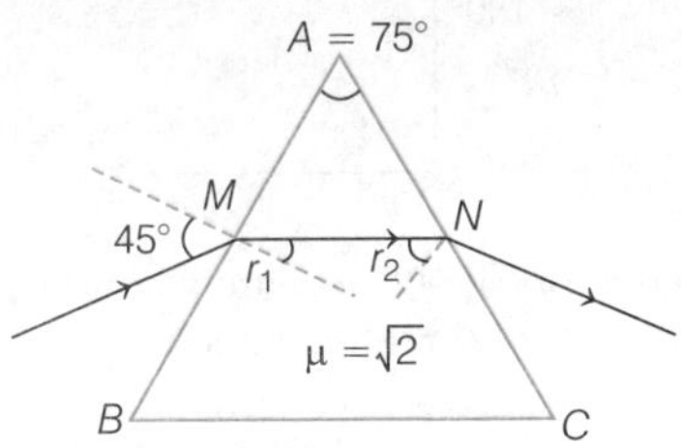

In the ray diagram shown in figure, find total deviation by prism.

Sol. Deviation by a prism is given by

$$\delta = (i_1 + i_2) - A \quad \text{...(i)}$$

Here, $i_1 = 45°$ and $A = 75°$

Therefore, the main objective is to find i_2 and this angle i_2 can be obtained under following three steps.

(i) Applying Snell's law at point M, we have

$\mu = \dfrac{\sin i_1}{\sin r_1}$ or $\sqrt{2} = \dfrac{\sin 45°}{\sin r_1}$

Solving this equation, we get $r_1 = 30°$

(ii) $r_1 + r_2 = A$

$\therefore 30° + r_2 = 75°$

$\therefore r_2 = 45°$

(iii) Further applying Snell's law at N,

$\mu = \dfrac{\sin i_2}{\sin r_2}$

$\Rightarrow \sqrt{2} = \dfrac{\sin i_2}{\sin 45°}$

Solving this equation, we get $i_2 = 90°$

Now, substituting the values in Eq. (i), we have

$\delta = 45° + 90° - 75°$

$= 60°$ **Ans.**

Example 7 **Based on the condition of no emergence from face AC**

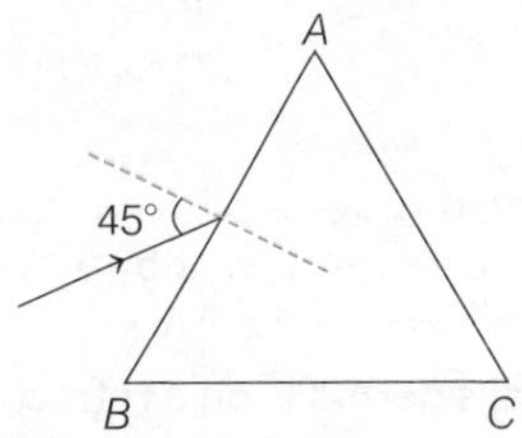

In the figure shown, if:

$A = 110°, B = 20°, C = 50°, i_1 = 45°$ and $\mu = \sqrt{2}$

then find the total deviation by prism.

Sol. $\theta_C = \sin^{-1}\left(\dfrac{1}{\mu}\right) = \sin^{-1}\left(\dfrac{1}{\sqrt{2}}\right) = 45°$

Here, $A > 2\theta_C$

Therefore, TIR will take place at AC and the ray of light emerges from the prism as shown in figure.

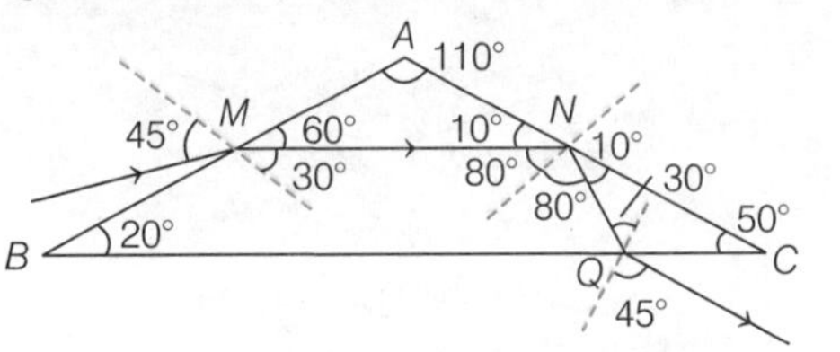

Applying, $\mu = \dfrac{\sin i}{\sin r}$ at M and Q, we can find the respective angles as shown in figure.

Now, deviation at M is clockwise, deviation at N is clockwise but deviation at Q is anti-clockwise.

$\therefore \delta_{Total} = \delta_M + \delta_N - \delta_Q$

$= (45° - 30°) + (180° - 2 \times 80°) - (45° - 30°)$

$= 20°$ **Ans.**

INTRODUCTORY Exercise

1. The prism shown in figure has a refractive index of 1.60 and the angles A are 30°. Two light rays P and Q are parallel as they enter the prism. What is the angle between them after they emerge? $[\sin^{-1}(0.8) = 53°]$

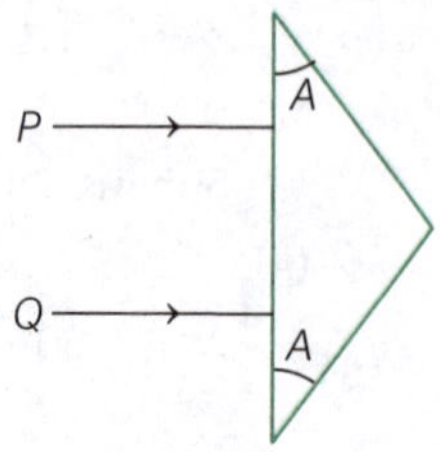

2. A glass vessel in the shape of a triangular prism is filled with water, and light is incident normally on the face xy. If the refractive indices for water and glass are 4/3 and 3/2 respectively, total internal reflection will occur at the glass-air surface xz only for $\sin\theta$ greater than

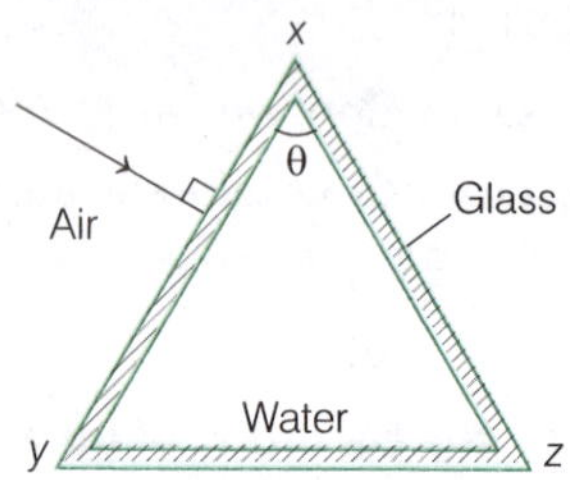

A 1/2 B 2/3
C 3/4 D 8/9
E 16/27.

3. A light ray going through a prism with the angle of prism 60°, is found to deviate at least by 30°. What is the range of the refractive index of the prism?

4. A ray of light falls normally on a refracting face of a prism. Find the angle of prism if the ray just fails to emerge from the prism ($\mu = 3/2$).

5. A ray of light is incident at an angle of 60° on one face of a prism which has an angle of 30°. The ray emerging out of the prism makes an angle of 30° with the incident ray. Show that the emergent ray is perpendicular to the face through which it emerges and calculate the refractive index of the material of prism.

6. A ray of light passing through a prism having refractive index $\sqrt{2}$ suffers minimum deviation. It is found that the angle of incidence is double the angle of refraction within the prism. What is the angle of prism?

7. Light is incident at an angle i on one planar end of a transparent cylindrical rod of refractive index μ. Find the least value of μ so that the light entering the rod does not emerge from the curved surface of the rod irrespective of the value of i.

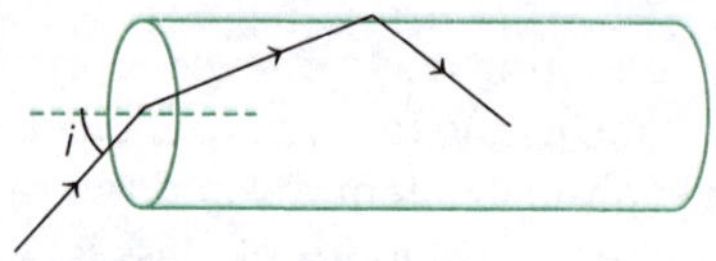

8. The refractive index of the material of a prism of refracting angle 45° is 1.6 for a certain monochromatic ray. What will be the minimum angle of incidence of this ray on the prism so that no TIR takes place as the ray comes out of the prism.

Answers

1. 45°	2. C	3. $\mu \le \sqrt{2}$	4. $A = \sin^{-1}\left(\frac{2}{3}\right)$
5. $\mu = \sqrt{3}$	6. $A = 90°$	7. $\mu \ge \sqrt{2}$	8. $\sin^{-1}(0.17)$

See hints on pages 161-162.

Important POINTS

Deviation

1. **In reflection** The deviation is given by

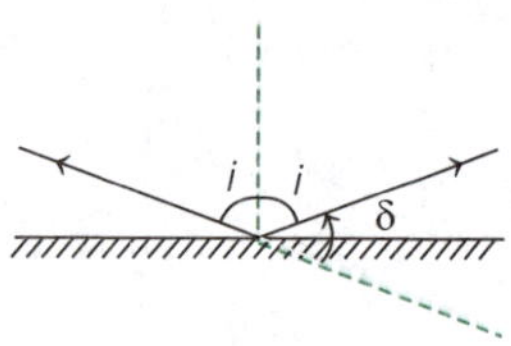

$$\delta = 180° - 2i$$

Therefore, δ *versus* i graph is a straight line.

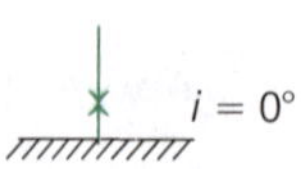

The range of i is from 0° to 90°.

At $i = 0°, \delta = 180°$

At $i = 90°, \delta = 0°$

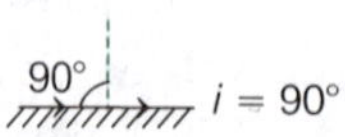

δ *versus* i graph is as shown below:

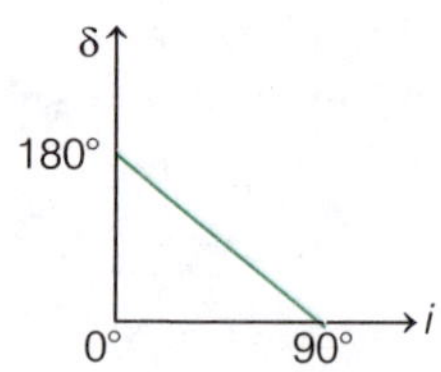

2. Two plane mirrors at 90°, deviate all rays by 180° from their original path after two reflections.

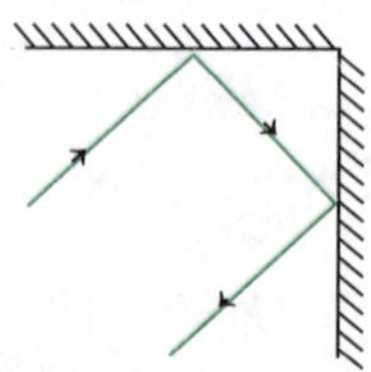

3. In refraction Deviation is given by

$$\boxed{\delta = i - r} \qquad \text{(where, } i > r\text{)}$$

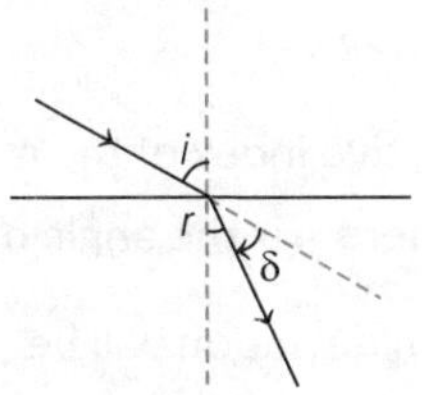

Note *(i) To plot δ versus i graph, first we will have to convert r into i with the help of Snell's law, otherwise there are three variables in the equation,*

$$\delta = i - r$$

(ii) In general, deviation in reflection is more than the deviation in refraction.

4. Deviation by a sphere after two refractions is

$$\delta = 2(i - r)$$

This can be proved as under :

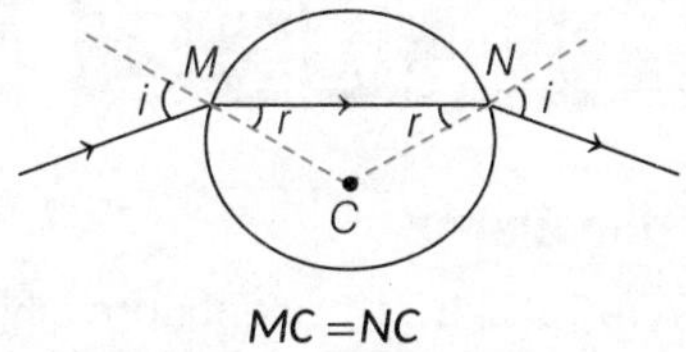

$MC = NC$

Therefore, both angles inside the sphere are same $(= r)$. Hence, angles outside the sphere will also be same $(= i)$. Deviation at M as well as N is clockwise.

$$\therefore \quad \delta = \delta_M + \delta_N = (i - r) + (i - r) \text{ or } \delta = 2(i - r)$$

5. Deviation by a prism

$$\boxed{\delta = (i_1 + i_2) - A}$$

If A and i_1 are small, then

$$\boxed{\delta \approx (\mu - 1)A}$$

Example 8 **Theory**

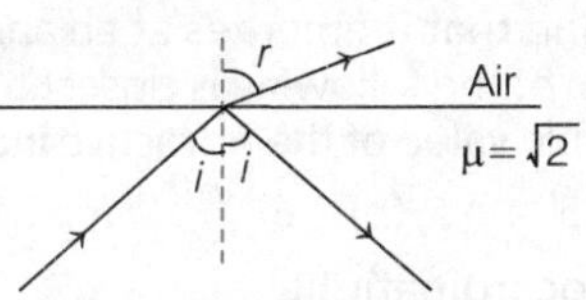

In the figure, i is increased from 0° to 90°. But ray of light is travelling from denser to rarer medium. Therefore, TIR will take place when $i > \theta_C$, where

$$\theta_C = \sin^{-1}\left(\frac{1}{\mu}\right) = \sin^{-1}\left(\frac{1}{\sqrt{2}}\right) = 45^\circ$$

From 0° – 45°, refraction and reflection both will take place. After 45°, only reflection will take place.

Question Plot δ *versus* i graph between incident ray and refracted ray, for $i \le 45^\circ$ and with reflected ray for $i \ge 45^\circ$.

Sol. For $i \le 45^\circ$

$$\delta = \delta_{\text{Refraction}} = r - i \qquad \text{(as } r > i\text{)}$$

Applying Snell's law, we have

$$\mu = \frac{\sin r}{\sin i} \quad \text{or} \quad \sqrt{2} = \frac{\sin r}{\sin i}$$

$$\therefore \quad r = \sin^{-1}(\sqrt{2} \sin i)$$

Substituting this value of r in the equation, we have

$$\delta = \sin^{-1}(\sqrt{2} \sin i) - i \qquad \ldots\text{(i)}$$

Now, variables are only two δ and i but this is not a known equation.

So, we can find some of the coordinates from where graph must pass.

At $i = 0^\circ$, $\delta = 0^\circ$

At $i = 45^\circ = \theta_C$, $\delta = 45^\circ$

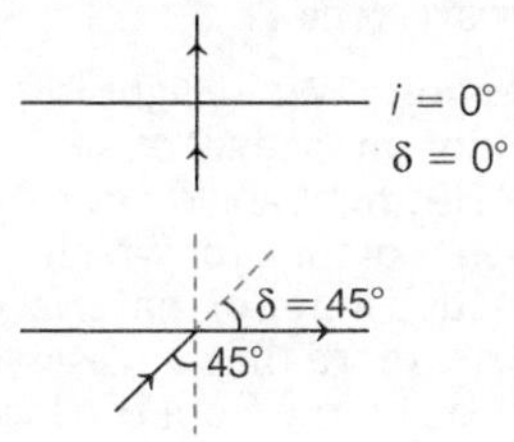

For $i \ge 45^\circ$

$$\delta = \delta_{\text{Reflection}}$$

$$\therefore \quad \delta = 180^\circ - 2i$$

Now, δ *versus* i graph is a straight line.

At $i = 45^\circ$, $\delta = 90^\circ$

At $i = 90^\circ$, $\delta = 0^\circ$

Now, δ *versus* i graph is as shown in figure.

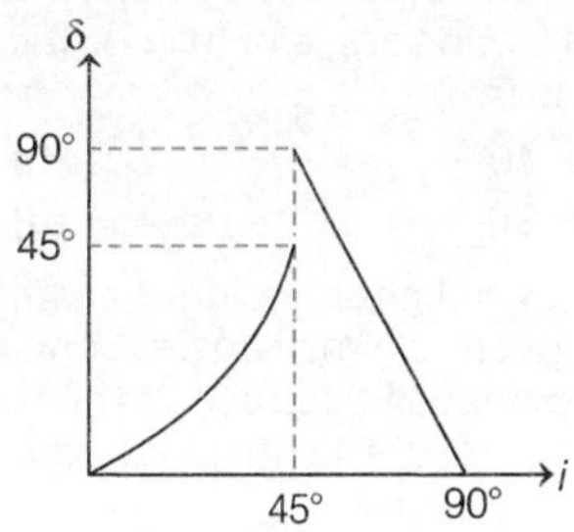

Note *At* $\quad i = 45^\circ = \theta_C$

$$\delta_{\text{Refraction}} = 45^\circ$$

but $\quad \delta_{\text{Reflection}} = 90^\circ$

This is because deviation in reflection is more than deviation in refraction.

MODULE 8 Exercise

Fill in the Blanks

1. A ray of light is incident normally on one of the faces of a prism of apex angle 30° and refractive index $\sqrt{2}$. The angle of deviation of the ray is ... degrees. **(1997 JEE)**

2. A ray of light undergoes deviation of 30° when incident on an equilateral prism of refractive index $\sqrt{2}$. The angle made by the ray inside the prism with the base of the prism is .... **(1992 JEE)**

True/False

3. A beam of white light passing through a hollow prism give no spectrum. **(1983 JEE)**

Assertion and Reason

See directions on page 11.

4. **Assertion :** White light is incident on face AB of an isosceles right angled prism as shown. Colours, for which refractive index of material of prism is more than 1.414, will be able to emerge from the face AC.

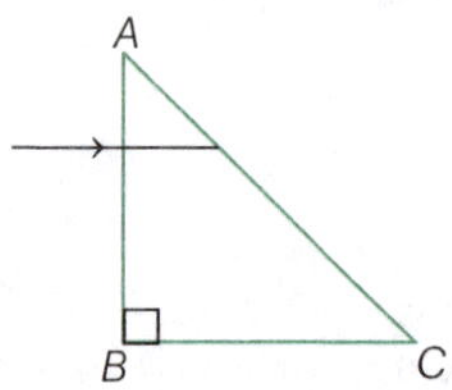

Reason : Total internal reflection cannot take place for the light travelling from a rarer medium to a denser medium.

Single Correct Option

5. A prism of apex angle $A = 60°$ has the refractive index $\mu = \sqrt{2}$. The angle of incidence for minimum deviation is

(a) 30° (b) 45°
(c) 60° (d) None of these

6. For no TIR to take place, a prism can have a maximum refracting angle of (θ_C = critical angle for the material of prism)

(a) 60° (b) θ_C
(c) $2\theta_C$ (d) slightly less than 180°

7. A ray of light is incident at small angle I on the surface of prism of small angle A and emerges normally from the opposite surface. If the refractive index of the material of the prism is μ, the angle of incidence is nearly equal to

(a) $\frac{A}{\mu}$ (b) $\frac{A}{2\mu}$ (c) μA (d) $\mu A/2$

8. For refraction through a small angled prism, the angle of minimum deviation

(a) increases with increase in refractive index of a prism
(b) will be 2δ for a ray of refractive index 2.4 if it is δ for a ray of refractive index 1.2
(c) is directly proportional to the angle of the prism
(d) will decrease with increase in refractive index of the prism

9. If the refractive index of the material of a prism is $\cot\left(\frac{A}{2}\right)$, where A is the angle of prism, then the angle of minimum deviation will be **(2024 Main)**

(a) $\pi - 2A$ (b) $\frac{\pi}{2} - A$ (c) $\pi - A$ (d) $\frac{\pi}{2} - 2A$

10. A monochromatic light is incident at a certain angle on an equilateral triangular prism and suffers minimum deviation. If the refractive index of the material of the prism is $\sqrt{3}$, then the angle of incidence is **(2019 Main)**

(a) 45° (b) 90° (c) 60° (d) 30°

11. In an experiment for determination of refractive index of glass of a prism by i-δ plot, it was found that a ray incident at an angle 35° suffers a deviation of 40° and that it emerges at an angle 79°. In that case, which of the following is closest to the maximum possible value of the refractive index? **(2016 Main)**

(a) 1.5 (b) 1.6 (c) 1.7 (d) 1.8

12. Monochromatic light is incident on a glass prism of angle A. If the refractive index of the material of the prism is μ, a ray incident at an angle θ, on the face AB would get transmitted through the face AC of the prism provided **(2015 Main)**

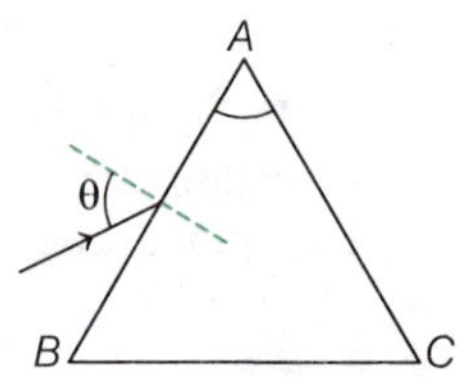

(a) $\theta < \cos^{-1}\left[\mu \sin\left\{A + \sin^{-1}\left(\frac{1}{\mu}\right)\right\}\right]$

(b) $\theta < \sin^{-1}\left[\mu \sin\left\{A - \sin^{-1}\left(\frac{1}{\mu}\right)\right\}\right]$

(c) $\theta > \cos^{-1}\left[\mu \sin\left\{A + \sin^{-1}\left(\frac{1}{\mu}\right)\right\}\right]$

(d) $\theta > \sin^{-1}\left[\mu \sin\left\{A - \sin^{-1}\left(\frac{1}{\mu}\right)\right\}\right]$

13. The graph between angle of deviation (δ) and angle of incidence (i) for a triangular prism is represented by **(2013 Main)**

(a)
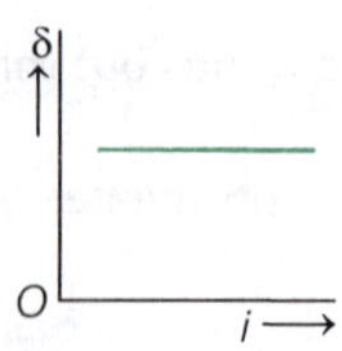

(b)
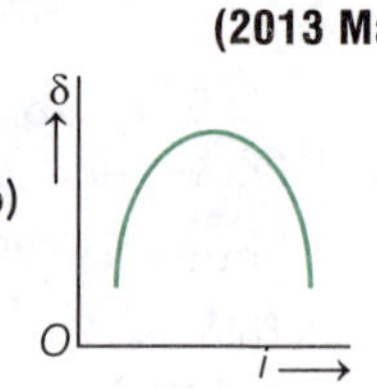

(c)
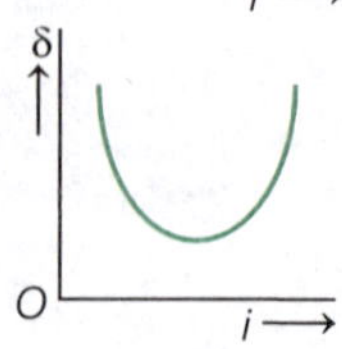

(d)
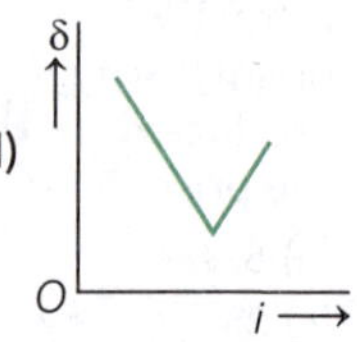

14. Two beams of red and violet colours are made to pass separately through a prism (angle of the prism is 60°). In the position of minimum deviation, the angle of refraction will be **(2008 JEE)**

(a) 30° for both the colours
(b) greater for the violet colour
(c) greater for the red colour
(d) equal but not 30° for both the colours

15. A ray of light is incident on an equilateral glass prism placed on a horizontal table. For minimum deviation which of the following is true? **(2004 JEE)**

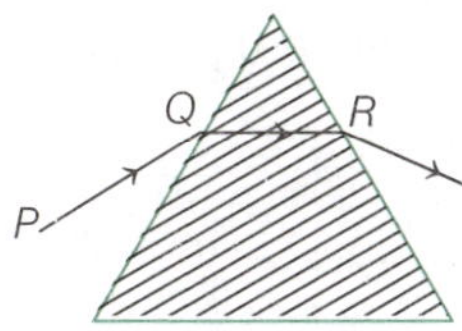

(a) PQ is horizontal (b) QR is horizontal
(c) RS is horizontal
(d) Either PQ or RS is horizontal

16. An isosceles prism of angle 120° has a refractive index 1.44. Two parallel rays of monochromatic light enter the prism parallel to each other in air as shown. The rays emerging from the opposite face **(1995 JEE)**

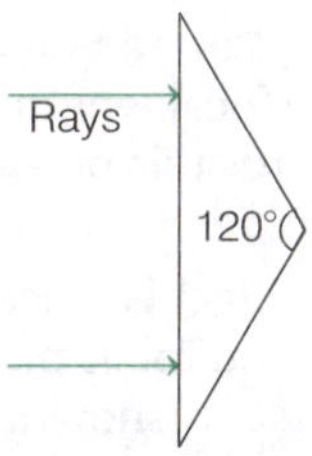

(a) are parallel to each other
(b) are diverging
(c) make an angle $2[\sin^{-1}(0.72) - 30°]$ with each other
(d) make an angle $2\sin^{-1}(0.72)$ with each other

17. A beam of light consisting of red, green and blue colours is incident on a right-angled prism. The refractive indices of the material of the prism for the above red, green and blue wavelengths are 1.39, 1.44 and 1.47 respectively. The prism will **(1989 JEE)**

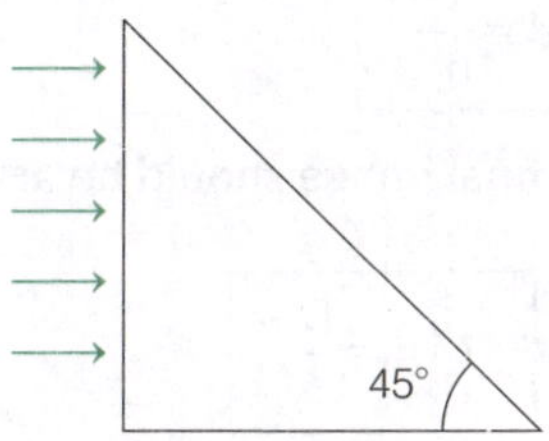

(a) separate the red colour from the green and blue colours
(b) separate the blue colour from the red and green colours
(c) separate all the three colours from one another
(d) not separate even partially any colour from the other two colours.

18. A thin prism P_1 with angle 4° and made from glass of refractive index 1.54 is combined with another thin prism P_2 made from glass of refractive index 1.72 to produce dispersion without deviation. The angle of the prism P_2 is **(1990 JEE)**

(a) 5.33° (b) 4°
(c) 3° (d) 2.6°

Subjective Questions

19. Light is incident from glass $\left(\mu_g = \frac{3}{2}\right)$ to water $\left(\mu_w = \frac{4}{3}\right)$. Find the range of the angle of deviation for refracted light.

20. In an equilateral prism of $\mu = 1.5$, the condition for minimum deviation is fulfilled. If face AC is polished

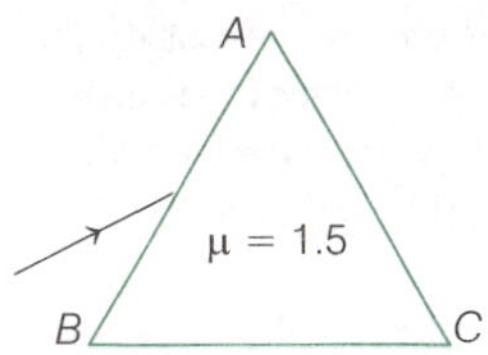

(a) Find the net deviation.
(b) If the system is placed in water what will be the net deviation for same angle of incidence? Refractive index of water $= \frac{4}{3}$.

Integer Type Questions

21. The refractive index of a transparent liquid filled in an equilateral hollow prism is $\sqrt{2}$. The angle of minimum deviation for the liquid will be .... **(2023 Main)**

22. A thin prism of angle 6° and refractive index for yellow light (n_Y) 1.5 is combined with another prism of angle 5° and $n_Y = 1.55$. The combination produces no dispersion. The net average deviation (δ) produced by the combination is $\left(\frac{1}{x}\right)^\circ$. The value of x is **(2022 Main)**

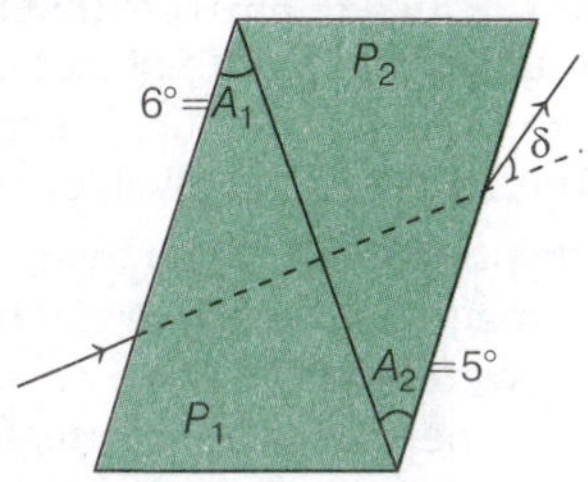

23. A deviation of 2° is produced in the yellow ray when prism of crown and flint glass are achromatically combined. Taking dispersive powers of crown and flint glass as 0.02 and 0.03 respectively and refractive index for yellow light for these glasses are 1.5 and 1.6, respectively. The refracting angles for crown glass prism will be ......° (in degree).
(Round off to the nearest integer) **(2021 Main)**

Answers

1. (15)	**2.** Zero	**3.** (True)	**4.** (d)	**5.** (b)
6. (c)	**7.** (c)	**8.** (a)	**9.** (a)	**10.** (c)
11. (a)	**12.** (d)	**13.** (c)	**14.** (a)	**15.** (b)
16. (c)	**17.** (a)	**18.** (c)	**19.** 0 to $\cos^{-1}(8/9)$	
20. (a) 157.2° (b) 157.2°		**21.** (30)	**22.** (4)	**23.** (12)

See hints on pages 162-166.

MODULE 9

Optical Instruments

Optical instruments are used to assist the eye in viewing an object. Our eye lens has a power to adjust its focal length to see the nearer objects. This process of adjusting focal length is called accommodation. However, if the object is brought too close to the eye, the focal length cannot be adjusted to form the image on the retina. Thus, there is a minimum distance for the clear vision of an object. This distance is called **least distance of distinct vision (+D).** For normal eye this distance is generally taken to be 25 cm.

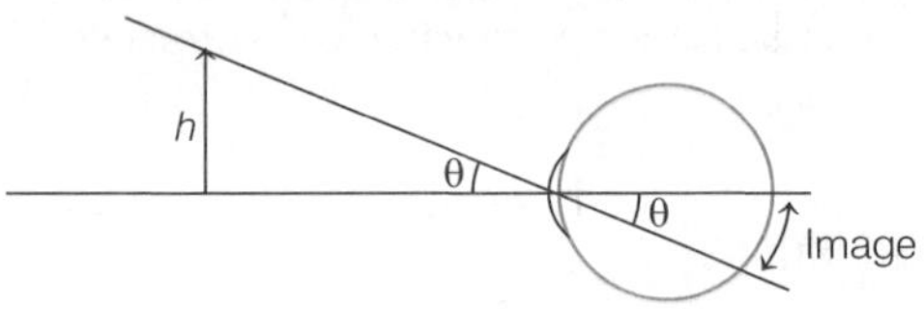

Visual angle The size of an object as sensed by us is related to the size of the image formed on the retina.

The size of the image on the retina is roughly proportional to the angle subtended by the object on the eye. This angle is known as the visual angle. Optical instruments are used to increase this angle artificially in order to improve the clarity.

Magnifying power (*M*) Magnifying power is the factor by which the image on the retina can be enlarged by using the microscope or telescope. For a microscope and for a telescope the definition of *M* is slightly different.

For a microscope, M

$$= \frac{\text{Visual angle formed by final image}}{\text{Visual angle formed by the object when kept at distance } D}$$

For a telescope, M

$$= \frac{\text{Visual angle formed by final image}}{\text{Visual angle subtended by the object directly when seen from naked eye}}$$

Note that M is different from linear magnification $m\left(=\pm\frac{v}{u}\right)$ which is the ratio of height of image to that of object while M is the ratio of apparent increase in size of image seen by the eye. Unit of M is X, thus we write an angular magnification of 10 as 10X.

Simple microscope To view an object with naked eyes, the object must be placed between D and infinity. The maximum angle is subtended when it is placed at D.

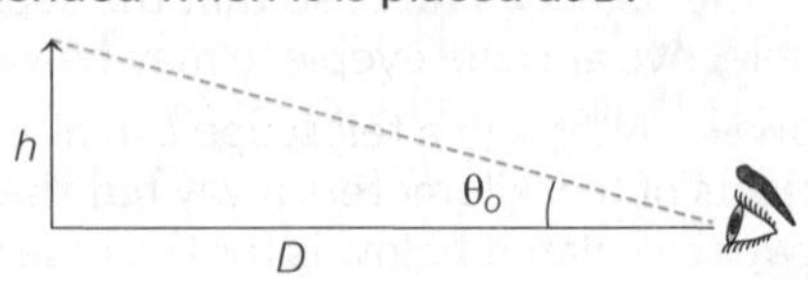

Say this angle is θ_o. Then, $\theta_o = \frac{h}{D}$

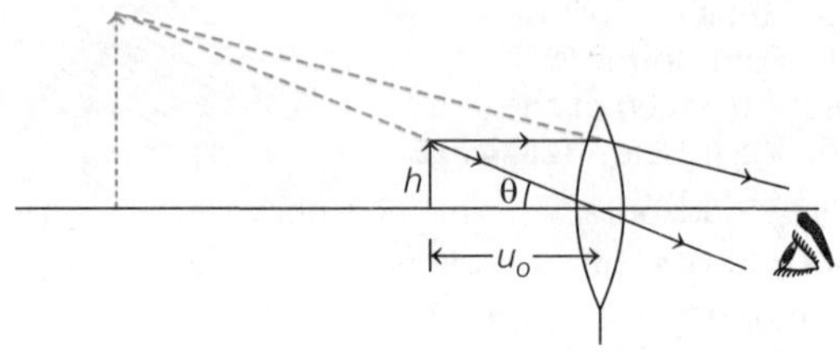

This angle can be further increased if a converging lens of short focal length is placed just in front of the eye. The lens used for this purpose is called simple microscope or a magnifier.

The object is placed at a distance u_o from the lens (between pole and focus of lens). The virtual magnified image is formed as shown. This image subtends a visual angle say θ on the eye. Then,

$$\boxed{\theta = \frac{h}{u_o}}$$

From the definition of magnifying power for a microscope,

$$M = \frac{\theta}{\theta_o} = \frac{h/u_o}{h/D}$$

$$\therefore \qquad \boxed{M = \frac{D}{u_o}}$$

For relaxed eye The final image should be at infinity. Thus, $u_o = f$

$$\therefore \qquad \boxed{M_\infty = \frac{D}{f}}$$

This is also called magnifying power for normal adjustment. We can see that $M_\infty > 1$ if $f < D$.

Magnifying power when final image is at *D* Suppose, the final virtual image is formed at a distance D. Then, from the equation $\frac{1}{v} - \frac{1}{u} = \frac{1}{f}$,

we have

$$\frac{1}{-D} + \frac{1}{u_o} = \frac{1}{f} \quad \text{or} \quad \frac{1}{u_o} = \frac{1}{D} + \frac{1}{f}$$

Substituting this value in the equation, $M = \frac{D}{u_o}$, we have

$$M_D = 1 + \frac{D}{f}$$

Note (i) *That $M_D > M_\infty$, i.e. when final image is formed at 25 cm, angular magnification is increased but eye is most strained. On the other hand when final image is at infinity, angular magnification is slightly less but eye is relaxed. So, the choice is yours whether you want to see bigger size with strained eye or smaller size with relaxed eye.*

(ii) *That M can be increased by decreasing f, but due to several other aberrations the image becomes too defective at large magnification with a simple microscope. Roughly speaking a magnification upto 4 is trouble free.*

Compound Microscope Figure shows a simplified version of a compound microscope. It consists of two converging lenses arranged coaxially. The one facing the object is called objective and the one close to eye is called eyepiece. The objective has a smaller aperture and smaller focal length than those of the eyepiece.

The separation between the objective and the eyepiece (called the length of the microscope *L*) can be varied by appropriate screws fixed on the panel of microscope.

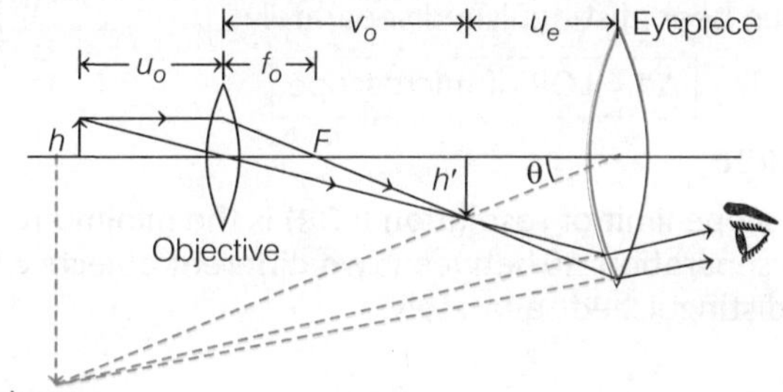

The object is placed beyond first focus of objective, so that an inverted and real image (intermediate image) is formed by the objective. This intermediate image acts as an object for the eyepiece and lies between first focus and pole of eye piece. The final magnified virtual image is formed by the eyepiece. Let θ be the angle subtended by the final image on the eye, then,

$$\theta = \frac{h'}{u_e}$$

Here, *h'* is the height of the first image and u_e is its distance from the eyepiece.

Further $$\theta_o = \frac{h}{D}$$

∴ Magnifying power of the compound microscope will be

$$M = \frac{\theta}{\theta_o} = \frac{h'}{u_e} \times \frac{D}{h} = \left(\frac{h'}{h}\right)\left(\frac{D}{u_e}\right)$$

Here, $\frac{h'}{h}$ is the linear magnification by the objective. Thus,

$$\frac{h'}{h} = |m_0| = \frac{v_0}{u_0}$$

∴ $$\boxed{M = \frac{v_0}{u_0}\left(\frac{D}{u_e}\right)}$$

Length of the microscope will be

$$\boxed{L = v_0 + u_e}$$

For relaxed eye For relaxed eye final image should be at infinity. Or,

$$\boxed{u_e = f_e \quad \therefore \quad M_\infty = \frac{v_0}{u_0}\frac{D}{f_e}}$$

and $$\boxed{L_\infty = v_0 + f_e}$$

Final image at *D* When the final image (by eyepiece) is formed at *D*. Then, by the formula $\frac{1}{v} - \frac{1}{u} = \frac{1}{f}$ we have

$$\frac{1}{-D} + \frac{1}{u_e} = \frac{1}{f_e}$$

∴ $$\frac{1}{u_e} = \frac{1}{D} + \frac{1}{f_e}$$

or $$u_e = \frac{Df_e}{D + f_e}$$

Thus, $$M_D = \frac{v_0}{u_0}\left(1 + \frac{D}{f_e}\right)$$

and $$L_D = v_0 + \frac{Df_e}{D + f_e}$$

Telescopes A microscope is used to view the objects placed close to it. To look at distant objects such as a star, a planet or a distant tree etc., we use telescopes. There are three types of telescopes in use.

(i) Astronomical telescope,

(ii) Terrestrial telescope and

(iii) Galilean telescope.

Questions are asked only from astronomical telescope. So, we are discussing only astronomical telescope.

Astronomical telescope Figure shows the construction and working of an astronomical telescope.

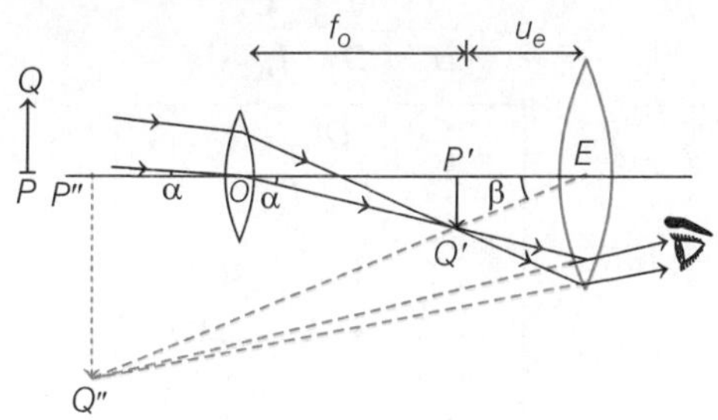

It consists of two converging lenses placed coaxially. The one facing the distant object is called the objective and has a large aperture and large focal length. The other is called the eyepiece, as the eye is placed close to it. The eyepiece tube can slide within the objective tube, so that the separation between the objective and the eyepiece may be varied.

Magnifying power Although a telescope can also be used to view the objects of few kilometers away but the magnifying power calculated below is for the case when object is at infinity. Rays coming from the object in that case will be almost parallel.

The image formed by objective will be at its second focus. This image called the intermediate image will act as the object for eyepiece. This usually lies between pole and first focus of eyepiece. So that eyepiece forms a virtual and magnified image of it.

$|\alpha|$ = angle subtended by object on objective (or you can say at eye)

$$= \frac{P'Q'}{f_o}$$

$|\beta|$=angle subtended by final image at eyepiece (or at eye)

$$= \frac{P'Q'}{u_e}$$

From the definition of magnifying power (for telescope),

$$M = \frac{|\beta|}{|\alpha|} = \frac{f_o}{u_e}$$

or

$$\boxed{M = \frac{f_o}{u_e}}$$

and length of telescope,

$$\boxed{L = f_o + u_e}$$

For relaxed eye For relaxed eye, intermediate image should lie at first focus of eyepiece or

$$u_e = f_e$$

$$\therefore \quad \boxed{M_\infty = \frac{f_o}{f_e} \quad \text{and} \quad L_\infty = f_o + f_e}$$

Final image at D When the final image is at D, then using the formula $\frac{1}{v} - \frac{1}{u} = \frac{1}{f}$ for eyepiece we have,

$$\frac{1}{-D} + \frac{1}{u_e} = \frac{1}{f_e}$$

$$\therefore \quad \frac{1}{u_e} = \frac{1}{D} + \frac{1}{f_e}$$

or

$$u_e = \frac{Df_e}{D + f_e}$$

Therefore,

$$M_D = \frac{f_o}{f_e}\left(1 + \frac{f_e}{D}\right)$$

and

$$L_D = f_o + \frac{Df_e}{D + f_e}$$

Note *(i) In all above formulae of M, we are considering only the magnitude of M.*

(ii) For telescopes, formulae have been derived when the object is at infinity. For the object at some finite distance different formulae will have to be derived.

(iii) Given below are formulae derived above of M and L in tabular form.

Table

Name of optical instruments	M	L	M_∞	M_D	L_∞	L_D
Simple microscope	$\frac{D}{u_o}$	—	$\frac{D}{f}$	$1 + \frac{D}{f}$	—	—
Compound microscope	$\frac{v_o}{u_o}\frac{D}{u_e}$	$v_o + u_e$	$\frac{v_o}{u_o}\frac{D}{f_e}$	$\frac{v_o}{u_o}\left(1 + \frac{D}{f_e}\right)$	$v_o + f_e$	$v_o + \frac{Df_e}{D + f_e}$
Astronomical telescope	$\frac{f_o}{u_e}$	$f_o + u_e$	$\frac{f_o}{f_e}$	$\frac{f_o}{f_e}\left(1 + \frac{f_e}{D}\right)$	$f_o + f_e$	$f_o + \frac{Df_e}{D + f_e}$

Limit of Resolution (LOR)

Microscope

For micriscope limit of resolution (LOR) is defined as the minimum distance Δd between two objects which can been distinguished separately

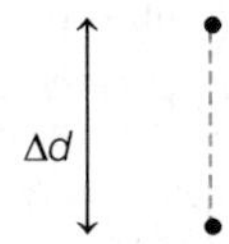

$$\boxed{\Delta d = \text{LOR of microscope}}$$

Telescope

For telescope limit of resolution (LOR) is the minimum angular separation $\Delta\theta$ between two different objects which can be distinguished separately.

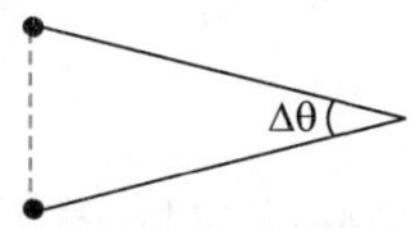

$$\boxed{\Delta\theta = \text{LOR of telescope}}$$

Resolving Power (R)

(i) Resolving power (R) is reciprocal of LOR.

(ii) LOR should be small and R should be large. The greater the value of R, the smaller the minimum distance Δd.

Microscope

$$\boxed{R = \frac{1}{\text{LOR}} = \frac{1}{\Delta d} = \frac{\mu \sin\theta}{0.61\,\lambda} = \frac{(\text{N.A})}{0.61\,\lambda}}$$

Here μ is the refractive index between the object and the objective and the angle θ is the angle subtended by a radius of the objective on one of the objects. $\mu \sin\theta$ is called numerical aperture (N.A).

Note *(i) For increasing resolving power of a microscope, electron microscope is used. In electron microscope small de-Broglie wavelength of an electron is used which is given by the following formula,*

$$\boxed{\lambda\,(\text{in } A^\circ) = \sqrt{\frac{150}{V\,(\text{in volt})}}}$$

Here V is the potential difference by which electron is accelerated.

(ii) In the above formula we have seen that $R \propto \mu$. Therefore some oil is used between object and objective

Telescope

$$R = \frac{1}{\Delta\theta} = \frac{a}{1.22\,\lambda}$$

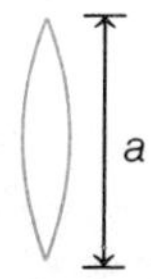

Here a is the diameter of the objective. Since $R \propto a$, that is why, telescopes with larger objective aperture are used.

Note *Distant objects are seen with the help of telescopes. So, after finding LOR or $\Delta\theta$ we can also find minimum distance Δd between two objects which can be distinguished. separately.*

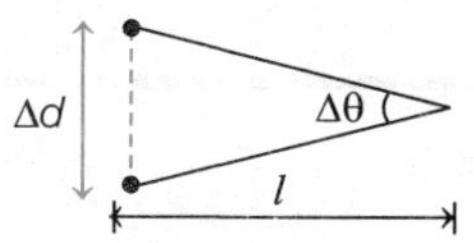

$$\Delta d = l\,(\Delta\theta)$$

Here l is the distance between earth (if telescope is kept on earth) and moon (if two objects are on moon)

Example 1 The value of numerical aperature of the objective lens of a microscope is 1.25. If light of wavelength 5000 Å is used, the minimum separation between two points, to be seen as distinct, will be

(a) 0.48 μm (b) 0.38 μm (c) 0.24 μm (d) 0.12 μm

Sol. For a microscope,

$$R = \frac{1}{\Delta d} = \frac{(\text{N.A})}{0.61\,\lambda}$$

$$\therefore \quad \Delta d = \frac{0.61\,\lambda}{(\text{N.A})} = \frac{0.61 \times 5 \times 10^{-7}}{1.25}$$

$$= 0.24 \times 10^{-6}\ \text{m} = 0.24\ \mu\text{m}$$

∴ The correct option is (c).

Example 2 An astronomical telescope has an angular magnification of magnitude 5 for distant objects. The separation between the objective and eyepiece is 36 cm and the final image is formed at infinity. Determine the focal length of objective and eyepiece.

Sol. For final image at infinity,

$$M_\infty = \frac{f_o}{f_e} \quad \text{and} \quad L_\infty = f_o + f_e$$

$$\therefore \quad 5 = \frac{f_o}{f_e} \qquad \text{...(i)}$$

$$\text{and} \quad 36 = f_o + f_e \qquad \text{...(ii)}$$

Solving these two equations, we have

$f_o = 30$ cm and $f_e = 6$ cm **Ans.**

Example 3 A telescope has an objective of focal length 50 cm and an eyepiece of focal length 5 cm. The least distance of distinct vision is 25 cm. The telescope is focused for distinct vision on a scale 2 m away from the objective. Calculate (a) magnification produced and (b) separation between objective and eyepiece.

Sol. Given, $f_o = 50$ cm and $f_e = 5$ cm

Note *Here, object is placed at finite distance from the objective. Hence, formulae derived for angular magnification M cannot be applied directly as they have been derived for the object to be at infinity. Here, it will be difficult to find angular magnification. So, only linear magnification can be obtained.*

For objective $\frac{1}{v_o} - \frac{1}{-200} = \frac{1}{50}$

$$\therefore \quad v_o = \frac{200}{3}\ \text{cm}$$

$$m_o = \frac{v_o}{u_o} = \frac{(200/3)}{-200} = -\frac{1}{3}$$

For eyepiece $\frac{1}{-25} - \frac{1}{u_e} = \frac{1}{5}$

$$\therefore \quad u_e = -\frac{25}{6}\ \text{cm}$$

$$\text{and} \quad m_e = \frac{v_e}{u_e} = \frac{-25}{-(25/6)} = 6$$

(a) Magnification, $m = m_o \times m_e = -2$ **Ans.**

(b) Separation between objective and eyepiece,

$$L = v_o + |u_e| = \frac{200}{3} + \frac{25}{6} = \frac{425}{6} = 70.83\ \text{cm} \qquad \textbf{Ans.}$$

Example 4 The focal lengths of the objective and the eyepiece of a compound microscope are 2.0 cm and 3.0 cm respectively. The distance between the objective and the eyepiece is 15.0 cm. The final image formed by the eyepiece is at infinity. The two lenses are thin. The distance in cm of the object and the image produced by the objective, measured from the objective lens, are respectively **(1995 JEE)**

(a) 2.4 and 12.0 (b) 2.4 and 15.0
(c) 2.0 and 12.0 (d) 2.0 and 3.0

Sol. Since, the final image is formed at infinity, the image formed by the objective will be at the first focus of the eyepiece, which is 3.0 cm. The image formed by the objective will be at a distance of 12.0 cm (= 15.0 cm − 3.0 cm) from the objective.

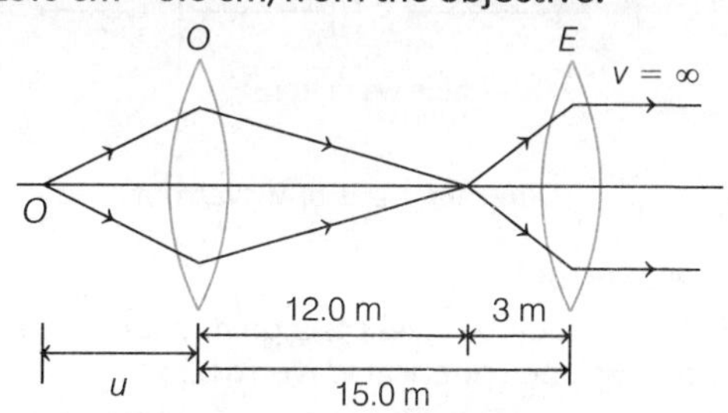

If u is the distance of the object from the objective, we have

$$\Rightarrow \quad \frac{1}{v} - \frac{1}{u} = \frac{1}{f}$$

$$\therefore \quad \frac{1}{12} - \frac{1}{-u} = \frac{1}{2}$$

$$u = 2.4\ \text{cm}$$

Example 5 Diameter of the objective lens of a telescope is 250 cm. For light of wavelength 600 nm coming from a distant object, the limit of resolution of the telescope is close to **(2019 Main)**

(a) 3.0×10^{-7} rad (b) 2.0×10^{-7} rad

(c) 1.5×10^{-7} rad (d) 4.5×10^{-7} rad

Sol. Limit of resolution for a telescope is

$$\theta_R = \frac{1.22\,\lambda}{a}$$

Here, $a = 250$ cm

$$= 250 \times 10^{-2}\ \text{m}$$

and $\lambda = 600\ \text{nm} = 600 \times 10^{-9}\ \text{m}$

So, limit of resolution is

$$\theta_R = \frac{1.22 \times 600 \times 10^{-9}}{250 \times 10^{-2}}$$

$$= 2.93 \times 10^{-7}\ \text{rad}$$

$$\approx 3 \times 10^{-7}\ \text{rad}$$

Important POINTS

1. Wavefront

- Wavefront is defined as locus of all points having same phase at a given instant of time.
- The shape of wavefront depends on the shape of the source of disturbance.
- A wavefront is always normal to the light rays.
- A wavefront does not propagate in the backward direction.

There are 3 types of wavefronts :

(a) Spherical wavefront

(b) Cylindrical wavefront

(c) Plane wavefront

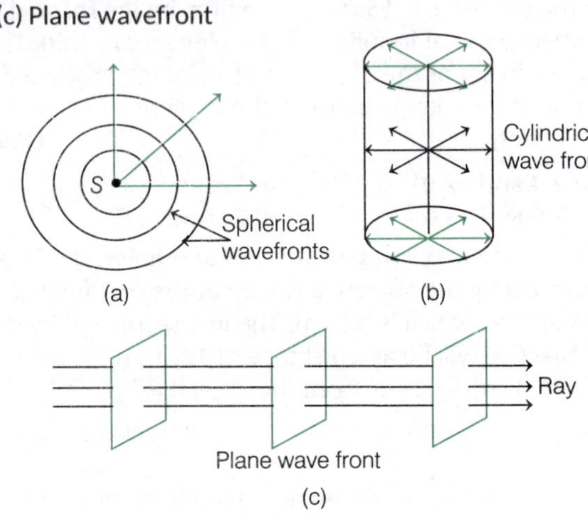

Different types of wavefront

Spherical Wavefront

- When the source of light is a point source, the wavefront formed will be spherical wavefront.
- Point source means the source of light is so small that it is considered as point.

Cylindrical Wavefront

- When the source of disturbance is a slit (i.e. line source) then the wavefront is cylindrical because all the points are equidistant from the source and they lie on the surface of the cylinder.

Plane Wavefront

- When the small part of a spherical or cylindrical wavefront originates from a distant source like infinity then the wavefront which is obtained is known as plane wavefront.
- For example, rays coming from infinity like sun.

2. Huygen's Principle

This principle states in detail how and where waves propagate. According to Huygens' principle.

(i) Every point on a given wavefront may be considered as source of secondary wavelets which spread out with the speed of light in that medium and

(ii) The new wavefront is the forward envelope of the secondary wavelets at that instant.

Huygen's construction for a spherical and plane wavefront is shown in figures (a) and (b).

Let AB represent a given wavefront at a time $t = 0$. According to Huygen's principle, every point on AB acts as source of secondary wavelets which travel with the speed of light c.

To find the position of the wavefront after a time t, circles are drawn with points P, Q, R... etc. as centres on AB and radii equal to ct. These are the traces of secondary wavelets.

The arc $A_1 B_1$ drawn as a forward envelope of the small circles is the new wavefront at that instant.

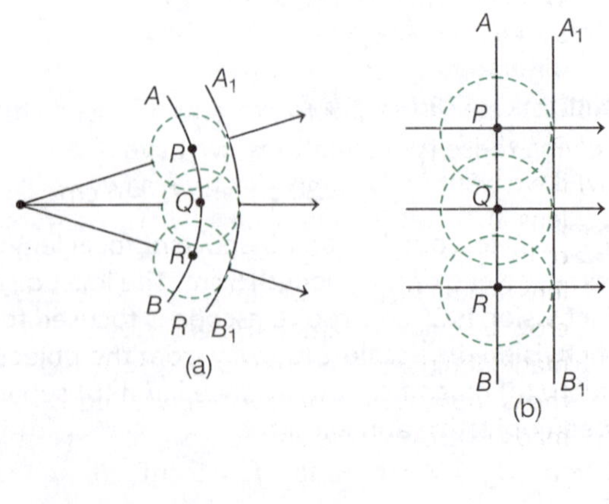

3. Defects of images

Actual image formed by an optical system is usually imperfect. The defects of images are called **aberrations.** The defect may be due to light or optical system. If the defect is due to light, it is called **chromatic aberration,** and if due to optical system, **monochromatic aberration.**

(a) **Chromatic aberration** The image of an object formed by a lens is usually coloured and blurred. This defect of image is called chromatic aberration. This defect arises due to the fact that focal length of a lens is different for different colours.

For a lens,

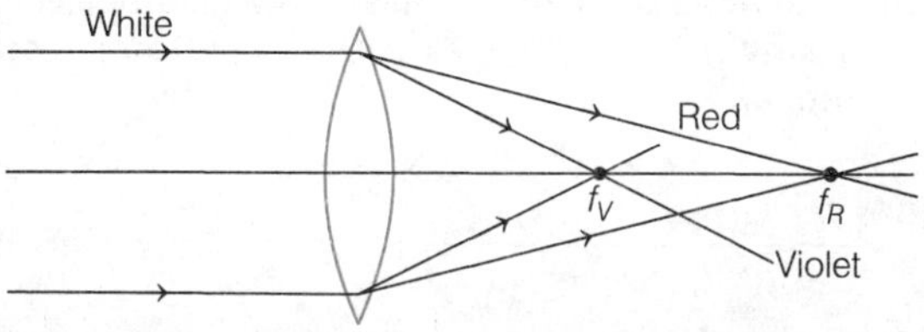

$$\frac{1}{f}=(\mu-1)\left(\frac{1}{R_1}-\frac{1}{R_2}\right)$$

As μ is maximum for violet while minimum for red, violet is focused nearest to the lens while red farthest from it.

The difference between f_R and f_V is a measure of longitudinal chromatic aberration. Thus,

$$\text{LCA}=f_R-f_V$$

Condition of achromatism To get achromatism, we use a pair of two lenses in contact. For two thin lenses in contact we have,

$$\boxed{\frac{\omega_1}{f_1}+\frac{\omega_2}{f_2}=0}$$

This is the **condition of achromatism.** From the condition of achromatism, following conclusions can be drawn:

(i) As ω_1 and ω_2 are positive quantities, f_1 and f_2 should have opposite signs, i.e. if one lens is convex, the other must be concave.

(ii) If $\omega_1=\omega_2$, means both the lenses are of same material. Then,

$$\frac{1}{f_1}+\frac{1}{f_2}=0 \quad \text{or} \quad \frac{1}{F}=0 \quad \text{or} \quad F=\infty$$

Thus, the combination behaves as a plane glass plate. So, we can conclude that both the lenses should be of different materials or $\omega_1 \neq \omega_2$

(iii) Dispersive power of crown glass (ω_C) is less than that of flint glass (ω_F).

(iv) If we want the combination to behave as a convergent lens, then convex lens should have lesser focal length or its dispersive power should be more. Thus, convex lens should be made of flint glass and concave lens of crown. Thus, combination is converging if convex is made of flint glass and concave of crown. Similarly, for the combination to behave as diverging lens, convex is made of crown glass and concave of flint glass.

(b) **Monochromatic aberration** This is the defect in image due to optical system. Monochromatic aberration is of many types such as, spherical, coma, distortion, curvature and astigmatism. Here, we shall limit ourselves to spherical aberration only.

Spherical aberration Spherical aberration arises due to spherical nature of lens (or mirror).

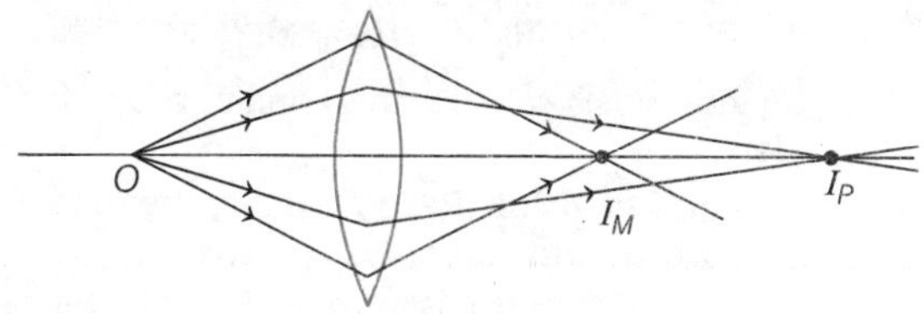

The paraxial rays (close to optic axis) get focused at I_P and marginal rays (away from the optic axis) are focused at I_M. Thus, image of a point object O is not a point.

The inability of the lens to form a point image of an axial point object is called spherical aberration. Spherical aberration can never be eliminated but can be minimised by the following methods:

(i) **By using stops** By using stops, either paraxial or marginal rays are cut-off.

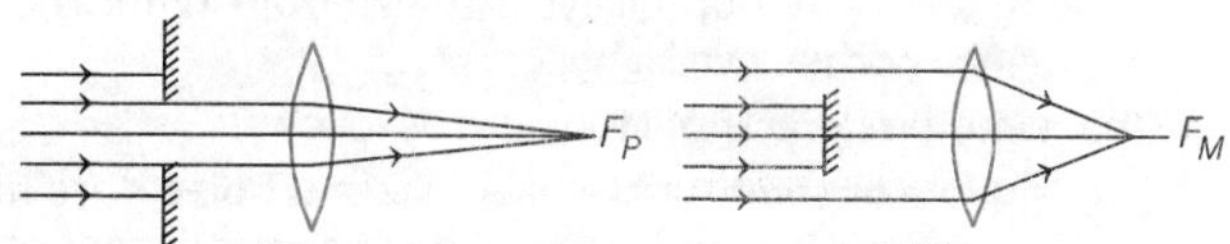

(A) (B)

(ii) **Using two thin lenses separated by a distance** Two thin lenses separated by a distance $d=f_2-f_1$ has the minimum spherical aberration.

(iii) **Using parabolic mirrors** If spherical mirror is replaced by parabolic mirror, spherical aberration is minimised.

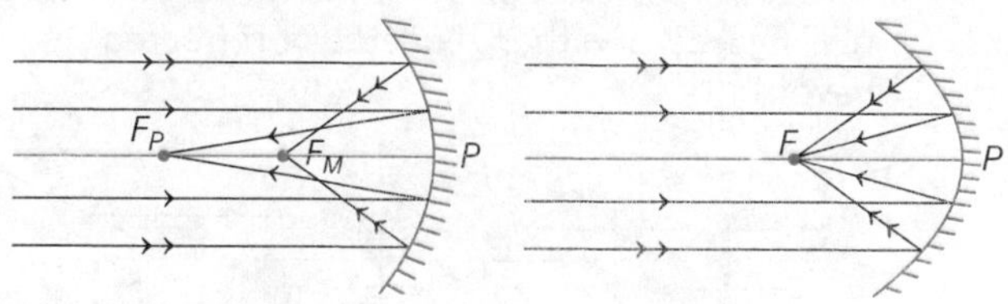

(A) Spherical mirror (B) Parabolic mirror

(iv) **Using lens of large focal length** It has been found that spherical aberration varies inversely as the cube of the focal length. So, if f is large, spherical aberration will be reduced.

(v) **Using plano-convex lens** In case of plano-convex lens, spherical aberration is minimised, if its curved surface faces the incident or emergent ray whichever is more parallel.

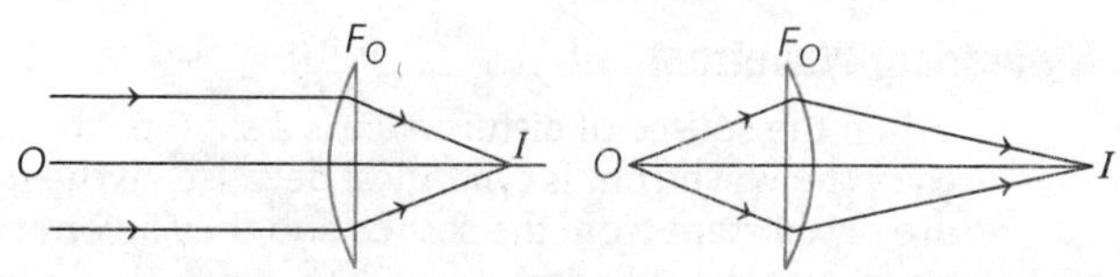

(A) Telescope (B) Microscope

This is why in telescope, the curved surface faces the object while in microscope curved surface is towards the image.

(vi) **Using crossed lens** For a single lens with object at infinity, spherical aberration is found to be minimum when R_1 and R_2 have the following ratio,

$$\frac{R_1}{R_2}=\frac{2\mu^2-\mu-4}{\mu(2\mu+1)}$$

A lens which satisfies this condition is called a crossed lens.

Defects of vision Regarding eye, the following points are worthnoting:

(a) The human eye is most sensitive to yellow-green light ($\lambda = 5550$ Å).

(b) The persistance of vision is $\frac{1}{10}$ sec, i.e. if time interval between two consecutive light pulses is less than 0.1 sec, eye cannot distinguish them separately.

(c) By the eye-lens, real, inverted and diminished image is formed on retina.

(d) While testing your eye through reading chart if doctor finds it to 6/12, it implies that you can read a letter from 6 m which the normal eye can read from 12 m. Thus, 6/6 means normal eye sight.

The common defects of vision are as follows:

(i) **Myopia or short-sightedness** Distant objects are not clearly visible in this defect. The image of distant object is formed before the retina.

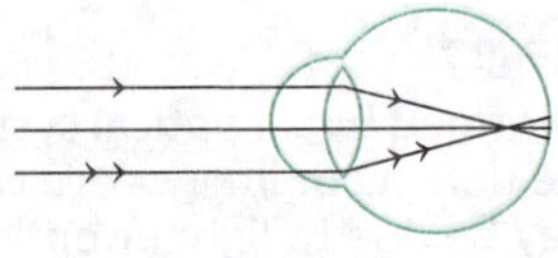

(A) Defected eye

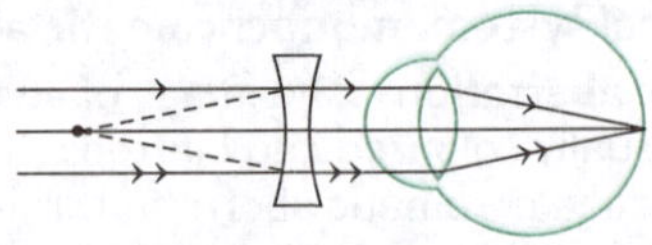

(B) Corrected eye

The defect can be remedied by using a concave lens.

(ii) **Hyperopia or far-sightedness** The near objects are not clearly visible. Image of near object is formed behind the retina.

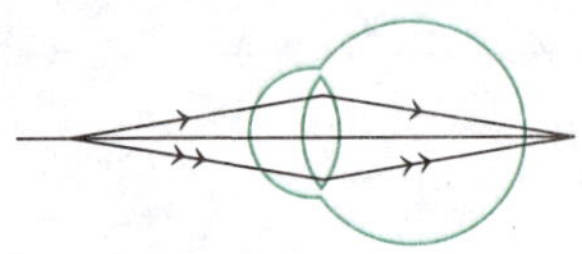

(A) Defected eye

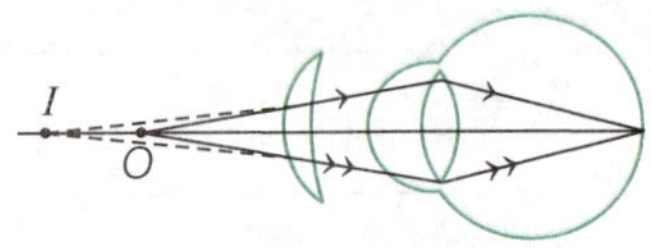

(B) Corrected eye

This defect is remedied by using a convex lens.

(iii) **Presbyopia** In it both near and far objects are not clearly visible. This is remedied either by using two separate lenses or by using single spectacle having bifocal lenses.

(iv) **Astigmatism** In this defect, eye cannot see objects in two orthogonal (perpendicular) directions clearly simultaneously. This defect is remedied by using cylindrical lens.

Example 6 Give some examples of wavefronts through figures only in case of reflection and refraction.

Sol. Here are some examples of incident wavefronts (plane in all figures) and then reflected or refracted wavefronts.

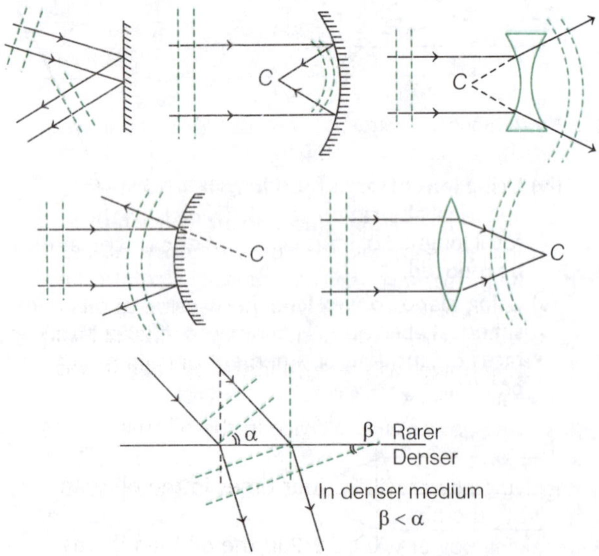

Example 7 From Huygen's principle, prove law of reflection $\angle i = \angle r$.

Sol.

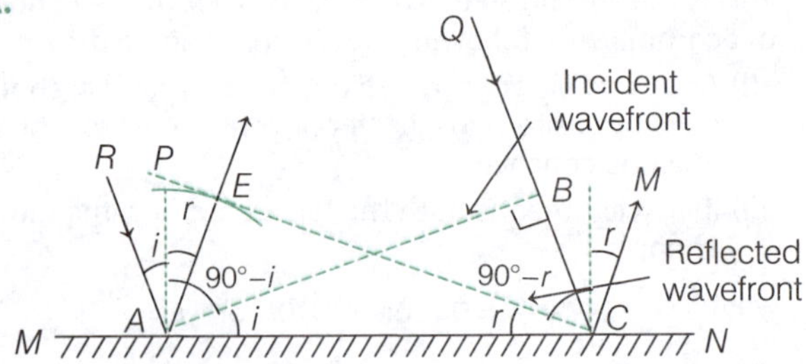

MN : Plane mirror, RA and QC : Incident rays, AP : Normal to MN at point A,

AB : Incident wavefront, i : Angle of incident, CE : Reflected wavefront, r : Angle of reflection.

When wavefront AB is incident on the mirror, point A first becomes a secondary source and emits secondary waves in the same medium. If T is the time taken by the incident wavefront to travel from B to C, then $BC = vT$. During this time, the secondary wave originating at A covers the same distance, so that the secondary spherical wavelet has a radius vT at time T.

To construct the reflected wavefront, a circular arc of radius vT is drawn from point A. Draw a tangent EC to the secondary wavelet.

The arrow AE shows the direction of propagation of the reflected wave. CM is also in reflected direction.

$\angle RAP = i$ = angle of incidence and $\angle PAE = r$ = angle of reflection

In ΔABC and ΔAEC,

AC is common and $\angle ABC = \angle AEC = 90°$

$\therefore$ ΔABC and ΔAEC are congruent.

$\therefore$ $\angle ACE = \angle BAC$

$\therefore$ $i = r$

Thus, the angle of incidence is equal to the angle of reflection.

This is the law of reflection.

Example 8 Using Huygen's principle prove law of refraction.

Sol.

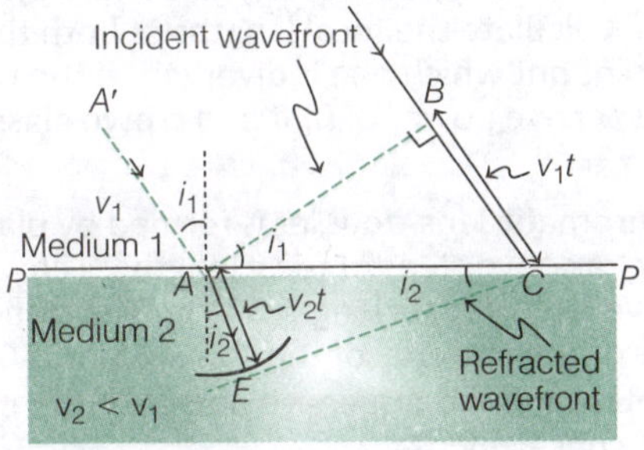

Let v_1 and v_2 represent the speed of light in medium 1 and medium 2, respectively.

Let wavefront AB be incident on the interface at an angle i_1. If t is the time taken by the wavefront to travel distance BC, i.e. $BC = v_1t$.

Draw circle of radius v_2t from point A in the second medium. CE is the tangent plane drawn from point C on to the circle. CE is the refracted wavefront.

$AE = v_2t$.

Consider ΔABC and ΔAEC,

$$\sin i_1 = \frac{BC}{AC} = \frac{v_1t}{AC}$$

$$\Rightarrow \quad \sin i_2 = \frac{AE}{AC} = \frac{v_2t}{AC}$$

$$\Rightarrow \quad \frac{\sin i_1}{\sin i_2} = \frac{v_1}{v_2} \quad \text{...(i)}$$

For medium 1, $v_1 = \dfrac{c}{\mu_1}$

For medium 2, $v_2 = \dfrac{c}{\mu_2}$

Substituting in equation (i), we have

$$\frac{\sin i_1}{\sin i_2} = \frac{c/\mu_1}{c/\mu_2} = \frac{\mu_2}{\mu_1}$$

or $\mu_1 \sin i_1 = \mu_2 \sin i_2$

This is nothing but Snell's law of refraction.

MODULE 9 Exercise

Fill in the Blank

1. The resolving power of electron microscope is higher than that of an optical microscope because the wavelength of electrons is ...... than the wavelength of visible light. **(1992 JEE)**

Single Correct Option

2. An achromatic convergent doublet of two lenses in contact has a power of +2D. The convex lens has a power +5D. What is the ratio of the dispersive powers of the convergent and divergent lenses?
(a) 2 : 5 (b) 3 : 5
(c) 5 : 2 (d) 5 : 3

3. A person has been using spectacles of power −1.0 dioptre for distant vision and a separate reading glass of power 2.0 dioptres. What is the least distance of distinct vision for this person **(2023 Main)**
(a) 50 cm (b) 30 cm
(c) 10 cm (d) 40 cm

4. In a reflecting telescope, a secondary mirror is used to **(2023 Main)**
(a) remove spherical aberration
(b) reduce the problem of mechanical support
(c) make chromatic aberration zero
(d) move the eyepiece outside the telescopic tube

5. A microscope was initially placed in air (refractive index 1). It is then immersed in oil (refractive index 2). For a light whose wavelength in air is λ, calculate the change of microscope's resolving power due to oil and choose the correct option. **(2022 Main)**
(a) Resolving power will be 1 / 4 in the oil than it was in the air.
(b) Resolving power will be twice in the oil than it was in the air.
(c) Resolving power will be four times in the oil than it was in the air.
(d) Resolving power will be 1/2 in the oil than it was in the air.

6. The aperture of the objective is 24.4 cm. The resolving power of this telescope, if a light of wavelength 2440 Å is used to see the object will be **(2022 Main)**

(a) 8.1×10^6 (b) 10.0×10^7
(c) 8.2×10^5 (d) 1.0×10^{-8}

7. Calculate the limit of resolution of a telescope with objective having a diameter of 200 cm, if it has to detect light of wavelength 500 nm coming from a star. **(2019 Main)**

(a) 610×10^{-9} rad (b) 305×10^{-9} rad
(c) 457.5×10^{-9} rad (d) 152.5×10^{-9} rad

8. An observer looks at a distant tree of height 10 m with a telescope of magnifying power of 20. To observer the tree appears **(2016 Main)**

(a) 10 times taller (b) 10 times nearer
(c) 20 times taller (d) 20 times nearer

9. The focal lengths of objective lens and eye lens of a Galilean telescope are respectively 30 cm and 3.0 cm. Telescope produces virtual, erect image of an object situated far away from it at least distance of distinct vision from the eye lens. In this condition, the magnifying power of the Galilean telescope should be **(2014 Main)**

(a) +11.2 (b) −11.2 (c) −8.8 (d) +8.8

10. An eye specialist prescribes spectacles having combination of convex lens of focal length 40 cm in contact with a concave lens of focal length 25 cm. The power of this lens combination in diopters is **(1997 JEE)**

(a) + 1.5 (b) − 1.5
(c) + 6.67 (d) − 6.67

11. The focal lengths of the objective and the eyepiece of a compound microscope are 2.0 cm and 3.0 cm respectively. The distance between the objective and the eyepiece is 15.0 cm. The final image formed by the eyepiece is at infinity. The two lenses are thin. The distance in cm of the object and the image produced by the objective, measured from the objective lens, are respectively **(1995 JEE)**

(a) 2.4 and 12.0 (b) 2.4 and 15.0
(c) 2.0 and 12.0 (d) 2.0 and 3.0

12. An astronomical telescope has an angular magnification of magnitude 5 for far objects. The separation between the objective and the eyepiece is 36 cm and the final image is formed at infinity. The focal length f_o of the objective and the focal lengt of the eyepiece are **(1989**

(a) $f_o = 45$ cm and $f_e = -9$ cm
(b) $f_o = 50$ cm and $f_e = 10$ cm
(c) $f_o = 7.2$ cm and $f_e = 5$ cm
(d) $f_o = 30$ cm and $f_e = 6$ cm

Multiple Correct Options

13. A planet is observed by an astronomical refractin telescope having an objective of focal length 16 n and an eyepiece of focal length 2 cm **(1992**

(a) the distance between the objective and the eyepiece is 16.02 m
(b) the angular magnification of the planet is − 80
(c) the image of the planet is inverted
(d) the objective is larger than the eyepiece

Subjective Questions

14. An achromatic convergent lens of focal length 150 cm is made by combining flint and crown glass lenses. Calculate the focal lengths of both the lenses and point out which one is divergent if the ratio of the dispersive power of flint and crown glasses is 3 : 2.

15. An achromatic lens-doublet is formed by placing in contact a convex lens of focal length 20 cm and a concave lens of focal length 30 cm. The dispersive power of the material of the convex lens is 0.18.
(a) Determine the dispersive power of the material of the concave lens.
(b) Calculate the focal length of the lens-doublet.

16. There is a telescope whose objective has a diameter $D = 5.0$ cm. Find the resolving power of the objective and the minimum separation between two points at a distance $l = 3.0$ km from the telescope, which it can resolve (assume $\lambda = 0.55\ \mu m$). **(Irodov 5.146)**

17. Calculate the minimum separation between two points on the Moon which can be resolved by a reflecting telescope with mirror diameter 5m. The wavelength of light is assumed to be equal to $\lambda = 0.55\ \mu m$. **(Irodov 5.147)**

18. There is a microscope whose objective's numerical aperture is $\sin \alpha = 0.24$, where α is the half-angle subtended by the objective's rim. Find the minimum separation resolved by this microscope when an object is illuminated by light with wavelength $\lambda = 0.55\ \mu m$. **(Irodov 5.149)**

Answers

1. (Less) **2.** (b) **3.** (b) **4.** (d) **5.** (b) **6.** (c) **7.** (b) **8.** (d) **9.** (b) **10.** (b)
11. (a) **12.** (d) **13.** (a,b,c,d) **14.** 50 cm, –75 cm, divergent lens is of flint glass **15.** (a) 0.27 (b) 60 cm
16. (a) $R = 7.45 \times 10^4$ (b) $\Delta y_{min} = 4$ cm **17.** $\Delta y_{min} \approx 50$ m **18.** $d_{min} = 1.4\ \mu m$

See hints on pages 166-168.

Unit Exercise (Cumulative)

Level 1

Fill in the Blank

1. A slab of material of refractive index 2 shown in figure has a curved surface *APB* of radius of curvature 10 cm and a plane surface *CD*. On the left of *APB* is air and on the right of *CD* is water with refractive indices as given in the figure. An object *O* is placed at a distance of 15 cm from the pole *P* as shown. The distance of the final image of *O* from *P*, as viewed from the left is .... **(1991 JEE)**

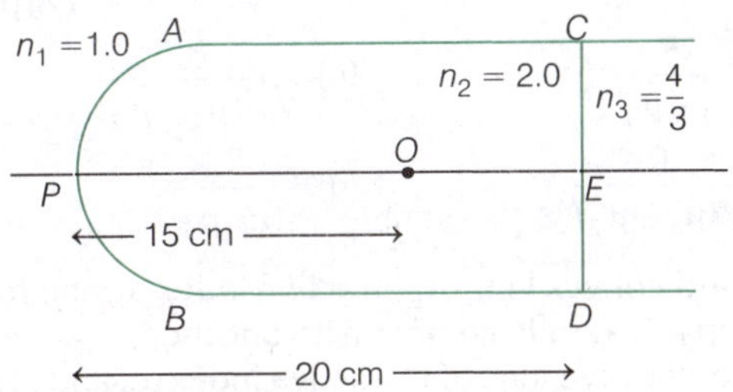

Single Correct Option

2. White light is incident from under water on the water-air interface. If the angle of incidence is slowly increased from zero, the emergent beam coming out into the air will turn from
   (a) white to violet (b) white to red
   (c) white to black (d) None of these

3. An optical system consists of a thin convex lens of focal length 30 cm and a plane mirror placed 15 cm behind the lens. An object is placed 15 cm in front of the lens. The distance of the final image from the object is
   (a) 60 cm (b) 30 cm
   (c) 75 cm (d) 45 cm

4. A thin convex lens of focal length 30 cm is placed in front of a plane mirror. An object is placed at a distance *x* from the lens (not in between lens and mirror) so that its final image coincides with itself. Then, the value of *x* is
   (a) 15 cm (b) 30 cm
   (c) 60 cm (d) Insufficient data

5. One side of a glass slab is silvered as shown in the figure. A ray of light is incident on the other side at angle of incidence 45°. Refractive index of glass is given as $\sqrt{2}$. The deflection suffered by the ray when it comes out of the slab is

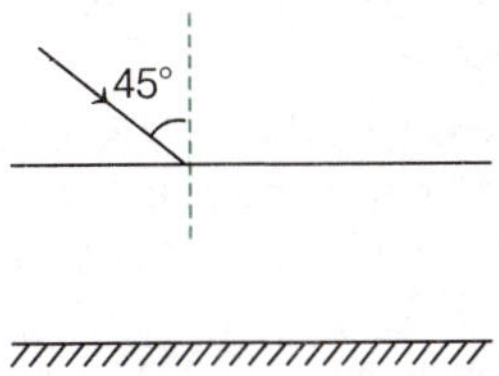

   (a) 90° (b) 180°
   (c) 120° (d) 45°

6. In Fig. (i), a lens of focal length 10 cm is shown. It is cut into two parts and placed as shown in Fig. (ii). An object *AB* of height 1 cm is placed at a distance of 7.5 cm. The height of the image will be

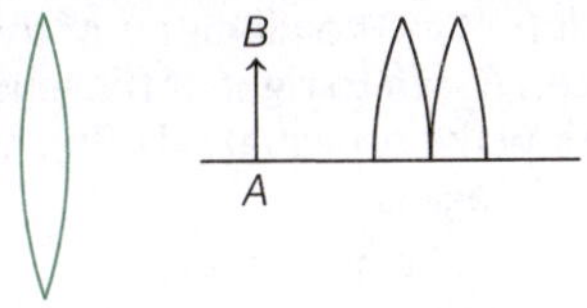

(i) (ii)

   (a) 2 cm
   (b) 1 cm
   (c) 1.5 cm
   (d) 3 cm

7. From the figure shown, establish a relation between μ_1, μ_2 and μ_3

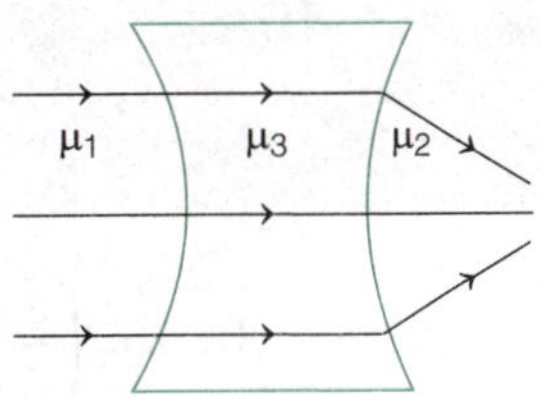

   (a) $\mu_1 < \mu_2 < \mu_3$
   (b) $\mu_3 < \mu_2; \mu_3 = \mu_1$
   (c) $\mu_3 > \mu_2; \mu_3 = \mu_1$
   (d) $\mu_1 > \mu_2 > \mu_3$

8. When light of wavelength λ is incident on an equilateral prism, kept on its minimum deviation position, it is found that the angle of deviation equals the angle of the prism itself. The refractive index of the material of the prism for the wavelength λ is
   (a) $\sqrt{3}$ (b) $\sqrt{3/2}$
   (c) 2 (d) $\sqrt{2}$

9. In the figure, an air lens of radii of curvature 10 cm ($R_1 = R_2 = 10$ cm) is cut in a cylinder of glass $\left(\mu = \dfrac{3}{2}\right)$. The focal length and the nature of the lens is

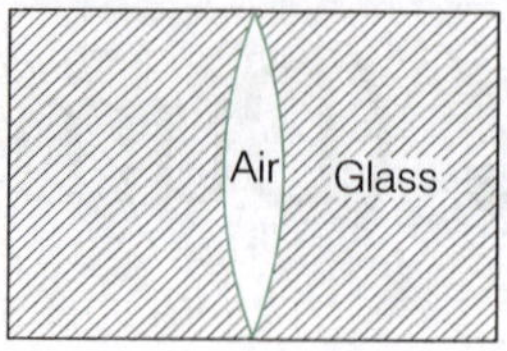

(a) 15 cm, concave
(b) 15 cm, convex
(c) ∞, neither concave nor convex
(d) 10 cm, concave

10. In a plano-convex lens the radius of curvature of the convex lens is 10 cm. If the plane side is polished, then the focal length of this combination will be (Refractive index = 1.5)
(a) 20.5 cm (b) 10 cm (c) 15.5 cm (d) 5 cm

11. A convex lens forms an image of an object on a screen 30 cm from the lens. When the lens is moved 90 cm towards the object, the image is again formed on the screen. Then, the focal length of the lens is
(a) 13 cm (b) 24 cm (c) 33 cm (d) 40 cm

12. A point object O is placed on the principal axis of a convex lens of focal length $f = 20$ cm at a distance of 40 cm to the left of it. The diameter of the lens is 10 cm. An eye is placed 60 cm to right of the lens and a distance h below the principal axis. The maximum value of h to see the image is
(a) 7.5 cm (b) 2.5 cm (c) 5 cm (d) 10 cm

13. A plane mirror is placed horizontally inside water ($\mu = 4/3$). A ray falls normally on it. Then, mirror is rotated through an angle θ. The minimum value of θ for which the ray does not come out of the water surface, is

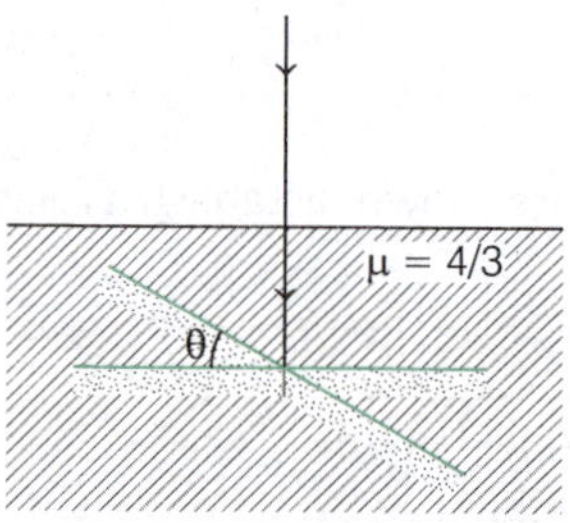

(a) $\pi/4$ (b) $\sin^{-1}\left(\dfrac{3}{4}\right)$
(c) $\dfrac{1}{2}\sin^{-1}\left(\dfrac{3}{4}\right)$ (d) $2\sin^{-1}\left(\dfrac{3}{4}\right)$

14. A glass prism of refractive index 1.5 is immersed in water of refractive index 4/3. A light ray incident normally on face AB is totally reflected at face AC if

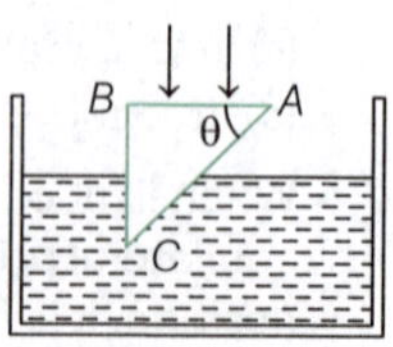

(a) $\sin\theta > 8/9$
(b) $\sin\theta < 2/3$
(c) $\sin\theta = \sqrt{3}/2$
(d) $2/3 < \sin\theta \le 8/9$

15. A thin lens, made of glass of refractive index 3/2, produces a real and magnified image of an object in air. If the whole system, maintaining the same distance between the object and the lens, is immersed in water (RI = 4/3), then the image formed will be
(a) real, magnified (b) real, diminished
(c) virtual, magnified (d) virtual, diminished

16. The maximum value of refractive index of a prism which permits the transmission of light through it when the refracting angle of the prism is 90°, is given by
(a) 1.500 (b) 1.414
(c) 2.000 (d) 1.732

17. One plano-convex and one plano-concave lens of same radius of curvature R but of different materials are joined side by side as shown in the figure. If the refractive index of the material of 1 is μ_1 and that of 2 is μ_2, then the focal length of the combination is **(2019 Main)**

(a) $\dfrac{2R}{\mu_1 - \mu_2}$ (b) $\dfrac{R}{2-(\mu_1 - \mu_2)}$
(c) $\dfrac{R}{2(\mu_1 - \mu_2)}$ (d) $\dfrac{R}{\mu_1 - \mu_2}$

18. A plano-convex lens of refractive index μ_1 and focal length f_1 is kept in contact with another plano-concave lens of refractive index μ_2 and focal length f_2. If the radius of curvature of their spherical faces is R each and $f_1 = 2f_2$, then μ_1 and μ_2 are related as **(2019 Main)**
(a) $3\mu_2 - 2\mu_1 = 1$
(b) $2\mu_2 - \mu_1 = 1$
(c) $2\mu_1 - \mu_2 = 1$
(d) $\mu_1 + \mu_2 = 3$

19. Diameter of the flat surface of a circular plano-convex lens is 6 cm and thickness at the centre is 3 mm. The radius of curvature of the curved part is
(a) 15 cm
(b) 20 cm
(c) 30 cm
(d) 10 cm

20. A diverging lens with magnitude of focal length 25 cm is placed at a distance of 15 cm from a converging lens of magnitude of focal length 20 cm. A beam of parallel light falls on the diverging lens. The final image formed is **(2017 Main)**
(a) virtual and at a distance of 40 cm from convergent lens
(b) real and at a distance of 40 cm from the divergent lens
(c) real and at a distance of 6 cm from the convergent lens
(d) real and at a distance of 40 cm from convergent lens

21. A thin convex lens made from crown glass ($\mu = 3/2$) has focal length f. When it is measured in two different liquids having refractive indices 4/3 and 5/3. It has the focal lengths f_1 and f_2, respectively. The correct relation between the focal length is **(2014 Main)**

(a) $f_1 = f_2 < f$
(b) $f_1 > f$ and f_2 becomes negative
(c) $f_2 > f$ and f_1 becomes negative
(d) f_1 and f_2 both become negative

22. The image of an object, formed by a plano-convex lens at a distance of 8 m behind the lens, is real and is one-third the size of the object. The wavelength of light inside the lens is 2/3 times the wavelength in free space. The radius of the curved surface of the lens is **(2013 Adv.)**

(a) 1 m (b) 2 m (c) 3 m (d) 6 m

23. Two light rays 1 and 2 are incident on two faces AB and AC on an isosceles prism as shown in the figure. The rays emerge from the side BC. Then,

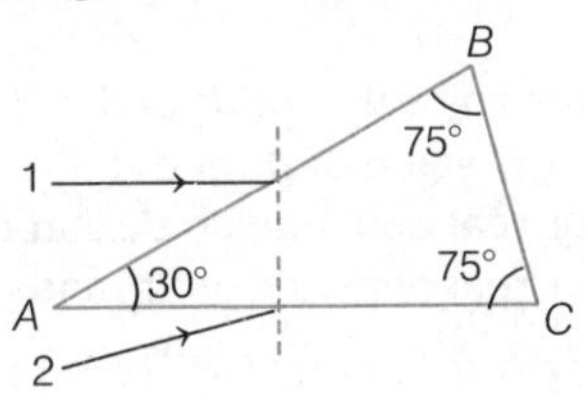

(a) minimum deviation of ray 1 > minimum deviation of ray 2
(b) minimum deviation of ray 1 < minimum deviation of ray 2
(c) minimum deviation of ray 1 = minimum deviation of ray 2
(d) Cannot be determined

24. A bi-convex lens is formed with two thin plano-convex lenses as shown in the figure. Refractive index n of the first lens is 1.5 and that of the second lens is 1.2. Both the curved surfaces are of the same radius of curvature $R = 14$ cm.

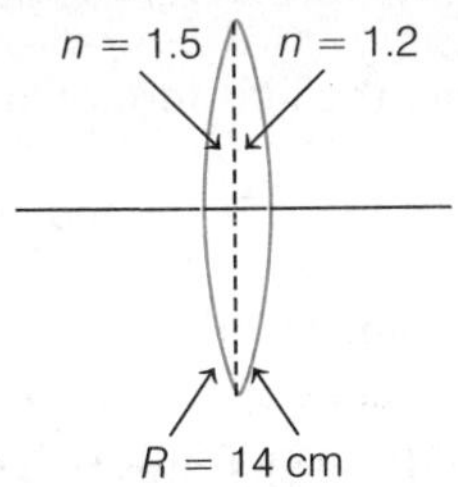

For this bi-convex lens, for an object distance of 40 cm, the image distance will be **(2012 JEE)**

(a) -280.0 cm (b) 40.0 cm
(c) 21.5 cm (d) 13.3 cm

25. A convex lens is in contact with concave lens. The magnitude of the ratio of their focal length is 3/2. Their equivalent focal length is 30 cm. What are their individual focal lengths? **(2005 JEE)**

(a) -75, 50 (b) -10, 15 (c) 75, 50 (d) -15, 10

26. The size of the image of an object, which is at infinity, as formed by a convex lens of focal length 30 cm is 2 cm. If a concave lens of focal length 20 cm is placed between the convex lens and the image is at a distance of 26 cm from the convex lens, calculate the new size of the image. **(2003 JEE)**

(a) 1.25 cm (b) 2.5 cm (c) 1.05 cm (d) 2 cm

27. A hollow double concave lens is made of very thin transparent material. It can be filled with air or either of two liquids L_1 or L_2 having refracting indices n_1 and n_2 respectively ($n_2 > n_1 > 1$). The lens will diverge a parallel beam of light if it is filled with **(2000 JEE)**

(a) air and placed in air (b) air and immersed in L_1
(c) L_1 and immersed in L_2 (d) L_2 and immersed in L_1

28. A diminished image of an object is to be obtained on a screen 1.0 m from it. This can be achieved by placing **(1995 JEE)**

(a) a plane mirror
(b) a convex mirror of suitable focal length
(c) a convex lens of focal length less than 0.25 m
(d) a concave lens of suitable focal length

29. A plano-convex thin lens of focal length 10 cm is silvered at its plane surface. The distance d at which an object must be kept in order to get its image on itself is

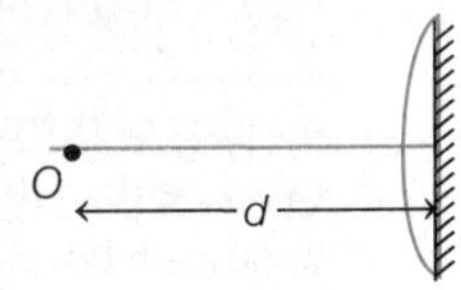

(a) 5 cm (b) 20 cm (c) 10 cm (d) 2.5 cm

30. A point object is placed at a distance of 20 cm from a thin plano-convex lens of focal length 15 cm. The plane surface of the lens is now silvered. The image created by the system is at **(2006 JEE)**

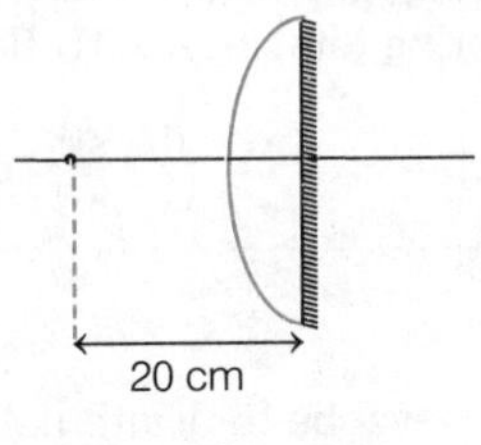

(a) 60 cm to the left of the system
(b) 60 cm to the right of the system
(c) 12 cm to the left of the system
(d) 12 cm to the right of the system

31. A parallel beam of light strikes a piece of transparent glass having cross-section as shown in the figure below. Correct shape of the emergent wavefront will be (figures are schematic and not drawn to scale) **(2020 Adv.)**

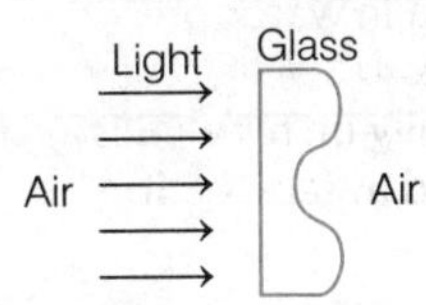

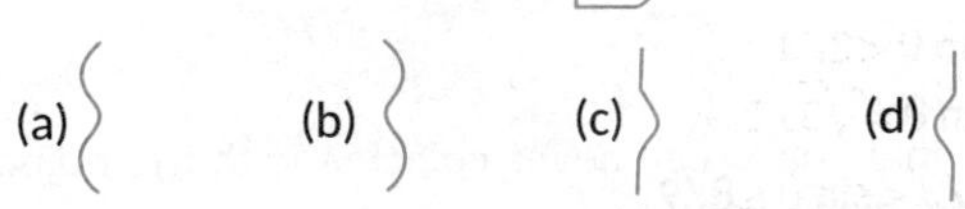

32. There is a small black dot at the centre C of a solid glass sphere of refractive index μ. When seen from outside, the dot will appear to be located

(a) away from the C for all values of μ
(b) at C for all values of μ
(c) at C for $\mu = 1.5$, but away from C for μ not equal to 1.5
(d) at C for $2 < \mu < 1.5$

33. How much water should be filled in a container of height 21 cm, so that it appears half filled to the observer when viewed from the top of the container ($\mu = 4/3$).

(a) 8 cm (b) 10.5 cm (c) 12 cm (d) 14 cm

34. Optic axis of a thin equi-convex lens is the x-axis. The co-ordinates of a point object and its image are (– 40 cm, 1 cm) and (50 cm, – 2 cm), respectively. Lens is located at

(a) $x = 20$ cm (b) $x = -30$ cm
(c) $x = -10$ cm (d) origin

35. A thin plano-convex lens acts like a concave mirror of radius of curvature 20 cm when its plane surface is silvered. The radius of curvature of the curved surface if index of refraction of its material is 1.5 will be

(a) 40 cm (b) 30 cm (c) 10 cm (d) 20 cm

36. A light source S is placed at the centre of a glass sphere of radius R and refractive index μ. The maximum angle θ with the x-axis (as shown in the figure) an incident light ray can make without suffering total internal reflection is

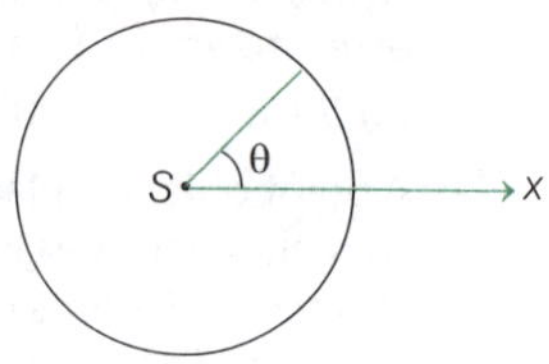

(a) $\cos^{-1}\left(\frac{1}{\mu}\right)$ (b) $\sin^{-1}\left(\frac{1}{\mu}\right)$

(c) $\tan^{-1}\left(\frac{1}{\mu}\right)$

(d) there will never be total internal reflection

37. A point object O is placed at a distance of 20 cm from a convex lens of focal length 10 cm as shown in the figure. At what distance x from the lens should a convex mirror of focal length 60 cm, be placed so that final image coincide with the object?

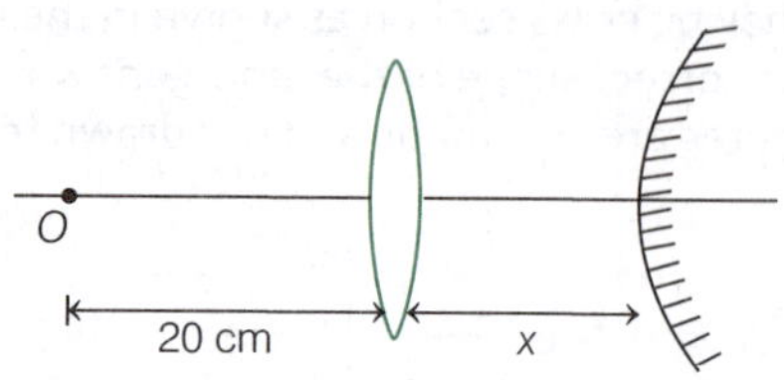

(a) 10 cm
(b) 40 cm
(c) 20 cm
(d) Final image can never coincide with the object in the given conditions

38. Distance of an object from the first focus of an equi-convex lens is 10 cm and the distance of its real image from second focus is 40 cm. The focal length of the lens is

(a) 25 cm (b) 10 cm (c) 20 cm (d) 40 cm

39. A convex spherical refracting surface separates two media glass and air ($\mu_g = 1.5$). If the image is to be real, at what minimum distance u should the object be placed in air if R is the radius of curvature

(a) $u > 3R$ (b) $u > 2R$
(c) $u < 4R$ (d) $u < R$

40. Two diverging lenses are kept as shown in figure. The final image formed will be

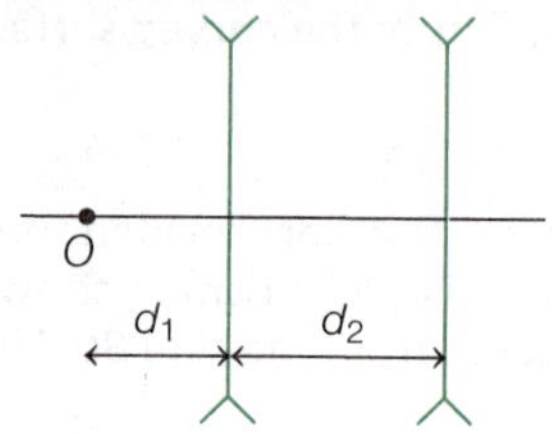

(a) virtual for any value of d_1 and d_2
(b) real for any value of d_1 and d_2
(c) virtual or real depends on d_1 and d_2 only
(d) virtual or real depends on d_1 and d_2 and also on the focal lengths of the lens

41. In the figure shown, a point object O is placed in air on the principal axis. The radius of curvature of the spherical surface is 60 cm. I is the final image formed after all reflections and refractions.

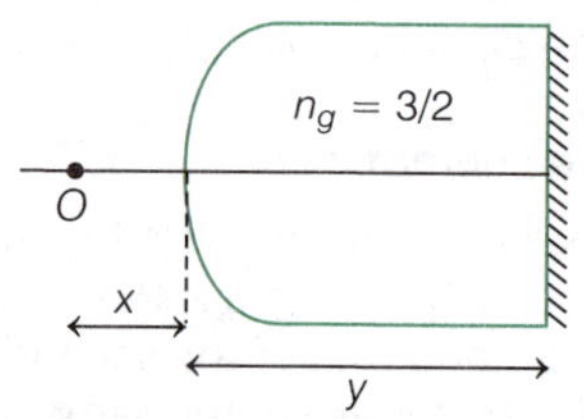

(a) If $x = 120$ cm, then I is formed on O for any value of y
(b) If $x = 240$ cm, then I is formed on O only if $y = 360$ cm
(c) If $x = 240$ cm, then I is formed on O for any value of y
(d) None of the above

42. In the figure, a point object O is placed in air. A spherical boundary separates two media of radius of curvature 1.0 m. AB is principal axis. The separation between the images formed due to refraction from two halves of the spherical surface is

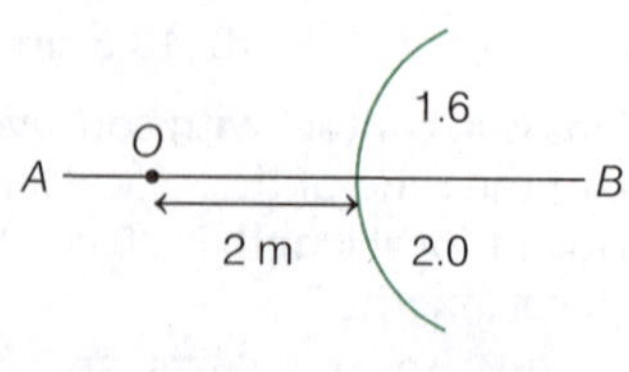

(a) 12 m (b) 20 m (c) 14 m (d) 10 m

43. If the distances of an object and its virtual image from the focus of a convex lens of focal length f are 1 cm each, then f is

(a) 4 cm (b) $(\sqrt{2}+1)$ cm

(c) $2\sqrt{2}$ cm (d) $(2+\sqrt{2})$ cm

44. To remove myopia (short sightedness) a lens of power 0.66 D is required. The distant point of the eye is approximately

(a) 100 cm (b) 151.5 cm (c) 50 cm (d) 25 cm

Multiple Correct Options

45. Which of the following form(s) a virtual and erect image for all positions of the object ? **(1996 JEE)**

(a) Convex lens (b) Concave lens

(c) Convex mirror (d) Concave mirror

46. A converging lens is used to form an image on a screen. When the upper half of the lens is covered by an opaque screen **(1986 JEE)**

(a) half of the image will disappear

(b) complete image will be formed

(c) intensity of the image will increase

(d) intensity of the image will decrease

Match the Columns

47. An optical component and an object S placed along its optic axis are given in Column I. The distance between the object and the component can be varied. The properties of images are given in Column II. Match all the properties of images from Column II with the appropriate components given in Column I. **(2008 JEE)**

	Column I		Column II
(A)	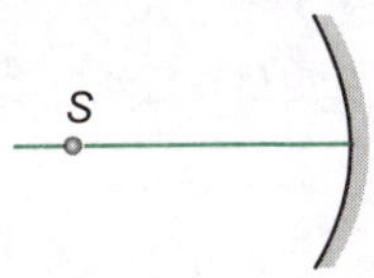	(p)	Real image
(B)	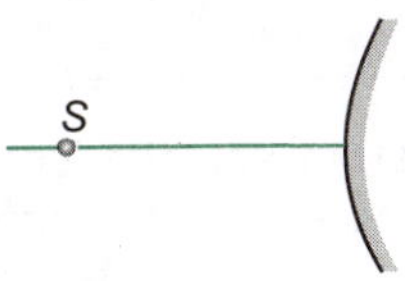	(q)	Virtual image
(C)	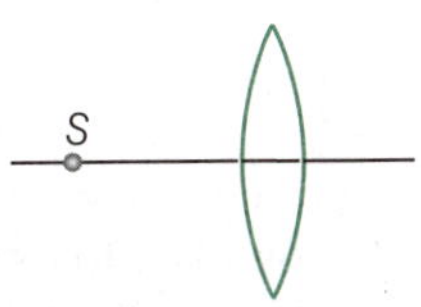	(r)	Magnified image
(D)	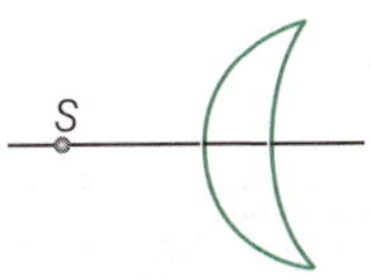	(s)	Image at infinity

Subjective Questions

48. Figure shows the optical axis of a lens, the point source of light A and its virtual image A'. Trace the rays to find the position of the lens and of its principal focus. What type of lens is it?

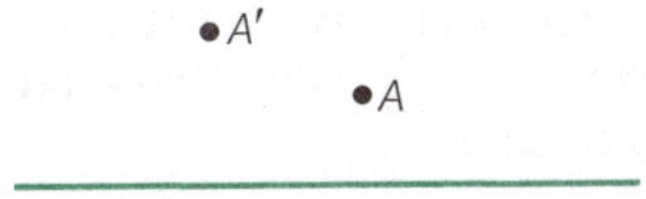

49. Solve the problem similar to the previous one if A and A' are interchanged.

50. A plate with plane parallel faces having refractive index 1.8 rests on a plane mirror. A light ray is incident on the upper face of the plate at 60°. How far from the entry point will the ray emerge after reflection by the mirror. The plate is 6 cm thick.

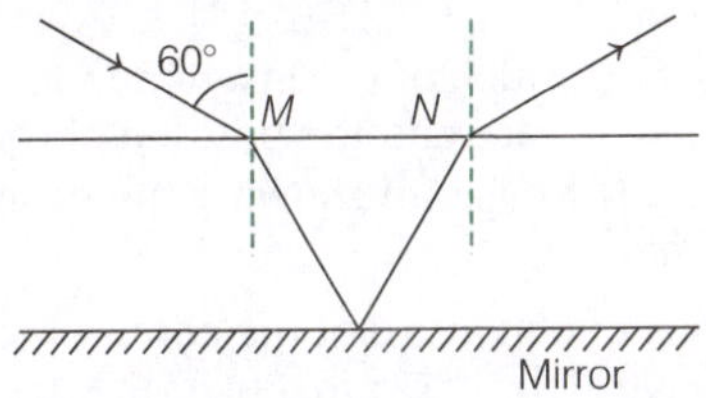

51. In a certain spectrum produced by a glass prism of dispersive power 0.0305, it is found that the refractive index for the red ray is 1.645 and that for the violet ray is 1.665. What is the refractive index for the yellow ray?

52. Find the position of final image of an object O as shown in figure.

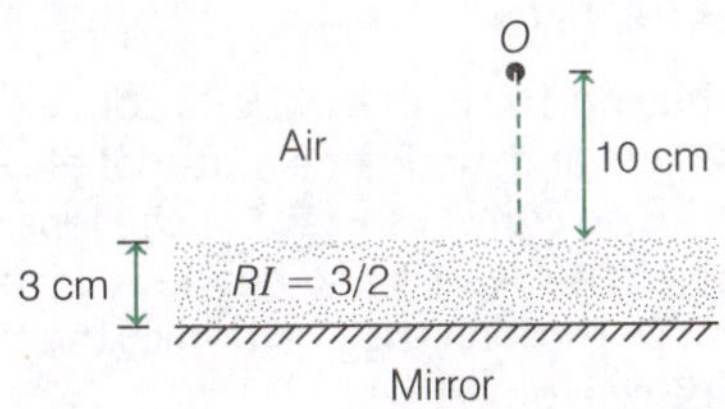

53. Determine the position of the image produced by an optical system consisting of a concave mirror with a focal length of 10 cm and a convergent lens with a focal length of 20 cm. The distance from the mirror to the lens is 30 cm and from the lens to the object is 40 cm. Consider only two steps. Plot the image.

54. A parallel beam of light is incident on a system consisting of three thin lenses with a common optical axis. The focal lengths of the lenses are equal to $f_1 = +10$ cm and $f_2 = -20$ cm, and $f_3 = +9$ cm respectively. The distance between the first and the second lens is 15 cm and between the second and the third is 5 cm. Find the position of the point at which the beam converges when it leaves the system of lenses.

55. A point source of light S is placed at the bottom of a vessel containing a liquid of refractive index 5/3. A person is viewing the source from above the surface. There is an opaque disc of radius 1 cm floating on the surface. The centre of the disc lies vertically above the source S. The liquid from the vessel is gradually drained out through a tap. What is the maximum height of the liquid for which the source cannot at all be seen from above?

56. A ray of light travelling in glass ($\mu_g = 3/2$) is incident on a horizontal glass-air surface at the critical angle θ_C. If a thin layer of water ($\mu_w = 4/3$) is now poured on the glass-air surface. At what angle will the ray of light emerges into water at glass-water surface?

57. A parallel beam of light travelling in water (refractive index $= 4/3$) is refracted by a spherical air bubble of radius 2 mm situated in water. Assuming the light rays to be paraxial. **(1988 JEE)**

(a) Find the position of the image due to refraction at the first surface and the position of the final image.

(b) Draw a ray diagram showing the positions of both the images.

58. The radius of curvature of the convex face of a planoconvex lens is 12 cm and its $\mu = 1.5$. **(1979 JEE)**

(a) Find the focal length of the lens.

The plane face of the lens is now silvered.

(b) At what distance from the lens will parallel rays incident on the convex surface converge ?

(c) Sketch the ray diagram to locate the image, when a point object is placed on the axis 20 cm from the lens.

(d) Calculate the image distance when the object is placed as in (c).

59. A pin is placed 10 cm in front of a convex lens of focal length 20 cm and made of a material of refractive index 1.5. The convex surface of the lens farther away from the pin is silvered and has a radius of curvature of 22 cm. Determine the position of the final image. Is the image real or virtual? **(1978 JEE)**

60. A ray of light is incident at an angle of 60° on one face of a prism which has an angle of 30°. The ray emerging out of the prism makes an angle of 30° with the incident ray. Show that the emergent ray is perpendicular to the face through which it emerges and calculate the refractive index of the material of the lens. **(1978 JEE)**

61. A point source is located at a distance of 20 cm from the front surface of a symmetrical glass biconvex lens. The lens is 5.0 cm thick and the curvature radius of its surfaces is 5.0 cm. How far beyond the rear surface of this lens is the image of the source formed? $\mu_g = 1.5$. **(Irodov 5.31)**

62. A source of light is located at a distance $d = 90$ cm from a screen. A thin converging lens provides the sharp image of the source when placed between the source of light and the screen at two positions. Determine the focal length of the lens if

(a) the distance between the two positions of the lens is $x = 30$ cm

(b) the transverse dimensions of the image at one position of the lens are $\eta = 4.0$ greater than those at the other position. **(Irodov 5.36)**

63. There are two thin symmetrical lenses: one is converging, with refractive index $\mu_1 = 1.70$, and the other is diverging with refractive index $\mu_2 = 1.51$. Both lenses have the same curvature radius of their surfaces equal to $R = 10$ cm. The lenses were put close together and submerged into water. What is the focal length of this system in water? $\mu_w = \frac{4}{3}$. **(Irodov 5.40)**

Integer Type Questions

64. Image of an object approaching a convex mirror of radius of curvature 20 m along its optical axis is observed to move from $\frac{25}{3}$ m to $\frac{50}{7}$ m in 30 s. What is the speed of the object in km h^{-1}? **(2010 JEE)**

65. As shown in the figure, a combination of a thin plano concave lens and a thin plano convex lens is used to image an object placed at infinity. The radius of curvature of both the lenses is 30 cm and refractive index of the material for both the lenses is 1.75. Both the lenses are placed at distance of 40 cm from each other. Due to the combination, the image of the object is formed at distance x =........ cm, from concave lens. **(2023 Main)**

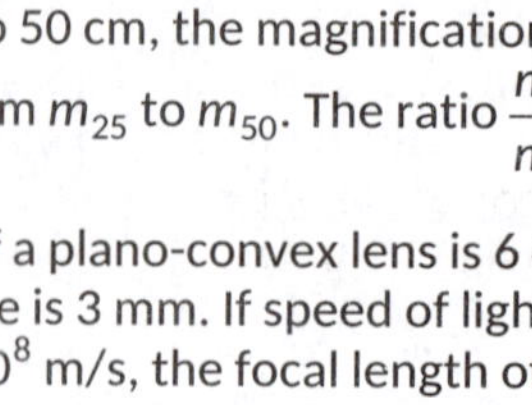

66. The focal length of a thin biconvex lens is 20 cm. When an object is moved from a distance of 25 cm in front of it to 50 cm, the magnification of its image changes from m_{25} to m_{50}. The ratio $\frac{m_{25}}{m_{50}}$ is .... . **(2010 JEE)**

67. Diameter of a plano-convex lens is 6 cm and thickness at the centre is 3 mm. If speed of light in material of lens is 2×10^8 m/s, the focal length of the lens is **(2013 Main)**

(a) 15 cm
(b) 20 cm
(c) 30 cm
(d) 10 cm

Level 2

Single Correct Option

68. A parallel narrow beam of light is incident on the surface of a transparent hemisphere of radius R and refractive index $\mu = 1.5$ as shown. The position of the image formed by refraction from the spherical surface only is

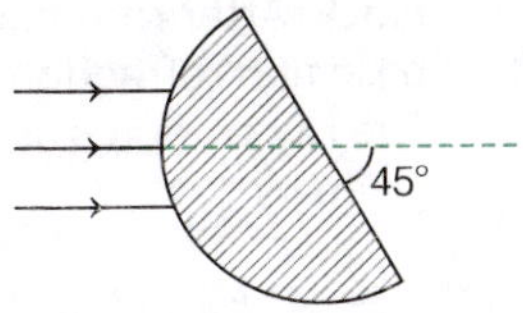

(a) $\frac{R}{2}$ (b) $3R$ (c) $\frac{R}{3}$ (d) $2R$

69. Consider the situation as shown in figure. The point O is the centre. The light ray forms an angle of 60° with the normal. The normal makes an angle 60° with the horizontal and each mirror makes an angle 60° with the normal. The value of refractive index of that spherical portion so that light ray retraces its path is

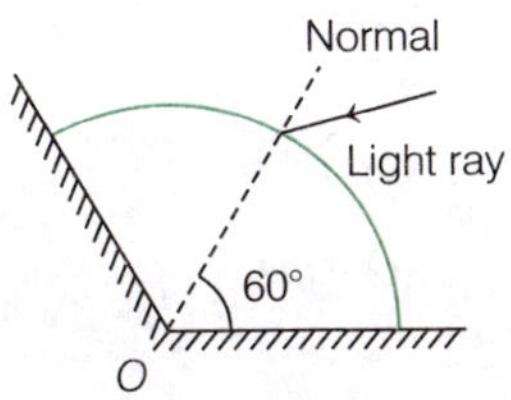

(a) $\sqrt{2}$ (b) $\frac{2}{\sqrt{3}}$ (c) $\frac{3}{2}$ (d) $\sqrt{3}$

70. The figure shows an equi-convex lens. What should be the condition of the refractive indices so that the lens becomes diverging?

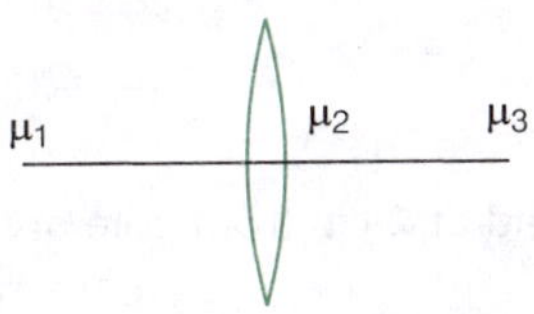

(a) $2\mu_3 > \mu_1 - \mu_2$ (b) $2\mu_2 < \mu_1 + \mu_3$
(c) $2\mu_2 > 2\mu_1 - \mu_3$ (d) None of these

71. An object is kept at a distance of 16 cm from a thin lens and the image formed is real. If the object is kept at a distance of 6 cm from the same lens, the image formed is virtual. If the sizes of the image formed are equal, the focal length of the lens will be

(a) 19 cm (b) 17 cm (c) 21 cm (d) 11 cm

72. A ray of light makes normal incidence on the diagonal face of a right angled prism as shown in figure. If $\theta = 37°$, then the angle of deviation after second step (from AB) is ($\sin 37° = 3/5$)

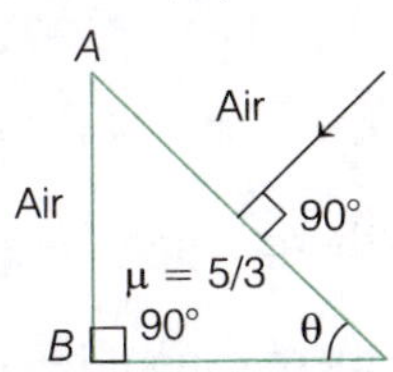

(a) 53° (b) 74°
(c) 106° (d) 90°

73. Refractive index of a prism is $\sqrt{\frac{7}{3}}$ and the angle of prism is 60°. The limiting angle of incidence of a ray that will be transmitted through the prism is approximately

(a) 30° (b) 45°
(c) 15° (d) None of these

74. In the figure, ABC is the cross-section of a right angled prism and $BCDE$ is the cross-section of a glass slab. The value of θ so that light incident normally on the face AB does not cross the face BC is (Given $\sin^{-1} 3/5 = 37°$)

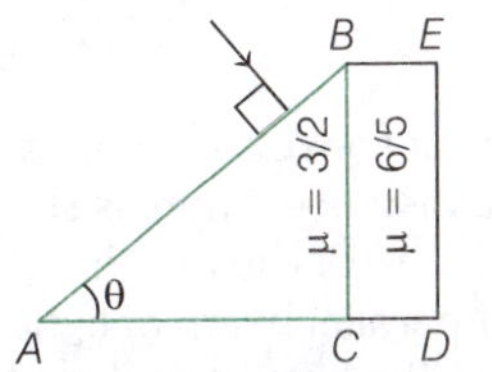

(a) $\theta < 37°$
(b) $\theta < 53°$
(c) $\theta \geq 37°$
(d) $\theta \geq 53°$

75. An object O is kept in air in front of a thin plano-convex lens of radius of curvature 10 cm. Its refractive index is 3/2 and the medium towards right of the plane surface is water of refractive index 4/3. What should be the distance x of the object so that the rays become parallel finally?

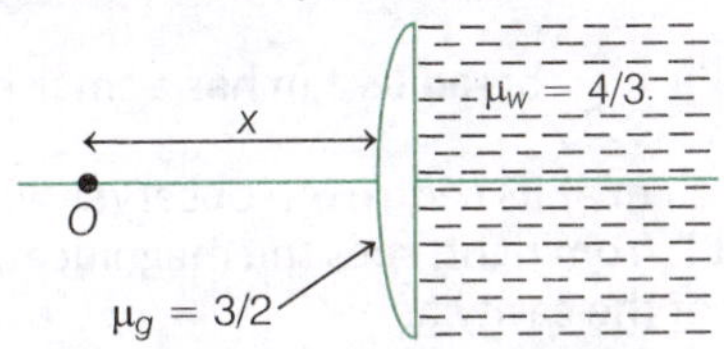

(a) 5 cm
(b) 10 cm
(c) 20 cm
(d) 15 cm

76. If a symmetrical bi-concave thin lens is cut into two identical halves, and they are placed in different ways as shown, then

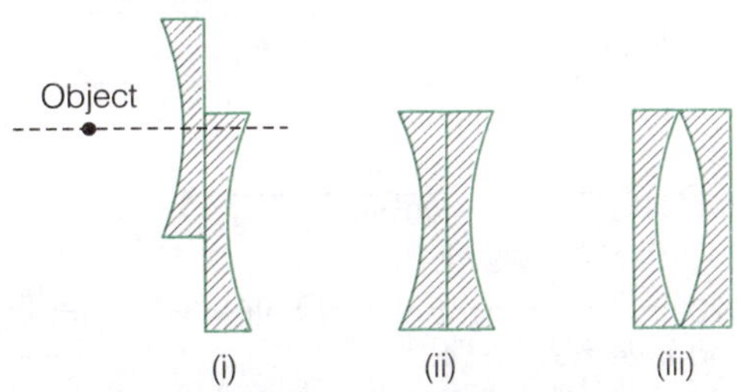

(a) three images will be formed in case (i)
(b) two images will be formed in case (ii)
(c) the ratio of focal lengths in (ii) and (iii) is 1
(d) the ratio of focal lengths in (ii) and (iii) is 2

77. If an object is placed at A $(OA > f)$; where f is the focal length of the lens, the image is formed at B. A perpendicular is erected at O and C is chosen on it such that the angle $\angle BCA$ is a right angle. Then, the value of f will be

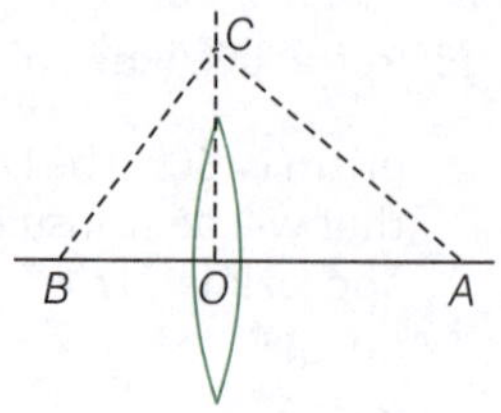

(a) $\dfrac{AB}{OC^2}$ (b) $\dfrac{(AC)(BC)}{OC}$

(c) $\dfrac{OC^2}{AB}$ (d) $\dfrac{(OC)(AB)}{AC+BC}$

78. If the optic axis of convex and concave lenses are separated by a distance 5 mm as shown in the figure. Find the coordinate of the final image formed by the combination if parallel beam of light is incident on lens. Origin is at the optical centre of convex lens

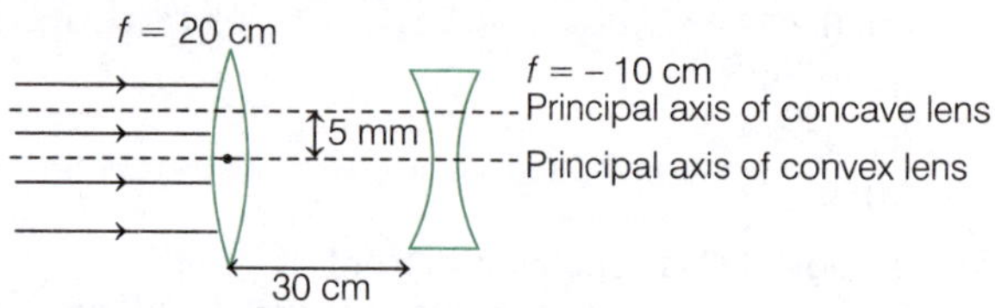

(a) (25 cm, 0.5 cm)
(b) (25 cm, 0.25 cm)
(c) (25 cm, –0.5 cm)
(d) (25 cm, –2.5 cm)

79. A sphere $\left(\mu = \dfrac{4}{3}\right)$ of radius 1 m has a small cavity of diameter 1 cm at its centre. An observer who is looking at it from right, sees the magnification of diameter of the cavity as

(a) $\dfrac{4}{3}$ (b) $\dfrac{3}{4}$ (c) 1 (d) 0.5

80. An equi-convex lens of $\mu = 1.5$ and $R = 20$ cm is cut into two equal parts along its axis. Two parts are then separated by a distance of 120 cm (as shown in figure). An object of height 3 mm is placed at a distance of 30 cm to the left of first half lens. The final image will be formed at

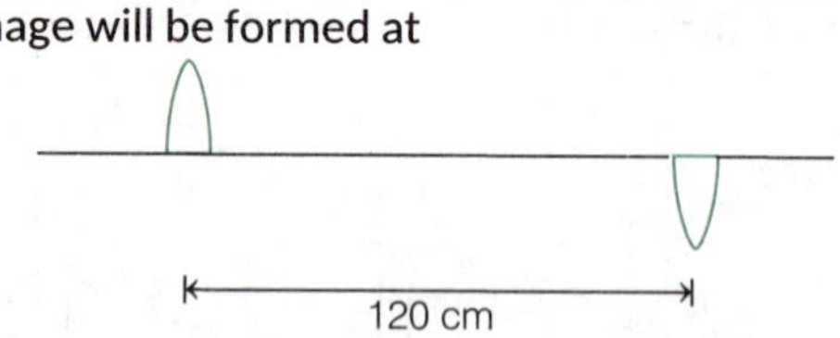

(a) 120 cm to the right of first half lens, 3 mm in size and inverted
(b) 150 cm to the right of first half lens, 3 mm in size and erect
(c) 120 cm to the right of first half lens, 4 mm in size and inverted
(d) 150 cm to the right of first half lens, 4 mm in size and erect

81. A cubical block of glass of refractive index n_1 is in contact with the surface of water of refractive index n_2. A beam of light is incident on vertical face of the block. After refraction a total internal reflection at the base and refraction at the opposite face take place. The ray emerges at angle θ as shown. The value of θ is given by

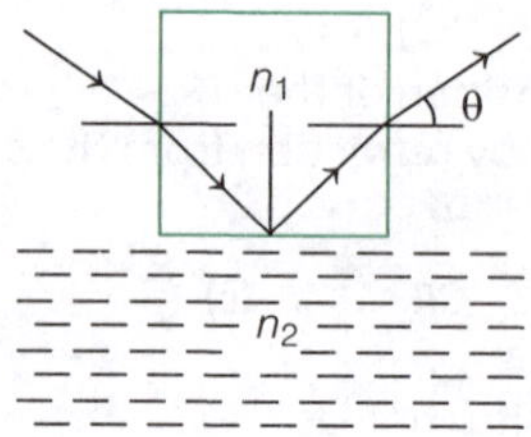

(a) $\sin\theta < \sqrt{n_1^2 - n_2^2}$ (b) $\cos\theta < \sqrt{n_1^2 - n_2^2}$

(c) $\sin\theta < \dfrac{1}{\sqrt{n_1^2 - n_2^2}}$ (d) $\cos\theta < \dfrac{1}{\sqrt{n_1^2 - n_2^2}}$

82. A concave mirror of focal length 2 cm is placed on a glass slab as shown in the figure. The image of point object O formed due to reflection at mirror and then refraction by the slab

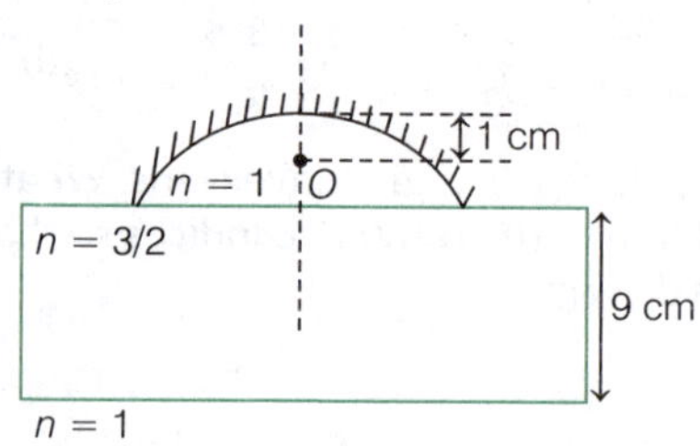

(a) is virtual and at 2 cm from pole of the concave mirror
(b) is virtual and on the pole of mirror
(c) is real and on the object itself
(d) None of the above

83. Two refracting media are separated by a spherical interface as shown in the figure. AB is the principal axis, μ_1 and μ_2 are the refractive indices of medium of incidence and medium of refraction respectively. Choose the correct option.

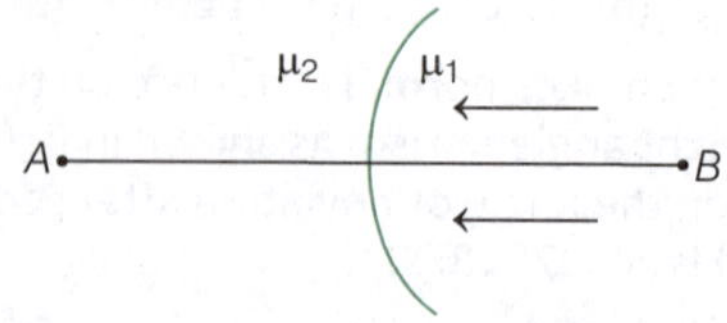

(a) if $\mu_2 > \mu_1$, then there cannot be a real image of real object
(b) if $\mu_2 > \mu_1$, then there cannot be a real image of virtual object
(c) if $\mu_1 > \mu_2$, then there cannot be a real image of virtual object
(d) if $\mu_1 > \mu_2$, then there cannot be a virtual image of virtual object

84. A circular beam of light (diameter $= d$) falls on a plane surface of a liquid. The angle of incidence is 45° and refractive index of the liquid is μ. The diameter of the refracted beam is

(a) d (b) $(\mu - 1)\, d$

(c) $\frac{\sqrt{2\mu^2 - 1}}{\mu} d$ (d) $\frac{\sqrt{\mu^2 - 1}}{\mu} d$

85. A convex lens of focal length 30 cm forms a real image three times larger than the object on a screen. Object and screen are moved until the image becomes twice the size of the object. If the shift of the object is 5 cm, then the shift of screen is

(a) 30 cm (b) 14 cm (c) 18 cm (d) 16 cm

86. A concave mirror is placed at the bottom of an empty tank with face upwards and axis vertical. When sunlight falls normally on the mirror, it is focussed at distance of 32 cm from the mirror. If the tank is filled with water $\left(\mu = \frac{4}{3}\right)$ upto a height of 20 cm, then the sunlight will now get focussed at

(a) 16 cm above water level

(b) 9 cm above water level

(c) 24 cm below water level

(d) 9 cm below water level

87. The graph shows how the inverse of magnification $\frac{1}{m}$ produced by a convex thin lens varies with object distance u. What was the focal length of the lens used?

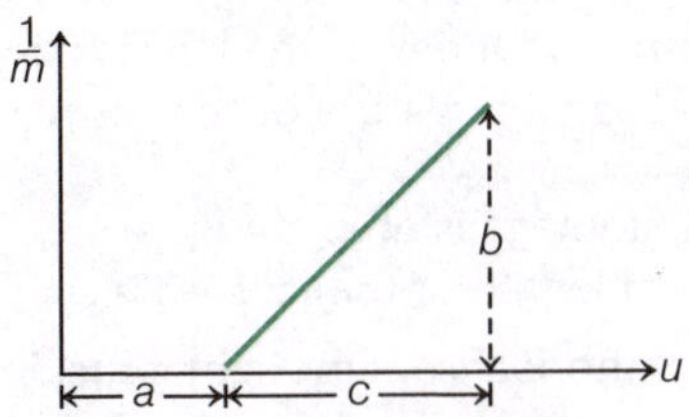

(a) $\frac{b}{c}$ (b) $\frac{b}{ca}$ (c) $\frac{bc}{a}$ (d) $\frac{c}{b}$

88. A ball is dropped from a height of 20 m above the surface of water in a lake. The refractive index of water is 4/3. A fish inside the lake, in the line of fall of the ball, is looking at the ball. At an instant, when the ball is 12.8 m above the water surface, the fish sees the speed of ball as $(g = 10 \text{ m/s}^2)$

(a) 9 m/s (b) 12 m/s (c) 16 m/s (d) 21.33 m/s

89. The diagram shown in figure represents a wavefront AB which passes from air to another transparent medium and produces a new wavefront CD after refraction.

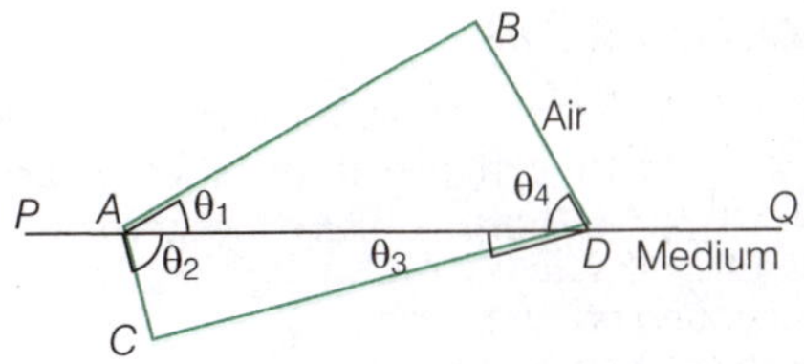

The refractive index of the medium is (PQ is the boundary between air and the medium)

(a) $\frac{\cos \theta_1}{\cos \theta_3}$ (b) $\frac{\cos \theta_4}{\cos \theta_1}$ (c) $\frac{\sin \theta_1}{\sin \theta_3}$ (d) $\frac{\sin \theta_2}{\sin \theta_3}$

90. A ray of light travels from an optically denser medium towards rarer medium. The critical angle for the two media is C. The maximum possible angle of deviation of the ray is

(a) $\frac{\pi}{2} - C$ (b) $\frac{\pi}{2} - 2C$ (c) $2C$ (d) $\frac{\pi}{2} + C$

91. A spherical surface of radius of curvature R, separates air (refractive index 1.0) from glass (refractive index 1.5). The centre of curvature is in the glass. A point object P placed in air is found to have a real image Q in the glass. The line PQ cuts the surface at a point O and $PO = OQ$. The distance PO is equal to

(a) 5 R (b) 3 R (c) 2 R (d) 1.5 R

92. A convex lens (of focal length 20 cm) and a concave mirror, having their principal axes along the same lines, are kept 80 cm apart from each other. The concave mirror is to the right of the convex lens. When an object is kept at a distance of 30 cm to the left of the convex lens, its image remains at the same position even if the concave mirror is removed. The maximum distance of the object for which this concave mirror, by itself would produce a virtual image would be **(2019 Main)**

(a) 25 cm (b) 20 cm

(c) 10 cm (d) 30 cm

93. A thin convex lens L (refractive index = 1.5) is placed on a plane mirror M. When a pin is placed at A, such that $OA = 18$ cm, its real inverted image is formed at A itself, as shown in figure. When a liquid of refractive index μ_l is put between the lens and the mirror, the pin has to be moved to A', such that $OA' = 27$ cm, to get its inverted real image at A' itself. The value of μ_l will be **(2019 Main)**

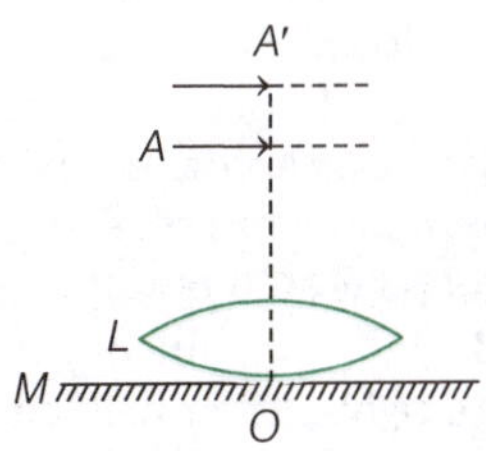

(a) $\sqrt{3}$ (b) $\sqrt{2}$ (c) 4/3 (d) 3/2

Multiple Correct Options

94. n number of identical equilateral prisms are kept in contact as shown in figure. If deviation through a single prism is δ. Then, (n, m are integers)

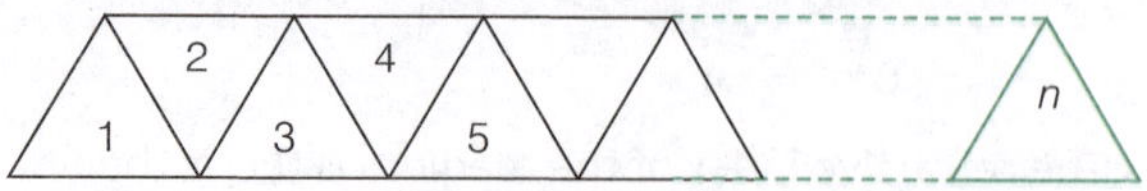

(a) if $n=2m$, deviation through n prisms is zero
(b) if $n=2m+1$, deviation through system of n prisms is δ
(c) if $n=2m$, deviation through system of n prisms is δ
(d) if $n=2m+1$, deviation through system of n prisms is zero

95. A ray of monochromatic light is incident on the plane surface of separation between two media x and y with angle of incidence i in the medium x and angle of refraction r in the medium y. The graph shows the relation between $\sin i$ and $\sin r$.

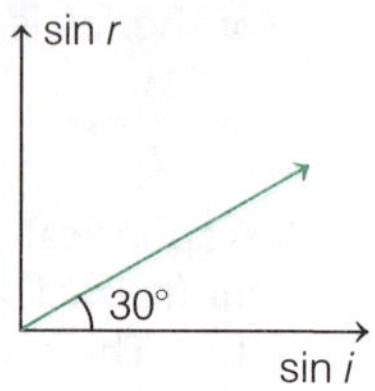

(a) The speed of light in the medium y is $\sqrt{3}$ times than in medium x
(b) The speed of light in the medium y is $\frac{1}{\sqrt{3}}$ times than in medium x
(c) The total internal reflection can take place when the incidence is in x
(d) The total internal reflection can take place when the incidence is in y

96. Which of the following statement(s) is/are true?
(a) In vacuum the speed of red colour is more than that of violet colour
(b) An object in front of a mirror is moved towards the pole of a spherical mirror from infinity, it is found that image also moves towards the pole. The mirror must be convex
(c) There exist two angles of incidence in a prism for which angles of deviation are same except minimum deviation
(d) A ray travels from a rarer medium to denser medium. There exist three angles of incidence for which the deviation is same

97. A lens of focal length f is placed in between an object and screen at a distance D. The lens forms two real images of object on the screen for two of its different positions, a distance x apart. The two real images have magnifications m_1 and m_2 respectively ($m_1 > m_2$). Choose the correct statement(s).
(a) $m_1 m_2 = -1$ (b) $m_1 m_2 = 1$
(c) $f = \frac{D^2 - x^2}{4D}$ (d) $D > 4f$

98. Which of the following quantities increase when wavelength of light is increased? Consider only the magnitudes.
(a) The power of a converging lens
(b) The focal length of a converging lens
(c) The power of a diverging lens
(d) The focal length of a diverging lens

99. A glass beaker has a solid, plano-convex base of refractive index 1.60, as shown in the figure. The radius of curvature of the convex surface (SPU) is 9 cm, while the planar surface (STU) acts as a mirror. This beaker is filled with a liquid of refractive index n up to the level QPR. If the image of a point object O at a height of h (OT in the figure) is formed onto itself, then which of the following option(s) is(are) correct? **(2024 Adv.)**

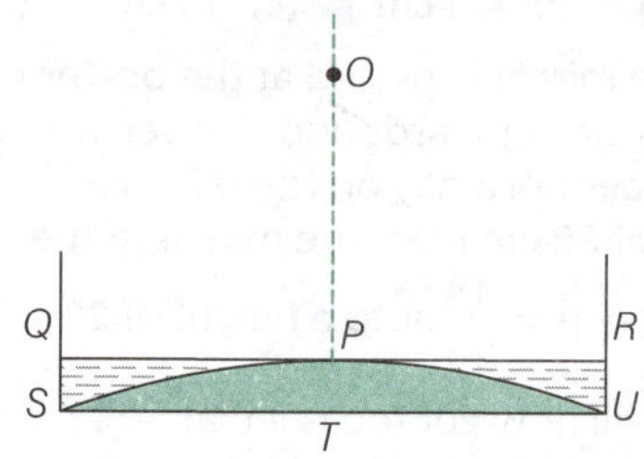

(a) For $n=1.42$, $h=50$ cm (b) For $n=1.35$, $h=36$ cm
(c) For $n=1.45$, $h=65$ cm (d) For $n=1.48$, $h=85$ cm

100. A plano-convex lens is made of material of refractive index n. When a small object is placed 30 cm away in front of the curved surface of the lens, an image of double the size of the object is produced. Due to reflection from the convex surface of the lens, another faint image is observed at a distance of 10 cm away from the lens. Which of the following statement(s) is (are) true? **(2016 Adv.)**
(a) The refractive index of the lens is 2.5
(b) The radius of curvature of the convex surface is 45 cm
(c) The faint image is erect and real
(d) The focal length of the lens is 20 cm

101. A ray OP of monochromatic light is incident on the face AB of prism $ABCD$ near vertex B at an incident angle of 60° (see figure). If the refractive index of the material of the prism is $\sqrt{3}$, which of the following is (are) correct? **(2010 JEE)**

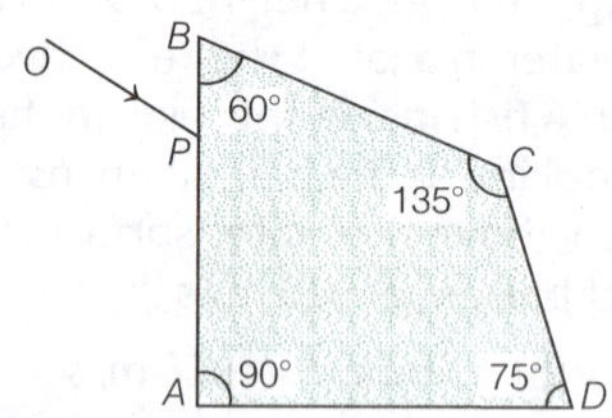

(a) The ray gets totally internally reflected at face CD
(b) The ray comes out through face AD
(c) The angle between the incident ray and the emergent ray is 90°
(d) The angle between the incident ray and the emergent ray is 120°

Passage Based Questions

Passage 1 (Q. No. 102 to 104)

A plano-convex lens P and a concavo-convex lens Q are in contact as shown in figure. The refractive index of the material of the lens P and Q is 1.8 and 1.2 respectively. The radius of curvature of the concave surface of the lens Q is double the radius of curvature of the convex surface. The convex surface of Q is silvered.

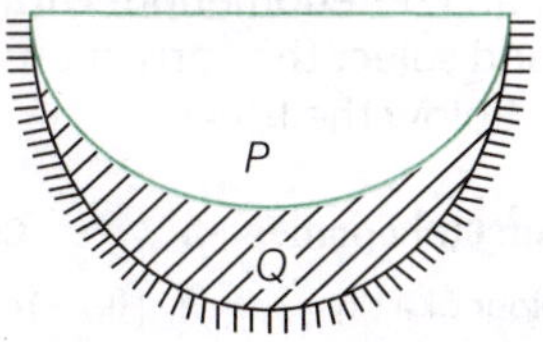

102. An object is placed on the principal axis at a distance 10 cm from the plane surface. The image is formed at a distance 40 cm from the plane surface on the same side. The focal length of the system is

(a) -8 cm (b) 8 cm

(c) $-\frac{40}{3}$ cm (d) $\frac{40}{3}$ cm

103. The radius of curvature of common surface is

(a) 48 cm (b) 24 cm

(c) 12 cm (d) 8 cm

104. If the plane surface of P is silvered as shown in figure, the system acts as

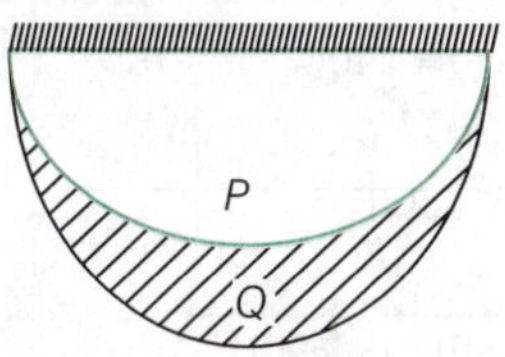

(a) convex mirror of focal length 24 cm

(b) concave mirror of focal length 8 cm

(c) concave mirror of focal length 24 cm

(d) convex mirror of focal length 8 cm

Passage 2 (Q. No 105 to 107)

The figure shows a surface XY separating two transparent media, medium-1 and medium-2. The lines ab and cd represent wavefronts of a light wave travelling in medium-1 and incident on XY. The lines ef and gh represent wavefronts of the light wave in medium-2 after refraction. **(2007 JEE)**

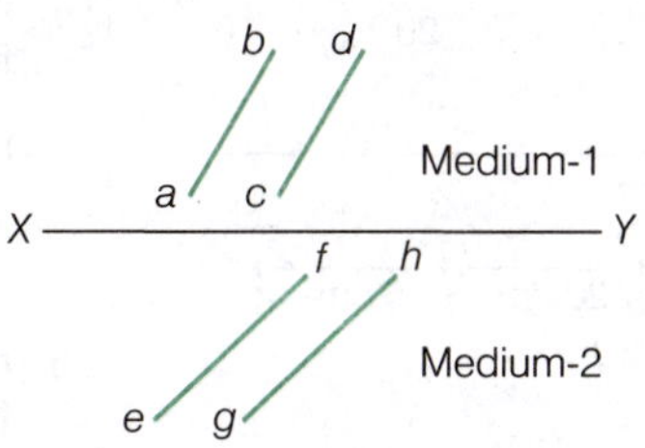

105. Light travels as a

(a) parallel beam in each medium

(b) convergent beam in each medium

(c) divergent beam in each medium

(d) divergent beam in one medium and convergent beam in the other medium

106. The phases of the light wave at c, d, e and f are ϕ_c, ϕ_d, ϕ_e and ϕ_f respectively. It is given that $\phi_c \neq \phi_f$

(a) ϕ_c cannot be equal to ϕ_d

(b) ϕ_d can be equal to ϕ_e

(c) $(\phi_d - \phi_f)$ is equal to $(\phi_c - \phi_e)$

(d) $(\phi_d - \phi_c)$ is not equal to $(\phi_f - \phi_e)$

107. Speed of light is

(a) the same in medium-1 and medium-2

(b) larger in medium-1 than in medium-2

(c) larger in medium-2 than in medium-1

(d) different at b and d

Match the Columns

108. Match the following two columns for a convex lens corresponding to object position shown in Column I.

	Column I		Column II
(a)	Between O and F_1	(p)	Real
(b)	Between F_1 and $2F_1$	(q)	Virtual
(c)	Between O and F_2	(r)	Erect
(d)	Between F_2 and $2F_2$	(s)	Inverted

Note *O → optical centre, F_1 → first focus and F_2 → second focus.*

109. Match the following two columns for a concave lens corresponding to object position shown in Column II.

	Column I		Column II
(a)	Between O and F_1	(p)	Real
(b)	Between F_1 and $2F_1$	(q)	Virtual
(c)	Between O and F_2	(r)	Erect
(d)	Between F_2 and $2F_2$	(s)	Inverted

110. Match the following two columns corresponding to single refraction from plane surface. In all cases shown in Column I, $\mu_1 > \mu_2$.

	Column I		Column II
(a)	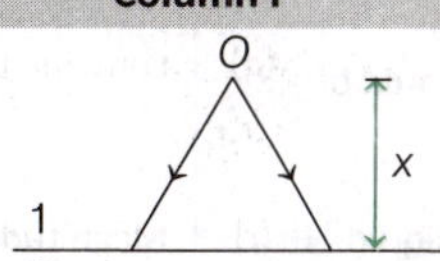	(p)	Image distance greater than x from plane surface
(b)	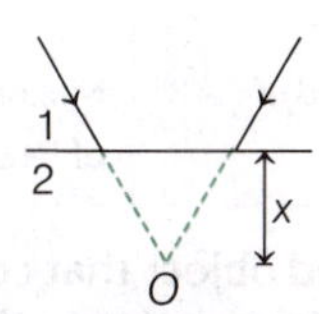	(q)	Image distance less than x from plane surface

	Column I		Column II
(c)	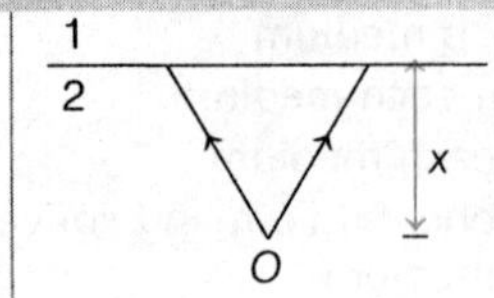	(r)	Real image
(d)	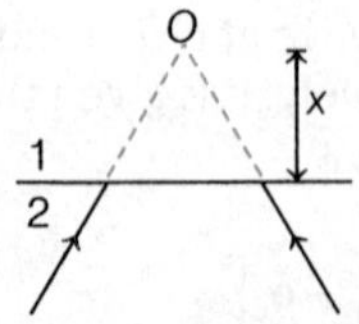	(s)	Virtual image

111. Match the following two columns.

	Column I		Column II
(a)	Air 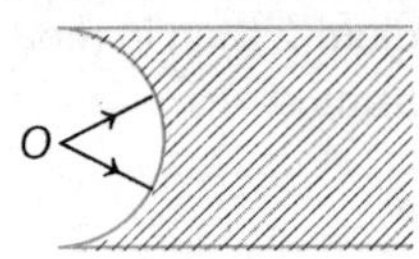	(p)	Real image
(b)	Air 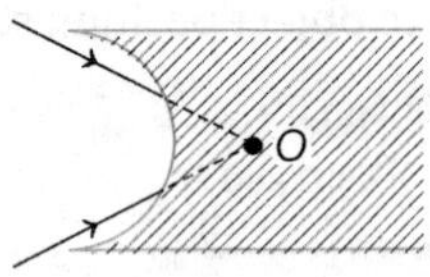	(q)	Virtual image
(c)	Air 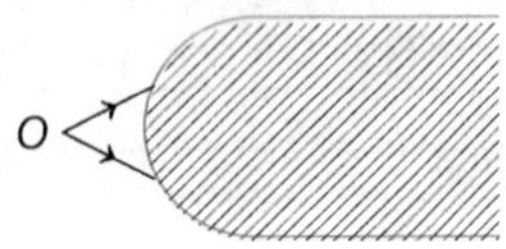	(r)	May be real or virtual image
(d)	Air 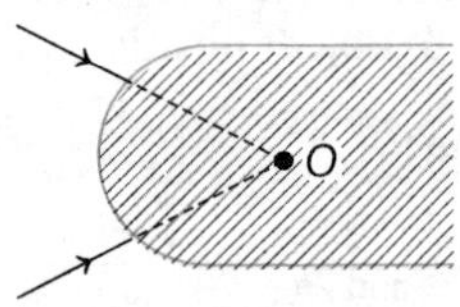	(s)	Image is at infinity

112. A convex lens L_1 and a concave lens L_2 have refractive index 1.5. Match the following two columns.

	Column I		Column II
(a)	L_1 is immersed in a liquid of refractive index 1.4	(p)	Lens will behave as convex lens
(b)	L_1 is immersed in a liquid of refractive index 1.6	(q)	Lens will behave as concave lens
(c)	L_2 is immersed in a liquid of refractive index 1.4	(r)	Magnitude of power of lens will increase
(d)	L_2 is immersed in a liquid of refractive index 1.6	(s)	Magnitude of power of lens will decrease

113. Consider a linear extended object that could be real or virtual with its length at right angles to the optic axis of a lens. With regard to image formation by lenses.

	Column I		Column II
(a)	Image of the same size as the object	(p)	Concave lens in case of real object
(b)	Virtual image of a size greater than the object	(q)	Convex lens in case of real object
(c)	Real image of a size smaller than the object	(r)	Concave lens in case of virtual object
(d)	Real and magnified image	(s)	Convex lens in case of virtual object

114. Match Column I (Phenomenon) with Column II (Principle) and select the correct answer using the codes given below the lists.

	Column I (Phenomenon)		Column II (Principle)
(a)	Blue colour of a sky	(p)	Total internal reflection
(b)	Glittering of diamond	(q)	Dispersion of light
(c)	Formation of rainbow	(r)	Scattering of light
(d)	In the evening when the sun goes down below the horizon, it continues to remain visible for sometime	(s)	Refraction of light

115. Column-I contains four combinations of two lenses (1 and 2) whose focal lengths (in cm) are indicated in the figures. In all cases, the object is placed 20 cm from the first lens on the left, and the distance between the two lenses is 5 cm. Column-II contains the positions of the final images.

	Column I		Column II
I	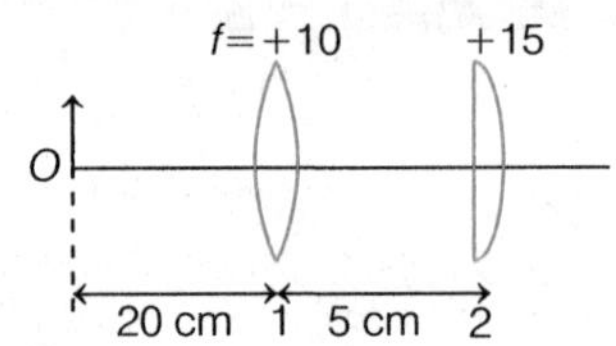	(P)	Final image is formed at 7.5 cm on the right side of lens 2.
II	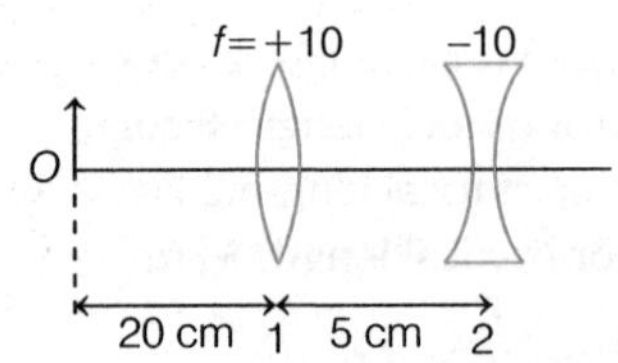	(Q)	Final image is formed at 60.0 cm on the right side of lens 2.
III	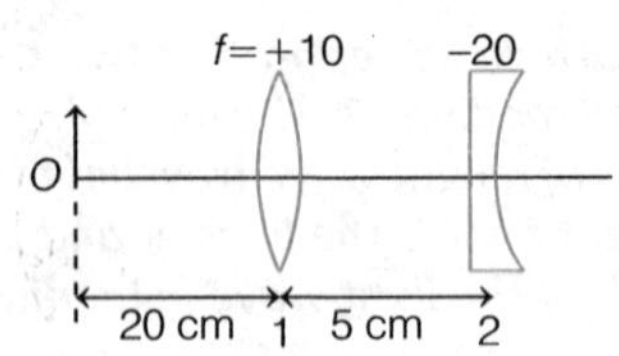	(R)	Final image is formed at 30.0 cm on the left side of lens 2.
IV	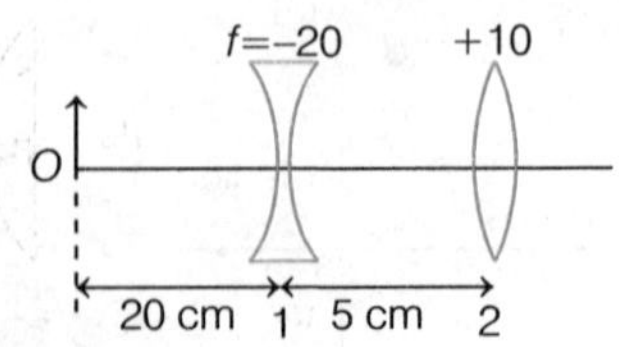	(S)	Final image is formed at 6.0 cm on the right side of lens 2.
		(T)	Final image is formed at 30.0 cm on the right side of lens 2.

Which one of the following options is correct? **(2022 Adv.)**

	I	II	III	IV		I	II	III	IV
(a)	P	R	Q	T	(b)	Q	P	T	S
(c)	P	T	R	Q	(d)	T	S	Q	R

116. Four combinations of two thin lenses are given in Column I. The radius of curvature of all curved surfaces is r and the refractive index of all the lenses is 1.5. Match lens combinations in Column I with their focal length in Column II and select the correct answer using the codes given below the lists. **(2014 Adv.)**

Column I		Column II	
(a)	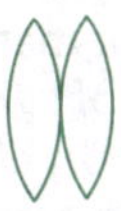	(p)	$2r$
(b)		(q)	$r/2$
(c)		(r)	$-r$
(d)	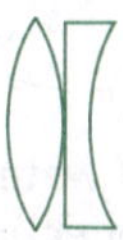	(s)	r

(a) A-p, B-q, C-r, D-s (b) A-q, B-s, C-r, D-p
(c) A-s, B-p, C-q, D-r (d) A-q, B-p, C-r, D-s

117. Two transparent media of refractive indices μ_1 and μ_3 have a solid lens shaped transparent material of refractive index μ_2 between them as shown in figures in **Column II**. A ray traversing these media is also shown in the figures. In **Column I** different relationships between μ_1, μ_2 and μ_3 are given. Match them to the ray diagram shown in **Column II**. **(2010 JEE)**

Column I		Column II	
(A)	$\mu_1 < \mu_2$	(p)	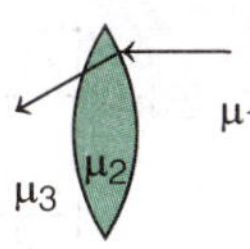
(B)	$\mu_1 > \mu_2$	(q)	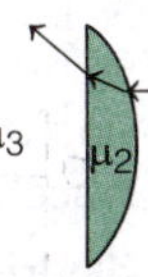
(C)	$\mu_2 = \mu_3$	(r)	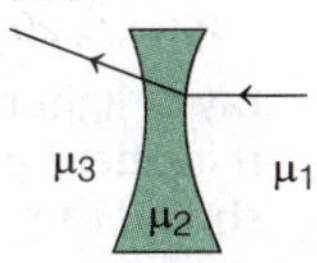
(D)	$\mu_2 > \mu_3$	(s)	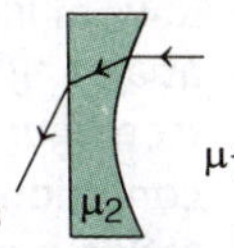
		(t)	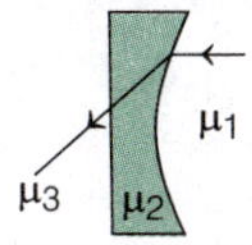

Subjective Questions

118. A lens with a focal length of $f = 30$ cm produces on a screen a sharp image of an object that is at a distance of $a = 40$ cm from the lens. A plane parallel plate with thickness of $d = 9$ cm is placed between the lens and the object perpendicular to the optical axis of the lens. Through what distance should the screen be shifted for the image of the object to remain distinct? The refractive index of the glass of the plate is $\mu = 1.8$.

119. One side of radius of curvature $R_2 = 120$ cm of a convexo-convex lens of material of refractive index $\mu = 1.5$ and focal length $f_1 = 40$ cm is slivered. It is placed on a horizontal surface with silvered surface in contact with it. Another convex lens of focal length $f_2 = 20$ cm is fixed coaxially $d = 10$ cm above the first lens. A luminous point object O on the axis gives rise to an image coincident with it. Find its height above the upper lens.

120. A thin glass lens of refractive index $\mu_2 = 1.5$ behaves as an interface between two media of refractive indices $\mu_1 = 1.4$ and $\mu_3 = 1.6$ respectively. Determine the focal length of the lens for the shown arrangement of radius of curvature of both the surfaces 20 cm.

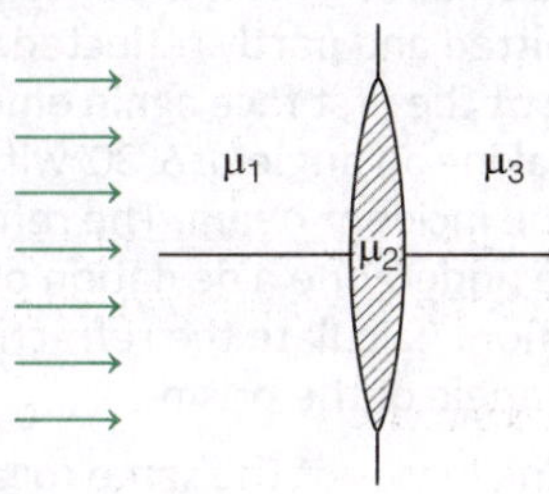

121. A glass hemisphere of radius 10 cm and $\mu = 1.5$ is silvered over its curved surface. There is an air bubble in the glass 5 cms from the plane surface along the axis. Find the position of the images of this bubble seen by observer looking along the axis into the flat surface of the atmosphere.

122. An equilateral prism of flint glass ($\mu_g = 3/2$) is placed inside water ($\mu_w = 4/3$).

(a) At what angle should a ray of light fall on the face of the prism so that inside the prism the ray is perpendicular to the bisector of the angle of the prism.

(b) Through what angle will the ray turn after passing through both faces of the prism?

123. Rays of light fall on the plane surface of a half cylinder at an angle 45° in the plane perpendicular to the axis (see figure). Refractive index of glass is $\sqrt{2}$. Discuss the condition that the rays do not suffer total internal reflection.

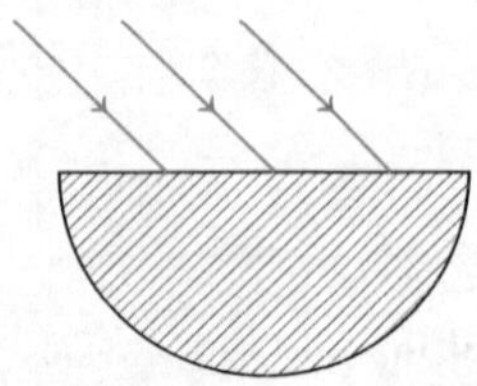

124. The figure shows an arrangement of an equi-convex lens and a concave mirror. A point object O is placed on the principal axis at a distance 40 cm from the lens such that the final image is also formed at the position of the object. If the radius of curvature of the concave mirror is 80 cm, find the distance d. Also draw the ray diagram. The focal length of the lens in air is 20 cm.

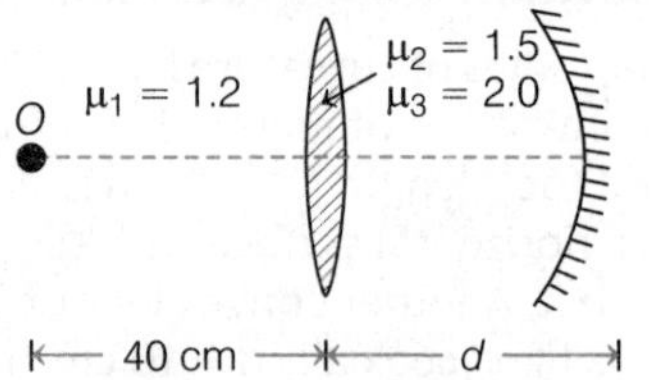

125. A convex lens is held 45 cm above the bottom of an empty tank. The image of a point at the bottom of a tank is formed 36 cm above the lens. Now, a liquid is poured into the tank to a depth of 40 cm. It is found that the distance of the image of the same point on the bottom of the tank is 48 cm above the lens. Find the refractive index of the liquid.

126. A parallel beam of light falls normally on the first face of a prism of a small angle. At the second face it is partly transmitted and partly reflected. The reflected beam striking at the first face again emerges from it in a direction making an angle of 6°30′ with the reversed direction of the incident beam. The refracted beam is found to have undergone a deviation of 1°15 from the original direction. Calculate the refractive index of the glass and the angle of the prism.

127. Two converging lenses of the same focal length f are separated by a distance $2f$. The axis of the second lens is inclined at angle $\theta = 60°$ with respect to the axis of the first lens. A parallel paraxial beam of light is incident from left side of the lens. Find the coordinates of the final image with respect to the origin of the first lens.

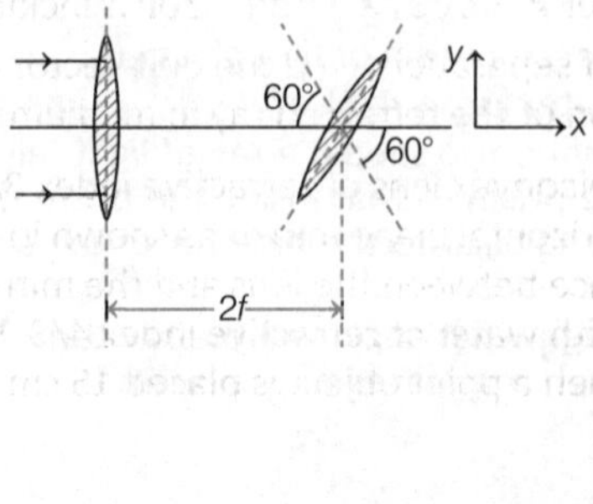

128. A thin converging lens of focal length $f = 1.5$ m is placed along y-axis such that its optical centre coincides with the origin. A small light source S is placed at $(-2.0 \text{ m}, 0.1 \text{ m})$. Where should a plane mirror inclined at an angle θ, be placed such that y-coordinate of final image is 0.3 m, i.e. find d. Also find x-coordinate of final image ($\tan\theta = 0.3$).

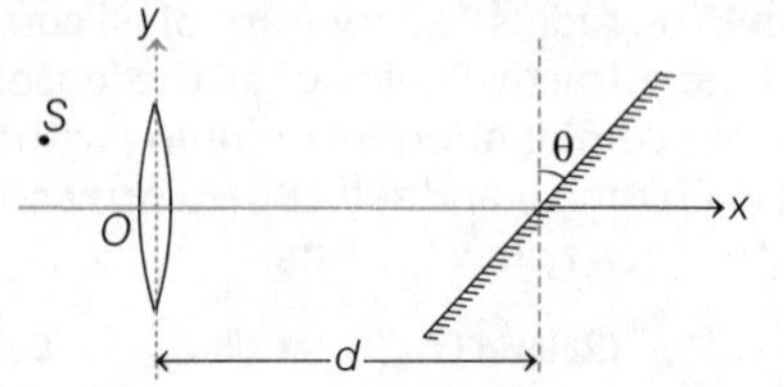

129. A spherical ball of transparent material has index of refraction μ. A narrow beam of light AB is aimed as shown. What must the index of refraction be in order that the light is focused at the point C on the opposite end of the diameter from where the light entered? Given that $x << R$.

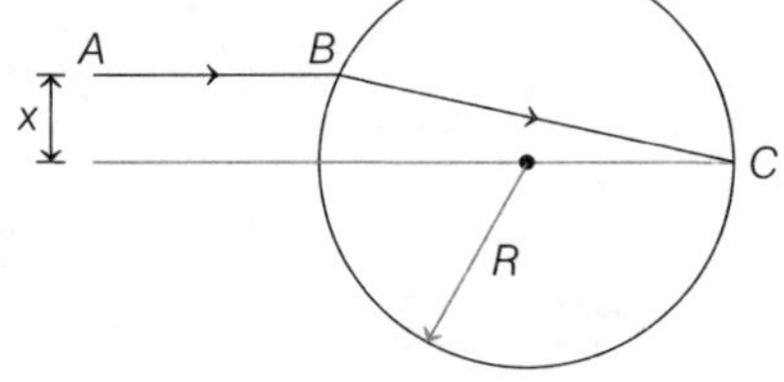

130. A ray incident on a droplet of water at an angle of incidence i undergoes two reflections (not total) and emerges. If the deviation suffered by the ray is minimum and the refractive index of the droplet be μ, then show that $\cos i = \sqrt{\dfrac{\mu^2 - 1}{8}}$.

131. A convex lens of focal length 15 cm is split into two halves and the two halves are placed at a separation of 120 cm. Between the two halves of convex lens a plane mirror is placed horizontally and at a distance of 4 mm below the principal axis of the lenses. An object of length 2 mm is placed at a distance of 20 cm from one half lens as shown in figure.

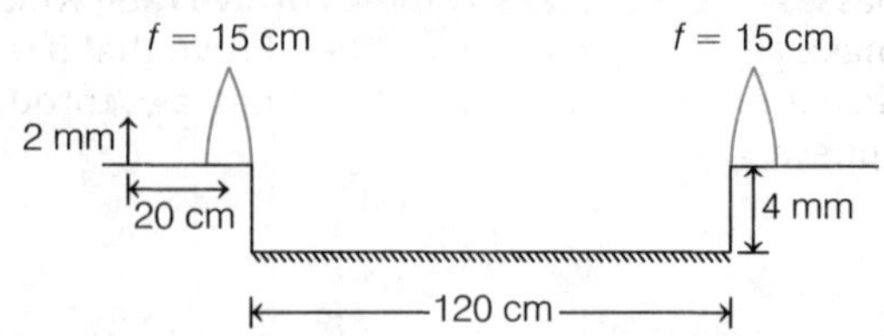

(a) Find the position and size of the final image.
(b) Trace the path of rays forming the image.

132. A cylindrical glass rod of radius 0.1 m and refractive index $\sqrt{3}$ lies on a horizontal plane mirror. A horizontal ray of light moving perpendicular to the axis of the rod is incident on it. At what height from the mirror should the ray be incident so that it leaves the rod at a height of 0.1 m above the plane mirror? At what centre to centre distance a second similar rod, parallel to the first, be placed on the mirror, such that the emergent ray from the second rod is in line with the incident ray on the first rod?

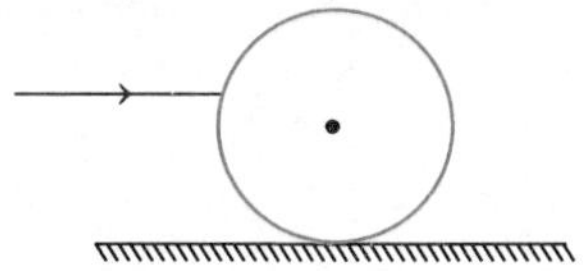

133. A transparent solid sphere of radius 2 cm and density ρ floats in a transparent liquid of density 2ρ kept in a beaker. The bottom of the beaker is spherical in shape with radius of curvature 8 cm and is silvered to make it concave mirror as shown in the figure. When an object is placed at a distance of 10 cm directly above the centre of the sphere C, its final image coincides with it. Find h (as shown in the figure), the height of the liquid surface in the beaker from the apex of the bottom. Consider the paraxial rays only. The refractive index of the sphere is 3/2 and that of the liquid is 4/3.

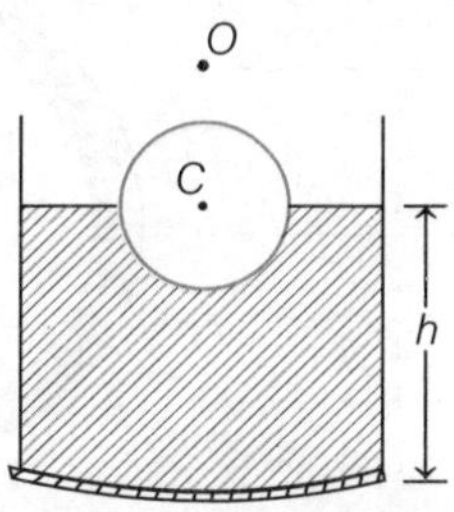

134. A hollow sphere of glass of refractive index μ has a small mark on its interior surface which is observed from a point outside the sphere on the side opposite the centre. The inner cavity is concentric with external surface and the thickness of the glass is everywhere equal to the radius of the inner surface. Prove that the mark will appear nearer than it really is, by a distance $\frac{(\mu - 1)R}{(3\mu - 1)}$, where R is the radius of the inner surface.

135. A ray of light is refracted through a sphere whose material has a refractive index μ in such a way that it passes through the extremities of two radii which make an angle β with each other. Prove that if α is the deviation of the ray caused by its passage through the sphere, then

$$\cos\left(\frac{\beta - \alpha}{2}\right) = \mu \cos\left(\frac{\beta}{2}\right)$$

136. A man of height 2.0 m is standing on a level road where because of temperature variation the refractive index of air is varying as $\mu = \sqrt{1 + ay}$, where y is height from road. If $a = 2.0 \times 10^{-6} \text{m}^{-1}$. Then, find distant point that he can see on the road.

137. A glass rod has ends as shown in figure. The refractive index of glass is μ. The object O is at a distance $2R$ from the surface of larger radius of curvature. The distance between apexes of ends is $3R$. Find the distance of image formed of the point object from right hand vertex. What is the condition to be satisfied if the image is to be real?

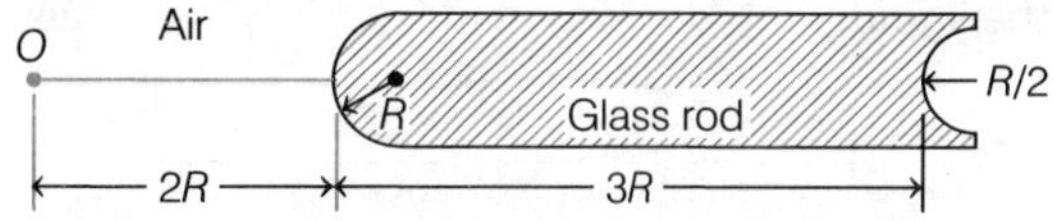

138. An object is approaching a thin convex lens of focal length 0.3 m with a speed of 0.01 m/s. Find the magnitudes of the rates of change of position and lateral magnification of image when the object is at a distance of 0.4 m from the lens. **(2004 JEE)**

139. A ray of light travelling in air is incident at grazing angle (Incident angle $= 90°$) on a long rectangular slab of a transparent medium of thickness $t = 1.0$ m. The point of incidence is the origin $A(0,0)$. The medium has a variable index of refraction $n(y)$ given by $n(y) = [ky^{3/2} + 1]^{1/2}$ where $k = 1.0 (\text{m})^{-3/2}$.
The refractive index of air is 1.0. **(1995 JEE)**
(a) Obtain a relation between the slope of the trajectory of the ray at a point $B(x, y)$ in the medium and the incident angle at that point.
(b) Obtain an equation for the trajectory $y(x)$ of the ray in the medium.
(c) Determine the coordinates (x_1, y_1) of the point P, where the ray intersects the upper surface of the slab-air boundary.
(d) Indicate the path of the ray subsequently.

140. Figure shows an irregular block of material of refractive index $\sqrt{2}$. A ray of light strikes the face AB as shown in the figure. After refraction it is incident on a spherical surface CD of radius of curvature 0.4 m and enters a medium of refractive index 1.514 to meet PQ at E. Find the distance OE upto two places of decimal. **(2004 JEE)**

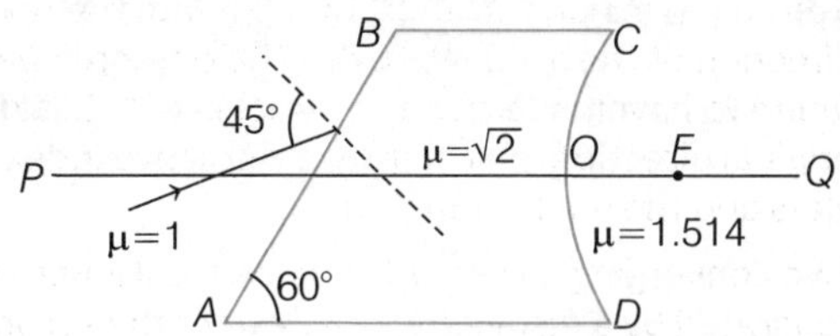

141. The XY-plane is the boundary between two transparent media. Medium-1 with $z \geq 0$ has a refractive index $\sqrt{2}$ and medium-2 with $z \leq 0$ has a refractive index $\sqrt{3}$. A ray of light in medium-1 given by vector $\mathbf{A} = 6\sqrt{3}\,\hat{\mathbf{i}} + 8\sqrt{3}\,\hat{\mathbf{j}} - 10\hat{\mathbf{k}}$ is incident on the plane of separation. Find the unit vector in the direction of the refracted ray in medium-2. **(1999 JEE)**

142. A thin biconvex lens of refractive index 3/2 is placed on a horizontal plane mirror as shown in the figure. The space between the lens and the mirror is then filled with water of refractive index 4/3. It is found that when a point object is placed 15 cm above the

lens on its principal axis, the object coincides with its own image. On repeating with another liquid, the object and the image again coincide at a distance 25 cm from the lens. Calculate the refractive index of the liquid. **(2001 JEE)**

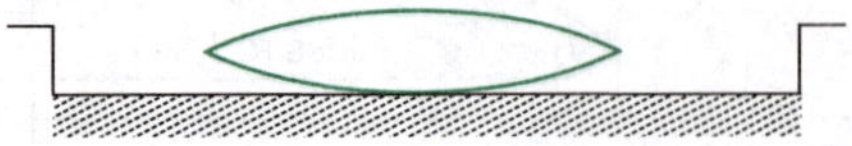

143. A convex lens of focal length 15 cm and a concave mirror of focal length 30 cm are kept with their optic axis *PQ* and *RS* parallel but separated in vertical direction by 0.6 cm as shown.

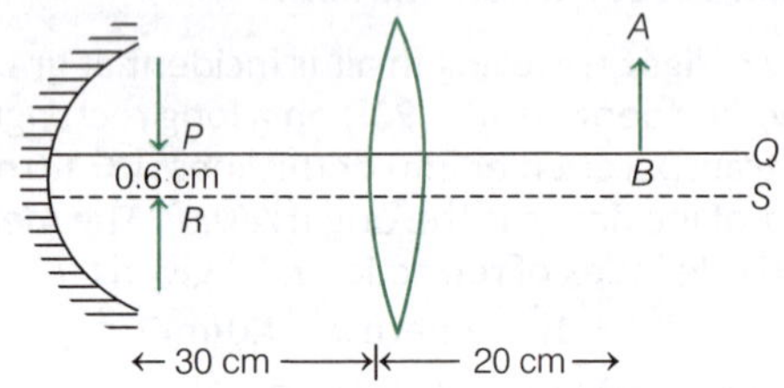

The distance between the lens and mirror is 30 cm. An upright object *AB* of height 1.2 cm is placed on the optic axis *PQ* of the lens at a distance of 20 cm from the lens. If *A′B′* is the image after refraction from the lens and the reflection from the mirror, find the distance of *A′B′* from the pole of the mirror and obtain its magnification. Also locate positions of *A′* and *B′* with respect to the optic axis *RS*. **(2000 JEE)**

144. A prism of refractive index n_1 and another prism of refractive index n_2 are stuck together with a gap as shown in the figure. The angles of the prism are as shown. n_1 and n_2 depend on λ, the wavelength of light according to :

$$n_1 = 1.20 + \frac{10.8 \times 10^4}{\lambda^2}$$

and $$n_2 = 1.45 + \frac{1.80 \times 10^4}{\lambda^2}$$

where λ is in nm. **(1998 JEE)**

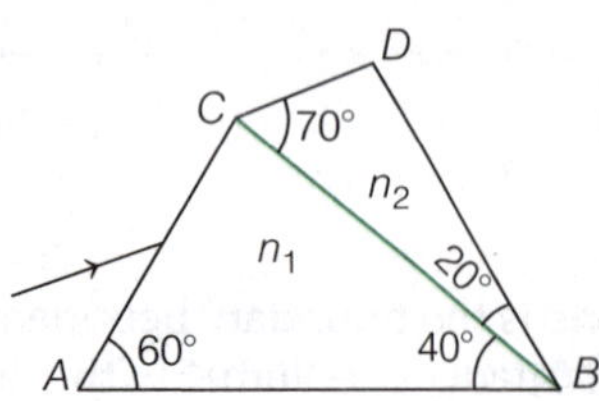

(a) Calculate the wavelength λ_0 for which rays incident at any angle on the interface *BC* pass through without bending at that interface.

(b) For light of wavelength λ_0, find the angle of incidence *i* on the face *AC* such that the deviation produced by the combination of prisms is minimum.

145. A right angled prism (45°-90°-45°) of refractive index *n* has a plane of refractive index n_1 ($n_1 < n$) cemented to its diagonal face. The assembly is in air. The ray is incident on *AB*.

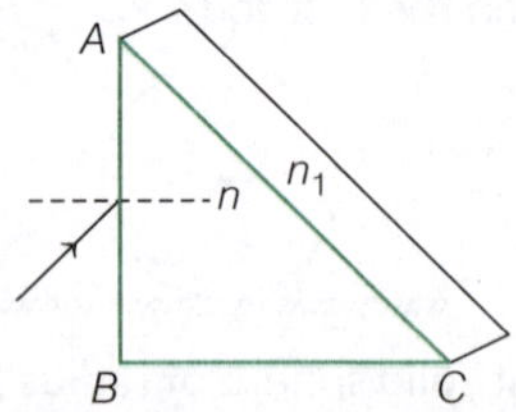

(a) Calculate the angle of incidence at *AB* for which the ray strikes the diagonal face at the critical angle. **(1996 JEE)**

(b) Assuming $n = 1.352$, calculate the angle of incidence at *AB* for which the refracted ray passes through the diagonal face undeviated.

146. In the figure, light is incident on a thin lens as shown. The radius of curvature for both the surfaces is *R*. Determine the focal length of this system. **(2003 JEE)**

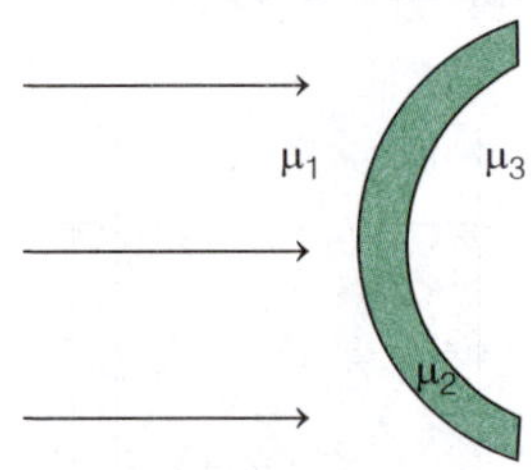

147. A thin equiconvex lens of glass of refractive index $\mu = 3/2$ and of focal length 0.3 m in air is sealed into an opening at one end of a tank filled with water $\mu = 4/3$. On the opposite side of the lens, a mirror is placed inside the tank , as shown in figure. The separation between the lens and the mirror is 0.8 m. A small object is placed outside the tank in front of lens. Find the position (relative to the lens) of the image of the object formed by the system. **(1997 JEE)**

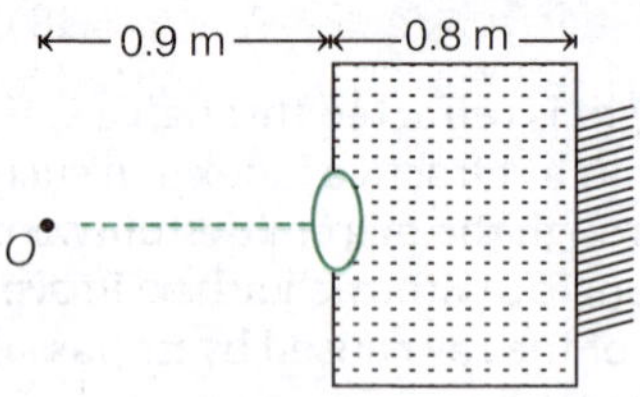

148. A plano-convex lens has a thickness of 4 cm. When placed on a horizontal table, with the curved surface in contact with it, the apparent depth of the bottom most point of the lens is found to be 3 cm. If the lens is inverted such that the plane face is in contact with the table, the apparent depth of the centre of the plane face is found to be 25/8 cm. Find the focal length of the lens. Assume thickness to be negligible while finding its focal length. **(1984 JEE)**

149. The convex surface of a thin concavo-convex lens of glass of refractive index 1.5 has a radius of curvature 20 cm. The concave surface has a radius of curvature 60 cm. The convex side is silvered and placed on a horizontal surface. **(1981 JEE)**

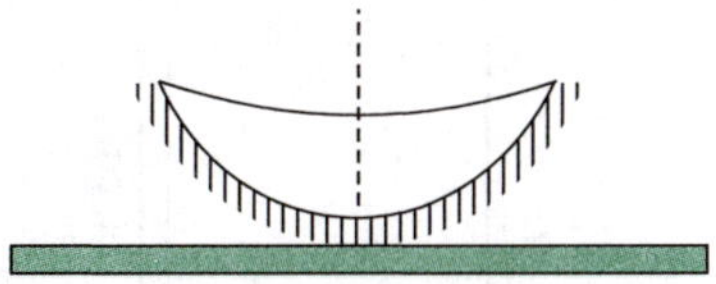

(a) Where should a pin be placed on the optic axis such that its image is formed at the same place?

(b) If the concave part is filled with water of refractive index 4/3, find the distance through which the pin should be moved, so that the image of the pin again coincides with the pin.

150. Two optical media have a plane boundary between them. Suppose θ_{1cr} is the critical angle of incidence of a beam and θ_1 is the angle of incidence at which the refracted beam is perpendicular to the reflected one (the beam is assumed to come from an optically denser medium). Find the relative refractive index of these media if $\sin\theta_{1cr}/\sin\theta_1 = 1.28$. **(Irodov 5.16)**

151. Find the minimum and maximum deflection angles for a light ray passing through a glass prism with refracting angle $\theta = 60°$. **(Irodov 5.22)**

152. A light ray composed of two monochromatic components passes through a trihedral prism with refracting angle $A = 60°$. Find the angle $\Delta\theta$ between the components of the ray after its passage through the prism if their respective indices of refraction are equal to 1.515 and 1.520. The prism is oriented to provide the least deflection angle. **(Irodov 5.24)**

153. A thin converging lens with focal length $f = 25$ cm makes the image of an object on a screen at a distance $l = 5.0$ m from lens. Then the screen was brought closer to the lens by a distance $\Delta l = 18$ cm. By what distance should the object be shifted for its image to become sharp again? **(Irodov 5.35)**

154. Figure illustrates an aligned system consisting of three thin lenses. The system is located in air. Determine:

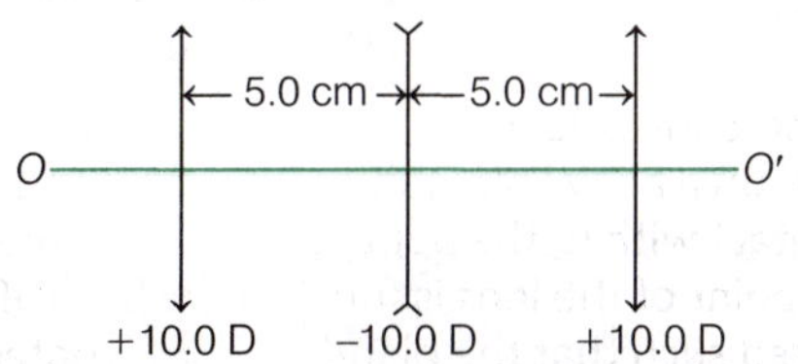

(a) the position of the point of convergence of a parallel ray incoming from the left after passing through the system

(b) the distance between the first lens and a point lying on the axis to the left of the system, at which that point and its image are located symmetrically with respect to the lens system. **(Irodov 5.42)**

155. Find the optical power and the focal lengths

(a) of a thin glass lens in liquid with refractive index $\mu_l = 1.7$ if its optical power in air is -5.0 D

(b) of a thin symmetrical biconvex glass lens, with air on one side and water on the other side, if the optical power of that lens in air is $+10$ D. $\mu_g = 1.5$ and $\mu_w = \frac{4}{3}$. **(Irodov 5.43)**

Note *Assume that light is incident from air side.*

156. In figure, a fish watcher watches a fish through a 3.0 cm thick glass wall of a fish tank. The watcher is in level with the fish; the index of refraction of the glass is 8/5 and that of the water is 4/3.

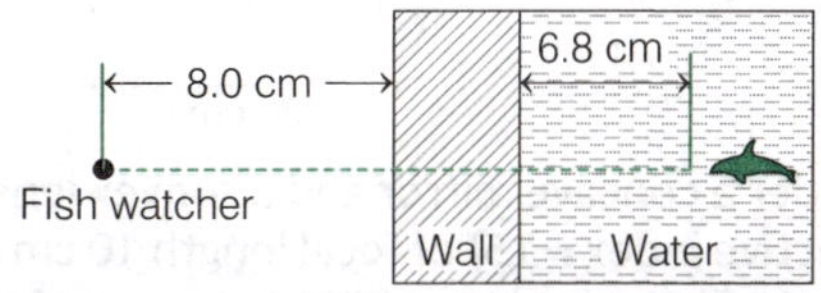

(a) To the fish, how far away does the watcher appear to be?

(b) To the watcher, how far away does the fish appear to be?

Integer Type Questions

157. An object and a concave mirror of focal length $f = 10$ cm both move along the principal axis of the mirror with constant speeds. The object moves with speed $v_0 = 15$ cm s^{-1} towards the mirror with respect to a laboratory frame. The distance between the object and the mirror at a given moment is denoted by u. When $u = 30$ cm, the speed of the mirror v_m is such that the image is instantaneously at rest with respect to the laboratory frame and the object forms a real image. The magnitude of v_m is .... cm s^{-1}. **(2022 Adv.)**

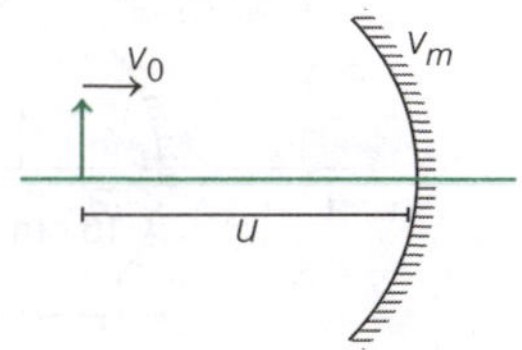

158. The XY-plane be taken as the boundary between two transparent media M_1 and M_2. M_1 in $Z \geq 0$ has a refractive index of $\sqrt{2}$ and M_2 with $Z < 0$ has a refractive index of $\sqrt{3}$. A ray of light travelling in M_1 along the direction given by the vector $\mathbf{A} = 4\sqrt{3}\hat{\mathbf{i}} - 3\sqrt{3}\hat{\mathbf{j}} - 5\hat{\mathbf{k}}$, is incident on the plane of separation. The value of difference between the angle of incident in M_1 and the angle of refraction in M_2 will be .... ° (in degree). **(2022 Main)**

159. An object is placed on the principal axis of convex lens of focal length 10 cm as shown. A plane mirror is placed on the other side of lens at a distance of 20 cm. The image produced by the plane mirror is 5 cm inside the mirror. The distance of the object from the lens is .... cm. **(2023 Main)**

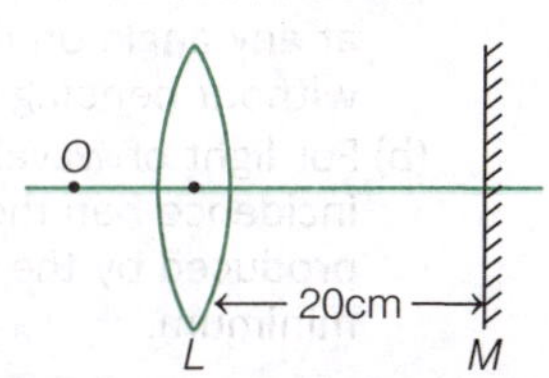

160. An optical arrangement consists of two concave mirrors M_1 and M_2 and a convex lens L, with a common principal axis, as shown in the figure. The focal length of L is 10 cm. The radii of curvature of M_1 and M_2 are 20 cm and 24 cm, respectively. The distance between L and M_2 is 20 cm. A point object S is placed at the mid-point between L and M_2 on the axis. When the distance between L and M_1 is $n/7$ cm, one of the images coincide with S. The value of n is ...... **(2023 Adv.)**

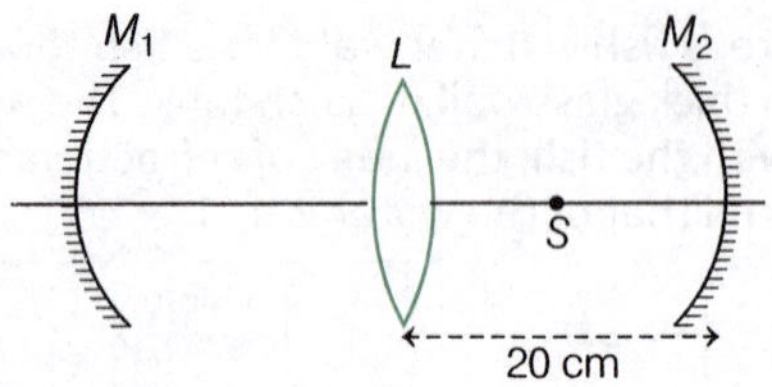

161. Consider a concave mirror and a convex lens (refractive index = 1.5) of focal length 10 cm each, separated by a distance of 50 cm in air (refractive index = 1) as shown in the figure. An object is placed at a distance of 15 cm from the mirror. Its erect image formed by this combination has magnification M_1. When the set-up is kept in a medium of refractive index $\frac{7}{6}$, the magnification becomes M_2.

The magnitude $\left|\frac{M_2}{M_1}\right|$ is .... **(2015 Adv.)**

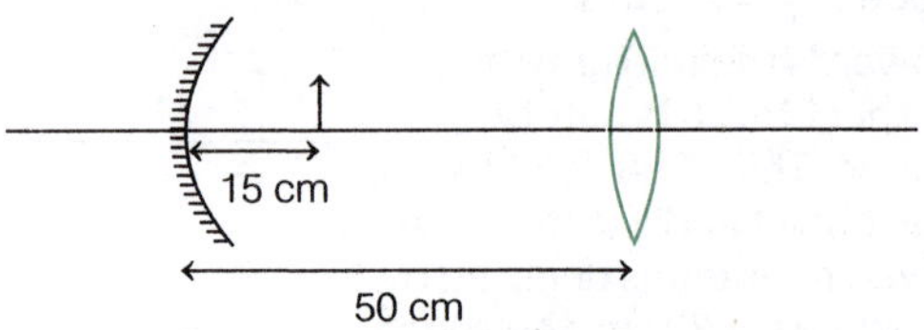

162. As shown in the figure, a plane mirror is fixed at a height of 50 cm from the bottom of a tank containing water $\left(\mu = \frac{4}{3}\right)$. The height of water in the tank is 8 cm. A small bulb is placed at the bottom of the water tank. The distance of image of the bulb formed by mirror from the bottom of the tank is .... cm. **(2023 Main)**

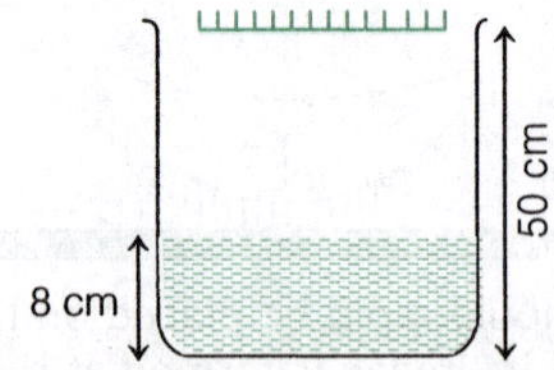

163. Sunlight of intensity 1.3 k Wm^{-2} is incident normally on a thin convex lens of focal length 20 cm. Ignore the energy loss of light due to the lens and assume that the lens aperture size is much smaller than its focal length. The average intensity of light, in k Wm^{-2}, at a distance 22 cm from the lens on the other side is .... **(2018 Adv.)**

164. Water (with refractive index $= \frac{4}{3}$) in a tank is 18 cm deep. Oil of refractive index $\frac{7}{4}$ lies on water making a convex surface of radius of curvature $R = 6$ cm as shown. Consider oil to act as a thin lens. An object S is placed 24 cm above water surface. The location of its image is at x cm above the bottom of the tank. Then x is .... **(2011 JEE)**

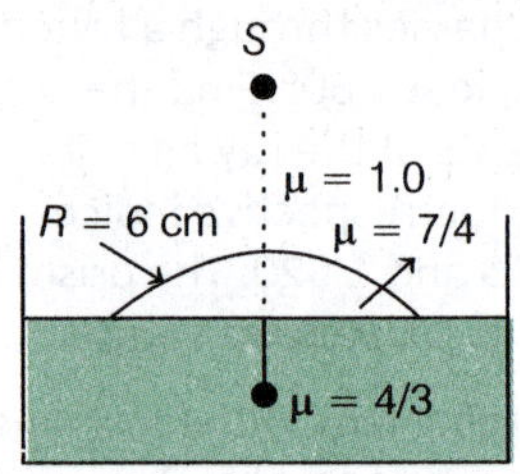

Answers

Level 1

1. 30 cm **2.** (c) **3.** (d) **4.** (b) **5.** (a) **6.** (a) **7.** (b) **8.** (a) **9.** (a) **10.** (b)
11. (b) **12.** (b) **13.** (c) **14.** (a) **15.** (c) **16.** (b) **17.** (d) **18.** (c) **19.** (a) **20.** (d)
21. (b) **22.** (c) **23.** (c) **24.** (b) **25.** (d) **26.** (b) **27.** (d) **28.** (c) **29.** (c) **30.** (c)
31. (a) **32.** (b) **33.** (d) **34.** (c) **35.** (c) **36.** (d) **37.** (c) **38.** (c) **39.** (b) **40.** (a)
41. (a) **42.** (a) **43.** (b) **44.** (b) **45.** (b, c) **46.** (b, d) **47.** (A) p,q,r,s (B) q (C) p,q,r,s (D) p,q,r,s
48. Lens is convex **49.** Lens is concave **50.** 6.6 cm **51.** $\mu_y = 1.656$ **52.** 11 cm behind mirror
53. 5 cm from mirror towards the lens **54.** Ray will become parallel to the optic axis **55.** $\frac{4}{3}$ cm **56.** $\sin^{-1}(3/4)$
57. (a) $v_1 = -6$ mm, $v_2 = -5$ mm **58.** (a) 24 cm (b) 12 cm (c) See the hints (d) 30 cm **59.** 10.8 cm, real **60.** $\sqrt{3}$
61. 6.25 cm **62.** (a) $f = 20$ cm (b) $f = 20$ cm **63.** $F = 35$ cm **64.** (3) **65.** (120) **66.** (6)

Level 2

67. (c) **68.** (b) **69.** (d) **70.** (b) **71.** (d) **72.** (b) **73.** (a) **74.** (a) **75.** (c) **76.** (c)
77. (c) **78.** (b) **79.** (a) **80.** (b) **81.** (a) **82.** (d) **83.** (d) **84.** (c) **85.** (a) **86.** (b)
87. (d) **88.** (c) **89.** (c) **90.** (a) **91.** (a) **92.** (c) **93.** (c) **94.** (a,b) **95.** (b,d) **96.** (b,c)
97. (b,c,d) **98.** (b,d) **99.** (a,b) **100.** (a,d) **101.** (a,b,c) **102.** (a) **103.** (a) **104.** (c) **105.** (a) **106.** (c)
107. (b) **108.** ($a \to q,r$; $b \to p,s$; $c \to p,r$; $d \to p,r$) **109.** ($a \to p,r$; $b \to q,s$; $c \to q,r$; $d \to q,r$)
110. ($a \to q,s$; $b \to q,r$; $c \to p,s$; $d \to p,r$) **111.** ($a \to q$; $b \to r$; $c \to r$; $d \to p$)
112. ($a \to p,s$; $b \to q,s$; $c \to q,s$; $d \to p,s$) **113.** ($a \to q,r$; $b \to q,r$; $c \to q,r$; $d \to q,r$)
114. ($a \to r$; $b \to p$; $c \to q$; $d \to s$) **115.** (a) **116.** (b) **117.** ($a \to p,r$; $b \to q,s,t$; $c \to p,r,t$; $d \to q,s$)
118. 60 cm away from the lens **119.** 10 cm **120.** $f = \infty$
121. First image at a distance of 3.33 cm from flat surface and the second at infinity **122.** (a) 34.2° (b) 8.4°
123. Maximum distance of the incident rays from the centre should be $\sqrt{\frac{2}{3}}R$, where R is the radius of hemisphere
124. 30 cm **125.** 1.37 **126.** $A = 2°$, $\mu = 1.62$ **127.** (0,0) **128.** $d = 5.0$ m, x co-ordinate of final image = 4.0 m
129. $\mu = 2$ **131.** (a) Final image is at a distance of 20 cm behind the second half lens and at a distance of 2/3 mm above the principal axis. The size of image is 2 mm and is inverted as compared to the given object **132.** 0.186 m, 0.315 m
133. $h \approx 15$ cm **136.** $x_{max} = 2000$ m = 2 km **137.** Distance = $\frac{R(9 - 4\mu)}{(10\mu - 9)(\mu - 2)}$, for final image to be real μ should lie between 2 and 2.25 **138.** 0.09 m/s, 0.3 s^{-1} **139.** (a) Slope = cot i (b) $4y^{\frac{1}{4}} = x$ (c) (4.0 m, 1.0 m) (d) See the hint
140. 6.06 m **141.** $\frac{1}{5\sqrt{2}}(3\hat{i} + 4\hat{j} - 5\hat{k})$ **142.** (1.6) **143.** 15 cm towards right, $-\frac{3}{2}$ **144.** (a) 600 nm (b) 60°
145. (a) $i_1 = \sin^{-1}\left[\frac{1}{\sqrt{2}}\left(\sqrt{n^2 - n_1^2} - n_1\right)\right]$ (b) 73° **146.** $\left(\frac{\mu_3 R}{\mu_3 - \mu_1}\right)$ **147.** 0.9 m to the right of lens
148. 75 cm **149.** (a) 15 cm (b) 1.16 cm **150.** $\frac{\mu_1}{\mu_2} \approx 1.25$
151. Minimum deviation = 37° and maximum deviation = 58° **152.** $\Delta\theta = 0.44°$ **153.** $S = 0.5$ mm
154. (a) $v = +3.3$ cm, (b) $x = 16.67$ cm **155.** (a) $P_{liquid} = 1.17$ D, $f_{liquid} = 85$ cm (b) $f = 20$ cm or 0.2 m, $P = 5$ D
156. (a) 20.0 cm (b) 14.975 cm **157.** (3) **158.** (15) **159.** (30) **160.** (80, 150, 220) **161.** (7)
162. (98) **163.** (130) **164.** (2)

See hints on pages 168-196.

Hints & SOLUTIONS

Module 1.

1. $v = \frac{c}{\mu} = \frac{3 \times 10^8}{(4/3)} = 2.25 \times 10^8$ m/s

2. As, refractive index,

$$\mu = \frac{\text{speed of light in air}}{\text{speed of light in medium}}$$

So, speed of light in a medium,

$$v = \frac{c}{\mu}$$

Hence, for medium A and B,

$$v_A = \frac{c}{\mu_A} \text{ and } v_B = \frac{c}{\mu_B}$$

Time taken by light to cross some thickness x is (speed = distance / time)

$$t_1 = \frac{x}{(c/\mu_A)} \text{ and } t_2 = \frac{x}{(c/\mu_B)}$$

Hence, $t_2 - t_1 = \frac{\mu_B \cdot x}{c} - \frac{\mu_A \cdot x}{c}$

$\Rightarrow \quad t_2 - t_1 = \frac{x}{c}(\mu_B - \mu_A)$

Now given, $\frac{\mu_A}{\mu_B} = \frac{1}{2}$

$\Rightarrow \quad \mu_B = 2\mu_A$

and $\quad t_2 - t_1 = 5 \times 10^{-10}$ s

Substituting these values we get,

$$5 \times 10^{-10} = \frac{x}{c}(2\mu_A - \mu_A)$$

$\Rightarrow \quad x = 5 \times 10^{-10} \times \frac{c}{\mu_A} \quad [\because c = 3 \times 10^8 \text{ m/s}]$

But $\frac{c}{\mu_A} = v_A$

$\Rightarrow \quad x = 5 \times 10^{-10} \times v_A$ (m)

3. ${}_1\mu_2 \times {}_2\mu_3 \times {}_3\mu_1 = 1$

$\therefore \quad \frac{4}{3} \times \frac{3}{2} = \frac{1}{{}_3\mu_1} = {}_1\mu_3$ or ${}_1\mu_3 = 2$

4. $\mu = \frac{c}{v} = \frac{c}{f\lambda} = \frac{3 \times 10^8}{6 \times 10^{14} \times 300 \times 10^{-9}} = 1.67$

5. $t_1 = \frac{l}{v_1} = \frac{l}{c/\mu_1} = \frac{\mu_1 l}{e}$

$\Rightarrow \quad t_2 = \frac{\mu_2 l}{c}$

$\therefore \quad t_2 - t_1 = (\mu_2 - \mu_1)\frac{l}{c}$

$$= \frac{(1.63 - 1.47)(20)}{3 \times 10^8}$$

$$= 1.07 \times 10^{-8} \text{ s}$$

6. (a) $t_1 = \frac{l}{v_1} = \frac{l}{c/n_1} = \frac{n_1 l}{c} = \text{minimum}$

$$= \frac{1.2 \times 10^{-6}}{3 \times 10^8}$$

$$= 4 \times 10^{-15} \text{ s}$$

(b) $\lambda = \frac{\lambda_0}{n}$

Number of wavelengths across any film,

$$N = \frac{l}{\lambda} = \frac{ln}{\lambda_0}$$

Module 2.

1. $\lambda_{medium} = \frac{\lambda_{air}}{\mu} = \frac{6000}{1.5} = 4000$ Å

$$f = \frac{v_{air}}{\lambda_{air}} = \frac{v_{medium}}{\lambda_{medium}} = \frac{3.0 \times 10^8}{6.0 \times 10^{-7}}$$

$$= 5.0 \times 10^{14} \text{ Hz}$$

Frequency remains unchanged

2. $v = \frac{c}{\mu} = \frac{3 \times 10^8}{1.5} = 2.0 \times 10^8$ m / s

$$\lambda = \frac{v}{f} = \frac{2.0 \times 10^8}{5.0 \times 10^{14}} = 4.0 \times 10^{-7} \text{ m}$$

3. Frequency does not change during refraction, but wavelength and speed decrease in a denser (here water) medium.

4. $\mu_1 \sin i_1 = \mu_3 \sin i_3$

$\therefore \quad \mu_1 \sin i = \mu_3 \sin r$ or $\frac{\sin i}{\sin r} = \frac{\mu_3}{\mu_1}$

5. From Snell's law,

$$\mu \sin i = \mu_4 \sin x$$

$\therefore \quad \sin x = \frac{\mu}{\mu_4} \sin i$

6. $n_1 \sin i_1 = n_3 \sin i_3$

$\therefore \quad (1)(\sin 45°) = \sqrt{2} \sin i_3$

$\Rightarrow \quad \sin i_3 = \frac{1}{2}$ or $i_3 = 30°$

7. $n = \frac{\sin i}{\sin(i/2)} = \frac{2\sin(i/2)\cos(i/2)}{\sin(i/2)}$

Solving we get, $i = 2\cos^{-1}(n/2)$

8. $\mu_g \sin i = \mu_a \sin 90° = 1$

$\therefore \quad \mu_g = \dfrac{1}{\sin i}$

9. $\mu_1 \sin i_1 = \mu_2 \sin i_2$

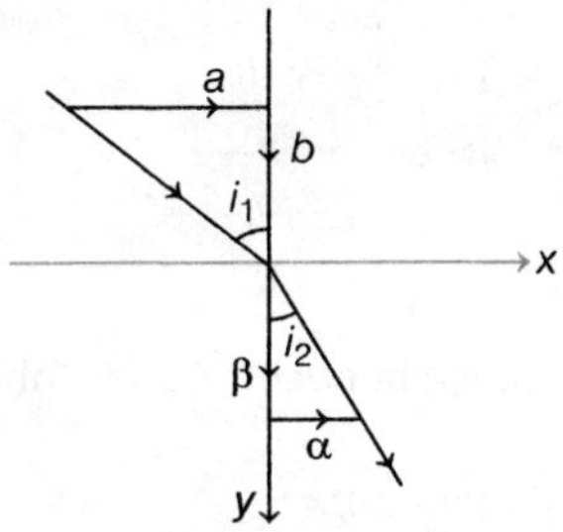

$$\therefore \quad \frac{\mu_1 a}{\sqrt{a^2+b^2}} = \frac{\mu_2 \alpha}{\sqrt{\alpha^2+\beta^2}}$$

$$\sqrt{a^2+b^2} = \sqrt{\alpha^2+\beta^2} = 1$$

$$\therefore \quad \mu_1 a = \mu_2 \alpha$$

10. Let $2i$ be angle of incidence, then according to Snell's law

$\Rightarrow \quad 1 \sin 2i = \sqrt{2n} \sin i$

$\Rightarrow \quad 2 \sin i \cos i = \sqrt{2n} \sin i$

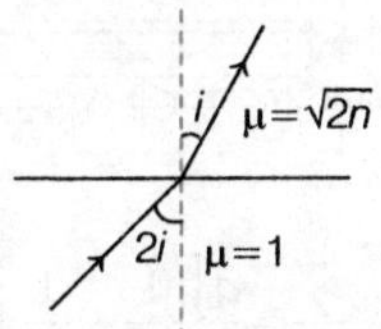

$$\Rightarrow \quad \cos i = \sqrt{\frac{n}{2}} \Rightarrow i = \cos^{-1}\left(\sqrt{\frac{n}{2}}\right)$$

$$\Rightarrow \quad 2i = 2\cos^{-1}\left(\sqrt{\frac{n}{2}}\right)$$

11. On going from rare medium to denser medium frequency remain unchanged, whereas speed and wavelength decreases because $v \propto \frac{1}{\mu}$ and $\lambda \propto \frac{1}{\mu}$.

12. Applying Snell's law at B and C,

$\mu \sin i = \text{constant}$ or

$\mu_1 \sin i_B = \mu_4 \sin i_C$

But $\quad AB \parallel CD$

$\therefore \quad i_B = i_C$ or $\mu_1 = \mu_4$

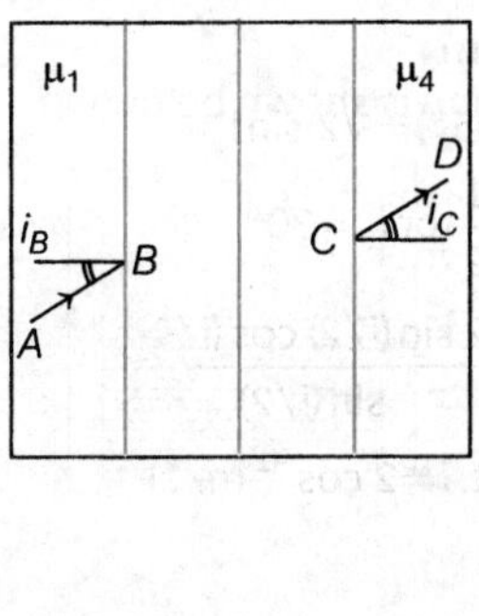

13. $${}_1\mu_2 = \frac{\mu_2}{\mu_1} = \frac{\sin i_1}{\sin i_2} = \frac{\sin 60°}{\sin 30°} = \sqrt{3}$$

14. $${}_1\mu_2 = 1.5 = \frac{\lambda_1}{\lambda_2}$$

15.

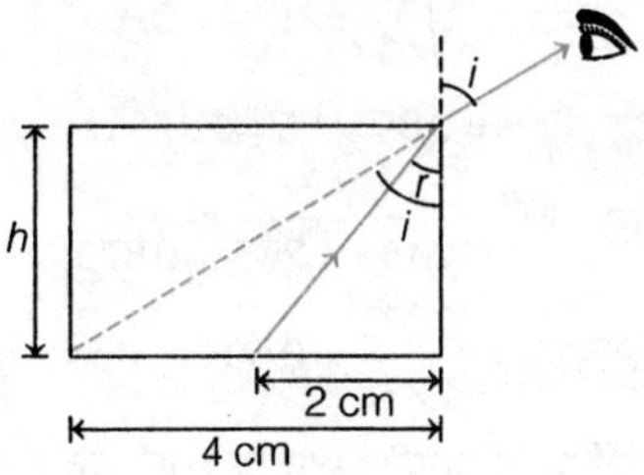

Applying, $\mu = \dfrac{\sin i}{\sin r}$ we get

$$\frac{4}{3} = \frac{4/\sqrt{16+h^2}}{2/\sqrt{4+h^2}}$$

Solving this equation we get,

$$h = 2.4 \text{ cm}$$

16.

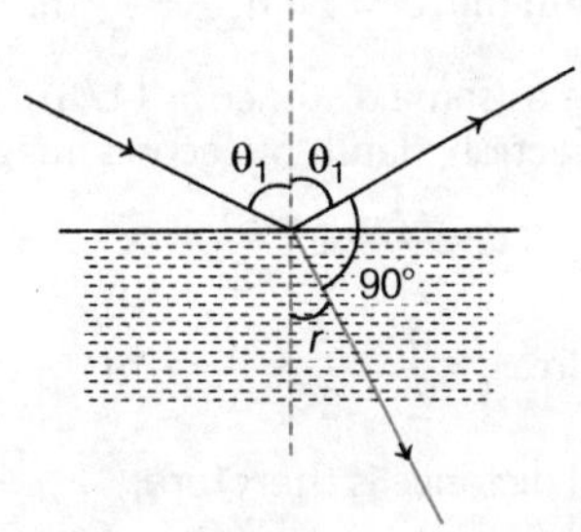

$$\theta_1 + 90° + r = 180°$$

$$\therefore \quad r = 90° - \theta_1$$

Now, refractive index of water,

$$\mu = \frac{\sin \theta_1}{\sin r}$$

or $$\frac{4}{3} = \frac{\sin \theta_1}{\sin(90° - \theta_1)} = \frac{\sin \theta_1}{\cos \theta_1} = \tan \theta_1$$

$$\Rightarrow \quad \theta_1 = \tan^{-1}\left(\frac{4}{3}\right)$$

or $\quad \theta_1 = 53°$

17. According to Snell's law,

$$\sin 60° = \frac{4}{3} \sin r$$

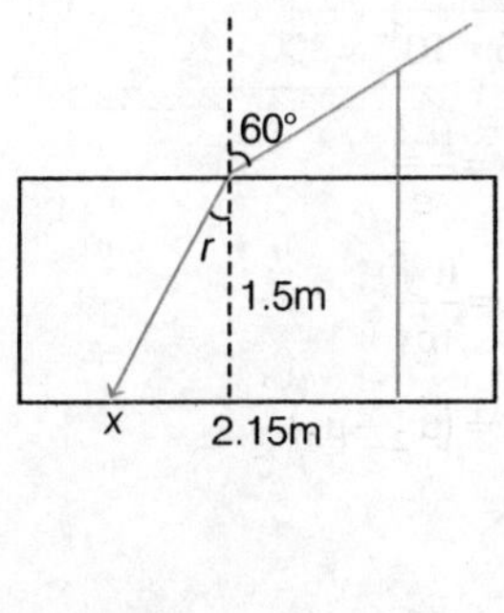

$$\sin r = \frac{3}{4} \times \frac{\sqrt{3}}{2} = \frac{3\sqrt{3}}{8} \quad \text{...(i)}$$

$$\cos r = \sqrt{1 - \frac{27}{64}} = \frac{\sqrt{37}}{8} = 0.75$$

$$\tan r = \sqrt{\frac{27}{37}} \Rightarrow \frac{x}{1.5} = 0.85$$

$$x = 0.85 \times 1.5 = 1.275 \text{ m}$$

$$\tan 30° = \frac{y}{2.15 - 1.275} = \frac{y}{0.875}$$

$$y = \frac{0.875}{1.732} = 0.50$$

So length of pole above water surface

$$= 0.50 \text{ m} = 50 \text{ cm}$$

Module 3.

1. $h' = \mu h = \frac{4}{3} \times 18 = 24 \text{ m}$

2. $h_{app} = \mu h = \frac{4}{3} \times 2 = \frac{8}{3} \text{ m}$

Distance from mirror $= 1 + h_{app} = \frac{11}{3}$ m. So, mirror will make image at same distance (=11/3 m from itself). Now in third refraction, depth of second image,

$$d = \frac{11}{3} + 1 = \frac{14}{3} \text{ m}$$

$$d_{app} = \frac{d}{\mu} = \frac{14}{3} \times \frac{3}{4} = \frac{7}{2} \text{ m}$$

The desired distance is therefore,

$$(d_{app} + h) \quad \text{or} \quad \left(\frac{7}{2} + 2\right) \text{ m}$$

$$\text{or} \quad \frac{11}{2} \text{ m}$$

3. $d_{app} = \frac{d}{(n_1/n_2)}$

$$\therefore \quad d = \frac{n_2}{n_1} d_{app}$$

$$-\frac{d}{dt}(d) = \frac{n_2}{n_1}\left(-\frac{d}{dt} d_{app}\right) = \left(\frac{n_2}{n_1}\right) x$$

$$\frac{dv}{dt} = A\left[-\frac{d}{dt}(d)\right] = \frac{x \, \pi R^2 \, n_2}{n_1}$$

4.

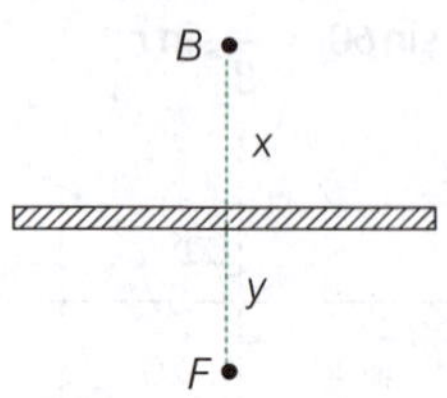

$$h_1 = x + \frac{y}{\mu} \quad \text{...(i)}$$

$$h_2 = y + \mu x \quad \text{...(ii)}$$

Eq. (i) can be written as

$$\frac{\mu x + y}{\mu} = h_1 \quad \text{or} \quad \frac{h_2}{\mu} = h_1 \quad \text{or} \quad \mu = \frac{h_2}{h_1}$$

5. Fish is observer and bird is object.

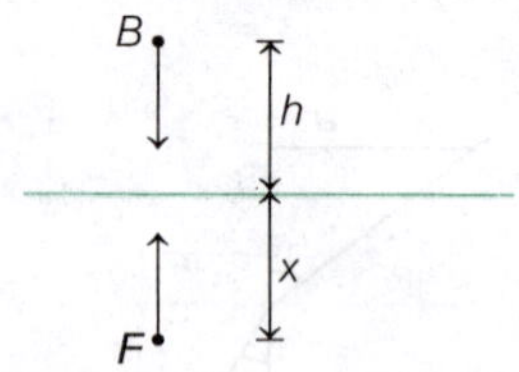

Apparent distance between F and B at some instant will be

$$y = (x + \mu h)$$

$$\left(-\frac{dy}{dt}\right) = \left(-\frac{dx}{dt}\right) + \mu\left(-\frac{dh}{dt}\right)$$

$$9 = 3 + \frac{4}{3}\left(-\frac{dh}{dt}\right)$$

$$\therefore \quad -\frac{dh}{dt} = 4.5 \text{ m/s}$$

6. The given situation is

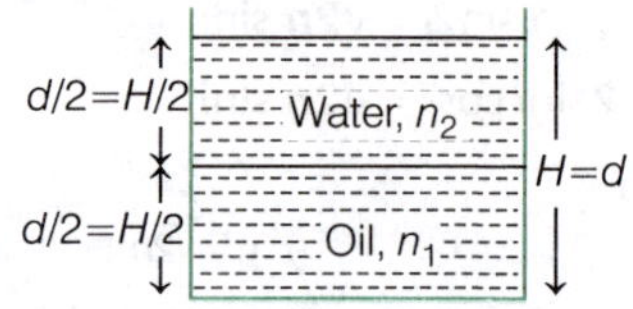

$$d_{app} = \frac{\frac{d}{2}}{n_2} + \frac{\frac{d}{2}}{n_1} = \frac{d}{2}\left[\frac{1}{n_2} + \frac{1}{n_1}\right]$$

$$= \frac{d}{2}\left[\frac{n_1 + n_2}{n_1 n_2}\right] = \frac{d}{2}\left(\frac{n_1 + n_2}{n_1 n_2}\right)$$

7. Let height of liquid filled in bucket be h. To see image, a microscope should be focussed at that point where image is formed.

Apparent depth, $d_{app} = \frac{d}{\mu} = \frac{h}{\frac{5}{3}} = \frac{3h}{5}$

Shift in position of image = Original position − Apparent depth

$$\text{Shift} = h - \frac{3h}{5} = \frac{2h}{5}$$

Given that Shift = 30 cm

$$\therefore \quad 30 = \frac{2}{5} h \Rightarrow h = \frac{30 \times 5}{2} = 75 \text{ cm}$$

8. Given, situation is shown below

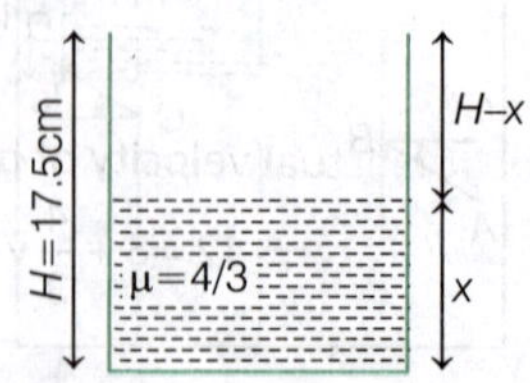

For an observer outside the water, height of water

$$= \frac{x}{\mu_w} = \frac{x}{(4/3)} = \frac{3x}{4}$$

Now, $\frac{3x}{4} = \frac{17.5}{2} \Rightarrow x = \frac{35}{3} = 11.7$ cm

9. $v = \sqrt{2gh} = \sqrt{2 \times 10 \times 7.2} = 12\ \text{ms}^{-1}$

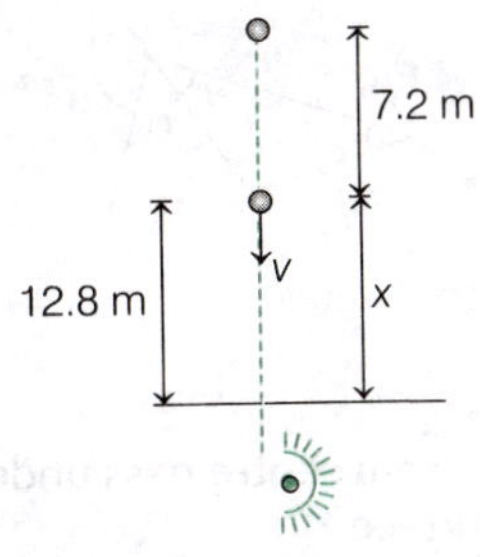

In this case when eye is inside water,

$$x_{app.} = \mu x \Rightarrow \frac{dx_{app.}}{dt} = \mu \cdot \frac{dx}{dt}$$

or $$v_{app.} = \mu v = \frac{4}{3} \times 12 = 16\text{ms}^{-1}$$

10. (a) $d_{app} = 10 + \frac{10}{1.5} = \frac{50}{3}$ cm

(b) $h_{app.} = 10 + (1.5)(10) = 25$ cm

11.

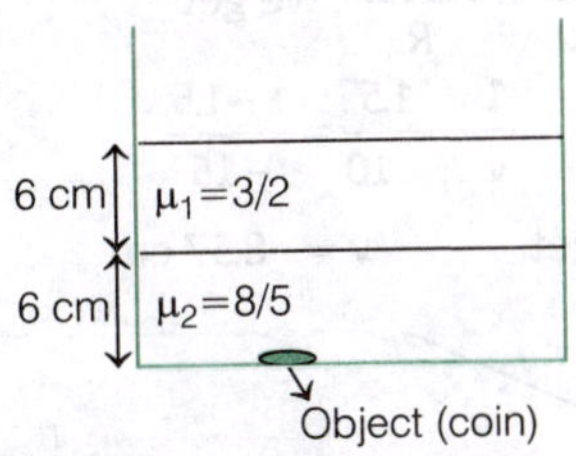

$$\text{Apparent depth} = \frac{h_1}{\mu_{rel\,1}} + \frac{h_2}{\mu_{rel\,2}}$$

$$= \frac{6}{3/2} + \frac{6}{8/5} = 4 + \frac{15}{4}$$

$$= \frac{31}{4}\ \text{cm} = \frac{\alpha}{4}\ \text{cm} \quad \text{(given)}$$

$$\alpha = 31$$

12. The given situation is shown below $d_{app} = d_1 + \mu d$

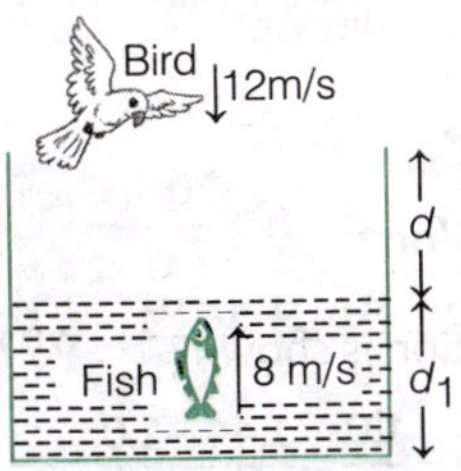

Suppose v be the actual velocity of bird.

$$\Rightarrow \quad v_{upp} = v_1 + \mu v \Rightarrow 12 = 8 + \frac{4}{3}v$$

$$\Rightarrow \quad v = 3\ \text{m/s}$$

Module 4.

1. Shift due to a slab $= \left(1 - \frac{1}{\mu}\right)t$ is in the direction of ray of light. Hence, Ram appears nearer to Anoop by that much distance.

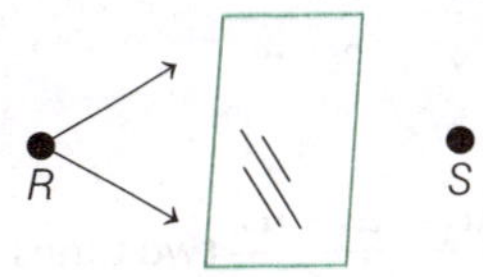

2. $d_{app.} = \frac{d}{\mu}$

μ of red is least. So, $d_{app.}$ for red is maximum. So, they appear to be raised least.

3. Image is coinciding with P. Hence, P is placed at centre of curvature. Glass slab will produce shift the object at a distance of $\left(1 - \frac{1}{\mu}\right)t$ towards the mirror. So, we will have to shift the object by the same distance away from the mirror.

4. $$\text{Shift} = \left(1 - \frac{\mu_{medium}}{\mu_{slab}}\right)t$$

$$= \left[1 - \frac{4/3}{3/2}\right] \times 36 = 4\ \text{cm}$$

5. $$\text{Shift} = \left(1 - \frac{1}{\mu}\right)t = \left(1 - \frac{2}{3}\right)(6) = 2\ \text{cm}$$

For mirror, object distance $= 50 - 2 = 48$ cm.

So, mirror will make image at a distance 48 cm behind it.

In return journey of ray of light, we will have to farther take 2 cm shift in the direction of ray of light.

So, image distance as observed by observer

$$= (50 + 48) - 2 = 96\ \text{cm}$$

6. $$\text{Total shift} = \left(1 - \frac{1}{\mu_1}\right)t_1 + \left(1 - \frac{1}{\mu_2}\right)t_2$$

$$= \left(1 - \frac{2}{3}\right)10 + \left(1 - \frac{1}{2}\right)10$$

$$= \frac{25}{3}\ \text{cm}$$

$$\therefore \text{Image distance} = 50 - \frac{25}{3} = \frac{125}{3}\ \text{cm}$$

Module 5.

1. Applying, $$\frac{\mu_2}{v} - \frac{\mu_1}{u} = \frac{\mu_2 - \mu_1}{R}$$

$$\therefore \quad \frac{1}{v} - \frac{3/2}{+30} = \frac{1 - 3/2}{+20}$$

or $$\frac{1}{v} = \frac{1}{20} - \frac{3}{40}$$

$$\therefore \quad v = 40\ \text{cm}$$

2. Applying $\frac{\mu_2}{v} - \frac{\mu_1}{u} = \frac{\mu_2 - \mu_1}{R}$, we have

$$\frac{3/2}{v} - \frac{1}{-15} = \frac{3/2 - 1}{+30}$$

$$\therefore \quad \frac{3}{2v} = \frac{1}{60} - \frac{1}{15} = -\frac{1}{20}$$

$$\therefore \quad v = -30 \text{ cm}$$

3. $R = 10$ cm

Applying $\frac{\mu_2}{v} - \frac{\mu_1}{u} = \frac{\mu_2 - \mu_1}{R}$ two times

$$\frac{1}{v} - \frac{1.5}{-50} = \frac{1 - 1.5}{-10} \quad \text{or} \quad v = 50$$

$$MN = d$$

$$MI_1 = 50 \text{ cm}$$

$$NI_1 = (d - 50) \text{ cm}$$

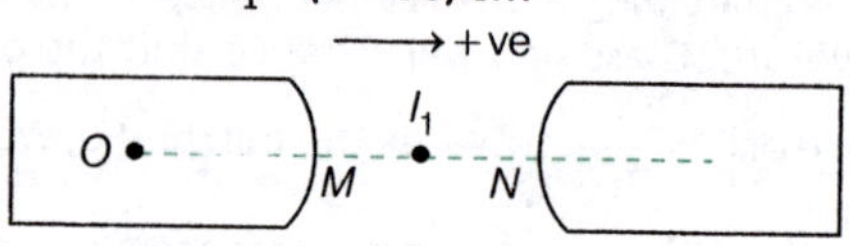

Again, $\frac{1.5}{\infty} - \frac{1}{-(d-50)} = \frac{1.5 - 1}{10}$

$$\Rightarrow \quad d = 70 \text{ cm}$$

4. The given condition is shown in the figure below

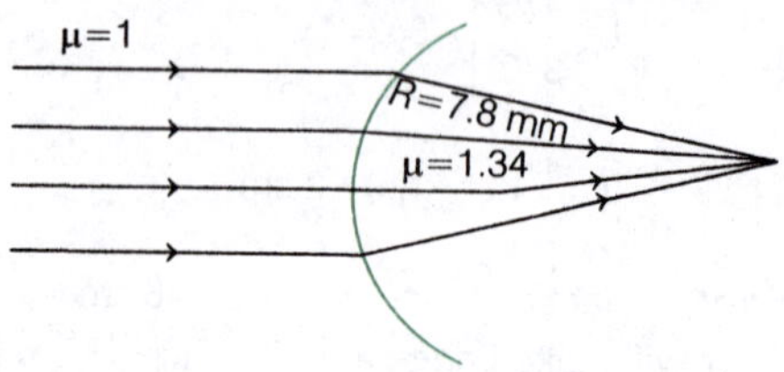

where, a parallel beam of light is coming from air ($\mu = 1$) to a spherical surface (eye) of refractive index 1.34. Radius of curvature of this surface is 7.8 mm.

From the image formation formula for spherical surface, i.e. relation between object, image and radius of curvature.

$$\frac{\mu_r}{v} - \frac{\mu_i}{u} = \frac{\mu_r - \mu_i}{R} \quad \text{... (i)}$$

Given, $\mu_r = 1.34$, $\mu_i = 1$, and $R = 7.8$

Substituting the given values, we get

$$\frac{1.34}{v} + \frac{1}{\infty} = \frac{1.34 - 1}{7.8}$$

or $$\frac{1.34}{v} = \frac{0.34}{7.8}$$

$$\Rightarrow \quad v = \frac{1.34 \times 7.8}{0.34} \text{ mm}$$

$$\Rightarrow \quad v = \frac{4}{3} \times 3 \times 7.8 \text{ mm}$$

($\because$ approximately $1.34 = 4/3$ and $0.34 = 1/3$)

$$\Rightarrow \quad v = 31.2 \text{ mm or } 3.12 \text{ cm}$$

5. $\sqrt{3} = \frac{\sin 60^\circ}{\sin r}$

$$\therefore \quad r = 30^\circ$$

The asked angle,

$$\theta = 180^\circ - i - r = 90^\circ$$

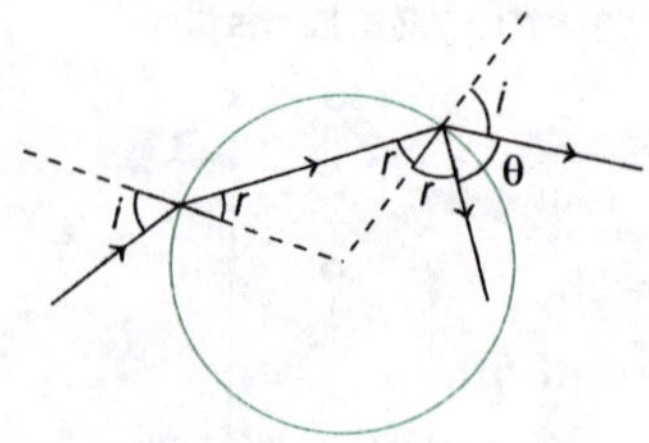

6. All rays starting from centre pass undeviated as they fall normal to the surface.

7.

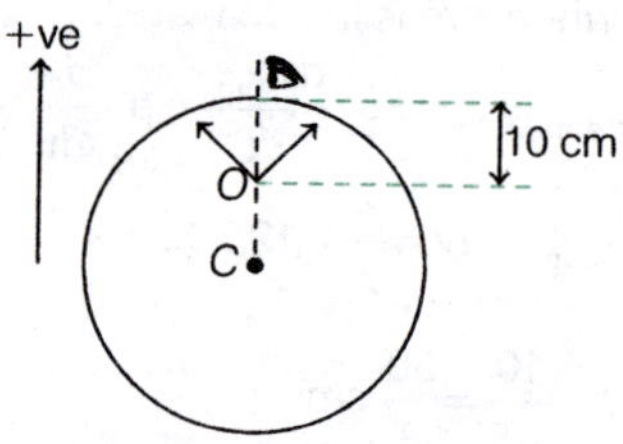

Using $\frac{\mu_2}{v} - \frac{\mu_1}{u} = \frac{\mu_2 - \mu_1}{R}$, we get

$$\frac{1}{v} - \frac{1.5}{-10} = \frac{1 - 1.5}{-15}$$

Solving, we get $\quad v = -8.57$ cm

8.

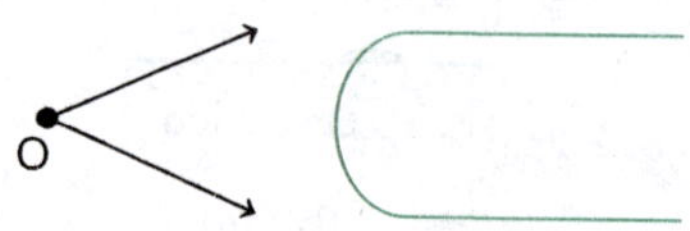

(a) Using $\frac{\mu_2}{v} - \frac{\mu_1}{u} = \frac{\mu_2 - \mu_1}{R}$, we get

$$\frac{1.5}{v} - \frac{1.0}{-20} = \frac{1.5 - 1.0}{+6}$$

Solving, we get $\quad v = +45$ cm

Similarly other parts can be solved.

9.

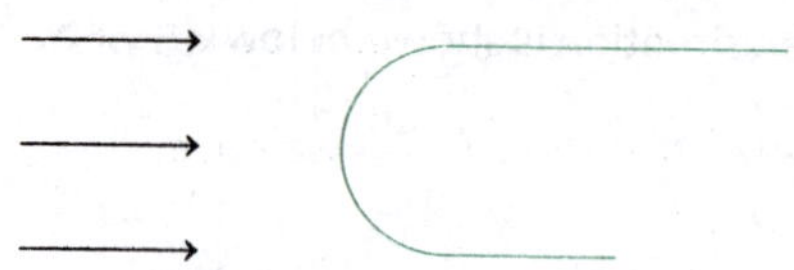

Using the equation

$$\frac{\mu_2}{v} - \frac{\mu_1}{u} = \frac{\mu_2 - \mu_1}{R}, \quad \text{we get}$$

$$\frac{1.44}{v} - \frac{1.0}{\infty} = \frac{1.44 - 1.0}{+1.25}$$

$$\therefore \quad v = 4.0 \text{ cm}$$

10.

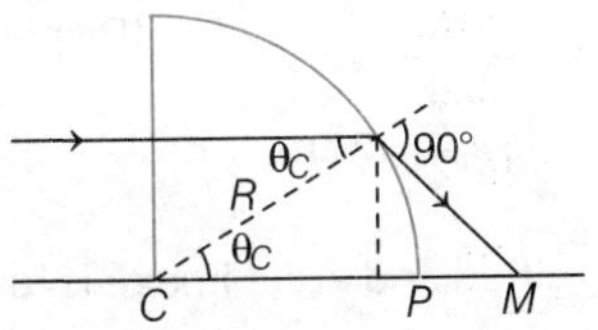

$$\theta_C = \sin^{-1}\left(\frac{1}{n}\right) = \sin^{-1}\left(\frac{2}{3}\right) = 41.8°$$

$$CM = R \sec\theta_C = \frac{R}{\cos\theta_C}$$

$$= \frac{5\,\text{cm}}{\cos 41.8°} = 6.7\text{ cm}$$

$$\therefore \quad PM = CM - CP = (6.7 - 5.0)$$

$$= 1.7\text{ cm}$$

Note *In critical case, angle in denser medium is θ_C and in rarer medium 90°.*

11.

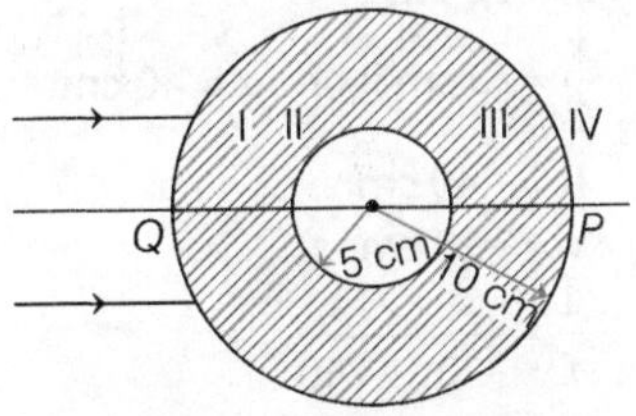

Apply $\frac{\mu_2}{v} - \frac{\mu_1}{u} = \frac{\mu_2 - \mu_1}{R}$ four times,

We have $\frac{1.5}{v_1} - \frac{1.0}{\infty} = \frac{1.5 - 1.0}{+10}$

$$\therefore \quad v_1 = +30\text{ cm}$$

$$\frac{1.0}{v_2} - \frac{1.5}{+25} = \frac{1.0 - 1.5}{-5.0}$$

$$v_2 = -6.25\text{ cm}$$

$$\frac{1.5}{v_3} - \frac{1.0}{-3.75} = \frac{1.5 - 1.0}{-5.0}$$

$$v_3 = -4.1\text{ cm}$$

$$\frac{1.0}{v_4} - \frac{1.5}{-9.1} = \frac{1.0 - 1.5}{-10}$$

$$\Rightarrow \quad v_4 = -4.67\text{ cm}$$

$\therefore$ Final image is at 4.67 cm to the left of P.

12. Applying $\frac{\mu_2}{v} = \frac{\mu_1}{u} = \frac{\mu_2 - \mu_1}{R}$ we have,

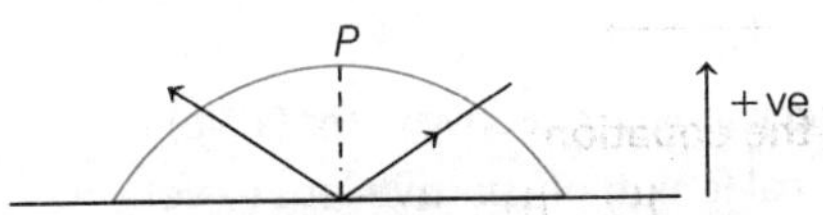

$$\frac{1.0}{v} - \frac{1.6}{-3.0} = \frac{1.0 - 1.6}{-5.0}$$

Solving we get, $\quad v = -2.42$ cm

This is distance from P (downwards).

$\therefore$ Distance from observer $= 5 + 2.42$

$$= 7.42\text{ cm}$$

13. Applying $\frac{\mu_2}{v} - \frac{\mu_1}{u} = \frac{\mu_2 - \mu_1}{R}$

First on plane surface

$$\frac{1.5}{AI_1} - \frac{1}{-mR} = \frac{1.5 - 1}{\infty} = 0 \qquad (R = \infty)$$

$$\therefore \quad AI_1 = -(1.5\,mR)$$

Then, on curved surface

$$\frac{1}{\infty} - \frac{1.5}{-(1.5\,mR + R)} = \frac{1 - 1.5}{-R}$$

[$v = \infty$, because final image is at infinity]

$$\Rightarrow \quad \frac{1.5}{(1.5\,m + 1)R} = \frac{0.5}{R}$$

$$\Rightarrow \quad 3 = 1.5m + 1$$

$$\Rightarrow \quad \frac{3}{2}m = 2 \Rightarrow m = \frac{4}{3}$$

14. Given, $n_1 = 1$

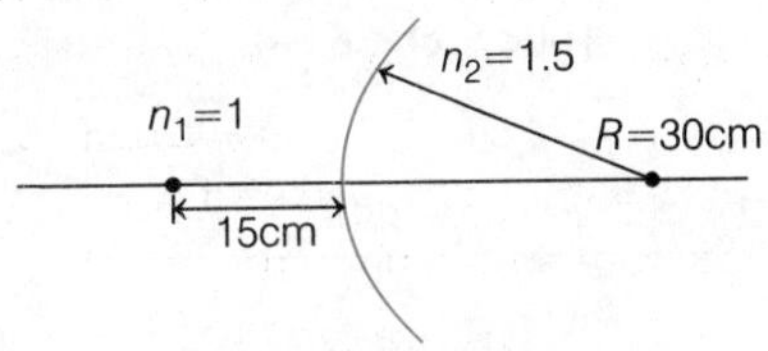

Using refraction formula,

$$\frac{n_2}{v} - \frac{n_1}{u} = \frac{n_2 - n_1}{R}$$

We get, $\frac{1.5}{v} - \frac{1}{(-15)} = \frac{1.5 - 1}{30}$

$$\Rightarrow \quad v = -30\text{ cm}$$

(Negative sign shows image is formed on same side as that of object)

Module 6.

Introductory Exercise

1. $\frac{1}{v} - \frac{1}{u} = \frac{1}{f} = (\mu - 1)\left(\frac{1}{R_1} - \frac{1}{R_2}\right)$

$$\therefore \quad \frac{1}{-20} - \frac{1}{-60} = (1.65 - 1)\left(\frac{1}{-R} - \frac{1}{+R}\right)$$

Solving we get, $\quad R = 39$ cm

2. $\frac{1}{-50} - \frac{1}{u} = \frac{1}{+30}$

Solving, we get $u = -18.75$ cm

$$m = \frac{v}{u} = \frac{(-50)}{(-18.75)} = 2.67$$

$$I = m(O) = 2.67 \times 2 = 5.33\text{ cm}$$

3.

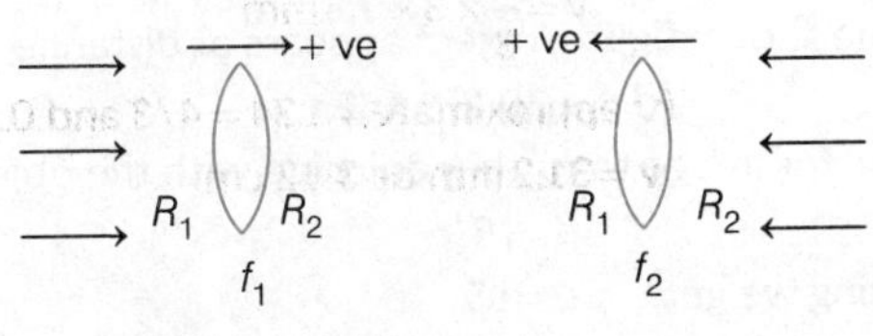

$$\frac{1}{f_1}=(\mu-1)\left(\frac{1}{+R_1}-\frac{1}{-R_2}\right) \quad ...(i)$$

$$\frac{1}{f_2}=(\mu-1)\left(\frac{1}{+R_2}-\frac{1}{-R_1}\right) \quad ...(ii)$$

Solving these two equations, we can see that $f_1=f_2$.

4.

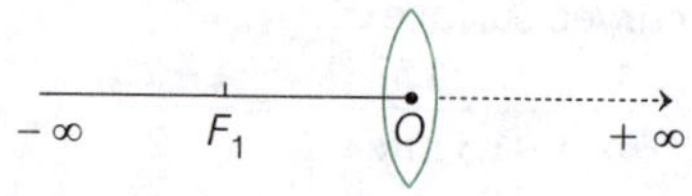

When object is moved from O to F_1, its virtual, erect and magnified image should vary from O to $-\infty$.

5. (a) $\frac{1}{f}=\left(\frac{1.3}{1.8}-1\right)\left(\frac{1}{-20}-\frac{1}{+20}\right)$

$\therefore \quad f=+36$ cm

(b) Between O and F_1 image is virtual. Hence, for real image.

$|u|<f$ or 36 cm

6.

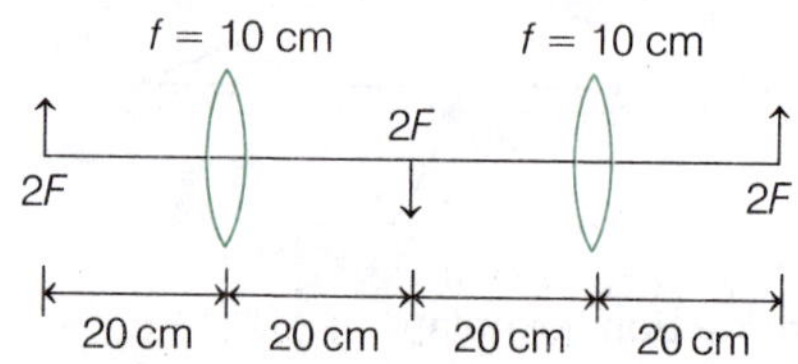

7. $\because \quad \frac{1}{v}-\frac{1}{u}=\frac{1}{f}$

Differentiating this equation, we get

$-v^{-2}\cdot dv+u^{-2}\cdot du=0 \quad$ (as $f=$ constant)

$\therefore \quad dv=\left(-\frac{v^2}{u^2}\right)\cdot du$

8. It is just like a concave mirror.

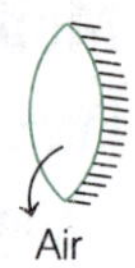

$|f|=0.2$ m

$\therefore \quad |R|=0.4$ m

Focal length of this equivalent mirror is

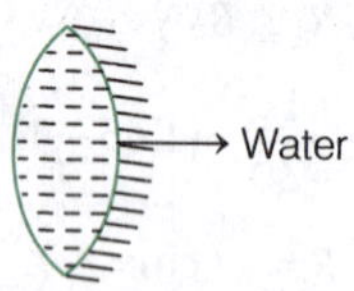

$$\frac{1}{F}=\frac{2(\mu_2/\mu_1)}{R_2}-\frac{2(\mu_2/\mu_1-1)}{R_1} \quad \text{(extra points)}$$

$$=\frac{2(4/3)}{-0.4}-\frac{2(4/3-1)}{+0.4}$$

or $\quad F=-0.12$ m or -12 cm

9. $|R|=0.5$ m (from first case)

In the shown figure, object appears at distance

$d=\mu_e(0.2)+0.2$

Now, for image to further coincide with the object,

$d=|R|$

Solving we get, $\mu_e=1.5$

10. $O=\sqrt{I_1I_2}$ (Displacement method)

$=\sqrt{6\times\frac{2}{3}}=2$ cm

11. Virtual, magnified and erect image is formed by convex lens.

Let $\quad u=-x$

Then, $\quad v=-3x$

Now, $\quad \frac{1}{-3x}-\frac{1}{-x}=\frac{1}{+12}$

$\therefore \quad x=8$ cm

Distance between object and image

$=3x-x=2x=16$ cm

12. Diminished erect image is formed by concave lens.

Let $\quad u=-x$, then $v=-\frac{x}{2}$

Now, $|u|-|v|=20$ cm

$\therefore \quad \frac{x}{2}=20$ cm or $x=40$ cm

$\therefore \quad u=-40$ cm

and $\quad v=-20$ cm

$\frac{1}{f}=\frac{1}{-20}-\frac{1}{-40}$

or $\quad f=-40$ cm

13. If an object is placed at focus of lens ($=10$ cm), rays become parallel and fall normal on plane mirror. So, rays retrace their path.

Exercise

1. At I_1, second focus of convex lens coincides with first focus of concave lens. Hence, rays will become parallel to the optic axis after refraction from both the lenses

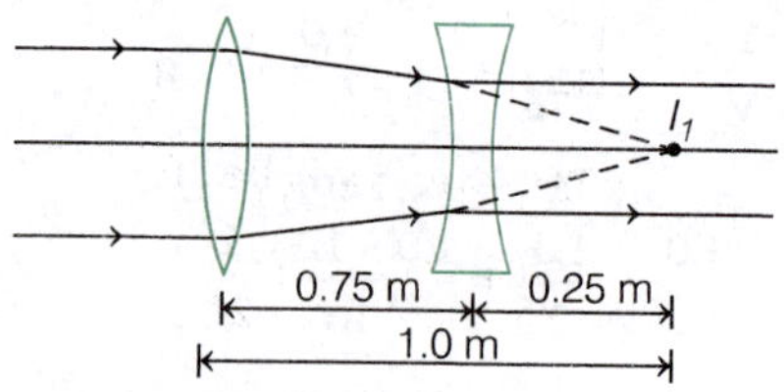

2. Theory based question.

3. Image is formed at second focus (not the first focus).

4. $\frac{1}{F}=\frac{1}{f_1}+\frac{1}{f_2}$

$f_1=$ Focal length of convex lens (+ ve)

$f_2=$ Focal length of concave lens (– ve)

If $f_1>|f_2|$, then F comes out to be negative. So, it becomes a diverging lens.

Negative power of a diverging lens is just for its diverging lens, nothing else.

5. If medium on both sides of the lens is same, then it doesn't matter, which side the object is kept.

6. $\frac{1}{f}=(\mu-1)\left(\frac{1}{R}-\frac{1}{R}\right)$

$$f=\infty$$

$$\therefore \quad P=\frac{1}{f}=0$$

7. When a diverging lens is immersed in a liquid, its diverging power will either decrease or it will become converging.

8. If λ is more, μ will be less as per Cauchy's formula $\left(\mu=A+\frac{B}{\lambda^2}\right)$. Therefore, focal length will be more.

9. Let image is n times in size.

Then, $$\frac{1}{-12n}-\frac{1}{-12}=\frac{1}{f} \quad \text{...(i)}$$

$$\frac{1}{+20n}-\frac{1}{-20}=\frac{1}{f} \quad \text{...(ii)}$$

Solving these two equations, we get

$$f=16 \text{ cm}$$

10. $\frac{1}{f}=P=(\mu-1)\left(\frac{1}{R_1}-\frac{1}{R_2}\right)$

$$=(1.6-1)\left(\frac{1}{0.1}-\frac{1}{-0.1}\right)=+12\text{D}$$

11. $$\frac{1}{0.2}=(1.5-1)\left(\frac{1}{R_1}-\frac{1}{R_2}\right) \quad \text{...(i)}$$

$$\frac{1}{-0.5}=\left(\frac{1.5}{\mu}-1\right)\left(\frac{1}{R_1}-\frac{1}{R_2}\right) \quad \text{...(ii)}$$

Here, $\mu=$ refractive index of medium or liquid.
Dividing Eq. (i) by Eq. (ii), we get

$$-5=\frac{1}{(1.5/\mu)-1} \quad \text{or} \quad \mu=\frac{15}{8}$$

12. Focal length of any one part will be $2f$.

$$\therefore \quad \frac{1}{F}=\frac{1}{2f}+\frac{1}{2f}+\frac{1}{2f}+\frac{1}{2f}$$

or $$F=\frac{f}{2}$$

13. $\frac{1}{F}=\frac{1}{f_1}+\frac{1}{f_2}-\frac{d}{f_1f_2}$

To behave like concave lens, F should be negative.

So, $$\frac{d}{f_1f_2}>\frac{1}{f_1}+\frac{1}{f_2}$$

or $$\frac{d}{f_1f_2}>\frac{f_1+f_2}{f_1f_2}$$

or $$d>(f_1+f_2) \text{ or } 30 \text{ cm}$$

14. Using the lens formula, we have

$$\frac{1}{v}-\frac{1}{-(f+x)}=\frac{1}{f}$$

$$\therefore \quad \frac{1}{v}=\frac{1}{f}-\frac{1}{(f+x)}$$

$$=\frac{f+x-f}{f(f+x)}=\left(\frac{x}{f+x}\right)\left(\frac{1}{f}\right)$$

$$m=-\frac{v}{u}=-\frac{\left(\frac{f+x}{x}\right)(f)}{-(f+x)}=\frac{f}{x}$$

15. $\frac{1}{F}=\frac{1}{f_1}+\frac{1}{f_2}-\frac{d}{f_1f_2}$

$$=\frac{f_1+f_2}{f_1f_2}-\frac{d}{f_1f_2}$$

$$\frac{1}{F}=\frac{(f_1+f_2)-d}{f_1f_2}$$

$$\therefore \quad F=\frac{f_1f_2}{(f_1+f_2)-d} \quad \text{...(i)}$$

If d is doubled, focal length is doubled or denominator becomes half.

$$\therefore \quad (f_1+f_2)-2d=\frac{1}{2}[(f_1+f_2)-d]$$

or $$(f_1+f_2)=3d$$

Substituting in Eq. (i), we have

Originally, $F=\frac{f_1f_2}{(f_1+f_2)-d}=\frac{f_1f_2}{3d-d}=\frac{f_1f_2}{2d}$

When d is made 4 times.

$$F'=\frac{f_1f_2}{(f_1+f_2)-4d}=\frac{f_1f_2}{3d-4d}=-\frac{f_1f_2}{d}$$

$$=-2F$$

16. $\frac{1}{24}=(1.5-1)\left(\frac{1}{R}-\frac{1}{2R}\right)$

$$R=6 \text{ cm}$$

$$\therefore \quad 2R=12 \text{ cm}$$

17. Image formed by convex lens l_1 should coincide at C_1, the centre of curvature C of convex mirror.

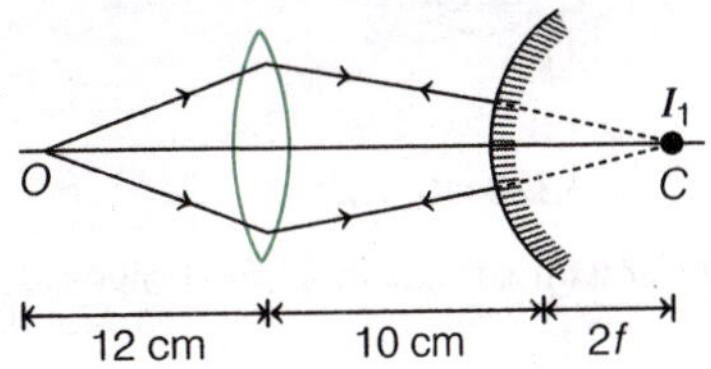

For convex lens,

$$\frac{1}{+(10+2f)}-\frac{1}{-12}=\frac{1}{+10}$$

Solving this equation we get, $f=25$ cm

18. For convex lens,

$$\frac{1}{v}-\frac{1}{-12}=\frac{1}{+20}$$

$$\Rightarrow \quad v=-30 \text{ cm}$$

This image I_1 is therefore, (30 + 10) cm or 40 cm towards left of plane mirror. Therefore, second image I_2 (by the plane mirror) will be formed 40 cm behind the mirror.

19. We know that,

$P_{eq} = \Sigma P_i$ (equivalent power of combination of lens)

All lenses are identical.

$$\therefore \quad 5P = 25\,\text{D} \Rightarrow P = 5\,\text{D}$$

Power of 1 lens = 5 D

Using relation, $P = \dfrac{1}{f}$

$$f = \frac{1}{P} = \frac{1}{5}\,\text{m} = 20\,\text{cm}$$

Hence, focal length is 20 cm.

20. Given, position of object,

$$u = -2.4\,\text{m} = -240\,\text{cm}$$

Position of image, $v = 12$ cm

Thickness of glass plate, $t = 1$ cm

By using lens formula, $\dfrac{1}{v} - \dfrac{1}{u} = \dfrac{1}{f}$

$$\frac{1}{12} - \frac{1}{-240} = \frac{1}{f} \Rightarrow f = \frac{240}{21}\,\text{cm}$$

The shift produced by the glass plate,

$$d = t\left(1 - \frac{1}{\mu}\right) = 1\left(1 - \frac{1}{1.5}\right) \qquad (\because \mu = 1.5)$$

$$= 1/3\,\text{cm}$$

Hence, position of final image will become

$$v' = v - \frac{1}{3} = 12 - \frac{1}{3} = \frac{35}{3}\,\text{cm}$$

According to given situation,

$$\frac{1}{f} = \frac{1}{v'} - \frac{1}{u'} \Rightarrow \frac{1}{u'} = \frac{1}{v'} - \frac{1}{f}$$

$$= \frac{1}{35/3} - \frac{1}{240/21}$$

$$\Rightarrow \frac{1}{u'} = \frac{3}{35} - \frac{21}{24}$$

$$\Rightarrow u' = -560\,\text{cm}$$

Hence, shift will be

$$\Delta d = u' - u = 560 - 240$$

$$= 320\,\text{cm} = 3.2\,\text{m}$$

21. Given a convex lens is cut into two halves along its principal axis.

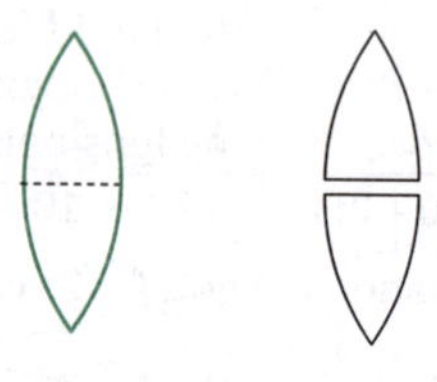

Further any one piece (out of the 2 halves) is cut into 2 halves perpendicular to the principal axis.

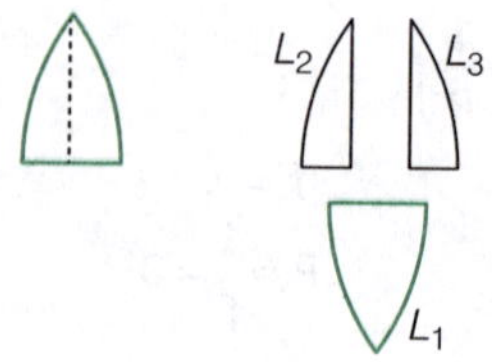

$$\text{Power, } P = \frac{1}{f} = (\mu - 1)\left[\frac{1}{R_1} - \frac{1}{R_2}\right]$$

$$\text{For } L_1, \frac{1}{f_1} = (\mu - 1)\left[\frac{1}{R_1} - \frac{1}{R_2}\right]$$

$$\Rightarrow P_1 = (\mu - 1)\left[\frac{1}{R} - \frac{1}{-R}\right] \qquad (\because R_1 = R, R_2 = -R)$$

$$= (\mu - 1)\left(\frac{2}{R}\right) = P \qquad \text{...(i)}$$

$$\text{For } L_2, \frac{1}{f_2} = (\mu - 1)\left[\frac{1}{R} - \frac{1}{\infty}\right] \qquad (\because R_1 = R \text{ and } R_2 = \infty)$$

$$\Rightarrow P_2 = \frac{\mu - 1}{R} = \frac{P}{2} \qquad \text{[From Eq. (i)] ...(ii)}$$

$$\text{For } L_3, \frac{1}{f_3} = (\mu - 1)\left[-\frac{1}{(-R)}\right]$$

$$\Rightarrow P_3 = \frac{\mu - 1}{R} = \frac{P}{2} \qquad (\because R_1 = \infty \text{ and } R_2 = -R) \text{...(iii)}$$

22. Focal length of convex lens f_1,

$$\therefore \quad \frac{1}{f_1} = (\mu - 1)\left[\frac{1}{R_1} - \frac{1}{R_2}\right]$$

$$= (1.5 - 1)\left[\frac{1}{20} - \left(\frac{1}{-20}\right)\right]$$

$$\Rightarrow \quad f_1 = +20\,\text{cm}$$

Focal length of concave lens f_2,

$$\therefore \quad \frac{1}{f_2} = (\mu - 1)\left[\frac{1}{R_1} - \frac{1}{R_2}\right]$$

$$\frac{1}{f_2} = (1.5 - 1)\left[-\frac{1}{20} - \frac{1}{20}\right] = \frac{1}{-20}$$

$$\Rightarrow \quad f_2 = -20\,\text{cm}$$

For lens 1

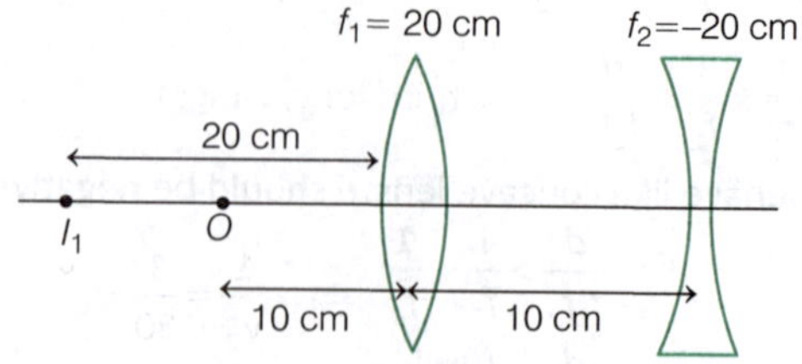

$$\frac{1}{v} - \frac{1}{u} = \frac{1}{f} \Rightarrow v = -20\,\text{cm}$$

$$m_1 = \frac{v}{u} = \frac{-20}{-10} = 2$$

For lens 2

$u = -30$ cm, $f = -20$ cm,

$$\frac{1}{v} - \frac{1}{u} = \frac{1}{f} \Rightarrow v = -12 \text{ cm}$$

$$m_2 = \frac{v}{u} = \frac{-12}{-30} = \frac{2}{5}$$

Net magnification,

$$m = m_1 m_2 = 2 \times \frac{2}{5} = \frac{4}{5} = 0.8$$

23. Given, focal length of first lens,

$$f_1 = +10 \text{ cm}$$

Focal length of second lens,

$$f_2 = -10 \text{ cm}$$

Focal length of third lens,

$$f_3 = +30 \text{ cm}$$

Object distance from first lens,

$$u_1 = -30 \text{ cm}$$

Using lens formula for first lens, we get

$$\frac{1}{f_1} = \frac{1}{v_1} - \frac{1}{u_1}$$

$$\Rightarrow \frac{1}{-10} = \frac{1}{v_1} - \frac{1}{-30}$$

$$\Rightarrow \frac{1}{v_1} = \frac{1}{10} - \frac{1}{30} = \frac{2}{30}$$

$$\Rightarrow v_1 = 15 \text{ cm}$$

Thus, the image formed by first lens is 15 cm to the right of first lens.

The object distance for second lens will be

$$u_2 = 15 \text{ cm} - 5 \text{ cm} = 10 \text{ cm}$$

Using lens formula for first lens, we get

$$\frac{1}{f_2} = \frac{1}{v_2} - \frac{1}{u_2}$$

$$\Rightarrow \frac{1}{-10} = \frac{1}{v_2} - \frac{1}{10}$$

$$\Rightarrow \frac{1}{v_2} = \frac{1}{-10} + \frac{1}{10} = 0$$

$$\Rightarrow v_2 = \infty$$

Thus, the object distance for third lens,

$$u_3 = \infty$$

Using lens formula for third lens, we get

$$\frac{1}{f_3} = \frac{1}{v_3} - \frac{1}{u_3}$$

$$\Rightarrow \frac{1}{30} = \frac{1}{v_3} - \frac{1}{\infty} \Rightarrow \frac{1}{v_3} = \frac{1}{30}$$

$$v_3 = 30 \text{ cm}$$

The final image will form 30 cm from the third lens.

The distance of final image from object will be $30 + 10 + 5 + 30 = 75$ cm.

Thus, the distance of final image formed from object O is 75 cm.

24. For lens A, object distance,

$$u = -20 \text{ cm}$$

Focal length, $f = +5$ cm

From lens formula, $\frac{1}{v} - \frac{1}{u} = \frac{1}{f}$

We have, $\frac{1}{v} = \frac{1}{5} - \frac{1}{20}$

$$\frac{1}{v} = \frac{20-5}{20 \times 5} = \frac{15}{100}$$

$$v = \frac{20}{3} \text{ cm}$$

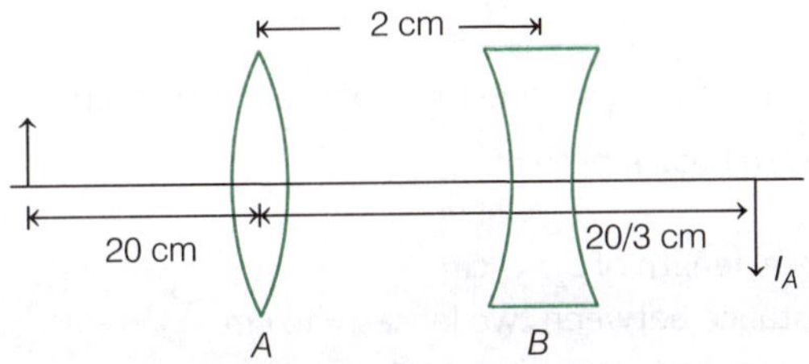

For lens B, image of A is object for B.

$$\therefore \quad u = \frac{20}{3} - 2 = +\frac{14}{3} \text{ cm}$$

$$f = -5 \text{ cm}$$

Now, from lens formula, we have

$$\frac{1}{v} - \frac{1}{u} = \frac{1}{f}$$

$$\Rightarrow \frac{1}{v} = \frac{1}{-5} + \frac{3}{14} = \frac{15-14}{5 \times 14}$$

$$\Rightarrow v = 70 \text{ cm}$$

Hence, image is on right of lens B and is real in nature.

25. $f = \dfrac{d^2 - x^2}{4d}$ (displacement method)

$$f = 16 \text{ cm}, x = 60 \text{ cm}$$

Substituting the values, we get

$$d = 100 \text{ cm}$$

26. (a) $\dfrac{1}{f} = (\mu - 1)\left(\dfrac{1}{R_1} - \dfrac{1}{R_2}\right)$

$$\therefore \quad f \propto \left(\frac{1}{\mu - 1}\right)$$

or $$\frac{f_1}{f_2} = \frac{\mu_2 - 1}{\mu_1 - 1} = \frac{1.7 - 1.0}{1.5 - 1.0} = 1.4$$

(b) If refractive index of the liquid (or the medium) is greater than the refractive index of lens it changes its nature or converging lens behaves as diverging.

27.

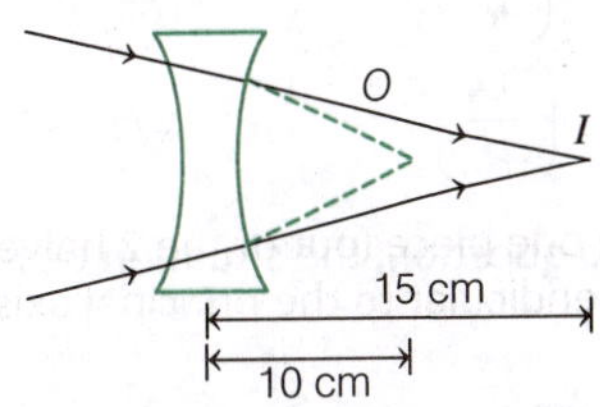

Using $\frac{1}{f}=\frac{1}{v}-\frac{1}{u}$,

or $\frac{1}{f}=\frac{1}{+15}-\frac{1}{+10}$

Solving, we get $f=-30$ cm

28.

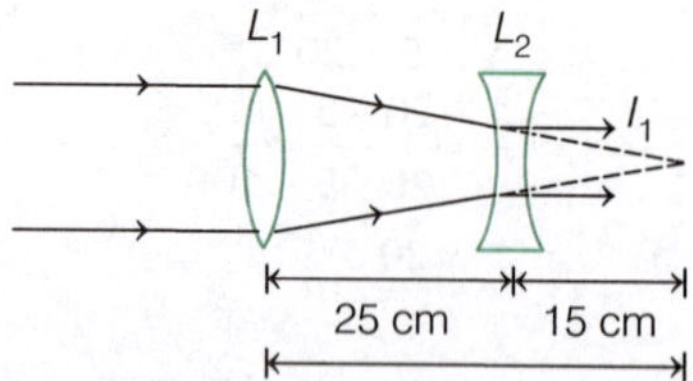

I_1 is formed at second focus of L_1 and first focus of L_2.

29. Given focal length of

$$L_1=24 \text{ m}$$

Focal length of $L_2=9$ cm

distance between two lenses $=10$ cm

According to question, for L_1

$$\frac{1}{v}+\frac{1}{6}=\frac{1}{24} \Rightarrow v=-8 \text{ cm}$$

For L_2 $\frac{1}{v}+\frac{1}{18}=\frac{1}{9} \Rightarrow \frac{1}{v}=\frac{1}{18}$

$\Rightarrow$ $v=18$ cm

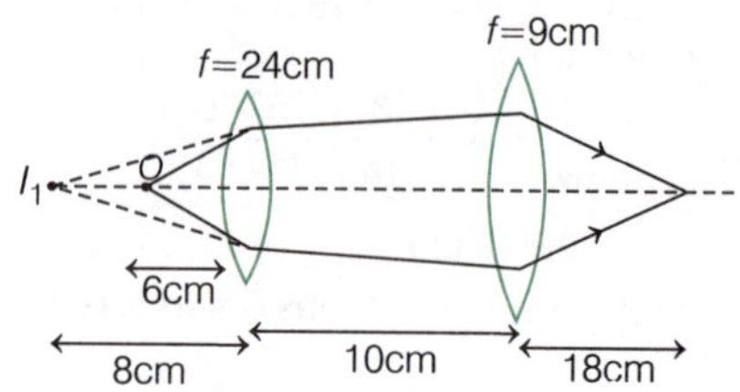

30. $\frac{1}{f}=\left(\frac{\mu_l}{\mu_m}-1\right)\left(\frac{1}{R}-\frac{1}{-R}\right)$

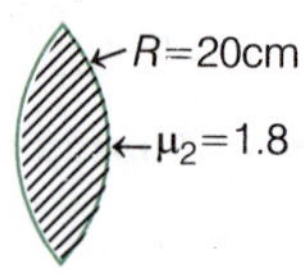

$$P_l=\frac{2}{R}\left[\frac{1.8}{1}-1\right]$$

$$P_l=\frac{2}{R}\times 0.8$$

$$P_l=\frac{1.6}{R} \quad \text{...(i)}$$

Now, $P_2=\frac{2}{R}\left[\frac{1.8}{1.5}-1\right]$

$$P_2=\frac{2}{R}\left[\frac{0.3}{1.5}\right]=\frac{2}{R}\times\frac{3}{15}=\frac{2}{5R}$$

$$\frac{P_{air}}{P_{liquid}}=\frac{P_1}{P_2}=\frac{\left(\frac{1.6}{R}\right)}{\left(\frac{0.4}{R}\right)}=\frac{4}{1}=\frac{x}{1}$$

31. According to question, the situation described is given below

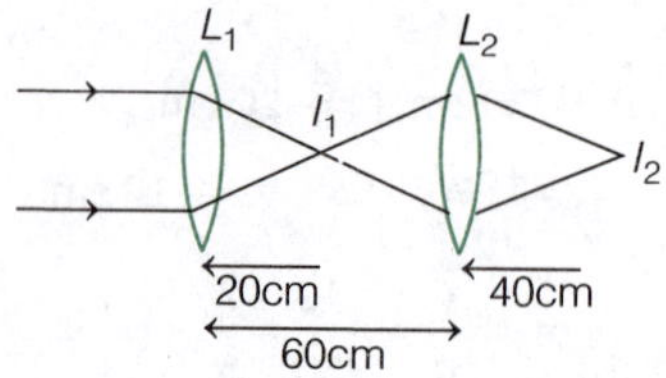

For L_1; $\frac{1}{v}-\frac{1}{u}=\frac{1}{f}$

$\Rightarrow$ $\frac{1}{v}-\frac{1}{\infty}=\frac{1}{f}$ $(\because f=20 \text{ cm})$

$\therefore$ $v=f$

For L_2; $I_1\rightarrow$ object and $I_2\rightarrow$ image

$\Rightarrow$ $u=-40$ cm and $f=20$ cm

$$\frac{1}{v}-\frac{1}{u}=\frac{1}{f} \Rightarrow \frac{1}{v}-\frac{1}{(-40)}=\frac{1}{20}$$

$\Rightarrow$ $\frac{1}{v}=\frac{1}{20}-\frac{1}{40}=\frac{6-3}{120}$

$\Rightarrow$ $\frac{1}{v}=\frac{3}{120}=\frac{1}{40} \Rightarrow v=40$ cm

Hence, the distance from

$$L_1=60+40=100 \text{ cm}$$

32. Given $f=10 \text{ cm}=0.1$ m

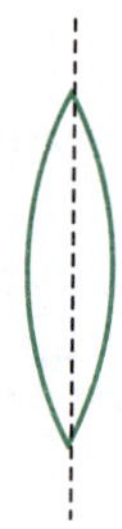

$$P_1+P_2=P=\frac{1}{f}$$

$$2P_1=\frac{1}{0.1}$$

$$P_1=\frac{1}{0.2} \Rightarrow P_1=\frac{10}{2}$$

$\Rightarrow$ $P_1=5$D

Module 7.

1. Theory based question.

2. Critical angle,

$$\sin C=\frac{1}{\mu}$$

$\therefore$ $C=\sin^{-1}\left(\frac{1}{\mu}\right)$

and μ decreases with increase in λ. Yellow, orange and red have larger wavelength than green, so μ will be less for these rays, so critical angle for these rays will be high, hence if green is just totally internally reflected then yellow, orange and red rays will emerge out.

3. $r_1=i$ and $r_2=90°-r_1=90°-i$

Now, $\mu_R \sin i_R=\mu_D \sin i_D$

or $\frac{\mu_R}{\mu_D}=\sin\theta_C=\frac{\sin i_D}{\sin i_R}=\frac{\sin i}{\sin(90°-i)}$

or $\sin\theta_C=\frac{\sin i}{\cos i}=\tan i$

$\Rightarrow$ $\theta_C=\sin^{-1}(\tan i)$

4. $\mu_A > \mu_B$

$$\Rightarrow \quad C_1 < C_2$$

$$\mu_B > \mu_C$$

$$\Rightarrow \quad C_2 < C_3$$

$$\mu_C < \mu_A \quad \Rightarrow \quad C_3 > C_1$$

The correct relation is therefore (d).

5. $\sin i_c = \dfrac{\mu_r}{\mu_d}$

$$i_c = 45 \qquad \text{[Given]}$$

$$\sin 45° = \frac{\mu_r}{\mu_d}$$

$$\Rightarrow \quad \frac{\mu_r}{\mu_d} = \frac{1}{\sqrt{2}}$$

We know,

$$v \propto \frac{1}{\mu} \quad \Rightarrow \quad \frac{v_d}{v_r} = \frac{\mu_r}{\mu_d}$$

$$\frac{v_d}{3 \times 10^8} = \frac{1}{\sqrt{2}} \quad \Rightarrow \quad v_d = \frac{3 \times 10^8}{\sqrt{2}}$$

$$v_d = 3 \times 0.7 \times 10^8$$

$$v_d = 2.12 \times 10^8 \text{ m/s}$$

6. According to Snell's law $n_d \sin i_c = n_r \sin 90°$

$$\sin i_c = \frac{n_r}{n_d} = \frac{v_d}{v_r} \qquad \left(\because v = \frac{c}{n}\right)$$

$$\Rightarrow \quad \sin i_c = \frac{1.5 \times 10^8}{2 \times 10^8} = \frac{1.5}{2}$$

$$\Rightarrow \quad \sin i_c = \frac{3}{4}$$

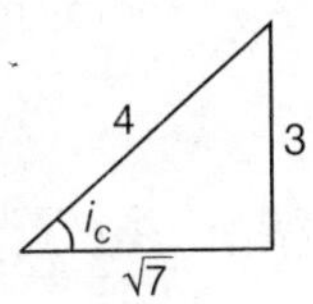

$$\Rightarrow \quad \tan i_c = \frac{3}{\sqrt{4^2 - 3^2}} \Rightarrow \frac{3}{\sqrt{7}}$$

The critical angle between them, $i_c = \tan^{-1}\left(\dfrac{3}{\sqrt{7}}\right)$.

7. We know that,

$$\sin C = \frac{\mu_r}{\mu_d} \text{ and } \mu \propto \frac{1}{V} \Rightarrow \frac{\mu_r}{\mu_d} = \frac{v_d}{v_r}$$

$$= \frac{1.5 \times 10^{10}}{2 \times 10^{10}} = \frac{3}{4}$$

So, $\sin C = \dfrac{3}{4} \quad \Rightarrow \quad C = \sin^{-1}\left(\dfrac{3}{4}\right)$

Therefore, for total internal reflection,

$$\theta > c \quad \Rightarrow \quad \theta > \sin^{-1}\left(\frac{3}{4}\right)$$

8. Given, refractive index, $\mu = \dfrac{4}{3}$

By using Snell's law,

$$\mu = \frac{\sin i}{\sin r}$$

$$\Rightarrow \quad \frac{4}{3} = \frac{\sin\theta}{\sin\theta'} \qquad \text{...(i)}$$

From diagram,

$$\theta'' = 90 - \theta'$$

For total internal reflection,

$$\frac{1}{\mu} = \sin\theta''$$

$$\Rightarrow \quad \sin(90 - \theta') = \frac{3}{4}$$

$$\Rightarrow \quad \cos\theta' = \frac{3}{4}$$

Since, $\quad \sin\theta' = \sqrt{1 - \cos^2\theta'}$

$$\Rightarrow \quad \sin\theta' = \sqrt{1 - \left(\frac{3}{4}\right)^2} = \sqrt{\frac{7}{16}} = \frac{\sqrt{7}}{4}$$

Putting this value in Eq. (i), we get

$$\frac{4}{3} = \frac{\sin\theta \times 4}{\sqrt{7}}$$

$$\Rightarrow \quad \sin\theta = \frac{\sqrt{7}}{3} \quad \Rightarrow \quad \theta = \sin^{-1}\left(\frac{\sqrt{7}}{3}\right)$$

The maximum value of θ is $\sin^{-1}\left(\dfrac{\sqrt{7}}{3}\right)$.

9. $\mu_1 \sin\theta = \mu_2 \sin\alpha \qquad \text{...(i)}$

For TIR

$$\mu_2 (\sin(90 - \alpha)) > \mu_1 \qquad \text{...(ii)}$$

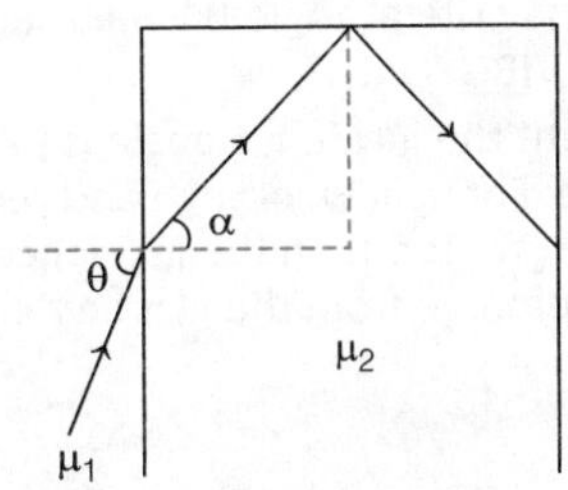

From Eq. (i)

$$\sin\alpha = \frac{\mu_1}{\mu_2}\sin\theta$$

$$\cos\alpha = \sqrt{1 - \frac{\mu_1^2}{\mu_2^2}\sin^2\theta}$$

Now in Eq. (ii)

$$\sin(90 - \alpha) > \frac{\mu_1}{\mu_2}, \ \cos\alpha > \frac{\mu_1}{\mu_2}$$

$$\sqrt{1 - \frac{\mu_1^2}{\mu_2^2}\sin^2\theta} > \frac{\mu_1}{\mu_2}$$

$$\Rightarrow \quad \sin\theta < \sqrt{\frac{\mu_2^2}{\mu_1^2} - 1}$$

$$\theta < \sin^{-1}\left(\sqrt{\frac{\mu_2^2}{\mu_1^2} - 1}\right)$$

10. Critical angle from region III to region IV

$$\sin\theta_C = \frac{n_0/8}{n_0/6} = \frac{3}{4}$$

Now, applying Snell's law in region I and region III

$$n_0 \sin\theta = \frac{n_0}{6}\sin\theta_C$$

or $$\sin\theta = \frac{1}{6}\sin\theta_C = \frac{1}{6}\left(\frac{3}{4}\right) = \frac{1}{8}$$

$\Rightarrow$ $$\theta = \sin^{-1}\left(\frac{1}{8}\right)$$

11. Since $\theta < \theta_c$, both reflection and refraction will take place. From the figure we can see that angle between reflected and refracted rays α is less than $180° - 2\,\theta$.

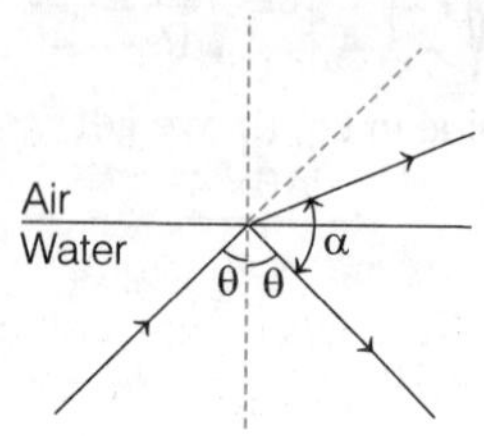

12. Critical angle $\theta_C = \sin^{-1}\left(\frac{1}{\mu}\right)$

Wavelength increases in the sequence of VIBGYOR. According to Cauchy's formula refractive index (μ) decreases as the wavelength increases. Hence the refractive index will increase in the sequence of ROYGBIV. The critical angle θ_C will thus increase in the same order VIBGYOR.

For green light the incidence angle is just equal to the critical angle. For yellow, orange and red the critical angle will be greater than the incidence angle. So, these colours will emerge from the glass air interface.

13.

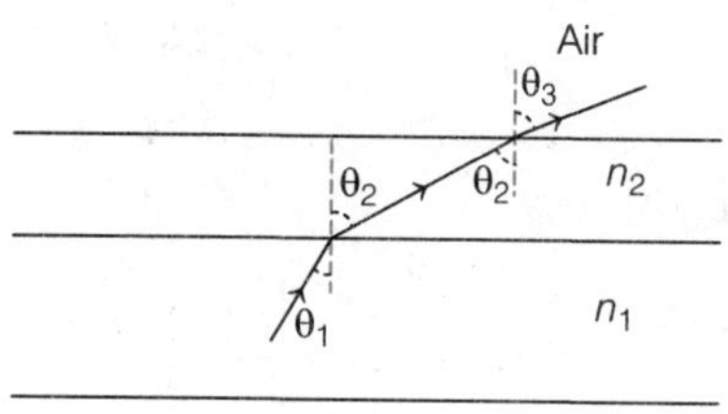

$$\sin\theta > \frac{1}{n_1} \quad \text{(Given)}$$

i.e. $$\sin\theta_1 > \frac{1}{n_1}$$

$$n_1\sin\theta_1 = n_2\sin\theta_2 \Rightarrow \sin\theta_2 = \frac{n_1\sin\theta_1}{n_2}$$

If $n_1 = n_2$, then $\theta_2 = \theta_1$

$$n_2\sin\theta_2 = (1)\sin\theta_3$$

$$\sin\theta_3 = n_2\sin\theta_2 = n_1\sin\theta_1$$

$$\sin\theta_1 = \frac{\sin\theta_3}{n_1} > \frac{1}{n_1}$$

$$\sin\theta_3 > 1$$

$$\theta_3 > 90°$$

This means ray cannot enter air.

For $n_1 > n_2$; $\sin\theta_1 = \frac{n_2}{n_1}\sin\theta_2 > \frac{1}{n_1}$

$$\sin\theta_2 > \frac{1}{n_2}$$

For surface 2 – air interface

$$n_2\sin\theta_2 = \sin\theta_3$$

$$\sin\theta_2 = \frac{\sin\theta_3}{n_2} > \frac{1}{n_2}$$

$$\theta_2 > 90°$$

It means ray is reflected back in medium-2

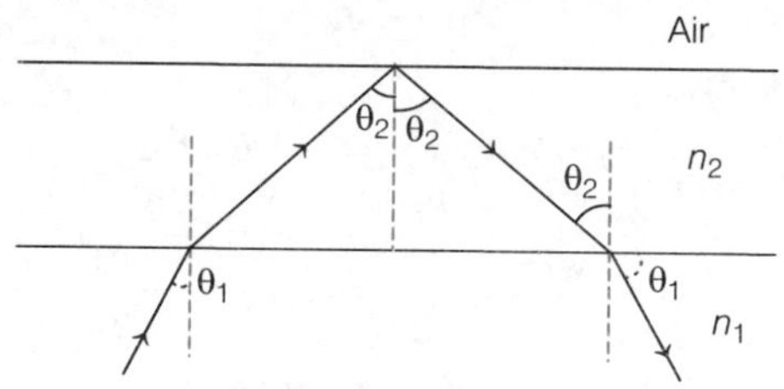

For surface 1 and surface 2 interface

$$n_2\sin\theta_2 = n_1\sin\theta_1$$

$$\sin\theta_{2C} = \frac{n_1}{n_2}$$

θ_{2C} : critical angle

For ray to enter medium-1

$$\theta_2 < \theta_{2C}$$

$$\sin\theta_2 < \sin 2\theta_C$$

$$\frac{n_1}{n_2}\sin\theta_1 < \frac{n_1}{n_2}$$

$$\sin\theta_1 < 1$$

$\theta_1 < 90°$, which is true.

Hence, ray enters medium-1

For $$n_2 > n_1$$

$$\frac{n_2}{n_1}\sin\theta_2 > \frac{n_2}{n_1}$$

$$\sin\theta_2 > \frac{1}{n_2}$$

For surface 2 – air interface

$$n_2\sin\theta_2 = \sin\theta_3$$

$$\sin\theta_2 = \frac{\sin\theta_3}{n_2} > \frac{1}{n_2}$$

$$\theta_2 > 90$$

It means ray is reflected back in medium-2

$$n_2\sin\theta_2 = n_1\sin\theta_1$$

$$\sin\theta_1 = \frac{n_2}{n_1}\sin\theta_2$$

$$\sin\theta_{2C} = \frac{n_1}{n_2};\ \theta_{2C} \rightarrow \text{critical angle}$$

For ray to enter medium-1

$$\theta_2 < \theta_{2C}$$
$$\sin\theta_2 < \sin\theta_{2C}$$
$$\frac{n_1}{n_2}\sin\theta_1 < \frac{n_1}{n_2}$$
$$\sin\theta_1 < 1$$

$\theta_1 < 90°$, which is true.

Hence, ray enters medium-1

Let, $n_2 = 1$

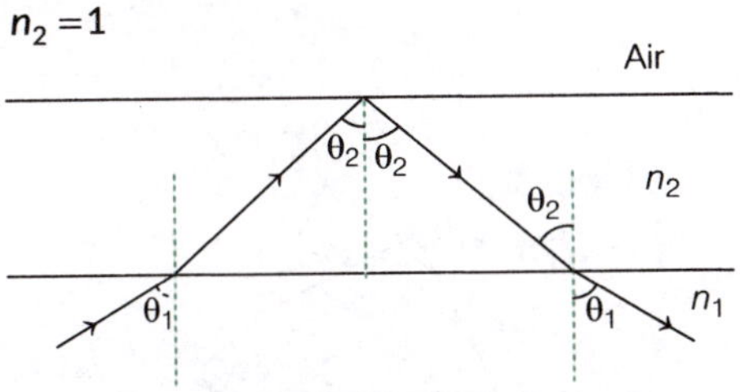

$$n_1 \sin\theta_1 = n_2 \sin\theta_2 \Rightarrow n_2 = 1$$
$$n_1 \sin\theta_1 = \sin\theta_2$$
$$\sin\theta_1 = \frac{\sin\theta_2}{n_1} > \frac{1}{n_1}$$
$$\sin\theta_2 > 1 \Rightarrow \theta_2 = 90°$$

$\therefore$ Ray is reflected back in medium.

14. For total internal reflection to take place

Angle of incidence, $i >$ critical angle, θ_C

or $\quad \sin i > \sin\theta_C$ or $\sin 45° > 1/n$

or $\quad \frac{1}{\sqrt{2}} > \frac{1}{n}$ or $n > \sqrt{2}$ or $n > 1.414$

Therefore, possible values of n can be 1.5 or 1.6 in the given options.

15. (a) $\mu = \frac{343}{1498} = 0.229$

(b) $\theta_C = \sin^{-1}(0.229) = 13.2°$

16.

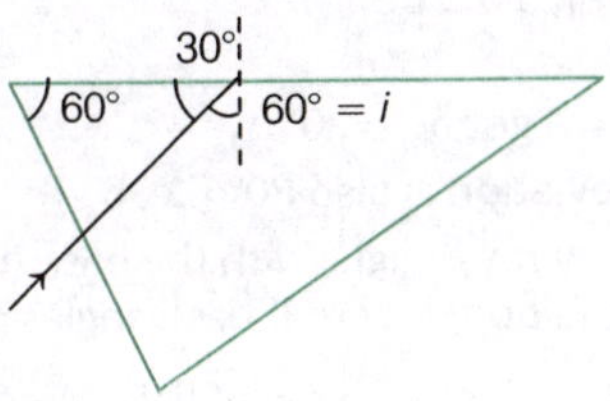

Critical angle $= i = 60° = \theta_C$

$$\sin\theta_C = \frac{\mu_R}{\mu_D} \Rightarrow \sin 60° = \frac{\mu}{\sqrt{3}}$$

Solving we get, $\mu = 1.5$

17. (a) $\mu_1 \sin i_1 = \mu_2 \sin i_2 = \mu_2 \sin\theta_C$

$$(1.6)\sin\theta = (1.80)\left(\frac{1.30}{1.80}\right)$$

$$\therefore \quad \theta = \sin^{-1}\left(\frac{13}{16}\right)$$

(b) If θ is decreased, then i_2 will decrease from the value θ_C. Hence, refraction will take place in medium-3.

Module 8.

Introductory Exercise

1.

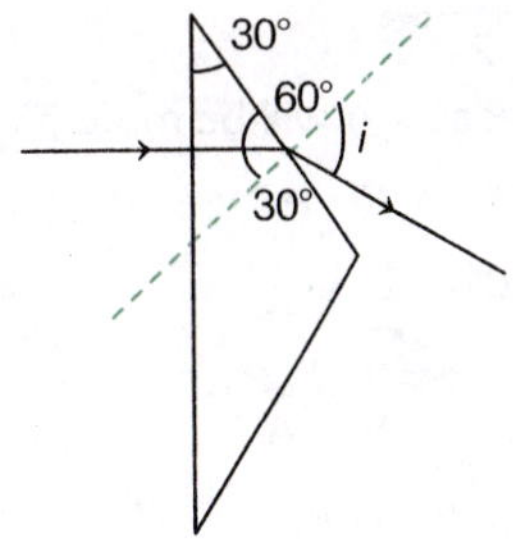

$$\mu = \frac{\sin i}{\sin 30°}$$

$$\therefore \quad \sin i = \mu \sin 30°$$
$$= (1.6)\left(\frac{1}{2}\right) = 0.8$$

$$\therefore \quad i = 53°$$

P ray deviates from its original path by an angle,

$$\delta = i - 30° = 23°$$

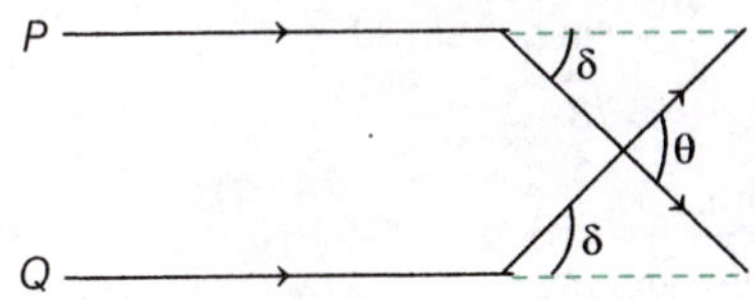

$\therefore$ Angle between two rays, $\theta = 2\delta$
$= 46°$

2.

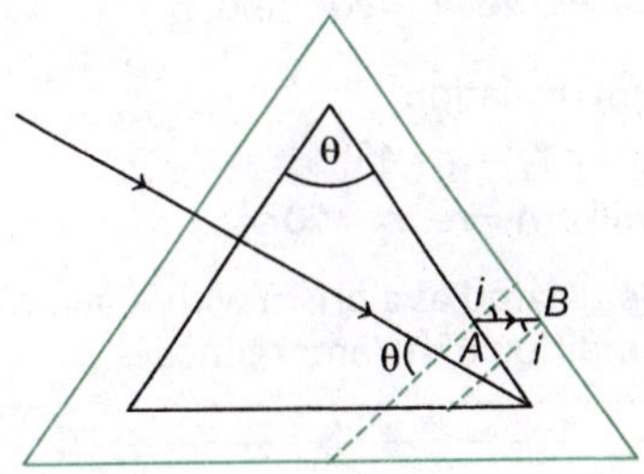

$$i = \theta_C$$

$$\therefore \quad \sin i = \sin\theta_C = \frac{1}{\mu_g} = \frac{2}{3}$$

Applying Snell's law at point A,

We have

$$\mu_w \sin\theta = \mu_g \sin i$$

$$\therefore \quad \frac{4}{3}\sin\theta = \frac{3}{2} \times \frac{2}{3}$$

$$\therefore \quad \sin\theta = \frac{3}{4}$$

3. Given, $A = 60°$ and $\delta = 30°$

We know that,

$$\mu = \frac{\sin\left(\frac{A + \delta_m}{2}\right)}{\sin(A/2)} = \frac{\sin\frac{60° + \delta_m}{2}}{\sin 30°} = 2\sin\frac{60° + \delta_m}{2}$$

Since, one ray has been found out which has deviated by 30°, the angle of minimum deviation should be either equal or less than 30°. (It cannot be more than 30°).

So, $\mu \le 2\sin\frac{60°+\delta_m}{2}$

(because μ will be more if δ_m will be more)

Or, $\mu \le 2\times 1/\sqrt{2}$ or, $\mu \le \sqrt{2}$

4. $i_1 = 0° \Rightarrow r_1 = 0°$

or $r_2 = A$

Now, $r_2 = \theta_C = A$

$\therefore$ $\sin A = \sin\theta_C = \frac{1}{\mu} = \frac{2}{3}$

or $A = \sin^{-1}\left(\frac{2}{3}\right)$

5. $\delta = i_1 + i_2 - A$

$30° = 60° + i_2 - 30°$

$\therefore$ $i_2 = 0$ or $r_2 = 0$ **Hence proved.**

$\Rightarrow$ $r_1 = A = 30°$

Now, $\mu = \frac{\sin i_1}{\sin r_1} = \frac{\sin 60°}{\sin 30°}$

$= \sqrt{3}$

6. $\sqrt{2} = \frac{\sin i_1}{\sin(i_1/2)}$

$= \frac{2\sin(i_1/2)\cos(i_1/2)}{\sin(i_1/2)}$

Solving this, we get $i_1 = 90°$ and $r_1 = \frac{i_1}{2} = 45°$

At minimum deviation,

$r_2 = r_1 = 45°$

$\therefore$ $A = r_1 + r_2 = 90°$

7. *ABC* can be treated as a prism with angle of prism $A = 90°$. Condition of no emergence is

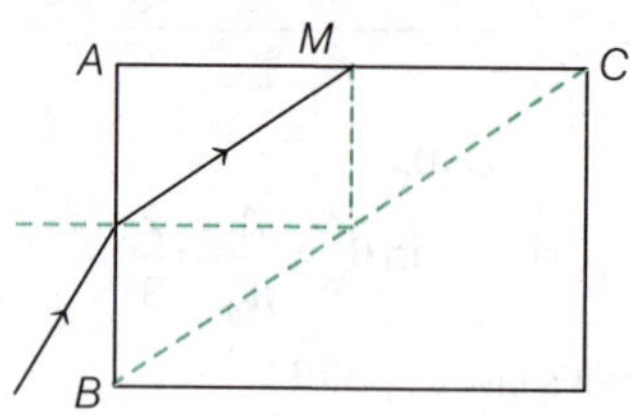

$A \ge 2\theta_C$

or $\sin\theta_C \le \sin\left(\frac{A}{2}\right)$

or $\frac{1}{\mu} \le \sin 45°$

or $\frac{1}{\mu} \le \frac{1}{\sqrt{2}}$

$\therefore$ $\mu \ge \sqrt{2}$

8. $\theta_C = \sin^{-1}\left(\frac{1}{\mu}\right) = \sin^{-1}\left(\frac{1}{1.6}\right) = 38.7°$

$r_2 = \theta_C = 38.7°$

$\therefore$ $r_1 = A - r_2 = 45° - 38.7° = 6.3°$

Now applying, $\mu = \frac{\sin i_1}{\sin r_1}$

we can find i_1.

Exercise

1.

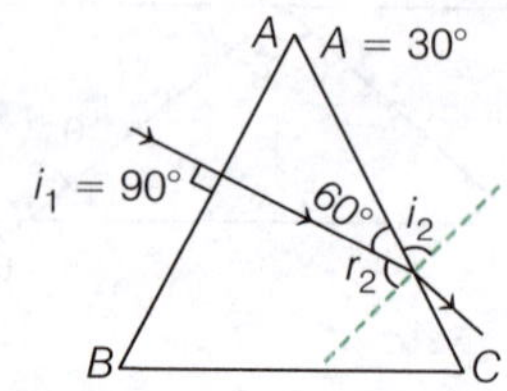

Ray falls normally on the face *AB*. Therefore, it will pass undeviated through *AB*.

$\therefore$ $r_2 = 90° - 60° = 30°$

According to Snell's law,

$\mu = \sqrt{2} = \frac{\sin i_2}{\sin r_2}$

$i_2 = 45°$

Deviation $= i_2 - r_2 = 45° - 30° = 15°$

(Deviation at face *AC* only)

2. Let δ_m be the angle of minimum deviation. Then

$\mu = \frac{\sin\left(\frac{A+\delta_m}{2}\right)}{\sin(A/2)}$ ($A = 60°$ for an equilateral prism)

$\therefore$ $\sqrt{2} = \frac{\sin\left(\frac{60°+\delta_m}{2}\right)}{\sin\left(\frac{60°}{2}\right)}$

Solving this we get $\delta_m = 30°$

The given deviation is also 30° (i.e. δ_m)

Angle made by ray of light with the base (under minimum deviation condition) is zero if base angles are equal.

3. Through a thin glass slab ray of light almost passes undeviated. When white light travels from air into the hollow prism, there is no change of medium, as prism has air inside it. Thus, a beam of white light does not give a spectrum on passing through a hollow prism.

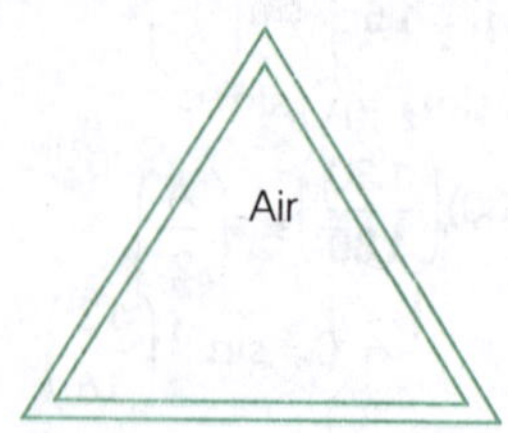

4. $i = 45°$

For $\mu > \sqrt{2}$ or 1.414

$\Rightarrow$ $\theta_C < 45°$

$\therefore$ They get TIR on face AC.

5. At minimum deviation,

$$r_1 = r_2 = \frac{A}{2} = 30°$$

Now using, $\mu = \dfrac{\sin i_1}{\sin r_1}$

or $\sqrt{2} = \dfrac{\sin i_1}{\sin 30°}$

We get $i_1 = 45°$

6. Condition of no emergence from opposite face is

$$A > 2\theta_C$$

7. $r_2 = 0, r_1 = A$

$$\mu = \frac{\sin i_1}{\sin r_1} \approx \frac{i_1}{r_1} = \frac{i_1}{A}$$

$\Rightarrow$ $i_1 = \mu A$

8. $\mu = \dfrac{\sin\left(\dfrac{A+\delta_m}{2}\right)}{\sin(A/2)}$

For small angled prism, $\sin\dfrac{A}{2} \approx \dfrac{A}{2}$

$\therefore$ $\sin\left(\dfrac{A+\delta_m}{2}\right) = \dfrac{\mu A}{2}$

With increase in μ, $\sin\left(\dfrac{A+\delta_m}{2}\right)$ will increase. Hence, δ_m will increase.

9. By Snell's law

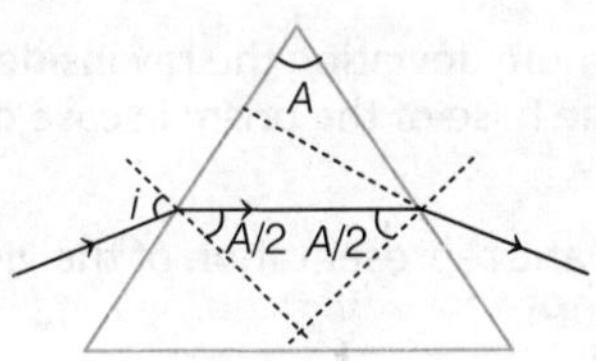

$$1 \sin i = \mu \sin\frac{A}{2}$$

$$\sin i = \mu \sin\left(\frac{A}{2}\right) \text{ and } \mu = \cot\frac{A}{2}$$

$$\sin i = \cot\left(\frac{A}{2}\right) \cdot \sin\left(\frac{A}{2}\right)$$

$$\sin i = \frac{\cos\left(\frac{A}{2}\right)}{\sin\left(\frac{A}{2}\right)} \cdot \sin\left(\frac{A}{2}\right)$$

$$\sin i = \cos\left(\frac{A}{2}\right)$$

$$\sin i = \sin\left(\frac{\pi}{2} - \frac{A}{2}\right)$$

$$i = \frac{\pi}{2} - \frac{A}{2}$$

$$2i = \pi - A$$

$$\delta_{min} = 2i - A = \pi - A - A$$

$$= \pi - 2A$$

Alternate Solution

$$\mu = \frac{\sin\left(\frac{A+\delta_{min}}{2}\right)}{\sin\left(\frac{A}{2}\right)}$$

$$\cot\frac{A}{2} = \frac{\sin\left(\frac{A+\delta_{min}}{2}\right)}{\sin\left(\frac{A}{2}\right)}$$

$$\frac{\cos\frac{A}{2}}{\sin\left(\frac{A}{2}\right)} = \frac{\sin\left(\frac{A+\delta_{min}}{2}\right)}{\sin\left(\frac{A}{2}\right)}$$

$$\cos\left(\frac{A}{2}\right) = \sin\left(\frac{\pi}{2} - \frac{A}{2}\right) = \sin\left(\frac{A+\delta_{min}}{2}\right)$$

$$\frac{\pi}{2} - \frac{A}{2} = \frac{A+\delta_{min}}{2}$$

$$\frac{\pi}{2} - \frac{A}{2} = \frac{A}{2} + \frac{\delta_{min}}{2}$$

$\Rightarrow$ $\delta_{min} = (\pi - 2A)$

10. Given, refractive index of material of prism $n = \sqrt{3}$, prism angle $A = 60°$

Using prism formula,

$$n = \frac{\sin\left(\frac{A+\delta}{2}\right)}{\sin\left(\frac{A}{2}\right)}$$

$\Rightarrow$ $\sqrt{3} = \dfrac{\sin\left(\dfrac{60+\delta}{2}\right)}{\sin 30°}$

$\Rightarrow$ $\sin\left(\dfrac{60+\delta}{2}\right) = \dfrac{\sqrt{3}}{2}$

$\Rightarrow$ $\sin\left(\dfrac{60+\delta}{2}\right) = \sin 60°$

or $\dfrac{60+\delta}{2} = 60$

or angle of minimum deviation $\delta = 60°$

Incident angle,

$$i = \frac{60+\delta}{2} = 60°$$

Alternate solution

For minimum deviation, ray should pass symmetrically (i.e. parallel to the base of the equilateral prism)

$\Rightarrow$ From geometry of given figure, we have, $r = 30°$

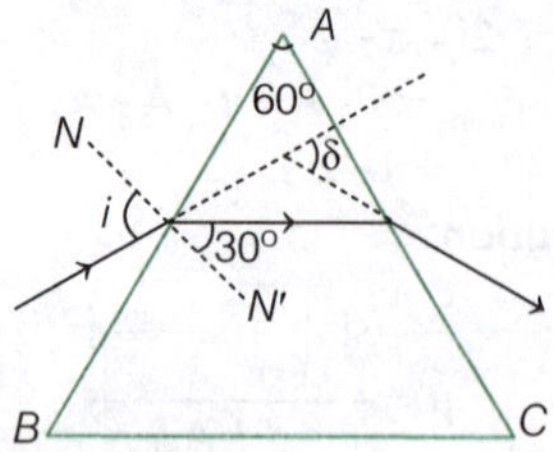

Using Snell's law, $n = \frac{\sin i}{\sin r}$

$$\sin i = n \sin r = \sqrt{3} \sin 30°$$

$$\Rightarrow \qquad \sin i = \frac{\sqrt{3}}{2} \text{ or } i = 60°$$

11. $\delta = (i_1 + i_2) - A$

$$\Rightarrow \qquad 40° = (35° + 79°) - A$$

$$\Rightarrow \qquad A = 74°$$

Now, we know that

$$\mu = \frac{\sin\left(\frac{A + \delta_m}{2}\right)}{\sin\left(\frac{A}{2}\right)}$$

It we take the given deviation as the minimum deviation then,

$$\mu = \frac{\sin\left(\frac{74° + 40°}{2}\right)}{\sin\left(\frac{74°}{2}\right)} = 1.51$$

The given deviation may or may not be the minimum deviation. Rather it will be less than this value. Therefore, μ will be less than 1.51.

Hence, maximum possible value of refractive index is 1.51.

12.

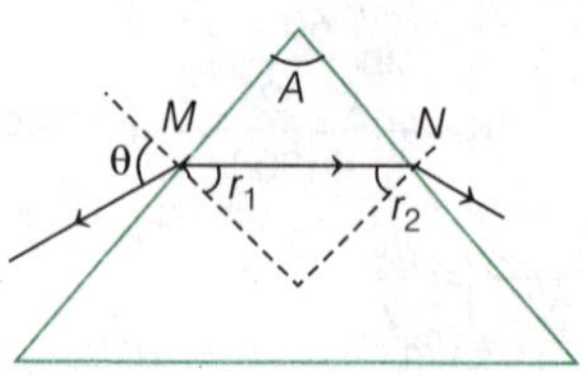

Applying Snell's law at M, $\mu = \frac{\sin\theta}{\sin r_1}$

$$\therefore \quad r_1 = \sin^{-1}\left(\frac{\sin\theta}{\mu}\right) \text{ or } \sin r_1 = \frac{\sin\theta}{\mu}$$

Now, $r_2 = A - r_1 = A - \sin^{-1}\left(\frac{\sin\theta}{\mu}\right)$

Ray of light would get transmitted from face AC if

$$r_2 < \theta_c \quad \text{or} \quad A - \sin^{-1}\left(\frac{\sin\theta}{\mu}\right) < \theta_c$$

where, $\qquad \theta_c = \sin^{-1}(1/\mu)$

$$\therefore \qquad \sin^{-1}\left(\frac{\sin\theta}{\mu}\right) > A - \theta_c$$

$$\text{or} \qquad \frac{\sin\theta}{\mu} > \sin(A - \theta_c)$$

$$\therefore \qquad \theta > \sin^{-1}[\mu \sin(A - \theta_c)]$$

$$\text{or} \qquad \theta > \sin^{-1}\left[\mu \sin\left\{A - \sin^{-1}\left(\frac{1}{\mu}\right)\right\}\right]$$

13. We know that the angle of deviation depends upon the angle of incidence. If we determine experimentally, the angles of deviation corresponding to different angles of incidence and then plot i (on-X-axis) and δ (on-Y-axis), we get a curve as shown in figure.

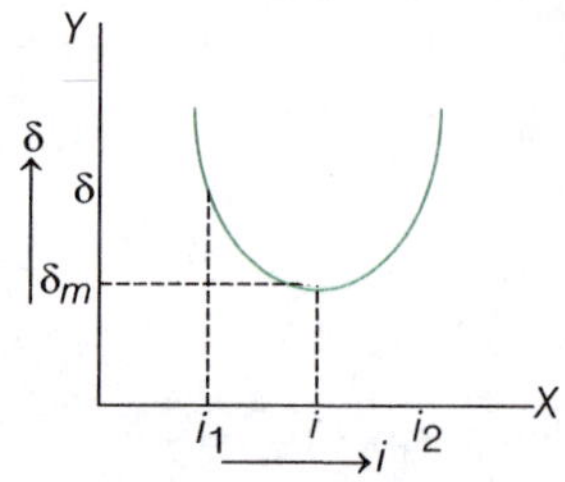

Clearly if angle of incidence is gradually increased, from a small value, the angle of deviation first decreases, becomes minimum for a particular angle of incidence and then begins to increase.

14. At minimum deviation $(\delta = \delta_m)$:

$$r_1 = r_2 = \frac{A}{2} = \frac{60°}{2} = 30° \qquad \text{(For both colours)}$$

15. During minimum deviation the ray inside the prism is parallel to the base of the prism in case of an equilateral prism.

16. The diagramatic representation of the given problem is shown in figure.

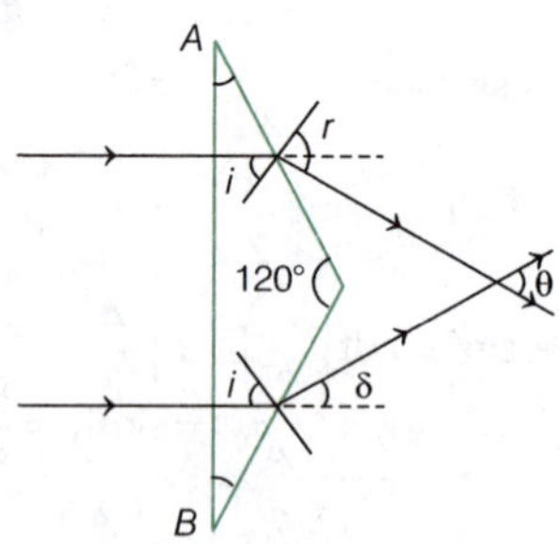

From figure it follows that

$$\angle i = \angle A = 30°$$

From Snell's law, $n_1 \sin i = n_2 \sin r$

or $\quad \sin r = \dfrac{1.44 \sin 30°}{1} = 0.72$

Now, $\quad \angle\delta = \angle r - \angle i = \sin^{-1}(0.72) - 30°$

$\therefore \quad \theta = 2(\angle\delta) = 2\{\sin^{-1}(0.72) - 30°\}$

17. The colours for which $i > \theta_c$, will get total internal reflection : $i > \theta_c$ or $\sin i > \sin\theta_c$

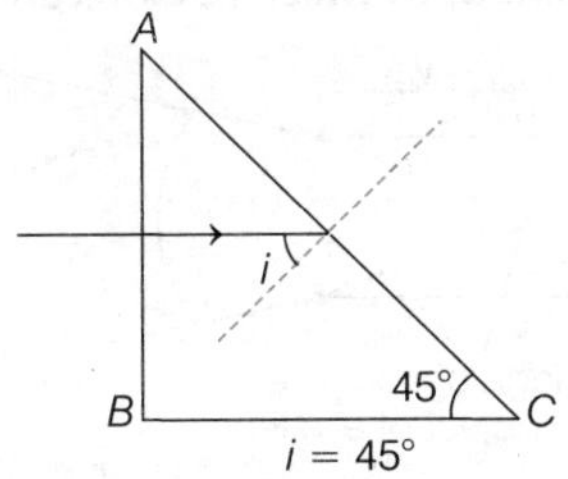

or $\quad \sin 45° > \dfrac{1}{\mu}$

or $\quad \dfrac{1}{\sqrt{2}} > \dfrac{1}{\mu}$

or for which $\mu > \sqrt{2}$

or $\mu > 1.414$

Hence, the rays for which $\mu > 1.414$ will get TIR.

For green and blue $\mu > 1.414$, so they will suffer TIR on face AC. Only red comes out from this face.

18. Deviation $\delta = (\mu - 1)A$

Given, $\quad \delta_{net} = 0$

$\therefore \quad (\mu_1 - 1)A_1 = (\mu_2 - 1)A_2$

or $\quad A_2 = \dfrac{(\mu_1 - 1)}{(\mu_2 - 1)} A_1$

$= \dfrac{(1.54 - 1)}{(1.72 - 1)}(4°) = 3°$

19. $\theta_C = \sin^{-1}\left(\dfrac{\mu_R}{\mu_D}\right) = \sin^{-1}\left(\dfrac{4/3}{3/2}\right) = \sin^{-1}(8/9)$

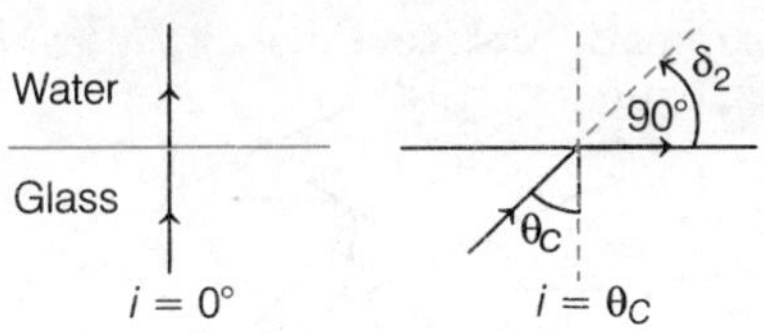

$\therefore \quad \delta_1 = 0°$

$\therefore \quad \delta_2 = 90° - \theta_C$

$\cos\delta_2 = \cos(90° - \theta_C) = \sin\theta_C = \dfrac{8}{9}$

$\therefore \quad \delta_2 = \cos^{-1}\left(\dfrac{8}{9}\right)$

20. At minimum deviation,

$$r_1 = r_2 = \frac{A}{2} = 30°$$

Applying $\quad \mu = \dfrac{\sin i_1}{\sin r_1}$ or $1.5 = \dfrac{\sin i_1}{\sin 30°}$

We get $\quad i_1 = 48.6°$

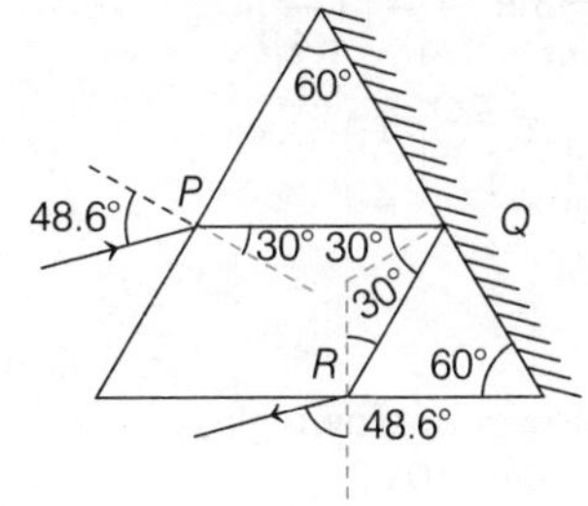

$$\delta_{Total} = \delta_P + \delta_Q + \delta_R$$
$$= (48.6° - 30°) + (180° - 2 \times 30°) + (48.6° - 30°)$$
$$= 157.2°$$

(b) $\dfrac{4}{3}\sin(48.6°) = 1.5 \sin r_1$

Solving we get, $r_1 = 41.8°$

$r_2 = 60° - r_1 = 18.2°$

$r_3 = 60° - r_2 = 41.8°$

$\therefore \quad i_3 = 48.6°$

Hence,

$\delta_{Total} = (48.6° - 41.8°) + (180° - 2 \times 18.2°) + (48.6° - 41.8°)$

$= 157.2°$

21. Given, for equilateral prism,

$$A = 60°, \mu = \sqrt{2}$$

We know that, $\mu = \dfrac{\sin\left(\dfrac{A + \delta_m}{2}\right)}{\sin\dfrac{A}{2}}$

$\Rightarrow \quad \sqrt{2} = \dfrac{\sin\left(\dfrac{60° + \delta_m}{2}\right)}{\sin 30°}$

$\Rightarrow \quad \sin\left(\dfrac{A + \delta_m}{2}\right) = \dfrac{1}{\sqrt{2}} = \sin 45°$

$\Rightarrow \quad \dfrac{A + \delta_m}{2} = 45°$

$\Rightarrow \quad \delta_m = 90° - A = 90 - 60° = 30°$

22. We know that, condition for deviation without dispersion is given by

$(n_{Y_1} - 1)A_1\omega_1 = (n_{Y_2} - 1)A_2\omega_2$

$\Rightarrow \quad (1.5 - 1)6\omega_1 = (1.55 - 1)5\omega_2$

$\Rightarrow \quad 0.5 \times 6\omega_1 = 0.55 \times 5\omega_2$

$\Rightarrow \quad 3\omega_1 = 2.75\omega_2$

$\Rightarrow \quad \dfrac{\omega_1}{\omega_2} = \dfrac{2.75}{3}$

Now, net deviation

$$= \delta_{net} = (n_{Y_1} - 1)A_1\left[1 - \frac{\omega_1}{\omega_2}\right]$$

$$=(1.5-1)\,6\left[1-\frac{2.75}{3}\right]$$

$$=3\times\frac{0.25}{3}=\left(\frac{1}{4}\right)^0$$

$\therefore \quad \delta_{net}=\left(\frac{1}{x}\right)^0=\left(\frac{1}{4}\right)^0$

$\therefore \quad x=4$

23. Given,

Dispersive power of crown glass,

$$\omega_1=0.02$$

Dispersive power of flint glass,

$$\omega_2=0.03$$

Refractive index of yellow light,

for crown glass, $\mu_1=1.5$ and

for flint glass, $\mu_2=1.6$

This is a case of achromatic combination.

$\therefore \quad \theta_{net}=0$

$\Rightarrow \quad \theta_1-\theta_2=0$

$\Rightarrow \quad \theta_1=\theta_2$

$\Rightarrow \quad \omega_1\delta_1=\omega_2\delta_2 \quad [\because \theta=\omega\delta] \quad$ ...(i)

and $\quad \delta_{net}=\delta_1-\delta_2=2^\circ \quad$ ... (ii)

From Eqs. (i) and (ii), we get

$$\delta_1-\frac{\omega_1\delta_1}{\omega_2}=2^\circ$$

$\Rightarrow \quad \delta_1\left(1-\frac{\omega_1}{\omega_2}\right)=2^\circ$

$\Rightarrow \quad \delta_1\left(1-\frac{2}{3}\right)=2^\circ$

$\Rightarrow \quad \delta_1=6^\circ$

Also, $\quad \delta_1=(\mu_1-1)A_1$

$\Rightarrow \quad 6^\circ=(1.5-1)A_1$

$\Rightarrow \quad A_1=12^\circ$

$\therefore$ The refracting angle for crown glass prism will be 12°.

Module 9.

1. The resolving power of a microscope is inversely proportional to the wavelength of the wave used. de-Broglie matter wave is used in case of an electron microscope whose wavelength is less than the wavelength of visible light used in optical microscope.

2. $P_1+P_2=P$

$\therefore \quad 5+P_2=2 \quad (P_1=+5\,D)$

or $\quad P_2=-3$

$$P\propto\frac{1}{f} \Rightarrow \frac{P_1}{P_2}=\frac{f_2}{f_1}$$

or $\quad \frac{5}{-3}=\frac{f_2}{f_1} \Rightarrow \frac{f_1}{f_2}=-\frac{3}{5}$

Now, $\quad \frac{\omega_1}{f_1}+\frac{\omega_2}{f_2}=0 \Rightarrow \frac{\omega_1}{\omega_2}=-\frac{f_1}{f_2}=\frac{3}{5}$

3. Given, power of lens used for distant $(u=\infty)$ vision is, $P_1=-1.0\,D$

$\Rightarrow$ Focal length of lens used $f_1=-100$ cm

$$\left(\because f\,(\text{cm})=\frac{100}{P(\text{in D})}\right)$$

So, image of distant object must be formed with in the far point (point upto which person can see).

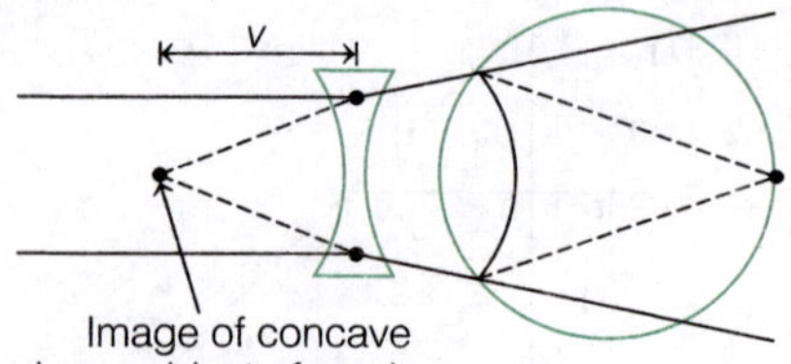

Image of concave lens=object of eye lens

For concave lens; $\frac{1}{v}-\frac{1}{u}=\frac{1}{f_1}$

$$u=\infty,\ v=?,\ f_1=-100\text{ cm}$$

$\Rightarrow \quad \frac{1}{v}=-\frac{1}{100}$

or $\quad v=-100$ cm

Now, person is using a lens of power +2D for reading.

Focal length of convex lens used

$$=f_2=\frac{100}{P(\text{in D})}=+50\text{ cm}$$

Now, if distance of distinct vision is x, then image of x must be formed at 100 cm from eye.

$$u=-x,\ v=-100\text{ cm}$$

$$f=50\text{ cm}$$

$$\frac{1}{-100}-\frac{1}{-x}=\frac{1}{50}$$

$\Rightarrow \quad \frac{1}{x}=\frac{1}{50}+\frac{1}{100}=\frac{3}{100}$

$$x=\frac{100}{3}=33.33\text{ cm.}$$

Nearest answer is 30 cm.

4.

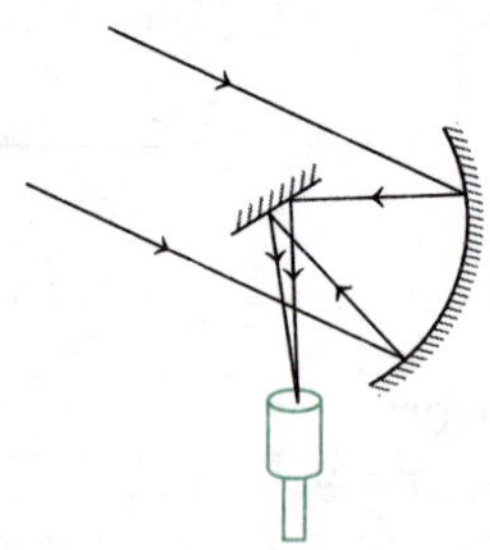

In a reflecting telescope secondary mirror turns light towards eyepiece which is outside the telescope tube.

5. $(RP)_{air}=\frac{2\sin\theta}{1.22\lambda}$

$$(RP)_{oil}=\frac{2\sin\theta}{1.22\lambda_{oil}}=\frac{2\sin\theta\times\mu}{1.22\lambda}$$

$(RP)_{oil}=(RP)_{air}\times 2$

6. Resolving power is given by

$$RP = \frac{d}{1.22\lambda} = \frac{24.4 \times 10^{-2}}{1.22 \times 2440 \times 10^{-10}}$$

$$= 8.2 \times 10^5$$

7. For a telescope, limit of resolution is given by $\Delta\theta = \frac{1.22\lambda}{D}$

Here, $\lambda = 500 \text{ nm} = 500 \times 10^{-9}$ m,

$D = 200 \text{ cm} = 200 \times 10^{-2}$ m

So, limit of resolution is

$$\Delta\theta = \frac{1.22 \times 500 \times 10^{-9}}{200 \times 10^{-2}}$$

$$= 305 \times 10^{-9} \text{ rad}$$

8. Telescope revolves and brings objects closer. Hence, telescope with magnifying power of 20, the tree appears 20 times nearer.

9. Given, Focal length of objective of telescope $f_0 = 30$ cm

focal length of eyepiece, $f_e = 3.0$ cm

Magnifying power, $M = ?$

Magnifying power of the Galilean telescope,

$$M_D = \frac{f_0}{f_e}\left(1 - \frac{f_e}{D}\right) = \frac{30}{3}\left(1 - \frac{3}{25}\right) \quad (\because D = 25 \text{ cm})$$

$$= 10 \times \frac{22}{25} = 8.8 \text{ cm}$$

10. The focal length of combination is given by

$$\frac{1}{F} = \frac{1}{40} - \frac{1}{25} \left(\frac{1}{F} = \frac{1}{F_1} + \frac{1}{F_2}\right)$$

or $\quad F = -\frac{200}{3} \text{ cm} = -\frac{2}{3} \text{ m}$

∴ Power of the combination in dioptres,

$$P = -\frac{3}{2} \quad \left[P = \frac{1}{F(\text{m})}\right]$$

$$= -1.5$$

11.

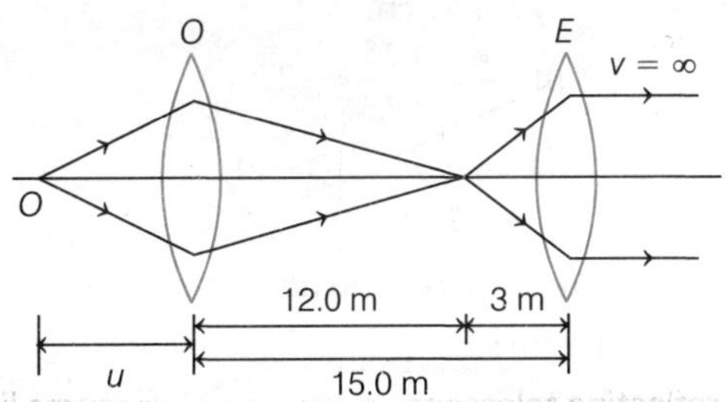

Since, the final image is formed at infinity, the image formed by the objective will be at the focal point of the eyepiece, which is 3.0 cm. The image formed by the objective will be at a distance of 12.0 cm (= 15.0 cm − 3.0 cm) from the objective.

If u is the distance of the object from the objective, we have

$$\Rightarrow \quad \frac{1}{v} - \frac{1}{u} = \frac{1}{f}$$

$$\Rightarrow \quad \frac{1}{12} - \frac{1}{-u} = \frac{1}{2}$$

$$u = 2.4 \text{ cm}$$

12. $L_\infty = f_o + f_e = 36$ ...(i)

Further angular magnification is given as 5. Therefore,

$$M_\infty = \frac{f_o}{f_e} = 5 \quad \text{...(ii)}$$

Solving Eqs. (i) and (ii), we get

$$f_o = 30 \text{ cm and } f_e = 6 \text{ cm}$$

13. Distance between objective and eyepiece

$$L = f_o + f_e = (16 + 0.02) \text{ m} = 16.02 \text{ m}$$

Angular magnification

$$M = -f_o/f_e = -16/0.02 = -800$$

Image is inverted and objective is larger than the eyepiece.

14. $\frac{\omega_1}{f_1} + \frac{\omega_2}{f_2} = 0$

$$\therefore \quad \left|\frac{\omega_1}{\omega_2}\right| = \left|\frac{f_1}{f_2}\right|$$

Let 1-stands for flint glass and 2-stands for crown glass. Then,

$$\left|\frac{f_1}{f_2}\right| = \frac{3}{2} \text{ or } |f_1| = 1.5\,|f_2|$$

Focal length of flint glass is more. So, its power is less. Combined focal length (and hence combined power) is positive. So, convex lens (converging lens) should be made up of crown glass (having more positive power).

Now, $\quad \frac{1}{F} = \frac{1}{f_1} + \frac{1}{f_2}$

$$\therefore \quad \frac{1}{150} = \frac{1}{-1.5f} + \frac{1}{f}$$

Solving this equation, we get

$$f_2 = f = 50 \text{ cm and}$$

$$f_1 = -1.5f = -75 \text{ cm}$$

15. (a) $\frac{\omega_1}{f_1} + \frac{\omega_2}{f_2} = 0$

$$\therefore \quad \omega_2 = \left(-\frac{f_2}{f_1}\right)\omega_1 = -\frac{(-30)}{(+20)}(0.18) = 0.27$$

(b) $\frac{1}{F} = \frac{1}{f_1} + \frac{1}{f_2} = \frac{1}{20} - \frac{1}{30}$

or $\quad F = +60$ cm

16. (a) Resolving power of telescope is given by

$$R = \frac{D}{1.22\lambda} = \frac{5.0 \times 10^{-2}}{1.22 \times 0.55 \times 10^{-6}}$$

or $\quad R = 7.45 \times 10^4$

(b) The smallest angular separation between two objects which can be seen separately.

$$\Delta\theta = \frac{1}{R} = \frac{\Delta y_{min}}{l}$$

$$\therefore \quad \Delta y_{min} = \frac{l}{R} = \frac{3.0 \times 10^3}{7.45 \times 10^4} \text{ m}$$

$$= 0.04 \text{ m} \quad \text{or} \quad \Delta y_{min} = 4 \text{ cm}$$

17. As discussed in the above solution,

$$\Delta y_{min} = \frac{l}{R} = \frac{l(1.22\lambda)}{D} \quad \text{...(i)}$$

Here l is distance of moon from earth $= 3.84 \times 10^8$ m

Substituting the values in equation (i), we get

$$\Delta y_{min} \approx 50 \text{ m}$$

18. $$d_{min} = \frac{0.61\lambda}{\text{NA}} \quad \text{...(i)}$$

where NA = numerical aperture

$$= \sin\alpha = 0.24$$

Substituting in Eq. (i), we get

$$d_{min} = 1.4\,\mu\text{m}$$

Unit Exercise (Cumulative)

Level 1

1. Rays starting from O will suffer single refraction from spherical surface APB. Therefore, applying

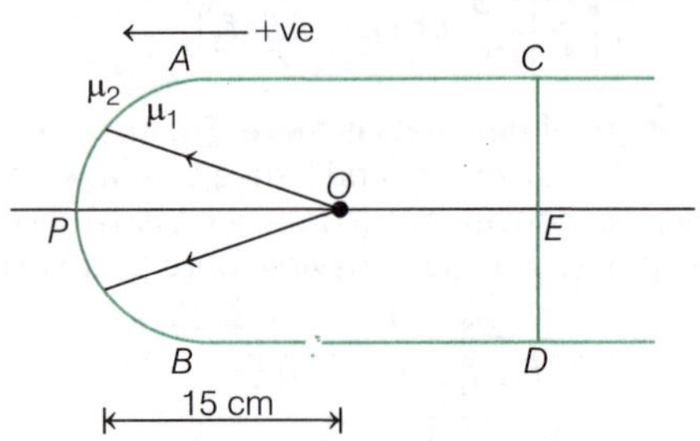

$$\frac{\mu_2}{v} - \frac{\mu_1}{u} = \frac{\mu_2 - \mu_1}{R}$$

$$\frac{1.0}{v} - \frac{2.0}{-15} = \frac{1.0 - 2.0}{-10}$$

$$\frac{1}{v} = \frac{1}{10} - \frac{1}{7.5}$$

or $$v = -30 \text{ cm}$$

Therefore, image of O will be formed at 30 cm to the right of P. Note that image will be virtual. There will be no effect of CED.

2. After a certain angle all colours get total internally reflected.

3. Lens formula:

$$\frac{1}{v_1} - \frac{1}{-15} = \frac{1}{30}$$

$$\Rightarrow \quad v_1 = -30 \text{ cm}$$

Mirror formula:

$$v_2 = -u_2 = -(-45) = 45 \text{ cm}$$

Lens formula:

$$\frac{1}{v_3} - \frac{1}{-60} = \frac{1}{30}$$

$$\therefore \quad v_3 = +60 \text{ cm}$$

Hence, distance of final image from object

$$= 60 - 15 = 45 \text{ cm}$$

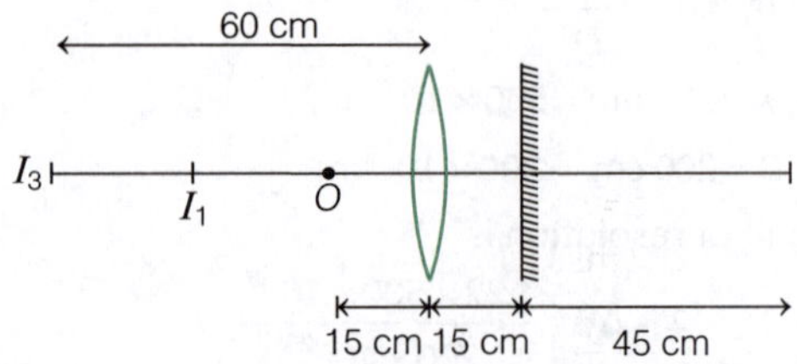

4. If object is placed at focus of convex lens, rays become parallel and they are incident normally on plane mirror. So, ray of light will retrace its path.

5. $$\mu = \frac{\sin i}{\sin r}$$

$$\Rightarrow \quad \sqrt{2} = \frac{\sin 45^\circ}{\sin r} \quad \text{or} \quad r = 30^\circ$$

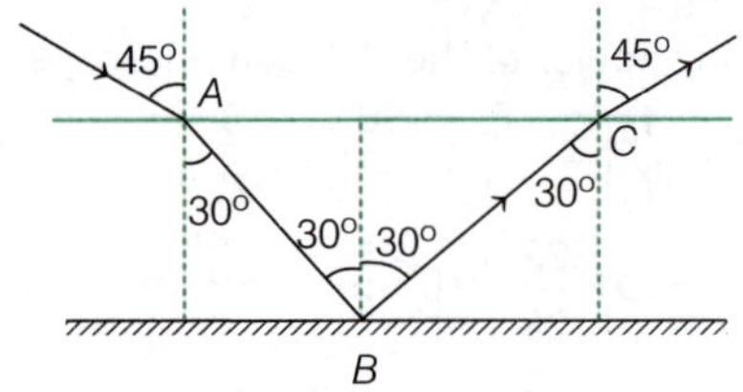

$$\delta_{Total} = \delta_A - \delta_B + \delta_C$$

$$= (45^\circ - 30^\circ) - [180^\circ - 2(30^\circ)] + (45^\circ - 30^\circ)$$

$$= -90^\circ \quad \text{or} \quad |\delta_{Total}| = 90^\circ$$

6. $$\frac{1}{F} = \frac{1}{f_1} + \frac{1}{f_2} = \frac{1}{10} + \frac{1}{10}$$

$$\therefore \quad F = 5 \text{ cm}$$

$$\frac{1}{v} - \frac{1}{-7.5} = \frac{1}{+5}$$

$$\therefore \quad v = +15 \text{ cm}$$

$$m = \frac{v}{u} = \frac{+15}{-7.5} = -2$$

$$I = mO = (-2)(1 \text{ cm})$$

$$= -2 \text{ cm}$$

7. Between 1 and 3 there is no deviation.

Hence $\mu_1 = \mu_3$

Between 3 and 2

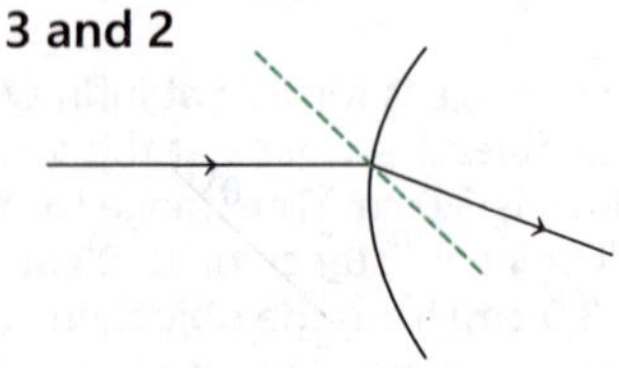

Ray to light binds towards normal. Hence,

$$\mu_2 > \mu_3.$$

8. $A = \delta_m = 60° \Rightarrow \mu = \dfrac{\sin\left(\dfrac{A+\delta_m}{2}\right)}{\sin(A/2)}$

9. For air lens in glass,

$$\frac{1}{f} = ({}_g\mu_a - 1)\left(\frac{1}{R_1} - \frac{1}{R_2}\right)$$

$$= \left(\frac{2}{3} - 1\right)\left[\frac{1}{10} - \left(-\frac{1}{10}\right)\right]$$

$\Rightarrow \quad f = -15$ cm

So, nature of lens is diverging (concave).

10. Apply $\dfrac{1}{f} = \dfrac{2(\mu_2/\mu_1)}{R_2} + \dfrac{2(\mu_2/\mu_1 - 1)}{R_1}$

11.
$$\frac{1}{30} - \frac{1}{-u} = \frac{1}{f}$$

or $\quad \dfrac{1}{30} + \dfrac{1}{u} = \dfrac{1}{f} \quad$ ...(i)

Similarly, $\dfrac{1}{120} + \dfrac{1}{u - 90} = \dfrac{1}{f} \quad$ ...(ii)

Solving these two equations, we get

$f = 24$ cm

12.

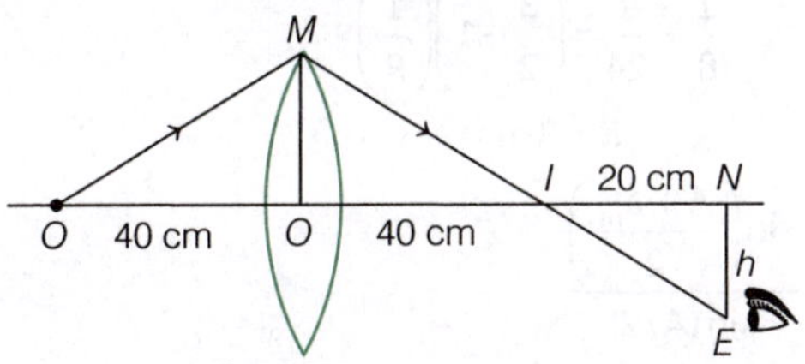

$f = 20$ cm

$$\frac{h}{MO} = \frac{20}{40}$$

$$\Rightarrow \quad h = \frac{MO}{2} = \frac{5}{2} = 2.5 \text{ cm}$$

13. The reflected ray will rotate by an angle 2θ. For TIR to take place at water-air boundary,

$$\sin 2\theta > \sin\theta_C \text{ or } \sin 2\theta > \frac{1}{\mu}$$

$$\therefore \quad \theta > \frac{1}{2}\sin^{-1}\left(\frac{3}{4}\right)$$

14. Critical angle between glass and water,

$$\sin\theta_C = \frac{\mu_w}{\mu_g} = \frac{4/3}{3/2} = \frac{8}{9}$$

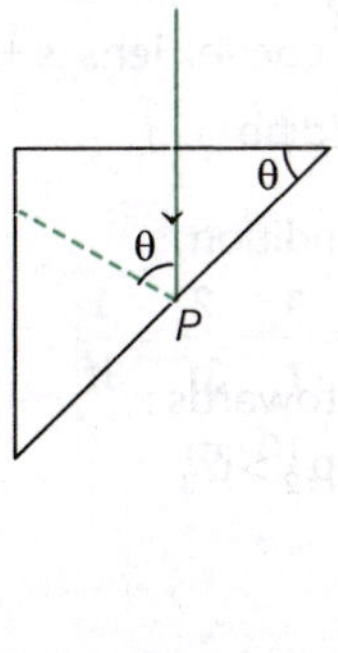

Now, total internal reflection will take place on face AC, if

$$\sin\theta > \sin\theta_c \text{ or } \sin\theta > \frac{8}{9}$$

15. In air, object lies between F and $2F$.

In liquid, focal length will become 4 times. So, object will now lie between optical centre and focus.

16. Condition of no emergence,

$$A > 2\theta_C$$

$$\therefore \quad \theta_C < \frac{A}{2} \text{ or } 45°$$

$$\therefore \quad \sin\theta_C \text{ or } \frac{1}{\mu} < \sin 45° \text{ or } \frac{1}{\sqrt{2}}$$

For no emergence, $\mu > \sqrt{2}$

17. Focal length of a lens is given as

$$\frac{1}{f} = (\mu_1 - 1)\left(\frac{1}{R_1} - \frac{1}{R_2}\right)$$

$\therefore$ Focal length of plano-convex lens, i.e. lens 1,

$R_1 = \infty$ and $R = -R$

$\Rightarrow \quad \dfrac{1}{f_1} = \dfrac{\mu_1 - 1}{R}$ or $f_1 = \dfrac{R}{(\mu_1 - 1)} \quad$ ...(i)

Similarly, focal length of plano-concave lens, i.e. lens 2,

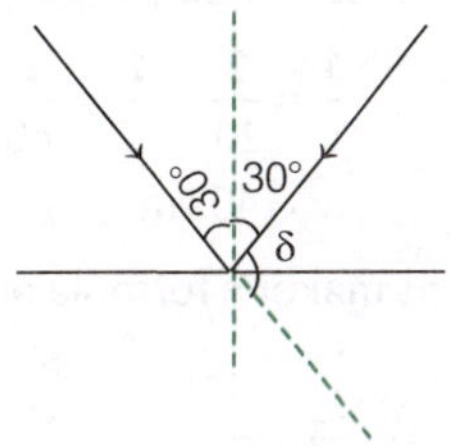

$R_1 = -R$ and $R_2 = \infty$

$$\Rightarrow \quad \frac{1}{f_2} = -\frac{(\mu_2 - 1)}{R}$$

or $\quad f_2 = \dfrac{-R}{(\mu_2 - 1)} \quad$ ...(ii)

From Eqs. (i) and (ii), net focal length is

$$\frac{1}{f} = \frac{\mu_1 - 1}{R} - \frac{\mu_2 - 1}{R} = \frac{\mu_1 - \mu_2}{R}$$

$$\Rightarrow \quad f = \frac{R}{\mu_1 - \mu_2}$$

18.
$$\frac{1}{f_1} = (\mu_1 - 1)\left[\frac{1}{\infty} - \frac{1}{-R}\right] = \frac{\mu_1 - 1}{R}$$

$$\frac{1}{f_2} = (\mu_2 - 1)\left[\frac{1}{4R} - \frac{1}{\infty}\right] = \frac{\mu_2 - 1}{R}$$

$$\frac{1}{f_1} = \frac{1}{2f_2}$$

$$\Rightarrow \quad \frac{\mu_1 - 1}{R} = \frac{\mu_2 - 1}{2R}$$

$$\Rightarrow 2\mu_1 - \mu_2 = 1$$

19. $MC = QC - QM = (R - 0.3)$ cm

$$PC^2 = MC^2 + PM^2$$
$$R^2 = (R - 0.3)^2 + (3)^2$$

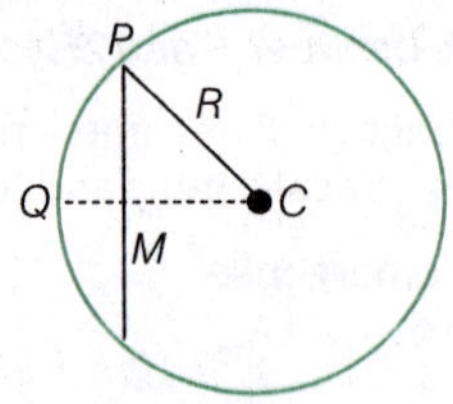

Solving this equation, we get

$$R = 15 \text{ cm}$$

20.

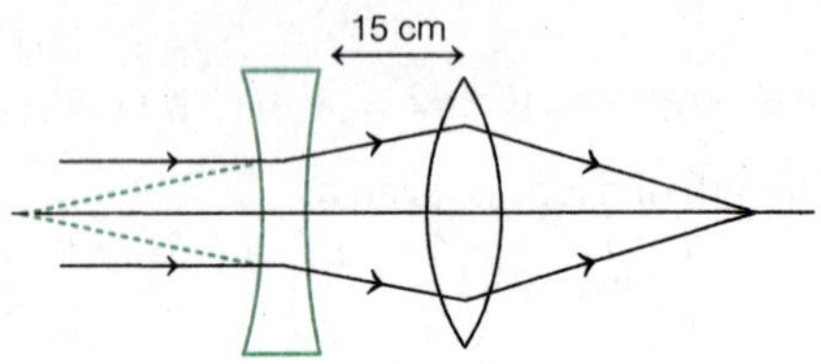

Here, $f_1 = -25$ cm, $f_2 = 20$ cm

For diverging lens, $v = -25$ cm

For converging lens, $u = -(15 + 25) = -40$ cm

$$\therefore \quad \frac{1}{v} - \frac{1}{-40} = \frac{1}{+20}$$
$$\Rightarrow \quad \frac{1}{v} = \frac{1}{20} - \frac{1}{40} = \frac{1}{40}$$
$$\Rightarrow \quad v = 40 \text{ cm}$$

21. It is based on lens maker's formula and its magnification.

i.e. $\frac{1}{f} = (\mu - 1)\left(\frac{1}{R_1} - \frac{1}{R_2}\right)$

According to lens maker's formula, when the lens in the air.

$$\frac{1}{f} = \left(\frac{3}{2} - 1\right)\left(\frac{1}{R_1} - \frac{1}{R_2}\right)$$
$$\frac{1}{f} = \frac{1}{2x}$$
$$\Rightarrow \quad f = 2x$$

Here, $\left(\frac{1}{x} = \frac{1}{R_1} - \frac{1}{R_2}\right)$

In case of liquid, where refractive index is 4/3 and 5/3, we get

Focal length in first liquid

$$\frac{1}{f_1} = \left(\frac{\mu_g}{\mu_{l_1}} - 1\right)\left(\frac{1}{R_1} - \frac{1}{R_2}\right)$$
$$\Rightarrow \quad \frac{1}{f_1} = \left(\frac{\frac{3}{2}}{\frac{4}{3}} - 1\right)\frac{1}{x}$$

$\Rightarrow f_1$ is positive.

$$\frac{1}{f_1} = \frac{1}{8x} = \frac{1}{4(2x)} = \frac{1}{4f}$$
$$\Rightarrow \quad f_1 = 4f$$

Focal length in second liquid

$$\frac{1}{f_2} = \left(\frac{\mu_g}{\mu_{l_2}} - 1\right)\left(\frac{1}{R_1} - \frac{1}{R_2}\right)$$
$$\Rightarrow \quad \frac{1}{f_2} = \left(\frac{\frac{3}{2}}{\frac{5}{3}} - 1\right)\left(\frac{1}{x}\right)$$

$\Rightarrow f_2$ is negative.

22. $\mu = \frac{\lambda_{air}}{\lambda_{medium}} = \frac{1}{(2/3)} = \frac{3}{2}$

Further, $|m| = \frac{1}{3} = \left|\frac{v}{u}\right|$

$$\therefore \quad |v| = \frac{|u|}{3}$$

$\Rightarrow \quad u = -24$ m (Real object)

$\therefore \quad v = +8$ m (Real image)

Now, $\frac{1}{v} - \frac{1}{u} = \frac{1}{f} = (\mu - 1)\left(\frac{1}{+R} - \frac{1}{\infty}\right)$

$$\therefore \quad \frac{1}{8} + \frac{1}{24} = \left(\frac{3}{2} - 1\right)\left(\frac{1}{R}\right)$$
$$\therefore \quad R = 3 \text{ m}$$

23. $\mu = \frac{\sin\left(\frac{A + \delta_m}{2}\right)}{\sin(A/2)}$

μ and A for both rays are same. Hence, value of δ_m is also same for both rays.

24. Using the lens formula,

$$\frac{1}{v} - \frac{1}{u} = \frac{1}{F} = \frac{1}{f_1} + \frac{1}{f_2}$$

or $\frac{1}{v} = \frac{1}{u} + \frac{1}{f_1} + \frac{1}{f_2}$

$$= \frac{1}{u} + (n_1 - 1)\left(\frac{1}{R_1} - \frac{1}{R_2}\right) + (n_2 - 1)\left(\frac{1}{R_1'} - \frac{1}{R_2'}\right)$$

Substituting the values, we get

$$\frac{1}{v} = \frac{1}{-40} + (1.5 - 1)\left(\frac{1}{14} - \frac{1}{\infty}\right) + (1.2 - 1)\left(\frac{1}{\infty} - \frac{1}{-14}\right)$$

Solving this equations, we get

$$v = +40 \text{ cm}$$

25. Let focal length of convex lens is $+f$, then focal length of concave lens would be $-\frac{3}{2}f$.

From the given condition,

$$\frac{1}{30} = \frac{1}{f} - \frac{2}{3f} = \frac{1}{3f}$$
$$\therefore \quad f = 10 \text{ cm}$$

Therefore, focal length of convex lens $= + 10$ cm
and that of concave lens $= - 15$ cm

26. Image formed by convex lens at I_1 will act as a virtual object for concave lens. For concave lens

$$\frac{1}{v} - \frac{1}{u} = \frac{1}{f}$$

or
$$\frac{1}{v} - \frac{1}{4} = \frac{1}{-20}$$

or
$$v = 5 \text{ cm}$$

Magnification for concave lens

$$m = \frac{v}{u} = \frac{5}{4} = 1.25$$

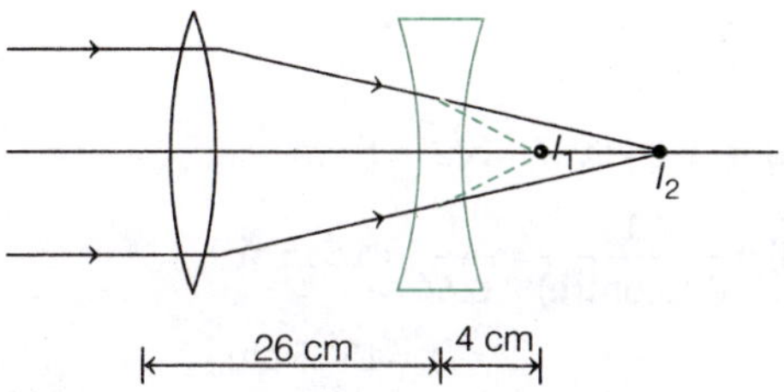

As size of the image at I_1 is 2 cm. Therefore, size of image at I_2 will be $2 \times 1.25 = 2.5$ cm.

27. The lens makers' formula is

$$\frac{1}{f} = \left(\frac{n_L}{n_m} - 1\right)\left(\frac{1}{R_1} - \frac{1}{R_2}\right)$$

where, n_L = Refractive index of lens and n_m = Refractive index of medium.

In case of double concave lens, R_1 is negative and R_2 is positive.

Therefore, $\left(\frac{1}{R_1} - \frac{1}{R_2}\right)$ will be negative.

For the lens to be diverging in nature, focal length f should be negative or $\left(\frac{n_L}{n_m} - 1\right)$ should be positive or

$n_L > n_m$.

Since $n_2 > n_1$ (given), therefore the lens should be filled with L_2 and immersed in L_1.

28. Image can be formed on the screen if it is real. Real image of reduced size can be formed by a concave mirror or a convex lens.

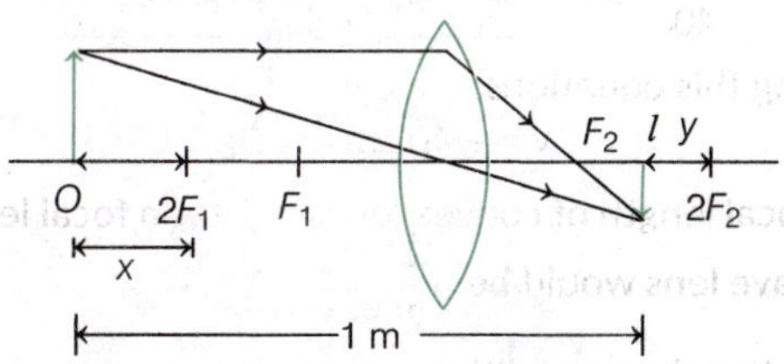

A diminished real image is formed by a convex lens when the object is placed beyond $2f$ and the image of such object is formed between f and $2f$ on other side.

Thus, $\quad d > (2f + 2f) \quad (x > y)$

or $\quad 4f < 0.1$ m

or $\quad f < 0.25$ m

29. If object is placed at focus of plano-convex lens, then it will make rays parallel. Now, these rays fall normal on plane mirror. So, they retrace their path.

30. Refraction from lens :

$$\frac{1}{v_1} - \frac{1}{-20} = \frac{1}{15}$$

$\therefore \quad v = 60 \text{ cm} \quad \overrightarrow{+\text{ve direction}}$

i.e. first image is formed at 60 cm to the right of lens system.

Reflection from mirror

After reflection from the mirror, the second image will be formed at a distance of 60 cm to the left of lens system.

Refraction from lens

$$\frac{1}{v_3} - \frac{1}{60} = \frac{1}{15} \qquad \longleftarrow +\text{ve direction}$$

or $\quad v_3 = 12$ cm

Therefore, the final image is formed at 12 cm to the left of the lens system.

31. Clearly middle part of glass is diverging and upper and lower part are converging, so correct shape of the emergent wavefront is as shown in the figure.

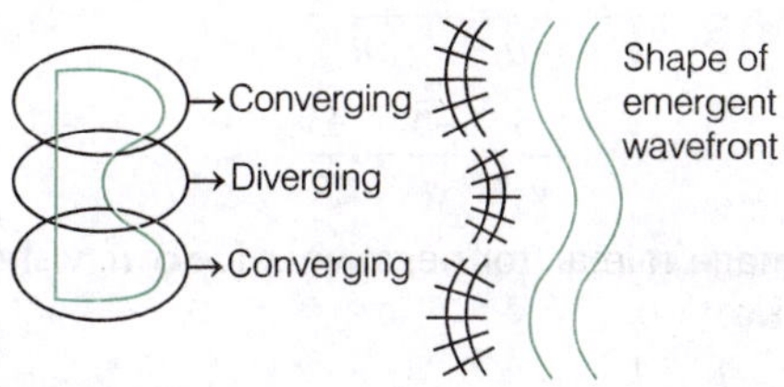

32. If object is placed at centre of the sphere, then all rays starting from C fall normal on spherical surface and pass understand.

33. $\frac{h}{\mu} = \frac{21}{2}$ or $\frac{h}{(4/3)} = \frac{21}{2}$

Solving, we get $h = 14$ cm.

34. $m = -\frac{2\text{cm}}{1\text{cm}} = -2$

$\Rightarrow \quad |v| = m|u|$

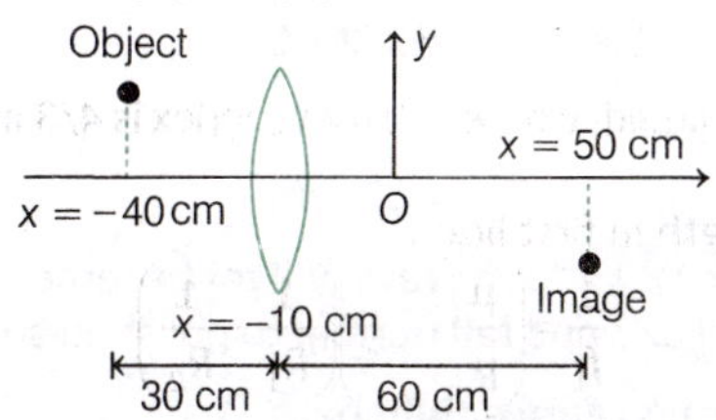

35. Using the equation,

$$\frac{1}{F} = \frac{2(\mu_2/\mu_1)}{R_2} - 2\frac{(\mu_2/\mu_1 - 1)}{R_1}$$

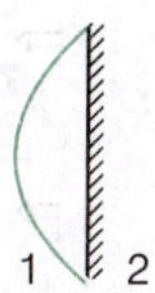

we get

$$\frac{1}{-10}=\frac{2(1.5)}{\infty}-\frac{1(1.5-1)}{R_1} \qquad \left(\text{as } F=\frac{R}{2}\right)$$

Solving, we get $R_1 = 10$ cm.

36. $\angle i = 0°$ for all values of θ, as the rays fall normal to sphere at all points.

37.

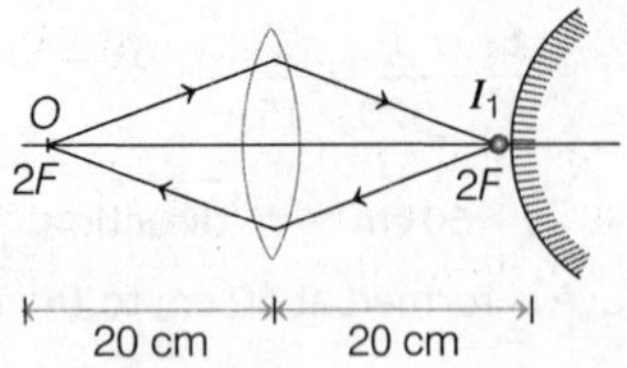

38. Using $\frac{1}{v}-\frac{1}{u}=\frac{1}{f}$, we get

$$\frac{1}{+(f+40)}-\frac{1}{-(f+10)}=\frac{1}{+f}$$

Solving this equation, we get

$$f=+20 \text{ cm}$$

39.

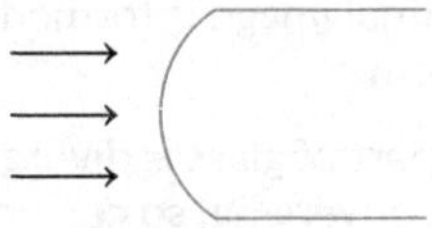

$$\frac{1.5}{v}-\frac{1.0}{-u}=\frac{1.5-1.0}{+R}$$

or $$\frac{1.5}{v}=\frac{-1}{u}+\frac{1}{2R}$$

For image to real (for negative value of u) v should be positive.

Hence, $\frac{1}{u}<\frac{1}{2R}$

or $u>2R$.

40. $\frac{1}{F}=\frac{1}{f_1}+\frac{1}{f_2}-\frac{d_2}{f_1/f_2}$

f_1 and f_2 both are negative. Hence, F is also negative. Object is real so combined lens (having negative focal length) will always make, its virtual image.

41. Using $\frac{\mu_2}{u}-\frac{\mu_1}{u}=\frac{\mu_2-\mu_1}{R}$ we get

$$\frac{3/2}{\infty}-\frac{1.0}{-x}=\frac{3/2-1}{+60}$$

$\therefore$ $x=120$ cm

Hence for $x=120$ cm, rays of light become parallel to principal axis and fall normal to polished surface.

Hence, rays retrace their path.

42. $$\frac{1.6}{v_1}-\frac{1.0}{-2}=\frac{1.6-1.0}{+1.0}$$

$\Rightarrow$ $v_1=16$ m

$$\frac{2.0}{v_2}-\frac{1.0}{-2}=\frac{2.0-1.0}{+1.0}$$

$\therefore$ $v_2=4$ m

$$I_2I_2=v_1-v_2$$
$$=12 \text{ m}$$

43. $$\frac{1}{-(f+1)}-\frac{1}{-(f-1)}=\frac{1}{f}$$

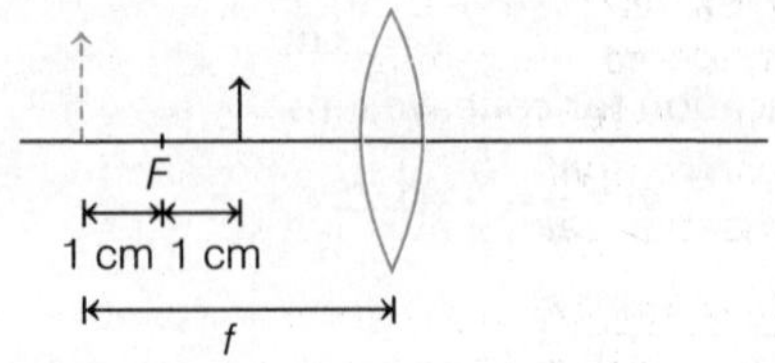

Solving, we get $f=(\sqrt{2}+1)$ cm

44. $f(\text{m})=\frac{1}{P\ (\text{Dioptre})}=\frac{1}{0.66}=1.515$ m

or $f=151.5$ cm

For short sightedness we need a concave lens so that images of all objects lie between O and F_2 or between O and f. Here, f is 151.5 cm. So, distant point of the eye is approximately 151.5 cm.

45. For a lens $\frac{1}{v}-\frac{1}{u}=\frac{1}{f}$,

i.e. $\frac{1}{v}=\frac{1}{f}+\frac{1}{u}$

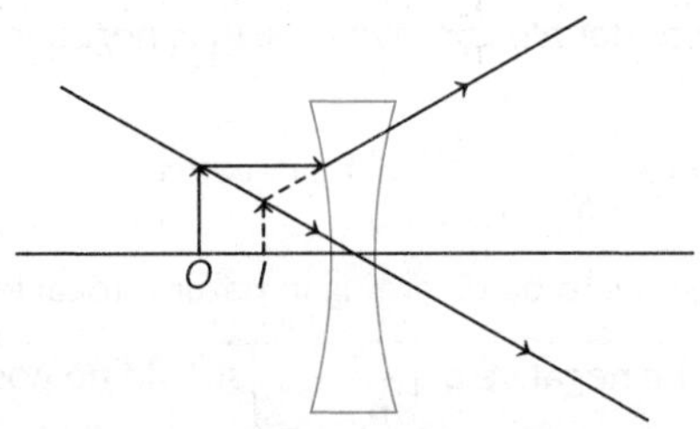

For a concave lens, f and u are negative, i.e. v will always be negative and image will always be virtual.

For a mirror :

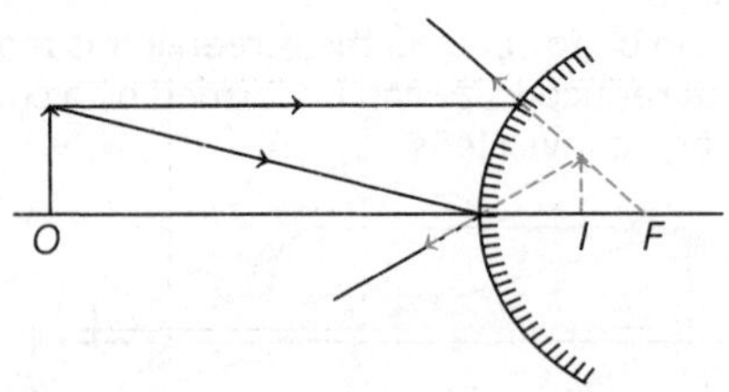

$$\frac{1}{v}+\frac{1}{u}=\frac{1}{f} \text{ i.e. } \frac{1}{v}=\frac{1}{f}-\frac{1}{u}$$

Here, f is positive and u is negative for a convex mirror. Therefore, v is always positive and image is always virtual.

46. When upper half of the lens is covered, image is formed by the rays coming from lower half of the lens. Or image will be formed by less number of rays.

Therefore, intensity of image will decrease. But complete image will be formed.

47. For concave mirror, a real object can real/virtual, magnified/diminished image. Image location can be at infinity too.
For convex mirror, a real object always form virtual, diminished and erect image located between pole and focus. For convex lens or plano-convex lens, a real object can real/virtual, magnified/diminished image. Image location can be at infinity too.

48. First draw a ray AA' until it intersects with the principal optical axis and find the centre of the lens C. Since, the virtual image is magnified, the lens is convex.

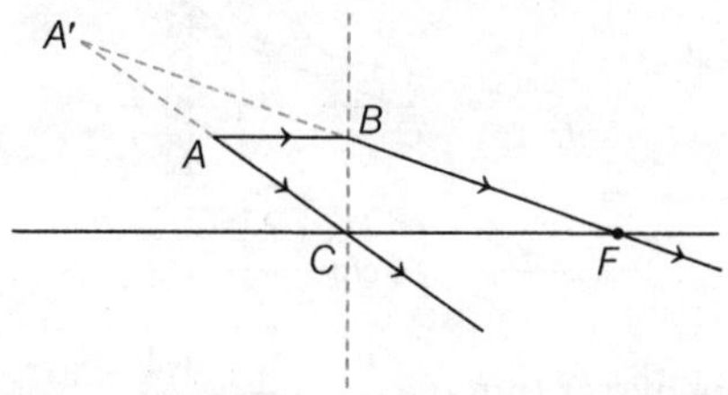

Draw a ray AB parallel to the principal optical axis. It is refracted by the lens so that it passes through its focus and its continuation passes through the virtual image. The ray $A'B$ intersects the principal optical axis at point F, the focus of the lens.

49. The paths of the rays are shown in figure. Since, the virtual image is diminished, the lens is concave.

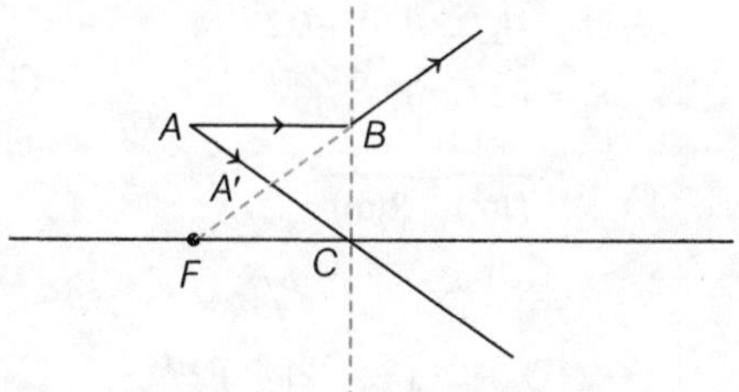

50. $\mu = \dfrac{\sin i}{\sin r}$

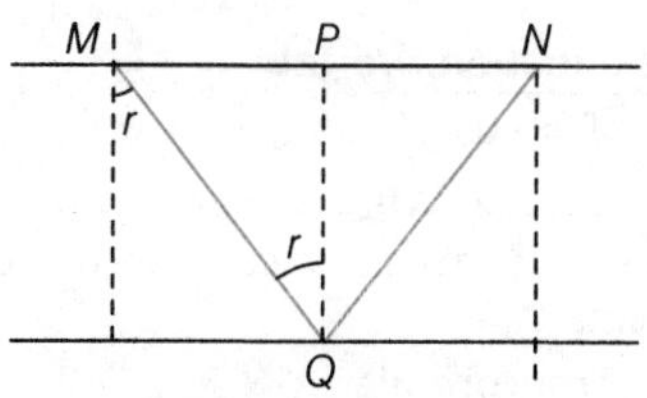

$$1.8 = \frac{\sin 60°}{\sin r}$$

Solving, we get $r = 28.8°$

$$MP = PQ \tan r$$

$$\therefore \quad MN = 2(MP) = 2PQ \cdot \tan r$$
$$= 2 \times 6 \times \tan 28.8°$$
$$= 6.6 \text{ cm}$$

$$\mu = \frac{\sin 45°}{\sin r} = \frac{4}{3}$$

51. Dispersion power,

$$\omega = \frac{\mu_v - \mu_r}{\mu_y - 1}$$

52. For plane surface, $h_{app} = \mu h = \frac{3}{2} \times 10 = 15 \text{ cm}$

This first image is at a distance, $(15 + 3)$ cm from the plane mirror. So, mirror will make its second image at a distance 18 cm below the mirror or 21 cm below the plane surface.

Now further applying,

$$d_{app} = \frac{d}{\mu} = \frac{21}{1.5} = 14 \text{ cm}$$

below the plane surface or 11 cm behind the mirror.

53. Object is placed at distance $2f$ from the lens. Hence, image is also formed at distance $2f$ on other side. For mirror,

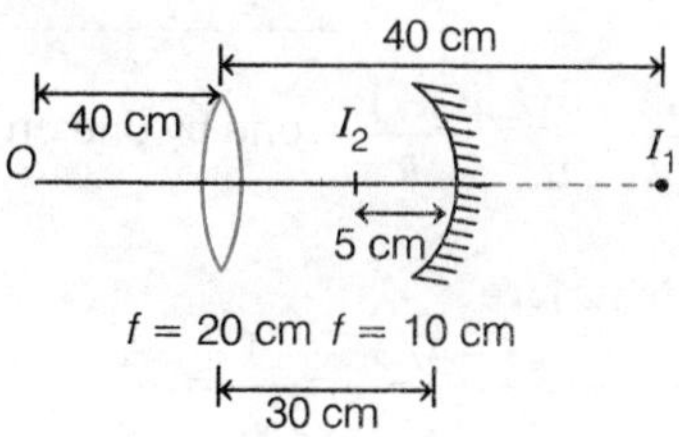

$$\frac{1}{v} + \frac{1}{+10} = \frac{1}{-10}$$

$$\therefore \quad v = -5 \text{ cm}$$

Ray diagram is as shown below.

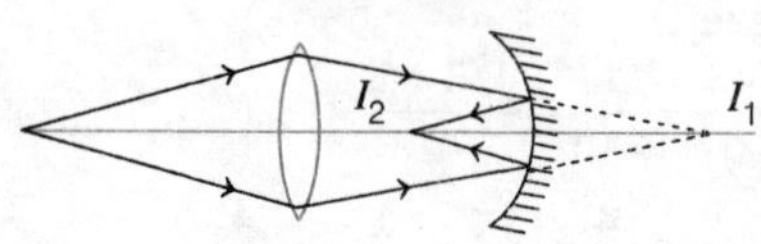

54. For second lens,

$$\frac{1}{v} - \frac{1}{-5} = \frac{1}{-20}$$

$$\Rightarrow \quad v = -4 \text{ cm}$$

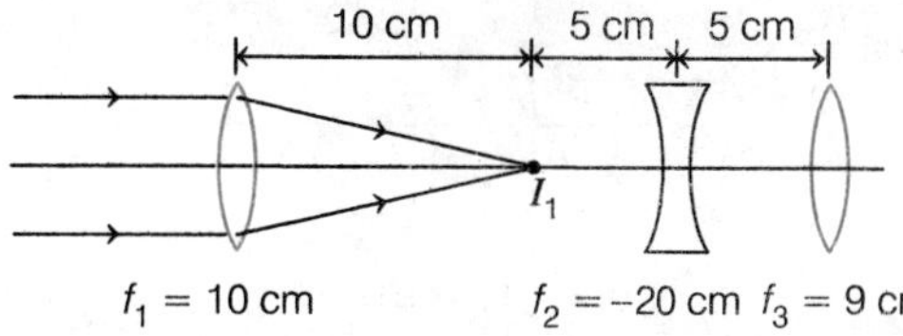

For third lens,

$$\frac{1}{v} - \frac{1}{-(4+9)} = \frac{1}{+9}$$

$$\therefore \quad v = \infty$$

55. See the result of example-1 of module-7.

$$R = \frac{h}{\sqrt{\mu^2 - 1}}$$

$$h = R\sqrt{\mu^2 - 1}$$
$$= (1 \text{ cm})\sqrt{(5/3)^2 - 1}$$
$$= \frac{4}{3} \text{ cm}$$

56. $\sin\theta_C = \frac{1}{\mu_1} = \frac{2}{3}$

Now, $\mu_1 \sin i_1 = \mu_2 \sin i_2$

or $\mu_1 \sin\theta_C = \mu_2 \sin\theta$

$\therefore \left(\frac{3}{2}\right)\left(\frac{2}{3}\right) = \left(\frac{4}{3}\right)\sin\theta$

or $\theta = \sin^{-1}\left(\frac{3}{4}\right)$

57.

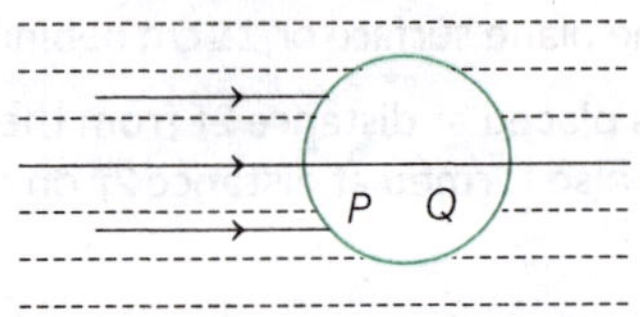

Applying $\frac{\mu_2}{v} - \frac{\mu_1}{u} = \frac{\mu_2 - \mu_1}{R}$, one by one on two spherical surfaces.

First on left surface

$$\frac{1}{v_1} - \frac{4/3}{\infty} = \frac{1 - 4/3}{+2} \Rightarrow \frac{1}{v_1} = -\frac{1}{6}$$

$\Rightarrow \quad v_1 = -6 \text{ mm}$

i.e. first image will be formed at 6 mm towards left of P.

Second on right surface

Now, distance of first image I_1 from Q will be 10 mm (towards left).

$$\frac{4/3}{v_2} - \frac{1}{-10} = \frac{4/3 - 1}{-2}$$

$$\Rightarrow \quad \frac{4}{3v_2} = -\frac{1}{6} - \frac{1}{10} = -\frac{4}{15}$$

$\Rightarrow \quad v_2 = -5 \text{mm}$

(b) The ray diagram is shown in figure.

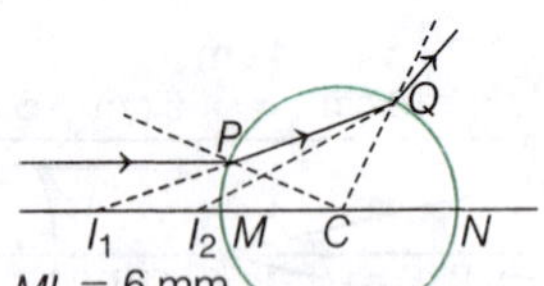

$MI_1 = 6$ mm
$NI_2 = 5$ mm

58. (a) $\frac{1}{f} = (\mu - 1)\left(\frac{1}{R_1} - \frac{1}{R_2}\right)$

$\because$ Radium (R_1) for convex face and radius (R_2) for plane face

$$= (1.5 - 1)\left(\frac{1}{12} - \frac{1}{\infty}\right) = \frac{1}{24}$$

$\therefore \quad f = +24$ cm

(b) The system will behave like a mirror of power given by

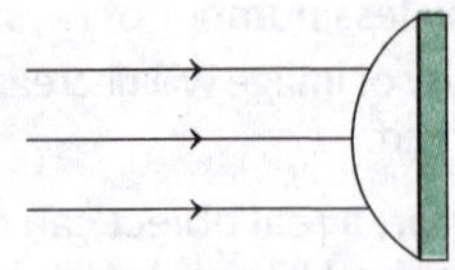

$$P = 2P_L + P_M$$

$$\therefore \quad -\frac{1}{f(\text{m})} = 2\left(\frac{1}{0.24}\right) + 0$$

$\therefore \quad f = -0.12 \text{ m} = -12$ cm

Hence, the system will behave like a concave mirror of focal length 12 cm. Therefore, parallel rays will converge at a distance of 12 cm (to the left) of the system.

(c)

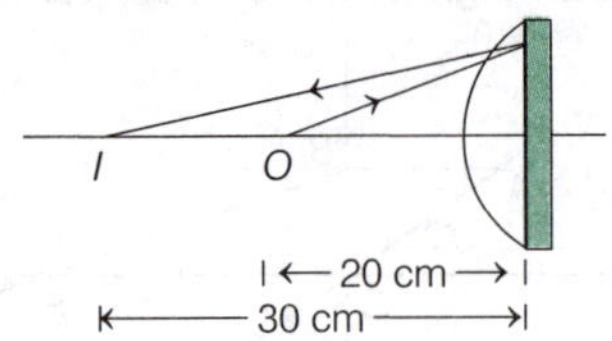

(d) Using mirror formula $\frac{1}{v} + \frac{1}{-20} = \frac{-1}{12}$

Solving, we get $v = -30$ cm.

Therefore the image will be formed at a distance of 30 cm to the left of system.

59. The given system behaves like a mirror of power given by $P = 2P_L + P_M$

$$\Rightarrow \quad -\frac{1}{f} = 2\left(\frac{1}{0.2}\right) + \left(\frac{-2}{-0.22}\right)$$

As $\quad P_L = 1/f(\text{m})$

and $\quad P_M = \frac{-1}{f(\text{m})} = \frac{-2}{R(\text{m})}$

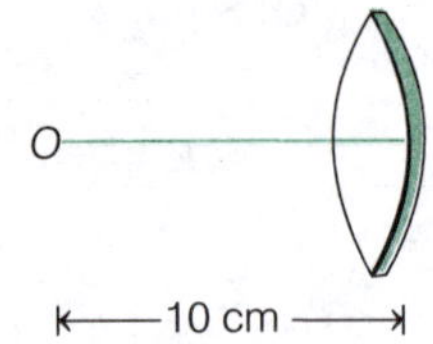

Solving this equation, we get

$$f = -0.052 \text{ m}$$
$$= -5.2 \text{ cm}$$

i.e. the system behaves as a concave mirror of focal length 5.2 cm.

Using the mirror formula

$$\frac{1}{v} + \frac{1}{u} = \frac{1}{f}, \text{ we have}$$

$$\frac{1}{v} - \frac{1}{10} = -\frac{1}{5.2}$$

$\Rightarrow \quad v = -10.8$ cm

i.e. real image will be formed at a distance of 10.8 cm.

60. Given $i_1 = 60°, A = 30°, \delta = 30°$

From the relation

$$\delta = (i_1 + i_2) - A$$

we have, $i_2 = 0°$

i.e. the ray is perpendicular to the face from which it emerges.

Further, $i_2 = 0°$

$\therefore \quad r_2 = 0°$

$$r_1 + r_2 = A \Rightarrow r_1 = A = 30°$$

$$\mu = \frac{\sin i_1}{\sin r_1} = \frac{\sin 60°}{\sin 30°} = \sqrt{3}$$

61.

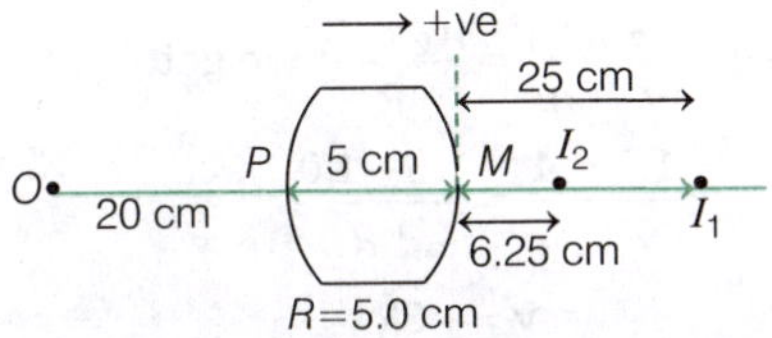

Applying $\frac{\mu_2}{v} - \frac{\mu_1}{u} = \frac{\mu_2 - \mu_1}{R}$ two times,

$$\frac{1.5}{v_1} - \frac{1.0}{-20} = \frac{1.5 - 1.0}{+5.0}$$

$\Rightarrow \quad v_1 = PI_1 = +30$ cm

Further,

$$\frac{1.0}{v_2} - \frac{1.5}{+25} = \frac{1.0 - 1.5}{-5.0}$$

$\Rightarrow \quad v_2 = MI_2 = 6.25$ cm

62. (a) It is based on the principle of displacement method of finding focal length of a convex lens. Focal length is given by,

$$f = \frac{d^2 - x^2}{4d} = \frac{(90)^2 - (30)^2}{4 \times 90} = 20 \text{ cm}$$

$\therefore \quad f = 20$ cm

(b) In displacement method, we know that object length,

$$O = \sqrt{I_1 I_2}$$

Let $I_2 = 4I_1$

Then $O = 2I_1$

or $\quad \frac{I_1}{O} = |m_1| = 2 = \left|\frac{v_1}{u_1}\right|$

or $\quad |v_1| = 2|u_1|$

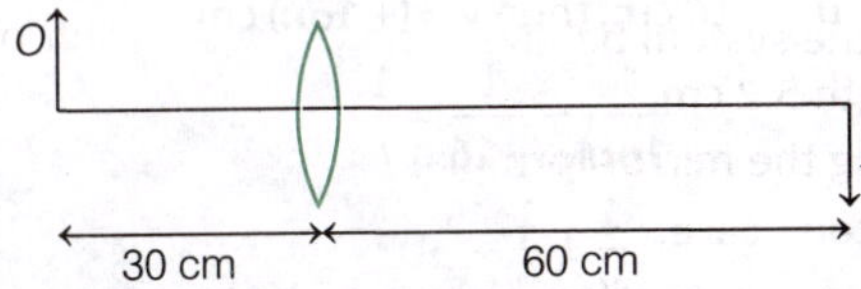

Applying lens formula, $\frac{1}{v} - \frac{1}{u} = \frac{1}{f}$, we have

$$\frac{1}{f} = \frac{1}{60} + \frac{1}{30}$$

or $\quad f = 20$ cm

63.

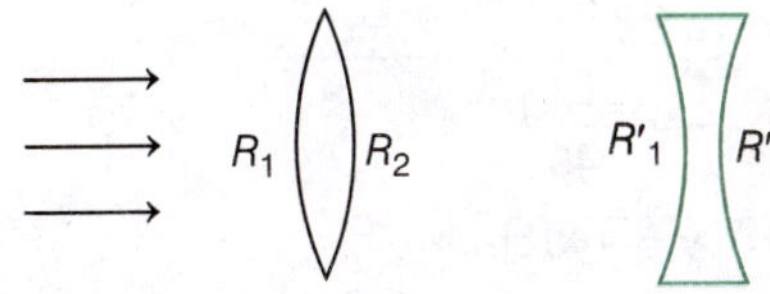

$$\frac{1}{F} = \frac{1}{f_1} + \frac{1}{f_2}$$

$$= \left(\frac{\mu_1}{\mu_w} - 1\right)\left(\frac{1}{R_1} - \frac{1}{R_2}\right) + \left(\frac{\mu_2}{\mu_w} - 1\right)\left(\frac{1}{R_1'} - \frac{1}{R_2'}\right)$$

$$= \left(\frac{1.7}{4/3} - 1\right)\left[\frac{1}{10} - \frac{1}{(-10)}\right] + \left(\frac{1.51}{4/3} - 1\right)\left(\frac{1}{-10} - \frac{1}{10}\right)$$

Solving this equation, we get

$$F = 35 \text{ cm}$$

64. Using mirror formula twice,

$$\frac{1}{+25/3} + \frac{1}{-u_1} = \frac{1}{+10}$$

or $\quad \frac{1}{u_1} = \frac{3}{25} - \frac{1}{10}$

or $\quad u_1 = 50$ m

and $\quad \frac{1}{(+50/7)} + \frac{1}{-u_2} = \frac{1}{+10}$

$\therefore \quad \frac{1}{u_2} = \frac{7}{50} - \frac{1}{10}$

or $\quad u_2 = 25$ m

Speed of object $= \frac{u_1 - u_2}{\text{time}} = \frac{25}{30}$ ms^{-1}

$= 3$ kmh^{-1}

65. Using lens maker's formula,

$$\frac{1}{f} = (\mu - 1)\left(\frac{1}{R_1} - \frac{1}{R_2}\right)$$

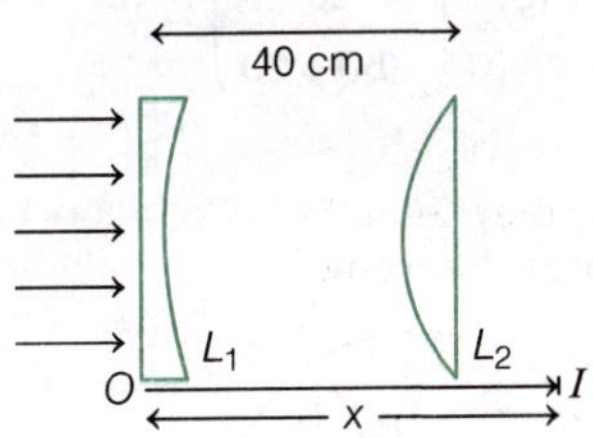

For lens, $L_1 \Rightarrow R_1 = \infty, R_2 = 30$ cm

$$\mu = 1.75$$

So, $\quad \frac{1}{f_1} = 0.75\left(-\frac{1}{30}\right) = -\frac{1}{40}$

or $\quad f_1 = -40$ cm

For lens L_2, $R_1 = +30$ cm, $R_2 = \infty$ and $\mu = 1.75$

So, $\quad \frac{1}{f_2} = 0.75\left(\frac{1}{30}\right) = 40$ cm

Now, in given situation, for lens L_1,

$$u = \infty, f_1 = -40 \text{ cm}, v = ?$$

Using, $\frac{1}{v}-\frac{1}{u}=\frac{1}{f}$,

we have $\frac{1}{v}=\frac{1}{-40}$

$\Rightarrow \quad v=-40$ cm.

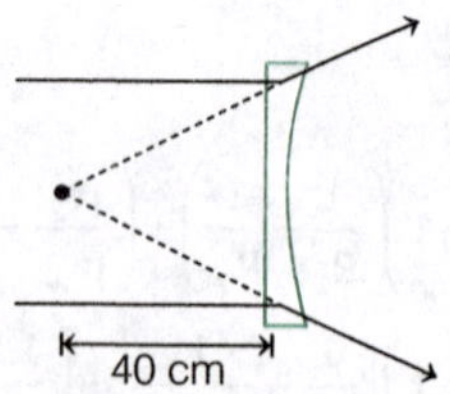

Now for lens L_2,

$u=-80$ cm, $v=?$, $f=40$ cm

So, $\frac{1}{v}-\frac{1}{-80}=\frac{1}{40}$

or $\quad \frac{1}{v}=\frac{1}{40}-\frac{1}{80}=\frac{1}{80}$

or $\quad v=80$ cm

So, distance of image from plano concave (L_1) lens is $80+40=120$ cm.

66. $\frac{1}{v}-\frac{1}{u}=\frac{1}{f}$

or $\quad \frac{u}{v}-1=\frac{u}{f}$

or $\quad \frac{u}{v}=\left(\frac{u+f}{f}\right)$

$\Rightarrow \quad m=\frac{v}{u}=\left(\frac{f}{u+f}\right)$

$$\Rightarrow \quad \frac{m_{25}}{m_{50}}=\frac{\left(\frac{20}{-25+20}\right)}{\left(\frac{20}{-50+20}\right)}=6$$

Level 2

67. By Pythagoras theorem

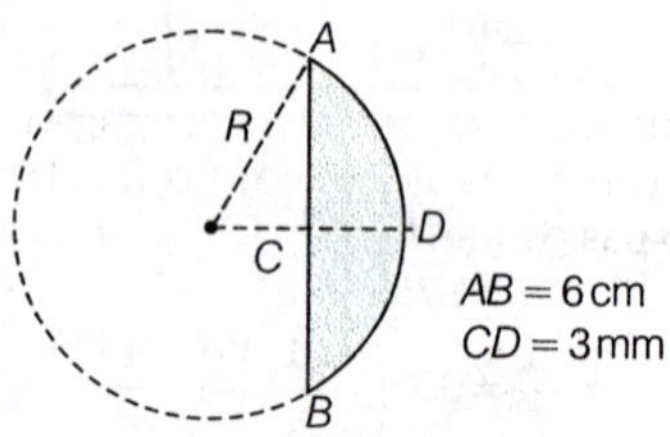

$R^2=(3)^2+(R-0.3)^2$

$\Rightarrow \quad R \approx 15$ cm

Refractive index of material of lens

$\mu=c/v$

Here $c=$ speed of light in vacuum

$=3\times 10^8$ m/s

$v=$ speed of light in material of lens

$=2\times 10^8 \text{ m/s}=\frac{3\times 10^8}{2\times 10^8}=\frac{3}{2}$

From lens maker's formula

$\frac{1}{f}=(\mu-1)\left(\frac{1}{R_1}-\frac{1}{R_2}\right)$

Here, $R_1=R$ and $R_2=\infty$ (For plane surface)

$\frac{1}{f}=\left(\frac{3}{2}-1\right)\left(\frac{1}{15}\right)$

$\Rightarrow \quad f=30$ cm

68. Applying, $\frac{\mu_2}{v}-\frac{\mu_1}{u}=\frac{\mu_2-\mu_1}{R}$ we get,

$\frac{1.5}{v}-\frac{1}{\infty}=\frac{1.5-1.0}{+R}$

$\therefore \quad v=+3R$

69.

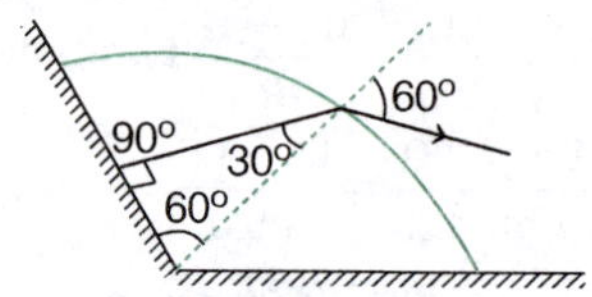

$\mu=\frac{\sin 60°}{\sin 30°}=\sqrt{3}$

70. Refraction from first surface,

$\frac{\mu_2}{v_1}-\frac{\mu_1}{\infty}=\frac{\mu_2-\mu_2}{+R}$

Refraction from second surface,

$\frac{\mu_3}{f}-\frac{\mu_2}{v_1}=\frac{\mu_3-\mu_2}{-R}$ (as $v_2=f$)

Adding these two equations, we get

$\frac{\mu_3}{f}=\frac{\mu_2-\mu_1}{R}-\frac{\mu_3-\mu_2}{R}$

Lens becomes diverging if f is negative or

$\mu_3-\mu_2>\mu_2-\mu_1$

or $\quad \mu_3+\mu_1>2\mu_2$

Same result is obtained if parallel beam of light is incident from RHS.

71. In first case,

$u=-16$ cm, then $v=(+16n)$ cm

$\therefore \quad \frac{1}{16n}-\frac{1}{-16}=\frac{1}{f}$ ...(i)

In second case,

$u=-6$ cm, then $v=-(6n)$ cm

$\therefore \quad \frac{1}{-6n}-\frac{1}{-6}=\frac{1}{f}$ ...(ii)

Solving these two equations, we get

$f=11$ cm

72. From geometry we can find that

$$r_2 = 53°$$

$$\theta_C = \sin^{-1}\left(\frac{1}{\mu}\right) = 37°$$

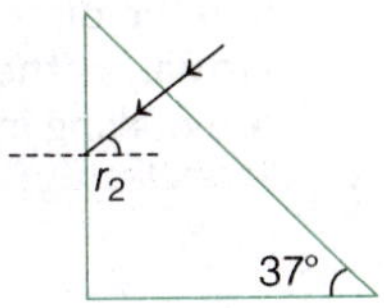

Since, $r_2 > \theta_C$, TIR will take place on the face AB

$$\delta = \delta_{AC} + \delta_{AB} = 0 + 180° - 2r_2$$

$$= 180° - 2 \times 53° = 74°$$

73. $\theta_C = \sin^{-1}\left(\frac{1}{\mu}\right)$

$$= \sin^{-1}\left(\sqrt{\frac{3}{7}}\right) = 40.9°$$

$$r_2 = \theta_C = 40.9°$$

$$r_1 = A - r_2 = 19.1°$$

$$\mu = \frac{\sin i_1}{\sin r_1}$$

$$\sqrt{\frac{7}{3}} = \frac{\sin i_1}{\sin r_1}$$

Solving this equation, we get $i_1 = 30°$

74. $\sin \theta_C = \frac{\mu_R}{\mu_D} = \frac{6/5}{3/2} = \frac{4}{5}$

$$r_1 = 0°$$

$\Rightarrow$ $r_2 = \angle B = 90° - \theta$

Now, $r_2 > \theta_c$

or $\sin r_2 > \sin \theta_C$

$\therefore$ $\sin(90° - \theta) > \frac{4}{5}$

or $\cos\theta > \frac{4}{5}$ ...(i)

$$\cos 37° = \frac{4}{5}$$

From Eq. (i), we see that

$$\theta < 37°$$

75. From the first refraction, rays should become parallel. Or, image should formed at infinity.

Applying,

$$\frac{\mu_2}{u} - \frac{\mu_1}{u} = \frac{\mu_2 - \mu_1}{R}$$

$$\frac{3/2}{\infty} - \frac{1.0}{-x} = \frac{3/2 - 1.0}{+10}$$

Solving, we get

$$x = 20 \text{ cm}$$

76. (a) Two images are formed in case (i).

(b) One image is formed in case (ii).

(c) $\frac{1}{f_2} = (\mu - 1)\left(\frac{1}{-R} - \frac{1}{R}\right) = -\frac{2}{R}(\mu - 1)$ ...(i)

$$\frac{1}{f_3} = \frac{1}{F_1} + \frac{1}{F_2}$$

$$= (\mu - 1)\left(\frac{1}{\infty} - \frac{1}{R}\right) + (\mu - 1)\left(\frac{1}{-R} - \frac{1}{\infty}\right) \quad \text{...(ii)}$$

From Eqs. (i) and (ii), we can see that $f_2 = f_3$.

77. $\frac{1}{f} = \frac{1}{OB} - \frac{1}{-OA} = \frac{1}{OB} + \frac{1}{OA}$

$$f = \frac{(OA)(OB)}{AB + OB}$$

$\therefore$ $f = \frac{(OA)(OB)}{AB}$ ...(i)

Now, $AB^2 = AC^2 + BC^2$

or $(OA + OB)^2 = AC^2 + BC^2$

or $OA^2 + OB^2 + 2(OA)(OB) = AC^2 + BC^2$

$\therefore$ $(AC^2 - OC^2) + (BC^2 - OC^2) + 2(OA)(OB) = AC^2 + BC^2$

Solving, we get

$$(OA)(OB) = OC^2$$

Substituting in Eq. (i), we get

$$f = \frac{OC^2}{AB}$$

78. For concave lens,

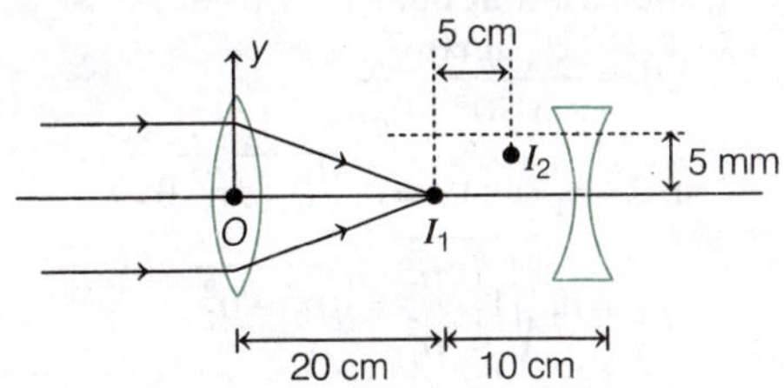

$$\frac{1}{v} = \frac{1}{-10} = -\frac{1}{10}$$

$\Rightarrow$ $v = -5$ cm

$$m = \frac{v}{u} = \frac{(-5\text{ cm})}{(-10\text{ cm})} = \frac{1}{2}$$

$$X_{I_2} = 20 + 5 = 25 \text{ cm}$$

$$Y_{I_2} = (5\text{ mm})\left(\frac{1}{2}\right) = 2.5 \text{ mm}$$

$$= 0.25 \text{ cm}$$

79. Cavity of placed at centre. Hence, image of cavity is also formed at centre, as all rays fall normal to surface at all points. (so pass undeviated).

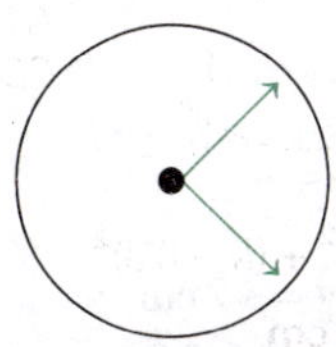

Now, $m = \left(\frac{\mu_1}{\mu_2}\right)\left(\frac{v}{u}\right)$

$$= \frac{(4/3)}{1}\left(\frac{1\text{ m}}{1\text{ m}}\right) = \frac{4}{3}$$

80. $\frac{1}{f} = (1.5 - 1)\left(\frac{1}{20} - \frac{1}{-20}\right)$

$\Rightarrow \quad f = +20$ cm

$$\frac{1}{v_1} - \frac{1}{-30} = \frac{1}{+20}$$

$\therefore \quad v_1 = +60$ cm

$$m_1 = \frac{v_1}{u_1} = \frac{+60}{-30} = -2$$

For second lens,

$$\frac{1}{v_2} - \frac{1}{-60} = \frac{1}{+20}$$

$$v_2 = +30 \text{ cm}$$

$$m_2 = \frac{v_2}{u_2} = \frac{(+30)}{(-60)} = -\frac{1}{2}$$

$$m = m_1 m_2 = 1$$

Final image is 30 cm to the right of second lens or 150 cm to the right of first lens.

$$m = 1$$

Hence, image height = object height

$= 3$ mm

81. Applying Snell's law at point M, we get

$$n_1 = \frac{\sin\theta}{\sin(90° - \theta_C)}$$

or $\quad \sin\theta = n_1 \cos\theta_C = n_1\sqrt{1 - \sin^2\theta_C}$

$$= n_1\sqrt{1 - \frac{n_2^2}{n_1^2}} = \sqrt{n_1^2 - n_2^2}$$

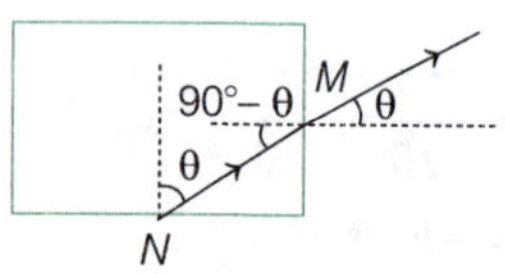

If angle of θ is less than this value, then angle of incidence at N will be greater than θ_C. Hence, TIR will take place at N.

82. Reflection from the concave mirror, I_1

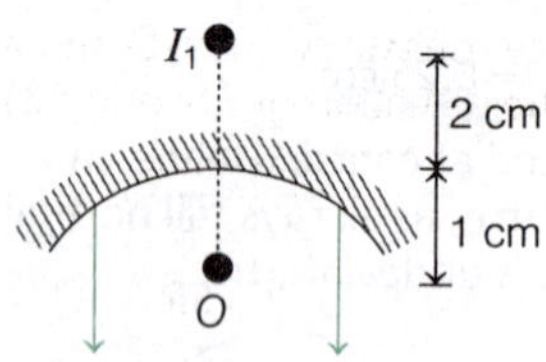

$$\frac{1}{v} + \frac{1}{-1} = \frac{1}{-2}$$

$\Rightarrow \quad v = +2$ cm

Shift due to slab $= \left(1 - \frac{1}{n}\right)t$

$= (1 - 2/3)(9 \text{ cm})$

$= 3$ cm

Now, slab will make next image at a distance 3 cm from I_1 in the direction of ray of light, i.e. at O itself but it is virtual, as the ray of light has crossed the slab and we are making image behind the slab.

83.

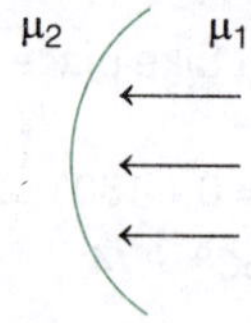

$$\frac{\mu_2}{v} - \frac{\mu_1}{u} = \frac{\mu_2 - \mu_1}{-R}$$

$$\therefore \quad \frac{\mu_2}{v} = \frac{\mu_1 - \mu_2}{R} + \frac{\mu_1}{u}$$

If $\mu_1 > \mu_2$ and u is positive (i.e. virtual object), then v is always positive or image is always real.

84. $AB = \frac{d}{\cos i} = \frac{d'}{\cos r}$

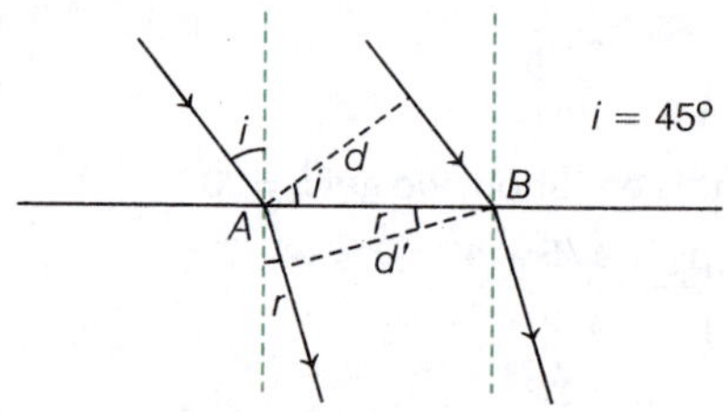

$$\therefore \quad d' = \frac{\cos r}{\cos i} d \qquad \text{...(i)}$$

Further, $\quad \sin r = \frac{\sin i}{\mu} = \frac{1}{\sqrt{2}\mu}$

Hence, $\quad \cos r = \sqrt{1 - \frac{1}{2\mu^2}} = \frac{\sqrt{2\mu^2 - 1}}{\sqrt{2}\mu}$

Substituting in Eq. (i), we have

$$d' = \frac{\sqrt{2\mu^2 - 1}}{\mu} \cdot d$$

85. $\frac{1}{3x} - \frac{1}{-x} = \frac{1}{+30}$

$\therefore \quad x = 40$ cm and $3x = 120$ cm

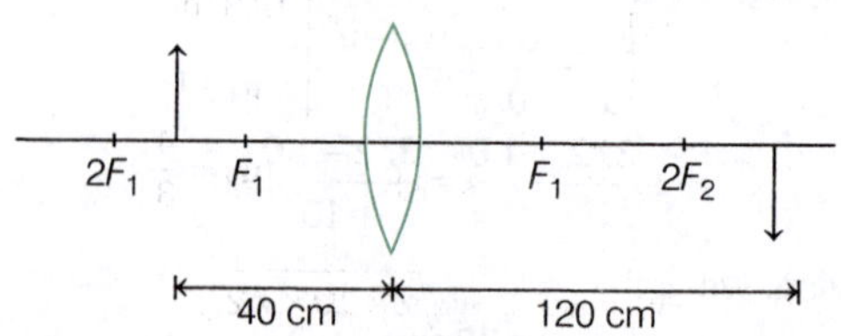

To decrease the magnification object should be moved towards $2F_1$.

Hence, image will move towards $2F_2$. Let displacement is y. Then,

$$2(40 + 5) = (120 - y)$$

$\therefore \quad y = 30$ cm

86. In first case when sun is at infinity, i.e.

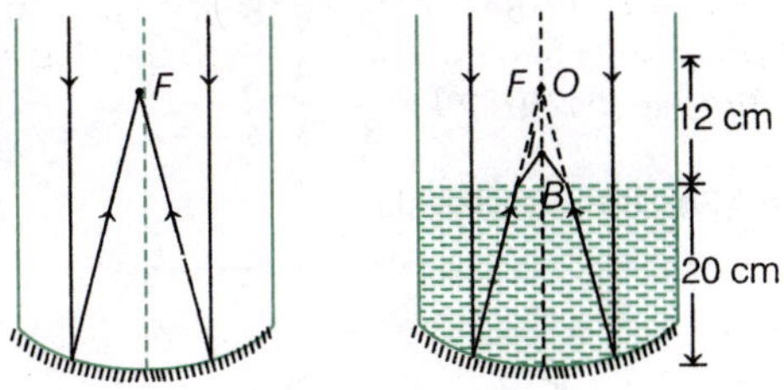

$$u = \infty$$

$$\frac{1}{f} = \frac{1}{-32} + \frac{1}{(-\infty)}$$

$\therefore$ $$f = -32 \text{ cm}$$

When water is filled in that tank upto a height of 20 cm, the image formed by the mirror will act as virtual object O for water surface.

$\therefore$ $$BI = BO \times \frac{3}{4}$$

$$= 12 \times \frac{3}{4} = 9 \text{ cm}$$

87. $\frac{1}{v} - \frac{1}{-u} = \frac{1}{+f}$

$\therefore$ $$v = \frac{uf}{u - f}$$

or $$\frac{v}{u} = m = \frac{f}{u - f}$$

$\therefore$ $$\frac{1}{m} = \left(\frac{1}{f}\right)u - 1$$

Comparing this with equation of straight line, $\frac{1}{f}$ is the slope of line, which is $\frac{b}{c}$.

$\therefore$ $$f = \frac{c}{b}$$

88.

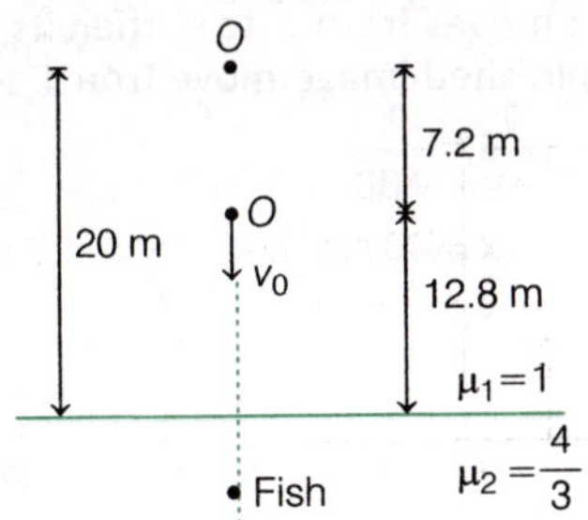

$$v_0 = \sqrt{2as} = \sqrt{2 \times 10 \times 7.2}$$

$$= 12 \text{ m/s} = \text{Object speed}$$

Image distance,

$$v = \frac{\mu_2}{\mu_1} u = \frac{4/3}{1} u$$

$\Rightarrow$ $$\frac{dv}{dt} = \frac{4}{3} \frac{du}{dt}$$

or $$v_I = \frac{4}{3} v_0 = \frac{4}{3} \times 12$$

$$= 16 \text{ m/s} = \text{Image speed.}$$

89. $\mu = \frac{\sin \theta_1}{\sin \theta_3}$

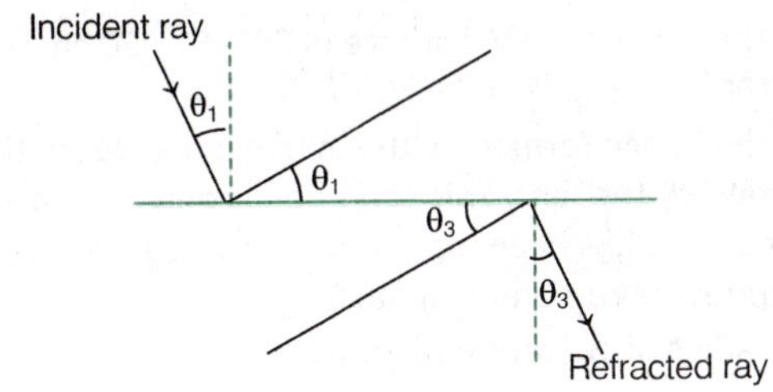

90. When the ray passes into the rarer medium, the deviation is $\delta = \phi - \theta$. This can have a maximum value of $\left(\frac{\pi}{2}\right) - C$

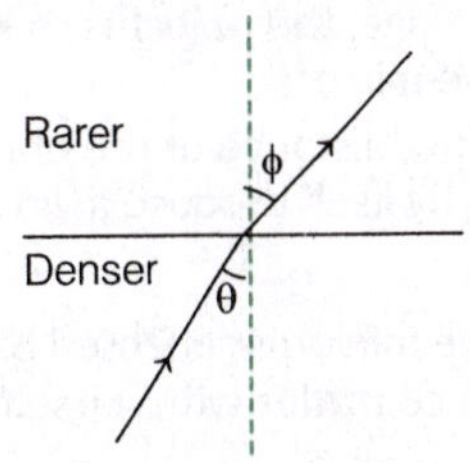

For $\theta = C$ and $\phi = \frac{\pi}{2}$

91. Let us say $PO = OQ = X$

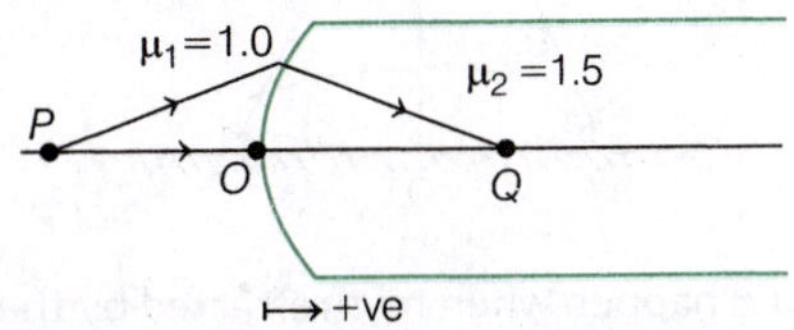

Applying $\frac{\mu_2}{v} - \frac{\mu_1}{u} = \frac{\mu_2 - \mu_1}{R}$

Substituting the values with sign

$$\frac{1.5}{+X} - \frac{1.0}{-X} = \frac{1.5 - 1.0}{+R}$$

(Distances are measured from O and are taken as positive in the direction of ray of light)

$\therefore$ $$\frac{2.5}{X} = \frac{0.5}{R}$$

$\therefore$ $$X = 5R$$

92. The given situation can be drawn as shown below

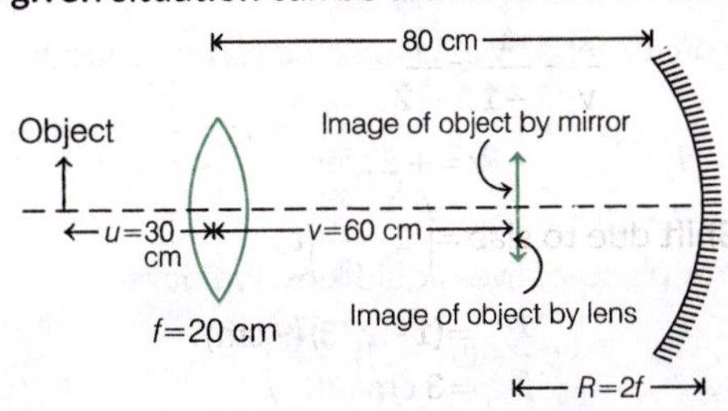

For lens formula, $\frac{1}{v}-\frac{1}{u}=\frac{1}{f}$

Substituting given values, we get

$$\frac{1}{v}-\frac{1}{-30}=\frac{1}{20}$$

$\Rightarrow$ $$v=60 \text{ cm}$$

So, this image is at a distance of $80-60=20$ cm from the mirror.

As, the image formed by the mirror coincides with image formed by the lens. This condition is only possible, if any object that has been placed in front of concave mirror is at centre of curvature, i.e. at $2f$.

So, radius of curvature of mirror is

$$R=20 \text{ cm}$$

$\therefore$ Focal length of mirror,

$$f=\frac{R}{2}=10 \text{ cm}$$

As, for virtual image, the object is to kept between pole and focus of the mirror.

$\therefore$ The maximum distance of the object for which this concave mirror by itself produce a virtual image would be 10 cm.

93. Light from plane mirror is reflected back on it's path, so that image of A coincides with A itself.

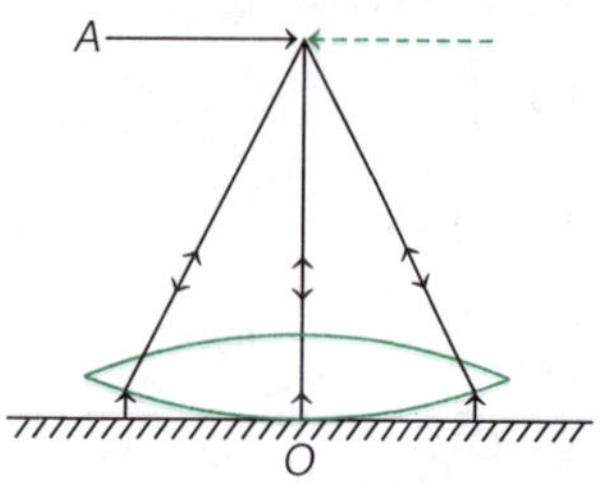

This would happen when rays refracted by the convex lens falls normally on the plane mirror, i.e. the refracted rays form a beam parallel to principal axis of the lens. Hence, the object would then be considered at the focus of convex lens.

$\therefore$ Focal length of curvature of convex lens is, $f_1=18$ cm

With liquid between lens and mirror, image is again coincides with object, so the second measurement is focal length of combination of liquid lens and convex lens.

$\therefore$ $$\frac{1}{f_1}+\frac{1}{f_2}=\frac{1}{f_{eq}} \Rightarrow \frac{1}{18}+\frac{1}{f_2}=\frac{1}{27}$$

$\Rightarrow$ $$f_2=-54 \text{ cm}$$

For convex lens by lens maker's formula, we have

$$\frac{1}{f}=(\mu-1)\left(\frac{2}{R}\right) \Rightarrow \frac{1}{18}=0.5\times\frac{2}{R}$$

$\Rightarrow$ $R=18$ cm

and for plano-convex liquid lens, we have

$$\frac{1}{f}=(\mu_l-1)\left(\frac{-1}{R}\right)$$

$\Rightarrow$ $$-\frac{1}{54}=(\mu_l-1)\left(\frac{-1}{18}\right)$$

$\Rightarrow$ $$\mu_l=1+\frac{1}{3}=\frac{4}{3}$$

94. For $n=2m$, it is just like slab.

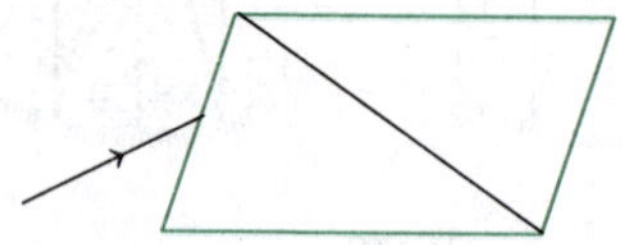

$\therefore$ Deviation $=0$

For $n=2m+1$, it is just like an identical prism of larger size.

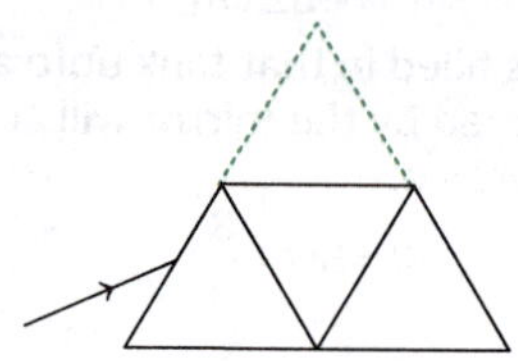

95. $\frac{\sin i_1}{\sin i_2}=\frac{v_1}{v_2}$

$\therefore$ $$\frac{\sin r}{\sin i}=\text{slope}=\frac{1}{\sqrt{3}}=\frac{v_y}{v_x}$$

$\therefore$ $$v_y=\frac{v_x}{\sqrt{3}}$$

Speed of light in medium-y is less. So, it is denser. TIR takes place when ray of travels from denser to rarer medium.

96. (a) If vacuum speed of light of all colours is same.

(b)

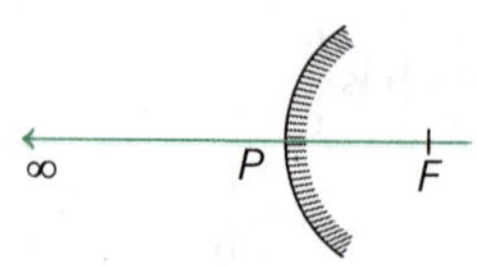

If object moves from ∞ to P, then its virtual, erect and diminished image move from F to P.

(c)

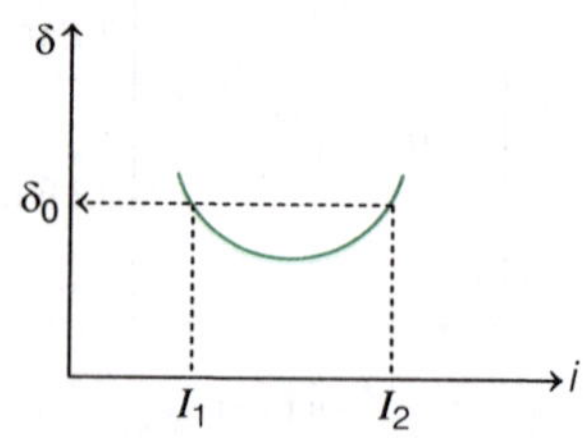

97. Displacement method of finding focal length of convex lens.

98. With increase in wavelength, refractive index gets decreased.

99. Combination is acted as mirror of local length f and object is kept at its centre $\Rightarrow h=2|f|$

$$\frac{1}{f}=\frac{2}{f_m}-\frac{2}{f_l}$$

$$\Rightarrow \quad \frac{1}{f}=\frac{1}{\infty}-2\times\left[(1.6-1)\left(\frac{1}{9}\right)+(n-1)\left(-\frac{1}{9}\right)\right]$$

$$\frac{1}{f}=-2\left[\frac{0.6+1-n}{9}\right]$$

$$\Rightarrow \quad f=\frac{-9}{2(1.6-n)}$$

$$h=2|f| \quad \Rightarrow \quad h=\frac{9}{1.6-n}$$

(a) $n=1.42 \Rightarrow h=\frac{9}{1.6-1.42}=\frac{9}{0.18}=50$ cm

(b) $n=1.35 \Rightarrow h=36$ cm

(c) $n=1.45 \Rightarrow h=60$ cm

(d) $n=1.48 \Rightarrow h=75$ cm

$\therefore$ The correct options are (a) and (b).

100. Case 1

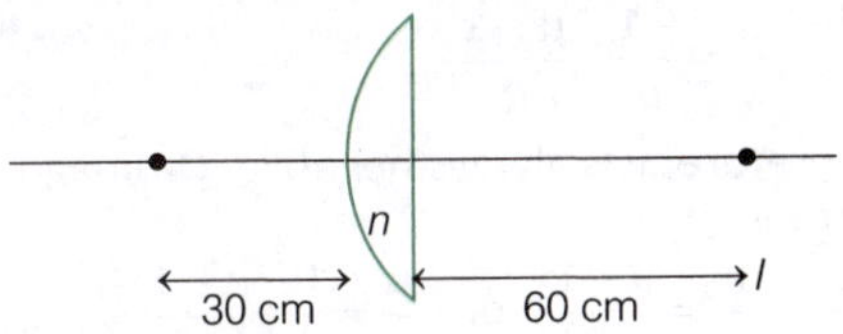

Using lens formula,

$$\frac{1}{60}+\frac{1}{30}=\frac{1}{f_1}$$

$$\Rightarrow \quad \frac{1}{f_1}=\frac{1}{60}+\frac{2}{60}$$

$$\Rightarrow \quad f_1=20 \text{ cm}$$

Further, $\frac{1}{f_1}=(n-1)\left(\frac{1}{R}-\frac{1}{\infty}\right)$

$$\Rightarrow \quad f_1=\frac{R}{n-1}=+20 \text{ cm}$$

Case 2

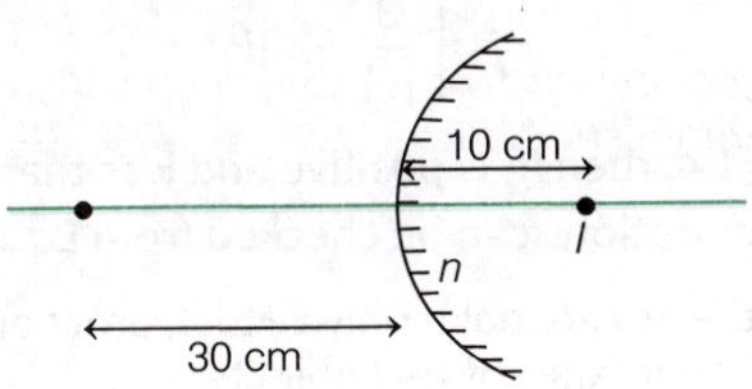

Using mirror formula

$$\frac{1}{10}-\frac{1}{30}=\frac{1}{f_2}$$

$$\Rightarrow \quad f_2=15=\frac{R}{2}$$

$$\Rightarrow \quad R=30$$

$$\therefore \quad R=30 \text{ cm}$$

$$\Rightarrow \quad \frac{R}{n-1}=20 \text{ cm}$$

Solving this equation with $R=30$ cm,

we get $n=2.5$.

101. $\sqrt{3}=\frac{\sin 60^\circ}{\sin r}$

$$\therefore \quad r=30^\circ$$

$$\theta_C=\sin^{-1}\left(\frac{1}{\sqrt{3}}\right)$$

or $$\sin\theta_C=\frac{1}{\sqrt{3}}$$

$$=0.577$$

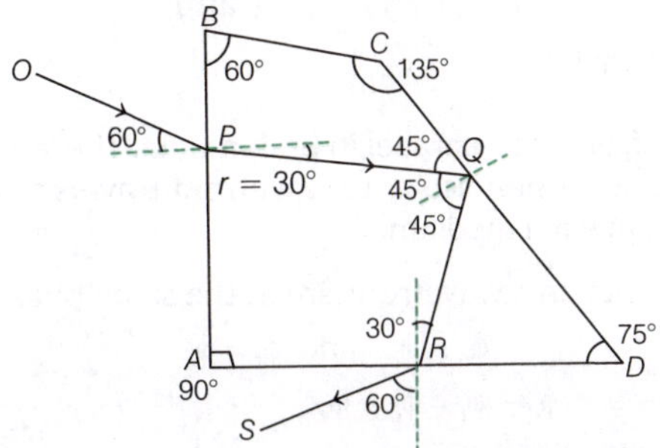

At point Q, angle of incidence inside the prism is $i=45°$.

Since $\sin i=\frac{1}{\sqrt{2}}$ is greater than $\sin\theta_C=\frac{1}{\sqrt{3}}$, ray gets totally internally reflected at face CD. Path of ray of light after point Q is shown in figure.

From the figure, we can see that angle between incident ray OP and emergent ray RS is 90°.

102. Using the mirror formula,

$$\frac{1}{f}=\frac{1}{v}+\frac{1}{u}=\frac{1}{-40}-\frac{1}{10}$$

Solving we get,

$$f=-8 \text{ cm}$$

103. Focal length of lenses is

$$\frac{1}{F}=(1.8-1)\left(\frac{1}{\infty}-\frac{1}{-2R}\right)+(1.2-1)\left(\frac{1}{-2R}-\frac{1}{-R}\right)$$

$$F=2R$$

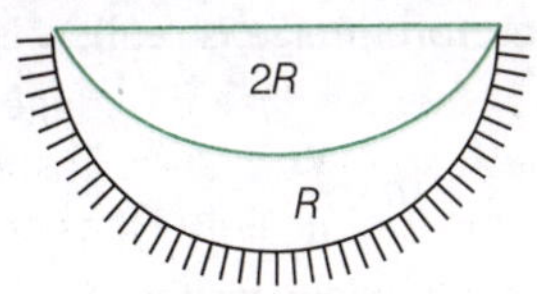

Now combined power of system,

$$P=2P_L+P_m$$

or $$-\frac{1}{f}=2P_L+P_m$$

or $$\frac{1}{8}=2\left(\frac{1}{2R}\right)+\frac{2}{R}$$

or $$R=24 \text{ cm}$$

$\therefore$ Radius of curvature of common surface

$$=2R=48 \text{ cm}$$

104. Combined focal length of lens,

$$\frac{1}{f}=(1.2-1)\left(\frac{1}{+24}-\frac{1}{+48}\right)+(1.8-1)\left(\frac{1}{+48}-\frac{1}{\infty}\right)$$

$$=\frac{1}{48}$$

Now, combined power of system

$$P=2P_L+P_M$$

$$\therefore \quad -\frac{1}{F}=2\left(\frac{1}{f}\right)+\infty=2\left(\frac{1}{48}\right)$$

$$\therefore \quad F=-24 \text{ cm}$$

105. Wavefronts are parallel in both media. Therefore, light which is perpendicular to wavefront travels as a parallel beam in each medium.

106. All points on a wavefront are at the same phase.

$$\therefore \quad \phi_d=\phi_c \text{ and } \phi_f=\phi_e$$

$$\therefore \quad \phi_d-\phi_f=\phi_c-\phi_e$$

107. Ray of light which is perpendicular to wavefront bends towards the normal in medium-2 during refraction. So, medium-2 is denser or its speed in medium-1 is more.

108. (c) and (d) $\frac{1}{v}-\frac{1}{u}=\frac{1}{f}$

$$\therefore \quad \frac{1}{v}=\frac{1}{u}+\frac{1}{f}$$

Between O and F_2 or between F_2 and $2F_2$, u is positive. So, v is also positive.

$$\therefore \quad m=\frac{u}{v} \text{ is positive}$$

Therefore, image is real (as v is positive) and erect (as m is also positive).

109. (a) $\frac{1}{v}-\frac{1}{u}=\frac{1}{-f}$

$$\therefore \quad \frac{1}{u}=\frac{1}{u}-\frac{1}{f}$$

Between O and F_1, u is positive and less than f. So, v is positive (therefore image is real).

Further from

$$m=\frac{v}{u}$$

We can see that m is allow positive. So, it is erect also.

(b) $\frac{1}{v}-\frac{1}{u}=\frac{1}{-f}$

$$\therefore \quad \frac{1}{v}=\frac{1}{u}-\frac{1}{f}$$

Between F_1 and $2F_1$, μ positive and greater than f. So, v negative (therefore image is virtual).

Further from

$$m=\frac{v}{u}$$

We can see that m is negative so, image is inverted.

110. (a) and (b)

$$v=\frac{\mu_2}{\mu_1}u$$

$$\Rightarrow \quad |v|<|u|$$

$$\text{as} \quad \mu_1>\mu_2$$

i.e v and u are of same sign.

Or they are on same side of plane surface. From plane surface, if object is real, image is virtual and *vice-versa*.

(c) and (d)

$$v=\frac{\mu_1}{\mu_2}u$$

$$\Rightarrow \quad |v|>|u|$$

Other explanations are same.

111. (a) $\frac{\mu}{v}-\frac{1}{-u}=\frac{\mu-1}{-R}$

$$\therefore \quad \frac{\mu}{v}=\frac{-1}{u}-\frac{\mu-1}{R}$$

Therefore, v is always negative. Or image is always virtual.

(b) $\frac{\mu}{v}-\frac{1}{+u}=\frac{\mu-1}{-R}$ or $\frac{\mu}{v}=\frac{1}{u}-\frac{\mu-1}{R}$

So, v may be positive or negative. Hence, image may be real or virtual.

Same logic can be applied for two options. For them R is positive. In option (c), u is negative and in option (d) u is positive.

112. $\frac{1}{f_1}$ or $P_1=(1.5-1)\left(\frac{1}{R_1}-\frac{1}{R_2}\right)$ ...(i)

$\frac{1}{f_2}$ or $P_2=\left(\frac{1.5}{\mu_e}-1\right)\left(\frac{1}{R_1}-\frac{1}{R_2}\right)$ ...(ii)

Dividing Eq. (ii) by Eq. (i), we get

$$P_2=\left(\frac{3}{\mu_e}-2\right)P_1 \quad \text{...(iii)}$$

(a) $\mu_e=1.4$, then P_2 is positive and less than P_1.

Other options can be checked from Eq. (iii).

113. Concave lens can make only virtual, erect and diminished images of real objects.

Convex lens can make real, inverted and diminished size or real inverted and magnified or virtual, erect and magnified images of real objects.

Rest type of cases are possible with virtual, objects.

114. Theory based question.

115. (I) $\frac{1}{v}-\frac{1}{u}=\frac{1}{f} \Rightarrow v=\frac{uf}{u+f}$

$$\therefore \quad v_1=\frac{(-20)(10)}{(-20)+(10)}$$

$$=+20 \text{ cm}$$

$$u_2=+15 \text{ cm}$$

$$v_2=\frac{(15)(15)}{(15)+(15)}=+7.5\text{ cm}$$

(II) $v_1=+20$ cm; $u_2=+15$ cm

$$v_2=\frac{(15)(-10)}{(15)+(-10)}=-30\text{ cm}$$

(III) $v_1=+20$ cm $\Rightarrow u_2=+15$ cm

$$v_2=\frac{(15)(-20)}{(15)+(-20)}=60\text{ cm}$$

(IV) $v_1=\frac{(-20)(-20)}{(-20)+(-20)}=-10$ cm

$$u_2=-15\text{ cm}$$

$$v_2=\frac{(-15)(10)}{(-15)+(10)}=30\text{ cm}$$

116. (A) $\frac{1}{f}=\left(\frac{3}{2}-1\right)\left(\frac{1}{r}+\frac{1}{r}\right)=\frac{1}{r}$

$\Rightarrow f=r$

$\Rightarrow \frac{1}{f_{eq}}=\frac{1}{f}+\frac{1}{f}=\frac{2}{r}$

$\Rightarrow f_{eq}=\frac{r}{2}$

$\therefore$ A $\rightarrow$ q

(B) $\frac{1}{f}=\left(\frac{3}{2}-1\right)\left(\frac{1}{r}\right)\Rightarrow f=2r$

$\Rightarrow \frac{1}{f_{eq}}=\frac{1}{2r}+\frac{1}{2r}\Rightarrow f_{eq}=r$

$\therefore$ B $\rightarrow$ s

(C) $\frac{1}{f}=\left(\frac{3}{2}-1\right)\left(-\frac{1}{r}\right)=-\frac{1}{2r}$

$\Rightarrow f=-2r$

$\Rightarrow \frac{1}{f_{eq}}=\frac{1}{f}+\frac{1}{f}=-\frac{2}{2r}$

$\Rightarrow f_{eq}=-r$

$\therefore$ C $\rightarrow$ r

(D) $\Rightarrow \frac{1}{f_{eq}}=\frac{1}{r}+\frac{1}{-2r}=\frac{1}{2r}$

$\Rightarrow f_{eq}=2r$

$\therefore$ D $\rightarrow$ p

117. Ray of light bends towards normal in travelling from rarer to denser medium.

118. Using lens formula, $\frac{1}{v}-\frac{1}{u}=\frac{1}{f}$

$$\frac{1}{v_1}-\frac{1}{-40}=\frac{1}{30}$$

$\therefore$ $v_1=120$ cm

Shift due to the slab,

$$\Delta x=\left(1-\frac{1}{\mu}\right)d=\left(1-\frac{1}{1.8}\right)9=4\text{ cm}$$

$\therefore$ $u'=-(40-\Delta x)=-36$ cm

$\therefore$ $\frac{1}{v_2}-\frac{1}{-36}=\frac{1}{30}$

$\therefore$ $v_2=180$ cm

Therefore, we will have to shift the screen a distance $x=v_2-v_1=60$ cm away from lens. **Ans.**

119. $\frac{1}{40}=(1.5-1)\left(\frac{1}{120}+\frac{1}{R_1}\right)$

Solving we get, $R_2=24$ cm

Applying lens formula, for L_2

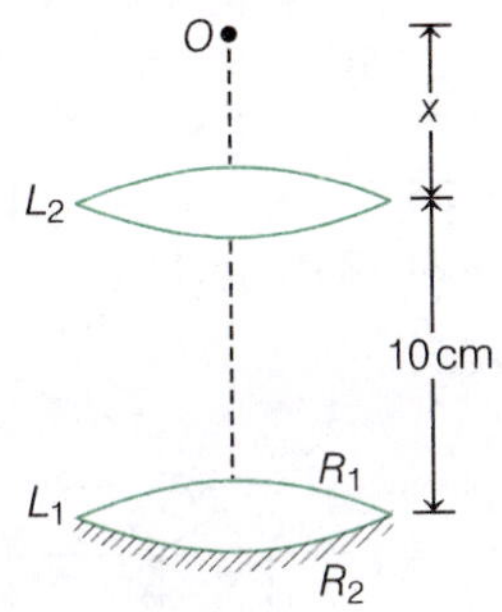

$$\frac{1}{v_1}+\frac{1}{x}=\frac{1}{20} \quad \text{...(i)}$$

Using $\frac{\mu_2}{v}-\frac{\mu_1}{u}=\frac{\mu_2-\mu_1}{R}$ for unsilvered side of L_1.

$$\frac{1.5}{-120}-\frac{1.0}{v_1-10}=\frac{1.5-1.0}{24} \quad \text{...(ii)}$$

Solving Eqs. (i) and (ii), we get $x=10$ cm **Ans.**

120. Using $\frac{\mu_2}{v}-\frac{\mu_1}{u}=\frac{\mu_2-\mu_1}{R}$, twice with $u=\infty$,

we have $\frac{1.5}{v_1}=\frac{1.5-1.4}{+20}$ ...(i)

$$\frac{1.6}{v_2}-\frac{1.5}{v_1}=\frac{1.6-1.5}{-20} \quad \text{...(ii)}$$

Solving Eqs. (i) and (ii), we get $f=v_2=\infty$, i.e. the system behaves like a glass plate.

121. First image will be formed by direct rays 1 and 2, etc.

$$PI_1=\frac{PO}{\mu}=\frac{5}{1.5}=3.33\text{ cm} \quad \textbf{Ans.}$$

Second image will be formed by reflected rays 3 and 4, etc.

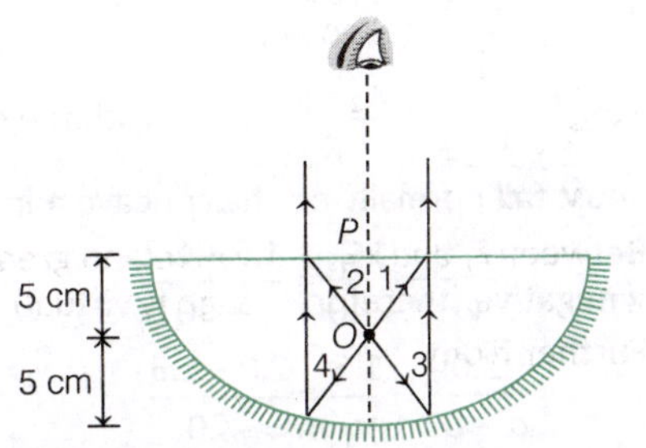

Object is placed at the focus of the mirror. Hence, I_2 is formed at infinity.

122. (a) Applying Snell's law at D,

$$\frac{4}{3}\sin i=\frac{3}{2}\sin 30°$$

$$\therefore \quad i=34.2° \qquad \textbf{Ans.}$$

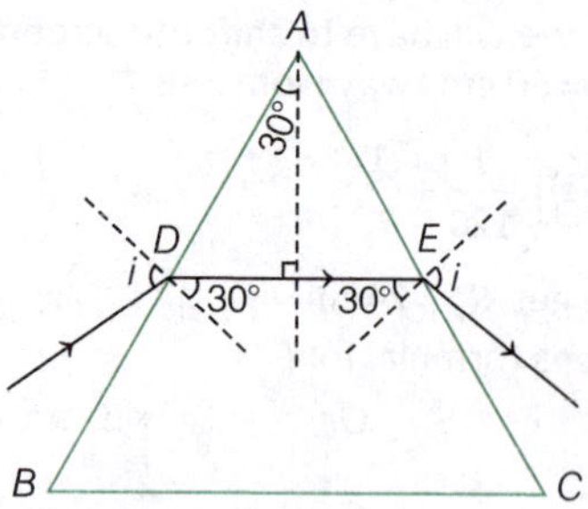

(b) $\delta=\delta_D+\delta_E=2\delta_D$

$$=2(i-30°)=8.4° \qquad \textbf{Ans.}$$

123. $\sqrt{2}=\dfrac{\sin 45°}{\sin r}$

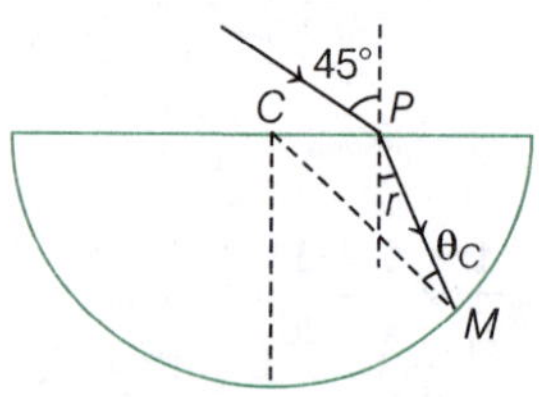

$$r=30°$$

$$\theta_C=\sin^{-1}\left(\frac{1}{\mu}\right)=45°$$

Applying sine law in ΔCPM,

$$\frac{CP}{\sin\theta_C}=\frac{CM}{\sin(90°+r)}$$

$$\therefore \quad \frac{CP}{(1/\sqrt{2})}=\frac{R}{\cos r} \qquad [R=\text{radius}]$$

$$\therefore \quad CP=\sqrt{\frac{2}{3}}R$$

As we move away from C, angle PMC will increase.

Therefore, $CP \not> \sqrt{\frac{2}{3}}R$. Same is the case on left side of C.

124. $\dfrac{1}{20}=(1.5-1)\left(\dfrac{1}{R}-\dfrac{1}{-R}\right)$

$$\therefore \quad R=20\text{ cm}$$

Applying $\dfrac{\mu_2}{v}-\dfrac{\mu_1}{u}=\dfrac{\mu_2-\mu_1}{R}$ twice with the condition that rays must fall normally on the concave mirror.

$$\frac{1.5}{v_1}-\frac{1.2}{-40}=\frac{1.5-1.2}{+20} \qquad \text{...(i)}$$

$$\frac{2.0}{d-80}-\frac{1.5}{v_1}=\frac{2.0-1.5}{-20} \qquad \text{...(ii)}$$

Solving Eqs. (i) and (ii), we get

$$d=30\text{ cm} \qquad \textbf{Ans.}$$

and $\quad v_1=-100$ cm

The ray diagram is as shown in figure.

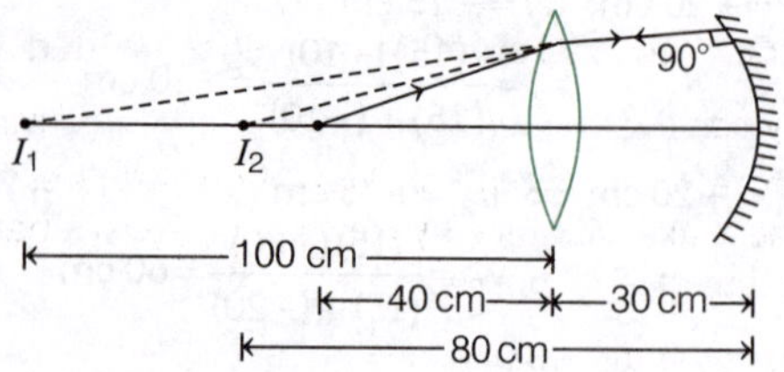

125. Using lens formula,

$$\frac{1}{36}-\frac{1}{-45}=\frac{1}{f}$$

$$\therefore \quad f=20\text{ cm}$$

In the second case, let μ be the refractive index of the liquid, then

$$\frac{1}{48}-\frac{1}{-\left(5+\dfrac{40}{\mu}\right)}=\frac{1}{20}$$

Solving this, we get

$$\mu=1.37 \qquad \textbf{Ans.}$$

126. As the angles are small we can take,

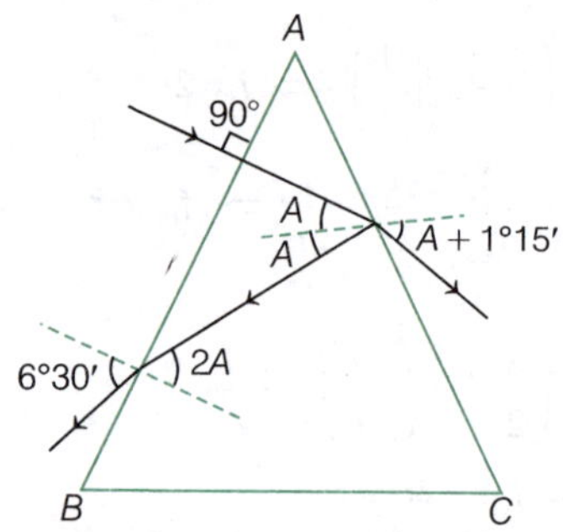

$$\sin\theta\approx\theta$$

Now, $\quad \mu=\dfrac{A+1°15'}{A}=\dfrac{6°30'}{2A}$

Solving this equation, we get

$$A=2°$$

and $\quad \mu=1.62 \qquad$ **Ans.**

127. Using lens formula for L_2,

$$\frac{1}{v}-\frac{1}{-f/2}=\frac{1}{f} \quad \text{or} \quad v=-f$$

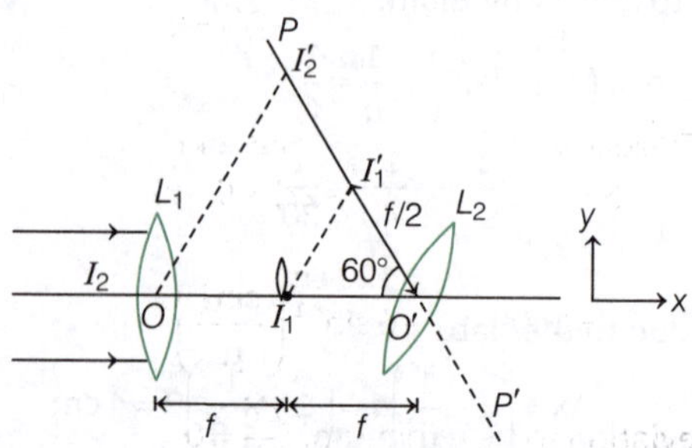

This f length will be along PP' from point O' (towards P).

$\therefore \quad O'I_2' = f$

On x-axis this distance will be $f \sec 60° = 2f$.

Since, $OO' = 2f$, therefore image will be formed at origin.

Note *A ray passing through O and then O′ goes undeviated.*

Therefore, I_1 and I_2 both should be on this line, which is also the x-axis. That's why for final image we have taken projection of $O'I_2'$ on x-axis.

128. For the lens, $u = -2.0$ m, $f = +1.5$ m

$$\therefore \quad \frac{1}{v} - \frac{1}{-2.0} = \frac{1}{1.5}$$

or $v = 6.0$ m

$$m = \frac{6.0}{-2.0} = -3.0$$

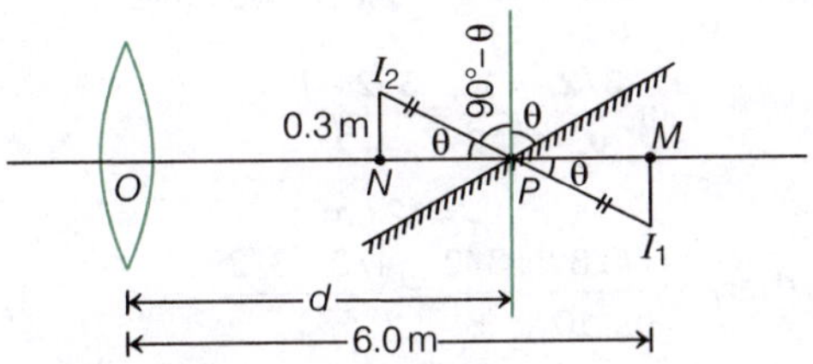

Therefore, y-coordinate of image formed by lens is $m\,(0.1) = -0.3$ m.

$$\frac{0.3}{NP} = \tan\theta = 0.3$$

$\therefore \quad NP = MP = 1.0$ m

or $d = 6.0 - 1.0$

$= 5.0$ m **Ans.**

and x-coordinate of final image I_2 is

$x = d - 1.0 = 4.0$ m **Ans.**

129. $BO = OC$

$\therefore \quad \angle OBC = \angle BCO = r$ (say)

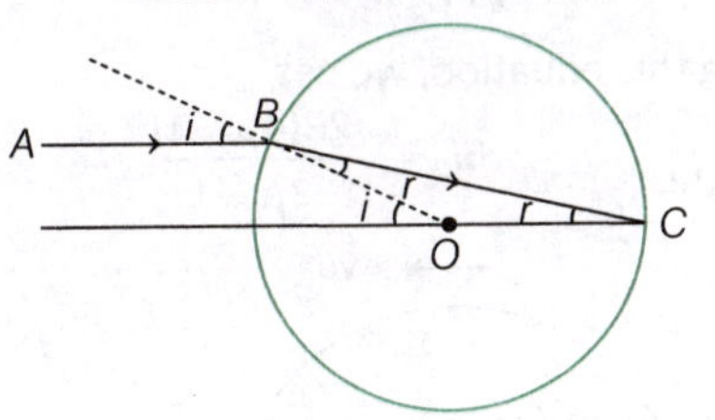

Let angle of incidence be i,

$i = r + r = 2r$ (external angle)

$$\therefore \quad \mu = \frac{\sin i}{\sin r} = \frac{\sin 2r}{\sin r} \approx \frac{2r}{r} = 2$$ **Ans.**

130. $\delta_{Total} = \delta_{Refraction} + 2\delta_{Reflection} + \delta_{Refraction}$

or $\delta = (i - r) + 2(180° - 2r) + (i - r)$

$= 360° + 2i - 6r$

$$= 360° + 2i - 6\sin^{-1}\left(\frac{\sin i}{\mu}\right)$$

For deviation to be minimum, $\dfrac{d\delta}{di} = 0$

By putting first derivative of δ (w.r.t. i) equal to zero, we get the desired result.

131. (a) For refraction at first half lens $\left(\frac{1}{v} - \frac{1}{u} = \frac{1}{f}\right)$

$$\frac{1}{v} - \frac{1}{-20} = \frac{1}{15}$$

$\therefore \quad v = 60$ cm

Magnification, $m = \dfrac{v}{u} = \dfrac{60}{-20} = -3$

The image formed by first half lens is shown in figure (a).

$AB = 2$ mm, $A_1B_1 = 6$ mm, $AO_1 = 20$ cm, $O_1F = 15$ cm and $O_1A_1 = 60$ cm.

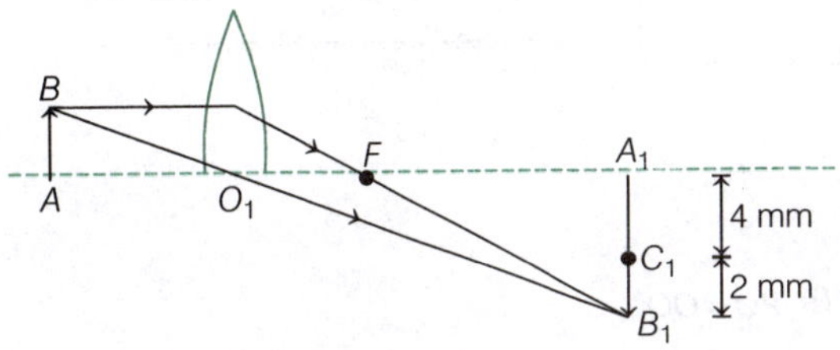

Point B_1 is 6 mm below the principal axis of the lenses. Plane mirror is 4 mm below it.

Hence, 4 mm length of A_1B_1 (i.e. A_1C_1) acts as real object for mirror. Mirror forms its virtual image A_2C_2. 2 mm length of A_1B_1 (i.e. C_1B_1) acts as virtual object for mirror. Real image C_2B_2 is formed of this part. Image formed by plane mirror is shown in figure (b).

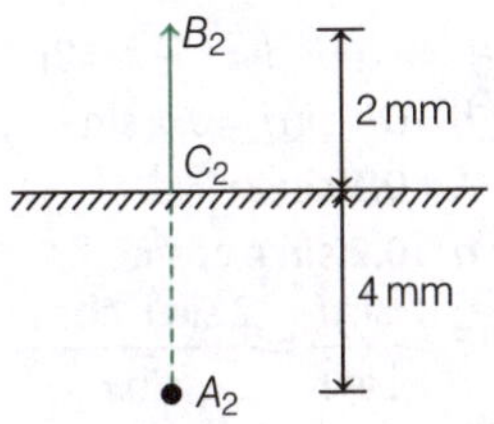

(b)

For the second half lens, $\dfrac{1}{v} - \dfrac{1}{-60} = \dfrac{1}{15}$

$\therefore \quad v = +20$

$$m = \frac{v}{u} = \frac{20}{-60} = -\frac{1}{3}$$

So, length of final image

$$A_3B_3 = \frac{1}{3}A_2B_2 = 2\text{ mm}$$

Point B_2 is 2 mm below the optic axis of second half lens. Hence, its image B_3 is formed 2/3 mm above the principal axis. Similarly, point A_2 is 8 mm below the principal axis. Hence, its image is 8/3 mm above it. Therefore, image is at a distance of 20 cm behind the second half lens and at a distance of 2/3 mm above the principal axis. The size of image is 2 mm and is inverted as compared to the given object. Image formed by second half lens is shown in figure (c).

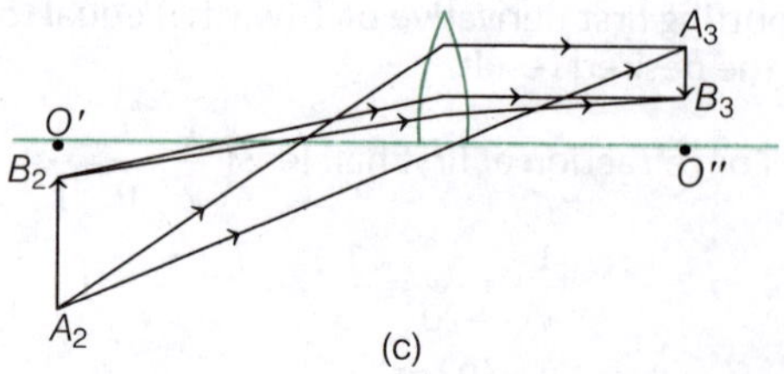

(c)

(b) Ray diagram for final image is shown in figure (d).

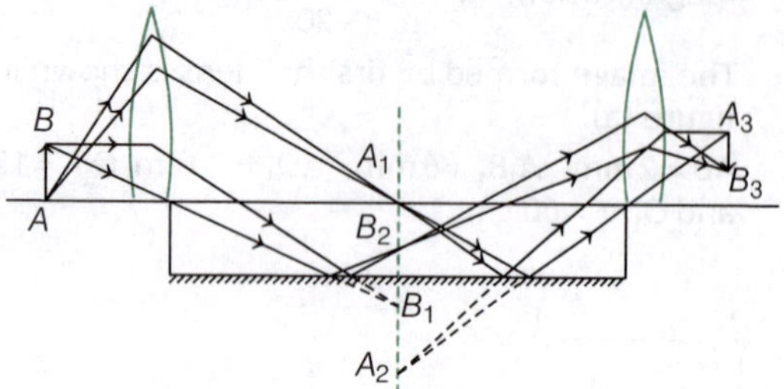

(d)

132. (i) $PO = OQ$

$\therefore \qquad \angle OPQ = \angle OQP = r$ (say)

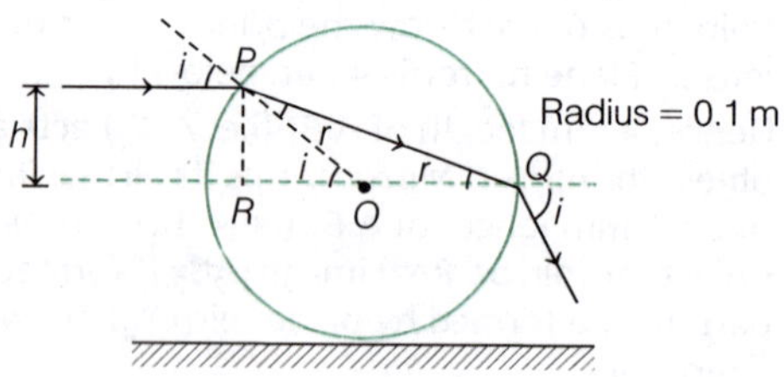

Also, $\qquad i = r + r = 2r$

In ΔPOR, $h = OP \sin i = 0.1 \sin i$

$= 0.1 \sin 2r$

or $\qquad h = 0.2 \sin r \cos r \qquad$ ...(i)

Also, $\qquad \sqrt{3} = \dfrac{\sin i}{\sin r} = \dfrac{2 \sin r \cos r}{\sin r}$

$= 2 \cos r$

$\therefore \qquad r = 30°$

Substituting in Eq. (i), we get

$$h = 0.2 \times \frac{1}{2} \times \frac{\sqrt{3}}{2}$$

$= 0.086$ m

Hence, height from the mirror is

$0.1 + 0.086 = 0.186$ m

(ii) Use the principle of reversibility.

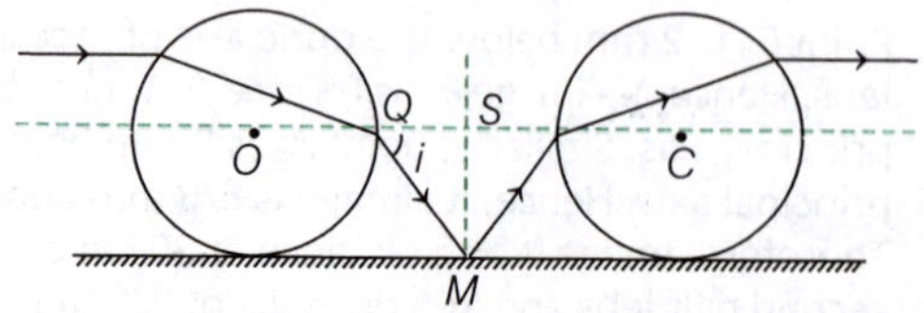

$$i = 2r = 60°$$

Now, $\qquad \dfrac{QS}{MS} = \cot i = \cot 60° = \dfrac{1}{\sqrt{3}}$

$\therefore \qquad QS = \dfrac{MS}{\sqrt{3}} = \dfrac{0.1}{\sqrt{3}}$

$\therefore$ The desired distance,

$$OC = 2 \times 0.1 + \frac{2 \times 0.1}{\sqrt{3}}$$

$= 0.315$ m **Ans.**

133. $\dfrac{V_i}{V} = \dfrac{\rho_S}{\rho_L} = \dfrac{\rho}{2\rho} = \dfrac{1}{2}$

i.e. half the sphere is inside the liquid. For the image to coincide with the object light should fall normally on the sphere.

Using $\dfrac{\mu_2}{v} - \dfrac{\mu_1}{u} = \dfrac{\mu_2 - \mu_1}{R}$ twice, we have

$$\frac{3/2}{v_1} - \frac{1}{-8} = \frac{3/2 - 1}{+2}$$

$\therefore \qquad v_1 = 12$ cm

Further, $\qquad \dfrac{4/3}{h - 10} - \dfrac{3/2}{8} = \dfrac{4/3 - 3/2}{-2}$

Solving this equation, we get

$h \approx 15$ cm **Ans.**

134. We have to see the image of O from the other side.

Applying, $\dfrac{\mu_2}{v} - \dfrac{\mu_1}{u} = \dfrac{\mu_2 - \mu_1}{R}$ twice, we have

$$\frac{\mu}{AI_1} - \frac{1}{-2R} = \frac{\mu - 1}{-R}$$

$\therefore \qquad AI_1 = \dfrac{2\mu R}{1 - 2\mu}$

Further, $\qquad \dfrac{1}{BI_2} - \dfrac{\mu}{(AI_1 - R)} = \dfrac{1 - \mu}{-R}$

Solving this equation, we get

$$BI_2 = -\frac{2R(4\mu - 1)}{3\mu - 1}$$

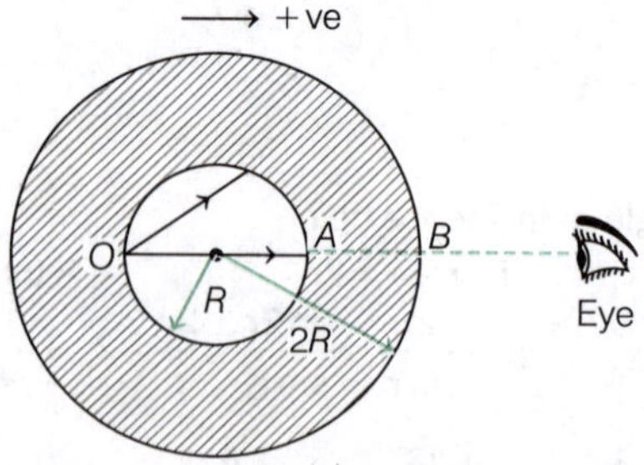

$\therefore$ Distance between the final image and object is

$$d = 3R - \frac{2R(4\mu - 1)}{3\mu - 1}$$

$$= \frac{(\mu - 1)R}{(3\mu - 1)}$$ **Hence proved.**

135. $\delta_{Total} = \delta_P + \delta_Q$

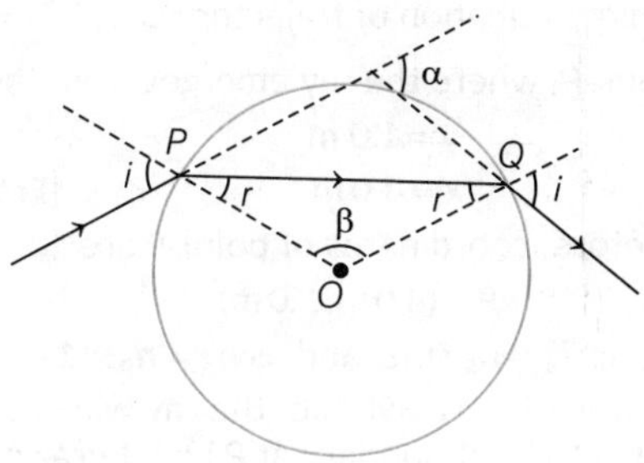

$$\therefore \quad \alpha = (i - r) + (i - r)$$

or $$i - r = \frac{\alpha}{2} \quad \text{...(i)}$$

Further, in ΔOPQ,

$$r + r + \beta = 180^\circ$$

$$\therefore \quad r = 90^\circ - \frac{\beta}{2} \quad \text{...(ii)}$$

From Eq. (i),

$$i = r + \frac{\alpha}{2} = 90^\circ + \left(\frac{\alpha - \beta}{2}\right) \quad \text{...(iii)}$$

$$\mu = \frac{\sin i}{\sin r} = \frac{\sin\left[90^\circ + \left(\frac{\alpha-\beta}{2}\right)\right]}{\sin\left(90^\circ - \frac{\beta}{2}\right)}$$

$$= \frac{\cos\left(\frac{\beta - \alpha}{2}\right)}{\cos\left(\frac{\beta}{2}\right)}$$

or $$\cos\left(\frac{\beta - \alpha}{2}\right) = \mu \cos\frac{\beta}{2}$$ **Hence proved**

136. $\theta = 90^\circ - i$

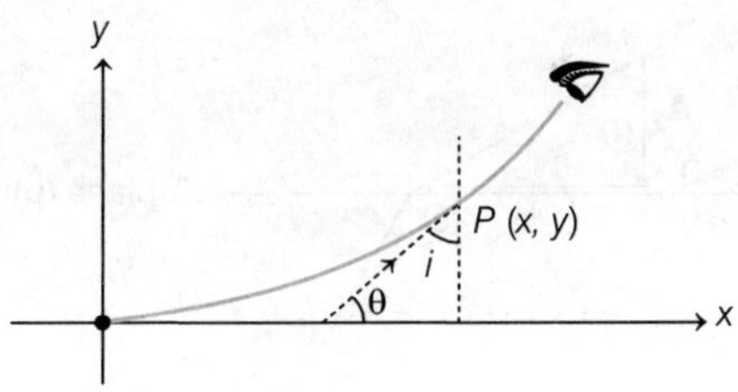

$$\tan\theta = \cot i$$

or $$\frac{dy}{dx} = \cot i \quad \text{...(i)}$$

$$\mu_O \sin i_O = \mu_P \sin i_P$$

(i) $$\sin 90^\circ = (\sqrt{1 + ay}) \sin i$$

$$\therefore \quad \sin i = \frac{1}{\sqrt{1 + ay}}$$

$$\therefore \quad \cot i = \sqrt{ay} = \frac{dy}{dx}$$

$$\therefore \quad \int_0^y \frac{dy}{\sqrt{ay}} = \int_0^x dx$$

or $$x = 2\sqrt{\frac{y}{a}}$$

Substituting $y = 2$ m,

and $a = 2.0 \times 10^{-6}\ \text{m}^{-1}$

We get $x_{max} = 2000\ \text{m} = 2\ \text{km}$ **Ans.**

137. Applying, $\frac{\mu_2}{v} - \frac{\mu_1}{u} = \frac{\mu_2 - \mu_1}{R}$ twice, we have

$$\frac{\mu}{v_1} - \frac{1}{-2R} = \frac{\mu - 1}{R}$$

$$\therefore \quad v_1 = \frac{2\mu R}{2\mu - 3}$$

Further, $$\frac{1}{v_2} - \frac{\mu}{-(3R - v_1)} = \frac{1 - \mu}{R/2}$$

$$\therefore \quad v_2 = \frac{R(9 - 4\mu)}{(10\mu - 9)(\mu - 2)}$$ **Ans.**

Final image is real if, $v_2 > 0$.

As $10\mu - 9$ is always positive ($\mu > 1$). Therefore, for $v_2 > 0$, either $(9 - 4\mu)$ and $(\mu - 2)$ both should be greater than zero or both should be less than zero. For the first condition (when both > 0) $2 < \mu < 2.25$ and for the second condition (when both < 0), $\mu < 2$ and $\mu > 2.25$ which is not possible. Hence, μ should lie between 2 and 2.25.

138. Differentiating the lens formula, $\frac{1}{v} - \frac{1}{u} = \frac{1}{f}$ with respect to time, we get

$$-\frac{1}{v^2} \cdot \frac{dv}{dt} + \frac{1}{u^2} \cdot \frac{du}{dt} = 0 \quad (\text{as } f = \text{constant})$$

$$\therefore \quad \left(\frac{dv}{dt}\right) = \left(\frac{v^2}{u^2}\right) \cdot \frac{du}{dt} \quad \text{...(i)}$$

Further, substituting proper values in lens formula, we have

$$\frac{1}{v} + \frac{1}{0.4} = \frac{1}{0.3} \quad (u = -0.4\ \text{m}, f = 0.3\ \text{m})$$

or $$v = 1.2\ \text{m}$$

Putting the values in Eq. (i), we get magnitude of rate of change of position of image = 0.09 m/s

Lateral magnification, $m = \frac{v}{u}$

$$\therefore \quad \frac{dm}{dt} = \frac{u.\frac{dv}{dt} - v.\frac{du}{dt}}{u^2}$$

$$= \frac{(-0.4)(0.09) - (1.2)(0.01)}{(0.4)^2}$$

$$= -0.3\ /\text{s}$$

$\therefore$ Magnitude of rate of change of lateral magnification $= 0.3\ /\text{s}$

139. Refractive index is a function of y. It varies along Y-axis i.e. the boundary separating two media is parallel to X-axis or normal at any point will be parallel to Y-axis.

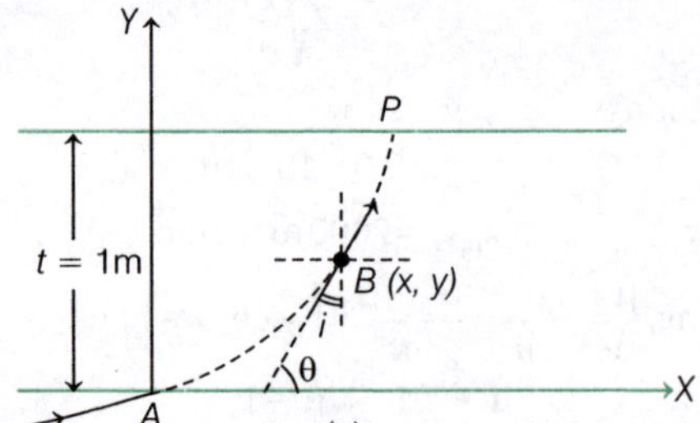

(a)

Secondly, refractive index increases as y is increased. Therefore, ray of light is travelling from rarer to denser medium i.e. it will bend towards the normal and shape of its trajectory will be as shown below.

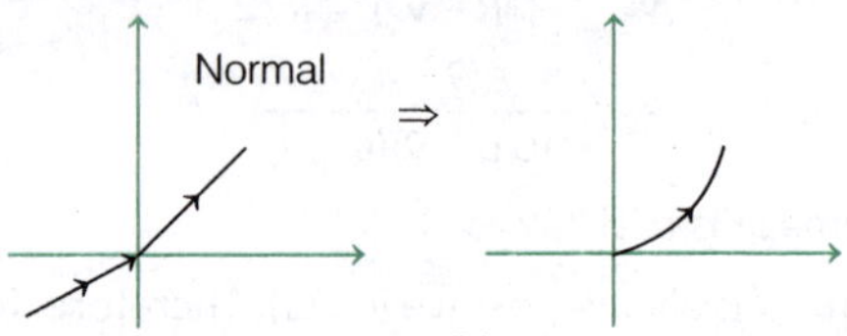

(b)

Now, refer to figure (a)

Let i be the angle of incidence at any point B on its path

$$\theta = 90° - i$$

or $\tan\theta = \tan(90° - i) = \cot i$

or slope $= \cot i$

(b) but $\tan\theta = \dfrac{dy}{dx}$

$$\therefore \quad \frac{dy}{dx} = \cot i \qquad \text{... (i)}$$

Applying Snell's law at A and B

$$n_A \sin i_A = n_B \sin i_B$$

$\Rightarrow$ $n_A = 1$ because $y = 0$

$\sin i_A = 1$ because

$i_A = 90°$ (Grazing incidence)

$$n_B = \sqrt{ky^{3/2} + 1}$$

$$= \sqrt{y^{3/2} + 1}$$

because $k = 1.0\,(\text{m})^{-3/2}$

$$\therefore \quad (1)(1) = \sqrt{(y^{3/2} + 1)}\ \sin i$$

$$\Rightarrow \quad \sin i = \frac{1}{\sqrt{y^{3/2} + 1}}$$

$$\therefore \quad \cot i = \sqrt{y^{3/2}} \text{ or } y^{3/4} \qquad \text{... (ii)}$$

Equating Eqs. (i) and (ii), we get

$$\frac{dy}{dx} = y^{3/4}$$

or $y^{-3/4} dy = dx$

or $\int_0^y y^{-3/4} dy = \int_0^x dx$

or $4y^{1/4} = x$ ... (iii)

The required equation of trajectory is $4y^{1/4} = x$.

(c) At point P, where the ray emerges from the slab

$y = 1.0$ m

$\therefore$ $x = 4.0$ m [From Eq. (iii)]

Therefore, coordinates of point P are

$$P = (4.0\,\text{m}, 1.0\,\text{m})$$

(d) As $n_A \sin i_A = n_P \sin i_p$ and as $n_A = n_P = 1$

Therefore, $i_P = i_A = 90°$ i.e. the ray will emerge parallel to the boundary at P i.e. at grazing emergence.

140. Applying Snell's law on face AB,

$$(1) \sin 45° = (\sqrt{2}) \sin r$$

$$\therefore \quad \sin r = \frac{1}{2}$$

$$\Rightarrow \quad r = 30°$$

i.e. ray becomes parallel to AD inside the block.

Now applying,

$$\frac{\mu_2}{v} - \frac{\mu_1}{u} = \frac{\mu_2 - \mu_1}{R} \text{ on face } CD,$$

$$\Rightarrow \quad \frac{1.514}{OE} - \frac{\sqrt{2}}{\infty} = \frac{1.514 - \sqrt{2}}{0.4}$$

Solving this equation, we get

$$OE = 6.06 \text{ m}$$

141. Let us take $\mathbf{A} = \mathbf{A}_1 + \mathbf{A}_2$

Here $\mathbf{A}_1 = (6\sqrt{3}\,\hat{\mathbf{i}} + 8\sqrt{3}\,\hat{\mathbf{j}})$, a vector in XY-plane

$$A_1 \text{ or } |\mathbf{A}_1| = \sqrt{(6\sqrt{3})^2 + (8\sqrt{3})^2}$$

$$= 10\sqrt{3} \text{ units}$$

$$\mathbf{A}_2 = -10\,\hat{\mathbf{k}}$$

A_2 or $|\mathbf{A}_2| = 10$ units

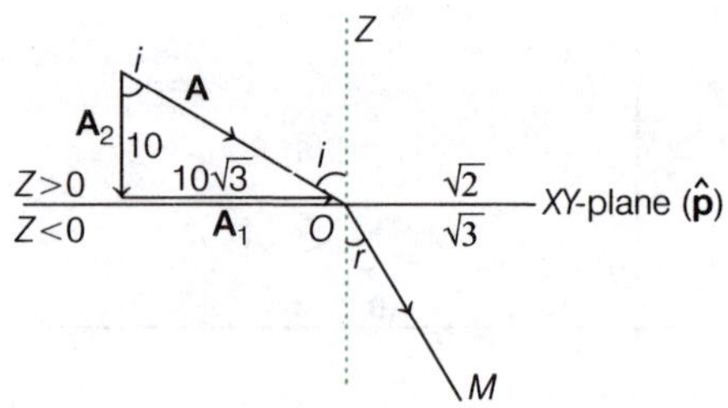

$$\sin i = \frac{10\sqrt{3}}{\sqrt{(10)^2 + (10\sqrt{3})^2}} = \frac{\sqrt{3}}{2}$$

$$\Rightarrow \quad i = 60°$$

Applying Snell's law at O,

$$\sqrt{2} \sin i = \sqrt{3} \sin r$$

Putting the value of $\sin i$, we get

$$r = 45°$$

Let $\hat{\mathbf{p}}$ is a unit vector in the direction of $\mathbf{A}_1$, then

$$\hat{\mathbf{p}} = \frac{\mathbf{A}_1}{A_1} = \frac{1}{10\sqrt{3}}(6\sqrt{3}\,\hat{\mathbf{i}} + 8\sqrt{3}\,\hat{\mathbf{j}})$$

Now, we have to find a unit vector (having magnitude 1) in the direction of OM and let this is $\hat{\mathbf{n}}$. Then

$$\hat{\mathbf{n}} = (1 \sin r)\hat{\mathbf{p}} + (1 \cos r)(-\hat{\mathbf{k}}) \qquad (r = 45°)$$

$$= \frac{1}{\sqrt{2}}\frac{1}{10\sqrt{3}}(6\sqrt{3}\,\hat{\mathbf{i}} + 8\sqrt{3}\,\hat{\mathbf{j}}) - \frac{1}{\sqrt{2}}\hat{\mathbf{k}}$$

$$= \frac{1}{5\sqrt{2}}(3\hat{\mathbf{i}} + 4\hat{\mathbf{j}} - 5\hat{\mathbf{k}})$$

142. Let R be the radius of curvature of both the surfaces of the equi-convex lens. In the first case :

Let f_1 be the focal length of equi-convex lens of refractive index μ_1 and f_2 the focal length of plano-concave lens of refractive index μ_2. The focal length of the combined lens system will be given by

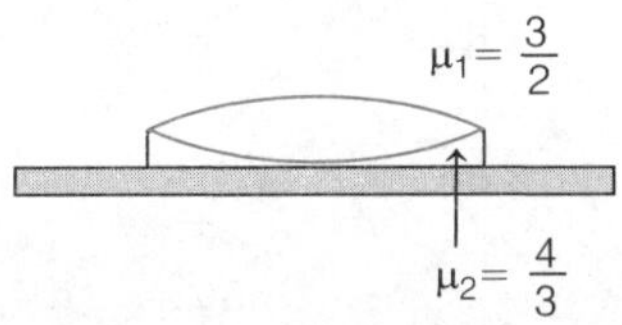

$$\frac{1}{f} = \frac{1}{f_1} + \frac{1}{f_2}$$

$$= (\mu_1 - 1)\left(\frac{1}{R} - \frac{1}{-R}\right) + (\mu_2 - 1)\left(\frac{1}{-R} - \frac{1}{\infty}\right)$$

$$= \left(\frac{3}{2} - 1\right)\left(\frac{2}{R}\right) + \left(\frac{4}{3} - 1\right)\left(-\frac{1}{R}\right)$$

$$= \frac{1}{R} - \frac{1}{3R} = \frac{2}{3R} \quad \text{or} \quad f = \frac{3R}{2}$$

Now, image coincides with the object when ray of light retraces its path or it falls normally on the plane mirror. This is possible only when object is at focus of the lens system.

Hence, $f = 15$ cm

or $\quad \frac{3R}{2} = 15$ cm or $R = 10$ cm

In the second case, let μ be the refractive index of the liquid filled between lens and mirror and let f' be the focal length of new lens system. Then,

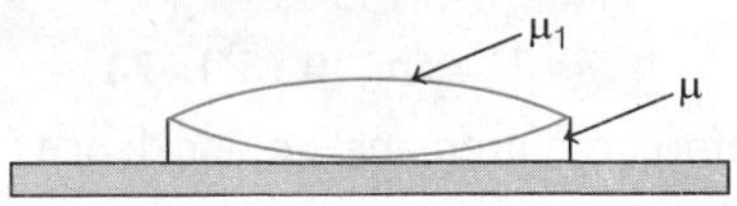

$$\frac{1}{f'} = (\mu_1 - 1)\left(\frac{1}{R} - \frac{1}{-R}\right) + (\mu - 1)\left(\frac{1}{-R} - \frac{1}{\infty}\right)$$

$$\Rightarrow \quad \frac{1}{f'} = \left(\frac{3}{2} - 1\right)\left(\frac{2}{R}\right) - \frac{(\mu - 1)}{R}$$

$$\Rightarrow \quad = \frac{1}{R} - \frac{\mu - 1}{R} = \frac{(2 - \mu)}{R}$$

$$\therefore \quad f' = \frac{R}{2 - \mu} = \frac{10}{2 - \mu} \qquad (\because R = 10 \text{ cm})$$

Now, the image coincides with object when it is placed at 25 cm distance.

Hence,

$$f' = 25$$

$$\Rightarrow \quad \frac{10}{2 - \mu} = 25$$

$$\Rightarrow \quad 50 - 25\mu = 10$$

$$\Rightarrow \quad 25\mu = 40$$

$$\therefore \quad \mu = \frac{40}{25} = 1.6$$

$$\Rightarrow \quad \mu = 1.6$$

143. Rays coming from object AB first refract from the lens and then reflect from the mirror.

Refraction from the lens

Given, $\quad u = -20$ cm, $f = +15$ cm

Using lens formula, $\frac{1}{v} - \frac{1}{u} = \frac{1}{f}$

$$\Rightarrow \quad \frac{1}{v} - \frac{1}{-20} = \frac{1}{15}$$

$$\therefore \quad v = +60 \text{ cm}$$

and linear magnification,

$$m_1 = \frac{v}{u} = \frac{+60}{-20} = -3$$

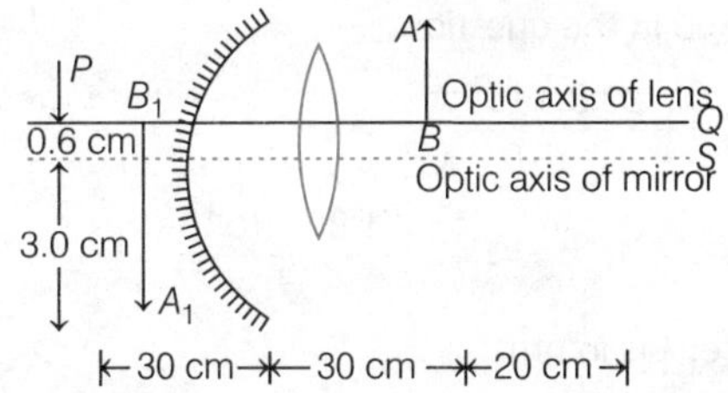

i.e. first image formed by the lens will be at 60 cm from it (or 30 cm from mirror) towards left and 3 times magnified but inverted. Length of first image A_1B_1 would be $1.2 \times 3 = 3.6$ cm (inverted).

Reflection from mirror

Image formed by lens (A_1B_1) will behave like a virtual object for mirror at a distance of 30 cm from it as shown. Therefore $u = +30$ cm, $f = -30$ cm.

Using mirror formula, $\frac{1}{v} + \frac{1}{u} = \frac{1}{f}$

$$\Rightarrow \quad \frac{1}{v} + \frac{1}{30} = -\frac{1}{30}$$

$$\Rightarrow \quad v = -15 \text{ cm}$$

and linear magnification,

$$m_2 = -\frac{v}{u} = -\frac{-15}{+30} = +\frac{1}{2}$$

i.e. final image $A'B'$ will be located at a distance of 15 cm from the mirror (towards right) and since magnification is $+\frac{1}{2}$, length of final image would be $3.6 \times \frac{1}{2} = 1.8$ cm.

$$\therefore \quad A'B' = 1.8 \text{ cm}$$

Point B_1 is 0.6 cm above the optic axis of mirror, therefore, its image B' would be $(0.6)\left(\frac{1}{2}\right) = 0.3$ cm above optic axis. Similarly, point A_1 is 3 cm below the optic axis, therefore, its image A' will be $3 \times \frac{1}{2} = 1.5$ cm below the optic axis as shown below

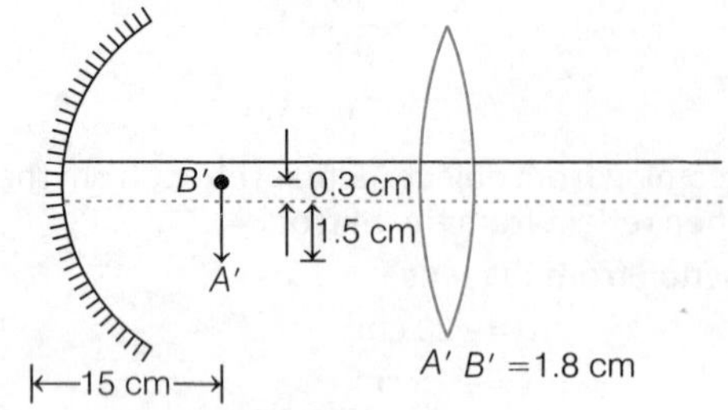

Total magnification of the image,

$$m = m_1 \times m_2 = (-3)\left(+\frac{1}{2}\right) = -\frac{3}{2}$$

$$\therefore \quad A'B' = (m)(AB) = \left(-\frac{3}{2}\right)(1.2)$$

$$= -1.8 \text{ cm}$$

Note that, there is no need of drawing the ray diagram if not asked in the question.

144. $n_1 = 1.20 + \dfrac{10.8 \times 10^4}{\lambda^2}$

and $\quad n_2 = 1.45 + \dfrac{1.80 \times 10^4}{\lambda^2}$

Here, λ is in nm.

(a) The incident ray will not deviate at BC if $n_1 = n_2$

$$\Rightarrow 1.20 + \frac{10.8 \times 10^4}{\lambda_0^2} = 1.45 + \frac{1.80 \times 10^4}{\lambda_0^2}$$

$$\Rightarrow \quad \frac{9 \times 10^4}{\lambda_0^2} = 0.25$$

$$\Rightarrow \quad \lambda_0 = \frac{3 \times 10^2}{0.5}$$

$$\Rightarrow \quad \lambda_0 = 600 \text{ nm}$$

(b) The given system is a part of an equilateral prism of prism angle 60° as shown in given figure.

145. Critical angle θ_c at face AC will be given by

$$\theta_c = \sin^{-1}\left(\frac{n_1}{n}\right)$$

$$\Rightarrow \quad \sin\theta_c = \frac{n_1}{n}$$

Now, it is given that $r_2 = \theta_c$

$$\therefore \quad r_1 = A - r_2 = (45° - \theta_c)$$

Applying Snell's law at face AB, we have

$$n = \frac{\sin i_1}{\sin r_1}$$

$$\Rightarrow \quad \sin i_1 = n \sin r_1$$

$$\therefore \quad i_1 = \sin^{-1}(n \sin r_1)$$

Substituting value of r_1, we get

$$i_1 = \sin^{-1}\{n \sin(45° - \theta_c)\}$$

$$= \sin^{-1}\{n(\sin 45° \cos\theta_c - \cos 45° \sin\theta_c)\}$$

$$= \sin^{-1}\left\{\frac{n}{\sqrt{2}}\left(\sqrt{1 - \sin^2\theta_c} - \sin\theta_c\right)\right\}$$

$$= \sin^{-1}\left\{\frac{n}{\sqrt{2}}\left(\sqrt{1 - \frac{n_1^2}{n^2}} - \frac{n_1}{n}\right)\right\}$$

$$i_1 = \sin^{-1}\left\{\frac{1}{\sqrt{2}}\left(\sqrt{n^2 - n_1^2} - n_1\right)\right\}$$

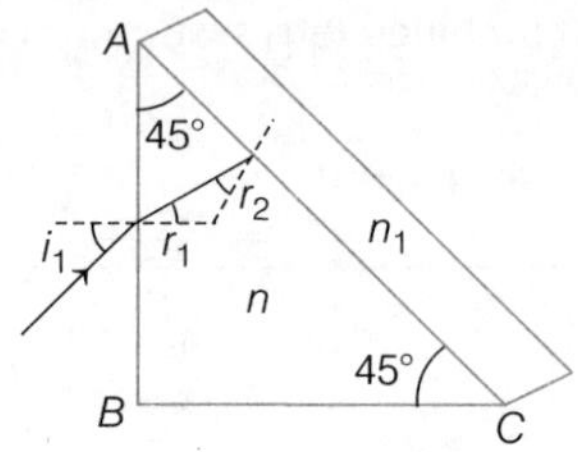

Therefore, required angle of incidence (i_1) at face AB for which the ray strikes at AC at critical angle is

$$i_1 = \sin^{-1}\left\{\frac{1}{\sqrt{2}}\left(\sqrt{n^2 - n_1^2} - n_1\right)\right\}$$

(b) The ray will pass undeviated through face AC when either $n_1 = n$ or $r_2 = 0°$ i.e. ray falls normally on face AC.

Here $n_1 \neq n$ (because $n_1 < n$ is given)

$$\therefore \quad r_2 = 0°$$

$$\Rightarrow \quad r_1 = A - r_2$$

$$= 45° - 0° = 45°$$

Now applying Snell's law at face AB, we have

$$n = \frac{\sin i_1}{\sin r_1} \Rightarrow 1.352 = \frac{\sin i_1}{\sin 45°}$$

$$\therefore \quad \sin i_1 = (1.352)\left(\frac{1}{\sqrt{2}}\right)$$

$$\Rightarrow \quad \sin i_1 = 0.956$$

$$\therefore \quad i_1 = \sin^{-1}(0.956) \approx 73°$$

Therefore, required angle of incidence is $i = 73°$

146. For refraction at first surface,

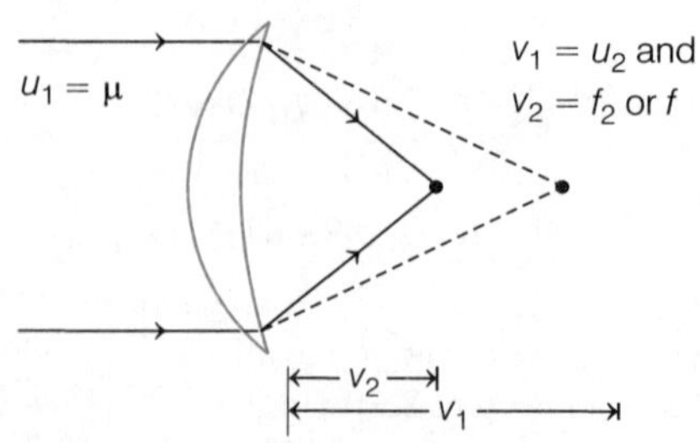

$$\frac{\mu_2}{v_1} - \frac{\mu_1}{-\infty} = \frac{\mu_2 - \mu_1}{+R} \quad \text{...(i)}$$

For refraction at second surface,

$$\frac{\mu_3}{v_2}-\frac{\mu_2}{v_1}=\frac{\mu_3-\mu_2}{+R} \quad \text{... (ii)}$$

Adding Eqs. (i) and (ii), we get

$$\frac{\mu_3}{v_2}=\frac{\mu_3-\mu_1}{R}$$

$$\Rightarrow \quad v_2=\frac{\mu_3 R}{\mu_3-\mu_1}$$

Therefore, focal length of the given lens system is

$$\frac{\mu_3 R}{\mu_3-\mu_1}$$

147. From lens maker's formula,

$$\frac{1}{f}=(\mu-1)\left(\frac{1}{R_1}-\frac{1}{R_2}\right)$$

we have

$$\frac{1}{0.3}=\left(\frac{3}{2}-1\right)\left(\frac{1}{R}-\frac{1}{-R}\right) \quad \text{(Here, } R_1=R \text{ and } R_2=-R)$$

$$\Rightarrow \quad R=0.3$$

Now applying, $\frac{\mu_2}{v}-\frac{\mu_1}{u}=\frac{\mu_2-\mu_1}{R}$ at air glass surface,

we get

$$\frac{3/2}{v_1}-\frac{1}{-(0.9)}=\frac{3/2-1}{0.3}$$

$$\therefore \quad v_1=2.7\text{ m}$$

i.e. first image I_1 will be formed at 2.7 m from the lens. This will act as the virtual object for glass water surface. Therefore, applying $\frac{\mu_2}{v}-\frac{\mu_1}{u}=\frac{\mu_2-\mu_1}{R}$ at glass water surface, we have

$$\frac{4/3}{v_2}-\frac{3/2}{2.7}=\frac{4/3-3/2}{-0.3}$$

$$\therefore \quad v_2=1.2\text{ m}$$

i.e. second image I_2 is formed at 1.2 m from the lens or 0.4 m from the plane mirror. This will act as a virtual object for mirror. Therefore, third real image I_3 will be formed at a distance of 0.4 m in front of the mirror after reflection from it. Now this image will work as a real object for water-glass interface. Hence, applying

$$\frac{\mu_2}{v}-\frac{\mu_1}{u}=\frac{\mu_2-\mu_1}{R}$$

we get, $$\frac{3/2}{v_4}-\frac{4/3}{-(0.8-0.4)}=\frac{3/2-4/3}{0.3}$$

$$\therefore \quad v_4=-0.54\text{ m}$$

i.e. fourth image is formed to the right of the lens at a distance of 0.54 m from it. Now finally applying the same formula for glass-air surface,

$$\frac{1}{v_5}-\frac{3/2}{-0.54}=\frac{1-3/2}{-0.3}$$

$$\therefore \quad v_5=-0.9\text{ m}$$

i.e. position of final image is 0.9 m relative to the lens (rightwards) or the image is formed 0.1 m behind the mirror.

148. Refer figure (a)

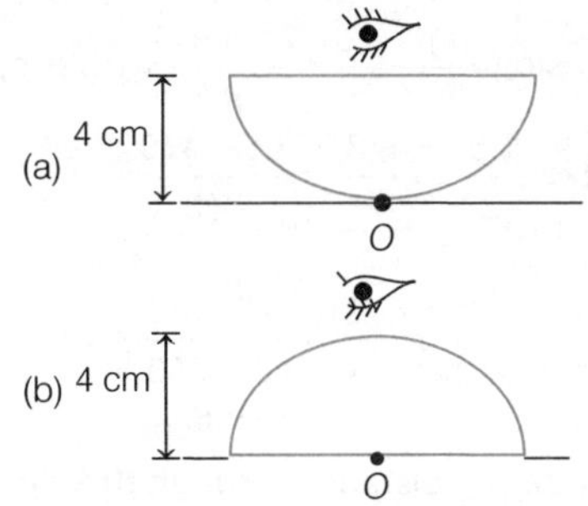

In this case refraction of the rays starting from O takes place from a plane surface. So, we can use

$$d_{app}=\frac{d_{actual}}{\mu} \quad \text{or} \quad 3=\frac{4}{\mu} \quad \text{or} \quad \mu=\frac{4}{3}$$

Refer figure (b)

In this case refraction takes place from a spherical surface. Hence, applying

$$\frac{\mu_2}{v}-\frac{\mu_1}{u}=\frac{\mu_2-\mu_1}{R}$$

we have, $$\frac{1}{(-25/8)}-\frac{4/3}{-4}=\frac{1-4/3}{-R}$$

or $$\frac{1}{3R}=\frac{1}{3}-\frac{8}{25}=\frac{1}{75}$$

$$\therefore \quad R=25\text{ cm}$$

Now, to find the focal length we will use the lens Maker's formula

$$\frac{1}{f}=(\mu-1)\left(\frac{1}{R_1}-\frac{1}{R_2}\right)$$

$$=\left(\frac{4}{3}-1\right)\left(\frac{1}{\infty}-\frac{1}{-25}\right)=\frac{1}{75}$$

$$\therefore \quad f=75\text{ cm}$$

149. (a) Image of object will coincide with it if ray of light after refraction from the concave surface fall normally on concave mirror so formed by silvering the convex surface. Or image after refraction from concave surface should form at centre of curvature of concave mirror or at a distance of 20 cm on same side of the combination. Let x be the distance of pin from the given optical system.

Applying, $$\frac{\mu_2}{v}-\frac{\mu_1}{u}=\frac{\mu_2-\mu_1}{R}$$

With proper signs, $$\frac{1.5}{-20}-\frac{1}{-x}=\frac{1.5-1}{-60}$$

or $$\frac{1}{x}=\frac{3}{40}-\frac{1}{120}=\frac{8}{120}$$

$$\Rightarrow \quad x=\frac{120}{8}=15\text{ cm}$$

(b) Now, before striking with the concave surface, the ray is first refracted from a plane surface. So, let x be the distance of pin, then the plane surface will form its image at a distance $\frac{4}{3}x$

Now, using $\frac{\mu_2}{v} - \frac{\mu_1}{u} = \frac{\mu_2 - \mu_1}{R}$ with proper signs,

we have $\frac{1.5}{-20} - \frac{4/3}{-\frac{4x}{3}} = \frac{1.5 - 4/3}{-60}$

or $\frac{1}{x} = \frac{3}{40} - \frac{1}{360}$

or $x = 13.84$ cm

Let Δx be the distance through the pin moved.

$\therefore \quad \Delta x = x_1 - x_2$

$= 15 \text{ cm} - 13.84 \text{ cm}$

$= 1.16$ cm (downwards)

150.

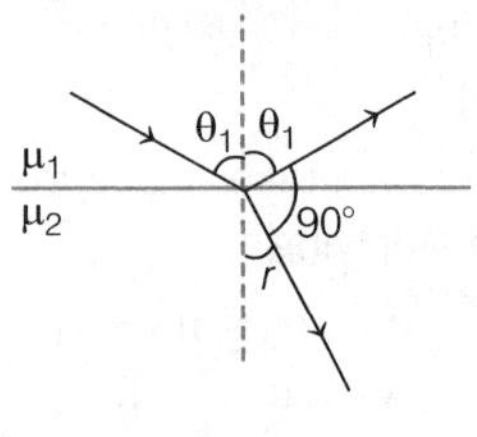

$$\sin \theta_{1cr} = \frac{\mu_R}{\mu_D} = \frac{\mu_2}{\mu_1} \quad \text{...(i)}$$

$$\theta_1 + 90° + r = 180°$$

$$\therefore \quad r = 90° - \theta_1$$

Now, applying Snell's law,

$$\mu_1 \sin \theta_1 = \mu_2 \sin r = \mu_2 \sin(90° - \theta_1) = \mu_2 \cos \theta_1$$

$$\therefore \quad \tan \theta_1 = \frac{\mu_2}{\mu_1} \quad \text{...(ii)}$$

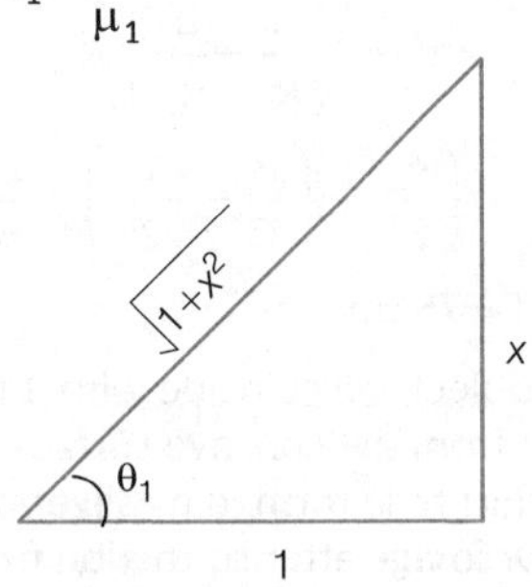

Now let us take $\frac{\mu_2}{\mu_1} = x$

$\therefore \quad \sin \theta_{1cr} = x$

Now, given that :

$$\frac{\sin \theta_{1cr}}{\sin \theta_1} = 1.28 = \frac{x}{x/\sqrt{1+x^2}} = \sqrt{1+x^2}$$

Solving this equation, we get

$$\frac{\mu_2}{\mu_1} = x = 0.8$$

$$\frac{\mu_1}{\mu_2} \approx 1.25$$

151. Minimum deflection angle

Using the equation,

$$\mu = \frac{\sin\left(\frac{A + \delta_m}{2}\right)}{\sin\left(\frac{A}{2}\right)}$$

We can find value of minimum deviation angle δ_m.

Maximum deflection angle

Maximum deflection occurs for $i_1 = 90°$.

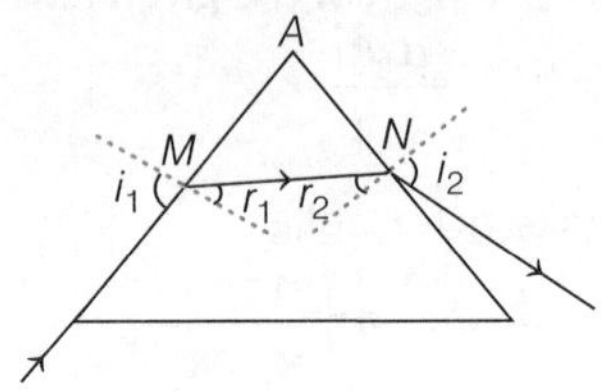

Here, $\angle A = 60°$

$$\sin \theta_{cr} = \frac{1}{\mu}$$

When angle in air is $90°$ ($i_1 = 90°$), angle in medium is critical ($r_1 = \theta_{cr}$).

Further, $r_1 + r_2 = A$

$\Rightarrow \quad r_2 = A - r_1 = A - \theta_{cr}$

Now applying Snell's law at M,

$$\mu = \frac{\sin i_2}{\sin r_2}$$

We can also find i_2.

Finally deflection is given by,

$$\delta = (i_1 + i_2) - A$$

Note *Deviation will be maximum at $i_1 = 90°$, this we can conclude from δ versus i graph of a prism.*

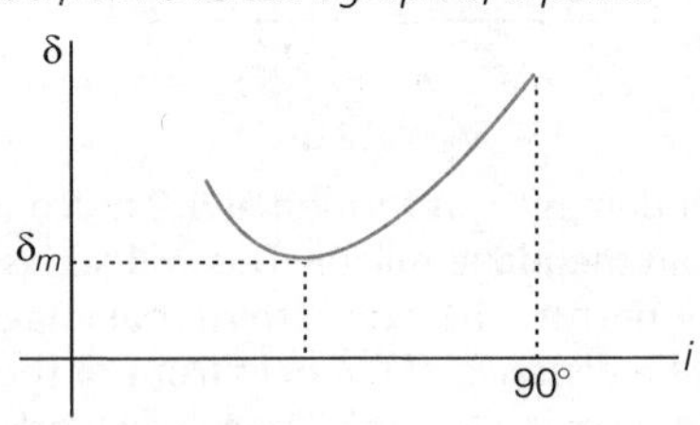

152. Let us denote minimum deviation by θ. Then we can write,

$$\mu = \frac{\sin\left(\frac{A+\theta}{2}\right)}{\sin\left(\frac{A}{2}\right)} \quad \text{...(i)}$$

Here, A is constant, μ and θ are variables.

Since difference in μ is given very small, so after differentiating, we can write the above equation as,

$$d\mu = \frac{\cos\left(\frac{A+\theta}{2}\right)}{2\sin\left(\frac{A}{2}\right)} d\theta$$

or $$\Delta\mu = \frac{\cos\left(\frac{A+\theta}{2}\right)}{2\sin\left(\frac{A}{2}\right)}\Delta\theta \quad \text{...(ii)}$$

From equation (i), we get

$$\sin\left(\frac{A+\theta}{2}\right) = \mu \sin\left(\frac{A}{2}\right)$$

$$\therefore \quad \cos\left(\frac{A+\theta}{2}\right) = \sqrt{1-\mu^2\sin^2\left(\frac{A}{2}\right)}$$

Substituting in equation (ii), we get

$$\Delta\theta = \frac{2\sin\left(\frac{A}{2}\right)\Delta\mu}{\sqrt{1-\mu^2\sin^2\left(\frac{A}{2}\right)}}$$

Putting the proper values, we get

$$\Delta\theta \approx 0.44°$$

153.

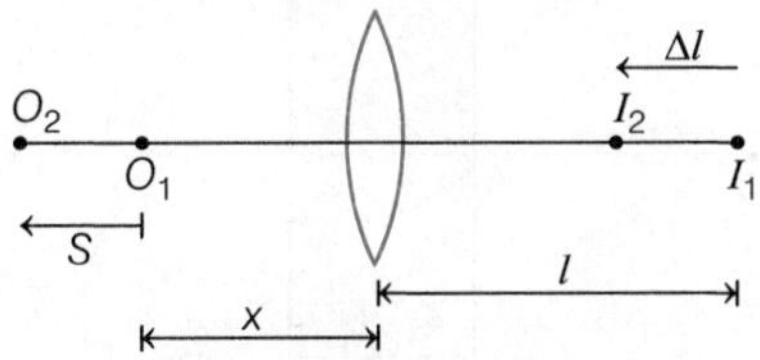

$l = 5\text{ m} = 500\text{ cm}, \Delta l = 18.0\text{ cm}$ (Given)

In the question S is asked.

Using lens formula $\frac{1}{v} - \frac{1}{u} = \frac{1}{f}$ two times,

$$\frac{1}{l} + \frac{1}{x} = \frac{1}{f} \quad \text{...(i)}$$

and $$\frac{1}{(l-\Delta l)} + \frac{1}{S+x} = \frac{1}{f} \quad \text{...(ii)}$$

We have two unknowns x and S. Solving two equations, we get

$$S = 0.5\text{ mm}$$

Alternate method

$$\frac{1}{f} = \frac{1}{v} - \frac{1}{u}$$

$$\Rightarrow \quad \frac{1}{25} = \frac{1}{500} - \frac{1}{-u}$$

$$\Rightarrow \quad u = 26.32\text{ cm}$$

Now $|\Delta u| = \left|\frac{u^2}{v^2}\right| |\Delta v|$

$$= \left(\frac{26.32}{500}\right)^2 (18)\text{ cm}$$

$$= 0.05\text{ cm}$$

$$= 0.5\text{ mm}$$

154. (a) Focal length of a lens in cm is given by,

$$f = \frac{100}{P\,(\text{dioptre})}$$

In the given figure,

$$f_3 = f_1 = \frac{100}{10} = 10\text{ cm}$$

$$f_2 = \frac{100}{-10} = -10\text{ cm}$$

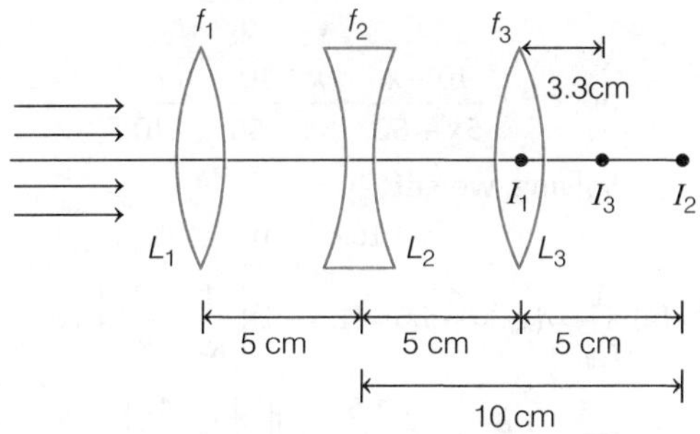

First image I_1 is formed at second focus (or principal focus) of L_1 or at 10 cm to its right hand side (or at optical centre of L_3).

This will behave as a virtual object for L_2.

Applying lens formula, $\frac{1}{v} - \frac{1}{u} = \frac{1}{f}$ for L_2,

$$\frac{1}{v} - \frac{1}{+5} = \frac{1}{-10}$$

$$\therefore \quad v = +10\text{ cm}$$

I_2 is as shown in figure. Now this will behave as virtual object for L_3.

Again applying lens formula for L_3,

$$\frac{1}{v} - \frac{1}{+5} = \frac{1}{10}$$

$$\therefore \quad v = +3.3\text{ cm}$$

(b)

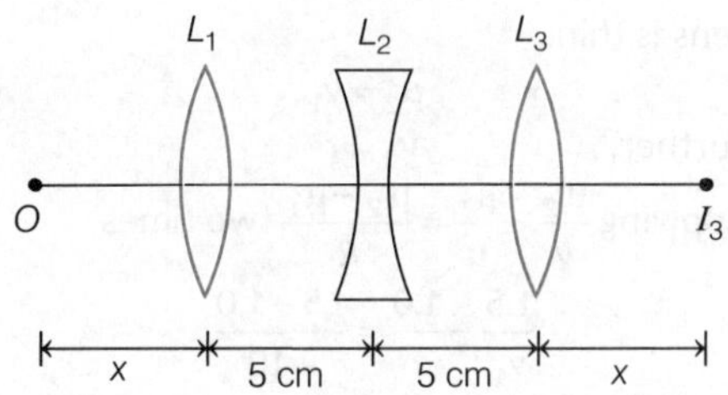

Symmetrical to lens system means if object is at a distance x to the left of L_1 then final image I_3 is also at a distance x to the right hand side of L_3.

Applying lens formula for L_1,

$$\frac{1}{v_1} - \frac{1}{-x} = \frac{1}{10}$$

$$\therefore \quad v_1 = \frac{10x}{x-10} \quad \text{...(i)}$$

Applying lens formula for L_3,

$$\frac{1}{x} - \frac{1}{u_3} = \frac{1}{10}$$

$$\therefore \quad u_3 = \frac{10x}{10-x}$$

$$u_2 = v_1 - 5 = \frac{10x}{x-10} - 5 = \frac{5x+50}{x-10}$$

$$v_2 = u_3 + 5 = \frac{10x}{10-x} + 5 = \frac{5x+50}{10-x}$$

Applying lens formula for L_2,

$$\frac{1}{v_2} - \frac{1}{u_2} = \frac{1}{f_2}$$

or $$\frac{10-x}{5x+50} - \frac{x-10}{5x+50} = \frac{1}{-10}$$

Solving, we get

$$x = 16.67 \text{ cm}$$

155. (a) $$\frac{1}{f_{air}} = P_{air} = -5.0 = (1.5-1)\left(\frac{1}{R_1} - \frac{1}{R_2}\right) \quad ...(i)$$

$$\frac{1}{f_{liquid}} = P_{liquid} = \left(\frac{1.5}{1.7} - 1\right)\left(\frac{1}{R_1} - \frac{1}{R_2}\right) \quad ...(ii)$$

Dividing Eq. (ii) by Eq. (i), we get

$$P_{liquid} = 1.17 \text{ D}$$

Focal length in liquid (in metre),

$$f_{liquid} = \frac{1}{1.17} = 0.85 \text{ m} \quad \text{or} \quad f_{liquid} = 85 \text{ cm}$$

(b) In air, $\frac{1}{f} = P = 10 = (1.5-1)\left[\frac{1}{R} - \frac{1}{-R}\right]$

Solving this, we get

$$R = 0.1 \text{ m} \quad \text{or} \quad 10 \text{ cm}$$

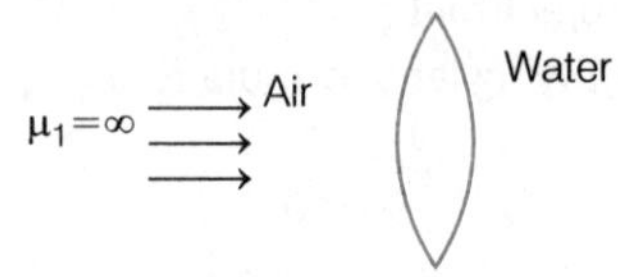

Lens is thin,

$\therefore$ $$u_2 = v_1$$

Further, $$v_2 = f$$

Applying $\frac{\mu_2}{v} - \frac{\mu_1}{u} = \frac{\mu_2 - \mu_1}{R}$ two times,

$$\frac{1.5}{v_1} - \frac{1.0}{\infty} = \frac{1.5-1.0}{+10} \quad ...(i)$$

$$\frac{4/3}{f} - \frac{1.5}{v_1} = \frac{4/3-1.5}{-10} \quad ...(ii)$$

Adding Eqs. (i) and (ii), we get

$$\frac{4}{3f} = \frac{1}{20} + \frac{1}{60}$$

$\therefore$ $$f = 20 \text{ cm} \quad \text{or} \quad 0.2 \text{ m}$$

$$P = \frac{1}{f\text{(metre)}} = \frac{1}{0.2} \quad \text{or} \quad P = 5 \text{ D}$$

156. (a) $OA = 8.0$ cm

$\therefore$ $$AI_1 = (n_g)(OA)$$

$$= \left(\frac{8}{5}\right)(8.0) = 12.8 \text{ cm}$$

For refraction at EG ($R = \infty$), using

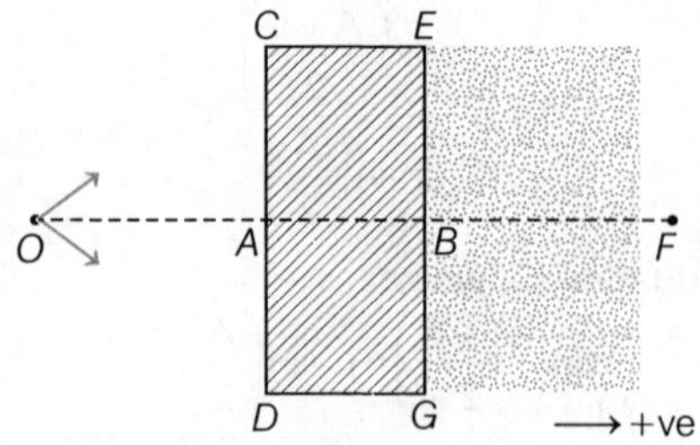

$$\frac{n_2}{v} - \frac{n_1}{u} = \frac{n_2 - n_1}{R}$$

$\therefore$ $$\frac{4/3}{BI_2} - \frac{8/5}{-(12.8+3)} = 0$$

$\therefore$ $$BI_2 = -(15.8)(4/3)(5/8) = -13.2 \text{ cm}$$

$\therefore$ $$FI_2 = 13.2 + 6.8 = 20.0 \text{ cm}$$ **Ans.**

(b) **For face *EF***

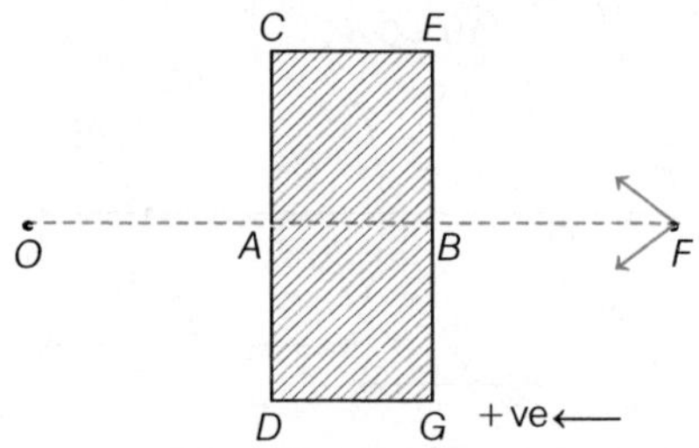

$$\frac{8/5}{BI_1} - \frac{4/3}{-6.8} = 0$$

$\therefore$ $$BI_1 = -(6.8)(8/5)(3/4)$$
$$= -8.16 \text{ cm}$$

For face *CD*

$$\frac{1.0}{AI_2} - \frac{8/5}{-11.16} = 0$$

$\therefore$ $$AI_2 = -(11.16)(5/8) = -6.975 \text{ cm}$$

$\therefore$ $$FI_2 = 8 + 6.975$$
$$= 14.975 \text{ cm}$$ **Ans.**

157.

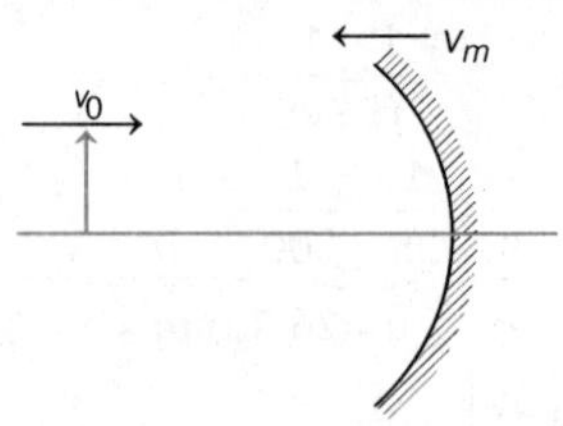

Let

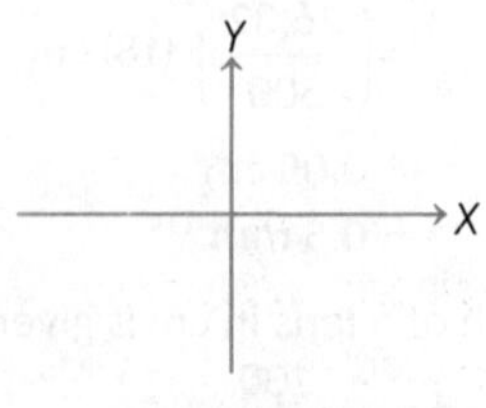

$u = -30$ cm; $f = -10$ cm

$\therefore \quad \frac{1}{v}+\frac{1}{u}=\frac{1}{f}$

$\Rightarrow \quad \frac{1}{v}-\frac{1}{30}=\frac{1}{-10}$

or $\quad v=-15$ cm

Further, $\quad \frac{1}{v}+\frac{1}{u}=\frac{1}{f}$

Differentiating w.r.t. time, we get

$$\frac{du}{dt}=-\frac{v^2}{u^2}\frac{du}{dt}$$

$$\mathbf{v}_{IM}=-\left(\frac{v}{u}\right)^2 \mathbf{v}_{OM}$$

Given, $\mathbf{v}_I=0$

$$\mathbf{v}_I-\mathbf{v}_M=-\left(\frac{-15}{-30}\right)^2(\mathbf{v}_{OM})$$

$\Rightarrow \quad \mathbf{v}_I-\mathbf{v}_M=-\frac{1}{4}\mathbf{v}_O+\frac{1}{4}\mathbf{v}_M$

Since, $\quad \mathbf{v}_O=15\text{ cm/s }\hat{\mathbf{i}}$

and $\quad \mathbf{v}_I=0$

$\therefore \quad \frac{5}{4}\mathbf{v}_M=\frac{\mathbf{v}_O}{4}$

$\Rightarrow \quad \mathbf{v}_M=\frac{\mathbf{v}_O}{4}=\frac{15\text{ cm/s }\hat{\mathbf{i}}}{5}$

$=3\text{ cm/s }\hat{\mathbf{i}}$

$\Rightarrow \quad |\mathbf{v}_M|=3$

158. Since, the ray is going from rarer to denser medium as shown in the situation accordingly the refracted ray will bend towards the normal.

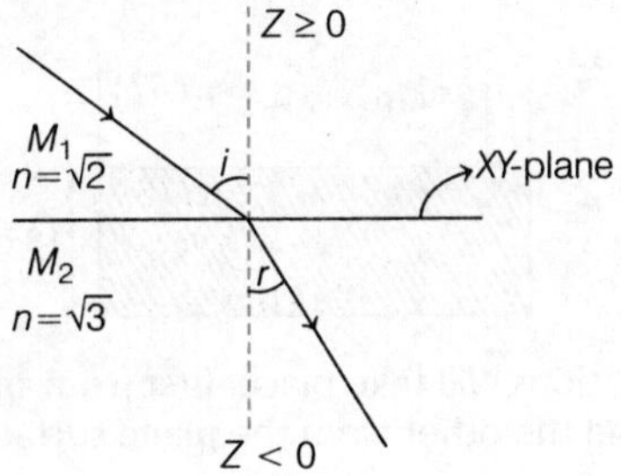

$$i=\cos^{-1}\left(\frac{A_Z}{A}\right)=\cos^{-1}\left[\frac{5}{\sqrt{(4\sqrt{3})^2+(3\sqrt{3})^2+(5)^2}}\right]$$

$\Rightarrow \quad i=\cos^{-1}\left(\frac{5}{10}\right)$

$\Rightarrow \quad i=\cos^{-1}\left(\frac{1}{2}\right)$

$\Rightarrow \quad i=60°$

Now, $\quad n_1 \sin i=n_2 \sin r$

$\Rightarrow \quad \sqrt{2}\sin 60°=\sqrt{3}\sin r$

$$\sqrt{2}\times\frac{\sqrt{3}}{2}=\sqrt{3}\sin r$$

$\Rightarrow \quad \sin r=\frac{1}{2}\times\sqrt{2}=\frac{1}{\sqrt{2}}$

$\Rightarrow \quad r=45°$

$\therefore \quad i-r=(60-45)^\circ=15°$

159. Focal length of convex lens,

$$f=10\text{ cm}$$

Since, image produced by the plane mirror is 5 cm inside the mirror.

Hence, distance image formed by the convex mirror,

$$v=20-5=15\text{ cm}$$

$\therefore$ By lens formula,

$$\frac{1}{v}-\frac{1}{u}=\frac{1}{f}$$

$\Rightarrow \quad \frac{1}{u}=\frac{1}{v}-\frac{1}{f}$

$$=\frac{1}{15}-\frac{1}{10}=-\frac{1}{30}$$

$\Rightarrow \quad u=-30$ cm

Thus, distance of the object from the lens is 30 cm.

160.

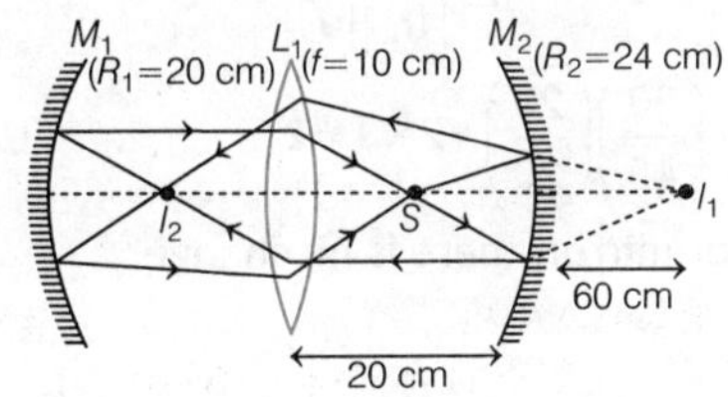

For reflection from M_2

$$\frac{1}{v}+\frac{1}{(-10)}=\frac{1}{(-12)}$$

$$\frac{1}{v}=\frac{1}{10}-\frac{1}{12}$$

$$v=+60\text{ cm (for } I_1)$$

For refraction from L

$$\frac{1}{v}-\frac{1}{u}=\frac{1}{f}$$

$$\frac{1}{v}-\frac{1}{(-80)}=\frac{1}{10}$$

$$v=+\frac{80}{7}\text{ (For } I_2)$$

This image should be at focus of M_1.

$\therefore \quad \frac{20}{2}+\frac{80}{7}=\frac{n}{7}$

$\Rightarrow \quad n=150$

Also, if I_2 is formed at pole of M_1, then $\frac{n}{7}=\frac{80}{7}$

$\Rightarrow \quad n=80$

and further if I_2 is formed at centre of curvature of M_1, then

$$\frac{n}{7}=\frac{80}{7}+20$$

$\therefore \quad n=220$

161. Case I

Reflection from mirror

$$\frac{1}{f}=\frac{1}{v}+\frac{1}{u} \Rightarrow \frac{1}{-10}=\frac{1}{v}+\frac{1}{-15}$$

$$\Rightarrow \quad v=-30$$

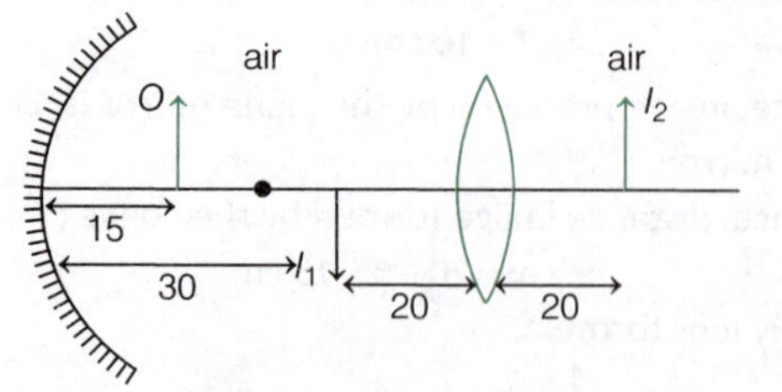

For lens

$$\frac{1}{f}=\frac{1}{v}-\frac{1}{u}$$

$$\Rightarrow \quad \frac{1}{10}=\frac{1}{v}-\frac{1}{-20}$$

$$v=20$$

$$|M_1|=\left|\frac{v_1}{u_1}\right|\left|\frac{v_2}{u_2}\right|$$

$$=\left(\frac{30}{15}\right)\left(\frac{20}{20}\right)=2\times 1=2 \quad \text{(in air)}$$

Case II For mirror, there is no change.

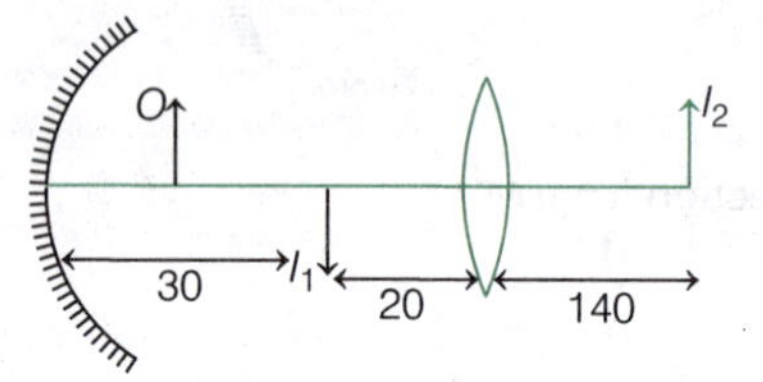

For lens, $\frac{1}{f_{air}}=\left(\frac{3/2}{1}-1\right)\left(\frac{1}{R_1}-\frac{1}{R_2}\right)$

$$\frac{1}{f_{medium}}=\left(\frac{3/2}{7/6}-1\right)\left(\frac{1}{R_1}-\frac{1}{R_2}\right)$$

with $f_{air}=10$ cm

We get $\frac{1}{f_{medium}}=\frac{4}{70}\ \text{cm}^{-1}$

$$\frac{1}{v}-\frac{1}{(-20)}=\frac{4}{70}$$

$$\Rightarrow \quad \frac{1}{v}=\frac{4}{70}-\frac{1}{20}$$

$$\Rightarrow v=140$$

$$|M_2|=\left|\frac{v_1}{u_1}\right|\left|\frac{v_2}{u_2}\right|$$

$$=\left(\frac{30}{15}\right)\left(\frac{140}{20}\right)=14$$

$$\Rightarrow \quad \frac{|M_2|}{|M_1|}=\frac{14}{2}=7$$

162.

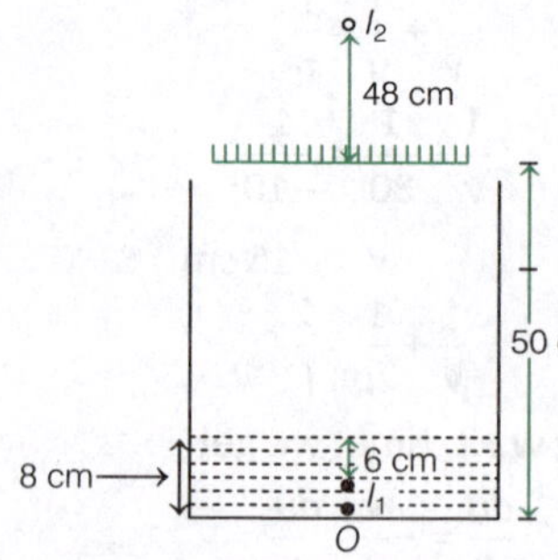

Apparent depth of $O=\frac{d}{\mu}=6$

Distance between O and

$$I_2=48+50=98 \text{ cm}$$

163.

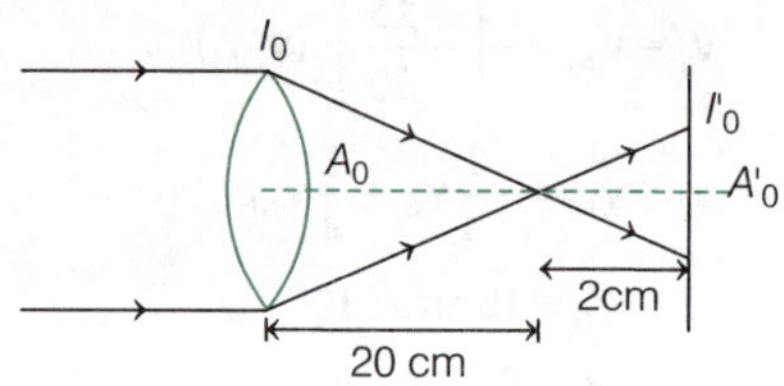

$$\frac{A'_0}{A_0}=\left(\frac{2}{20}\right)^2=\frac{1}{100}$$

$$\Rightarrow \quad A'_0=\frac{A_0}{100}$$

$$\Rightarrow \quad P=I_0A_0=I_0'A_0'$$

$$\Rightarrow \quad I'_0=\frac{I_0A_0}{\frac{A_0}{100}}=100I_0=130\ \text{kW/m}^2$$

164.

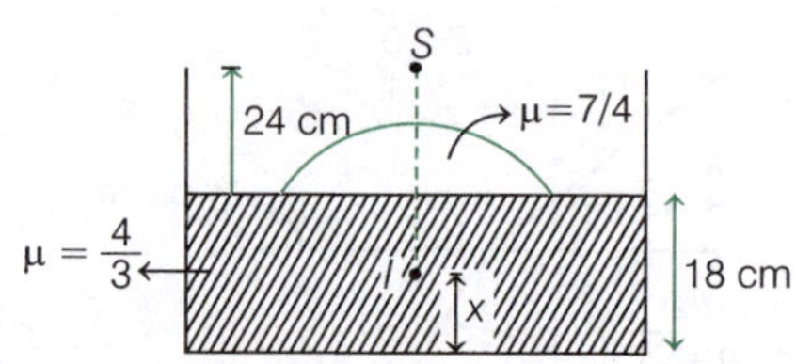

Two refractions will take place, first from spherical surface and the other from the plane surface.

So, applying $\frac{\mu_2}{v}-\frac{\mu_1}{u}=\frac{\mu_2-\mu_1}{R}$ two times with proper sign convention.

Ray of light is travelling downwards. Therefore, downward direction is taken as positive direction.

$$\frac{7/4}{v}-\frac{1.0}{-24}=\frac{7/4-1.0}{+6} \quad \text{...(i)}$$

$$\frac{4/3}{(18-x)}-\frac{7/4}{v}=\frac{4/3-7/4}{\infty} \quad \text{...(ii)}$$

Solving these equations, we get,

$$x=2\ \text{cm}$$

$\therefore$ Answer is 2.

UNIT-10

INTERFERENCE, DIFFRACTION AND POLARIZATION OF LIGHT

Learning Modules

1. Interference
2. Young's Double Slit Experiment (YDSE)
3. Diffraction
4. Polarization of Light

MODULE 1

Interference

Principle of Superposition

Suppose there are two sources of waves S_1 and S_2.

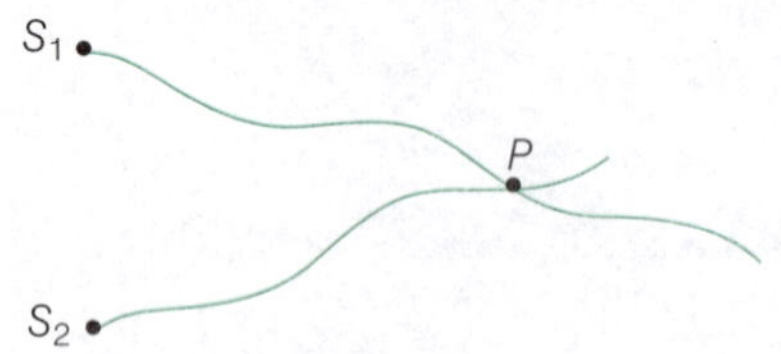

Now, the two waves from S_1 and S_2 meet at some point (say P). Then, according to principle of superposition net displacement at P (from its mean position) at any time is given by

$$\boxed{y = y_1 + y_2}$$

Here, y_1 and y_2 are the displacements of P due to two waves individually.

For example, suppose at 9 AM, displacement of P above its mean position should be 6 mm accordingly to wave-1 and at the same time its displacement should be 2 mm below its mean position accordingly to wave-2, then at 9 AM net displacement of P will be 4 mm above its mean position.

Now, based upon the principle of superposition we have two phenomena in physics, interference and beats. Stationary waves (or standing waves) and Young's double slit experiment (or YDSE) are two examples of interference.

Based on principle of superposition means two or more than two waves meet at one point or several points and at every point net displacement is $y = y_1 + y_2$ or $y = y_1 + y_2 + y_3$ etc.

Resultant Amplitude and Intensity due to Coherent Sources

As we have seen that the two waves from two sources S_1 and S_2 were meeting at point P. Suppose they meet at P in a phase difference $\Delta\phi$ (or ϕ). If this phase difference remains constant with time, then sources are called coherent, otherwise incoherent.

For sources to be coherent, the frequencies (f, ω or T) of the two sources must be same. This can be understood by the following example.

Suppose the phase difference is 0°. It means they are in same phase. Both reaches their extremes ($+A$ or $-A$) simultaneously. They cross their mean positions (in the same direction) simultaneously. Now, if we want their phase difference to remain constant or we want that the above situation is maintained all the time, then obviously their time periods (or frequencies) must be same.

Resultant Amplitude

1. Consider the superposition of two sinusoidal waves of same frequency (means sources are coherent) at some point. Let us assume that the two waves are travelling in the same direction with same velocity. The equation of the two waves reaching at a point can be written as

$$y_1 = A_1 \sin(kx - \omega t)$$

and $$y_2 = A_2 \sin(kx - \omega t + \phi)$$

The resultant displacement of the point where the waves meet, is

$$y = y_1 + y_2$$
$$= A_1 \sin(kx - \omega t) + A_2 \sin(kx - \omega t + \phi)$$
$$= A_1 \sin(kx - \omega t) + A_2 \sin(kx - \omega t)\cos\phi + A_2 \cos(kx - \omega t)\sin\phi$$
$$= (A_1 + A_2 \cos\phi)\sin(kx - \omega t) + A_2 \sin\phi \cos(kx - \omega t)$$
$$= A\cos\theta \sin(kx - \omega t) + A\sin\theta\cos(kx - \omega t)$$

or $$y = A\sin(kx - \omega t + \theta)$$

Here, $$A_1 + A_2\cos\phi = A\cos\theta$$

and $$A_2 \sin\phi = A\sin\theta$$

or $$A^2 = (A_1 + A_2\cos\phi)^2 + (A_2\sin\phi)^2$$

or $$\boxed{A = \sqrt{A_1^2 + A_2^2 + 2A_1A_2\cos\phi}} \quad \ldots\text{(i)}$$

and $$\tan\theta = \frac{A\sin\theta}{A\cos\theta} = \frac{A_2\sin\phi}{A_1 + A_2\cos\phi}$$

2. The above result can be obtained by graphical method also. Assume a vector $\mathbf{A}_1$ of length A_1 to represent the amplitude of first wave.

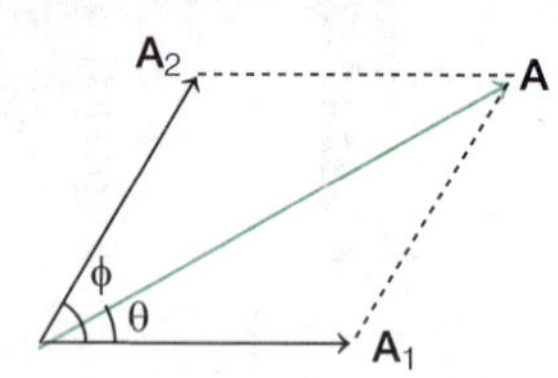

Another vector $\mathbf{A}_2$ of length A_2, making an angle ϕ with $\mathbf{A}_1$ represent the amplitude of second wave. The resultant of $\mathbf{A}_1$ and $\mathbf{A}_2$ represents the amplitude of resulting function y. The angle θ represents the phase difference between the resulting function and the first wave.

Resultant Intensity

Previously we have read that intensity of a wave is given by

$$I = \frac{1}{2}\rho\omega^2 A^2 v \quad \text{or} \quad I \propto A^2$$

So, if ρ, ω and v are same for the both interfering waves then Eq. (i) can also be written as

$$I = I_1 + I_2 + 2\sqrt{I_1 I_2}\cos\phi \quad ...(ii)$$

Here, proportionality constant (in $I \propto A^2$) cancels out on right hand side and left hand side.

Note *(i) Eqs. (i) and (ii) are two equations for finding resultant amplitude and resultant intensity at some point due to two coherent sources.*

(ii) In the above equations ϕ is the constant phase difference at that point as the sources are coherent. Value of this constant phase difference will be different at different points.

(iii) The special case of above two equations is, when the individual amplitudes (or intensities) are equal.

or $A_1 = A_2 = A_0$ *(say)*

$\therefore$ $I_1 = I_2 = I_0$ *(say)*

In this case, Eqs. (i) and (ii) become

$$A = 2A_0 \cos\frac{\phi}{2} \quad ...(iii)$$

and

$$I = 4I_0 \cos^2\frac{\phi}{2} \quad ...(iv)$$

(iv) From Eqs. (i) to (iv), we can see that, for given values of A_1, A_2, I_1 and I_2 the resultant amplitude and the resultant intensity are the functions of only ϕ.

(v) If three or more than three waves (due to coherent sources) meet at some point then there is no direct formula for finding resultant amplitude or resultant intensity. In this case, first of all we will find resultant amplitude by vector method (either by using polygon law of vector addition or component method) and then by the relation $I \propto A^2$, we can also determine the resultant intensity.

For example, if resultant amplitude comes out to be $\sqrt{2}$ times then resultant intensity will become two times.

Interference

For interference phenomena to take place, sources must be coherent. So, phase difference at some point should remain constant. Value of this constant phase difference will be different at different points. And since the sources are coherent, therefore following four equations can be applied for finding resultant amplitude and intensity (in case of two sources)

$$A = \sqrt{A_1^2 + A_2^2 + 2A_1A_2\cos\phi} \quad ...(i)$$

$$I = I_1 + I_2 + 2\sqrt{I_1 I_2}\cos\phi \quad ...(ii)$$

$$A = 2A_0\cos\frac{\phi}{2} \quad (\text{if } A_1 = A_2 = A_0) \quad ...(iii)$$

$$I = 4I_0\cos^2\frac{\phi}{2} \quad (\text{if } I_1 = I_2 = I_0) \quad ...(iv)$$

For given values of A_1, A_2, I_1 and I_2 the resultant amplitude and resultant intensity are the functions of only ϕ.

Now, suppose S_1 and S_2 are two coherent sources, then we can see that the two waves are meeting at several points (P_1, P_2, P_3 ... etc). At different points path difference Δx will be different and therefore phase difference $\Delta\phi$ or ϕ will also be different. Because the phase difference depends on the path difference ($\Delta\phi$ or $\phi = \frac{2\pi}{\lambda}\cdot\Delta x$).

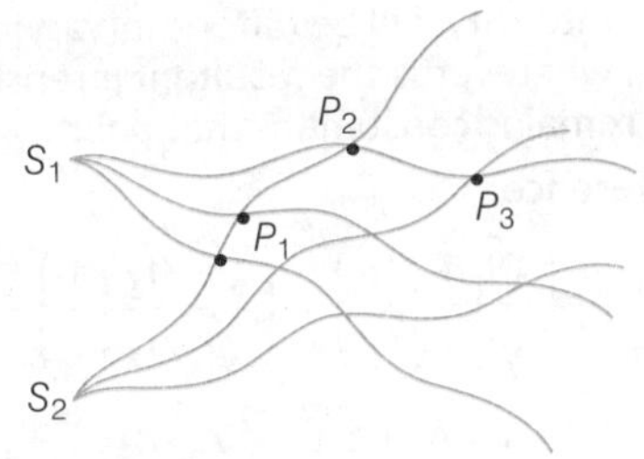

And since phase difference at different points is different, therefore from the above four equations we can see that resultant amplitude and intensity will also be different. But whatever is the intensity at some point, it will remain constant at that point because the sources are coherent and the phase difference is constant at that point.

Constructive Interference

These are the points where resultant amplitude or intensity is maximum or

$A_{max} = A_1 + A_2$ [from Eq. (i)]

or $A_{max} = \pm 2A_0$ [from Eq. (iii)]

and $I_{max} = (\sqrt{I_1} + \sqrt{I_2})^2$ [from Eq. (ii)]

or $I_{max} = 4I_0$ [from Eq. (iv)]

These are the points where, $\cos\phi = +1$ [from Eqs. (i) or (ii)]

or $\phi = 0, 2\pi, 4\pi, ..., 2n\pi$ (where $n = 0, 1, 2$)

$\therefore$ $\Delta x = 0, \lambda, 2\lambda, ..., n\lambda$ $\left[\text{as } \Delta x = \phi\left(\frac{\lambda}{2\pi}\right)\right]$

Destructive Interference

These are the points where resultant amplitude or intensity is minimum or

$A_{min} = A_1 \sim A_2$ [from Eq. (i)]

or $A_{min} = 0$ [from Eq. (iii)]

and $I_{min} = (\sqrt{I_1} - \sqrt{I_2})^2$ [from Eq. (ii)]

or $I_{min} = 0$ [from Eq. (iv)]

These are the points where, $\cos\phi = -1$ [from Eqs. (i) or (ii)]

or $\phi = \pi, 3\pi .. (2n-1)\pi$ (where $n = 1, 2...$)

$\therefore$ $\Delta x = \frac{\lambda}{2}, \frac{3\lambda}{2} .. (2n-1)\frac{\lambda}{2}$ $\left[\text{as } \Delta x = \phi\left(\frac{\lambda}{2\pi}\right)\right]$

Important POINTS

- In amplitude, it hardly matters whether it is $+2A_0$ or $-2A_0$. This is the reason we have taken, $A_{max} = \pm 2A_0$
- In interference, two or more than two waves from coherent sources meet at several points. At different points Δx, $\Delta\phi$ or ϕ, resultant amplitude and therefore resultant intensity will be different (varying from I_{max} to I_{min}). But, whatever is the resultant intensity at some point, it remains constant at that point.
- In interference,

$$\frac{I_{max}}{I_{min}} = \left(\frac{\sqrt{I_1}+\sqrt{I_2}}{\sqrt{I_1}-\sqrt{I_2}}\right)^2 = \left(\frac{\sqrt{I_1/I_2}+1}{\sqrt{I_1/I_2}-1}\right)^2$$

$$= \left(\frac{A_1/A_2+1}{A_1/A_2-1}\right)^2 = \left(\frac{A_1+A_2}{A_1-A_2}\right)^2 = \left(\frac{A_{max}}{A_{min}}\right)^2$$

- **Coherent sources** In order to produce a stable interference pattern the individual waves must maintain a **constant phase** relationship with one another, i.e. the two interfering sources must emit waves having a constant phase difference between them.

  If the phase difference between two sources does not remain constant, then the places of maxima and minima shift. In case of mechanical waves it is possible to keep a constant phase relationship between two different sources. But in case of light two different light sources can't be coherent This is because of the way light is emitted. In ordinary light sources, atoms gain excess energy by thermal agitation or by impact with accelerated electrons. An atom that is 'excited' in such a way begins to radiate energy and continues until it has lost all the energy it can, typically in a time of the order of 10^{-8} s.

  The many atoms in a source ordinarily radiate in an unsynchronized and random phase relationship, and the light that is emitted from two such sources has no definite phase relationship. Hence, to obtain a stable interference in light a single source is split into two coherent sources.

  Following are shown some of the methods by which we can split a single light source into two.

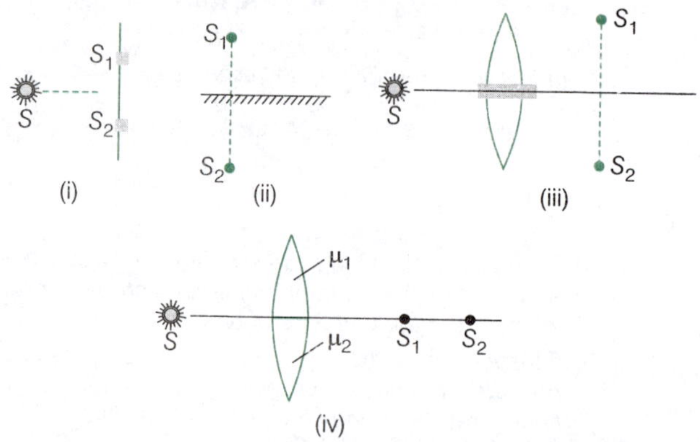

Example 1 In interference, two individual amplitudes are A_0 each and the intensity is I_0 each. Find resultant amplitude and intensity at a point, where:

(a) phase difference between two waves is 60°

(b) path difference between two waves is $\dfrac{\lambda}{3}$.

Sol. (a) Substituting $\phi = 60°$ in the equations,

$$A = 2A_0 \cos\frac{\phi}{2} \quad \text{and} \quad I = 4I_0 \cos^2\frac{\phi}{2}$$

We get, $A = \sqrt{3}A_0$ and $I = 3I_0$ **Ans.**

(b) Given, $\Delta x = \dfrac{\lambda}{3}$

$$\therefore \quad \phi \text{ or } \Delta\phi = \left(\frac{2\pi}{\lambda}\right)\cdot\Delta x$$

$$= \left(\frac{2\pi}{\lambda}\right)\left(\frac{\lambda}{3}\right) = \frac{2\pi}{3} \text{ or } 120°$$

Now, substituting $\phi = 120°$ in the above two equations, we get

$A = A_0$ and $I = I_0$ **Ans.**

Example 2 Three waves from three coherent sources meet at some point. Resultant amplitude of each is A_0. Intensity corresponding to A_0 is I_0. Phase difference between first wave and the second wave is 60°. Path difference between first wave and the third wave is $\dfrac{\lambda}{3}$. The first wave lags behind in phase angle from second and the third wave. Find resultant intensity at this point.

Sol. Here, the sources are three. So, we don't have any direct formula for finding the resultant intensity. First we will find the resultant amplitude by vector method and then, by using the relation $I \propto A^2$, we can also find the resulting intensity.

Further, a path difference of $\dfrac{\lambda}{3}$ is equivalent to a phase difference of 120° ($\Delta\phi$ or $\phi = \dfrac{2\pi}{\lambda}\cdot\Delta x$).

Hence, the phase difference between first and second is 60° and between first and third is 120°. So, vector diagram for amplitudes is as shown below.

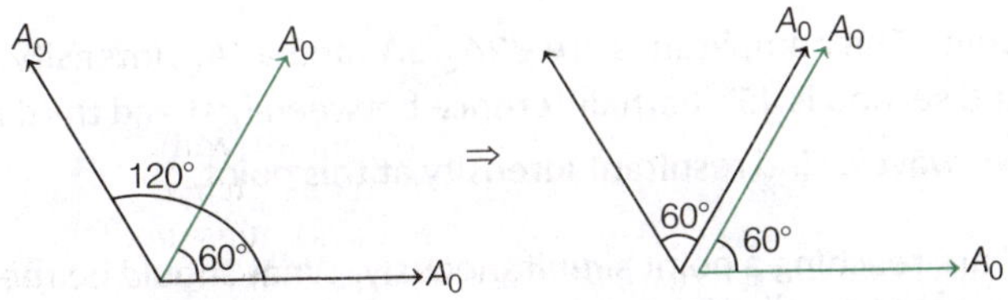

Now, resultant of first and third acting at 120° is also A_0 (as $A = 2A_0 \cos\frac{\phi}{2}$ and $\phi = 120°$) and since the first and third are equal, so this resultant A_0 passes through the bisector line of these two or in the direction of second amplitude vector. Therefore, the resultant amplitude is

$$A = A_0 + A_0 = 2A_0$$

and the resultant intensity is

$$I = 4I_0 \qquad (\text{as } I \propto A^2)$$ **Ans.**

Example 3 Two waves of equal frequencies have their amplitudes in the ratio of 3 : 5. They are superimposed on each other. Calculate the ratio of maximum and minimum intensities of the resultant wave.

Sol. Given, $\frac{A_1}{A_2} = \frac{3}{5}$

$$\frac{I_{max}}{I_{min}} = \left(\frac{A_1 + A_2}{A_1 - A_2}\right)^2 = \left(\frac{3+5}{3-5}\right)^2$$

$$= \frac{16}{1}$$ **Ans.**

Example 4 In interference, $\frac{I_{max}}{I_{min}} = \alpha$, find

(a) $\frac{A_{max}}{A_{min}}$ (b) $\frac{A_1}{A_2}$ (c) $\frac{I_1}{I_2}$

Sol. (a) $\frac{A_{max}}{A_{min}} = \sqrt{\frac{I_{max}}{I_{min}}} = \sqrt{\alpha}$ **Ans.**

(b) $\frac{A_{max}}{A_{min}} = \sqrt{\alpha} = \frac{A_1 + A_2}{A_1 - A_2}$

$$= \frac{A_1/A_2 + 1}{A_1/A_2 - 1}$$

Solving this equation, we get

$$\frac{A_1}{A_2} = \frac{\sqrt{\alpha}+1}{\sqrt{\alpha}-1}$$ **Ans.**

(c) $\frac{I_1}{I_2} = \left(\frac{A_1}{A_2}\right)^2 = \left(\frac{\sqrt{\alpha}+1}{\sqrt{\alpha}-1}\right)^2$ **Ans.**

MODULE 1 Exercise

Single Correct Option

1. Three coherent waves having amplitudes 12 mm, 6 mm and 4 mm arrive at a given point with successive phase difference of $\pi/2$. Then, the amplitude of the resultant wave is

(a) 7 mm (b) 10 mm
(c) 5 mm (d) 4.8 mm

2. The ratio of maximum to minimum intensity due to superposition of two waves is $\frac{49}{9}$. Then, the ratio of the intensity of component waves is

(a) $\frac{25}{4}$ (b) $\frac{5}{4}$
(c) $\frac{25}{6}$ (d) $\frac{7}{5}$

3. Two coherent sources of intensity ratio β^2 interfere. Then, the value of $(I_{max} - I_{min})/(I_{max} + I_{min})$ is

(a) $\frac{1+\beta}{\sqrt{\beta}}$ (b) $\sqrt{\frac{1+\beta}{\beta}}$
(c) $\frac{1+\beta}{\beta}$ (d) None of these

4. Two coherent sources of light interfere. The intensity ratio of two sources is 1 : 4. For this interference pattern if the value of $\frac{I_{max} + I_{min}}{I_{max} - I_{min}}$ is equal to $\frac{2\alpha + 1}{\beta + 3}$, then $\frac{\alpha}{\beta}$ will be **(2022, 2021 Main)**

(a) 1.5 (b) 2
(c) 0.5 (d) 1

5. Two beams of light having intensities I and $4I$ interfere to produce a fringe pattern on a screen. The phase difference between the beams is $\pi/2$ at point A and π at point B. Then the difference between resultant intensities at A and B is **(2001 JEE)**

(a) $2I$ (b) $4I$
(c) $5I$ (d) $7I$

Subjective Questions

6. In interference, two individual amplitudes are 5 units and 3 units. Find

(a) $\frac{A_{max}}{A_{min}}$ (b) $\frac{I_{max}}{I_{min}}$

7. Three waves due to three coherent sources meet at one point. Their amplitudes are $\sqrt{2}A_0$, $3A_0$ and $\sqrt{2}A_0$. Intensity corresponding to A_0 is I_0. Phase difference between first and second is 45°. Path difference between first and third is $\frac{\lambda}{4}$. In phase angle, first wave lags behind from the other two waves. Find resultant intensity at this point.

8. Two waves of the same frequency and same amplitude 'a' are reaching a point simultaneously. What should be the phase difference between the waves so that the amplitude of the resultant wave be :
(i) $2a$ (ii) $\sqrt{2}\,a$ (iii) a (iv) zero

9. Two coherent sources A and B of radio waves are 5.00 m apart. Each source emits waves with wavelength 6.00 m. Consider the points along the line between the two sources. At what distances, if any, from A is the interference (a) constructive (b) destructive?

Integer Type Question

10. Two light beams of intensities $4I$ and $9I$ interfere on a screen. The phase difference between these beams on the screen at point A is zero and at point B is π. The difference of resultant intensities, at the point A and B, will be ________ I. **(2022 Main)**

Answers

1. (b) 2. (a) 3. (d) 4. (b) 5. (b) 6. (a) 4 : 1 (b) 16 : 1 7. 25 I_0
8. (i) 0° (ii) 90° (iii) 120° (iv) 180° 9. (a) 2.50 m (b) 1.0 m, 4.0 m 10. (24)

See hints on pages 241-242.

MODULE 2

Young's Double Slit Experiment (YDSE)

(i) YDSE is an experiment (or an example) of interference in light.

(ii) For interference, two coherent sources are required and in light two different light sources are never coherent. Therefore, a single source S is split into two sources as shown below.

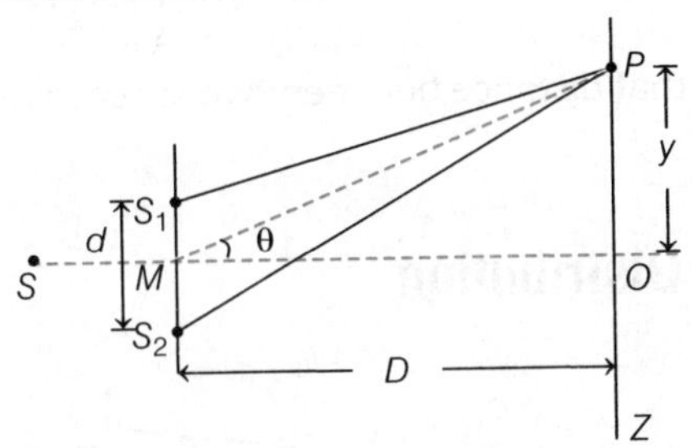

(iii) Z is a two-dimensional screen and OP is the centre line of this screen. On different points of this screen, two rays of light (from two coherent sources S_1 and S_2) will interfere. At different points of the screen path difference (and therefore) phase difference will be different. Therefore, resultant intensity will be different. But whatever is the resultant intensity at any point, it remains constant at that point.

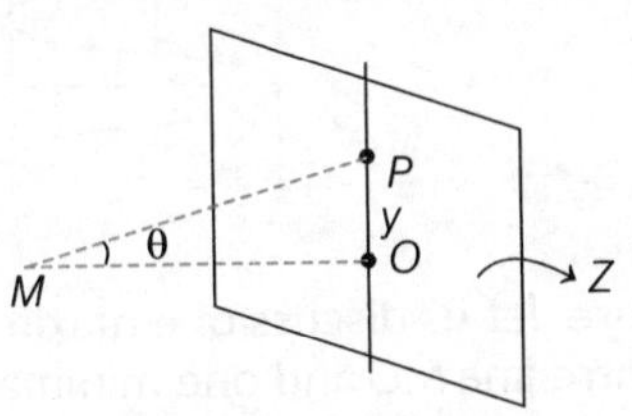

(iv) Mathematically, we will find the resultant intensity at any point on the centre line OP of the screen. So, it will have only one variable y (or θ).

(v) The order of λ, d and D is normally

$$\lambda << d << D$$

(vi) Since $d << D$, we can assume that intensities at P due to independent sources S_1 and S_2 are almost equal, or

$$I_1 \approx I_2 = I_0 \quad \text{(say)}$$

Therefore, for resultant intensity we can apply

$$\boxed{I = 4I_0 \cos^2 \frac{\phi}{2}} \quad \ldots\text{(i)}$$

(vii) In YDSE, our main objective is to find resultant intensity at a general point P on the centre line of the screen. Point P can be generalised in the following four ways.

(a) Directly phase difference ϕ (between two rays interfering at P) can be given. This is the simplest one. As, we can directly apply

$$I = 4I_0 \cos^2 \frac{\phi}{2}$$

for the resultant intensity.

(b) Path difference Δx (between two interfering rays) can be given at P. In this case, first we will convert Δx into phase difference ϕ by the relation,

$$\phi = \frac{2\pi}{\lambda} \Delta x$$

and then, we will apply

$$I = 4I_0 \cos^2 \frac{\phi}{2}$$

(c) Distance OP or y-coordinate of point P can be given.

(d) Angular position θ of point P will be given.

Note *In last two cases, first we will find the path difference Δx in terms of y and θ and then we will find the resultant intensity.*

Path Difference in Terms of y and θ

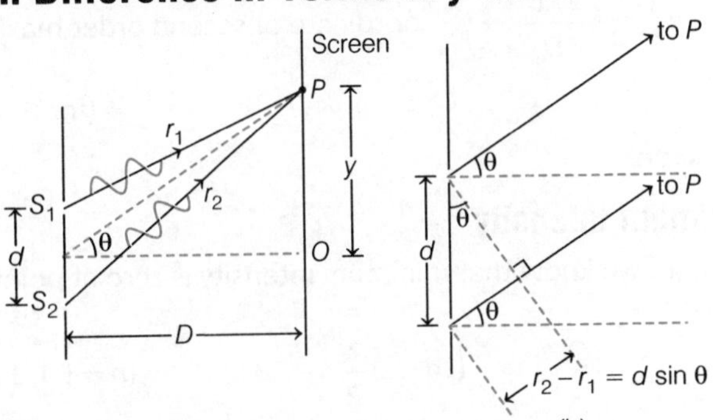

(a) (b)

Fig. (a) To reach P, the light waves from S_1 and S_2 must travel different distances. (b) The path difference between the two rays is $d \sin \theta$.

Figure shows the light waves from S_1 and S_2 meeting at an arbitrary point P on the screen. Since, $D >> d$, the two light rays are approximately parallel, with a path difference,

$$\Delta x = S_2P - S_1P$$

$$\boxed{\Delta x \approx d \sin\theta} \quad \ldots\text{(ii)}$$

This is basically the expression of Δx in terms of θ.

If θ is small, then

$$\sin\theta \approx \tan\theta = \frac{y}{D}$$

Substituting in Eq. (ii), we get

$$\boxed{\Delta x = \frac{yd}{D}} \quad \text{...(iii)}$$

This is the expression of path difference Δx in terms of y.

Maximum and Minimum Intensity

Maximum Intensity

In Eq. (i), we know that maximum intensity is $4I_0$ at points where

$$\Delta x = n\lambda \qquad (n = 0, \pm 1, \pm 2 \ldots)$$

or $$d \sin\theta = n\lambda$$

or $$\frac{yd}{D} = n\lambda$$

or $$\boxed{y = \frac{n\lambda D}{d} = Y_n} \quad \ldots\text{(iv)}$$

Here, Y_n may be called as y-coordinate (with respect to point O) of nth order maxima, where

$$n = 0, \pm 1, \pm 2 \ldots$$

For example,

$Y_0 = 0 \rightarrow y$-coordinate of zero order maxima (for $n = 0$)

Y_1 or $Y_1' = \pm \frac{\lambda D}{d} \rightarrow y$ - coordinate of first order maxima

(for $n = \pm 1$)

Y_2 or $Y_2' = \pm \frac{2\lambda D}{D} \rightarrow y$ - coordinate of second order maxima

(for $n = \pm 2$)

and so on.

Minimum Intensity

In Eq. (i), we know that minimum intensity is zero at points where

$$\Delta x = (2n - 1)\frac{\lambda}{2} \qquad (n = \pm 1, \pm 2 \ldots)$$

or $$d \sin\theta = (2n - 1)\frac{\lambda}{2}$$

or $$\frac{yd}{D} = (2n - 1)\frac{\lambda}{2}$$

or $$\boxed{y = \frac{(2n - 1)\lambda D}{2d} = y_n} \quad \ldots\text{(v)}$$

Here, y_n may be called as y-coordinate (with respect to point O) of nth order minima, where $n = \pm 1, \pm 2 \ldots$

For example,

y_1 or $y_1' = \pm \frac{\lambda D}{2d} \rightarrow y$-coordinate of first order minima

(for $n = \pm 1$)

y_2 or $y_2' = \pm \frac{3\lambda D}{2d} \rightarrow y$ - coordinate of second order minima

(for $n = \pm 2$)

and so on.

Fringe Width (ω)

Distance between two adjacent maximas or minimas (or bright/dark fringes) is called the fringe width. Thus,

$\omega = Y_n - Y_{n-1} =$ distance between two adjacent maximas

$$= \frac{n\lambda D}{d} - \frac{(n-1)\lambda D}{d} = \frac{\lambda D}{d}$$

or $$\boxed{\omega = \frac{\lambda D}{d}} \quad \ldots\text{(vi)}$$

We can see that distance between two successive minima is also $\frac{\lambda D}{d}$.

Intensity Distribution

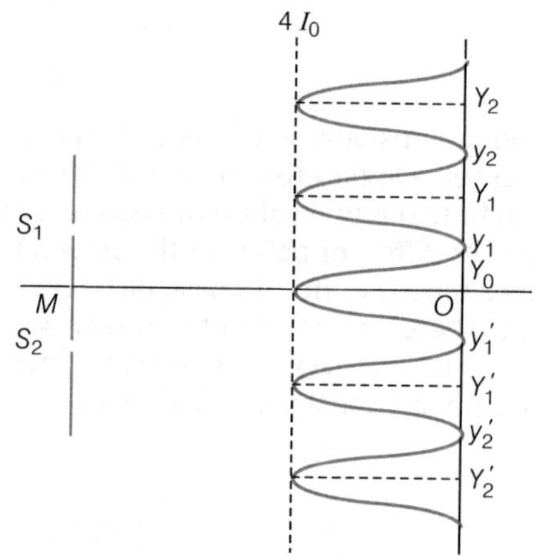

In the shown figure, let us discuss one maxima (say Y_2) on upper side of centre line MO and one minima (say y_2') on lower side.

Y_2 This may be called second order maxima on upper side of line MO. Here, the intensity is $4I_0$. Path difference is

$$\Delta x = S_2P - S_1P = 2\lambda$$

and the phase difference is 4π. Further, y-coordinate of this point is

$$y = \frac{2\lambda D}{d} = 2\omega$$

y_2' This may be called the second order minima on lower side of line MO. Here, the intensity is zero. Path difference is

$$\Delta x = S_1P - S_2P = \frac{3\lambda}{2}$$

and the phase difference is 3π. Further, y-coordinate of this point is

$$y = -\frac{3\lambda D}{2d} = -\frac{3}{2}\omega$$

Intensity Variation within One Fringe

Let us first make the following table corresponding to this point.

Table 1.

Intensity	Amplitude $A \propto \sqrt{I}$	Phase difference (ϕ) $A = 2A_0 \cos\frac{\phi}{2}$	Path difference $\Delta x = \frac{\lambda}{2\pi}\phi$	y-coordinate $\Delta x = \frac{yd}{D}$ $\Rightarrow y = \Delta x\left(\frac{D}{d}\right)$
$4I_0$	$2A_0$	0	0	0
$3I_0$	$\sqrt{3}A_0$	$\frac{\pi}{3}$ or 60°	$\lambda/6$	$\lambda D/6d = \omega/6$
$2I_0$	$\sqrt{2}A_0$	$\frac{\pi}{2}$ or 90°	$\lambda/4$	$\lambda D/4d = \omega/4$
I_0	A_0	$\frac{2\pi}{3}$ or 120°	$\lambda/3$	$\lambda D/3d = \omega/3$
0	0	π or 180°	$\lambda/2$	$\lambda D/2d = \omega/2$

Now, according to above table we can make the following figure.

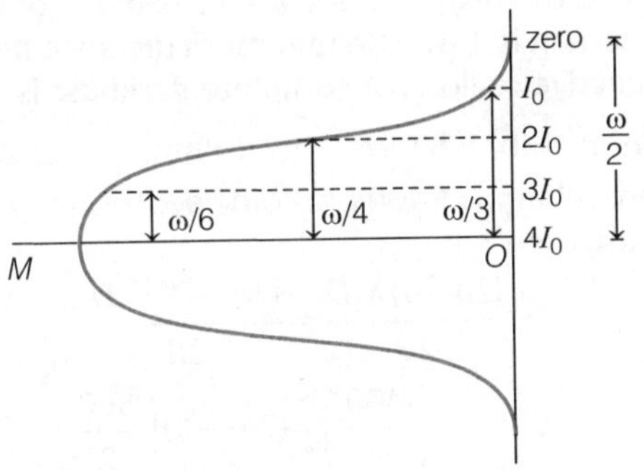

Example 1 In YDSE, the two slits are separated by 0.1 mm and they are 0.5 m from the screen. The wavelength of light used is 5000 Å. Find the distance between 7th maxima and 11th minima on the upper side of screen.

Sol. Given, $d = 0.1 \text{ mm} = 10^{-4}$ m, $D = 0.5$ m and $\lambda = 5000 \text{ Å} = 5.0 \times 10^{-7}$ m

$$\Delta y = y_{11} - Y_7 = \frac{(2 \times 11 - 1)\lambda D}{2d} - \frac{7\lambda D}{d}$$

or $$\Delta y = \frac{7\lambda D}{2d} = \frac{7 \times 5.0 \times 10^{-7} \times 0.5}{2 \times 10^{-4}}$$

$$= 8.75 \times 10^{-3} \text{ m}$$

$$= 8.75 \text{ mm}$$ **Ans.**

Example 2 Maximum intensity in YDSE is I_0. Find the intensity at a point on the screen where

(a) the phase difference between the two interfering beams is $\frac{\pi}{3}$.

(b) the path difference between them is $\frac{\lambda}{4}$.

Sol. (a) We know that

$$I = I_{max} \cos^2\left(\frac{\phi}{2}\right)$$

Here, I_{max} is I_0 (i.e. intensity due to independent sources is $I_0/4$). Therefore, at

$$\phi = \frac{\pi}{3} \text{ or } \frac{\phi}{2} = \frac{\pi}{6}$$

$$I = I_0 \cos^2\left(\frac{\pi}{6}\right) = \frac{3}{4}I_0$$ **Ans.**

(b) Phase difference corresponding to the given path difference $\Delta x = \frac{\lambda}{4}$ is

$$\phi = \left(\frac{2\pi}{\lambda}\right)\left(\frac{\lambda}{4}\right) = \frac{\pi}{2} \text{ or } \frac{\phi}{2} = \frac{\pi}{4}$$

$$\therefore \quad I = I_0 \cos^2\left(\frac{\pi}{4}\right) = \frac{I_0}{2}$$ **Ans.**

Dependence of Fringe Width on λ

Fringe width (ω) is given by

$$\omega = \frac{\lambda D}{d} \text{ or } \boxed{\omega \propto \lambda}$$

Two conclusions can be drawn from this relation.

(i) If YDSE apparatus is immersed in a liquid of refractive index μ, then wavelength of light and hence, fringe width decreases μ times.

(ii) If white light is used in place of a monochromatic light then coloured fringes are obtained on the screen with red fringes of larger size than that of violet, because $\lambda_{red} > \lambda_{violet}$.

But note that centre is still white because path difference at point O is zero for all colours. Hence, all the wavelengths interfere constructively at O. So they produce white light at O. At other points light will interfere destructively for those wavelengths for whom path difference is $\lambda/2, 3\lambda/2,$... etc. and they will interfere constructively for the wavelengths for whom path difference is λ, 2λ,...etc.

This point can be explained as below :

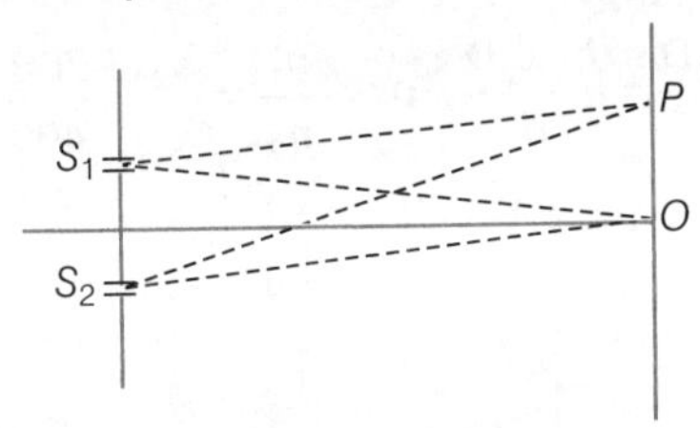

In YDSE let us take a bichromatic light (having two wavelengths). Suppose one wavelength is $\lambda_1 = \lambda$ and the other wavelength is $\lambda_2 = 2\lambda$. At point O,

$S_1O = S_2O \Rightarrow \Delta x = O$ for both wavelengths. Therefore, both wavelengths interfere constructively.

At any other point (say at P) $S_1P \neq S_2P \Rightarrow \Delta x \neq O$ and suppose $\Delta x = \lambda$. Then, this Δx is

$$\Delta x = \lambda_1 \quad \text{and} \quad \Delta x = \frac{\lambda_2}{2}$$

Therefore at P, wavelength λ_1 interferes constructively and λ_2 destructively. Same is the case with white light. At point O, all wavelengths interfere constructively. Therefore, white is produced. At any other point some of the wavelengths interfere constructively, (produce $4I_0$) some destructively (produce zero intensity) and rest intermediately (between zero to $4I_0$ intensity).

Example 3 White light is used to illuminate the two slits in a Young's double slit experiment. The separation between the slits is b and the screen is at a distance d ($>>b$) from the slits. At a point on the screen directly in front of one of the slits, certain wavelengths are missing. Some of these missing wavelengths are **(1984 JEE)**

(a) $\lambda = b^2/d$ (b) $\lambda = 2b^2/d$ (c) $\lambda = b^2/3d$ (d) $\lambda = 2b^2/3d$

Sol. At P (directly in front of S_1) $y = b/2$

$$\therefore \text{ Path difference}, \Delta x = S_2P - S_1P = \frac{y \cdot (b)}{d} = \frac{\left(\frac{b}{2}\right)(b)}{d} = \frac{b^2}{2d}$$

Those wavelengths will be missing at P for which

$$\Delta x = \frac{\lambda_1}{2}, \frac{3\lambda_2}{2}, \frac{5\lambda_3}{2} \ldots$$

$$\therefore \quad \lambda_1 = 2\Delta x = \frac{b^2}{d}$$

$$\lambda_2 = \frac{2\Delta x}{3} = \frac{b^2}{3d}$$

$$\lambda_3 = \frac{2\Delta x}{5} = \frac{b^2}{5d}$$

Therefore, the correct options are (a) and (c).

Example 4 Bichromatic light is used in YDSE having wavelengths $\lambda_1 = 400$ nm and $\lambda_2 = 700$ nm. Find minimum order of bright fringe of λ_1 which overlaps with bright fringe of λ_2.

Sol. Let n_1 bright fringe of λ_1 overlaps with n_2 bright fringe of λ_2. Then,

$$\frac{n_1\lambda_1 D}{d} = \frac{n_2\lambda_2 D}{d} \quad \text{or} \quad \frac{n_1}{n_2} = \frac{\lambda_2}{\lambda_1} = \frac{700}{400} = \frac{7}{4}$$

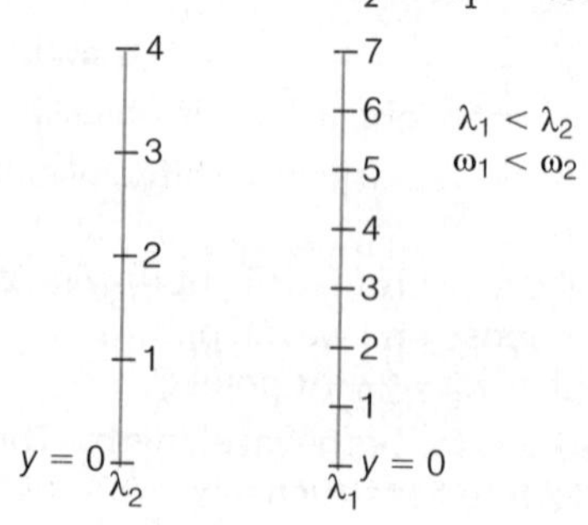

The ratio $\frac{n_1}{n_2} = \frac{7}{4}$ implies that 7th bright fringe of λ_1 will overlap with 4th bright fringe of λ_2.

Similarly, 14th of λ_1 will overlap with 8th of λ_2 and so on.

So, the minimum order of λ_1 which overlaps with λ_2 is 7.

Note *In the above example,*

$$\frac{n_1}{n_2} = \frac{7}{4}, \frac{14}{8}, \frac{21}{12} \text{ etc.}$$

So, to overlap maximas, we can take either of the ratios $\frac{7}{4}$ *or* $\frac{14}{8}$ *or* $\frac{21}{12}$ *etc.*

But in the next example, we will see that if we wish to overlap minimas we cannot take each successive ratio. The reason behind this is that order of fringe n (whether it is order of maxima or minima) should always be an integer.

Example 5 In YDSE, bichromatic light of wavelengths 400 nm and 560 nm are used. The distance between the slits is 0.1 mm and the distance between the plane of the slits and the screen is 1 m. The minimum distance between two successive regions of complete darkness is **(2004 JEE)**

(a) 4 mm (b) 5.6 mm (c) 14 mm (d) 28 mm

Sol. Let nth minima of 400 nm coincides with mth minima of 560 nm, then

$$\frac{(2n-1)\lambda_1 D}{2d} = \frac{(2m-1)\lambda_2 D}{2d}$$

$$\text{or} \quad (2n-1)\left(\frac{400}{2}\right) = (2m-1)\left(\frac{560}{2}\right)$$

$$\frac{2n-1}{2m-1} = \frac{7}{5} \text{ or } \frac{14}{10} \text{ or } \frac{21}{15}$$

If we take the first ratio, then $n = 4$ and $m = 3$.

If we take the second ratio, then $n = 7.5$ and $m = 5.5$.

This is not acceptable. If we take the third ratio, then $n = 11$ and $m = 8$ i.e. 4th minima of 400 nm coincides with 3rd minima of 560 nm.

Location of this minima is

$$y_1 = \frac{(2 \times 4 - 1)(1000)(400 \times 10^{-6})}{2 \times 0.1} = 14 \text{ mm}$$

At the same time 11th minima of 400 nm is coinciding with 8th minima of 560 nm.

Location of this minima is

$$y_2 = \frac{(2 \times 11 - 1)(1000)(400 \times 10^{-6})}{2 \times 0.1} = 42 \text{ mm}$$

$\therefore$ Required distance $= y_2 - y_1 = 28$ mm **Ans.**

$\therefore$ The correct option is (d).

Path Difference Produced by a Slab

Consider two light rays 1 and 2 moving in air parallel to each other. If a slab of refractive index μ and thickness t is inserted between the path of one of the rays, then a path difference

$$\boxed{\Delta x = (\mu - 1)\,t} \qquad \text{...(i)}$$

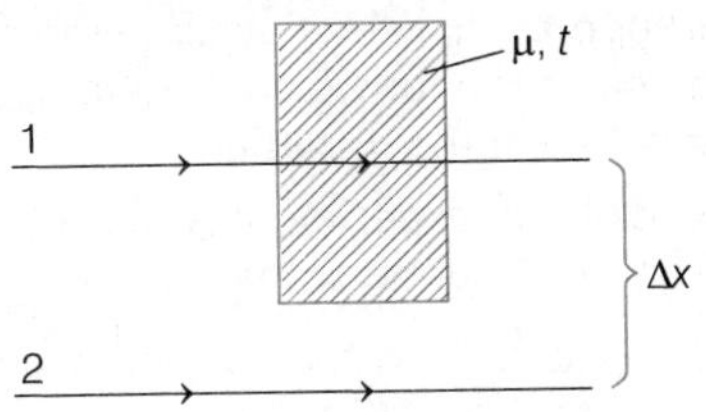

is produced between them. This can be shown as below :

$$\text{Speed of light in air} = c$$

$$\text{Speed of light in medium} = \frac{c}{\mu}$$

Time taken by ray 1 to cross the slab, $t_1 = \dfrac{t}{c/\mu} = \dfrac{\mu t}{c}$

and time taken by ray 2 to cross the same thickness t in air will be,

$$t_2 = \frac{t}{c}$$

as $\qquad t_1 > t_2$

Difference in time $\quad \Delta t = t_1 - t_2 = (\mu - 1)\dfrac{t}{c}$

During this time ray 2 will travel an extra distance, $\Delta x = (\Delta t)\, c = (\mu - 1)\, t$, which is same as Eq. (i).

EXERCISE 1 A slab of thickness t and refractive index μ_2 is kept in a medium of refractive index μ_1 ($<\mu_2$). Prove that, if two rays parallel to each other passes through such a system, with one ray passing through the slab, then the path difference produced between them due to the slab will be:

$$\boxed{\Delta x = \left(\frac{\mu_2}{\mu_1} - 1\right) t}$$

EXERCISE 2

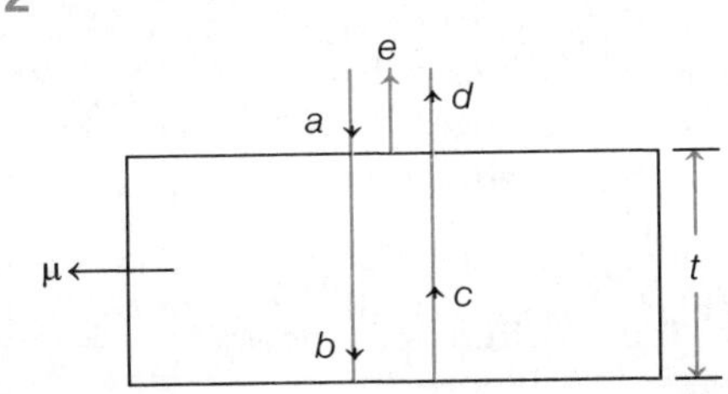

In the figure shown, a is the incident ray, e is reflected from top surface of the slab but d comes after reflecting from bottom surface. Then, prove that path difference between e and d is

$$\boxed{\Delta x = 2\mu t}$$

Note *that all rays a, b, c, d and e are in one line. For better understanding they are shown separately.*

Shifting of Fringes

Suppose a glass slab of thickness t and refractive index μ is inserted onto the path of the ray emanating from source S_1, then the whole fringe pattern shifts upwards by a distance $\dfrac{(\mu - 1)\, tD}{d}$. This can be proved as below :

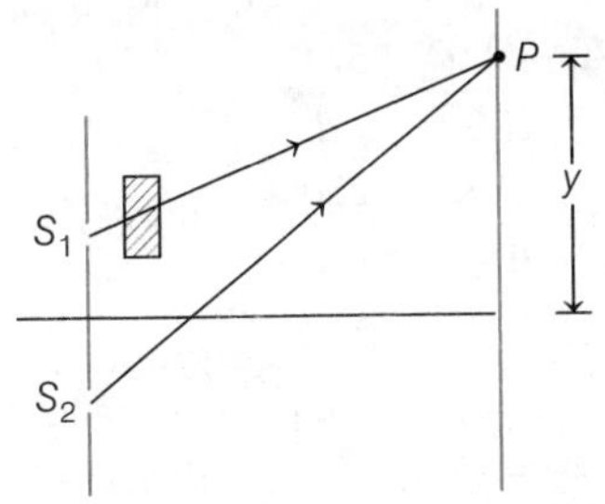

Geometric path difference between S_2P and S_1P is

$$\Delta x_1 = S_2P - S_1P = \frac{yd}{D}$$

Path difference produced by the glass slab,

$$\Delta x_2 = (\mu - 1)\, t$$

Note *Due to the glass slab path of ray 1 gets increased by Δx_2.*

Therefore, net path difference between the two rays is,

$$\Delta x = \Delta x_1 - \Delta x_2 \quad \text{or} \quad \Delta x = \frac{yd}{D} - (\mu - 1)\, t$$

For n^{th} order maxima on upper side,

$$\Delta x = n\lambda \quad \text{or} \quad \frac{yd}{D} - (\mu - 1)\, t = n\lambda$$

$$\therefore \qquad y = \frac{n\lambda D}{d} + \frac{(\mu - 1)\, tD}{d} = Y_n$$

Earlier, without slab it was $\dfrac{n\lambda D}{d}$

$$\therefore \qquad \boxed{\text{Shift} = \frac{(\mu - 1)tD}{d}} \qquad \text{...(ii)}$$

Following three points are important with regard to Eq. (ii).

(a) Shift is independent of n, (the order of the fringe), i.e.
shift of zero order maximum = shift of 7th order maximum
or shift of 5th order maximum = shift of 9th order minimum and so on

(b) Shift is independent of λ, i.e. if white light is used then,
shift of red colour fringe = shift of violet colour fringe

(c) Number of fringes shifted $= \dfrac{\text{shift}}{\text{fringe width}}$

$$= \frac{(\mu - 1)\, t D/d}{\lambda D/d} = \frac{(\mu - 1)t}{\lambda}$$

These numbers are inversely proportional to λ. This is because shift is same for all colours but fringe width of the colour having smaller value of λ is small, so more number of fringes will shift for this colour.

Example 6 In YDSE, find the thickness of a glass slab ($\mu = 1.5$) which should be placed in front of the upper slit S_1 so that the central maximum now lies at a point where 5th bright fringe was lying earlier (before inserting the slab). Wavelength of light used is 5000 Å.

Sol. According to the question,

$$\text{Shift} = 5 \text{ (fringe width)}$$

$$\therefore \quad \frac{(\mu - 1)\,tD}{d} = \frac{5\lambda D}{d}$$

$$\therefore \quad t = \frac{5\lambda}{\mu - 1} = \frac{25000}{1.5 - 1} = 50000 \text{ Å} \qquad \textbf{Ans.}$$

Example 7 Interference fringes are produced by a double slit arrangement and a piece of plane parallel glass of refractive index 1.5 is placed in the path of one of the interfering beam. If the fringes are displaced through 30 fringe widths for light of wavelength 6×10^{-5} cm, find the thickness of the plate.

Sol. Path difference due to the glass slab,

$$\Delta x = (\mu - 1)t$$

Thirty fringes are displaced due to the slab. Hence,

$$\Delta x = 30\lambda$$

$$\Rightarrow \quad (\mu - 1)t = 30\lambda$$

$$\therefore \quad t = \frac{30\lambda}{\mu - 1} = \frac{30 \times 6 \times 10^{-5}}{1.5 - 1}$$

$$= 3.6 \times 10^{-3} \text{ cm} \qquad \textbf{Ans.}$$

INTRODUCTORY Exercise

1. Explain why two flashlights held close together do not produce an interference pattern on a distant screen?
2. Why it is easier to perform interference experiments with a laser light than with an ordinary light source?
3. In YDSE, $D = 1.2$ m and $d = 0.25$ cm, the slits are illuminated with coherent 600 nm light. Calculate the distance y above the central maximum for which the average intensity on the screen is 75% of the maximum.
4. Slit 1 of a double slit experiment is wider than slit 2, so that the light from slit 1 has an amplitude three times that of the light from slit 2. Show that equation $I = I_{max} \cos^2 \frac{\phi}{2}$ is replaced by the equation,
$$I = \left(\frac{I_{max}}{4}\right)\left(1 + 3\cos^2 \frac{\phi}{2}\right)$$
5. In a two-slit interference pattern, the maximum intensity is I_0.
   (a) At a point in the pattern where the phase difference between the waves from the two slits is 60°, what is the intensity?
   (b) What is the path difference for 480 nm light from the two slits at a point where the phase angle is 60°?

Answers

1. Because they are incoherent
2. Because they are highly coherent
3. 48.0 μm 5. (a) 0.75 I_0 (b) 80 nm

See hints on page 242.

Important POINTS

1. In YDSE, if one slit is closed then we will not get interference on screen and intensity at every point is almost uniform ($= I_0$) and this intensity is due to only one slit.
2. In YDSE, if both sources are incoherent, then again we will not get interference and intensity at every point is again uniform ($= I_1 + I_2$ or $2I_0$).
3. In YDSE, if width of one slit is slightly increased then I_{max} and I_{min} both will increase. This is because intensity due to the slit of increased width will increase or
$$I_1 = I_0 \text{ but } I_2 = nI_0 \qquad \text{(where } n > 1)$$
$$\therefore \quad I_{min} = (\sqrt{I_1} - \sqrt{I_2})^2 > 0$$
$$\text{and} \quad I_{max} = (\sqrt{I_1} + \sqrt{I_2})^2 > 4I_0$$
4. **Shape of fringes on complete screen** Until now, we have discussed the fringe pattern on the centre line of the screen. On this centre line maximas (like Y_0, Y_1, Y_2 etc.) or minimas (like y_1, y_2 etc.) are just points.

   But on the whole screen fringes make a curve and this curve is a locus of points where path difference from two slits is a constant. Or
$$\Delta x = S_1P - S_2P = C \qquad \ldots\text{(i)}$$
   $C = 0$, gives Y_0 fringe. Similarly, $C = \pm\lambda$ gives Y_1 or Y_1' fringe etc. Now on the centre line, Δx was a function of only one variable coordinate $y\left(\Delta x = \frac{yd}{D}\right)$. But on the whole screen it will become a function of two variable coordinates (say y and z). Therefore, Eq. (i) becomes
$$\Delta x = f(y, z) = C$$
   After proper calculations, we can show that this comes out to be a family of curves of hyperbolas. Thus, on the complete screen, fringes are of the shape of hyperbolas.

   For $C = 0$, this hyperbola converts into a straight line.

   Hence, only Y_0 fringe is a straight line. The fringe pattern is as shown in figure.

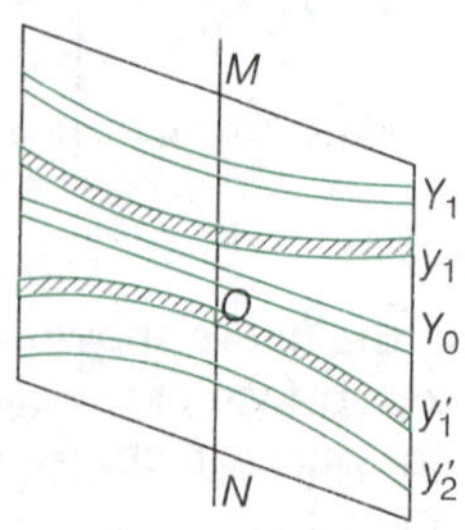

   MN is the centre line of screen,

   on Y_0 fringe, $\Delta x = S_1P - S_2P = 0$

   on Y_1 fringe, $\Delta x = S_2P - S_1P = \lambda$

   on Y_1' fringe, $\Delta x = S_1P - S_2P = \lambda$

   and so on

Typed Problems

Based on YDSE

Note *Unless mentioned in the question consider two sources S_1 and S_2 as coherent.*

Type 1. *Based on interference by thin films.*

Concept

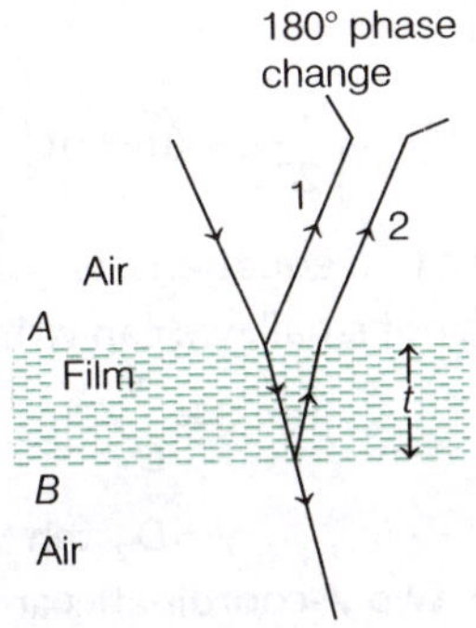

Consider a film of uniform thickness t and index of refraction μ, as shown in figure. Let us assume that the light rays travelling in air are nearly normal to the two surfaces of the film. To determine whether the reflected rays interfere constructively or destructively, we first note the following facts.

(i) The wavelength of light in a medium whose refractive index is μ, is

$$\lambda_\mu = \frac{\lambda}{\mu}$$

where, λ is the wavelength of light in vacuum (or air).

(ii) If a wave is reflected from a denser medium, it undergoes a phase change of 180°. Let us apply these rules to the film shown in figure. The path difference between the two rays 1 and 2 is 2t while the phase difference between them is 180°. Hence, condition of **constructive** interference will be

$$2t = (2n-1)\frac{\lambda_\mu}{2} \qquad (n = 1, 2, 3, \ldots)$$

or
$$2\,\mu t = \left(n - \frac{1}{2}\right)\lambda \qquad \left(\text{as } \lambda_\mu = \frac{\lambda}{\mu}\right)$$

Similarly, condition of **destructive** interference will be

$$2\,\mu t = n\lambda \qquad (n = 0, 1, 2, \ldots)$$

Note *Where there is a phase difference of π between two interfering rays, conditions (of path difference) of maximas and minimas are interchanged.*

Ex. 1 Calculate the minimum thickness of a soap bubble film ($\mu = 1.33$) that results in constructive interference in the reflected light if the film is illuminated with light whose wavelength in free space is $\lambda = 600$ nm.

Sol. For constructive interference in case of soap film,

$$2\mu t = \left(n - \frac{1}{2}\right)\lambda \qquad (n = 1, 2, 3, \ldots)$$

For minimum thickness t,

$$n = 1$$

or
$$2\mu t = \frac{\lambda}{2} \quad \text{or} \quad t = \frac{\lambda}{4\mu} = \frac{600}{4 \times 1.33}$$

$$= 112.78 \text{ nm}$$ **Ans.**

Ex. 2 In solar cells, a silicon solar cell ($\mu = 3.5$) is coated with a thin film of silicon monoxide SiO ($\mu = 1.45$) to minimize reflective losses from the surface. Determine the minimum thickness of SiO that produces the least reflection of a wavelength of 550 nm. Assume approximately normal incidence.

Sol. The reflected light is a minimum when rays 1 and 2 (shown in figure) meet the condition of destructive interference.

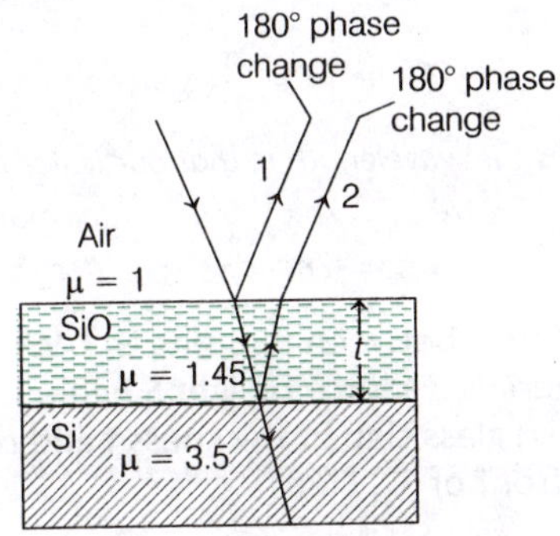

Note *Both rays undergo a 180° phase change upon reflection from denser media. The net change in phase due to reflection is therefore zero, and the condition for a reflection minimum requires a path difference of $\lambda_\mu/2$. Hence,*

$$2t = \frac{\lambda}{2\mu} \quad \text{or} \quad t = \frac{\lambda}{4\mu} = \frac{550}{4\,(1.45)}$$

$$= 94.8 \text{ nm}$$ **Ans.**

Type 2. *Based on conditions of maxima or minima.*

Concept

(i) In the problems of YDSE, our first task is to find the path difference. Let us take a typical case. In the figure shown, path of ray 1 is more than path of ray 2 by a distance,

$$\Delta x_1 = d \sin\alpha$$

and
$$\Delta x_2 = (\mu_1 - 1)\,t_1$$

and path of ray 2 is greater than path of ray 1 by a distance,

$$\Delta x_3 = \frac{yd}{D} \quad \text{and} \quad \Delta x_4 = (\mu_2 - 1)\,t_2$$

Therefore, net path difference is

$$\Delta x_{net} = (\Delta x_1 + \Delta x_2) \sim (\Delta x_3 + \Delta x_4)$$

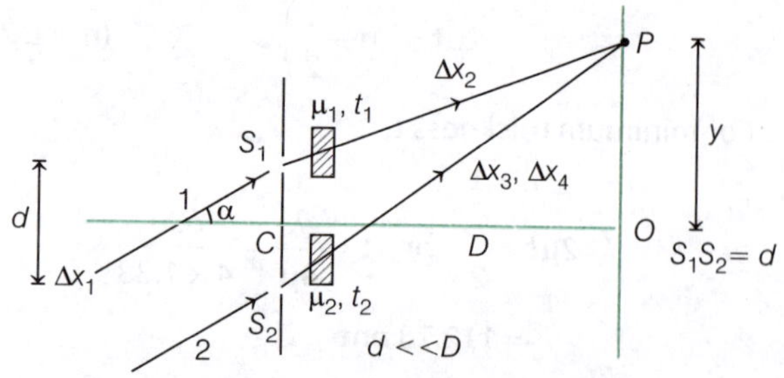

(ii) Once the path difference is known, put

$$\Delta x_{net} = n\lambda \quad \text{(for maximum intensity)}$$

and $$\Delta x_{net} = (2n-1)\frac{\lambda}{2} \quad \text{(for minimum intensity)}$$

Note *If medium is not air or medium is different on two sides of the slits, then for conditions of maxima/minima, phase difference between two interfering beams is more important rather than the path difference. For phase difference, we will use*

$$\Delta\phi \text{ or } \phi = \frac{2\pi}{\lambda}(\Delta x)$$

(Here, λ is the wavelength in that particular medium.)

So, $\Delta\phi_{net} = 2n\pi$ *(for maximum intensity)*

and $\Delta\phi_{net} = (2n-1)\pi$ *(for minimum intensity)*

Ex. 3 Distance between two slits is d. Wavelength of light is λ. There is a source of light S behind S_2 at a distance D_1. A glass slab of thickness t and refractive index μ is kept in front of S_1. Find

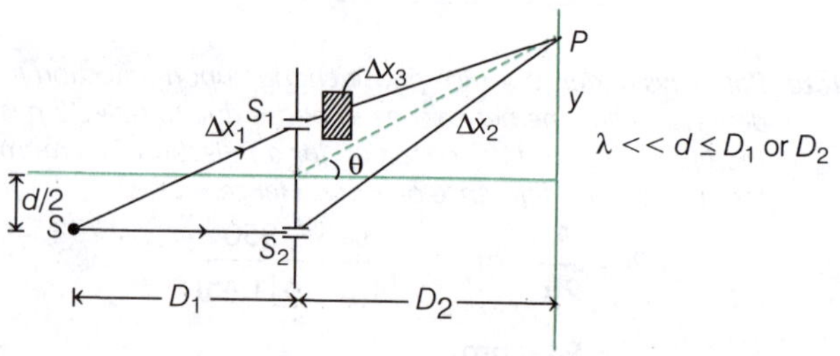

(a) Net path difference at point P at an angular position θ.

(b) Write the equation for finding two angular positions corresponding to second order minima (y_2 and y_2').

(c) If θ in part (b) does not come out to be small, then find two y-coordinates corresponding to them.

Sol. (a) $\Delta x_1 = SS_1 - SS_2 = \frac{(d/2)(d)}{D_1}$ $\left(\text{Using } \Delta x = \frac{yd}{D}\right)$

$$= \frac{d^2}{2D_1}$$

$$\Delta x_2 = d \sin\theta$$

$$\Delta x_3 = (\mu - 1)t$$

$\therefore$ $$\Delta x_{net} = (\Delta x_1 + \Delta x_3) \sim \Delta x_2 = \left\{\frac{d^2}{2D_1} + (\mu-1)t\right\} \sim d\sin\theta$$

(b) Corresponding to second order minima, net path difference should be $\frac{3\lambda}{2}$. So, let θ_1 and θ_2 be the two angular positions, then

$$\left\{\frac{d^2}{2D_1} + (\mu-1)t\right\} - d\sin\theta_1 = \frac{3\lambda}{2}$$

and $$d\sin\theta_2 - \left\{\frac{d^2}{2D_1} + (\mu-1)t\right\} = \frac{3\lambda}{2}$$

From these two equations, we can find θ_1 and θ_2.

(c) Even if θ is not small, we can write

$$\tan\theta = \frac{y}{D_2}$$

$\therefore$ $$y = D_2 \tan\theta$$

Therefore, two y-coordinates are

$$y_1 = D_2 \tan\theta_1$$

and $$y_2 = D_2 \tan\theta_2$$

Ex. 4 In the figure shown, a parallel beam of light (of wavelength λ_1 in medium μ_1) is incident at an angle θ. Distance $S_1O = S_2O$. Distance between the slits is d.

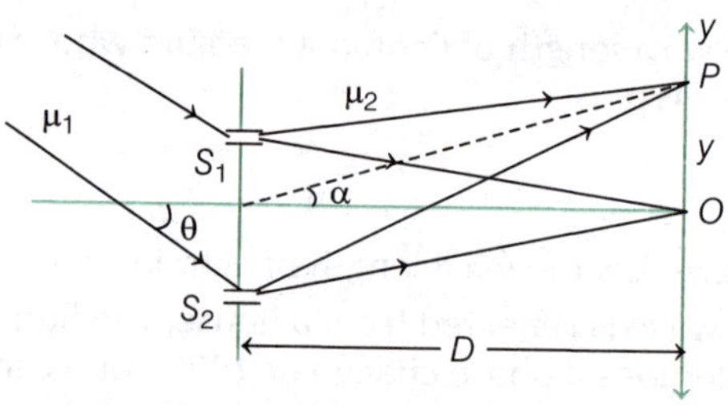

Using $d = 1$ mm, $D = 1$ m, $\theta = 30°$, $\lambda_1 = 0.3$ mm, $\mu_1 = 4/3$ and $\mu_2 = 10/9$, find

(a) the y-coordinate of the point where the total phase difference between the interfering waves is zero.

(b) If the intensity due to each light wave at point O is I_0, then find the resultant intensity at O.

(c) Find y-coordinate of the nearest maxima above O.

Sol. (a) Wavelength of light in air,

$$\lambda_0 = \mu_1\lambda_1 = 0.4 \text{ mm}$$

Wavelength of light in medium-2,

$$\lambda_2 = \frac{\lambda_0}{\mu_2} = \frac{0.4}{(10/9)} = 0.36 \text{ mm}$$

Let net phase difference at some angle α is zero, then

$$\Delta\phi_1 + \Delta\phi_2 = 0$$

or $$\frac{2\pi}{\lambda_1}(\Delta x_1) + \frac{2\pi}{\lambda_2}(\Delta x_2) = 0$$

or $$\frac{\Delta x_1}{\lambda_1} + \frac{\Delta x_2}{\lambda_2} = 0$$

or $$\frac{d \sin\theta}{\lambda_1} + \frac{d \sin\alpha}{\lambda_2} = 0$$

$\therefore$ $$\sin \alpha = -\frac{\lambda_2}{\lambda_1} \sin \theta$$

$$= -\frac{0.36}{0.4} \times \frac{1}{2} = -0.45$$

$\therefore$ $$\alpha \approx -26.74°$$

$$y = D \tan \alpha$$

$$= (1 \text{ m}) \tan(-26.74°)$$

$$\approx -\frac{1}{2} \text{ m}$$ **Ans.**

(b) At O, net phase difference,

$$\Delta\phi \text{ or } \phi = \left(\frac{2\pi}{\lambda_1}\right) \Delta x_1$$

$$= \frac{2\pi}{\lambda_1} (d \sin \theta)$$

$$= \frac{2\pi}{0.3} (1) \sin 30°$$

$$= \frac{10\pi}{3} = 600°$$

Using the equation

$$I = 4 I_0 \cos^2 \frac{\phi}{2}, \text{ we have}$$

$$I = 4 I_0 \cos^2 (300°)$$

$$= I_0$$ **Ans.**

(c) At O, phase difference $\Delta\phi_1$ is $\frac{10\pi}{3}$ which is greater than 2π but less than 4π. So, to make it 4π, we must have

$$\Delta\phi_1 + \Delta\phi_2 = 4\pi$$

$$\Delta\phi_2 = 4\pi - \frac{10\pi}{3} = \frac{2\pi}{3}$$

$$\Delta\phi_2 = \frac{2\pi}{3} = \frac{2\pi}{\lambda_2} (\Delta x_2) = \frac{2\pi}{\lambda_2} (d \sin \alpha)$$

or $$\sin \alpha = \frac{\lambda_2}{3d} = \frac{0.36}{3 \times 1} = 0.12$$

$\therefore$ $$\alpha \approx 6.89°$$

Now, $$y = D \tan \alpha$$

$$= (1 \text{ m}) \tan (6.89°)$$

$$= 0.12 \text{ m}$$ **Ans.**

Type 3. *Based on the concept of $\Delta x = d \cos\theta$ and number of maximas or minimas on the screen.*

Concept

(i) If the slits are vertical [as in figure (a)], path difference is

$$\Delta x = d \sin\theta$$

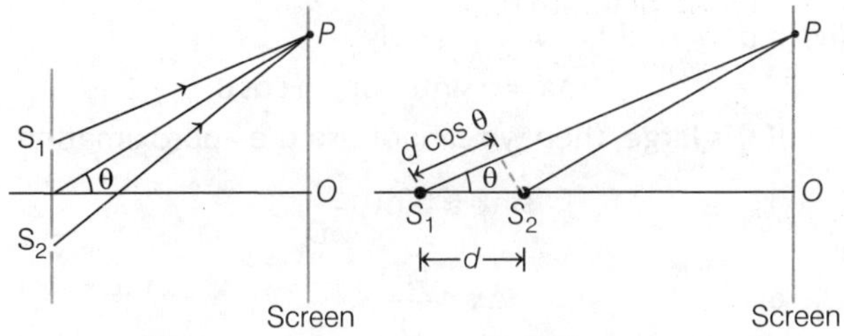

(a) (b)

This path difference increases as θ increases. Hence, order of (let bright) fringe ($d \sin\theta = n\lambda$ or $n = \frac{d \sin\theta}{\lambda}$) increases as we move away from point O on the screen.

Opposite is the case when the slits are horizontal [as in figure (b)]. Here, path difference is

$$\Delta x = d \cos\theta$$

This path difference decreases as θ increases. Hence, order of fringe $\left(n = \frac{d \cos\theta}{\lambda}\right)$ decreases as we move away from point O.

See the figure below,

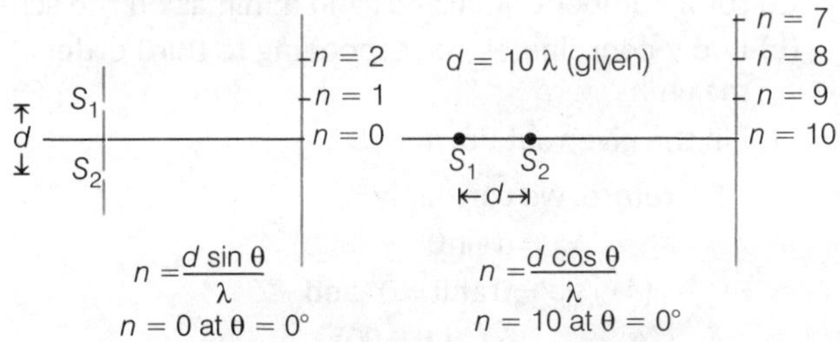

(ii) Sometimes maximum number of maximas or minimas are asked in the question which can be obtained on the screen. For this, we use the fact that value of $\sin\theta$ (or $\cos\theta$) can't be greater than 1. For example, in the first case when the slits are vertical,

$$d \sin\theta = n\lambda \quad \text{or} \quad \sin\theta = \frac{n\lambda}{d} \quad \text{(for maximum intensity)}$$

$$\sin\theta \not> 1$$

$\therefore$ $$\frac{n\lambda}{d} \not> 1 \quad \text{or} \quad n \not> \frac{d}{\lambda}$$

Suppose in some question $\frac{d}{\lambda}$ is 4.6, then total number of maximas on the screen will be 9. Corresponding to $n = 0, \pm 1, \pm 2, \pm 3$ and ± 4.

(iii) Number of maximas or minimas are normally asked when λ is of the order of d. In this case, fringe size will be large and limited number of maximas and minimas will be obtained on the screen. If $\lambda << d$, then fringe size $\left(\omega = \frac{\lambda D}{d}\right)$ is very small (of the order of μm). So, millions of fringes can be obtained on the screen. So, number of maximas or minimas are normally not asked.

(iv) If $d << D$, then we can apply

$$\Delta x = d\sin\theta \quad \text{or} \quad d\cos\theta$$

If θ is large, then we cannot use the approximation

$$\sin\theta \approx \tan\theta = \frac{y}{D}$$

or $$\Delta x = \frac{yd}{D}$$

But we can use $\tan\theta = \frac{y}{D}$

or $$y = D\tan\theta$$

Ex. 5 In the YDSE apparatus shown in figure, $d << D$ and $d = 6\lambda$. Find

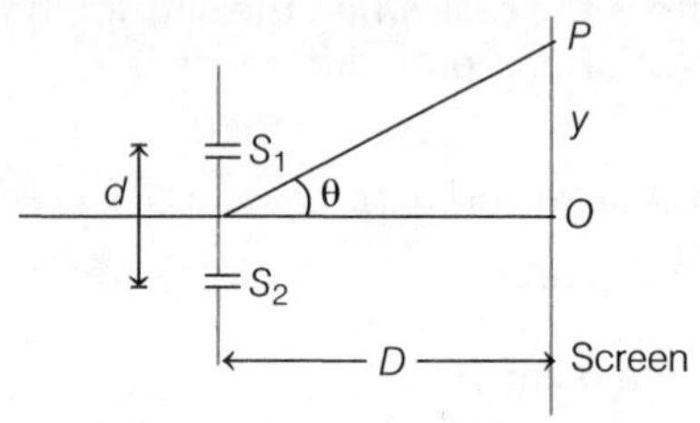

(a) total number of maximas and minimas on the screen

(b) two y-coordinates corresponding to third order maxima

Sol. (a) In the given set up, $d << D$

Therefore, we can apply

$$\Delta x = d\sin\theta$$

$$(\Delta x)_{min} = 0 \text{ at } \theta = 0° \text{ and}$$

$$(\Delta x)_{max} = 6\lambda \text{ at } \theta = 90°$$

Therefore, total number of maximas are **eleven** corresponding to,

$$\Delta x = 0, \pm\lambda, \pm 2\lambda, \pm 3\lambda, \pm 4\lambda \text{ and } \pm 5\lambda$$

Note *$\Delta x = 6\lambda$ will also produce maxima but it is corresponding to $\theta = 90°$ and in the figure, we can see that $\theta = 90°$ point lies outside the screen. So, we will have to ignore this maxima. Similarly, total number of minimas are* ***twelve*** *corresponding to :*

$\Delta x = \pm 0.5\lambda, \pm 1.5\lambda, \pm 2.5\lambda, \pm 3.5\lambda, \pm 4.5\lambda$ *and* $\pm 5.5\lambda$

(b) Third order maxima lies at

$$\Delta x = \pm 3\lambda$$

$\therefore$ $$d\sin\theta = \pm 3\lambda$$

or $$6\lambda\sin\theta = \pm 3\lambda$$

or $$\sin\theta = \pm\frac{1}{2}$$

or $$\theta = \pm 30°$$

Now, $$\frac{y}{D} = \tan\theta$$

and $$y = D\tan\theta$$

$\therefore$ $$y = \pm D\tan 30°$$

or $$y = \pm\frac{D}{\sqrt{3}}$$ **Ans.**

Ex. 6 In the set up shown in figure $d << D$ and $d = 4\lambda$, find

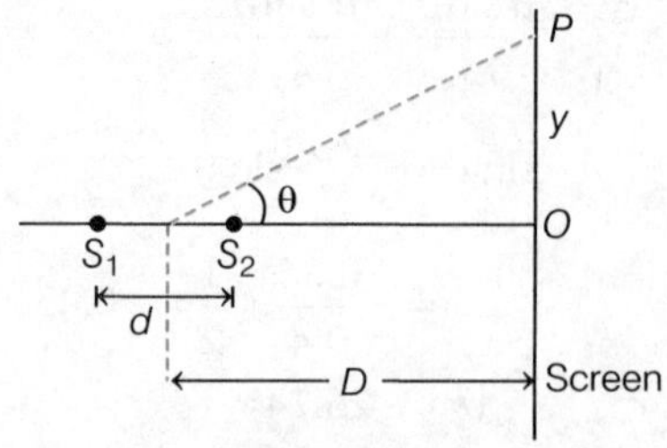

(a) total number of maximas and minimas on the screen

(b) y-coordinates corresponding to minima nearest to O.

Sol. (a) In the given set up, $d << D$, therefore we can use

$$\Delta x = d\cos\theta$$

$$(\Delta x)_{min} = 0 \text{ at } \theta = 90°$$

$$(\Delta x)_{max} = d = 4\lambda \text{ at } \theta = 0°$$

Therefore, total number of maximas are **seven** corresponding to

$$\Delta x = 4\lambda, \pm 3\lambda, \pm 2\lambda \text{ and } \pm\lambda$$

Note *$\Delta x = 0$ also produce maxima. But this is corresponding to $\theta = 90°$, which does not lie on screen.*

Similarly, total number of minimas are **eight** corresponding to

$$\Delta x = \pm 3.5\lambda, \pm 2.5\lambda, \pm 1.5\lambda \text{ and } \pm 0.5\lambda$$

(b) Minima nearest to O are corresponding to

$$\Delta x = \pm 3.5\lambda$$

$\therefore$ $$d\cos\theta = \pm 3.5\lambda$$

or $$4\lambda\cos\theta = \pm 3.5\lambda$$

or $$\theta = \pm\cos^{-1}\left(\frac{3.5\lambda}{4\lambda}\right)$$

or $$\theta = \pm\cos^{-1}\left(\frac{7}{8}\right)$$

Now, $$\frac{y}{D} = \tan\theta \Rightarrow y = D\tan\theta$$

$\therefore$ $$y = \pm D\tan\left\{\cos^{-1}\left(\frac{7}{8}\right)\right\}$$ **Ans.**

Ex. 7 There is a large circle (not a screen this time) around two coherent sources S_1 and S_2 kept at a distance $d = 3.4\lambda$.

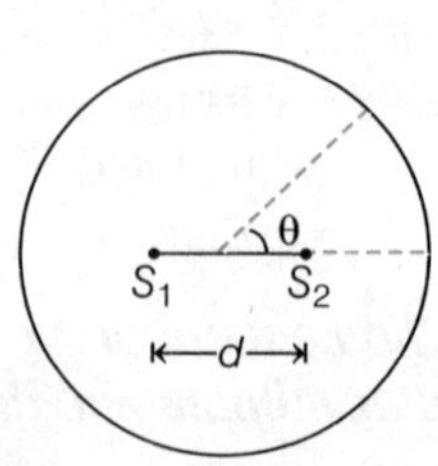

(a) Find total number of maximas on this circle.

(b) Four angular positions corresponding to third order maxima on this circle.

Sol. (a) Since, radius of circle >> d, therefore we can apply

$$\Delta x = d\cos\theta$$

Corresponding to given figure

$$(\Delta x)_{min} = 0 \text{ at } \theta = 90^\circ$$

and $$(\Delta x)_{max} = d = 3.4\lambda \text{ at } \theta = 0^\circ$$

Note *This time, $\theta = 90^\circ$ lies on the circle. Therefore, $\Delta x = 0$ corresponding to zero order maxima lie on the given circle (two in numbers). Hence, the total number of maximas are fourteen as shown below.*

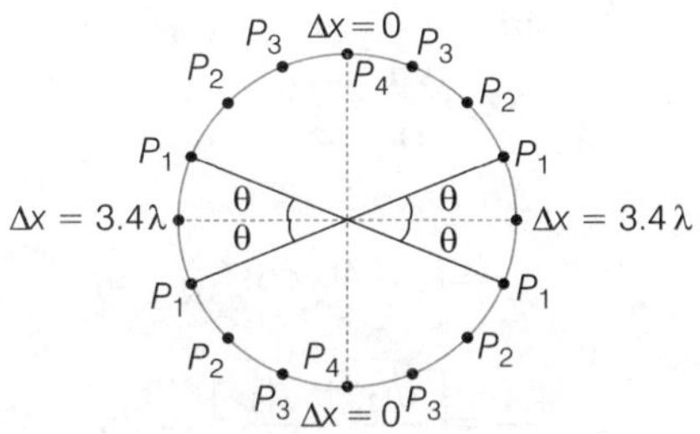

At P_1, $\Delta x = 3\lambda$

At P_2, $\Delta x = 2\lambda$

At P_3, $\Delta x = \lambda$

At P_4, $\Delta x = 0$

(b) Corresponding to third order maxima, (At P_1)

$$\Delta x = 3\lambda$$

or $$d\cos\theta = 3\lambda$$

or $$3.4\cos\theta = 3\lambda$$

$\therefore$ $$\theta = \cos^{-1}\left(\frac{3}{3.4}\right)$$ **Ans.**

Four angular positions are as shown in figure.

Note *At $\theta = 0^\circ$, $\Delta x = d = 3.4\lambda$. So, this is neither a maxima nor a minima.*

EXERCISE Find number of minimas on the circle in the above problem.

Type 4. *When one of the interfering rays is reflected from a denser medium.*

Concept

In the shown figure, a virtual image S_2 is formed of the real source S_1. Further, $\lambda << d << D$. At any point T on the screen two rays interfere. One is direct from S_1 and other is reflected (or we can assume that it comes from S_2) from a denser medium. So, they will have a phase difference of π or 180° between them.

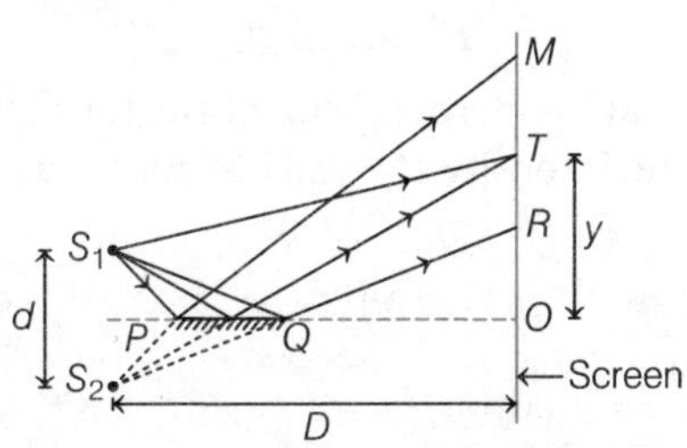

Whenever there exists a phase difference of π between the two interfering beams of light, conditions of maximas and minimas of path difference are interchanged, i.e.

$$\Delta x = n\lambda \quad \text{(for minimum intensity)}$$

and $$\Delta x = (2n-1)\,\lambda/2 \quad \text{(for maximum intensity)}$$

Further, $PQRM$ is the field of view corresponding to S_2 and the plane mirror. Or all reflected rays fall on this region. So, interference will be obtained only between M and R on the screen. Fringe width is still,

$$\omega = \frac{\lambda D}{d}$$

$\therefore$ Total number of fringes obtained on the screen will be

$$N = \frac{MR}{\omega}$$

Suppose OT is $$y = \frac{n\lambda D}{d} \quad \text{(where, } n \text{ is an integer)}$$

$$= n\omega$$

and T lies between M and R, then it will become a dark fringe because conditions of maxima and minima have been interchanged.

Ex. 8 A source of light of wavelength 5000 Å is placed as shown in figure. Considering interference of direct and reflected rays, determine the position of the region where the fringes will be visible and calculate the number of fringes.

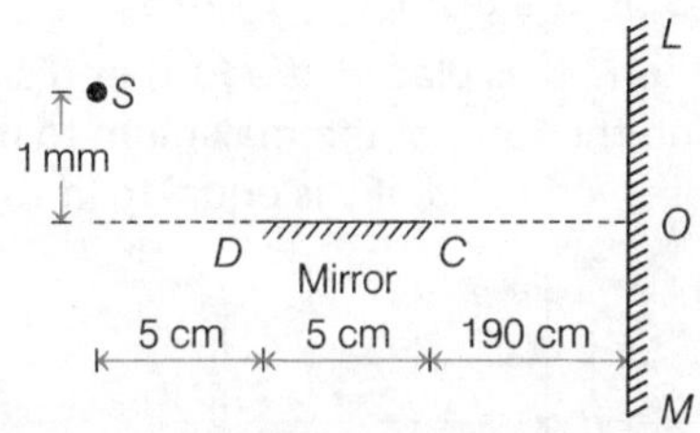

Sol. Interference will be obtained between direct rays from S and reflected rays from S' (image of S on mirror).

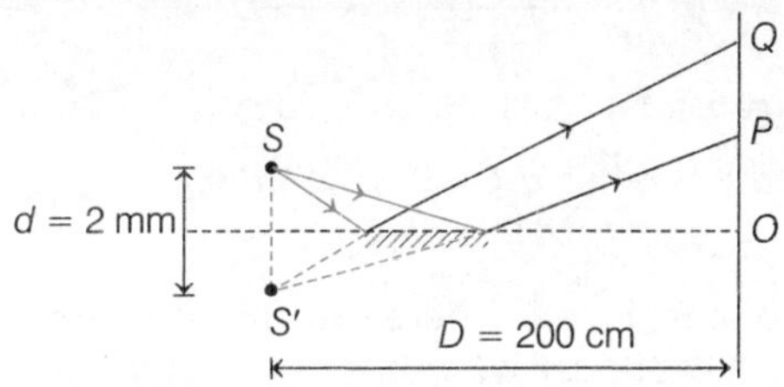

Since, the reflected rays will lie between region P and Q on the screen. So, interference is obtained in this region only. From geometry will can show that,

$$OP = 1.9 \text{ cm} \quad \text{and} \quad OQ = 3.9 \text{ cm}$$

$\therefore$ $$PQ = 2 \text{ cm}$$ **Ans.**

Fringe width, $$\omega = \frac{\lambda D}{d} = \frac{(5000\times 10^{-8})(200)}{(2\times 10^{-1})} \text{ cm}$$

$$= 0.05 \text{ cm}$$

$\therefore$ Total number of fringes in the region PQ,

$$N = \frac{PQ}{\omega} = \frac{2}{0.05} = 40 \qquad \textbf{Ans.}$$

Type 5. *Based on conditions of double interference.*

Concept

On screen-1 interference takes place first time and intensity varies between 0 and $4I_0$. There are further two slits on screen-1 at S_3 and S_4. Therefore, second time interference takes place on screen-2 due to two rays of light from S_3 and S_4.

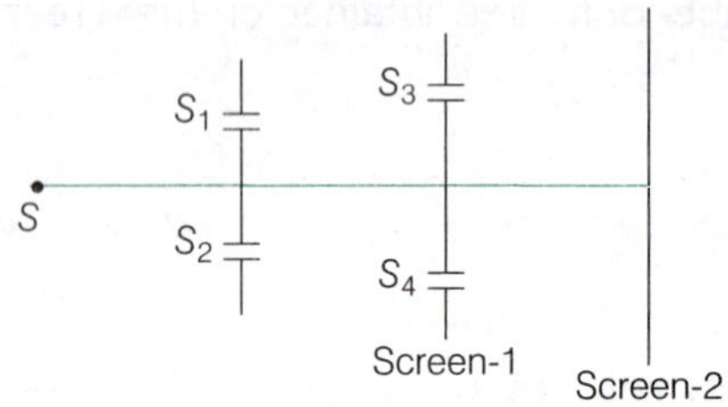

Ex. 9 Consider the situation shown in figure. The two slits S_1 and S_2 placed symmetrically around the centre line are illuminated by a monochromatic light of wavelength λ. The separation between the slits is d. The light transmitted by the slits falls on a screen M_1 placed at a distance D from the slits. The slit S_3 is at the centre line and the slit S_4 is at a distance y from S_3.

Another screen M_2 is placed at a further distance D away from M_1. Find the ratio of the maximum to minimum intensity observed on M_2 if y is equal to ($d << D$).

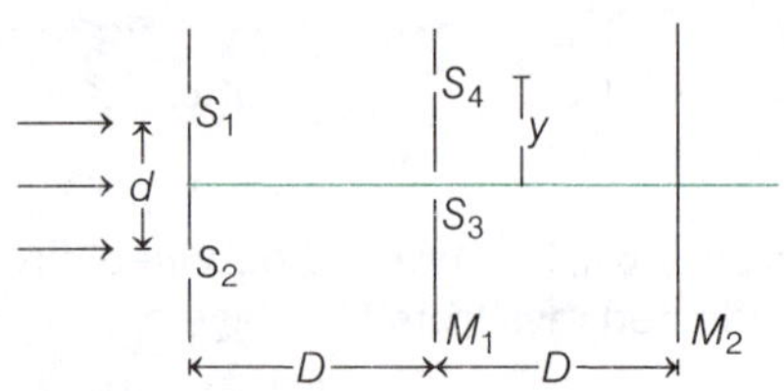

(a) $\frac{\lambda D}{2d}$ (b) $\frac{\lambda D}{d}$ (c) $\frac{\lambda D}{4d}$

Sol. $S_1S_3 = S_2S_3$

$\therefore$ Δx at S_3 is zero. Therefore, intensity at S_3 will be $4I_0$. Let us call it I_1. Thus,

$$I_{S_3} = I_1 = 4I_0$$

Now, I_{S_4} (or I_2) depends on the value of y.

(a) When $y = \frac{\lambda D}{2d}$

$$\Delta x = \frac{yd}{D} = \frac{\lambda}{2}$$

$$\therefore \quad I_{S_4} = I_2 = 0$$

$$\text{or} \quad \frac{I_{max}}{I_{min}} = \left(\frac{\sqrt{I_1} + \sqrt{I_2}}{\sqrt{I_1} - \sqrt{I_2}}\right)^2 = 1 \qquad \textbf{Ans.}$$

(b) When $y = \frac{\lambda D}{d}$

$$\Delta x = \frac{yd}{D} = \lambda$$

$$\therefore \quad I_{S_4} = I_2 = 4I_0$$

$$\text{or} \quad \frac{I_{max}}{I_{min}} = \left(\frac{\sqrt{I_1} + \sqrt{I_2}}{\sqrt{I_1} - \sqrt{I_2}}\right)^2 = \infty$$

(c) When $y = \frac{\lambda D}{4d}$

$$\Delta x = \frac{yd}{D} = \frac{\lambda}{4}$$

$$\Rightarrow \quad \Delta\phi \text{ or } \phi = 90°$$

$$\therefore \quad I_{S_4} = I_2 = 4I_0 \cos^2 \frac{\phi}{2} = 2I_0$$

$$\text{or} \quad \frac{I_{max}}{I_{min}} = \left(\frac{\sqrt{I_1} + \sqrt{I_2}}{\sqrt{I_1} - \sqrt{I_2}}\right)^2 = 34 \qquad \textbf{Ans.}$$

Ex. 10 Consider the arrangement shown in figure. By some mechanism, the separation between the slits S_3 and S_4 can be changed. The intensity is measured at the point P which is at the common perpendicular bisector of S_1S_2 and S_3S_4. When $z = \frac{D\lambda}{2d}$, the intensity measured at P is I. Find the intensity when z is equal to

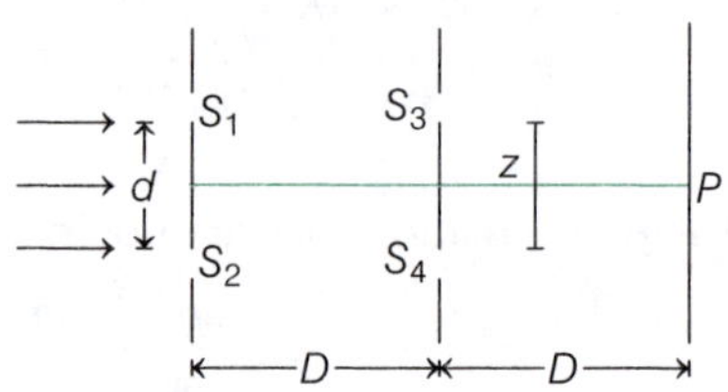

(a) $\frac{D\lambda}{d}$ (b) $\frac{3D\lambda}{2d}$ (c) $\frac{2D\lambda}{d}$

Sol. $|y_{S_3}| = |y_{S_4}| = \frac{z}{2} = y$ (say)

$$\text{When} \quad z = \frac{D\lambda}{2d}, \ \frac{z}{2} = y = \frac{D\lambda}{4d}$$

$$\therefore \quad \Delta x = \frac{yd}{D} = \frac{\lambda}{4}$$

and we have seen in the above example that, at $\Delta x = \frac{\lambda}{4}$, intensity is $2I_0$.

$$\therefore \quad I_{S_3} = I_{S_4} = 2I_0$$

Now, P is at the perpendicular bisector of S_3S_4. Therefore, intensity at P will be four times of $2I_0$ or $8I_0$.

$$\therefore \quad 8I_0 = I \qquad \text{(Given)}$$

$$\text{Hence,} \quad I_0 = \frac{I}{8}$$

(a) When $z = \frac{D\lambda}{d}$

$$y = \frac{z}{2} = \frac{D\lambda}{2d}$$

$$\therefore \quad \Delta x = \frac{yd}{D} = \frac{\lambda}{2}$$

or $\quad I_{S_3} = I_{S_4} = 0$

Hence, $\quad I_P = 0$ **Ans.**

(b) When $z = \frac{3D\lambda}{2d}$

$$\Rightarrow \quad y = \frac{z}{2} = \frac{3D\lambda}{4d}$$

$$\Delta x = \frac{yd}{D} = \frac{3\lambda}{4}$$

$$\therefore \quad \Delta\phi \text{ or } \phi = \frac{2\pi}{\lambda}(\Delta x) = \frac{3\pi}{2}$$

Using $\quad I = 4I_0 \cos^2 \frac{\phi}{2}$

We have, $\quad I_{S_3} = I_{S_4} = 2I_0$

$$\therefore \quad I_P = 4(2I_0) = 8I_0 = I$$ **Ans.**

(c) When $z = \frac{2D\lambda}{d}$

$$y = \frac{z}{2} = \frac{D\lambda}{d}$$

$$\therefore \quad \Delta x = \frac{yd}{D} = \lambda$$

$$\therefore \quad I_{S_3} = I_{S_4} = 4I_0$$

$$I_P = 4(4I_0) = 16 I_0$$

$$= 2I$$ **Ans.**

Type 6. *When no approximation can be taken in finding the path difference.*

Concept

If D is not very very greater than d, then we cannot apply $\Delta x = d \sin\theta$ or $d\cos\theta$ or $\frac{yd}{D}$. In this case, we will have to find the path difference by using geometry.

Ex. 11 Two coherent point sources S_1 and S_2 emit light of wavelength λ. The separation between sources is 2λ. Consider a line passing through S_2 and perpendicular to the line S_1S_2. What is the smallest distance on this line from S_2 where a minimum of intensity occurs?

Sol. At S_2, $\Delta x = 2\lambda$

Therefore, the minima closest to S_2 will be corresponding to the path difference $\Delta x = \frac{3\lambda}{2}$. Suppose this point is P at a distance y from S_2. Then,

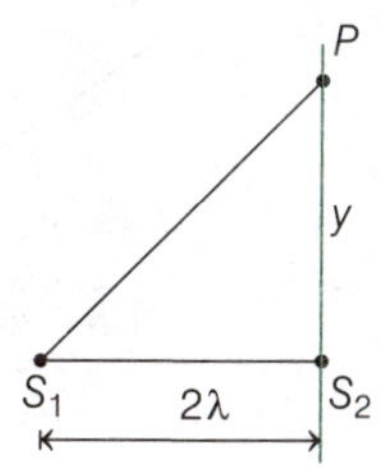

$$S_1P - S_2P = \frac{3\lambda}{2}$$

$$\sqrt{y^2 + (S_1S_2)^2} - y = \frac{3\lambda}{2}$$

or $$\sqrt{y^2 + (2\lambda)^2} = \left(y + \frac{3\lambda}{2}\right)$$

Squaring and then solving this equation, we get

$$y = \frac{7\lambda}{12}$$ **Ans.**

Miscellaneous Examples

Ex. 12 Figure shows three equidistant slits illuminated by a monochromatic parallel beam of light. Let $BP_0 - AP_0 = \lambda/3$ and $D >> \lambda$

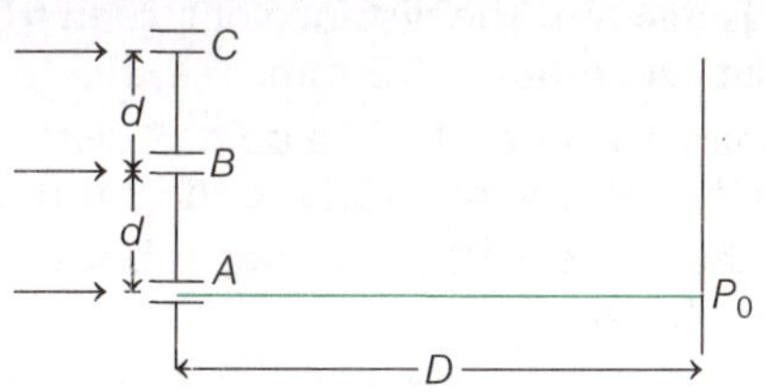

(a) Show that $d = \sqrt{2\lambda D/3}$

(b) Show that the intensity at P_0 is three times the intensity due to any of the three slits individually.

Sol. (a) Given, $\quad BP_0 - AP_0 = \lambda/3$

$$\therefore \quad \sqrt{D^2 + d^2} - D = \frac{\lambda}{3}$$

or $$\sqrt{D^2 + d^2} = \left(D + \frac{\lambda}{3}\right)$$

Squaring both sides, we get

$$D^2 + d^2 = D^2 + \frac{\lambda^2}{9} + \frac{2D\lambda}{3}$$

Since $\lambda << D$, we can ignore the term $\frac{\lambda^2}{9}$. By ignoring this term, we get the desired result.

$$d = \sqrt{\frac{2\lambda D}{3}}$$

(b) Given, $\quad BP_0 - AP_0 = \Delta x_{12} = \frac{\lambda}{3}$

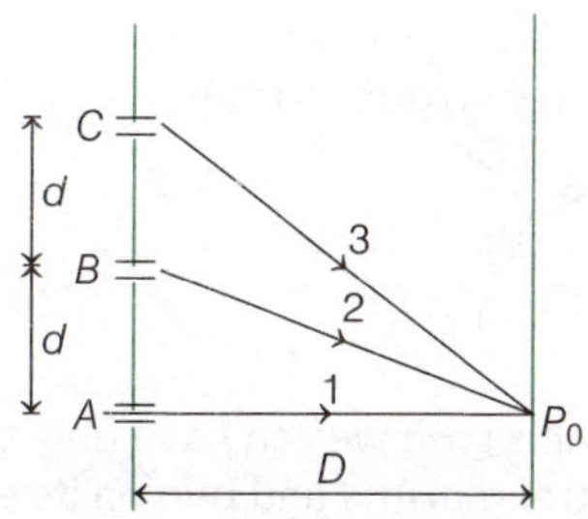

$$\therefore \quad \Delta\phi_{12} \text{ or } \phi_{12} = 120°$$

Now, $CP_0 - AP_0 = \Delta x_{13} = \sqrt{(2d)^2 + D^2} - D$

$$= D\left[1 + \left(\frac{2d}{D}\right)^2\right]^{\frac{1}{2}} - D$$

$$\approx D\left[1 + \frac{1}{2} \times \frac{4d^2}{D^2}\right] - D = \frac{2d^2}{D}$$

Substituting, $d = \sqrt{\frac{2\lambda D}{3}}$ or $d^2 = \frac{2\lambda D}{3}$

We get, $\Delta x_{13} = \frac{4}{3}\lambda$

$\therefore$ $\Delta\phi_{13}$ or $\phi_{13} = \frac{4}{3}(360°) = 480°$

$$= 480° - 360° = 120°$$

Now, we know that in case of coherent sources amplitudes are first added by vector method. So, let individual amplitude is A_0.

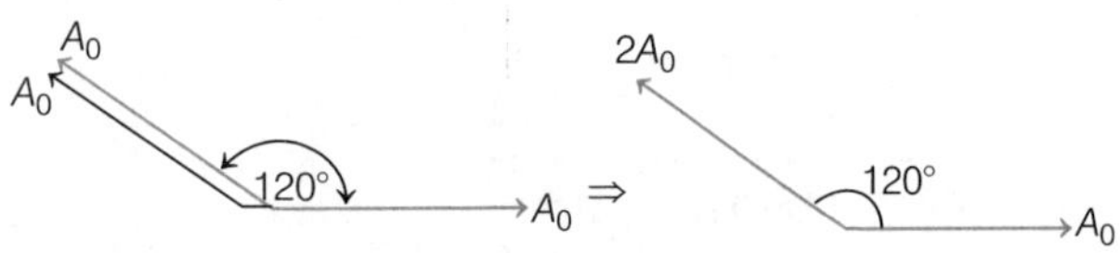

The resultant amplitude will be given by

$$A = \sqrt{A_0^2 + (2A_0)^2 + 2(A_0)(2A_0)\cos 120°}$$

$$= \sqrt{3}\,A_0$$

$$I \propto A^2$$

and amplitude has become $\sqrt{3}$ times, therefore resultant intensity will become 3 times.

Ex. 13 Young's double slit experiment is carried out using microwaves of wavelength $\lambda = 3$ cm. Distance between the slits is $d = 5$ cm and the distance between the plane of slits and the screen is $D = 100$ cm.

(a) Find total number of maximas and

(b) their positions on the screen.

Sol. (a) The maximum path difference that can be produced $d\sin 90° = d = 5$ cm.

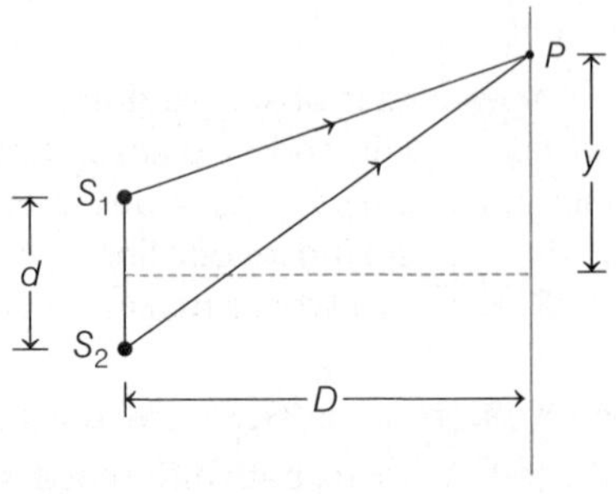

Thus, in this case we can have only three maximas, one central maxima and two on its either side for a path difference of λ or 3 cm.

(b) For maximum intensity at P,

$$S_2P - S_1P = \lambda$$

or $\sqrt{(y + d/2)^2 + D^2} - \sqrt{(y - d/2)^2 + D^2} = \lambda$

Substituting $d = 5$ cm, $D = 100$ cm and $\lambda = 3$ cm we get,

$$y = \pm 75 \text{ cm}$$

Thus, the three maximas will be at

$$y = 0$$

and $y = \pm 75$ cm **Ans.**

Ex. 14 Two coherent sources are 0.3 mm apart. They are 0.9 m away from the screen. The second dark fringe is at a distance of 0.3 cm from the centre. Find the distance of fourth bright fringe from the centre. Also, find the wavelength of light used.

Sol. Given, $d = 0.3 \times 10^{-3}$ m, $D = 0.9$ m

$$\frac{3\lambda D}{2d} = 0.3 \times 10^{-2} \text{ cm}$$

(the distance of second dark fringe)

$$\therefore \quad \frac{\lambda D}{d} = (0.3 \times 10^{-2})\left(\frac{2}{3}\right)$$

$$= 0.2 \times 10^{-2} \text{ m} = 0.2 \text{ cm}$$

(i) Distance of fourth bright fringe from centre $= \frac{4\lambda D}{d}$

$$= 0.8 \text{ cm}$$ **Ans.**

(ii) $$\lambda = \left(\frac{d}{D}\right)(0.2 \times 10^{-2}) \text{ m}$$

$$= \left(\frac{0.3 \times 10^{-3}}{0.9}\right)(0.2 \times 10^{-2})$$

$$= 6.67 \times 10^{-7} \text{ m}$$ **Ans.**

Ex. 15 In a Young's double slit set up, the wavelength of light used is 546 nm. The distance of screen from slits is 1 m. The slit separation is 0.3 mm.

(a) Compare the intensity at a point P distant 10 mm from the central fringe where the intensity is I_0.

(b) Find the number of bright fringes between P and the central fringe.

Sol. Given, $\lambda = 546$ nm $= 5.46 \times 10^{-7}$ m, $D = 1.0$ m and $d = 0.3$ mm $= 0.3 \times 10^{-3}$ m

(a) At a distance $y = 10$ mm $= 10 \times 10^{-3}$ m, from central fringe, the path difference will be

$$\Delta x = \frac{yd}{D} = \frac{(10 \times 10^{-3})(0.3 \times 10^{-3})}{1.0}$$

$$= 3.0 \times 10^{-6} \text{ m}$$

The corresponding phase difference between the two interfering beams will be

$$\phi = \frac{2\pi}{\lambda} \cdot \Delta x$$

$$= \left(\frac{2\pi}{5.46 \times 10^{-7}}\right)(3.0 \times 10^{-6}) \text{ radian}$$

$$= 1978°$$

$$\therefore \quad \frac{\phi}{2} = 989°$$

$$\therefore \quad I = I_0 \cos^2 \frac{\phi}{2}$$

$$= I_0 \cos^2 (989)$$

$$= 3.0 \times 10^{-4} I_0$$ **Ans.**

(b) Fringe width, $\omega = \frac{\lambda D}{d} = \frac{(5.46 \times 10^{-7})(1.0)}{0.3 \times 10^{-3}}$ m

$$= 1.82 \text{ mm}$$

Since, $\frac{y}{\omega} = \frac{10}{1.82} = 5.49$

Therefore, number of bright fringes between P and central fringe will be 5 (excluding the central fringe). **Ans.**

Ex. 16 In a double slit pattern ($\lambda = 6000$ Å), the first order and tenth order maxima fall at 12.50 mm and 14.75 mm from a particular reference point. If λ is changed to 5500 Å, find the position of zero order and tenth order fringes, other arrangements remaining the same.

Sol. Given,

$$9\omega = (14.75 - 12.50) \text{ mm} = 2.25 \text{ mm}$$

$\therefore$ Fringe width, $\omega = 0.25$ mm

When the wavelength is changed from 6000 Å to 5500 Å, the new fringe width will become,

$$\omega' = \left(\frac{5500}{6000}\right)\omega = \left(\frac{5500}{6000}\right)(0.25)$$

(as fringe width $\propto \lambda$)

$$\therefore \quad \omega' = 0.23 \text{ mm}$$

The position of central (or zero order) maxima will remain unchanged. Earlier it was at a position,

$$Y_0 = Y_1 - \omega = (12.50 - 0.25) = 12.25 \text{ mm}$$ **Ans.**

The new position of tenth order maxima will be

$$Y_{10} = Y_0 + 10\omega' = (12.25) + (10)(0.23) = 14.55 \text{ mm}$$ **Ans.**

Ex. 17 Two coherent narrow slits emitting light of wavelength λ in the same phase are placed parallel to each other at a small separation of 2λ. The light is collected on a screen S which is placed at a distance $D (>> \lambda)$ from the slit S_1 as shown in figure. Find the finite distance x such that the intensity at P is equal to intensity at O.

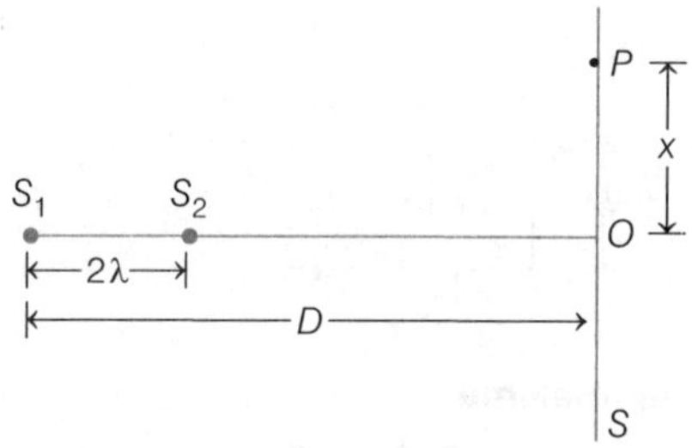

Sol. Path difference at O,

$$S_1O - S_2O = 2\lambda$$

i.e. maximum intensity is obtained at O. Next maxima will be obtained at point P where,

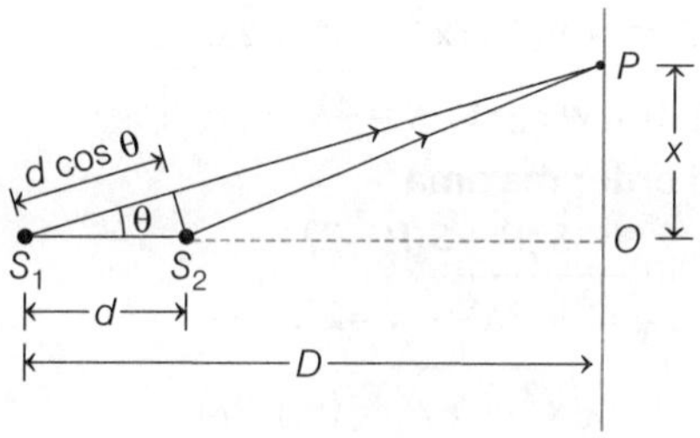

$$S_1P - S_2P = \lambda$$

or $\quad d \cos\theta = \lambda$

or $\quad 2\lambda \cos\theta = \lambda$

or $\quad \cos\theta = \frac{1}{2}$

$\therefore \quad \theta = 60°$

Now in ΔS_1PO, $\frac{PO}{S_1O} = \tan\theta$

or $\quad \frac{x}{D} = \tan 60° = \sqrt{3}$

$\therefore \quad x = \sqrt{3}D$ **Ans.**

Note *At point O, path difference is 2λ, i.e. we get second order maxima. At point P, where path difference is λ (i.e $x = \sqrt{3}D$) we get first order maxima. The next, i.e. zero order maxima will be obtained where path difference, i.e. $d\cos\theta = 0$ or $\theta = 90°$. At $\theta = 90°$, $x = \infty$. So, our answer, i.e. finite distance of x should be $x = \sqrt{3}D$, corresponding to first order maxima.*

Ex. 18 An interference is observed due to two coherent sources S_1 placed at origin and S_2 placed at $(0, 3\lambda, 0)$. Here, λ is the wavelength of the sources. A detector D is moved along the positive x-axis. Find x-coordinates on the x-axis (excluding $x = 0$ and $x = \infty$) where maximum intensity is observed.

Sol. At $x = 0$, path difference is 3λ. Hence, third order maxima will be obtained. At $x = \infty$, path difference is zero. Hence, zero order maxima is obtained. In between, first and second order maxima will be obtained.

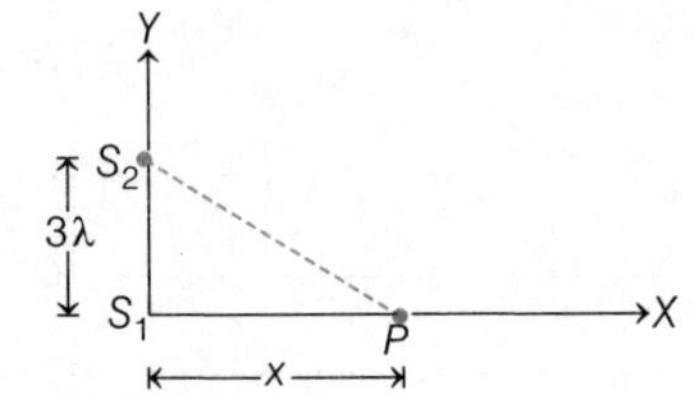

First order maxima

$$S_2P - S_1P = \lambda$$

or $$\sqrt{x^2 + 9\lambda^2} - x = \lambda$$

or $$\sqrt{x^2 + 9\lambda^2} = x + \lambda$$

Squaring on both sides, we get

$$x^2 + 9\lambda^2 = x^2 + \lambda^2 + 2x\lambda$$

Solving this, we get $x = 4\lambda$

Second order maxima

$$S_2P - S_1P = 2\lambda$$

or $$\sqrt{x^2 + 9\lambda^2} - x = 2\lambda$$

or $$\sqrt{x^2 + 9\lambda^2} = (x + 2\lambda)$$

Squaring on both sides, we get

$$x^2 + 9\lambda^2 = x^2 + 4\lambda^2 + 4x\lambda$$

Solving, we get $x = \frac{5}{4}\lambda = 1.25\lambda$

Hence, the desired x-coordinates are

$$x = 1.25\lambda$$

and $$x = 4\lambda$$ **Ans.**

Note *(i) As we move along positive x-axis (from origin) order of maxima decreases from n = 3 to n = 0.*

(ii) Here, we cannot take the path difference $d\cos\theta$ or $d\sin\theta$. Think why?

Ex. 19 In a Young's double slit experiment, the light sources is at distance $l_1 = 20\ \mu m$ and $l_2 = 40\ \mu m$ from the main slit. The light of wavelength $\lambda = 500$ nm is incident on slits separated at a distance 10 μm. A screen is placed at a distance $D = 2$ m away from the slits as shown in figure. Find

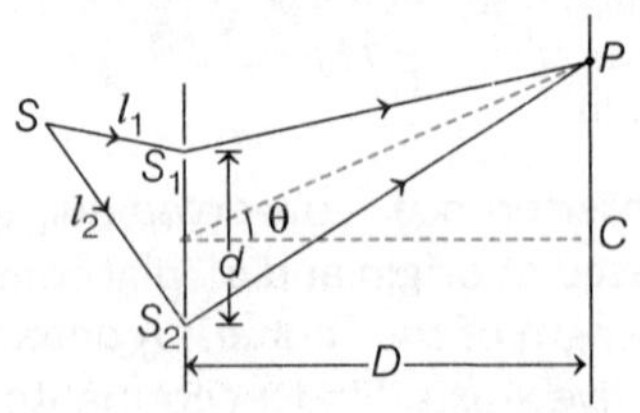

(a) the values of θ relative to the central line where maxima appear on the screen?
(b) how many maxima can be obtained?
(c) what should be the minimum thickness of a slab of refractive index 1.5 placed on the path of one of the ray so that minima occurs at C?

Sol. (a) The optical path difference between the beams arriving at P,

$$\Delta x = (l_2 - l_1) + d\sin\theta$$

The condition for maximum intensity is

$$\Delta x = n\lambda \qquad [n = 0, \pm 1, \pm 2, \ldots]$$

Thus, $$\sin\theta = \frac{1}{d}[\Delta x - (l_2 - l_1)]$$

$$= \frac{1}{d}[n\lambda - (l_2 - l_1)]$$

$$= \frac{1}{10 \times 10^{-6}}[n \times 500 \times 10^{-9} - 20 \times 10^{-6}]$$

$$= 2\left[\frac{n}{40} - 1\right]$$

Hence, $$\theta = \sin^{-1}\left[2\left(\frac{n}{40} - 1\right)\right]$$ **Ans.**

(b) $|\sin\theta| \le 1$

$\therefore$ $$-1 \le 2\left[\frac{n}{40} - 1\right] \le 1$$

or $$-20 \le (n - 40) \le 20$$

or $$20 \le n \le 60$$

Hence, number of maximas will be 41 between $n = 20$ and $n = 60$, if we take all maximas corresponding to $\theta = \pm 90°$ also.

(c) At C, phase difference $\phi = \left(\frac{2\pi}{\lambda}\right)(l_2 - l_1)$

$$= \left(\frac{2\pi}{500 \times 10^{-9}}\right)(20 \times 10^{-6})$$

$$= 80\pi$$

Hence, maximum intensity will appear at C. For minimum intensity at C,

$$(\mu - 1)t = \frac{\lambda}{2}$$

or $$t = \frac{\lambda}{2(\mu - 1)} = \frac{500 \times 10^{-9}}{2 \times 0.5}$$

$$= 500 \text{ nm}$$ **Ans.**

MODULE 2 Exercise

Fill in the Blank

1. In Young's double-slit experiment, the two slits act as coherent sources of equal amplitude A and of wavelength λ. In another experiment with the same set-up the two slits are sources of equal amplitude A and wavelength λ, but are incoherent. The ratio of the intensity of light at the mid-point of the screen in the first case to that in the second case is .... **(1986 JEE)**

True/False

2. In a Young's double slit experiment performed with a source of white light, only black and white fringes are observed. **(1987 JEE)**

3. Two slits in a Young's double slit experiment are illuminated by two different sodium lamps emitting light of the same wavelength. No interference pattern will be observed on the screen. **(1984 JEE)**

Assertion and Reason

See directions on page 11.

4. **Assertion :** In the figure shown, zero order maxima will lie above the point O.

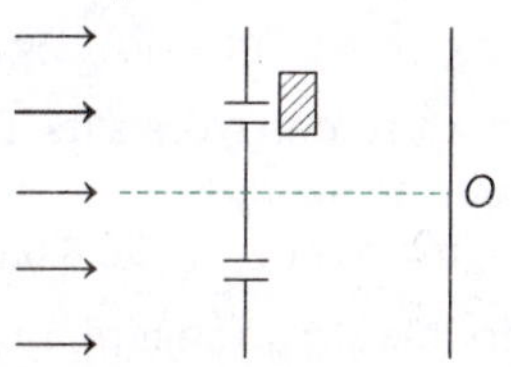

Reason : Zero order maxima normally means a point where path difference is zero.

5. **Assertion :** If width of one slit in Young's double slit experiment is slightly increased, then maximum and minimum both intensities will increase.

Reason : Intensity reaching from that slit on screen will slightly increase.

6. **Assertion :** Two coherent sources S_1 and S_2 are placed in front of a screen as shown in figure. At point P, 10th order maxima is obtained . Then, 11th order maxima will be obtained above P.

Reason : For 11th order maxima path difference should be more.

Single Correct Option

7. Interference was observed in interference chamber when air is present. Now, the chamber is evacuated and if the same light is used, then for the same arrangement
(a) no interference pattern will be obtained
(b) exactly same interference pattern will be obtained with better contrast
(c) the fringe width is slightly decreased
(d) the fringe width is slightly increased

8. In Young's double slit experiment, distance between two sources is 0.1 mm. The distance of screen from the sources is 20 cm. Wavelength of light used is 5460 Å. Then, angular position of first dark fringe is approximately
(a) 0.08° (b) 0.16°
(c) 0.20° (d) 0.32°

9. Young's double slit experiment is made in a liquid. The tenth bright fringe in liquid lies in screen where 6th dark fringe lies in vacuum. The refractive index of the liquid is approximately
(a) 1.8 (b) 1.54
(c) 1.67 (d) 1.2

10. A plane monochromatic light wave falls normally on a diaphragm with two narrow slits separated by 2.5 mm. The fringe pattern is formed on a screen 100 cm behind the diaphragm. By what distance will these fringes be displaced, when one of the slits is covered by a glass plate ($\mu = 1.5$) of thickness 10 μm?
(a) 2 mm (b) 1 mm
(c) 3 mm (d) 4 mm

11. In Young's double slit experiment, 60 fringes are observed in the central view zone with light of wavelength 4000 Å . The number of fringes that will be observed in the same view zone with the light of wavelength 6000 Å, is
(a) 40 (b) 90
(c) 60 (d) None of these

12. In a two slit experiment with monochromatic light, fringes are obtained on a screen placed at some distance from the slits . If the screen is moved by 5×10^{-2} m, towards the slits, the change in fringe width is 3×10^{-5} m. If separation between the slits is 10^{-3} m, the wavelength of light used is
(a) 6000 Å
(b) 5000 Å
(c) 3000 Å
(d) 4500 Å

13. A beam of light parallel to central line AB is incident on the plane of slits . The number of minima obtained on the large screen is n_1. Now, if the beam is tilted by some angle ($\neq 90°$) as shown in figure, then the number of minima obtained is n_2. Then,

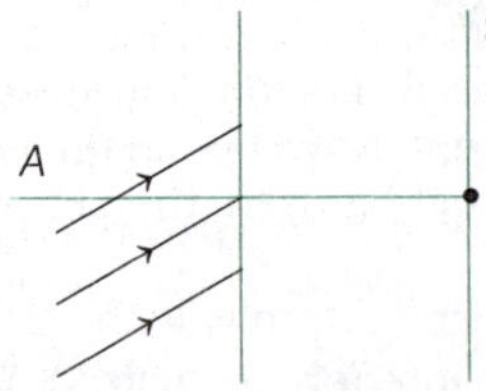

(a) $n_1 = n_2$ (b) $n_1 > n_2$
(c) $n_2 > n_1$ (d) n_2 will be zero

14. Young's double slit experiment is performed with blue and green light of wavelengths 4360 Å and 5460 Å, respectively. If x is the distance of 4th maxima from the central one, then

(a) x (blue) $= x$ (green) (b) x (blue) $> x$ (green)
(c) x (blue) $< x$ (green) (d) $\frac{x \text{ (blue)}}{x \text{ (green)}} = \frac{5460}{4360}$

15. In a Young's double-slit experiment D equals the distance of screen and d is the separation between the slits. The distance of the nearest point to the centre maximum where the intensity is same as that due to a single slit, is equal to

(a) $\frac{D\lambda}{4d}$ (b) $\frac{D\lambda}{2d}$
(c) $\frac{D\lambda}{3d}$ (d) $\frac{2D\lambda}{3d}$

16. In Young's double slit experiment, the angular width of a fringe formed on a distant screen is 1°, the wavelength of light used is 6000 Å. The spacing between the slits is

(a) 6×10^{-7} m (b) 6.8×10^{-5} m
(c) 3.4×10^{-5} m (d) 3.4×10^{-4} m

17. In the Young's double-slit experiment, the intensity of light at a point on the screen where the path difference is λ is K, (λ being the wave length of light used). The intensity at a point where the path difference is $\lambda/4$, will be

(a) K (b) $K/4$
(c) $K/2$ (d) Zero

18. In the Young's double slit experiment, the intensities at two points P_1 and P_2 on the screen are respectively I_1 and I_2. If P_1 is located at the centre of a bright fringe and P_2 is located at a distance equal to a quarter of fringe width from P_1, then $\frac{I_1}{I_2}$ is

(a) 2 (b) 3
(c) 4 (d) None of these

19. The width of fringe is 2 mm on the screen in a double slits experiment for the light of wavelength of 400 nm. The width of the fringe for the light of wavelength 600 nm will be **(2023 Main)**

(a) 1.33 mm (b) 2 mm (c) 4 mm (d) 3 mm

20. The ratio of intensities at two points P and Q on the screen in a Young's double slit experiment where phase difference between two waves of same amplitude are $\frac{\pi}{3}$ and $\frac{\pi}{2}$, respectively are **(2023 Main)**

(a) 2 : 3 (b) 3 : 1
(c) 3 : 2 (d) 1 : 3

21. In Young's double slits experiment, the position of 5th bright fringe from the central maximum is 5 cm. The distance between slits and screen is 1 m and wavelength of used monochromatic light is 600 nm. The separation between the slits is **(2023 Main)**

(a) 36 μm (b) 48 μm (c) 12 μm (d) 60 μm

22. In Young's double slit experiment, two slits are illuminated with a light of wavelength 800 nm. The line joining A_1P is perpendicular to A_1A_2 as shown in the figure. If the first minimum is detected at P, the value of slits separation a will be :

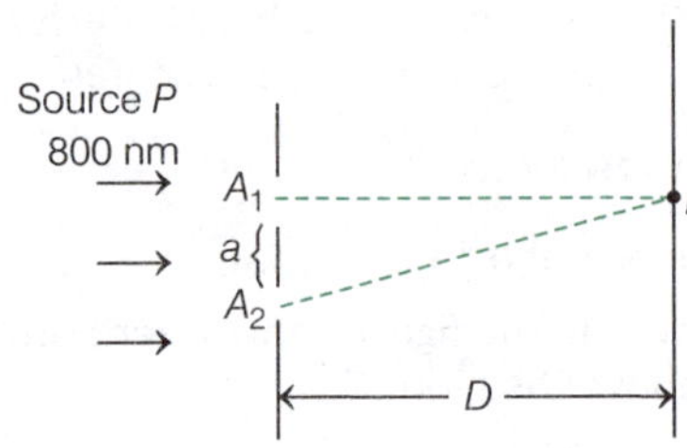

(The distance of screen from slits, $D = 5$ cm) **(2023 Main)**

(a) 0.5 mm (b) 0.1 mm (c) 0.4 mm (d) 0.2 mm

23. In Young's double slit arrangement, slits are separated by a gap of 0.5 mm, and the screen is placed at a distance of 0.5 m from them. The distance between the first and the third bright fringe formed when the slits are illuminated by a monochromatic light of 5890 Å is **(2021 Main)**

(a) 1178×10^{-9} m (b) 1178×10^{-6} m
(c) 1178×10^{-12} m (d) 5890×10^{-7} m

24. In Young's double slit experiment, light of 500 nm is used to produce an interference pattern. When the distance between the slits is 0.05 mm, the angular width (in degrees) of the fringes formed on the distant screen is close to **(2020 Main)**

(a) 0.17° (b) 0.57° (c) 1.7° (d) 0.07°

25. In a double slit experiment, when a thin film of thickness t having refractive index μ is introduced in front of one of the slits, the maximum at the centre of the fringe pattern shifts by one fringe width. The value of t is (λ is the wavelength of the light used) **(2019 Main)**

(a) $\frac{2\lambda}{(\mu-1)}$ (b) $\frac{\lambda}{2(\mu-1)}$
(c) $\frac{\lambda}{(\mu-1)}$ (d) $\frac{\lambda}{(2\mu-1)}$

26. In a Young's double slit experiment, the ratio of the slits' widths is 4 : 1. The ratio of the intensity of maxima to minima, close to the central fringe on the screen, will be **(2019 Main)**
(a) 4 : 1
(b) 25 : 9
(c) 9 : 1
(d) $(\sqrt{3}+1)^4 : 16$

Multiple Correct Options

27. In the Young's double slit experiment, the interference pattern is found to have an intensity ratio between the bright and dark fringes as 9. This implies that **(1982 JEE)**
(a) the intensities at the screen due to the two slits are 5 units and 4 units respectively
(b) the intensities at the screen due to the two slits are 4 units and 1 unit respectively
(c) the amplitude ratio is 3
(d) the amplitude ratio is 2

Subjective Questions

28. A Young's double slit apparatus has slits separated by 0.25 mm and a screen 48 cm away from the slits. The whole apparatus is immersed in water and the slits are illuminated by the red light ($\lambda = 700$ nm in vacuum). Find the fringe width of the pattern formed on the screen. ($\mu_w = 4/3$)

29. In a double slit experiment, the distance between the slits is 5.0 mm and the slits are 1.0 m from the screen. Two interference patterns can be seen on the screen one due to light with wavelength 480 nm, and the other due to light with wavelength 600 nm. What is the separation on the screen between the third order bright fringes of the two interference patterns?

30. Coherent light with wavelength 600 nm passes through two very narrow slits and the interference pattern is observed on a screen 3.00 m from the slits. The first order bright fringe is at 4.94 mm from the centre of the central bright fringe. For what wavelength of light will the first order dark fringe be observed at this same point on the screen?

31. Two very narrow slits are spaced 1.80 μm apart and are placed 35.0 cm from a screen. What is the distance between the first and second dark lines of the interference pattern when the slits are illuminated with coherent light of $\lambda = 550$ nm? (Hint : The angle θ is not small).

32. In a Young's double slit set up, the wavelength of light used is 546 nm. The distance of screen from slits is 1 m. The slit separation is 0.3 mm.
(a) Compare the intensity at a point P distant 10 mm from the central fringe where the intensity is I_0.
(b) Find the number of bright fringes between P and the central fringe.

33. What is the thinnest film of coating with $n = 1.42$ on glass ($n = 1.52$) for which destructive interference of the red component (650 nm) of an incident white light beam in air can take place by reflection?

34. Determine what happens to the double slit interference pattern if one of the slits is covered with a thin, transparent film whose thickness is $\frac{\lambda}{2(\mu - 1)}$, where λ is the wavelength of the incident light and μ is the index of refraction of the film.

Answers

1. 2 : 1 **2.** (False) **3.** (True) **4.** (b) **5.** (a) **6.** (d) **7.** (d) **8.** (b) **9.** (a) **10.** (a)
11. (a) **12.** (a) **13.** (a) **14.** (c) **15.** (c) **16.** (c) **17.** (c) **18.** (a) **19.** (d) **20.** (c)
21. (d) **22.** (d) **23.** (b) **24.** (b) **25.** (c) **26.** (c) **27.** (b,d) **28.** 1.0 mm **29.** 0.072 mm
30. 1200 nm **31.** 12.6 cm **32.** (a) $I_p = 3.0 \times 10^{-4}\ I_0$ (b) Five **33.** 114 nm
34. Bright and dark fringes interchange positions

See hints on pages 242-245.

MODULE 3

Diffraction

What is Diffraction?

Diffraction of light is defined as the bending of light around corners such that it spreads out and illuminates areas where a shadow is expected. In general, it is hard to separate diffraction from interference since both occur simultaneously.

The silver lining which we witness in the sky is caused due to diffraction of light. When the sunlight passes through or encounters the cloud, a silver lining is seen in the sky.

What is Single Slit Diffraction?

In the single slit diffraction experiment, we can observe the bending phenomenon of light or diffraction that causes light from a coherent source to interfere with itself and produce a distinctive pattern on the screen called the diffraction pattern.

Diffraction is evident when the sources are small enough that they are relatively the size of the wavelength of light. You can see this effect in the diagram below. For large slits, the spreading out is small and generally unnoticeable.

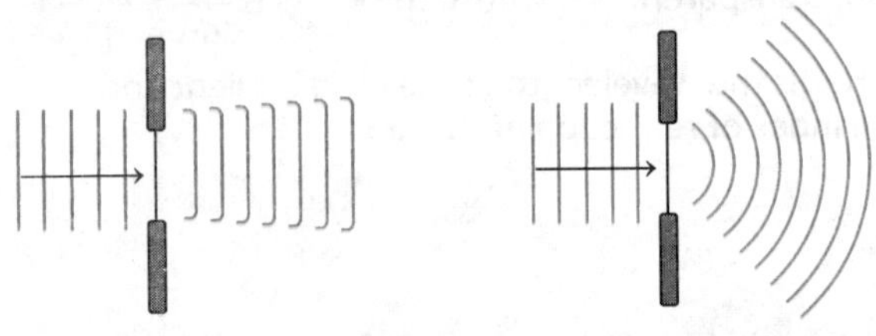

Wide gap Small diffraction effect   **Narrow gap** Large diffraction effect

Fresnel and Fraunhofer Diffraction

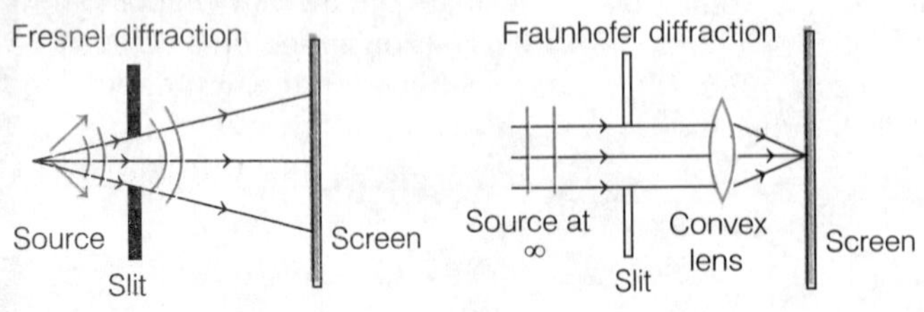

Diffraction is of two types :

Fresnel Diffraction	Fraunhofer Diffraction
It is the type of diffraction that occurs when the light source lies at a finite distance from the slit i.e. the source of light and screen is kept at a finite distance from the diffracting system.	It is the type of diffraction that occurs when a plane wavefront is incident on the slit and the wavefront emerging from the slit is also plane i.e. the source of light and the screen on which the diffraction pattern is obtained are at an infinite distance from the diffracting system.
Cylindrical or spherical wavefront is considered.	Plane wavefront is considered.
Fresnel diffraction patterns on flat surfaces.	Fraunhofer diffraction patterns on spherical surfaces.

Note *In this module, we restrict our attention to Fraunhofer diffraction.*

Diffraction from a Narrow Slit

Until now, we have assumed that slits are point sources of light. In this section, we abandon that assumption and see how the finite width of slits is the basis for understanding Fraunhofer diffraction.

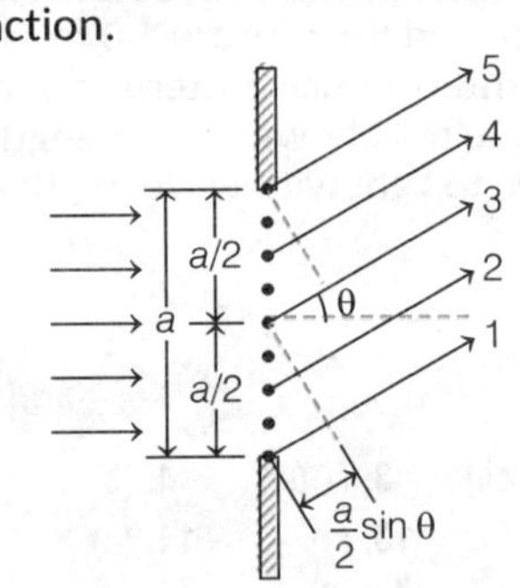

Diffraction of light by a narrow slit of width a. Each portion of the slit acts as a point source of light waves. The path difference between rays 1 and 3 or between rays 2 and 4 is $(a/2)\sin\theta$ (drawing not to scale).

We can deduce some important features of this phenomenon by examining waves coming from various portions of the slit, as shown in figure. According to Huygens's principle, **each portion of the slit acts as a source of light waves.**

Hence, light from one portion of the slit can interfere with light from another portion, and the resultant light intensity on a viewing screen depends on the direction θ.

To analyze the diffraction pattern, it is convenient to divide the slit into two halves, as shown in figure. Keeping in mind that all the waves are in phase as they leave the slit, consider rays 1 and 3. As these two rays travel toward a viewing screen far to the right of the above figure, ray 1 travels farther than ray 3 by an amount equal to the path difference $(a/2)\sin\theta$, where a is the width of the slit. Similarly, the path difference between rays 2 and 4 is also $(a/2)\sin\theta$.

If this path difference is exactly half a wavelength (corresponding to a phase difference of 180°), then the two waves cancel each other and destructive interference results. This is true for any two rays that originate at points separated by half the slit width because the phase difference between two such points is 180°. Therefore, waves from the upper half of the slit interfere destructively with waves from the lower half when

$$\frac{a}{2}\sin\theta = \frac{\lambda}{2} \quad \text{or} \quad \sin\theta = \frac{\lambda}{a}$$

If we divide the slit into four equal parts and use similar reasoning, we find that the viewing screen is also dark when

$$\sin\theta = \frac{2\lambda}{a}$$

Likewise, we can divide the slit into six equal parts and show that darkness occurs on the screen when

$$\sin\theta = \frac{3\lambda}{a}$$

Therefore, the general condition for destructive interference is

$$\boxed{\sin\theta = m\frac{\lambda}{a}} \qquad m = \pm 1, \pm 2, \pm 3, \ldots \qquad \ldots\text{(i)}$$

This equation gives the values of θ for which the diffraction pattern has zero light intensity that is, when a dark fringe is formed. However, it tells us nothing about the variation in light intensity along the screen. The general features of the intensity distribution are shown in below figure.

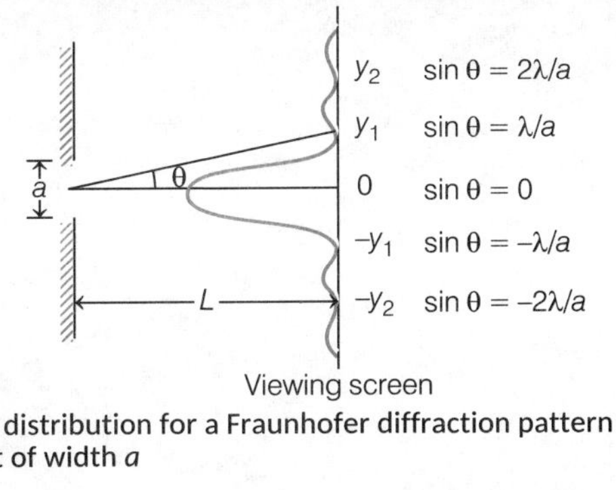

Intensity distribution for a Fraunhofer diffraction pattern from a single slit of width a

A broad central bright fringe is observed; this fringe is flanked by much weaker bright fringes alternating with dark fringes.

The various dark fringes occur at the values of θ that satisfy Eq. (i). Each bright fringe peak lies approximately halfway between its bordering dark fringe minima. Note that the central bright maximum is twice as wide as the secondary maxima.

Intensity of Single Slit Diffraction Patterns

The proof is beyond our syllabus, we are just writing here the intensity at angle θ.

$$I = I_0\left[\frac{\sin\beta/2}{\beta/2}\right]^2$$

Here, $$\frac{\beta}{2} = \frac{\pi a \sin\theta}{\lambda}$$

or $$\boxed{I = I_0\left[\frac{\sin(\pi a \sin\theta/\lambda)}{(\pi a \sin\theta)/\lambda}\right]^2} \qquad \text{(at angle } \theta)$$

Here, I_0 is the intensity at $\theta = 0°$ (the central maximum).

From this result, we see that minima occurs when

$$\frac{\pi a \sin\theta}{\lambda} = m\pi \quad \text{or} \quad \sin\theta = m\frac{\lambda}{a}$$

$m = \pm 1, \pm 2, \ldots$

This is in agreement with Eq. (i).

Note *That* $\sin\theta = 0$, *corresponds to central maxima while* $\frac{\pi a \sin\theta}{\lambda} = \pi$, *corresponds to first minima.*

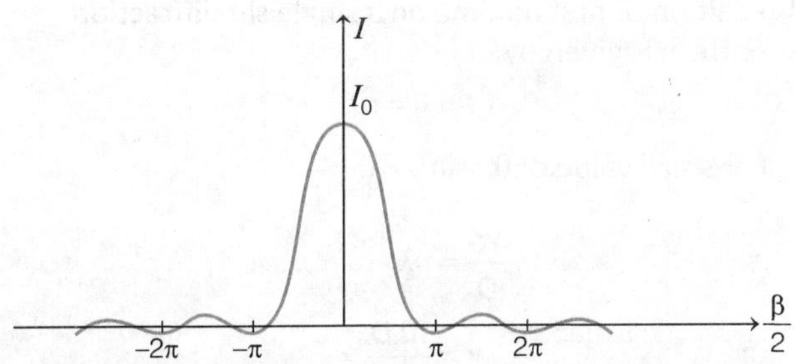

Example 1 A beam of light of wavelength 600 nm from a distant source falls on a single slit 1.0 mm wide and the resulting diffraction pattern is observed on a screen 2 m away. What is the distance between the first dark fringe on either side of the central bright fringe?

Sol. For the diffraction at a single slit, the position of minima is given by

$$a\sin\theta = n\lambda$$

For small value of θ, $\sin\theta \approx \theta = \dfrac{y}{D}$

$$\therefore \quad a\frac{y}{D} = \lambda \quad \text{or} \quad y = \frac{D}{a}\lambda$$

Substituting the values, we have

$$y = \frac{2 \times 6 \times 10^{-7}}{1 \times 10^{-3}} = 1.2 \times 10^{-3} \text{ m}$$

$$= 1.2 \text{ mm}$$

$\therefore$ Distance between first minima on either side of central maxima $= 2y = 2.4$ mm **Ans.**

Example 2 A parallel beam of monochromatic light of wavelength 450 nm passes through a slit of width 0.2 mm. Find the angular divergence in which most of the light is diffracted.

Sol. Most of the light is diffracted between the two first order minimas. One on upper side and the other at lower side. These minimas occur at angle given by

$$a \sin \theta = \pm n\lambda$$

$$\therefore \quad \sin \theta = \pm \frac{\lambda}{a}$$

$$= \pm \frac{450 \times 10^{-9}}{0.2 \times 10^{-3}}$$

$$= \pm 2.25 \times 10^{-3} \text{ rad}$$

$\therefore$ The angular divergence $= 4.5 \times 10^{-3}$ rad. **Ans.**

Example 3 A screen is placed 50 cm from a single slit, which is illuminated with 6000 Å light. If distance between the first and third minima in the diffraction pattern is 3.0 mm, what is the width of the slit?

Sol. Position of first minima on a single slit diffraction pattern is given by

$$a \sin \theta = n\lambda$$

For small value of θ, $\sin\theta \approx \theta = \frac{y}{D}$

$$\therefore \quad \frac{ya}{D} = n\lambda$$

$$\text{or} \quad y = \frac{n\lambda D}{a}$$

$\therefore$ Distance between third order minima and first order minima will be

$$\Delta y = y_3 - y_1 = \frac{(3-1)(\lambda D)}{a} = \frac{2\lambda D}{a}$$

Substituting the values, we have

$$\Delta y = \frac{(2)(6 \times 10^{-7})(0.5)}{3 \times 10^{-3}}$$

$$= 2 \times 10^{-4} \text{ m}$$

$$= 0.2 \text{ mm}$$ **Ans.**

Example 4 In a single slit diffraction experiment first minima for $\lambda_1 = 660$ nm coincides with first maxima for wavelength λ_2. Calculate the value of λ_2.

Sol. Position of minima in diffraction pattern is given by

$$a \sin \theta = n\lambda$$

For first minima of λ_1, we have

$$a \sin \theta_1 = (1)\lambda_1$$

$$\text{or} \quad \sin \theta_1 = \frac{\lambda_1}{a} \qquad \text{...(i)}$$

The first maxima approximately lies between first and second minima. For wavelength λ_2, its position will be

$$a \sin \theta_2 = \frac{3}{2}\lambda_2$$

$$\therefore \quad \sin \theta_2 = \frac{3\lambda_2}{2a} \qquad \text{...(ii)}$$

The two will coincide if

$$\theta_1 = \theta_2$$

$$\text{or} \quad \sin \theta_1 = \sin \theta_2$$

$$\therefore \quad \frac{\lambda_1}{a} = \frac{3\lambda_2}{2a}$$

$$\text{or} \quad \lambda_2 = \frac{2}{3}\lambda_1 = \frac{2}{3} \times 660 \text{ nm}$$

$$= 440 \text{ nm}$$ **Ans.**

MODULE 3 Exercise

Fill in the Blank

1. A slit of width d is placed in front of a lens of focal length 0.5 m and is illuminated normally with light of wavelength 5.89×10^{-7} m. The first diffraction minima on either side of the central diffraction maximum are separated by 2×10^{-3} m. The width d of the slit is ...... m. **(1997 JEE)**

Single Correct Option

2. The main difference in the phenomenon of interference and diffraction is that
   (a) diffraction is due to interaction of light from the same wavefront, whereas interference is the interaction of waves from two isolated sources
   (b) diffraction is due to interaction of light from same wavefront, whereas the interference is the interaction of two waves derived from two incoherent sources
   (c) diffraction is due to interaction of waves derived from the same source, whereas the interference is the bending of light from the same wavefront
   (d) diffraction is caused by the reflected waves from a source, whereas interference is caused due to refraction of waves from a source

3. In the diffraction pattern of single slit under bichromatic illumination, the first minimum with the wavelength λ_1 is found to be coincident with the third minimum at λ_2. So,
   (a) $\lambda_1 = 3\lambda_2$ (b) $3\lambda_1 = \lambda_2$
   (c) $\lambda_1 = 3.5\lambda_2$ (d) None of these

4. A single slit of width a is illuminated by a monochromatic light of wavelength 600 nm. The value of a for which first minimum appears at $\theta = 30°$ on the screen will be **(2023 Main)**
   (a) 1.2 μm (b) 3 μm (c) 0.6 μm (d) 1.8 μm

5. Consider the diffraction pattern obtained from sunlight incident on a pinhole 0.1 μm. If the diameter of the pinhole is slightly increased, it will affect the diffraction pattern such that **(2021 Main)**
   (a) Its size decreases, and intensity decreases
   (b) Its size increases, and intensity increases
   (c) Its size increases, but intensity decreases
   (d) Its size decreases, and intensity increases

6. The angular width of the central maximum in a single slit diffraction pattern is 60°. The width of the slit is 1 μm. The slit is illuminated by monochromatic plane waves. If another slit of same width is made near it, Young's fringes can be observed on a screen placed at a distance 50 cm from the slits. If the observed fringe width is 1 cm, what is the slit separation distance? (i.e. distance between the centres of each slit.) **(2018 Main)**
   (a) 100 μm (b) 25 μm
   (c) 50 μm (d) 75 μm

7. Yellow light is used in a single slit diffraction experiment with slit width of 0.6 mm. If yellow light is replaced by X-rays, then the observed pattern will reveal **(1999 JEE)**
   (a) that the central maximum is narrower
   (b) more number of fringes
   (c) less number of fringes
   (d) no diffraction pattern

8. A parallel monochromatic beam of light is incident normally on a narrow slit. A diffraction pattern is formed on a screen placed perpendicular to the direction of the incident beam. At the first minimum of the diffraction pattern, the phase difference between the rays coming from the two edges of the slit is **(1998 JEE)**
   (a) zero (b) $\pi/2$
   (c) π (d) 2π

9. A narrow slit of width 1 mm is illuminated by monochromatic light of wavelength 600 nm. The distance between the first minima on either side of a screen at a distance of 2 m is **(1994 JEE)**
   (a) 1.2 cm (b) 1.2 mm
   (c) 2.4 cm (d) 2.4 mm

Answers

1. 2.945×10^{-4} m **2.** (a) **3.** (a) **4.** (a) **5.** (d) **6.** (b) **7.** (d) **8.** (d) **9.** (d)

See hints on pages 245-246.

Polarization of Light

(i) Polarization is a characteristic of all transverse waves.

(ii) Oscillation which takes place in a transverse wave in many different directions is said to be unpolarized.

(iii) In an unpolarized transverse wave, oscillations may take place at right angles to the direction in which the wave travels.

(iv) Electromagnetic waves such as light exhibit polarization.

(v) Sound waves do not exhibit polarization as they are longitudinal in nature.

(vi) In an electromagnetic wave we know that electric and magnetic fields oscillate in mutually perpendicular direction to propagation of wave.

Further, magnitude of electric field is very-very greater than magnitude of magnetic field ($E >> B$), so we are mainly concerned with the polarization of electric field.

An unpolarized light can be polarized by passing it through a polaroid as shown below,

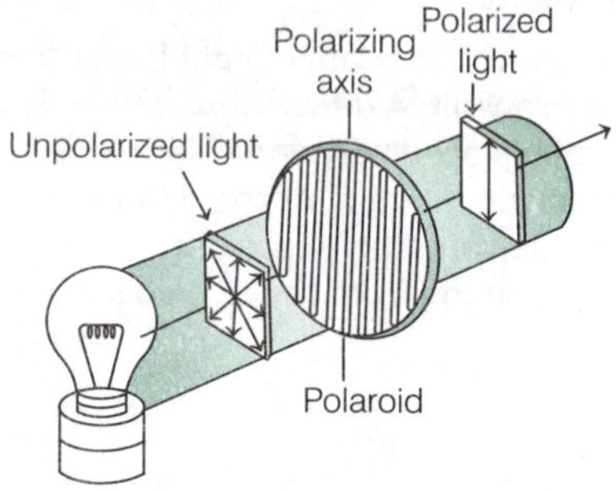

Polarization of Light

Polaroids

Plane sheets in the shape of circular discs called polaroids have long chain of hydrocarbons. The direction perpendicular to the chains is called the transmission axis of the polaroid.

When light falls perpendicular on the polaroid, the transmitted light becomes linearly polarized with E-vector parallel to the transmission axis.

Note *If an unpolarized light of intensity I_0 falls on a polaroid then intensity of linearly polarized light after transmitting from the polaroid remains $I_0/2$.*

Analyzer

This is another polaroid kept after the first polaroid.

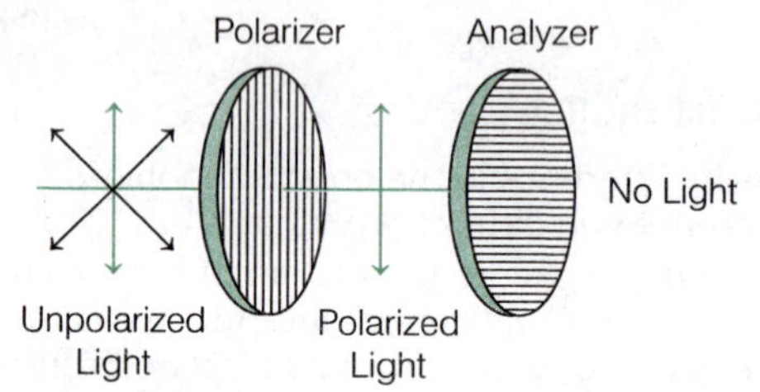

In the figure, transmission axes of polarizer and analyzer are mutually perpendicular. So, intensity of light after the analyzer is zero.

Law of Malus

If linearly polarized light of intensity I_0 falls on an analyzer and angle between E-Vector of linearly polarized light and transmission axis of polarizer is θ, then intensity of light after passing through the analyzer is given by

$$I = I_0 \cos^2 \theta$$

This is called law of Malus.

Now we can see that angle θ is 90° in above figure. So intensity of light after passing through the analyzer is zero.

Now let us come to the following figure,

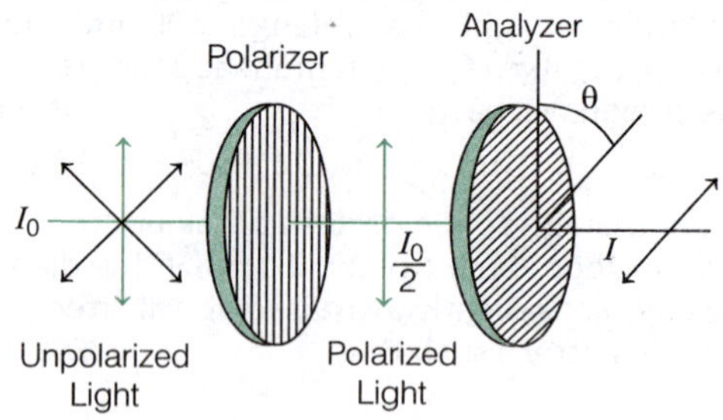

Suppose I_0 is the intensity of unpolarized light, then intensity after polarizer will become $\frac{I_0}{2}$ and finally the intensity after analyzer will become $I = \frac{I_0}{2} \cos^2 \theta$.

Polarization by Reflection and Refraction

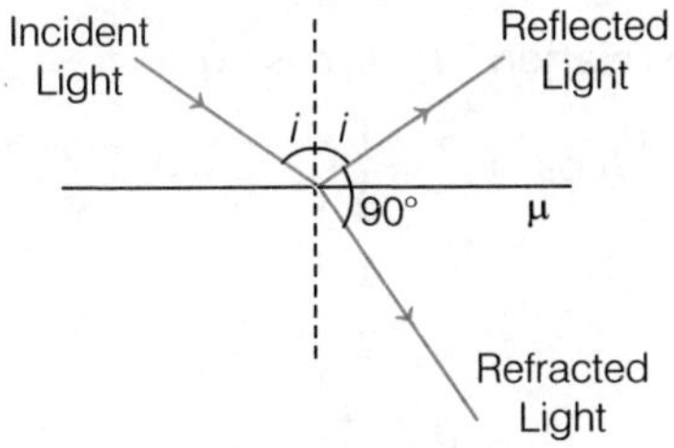

At Brewster's angle reflected and refracted rays are mutually perpendicular

Consider a light beam from air incident on the surface of a transparent medium of refractive index μ. The reflected and the refracted rays are partially polarized. At angle of incidence given by:

$$\tan i = \mu \quad \text{or} \quad i = \tan^{-1}(\mu)$$

reflected light is completely polarized. The angle i given by the above equation is called **Brewster angle** and the above equation itself is known as Brewster's law.

Note that the refracted ray is never completely polarized.

Example 1 Prove that at Brewster's angle reflected and refracted rays are mutually perpendicular.

Sol.

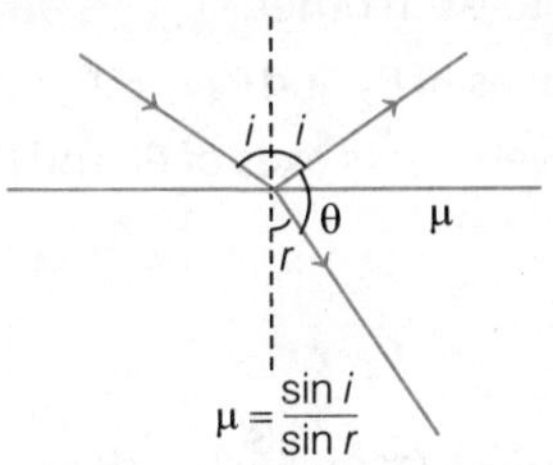

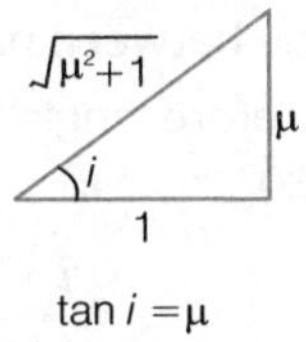

$$\therefore \quad \sin r = \frac{\sin i}{\mu}$$

$$= \frac{\mu/\sqrt{\mu^2+1}}{\mu} = \frac{1}{\sqrt{\mu^2+1}} = \cos i$$

$$\therefore \quad r = 90° - i$$

or $\quad r + i = 90°$ ...(i)

In the figure, we can see that

$$i + r + \theta = 180° \quad \text{...(ii)}$$

From Eqs. (i) and (ii), we can see that

$$\theta = 90°$$ **Hence proved.**

Polarization by Scattering

When a beam of white light passes through a medium consisting of small particles of size of the order of the wavelength of light (dust, smoke, air molecules), then the light scatters in all directions and the particles causing scattering are called **scatterers**. The scattering of light is, infact, absorption and re-radiation of light by the scatterers.

It has been see that if unpolarized light is scattered then the scattered light is partially polarized.

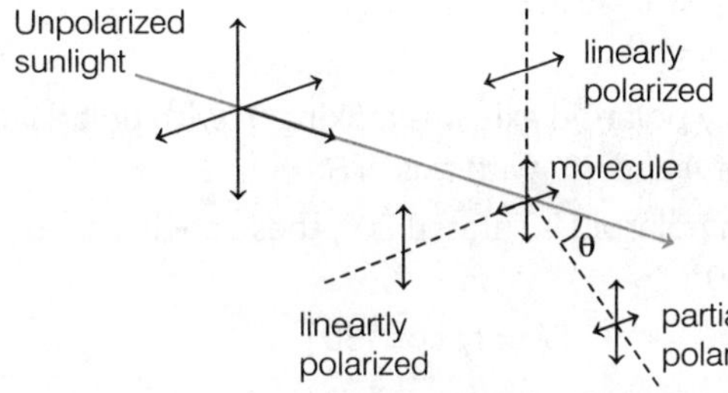

At $\theta = 90°$ as shown in above figure light is totally plane polarized. At all other angles the light is partially plane polarized.

Interesting Fact

Human eye can't distinguish between an unpolarized and a polarized light but the eyes of a bee can detect the difference.

Example 2 When light of a particular wavelength falls on a plane surface at an angle of incidence 60°, then the reflected light becomes completely plane polarised. Find the refractive index of surface material and the angle of refraction through it.

Sol. Using Brewster's law, $\mu = \tan i = \tan 60° = \sqrt{3}$

At this condition, $i + r = 90°$

$$\therefore \quad r = 90° - 60°$$

Angle of refraction, $r = 30°$

Example 3 A beam of unpolarised light of intensity I_0 is passed through a polaroid A and then through another polaroid B which is oriented so that its principal plane makes an angle of 45° relative to that of A. The intensity of the emergent light is **(2013 Main)**

(a) I_0 (b) $I_0/2$ (c) $I_0/4$ (d) $I_0/8$

Sol. Relation between intensities is

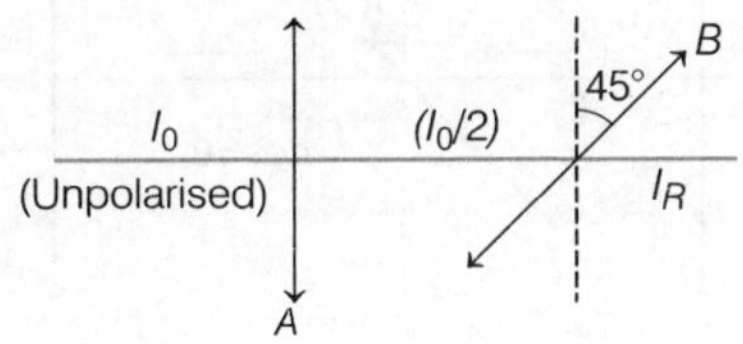

After passing from A, intensity will remain $\frac{I_0}{2}$.

$$I_R = \left(\frac{I_0}{2}\right)\cos^2(45°) = \frac{I_0}{2} \times \frac{1}{2} = \frac{I_0}{4}$$

So, the correct option is (c).

Example 4 Two beams, A and B, of plane polarised light with mutually perpendicular planes of polarisation are seen through a polaroid. From the position when the beam A has maximum intensity (and beam B has zero intensity), a rotation of polaroid through 30° makes the two beams appear equally bright. If the initial intensities of the two beams are I_A and I_B respectively, then I_A/I_B equals **(2014 Main)**

(a) 3 (b) 3/2 (c) 1 (d) 1/3

Sol. $I = I_0 \cos^2 \theta$

Initially polaroid axis was making 0° with polarisation axis of A and 90° with axis of B.

When polaroid is rotated 30°, these angles become 30° and 60°.

Now, $I'_A = I_A \cos^2 30°$

$I'_B = I_B \cos^2 60°$

As, $I'_A = I'_B$

$$I_A \cos^2 30° = I_B \cos^2 60°$$

$$\Rightarrow \quad I_A \frac{3}{4} = I_B \frac{1}{4}$$

$$\Rightarrow \quad \frac{I_A}{I_B} = \frac{1}{3}$$

So, the correct option is (d).

Example 5 Unpolarised light of intensity I passes through an ideal polariser A. Another identical polariser B is placed behind A. The intensity of light beyond B is found to be $\frac{I}{2}$. Now, another identical polariser C is placed between A and B. The intensity beyond B is now found to be $\frac{I}{8}$. The angle between polariser A and C is **(2018 Main)**

(a) 60° (b) 0°
(c) 30° (d) 45°

Sol. After passing through A intensity will remain $\frac{I}{2}$.

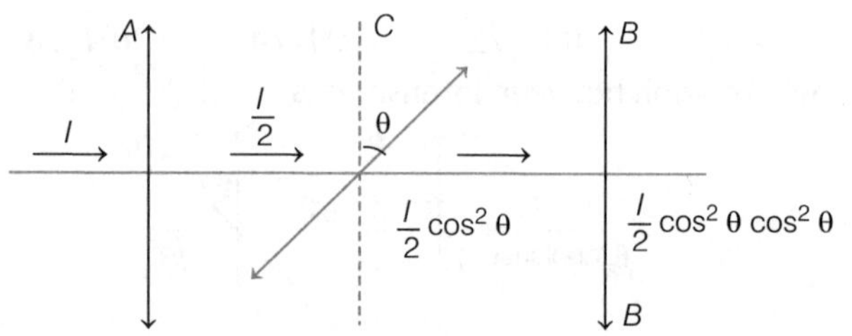

Since, intensity after B is also $\frac{I}{2}$.

Therefore, axes of A and B are parallel.

Using the relation, $I = I_0 \cos^2 \theta$

We have, $\frac{I}{2}(\cos^2 \theta)^2 = \frac{I}{8}$

$$\Rightarrow \quad \cos^2 \theta = \frac{1}{2}$$

$$\text{or} \quad \cos \theta = \frac{1}{\sqrt{2}}$$

$$\Rightarrow \quad \theta = 45°$$

So, the correct option is (d).

Example 6 A system of three polarisers P_1, P_2, P_3 is set up such that the pass axis of P_3 is crossed with respect to that of P_1. The pass axis of P_2 is inclined at 60° to the pass axis of P_3. When a beam of unpolarised light of intensity I_0 is incident on P_1, the intensity of light transmitted by the three polarisers is I. The ratio (I_0 / I) equals (nearly) **(2018 Main)**

(a) 5.33 (b) 16.00
(c) 10.67 (d) 1.80

Sol. Angle between pass axes of P_1 and P_3 is 90° as they are crossed with respect to each other.

Angle between pass axes of P_2 and P_3 is 60°.

Therefore, angle between pass axes of P_1 and P_2 should be 30°.

$$I_1 = \frac{I_0}{2}$$

$$I_2 = \frac{I_0}{2} \cos^2 (30°) = \frac{3I_0}{8}$$

$$I_3 = \frac{3I_0}{8} \cos^2 (60°) = \frac{3I_0}{32}$$

$$\therefore \quad I = \frac{3I_0}{32}$$

$$\therefore \quad \frac{I_0}{I} = \frac{32}{3} = 10.67$$

So, the correct option is (c).

MODULE 4 Exercise

Statement Type Question

1. Given below are two statements.

Statement I If the Brewster's angle for the light propagating from air to glass is θ_B, then the Brewster's angle for the light propagating from glass to air is $\frac{\pi}{2} - \theta_B$.

Statement II The Brewster's angle for the light propagating from glass to air is $\tan^{-1}(\mu_g)$, where μ_g is the refractive index of glass. **(2023 Main)**

In the light of the above statements, choose the correct answer from the options given below.

(a) Statement I is false but Statement II is true.
(b) Statement I is true but Statement II is false.
(c) Both Statement I and Statement II are false.
(d) Both Statement I and Statement II is true.

Single Correct Option

2. n polarising sheets are arranged such that each makes an angle 45° with the preceeding sheet. An unpolarised light of intensity I is incident into this arrangement. The output intensity is found to be $I/64$. The value of n will be **(2023 Main)**

(a) 3 (b) 6 (c) 4 (d) 5

3. Two polaroids A and B are placed in such a way that the pass-axis of polaroids are perpendicular to each other. Now, another polaroid C is placed between A and B bisecting angle between them. If intensity of unpolarised light is I_0 then intensity of transmitted light after passing through polaroid B will be **(2023 Main)**

(a) $I_0/8$ (b) $I_0/2$ (c) Zero (d) $I_0/4$

4. An unpolarised light beam of intensity $2I_0$ is passed through a polaroid P and then through another polaroid Q which is oriented in such a way that its passing axis makes an angle of 30° relative to that of P. The intensity of the emergent light is **(2022 Main)**

(a) $\frac{I_0}{4}$ (b) $\frac{I_0}{2}$
(c) $\frac{3I_0}{4}$ (d) $\frac{3I_0}{2}$

5. A beam of plane polarised light of large cross-sectional area and uniform intensity of 3.3 Wm^{-2} falls normally on a polariser (cross-sectional area 3×10^{-4} m^2) which rotates about its axis with an angular speed of 31.4 rad/s. The energy of light passing through the polariser per revolution, is close to **(2020 Main)**

(a) 1.0×10^{-5} J (b) 1.0×10^{-4} J
(c) 1.5×10^{-4} J (d) 5.0×10^{-4} J

6. Consider a tank made of glass (refractive index 1.5) with a thick bottom. It is filled with a liquid of refractive index μ. A student finds that, irrespective of what the incident angle i (see figure) is for a beam of light entering the liquid, the light reflected from the liquid glass interface is never completely polarised. For this to happen, the minimum value of μ is **(2019 Main)**

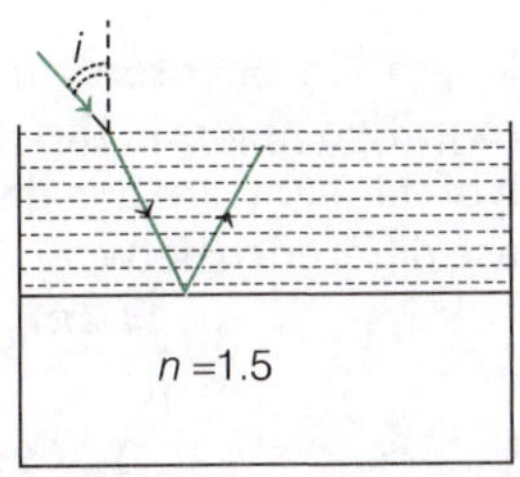

(a) $\sqrt{\frac{5}{3}}$ (b) $\frac{3}{\sqrt{5}}$
(c) $\frac{5}{\sqrt{3}}$ (d) $\frac{4}{3}$

Answers

1. (b) 2. (b) 3. (a) 4. (c) 5. (b) 6. (b)

See hints on pages 246-247.

Unit Exercise (Cumulative)

Level 1

Assertion and Reason

See directions on page 11.

1. **Assertion :** In the YDSE apparatus shown in figure $d << D$ and $\frac{d}{\lambda} = 4$, then second order maxima will be obtained at $\theta = 30°$.

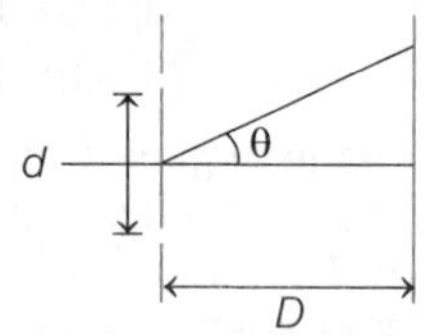

Reason : Total seven maximas will be obtained on screen.

Single Correct Option

2. Light of wavelength λ in air enters a medium of refractive index μ. Two points in this medium, lying along the path of this light, are at a distance of x apart. The phase difference between these points is

(a) $\mu\left(\frac{2\pi}{\lambda}\right)x$ (b) $\frac{1}{\mu}\left(\frac{2\pi}{\lambda}\right)x$

(c) $(\mu-1)\left(\frac{2\pi}{\lambda}\right)x$ (d) $\frac{1}{\mu-1}\left(\frac{2\pi}{\lambda}\right)x$

3. In a double-slit experiment, green light (5303 Å) falls on a double slit having a separation of 19.44 μ-m and a width of 4.05 μ-m. The number of bright fringes between the first and the second diffraction minima is **(2019 Main)**

(a) 5 (b) 10 (c) 9 (d) 4

4. If two sources (each having intensity I_0) have a randomly varying phase difference $\phi(t)$, the resultant intensity will be given by

(a) $4I_0$ (b) $I_0/2$ (c) $2I_0$ (d) $I_0/\sqrt{2}$

5. Consider a Young's double slit experiment as shown in figure

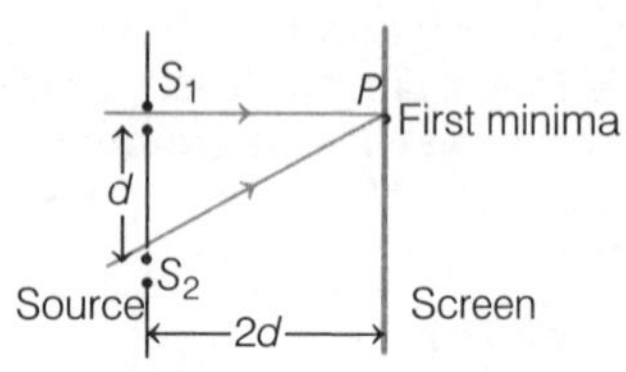

What should be the slit separation d in terms of wavelength λ such that the first minimum occurs directly in front of the slit (S_1) ? **(2019 Main)**

(a) $\frac{\lambda}{2(5-\sqrt{2})}$ (b) $\frac{\lambda}{(5-\sqrt{2})}$

(c) $\frac{\lambda}{2(\sqrt{5}-2)}$ (d) $\frac{\lambda}{(\sqrt{5}-2)}$

6. In a Young's double slit experiment with slit separation 0.1 mm, one observes a bright fringe at angle $\frac{1}{40}$ rad by using light of wavelength λ_1. When the light of the wavelength λ_2 is used, a bright fringe is seen at the same angle in the same set up. Given that λ_1 and λ_2 are in visible range (380 nm to 740 nm), their values are **(2019 Main)**

(a) 380 nm, 525 nm (b) 400 nm, 500 nm

(c) 380 nm, 500 nm (d) 625 nm, 500 nm

7. In a Young's double slit experiment, the slits are placed 0.320 mm apart. Light of wavelength $\lambda = 500$ nm is incident on the slits. The total number of bright fringes that are observed in the angular range $-30° \le \theta \le 30°$ is **(2019 Main)**

(a) 320 (b) 321 (c) 640 (d) 641

8. In a Young's double slit experiment, slits are separated by 0.5 mm and the screen is placed 150 cm away. A beam of light consisting of two wavelengths, 650 nm and 520 nm, is used to obtain interference fringes on the screen. The least distance from the common central maximum to the point where the bright fringes due to both the wavelengths coincide, is **(2017 Main)**

(a) 7.8 mm (b) 9.75 mm (c) 15.6 mm (d) 1.56 mm

9. In the Young's double slit experiment using a monochromatic light of wavelength λ the path difference (in terms of an integer n) corresponding to any point having half the peak intensity is **(2013 Adv.)**

(a) $(2n+1)\frac{\lambda}{2}$ (b) $(2n+1)\frac{\lambda}{4}$

(c) $(2n+1)\frac{\lambda}{8}$ (d) $(2n+1)\frac{\lambda}{16}$

10. Young's double slit experiment is carried out by using green, red and blue light, one colour at one time. The fringe widths recorded are β_G, β_R and β_B respectively. Then, **(2012 JEE)**

(a) $\beta_G > \beta_B > \beta_R$ (b) $\beta_B > \beta_G > \beta_R$

(c) $\beta_R > \beta_B > \beta_G$ (d) $\beta_R > \beta_G > \beta_B$

11. In Young's double slit experiment intensity at a point is (1/4) of the maximum intensity. Angular position of this point is **(2005 JEE)**

(a) $\sin^{-1}\left(\frac{\lambda}{d}\right)$ (b) $\sin^{-1}\left(\frac{\lambda}{2d}\right)$ (c) $\sin^{-1}\left(\frac{\lambda}{3d}\right)$ (d) $\sin^{-1}\left(\frac{\lambda}{4d}\right)$

12. Two coherent point sources S_1 and S_2 are separated by a small distance d as shown. The fringes obtained on the screen will be

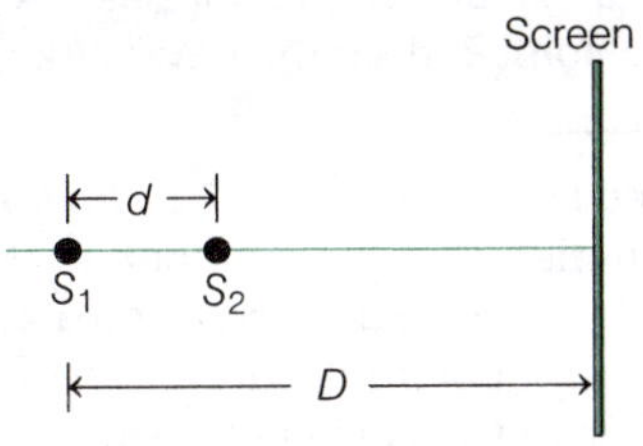

(a) points (b) straight lines
(c) semi-circle (d) concentric circles

13. In Young's double slit experiment, the separation between the slits is halved and the distance between the slits and the screen is doubled. The fringe width is **(1981 JEE)**

(a) unchanged (b) halved
(c) doubled (d) quadrupled

Subjective Questions

14. Consider an interference experiment using eight equally spaced slits. Determine the smallest phase difference in the waves from adjacent slits such that the resultant wave has zero amplitude.

15. A radio transmitting station operating at a frequency of 120 MHz has two identical antennas that radiate in phase. Antenna B is 9.00 m to the right of antenna A. Consider point P between the antennas and along the line connecting them, a horizontal distance x to the right of antenna A. For what values of x will constructive interference occur at point P ?

16. Coherent light from a sodium-vapour lamp is passed through a filter that blocks everything except for light of a single wavelength. It then falls on two slits separated by 0.460 mm. In the resulting interference pattern on a screen 2.20 m away, adjacent bright fringes are separated by 2.82 mm. What is the wavelength?

17. Two slits 4.0×10^{-6} m apart are illuminated by light of wavelength 600 nm. What is the highest order fringe in the interference pattern?

18. Interference pattern with Young's double slits 1.5 mm apart are formed on a screen at a distance 1.5 m from the plane of slits. In the path of the beam of one of the slits, a transparent film of 10 micron thickness and of refractive index 1.6 is interposed while in the path of the beam from the other slit a transparent film of 15 micron thickness and of refractive index 1.2 is interposed. Find the displacement of the fringe pattern.

19. In a Young's double slit experiment using monochromatic light, the fringe pattern shifts by a certain distance on the screen when a mica sheet of refractive index 1.6 and thickness 1.964 microns is introduced in the path of one of the interfering waves. The mica sheet is then removed and the distance between the slits and screen is doubled. It is found that the distance between successive maxima (or minima) now is the same as observed fringe shift upon the introduction of the mica sheet. Calculate the wavelength of the monochromatic light used in the experiment.

20. Interference effects are produced at point P on a screen as a result of direct rays from a 500 nm source and reflected rays from a mirror, as shown in figure. If the source is 100 m to the left of the screen and 1.00 cm above the mirror, find the distance y (in milimetres) to the first dark band above the mirror.

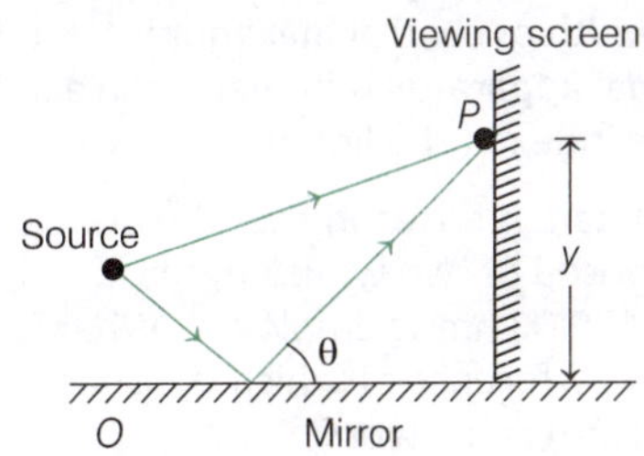

21. A glass plate ($n = 1.53$) that is 0.485 μm thick and surrounded by air is illuminated by a beam of white light normal to the plate.
(a) What wavelengths (in air) within the limits of the visible spectrum ($\lambda = 400$ to 700 nm) are intensified in the reflected beam?
(b) What wavelengths within the visible spectrum are intensified in the transmitted light?

22. An oil film covers the surface of a small pond. The refractive index of the oil is greater than that of water. At one point on the film, the film has the smallest non-zero thickness for which there will be destructive interference in the reflected light when infrared radiation with wavelength 800 nm is incident normal to the film. When this film is viewed at normal incidence at this same point, for what visible wavelengths, if any, will there be constructive interference? (Visible light has wavelengths between 400 nm and 700 nm)

23. A possible means for making an airplane invisible to radar is to coat the plane with an anti reflective polymer. If radar waves have a wavelength of 3.00 cm and the index of refraction of the polymer is $\mu = 1.5$. How thick is the oil film? Refractive index of the material of airplane wings is greater than the refractive index of polymer.

24. A narrow monochromatic beam of light of intensity I is incident on a glass plate as shown in figure. Another identical glass plate is kept close to the first one-and parallel to it. Each glass plate reflects 25 per cent of the light incident on it and transmits the remaining. Find the ratio of the minimum and maximum intensities in the interference pattern formed by the two beams obtained after one reflection at each plate. **(1990 JEE)**

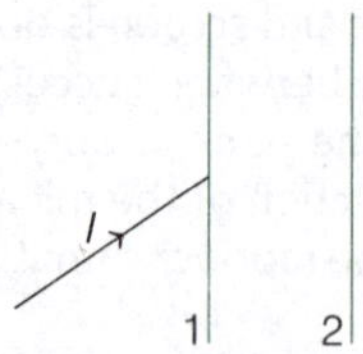

25. Angular width of central maximum in the Fraunhofer diffraction pattern of a slit is measured. The slit is illuminated by light of wavelength 6000 Å. When the slit is illuminated by light of another wavelength, the angular width decreases by 30%. (a) Calculate the wavelength of this light. (b) The same decrease in the angular width of central maximum is obtained when the original apparatus is immersed in a liquid. Find the refractive index of the liquid. **(1996 JEE)**

26. In a two-beam interferometer the orange mercury line composed of two wavelengths $\lambda_1 = 576.97$ nm and $\lambda_2 = 579.03$ nm is employed. What is the least order of interference at which the sharpness of the fringe pattern is the worst? **(Irodov 5.93)**

27. Light with wavelength $\lambda = 0.50\ \mu$m falls on a slit of width $b = 10\ \mu$m at an angle $\theta_0 = 30°$ to its normal. Find the angular position of the first minima located on both sides of the central Fraunhofer maximum. **(Irodov 5.121)**

Integer Type Questions

28. Two wavelengths λ_1 and λ_2 are used in Young's double slit experiment. $\lambda_1 = 450$ nm and $\lambda_2 = 650$ nm. The minimum order of fringe produced by λ_2 which overlaps with the fringe produced by λ_1 is n. The value of n is...... . **(2024 Main)**

29. In a Young's double slit experiment, the intensities at two points, for the path differences $\frac{\lambda}{4}$ and $\frac{\lambda}{3}$ (λ being the wavelength of light used) are I_1 and I_2 respectively. If I_0 denotes the intensity produced by each one of the individual slits, then $\frac{I_1 + I_2}{I_0} =$ .... **(2023 Main)**

30. White light is passed through a double slit and interference is observed on a screen 1.5 m away. The separation between the slits is 0.3 mm. The first violet and red fringes are formed 2.0 mm and 3.5 mm away from the central white fringes. The difference in wavelengths of red and violet light is .... nm. **(2021 Main)**

31. Orange light of wavelength 6000×10^{-10} m illuminates a single slit of width 0.6×10^{-4} m. The maximum possible number of diffraction minima produced on both sides of the central maximum is .... **(2022 Main)**

32. A point source S emits unpolarised light uniformly in all directions. At two points A and B, the ratio $r = I_A / I_B$ of the intensities of light is 2. If a set of two polaroids having 45° angle between their pass-axes is placed just before point B, then the new value of r will be ____________ . **(2024 Adv.)**

33. Unpolarised light of intensity 32 Wm^{-2} passes through the combination of three polaroids such that the pass axis of the last polaroid is perpendicular to that of the pass axis of first polaroid. If intensity of emerging light is 3 Wm^{-2}, then the angle between pass axis of first two polaroids is .... ° . **(2023 Main)**

Level 2

Single Correct Option

34. The intensity of each of the two slits in Young's double slit experiment is I_0. Calculate the minimum separation between the two points on the screen where intensities are $2I_0$ and I_0. Given, the fringe width equal to β.
(a) $\frac{\beta}{4}$ (b) $\frac{\beta}{3}$
(c) $\frac{\beta}{12}$ (d) None of these

35. In Young's double slit experiment, the intensity of light at a point on the screen where path difference is λ is I. If intensity at another point is $I/4$, then possible path differences at this point are
(a) $\lambda/2, \lambda/3$ (b) $\lambda/3, 2\lambda/3$
(c) $\lambda/3, \lambda/4$ (d) $2\lambda/3, \lambda/4$

36. In a YDSE experiment, $d =$ mm, $\lambda = 6000$ Å and $D = 1$ m. The minimum distance between two points on screen having 75% intensity of the maximum intensity will be
(a) 0.50 mm (b) 0.40 mm (c) 0.30 mm (d) 0.20 mm

37. Let S_1 and S_2 be the two slits in Young's double slit experiment . If central maxima is observed at P and angle $S_1 P S_2 = \theta$, (θ is small) find the y-coordinates of the 3rd minima assuming the origin at the central maxima . (λ = wavelength of monochromatic light used).
(a) $\pm\frac{2\lambda}{\theta}$ (b) $\pm\frac{5\lambda}{2\theta}$
(c) $\pm\frac{5}{2}\lambda\theta$ (d) $\pm 2\lambda\theta$

38. In YDSE if a slab whose refractive index can be varied is placed in front of one of the slits . Then, the variation of resultant intensity at mid-point of screen with μ will be best represented by (μ is greater than or equal to 1)

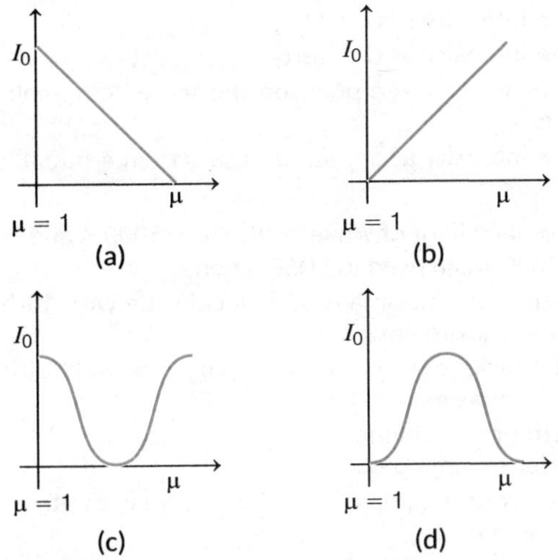

39. In YDSE, both slits produce equal intensities on the screen. A 100% transparent thin film is placed in front of one of the slits. Now, the intensity on the centre becomes 75% of the previous intensity. The wavelength of light is 6000 Å and refractive index of glass is 1.5. The minimum thickness of the glass slab is

(a) 0.2 μm (b) 0.3 μm
(c) 0.4 μm (d) 0.5 μm

40. YDSE is carried with two thin sheets of thickness 10.4 μm each and refractive index $\mu_1 = 1.52$ and $\mu_2 = 1.40$ covering the slits S_1 and S_2, respectively. If white light of range 400 nm to 780 nm is used, then which wavelength will form maxima exactly at point O, the centre of the screen

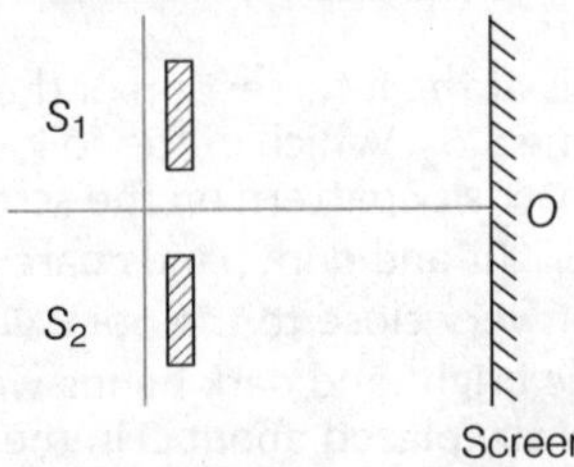

(a) 416 nm only (b) 624 nm only
(c) 416 nm and 624 nm only (d) None of these

41. Two light rays having the same wavelength λ in vacuum are in phase initially. Then, the first ray travels a path L_1 through a medium of refractive index n_1 while the second ray travels a path of length L_2 through a medium of refractive index n_2. The two waves are then combined to produce interference. The phase difference between the two waves is

(a) $\frac{2\pi}{\lambda}(L_2 - L_1)$ (b) $\frac{2\pi}{\lambda}(n_1L_1 - n_2L_2)$
(c) $\frac{2\pi}{\lambda}(n_2L_1 - n_1L_2)$ (d) $\frac{2\pi}{\lambda}\left(\frac{L_1}{n_1} - \frac{L_2}{n_2}\right)$

42. An interference is observed due to two coherent sources separated by a distance 5λ along positive y-axis, where λ is the wavelength of light. A detector D is moved along the positive x-axis. The number of points on the x-axis excluding the points $x = 0$ and $x = \infty$ at which resultant intensity will be maximum, are

(a) 4 (b) 5
(c) ∞ (d) zero

43. In Young's double-slit experiment, the y-coordinates of central maxima and 10th maxima are 2 cm and 5 cm respectively. When the YDSE apparatus is immersed in a liquid of refractive index 1.5, then corresponding y-coordinates will be

(a) 2 cm, 7.5 cm (b) 3 cm, 6 cm
(c) 2 cm, 4 cm (d) 4/3 cm, 10/3 cm

44. In Young's double-slit experiment how many maximas can be obtained on a screen (including the central maximum) on both sides of the central fringes if $\lambda = 2000$ Å and $d = 7000$ Å

(a) 12 (b) 7
(c) 18 (d) 4

45. Two ideal slits S_1 and S_2 are at a distance d apart and illuminated by light of wavelength λ passing through an ideal source slit S placed on the line through S_2 as shown. The distance between the planes of slits and the source slit is D.

A screen is held at a distance D from the plane of the slits. The minimum value of d for which there is darkness at O is

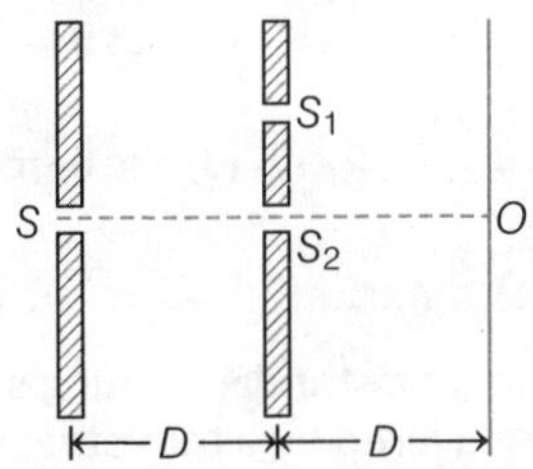

(a) $\sqrt{\frac{3\lambda D}{2}}$ (b) $\sqrt{\lambda D}$
(c) $\sqrt{\frac{\lambda D}{2}}$ (d) $\sqrt{3\lambda D}$

46. In the figure, Young's double-slit experiment is shown. Q is the position of the first bright fringe on the one side of O. P is the 11th bright fringe on the other side, as measured from Q. If the wavelength of the light used is 600 nm, then S_1B will be equal to

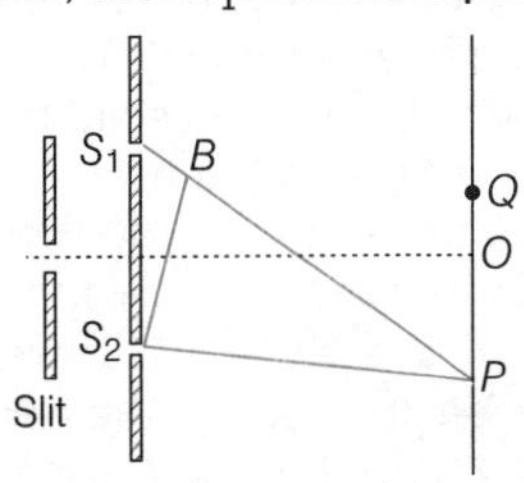

(a) 6×10^{-6} m (b) 6.6×10^{-6} m
(c) 3.138×10^{-7} m (d) 3.144×10^{-7} m

47. Two coherent light sources A and B are at a distance 3λ from each other (λ = wavelength of light used). The distance from A on the x-axis at which the interference is constructive is

(a) 3λ (b) 4λ (c) 3.5λ (d) 1.5λ

48. In the below diagram, CP represents a wavefront and AO and BP, the corresponding two rays. Find the condition of θ for constructive interference at P between the ray BP and reflected ray OP. **(2023 JEE)**

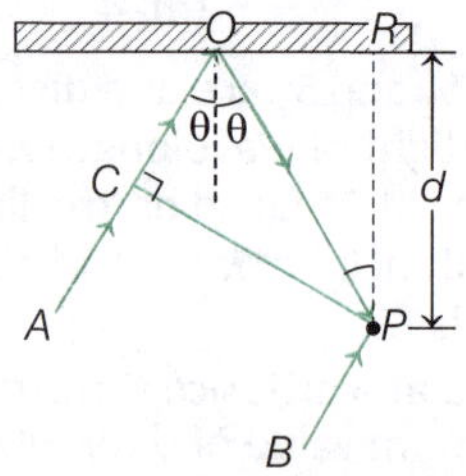

(a) $\cos\theta = \frac{3\lambda}{2d}$ (b) $\cos\theta = \frac{\lambda}{4d}$

(c) $\sec\theta - \cos\theta = \frac{\lambda}{d}$ (d) $\sec\theta - \cos\theta = \frac{4\lambda}{d}$

Multiple Correct Options

49. If one of the slit of a standard Young's double slit experiment is covered by a thin parallel sided glass slab so that it transmits only one-half the light intensity of the other, then
(a) the fringe pattern will get shifted towards the covered slit
(b) the fringe pattern will get shifted away from the covered slit
(c) the bright fringes will be less bright and the dark ones will be more bright
(d) the fringe width will remain unchanged

50. A parallel beam of light ($\lambda = 5000$ Å) is incident at an angle $\theta = 30°$ with the normal to the slit plane in a Young's double slit experiment. The intensity due to each slit is I_0. Point O is equidistant from S_1 and S_2. The distance between slits is 1 mm.

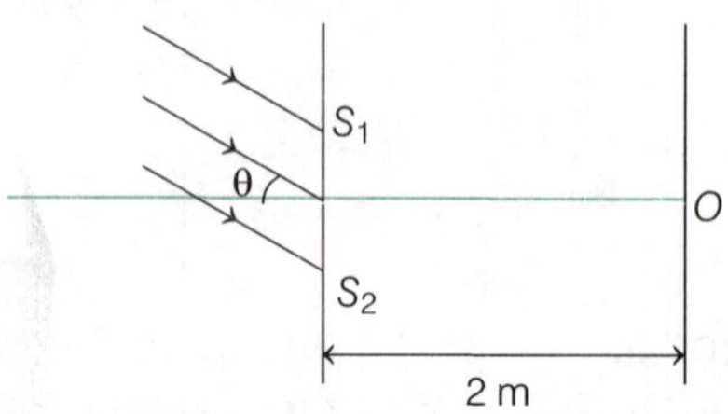

(a) The intensity at O is $4I_0$
(b) The intensity at O is zero
(c) The intensity at a point on the screen 4 mm above O is $4I_0$
(d) The intensity at a point on the screen 4 mm above O is zero

51. Bichromatic light of wavelengths $\lambda_1 = 5000$ Å and $\lambda_2 = 7000$ Å are used in YDSE. Then,
(a) 14th order maxima of λ_1 will coincide with 10th order maxima of λ_2
(b) 21st order maxima of λ_2 will coincide with 15th order maxima of λ_1
(c) 11th order minima of λ_1 will coincide with 8th order minima of λ_2
(d) 3rd order minima of λ_1 will coincide with 4th order minima of λ_2

52. While conducting the Young's double slit experiment, a student replaced the two slits with a large opaque plate in the xy-plane containing two small holes that act as two coherent point sources (S_1, S_2) emitting light of wavelength 600 nm. The student mistakenly placed the screen parallel to the xz-plane (for $z > 0$) at a distance $D = 3$ m from the mid-point of S_1S_2, as shown schematically in the figure. The distance between the sources is $d = 0.6003$ mm.

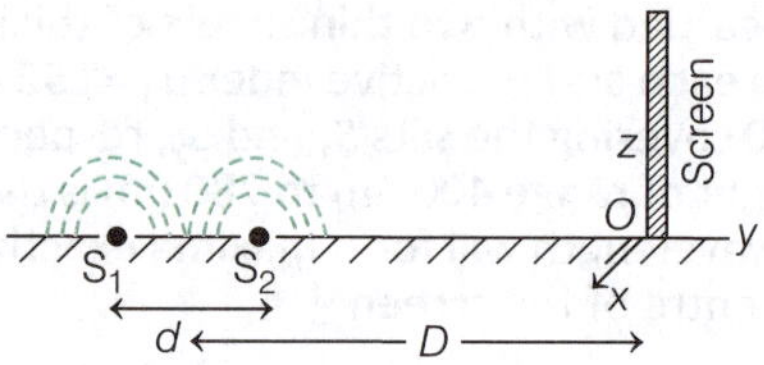

The origin O is at the intersection of the screen and the line joining S_1S_2. Which of the following is (are) true of the intensity pattern on the screen? **(2016 Adv.)**
(a) Straight bright and dark bands parallel to the X-axis
(b) The region very close to the point O will be dark
(c) Hyperbolic bright and dark bands with foci symmetrically placed about O in the x-direction
(d) Semi circular bright and dark bands centered at point

53. A light source, which emits two wavelength $\lambda_1 = 400$ nm and $\lambda_2 = 600$ nm, is used in a Young's double slit experiment. If recorded fringe widths for λ_1 and λ_2 are β_1 and β_2 and the number of fringes for them within a distance y on one side of the central maximum are m_1 are m_2 respectively, then **(2014 Adv.)**
(a) $\beta_2 > \beta_1$
(b) $m_1 > m_2$
(c) From the central maximum, 3rd maximum of λ_2 overlaps with 5 th minimum of λ_1
(d) The angular separation of fringes for λ_1 is greater than λ_2.

54. In a Young's double slit experiment, the separation between the two slits is d and the wavelength of the light is λ. The intensity of light falling on slit 1 is four

times the intensity of light falling on slit 2. Choose the correct choice (s). **(2008 JEE)**

(a) If $d = \lambda$, the screen will contain only one maximum

(b) If $\lambda < d < 2\lambda$, then at least one more maximum (besides the central maximum) will be observed on the screen

(c) If the intensity of light falling on slit 1 is reduced so that it becomes equal to that of slit 2, the intensities of the observed dark and bright fringes will increase

(d) If the intensity of light falling on slit 2 is increased so that it becomes equal to that of slit 1, the intensities of the observed dark and bright fringes will increase

55. In an interference arrangement similar to Young's double-slit experiment, the slits S_1 and S_2 are illuminated with coherent microwave sources, each of frequency 10^6 Hz. The sources are synchronized to have zero phase difference. The slits are separated by a distance $d = 150.0$ m. The intensity $I(\theta)$ is measured as a function of θ, where θ is defined as shown.

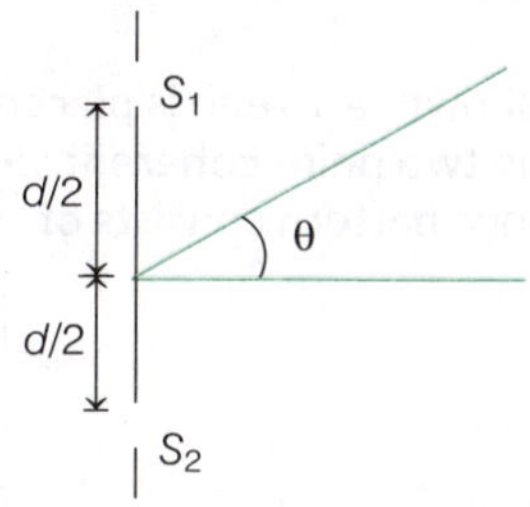

If I_0 is the maximum intensity, then $I(\theta)$ for $0 \le \theta \le 90°$ is given by **(1995 JEE)**

(a) $I(\theta) = \frac{I_0}{2}$ for $\theta = 30°$

(b) $I(\theta) = \frac{I_0}{4}$ for $\theta = 90°$

(c) $I(\theta) = I_0$ for $\theta = 0°$

(d) $I(\theta)$ is constant for all values of θ

Passage Based Questions

Passage (Q.56 to 57)

In a Young's double slit experiment, each of the two slits A and B, as shown in the figure, are oscillating about their fixed centre and with a mean separation of 0.8 mm. The distance between the slits at time t is given by $d = (0.8 + 0.04 \sin \omega t.)$ mm, where $\omega = 0.08$ rads^{-1}. The distance of the screen from the slits is 1 m and the wavelength of the light used to illuminate the slits is 6000 Å. The interference pattern on the screen changes with time, while the central bright fringe (zeroth fringe) remains fixed at point O. **(2024 Adv.)**

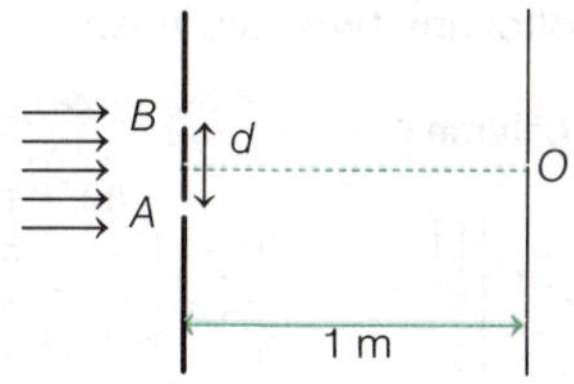

56. The 8th bright fringe above the point O oscillates with time between two extreme positions. The separation between these two extreme positions, in micrometre (μm), is ____________.

57. The maximum speed in μm/s at which the 8th bright fringe will move is ____________.

Match the Columns

58. Two waves from coherent sources meet at a point in a phase difference of ϕ. Both the waves have same intensities. Match the following two columns.

	Column I		Column II
(a)	If $\phi = 60°$	(p)	Resultant intensity will become four times
(b)	If $\phi = 90°$	(q)	Resultant intensity will become two times
(c)	If $\phi = 0°$	(r)	Resultant intensity will remain unchanged
(d)	If $\phi = 120°$	(s)	Resultant intensity will become three times

59. Two waves from coherent sources meet at a point in a path difference of Δx. Both the waves have same intensities. Match the following two columns.

	Column I		Column II
(a)	If $\Delta x = \lambda/3$	(p)	Resultant intensity will become three times
(b)	If $\Delta x = \lambda/6$	(q)	Resultant intensity will remain same
(c)	If $\Delta x = \lambda/4$	(r)	Resultant intensity will become two times
(d)	If $\Delta x = \lambda/2$	(s)	Resultant intensity will become zero.

60. In terms of fringe width ω, match the following two columns.

	Column I		Column II
(a)	Distance between central maxima and third order maxima	(p)	2.5 ω
(b)	Distance between central maxima and third order minima	(q)	3.0 ω
(c)	Distance between first minima and fourth order maxima	(r)	3.5 ω
(d)	Distance between second order maxima and fifth order minima	(s)	None of these

61. Match the following two columns.

	Column I		Column II
(a)	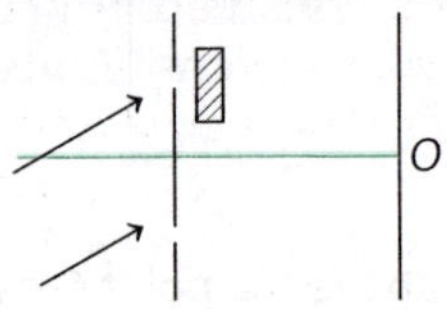	(p)	The zero order maxima will lie above point O
(b)	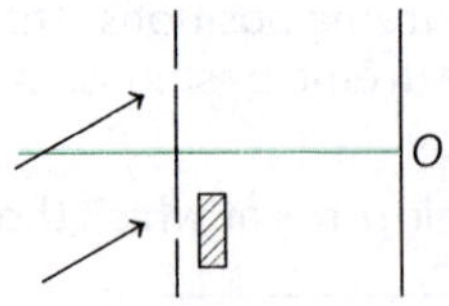	(q)	The zero order maxima will lie below point O
(c)	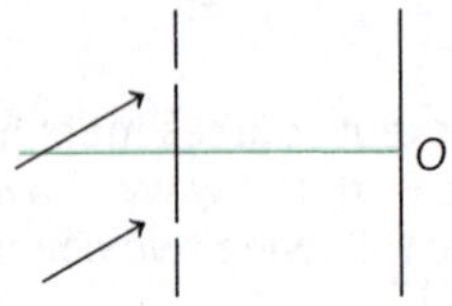	(r)	The zero order maxima may lie above or below point O
(d)	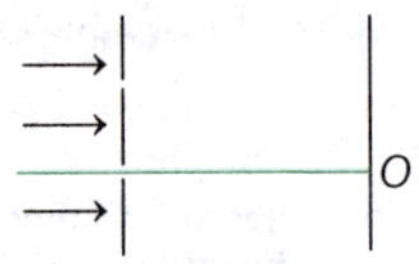	(s)	The zero order maxima may lie at point O

62. Column I shows four situations of standard Young's double slit arrangement with the screen placed far away from the slits S_1 and S_2. In each of these cases $S_1P_0 = S_2P_0$, $S_1P_1 - S_2P_1 = \frac{\lambda}{4}$ and $S_1P_2 - S_2P_2 = \lambda/3$, where λ is the wavelength of the light used. In the cases B, C and D, a transparent sheet of refractive index μ and thickness t is pasted on slit S_2. The thickness of the sheets are different in different cases. The phase difference between the light waves reaching a point P on the screen from the two slits is denoted by $\delta(P)$ and the intensity by $I(P)$. Match each situation given in Column I with the statement(s) in Column II valid for that situation. **(2009 JEE)**

	Column I			Column II
(a)		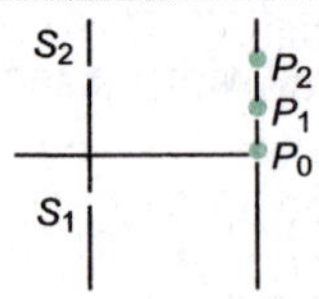	(p)	$\delta(P_0) = 0$
(b)	$(\mu - 1)t = \frac{\lambda}{4}$	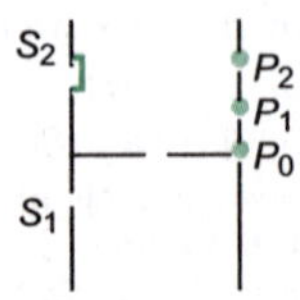	(q)	$\delta(P_1) = 0$
(c)	$(\mu - 1)t = \frac{\lambda}{2}$	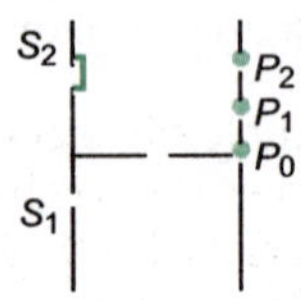	(r)	$I(P_1) = 0$
(d)	$(\mu - 1)t = \frac{3\lambda}{4}$	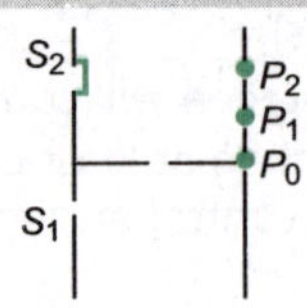	(s)	$I(P_0) > I(P_1)$
			(t)	$I(P_2) > I(P_1)$

Subjective Questions

63. A parallel beam of white light falls on a thin film whose refractive index is equal to 4/3. The angle of incidence $i = 53°$. What must be the minimum film thickness if the reflected light is to be coloured yellow (λ of yellow $= 0.6\ \mu$m) most intensively? ($\tan 53° = 4/3$)

64. A convergent lens with a focal length of $f = 10$ cm is cut into two halves that are then moved apart to a distance of $d = 0.5$ mm (a double lens). Find the fringe width on screen at a distance of 60 cm behind the lens if a point source of monochromatic light ($\lambda = 5000$ Å) is placed in front of the lens at a distance of $a = 15$ cm from it.

65. In the figure shown, a screen is placed normal to the line joining the two point coherent sources S_1 and S_2. The interference pattern consists of concentric circles.

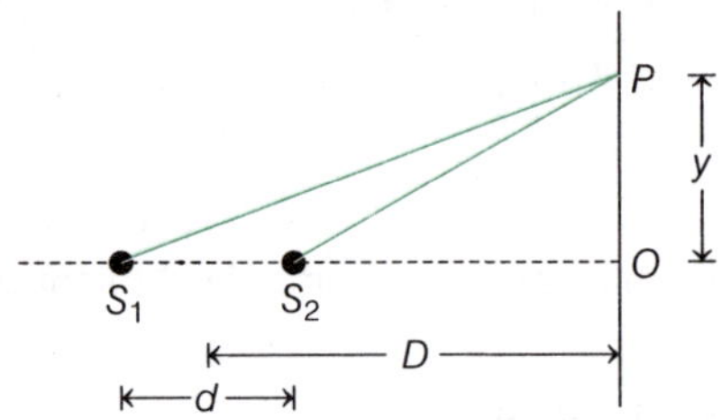

(a) Find the radius of the nth bright ring.

(b) If $d = 0.5$ mm, $\lambda = 5000$ Å and $D = 100$ cm, find the radius of the closest second bright ring.

(c) Also, find the value of n for this ring.

66. In the Young's double slit experiment, a point source of $\lambda = 5000$ Å is placed slightly above the central axis as shown in the figure.

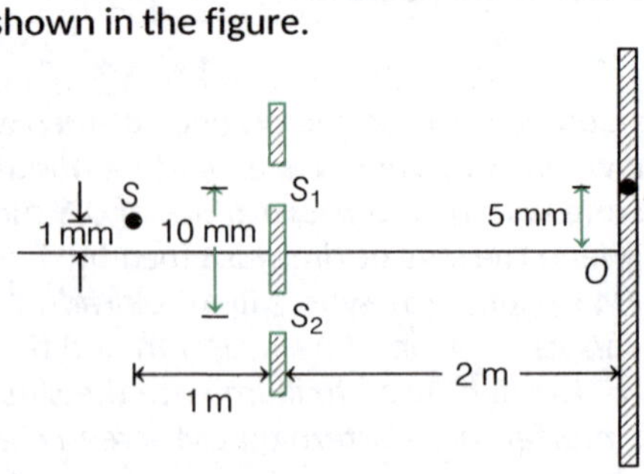

(a) Find the nature and order of the interference at the point P.

(b) Find the nature and order of the interference at O.

(c) Where should we place a film of refractive index $\mu = 1.5$ and what should be its thickness so that maxima of zero order is obtained at O?

67. Light of wavelength $\lambda = 500$ nm falls on two narrow slits placed a distance $d = 50 \times 10^{-4}$ cm apart, at an angle $\phi = 30°$ relative to the slits as shown in figure. On the lower slit a transparent slab of thickness 0.1 mm and refractive index $\frac{3}{2}$ is placed. The interference pattern is observed at a distance $D = 2$ m from the slits. Then, calculate

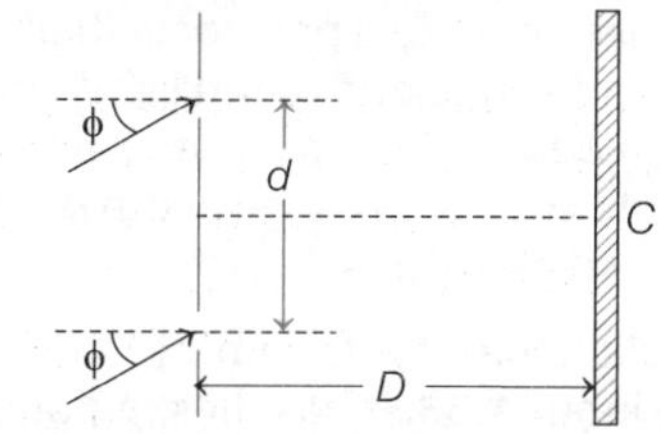

(a) position of the central maxima.
(b) the order of maxima at point C of screen.
(c) how many fringes will pass C, if we remove the transparent slab from the lower slit?

68. In the YDSE, the monochromatic source of wavelength λ is placed at a distance $\frac{d}{2}$ from the central axis (as shown in the figure), where d is the separation between the two slits S_1 and S_2.

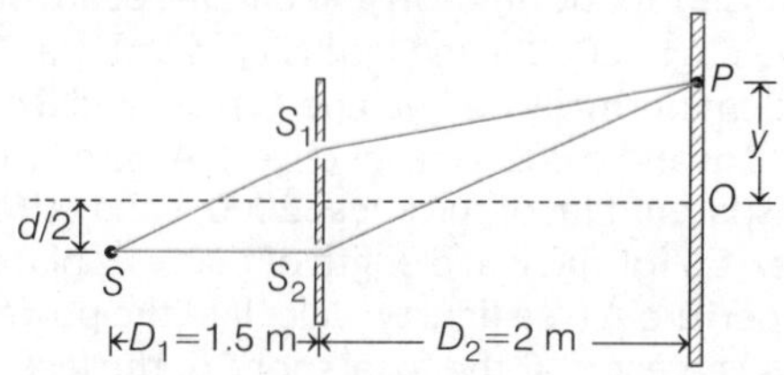

(a) Find the position of the central maxima.
(b) Find the order of interference formed at O.
(c) Now, S is placed on centre dotted line. Find the minimum thickness of the film of refractive index $\mu = 1.5$ to be placed in front of S_2 so that intensity at O becomes $\frac{3}{4}$th of the maximum intensity.
(Take, $\lambda = 6000$ Å ; $d = 6$ mm)

69. YDSE is carried out in a liquid of refractive index $\mu = 1.3$ and a thin film of air is formed in front of the lower slit as shown in the figure. If a maxima of third order is formed at the origin O, find the thickness of the air film. Find the positions of the fourth maxima. The wavelength of light in air is $\lambda_0 = 0.78\ \mu$m and $D/d = 1000$.

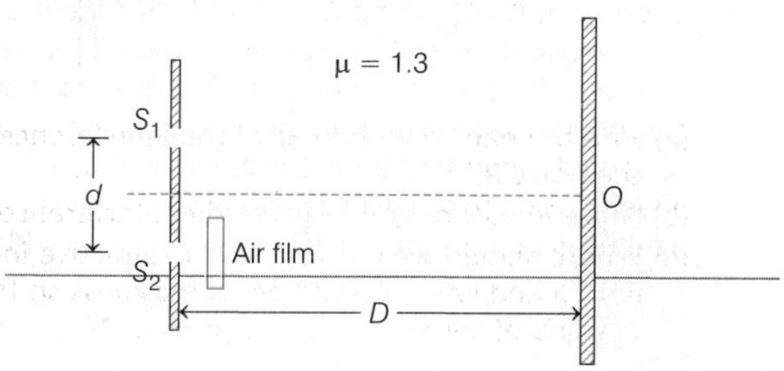

70. A point source S emitting light of wavelength 600 nm is placed at a very small height h above a flat reflecting surface AB (see figure). The intensity of the reflected light is 36% of the incident intensity. Interference fringes are observed on a screen placed parallel to the reflecting surface at a very large distance D from it.

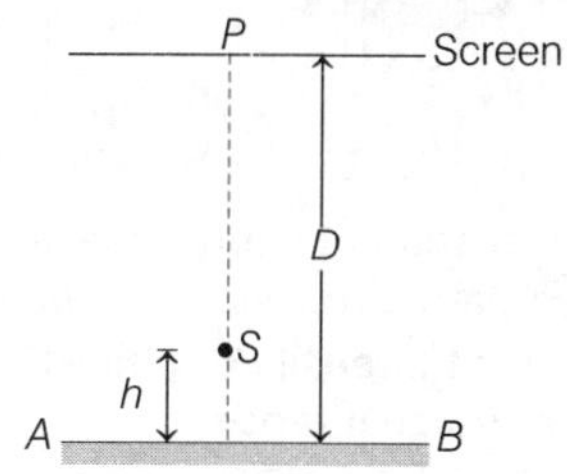

(2002 JEE)

(a) What is the shape of the interference fringes on the screen?
(b) Calculate the ratio of the minimum to the maximum intensities in the interference fringes formed near the point P (shown in the figure).
(c) If the intensity at point P corresponds to a maximum, calculate the minimum distance through which the reflecting surface AB should be shifted so that the intensity at P again becomes maximum.

71. A glass plate of refractive index 1.5 is coated with a thin layer of thickness t and refractive index 1.8. Light of wavelength λ travelling in air is incident normally on the layer. It is partly reflected at the upper and the lower surfaces of the layer and the two reflected rays interfere. Write the condition for their constructive interference. If $\lambda = 648$ nm, obtain the least value of t for which the rays interfere constructively. **(2000 JEE)**

72. A vessel $ABCD$ of 10 cm width has two small slits S_1 and S_2 sealed with identical glass plates of equal thickness. The distance between the slits is 0.8 mm. POQ is the line perpendicular to the plane AB and passing through O, the middle point of S_1 and S_2. A monochromatic light source is kept at S, 40 cm below P and 2 m from the vessel, to illuminate the slits as shown in the figure alongside. Calculate the position of the central bright fringe on the other wall CD with respect to the line OQ. Now, a liquid is poured into the vessel and filled upto OQ. The central bright fringe is found to be at Q. Calculate the refractive index of the liquid. **(2001 JEE)**

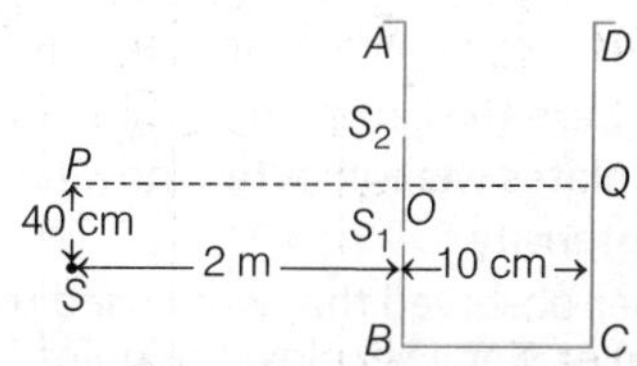

73. The Young's double slit experiment is done in a medium of refractive index 4/3. A light of 600 nm wavelength is falling on the slits having 0.45 mm separation. The lower slit S_2 is covered by a thin glass sheet of thickness 10.4 μm and refractive index 1.5. The interference pattern is observed on a screen placed 1.5 m from the slits as shown in the figure. **(1999 JEE)**

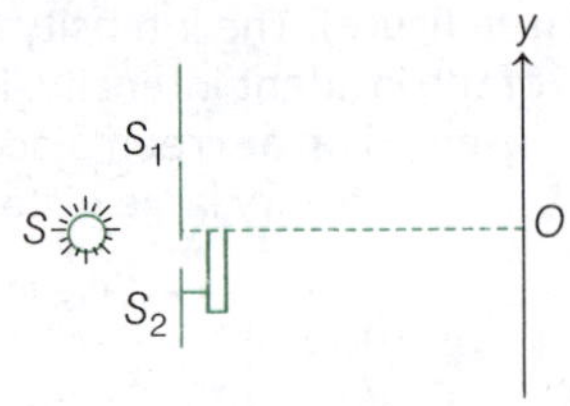

(a) Find the location of central maximum (bright fringe with zero path difference) on the Y-axis.

(b) Find the light intensity of point O relative to the maximum fringe intensity.

(c) Now, if 600 nm light is replaced by white light of range 400 to 700 nm, find the wavelengths of the light that form maxima exactly at point O.

(All wavelengths in the problem are for the given medium of refractive index 4/3. Ignore dispersion)

74. A coherent parallel beam of microwaves of wavelength $\lambda = 0.5$ mm falls on a Young's double slit apparatus. The separation between the slits is 1.0 mm. The intensity of microwaves is measured on a screen placed parallel to the plane of the slits at a distance of 1.0 m from it as shown in the figure.

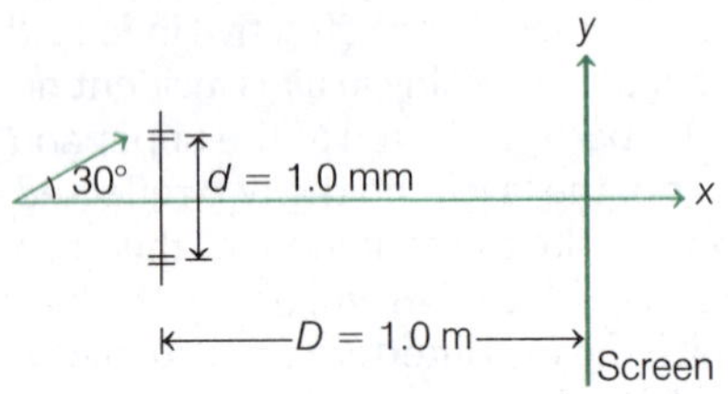

(1998 JEE)

(a) If the incident beam falls normally on the double slit apparatus, find the y-coordinates of all the interference minima on the screen.

(b) If the incident beam makes an angle of 30° with the x-axis (as in the dotted arrow shown in figure), find the y-coordinates of the first minima on either side of the central maximum.

75. In a Young's experiment, the upper slit is covered by a thin glass plate of refractive index 1.4, while the lower slit is covered by another glass plate, having the same thickness as the first one but having refractive index 1.7. Interference pattern is observed using light of wavelength 5400 Å. It is found that the point P on the screen, where the central maximum ($n = 0$) fall before the glass plates were inserted, now has 3/4 the original intensity.

It is further observed that what used to be the fifth maximum earlier lies below the point P while the sixth minima lies above P. Calculate the thickness of glass plate. (Absorption of light by glass plate may be neglected). **(1997 JEE)**

76. In Young's experiment, the source is red light of wavelength 7×10^{-7} m. When a thin glass plate of refractive index 1.5 at this wavelength is put in the path of one of the interfering beams, the central bright fringe shifts by 10^{-3} m to the position previously occupied by the 5th bright fringe. (a) Find the thickness of the plate. (b) When the source is now changed to green light of wavelength 5×10^{-7} m, the central fringe shifts to a position initially occupied by the 6th bright fringe due to red light. Find the refractive index of glass for green light. (c) Also estimate the change in fringe width due to the change in wavelength. **(1997 JEE)**

77. A double slit apparatus is immersed in a liquid of refractive index 1.33. It has slit separation of 1 mm and distance between the plane of slits and screen is 1.33 m. The slits are illuminated by a parallel beam of light whose wavelength in air is 6300 Å. **(1996 JEE)**

(a) Calculate the fringe width.

(b) One of the slits of the apparatus is covered by a thin glass sheet of refractive index 1.53. Find the smallest thickness of the sheet to bring the adjacent minimum on the axis.

78. In a modified Young's double slit experiment, a monochromatic uniform and parallel beam of light of wavelength 6000 Å and intensity $(10/\pi)$ Wm^{-2} is incident normally on two apertures A and B of radii 0.001 m and 0.002 m respectively. A perfectly transparent film of thickness 2000 Å and refractive index 1.5 for the wavelength of 6000Å is placed in front of aperture A (see figure). Calculate the power (in W) received at the focal spot F of the lens. The lens is symmetrically placed with respect to the apertures. Assume that 10% of the power received by each aperture goes in the original direction and is brought to the focal spot. **(1989 JEE)**

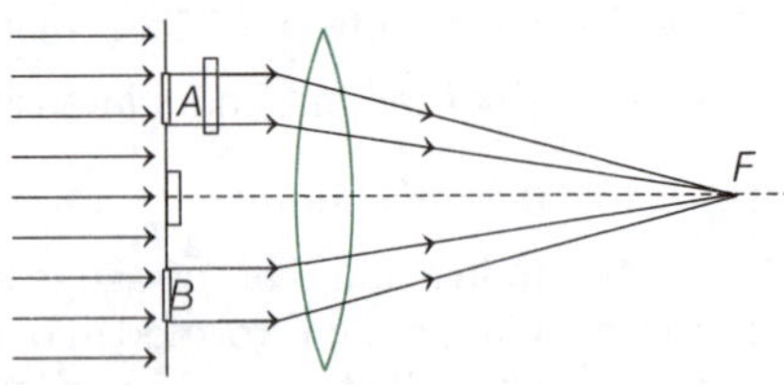

79. In Young's double slit experiment using monochromatic light, the fringe pattern shifts by a certain distance on the screen when a mica sheet of refractive index 1.6 and thickness 1.964 microns is introduced in the path of one of the interfering waves. The mica sheet is then removed and the distance between the slits and the screen is doubled. It is found that the distance between successive maxima (or minima) now is the same as the observed fringe shift upon the introduction of the mica sheet. Calculate the wavelength of the monochromatic light used in the experiment. **(1983 JEE)**

80. Two parallel beams of light P and Q (separation d) containing radiations of wavelengths 4000 Å and 5000Å (which are mutually coherent in each wavelength separately) are incident normally on a prism as shown in figure.

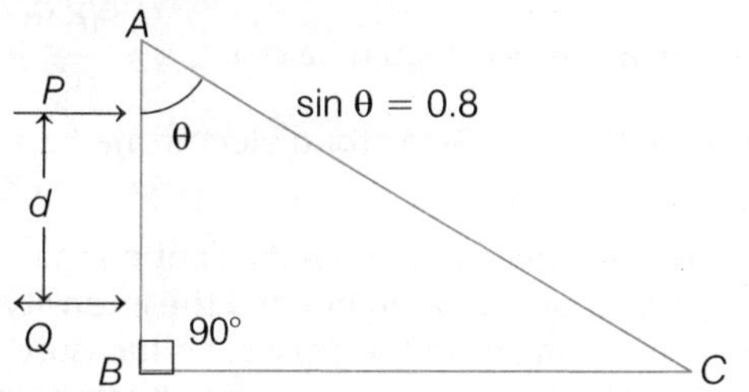

The refractive index of the prism as a function of wavelength is given by the relation, $\mu(\lambda) = 1.20 + \frac{b}{\lambda^2}$ where λ is in Å and b is positive constant. The value of b is such that the condition for total reflection at the face AC is just satisfied for one wavelength and is not satisfied for the other. **(1991 JEE)**

(a) Find the value of b.

(b) Find the deviation of the beams transmitted through the face AC.

(c) A convergent lens is used to bring these transmitted beams into focus. If the intensities of the upper and the lower beams immediately after transmission from the face AC, are $4I$ and I respectively, find the resultant intensity at the focus.

81. Screen S is illuminated by two point sources A and B. Another source C sends a parallel beam of light towards point P on the screen (see figure). Line AP is normal to the screen and the lines AP, BP and CP are in one plane. The distances AP and BP are 3m and 1.5m. The radiant powers of sources A and B are 90 W and 180 W respectively. The beam from C is of intensity 20 W/m^2. Calculate intensity at P on the screen. **(1982 JEE)**

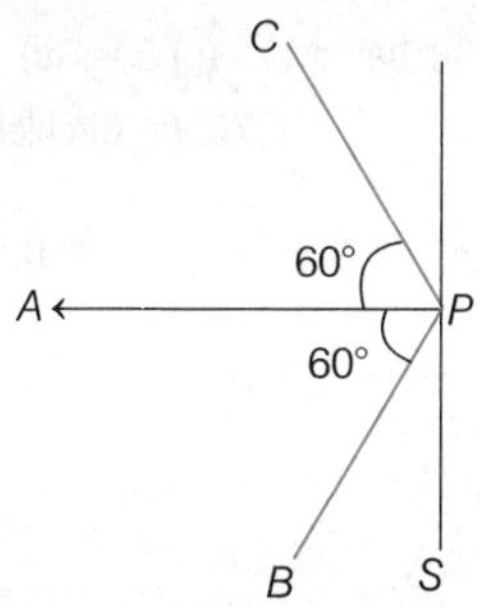

82. A system illustrated in figure consists of two coherent point sources 1 and 2 located as shown in the figure. The sources are separated by a distance d, the radiation wavelength is equal to λ. Taking into account that the oscillations of source 2 lag in phase behind the oscillations of source 1 by $\phi\ (\phi < \pi)$, find: **(Irodov 5.67)**

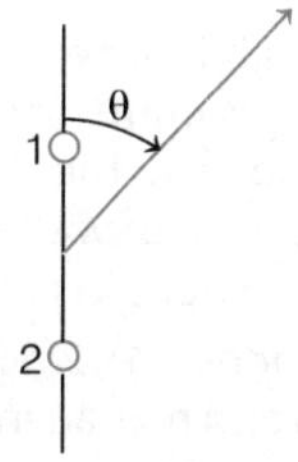

(a) the angles θ at which the radiation intensity is maximum

(b) the conditions under which the radiation intensity in the direction $\theta = \pi$ is maximum and in the opposite direction, minimum.

83. In Lloyd's mirror experiment (figure), a light wave emitted directly by the source S (narrow slit) interferes with the wave reflected from a mirror M. As a result, an interference fringe pattern is formed on the screen Sc. The source and the screen are separated by a distance $D = 100$ cm. At a certain position of the source, the fringe width on the screen was equal to $\omega = 0.25$ mm, and after the source was moved away from the screen plane by $\Delta h = 0.60$ mm, the fringe width decreased $\eta = 1.5$ times. Find the wavelength of light. **(Irodov 5.69)**

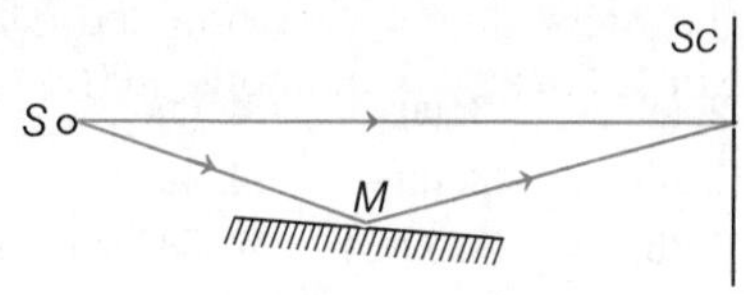

84. To decrease light losses due to reflection from the glass surface the latter is coated with a thin layer of substance whose refractive index $\mu' = \sqrt{\mu}$, where μ is the refractive index of the glass. In this case the amplitudes of electromagnetic oscillations reflected from both coated surfaces are equal. At what thickness of that coating is the glass reflectivity in the direction of the normal equal to zero for light with wavelength λ? **(Irodov 5.81)**

Integer Type Questions

85. In Young's double slit experiment, two slits S_1 and S_2 are d distance apart and the separation from slits to screen is D (as shown in figure). Now, if two transparent slabs of equal thickness 0.1 mm but refractive index 1.51 and 1.55 are introduced in the path of beam ($\lambda = 4000$ Å) from S_1 and S_2 respectively, the central bright fringe spot will shift by .... number of fringes.

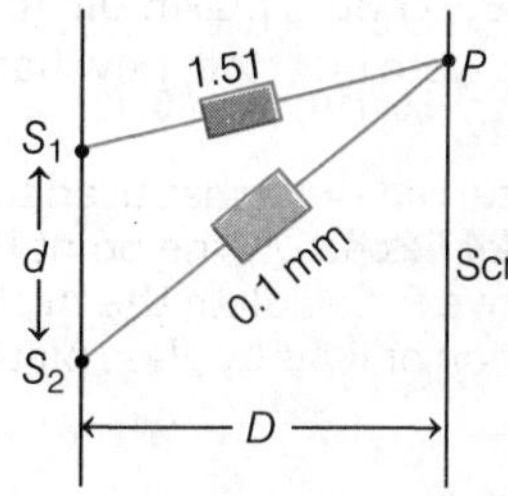

(2023 Main)

86. A Young's double slit interference arrangement with slits S_1 in air and S_2 is immersed in water (refractive index $= 4/3$) as shown in the figure. The positions of maxima on the surface of water are given by $x^2 = p^2m^2\lambda^2 - d^2$, where λ is the wavelength of light in air (refractive index $= 1$), $2d$ is the separation between the slits and m is an integer. The value of p is ………. **(2015 Adv.)**

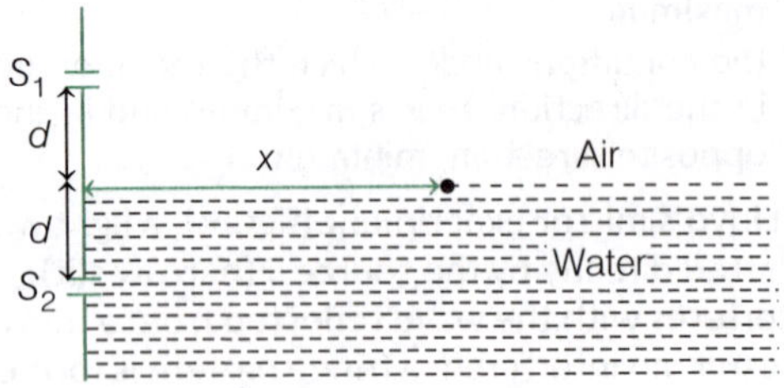

87. Unpolarised light is incident on the boundary between two dielectric media, whose dielectric constants are 2.8 (medium-1) and 6.8 (medium-2), respectively. To satisfy the condition, so that the reflected and refracted rays are perpendicular to each other, the angle of incidence should be $\tan^{-1}\left(1+\frac{10}{\theta}\right)^{1/2}$ the value of θ is …… .(Given for dielectric media, $\mu_r = 1$) **(2023 Main)**

88. An unpolarised light beam is incident on the polariser of a polarisation experiment and the intensity of light beam emerging from the analyser is measured as 100 lumens. Now, if the analyser is rotated around the horizontal axis (direction of light) by 30° in clockwise direction, the intensity of emerging light will be ……. lumens. **(2021 Main)**

Answers

Level 1

1. (b) **2.** (a) **3.** (a) **4.** (c) **5.** (c) **6.** (d) **7.** (d) **8.** (a) **9.** (b) **10.** (d)
11. (c) **12.** (d) **13.** (d) **14.** 45° **15.** 0.75 m, 2.0 m, 3.25 m, 4.50 m, 5.75 m, 7.0 m, 8.25 m
16. 590 nm **17.** (6) **18.** 3 mm **19.** 589 nm **20.** 2.5 mm **21.** (a) 424 nm, 594 nm (b) 495 nm **22.** 533 nm
23. 0.5 cm **24.** 1 : 49 **25.** (a) 4200 Å (b) 1.43 **26.** $n \approx 140$ **27.** 33° and 27° respectively **28.** (9) **29.** (3)
30. (300) **31.** (198) **32.** (8) **33.** (30)

Level 2

34. (c) **35.** (b) **36.** (d) **37.** (b) **38.** (c) **39.** (a) **40.** (c) **41.** (b) **42.** (a) **43.** (c)
44. (b) **45.** (c) **46.** (a) **47.** (b) **48.** (b) **49.** (a,c,d) **50.** (a,c) **51.** (a,c) **52.** (b,d) **53.** (a,b,c)
54. (a, b) **55.** (a,c) **56.** (601.5) **57.** (24) **58.** ($a\to s$; $b\to q$; $c\to p$; $d\to r$)
59. ($a\to q$; $b\to p$; $c\to r$; $d\to s$) **60.** ($a\to q$; $b\to p$; $c\to r$; $d\to p$) **61.** ($a\to p$; $b\to r, s$; $c\to p$; $d\to p$)
62. ($a\to p,s$; $b\to q$; $c\to t$; $d\to r,s,t$) **63.** 0.14 μm **64.** 0.1 mm **65.** (a) $D\sqrt{2\left(1-\frac{n\lambda}{d}\right)}$ (b) 6.32 cm (c) 998
66. (a) 70th order maxima (b) 20th order maxima (c) $t = 20\,\mu$m, in front of S_1 **67.** (a) At $\theta = 30°$ below C (b) 50 (c) 100
68. (a) 4 mm above O (b) 20 (c) 2000 Å **69.** (a) 7.8 μm (b) 4.2 mm, – 0.6 mm **70.** (a) Circular (b) $\frac{1}{16}$ (c) 300 nm
71. $\Delta x = 3.6t = \left(n-\frac{1}{2}\lambda\right)$ where $n = 1, 2, 3 \ldots$; 90 nm **72.** (2 cm, 1.0016) **73.** (a) 4.33 mm; (b) $I = \frac{3}{4}I_{max}$; (c) 650 nm and 433.33 nm
74. (a) $\pm$ 0.26 m, $\pm$ 1.13 m (b) $\frac{3}{\sqrt{7}}$ m and $\frac{1}{\sqrt{15}}$ m **75.** 9.3 μm **76.** (a) 7×10^{-6} m (b) 1.6 (c) -5.71×10^{-5} m
77. (a) 0.63 mm (b) 1.579 μm **78.** (7×10^{-6} W) **79.** (5892 Å) **80.** (a) 8.0×10^{5}(Å)^2 (b) 27.13° (c) 9I **81.** (13.97 W/m^2)
82. (a) $\cos\theta = (n - \phi/2\pi)\,\lambda/d$, $n = 0, \pm 1, \pm 2, \ldots$ (b) $\phi = \pi/2$, $d/\lambda = n + 1/4$, $n = 0, 1, 2, \ldots$ **83.** $\lambda = 0.6\,\mu$m
84. $t = \frac{\lambda(2n+1)}{4\sqrt{\mu}}$ **85.** (10) **86.** (3) **87.** (7) **88.** (75)

See hints on pages 247-264.

Hints & SOLUTIONS

Module 1.

1. $A = \sqrt{(8)^2 + (6)^2} = 10$ mm

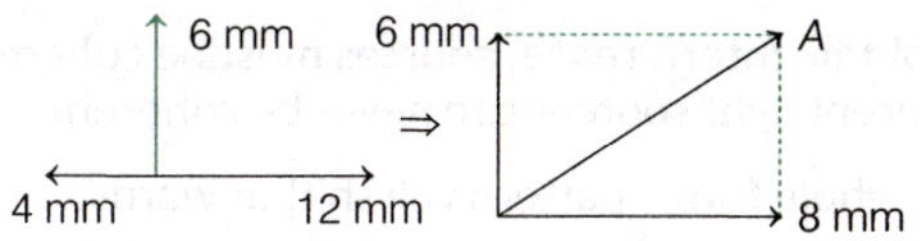

2. $\dfrac{I_{max}}{I_{min}} = \dfrac{(\sqrt{I_1/I_2}+1)^2}{(\sqrt{I_1/I_2}-1)^2} = \dfrac{49}{9}$

Solving, we get

$$\frac{I_1}{I_2} = \frac{25}{4}$$

3. $\dfrac{I_1}{I_2} = \beta^2$

So let, $I_2 = 1$ unit, then $I_1 = \beta$

$$I_{max} = (\sqrt{I_1} + \sqrt{I_2})^2 = (1+\beta)^2$$
$$I_{min} = (\sqrt{I_1} - \sqrt{I_2})^2 = (1-\beta)^2$$
$$= I_{max} - I_{min} = 4\beta$$
$$I_{max} + I_{min} = 2(1+\beta^2)$$

$\therefore$ The asked ratio is $\dfrac{2\beta}{1+\beta^2}$.

4. According to given situation,

$$\frac{I_1}{I_2} = \frac{1}{4} \Rightarrow I_2 = 4I_1$$
$$I_{max} = (\sqrt{I_1} + \sqrt{I_2})^2 = 9I_1$$
$$I_{min} = (\sqrt{I_1} - \sqrt{I_2})^2 = I_1$$
$$\therefore \frac{I_{max} + I_{min}}{I_{max} - I_{min}} = \frac{9I_1 + I_1}{9I_1 - I_1}$$
$$= \frac{10}{8} = \frac{5}{4} = \frac{2\alpha+1}{\beta+3}$$
$$\therefore \quad \frac{\alpha}{\beta} = \frac{2}{1} = 2$$

5. $I(\phi) = I_1 + I_2 + 2\sqrt{I_1 I_2}\cos\phi$ ...(i)

Here, $I_1 = I$ and $I_2 = 4I$

At point A, $\phi = \dfrac{\pi}{2}$

$\therefore \quad I_A = I + 4I = 5I$

At point B, $\phi = \pi$

$\therefore \quad I_B = I + 4I - 4I = I$

$\Rightarrow \quad I_A - I_B = 4I$

6. (a) $\dfrac{A_{max}}{A_{min}} = \dfrac{A_1 + A_2}{A_1 - A_2}$

(b) $\dfrac{I_{max}}{I_{min}} = \left(\dfrac{A_{max}}{A_{min}}\right)^2$

7. $\dfrac{\lambda}{4}$ path difference is equivalent to $90°$ phase difference

$$A_{net} = 5A_0 \Rightarrow I_{max} = 25\,I_0$$

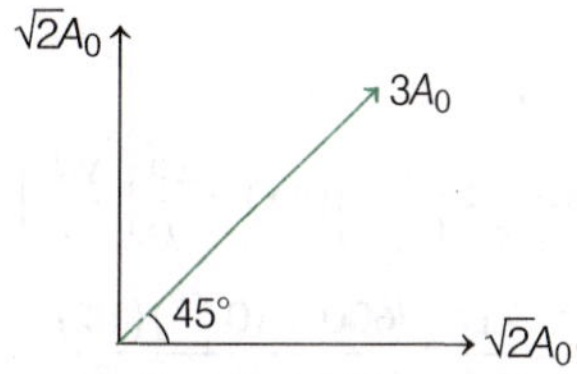

8. $a_R = 2a\cos\dfrac{\phi}{2}$

(i) For $a_R = 2a, \phi = 0°$

(ii) For $a_R = \sqrt{2}a, \phi = 90°$ etc

9. (a) At centre path difference is zero. Therefore, construction interference will be obtained.

(b) $\dfrac{\lambda}{2} = 3$ m. At a distance, where path difference is $\dfrac{\lambda}{2}$ or 3 m destructive interference will be obtained.

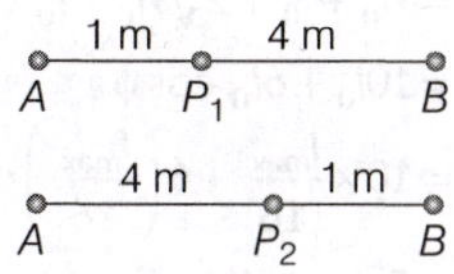

At P_1 $\quad BP_1 - AP_1 = 3\text{m} = \dfrac{\lambda}{2}$

At P_2 $\quad AP_2 - BP_2 = 3\,\text{m} = \dfrac{\lambda}{2}$

10. Given, $I_1 = 4I \Rightarrow I_2 = 9I$

At point A, $\Delta\phi_A = 0$

At point B, $\Delta\phi_B = \pi$

To find, $(I_A)_{resultant} - (I_B)_{resultant}$

But we know that, in interference when $\Delta\phi = 0$, then resultant intensity in maximum i.e.

$$(I_A)_{resultant} = I_{max}$$

and when $\Delta\phi = \pi$, then resultant intensity is minimum i.e.

$$(I_B)_{resultant} = I_{min}$$

$\therefore$We have to find, $(I_{max} - I_{min})$

Now,

$$I_{max} = (\sqrt{I_1} + \sqrt{I_2})^2 = (\sqrt{4I} + \sqrt{9I})^2$$
$$= 4I + 9I + 12I$$
$$\Rightarrow \quad I_{max} = 25I$$

Also,

$$I_{min} = (\sqrt{I_1} - \sqrt{I_2})^2 = (\sqrt{4I} - \sqrt{9I})^2$$

$$= 4I + 9I - 12I = I$$

$\Rightarrow \quad I_{min} = I$

$\therefore \; I_{max} - I_{min} = 25I - I = 24I$

Module 2.

Introductory Exercise

3. $I = I_{max} \cos^2 \frac{\phi}{2}$

$$\frac{3}{4} I_{max} = I_{max} \cos^2 \frac{\phi}{2} \quad \text{or} \quad \cos \frac{\phi}{2} = \frac{\sqrt{3}}{2}$$

$$\therefore \quad \frac{\phi}{2} = \frac{\pi}{6}$$

$$\therefore \quad \phi = \frac{\pi}{3} = \left(\frac{2\pi}{\lambda}\right)(\Delta x) = \frac{2\pi}{\lambda}\left(\frac{yd}{D}\right)$$

$$\therefore \quad y = \frac{\lambda D}{6d} = \frac{(600 \times 10^{-19})(1.2)}{(6)(0.25 \times 10^{-2})}$$

$$= 48 \times 10^{-6} \text{ m} = 48 \,\mu\text{m}$$

4. $A_1 = 3A_2$

So, $I_1 = 9I_2$

Let $A_2 = A_0$ and $I_2 = I_0$

Then, $A_1 = 3A_0$ and $I_1 = 9I_0$

$A_{max} = (A_1 + A_2) = 4A_0$ and $I_{max} = 16I_0$

Now,

$$I = I_1 + I_2 + 2\sqrt{I_1 I_2} \cos \phi$$

$$= 9I_0 + I_0 + 2\sqrt{9I_0 \times I_0} \cos \phi$$

$$= 10I_0 + 6I_0 \cos \phi$$

$$= 10 \times \frac{I_{max}}{16} + 6\left(\frac{I_{max}}{16}\right) \cos \phi$$

$$= \frac{5}{8} I_{max} + \frac{3}{8} I_{max} \cos \phi$$

$$= \frac{5}{8} I_{max} + \frac{3}{8} I_{max}\left(2\cos^2 \frac{\phi}{2} - 1\right)$$

$$= \frac{1}{4} I_{max} + \frac{3}{4} I_{max} \cdot \cos^2 \frac{\phi}{2}$$

$$= \frac{I_{max}}{4}\left(1 + 3\cos^2 \frac{\phi}{2}\right)$$

5. (a) $I = I_{max} \cos^2 \frac{\phi}{2}$

$$= I_0 \cos^2 30° \qquad (\text{as } \phi = 60°)$$

$$= \frac{3}{4} I_0$$

(b) 60° phase difference is equivalent to $\frac{\lambda}{6}$ path difference.

Exercise

1. In case of YDSE, at mid-point intensity will be $I_{max} = 4I_0$.

In the second case when sources are incoherent, the intensity will be

$$I = I_0 + I_0 = 2I_0$$

Therefore, the desired ratio is

$$\frac{4I_0}{2I_0} = 2$$

Here, I_0 is the intensity due to one slit.

2. With white light we get coloured fringes (not only black and white) with centre as white.

3. To obtain interference, sources must be coherent. Two different light sources can never be coherent.

4. The whole fringe pattern will shift upwards.

5. $I_{max} = (\sqrt{I_1} + \sqrt{I_2})^2$

and $I_{min} = (\sqrt{I_1} - \sqrt{I_2})^2$

When $I_1 = I_2 = I_0$, then

$$I_{max} = 4I_0 \text{ and } I_{min} = 0$$

When slit of one width is slightly increased, then intensity due to that slit becomes greater than I_0. In that case, we can see that

$$I_{max} > 4I_0 \text{ and } I_{min} > 0$$

6. At centre, path difference is maximum and this is equal to S_1S_2. Then, path difference decreases as we move away on the screen. So, order of fringe also decreases. Hence, 11th order maxima occurs before 10th order maxima.

7. Refractive index is slightly decreased. Therefore wavelength will increase.

Fringe width $\omega \propto \lambda$.

8. $d \sin \theta = \frac{\lambda}{2}$

$$\therefore \quad \theta = \sin^{-1}\left(\frac{\lambda}{2d}\right)$$

$$= \sin^{-1}\left(\frac{5460 \times 10^{-10}}{2 \times 0.1 \times 10^{-3}}\right)$$

$$= 0.16°$$

9. 6th dark fringe distance in vacuum = 10th bright fringe distance in liquid.

$$\therefore \quad 5.5\,\omega = 10\,\omega'$$

or

$$\frac{\omega}{\omega'} = \mu = \frac{10}{5.5} = 1.81$$

10. Shift $= \frac{(\mu - 1)tD}{d}$

$$= \frac{(1.5 - 1)(10 \times 10^{-6})(1.0)}{2.5 \times 10^{-3}}$$

$$= 2 \times 10^{-3} \text{ m} = 2 \text{ mm}$$

11. $\omega = \frac{\lambda D}{d}$ or $\omega \propto \lambda$

ω will increase $\frac{6000}{4000}$ or 1.5 times

Hence, number of fringes in same distance will decrease 1.5 times.

12. $\omega = \frac{\lambda D}{d}$

$\Rightarrow \quad \Delta\omega = \frac{\lambda(\Delta D)}{d}$

$\therefore \quad \lambda = \frac{(d)(\Delta\omega)}{\Delta D} = \frac{(10^{-3})(3\times 10^{-5})}{5\times 10^{-2}}$

$= 0.6\times 10^{-6}$ m

$= 6000$ Å

13. Only fringe pattern will shift. Number of fringes on screen will remain unchanged.

14. $\lambda_{blue} < \lambda_{green}$

$\therefore \quad \omega_{blue} < \omega_{green}$

15. $I = 4I_0 \cos^2 \frac{\phi}{2}$

Given, $\quad I = I_0$

$\therefore \quad \phi = \frac{2\pi}{3} = \frac{2\pi}{\lambda}\cdot \Delta x = \frac{2\pi}{\lambda}\left(\frac{yd}{D}\right)$

$\therefore \quad y = \frac{\lambda D}{3d}$

16. θ (in radian) $= \frac{\lambda}{d}$

$\therefore \quad d = \frac{\lambda}{\theta} = \frac{6\times 10^{-7}}{\pi/180}$

$= 3.4\times 10^{-5}$ m

17. $K = 4I_0,\ K' = 2I_0 = \frac{K}{2}$

18. $y = \frac{\omega}{4} = \frac{\lambda D}{4d} : \Delta x = \frac{yd}{D} = \frac{\lambda}{4} : \phi = \frac{2\pi}{\lambda}\cdot \Delta x = \frac{\pi}{2}$

$\frac{\phi}{2} = \frac{\pi}{4}$

Now, $I_2 = I_1 \cos^2 \frac{\phi}{2}$

or $\quad \frac{I_1}{I_2} = \frac{1}{\cos^2 \phi/2} = 2$

19. Fringe width in YDSE; $\beta = \frac{\lambda D}{d}$

So, (In same experimental set up)

$\frac{\beta_2}{\beta_1} = \lambda_2/\lambda_1$

$\Rightarrow \quad \beta_2 = \beta_1 \cdot \frac{\lambda_2}{\lambda_1}$

Here $\beta_1 = 2$ mm

$\lambda_2 = 600$ nm, $\lambda_1 = 400$ nm

$\therefore \quad \beta_2 = 2\,\text{mm} \times \frac{600\,\text{nm}}{400\,\text{nm}}$

$= \frac{2\times 6}{4}$ mm $= 3$ mm

20. For same amplitude,

$I_1 = I_2 = Ka^2 = I_0$

When, $\phi_1 = \pi/3$

$I_{0_1} = I_1 + I_2 + 2\sqrt{I_1 I_2}\cos\phi_1$

$I_{0_1} = I_0 + I_0 + 2I_0 \cos\frac{\pi}{3} = 3I_0$

When, $\phi_2 = \pi/2$

$I_{0_2} = I_1 + I_2 + 2\sqrt{I_1 I_2}\cos\phi_2$

$= 2I_0 + 2I_0\cos\frac{\pi}{2} = 2I_0$

Hence ratio, $\frac{I_{0_1}}{I_{0_2}} = \frac{3}{2}$

21. Given, $D = 1$ m

$\lambda = 600$ nm

$= 6\times 10^{-7}$ m

$x_5 = 5$ cm

$= 5\times 10^{-2}$ m

We know that position of nth bright fringe, $x_n = \frac{nD\lambda}{d}$

Here, $\quad n = 5$

$\therefore \quad x_5 = \frac{5D\lambda}{d}$

$\Rightarrow \quad d = \frac{5D\lambda}{x_5}$

$= \frac{5\times 1\times 6\times 10^{-7}}{5\times 10^{-2}}$

$= 60\,\mu$m

22. In given YDSE, first minimum occurs at P. When wavelength of light used is

$\lambda = 800$ nm

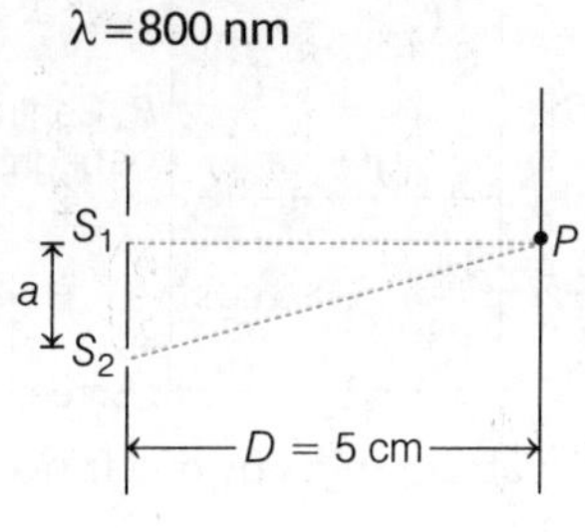

For 1st minima,

Path difference,

$S_2P - S_1P = \sqrt{(5+a)^2} - 5 = \frac{\lambda}{2}$

Taking cm unit for length

$\Rightarrow \quad \sqrt{(5+a)^2} - 5 = \frac{800\times 10^{-9}\times 100}{2}$

$\Rightarrow \quad \sqrt{(5+a)^2} = 5 + 4\times 10^{-5}$

On squaring, we get

$5^2 + a^2 + 10a = 5^2 + (4\times 10^{-5})^2 + 40\times 10^{-5}$

Neglecting $10\,a$ and $(4\times 10^{-5})^2$ being too small, we get

$$a^2 = 400 \times 10^{-6}$$

$$\Rightarrow \quad a = 20 \times 10^{-3} \text{ cm}$$

$$= 20 \times 10^{-3} \times 10 \text{ mm}$$

$$= 0.2 \text{ mm}$$

23. Given,

The distance of sources from the screen,

$$D = 0.5 \text{ m}$$

The distance between the slits,

$$d = 0.5 \text{ mm} = 0.0005 \text{ m}$$

The wavelength of the monochromatic light,

$$\lambda = 5890 \text{ Å}$$

$$= 5890 \times 10^{-10} \text{ m}$$

The distance between the first and the third bright fringe formed,

$$Y = 2\beta$$

As we know, $\beta = \dfrac{\lambda D}{d}$

Substituting the values in the above equation,

$$Y = 2\left(\frac{\lambda D}{d}\right) = 2\left(\frac{5890 \times 10^{-10} \times 0.5}{0.0005}\right)$$

$$= 1178 \times 10^{-6} \text{ m}$$

24. Angular fringe width

$$= \beta_0 = \frac{\lambda}{d} = \frac{500 \times 10^{-9}}{5 \times 10^{-5}}$$

$$= 10^{-2} \text{ Radian}$$

$$= 0.57°$$

25. As we know,

Path difference introduced by thin film,

$$\Delta = (\mu - 1)t \quad \text{...(i)}$$

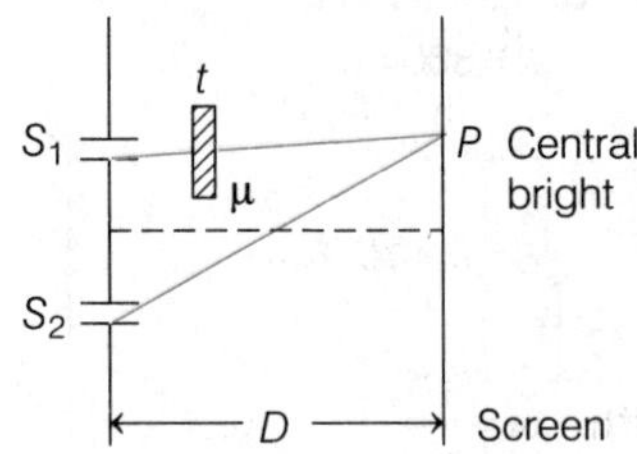

and if fringe pattern shifts by one fringe width, then path difference,

$$\Delta = 1 \times \lambda = \lambda \quad \text{...(ii)}$$

So, from Eqs. (i) and (ii), we get

$$(\mu - 1)t = \lambda$$

$$\Rightarrow \quad t = \frac{\lambda}{\mu - 1}$$

26. $I_1 = 4I_0, I_2 = I_0$

$$I_{max} = (\sqrt{I_1} + \sqrt{I_2})^2 = 9I_0$$

$$I_{min} = (\sqrt{I_1} - \sqrt{I_2})^2 = I_0$$

$$\Rightarrow \quad \frac{I_{max}}{I_{min}} = \frac{9}{1} = 9:1$$

27. $\dfrac{I_{max}}{I_{min}} = \dfrac{(\sqrt{I_1} + \sqrt{I_2})^2}{(\sqrt{I_1} - \sqrt{I_2})^2} = \left(\dfrac{\sqrt{I_1/I_2} + 1}{\sqrt{I_1/I_2} - 1}\right)^2 = 9$ (Given)

Solving this, we have $\dfrac{I_1}{I_2} = 4$

but $\quad I \propto A^2$

$$\therefore \quad \frac{A_1}{A_2} = 2$$

$\therefore$ Correct options are (b) and (d).

28. Wavelength in water, $\lambda' = \dfrac{\lambda}{\mu}$

Fringe width, $\quad \omega = \dfrac{\lambda' D}{d} = \dfrac{\lambda D}{\mu d}$

$$= \frac{(700 \times 10^{-9})(0.48)}{(4/3)(0.25 \times 10^{-3})}$$

$$= 10^{-3} \text{ m}$$

$$= 1 \text{ mm}$$

29. $\quad \text{Distance} = \dfrac{3\lambda_2 D}{d} - \dfrac{3\lambda_1 D}{d}$

$$= \frac{3(\lambda_2 - \lambda_1)D}{d}$$

$$= \frac{3 \times (600 - 480) \times 10^{-9} \times 1.0}{5.0 \times 10^{-3}}$$

$$= 7.2 \times 10^{-5} \text{ m}$$

$$= 0.072 \text{ mm}$$

30. $y = \omega_1 = \dfrac{\omega_2}{2}$

$$\therefore \quad \frac{\lambda_1 D}{d} = \frac{\lambda_2 D}{2d}$$

$$\Rightarrow \quad \lambda_2 = 2\lambda_1 = 1200 \text{ nm}$$

31. $d \sin \theta_1 = \dfrac{\lambda}{2}$

$$\sin \theta_1 = \frac{\lambda}{2d} = \frac{550 \times 10^{-9}}{2 \times 1.8 \times 10^{-6}}$$

$$\therefore \quad \theta_1 = 8.78°$$

$$\frac{y_1}{D} = \tan \theta_1$$

$$\therefore \quad y_1 = D \tan \theta_1$$

$$= 35 \tan 8.78° = 5.41 \text{ cm}$$

$$d \sin \theta_2 = \frac{3\lambda}{2}$$

$$\therefore \quad \sin \theta_2 = \frac{3\lambda}{2d} = \frac{3 \times 550 \times 10^{-9}}{2 \times 1.8 \times 10^{-6}}$$

$$\therefore \quad \theta_2 = 27.27°$$

$$\therefore \quad y_2 = D \tan \theta_2$$

$$= 35 \tan 27.27°$$

$$= 18 \text{ cm}$$

$$\Delta y = y_2 - y_1 = 12.6 \text{ cm}$$

32. (a) $\Delta x = \frac{yd}{D}$ and $\phi = \frac{2\pi}{\lambda} \cdot \Delta x$

$$= \frac{(2\pi)yd}{\lambda D} = \frac{(2\times 180)yd}{\lambda D} \text{ degree}$$

$$= \frac{360\times 0.3\times 10^{-3}\times 10\times 10^{-3}}{546\times 10^{-9}\times 1.0}$$

$$= 1978°$$

Now, $I = I_0 \cos^2 \frac{\phi}{2}$

$$= 2.97\times 10^{-4} I_0$$

$$\approx 3.0\times 10^{-4} I_0$$

(b) $\omega = \frac{\lambda D}{d}$

$\therefore$ Number of fringes between central fringe and P

$$N = \frac{y}{\omega} = \frac{yd}{\lambda D} = \frac{(10\times 10^{-3})(0.3\times 10^{-3})}{(546\times 10^{-9})(1.0)}$$

$$= 5.49$$

So, bright fringes are five.

33. 1 and 2 both are reflected from denser medium.

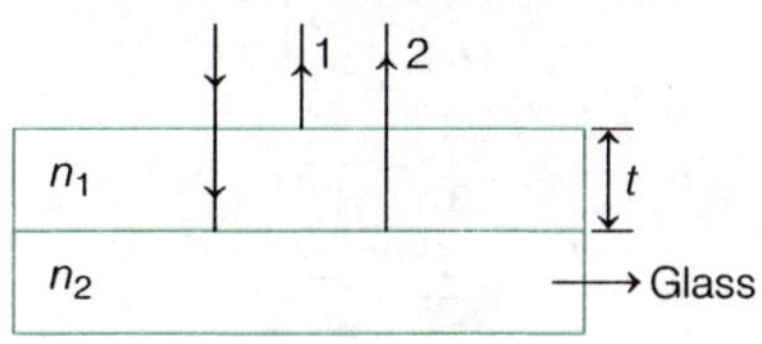

Hence,

$$2n_1 t = \frac{\lambda}{2} \text{ for first order minima}$$

or $$t_{min} = \frac{\lambda}{4n_1} = \frac{650}{4\times 1.42}$$

$$= 114 \text{ nm}$$

34. Path difference produced by slab,

$$\Delta x = (\mu - 1)t = \frac{\lambda}{2}$$

$\frac{\lambda}{2}$ path difference is equivalent to 180° phase difference.

Hence, maxima and minima interchange their positions.

Module 3.

1. Given

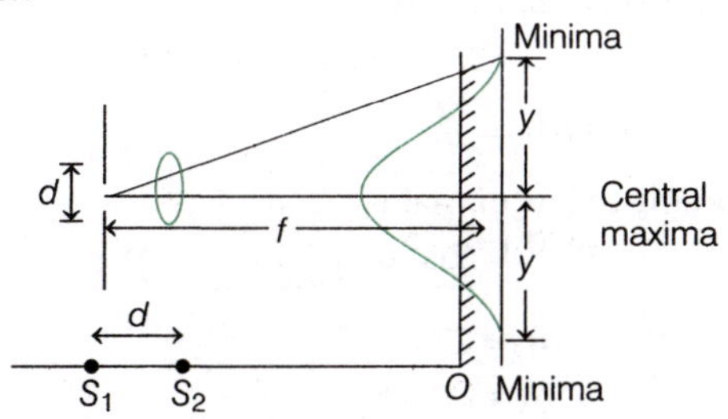

$$2y = 2\times 10^{-3} \text{ m}$$

$\Rightarrow$ $$y = 1\times 10^{-3} \text{ m}$$

First minima is obtained at

$$d \sin\theta = \lambda \text{ but } \sin\theta \approx \tan\theta = \frac{y}{f}$$

$\therefore$ $$d\left(\frac{y}{f}\right) = \lambda$$

$$d = \frac{\lambda f}{y} = \frac{5.89\times 10^{-7}\times 0.5}{1\times 10^{-3}}$$

$$= 2.945\times 10^{-4} \text{ m}$$

2. Theory based question.

3. At minima, $\sin\theta = m\frac{\lambda}{a}$

θ and a are same. Therefore,

$$(1)\lambda_1 = (3)\lambda_2$$

or $$\lambda_1 = 3\lambda_2$$

4. Given, $\lambda = 600 \text{ nm} = 6\times 10^{-7}$ m

According to given situation,

$$\frac{x}{D} = \sin\theta = \frac{\lambda}{a} \Rightarrow \sin\theta = \frac{\lambda}{a}$$

$$a = \frac{\lambda}{\sin\theta} = \frac{6\times 10^{-7}}{\sin 30°}$$

$$= 12\times 10^{-7} \text{ m}$$

$$= 1.2\times 10^{-6} \text{ m}$$

$$= 1.2 \, \mu\text{m}$$

5. $\because \sin\theta = \frac{1.22\lambda}{D}$, where D is opening diameter.

When opening size diameter of the pinhole is increased, the diffraction size decreases but intensity increases.

6. In single slit diffraction pattern,

$$\lambda = b\sin\theta$$

At $$\theta = 30°$$

$$\lambda = \frac{b}{2} = \frac{1\times 10^{-6}}{2}$$

$$= 5\times 10^{-7} \text{ m}$$

In YDSE,

fringe width, $\omega = \frac{\lambda D}{d}$

$\Rightarrow$ $$d = \frac{\lambda D}{\omega} = \frac{5\times 10^{-7}\times 0.5}{1\times 10^{-2}}$$

$$d = 25\times 10^{-6} \text{ m}$$

$$= 25 \, \mu\text{m}$$

7. Diffraction is obtained when the slit width is of the order of wavelength of light (or any electromagnetic wave) used.

Here, wavelength of X-rays (1-100 Å) << slit width (0.6 mm). Therefore, no diffraction pattern will be observed.

8. At first minima,

$$b\sin\theta = \lambda$$

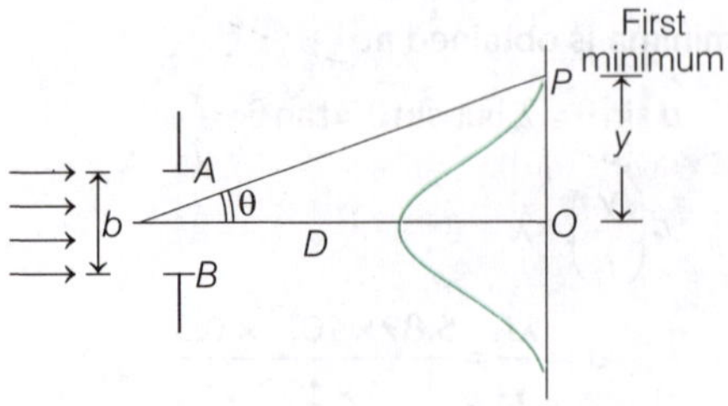

or $\quad b\theta = \lambda \quad$ or $\quad b\left(\frac{y}{D}\right) = \lambda$

or $\quad y = \frac{\lambda D}{b} \quad$ or $\quad \frac{yb}{D} = \lambda \quad$ ...(i)

Now, at P (First minima) path difference between the rays reaching from two edges (A and B) will be

$$\Delta x = \frac{yb}{D} \quad \left(\text{Compare with } \Delta x = \frac{yd}{D} \text{ in YDSE}\right)$$

or $\quad \Delta x = \lambda \quad$ [From Eq. (i)]

Corresponding phase difference (ϕ) will be

$$\phi = \left(\frac{2\pi}{\lambda}\right).\Delta x, \quad \phi = \frac{2\pi}{\lambda}.\lambda = 2\pi$$

9. For first dark fringe on either side $d \sin\theta = \lambda$

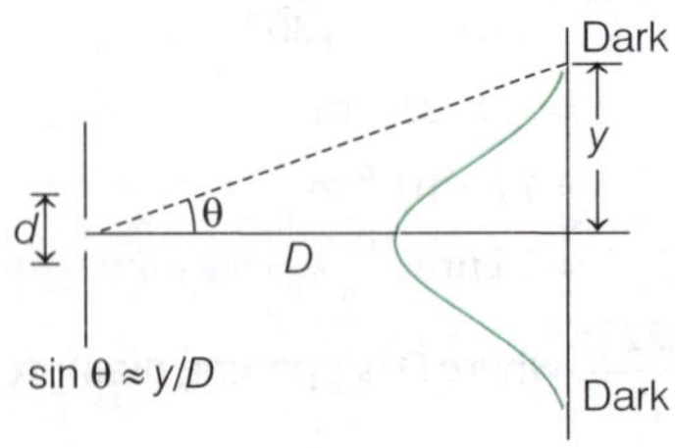

or $\quad \frac{dy}{D} = \lambda \Rightarrow y = \frac{\lambda D}{d}$

Therefore, distance between two dark fringes on either side

$$= 2y = \frac{2\lambda D}{d}$$

Substituting the values, we have

$$\text{Distance} = \frac{2(600 \times 10^{-6}\text{mm})(2 \times 10^{3}\text{mm})}{(1.0\text{ mm})}$$

$$= 2.4 \text{ mm}$$

Module 4.

1.

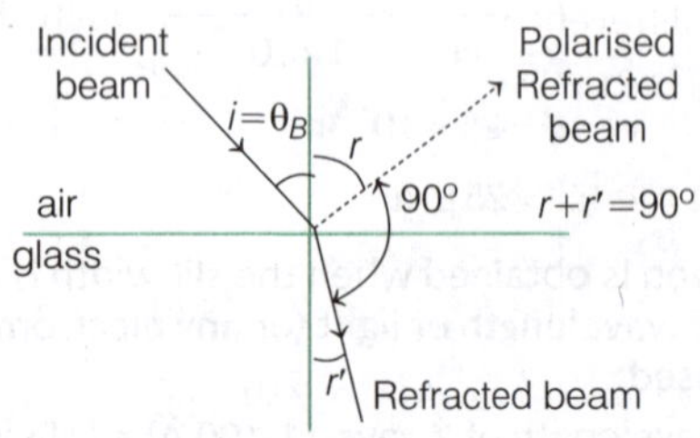

As, angle of incidence = angle of refraction

So, $\quad \theta_B + r' = 90°$

or $\quad r' = 90 - \theta_B = \frac{\pi}{2} - \theta_B$

So, Statement I is correct

Also, For light propagating from air to glass,

$$\mu_g = \frac{\sin i}{\sin r} = \frac{\sin\theta_B}{\sin\left(\frac{\pi}{2} - \theta_B\right)}$$

$$= \frac{\sin\theta_B}{\cos\theta_B} = \tan\theta_B$$

or $\quad \theta_B(\text{air to glass}) = \tan^{-1}(\mu_g)$

So, $\quad \theta_B(\text{glass to air}) = \tan^{-1}\left(\frac{1}{\mu_g}\right)$

Hence, Statement II is incorrect.

2. If an unpolarised light is converted into plane polarised light, then its intensity becomes half. $I = \frac{I_0}{2}$, where I_0 is intensity of unpolarised light.

According to Malus, $I = I_0 \cos^2\theta$,

$$I = \frac{I_0}{2} \quad [\cos^2 45 \times \cos^2 45 \times \ldots \times (n-1) \text{ times}]$$

$$\Rightarrow \quad \frac{I_0}{64} = \frac{I_0}{2} \times \left(\frac{1}{2}\right)^{n-1}$$

$$\Rightarrow \quad \frac{1}{32} = \frac{1}{2^{n-1}}$$

$$\Rightarrow \quad \frac{1}{2^5} = \frac{1}{2^{n-1}}$$

$\therefore \quad n - 1 = 5$

or $\quad n = 6$

3. As, we know that if an unpolarised light is converted into plane polarised light then intensity becomes half of incident intensity

i.e., $\quad I = \frac{I_0}{2}$

and from law of Malus, $I = I_0 \cos^2\theta$

After polaroid A, $I = \frac{I_0}{2}$

After polaroid C, $I = \left(\frac{I_0}{2}\right)\cos^2 45°$

$$= \frac{I_0}{4}$$

After polaroid B, $I = \frac{I_0}{4}\cos^2 45°$

$$= \frac{I_0}{8}$$

4. According to law of Malus,

$$I = I_0 \cos^2\theta$$

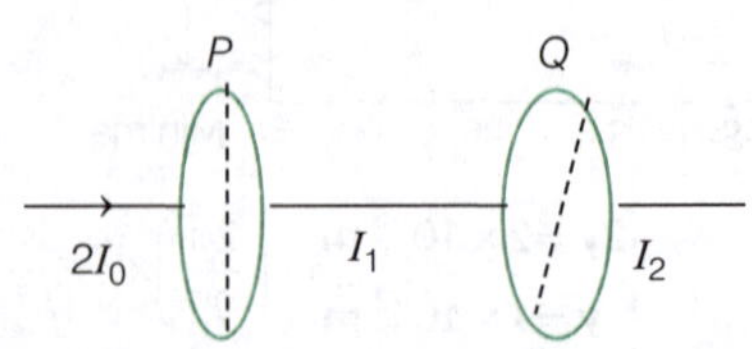

$$I_1 = \frac{1}{2}(2I_0)\cos^2 0 = I_0$$

$$I_2 = I_1 \cos^2 30°$$

$$I_0 \cdot \frac{3}{4} = \frac{3I_0}{4}$$

Hence, the intensity of the emergent light is $\frac{3I_0}{4}$.

5. Given, Intensity, $I_0 = 3.3\ \text{Wm}^{-2}$

Area, $A = 3 \times 10^{-4}\ \text{m}^2$

Angular speed, $\omega = 314.4$ rad/s

We know that

Average energy $= I_0 A < \cos^2\theta > T$

$\because \quad < \cos^2\theta > = \frac{1}{2}$

$$\therefore \text{Average energy} = \frac{(3.3)(3 \times 10^{-4})}{2} \times \frac{2\pi}{\omega}$$

$$\simeq 10^{-4}\ \text{J}$$

6. According to Brewster's law, refractive index of material (μ) is equal to tangent of polarising angle

$$\because \quad \tan i_b = \mu = \frac{1.5}{\mu}$$

$$\frac{1}{\mu} < \frac{1.5}{\sqrt{\mu^2 + (1.5)^2}} \qquad (\because \sin i_c < \sin i_b)$$

$$\therefore \quad \sin i_b = \frac{1.5}{\sqrt{\mu^2 + (1.5)^2}}$$

$$\Rightarrow \sqrt{\mu^2 + (1.5)^2} < 1.5 \times \mu$$

$$\Rightarrow \mu^2 + (1.5)^2 < (\mu \times 1.5)^2$$

$\Rightarrow \mu < \frac{3}{\sqrt{5}}$ i.e. minimum value of μ should be $\frac{3}{\sqrt{5}}$

Unit Exercise (Cumulative)

Level 1

1. $d \sin\theta = 2\lambda$ (for second order maxima)

$$\sin\theta = 2\frac{\lambda}{d} = 2 \times \frac{1}{4} = \frac{1}{2}$$

$$\therefore \quad \theta = 30°$$

For maxima, $d\sin\theta = n\lambda$

$$\therefore \quad n_{max} = \frac{d}{\lambda} = 4 \qquad (\text{for } \theta = 90°)$$

So, there are total 7 maxima corresponding to $n = 0, \pm 1, \pm 2$ and ± 3.

We cannot take $n = 4$, as it is for $\theta = 90°$, which is out of screen.

2. Wavelength in medium, $\lambda' = \frac{\lambda}{\mu}$

$$\Delta\phi = \left(\frac{2\pi}{\lambda'}\right)x = \frac{2\pi}{(\lambda/\mu)}$$

$$x = \frac{2\pi\mu x}{\lambda}$$

3. Here, wavelength of light used

$(\lambda) = 5303\ \text{Å}$

Distance between two slit

$(d) = 19.44\ \mu\text{m}$

Width of single slit (a)

$= 4.05\ \mu\text{m}$

Here, angular width between first and second diffraction minima

$$\theta \simeq \frac{\lambda}{a}$$

and angular width of a fringe due to double slit is

$$\theta' = \frac{\lambda}{d}$$

$\therefore$ Number of fringes between first and second diffraction minima,

$$n = \frac{\theta}{\theta'} = \frac{\lambda/a}{\lambda/d}$$

$$= \frac{d}{a} = \frac{19.44}{4.05} = 4.81$$

or $\quad n \simeq 5$

$\therefore$ 5 interfering bright fringes lie between first and second diffraction minima.

4. If two sources have a randomly varying phase difference ϕ, the resultant intensity will be $I_0 + I_0 = 2I_0$.

5. In the given case, figure for first minimum will be as shown below.

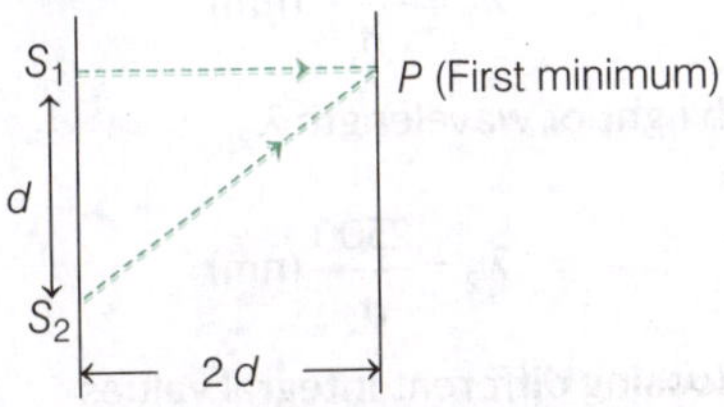

We know that condition for minimum in Young's double slit experiment is path difference,

$$\Delta x = (2n - 1)\lambda/2$$

For first minimum, $n = 1$

$$\Rightarrow \quad \Delta x = \lambda/2 \qquad \text{... (i)}$$

Path difference between the rays coming from virtual sources S_1 and S_2 at point 'P' will be

$$\Delta x = S_2P - S_1P \qquad \text{... (ii)}$$

From triangle S_1S_2P,

$$S_1P = 2d \qquad \text{...(iii)}$$

and $\quad (S_2P)^2 = (S_1S_2)^2 + (S_1P)^2$

$$= d^2 + (2d)^2$$

$$\Rightarrow \quad (S_2P^2) = 5d^2$$

or $\quad S_2P = \sqrt{5}\, d \qquad \text{...(iv)}$

Substituting the values from Eqs. (iii) and (iv) in Eq. (ii), we get

$$\Delta x = \sqrt{5}\, d - 2d \quad \text{...(v)}$$

From Eqs. (i) and (v), we get

$$\sqrt{5}\, d - 2d = \lambda / 2$$

$$\Rightarrow \quad d = \frac{\lambda}{2(\sqrt{5} - 2)}$$

6. $\Delta L = d \sin\theta$

For small value of θ; $\sin\theta \approx \theta$

So, path difference $= \Delta L = d\theta$

For a bright fringe at same angular position 'θ', both of the rays from slits S_1 and S_2 are in phase.

Hence, path difference is an integral multiple of wavelength of light used.

i.e., $\Delta L = n\lambda$

or $d\theta = n\lambda$

$$\Rightarrow \quad \lambda = \frac{d\theta}{n}$$

Here, $\theta = \frac{1}{40}$ rad, $d = 0.1$ mm

Hence, $\lambda = \frac{0.1}{40n}$ mm

$$= \frac{0.1 \times 10^{-3}\ \text{m}}{40n}$$

$$= \frac{0.1 \times 10^{-3} \times 10^{9}}{40n}\ \text{nm}$$

$$\Rightarrow \quad \lambda = \frac{2500}{n}\ \text{nm}$$

So, with light of wavelength λ_1, we have

$$\lambda_1 = \frac{2500}{n_1}\ \text{(nm)}$$

and with light of wavelength λ_2, we have

$$\lambda_2 = \frac{2500}{n_2}\ \text{(nm)}$$

Now, choosing different integral values for n_1 and n_2, (i.e., $n_1, n_2 = 1, 2, 3 \ldots$ etc) we find that for

$$n_1 = 4,\ \lambda_1 = \frac{2500}{4} = 625\ \text{(nm)}$$

and for $n_2 = 5$,

$$\lambda_2 = \frac{2500}{5} = 500\ \text{(nm)}$$

These values lie in given interval 500 nm to 625 nm.

7. $d \sin\theta = n\lambda$

$$(0.32 \times 10^{-3}) \sin 30° = n \times 500 \times 10^{-9}$$

$$\Rightarrow \quad n = 320$$

In range $-30° \le \theta \le 30°$

number of bright fringes

$$= 320 + 1 + 320 = 641$$

8. Let n_1 bright fringe of λ_1 is coinciding with n_2 bright fringe of λ_2, then

$$y_{n_1} = y_{n_2}$$

$$\Rightarrow \quad \frac{n_1 \lambda_1 D}{d} = \frac{n_2 \lambda_2 D}{d}$$

$$\Rightarrow \quad \frac{n_1}{n_2} = \frac{\lambda_2}{\lambda_1} = \frac{520}{650} = \frac{4}{5}$$

Therefore, 4th bright fringe of λ_1 is coinciding with 5th bright fringe of λ_2

Hence, distance from the central maxima is

$$y = \frac{n_1 \lambda_1 D}{d} = \frac{4 \times 650 \times 10^{-9} \times 1.5}{0.5 \times 10^{-3}}$$

$$= 7.8\ \text{mm}$$

9. $I = I_{max} \cos^2 \frac{\phi}{2}$ ...(i)

Given, $I = \frac{I_{max}}{2}$ ...(ii)

$\therefore$ From Eqs. (i) and (ii), we have

$$\phi = \frac{\pi}{2}, \frac{3\pi}{2}, \frac{5\pi}{2}$$

Or path difference,

$$\Delta x = \left(\frac{\lambda}{2\pi}\right) \cdot \phi$$

$$\therefore \quad \Delta x = \frac{\lambda}{4}, \frac{3\lambda}{4}, \frac{5\lambda}{4} \ldots, \left(\frac{2n+1}{4}\right)\lambda$$

10. Fringe width $\beta = \frac{\lambda D}{d}$

or $\beta \propto \lambda$

Now, $\lambda_R > \lambda_G > \lambda_B$

$\Rightarrow \quad \beta_R > \beta_G > \beta_B$

11. $I = I_{max} \cos^2\left(\frac{\phi}{2}\right)$

$$\therefore \quad \frac{I_{max}}{4} = I_{max} \cos^2 \frac{\phi}{2}$$

$$\cos \frac{\phi}{2} = \frac{1}{2} \text{ or } \frac{\phi}{2} = \frac{\pi}{3}$$

$$\therefore \quad \phi = \frac{2\pi}{3} = \left(\frac{2\pi}{\lambda}\right)\Delta x \quad \text{...(i)}$$

where $\Delta x = d \sin\theta$

Substituting in Eq. (i), we get

$$\sin\theta = \frac{\lambda}{3d} \text{ or } \theta = \sin^{-1}\left(\frac{\lambda}{3d}\right)$$

12. A fringe is a locus of points having constant path difference from the two coherent sources S_1 and S_2. It will be concentric circle.

13. Given, $\frac{D_2}{D_1} = 2$, $\frac{d_1}{d_2} = 2$

In double slit experiment, fringe width

$$\beta = \frac{\lambda D}{d}$$

$$\therefore \quad \frac{\beta_2}{\beta_1} = \left(\frac{D_2}{D_1}\right)\left(\frac{d_1}{d_2}\right) = (2)(2) = 4$$

$$\beta_2 = 4\beta_1$$

Hence, firnge width will become four times.

14.

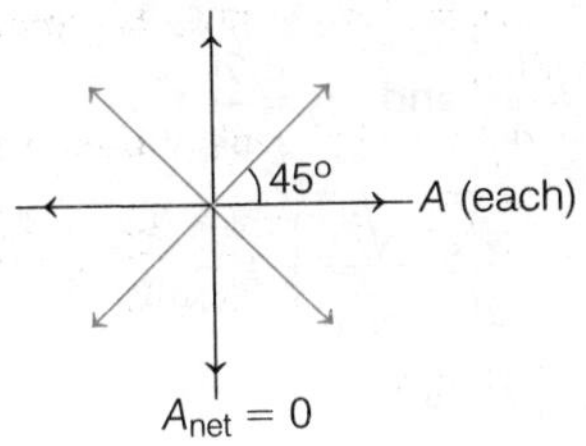

15. $\because \quad \lambda = \frac{c}{f} = \frac{3 \times 10^8}{120 \times 10^6} = 2.5 \text{ m}$

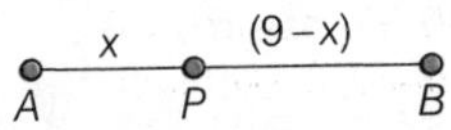

$$\Delta x = (BP - AP) = (9 - 2x) = n\lambda$$

$$\therefore \quad x = \frac{9 - n\lambda}{2} = \frac{9 - 2.5n}{2}$$

Now, substituting $n = 1, 2, \ldots$ etc.

We can find different values of x.

$x_1 = 3.25$ m for $n = 1$

$x_2 = 2.0$ m for $n = 2$

and $x_3 = 0.75$ m for $n = 3$

Similarly, we will get three points at same distance from other point B.

16. $\because \quad \omega = \frac{\lambda D}{d}$

$$\therefore \quad \lambda = \frac{\omega d}{D} = \frac{(2.82 \times 10^{-3})(0.46 \times 10^{-3})}{2.2}$$

$$= 0.589 \times 10^{-6} \text{ m}$$

$$\approx 590 \text{ nm}$$

17. $\Delta x = d \sin\theta = n\lambda$

$$n = \frac{d \sin\theta}{\lambda}$$

$$n_{max} = \frac{d}{\lambda} = \frac{4.0 \times 10^{-6}}{600 \times 10^{-9}}$$

$$= 6.66$$

Highest integer is 6.

18. Shift $= \frac{(\mu - 1)tD}{d}$

$$S_1 = \frac{(1.6 - 1)(10 \times 10^{-6})(1.5)}{1.5 \times 10^{-3}}$$

$$= 0.6 \times 10^{-2} \text{ m}$$

$$= 0.6 \text{ m}$$

$$S_2 = \frac{(1.2 - 1)(15 \times 10^{-6})(1.5)}{1.5 \times 10^{-3}}$$

$$= 0.3 \times 10^{-2} \text{ m}$$

$$= 0.3 \text{ cm}$$

$$= \Delta S = S_1 - S_2$$

$$= 0.3 \text{ cm}$$

$$= 3 \text{ mm}$$

19. $\frac{\lambda(2D)}{d} = \frac{(\mu - 1)tD}{d}$ (fringe width = shift)

$$\therefore \quad \lambda = \frac{(\mu - 1)t}{2}$$

$$= \frac{(1.6 - 1)(1.964 \times 10^{-6})}{2} \text{ m}$$

$$= 0.5892 \times 10^{-6} \text{ m} = 589 \text{ nm}$$

20. $\because \quad d = 2$ cm

$$\omega = \frac{\lambda D}{d} = \frac{(500 \times 10^{-9})(100)}{2 \times 10^{-2}}$$

$$= 2.5 \times 10^{-3} \text{ m} = 2.5 \text{ mm}$$

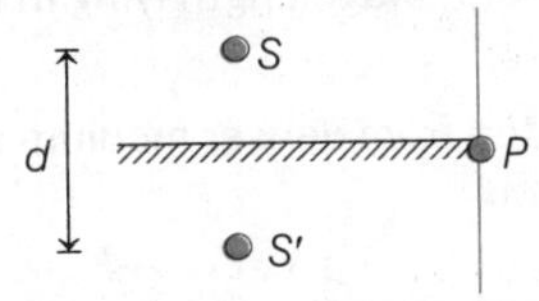

In this figure, P is in a dark fringe, as conditions of maxima and minima are interchanged.

Hence, next dark fringe will be obtained at a distance ω or 2.5 mm from P.

21. (a) Ray-1 is reflected from a denser medium and ray-2 by a rarer medium.

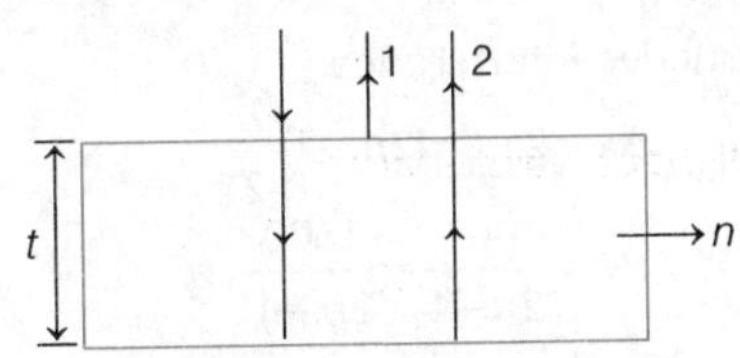

$$\Delta x = 2nt = (2m - 1)\frac{\lambda}{2} \text{ for maximum intensity}$$

$$\therefore \quad \lambda = \frac{4nt}{(2m - 1)}$$

$$= \frac{(4)(1.53)(485 \text{ nm})}{2m - 1}$$

$$= \left(\frac{2968}{2m - 1}\right) \text{nm}$$

For $m = 1, \lambda = 2968$ nm

For $m = 2, \lambda = 989$ nm

For $m = 3, \lambda = 594$ nm

For $n = 4, \lambda = 424$ nm

For $n = 5, \lambda = 329$ nm

Therefore, two wavelengths lying in the given range are 424 nm and 594 nm.

(b) Ray-1 and ray-2 are in same phase.

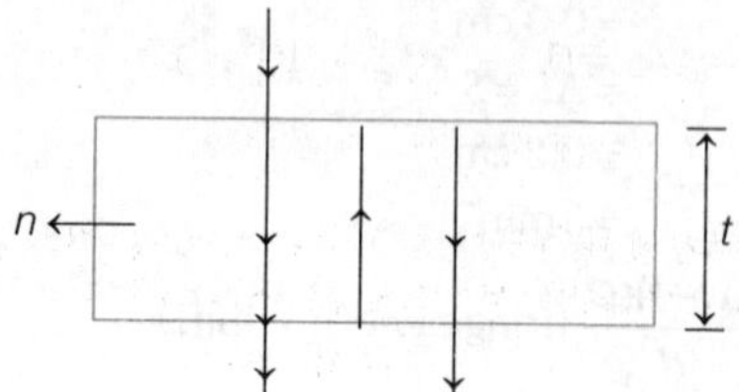

Hence,

$$\Delta x = 2nt = m\lambda \quad \text{(for maximum intensity)}$$

$$\therefore \quad \lambda = \frac{2nt}{m} = \frac{(2)(1.53)(485\,\text{nm})}{m} = \left(\frac{1484}{m}\right)\text{nm}$$

Substituting $m = 1, 2, 3 \cdots$ etc,

$\lambda_1 = 1484$ nm, $\lambda_2 = 742$ nm,

$\lambda_3 = 495$ nm, $\lambda_4 = 371$ nm etc.

Therefore, only wavelength lying in the given range is 495 nm.

22. Ray-1 is reflected from denser medium and ray-2 from denser medium.

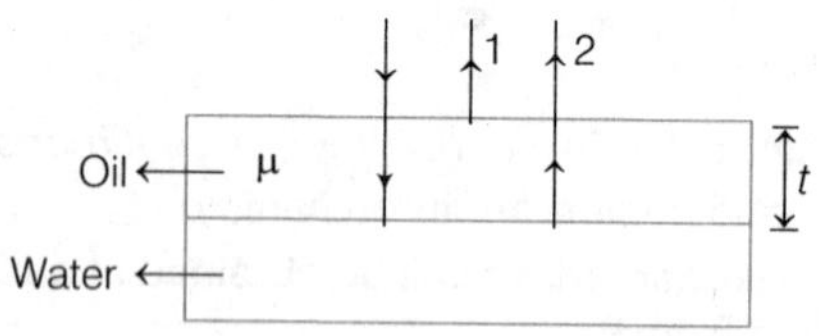

$\therefore \quad \Delta x = 2\mu t = \lambda = 800$ nm for destruction interference.

$\therefore \quad \mu t = 400$ nm

For constructive interference,

$$\Delta x = 2\mu t = (2n-1)\frac{\lambda}{2}$$

$$\therefore \quad \lambda = \frac{4\mu t}{2n-1} = \frac{1600}{2n-1}$$

For $n = 1, \lambda = 1600$ nm

For $n = 2, \lambda = 533$ nm

For $n = 3, \lambda = 320$ nm

The only wavelength lying in the given range is 533 nm.

23. $2\mu t = \lambda/2$

This is the condition for destructive interference.

$$\therefore \quad t = \frac{\lambda}{4\mu} = \frac{3.0}{4 \times 1.5} = 0.5 \text{ cm}$$

24. Each plate reflects 25% and transmits 75%.

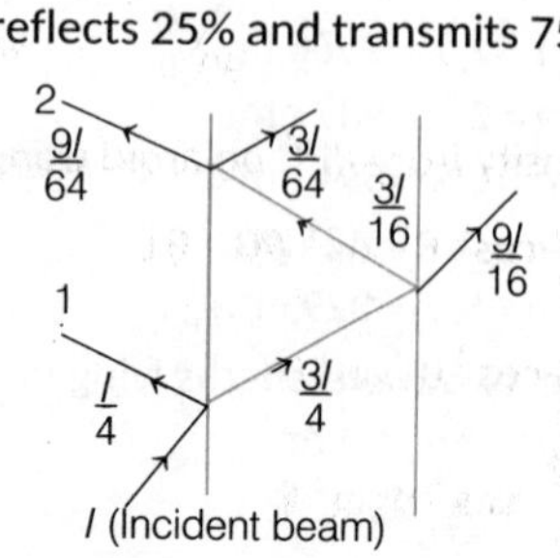

Incident beam has an intensity I. This beam undergoes multiple reflections and refractions. The corresponding intensity after each reflection and refraction (transmission) are shown in figure.

Interference pattern is to take place between rays 1 and 2.

$$I_1 = \frac{I}{4} \text{ and } I_2 = \frac{9I}{64}$$

$$\therefore \quad \frac{I_{min}}{I_{max}} = \left(\frac{\sqrt{I_1} - \sqrt{I_2}}{\sqrt{I_1} + \sqrt{I_2}}\right)^2 = \frac{1}{49}$$

25. Given, $\lambda = 6000$ Å

Let b be the width of slit and D the distance between screen and slit.

First minima is obtained at $b \sin\theta = \lambda$

or $\quad b\theta = \lambda$ as $\sin\theta \approx \theta$

or $\quad \theta = \dfrac{\lambda}{b}$

Angular width of first maxima

$$= 2\theta = \frac{2\lambda}{b} \propto \lambda$$

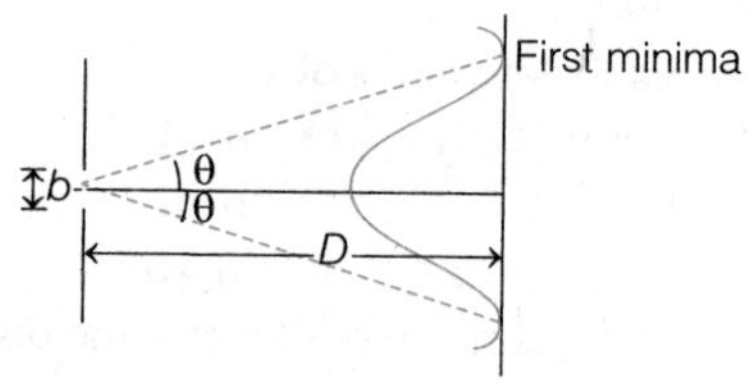

Angular width will decrease by 30% when λ is also decreased by 30%.

Therefore, new wavelength

$$\lambda' = \left\{(6000) - \left(\frac{30}{100}\right)6000\right\} \text{Å}$$

$$= 4200 \text{ Å}$$

(b) When the apparatus is immersed in a liquid of refractive index μ, the wavelength is decreased μ times. Therefore, $4200 \text{ Å} = \dfrac{6000 \text{ Å}}{\mu}$

$$\therefore \quad \mu = \frac{6000}{4200} \quad \text{or} \quad \mu = 1.429 \simeq 1.43$$

26. Sharpness of interference is the worst when maxima of one wavelength overlaps with the minima of the other wavelength.

$$\therefore \quad (2n-1)\frac{\lambda_2}{2} = n\lambda_1$$

$$\therefore \quad n = \frac{\lambda_2}{2(\lambda_2 - \lambda_1)}$$

Substituting the values, we get

$$n \approx 140$$

27. When light is incident normally,

then for minima,

$$b \sin\theta = n\lambda$$

In the given case,

$$b\sin\theta - b\sin\theta_0 = \pm n\lambda$$

For first minima, $n = 1$

$$\therefore \quad b\sin\theta - b\sin\theta_0 = +\lambda$$

After substituting the values we may find two values of θ, which come out to be 33° and 27° respectively.

28. Given, $\lambda_1 = 450\,\text{nm}, \lambda_2 = 650\,\text{nm}$

For overlap,

$$n_1\lambda_1 = n_2\lambda_2$$

$$\Rightarrow \quad \frac{\lambda_2}{\lambda_1} = \frac{n_1}{n_2}$$

$$\frac{n_1}{n_2} = \frac{650}{450} = \frac{13}{9}$$

$$n_2 = 9$$

The minimum order of fringe produced is 9.

29. $I = 4I_0\cos^2\frac{\phi}{2}$

$$\Delta\phi = \frac{2\pi}{\lambda} \times \Delta x$$

$$I_1 = 4I_0\cos^2\frac{\pi}{4} = 2I_0$$

$$I_2 = 4I_0\cos^2\frac{2\pi}{3} = I_0$$

$$\Rightarrow \quad \frac{I_0 + I_2}{I_0} = 3$$

30. In a Young's double slit experiment for interference pattern, the position of bright fringe is given by

$$y_n = \frac{n\lambda D}{d}$$

Here, $D = 1.5$ m, $d = 0.3 \times 10^{-3}$ m

and $\quad n = 1; \lambda = \frac{y_n d}{D}$

For first violet,

$$y_n = 2\,\text{mm} = 2 \times 10^{-3}\,\text{m}$$

$$\therefore \quad \lambda_{violet} = 2 \times 10^{-3}\frac{d}{D}$$

For first red,

$$y_n = 3.5\,\text{mm} = 3.5 \times 10^{-3}\,\text{m}$$

$$\lambda_{red} = 3.5 \times 10^{-3}\frac{d}{D}$$

The difference in wavelengths of red and violet light is

$$\Delta\lambda = \lambda_{red} - \lambda_{violet}$$

$$= 3.5 \times 10^{-3}\frac{d}{D} - 2 \times 10^{-3}\frac{d}{D}$$

$$= \frac{d}{D}(1.5) \times 10^{-3}$$

$$= \frac{0.3 \times 10^{-3}}{1.5} \times 1.5 \times 0^{-3}$$

$$= 0.3 \times 10^{-6}$$

$$= 0.3 \times 10^{-6} \times 10^{3} \times 10^{-3}$$

$$= 300 \times 10^{-9} = 300\,\text{nm}$$

31. For obtaining secondary minima at a point, path difference should be integral multiple of wavelength

$$\therefore \quad d\sin\theta = n\lambda$$

$$\Rightarrow \quad \sin\theta = \frac{n\lambda}{d}$$

For n to be maximum $\sin\theta = 1$

$$n = \frac{d}{\lambda} = \frac{6 \times 10^{-5}}{6 \times 10^{-7}} = 100$$

Total number of minima on one side

$$= 99$$

Total number of minima $= 198$.

32. **Case-I**

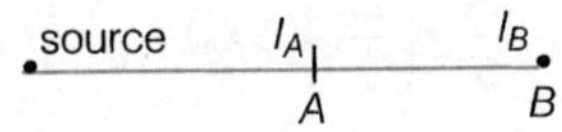

$$r = \frac{I_A}{I_B} = 2$$

Case-II

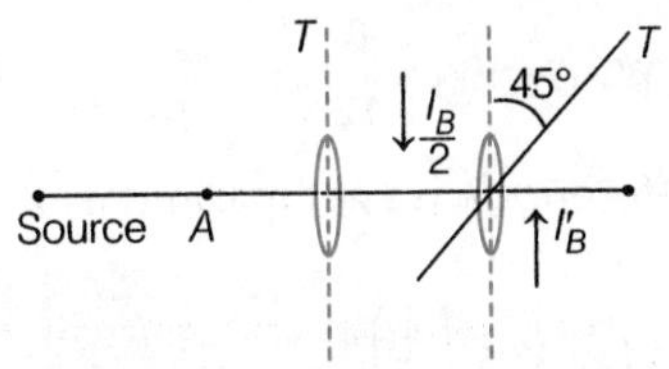

$$I'_B = \frac{I_B}{2}\cos^2 45° = \frac{I_B}{4}$$

Now, $\quad \frac{I_A}{I'_B} = \frac{I_A}{(I_B/4)} = 4\left(\frac{I_A}{I_B}\right) = 4 \times 2 = 8$

$\therefore$ The correct answer is 8.

33. The given situation is shown below.

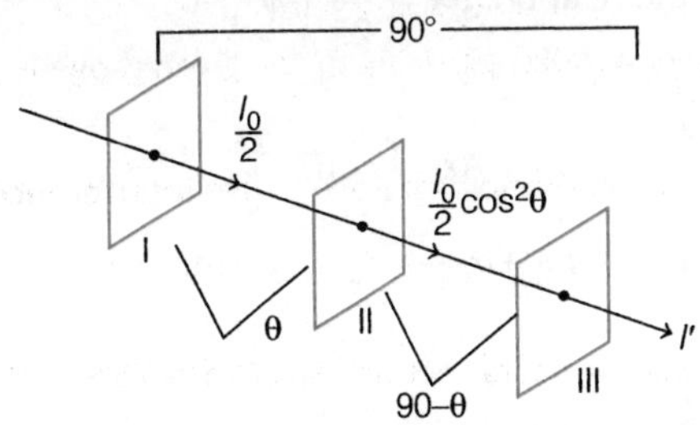

Output intensity from IIIrd polaroid using Malus Law, is

$$I' = \frac{I_0}{2}\cos^2\theta \cdot \cos^2(90 - \theta)$$

$$= \frac{I_0}{2}\cos^2\theta \cdot \sin^2\theta$$

$$\text{or,} \quad 3 = \frac{32}{2} \cdot \cos^2\theta\sin^2\theta$$

$$\Rightarrow \quad 3 = 4(4\cos^2\theta \sin^2\theta)$$

$$\Rightarrow \quad \frac{3}{4} = (\sin 2\theta)^2 \quad \text{or} \quad \sin 2\theta = \frac{\sqrt{3}}{2}$$

$$\Rightarrow \quad 2\theta = 60^\circ$$

$$\text{or} \quad \theta = 30^\circ$$

Level 2

34. $2I_0 = 4I_0 \cos^2\left(\frac{\phi_1}{2}\right)$

$$\therefore \quad \phi_1 = \frac{\pi}{2} = \left(\frac{2\pi}{\lambda}\right)(\Delta x_1) = \left(\frac{2\pi}{\lambda}\right)\left(\frac{y_1 d}{D}\right)$$

$$\therefore \quad y_1 = \frac{\lambda D}{4d} = \frac{\beta}{4}$$

Further, $I_0 = 4I_0 \cos^2\left(\frac{\phi_2}{2}\right)$

$$\therefore \quad \phi_2 = \frac{2\pi}{3} = \left(\frac{2\pi}{\lambda}\right)(\Delta x_2) = \left(\frac{2\pi}{\lambda}\right)\left(\frac{y_2 d}{D}\right)$$

$$\therefore \quad y_2 = \frac{\lambda D}{3d} = \frac{\beta}{3}$$

$$\Delta y = y_2 - y_1 = \frac{\beta}{12}$$

35. At path difference λ, we get maximum intensity.

$$\therefore \quad I_{max} = I$$

$$I_R = I_{max} \cos^2\left(\frac{\phi}{2}\right)$$

$$\therefore \quad \frac{I}{4} = I\cos^2\left(\frac{\phi}{2}\right) \quad \text{or} \quad \cos\left(\frac{\phi}{2}\right) = \pm\frac{1}{2}$$

$$\therefore \quad \frac{\phi}{2} = 60^\circ \text{ or } 120^\circ$$

$$\therefore \quad \phi = 120^\circ \text{ or } 240^\circ \text{ or } \frac{2\pi}{3} \text{ and } \frac{4\pi}{3}$$

From the relation, $\Delta x = \left(\frac{\lambda}{2\pi}\right)\cdot\phi$

We see that,

$$\Delta x = \frac{\lambda}{3} \text{ and } \frac{2\lambda}{3}$$

36. At points P, Q and R,

$$I = \frac{3}{4} I_{max} = I_{max} \cos^2\frac{\phi}{2}$$

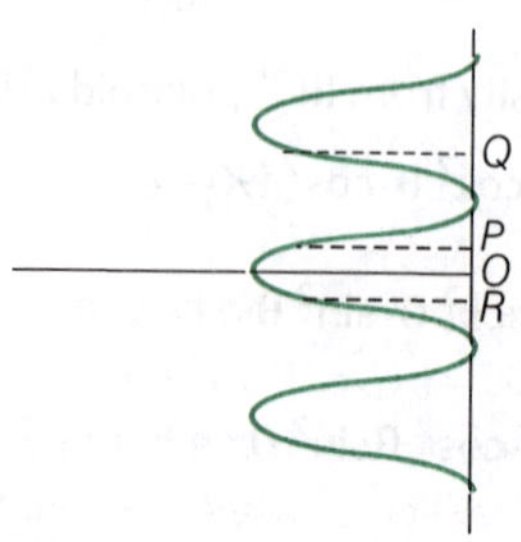

$$\therefore \quad \frac{\phi}{2} = \frac{\pi}{6} \text{ and } \frac{5\pi}{6}$$

$$\therefore \quad \phi = \frac{\pi}{3}$$

$$\text{and} \quad \frac{5\pi}{3} = \left(\frac{2\pi}{\lambda}\right)\Delta x = \left(\frac{2\pi}{\lambda}\right)\frac{yd}{D}$$

$$\therefore \quad y_1 = OP = \frac{\lambda D}{6d} = \frac{6000 \times 10^{-10} \times 1 \times 10^3}{6 \times 10^{-3}} \text{ mm}$$

$$= 0.1 \text{ mm}$$

$$y_2 = OQ = \frac{5\lambda D}{6d}$$

$$= 0.5 \text{ mm}$$

Now, the distance is either PR or 0.2 mm or PQ or 0.4 mm. Hence, the answer is 0.2 mm.

37. $\because \quad \theta = \frac{d}{D}$

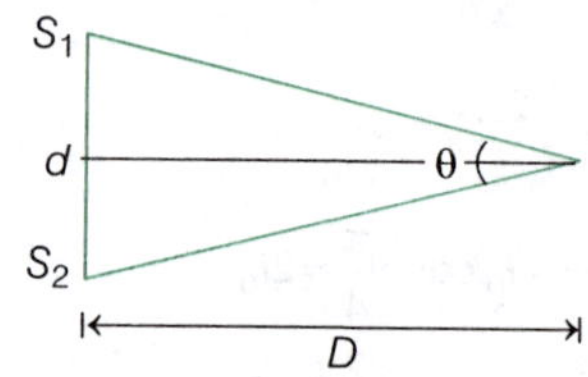

Third minima,

$$y = \pm 2.5\,\omega = \pm 2.5\left(\frac{\lambda D}{d}\right) = \pm\frac{2.5\lambda}{\theta}$$

38. Shift $= \frac{(\mu - 1)tD}{d}$

At $\mu = 1$, shift $= 0$

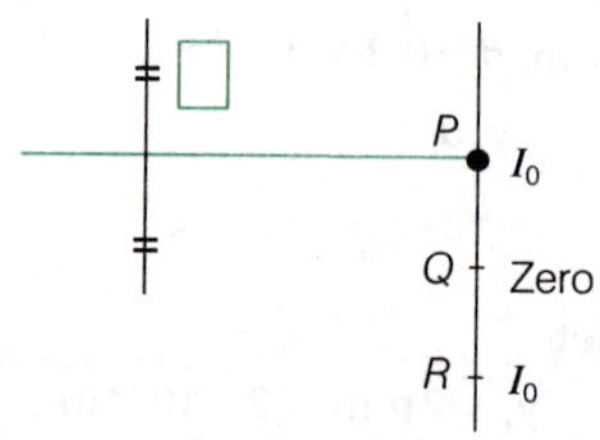

Therefore, intensity at centre is maximum or I_0.
As μ increases fringes shift upwards as shown in figure. So, intensity at P first decreases to zero (as Q reaches at P), then it further increases to I_0 (as point R reaches to P).

39. $\frac{3}{4} I_{max} = I_{max} \cos^2\frac{\phi}{2}$

$$\therefore \quad \frac{\phi}{2} = \frac{\pi}{6}$$

$$\text{or} \quad \phi = \frac{\pi}{3} = \left(\frac{2\pi}{\lambda}\right)(\Delta x) = \left(\frac{2\pi}{\lambda}\right)(\mu - 1)t$$

$$\therefore \quad t = \frac{\lambda}{6(\mu - 1)} = \frac{6000 \times 10^{-10}}{6(1.5 - 1)}$$

$$= 0.2 \times 10^{-6} \text{ m} = 0.2 \,\mu\text{m}$$

40. $\Delta x_1 = (\mu_1 - 1), \Delta x_2 = (\mu_2 - 1)t$

$$\therefore \quad \Delta x = (\mu_1 - \mu_2)t$$
$$= (1.52 - 1.40)(10400 \text{ nm})$$
$$= 1248 \text{ nm}$$

For maximum intensity,

$$\Delta x = 1248 = n\lambda$$
$$\therefore \quad \lambda = \frac{1248}{n} \qquad (n = 1, 2, 3 \cdots)$$

For $n = 2, \lambda = 624 \text{ nm}$

and for $n = 3, \lambda = 416 \text{ nm}$

41. $\Delta\phi = \left(\frac{2\pi}{\lambda / n_1}\right) L_1 - \left(\frac{2\pi}{\lambda / n_2}\right) L_2$

42. We will get four maximas corresponding to,

$$\Delta X = \lambda, 2\lambda, 3\lambda \text{ and } 4\lambda$$

Note *At $x = 0$, $\Delta x = 5\lambda$*
and at $x = \infty$, $\Delta x = 0$

43. Fringe width, $\beta = \frac{D\lambda}{d}$ i.e. $\beta \propto \lambda$

So, wavelength λ and hence fringe width β decreases 1.5 times when immersed in liquid. The distance between central maxima and 10th maxima is 3 cm in vacuum. When immersed in liquid it will reduce to 2 cm. Position of central maxima will not change while 10th maxima will be obtained at $y = 4$ cm.

44. For maximum intensity on the screen, path difference should be integer multiple of wavelength, i.e.

$$d \sin\theta = n\lambda$$
$$\sin\theta = \frac{n\lambda}{d} = \frac{n(2000)}{7000} = \frac{n}{3.5}$$

As, $(\sin\theta)_{max} = 1$

So, $n = 0, 1, 2, 3$

Thus, only seven maximas can be obtained on both sides of the screen.

45. Path difference between the waves reaching at P,

$$\Delta = \Delta_1 + \Delta_2$$

where, $\Delta_1 =$ initial path difference

$\Delta_2 =$ path difference between the waves after emerging from slits.

Now, $\Delta_1 = SS_1 - SS_2 = \sqrt{(D^2 + d^2)} - D$

and $\Delta_2 = S_1O - S_2O = \sqrt{(D^2 + d^2)} - D$

$$\therefore \quad \Delta = 2\{\sqrt{(D^2 + d^2)} - D\}$$
$$= 2\{(D^2 + d^2)^{1/2} - D\}$$
$$\approx 2\left\{\left(D + \frac{d^2}{2D}\right) - D\right\} \text{ from binomial expansion}$$
$$= \frac{d^2}{D}$$

For obtaining minima at O, Δ must be equal to $(2n - 1)\frac{\lambda}{2}$

i.e. $$\frac{d^2}{D} = (2n - 1)\frac{\lambda}{2}$$
$$\therefore \quad d^2 = \frac{(2n - 1)\lambda D}{2}$$
or $$d = \sqrt{\frac{(2n - 1)\lambda D}{2}}$$

For minimum distance, $n = 1$

So, $$d = \sqrt{\left(\frac{\lambda D}{2}\right)}$$

46. P is actually 10th maxima with respect to point O.

$$\therefore \quad S_1P - S_2P = 10\lambda$$
or $$S_1B = 10\lambda = 10 \times 600 \times 10^{-9} \text{ m} \qquad (S_2P \approx BP)$$
$$= 6 \times 10^{-6} \text{ m}$$

47. Suppose P be the point on x-axis, where constructive interference is obtained.

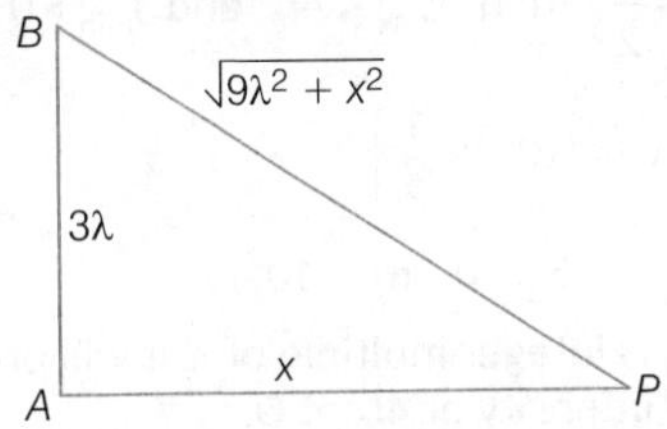

$$BP - AP = 2\lambda \text{ or } \lambda$$
$$\therefore \quad \sqrt{9\lambda^2 + x^2} - x = 2\lambda$$
$$\therefore \quad 9\lambda^2 + x^2 = x^2 + 4\lambda^2 + 4x\lambda$$
$$x = \frac{5\lambda}{4}$$

Further, $\sqrt{9\lambda^2 + x^2} - x = \lambda$

$$\therefore \quad 9\lambda^2 + x^2 = x^2 + \lambda^2 + 2x\lambda$$
$$\therefore \quad x = 4\lambda$$

48. $PR = d$

$$\therefore \quad PO = d\sec\theta$$
and $$CO = PO\cos 2\theta = d\sec\theta\cos 2\theta$$

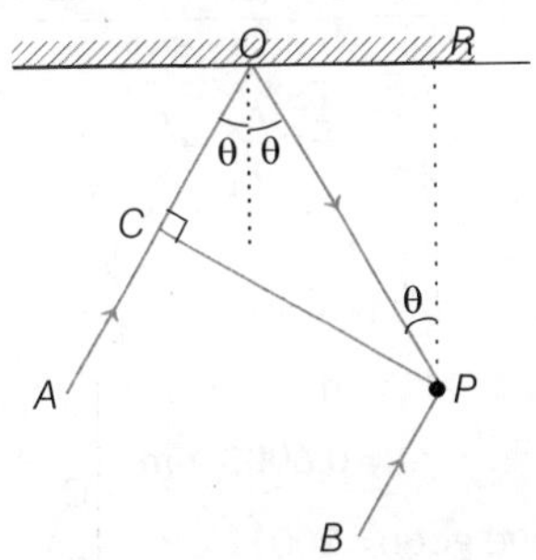

Path difference between the two rays is,

$$\Delta x = PO + OC = (d\sec\theta + d\sec\theta\cos 2\theta)$$

Phase difference between the two rays is

$\Delta\phi = \pi$ (one is reflected, while another is direct)

Therefore, condition for constructive interference should be

$$\Delta x = \frac{\lambda}{2}, \frac{3\lambda}{2} \ldots$$

or $$d \sec\theta (1 + \cos 2\theta) = \frac{\lambda}{2}$$

or $$\left(\frac{d}{\cos\theta}\right)(2\cos^2\theta) = \frac{\lambda}{2}$$

or $$\cos\theta = \frac{\lambda}{4d}$$

49. $I_{max} = (\sqrt{I_1} + \sqrt{I_2})^2$

$$I_{min} = (\sqrt{I_1} - \sqrt{I_2})^2$$

When $I_1 = I_2 = I_0$

$$I_{max} = 4I_0$$

and $I_{min} = 0$

When $I_2 = \frac{I_0}{2}$, then $I_{max} < 4I_0$ and $I_{min} > 0$

50. $\Delta x_0 = d\sin\theta = (10^{-3})\left(\frac{1}{2}\right)$

$$= 5 \times 10^{-4} \text{m} = (10^3)\,\lambda$$

Since, Δx_0 is integer multiple of λ, it will produce maximum intensity or $4I_0$ at O.

$$\omega = \frac{\lambda D}{d} = \frac{(5 \times 10^{-7})(2)}{(10^{-3})}$$

$$= 10^{-3} \text{m} = 1 \text{mm}$$

At 4 mm, we will get 4th order maxima.

51. For overlapping of maxima

$$\frac{n_1\lambda_1 D}{d} = \frac{n_2\lambda_2 D}{d}$$

or $$\frac{n_1}{n_2} = \frac{\lambda_2}{\lambda_1} = \frac{7}{5}, \frac{14}{10} \cdots$$

14th order maxima of λ_1 will coincide with 10th order maxima of λ_2.

For overlapping of minima

$$\frac{(2n_1 - 1)\lambda_1 D}{2d} = \frac{(2n_2 - 1)\lambda_2 D}{2d}$$

$\therefore$ $$\frac{2n_1 - 1}{2n_2 - 1} = \frac{\lambda_2}{\lambda_1} = \frac{7}{5}$$

(c) Option with $n_1 = 11$ and $n_2 = 8$ gives this ratio.

52. Path difference at $O = d$

$$= 0.6003 \text{ mm}$$

For $n\frac{\lambda}{2} = d$, we get $n = 2001$

As n is a whole number, the condition for minima is satisfied. Therefore O will be dark i.e., minima is formed at O. Also, as the screen is perpendicular to the plane containing the slits S_1, S_2, therefore fringes obtained will be semicircular (only top half of the screen is available).

53. We know that fringe width,

$$\beta = \frac{\lambda D}{d}$$

$\because$ $$\lambda_2 > \lambda_1$$

$\Rightarrow$ $$\beta_2 > \beta_1$$

Number of fringes in a given width

$$m \propto \frac{1}{\beta}$$

$\therefore$ $$m_1 > m_2$$

$$3 \times \frac{\lambda_2 D}{d} = \frac{(2 \times 5 - 1)}{2}\frac{D}{d}$$

$$3 \times 600 = 4.5 \times 400$$

Angular separation $\frac{\lambda}{d} \propto \lambda$

So it is geater for λ_2.

54. For $d = \lambda$, there will be only one central maxima.

For $\lambda < d < 2\lambda$, there will be three maximas on the screen corresponding to path difference,

$$\Delta x = 0$$

and $$\Delta x = \pm\lambda.$$

55. The intensity of light is

$$I(\theta) = I_0 \cos^2\left(\frac{\delta}{2}\right)$$

where, $\delta = \frac{2\pi}{\lambda}(\Delta x) = \left(\frac{2\pi}{\lambda}\right)(d\sin\theta)$

(a) For $\theta = 30°$

$$\lambda = \frac{c}{v} = \frac{3 \times 10^8}{10^6} = 300 \text{ m}$$

and $$d = 150 \text{ m}$$

$$\delta = \left(\frac{2\pi}{300}\right)(150)\left(\frac{1}{2}\right) = \frac{\pi}{2}$$

$\therefore$ $$\frac{\delta}{2} = \frac{\pi}{4}$$

$\therefore$ $$I(\theta) = I_0 \cos^2\left(\frac{\pi}{4}\right) = \frac{I_0}{2}$$ [option (a)]

(b) For $\theta = 90°$

$$\delta = \left(\frac{2\pi}{300}\right)(150)(1) = \pi$$

or $$\frac{\delta}{2} = \frac{\pi}{2} \text{ and } I(\theta) = 0$$

(c) For $\theta = 0°$, $\delta = 0$ or $\frac{\delta}{2} = 0$

$\therefore$ $$I(\theta) = I_0$$ [option (c)]

56. Position of 8th bright spot, $Y = 8\beta$

$$Y = 8\frac{\lambda D}{d} = 8 \times \frac{(600 \times 10^{-9})(1)}{(0.8 + 0.04\sin\omega t) \times 10^{-3}}$$

$$Y = \frac{4800\ \mu\text{m}}{0.8(1 + 0.05\sin\omega t)}$$

$$Y = 6000\ \mu\text{m}\,(1 + 0.05\sin\omega t)^{-1}$$

Using Binomial theorem,

$$Y = 6000\ \mu\text{m}\,(1 - 0.05\sin\omega t)$$

$$Y = 6000\,\mu\text{m} - 300\,\mu\text{m}\sin(\omega t)$$

Amplitude, $A = 300\ \mu\text{m}$

Separation between the two extreme positions $= 2A = 600\ \mu\text{m}$

Exact Calculation :

$$Y_{max} = \left(\frac{6000}{1-0.05}\right)\mu\text{m}$$

$$Y_{min} = \left(\frac{6000}{1+0.05}\right)\mu\text{m}$$

$$Y_{max} - Y_{min} = (6000)\left[\frac{1}{0.95} - \frac{1}{1.05}\right]\mu\text{m}$$

$$= (601.5)\ \mu\text{m}$$

57. $v = \dfrac{\delta y}{\delta t} = \dfrac{\delta}{\delta t}\left(\dfrac{8\lambda D}{d}\right)$

$$= -\frac{8\lambda D}{d^2}\frac{\delta d}{(\delta t)}$$

$$v = -\frac{8\lambda D}{d^2}(0.04\,\omega\cos\omega t) \times 10^{-3}$$

$$v_{max} = \frac{8\lambda D}{d^2} \times 4\omega \times 10^{-5}$$

$$= \frac{8 \times 6 \times 10^{-7} \times 1 \times 4 \times 8 \times 10^{-7}}{64 \times 10^{-8}}$$

$$= 24 \times 10^{-6}$$

$$= 24\,\mu\ \text{m/s}$$

58. $I = 4I_0\cos^2\left(\dfrac{\phi}{2}\right)$

59. $\phi = \dfrac{2\pi}{\lambda}\Delta x$ and then apply,

$$I = 4I_0\cos^2\left(\frac{\phi}{2}\right)$$

60.

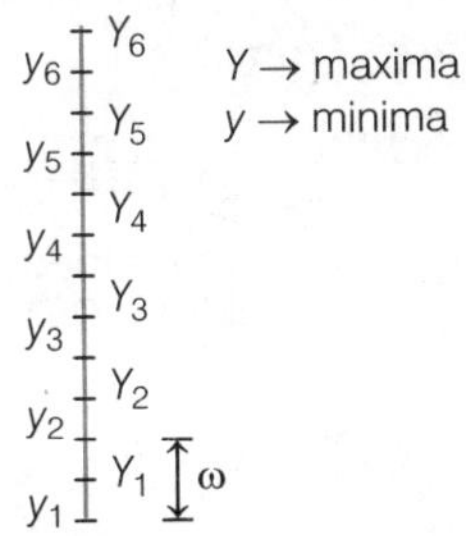

61. (a) Inclined rays and slab both will shift the fringe pattern upwards. So, zero order maxima will definitely lie about O.

(b) Inclined rays will shift the fringe pattern upwards, but slab will shift the fringe pattern downwards. Hence, zero order maxima may lie above O, below O or at O.

(c) Same explanations can be given for this option.

(d)

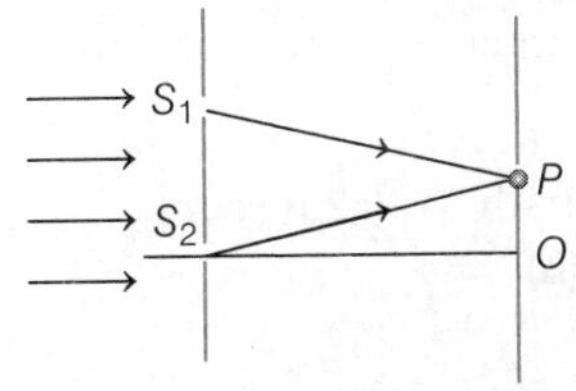

$\Delta X_p = 0$, where $S_1P = S_2P$

62. (A) → (p,s) → Intensity at P_0 is maximum. It will continuously decrease from P_0 towards P_2

(B) → (q) → Path difference due to slab will be compensated by geometrical path difference. Hence, $\delta(P_1) = 0$.

(C) → (t) → $\delta(P_0) = \dfrac{\lambda}{2}$, $\delta(P_1) = \dfrac{\lambda}{2} - \dfrac{\lambda}{4} = \dfrac{\lambda}{4}$ and

$\delta(P_2) = \dfrac{\lambda}{2} - \dfrac{\lambda}{3} = \dfrac{\lambda}{6}$. When path difference increases from 0 to $\dfrac{\lambda}{2}$, intensity will decrease from maximum to zero. Hence, in this case,

$$I(P_2) > I(P_1) > I(P_0)$$

(D) → (r, s, t,)

$$\delta(P_0) = \frac{3\lambda}{4}$$

$$\delta(P_1) = \frac{3\lambda}{4} - \frac{\lambda}{4} = \frac{\lambda}{2}$$

and $$\delta(P_2) = \frac{3\lambda}{4} - \frac{\lambda}{3} = \frac{5\lambda}{12}.$$

In this case $I(P_1) = 0$.

63. ∵ $\mu = \dfrac{\sin i}{\sin r}$

∴ $$\frac{4}{3} = \frac{\sin 53°}{\sin r} = \frac{4/5}{\sin r}$$

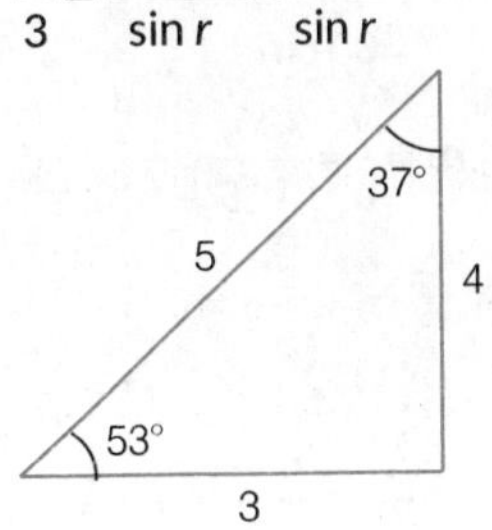

∴ $$\sin r = \frac{3}{5}$$

∴ $$r = 37°$$

Refer figure (a)

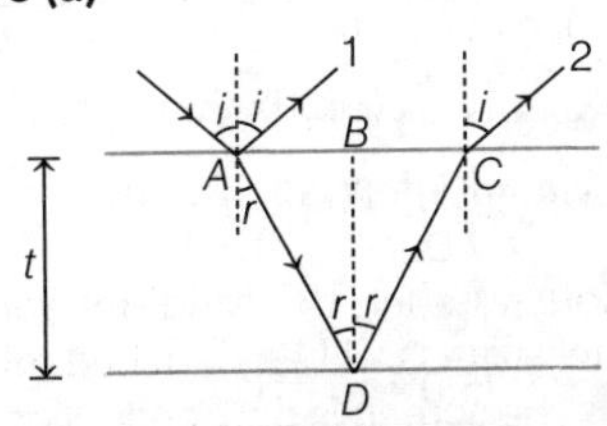

(a)

$$\Delta x_1 = \text{between 2 and } 1 = 2(AD)$$
$$= 2BD \sec r$$
$$= 2t \sec r$$

Their optical path $\Delta x_1 = 2\mu t \sec r$.

Refer figure (b)

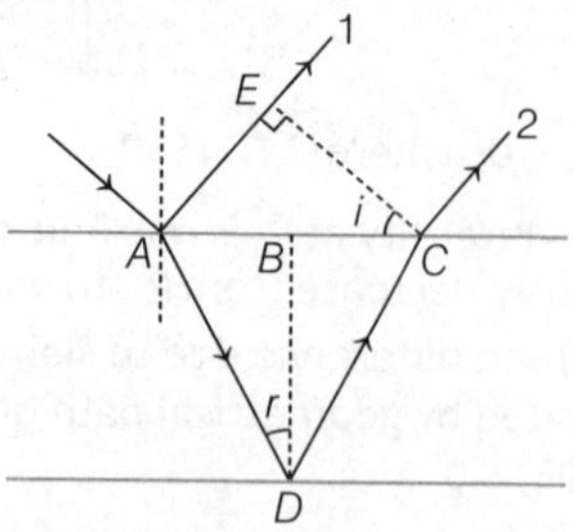

(b)

$$\Delta x_2 = AC \sin i = (2t \tan r) \sin i$$

$$\therefore \quad (\Delta x)_{net} = \Delta x_1 - \Delta x_2$$
$$= 2\mu t \sec r - 2t (\tan r)(\sin i)$$
$$= 2 \times \frac{4}{3} \times t \times \frac{5}{4} - 2 \times t \times \frac{3}{4} \times \frac{4}{5}$$
$$= \frac{32}{15} t$$

Phase difference between 1 and 2 is π.

$\therefore$ For constructive interference,

$$\frac{32}{15} t = \frac{\lambda}{2}$$

or
$$t = \frac{15\lambda}{64} = \frac{15 \times 0.6}{64}$$
$$= 0.14 \, \mu\text{m} \qquad \textbf{Ans.}$$

64. Applying lens formula, $\frac{1}{v} - \frac{1}{u} = \frac{1}{f}$

$$\frac{1}{v} + \frac{1}{15} = \frac{1}{10}$$

$$\therefore \quad v = 30 \text{ cm}$$

$$m = \frac{v}{u} = \frac{30}{-15} = -2$$

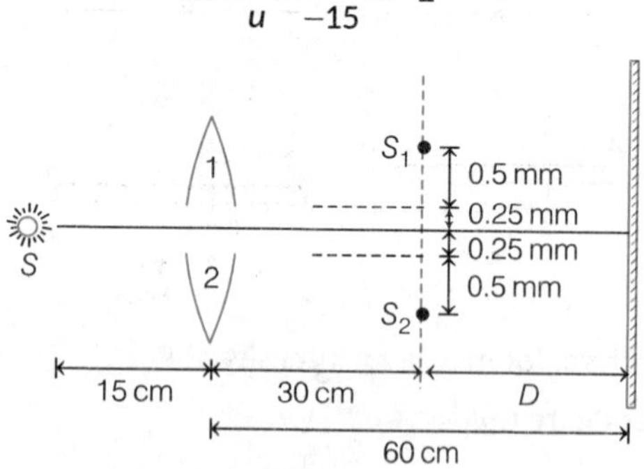

Distance between two slits,

$$d = 1.5 \text{ mm}, \; D = 30 \text{ cm}$$

Fringe width, $\omega = \frac{\lambda D}{d}$

$$= \frac{(5.0 \times 10^{-7})(0.3)}{(1.5 \times 10^{-3})}$$
$$= 10^{-4} \text{ m}$$
$$= 0.1 \text{ mm} \qquad \textbf{Ans.}$$

65. (a) $\because \quad \Delta x = d \cos \theta$

$$\cos \theta = 1 - \frac{\theta^2}{2} \qquad \text{(When } \theta \text{ is small)}$$

$$\therefore \quad \Delta x = d\left(1 - \frac{\theta^2}{2}\right)$$
$$= d\left(1 - \frac{y^2}{2D^2}\right)$$

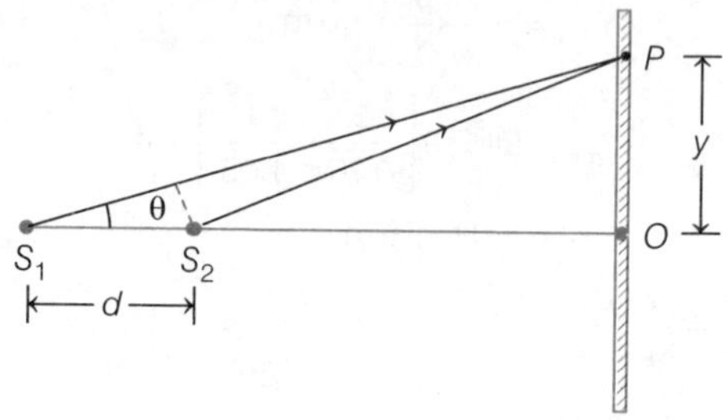

For nth maxima $\Delta x = n\lambda$

$\therefore \quad y = $ radius of nth bright ring

$$= D\sqrt{2\left(1 - \frac{n\lambda}{d}\right)} \qquad \textbf{Ans.}$$

(b) $d = 1000\lambda$

At O, $\Delta x = d = 1000\lambda$

i.e. at O, 1000 th order maxima is obtained.

Substituting $n = 998$ in, $y = D\sqrt{2\left(1 - \frac{n\lambda}{d}\right)}$

We get the radius of second closest ring

$$r = 6.32 \text{ cm} \qquad \textbf{Ans.}$$

(c) $n = 998$ **Ans.**

66. (a) The optical path difference between the two waves arriving at P is

$$\Delta x = \frac{y_1 d}{D_1} + \frac{y_2 d}{D_2} = \frac{(1)(10)}{10^3} + \frac{(5)(10)}{2 \times 10^3}$$
$$= 3.5 \times 10^{-2} \text{ mm}$$
$$= 0.035 \text{ mm}$$

As, $\Delta x = 70\lambda$

$\therefore$ 70th order maxima is obtained at P.

(b) At O, $\Delta x = \frac{y_1 d}{D_1} = 10^{-2}$ mm

$$= 0.01 \text{ mm}$$

As $\quad \Delta x = 20\lambda$

$\therefore$ 20th order maxima is obtained at O.

(c) $(\mu - 1)t = 0.01$ mm

$$\therefore \quad t = \frac{0.01}{1.5 - 1} = 0.02 \text{ mm}$$
$$= 20 \, \mu\text{m} \qquad \textbf{Ans.}$$

Since, the pattern has to be shifted upwards, therefore, the film must be placed in front of S_1.

67. (a) $d \sin\phi = \Delta x_1$

$= (50 \times 10^{-4}) \sin 30°$

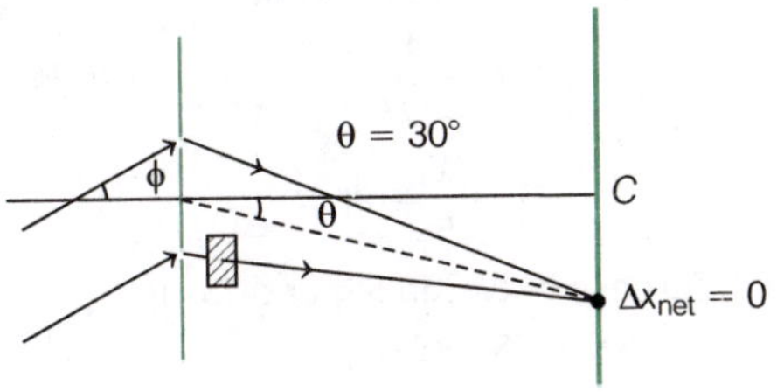

$= 2.5 \times 10^{-3}$ cm

$\Delta x_2 = (\mu - 1)t$

$= \left(\frac{3}{2} - 1\right)(0.01)$

$= 5.0 \times 10^{-3}$ cm

$\Delta x_2 - \Delta x_1 = 2.5 \times 10^{-3} \text{ cm} = \Delta x_1$ (also)

$\therefore$ Central maxima will be obtained at $\theta = 30°$ below C.

(b) **At C** $\quad \Delta X_{net} = 2.5 \times 10^{-3} \text{ cm} = n\lambda$

$$\therefore \quad n = \frac{2.5 \times 10^{-3}}{\lambda} = \frac{2.5 \times 10^{-3}}{500 \times 10^{-7}}$$

$= 50$ **Ans.**

(c) Number of fringes that will pass if we remove the slab

$$= \frac{\text{Path difference due to slab}}{\lambda}$$

$$= \frac{5 \times 10^{-3}}{500 \times 10^{-7}} = 100$$ **Ans.**

68. (a) $(\Delta x)_{net} = 0$

$$\therefore \quad \frac{y_1 d}{D_1} = \frac{y_2 d}{D_2}$$

$$\therefore \quad \frac{d/2}{1.5} = \frac{y}{2.0}$$

or $$y = \frac{d}{1.5} = \frac{6}{1.5}$$

$= 4$ mm **Ans.**

(b) At O, net path difference,

$$\Delta x = \frac{y_1 d}{D_1} = \frac{(d/2)(d)}{D_1}$$

$$= \frac{(6 \times 10^{-3})^2}{2 \times 1.5} = 12 \times 10^{-6} \text{ m}$$

$= 120 \times 10^{-7}$ m

$\lambda = 6000$ Å

$= 6 \times 10^{-7}$ m

As, $\Delta x = 20\lambda$, therefore at O bright fringe of order 20 will be obtained.

(c) $I = I_{max} \cos^2\left(\frac{\phi}{2}\right)$

$$\frac{3}{4} I_{max} = I_{max} \cos^2\left(\frac{\phi}{2}\right)$$

$$\therefore \quad \frac{\phi}{2} = \frac{\pi}{6}$$

$$\phi = \frac{\pi}{3} = \left(\frac{2\pi}{\lambda}\right)(\mu - 1)t$$

$$\therefore \quad t = \frac{\lambda}{6(\mu - 1)} = \frac{6000}{6(1.5 - 1)}$$

$= 2000$ Å **Ans.**

69. (a) $\left(1 - \frac{1}{\mu}\right)t = \frac{3\lambda}{\mu}$

$$\therefore \quad t = \frac{3\lambda}{(\mu - 1)} = \frac{3 \times 0.78}{1.3 - 1}$$

$= 7.8\,\mu$m **Ans.**

(b) **Upwards** $\quad \frac{yd}{D} - \left(1 - \frac{1}{\mu}\right)t = \frac{4\lambda}{\mu}$

Solving, we get $y = 4.2$ mm **Ans.**

Downwards $\quad t\left(1 - \frac{1}{\mu}\right) + \frac{yd}{D} = \frac{4\lambda}{\mu}$

Solving, we get $y = 0.6$ mm **Ans.**

70. (a) Shape of the interference fringes will be circular.

(b) Intensity of light reaching on the screen directly from the source, $I_1 = I_0$ (say) and intensity of light reaching on the screen after reflecting from the mirror is $I_2 = 36\%$ of $I_0 = 0.36\, I_0$

$$\therefore \quad \frac{I_1}{I_2} = \frac{I_0}{0.36 I_0} = \frac{1}{0.36} \text{ or } \sqrt{\frac{I_1}{I_2}} = \frac{1}{0.6}$$

$$\therefore \quad \frac{I_{min}}{I_{max}} = \frac{\left(\sqrt{\frac{I_1}{I_2}} - 1\right)^2}{\left(\sqrt{\frac{I_1}{I_2}} + 1\right)^2} = \frac{\left(\frac{1}{0.6} - 1\right)^2}{\left(\frac{1}{0.6} + 1\right)^2} = \frac{1}{16}$$

(c) Initially path difference at P between two waves reaching from S and S' is $2h$.

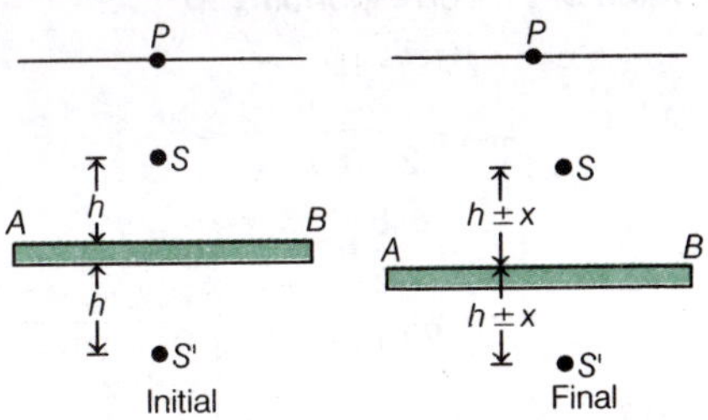

Therefore, for maximum intensity at P

$$2h = \left(n - \frac{1}{2}\right)\lambda \quad \text{... (i)}$$

Now, let the reflecting surface AB is displaced by x. Then, new path difference will be $2h + 2x$ or $2h - 2x$. So, again for maximum intensity at P.

$$2h + 2x = \left[n + 1 - \frac{1}{2}\right]\lambda \quad \text{... (ii)}$$

or $$2h - 2x = \left[n - 1 - \frac{1}{2}\right]\lambda \quad \text{... (iii)}$$

Solving Eqs. (i) and (ii) or Eqs. (i) and (iii), we get

$$x = \frac{\lambda}{2} = \frac{600}{2} = 300 \text{ nm}$$

Note *Here, we have taken the condition of maximum intensity at P as : Path difference* $\Delta x = \left(n - \frac{1}{2}\right)\lambda$

Because the reflected beam suffers a phase difference of π.

71. Incident ray AB is partly reflected as ray 1 from the upper surface and partly reflected as ray 2 from the lower surface of the layer of thickness t and refractive index $\mu_1 = 1.8$ as shown in figure. Path difference between the two rays would be

$$\Delta x = 2\mu_1 t = 2(1.8)t = 3.6t$$

Ray 1 is reflected from a denser medium, therefore, it undergoes a phase change of π, whereas the ray 2 gets reflected from a rarer medium, therefore, there is no change in phase of ray 2.

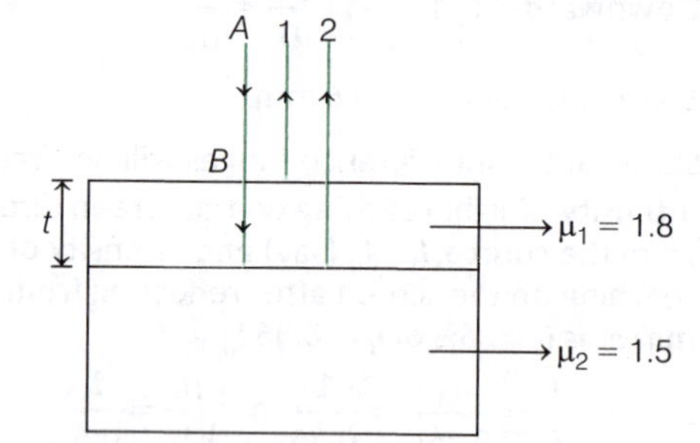

Hence, phase difference between rays 1 and 2 would be $\Delta\phi = \pi$. Therefore, condition of constructive interference will be

$$\Delta x = \left(n - \frac{1}{2}\right)\lambda \text{ where } n = 1, 2, 3...$$

or $$3.6t = \left(n - \frac{1}{2}\right)\lambda$$

Least value of t is corresponding to

$$n = 1$$

or $$t_{min} = \frac{\lambda}{2 \times 3.6}$$

or $$t_{min} = \frac{648}{7.2} \text{ nm}$$

or $$t_{min} = 90 \text{ nm}$$

74. (i) Given $y_1 = 40$ cm,

$$D_1 = 2 \text{ m} = 200 \text{ cm},$$

$$D_2 = 10 \text{ cm}$$

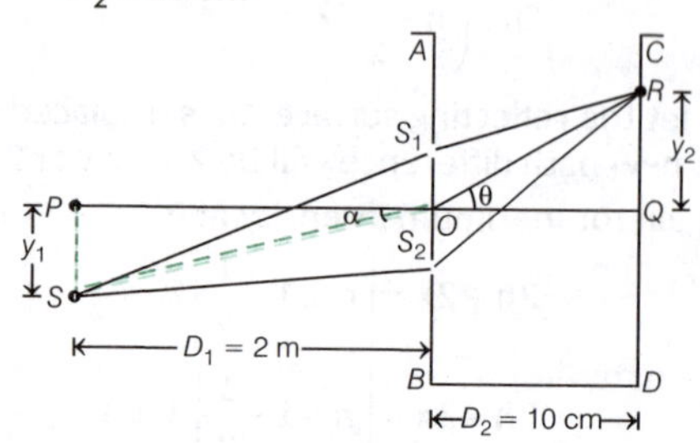

$$\tan\alpha = \frac{y_1}{D_1} = \frac{40}{200} = \frac{1}{5}$$

$\therefore$ $$\alpha = \tan^{-1}(1/5)$$

$$\sin\alpha = \frac{1}{\sqrt{26}}$$

$$\approx \frac{1}{5} = \tan\alpha$$

Path difference between SS_1 and SS_2 is

$$\Delta X_1 = SS_1 - SS_2$$

or $$\Delta X_1 = d\sin\alpha = (0.8 \text{ mm})\left(\frac{1}{5}\right)$$

or $$\Delta X_1 = 0.16 \text{ mm} \quad \text{...(i)}$$

Now, let at point R on the screen, central bright fringe is observed (*i.e.*, net path difference = 0).

Path difference between S_2R and S_1R would be

$$\Delta X_2 = S_2R - S_1R$$

or $$\Delta X_2 = d\sin\theta \quad \text{...(ii)}$$

Central bright fringe is observed where net path difference is zero.

or $$\Delta X_2 - \Delta X_1 = 0$$

$\Rightarrow$ $$\Delta X_2 = \Delta X_1$$

or $$d\sin\theta = 0.16$$

or $$(0.8)\sin\theta = 0.16$$

or $$\sin\theta = \frac{0.16}{0.8} = \frac{1}{5}$$

$$\tan\theta = \frac{1}{\sqrt{24}} \approx \sin\theta = \frac{1}{5}$$

Hence, $$\tan\theta = \frac{y_2}{D_2} = \frac{1}{5}$$

$\therefore$ $$y_2 = \frac{D_2}{5} = \frac{10}{5} = 2 \text{ cm}$$

Therefore, central bright fringe is observed at 2 cm above point Q on side CD.

(ii) $(\mu - 1)t = \Delta x_1$

$\therefore$ $$\mu = 1 + \frac{\Delta x_1}{t}$$

$$= 1 + \frac{0.16 \text{ mm}}{100 \text{ mm}} = 1.0016$$

73. Given, $\lambda = 600 \text{ nm} = 6 \times 10^{-7}$ m

$$d = 0.45 \text{ mm}$$

$$= 0.45 \times 10^{-3} \text{ m}$$

$$D = 1.5 \text{ m}$$

Thickness of glass sheet,

$$t = 10.4\,\mu\text{m} = 10.4 \times 10^{-6} \text{ m}$$

Refractive index of medium,

$$\mu_m = \frac{4}{3}$$

and refractive index of glass sheet,

$$\mu_g = 1.5$$

(a) Let central maximum is obtained at a distance y below point O. Then

$$\Delta x_1 = S_1P - S_2P = \frac{yd}{D}$$

Path difference due to glass sheet

$$\Delta x_2 = \left(\frac{\mu_g}{\mu_m} - 1\right)t$$

Position of central maximum Central maximum is defined as a point where net path difference is zero. So,

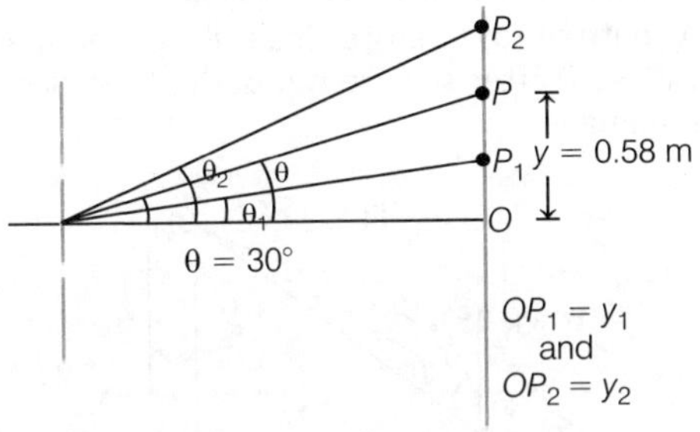

$$\Delta x_1 = \Delta x_2$$

or $\quad d \sin\alpha = d \sin\theta$ or $\theta = \alpha = 30°$

or $\quad \tan\theta = \dfrac{1}{\sqrt{3}} = \dfrac{y_0}{D}$

$\therefore \quad y_0 = \dfrac{1}{\sqrt{3}}\text{ m} \quad (D = 1\text{ m})$

$$y_0 = 0.58\text{ m}$$

At point P, $\quad \Delta x_1 = \Delta x_2$

Above point P, $\quad \Delta x_2 > \Delta x_1$

and Below point P, $\Delta x_1 > \Delta x_2$

Now, let P_1 and P_2 be the minimas on either side of central maxima. Then, for P_2

$$\Delta x_2 - \Delta x_1 = \frac{\lambda}{2}$$

or $\quad \Delta x_2 = \Delta x_1 + \dfrac{\lambda}{2} = \lambda + \dfrac{\lambda}{2} = \dfrac{3\lambda}{2}$

or $\quad d \sin\theta_2 = \dfrac{3\lambda}{2}$

or $\quad \sin\theta_2 = \dfrac{3\lambda}{2d} = \dfrac{(3)(0.5)}{(2)(1.0)} = \dfrac{3}{4}$

$\therefore \quad \tan\theta_2 = \dfrac{3}{\sqrt{7}} = \dfrac{y_2}{D}$

or $\quad y_2 = \dfrac{3}{\sqrt{7}} = 1.13\text{ m}$

Similarly by for P_1

$$\Delta x_1 - \Delta x_2 = \frac{\lambda}{2}$$

or $\quad \Delta x_2 = \Delta x_1 - \dfrac{\lambda}{2}$

$$= \lambda - \frac{\lambda}{2} = \frac{\lambda}{2}$$

or $\quad d \sin\theta_1 = \dfrac{\lambda}{2}$

or $\quad \sin\theta_1 = \dfrac{\lambda}{2d} = \dfrac{(0.5)}{(2)(1.0)} = \dfrac{1}{4}$

$\therefore \quad \tan\theta_1 = \dfrac{1}{\sqrt{15}} = \dfrac{y_1}{D}$

or $\quad y_1 = \dfrac{1}{\sqrt{15}}\text{ m} = 0.26\text{ m}$

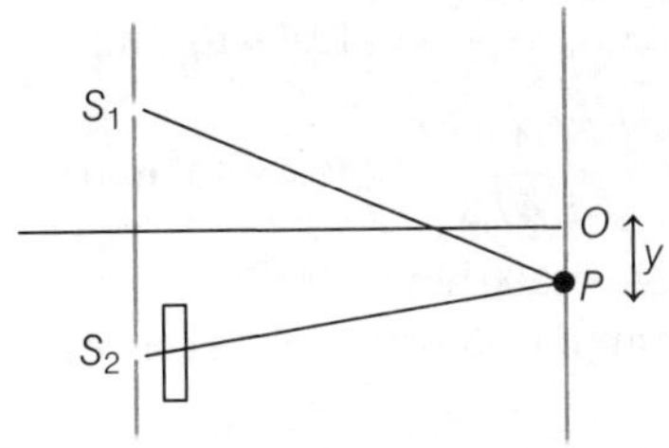

Therefore, y-coordinates of the first minima on either side of the central maximum are $y_1 = 0.26$ m and $y_2 = 1.13$ m.

Note *In this problem $\sin\theta \approx \tan\theta \approx \theta$ is not valid as θ is large.*

Net path difference will be zero when

$$\Delta x_1 = \Delta x_2$$

or $\quad \dfrac{yd}{D} = \left(\dfrac{\mu_g}{\mu_m} - 1\right)t$

$\therefore \quad y = \left(\dfrac{\mu_g}{\mu_m} - 1\right)\left(\dfrac{tD}{d}\right)$

Substituting the values, we have

$$y = \left(\frac{1.5}{4/3} - 1\right)\frac{10.4 \times 10^{-6}(1.5)}{0.45 \times 10^{-3}}$$

$$y = 4.33 \times 10^{-3}\text{ m}$$

or we can say $y = 4.33$ mm.

(b) At O, $\Delta x_1 = 0$ and $\Delta x_2 = \left(\dfrac{\mu_g}{\mu_m} - 1\right)t$

$\therefore$ Net path difference,

$$\Delta x = \Delta x_2$$

Corresponding phase difference, $\Delta\phi$ or ϕ

or $\quad \phi = \dfrac{2\pi}{\lambda} \cdot \Delta x$

Substituting the values, we have

$$\phi = \frac{2\pi}{6 \times 10^{-7}}\left(\frac{1.5}{4/3} - 1\right)(10.4 \times 10^{-6})$$

$$\phi = \left(\frac{13}{3}\right)\pi$$

Now, $\quad I(\phi) = I_{max}\cos^2\left(\dfrac{\phi}{2}\right)$

$\therefore \quad I = I_{max}\cos^2\left(\dfrac{13\pi}{6}\right)$

$$I = \frac{3}{4}I_{max}$$

(c) At O, path difference is

$$\Delta x = \Delta x_2 = \left(\frac{\mu_g}{\mu_m} - 1\right)t$$

For maximum intensity at O

$$\Delta x = n\lambda \text{ (Here } n = 1, 2, 3, \ldots)$$

$$\therefore \quad \lambda = \frac{\Delta x}{1}, \frac{\Delta x}{2}, \frac{\Delta x}{3} \ldots \text{ and so on}$$

$$\Delta x = \left(\frac{1.5}{4/3} - 1\right)(10.4 \times 10^{-6}\text{ m})$$

$$= \left(\frac{1.5}{4/3} - 1\right)(10.4 \times 10^{3}\text{ nm})$$

$$\Delta x = 1300 \text{ nm}$$

$\therefore$ Maximum intensity will be corresponding to

$$\lambda = 1300 \text{ nm}, \frac{1300}{2}\text{ nm},$$

$$\frac{1300}{3}\text{ nm}, \frac{1300}{4}\text{ nm} \ldots$$

$$= 1300 \text{ nm}, 650 \text{ nm},$$

$$433.33 \text{ nm}, 325 \text{ nm} \ldots$$

The wavelengths in the range 400 to 700 nm are 650 nm and 433.33 nm.

74. Given, $\lambda = 0.5$ mm, $d = 1.0$ mm, $D = 1$ m

(a) When the incident beam falls normally :

Path difference between the two rays S_2P and S_1P is

$$\Delta x = S_2P - S_1P \approx d \sin\theta$$

For minimum intensity,

$$d \sin\theta = (2n-1)\frac{\lambda}{2},$$

where $n = 1, 2, 3, \ldots$

$$\text{or} \quad \sin\theta = \frac{(2n-1)\lambda}{2d}$$

$$= \frac{(2n-1)0.5}{2 \times 1.0} = \frac{2n-1}{4}$$

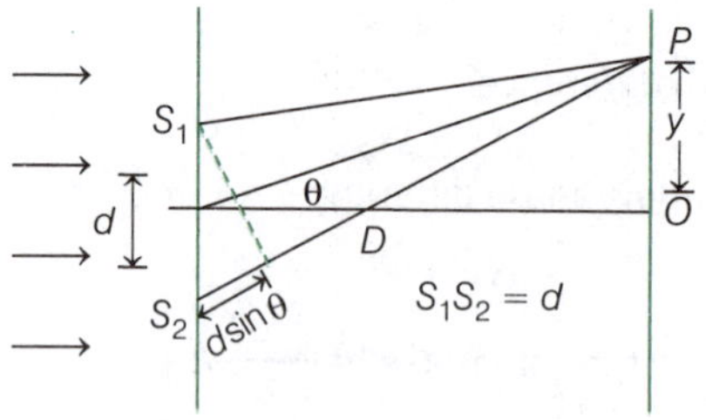

As $\sin\theta \le 1$ therefore $\dfrac{(2n-1)}{4} \le 1$

or $\quad n \le 2.5$

So, n can be either 1 or 2.

When $n = 1$, $\sin\theta_1 = \dfrac{1}{4}$

or $\quad \tan\theta_1 = \dfrac{1}{\sqrt{15}}$

$$n = 2, \sin\theta_2 = \frac{3}{4} \text{ or } \tan\theta_2 = \frac{3}{\sqrt{7}}$$

$$\therefore \quad y = D\tan\theta = \tan\theta \quad (D = 1\text{ m})$$

So, the position of minima will be

$$y_1 = \tan\theta_1 = \frac{1}{\sqrt{15}}\text{ m} = 0.26 \text{ m}$$

$$y_2 = \tan\theta_2 = \frac{3}{\sqrt{7}}\text{ m} = 1.13 \text{ m}$$

And as minima can be on either side of centre O. Therefore, there will be four minimas at positions ± 0.26 m and $\pm$ 1.13 m on the screen.

(b) Path difference before slits $= d \sin\phi$

Path difference after slits $= d\sin\theta$

As path of rays before slits is longer at S_1 and $S_2P > S_1P$ after slits, so net path difference for first minima is

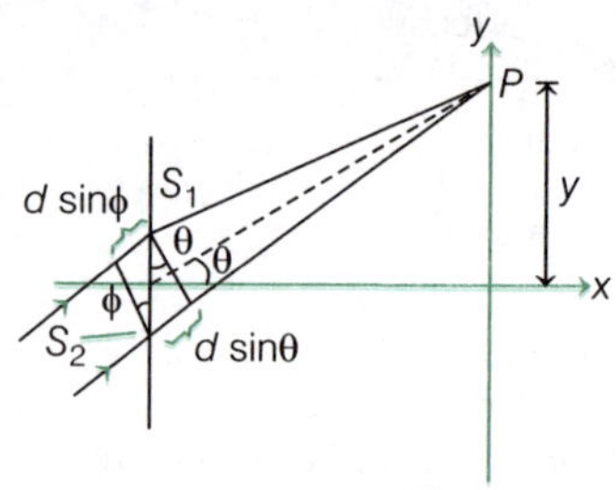

$$d\sin\theta - d\sin\phi = \pm\frac{\lambda}{2}$$

$$\sin\theta = \sin\phi \pm \frac{\lambda}{2}$$

$$= \sin 30° \pm \frac{0.5}{2 \times 1} = \frac{3}{4} \text{ or } \frac{1}{4}$$

$$\tan\theta = \frac{3}{\sqrt{7}} \text{ and } \frac{1}{\sqrt{15}}$$

So, the position of first minima on either side of central maxima is

$$y = D\tan\theta = \frac{3}{\sqrt{7}} \text{ and } \frac{1}{\sqrt{15}}\text{ m}$$

75. $\mu_1 = 1.4$ and $\mu_2 = 1.7$ and let t be the thickness of each glass plates.

Path difference at O, due to insertion of glass plates will be

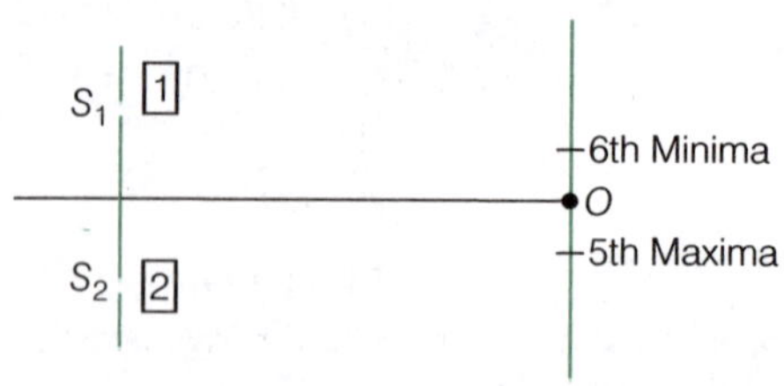

$$\Delta x = (\mu_2 - \mu_1)t$$

$$= (1.7 - 1.4)t = 0.3t \quad \ldots\text{(i)}$$

Now, since 5th maxima (earlier) lies below O and 6th minima lies above O,

this path difference should lie between 5λ and $5\lambda + \dfrac{\lambda}{2}$

So, let $\quad \Delta x = 5\lambda + \Delta \quad \ldots\text{(ii)}$

where $\quad \Delta < \dfrac{\lambda}{2}$

Due to the path difference Δx, the phase difference at O will be

$$\phi = \frac{2\pi}{\lambda}\Delta x = \frac{2\pi}{\lambda}(5\lambda + \Delta)$$

$$= \left(10\pi + \frac{2\pi}{\lambda}\cdot\Delta\right) \quad \text{...(iii)}$$

Intensity at O is given $\frac{3}{4}I_{max}$ and since

$$I(\phi) = I_{max}\cos^2\left(\frac{\phi}{2}\right)$$

$$\therefore \quad \frac{3}{4}I_{max} = I_{max}\cos^2\left(\frac{\phi}{2}\right)$$

or $$\frac{3}{4} = \cos^2\left(\frac{\phi}{2}\right) \quad \text{... (iv)}$$

From Eqs. (iii) and (iv), we find that

$$\Delta = \frac{\lambda}{6}$$

ie, $$\Delta x = 5\lambda + \frac{\lambda}{6} = \frac{31}{6}\lambda = 0.3\,t$$

$$\therefore \quad t = \frac{31\lambda}{6(0.3)} = \frac{(31)(5400\times10^{-10})}{1.8}$$

or $$t = 9.3\times10^{-6}\ \text{m}$$

$$= 9.3\ \mu\text{m}$$

76. (a) Path difference due to the glass slab,

$$\Delta x = (\mu - 1)t = (1.5 - 1)t = 0.5\,t$$

Due to this slab, 5 red fringes have been shifted upwards. Therefore,

$$\Delta x = 5\lambda_{red}$$

or $$0.5\,t = (5)(7\times10^{-7}\text{m})$$

$$\therefore \quad t = \text{thickness of glass slab}$$

$$= 7\times10^{-6}\ \text{m}$$

(b) Let μ' be the refractive index for green light then

$$\Delta x' = (\mu' - 1)\,t$$

Now the shifting is of 6 fringes of red light. Therefore,

$$\Delta x' = 6\lambda_{red}$$

$$\therefore \quad (\mu' - 1)\,t = 6\lambda_{red}$$

$$(\mu' - 1) = \frac{(6)(7\times10^{-7})}{7\times10^{-6}} = 0.6$$

$$\therefore \quad \mu' = 1.6$$

(c) In part (a), shifting of 5 bright fringes was equal to 10^{-3} m. Which implies that

$$5\omega_{red} = 10^{-3}\ \text{m} \quad (\text{Here, } \omega = \text{Fringe width})$$

$$\therefore \quad \omega_{red} = \frac{10^{-3}}{5}\text{m}$$

$$= 0.2\times10^{-3}\text{m}$$

Now since $\omega = \lambda D/d$ or $\omega \propto \lambda$

$$\therefore \quad \frac{\omega_{green}}{\omega_{red}} = \frac{\lambda_{green}}{\lambda_{red}}$$

$$\therefore \quad \omega_{green} = \omega_{red}\frac{\lambda_{green}}{\lambda_{red}}$$

$$= (0.2\times10^{-3})\left(\frac{5\times10^{-7}}{7\times10^{-7}}\right)$$

$$\omega_{green} = 0.143\times10^{-3}\text{m}$$

$$\therefore \quad \Delta\omega = \omega_{green} - \omega_{red}$$

$$= (0.143 - 0.2)\times10^{-3}\text{m}$$

$$\Delta\omega = -5.71\times10^{-5}\ \text{m}$$

77. Given, $\mu = 1.33$, $d = 1\,\text{mm}$, $D = 1.33\ \text{m}$,

$$\lambda = 6300\ \text{Å}$$

(a) Wavelength of light in the given liquid :

$$\lambda' = \frac{\lambda}{\mu} = \frac{6300}{1.33}\text{Å} \approx 4737\ \text{Å}$$

$$= 4737\times10^{-10}\ \text{m}$$

$$\therefore \quad \text{Fringe width, } \omega = \frac{\lambda' D}{d}$$

$$\omega = \frac{(4737\times10^{-10}\ \text{m})(1.33\text{m})}{(1\times10^{-3}\ \text{m})}$$

$$= 6.3\times10^{-4}\ \text{m}$$

$$\omega = 0.63\ \text{mm}$$

(b) Let t be the thickness of the glass slab. Path difference due to glass slab at centre O.

$$\Delta x = \left(\frac{\mu_{glass}}{\mu_{liquid}} - 1\right)t = \left(\frac{1.53}{1.33} - 1\right)t$$

or $$\Delta x = 0.15\,t$$

Now, for the intensity to be minimum at O, this path difference should be equal to $\frac{\lambda'}{2}$

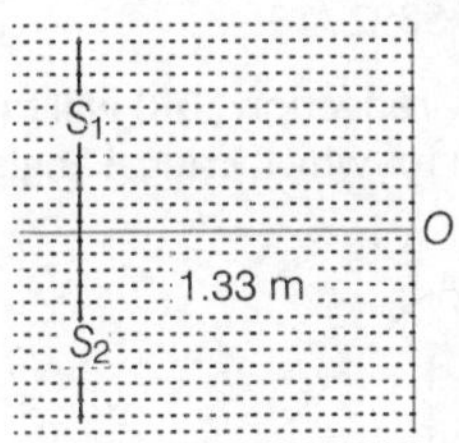

$$\therefore \quad \Delta x = \frac{\lambda'}{2} \quad \text{or } 0.15\,t = \frac{4737}{2}\ \text{Å}$$

$$\therefore \quad t = 15790\ \text{Å} \quad \text{or} \quad t = 1.579\ \mu\text{m}$$

78. Power received by aperture A,

$$P_A = I(\pi r_A^2) = \frac{10}{\pi}(\pi)(0.001)^2$$

$$= 10^{-5}\ \text{W}$$

Power received by aperture B,

$$P_B = I(\pi r_B^2) = \frac{10}{\pi}(\pi)(0.002)^2$$

$$= 4\times10^{-5}\ \text{W}$$

Only 10% of P_A and P_B goes to the original direction. Hence, 10% of $P_A = 10^{-6} = P_1$ (say) and 10% of $P_B = 4 \times 10^{-6} = P_2$ (say)

Path difference created by slab

$$\Delta x = (\mu - 1)t$$
$$= (1.5 - 1)(2000) = 1000 \text{ Å}$$

Corresponding phase difference,

$$\phi = \frac{2\pi}{\lambda} \cdot \Delta x = \frac{2\pi}{6000} \times 1000 = \frac{\pi}{3}$$

Now, resultant power at the focal point

$$P = P_1 + P_2 + 2\sqrt{P_1 P_2} \cos\phi$$
$$= 10^{-6} + 4 \times 10^{-6} + 2\sqrt{(10^{-6})(4 \times 10^{-6})} \cos\frac{\pi}{3}$$
$$= 7 \times 10^{-6} \text{ W}$$

79. Shifting of fringes due to introduction of slab in the path of one of the slits, comes out to be,

$$\Delta y = \frac{(\mu - 1)tD}{d} \qquad \text{...(i)}$$

Now, the distance between the screen and slits is doubled. Hence, the new fringe width will become.

$$\omega' = \frac{\lambda(2D)}{d} \qquad \text{...(ii)}$$

Given, $\Delta y = \omega'$

or $$\frac{(\mu - 1)tD}{d} = \frac{2\lambda D}{d}$$

$\therefore$ $$\lambda = \frac{(\mu - 1)t}{2}$$
$$= \frac{(1.6 - 1)(1.964 \times 10^{-6})}{2}$$
$$= 0.5892 \times 10^{-6} \text{ m}$$
$$= 5892 \text{ Å}$$

80. (a) Total internal reflection (TIR) will take place first for that wavelength for which critical angle is small or μ is large.

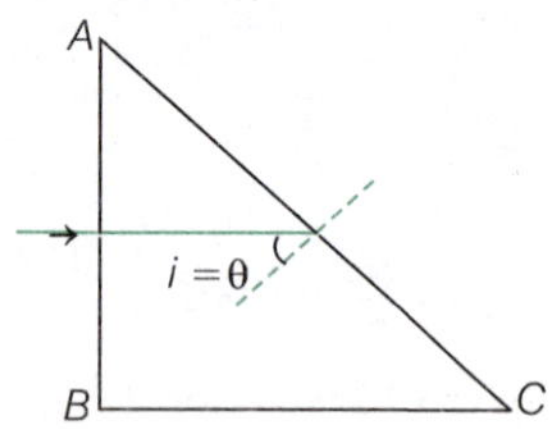

From the given expression of μ, it is more for the wavelength for which value of λ is less.

Thus, condition of TIR is just satisfied for 4000 Å.

$\Rightarrow$ for 4000Å or $\theta = \theta_c$

$\Rightarrow$ $\sin\theta = \sin\theta_c$

$\Rightarrow$ $0.8 = 1/\mu$ (for 4000Å)

$\Rightarrow$ $$0.8 = \frac{1}{1.20 + \dfrac{b}{(4000)^2}}$$

Solving this equation, we get

$$b = 8.0 \times 10^5 (\text{Å})^2$$

(b)

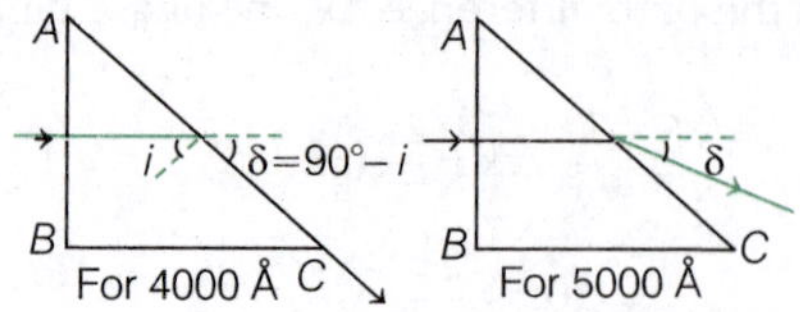

For, 4000 Å condition of TIR is just satisfied. Hence, it will emerge from AC, just grazingly.

$\Rightarrow$ $\delta_{4000\text{Å}} = 90° - i = 90° - \sin^{-1}(0.8) \approx 37°$

For 5000 Å, $\mu = 1.2 + \dfrac{b}{\lambda^2}$

$$= 1.2 + \frac{8.0 \times 10^5}{(5000)^2} = 1.232$$

Applying $\mu = \dfrac{\sin i_{air}}{\sin i_{medium}}$

$\Rightarrow$ $$1.232 = \frac{\sin i_{air}}{\sin\theta} = \frac{\sin i_{air}}{0.8}$$

$\Rightarrow$ $$i_{air} = 80.26°$$

$\therefore$ $$\delta_{5000\text{ Å}} = i_{air} - i_{medium}$$
$$= 80.26° - \sin^{-1}(0.8)$$
$$= 27.13°$$

(c)

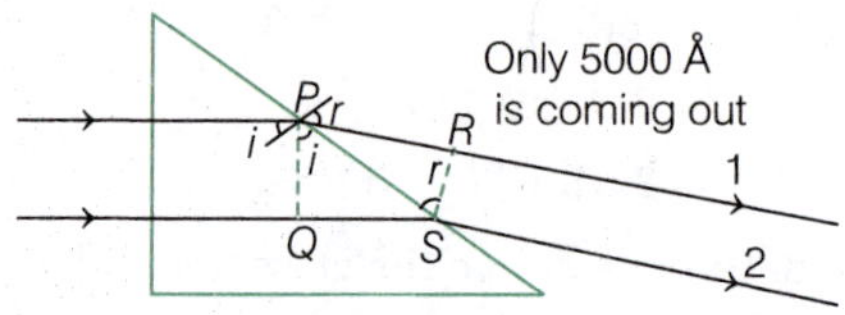

Path difference between rays 1 and 2

$$\Delta x = \mu(QS) - PR \qquad \text{...(i)}$$

Further, $\dfrac{QS}{PS} = \sin i$

$\Rightarrow$ $$\frac{PR}{PS} = \sin r$$

$\therefore$ $$\frac{PR/PS}{QS/PS} = \frac{\sin r}{\sin i} = \mu \Rightarrow \mu(QS) = PR$$

Substituting in Eq. (i), we get

$$\Delta x = 0$$

$\therefore$ Phase difference between rays 1 and 2 will be zero.

Or these two rays will interfere constructively. So, maximum intensity will be obtained from their interference.

$\Rightarrow$ $$I_{max} = (\sqrt{I_1} + \sqrt{I_2})^2$$
$$= (\sqrt{4I} + \sqrt{I})^2 = 9I$$

81. Resultant intensity at P

$$I_P = I_A + I_B + I_C$$
$$= \frac{P_A}{4\pi(PA)^2} + \frac{P_B}{4\pi(PB)^2}\cos 60° + I_C \cos 60°$$
$$= \frac{90}{4\pi(3)^2} + \frac{180}{4\pi(1.5)^2}\cos 60° + 20\cos 60°$$
$$= 0.79 + 3.18 + 10$$
$$= 13.97 \text{ W/m}^2$$

82. (a) Path difference at angle θ is

$$\Delta x = d\sin(90° - \theta) = d\cos\theta$$

Corresponding phase difference between 1 and 2 is

$$\phi' = \left(\frac{2\pi}{\lambda}\right).\Delta x$$

or $$\phi' = \left(\frac{2\pi}{\lambda}\right)d\cos\theta \qquad \text{(2 lags)}$$

$\therefore$ Net phase difference will be

$$\phi_{net} = \phi' + \phi = \left(\frac{2\pi}{\lambda}d\cos\theta\right) + \phi$$

For maximum intensity

$$\phi_{net} = 2n\pi,\ n = 0, \pm1, \pm2, \ldots$$

or $$\left(\frac{2\pi}{\lambda}d\cos\theta\right) + \phi = 2n\pi$$

or $$\theta = \cos^{-1}\left(n - \frac{\phi}{2\pi}\right)\frac{\lambda}{d} \qquad n = 0, \pm1, \pm2, \ldots$$

(b) In the direction $\theta = \pi$, path difference is

$$\Delta x = d$$

Hence corresponding phase difference is

$$\phi' = \left(\frac{2\pi}{\lambda}\right)\cdot\Delta x = \left(\frac{2\pi}{\lambda}\right)\cdot d \qquad \text{(1 lags)}$$

$\therefore$ Net phase difference is

$$\phi_{net} = \phi' - \phi = \left(\frac{2\pi}{\lambda}\right)\cdot d - \phi$$

For maximum intensity

$$\phi_{net} = 2n\pi,\ n = 0, \pm1, \pm2, \ldots$$

or $$\left(\frac{2\pi}{\lambda}\right)d - \phi = 2n\pi \qquad \ldots\text{(i)}$$

In the direction $\theta = 0°$, net phase difference is

$$\phi_{net} = \left(\frac{2\pi}{\lambda}\right)\cdot d + \phi$$

For minimum intensity

$$\phi_{net} = (2n+1)\pi,\ n = 0, \pm1, \pm2, \ldots$$

or $$\left(\frac{2\pi}{\lambda}\right)\cdot d + \phi = (2n+1)\pi \qquad \ldots\text{(ii)}$$

From equations (i) and (ii), we get

$$\phi = \frac{\pi}{2} \text{ and } \frac{d}{\lambda} = n + \frac{1}{4}$$

where $n = 0, \pm1, \pm2, \ldots$

Further explanation of answer :

$\theta = \pi$:

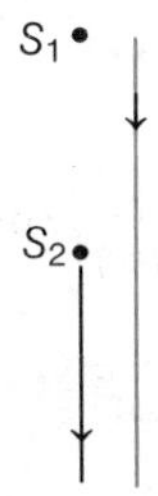

2 lags by ϕ;

$$2 \text{ leads by} \left(\frac{2\pi}{\lambda}\right)\Delta x = \frac{2\pi d}{\lambda}$$

$$\Delta\phi_{net} = \frac{2\pi}{\lambda}d - \phi \qquad \ldots\text{(iii)}$$

Condition $\phi = \frac{\pi}{2}$

$$\frac{d}{\lambda} = n + \frac{1}{4}$$

If $\phi = \frac{\pi}{2}$ and $\frac{d}{\lambda} = \frac{1}{4}$ for $n = 0$, then

$$\Delta\phi_{net} = 0 \text{ max.}$$

If $\phi = \frac{\pi}{2}$ and $\frac{d}{\lambda} = \frac{5}{4}$ for $n = 1$, then

$$\Delta\phi_{net} = 2\pi \text{ [from equation (iii)]} \qquad (\therefore \text{ max.})$$

If $\phi = \frac{\pi}{2}$ and $n = -1$, then

$$\Delta\phi_{net} = -2\pi \qquad (\therefore \text{ max.})$$

$\theta = 0°$:

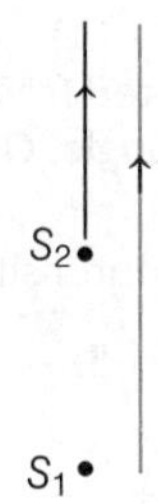

$$\Delta\phi_{net} = \frac{2\pi}{\lambda}d + \phi \qquad \ldots\text{(iv)}$$

Condition

$$\phi = \frac{\pi}{2}, \frac{d}{\lambda} = n + \frac{1}{4}$$

(i) $\boldsymbol{n = 0}$ $\Delta\phi_{net} = \pi$ [from equation (iv)] $\quad$ ($\therefore$ min)

(ii) $\boldsymbol{n = 1}$ $\Delta\phi_{net} = 3\pi$ [from equation (iv)] $\quad$ ($\therefore$ min)

(iii) $\boldsymbol{n = -1}$ $\Delta\phi_{net} = -\pi$ [from equation (iv)] $\quad$ ($\therefore$ min)

83.

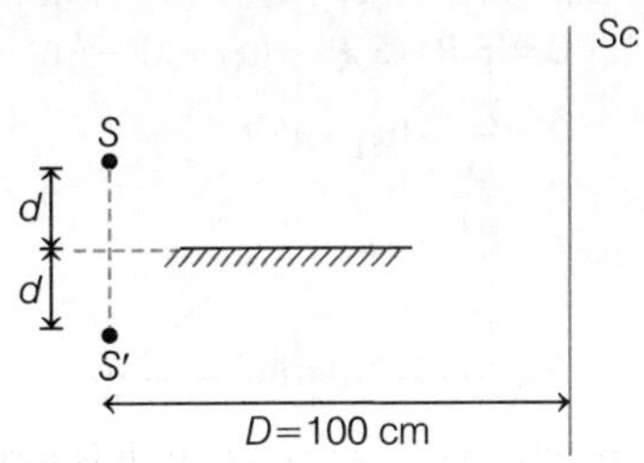

In the first case, fringe width,

$$\omega = \frac{\lambda D}{2d} \qquad \ldots\text{(i)}$$

In the second case,

$$\omega' = \frac{\omega}{1.5} = \frac{\lambda D}{2(d + \Delta h)} \qquad \ldots\text{(ii)}$$

From the first equation, we get

$$d = \frac{\lambda D}{2\omega} = \frac{\lambda(1.0)}{2(0.25\times10^{-3})}$$

or $$d = (2000\,\lambda)$$

Now substituting this value in equation (ii), we get

$$\frac{0.25\times 10^{-3}}{1.5}=\frac{\lambda(1.0)}{2(2000\lambda+0.6\times 10^{-3})}$$

$\Rightarrow \quad \lambda+0.3\times 10^{-6}=1.5\,\lambda$

or $\quad \lambda=0.6\times 10^{-6}\,\text{m}$

or $\quad \lambda=0.6\,\mu\text{m}$

84.

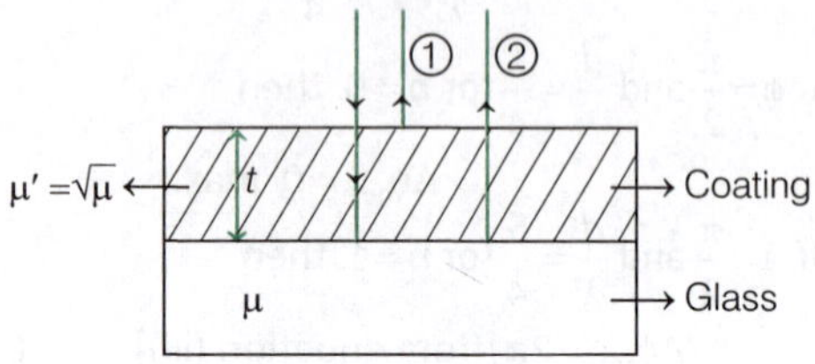

Path difference between 1 and 2,

$$\Delta x=2\mu' t=2\sqrt{\mu}\,t$$

$$\mu'<\mu$$

$\therefore$ Coating is rarer.

1 and 2 both are reflected from rarer medium. So, there is no change in phase angle. Or phase difference between 1 and 2 is zero.

For minimum (or zero) intensity,

$$\Delta x=(2n+1)\frac{\lambda}{2} \qquad (n=0,1,2,\ldots)$$

or $\quad 2\sqrt{\mu}\,t=(2n+1)\dfrac{\lambda}{2}$

$\therefore \quad t=\dfrac{\lambda(2n+1)}{4\sqrt{\mu}}$

85. Here, $\mu_1=1.51, t=0.1$ mm

$\mu_2=1.55,$

$\lambda=4000$ Å

Shifting central maxima

$$\Delta x=[S_1P+(\mu_1-1)t]-[S_2P+(\mu_2-1)t]$$

$$0=(S_1P-S_2P)+(\mu_1-1)t-(\mu_2-1)t$$

$$0=\frac{yd}{D}+(\mu_1-\mu_2)t$$

$\Rightarrow \quad (\mu_2-\mu_1)t=\dfrac{yd}{D}$

$$(1.55-1.51)\,(0.1\text{ mm})=y\times\frac{d}{D}$$

$$\frac{D}{d}(0.04\times 0.1)\times 10^{-3}=y \qquad \ldots\text{(i)}$$

Now, Fringe width

$\Rightarrow \quad \beta=\dfrac{\lambda D}{d}$

Number of fringes shifted

$$=\frac{y}{\beta}=\frac{4\times 10^{-6}}{4000\text{ Å}}=10$$

86.

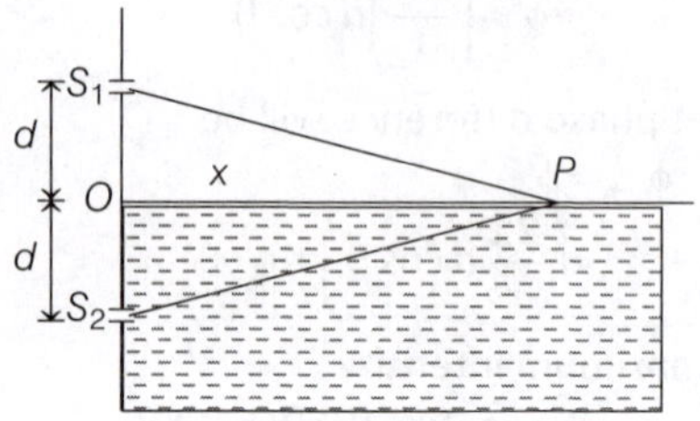

$$\mu(S_2P)-S_1P=m\lambda$$

$\Rightarrow \quad \mu\sqrt{d^2+x^2}-\sqrt{d^2+x^2}=m\lambda$

$\Rightarrow \quad (\mu-1)\sqrt{d^2+x^2}=m\lambda$

$\Rightarrow \quad \left(\dfrac{4}{3}-1\right)\sqrt{d^2+x^2}=m\lambda$

or $\quad \sqrt{d^2+x^2}=3m\lambda$

Squaring this equation we get,

$$x^2=9m^2\lambda^2-d^2$$

$\Rightarrow \quad p^2=9$

or $\quad p=3$

87. $\mu_1=\sqrt{2.8}, \mu_2=\sqrt{6.8}$

$$\mu_1\sin i=\mu_2\cos i$$

$$\tan i=\frac{\mu_2}{\mu_1}=\sqrt{\frac{6.8}{2.8}}$$

$$\tan i=\left(\frac{2.8+4}{2.8}\right)^{\frac{1}{2}}$$

$$i=\tan^{-1}\left(1+\frac{10}{7}\right)^{\frac{1}{2}}.$$

$\Rightarrow \quad \theta=7$

88. Given, $I_0=100$ lumens

When analyser is rotated through an angle θ, the intensity of light becomes

$$I=I_0\cos^2\theta=100\times\cos^2 30°$$

$$=100\times\left(\frac{\sqrt{3}}{2}\right)^2=75 \text{ lumens}$$

UNIT-11

MODERN PHYSICS – 1

Learning Modules

1. de-Broglie Wavelength of Matter Wave
2. Atomic Structure
3. X-Rays
4. Photoelectric Effect

MODULE 1

de-Broglie Wavelength of Matter Wave

The wave particle nature of electromagnetic waves, led de-Broglie (pronounced de Broy) to suggest that matter might also exhibit this duality and have wave properties. His ideas can be expressed quantitatively by first considering electromagnetic radiation. A photon of frequency f and wavelength λ has energy.

$$E = hf = \frac{hc}{\lambda}$$

By Einstein's energy mass relation, $E = mc^2$ the equivalent mass m of the photon is given by

$$m = \frac{E}{c^2} = \frac{hf}{c^2} = \frac{h}{\lambda c} \quad \text{...(i)}$$

or

$$\lambda = \frac{h}{mc} \text{ or } \frac{h}{p} \quad \text{...(ii)}$$

Here, p is the momentum of photon. By analogy de-Broglie suggested that a particle of mass m moving with speed v behaves in some ways like waves of wavelength λ given by

$$\lambda = \frac{h}{mv} = \frac{h}{p} \quad \text{...(iii)}$$

where, p is the momentum of the particle. Momentum is related to the kinetic energy by the equation,

$$p = \sqrt{2Km}$$

and a charge q when accelerated by a potential difference V gains a kinetic energy $K = qV$. Combining all these relations Eq. (iii) can be written as

$$\lambda = \frac{h}{mv} = \frac{h}{p} = \frac{h}{\sqrt{2Km}} = \frac{h}{\sqrt{2qVm}} \text{ (de-Broglie wavelength)} \quad \text{...(iv)}$$

de-Broglie Wavelength for an Electron

If an electron (charge $= e$) is accelerated by a potential difference of V volts, it acquires a kinetic energy,

$$K = eV$$

Substituting the values of h, m and q in Eq. (iv), we get a simple formula for calculating de-Broglie wavelength of an electron. This is

$$\lambda \text{ (in Å)} = \sqrt{\frac{150}{V \text{ (in volts)}}} \quad \text{...(v)}$$

Note *If an electron is accelerated by 1 volt, then its kinetic energy becomes 1 eV. Therefore, the above formula can also be written as*

$$\lambda \text{ (in Å)} = \sqrt{\frac{150}{KE \text{(in eV)}}}$$

Example 1 An electron is accelerated by a potential difference of 25 volt. Find the de-Broglie wavelength associated with it.

Sol. For an electron, de-Broglie wavelength is given by

$$\lambda = \sqrt{\frac{150}{V}} = \sqrt{\frac{150}{25}} = \sqrt{6} \approx 2.5 \text{ Å}$$ **Ans.**

Example 2 A particle of mass M at rest decays into two particles of masses m_1 and m_2 having non-zero velocities. The ratio of the de-Broglie wavelengths of the particles λ_1/λ_2 is **(1999 JEE)**

(a) m_1/m_2 (b) m_2/m_1 (c) 1 (d) $\sqrt{m_2}/\sqrt{m_1}$

Sol. From the law of conservation of momentum,

$$p_1 = p_2 \quad \text{(in opposite directions)}$$

Now, de-Broglie wavelength is given by

$$\lambda = \frac{h}{p}, \text{ where } h = \text{Planck constant}$$

Since magnitude of momentum (p) of both the particles is equal, therefore $\lambda_1 = \lambda_2$ or $\lambda_1/\lambda_2 = 1$

Therefore, the correct option is (c).

Example 3 The energy of a photon is equal to the kinetic energy of a proton. The energy of the photon is E. Let λ_1 be the de-Broglie wavelength of the proton and λ_2 be the wavelength of the photon. The ratio $\frac{\lambda_1}{\lambda_2}$ is proportional to **(2004 JEE)**

(a) E^0 (b) $E^{1/2}$ (c) E^{-1} (d) E^{-2}

Sol. $$\frac{\lambda_1}{\lambda_2} = \frac{\frac{h}{\sqrt{2mE}}}{\frac{hc}{E}} \text{ or } \frac{\lambda_1}{\lambda_2} \propto E^{1/2}$$

Therefore, the correct option is (b).

Example 4 An α-particle and a proton are accelerated from rest by a potential difference of 100 V. After this, their de-Broglie wavelengths are λ_α and λ_p respectively. The ratio $\frac{\lambda_p}{\lambda_\alpha}$, to the nearest integer, is **(2010 JEE)**

Sol. $\because$ $$\lambda = \frac{h}{p} = \frac{h}{\sqrt{2qVm}}$$

or $$\lambda \propto \frac{1}{\sqrt{qm}}$$

$$\frac{\lambda_p}{\lambda_\alpha} = \sqrt{\frac{q_\alpha}{q_p} \cdot \frac{m_\alpha}{m_p}}$$

$$= \sqrt{\frac{(2)(4)}{(1)(1)}} = 2.828$$

The nearest integer is 3.

$\therefore$ Answer is 3.

Example 5 The potential energy of a particle varies as

$$U(x) = E_0 \quad \text{for } 0 \le x \le 1$$
$$= 0 \quad \text{for } x > 1$$

For $0 \le x \le 1$, de-Broglie wavelength is λ_1 and for $x > 1$ the de-Broglie wavelength is λ_2. Total energy of the particle is $2E_0$. Find $\frac{\lambda_1}{\lambda_2}$. **(2005 JEE)**

Sol. For $0 \le x \le 1$, PE $= E_0$

$\therefore$ Kinetic energy K_1 = Total energy − PE

$$= 2E_0 - E_0 = E_0$$

$$\therefore \quad \lambda_1 = \frac{h}{\sqrt{2mE_0}} \quad \text{...(i)}$$

For $x > 1$, PE $= 0$

$\therefore$ Kinetic energy K_2 = Total energy $= 2E_0$

$$\therefore \quad \lambda_2 = \frac{h}{\sqrt{4mE_0}} \quad \text{...(ii)}$$

From Eqs. (i) and (i), we have

$$\frac{\lambda_1}{\lambda_2} = \sqrt{2}$$

Example 6 A proton is fired from very far away towards a nucleus with charge $Q = 120\,e$, where e is the electronic charge. It makes a closest approach of 10 fm to the nucleus. The de-Broglie wavelength (in units of fm) of the proton at its start is [Take the proton mass, $m_p = (5/3) \times 10^{-27}$ kg, $h/e = 4.2 \times 10^{-15}$ J-s/C, $\frac{1}{4\pi\varepsilon_0} = 9 \times 10^9$ m/F, 1 fm $= 10^{-15}$ m] **(2013 JEE)**

Sol. r = closest distance = 10 fm

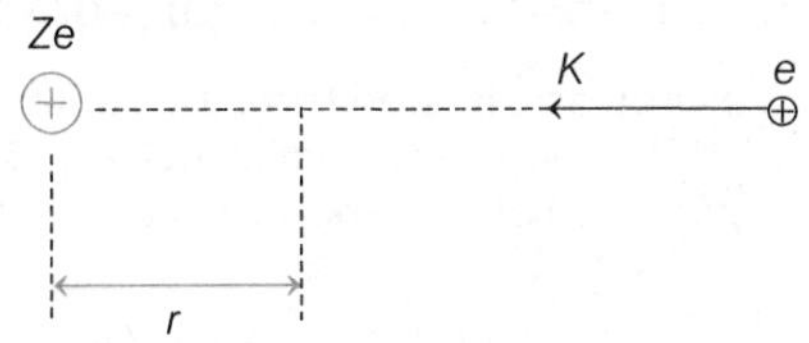

From energy conservation, we have

$$K_i + U_i = K_f + U_f$$

or $$K + 0 = 0 + \frac{1}{4\pi\varepsilon_0} \cdot \frac{q_1 q_2}{r}$$

or $$K = \frac{1}{4\pi\varepsilon_0} \cdot \frac{(120\,e)(e)}{r} \quad \text{...(i)}$$

de-Broglie wavelength,

$$\lambda = \frac{h}{\sqrt{2Km}} \quad \text{...(ii)}$$

Substituting the given values in above two equations, we get

$$\lambda = 7 \times 10^{-15}\text{ m}$$
$$= 7\text{ m}$$

MODULE 1 Exercise

Single Correct Option

1. If the de-Broglie wavelength of a proton is 10^{-13} m, the electric potential through which it must have been accelerated is
(a) 4.07×10^4 V (b) 8.15×10^4 V
(c) 8.15×10^3 V (d) 4.07×10^5 V

2. A proton accelerated through a potential difference of 100 V has de-Broglie wavelength λ_0. The de-Broglie wavelength of an α-particle, accelerated through 800 V is
(a) $\frac{\lambda_0}{\sqrt{2}}$ (b) $\frac{\lambda_0}{2}$ (c) $\frac{\lambda_0}{4}$ (d) $\frac{\lambda_0}{8}$

3. If E_1, E_2 and E_3 represent respectively the kinetic energies of an electron, an α-particle and a proton each having same de-Broglie wavelength, then
(a) $E_1 > E_3 > E_2$ (b) $E_2 > E_3 > E_1$
(c) $E_1 > E_2 > E_3$ (d) $E_1 = E_2 = E_3$

4. An electron of mass m when accelerated through a potential difference V has de-Broglie wavelength λ. The de-Broglie wavelength associated with a proton of mass M accelerated through the same potential difference will be
(a) $\lambda\frac{m}{M}$ (b) $\lambda\sqrt{\frac{m}{M}}$ (c) $\lambda\frac{M}{m}$ (d) $\lambda\sqrt{\frac{M}{m}}$

5. The ratio of the de-Broglie wavelength of proton and electron having same kinetic energy is
(Assume, $m_p = m_e \times 1849$) **(2023 Main)**
(a) 1 : 43 (b) 1 : 62
(c) 1 : 30 (d) 2 : 43

6. A proton and an α-particle are accelerated from rest by 2V and 4V potentials, respectively. The ratio of their de-Broglie wavelength is **(2023 Main)**
(a) 16 : 1 (b) 2 : 1
(c) 8 : 1 (d) 4 : 1

7. The de-Broglie wavelength of an electron having kinetic energy E is λ. If the kinetic energy of electron becomes $E/4$, then its de-Broglie wavelength will be **(2023 Main)**
(a) $\frac{\lambda}{2}$ (b) $\frac{\lambda}{\sqrt{2}}$ (c) 2λ (d) $\sqrt{2}\lambda$

8. The de-Broglie wavelength of a molecule in a gas at room temperature (300 K) is λ_1. If the temperature of the gas is increased to 600 K, then the de-Broglie wavelength of the same gas molecule becomes **(2023 Main)**
(a) $\frac{1}{\sqrt{2}}\lambda_1$ (b) $2\lambda_1$
(c) $\sqrt{2}\lambda_1$ (d) $\frac{1}{2}\lambda_1$

9. Proton (p) and electron (e) will have same de-Broglie wavelength when the ratio of their momentum is (assume, $m_p = 1849\, m_e$) **(2023 Main)**
(a) 1 : 1849 (b) 43 : 1
(c) 1 : 1 (d) 1 : 43

10. An α-particle, a proton and an electron have the same kinetic energy. Which one of the following is correct in case of their de-Broglie wavelength? **(2023 Main)**
(a) $\lambda_\alpha > \lambda_p > \lambda_e$ (b) $\lambda_\alpha > \lambda_p < \lambda_e$
(c) $\lambda_\alpha < \lambda_p < \lambda_e$ (d) $\lambda_\alpha = \lambda_p = \lambda_e$

11. An electron accelerated through a potential difference V_1 has a de-Broglie wavelength of λ. When the potential is changed to V_2, its de-Broglie wavelength increases by 50%. The value of $\left(\frac{V_1}{V_2}\right)$ is equal to **(2023 Main)**
(a) 4 (b) $\frac{9}{4}$ (c) 3 (d) $\frac{3}{2}$

12. The ratio of de-Broglie wavelength of an α particle and a proton accelerated from rest by the same potential is $\frac{1}{\sqrt{m}}$ the value of m is **(2023 Main)**
(a) 16 (b) 8 (c) 4 (d) 2

13. A proton moving with one tenth of velocity of light has a certain de-Broglie wavelength of λ. An alpha particle having certain kinetic energy has the same de-Broglie wavelength λ. The ratio of kinetic energy of proton and that of alpha particle is **(2023 Main)**
(a) 2 : 1 (b) 1 : 2
(c) 4 : 1 (d) 1 : 4

14. A nucleus A, with a finite de-Broglie wavelength λ_A, undergoes spontaneous fission into two nuclei B and C of equal mass. B flies in the same direction as that of A, while C flies in the opposite direction with a velocity equal to half of that of B. The de-Broglie wavelengths λ_B and λ_C of B and C respectively are **(2019 Main)**
(a) $2\lambda_A, \lambda_A$ (b) $\frac{\lambda_A}{2}, \lambda_A$ (c) $\lambda_A, 2\lambda_A$ (d) $\lambda_A, \frac{\lambda_A}{2}$

15. Two protons are having same kinetic energy. One proton enters a uniform magnetic field at right angles to it. Second proton enters a uniform electric field in the direction of field. After some time their de-Broglie wavelengths are λ_1 and λ_2, then
(a) $\lambda_1 = \lambda_2$
(b) $\lambda_1 < \lambda_2$
(c) $\lambda_1 > \lambda_2$
(d) some more information is required

Subjective Questions

16. Find the energy and momentum of a photon of ultraviolet radiation of 280 nm wavelength.
17. A small plate of a metal is placed at a distance of 2 m from a monochromatic light source of wavelength 4.8×10^{-7} m and power 1.0 Watt. The light falls normally on the plate. Find the number of photons striking the metal plate per square metre per second.
18. A proton and a deuteron are accelerated by same potential difference. Find the ratio of their de-Broglie wavelengths.
19. A deuteron and an α-particle have same kinetic energy. Find the ratio of their de-Broglie wavelengths.
20. Find the de-Broglie wavelengths of
    (a) a 46 g golf ball with a velocity of 30 m/s
    (b) an electron with a velocity of 10^7 m/s.
21. An electron has a de-Broglie wavelength of 2.80×10^{-10} m. Determine
    (a) the magnitude of its momentum,
    (b) its kinetic energy (in joule and in electron volt).
22. Find de-Broglie wavelength corresponding to the root-mean square velocity of hydrogen molecules at room temperature (20°C).

Answers

1. (b) **2.** (d) **3.** (a) **4.** (b) **5.** (a) **6.** (d) **7.** (c) **8.** (a) **9.** (c) **10.** (c)

11. (b) **12.** (b) **13.** (c) **14.** (b) **15.** (c) **16.** 4.6 eV, $2.45 \times 10^{-27} \frac{\text{kg-m}}{\text{s}}$

17. 4.82×10^{16} per m^2-s **18.** $\sqrt{2}$ **19.** $\sqrt{2}$ **20.** (a) 4.8×10^{-34} m (b) 7.12×10^{-11} m

21. (a) $2.37 \times 10^{-24} \frac{\text{kg-m}}{\text{s}}$ (b) 3.07×10^{-18} J = 19.2 eV **22.** 1.04 Å

See hints on pages 314-316.

MODULE 2

Atomic Structure

Every atom consists of a small nucleus of protons and neutrons with a number of electrons some distance away.

In the present article and in the next, our chief concern will be the structure of the atom, since it is this structure that is responsible for nearly all the properties of matter.In nineteenth century many models were present by different scientists, but ultimately the first theory of the atom to meet with any success was put forward in 1913 by Neils Bohr.

But before studying Bohr's model of atom let us have a look on other two models of the period one presented by J.J. Thomson in 1898 and the other by Ernest Rutherford in 1911.

J.J. Thomson suggested that atoms are just positively charged lumps of matter with electrons embedded in them like raisins in a fruit cake. Thomson's model called the 'plum pudding' model is illustrated in figure.

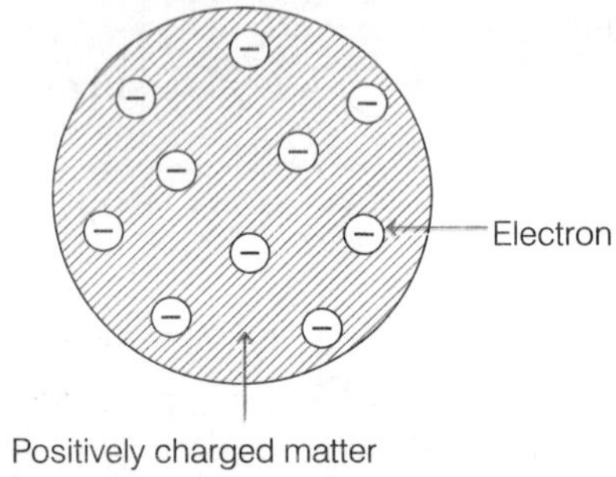

The Thomson model of the atom. The Rutherford scattering experiment showed it to be incorrect.

Thomson had played an important role in discovering the electron, his idea was taken seriously. But, the real atom turned out to be quite different.

Rutherford's Nuclear Atom

The nuclear atom is the basis of the modern theory of atomic structure and was proposed by Rutherford in 1911. He, with his two assistants Geiger and Marsden did an experiment in which they directed a narrow beam of α-particles onto gold foil about 1 μm thick and found that while most of the particles passed straight through, some were scattered appreciably and a very few about 1 in 8000 suffered deflection of more than 90°.

To account for this very surprising result Rutherford suggested that : "All the positive charge and nearly all the mass were concentrated in a very small volume or nucleus at the centre of the atom. The electrons were supposed to move in circular orbits round the nucleus (like planets round the sun). The electrostatic attraction between the two opposite charges provides the required centripetal force for such motion.

The large angle scattering of α-particles would then be explained by the strong electrostatic repulsion from the nucleus.

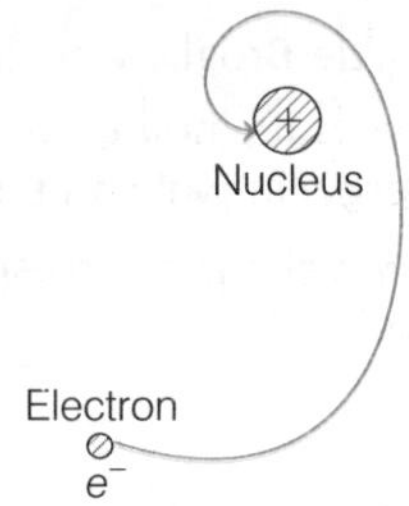

An atomic electron should, classically, spiral rapidly into the nucleus as it radiates energy due to its acceleration

Rutherford's model of the atom, although strongly supported by evidence for the nucleus, is inconsistent with classical physics. An electron moving in a circular orbit round a nucleus is accelerating and according to electromagnetic theory it should therefore, emit radiation continuously and thereby lose energy. If this happened, the radius of the orbit would decrease and the electron would spiral into the nucleus in a fraction of second. But atoms do not collapse. In 1913, an effort was made by Neils Bohr to overcome this paradox.

The Bohr Hydrogen Atom

After Neils Bohr obtained his doctorate in 1911, he worked under Rutherford for a while. In 1913, he presented a model of the hydrogen atom, which has one electron and one proton. He postulated that an electron moves only in certain circular orbits, called stationary orbits. In stationary orbits, electron does not emit radiation, contrary to the predictions of classical electromagnetic theory.

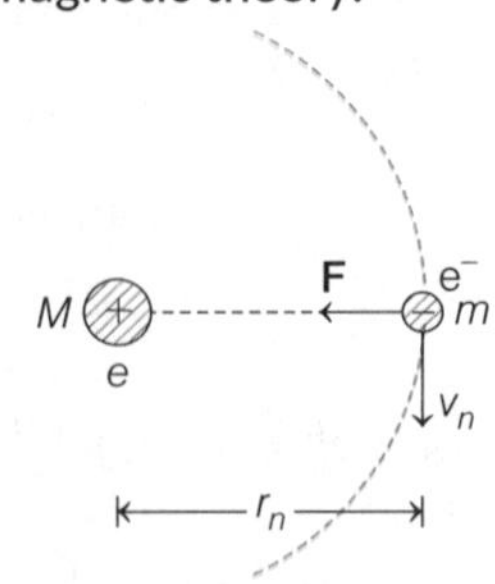

According to Bohr, there is a definite energy associated with each stable orbit and an atom radiates energy only when it makes a transition from one of these orbits to another.

The energy is radiated in the form of a photon with energy and frequency given by

$$\boxed{\Delta E = hf = E_i - E_f} \quad ...(i)$$

Bohr found that the magnitude of the electron's angular momentum is quantised, and this magnitude for the electron must be integral multiple of $\frac{h}{2\pi}$. The magnitude of the angular momentum is $L = mvr$ for a particle with mass m moving with speed v in a circle of radius r. So, according to Bohr's postulate,

$$mvr = \frac{nh}{2\pi} \quad (n = 1, 2, 3 \ldots)$$

Each value of n corresponds to a permitted value of the orbit radius, which we will denote by r_n and the corresponding speed v_n. The value of n for each orbit is called **principal quantum number** for the orbit. Thus,

$$\boxed{mv_n r_n = \frac{nh}{2\pi}} \quad ...(ii)$$

According to Newton's second law, a radially inward centripetal force of magnitude $F = \frac{mv^2}{r}$ is needed to the electron which is being provided by the electrical attraction between the positive proton and the negative electron.

Thus, $$\boxed{\frac{mv_n^2}{r_n} = \frac{1}{4\pi\varepsilon_0}\frac{e^2}{r_n^2}} \quad ...(iii)$$

Solving Eqs. (ii) and (iii), we get

$$r_n = \frac{\varepsilon_0 n^2 h^2}{\pi m e^2} \quad \left(\begin{array}{c} n\text{th orbit radius} \\ \text{in Bohr model}\end{array}\right) \quad ...(iv)$$

and $$v_n = \frac{e^2}{2\varepsilon_0 nh} \quad \left(\begin{array}{c} n\text{th orbit speed} \\ \text{in Bohr model}\end{array}\right) \quad ...(v)$$

The smallest orbit radius corresponds to $n = 1$. We'll denote this minimum radius, called the **Bohr radius** as a_0. Thus,

$$a_0 = \frac{\varepsilon_0 h^2}{\pi m e^2}$$

Substituting values of ε_0, h, π, m and e, we get

$$\boxed{a_0 = 0.529 \times 10^{-10}\ \text{m} = 0.529\ \text{Å}} \quad ...(vi)$$

Eq. (iv), in terms of a_0 can be written as

$$\boxed{r_n = n^2 a_0 \quad \text{or} \quad r_n \propto n^2} \quad ...(vii)$$

Similarly, substituting values of e, ε_0 and h with $n = 1$ in Eq. (v), we get

$$\boxed{v_1 = 2.19 \times 10^6\ \text{m/s} \approx \frac{c}{137}} \quad ...(viii)$$

This is the greatest possible speed of the electron in the hydrogen atom. Which is approximately equal to $c/137$, where c is the speed of light in vacuum.

Eq. (v), in terms of v_1 can be written as

$$\boxed{v_n = \frac{v_1}{n} \quad \text{or} \quad v_n \propto \frac{1}{n}} \quad ...(ix)$$

Energy levels Kinetic and potential energies K_n and U_n in nth orbit are

$$K_n = \frac{1}{2} mv_n^2 = \frac{me^4}{8\varepsilon_0^2 n^2 h^2}$$

and $$U_n = -\frac{1}{4\pi\varepsilon_0}\frac{(e)(e)}{r_n} = -\frac{me^4}{4\varepsilon_0^2 n^2 h^2}$$

The total energy E_n is the sum of the kinetic and potential energies.

$$E_n = K_n + U_n = -\frac{me^4}{8\varepsilon_0^2 n^2 h^2}$$

Substituting values of m, e, ε_0 and h with $n = 1$, we get the least energy of the atom in first orbit, which is -13.6 eV. Hence,

$$\boxed{E_1 = -13.6\ \text{eV}} \quad ...(x)$$

and $$\boxed{E_n = \frac{E_1}{n^2} = -\frac{13.6}{n^2}\ \text{eV}} \quad ...(xi)$$

Substituting $n = 2, 3, 4 \ldots$, etc., we get energies of atom in different orbits.

$$E_2 = -3.40\ \text{eV},\ E_3 = -1.51\ \text{eV}, \ldots E_\infty = 0$$

Ionization energy of the hydrogen atom is the energy required to remove the electron completely. In ground state ($n = 1$), energy of atom is -13.6 eV and energy corresponding to $n = \infty$ is zero. Hence, energy required to remove the electron from ground state is 13.6 eV.

Emission spectrum of hydrogen atom

Under normal conditions the single electron in hydrogen atom stays in ground state ($n = 1$). It is excited to some higher energy state when it acquires some energy from external source. But, it hardly stays there for more than 10^{-8} second.

A photon corresponding to a particular spectrum line is emitted when an atom makes a transition from an excited level to a lower excited level or the ground level.

Let n_i be the initial and n_f the final energy state, then depending on the final energy state following series are observed in the emission spectrum of hydrogen atom.

For the Lyman series $n_f = 1$, for Balmer series $n_f = 2$ and so on. The relation of the various spectral series to the energy levels and to electron orbits is shown in figure.

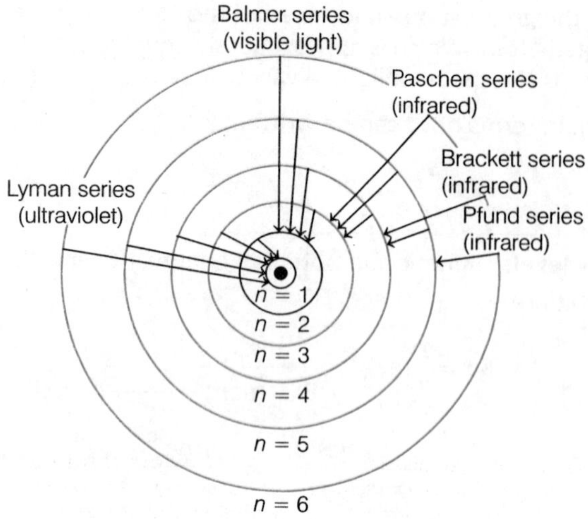

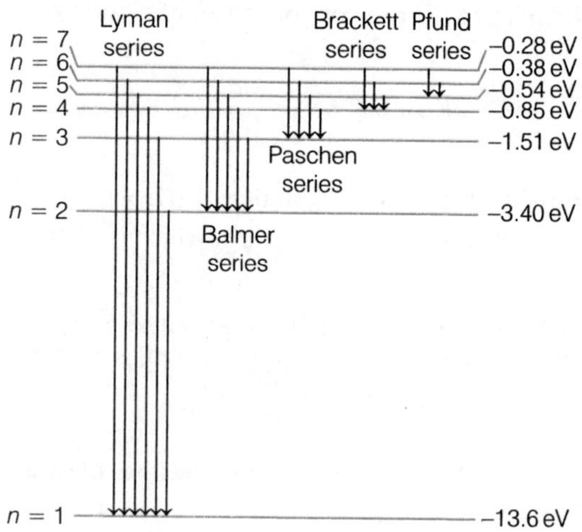

Wavelength of Photon Emitted in De-excitation

According to Bohr when an atom makes a transition from higher energy level to a lower energy level it emits a photon with energy equal to the energy difference between the initial and final levels. If E_i is the initial energy of the atom before such a transition, E_f is its final energy after the transition, and the photon's energy is $hf = \frac{hc}{\lambda}$, then conservation of energy gives

$$hf = \frac{hc}{\lambda} = E_i - E_f \quad \text{(energy of emitted photon)} \quad \text{...(xii)}$$

By 1913, the spectrum of hydrogen had been studied intensively. The visible line with longest wavelength, or lowest frequency is in the red and is called H_α, the next line, in the blue-green is called H_β and so on. In 1885, Johann Balmer, a swiss teacher found a formula that gives the wave lengths of these lines. This is now called the Balmer series. The Balmer's formula is

$$\frac{1}{\lambda} = R\left(\frac{1}{2^2} - \frac{1}{n^2}\right) \quad \text{...(xiii)}$$

Here, $n = 3, 4, 5 \ldots$, etc.

R = Rydberg constant $= 1.097 \times 10^7 \text{ m}^{-1}$

and λ is the wavelength of light/photon emitted during transition.

For $n = 3$, we obtain the wavelength of H_α line. Similarly, for $n = 4$, we obtain the wavelength of H_β line. For $n = \infty$, the smallest wavelength ($= 3646$ Å) of this series is obtained.

Using the relation $E = \frac{hc}{\lambda}$, we can find the photon energies corresponding to the wavelength of the Balmer series.

Multiplying Eq. (xiii) by hc, we find

$$E = \frac{hc}{\lambda} = hcR\left(\frac{1}{2^2} - \frac{1}{n^2}\right)$$

$$= \frac{Rhc}{2^2} - \frac{Rhc}{n^2} = E_n - E_2$$

This formula suggests that

$$E_n = -\frac{Rhc}{n^2}, \; n = 1, 2, 3 \ldots \quad \text{...(xiv)}$$

Comparing this with Eq. (xi) of the same article, we have

$$Rhc = 13.60 \text{ eV} \quad \text{...(xv)}$$

The wavelengths corresponding to other spectral series (Lyman, Paschen , etc.) can be represented by formula similar to Balmer formula.

Lyman series $\quad \frac{1}{\lambda} = R\left(\frac{1}{1^2} - \frac{1}{n^2}\right), n = 2, 3, 4 \ldots$

Paschen series $\quad \frac{1}{\lambda} = R\left(\frac{1}{3^2} - \frac{1}{n^2}\right), n = 4, 5, 6 \ldots$

Brackett series $\quad \frac{1}{\lambda} = R\left(\frac{1}{4^2} - \frac{1}{n^2}\right), n = 5, 6, 7 \ldots$

Pfund series $\quad \frac{1}{\lambda} = R\left(\frac{1}{5^2} - \frac{1}{n^2}\right), n = 6, 7, 8 \ldots$

The Lyman series is in the ultraviolet, and the Paschen, Brackett and Pfund series are in the infrared region.

Hydrogen Like Atoms

The Bohr model of hydrogen can be extended to hydrogen like atoms, i.e. one electron atoms such as singly ionized helium (He^+), doubly ionized lithium (Li^{+2}) and so on. In such atoms, the nuclear charge is $+Ze$, where Z is the atomic number, equal to the number of protons in the nucleus. The effect in the previous analysis is to replace e^2 everywhere by Ze^2. Thus, the equations for, r_n, v_n and E_n are altered as under

$$r_n = \frac{\varepsilon_0 n^2 h^2}{\pi m Z e^2} = \frac{n^2}{Z} a_0$$

or

$$r_n \propto \frac{n^2}{Z} \quad \text{...(i)}$$

where, $a_0 = 0.529$ Å (radius of first orbit of hydrogen atom)

$$v_n = \frac{Ze^2}{2\varepsilon_0 nh} = \frac{Z}{n}v_1 \quad \text{or} \quad v_n \propto \frac{Z}{n} \qquad \text{...(ii)}$$

where, $v_1 = 2.19 \times 10^6$ m/s

(speed of electron in first orbit of hydrogen atom)

$$E_n = -\frac{mZ^2e^4}{8\,\varepsilon_0^2 n^2 h^2} = \frac{Z^2}{n^2}E_1$$

or

$$E_n \propto \frac{Z^2}{n^2} \qquad \text{...(iii)}$$

where, $E_1 = -13.60$ eV

(energy of atom in first orbit of hydrogen atom)

Below figure compares the energy levels of H and He^+ which has $Z = 2$. H and He^+ have many spectrum lines that have almost the same wavelengths.

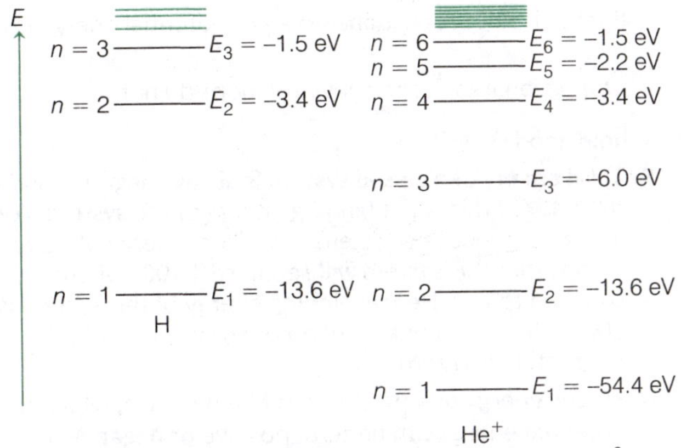

Energy levels of H and He^+. Because of the additional factor Z^2 in the energy expression, the energy of the He^+ ion with a given n is almost exactly four times that of the H-atom with the same n. There are small differences (of the order of 0.05%) because of the different masses.

Important POINTS

1. In hydrogen and hydrogen like atoms :
   Circumference of nth orbit $= n$ (de-Broglie wavelength of single electron in that orbit)

   Proof

   According to Bohr's assumption,

   $$L_n = n\left(\frac{h}{2\pi}\right) \quad \text{or} \quad mvr = n\left(\frac{h}{2\pi}\right)$$

   $$\therefore \quad (2\pi r) = n\left(\frac{h}{mv}\right)$$

   or circumference $= n$ (de-Broglie wavelength of electron)

2. $Rhc = 13.6$ eV
   Therefore, Rhc has the dimensions of energy or

   $$[Rhc] = [ML^2T^{-2}]$$

3. 1 Rhc is also called 1 Rydberg. It is not Rydberg constant R.
4. Bohr's theory is applicable for hydrogen and hydrogen like atoms/ions. For such types of atoms/ions number of electron is one. Although, atomic numbers may be different.
   e.g, For ${}_1H^1$, atomic number $Z = 1$,
   For He^+, atomic number $Z = 2$ and
   For Li^{+2}, atomic number $Z = 3$
   Although number of electron in each case is one.
5. In nth orbit of hydrogen and hydrogen like atoms :
   (a) $r \propto \frac{n^2}{Z}$ and $r \propto \frac{1}{m}$ (b) $v \propto \frac{Z}{n}$ and $v \propto m^0$
   (c) $E \propto \frac{Z^2}{n^2}$ and $E \propto m$ (d) $r_1^H = 0.529$ Å
   (e) $v_1^H = 2.19 \times 10^6 \text{ m/s} = \frac{c}{137}$ (f) $E_1^H = -13.6$ eV
   (g) $K = |E|$ and $U = 2E$

Note *With the help of above results, we can find any value in any orbit of hydrogen like atoms. In the above expressions, m is the mass of electron*

6. Total number of emission lines from some higher energy state n_1 to lower energy state $n_2 (< n_1)$ is given by $\frac{(n_1 - n_2)(n_1 - n_2 + 1)}{2}$.
   For example, total number of lines from $n_1 = n$ to $n_2 = 1$ are $\frac{n(n-1)}{2}$.
7. As the principal quantum number n is increased in hydrogen and hydrogen like atoms, some quantities are decreased and some are increased. The table given below shows which quantities are increased and which are decreased.

Table

Increased	Decreased
Radius	Speed
Potential energy	Kinetic energy
Total energy	Angular speed
Time period	Frequency
Angular momentum	

8. Whenever a force obeys inverse square law $\left(F \propto \frac{1}{r^2}\right)$ and potential energy is inversely proportional to $r \left(U \propto \frac{1}{r}\right)$, kinetic energy ($K$), potential energy ($U$) and total energy ($E$) have the following relationships.

   $$K = \frac{|U|}{2} \quad \text{and} \quad E = -K = \frac{U}{2}$$

If force is not proportional to $\frac{1}{r^2}$ or potential energy is not proportional to $\frac{1}{r}$, the above relations do not hold good.

9. Total energy of a closed system is always negative and the modulus of this is the binding energy of the system. For instance, suppose a system has a total energy of −100 J. It means that this system will separate if 100 J of energy is supplied to this. Hence, binding energy of this system is 100 J. Thus, total energy of an open system is either zero or greater than zero.
10. Kinetic energy of a particle can't be negative, while the potential energy can be zero, positive or negative. It basically depends on the reference point where we have taken it zero. It is customary to take zero potential energy when the electron is at infinite distance from the nucleus. In some problem, suppose we take zero potential energy in first orbit ($U_1 = 0$), then the modulus of actual potential energy in first orbit (when reference point was at infinity) is added in U and E in all energy states, while K remains unchanged. See example number 5.
11. In the transition from n_2 to $n_1 (< n_1)$. The wavelength of emitted photon can be given by the following shortcut formula,

$$\lambda (\text{in Å}) = \frac{12375}{E_{n_2} - E_{n_1}}$$

where, E_{n_1} and E_{n_2} are in eV. In general, E_n in eV is given by

$$E_n = -(13.6)\frac{Z^2}{n^2}$$

12. In hydrogen emission spectrum, Balmer series was first discovered as it lies in visible light.

Example 1 Using the known values for hydrogen atom, calculate

(a) radius of third orbit for Li^{+2}
(b) speed of electron in fourth orbit for He^+
(c) angular momentum of electron in 3rd orbit of He^+

Sol. (a) $Z = 3$ for Li^{+2}. Further we know that $r_n = \frac{n^2}{Z} a_0$

Substituting, $n = 3$, $Z = 3$ and $a_0 = 0.529$ Å

We have r_3 for $Li^{+2} = \frac{(3)^2}{(3)}(0.529)$ Å

$= 1.587$ Å **Ans.**

(b) $Z = 2$ for He^+. Also we know that

$$v_n = \frac{Z}{n} v_1$$

Substituting, $n = 4$, $Z = 2$

and $v_1 = 2.19 \times 10^6$ m/s

We get, v_4 for $He^+ = \left(\frac{2}{4}\right)(2.19 \times 10^6)$ m/s

$= 1.095 \times 10^6$ m/s **Ans.**

(c) $L_n = n\left(\frac{h}{2\pi}\right)$

For $n = 3$, $L_3 = 3\left(\frac{h}{2\pi}\right)$ **Ans.**

Note *This result is independent of the value of Z.*

Example 2 A doubly ionized lithium atom is hydrogen like with atomic number 3. Find the wavelength of the radiation required to excite the electron in Li^{++} from the first to the third Bohr orbit. The ionization energy of the hydrogen atom is 13.6 eV.

Sol. $\because$ $E_n = -\frac{Z^2}{n^2}(13.6 \text{ eV})$

By putting $Z = 3$, we have $E_n = -\frac{122.4}{n^2}$ eV

$$E_1 = -\frac{122.4}{(1)^2} = -122.4 \text{ eV}$$

and $$E_3 = -\frac{122.4}{(3)^2} = -13.6 \text{ eV}$$

$\therefore$ $\Delta E = E_3 - E_1 = 108.8$ eV

The corresponding wavelength is

$$\lambda = \frac{12375}{\Delta E \text{ (in eV)}} \text{ Å} = \frac{12375}{108.8} \text{ Å}$$

$= 113.74$ Å **Ans.**

Example 3 Find variation of angular speed and time period of single electron of hydrogen like atoms with n and Z.

Sol. Angular speed, $\omega = \frac{v}{r}$

Now, $v \propto \frac{Z}{n}$ and $r \propto \frac{n^2}{Z}$

$\therefore$ $\omega \propto \frac{(Z/n)}{(n^2/Z)}$

or $\omega \propto \frac{Z^2}{n^3}$ **Ans.**

Time period, $T = \frac{2\pi}{\omega}$ or $T \propto \frac{1}{\omega}$

$\therefore$ $T \propto \frac{n^3}{Z^2}$ **Ans.**

Example 4 Find kinetic energy, electrostatic potential energy and total energy of single electron in 2nd excited state of Li^{+2} atom.

Sol. $\because \; E_I^H = -13.6$ eV

Further, $E \propto \frac{Z^2}{n^2}$, For Li^{+2}, $Z = 3$

and for 2nd excited state $n = 3$

$$\therefore \quad E = -13.6\left(\frac{3}{3}\right)^2 = -13.6 \text{ eV} \quad \textbf{Ans.}$$

$$K = |E| = 13.6 \text{ eV} \quad \textbf{Ans.}$$

$$U = 2E = -27.2 \text{ eV} \quad \textbf{Ans.}$$

Note *In the above expressions E is the total energy, K is the kinetic energy and U is the potential energy.*

Example 5 Find the kinetic energy, potential energy and total energy in first and second orbit of hydrogen atom if potential energy in first orbit is taken to be zero.

Sol. $E_1 = -13.60$ eV, $K_1 = -E_1 = 13.60$ eV,

$U_1 = 2E_1 = -27.20$ eV

$$E_2 = \frac{E_1}{(2)^2} = -3.40 \text{ eV}, K_2 = 3.40 \text{ eV and}$$

$U_2 = -6.80$ eV

Now, $U_1 = 0$, i.e. potential energy has been increased by 27.20 eV. So, we will increase U and E in all energy states by 27.20 eV, while kinetic energy will remain unchanged. Changed values in tabular form are as under.

Table

Orbit	K (eV)	U (eV)	E (eV)
First	13.60	0	13.60
Second	3.40	20.40	23.80

Example 6 A small particle of mass m moves in such a way that the potential energy $U = ar^2$, where a is constant and r is the distance of the particle from the origin. Assuming Bohr model of quantization of angular momentum and circular orbits, find the radius of nth allowed orbit.

Sol. The force at a distance r is

$$F = -\frac{dU}{dr} = -2ar$$

Suppose r be the radius of nth orbit. Then, the necessary centripetal force is provided by the above force. Thus,

$$\frac{mv^2}{r} = |F| = 2ar \quad \text{...(i)}$$

Further, the quantization of angular momentum gives

$$mvr = \frac{nh}{2\pi} \quad \text{...(ii)}$$

Solving Eqs. (i) and (ii) for r, we get

$$r = \left(\frac{n^2h^2}{8\,am\,\pi^2}\right)^{\frac{1}{2}} \quad \textbf{Ans.}$$

Example 7 Calculate (a) the wavelength and (b) the frequency of the H_β line of the Balmer series for hydrogen.

Sol. (a) H_β line of Balmer series corresponds to the transition from $n = 4$ to $n = 2$ level.

Using Eq. (xiii), the corresponding wavelength for H_β line is

$$\frac{1}{\lambda} = (1.097 \times 10^7)\left(\frac{1}{2^2} - \frac{1}{4^2}\right)$$

$$= 0.2056 \times 10^7$$

$$\therefore \quad \lambda = 4.9 \times 10^{-7} \text{ m} \quad \textbf{Ans.}$$

(b) $$f = \frac{c}{\lambda} = \frac{3.0 \times 10^8}{4.9 \times 10^{-7}}$$

$$= 6.12 \times 10^{14} \text{ Hz} \quad \textbf{Ans.}$$

Example 8 Find the largest and shortest wavelengths in the Lyman series for hydrogen. In what region of the electromagnetic spectrum does each series lie?

Sol. The transition equation for Lyman series is given by

$$\frac{1}{\lambda} = R\left(\frac{1}{1^2} - \frac{1}{n^2}\right), \; n = 2, 3, \ldots$$

The largest wavelength is corresponding to $n = 2$

$$\therefore \quad \frac{1}{\lambda_{max}} = 1.097 \times 10^7\left(\frac{1}{1} - \frac{1}{4}\right)$$

$$= 0.823 \times 10^7$$

$$\therefore \quad \lambda_{max} = 1.2154 \times 10^{-7} \text{ m}$$

$$= 1215 \text{ Å} \quad \textbf{Ans.}$$

The shortest wavelength corresponds to $n = \infty$

$$\therefore \quad \frac{1}{\lambda_{min}} = 1.097 \times 10^7\left(\frac{1}{1} - \frac{1}{\infty}\right)$$

or $$\lambda_{min} = 0.911 \times 10^{-7} \text{ m}$$

$$= 911 \text{ Å} \quad \textbf{Ans.}$$

Both of these wavelengths lie in ultraviolet (UV) region of electromagnetic spectrum.

Example 9 In a hypothetical atom, mass of electron is doubled, value of atomic number is $Z = 4$. Find wavelength of emitted photon when this electron jumps from 3rd excited state to 2nd orbit.

Sol. $E \propto \frac{Z^2}{n^2} \propto m$

Mass is doubled, $Z = 4$ and 3rd excited state means $n = 4$, second orbit means $n = 2$. For these values, we have

$$E_4 = -13.6 \times 2\left(\frac{4}{4}\right)^2$$

$$= -27.2 \text{ eV}$$

and $E_2 = -13.6 \times 2\left(\frac{4}{2}\right)^2 = -108.8$ eV

$$\lambda(\text{in Å}) = \frac{12375}{\Delta E(\text{in eV})} = \frac{12375}{E_4 - E_2} = \frac{12375}{-27.2 + 108.8}$$

$\therefore$ $\lambda = 151.65$ Å **Ans.**

Example 10 Find de-Broglie wavelength of single electron in 2nd orbit of hydrogen atom by two methods.

Sol. Method 1 Kinetic energy of single electron in 2nd orbit is 3.4 eV using the equation,

$$\lambda = \sqrt{\frac{150}{\text{KE (in eV)}}} = \sqrt{\frac{150}{3.4}} = 6.64 \text{ Å}$$ **Ans.**

Method 2 Circumference of nth orbit $= n\lambda$

$\therefore$ $2\pi r = 2\lambda$

or $\lambda = \pi r$

Now, $r \propto n^2$

$r_1 = 0.529$ Å

$\therefore$ $\lambda = \pi(0.529)(2)^2$ Å

$= 6.64$ Å **Ans.**

INTRODUCTORY Exercise

1. As an electron makes a transition from an excited state to the ground state of a hydrogen like atom/ion **(2015 JEE)**
   (a) kinetic energy, potential energy and total energy decrease
   (b) kinetic energy decreases, potential energy increases but total energy remains same
   (c) kinetic energy and total energy decrease but potential energy increases
   (d) its kinetic energy increases but potential energy and total energy decrease
2. The wavelength of the first spectral line in the Balmer series of hydrogen atom is 6561 Å. The wavelength of the second spectral line in the Balmer series of singly ionized helium atom is **(2011 JEE)**
   (a) 1215 Å (b) 1640 Å (c) 2430 Å (d) 4687 Å
3. The largest wavelength in the ultraviolet region of the hydrogen spectrum is 122 nm. The smallest wavelength in the infrared region of the hydrogen spectrum (to the nearest integer) is **(2007 JEE)**
   (a) 802 nm (b) 823 nm (c) 1882 nm (d) 1648 nm
4. A photon collides with a stationary hydrogen atom in ground state inelastically. Energy of the colliding photon is 10.2 eV. After a time interval of the order of micro second another photon collides with same hydrogen atom inelastically with an energy of 15 eV. What will be observed by the detector? **(2005 JEE)**
   (a) 2 photons of energy 10.2 eV
   (b) 2 photons of energy 1.4 eV
   (c) One photon of energy 10.2 eV and an electron of energy 1.4 eV
   (d) One photon of energy 10.2 eV and another photon of energy 1.4 eV
5. A hydrogen atom and a Li^{2+} ion are both in the second excited state. If l_H and l_{Li} are their respective electronic angular momenta, and E_H and E_{Li} their respective energies, then **(2002 JEE)**
   (a) $l_H > l_{Li}$ and $|E_H| > |E_{Li}|$ (b) $l_H = l_{Li}$ and $|E_H| < |E_{Li}|$
   (c) $l_H = l_{Li}$ and $|E_H| > |E_{Li}|$ (d) $l_H < l_{Li}$ and $|E_H| < |E_{Li}|$
6. The transition from the state $n=4$ to $n=3$ in a hydrogen like atom results in ultraviolet radiation. Infrared radiation will be obtained in the transition **(2001 JEE)**
   (a) $2 \to 1$ (b) $3 \to 2$
   (c) $4 \to 2$ (d) $5 \to 4$
7. As per Bohr model, the minimum energy (in eV) required to remove an electron from the ground state of doubly ionized Li atom ($Z=3$) is **(1997 JEE)**
   (a) 1.51 (b) 13.6
   (c) 40.8 (d) 122.4
8. Consider the spectral line resulting from the transition $n=2 \to n=1$ in the atoms and ions given below. The shortest wavelength is produced by **(1983 JEE)**
   (a) hydrogen atom (b) deuterium atom
   (c) singly ionized helium (d) doubly ionized lithium
9. Find the longest wavelength present in the Balmer series of hydrogen.
10. Find the ionisation energy of a doubly ionized lithium atom.
11. A hydrogen atom is in a state with energy −1.51 eV. In the Bohr model, what is the angular momentum of the electron in the atom with respect to an axis at the nucleus?
12. The energy levels of a certain atom are shown in figure. If a photon of frequency f is emitted when there is an electron transition from $5E$ to E, what frequencies of photons could be produced by other energy level transitions?

Answers

1. (d) 2. (a) 3. (b) 4. (c)
5. (b) 6. (d) 7. (d) 8. (d)
9. 651 nm
10. 122.4 eV
11. 3.16×10^{-34} kg-m^2/s
12. $\frac{3f}{4}, \frac{f}{4}$

See hints on pages 316-317.

Miscellaneous Examples

Ex. 1 The electric potential between a proton and an electron is given by $V = V_0 \ln \frac{r}{r_0}$, where r_0 is a constant.

Assuming Bohr model to be applicable, write variation of r_n with n, being the principal quantum number. **(2003 JEE)**

(a) $r_n \propto n$ (b) $r_n \propto \frac{1}{n}$ (c) $r_n \propto n^2$ (d) $r_n \propto \frac{1}{n^2}$

Sol. $\because \quad U = eV = eV_0 \ln\left(\frac{r}{r_0}\right)$

$$|F| = \left|-\frac{dU}{dr}\right| = \frac{eV_0}{rr_0}$$

This force will provide the necessary centripetal force.

Hence, $$\frac{mv^2}{r} = \frac{eV_0}{rr_0} \text{ or } v = \sqrt{\frac{eV_0}{r_0 m}} \qquad \text{...(i)}$$

Moreover, $$mvr = \frac{nh}{2\pi} \qquad \text{...(ii)}$$

Dividing Eq. (ii) by Eq. (i), we have

$$mr = \left(\frac{nh}{2\pi}\right)\sqrt{\frac{mr_0}{eV_0}} \quad \text{or} \quad r_n \propto n$$

$\therefore$The correct option is (a).

Ex. 2 Imagine an atom made up of proton and a hypothetical particle of double the mass of the electron but having the same charge as the electron. Apply the Bohr atom model and consider all possible transitions of this hypothetical particle to the first excited level. The longest wavelength photon that will be emitted has wavelength λ (given in terms of the Rydberg constant R for the hydrogen atom) equal to **(2000 JEE)**

(a) 9/5R (b) 36/5R (c) 18/5R (d) 4/R

Sol. In hydrogen atom, $E_n = -\frac{Rhc}{n^2}$

Also, $E_n \propto m$

where, m is the mass of the electron.

Here, the electron has been replaced by a particle whose mass is double of an electron. Therefore, for this hypothetical atom energy in nth orbit will be given by

$$E_n = -\frac{2Rhc}{n^2}$$

The longest wavelength λ_{max} (or minimum energy) photon will correspond to the transition of particle from $n = 3$ to $n = 2$.

$$\therefore \quad \frac{hc}{\lambda_{max}} = E_3 - E_2 = 2Rhc\left(\frac{1}{2^2} - \frac{1}{3^2}\right)$$

This gives, $\lambda_{max} = 18/5R$

$\therefore$ The correct option is (c).

Ex. 3 The recoil speed of a hydrogen atom after it emits a photon is going from $n = 5$ state to $n = 1$ state is .... m/s. **(1997 JEE)**

Sol. From conservation of linear momentum,

|Momentum of recoil hydrogen atom| = |Momentum of emitted photon|

or $$mv = \frac{\Delta E}{c}$$

Here, $\Delta E = E_5 - E_1 = -13.6\left[\frac{1}{5^2} - \frac{1}{1^2}\right]$ eV

$= (13.6)\,(24/25)$ eV $= 13.056$ eV

$= 13.056 \times 1.6 \times 10^{-19}$ J $= 2.09 \times 10^{-18}$ J

and m = mass of hydrogen atom $= 1.67 \times 10^{-27}$ kg

$$\therefore \quad v = \frac{\Delta E}{mc} = \frac{2.09 \times 10^{-18}}{(1.67 \times 10^{-27})(3 \times 10^8)}$$

$v \approx 4.17$ m/s

Ex. 4 A hydrogen like atom (described by the Bohr model) is observed to emit six wavelengths, originating from all possible transitions between a group of levels. These levels have energies between -0.85 eV and -0.544 eV (including both these values). **(2002 JEE)**

(a) Find the atomic number of the atom.

(b) Calculate the smallest wavelength emitted in these transitions.

(Take, $hc = 1240$ eV-nm, ground state energy of hydrogen atom $= -13.6$ eV)

Sol. (a) Total 6 lines are emitted. Therefore,

$$\frac{n(n-1)}{2} = 6 \quad \text{or} \quad n = 4$$

So, transition is taking place between pth energy state and $(p+3)$th energy state.

$$E_p = -0.85 \text{ eV}$$

or $$-13.6\left(\frac{Z^2}{p^2}\right) = -0.85$$

or $$\frac{Z}{p} = 0.25 \qquad \text{...(i)}$$

Similarly, $$E_{p+3} = -0.544 \text{ eV}$$

or $$-13.6\frac{Z^2}{(p+3)^2} = -0.544$$

or $$\frac{Z}{(p+3)} = 0.2 \qquad \text{...(ii)}$$

Solving Eqs. (i) and (ii) for Z and m, we get

$p = 12$ and $Z = 3$ **Ans.**

(b) Smallest wavelength corresponds to maximum difference of energies which is obviously $E_{p+3} - E_p$

$$\therefore \quad \Delta E_{max} = -0.544 - (-0.85) = 0.306 \text{ eV}$$

$$\therefore \quad \lambda_{min} = \frac{hc}{\Delta E_{max}} = \frac{1240}{0.306}$$

$$= 4052.3 \text{ nm} \qquad \textbf{Ans.}$$

Ex. 5 A hydrogen like atom of atomic number Z is in an excited state of quantum number $2n$. It can emit a maximum energy photon of 204 eV. If it makes a transition to quantum state n, a photon of energy 40.8 eV is emitted. Find n, Z and the ground state energy (in eV) of this atom. Also calculate the minimum energy (in eV) that can be emitted by this atom during de-excitation. Ground state energy of hydrogen atom is –13.6 eV. **(2000 JEE)**

Sol. Let ground state energy (in eV) be E_1.

Then, from the given condition

$$E_{2n} - E_1 = 204 \text{ eV}$$

or $$\frac{E_1}{4n^2} - E_1 = 204 \text{ eV}$$

or $$E_1\left(\frac{1}{4n^2} - 1\right) = 204 \text{ eV} \qquad \text{...(i)}$$

and $$E_{2n} - E_n = 40.8 \text{ eV}$$

or $$\frac{E_1}{4n^2} - \frac{E_1}{n^2} = 40.8 \text{ eV}$$

or $$E_1\left(\frac{-3}{4n^2}\right) = 40.8 \text{ eV} \qquad \text{...(ii)}$$

From Eqs. (i) and (ii), we get

$$\frac{1 - \frac{1}{4n^2}}{\frac{3}{4n^2}} = 5 \quad \text{or} \quad 1 = \frac{1}{4n^2} + \frac{15}{4n^2}$$

or $$\frac{4}{n^2} = 1 \quad \text{or} \quad n = 2$$

From Eq. (ii),

$$E_1 = -\frac{4}{3} n^2 (40.8) \text{ eV} = -\frac{4}{3} (2)^2 (40.8) \text{ eV}$$

or $$E_1 = -217.6 \text{ eV}$$

$$E_1 = -(13.6) Z^2$$

$$\therefore \quad Z^2 = \frac{E_1}{-13.6} = \frac{-217.6}{-13.6} = 16$$

$$\therefore \quad Z = 4$$

$$E_{min} = E_{2n} - E_{2n-1} = \frac{E_1}{4n^2} - \frac{E_1}{(2n-1)^2}$$

$$= \frac{E_1}{16} - \frac{E_1}{9} = -\frac{7}{144} E_1$$

$$= -\left(\frac{7}{144}\right)(-217.6) \text{ eV}$$

$$\therefore \quad E_{min} = 10.58 \text{ eV}$$

Ex. 6 A hydrogen like atom (atomic number Z) is in a higher excited state of quantum number n. The excited atom can make a transition to the first excited state by successively emitting two photons of energy 10.2 eV and 17.0 eV, respectively. Alternatively, the atom from the same excited state can make a transition to the second excited state by successively emitting two photons of energies 4.25 eV and 5.95 eV, respectively. **(1994 JEE)**

Determine the values of n and Z.

(Ionization energy of H-atom = 13.6 eV)

Sol. From the given conditions,

$$E_n - E_2 = (10.2 + 17) \text{ eV} = 27.2 \text{ eV} \qquad \text{...(i)}$$

and $$E_n - E_3 = (4.25 + 5.95) \text{ eV} = 10.2 \text{ eV} \qquad \text{...(ii)}$$

Eq. (i) – Eq. (ii) gives

$$E_3 - E_2 = 17.0 \text{ eV}$$

or $$Z^2 (13.6)\left(\frac{1}{4} - \frac{1}{9}\right) = 17.0$$

$$\Rightarrow \quad Z^2 (13.6)(5/36) = 17.0$$

$$\Rightarrow \quad Z^2 = 9 \quad \text{or} \quad Z = 3$$

From Eq. (i),

$$Z^2 (13.6)\left(\frac{1}{4} - \frac{1}{n^2}\right) = 27.2$$

or $$(3)^2 (13.6)\left(\frac{1}{4} - \frac{1}{n^2}\right) = 27.2$$

or $$\frac{1}{4} - \frac{1}{n^2} = 0.222$$

or $$1/n^2 = 0.0278$$

or $$n^2 = 36 \Rightarrow n = 6$$

Ex. 7 The wavelength of the first line of Lyman series for hydrogen is identical to that of the second line of Balmer series for some hydrogen like ion x. Calculate energies of the first four levels of x.

Sol. Wavelength of the first line of Lyman series for hydrogen atom will be given by the equation

$$\frac{1}{\lambda_1} = R\left(\frac{1}{1^2} - \frac{1}{2^2}\right) = \frac{3R}{4} \qquad \text{...(i)}$$

The wavelength of second Balmer line for hydrogen like ion x is

$$\frac{1}{\lambda_2} = RZ^2\left(\frac{1}{2^2} - \frac{1}{4^2}\right) = \frac{3RZ^2}{16} \qquad \text{...(ii)}$$

Given that $\lambda_1 = \lambda_2$ or $\frac{1}{\lambda_1} = \frac{1}{\lambda_2}$

i.e. $$\frac{3R}{4} = \frac{3RZ^2}{16}$$

$\therefore$ $$Z = 2$$

i.e. x ion is He^+. The energies of first four levels of x are

$$E_1 = -(13.6)\,Z^2 = -54.4 \text{ eV}$$

$$E_2 = \frac{E_1}{(2)^2} = -13.6 \text{ eV}$$

$$E_3 = \frac{E_1}{(3)^2} = -6.04 \text{ eV}$$

and $$E_4 = \frac{E_1}{(4)^2} = -3.4 \text{ eV}$$ **Ans.**

Ex. 8 A moving hydrogen atom makes a head on collision with a stationary hydrogen atom. Before collision both atoms are in ground state and after collision they move together. What is the minimum value of the kinetic energy of the moving hydrogen atom, such that one of the atoms reaches one of the excited state?

Sol. Let K be the kinetic energy of the moving hydrogen atom and K', the kinetic energy of combined mass after collision.

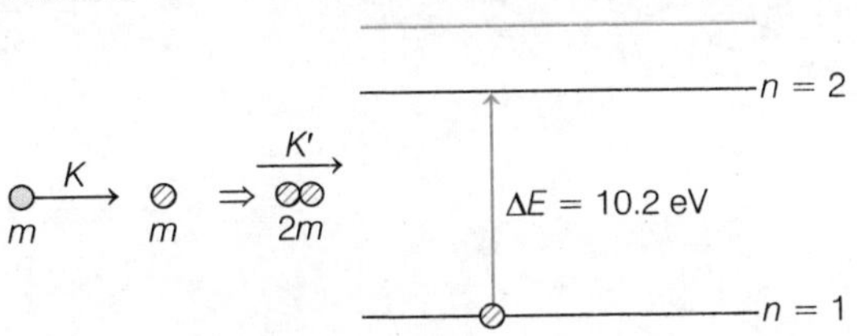

From conservation of linear momentum,

$$p = p' \quad \text{or} \quad \sqrt{2Km} = \sqrt{2K'\,(2m)}$$

or $$K = 2K' \qquad \text{...(i)}$$

From conservation of energy,

$$K = K' + \Delta E \qquad \text{...(ii)}$$

Solving Eqs. (i) and (ii), we get

$$\Delta E = \frac{K}{2}$$

Now, minimum value of ΔE for hydrogen atom is 10.2 eV.

or $$\Delta E \geq 10.2 \text{ eV}$$

$\therefore$ $$\frac{K}{2} \geq 10.2$$

$\therefore$ $$K \geq 20.4 \text{ eV}$$

Therefore, the minimum kinetic energy of moving hydrogen is 20.4 eV. **Ans.**

Ex. 9 An imaginary particle has a charge equal to that of an electron and mass 100 times the mass of the electron. It moves in a circular orbit around a nucleus of charge $+4e$. Take the mass of the nucleus to be infinite. Assuming that the Bohr model is applicable to this system.

(a) Derive an expression for the radius of nth Bohr orbit.

(b) Find the wavelength of the radiation emitted when the article jumps from fourth orbit to the second orbit.

Sol. (a) We have $$\frac{m_p v^2}{r_n} = \frac{1}{4\pi\varepsilon_0}\frac{Ze^2}{r_n^2} \qquad \text{...(i)}$$

The quantization of angular momentum gives

$$m_p v r_n = \frac{nh}{2\pi} \qquad \text{...(ii)}$$

Solving Eqs. (i) and (ii), we get

$$r = \frac{n^2h^2\varepsilon_0}{Z\pi m_p e^2}$$

Substituting $m_p = 100\,m$

where, m = mass of electron and $Z = 4$

We get, $$r_n = \frac{n^2h^2\varepsilon_0}{400\,\pi\, me^2}$$ **Ans.**

(b) As we know, $$E_1^H = -13.60 \text{ eV}$$

and $$E_n \propto \left(\frac{Z^2}{n^2}\right) m$$

For the given particle, $$E_4 = \frac{(-13.60)\,(4)^2}{(4)^2} \times 100$$

$$= -1360 \text{ eV}$$

and $$E_2 = \frac{(-13.60)\,(4)^2}{(2)^2} \times 100$$

$$= -5440 \text{ eV}$$

$$\Delta E = E_4 - E_2$$

$$= 4080 \text{ eV}$$

$\therefore$ $$\lambda \text{ (in Å)} = \frac{12375}{\Delta E \text{ (in eV)}} = \frac{12375}{4080}$$

$$= 3.0 \text{ Å}$$ **Ans.**

Ex. 10 The energy levels of a hypothetical one electron atom are given by

$$E_n = -\frac{18.0}{n^2} \text{ eV}$$

where $n = 1, 2, 3, \ldots$

(a) Compute the four lowest energy levels and construct the energy level diagram.

(b) What is the first excitation potential

(c) What wavelengths (Å) can be emitted when these atoms in the ground state are bombarded by electrons that have been accelerated through a potential difference of 16.2 V?

(d) If these atoms are in the ground state, can they absorb radiation having a wavelength of 2000 Å?

Sol. (a) $E_1 = \frac{-18.0}{(1)^2} = -18.0\text{ eV}$

$E_2 = \frac{-18.0}{(2)^2} = -4.5\text{ eV}$

$E_3 = \frac{-18.0}{(3)^2} = -2.0\text{ eV}$

and $E_4 = \frac{-18.0}{(4)^2} = -1.125\text{ eV}$

The energy level diagram is shown in figure.

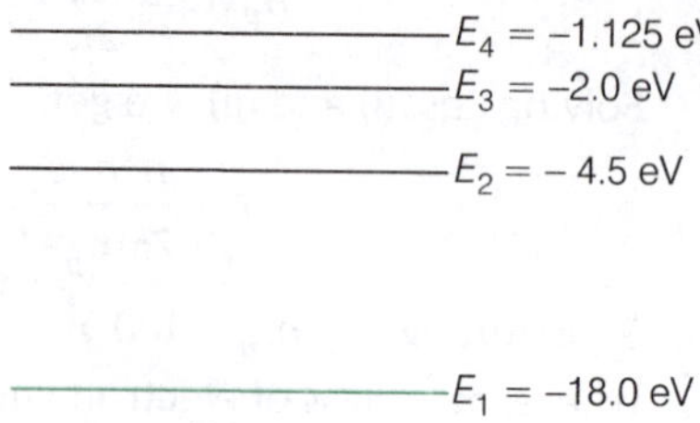

(b) $E_2 - E_1 = 13.5\text{ eV}$

$\therefore$ First excitation potential is 13.5 V.

(c) Energy of the electron accelerated by a potential difference of 16.2 V is 16.2 eV.

With this energy the electron can excite the atom from $n = 1$ to $n = 3$ as

$$E_4 - E_1 = -1.125 - (-18.0)$$
$$= 16.875\text{ eV} > 16.2\text{ eV}$$

and $E_3 - E_1 = -2.0 - (-18.0)$

$$= 16.0\text{ eV} < 16.2\text{ eV}$$

Now, $\lambda_{32} = \frac{12375}{E_3 - E_2} = \frac{12375}{-2.0-(-4.5)}$

$= 4950\text{ Å}$ **Ans.**

$\lambda_{31} = \frac{12375}{E_3 - E_1} = \frac{12375}{16} = 773\text{ Å}$ **Ans.**

and $\lambda_{21} = \frac{12375}{E_2 - E_1} = \frac{12375}{-4.5-(-18.0)}$

$= 917\text{ Å}$ **Ans.**

(d) No, the energy corresponding to $\lambda = 2000\text{ Å}$ is

$E = \frac{12375}{2000}$

$= 6.1875\text{ eV}$ **Ans.**

The minimum excitation energy is 13.5eV ($n = 1$ to $n = 2$).

MODULE 2 Exercise

Fill in the Blank

1. In the Bohr model of the hydrogen atom, the ratio of the kinetic energy to the total energy of the electron in a quantum state n is .... **(1992 JEE)**

Statement Type Question

2. Given below are two statements

Statement I : In hydrogen atom, the frequency of radiation emitted when an electron jumps from lower energy orbit (E_1) to higher energy orbit (E_2), is given as $hf = E_1 - E_2$.

Statement II : The jumping of electron from higher energy orbit (E_2) to lower energy orbit (E_1) is associated with frequency of radiation given as $f = (E_2 - E_1)/h$

In the light of the above statements, choose the correct options. **(2022 Main)**

(a) Both Statement I and Statement II are true.
(b) Both Statement I and Statement II are false.
(c) Statement I is true but Statement II is false.
(d) Statement I is false but Statement II is true.

Single Correct Option

3. Which of the folllowing products in a hydrogen atom are independent of the principal quantum number n?
(a) vr (b) Er
(c) Ev (d) None of these

4. What is the ratio of de-Broglie wavelength of electron in the second and third Bohr orbits in the hydrogen atoms?
(a) 2/3 (b) 3/2 (c) 4/3 (d) 3/4

5. The velocity of the electron in the first Bohr orbit as compared to that of light is about
(a) 1/300 (b) 1/500 (c) 1/137 (d) 1/187

6. The energy of an atom or ion in the first excited state is –13.6 eV. It may be
(a) He^+ (b) Li^{++}
(c) hydrogen (d) deuterium

7. If the potential energy of a hydrogen atom in the ground state is assumed to be zero, then total energy of $n = \infty$ is equal to
(a) 13.6 eV (b) 27.2 eV
(c) zero (d) None of these

8. In which of the following systems will the radius of the first orbit ($n = 1$) be minimum?
(a) Hydrogen atom
(b) Deuterium atom
(c) Singly ionized helium
(d) Doubly ionized lithium

9. The frequency of the first line in Lyman series in the hydrogen spectrum is ν. What is the frequency of the corresponding line in the spectrum of doubly ionized Lithium?
(a) ν (b) 3ν (c) 9ν (d) 2ν

10. Which energy state of doubly ionized lithium (Li^{++}) has the same energy as that of the ground state of hydrogen?
(a) $n=1$ (b) $n=2$ (c) $n=3$ (d) $n=4$

11. The radius of third stationary orbit of electron for Bohr's atom is R. The radius of fourth stationary orbit will be **(2024 Main)**
(a) $\frac{9}{16}R$ (b) $\frac{3}{4}R$ (c) $\frac{16}{9}R$ (d) $\frac{4}{3}R$

12. The energy of He^+ ion in its first excited state is, (The ground state energy for the hydrogen atom is -13.6 eV) **(2023 Main)**
(a) -27.2 eV (b) -3.4 eV (c) -54.4 eV (d) -13.6 eV

13. A small particle of mass m moves in such a way that its potential energy $U = \frac{1}{2}m\omega^2 r^2$, where ω is constant and r is the distance of the particle from origin. Assuming Bohr's quantization of momentum and circular orbit, the radius of nth orbit will be proportional to **(2023 Main)**
(a) $\frac{1}{n}$ (b) n (c) $\sqrt{n}$ (d) n^2

14. The angular momentum for the electron in Bohr's orbit is L. If the electron is assumed to revolve in second orbit of hydrogen atom, then the change in angular momentum will be **(2023 Main)**
(a) L (b) $\frac{L}{2}$ (c) Zero (d) $2L$

15. The energy levels of an hydrogen atom are shown below. The transition corresponding to emission of shortest wavelength is **(2023 Main)**

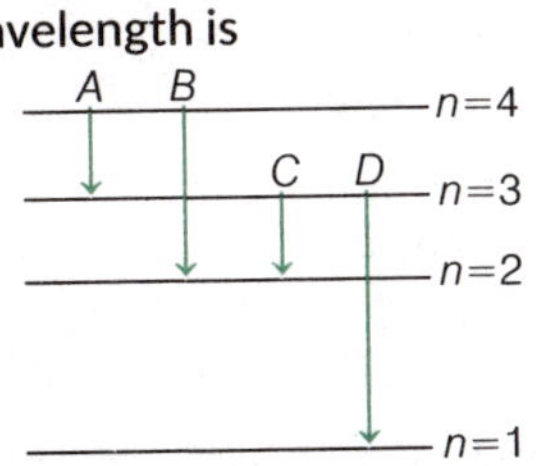

(a) D (b) A (c) C (d) B

16. A 12.5 eV electron beam is used to bombard gaseous hydrogen at room temperature. The number of spectral lines emitted will be **(2023 Main)**
(a) 1 (b) 3 (c) 2 (d) 4

17. An electron of a hydrogen like atom, having $Z = 4$, jumps from 4th energy state to 2nd energy state. The energy released in this process, will be
(given, $Rch = 13.6$ eV)
where, R = Rydberg constant, c = Speed of light in vacuum and h = Planck's constant **(2023 Main)**
(a) 13.6 eV (b) 10.5 eV (c) 40.8 eV (d) 3.4 eV

18. The energy levels of an atom is shown in figure.

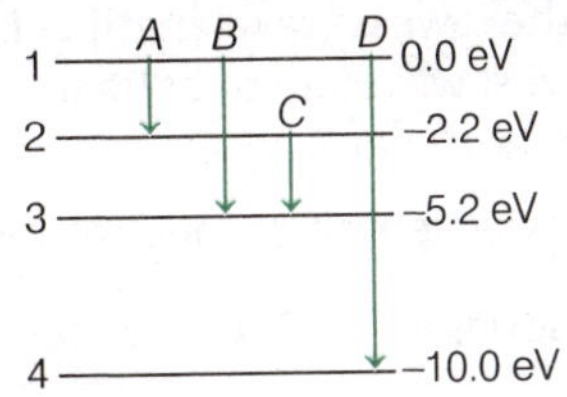

Which one of these transitions will result in the emission of a photon of wavelength 124.1 nm ?
(Given, $h = 6.62 \times 10^{-34}$ J-s) **(2023 Main)**
(a) A (b) C (c) D (d) B

Subjective Questions

19. In the Bohr model of the hydrogen atom, what is the de-Broglie wavelength for the electron when it is in
(a) the $n=1$ level?
(b) the $n=4$ level?

20. Hydrogen atom in its ground state is excited by means of monochromatic radiation of wavelength 1023 Å. How many different lines are possible in the resulting spectrum? Calculate the longest wavelength among them. You may assume the ionization energy of hydrogen atom as 13.6 eV.

21. A doubly ionized lithium atom is hydrogen like with atomic number 3. Find the wavelength of the radiation required to excite the electron in Li^{++} from the first to the third Bohr orbit (ionization energy of the hydrogen atom equals 13.6 eV).

22. Find the quantum number n corresponding to nth excited state of He^+ ion if on transition to the ground state the ion emits two photons in succession with wavelengths 108.5 nm and 30.4 nm. The ionization energy of the hydrogen atom is 13.6 eV.

23. The energy levels of a hypothetical one electron atom are shown in the figure.

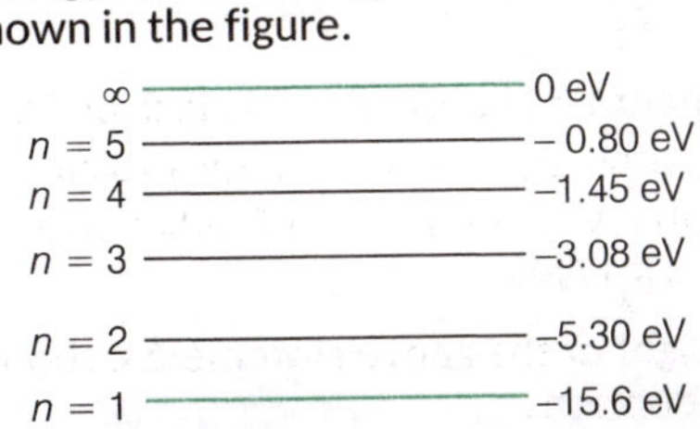

(a) Find the ionization potential of this atom.
(b) Find the short wavelength limit of the series terminating at $n=2$.
(c) Find the excitation potential for the state $n=3$.
(d) Find wave number of the photon emitted for the transition $n=3$ to $n=1$.

Integer Type Questions

24. A hydrogen atom changes its state from $n=3$ to $n=2$. Due to recoil, the percentage change in the wave length of emitted light is approximately 1×10^{-n}. The value of n is...... . [Given $Rhc=13.6$ eV, $hc=1242$ eV nm, $h=6.6\times10^{-34}$ Js mass of the hydrogen atom $=1.6\times10^{-27}$kg] **(2024 Main)**

25. If 917 Å be the lowest wavelength of Lyman series then the lowest wavelength of Balmer series will be .... Å. **(2023 Main)**

26. The ratio of wavelength of spectral lines H_α and H_β in the Balmer series is $\frac{x}{20}$. The value of x is .... **(2023 Main)**

27. The radius of 2nd orbit of He^+ of bohr's model is r_1 and that of fourth orbit of Be^{3+} is represented as r_2. Now, the ratio $\frac{r_2}{r_1}$ is x : 1. The value of x is .... **(2023 Main)**

28. The radius of fifth orbit of the Li^{++} is ......$\times 10^{12}$ m.

Take: radius of first orbit of hydrogen atom $=0.51$ Å **(2023 Main)**

29. Experimentally it is found that 12.8 eV energy is required to separate a hydrogen atom into a proton and an electron. So the orbital radius of the electron in a hydrogen atom is $\frac{9}{x}\times10^{-19}$ m. The value of the x is ..... . (1 eV $=1.6\times10^{-19}$ J, $\frac{1}{4\pi\varepsilon_0}=9\times10^9$ Nm²/C² and electronic charge $=1.6\times10^{-19}$ C) **(2023 Main)**

30. As per given figure A, B and C are the first, second and third energy levels of hydrogen atom, respectively. If the ratio of the two wavelengths $\left(\text{i.e. } \frac{\lambda_1}{\lambda_2}\right)$ is $\frac{7}{4n}$, then the value of n will be .... **(2023 Main)**

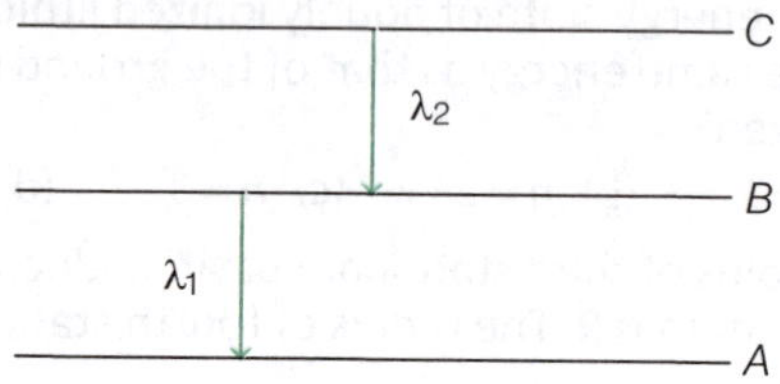

31. A light of energy 12.75 eV is incident on a hydrogen atom in its ground state. The atom absorbs the radiation and reaches to one of its excited states. The angular momentum of the atom in the excited state is $\frac{x}{\pi}\times10^{-17}$ eV-s. The value of x is ....

(Use $h=4.14\times10^{-15}$ eV-s, $c=3\times10^8$ms^{-1}). **(2023 Main)**

Answers

1. –1 **2.** (d) **3.** (b) **4.** (a) **5.** (c) **6.** (a) **7.** (b) **8.** (d) **9.** (c) **10.** (c)
11. (c) **12.** (d) **13.** (c) **14.** (a) **15.** (a) **16.** (b) **17.** (c) **18.** (c)
19. (a) 3.32×10^{-10} m (b) 1.33×10^{-9} m **20.** 3, 6513 Å **21.** Approximately 113 Å
22. $n=5$ **23.** (a) 15.6 volt (b) 2335 Å (c) 12.52 V (d) 1.01×10^7 m^{-1}
24. (7) **25.** (3668) **26.** (27) **27.** (2) **28.** (425) **29.** (16) **30.** (9.8) **31.** (828)

See hints on pages 317-321.

MODULE 3

X-Rays

Electromagnetic radiation with wavelengths from 0.1 Å to 100 Å falls into the category of X-rays. The boundaries of this category are not sharp. The shorter wavelength end overlaps gamma rays and the longer wavelength end overlaps ultraviolet rays.

Photoelectric effect (will be discussed later) provides convincing evidence that photons of light can transfer energy to electrons. Is the inverse process also possible? That is, can part or all of the kinetic energy of a moving electron be converted into a photon? Yes, it is possible.

In 1895 **Wilhelm Roentgen** found that a highly penetrating radiation of unknown nature is produced when fast moving electrons strike a target of high atomic number and high melting point. These radiations were given a name X-rays as their nature was unknown (in mathematics an unknown quantity is normally designated by X). Later, it was discovered that these are high energy photons (or electromagnetic waves).

Production of X-Rays Figure shows a diagram of a X-ray tube, called the coolidge tube. A cathode (a plate connected to negative terminal of a battery), heated by a filament through which an electric current is passed, supplies electrons by thermionic emission. The high potential difference V maintained between the cathode and a metallic target accelerate the electrons toward the later.

The face of the target is at an angle relative to the electron beam, and the X-rays that leave the target pass through the side of the tube. The tube is evacuated to permit the electrons to get to the target unimpedded.

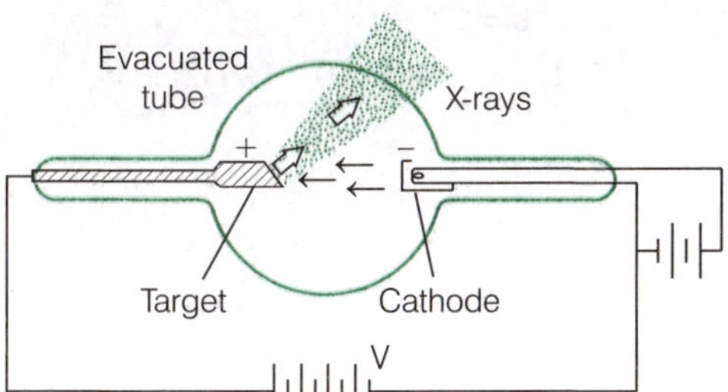

An X-ray tube. The higher the accelerating voltage V, the faster the electrons and the shorter the wavelengths of the X-rays

Continuous and characteristic X-rays

X-rays so produced by the coolidge tube are of two types, continuous and characteristic. While the former depends only on the accelerating voltage V, the later depends on the target used.

Continuous X-rays Electromagnetic theory predicts that an accelerated electric charge will radiate electromagnetic waves, and a rapidly moving electrons when suddenly brought to rest is certainly accelerated (of course negative). X-rays produced under these circumstances is given the German name **bremsstrahlung** (braking radiation). Energy loss due to bremsstrahlung is more important for electrons than for heavier particles because electrons are more violently accelerated when passing near nuclei in their paths. The continuous X-rays (or bremsstrahlung X-rays) produced at a given accelerating potential V vary in wavelength, but none has a wavelength shorter than a certain value λ_{min}. This minimum wavelength corresponds to the maximum energy of the X-rays which in turn is equal to the maximum kinetic energy qV or eV of the striking electrons. Thus,

$$\frac{hc}{\lambda_{min}} = eV \quad \text{or} \quad \lambda_{min} = \frac{hc}{eV}$$

After substituting values of h, c and e we obtain the following simple formula for λ_{min}.

$$\boxed{\lambda_{min} \text{ (in Å)} = \frac{12375}{V\text{(in volts)}}} \qquad ...(i)$$

Increasing V decreases λ_{min}. This wavelength is also known as the cut off wavelength or the threshold wavelength.

Characteristic X-rays The X-ray spectrum typically consists of a broad continuous band containing a series of sharp lines as shown in figure.

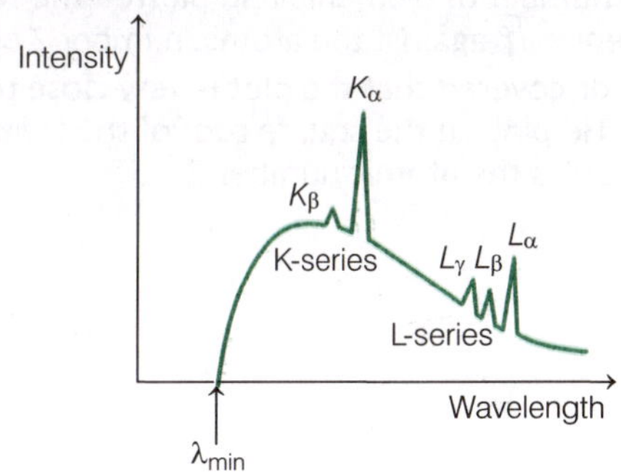

X-ray spectrum

As discussed above the continuous spectrum is the result of collisions between incoming electrons and atoms in the target. The kinetic energy lost by the electrons during the collisions emerges as the energy of the X-ray photons radiated from the target.

The sharp lines superimposed on the continuous spectrum are known as **characteristic X-rays** because they are characteristic of the target material. They were discovered in

1908, but their origin remained unexplained until the details of atomic structure, particularly the shell structure of the atom, were discovered.

Characteristic X-ray emission occurs when a bombarding electron that collides with a target atom has sufficient energy to remove an inner shell electron from the atom.

The vacancy created in the shell is filled when an electron from a higher level drops down into it. This transition is accompanied by the emission of a photon whose energy equals the difference in energy between the two levels.

Let us assume that the incoming electron has dislodged an atomic electron from the innermost shell-the *K* shell. If the vacancy is filled by an electron dropping from the next higher shell the *L* shell, the photon emitted has an energy corresponding to the K_α characteristic X-ray line.

If the vacancy is filled by an electron dropping from the *M* shell, the K_β line is produced. An L_α line is produced as an electron drops from the *M* shell to the *L*-shell, and an L_β line is produced by a transition from the *N*-shell to the *L*-shell.

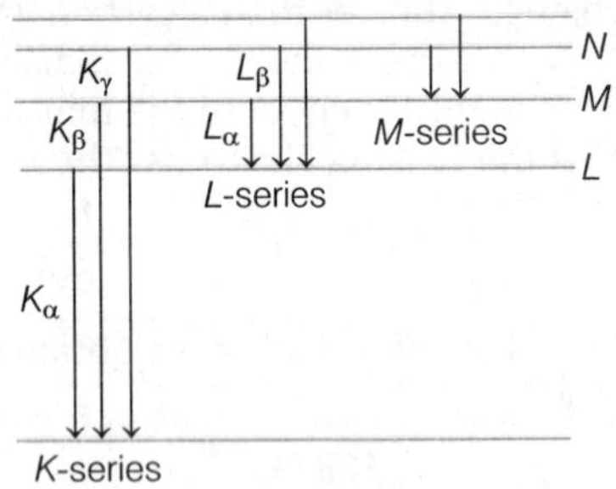

Moseley's Law for Characteristic Spectrum

Although multi-electron atoms cannot be analyzed with the Bohr model, Henery G.J. Moseley in 1914 made an effort towards this.

Moseley measured the frequencies of characteristic X-rays from a large number of elements and plotted the square root of the frequency $\sqrt{f}$ against the atomic number *Z* of the element. He discovered that the plot is very close to a straight line. He plotted the square root of the frequency of the K_α line *versus* the atomic number *Z*.

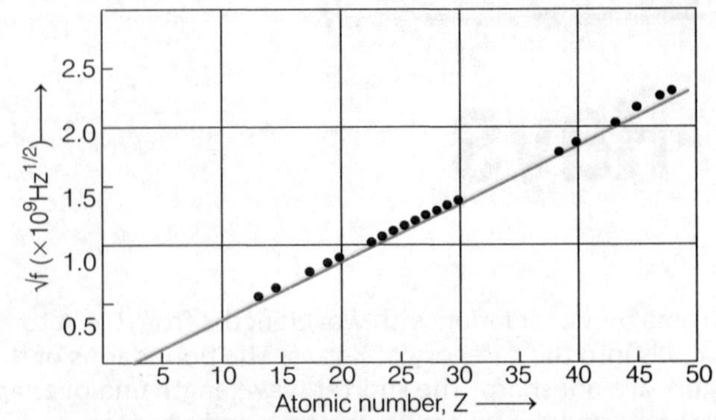

A plot of the square root of the frequency of the K_α lines *versus* atomic number using Moseley's data

Thus, Moseley's law of the frequency of K_α line is

$$\sqrt{f_{K_\alpha}} = a(Z-1) \qquad \text{...(ii)}$$

where, *a* is a constant that can be related to Bohr theory. The above law in general can be stated as under

$$\boxed{\sqrt{f} = a(Z-b)}$$

or

$$\boxed{\sqrt{f} \propto (Z-b)} \qquad \text{...(iii)}$$

For K_α line, $\Delta E = hf = Rhc(Z-1)^2\left(\frac{1}{1^2} - \frac{1}{2^2}\right)$

or $\sqrt{f} = \sqrt{\frac{3Rc}{4}}(Z-1)$

or $a = \sqrt{\frac{3Rc}{4}}$ and $b = 1$

After substituting values of *R* and *c*, we get

$$a = 4.98 \times 10^7 \ (\text{Hz})^{1/2}$$

Eq. (iii) can also be written as

$$f = a^2 (Z-b)^2 \qquad \text{...(iv)}$$

For K_α line, $a^2 = \frac{3Rc}{4} = (2.48 \times 10^{15} \text{ Hz})$

and $b = 1$

Hence, $f_{K_\alpha} = (2.48 \times 10^{15} \text{ Hz})(Z-1)^2$

Important POINTS

- In continuous X-ray spectrum, all wavelengths greater than λ_{min} are obtained. Characteristic X-ray spectrum is discrete. Certain fixed wavelengths like λ_{K_α}, λ_{K_β} etc. are obtained and these wavelengths are different for different target elements.

  The mixed spectrum of continuous and characteristic X-rays is as shown in figure.

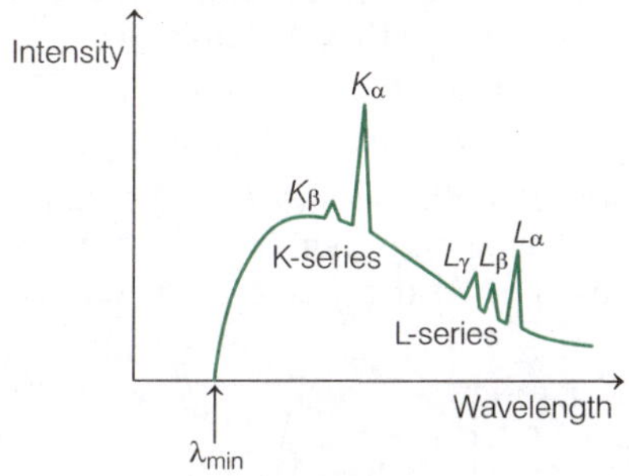

X-ray spectrum

- In general, if we compare between different series, then

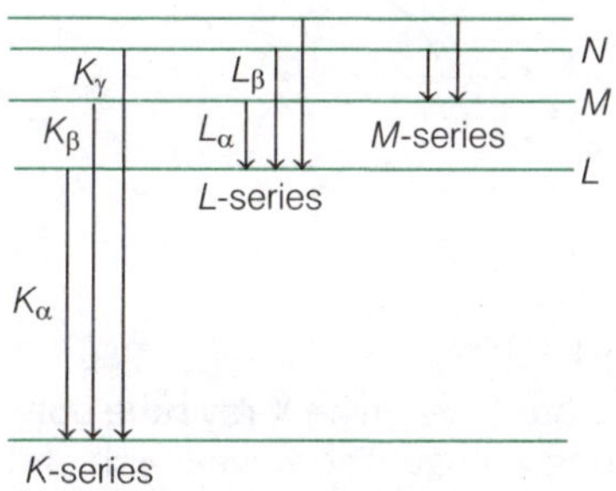

$$E_K > E_L > E_M \quad \text{or} \quad f_K > f_L > f_M \quad \text{or} \quad \lambda_K < \lambda_L < \lambda_M$$

And if we compare between α, β and γ, then

$$E_\alpha < E_\beta < E_\gamma \quad \text{or} \quad f_\alpha < f_\beta < f_\gamma \quad \text{or} \quad \lambda_\alpha > \lambda_\beta > \lambda_\gamma$$

- In Moseley's law,

$$\sqrt{f} \propto (Z - b)$$

$$b = 1 \quad \text{for} \quad K_\alpha \text{ line}$$

and $\quad b = 7.4 \quad \text{for} \quad L_\alpha$ line

Thus, $\sqrt{f} = 0$ at $Z = b = 1$ for K_α line

and $\sqrt{f} = 0$ at $Z = b = 7.4$ for K_β line

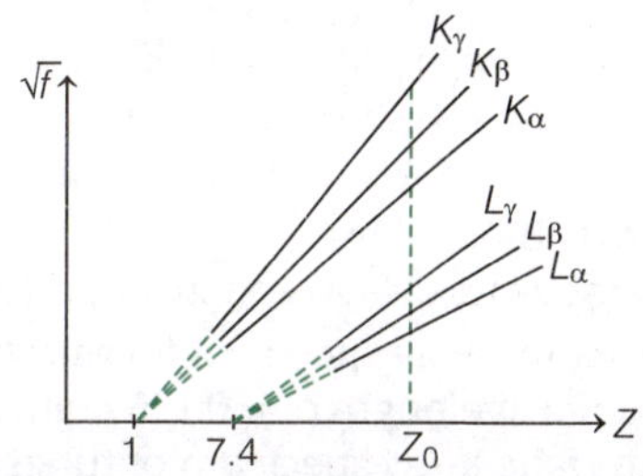

For lower atomic numbers lines are shown dotted. This is because X-rays are obtained only at high atomic numbers. Further, we can see that for a given atomic number (say Z_0).

$$\sqrt{f_K} > \sqrt{f_L}$$

- The target (or anode) used in the Coolidge tube should be of high melting point. This is because less than 0.5% of the kinetic energy of the electrons is converted into X-rays. The rest of the kinetic energy converts into internal energy of the target which simultaneously has to be kept cool by circulating oil or water.
- Atomic number of the target material should be high. This is because X-rays are high energy photons and as we have seen above energy of the X-rays increases as Z increases.
- X-rays are basically electromagnetic waves. So, they possess all the properties of electromagnetic waves.

Example 1 Find the cut off wavelength for the continuous X-rays coming from an X-ray tube operating at 40 kV.

Sol. Cut off wavelength λ_{min} is given by

$$\lambda_{min} \text{ (in Å)} = \frac{12375}{V(\text{in volts})} = \frac{12375}{40 \times 10^3}$$

$$= 0.31 \text{ Å} \qquad \textbf{Ans.}$$

Example 2 Use Moseley's law with $b = 1$ to find the frequency of the K_α X-rays of La ($Z = 57$) if the frequency of the K_α X-rays of Cu ($Z = 29$) is known to be 1.88×10^{18} Hz.

Sol. Using the equation, $\sqrt{f} = a(Z - b)$ $\qquad (b = 1)$

$$\frac{f_{La}}{f_{Cu}} = \left(\frac{Z_{La} - 1}{Z_{Cu} - 1}\right)^2 \quad \text{or} \quad f_{La} = f_{Cu}\left(\frac{Z_{La} - 1}{Z_{Cu} - 1}\right)^2$$

$$= 1.88 \times 10^{18}\left(\frac{57 - 1}{29 - 1}\right)^2$$

$$= 7.52 \times 10^{18} \text{ Hz} \qquad \textbf{Ans.}$$

Example 3 Electrons with de-Broglie wavelength λ fall on the target in an X-ray tube. The cut off wavelength of the emitted X-rays is **(2007 JEE)**

(a) $\lambda_0 = \frac{2mc\lambda^2}{h}$ (b) $\lambda_0 = \frac{2h}{mc}$

(c) $\lambda_0 = \frac{2m^2c^2\lambda^3}{h^2}$ (d) $\lambda_0 = \lambda$

Sol. Momentum of bombarding electrons,

$$p = \frac{h}{\lambda}$$

$\therefore$ Kinetic energy of bombarding electrons,

$$K = \frac{p^2}{2m} = \frac{h^2}{2m\lambda^2}$$

This is also maximum energy of X-ray photons.

Therefore, $\frac{hc}{\lambda_0} = \frac{h^2}{2m\lambda^2}$

or $\lambda_0 = \frac{2m\lambda^2 c}{h}$

$\therefore$ Correct option is (a).

Example 4 Electrons with energy 80 keV are incident on the tungsten target of an X-ray tube. *K*-shell electrons of tungsten have 72.5 keV ionisation energy. X-rays emitted by the tube contain only **(2000 JEE)**

(a) a continuous X-ray spectrum (Bremsstrahlung) with a minimum wavelength of ≈ 0.155 Å

(b) a continuous X-ray spectrum (Bremsstrahlung) with all wavelengths

(c) the characteristic X-ray spectrum of tungsten

(d) a continuous X-ray spectrum (Bremsstrahlung) with a minimum wavelength of ≈ 0.155 Å and the characteristic X-ray spectrum of tungsten

Sol. Minimum wavelength of continuous X-ray spectrum is given by

$$\lambda_{min} \text{ (in Å)} = \frac{12375}{E(\text{in eV})}$$

Here, E = energy of incident electrons (in eV)
= energy corresponding to minimum wavelength λ_{min} of X-ray

$\therefore$ $E = 80 \text{ keV} = 80 \times 10^3$ eV

$\therefore$ $\lambda_{min} \text{ (in Å)} = \frac{12375}{80 \times 10^3} \approx 0.155$

Also the energy of the incident electrons (80 keV) is more than the ionization energy of the *K*-shell electrons (i.e. 72.5 keV). Therefore, characteristic X-ray spectrum will also be obtained because energy of incident electron is high enough to knock out the electron from *K* or *L*-shells.

$\therefore$ The correct option is (d).

INTRODUCTORY Exercise

1. If λ_{Cu} is the wavelength of K_α, X-ray line of copper (atomic number 29) and λ_{Mo} is the wavelength of the K_α X-ray line of molybdenum (atomic number 42), then the ratio $\lambda_{Cu}/\lambda_{Mo}$ is close to **(2014 JEE)**
   (a) 1.99 (b) 2.14
   (c) 0.50 (d) 0.48

2. Which one of the following statements is **wrong** in the context of X-rays generated from an X-ray tube? **(2008 JEE)**
   (a) Wavelength of characteristic X-rays decreases when the atomic number of the target increases
   (b) Cut off wavelength of the continuous X-rays depends on the atomic number of the target
   (c) Intensity of the characteristic X-rays depends on the electrical power given to the X-ray tube
   (d) Cut off wavelength of the continuous X-rays depends on the energy of the electrons in the X-ray tube

3. K_α wavelength emitted by an atom of atomic number $Z = 11$ is λ. Find the atomic number for an atom that emits K_α radiation with wavelength 4λ **(2005 JEE)**
   (a) $Z = 6$ (b) $Z = 4$ (c) $Z = 11$ (d) $Z = 44$

4. The intensity of X-rays from a coolidge tube is plotted against wavelength λ as shown in the figure. The minimum wavelength found is λ_c and the wavelength of the K_α line is λ_k. As the accelerating voltage is increased **(2001 JEE)**

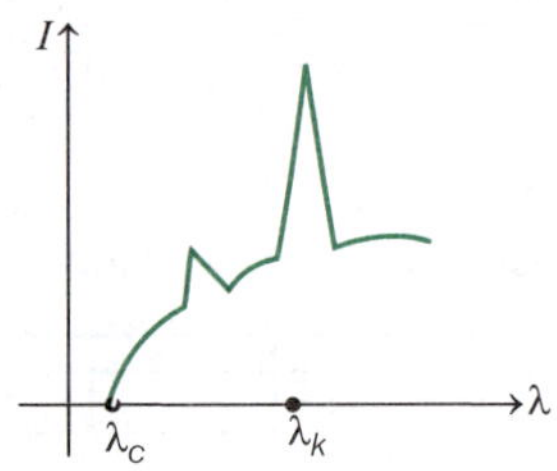

   (a) $\lambda_k - \lambda_c$ increases
   (b) $\lambda_k - \lambda_c$ decreases
   (c) λ_k increases
   (d) λ_k decreases

5. X-rays are produced in an X-ray tube operating at a given accelerating voltage. The wavelength of the continuous X-rays has values from **(JEE 1998)**
   (a) 0 to ∞
   (b) λ_{min} to ∞, where $\lambda_{min} > 0$
   (c) 0 to λ_{max}, where $\lambda_{max} < \infty$
   (d) λ_{min} to λ_{max}, where $0 < \lambda_{min} < \lambda_{max} < \infty$

6. Characteristic X-rays of frequency 4.2×10^{18} Hz are produced when transitions from *L*-shell to *K*-shell take place in a certain target material. Use Mosley's law to determine the atomic number of the target material. Given Rydberg constant $R = 1.1 \times 10^7 \text{ m}^{-1}$. **(2003 JEE)**

Answers

1. (b) 2. (b) 3. (a) 4. (a)
5. (b) 6. 42

See hints on page 321.

Miscellaneous Examples

Ex. 1 The potential difference applied to an X-ray tube is 5 kV and the current through it is 3.2 mA. Then, the number of electrons striking the target per second is **(2002 JEE)**

(a) 2×10^{16} (b) 5×10^{6} (c) 1×10^{17} (d) 4×10^{15}

Sol. $\because \quad i = \frac{q}{t} = \frac{ne}{t}$

$\therefore \quad n = \frac{it}{e}$

Substituting $i = 3.2 \times 10^{-3}$ A,

$e = 1.6 \times 10^{-19}$ C and $t = 1$ s

We get, $n = 2 \times 10^{16}$

$\therefore$ The correct answer is (a).

Ex. 2 X-rays are incident on a target metal atom having 30 neutrons. The ratio of nuclear radius of the target atom and ${}_2^4He$ is $(14)^{1/3}$. **(2005 JEE)**

(a) Find the mass number of target atom.

(b) Find the frequency of K_α line emitted by this metal.

Hint : Radius of a nucleus (r) has the following relation with mass number (A).

$$r \propto A^{1/3}$$

$(R = 1.1 \times 10^7 m^{-1}, c = 3 \times 10^8$ m/s)

Sol. (a) From the relation $r \propto A^{1/3}$,

We have, $\frac{r_2}{r_1} = \left(\frac{A_2}{A_1}\right)^{1/3}$

or $\left(\frac{A_2}{4}\right)^{1/3} = (14)^{1/3}$

$\therefore \quad A_2 = 56$

(b) $Z_2 = A_2 -$ number of neutrons

$= 56 - 30 = 26$

$$\therefore \quad f = Rc(Z-1)^2\left(\frac{1}{1^2} - \frac{1}{2^2}\right) = \frac{3Rc}{4}(Z-1)^2$$

Substituting the given values of R, c and Z, we get

$$f = 1.55 \times 10^{18} \text{ Hz}$$

Ex. 3 In Moseley's equation $\sqrt{f} = a(Z-b)$, a and b are constants. Find their values with the help of the following data.

Element	Z	Wavelength of K_α X-rays
Mo	42	0.71 Å
Co	27	1.785 Å

Sol. $\sqrt{f} = a(Z-b)$

or $\sqrt{\frac{c}{\lambda_1}} = a(Z_1 - b)$ ...(i)

and $\sqrt{\frac{c}{\lambda_2}} = a(Z_2 - b)$ ...(ii)

From Eqs. (i) and (ii), we have

$$\sqrt{c}\left[\frac{1}{\sqrt{\lambda_1}} - \frac{1}{\sqrt{\lambda_2}}\right] = a(Z_1 - Z_2) \quad \text{...(iii)}$$

Solving above three equations with

$c = 3.0 \times 10^8$ m/s,

$\lambda_1 = 0.71 \times 10^{-10}$ m

$\lambda_2 = 1.785 \times 10^{-10}$ m, $Z_1 = 42$

and $Z_2 = 27$, we get

$a = 5 \times 10^7 \text{ (Hz)}^{1/2}$

and $b = 1.37$ **Ans.**

Ex. 4 If an X-ray tube operates at the voltage of 10 kV, find the ratio of the de-Broglie wavelength of the incident electrons to the shortest wavelength of X-rays produced. The specific charge of electron is 1.8×10^{11} C/kg.

Sol. de-Broglie wavelength when a charge q is accelerated by a potential difference of V volts is

$$\lambda_b = \frac{h}{\sqrt{2qVm}} \quad \text{...(i)}$$

For cut off wavelength of X-rays, we have

$$qV = \frac{hc}{\lambda_m}$$

or $\lambda_m = \frac{hc}{qV}$ ...(ii)

From Eqs. (i) and (ii), we get

$$\frac{\lambda_b}{\lambda_m} = \frac{\sqrt{\frac{qV}{2m}}}{c}$$

For electron $\frac{q}{m} = 1.8 \times 10^{11}$ C/kg (given). Substituting the values the desired ratio is

$$\frac{\lambda_b}{\lambda_m} = \frac{\sqrt{\frac{1.8 \times 10^{11} \times 10 \times 10^3}{2}}}{3 \times 10^8} = 0.1$$ **Ans.**

MODULE 3 Exercise

Fill in the Blanks

1. A potential difference of 20 kV is applied across an X-ray tube. The minimum wavelength of X-rays generated is .... Å. **(1996 JEE)**

2. The wavelength of K_α, X-rays produced by an X-ray tube is 0.76 Å. The atomic number of the anode material of the tube is .... **(1996 JEE)**

3. In an X-ray tube, electrons accelerated through a potential difference of 15, 000 V strike a copper target. The speed of the emitted X-ray inside the tube is .... m/s. **(1992 JEE)**

4. The wavelength of the characteristic X-ray K_α line emitted by a hydrogen like element is 0.32 Å. The wavelength of the K_β line emitted by the same element will be .... **(1990 JEE)**

5. When the number of electrons striking the anode of an X-ray tube is increased the .... of the emitted X-rays increases, while when the speeds of the electrons striking the anode are increased the cut-off wavelength of the emitted X-rays .... **(1986 JEE)**

6. To produce characteristic X-rays using a tungsten target in an X-ray generator, the accelerating voltage should be greater than ...... V and the energy of the characteristic radiation is ...... eV. (The binding energy of the innermost electron in tungsten is 40 keV). **(1983 JEE)**

Assertion and Reason

See directions on page 11.

7. **Assertion :** If the accelerating potential in an X-ray tube is increased, the wavelengths of the characteristic X-rays do not change **(2007 JEE)**

   Reason : When an electron beam strikes the target in an X-ray tube, part of the kinetic energy is converted into X-ray energy.

8. **Assertion :** X-rays cannot be deflected by electric or magnetic fields.

   Reason : These are electromagnetic waves.

9. **Assertion :** X-rays cannot be obtained in the emission spectrum of hydrogen atom.

   Reason : Maximum energy of photons emitted from hydrogen spectrum is 13.6 eV.

Single Correct Option

10. An X-ray tube is operated at 18 kV. The maximum velocity of electron striking the target is
    (a) 8×10^7 m/s (b) 6×10^7 m/s
    (c) 5×10^7 m/s (d) None of these

11. In order that the short wavelength limit of the continuous X-ray spectrum be 1 Å, the potential difference through which an electron must be accelerated is
    (a) 124 kV (b) 1.24 kV (c) 12.4 kV (d) 1240 kV

12. The momentum of an X-ray photon with $\lambda = 0.5$ Å is
    (a) 13.26×10^{-26} kg-m/s
    (b) 1.326×10^{-26} kg-m/s
    (c) 13.26×10^{-24} kg-m/s
    (d) 13.26×10^{-22} kg-m/s

13. The operating potential in an X-ray tube is increased by 2%. The percentage change in the cut off wavelength is
    (a) 1% increase (b) 2% increase
    (c) 2% decrease (d) 1% decrease

14. The minimum wavelength of X-rays produced by electrons accelerated by a potential difference of V volt is equal to
    (a) $\frac{eV}{hc}$ (b) $\frac{eh}{cV}$ (c) $\frac{hc}{eV}$ (d) $\frac{cV}{eh}$

15. The wavelength of K_α, X-rays for lead isotopes Pb^{208}, Pb^{206}, Pb^{204} are λ_1, λ_2 and λ_3 respectively. Then,
    (a) $\lambda_1 = \lambda_2 > \lambda_3$ (b) $\lambda_1 > \lambda_2 > \lambda_3$
    (c) $\lambda_1 < \lambda_2 < \lambda_3$ (d) $\lambda_2 = \sqrt{\lambda_1 \lambda_3}$

16. Moseley's law for characteristic X-rays is $\sqrt{\nu} = a(Z - b)$. In this,
    (a) both a and b are independent of the material
    (b) a is independent but b depends on the material
    (c) b is independent but a depends on the material
    (d) both a and b depends on the material

Subjective Questions

17. For a given element the wavelength of the K_α-line is 0.71 nm and of the K_β-line it is 0.63 nm. Use this information to find wavelength of the L_α-line.

18. The energy of the $n = 2$ state in a given element is $E_2 = -2870$ eV. Given that the wavelengths of the K_α and K_β-lines are 0.71 nm and 0.63 nm respectively, determine the energies E_1 and E_3.

19. X-rays are produced in an X-ray tube by electrons accelerated through an electric potential difference of 50.0 kV. An electron makes three collisions in the target coming to rest and loses half its remaining kinetic energy in each of the first two collisions. Determine the wavelength of the resulting photons. (Neglecting the recoil of the heavy target atoms).

20. A voltage applied to an X-ray tube being increased $\eta = 1.5$ times, the short wave limit of an X-ray continuous spectrum shifts by $\Delta\lambda = 26$ pm. Find the initial voltage applied to the tube.

21. The electric current in an X-ray tube operating at 40 kV is 10 mA. Assume that on an average 1% of the total kinetic energy of the electrons hitting the target are converted into X-rays.
(a) What is the total power emitted as X-rays and
(b) How much heat is produced in the target every second?

Answers

1. (0.62) **2.** $Z = 41$ **3.** 3×10^8 **4.** 0.27 Å **5.** intensity, decrease **6.** 30×10^3, 30 k **7.** (b) **8.** (a)
9. (a) **10.** (a) **11.** (c) **12.** (c) **13.** (c) **14.** (c) **15.** (d) **16.** (a) **17.** 5.59 nm
18. $E_1 = -4613$ eV, $E_3 = -2649$ eV **19.** 49.5 pm, 99.0 pm **20.** 15865 V **21.** (a) 4 W (b) 396 J/s

See hints on pages 321-323.

MODULE 4

Photoelectric Effect

Emission of Electrons

At room temperature the free electrons move randomly within the conductor, but they don't leave the surface of the conductor due to attraction of positive charges. Some external energy is required to emit electrons from a metal surface. Minimum energy is required to emit the electrons which are just inside the surface of the conductor. This minimum energy is called the **work-function** (denoted by W) of the conductor. Work-function is the property of the metallic surface.

The energy required to liberate an electron from metal surface may arise from various sources such as heat, light, electric field etc. Depending on the nature of source of energy, the following methods are possible for emission of electrons:

(i) **Thermionic emission** The energy to the free electrons can be given by heating the metal. The electrons so emitted are known as **thermions**.

(ii) **Field emission** When a conductor is put under strong electric field, the free electrons on it experience an electric force in the opposite direction of field. Beyond a certain limit, electrons start coming out of the metal surface. Emission of electrons from a metal surface by this method is called the field emission.

(iii) **Secondary emission** Emission of electrons from a metal surface by the bombardment of high speed electrons or other particles is known as secondary emission.

(iv) **Photoelectric emission** Emission of free electrons from a metal surface by falling light (or any other electromagnetic wave which has an energy greater than the work-function of the metal) is called photoelectric emission. The electrons so emitted are called **photoelectrons**.

Photoelectric Effect

When light of an appropriate frequency (or correspondingly of an appropriate wavelength) is incident on a metallic surface, electrons are liberated from the surface. This observation is known as **photoelectric effect**. Photoelectric effect was first observed in 1887 by Hertz. For photoemission to take place, energy of incident light photons should be greater than or equal to the work-function of the metal.

or $$E \geq W \qquad \text{...(i)}$$

$\therefore$ $$hf \geq W \quad \text{or} \quad f \geq \frac{W}{h}$$

Here, $\frac{W}{h}$ is the minimum frequency required for the emission of electrons. This is known as threshold frequency f_0.

Thus, $$f_0 = \frac{W}{h} \quad \text{(threshold frequency)} \qquad \text{...(ii)}$$

Further, Eq. (i) can be written as

$$\frac{hc}{\lambda} \geq W \quad \text{or} \quad \lambda \leq \frac{hc}{W}$$

Here, $\frac{hc}{W}$ is the largest wavelength beyond which photoemission does not take place. This is called the threshold wavelength λ_0.

Thus, $$\lambda_0 = \frac{hc}{W} \quad \text{(threshold wavelength)} \qquad \text{...(iii)}$$

Hence, for the photoemission to take place either of the following conditions must be satisfied.

$$E \geq W \quad \text{or} \quad f \geq f_0 \quad \text{or} \quad \lambda \leq \lambda_0 \qquad \text{...(iv)}$$

Stopping Potential and Maximum Kinetic Energy of Photoelectrons

When the frequency f of the incident light is greater than the threshold frequency, some electrons are emitted from the metal with substantial initial speeds. Suppose E is the energy of light incident on a metal surface and W $(<E)$ the work-function of metal. As minimum energy is required to extract electrons from the surface, they will have the maximum kinetic energy which is $E - W$.

Thus, $$K_{max} = E - W \qquad \text{...(v)}$$

This value K_{max} can experimentally be found by keeping the metal plate P (from which electrons are emitting) at higher potential relative to an another plate Q placed in front of P. Some electrons after emitting from plate P, reach the plate Q despite the fact that Q is at lower potential and it is repelling the electrons from reaching in itself. This is because the electrons emitted from plate P possess some kinetic energy and due to this energy they reach the plate Q and current i flows in the circuit in the direction shown in figure.

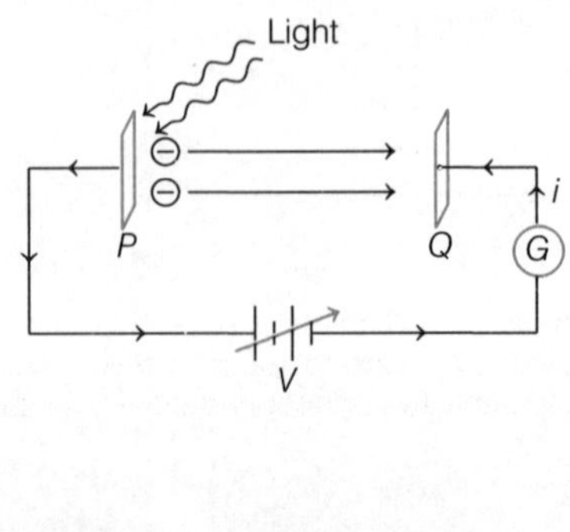

As the potential V is increased, the force of repulsion to the electrons gets increased and less number of electrons reach the plate Q and current in the circuit gets decreased. At a certain value V_0 electrons having maximum kinetic energy (K_{max}) also get stopped and current in the circuit becomes zero. This is called the **stopping potential**.

As an electron moves from P to Q, the potential decreases by V_0 and negative work $-eV_0$ is done on the (negatively charged) electron, the most energetic electron leaves plate P with kinetic energy $K_{max} = \frac{1}{2} mv_{max}^2$ and has zero kinetic energy at Q. Using the work energy theorem, we have

$$W_{ext} = -eV_0 = \Delta K = 0 - K_{max}$$

or

$$K_{max} = \frac{1}{2} mv_{max}^2 = eV_0 = E - W = hf - hf_0 = \frac{hc}{\lambda} - \frac{hc}{\lambda_0} \quad \text{...(vi)}$$

Photoelectric Current

Figure shows an apparatus used to study the variation of photocurrent i with the intensity and frequency of light falling on metal plate P. Photoelectrons are emitted from plate P which are being attracted by the positive plate Q and a photoelectric current i flows in the circuit, which can be measured by the galvanometer G.

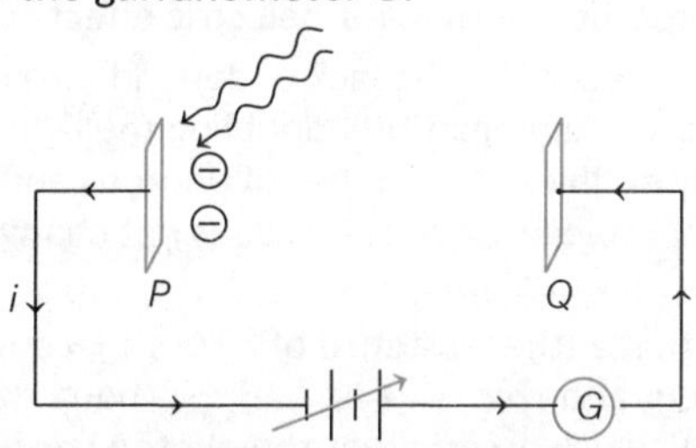

Figure (a) shows graphs of photocurrent as a function of potential difference V_{QP} for light of constant frequency and two different intensities. When V_{QP} is sufficiently large and positive the current becomes constant, showing that all the emitted electrons are being collected by the anode plate Q. The stopping potential difference $-V_0$ needed to reduce the current to zero is shown. If the intensity of light is increased, (or we can say the number of photons incident per unit area per unit time is increased) while its frequency is kept the same, the current becomes constant at a higher value, showing that more electrons are being emitted per unit time. But the stopping potential is found to be the same.

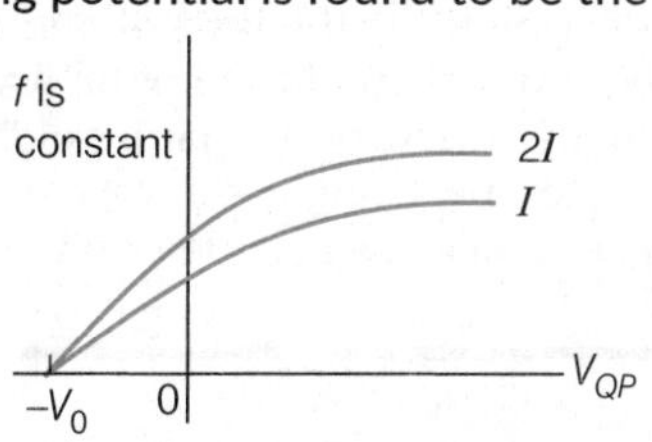

(a)

Photocurrent i as a function of the potential V_{QP} of the anode with respect to the cathode for a constant light frequency f, the stopping potential V_0 is independent of the light intensity I.

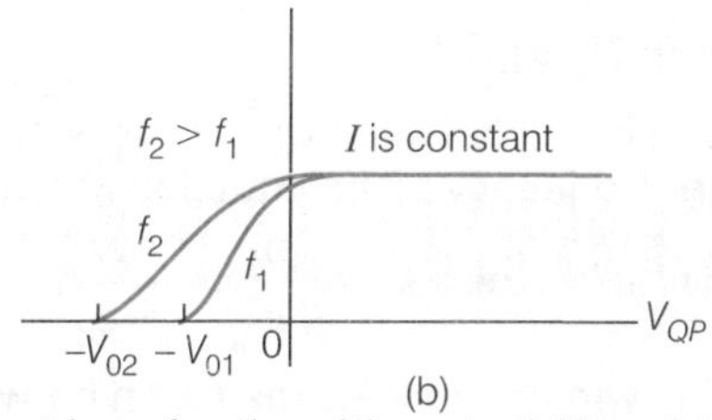

(b)

Photocurrent i as a function of the potential V_{QP} of the anode with respect to a cathode for two different light frequencies f_1 and f_2 with the same number of photons incident per unit area per unit time. The stopping potential V_0 (and therefore the maximum kinetic energy of the photoelectrons) increases with frequency.

Figure (b) shows current as a function of potential difference for two different frequencies with the same number of photons incident per unit area per unit time in each case. We see that when the frequency of the incident monochromatic light is increased, the stopping potential V_0 gets increased. Of course, V_0 turn out to be a linear function of the frequency f.

Graph between K_{max} and f

Let us plot a graph between maximum kinetic energy K_{max} of photoelectrons and frequency f of incident light. The equation between K_{max} and f is

$$K_{max} = hf - W$$

Comparing it with $y = mx + c$, the graph between K_{max} and f is a straight line with positive slope and negative intercept.

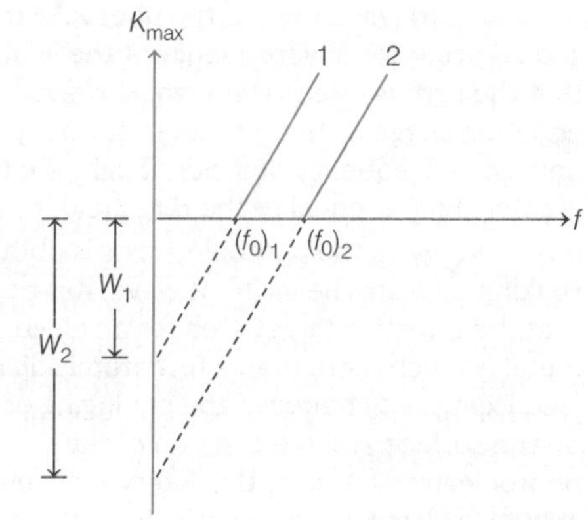

From the graph, we can note the following points

(i) $K_{max} = 0$ at $f = f_0$

(ii) Slope of the straight line is h, a universal constant, i.e. if graph is plotted for two different metals 1 and 2, slope of both the lines is same.

(iii) The negative intercept of the line is W, the work-function which is characteristic of a metal, i.e. intercepts for two different metals will be different. Further,

$$W_2 > W_1$$

$\therefore$ $(f_0)_2 > (f_0)_1$ [as $W = hf_0$]

Here, f_0 = threshold frequency

Graph between V_0 and f

Let us now plot a graph between the stopping potential V_0 and the incident frequency f. The equation between them is

$$eV_0 = hf - W \quad \text{or} \quad V_0 = \left(\frac{h}{e}\right)f - \left(\frac{W}{e}\right)$$

Again comparing with $y = mx + c$, the graph between V_0 and f is a straight line with positive slope $\frac{h}{e}$ (a universal constant) and negative intercept $\frac{W}{e}$ (which depends on the metal). The corresponding graph is shown in figure.

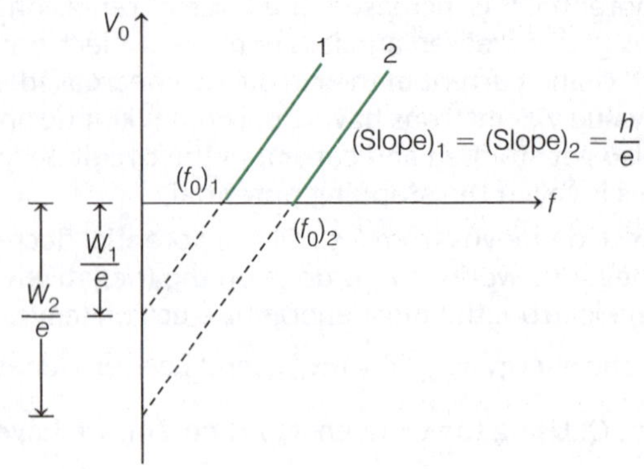

Important POINTS

- The major features of the photoelectric effect could not be explained by the wave theory of light which were later explained by Einstein's photon theory.
  - (i) Wave theory suggests that the kinetic energy of the photoelectrons should increase with the increase in intensity of light (here intensity means number of photons incident per unit area per unit time). However equation, $K_{max} = eV_0$ suggests that it is independent of the intensity of light.
  - (ii) According to wave theory, the photoelectric effect should occur for any frequency of the light, provided that the light is intense enough. However, the above equation suggests that photoemission is possible only when frequency of incident light is either greater than or equal to the threshold frequency f_0.
  - (iii) If the energy to the photoelectrons is obtained by soaking up from the incident wave, it is not likely that the effective target area for an electron in the metal is much more than a few atomic diameters. (see Example 1) between the impinging of the light on the surface and the ejection of the photoelectrons. During this interval the electron should be "soaking up" energy from the beam until it had accumulated enough energy to escape. However, no detectable time lag has ever been measured.
- **Einstein's photon theory** Einstein succeeded in explaining the photoelectric effect by making a remarkable assumption, that the energy in a light beam travels through space in concentrated bundles, called photons. The energy E of a single photon is given by

$$E = hf$$

Applying the photon concept to the photoelectric effect, Einstein wrote

$$hf = W + K_{max} \qquad \text{(already discussed)}$$

Consider how Einstein's photon hypothesis meets the three objections raised against the wave theory interpretation of the photoelectric effect.

As for objection 1 (the lack of dependence of K_{max} on the intensity of illumination), doubling the light intensity merely doubles the number of photons and thus doubles the photoelectric current, it does not change the energy of the individual photons

Objection 2 (the existence of a cutoff frequency) follows from equation $hf = W + K_{max}$. If K_{max} equals zero, We have $hf_0 = W$ which asserts that the photon has just enough energy to eject the photoelectrons and none extra to appear as kinetic energy. The quantity W is called the work-function of the substance. If f is reduced below f_0, the individual photons, no matter how many of them there are (that is, no matter how intense the illumination), will not have enough energy to eject photo electrons.

Objection 3 (the absence of a time lag) follows from the photon theory because the required energy is supplied in a concentrated bundle. It is not spread uniformly over a large area, as in the wave theory. Although, the photon hypothesis certainly fits the facts of photoelectricity, it seems to be in direct conflict with the wave theory of light. Our modern view of the nature of light is that it has a dual character, behaving like a wave under some circumstances and like a particle or photon under others.

Example 1 A metal plate is placed 5 m from a monochromatic light source whose power output is 10^{-3} W. Consider that the metal may collect its energy from a circular area of radius 10^{-9} m. The energy required to remove an electron through the metal surface is about 5.0 eV. Assuming light to be a wave, how long would it take for such a 'target' to soak up this much energy from such a light source.

Sol. The target area is $S_1 = \pi(10^{-9})^2 = \pi \times 10^{-18}$ m^2. The area of a 5 m sphere centered on the light source is, $S_2 = 4\pi(5)^2 = 100\,\pi\,\text{m}^2$. Thus, if the light source radiates uniformly in all directions the rate P at which energy falls on the target is given by

$$P = (10^{-3}\text{ watt})\left(\frac{S_1}{S_2}\right) = (10^{-3})\left(\frac{\pi \times 10^{-18}}{100 \times \pi}\right) = 10^{-23}\text{ J/s}$$

Assuming that all power is absorbed, the required time is

$$t = \frac{5 \times 1.6 \times 10^{-19}\text{ J}}{10^{-23}\text{ J/s}} = 8.0 \times 10^4\text{ s} \approx 22.22\text{ h}$$ **Ans.**

Example 2 The photoelectric work-function of potassium is 2.3 eV. If light having a wavelength of 2800 Å falls on potassium, find

(a) the kinetic energy in electron volts of the most energetic electrons ejected.

(b) the stopping potential in volts

Sol. Given, $W = 2.3$ eV, $\lambda = 2800$ Å

$$\therefore \quad E\text{ (in eV)} = \frac{12375}{\lambda\text{ (in Å)}} = \frac{12375}{2800} = 4.4\text{ eV}$$

(a) $K_{max} = E - W = (4.4 - 2.3)\text{ eV} = 2.1$ eV **Ans.**

(b) $K_{max} = eV_0$

$\therefore \quad 2.1\text{ eV} = eV_0 \quad \text{or} \quad V_0 = 2.1$ volt **Ans.**

Example 3 When a beam of 10.6 eV photons of intensity 2.0 W/m^2 falls on a platinum surface of area 1.0×10^{-4} m^2 and work-function 5.6 eV, 0.53% of the incident photons eject photoelectrons. Find the number of photoelectrons emitted per second and their minimum and maximum energies (in eV). Take 1 eV $= 1.6 \times 10^{-19}$ J.

Sol. Number of photoelectrons emitted per second

$$= \frac{\text{(Intensity)(Area)}}{\text{(Energy of each photon)}} \times \frac{0.53}{100}$$

$$= \frac{(2.0)(1.0 \times 10^{-4})}{(10.6 \times 1.6 \times 10^{-19})} \times \frac{0.53}{100}$$

$$= 6.25 \times 10^{11} \approx 22.22\text{ h}$$ **Ans.**

Minimum kinetic energy of photoelectrons, $K_{min} = 0$ and maximum kinetic energy is,

$$K_{max} = E - W = (10.6 - 5.6)\text{ eV} = 5.0\text{ eV}$$ **Ans.**

Example 4 Maximum kinetic energy of photoelectrons from a metal surface is K_0 when wavelength of incident light is λ. If wavelength is decreased to $\lambda/2$, the maximum kinetic energy of photoelectrons becomes

(a) $= 2K_0$ (b) $> 2K_0$ (c) $< 2K_0$

Sol. Using the equation,

$$K_{max} = E - W, \text{ we have}$$

$$K_0 = \frac{hc}{\lambda} - W \quad \text{...(i)}$$

with wavelength $\frac{\lambda}{2}$, suppose the maximum kinetic energy is K_0', then

$$K_0' = \frac{hc}{\lambda/2} - W = 2\frac{hc}{\lambda} - W$$

$$= 2\left(\frac{hc}{\lambda} - W\right) + W$$

but $\frac{hc}{\lambda} - W$ is K_0. Therefore,

$$K_0' = 2K_0 + W$$

or $$K_0' > 2K_0$$

$\therefore$ The correct option is (b). **Ans.**

Example 5 Intensity and frequency of incident light both are doubled. Then, what is the effect on stopping potential and saturation current.

Sol. By increasing the frequency of incident light energy of incident photons will increase. So, maximum kinetic energy of photoelectrons will also increase. Hence, stopping potential will increase.

Further, by doubling the frequency of incident light energy of each photon will be doubled. So, intensity itself becomes two times without increasing number of photons incident per unit area per unit time. Therefore, saturation current will remain unchanged.

Example 6 When a monochromatic point source of light is at a distance of 0.2 m from a photoelectric cell, the cut off voltage and the saturation current are respectively 0.6 V and 18.0 mA. If the same source is placed 0.6 m away from the photoelectric cell, then **(1992 JEE)**

(a) the stopping potential will be 0.2 V

(b) the stopping potential will be 0.6 V

(c) the saturation current will be 6.0 mA

(d) the saturation current will be 2.0 mA

Sol. (b) Stopping potential depends on two factors - one the energy of incident photons and work-function of the metal. By increasing the distance of source from the cell, neither of the two change. Therefore, stopping potential remains the same.

(d) Saturation current is directly proportional to the number of photons incident per unit area per unit time. For a point source, this factor $I \propto 1/r^2$

When distance is increased from 0.2 m to 0.6 m (three times), this factor and hence the saturation current will decrease 9 times, i.e. the saturation current will be reduced to 2.0 mA.

$\therefore$ The correct options are (b) and (d).

Note *5200 Å lies in visible range.*

Example 7 The threshold wavelength for photoelectric emission from a material is 5200 Å. Photoelectrons will be emitted when this material is illuminated with monochromatic radiation from a **(1982 JEE)**

(a) 50 W infrared lamp
(b) 1 W infrared lamp
(c) 50 W ultraviolet lamp
(d) 1 W ultraviolet lamp

Sol. For photoemission to take place, wavelength of incident light should be less than the threshold wavelength. Wavelength of ultraviolet light < 5200 Å while that of infrared radiation > 5200 Å.

$\therefore$ The correct options are (c) and (d).

Note *5200 Å lies in visible range.*

INTRODUCTORY Exercise

1. A metal surface is illuminated by light of two different wavelengths 248 nm and 310 nm. The maximum speeds of the photoelectrons corresponding to these wavelengths are u_1 and u_2, respectively. If the ratio $u_1 : u_2 = 2 : 1$ and $hc = 1240$ eV nm, the work-function of the metal is nearly **(2014 JEE)**
(a) 3.7 eV (b) 3.2 eV (c) 2.8 eV (d) 2.5 eV

2. The figure shows the variation of photocurrent with anode potential for a photosensitive surface for three different radiations. Let I_a, I_b and I_c be the intensities and f_a, f_b and f_c be the frequencies for the curves a, b and c, respectively **(2004 JEE)**

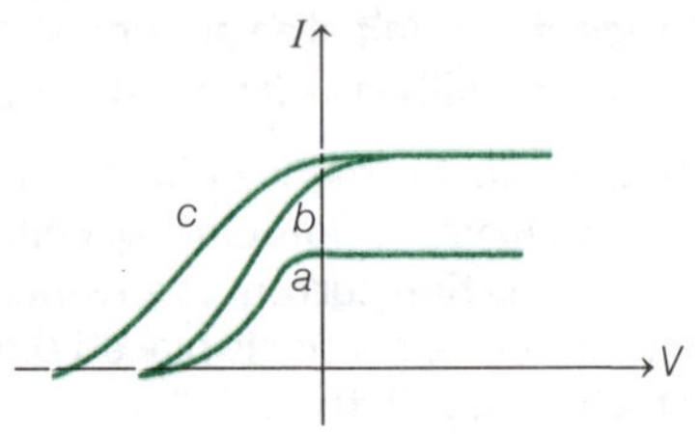

(a) $f_a = f_b$ and $I_a \neq I_b$ (b) $f_a = f_c$ and $I_a = I_c$
(c) $f_a = f_b$ and $I_a = I_b$ (d) $f_b = f_c$ and $I_b = I_c$

Note *Here intensity means number of photons incident per unit area per unit time.*

3. The work-function of a substance is 4.0 eV. The longest wavelength of light that can cause photoelectron emission from this substance is approximately **(1998 JEE)**
(a) 540 nm (b) 400 nm
(c) 310 nm (d) 220 nm

4. The maximum kinetic energy of photoelectrons emitted from a surface when photons of energy 6 eV fall on it is 4 eV. The stopping potential in volt is **(1997 JEE)**
(a) 2 (b) 4 (c) 6 (d) 10

5. Photoelectric effect supports quantum nature of light because **(1987 JEE)**
(a) there is a minimum frequency of light below which no photoelectrons are emitted
(b) the maximum kinetic energy of photoelectrons depends only on the frequency of light and not on its intensity
(c) even when the metal surface is faintly illuminated, the photoelectrons leave the surface immediately
(d) electric charge of the photoelectrons is quantised

6. Light of wavelength 2000 Å is incident on a metal surface of work-function 3.0 eV. Find the minimum and maximum kinetic energy of the photoelectrons.

7. Is it correct to say that K_{max} is proportional to f ? If not, what would a correct statement of the relationship between K_{max} and f ?

8. When a metal is illuminated with light of frequency f, the maximum kinetic energy of the photoelectrons is 1.2 eV. When the frequency is increased by 50%, the maximum kinetic energy increases to 4.2 eV. What is the threshold frequency for this metal?

Answers

1. (a) 2. (a) 3. (c) 4. (b)
5. (a) 6. Zero, 3.19 eV 7. $K_{max} \propto (f - f_0)$
8. 1.16×10^{15} Hz

See hints on page 323.

Miscellaneous Examples

Ex. 1 Stopping potential of 24, 100, 110 and 115 kV are measured for photoelectrons emitted from a certain element when it is radiated with monochromatic X-ray. If this element is used as a target in an X-ray tube, what will be the wavelength of K_α - line?

Sol. Stopping potentials are 24, 100, 110 and 115 kV, i.e. if the electrons are emitted from conduction band, maximum kinetic energy of photoelectrons would be 115×10^3 eV. If they are emitted from next inner shell, maximum kinetic energy of photoelectrons would be 110×10^3 eV and so on.

For photoelectrons of L- shell it would be 100×10^3 eV and for K-shell it is 24×10^3 eV. Therefore, difference between energy of L-shell and K-shell is

$$\Delta E = E_L - E_K$$
$$= (100 - 24) \times 10^3 \text{ eV}$$
$$= 76 \times 10^3 \text{ eV}$$

$\therefore$ Wavelength of K_α-line (transition of electron from L-shell to K-shell) is,

$$\lambda_{K_\alpha} \text{ (in Å)} = \frac{12375}{\Delta E \text{ (in eV)}} = \frac{12375}{76 \times 10^3} = 0.163 \text{ Å}$$ **Ans.**

Ex. 2 A monochromatic light source of frequency f illuminates a metallic surface and ejects photoelectrons. The photoelectrons having maximum energy are just able to ionize the hydrogen atoms in ground state. When the whole experiment is repeated with an incident radiation of frequency $\frac{5}{6}f$, the photoelectrons so emitted are able to excite the hydrogen atom beam which then emits a radiation of wavelength 1215 Å.

(a) What is the frequency of radiation?

(b) Find the work-function of the metal.

Sol. (a) Using Einstein's equation of photoelectric effect,

$$K_{max} = hf - W$$

Here, $K_{max} = 13.6$ eV

$\therefore$ $hf - W = 13.6$ eV ...(i)

Further, $h\left(\frac{5}{6}f\right) - W = \frac{12375}{1215} = 10.2$ eV ...(ii)

Solving Eqs. (i) and (ii), we have

$$\frac{hf}{6} = 3.4 \text{ eV or } f = \frac{(6)(3.4)(1.6 \times 10^{-19})}{(6.63 \times 10^{-34})}$$

$$= 4.92 \times 10^{15} \text{ Hz}$$ **Ans.**

(b) $W = hf - 13.6$ [from Eq. (i)]

$= 6(3.4) - 13.6 = 6.8$ eV **Ans.**

Ex. 3 The graph between $1/\lambda$ and stopping potential (V) of three metals having work-functions ϕ_1, ϕ_2 and ϕ_3 in an experiment of photoelectric effect is plotted as shown in the figure. Which of the following statement(s) is/are correct? (Here, λ is the wavelength of the incident ray). **(2006 JEE)**

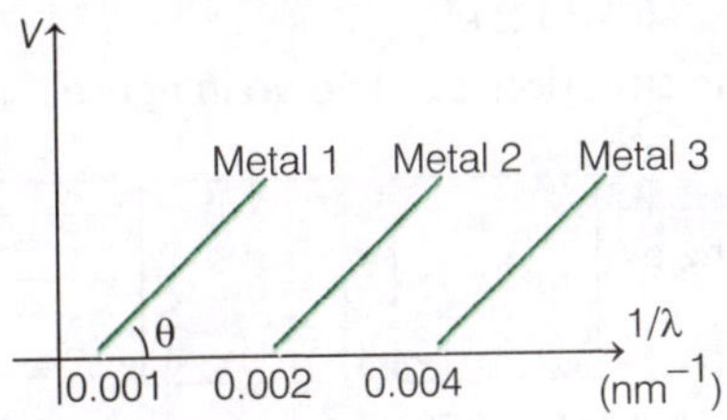

(a) Ratio of work-functions $\phi_1 : \phi_2 : \phi_3 = 1:2:4$

(b) Ratio of work-functions $\phi_1 : \phi_2 : \phi_3 = 4:2:1$

(c) $\tan\theta$ is directly proportional to hc/e, where h is Planck constant and c is the speed of light

(d) The violet colour light can eject photoelectrons from metals 2 and 3

Sol. From the relation,

$$eV = \frac{hc}{\lambda} - \phi \quad \text{or} \quad V = \left(\frac{hc}{e}\right)\left(\frac{1}{\lambda}\right) - \frac{\phi}{e}$$

This is equation of straight line. Slope is $\tan\theta = \frac{hc}{e}$.

Further $V = 0$ at $\phi = \frac{hc}{\lambda}$

$$\therefore \quad \phi_1 : \phi_2 : \phi_3 = \frac{hc}{\lambda_{01}} : \frac{hc}{\lambda_{02}} : \frac{hc}{\lambda_{03}}$$

$$= \frac{1}{\lambda_{01}} : \frac{1}{\lambda_{02}} : \frac{1}{\lambda_{03}}$$

$$= 0.001 : 0.002 : 0.004 = 1:2:4$$

$$\frac{1}{\lambda_{01}} = 0.001 \text{ nm}^{-1} \text{ or } \lambda_{01} = 10000 \text{ Å}$$

$$\frac{1}{\lambda_{02}} = 0.002 \text{ nm}^{-1} \text{ or } \lambda_{02} = 5000 \text{ Å}$$

$$\frac{1}{\lambda_{03}} = 0.004 \text{ nm}^{-1} \text{ or } \lambda_{03} = 2500 \text{ Å}$$

Violet colour has wavelength 4000 Å.

So, violet colour can eject photoelectrons from metal 1 and metal 2.

$\therefore$ The correct options are (a) and (c).

Ex. 4 A beam of light has three wavelengths 4144 Å, 4972 Å and 6216 Å with a total intensity of 3.6×10^{-3} Wm^{-2} equally distributed amongst the three wavelengths. The beam falls normally on an area 1.0 cm^2 of a clean metallic surface of work-function 2.3 eV. Assume that there is no loss of light by reflection and that each energetically capable photon ejects one electron. Calculate the number of photoelectrons liberated in two seconds. **(1989 JEE)**

Sol. Energy of photon having wavelength 4144 Å,

$$E_1 = \frac{12375}{4144} \text{ eV} = 2.99 \text{ eV}$$

Similarly, $E_2 = \frac{12375}{4972}$ eV $= 2.49$ eV and

$$E_3 = \frac{12375}{6216} \text{ eV} = 1.99 \text{ eV}$$

Since, only E_1 and E_2 are greater than the work-function $W = 2.3$ eV, only first two wavelengths are capable for ejecting photoelectrons. Given intensity is equally distributed in all wavelengths. Therefore, intensity corresponding to each wavelength is

$$\frac{3.6 \times 10^{-3}}{3} = 1.2 \times 10^{-3} \text{ W/m}^2$$

Or energy incident per second in the given area ($A = 1.0$ cm^2 $= 10^{-4}$ m^2) is

$$P = 1.2 \times 10^{-3} \times 10^{-4} = 1.2 \times 10^{-7} \text{ J/s}$$

Let n_1 be the number of photons incident per unit time in the given area corresponding to first wavelength. Then,

$$n_1 = \frac{P}{E_1} = \frac{1.2 \times 10^{-7}}{2.99 \times 1.6 \times 10^{-19}} = 2.5 \times 10^{11}$$

Similarly, $n_2 = \frac{P}{E_2} = \frac{1.2 \times 10^{-7}}{2.49 \times 1.6 \times 10^{-19}} = 3.0 \times 10^{11}$

Since, each energetically capable photon ejects one electron, total number of photoelectrons liberated in 2s.

$$= 2(n_1 + n_2) = 2(2.5 + 3.0) \times 10^{11}$$

$$= 1.1 \times 10^{12}$$ **Ans.**

Ex. 5 Two metallic plates A and B each of area $5\times10^{-4}\,m^2$, are placed parallel to each other at a separation of 1 cm. Plate B carries a positive charge of 33.7×10^{-12} C. A monochromatic beam of light, with photons of energy 5 eV each, starts falling on plate A at $t=0$, so that 10^{16} photons fall on it per square metre per second. Assume that one photoelectron is emitted for every 10^6 incident photons. Also assume that all the emitted photoelectrons are collected by plate B and the work-function of plate A remains constant at the value 2 eV.

Determine **(2002 JEE)**

(a) the number of photoelectrons emitted upto $t=10$ s,

(b) the magnitude of the electric field between the plates A and B at $t=10$ s and

(c) the kinetic energy of the most energetic photoelectrons emitted at $t=10$ s when it reaches plate B.

Neglect the time taken by the photoelectron to reach plate B.

(Take, $\varepsilon_0=8.85\times10^{-12}\,C^2/N\text{-}m^2$).

Sol. Area of plates, $=5\times10^{-4}\,m^2$

Distance between the plates, $d=1\text{ cm}=10^{-2}$ m

(a) Number of photoelectrons emitted upto $t=10$ s are

$$n=\frac{(\text{number of photons falling on unit area in unit time})\times(\text{area}\times\text{time})}{10^6}$$

$$=\frac{1}{10^6}[(10)^{16}\times(5\times10^{-4})\times(10)]$$

$$=5.0\times10^7$$ **Ans.**

(b) At time $t=10$ s,

Charge on plate A,

$$q_A=+ne=(5.0\times10^7)(1.6\times10^{-19})$$
$$=8.0\times10^{-12}\text{ C}$$

and charge on plate B,

$$q_B=(33.7\times10^{-12}-8.0\times10^{-12})$$
$$=25.7\times10^{-12}\text{ C}$$

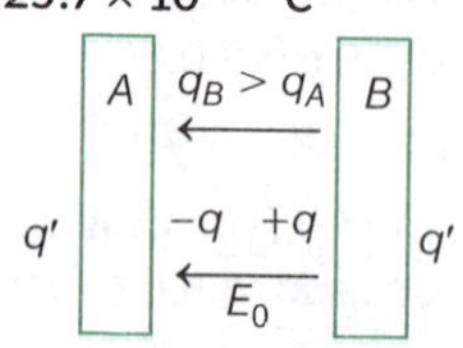

$$q'=\frac{q_{net}}{2}=\frac{q_A+q_B}{2}$$

$$q=q_B-q'=\frac{q_B-q_A}{2}$$

$\therefore$ Electric field between the plates, $E_0=\dfrac{\sigma}{\varepsilon_0}=\dfrac{q}{A\varepsilon_0}$

$$=\frac{(q_B-q_A)}{2A\varepsilon_0}$$

or $$E_0=\frac{(25.7-8.0)\times10^{-12}}{2\times(5\times10^{-4})(8.85\times10^{-12})}$$
$$=2\times10^3\text{ N/C}$$

(c) Energy of most energetic photoelectrons at plate A,

$$=E-W=(5-2)\text{ eV}=3\text{eV}$$

Increase in energy of photoelectrons

$$=(eE_0d)\text{ joule}=(E_0d)\text{ eV}$$
$$=(2\times10^3)(10^{-2})\text{ eV}=20\text{ eV}$$

Energy of photoelectrons at plate B

$$=(20+3)\text{ eV}=23\text{ eV}$$ **Ans.**

Ex. 6 Photoelectrons are emitted when 400 nm radiation is incident on a surface of work-function 1.9 eV. These photoelectrons pass through a region containing α-particles. A maximum energy electron combines with an α-particle to form a He^+ ion, emitting a single photon in this process. He^+ ions thus formed are in their fourth excited state. Find the energies in eV of the photons lying in the 2 to 4 eV range, that are likely to be emitted during and after the combination.

[Take, $h=4.14\times10^{-15}$ eV-s] **(1999 JEE)**

Sol. Given : work-function $W=1.9$ eV

Wavelength of incident light, $\lambda=400$ nm

$\therefore$ Energy of incident light, $E=\dfrac{hc}{\lambda}=3.1\text{ eV}$

(Substituting the values of h, c and λ)

Therefore, maximum kinetic energy of photoelectrons

$$K_{max}=E-W=(3.1-1.9)$$
$$=1.2\text{ eV}$$

Now, the situation is as shown in figure.

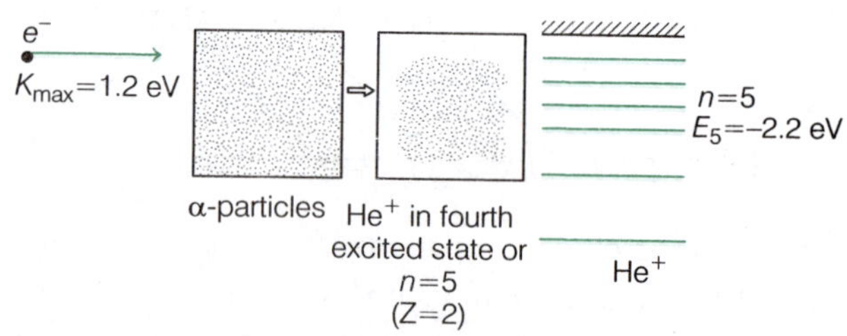

Energy of electron in 4th excited state of He^+ ($n=5$) will be

$$E_5=-13.6\frac{Z^2}{n^2}\text{ eV}$$

$$\Rightarrow\quad E_5=-(13.6)\frac{(2)^2}{(5)^2}=-2.2\text{ eV}$$

Therefore, energy released during the combination

$$=1.2-(-2.2)=3.4\text{ eV}$$

Similarly, energies in other energy states of He^+ will be

$$E_4=-13.6\frac{(2)^2}{(4)^2}=-3.4\text{ eV}$$

$$E_3 = -13.6 \frac{(2)^2}{(3)^2} = -6.04 \text{ eV}$$

$$E_2 = -13.6 \frac{(2)^2}{(2)^2} = -13.6 \text{ eV}$$

The possible transitions are

$$\Delta E_{5\to4} = E_5 - E_4 = 1.2 \text{ eV} < 2 \text{ eV}$$
$$E_{5\to3} = E_5 - E_3 = 3.84 \text{ eV}$$
$$\Delta E_{5\to2} = E_5 - E_2 = 11.4 \text{ eV} > 4 \text{ eV}$$
$$\Delta E_{4\to3} = E_4 - E_3 = 2.64 \text{ eV}$$
$$\Delta E_{4\to2} = E_4 - E_2 = 10.2 \text{ eV} > 4 \text{ eV}$$

Hence, the energy of emitted photons in the range of 2 eV and 4 eV are 3.4 eV during combination and 3.84 eV and 2.64 after combination.

Ex. 7 Light from a discharge tube containing hydrogen atoms falls on the surface of a piece of sodium. The kinetic energy of the fastest photoelectrons emitted from sodium is 0.73 eV. The work-function for sodium is 1.82 eV. **(1992 JEE)**

Find

(a) the energy of the photons causing the photoelectrons emission.

(b) the quantum numbers of the two levels involved in the emission of these photons.

(c) the change in the angular momentum of the electron in the hydrogen atom, in the above transition, and

(d) the recoil speed of the emitting atom assuming it to be at rest before the transition. (Ionization potential of hydrogen is 13.6 eV.)

Sol. (a) From Einstein's equation of photoelectric effect,

Energy of photons causing the photoelectric emission = Maximum kinetic energy of emitted electrons + work-function

or $E = K_{\max} + W = (0.73 + 1.82)$ eV

or $E = 2.55$ eV **Ans.**

(b) In case of a hydrogen atom,

$$E_1 = -13.6 \text{ eV}, E_2 = -3.4 \text{ eV}, E_3 = -1.5 \text{ eV}$$
$$E_4 = -0.85 \text{ eV}$$

Since, $E_4 - E_2 = 2.55$ eV

Therefore, quantum numbers of the two levels involved in the emission of these photons are 4 and 2 $(4 \to 2)$.

(c) Change in angular momentum in transition from 4 to 2 will be

$$\Delta L = L_2 - L_4$$
$$= 2\left(\frac{h}{2\pi}\right) - 4\left(\frac{h}{2\pi}\right)$$

or $$\Delta L = -\frac{h}{\pi}$$

(d) From conservation of linear momentum

|Momentum of hydrogen atom| = |Momentum of emitted photon|

or $mv = \frac{E}{c}$ (m = mass of hydrogen atom)

or $$v = \frac{E}{mc} = \frac{(2.55 \times 1.6 \times 10^{-19} \text{ J})}{(1.67 \times 10^{-27} \text{kg})(3.0 \times 10^8 \text{ m/s})}$$

$v = 0.814$ m/s **Ans.**

Ex. 8 In a photocell, the plates P and Q have a separation of 5 cm, which are connected through a galvanometer without any cell. Bichromatic light of wavelengths 4000 Å and 6000 Å are incident on plate Q whose work-function is 2.39 eV. If a uniform magnetic field B exists parallel to the plates, find the minimum value of B for which the galvanometer shows zero deflection.

Sol. Energy of photons corresponding to light of wavelength $\lambda_1 = 4000$ Å is

$$E_1 = \frac{12375}{4000} = 3.1 \text{ eV}$$

and that corresponding to $\lambda_2 = 6000$ Å is

$$E_2 = \frac{12375}{6000} = 2.06 \text{ eV}$$

As, $E_2 < W$

and $E_1 > W$ (W = work-function)

Photoelectric emission is possible with λ_1 only.

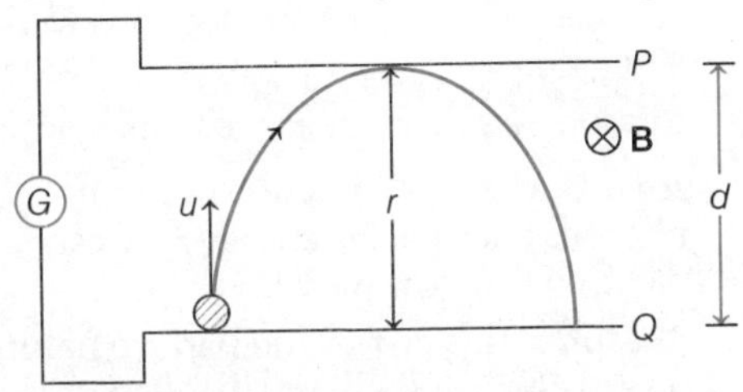

Photoelectrons experience magnetic force and move along a circular path. The galvanometer will indicate zero deflection if the photoelectrons just complete semicircular path before reaching the plate P.

Thus, $d = r = 5$ cm

$\therefore$ $r = 5 \text{ cm} = 0.05$ m

Further, $$r = \frac{mv}{Bq} = \frac{\sqrt{2Km}}{Bq}$$

$\therefore$ $$B_{\min} = \frac{\sqrt{2Km}}{rq}$$

Here, $K = K_{\max} = E_1 - W = (3.1 - 2.39) = 0.71$ eV

Substituting the values, we have

$$B_{\min} = \frac{\sqrt{2 \times 0.71 \times 1.6 \times 10^{-19} \times 9.109 \times 10^{-31}}}{(0.05)(1.6 \times 10^{-19})}$$
$$= 5.68 \times 10^{-5} \text{ T}$$ **Ans.**

MODULE 4 Exercise

Fill in the Blank

1. The maximum kinetic energy of electrons emitted in the photoelectric effect is linearly dependent on the .... of the incident radiation. **(1984 JEE)**

True/False

2. The kinetic energy of photoelectrons emitted by a photosensitive surface depends on the intensity of the incident radiation. **(1981 JEE)**

3. In a photoelectric emission process, the maximum energy of the photoelectrons increases with increasing intensity of the incident light. **(1986 JEE)**

Assertion and Reason

See directions on page 11.

4. **Assertion :** Photoelectric effect proves the particle nature of light.

   Reason : Photoemission starts as soon as light is incident on the metal surface, provided frequency of incident light is greater than or equal to the threshold frequency.

5. **Assertion :** If light continuously falls on a metal surface then emission of electrons will stop after some time.

   Reason : We cannot extract electrons from a metal.

6. **Assertion :** Work function of a metal is 8 eV. Two photons each having energy 5 eV cannot eject the electron from the metal.

   Reason : This proves the particle nature of light.

7. **Assertion :** We can increase the saturation current in photoelectric experiment without increasing the intensity of light.

   Reason : Intensity can be increased by increasing the frequency of incident photons.

Statement Type Questions

8. Given below are two statements

   Statement I Stopping potential in photoelectric effect does not depend on the power of the light source.

   Statement II For a given metal, the maximum kinetic energy of the photoelectron depends on the wavelength of the incident light. **(2023 Main)**

   In the light of above statements, choose the most appropriate answer from the options given below.
   (a) Both Statement I and Statement II are incorrect
   (b) Both Statement I and Statement II are correct
   (c) Statement I is correct but Statement II is incorrect
   (d) Statement I is incorrect but Statement II is correct

9. Given below are two statements.

   Statement I Out of microwaves, infrared rays and ultraviolet rays, ultraviolet rays are the most effective for the emission of electrons from a metallic surface.

   Statement II Above the threshold frequency, the maximum kinetic energy of photoelectrons is inversely proportional to the frequency of the incident light. **(2023 Main)**

Single Correct Option

10. Electromagnetic radiation of wavelength 3000 Å is incident on an isolated platinum surface of work-function 6.30 eV. Due to the radiation, the
    (a) sphere becomes positively charged
    (b) sphere becomes negatively charged
    (c) sphere remains neutral
    (d) maximum kinetic energy of the ejected photoelectrons would be 2.03 eV

11. Ultraviolet radiation of 6.2 eV falls on an aluminium surface (work-function = 4.2 eV). The kinetic energy in joule of the fastest electrons emitted is
    (a) 3.2×10^{-21} (b) 3.2×10^{-19}
    (c) 3.2×10^{-17} (d) 3.2×10^{-15}

12. Light of wavelength 330 nm falling on a piece of metal ejects electrons with sufficient energy with required voltage V_0 to prevent them from reaching a collector. In the same set up, light of wavelength 220 nm ejects electrons which require twice the voltage V_0 to stop them in reaching a collector. The numerical value of voltage V_0 is
    (a) $\frac{16}{15}$ V (b) $\frac{15}{16}$ V
    (c) $\frac{15}{8}$ V (d) $\frac{8}{15}$ V

13. Maximum kinetic energy of a photoelectron is E when the wavelength of incident light is λ. If energy becomes four times when wavelength is reduced to one-third, then work-function of the metal is
    (a) $\frac{3hc}{\lambda}$ (b) $\frac{hc}{3\lambda}$ (c) $\frac{hc}{\lambda}$ (d) $\frac{hc}{2\lambda}$

14. When a metallic surface is illuminated with monochromatic light of wavelength λ, the stopping potential is $5V_0$. When the same surface is illuminated with the light of wavelength 3λ, the stopping potential is V_0. Then, the work-function of the metallic surface is
    (a) $hc/6\lambda$ (b) $hc/5\lambda$
    (c) $hc/4\lambda$ (d) $2hc/4\lambda$

15. The threshold frequency for a certain photosensitive metal is ν_0. When it is illuminated by light of frequency $\nu = 2\nu_0$, the stopping potential for photoelectric current is V_0. What will be the stopping potential when the same metal is illuminated by light of frequency $\nu = 3\nu_0$?

(a) $1.5\,V_0$ (b) $2\,V_0$
(c) $2.5\,V_0$ (d) $3\,V_0$

16. Two identical photo-cathodes receive light of frequencies ν_1 and ν_2. If the velocities of the photoelectrons (of mass m) coming out are v_1 and v_2 respectively, then

(a) $v_1 - v_2 = \left[\frac{2h}{m}(\nu_1 - \nu_2)\right]^{1/2}$

(b) $v_1^2 - v_2^2 = \frac{2h}{m}(\nu_1 - \nu_2)$

(c) $v_1 + v_2 = \left[\frac{2h}{m}(\nu_1 - \nu_2)\right]^{1/2}$

(d) $v_1^2 + v_2^2 = \frac{2h}{m}(\nu_1 - \nu_2)$

17. The work functions of metals A and B are in the ratio $1:2$. If light of frequencies f and $2f$ are incident on metal surfaces of A and B respectively, the ratio of the maximum kinetic energies of photoelectron emitted is (f is greater than threshold frequency of A, $2f$ is greater than threshold frequency of B)

(a) $1:1$ (b) $1:2$ (c) $1:3$ (d) $1:4$

18. A convex lens of focal length 40 cm forms an image of an extended source of light on a photoelectric cell. A current I is produced. The lens is replaced by another convex lens having the same diameter but focal length 20 cm. The photoelectric current now is **(2024 Main)**

(a) I (b) $4I$ (c) $\frac{I}{2}$ (d) $2I$

19. Which figure shows the correct variation of applied potential difference V with photoelectric current I at two different intensities of light ($I_1 < I_2$) of same wavelengths? **(2024 Main)**

(a)
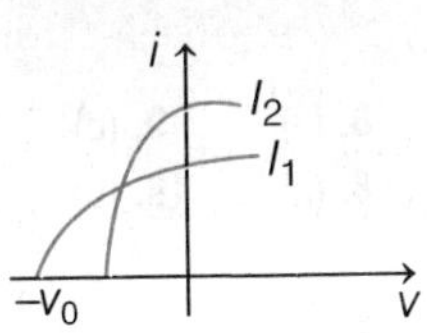

(b)
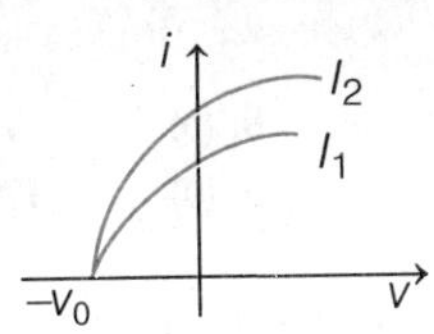

(c)
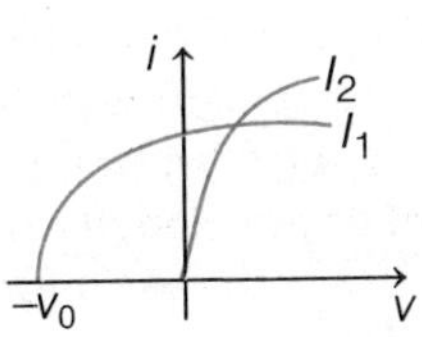

(d)
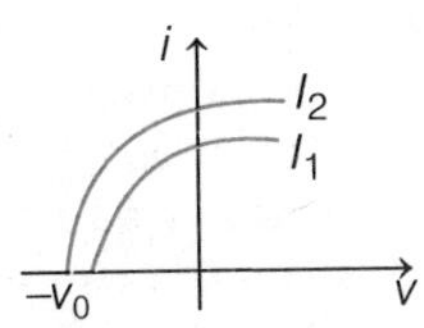

20. The difference between threshold wavelengths for two metal surfaces A and B having work function $\phi_A = 9$ eV and $\phi_B = 4.5$ eV in nm is
(Given, $hc = 1242$ eV-nm) **(2023 Main)**

(a) 264 (b) 276
(c) 540 (d) 138

21. A metallic surface is illuminated with radiation of wavelength λ, the stopping potential is V_0. If the same surface is illuminated with radiation of wavelength 2λ, the stopping potential becomes $V_0/4$. The threshold wavelength for this metallic surface will be **(2023 Main)**

(a) 3λ (b) $\frac{3}{2}\lambda$
(c) $\frac{\lambda}{4}$ (d) 4λ

22. The work functions of aluminium and Gold are 4.1 eV and 5.1 eV, respectively. The ratio of the slope of the stopping potential *versus* frequency plot for gold to that of aluminium is **(2023 Main)**

(a) 1.24 (b) 1.5 (c) 1 (d) 2

23. The variation of stopping potential (V_0) as a function of the frequency (ν) of the incident light for a metal is shown in figure. The work function of the surface is **(2023 Main)**

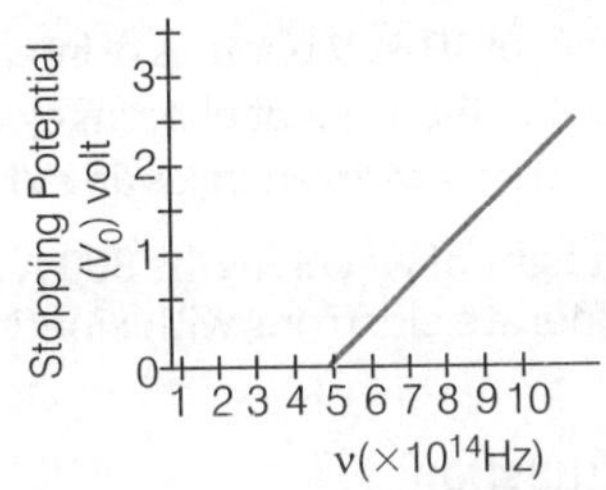

(a) 1.36 eV (b) 2.98 eV
(c) 18.6 eV (d) 2.07 eV

24. The threshold frequency of a metal is f_0. When the light of frequency $2f_0$ is incident on the metal plate, the maximum velocity of photoelectrons is v_1. When the frequency of incident radiation is increased to $5f_0$. The maximum velocity of photoelectrons emitted is v_2. The ratio of v_1 to v_2 is **(2023 Main)**

(a) $\frac{v_1}{v_2} = \frac{1}{4}$ (b) $\frac{v_1}{v_2} = \frac{1}{2}$ (c) $\frac{v_1}{v_2} = \frac{1}{8}$ (d) $\frac{v_1}{v_2} = \frac{1}{16}$

25. If the two metals A and B are exposed to radiation of wavelength 350 nm. The work functions of metals A and B are 4.8 eV and 2.2 eV. Then choose the correct option. **(2023 Main)**

(a) Both metals A and B will emit photoelectrons
(b) Metal B will not emit photoelectrons
(c) Both metals A and B will not emit photo electrons
(d) Metal A will not emit photoelectrons

Subjective Questions

26. 1.5 mW of 400 nm light is directed at a photoelectric cell. If 0.1% of the incident photons produce photoelectrons, find the current in the cell.

27. The stopping potential for the photoelectrons emitted from a metal surface of work-function 1.7eV is 10.4 V. Find the wavelength of the radiation used. Also, identify the energy levels in hydrogen atom, which will emit this wavelength.

28. What will be the maximum kinetic energy of the photoelectrons ejected from magnesium (for which the work-function $W = 3.7$ eV) when irradiated by ultraviolet light of frequency $1.5 \times 10^{15}\ s^{-1}$.

29. A metallic surface is irradiated with monochromatic light of variable wavelength. Above a wavelength of 5000 Å, no photoelectrons are emitted from the surface. With an unknown wavelength, stopping potential of 3 V is necessary to eliminate the photocurrent. Find the unknown wavelength.

30. A graph regarding photoelectric effect is shown between the maximum kinetic energy of electrons and the frequency of the incident light. On the basis of data as shown in the graph, calculate

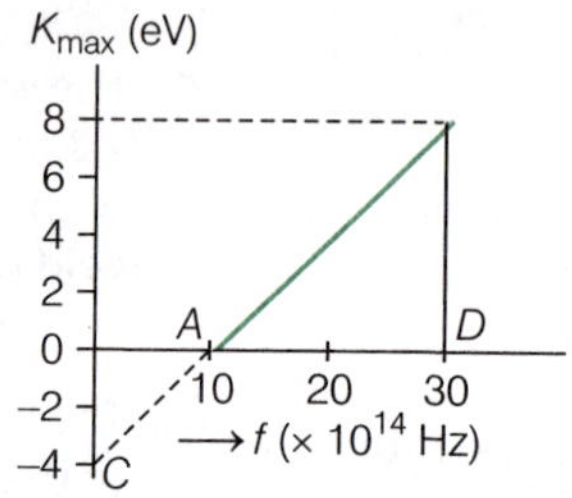

(a) threshold frequency (b) work-function (c) Planck constant

31. When a beam of 10.6 eV photons of intensity 2.0 W/m^2 falls on a platinum surface of area 1.0×10^{-4} m^2 and work function 5.6 eV. 0.53% of the incident photons eject photoelectrons. Find the number of photoelectrons emitted per second and their minimum and maximum energies (in eV). Take 1 eV $= 1.6 \times 10^{-19}$ J. **(2000 JEE)**

32. Ultraviolet light of wavelengths 800 Å and 700 Å when allowed to fall on hydrogen atoms in their ground state is found to liberate electrons with kinetic energy 1.8 eV and 4.0 eV respectively. Find the value of Planck's constant. **(1983 JEE)**

Integer Type Question

33. The work functions of silver and sodium are 4.6 and 2.3 eV, respectively. The ratio of the slope of the stopping potential *versus* frequency plot for silver to that of sodium is .... **(2013 Adv.)**

Answers

1. frequency **2.** False **3.** False **4.** (a) **5.** (c) **6.** (b) **7.** (a or b) **8.** (a) **9.** (c)
10. (c) **11.** (b) **12.** (c) **13.** (b) **14.** (a) **15.** (b) **16.** (b) **17.** (b) **18.** (a) **19.** (b)
20. (d) **21.** (a) **22.** (c) **23.** (d) **24.** (b) **25.** (d)
26. 0.48 μA **27.** 1022 Å, $n = 3$ to $n = 1$ **28.** 2.51 eV **29.** 2260 Å **30.** (a) 10^{15} Hz (b) 4eV (c) 6.4×10^{-34} J-s
31. $n = 6.25 \times 10^{11}$, 0, 0.5 eV **32.** $h \approx 6.6 \times 10^{-34}$ J-s **33.** (1)

See hints on pages 323-326.

Unit Exercise (Cumulative)

Level 1

Single Correct Option

1. The radius of an atom is approximately equal to
   (a) 10^{-8} cm (b) 10^{-4} cm
   (c) 10^{-10} cm (d) 10^{-6} cm

2. In Thomson's method of determining e/m of electrons
   (a) electric and magnetic fields are parallel to electron beam
   (b) electric and magnetic fields are perpendicular to each other and perpendicular to electron beam
   (c) magnetic field is parallel to the electron beam
   (d) electric field is parallel to the electron beam

3. In a sample of hydrogen like atoms all of which are in ground state, a photon beam containing photons of various energies is passed. In absorption spectrum, five dark lines are observed. The number of bright lines in the emission spectrum will be (assume that all transitions take place)
   (a) 21 (b) 10
   (c) 15 (d) None of these

4. The excitation energy of a hydrogen like ion to its first excited state is 40.8 eV. The energy needed to remove the electron from the ion in the ground state is
   (a) 54.4 eV (b) 62.6 eV
   (c) 72.6 eV (d) 58.6 eV

5. The longest wavelength of the Lyman series for hydrogen atom is the same as the wavelength of a certain line in the spectrum of He^+ when the electron makes a transition from $n \to 2$. The value of n is
   (a) 3 (b) 4 (c) 5 (d) 6

6. What should be the velocity of an electron so that its momentum becomes equal to that of a photon of wavelength 5200 Å?
   (a) 700 m/s
   (b) 1000 m/s
   (c) 1400 m/s
   (d) 2800 m/s

7. An electron with kinetic energy 5 eV is incident on a H-atom in its ground state. The collision
   (a) must be elastic
   (b) may be partially elastic
   (c) must be completely inelastic
   (d) may be completely inelastic

8. Find the binding energy of an electron in the ground state of a hydrogen like atom in whose spectrum the third Balmer line is equal to 108.5 nm.
   (a) 54.4 eV (b) 13.6 eV
   (c) 112.4 eV (d) None of these

9. An electron revolves round a nucleus of atomic number Z. If 32.4 eV of energy is required to excite an electron from the $n = 3$ state to $n = 4$ state, then the value of Z is
   (a) 5 (b) 6
   (c) 4 (d) 7

10. According to Moseley's law, the ratio of the slope of graph between $\sqrt{f}$ and Z for K_β and K_α is
    (a) $\sqrt{\frac{32}{27}}$ (b) $\sqrt{\frac{27}{32}}$ (c) $\sqrt{\frac{5}{36}}$ (d) $\sqrt{\frac{36}{5}}$

11. If E_n and L_n denote the total energy and the angular momentum of an electron in the nth orbit of Bohr atom, then
    (a) $E_n \propto L_n$ (b) $E_n \propto \frac{1}{L_n}$ (c) $E_n \propto L_n^2$ (d) $E_n \propto \frac{1}{L_n^2}$

12. The frequencies of K_α, K_β and L_α X-rays of a material are γ_1, γ_2 and γ_3 respectively. Which of the following relation holds good?
    (a) $\gamma_2 = \sqrt{\gamma_1 \gamma_3}$ (b) $\gamma_2 = \gamma_1 + \gamma_3$
    (c) $\gamma_2 = \frac{\gamma_1 + \gamma_3}{2}$ (d) $\gamma_3 = \sqrt{\gamma_1 \gamma_2}$

13. For the Bohr's first orbit of circumference $2\pi r$, the de-Broglie wavelength of revolving electron will be
    (a) $2\pi r$ (b) πr (c) $\frac{1}{2\pi r}$ (d) $\frac{1}{4\pi r}$

14. In a hypothetical Bohr hydrogen, the mass of the electron is doubled. The energy E_0 and radius r_0 of the first orbit will be (a_0 is the Bohr radius)
    (a) $E_0 = -27.2$ eV, $r_0 = a_0/2$
    (b) $E_0 = -27.2$ eV, $r_0 = a_0$
    (c) $E_0 = -13.6$ eV, $r_0 = a_0/2$
    (d) $E_0 = -13.6$ eV, $r_0 = a_0$

15. An electron makes a transition from orbit $n = 4$ to the orbit $n = 2$ of a hydrogen atom. The wave number of the emitted radiations (R = Rydberg's constant) will be
    (a) $\frac{16}{3R}$ (b) $\frac{2R}{16}$ (c) $\frac{3R}{16}$ (d) $\frac{4R}{16}$

16. The wavelength of radiation emitted is λ_0 when an electron jumps from the third to the second orbit of hydrogen atom. For the electron jump from the fourth to the second orbit of the hydrogen atom, the wavelength of radiation emitted will be

(a) $\frac{16}{25}\lambda_0$ (b) $\frac{20}{27}\lambda_0$ (c) $\frac{27}{20}\lambda_0$ (d) $\frac{25}{16}\lambda_0$

17. The electron in a hydrogen atom makes transition from M shell to L-shell. The ratio of magnitude of initial to final acceleration of the electron is

(a) 9 : 4 (b) 81 : 16 (c) 4 : 9 (d) 16 : 81

18. A beam of white light is incident normally on a plane surface absorbing 70% of the light and reflecting the rest. If the incident beam carries 20 W of power, the force exerted by it on the surface is

(a) 5.6×10^{-7} N (b) 2.6×10^{-7} N
(c) 1×10^{-7} N (d) None of these

19. An α-particle of 5 MeV energy strikes with a stationary nucleus of uranium at an scattering angle of 180°. The nearest distance upto which α-particle reaches the nucleus will be of the order of

(a) 1 Å (b) 10^{-10} cm (c) 10^{-12} cm (d) 10^{-15} cm

20. Hydrogen (H), deuterium (D), singly ionized helium (He^+) and doubly ionized lithium (Li^{++}) all have one electron around the nucleus. Consider $n = 2$ to $n = 1$ transition. The wavelengths of emitted radiations are $\lambda_1, \lambda_2, \lambda_3$ and λ_4 respectively. Then, approximately

(a) $\lambda_1 = \lambda_2 = 4\lambda_3 = 9\lambda_4$
(b) $4\lambda_1 = 2\lambda_2 = 2\lambda_3 = \lambda_4$
(c) $\lambda_1 = 2\lambda_2 = 2\sqrt{2}\lambda_3 = 3\sqrt{2}\lambda_4$
(d) $\lambda_1 = \lambda_2 = 2\lambda_3 = 3\sqrt{2}\lambda_4$

21. Speed of an electron in Bohr's 7th orbit for H-atom is 3.6×10^6 m/s. The corresponding speed of the electron in 3rd orbit, (in m/s) is **(2023 Main)**

(a) 3.6×10^6 (b) 1.8×10^6 (c) 8.4×10^6 (d) 7.5×10^6

22. A photon is emitted in transition from $n = 4$ to $n = 1$ level in hydrogen atom. The corresponding wavelength for this transition is (given, $h = 4 \times 10^{-15}$ eV-s) **(2023 Main)**

(a) 94.1 nm (b) 97.5 nm (c) 974 nm (d) 941 nm

23. Find the ratio of energies of photons produced due to transition of an election of hydrogen atom from its (i) second permitted energy level to the first level and (ii) the highest permitted energy level to the first permitted level. **(2022 Main)**

(a) 3 : 4 (b) 4 : 3 (c) 1 : 4 (d) 4 : 1

24. In an excited state of hydrogen like atom an electron has total energy of – 3.4 eV. If the kinetic energy of the electron is E and its de-Broglie wavelength is λ, then

(a) $\lambda = 6.6$ Å (b) $E = 3.4$ eV
(c) Both are correct (d) Both are wrong

25. The momentum of an electron revolving in nth orbit is given by **(2022 Main)**

(a) $\frac{nh}{2\pi r}$ (b) $\frac{nh}{2r}$ (c) $\frac{nh}{2\pi}$ (d) $\frac{2\pi r}{nh}$

26. Hydrogen atom from excited state comes to the ground by emitting a photon of wavelength λ. The value of principal quantum number n of the excited state will be **(2022 Main)**

(a) $\sqrt{\frac{\lambda R}{\lambda - 1}}$ (b) $\sqrt{\frac{\lambda R}{\lambda R - 1}}$ (c) $\sqrt{\frac{\lambda}{\lambda R - 1}}$ (d) $\sqrt{\frac{\lambda R^2}{\lambda R - 1}}$

27. A hydrogen atom in ground state absorbs 12.09 eV of energy. The orbital angular momentum of the electron is increased by **(2022 Main)**

(a) 1.05×10^{-34} J-s (b) 2.11×10^{-34} J-s
(c) 3.16×10^{-34} J-s (d) 4.22×10^{-34} J-s

28. The ratio for the speed of the electron in the 3rd orbit of He^+ to the speed of the electron in the 3rd orbit of hydrogen atom will be **(2022 Main)**

(a) 1 : 1 (b) 1 : 2 (c) 4 : 1 (d) 2 : 1

29. A ray of light of wavelength 5030 Å is incident on a totally reflecting surface. The momentum delivered by the ray is equal to

(a) 6.63×10^{-27} kg-m/s (b) 2.63×10^{-27} kg-m/s
(c) 1.25×10^{-24} kg-m/s (d) None of these

30. A particular hydrogen like ion emits radiation of frequency 2.92×10^{15} Hz when it makes transition from $n = 3$ to $n = 1$. The frequency in Hz of radiation emitted in transition from $n = 2$ to $n = 1$ will be **(2021 Main)**

(a) 0.44×10^{15} (b) 6.57×10^{15}
(c) 4.38×10^{15} (d) 2.46×10^{15}

31. If λ_1 and λ_2 are the wavelengths of the third member of Lyman and first number of the Paschen series respectively, then the value of $\lambda_1 : \lambda_2$ is **(2021 Main)**

(a) 1 : 3 (b) 7 : 108 (c) 7 : 135 (d) 1 : 9

32. The electron in a hydrogen atom first jumps from the third excited state to the second excited state and subsequently to the first excited state. The ratio of the respective wavelengths λ_1 / λ_2 of the photons emitted in this process is **(2019 Main)**

(a) 20/7 (b) 27/5 (c) 7/5 (d) 9/7

33. A particle of mass m moves in a circular orbit in a central potential field $U(r) = \frac{1}{2}kr^2$. If Bohr's quantization conditions are applied, radii of possible orbitals and energy levels vary with quantum number n as **(2019 Main)**

(a) $r_n \propto n, E_n \propto n$ (b) $r_n \propto n^2, E_n \propto \frac{1}{n^2}$
(c) $r_n \propto \sqrt{n}, E_n \propto n$ (d) $r_n \propto \sqrt{n}, E_n \propto \frac{1}{n}$

34. If the series limit frequency of the Lyman series is ν_L, then the series limit frequency of the Pfund series is **(2018 Main)**

(a) $\nu_L / 25$ (b) $16 \nu_L$ (c) $\frac{\nu_L}{16}$ (d) $\frac{\nu_L}{20}$

35. Some energy levels of a molecule are shown in the figure. The ratio of the wavelengths $r = \lambda_1 / \lambda_2$ is given by **(2017 Main)**

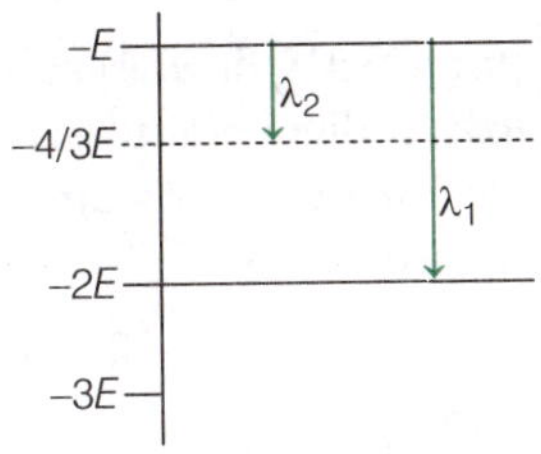

(a) $r = \frac{2}{3}$ (b) $r = \frac{3}{4}$ (c) $r = \frac{1}{3}$ (d) $r = \frac{4}{3}$

36. If the radius of first Bohr's orbit is x, then de-Broglie wavelength of electron in 3rd orbit is nearly

(a) $2\pi x$ (b) $6\pi x$
(c) $9x$ (d) $\frac{x}{3}$

37. In a hydrogen like atom electron makes transition from an energy level with quantum number n to another with quantum number $(n-1)$. If $n >> 1$, the frequency of radiation emitted is proportional to **(2013 Main)**

(a) $\frac{1}{n}$ (b) $\frac{1}{n^2}$ (c) $\frac{1}{n^4}$ (d) $\frac{1}{n^3}$

38. If the atom ${}_{100}Fm^{257}$ follows the Bohr's model and the radius of last orbit of ${}_{100}Fm^{257}$ is n times the Bohr radius, then find n **(2003 JEE)**

(a) 100 (b) 200
(c) 4 (d) 1/4

39. Magnetic moment of an electron in nth orbit of hydrogen atom is

(a) $\frac{neh}{\pi m}$ (b) $\frac{neh}{4\pi m}$
(c) $\frac{meh}{2\pi n}$ (d) $\frac{meh}{4\pi n}$

[where, m = mass of electron, h = Planck's constant]

40. An energy 24.6 eV is required to remove one of the electrons from a neutral helium atom. The energy in (eV) required to remove both the electrons from a neutral helium atom is **(1995 JEE)**

(a) 38.2 (b) 49.2 (c) 51.8 (d) 79.0

41. Consider an electron in a hydrogen atom, revolving in its second excited state (having radius 4.65 Å). The de-Broglie wavelength of this electron is **(2019 Main)**

(a) 3.5 Å (b) 6.6 Å
(c) 12.9 Å (d) 9.7 Å

42. When the voltage applied to an X-ray tube is increased from $V_1 = 10$ kV to $V_2 = 20$ kV, the wavelength difference between the K_α line and the short wavelength limit of the continuous X-ray spectrum increases by a factor 3. The atomic number of the target element is :

(a) 62 (b) 56
(c) 45 (d) 29

43. A particle A of mass m and initial velocity v collides with a particle B of mass $\frac{m}{2}$ which is at rest. The collision is head on, and elastic. The ratio of the de-Broglie wavelengths λ_A to λ_B after the collision is **(2017 Main)**

(a) $\frac{\lambda_A}{\lambda_B} = 2$ (b) $\frac{\lambda_A}{\lambda_B} = \frac{2}{3}$ (c) $\frac{\lambda_A}{\lambda_B} = \frac{1}{2}$ (d) $\frac{\lambda_A}{\lambda_B} = \frac{1}{3}$

44. For which of the following particle will it be most difficult to experimentally verify the de-Broglie relationship? **(2017 Main)**

(a) an electron (b) a proton
(c) an α-particle (d) a dust particle

45. Electrons are accelerated through a potential difference V and protons are accelerated through a potential difference 4 V. The de-Broglie wavelengths are λ_e and λ_p for electron and protons respectively. The ratio of $\frac{\lambda_e}{\lambda_p}$ is given by : (given, m_e is mass of electron and m_p is mass of proton). **(2013 Main)**

(a) $\frac{\lambda_e}{\lambda_p} = \sqrt{\frac{m_p}{m_e}}$ (b) $\frac{\lambda_e}{\lambda_p} = \sqrt{\frac{m_e}{m_p}}$

(c) $\frac{\lambda_e}{\lambda_p} = \frac{1}{2}\sqrt{\frac{m_p}{m_e}}$ (d) $\frac{\lambda_e}{\lambda_p} = 2\sqrt{\frac{m_p}{m_e}}$

46. A photon has the same wavelength as the de-Broglie wavelength of electron. Given that c = speed of light and v = speed of electron. Which of the following relation is correct?
[Here, E_e = Kinetic energy of electron, E_{ph} = energy of photon, p_e = momentum of electron and p_{ph} = momentum of photon]

(a) $\frac{E_e}{E_{ph}} = \frac{2c}{v}$ (b) $\frac{E_e}{E_{ph}} = \frac{v}{2c}$ (c) $\frac{p_e}{p_{ph}} = \frac{2c}{v}$ (d) $\frac{p_e}{p_{ph}} = \frac{c}{2v}$

47. In the Bohr's model of a hydrogen atom, the centripetal force is furnished by the coulomb attraction between the proton and the electron. If a_0 is the radius of the ground state orbit, m is the mass, e is the charge on electron and ε_0 is the permittivity of free space, the speed of the electron is

(a) $\frac{e}{\sqrt{\varepsilon_0 a_0 m}}$ (b) zero

(c) $\frac{e}{\sqrt{4\pi\varepsilon_0 a_0 m}}$ (d) $\frac{\sqrt{4\,\varepsilon_0 a_0 m}}{e}$

48. The intensity of light pulse travelling in an optical fibre decreases according to the relation $I = I_0 e^{-\alpha x}$. The intensity of light is reduced to 20% of its initial value after a distance x equal to

(a) $\ln(1/\alpha)$ (b) $\ln \alpha$ (c) $(\ln 5)/\alpha$ (d) $\ln(5/\alpha)$

49. From the photoelectric effect experiment, following observations are made. Identify which of these are correct?

A. The stopping potential depends only on the work function of the metal.
B. The saturation current increases as the intensity of incident light increases.
C. The maximum kinetic energy of a photoelectron depends on the intensity of the incident light.
D. Photoelectric effect can be explained using the wave theory of light.

Choose the correct answer from the options given below **(2023 Main)**

(a) B only (b) B and C only
(c) A, B and D (d) A, C and D

Note *Here, intensity means number of photons incident per unit area per unit time.*

50. The maximum kinetic energy of emitted electron is E when the light incident on the metals has wavelength λ. To double the kinetic energy, the incident light must have wavelength **(2022 Main)**

(a) $\dfrac{hc}{E\lambda - hc}$ (b) $\dfrac{hc\lambda}{E\lambda + hc}$ (c) $\dfrac{h\lambda}{E\lambda + hc}$ (d) $\dfrac{hc\lambda}{E\lambda - hc}$

51. The electric field at the point associated with a light wave is given by

$E = 200\,[\sin(6 \times 10^{15})t + \sin(9 \times 10^{15})t]\ \text{Vm}^{-1}$

Given, $h = 4.14 \times 10^{15}$ eVs)

If this light falls on a metal surface having a work function of 2.50 eV, the maximum kinetic energy of the photoelectrons will be **(2022 Main)**

(a) 1.90 eV (b) 3.27 eV
(c) 3.60 eV (d) 3.42 eV

52. Let K_1 and K_2 be the maximum kinetic energies of photoelectrons emitted when two monochromatic beams of wavelength λ_1 and λ_2, respectively are incident on a metallic surface. If $\lambda_1 = 3\lambda_2$ then **(2022 Main)**

(a) $K_1 > \dfrac{K_2}{3}$ (b) $K_1 < \dfrac{K_2}{3}$ (c) $K_1 = \dfrac{K_2}{3}$ (d) $K_2 = \dfrac{K_1}{3}$

53. When light of a given wavelength is incident on a metallic surface, the minimum potential needed to stop the emitted photoelectrons is 6.0 V. This potential drops to 0.6 V, if another source with wavelength four times that of the first one and intensity half of the first one is used. What are the wavelength of the first source and the work function of the metal, respectively? **(2022 Adv.)**

[Take, $\dfrac{hc}{e} = 1.24 \times 10^{-6}\ \text{JmC}^{-1}$]

(a) 1.72×10^{-7} m, 1.20 eV (b) 1.72×10^{-7} m, 5.60 eV
(c) 3.78×10^{-7} m, 5.60 eV (d) 3.78×10^{-7} m, 1.20 eV

54. When the wavelength of radiation falling on a metal is changed from 500 nm to 200 nm, the maximum kinetic energy of the photoelectrons becomes three times larger. The work function of the metal is close to **(2020 Main)**

(a) 0.81 eV (b) 1.02 eV (c) 0.52 eV (d) 0.61 eV

55. The stopping potential V_0 (in volt) as a function of frequency (ν) for a sodium emitter, is shown in the figure. The work function of sodium, from the data plotted in the figure, will be

(Take, Planck's constant $(h) = 6.63 \times 10^{-34}$ J-s, electron charge, $e = 1.6 \times 10^{-19}$ C] **(2019 Main)**

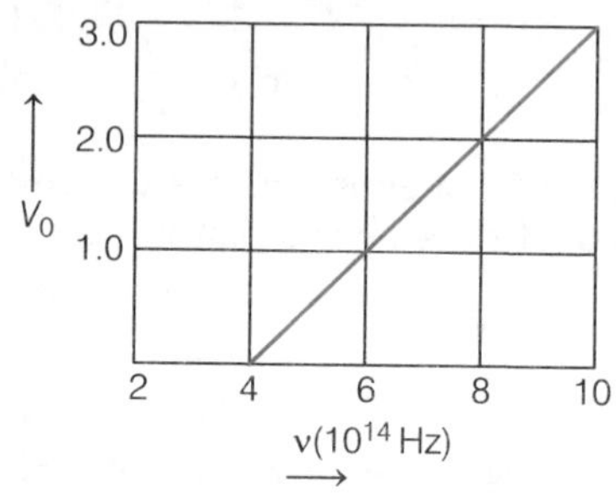

(a) 1.82 eV (b) 1.66 eV
(c) 1.95 eV (d) 2.12 eV

56. Radiation of wavelength λ, is incident on a photocell. The fastest emitted electron has speed v. If the wavelength is changed to $\dfrac{3\lambda}{4}$, the speed of the fastest emitted electron will be **(2016 Main)**

(a) $> v\left(\dfrac{4}{3}\right)^{1/2}$ (b) $< v\left(\dfrac{4}{3}\right)^{1/2}$

(c) $= v\left(\dfrac{4}{3}\right)^{1/2}$ (d) $= v\left(\dfrac{3}{4}\right)^{1/2}$

57. In a historical experiment to determine Planck's constant, a metal surface was irradiated with light of different wavelengths. The emitted photoelectron energies were measured by applying a stopping potential. The relevant data for the wavelength (λ) of incident light and the corresponding stopping potential (V_0) are given below : **(2016 Adv.)**

λ (μm)	V_0 (Volt)
0.3	2.0
0.4	1.0
0.5	0.4

Given that $c = 3 \times 10^8\ \text{ms}^{-1}$ and $e = 1.6 \times 10^{-19}$ C, Planck's constant (in units of J-s) found from such an experiment is)

(a) 6.0×10^{-34} (b) 6.4×10^{-34}
(c) 6.6×10^{-34} (d) 6.8×10^{-34}

58. The radiation corresponding to $3 \rightarrow 2$ transition of hydrogen atom falls on a metal surface to produce photoelectrons. These electrons are made to enter a magnetic field of 3×10^{-4} T. If the radius of the largest circular path followed by these electrons is 10.0 mm, the work function of the metal is close to **(2014 Main)**

(a) 1.8 eV (b) 1.1 eV (c) 0.8 eV (d) 1.6 eV

59. Photoelectric effect experiments are performed using three different metal plates p, q and r having work functions $\phi_p = 2.0$ eV, $\phi_q = 2.5$ eV and $\phi_r = 3.0$ eV, respectively. A light beam containing wavelengths of 550 nm, 450 nm and 350 nm with equal intensities illuminates each of the plates. The correct I-V graph for the experiment is **(2009 JEE)**

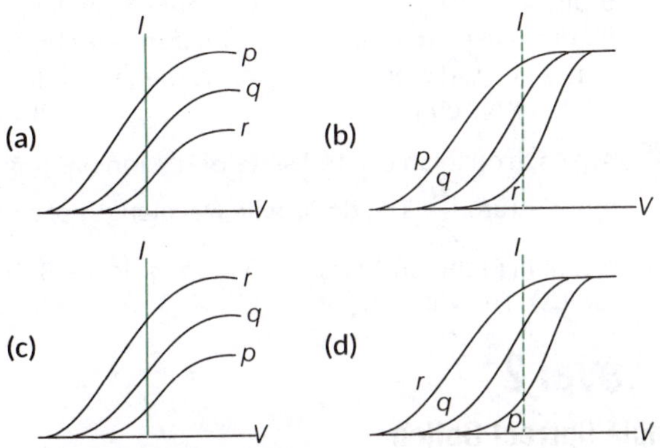

60. A metal target with atomic number $Z = 46$ is bombarded with a high energy electron beam. The emission of X-rays from the target is analysed. The ratio r of the wavelengths of the K_α-line and the cut-off is found to be $r = 2$. If the same electron beam bombards another metal target with $Z = 41$, the value of r will be **(2024 Adv.)**

(a) 2.53 (b) 1.27 (c) 2.24 (d) 1.58

Subjective Questions

61. A photon has momentum of magnitude 8.24×10^{-28} kg-m/s.
(a) What is the energy of this photon? Give your answer in joules and in electron volts.
(b) What is the wavelength of this photon? In what region of the electromagnetic spectrum does it lie?

62. A 75 W light source emits light of wavelength 600 nm.
(a) Calculate the frequency of the emitted light.
(b) How many photons per second does the source emit?

63. An excited nucleus emits a gamma-ray photon with energy of 2.45 MeV.
(a) What is the photon frequency?
(b) What is the photon wavelength?

64. (a) A proton is moving at a speed much less than the speed of light. It has kinetic energy K_1 and momentum p_1. If the momentum of the proton is doubled, so $p_2 = 2p_1$, how is its new kinetic energy K_2 related to K_1?
(b) A photon with energy E_1 has momentum p_1. If another photon has momentum p_2 that is twice p_1, how is the energy E_2 of the second photon related to E_1?

65. A parallel beam of monochromatic light of wavelength 500 nm is incident normally on a perfectly absorbing surface. The power through any cross-section of the beam is 10 W. Find
(a) the number of photons absorbed per second by the surface and
(b) the force exerted by the light beam on the surface.

66. A parallel beam of monochromatic light of wavelength 663 nm is incident on a totally reflecting plane mirror. The angle of incidence is 60° and the number of photons striking the mirror per second is 1.0×10^{19}. Calculate the force exerted by the light beam on the mirror.

67. A source emits monochromatic light of frequency 5.5×10^{14} Hz at a rate of 0.1 W. Of the photons given out, 0.15% fall on the cathode of a photocell which gives a current of 6 μA in an external circuit.
(a) Find the energy of a photon.
(b) Find the number of photons leaving the source per second.
(c) Find the percentage of the photons falling on the cathode which produce photoelectrons.

68. (a) An atom initially in an energy level with $E = -6.52$ eV absorbs a photon that has wavelength 860 nm. What is the internal energy of the atom after it absorbs the photon?
(b) An atom initially in an energy level with $E = -2.68$ eV emits a photon that has wavelength 420 nm. What is the internal energy of the atom after it emits the photon?

69. A silver ball is suspended by a string in a vacuum chamber and ultraviolet light of wavelength 2000 Å is directed at it. What electrical potential will the ball acquire as a result? Work function of silver is 4.3 eV.

70. A metallic surface is illuminated alternatively with light of wavelengths 3000 Å and 6000 Å. It is observed that the maximum speeds of the photoelectrons under these illuminations are in the ratio 3 : 1. Calculate the work-function of the metal and the maximum speed of the photoelectrons in two cases.

71. Light of wavelength 180 nm ejects photoelectrons from a plate of metal whose work-function is 2 eV. If a uniform magnetic field of 5×10^{-5} T be applied parallel to the plate, what would be the radius of the path followed by electrons ejected normally from the plate with maximum energy.

72. The electric field associated with a light wave is given by $E = E_0 \sin[(1.57 \times 10^7 \text{ m}^{-1})(x - ct)]$. Find the stopping potential when this light is used in an experiment on photoelectric effect with a metal having work-function 1.9 eV.

73. If the wavelength of the nth line of Lyman series is equal to the de-Broglie wavelength of electron in initial orbit of a hydrogen like element $(Z=11)$. Find the value of n. **(2005 JEE)**

74. Compose the expression for a quantity whose dimension is length, using velocity of light c, mass of a particle m and Planck's constant h. **(Irodov 5.280)**

Integer Type Questions

75. The wavelength of the radiation emitted is λ_0 when an electron jumps from the second excited state to the first excited state of hydrogen atom. If the electron jumps from the third excited state to the second orbit of the hydrogen atom the wavelength of the radiation emitted will be $\frac{20}{x}\lambda_0$. The value of x is ...... **(2023 Main)**

76. For a hydrogen atom, λ_1 and λ_2 are the wavelengths corresponding to the transitions 1 and 2, respectively as shown in figure. The ratio of λ_1 and λ_2 is $x/32$. The value of x is .... **(2023 Main)**

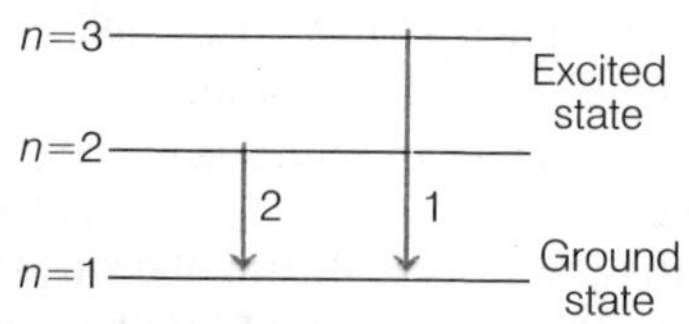

77. If the binding energy of a ground state electron in a hydrogen atom is 13.6 eV, then the energy required to remove the electron from the second excited state of Li^{2+} will be $x \times 10^{-1}$ eV. The value of x is .... **(2023 Main)**

78. $\sqrt{d_1}$ and $\sqrt{d_2}$ are the impact parameters corresponding to scattering angles 60° and 90° respectively, when an α-particle is approaching a gold nucleus. For $d_1 = x\, d_2$, the value of x will be .... **(2022 Main)**

79. In the hydrogen spectrum, λ is the wavelength of first transition line of Lyman series. The wavelength difference will be $a\lambda$ between the wavelength of 3rd transition line of Paschen series and that of 2nd transition line of Balmer series, where $a =$......... . **(2022 Main)**

80. A hydrogen atom in its first excited state absorbs a photon of energy $x \times 10^{-2}$ eV and exited to a higher energy state where the potential energy of electron is 1.08 eV. The value of x is .... **(2022 Main)**

81. The first three spectral lines of H-atom in the Balmer series are given $\lambda_1, \lambda_2, \lambda_3$ considering the Bohr atomic model. The wavelengths of first and third spectral lines(λ_1/λ_3) are related by a factor of approximately $x \times 10^{-1}$. The value of x to the nearest integer, is .... **(2021 Main)**

82. Consider a hydrogen-like ionised atom with atomic number Z with a single electron. In the emission spectrum of this atom, the photon emitted in the $n=2$ to $n=1$ transition has energy 74.8 eV higher than the photon emitted in the $n=3$ to $n=2$ transition. The ionisation energy of the hydrogen atom is 13.6 eV. The value of Z is .... **(2018 Adv.)**

83. A hydrogen atom in its ground state is irradiated by light of wavelength 970 Å. Taking $hc/e = 1.237 \times 10^{-6}$ eV - m and the ground state energy of hydrogen atom as -13.6 eV, the number of lines present in the emission spectrum is **(2016 Adv.)**

84. Consider a hydrogen atom with its electron in the nth orbit. An electromagnetic radiation of wavelength 90 nm is used to ionize the atom. If the kinetic energy of the ejected electron is 10.4 eV, then the value of n is ($hc = 1242$ eV nm) **(2015 Adv.)**

85. An electron in an excited state of Li^{2+} ion has angular momentum $\frac{3h}{2\pi}$. The de Broglie wavelength of the electron in this state is $p\pi a_0$ (where a_0 is the Bohr radius). The value of p is **(2015 Adv.)**

Level 2

Single Correct Option

86. If we assume only gravitational attraction between proton and electron in hydrogen atom and the Bohr quantization rule to be followed, then the expression for the ground state energy of the atom will be (the mass of proton is M and that of electron is m.)
(a) $\frac{G^2M^2m^2}{h^2}$
(b) $-\frac{2\pi^2G^2M^2m^3}{h^2}$
(c) $-\frac{2\pi^2GM^2m^3}{h^2}$
(d) None of these

87. An electron in a hydrogen atom makes a transition from first excited state to ground state. The magnetic moment due to circulating electron
(a) increases two times
(b) decreases two times
(c) increases four times
(d) remains same

88. An electron in a hydrogen atom makes a transition from first excited state to ground state. The equivalent current due to circulating electron
(a) increases 4 times
(b) decreases 4 times
(c) increases 8 times
(d) decreases 8 times

89. Let A_n be the area enclosed by the nth orbit in a hydrogen atom. The graph of $\ln(A_n/A_1)$ against $\ln(n)$
(a) will not pass through origin
(b) will be a straight line with slope 4
(c) will be a rectangular hyperbola
(d) will be a parabola

90. In the hydrogen atom, an electron makes a transition from $n = 2$ to $n = 1$. The magnetic field produced by the circulating electron at the nucleus

(a) decreases 16 times (b) increases 4 times
(c) decreases 4 times (d) increases 32 times

91. A stationary hydrogen atom emits photon corresponding to the first line of Lyman series. If R is the Rydberg constant and M is the mass of the atom, then the velocity acquired by the atom is

(a) $\frac{3Rh}{4M}$ (b) $\frac{4M}{3Rh}$ (c) $\frac{Rh}{4M}$ (d) $\frac{4M}{Rh}$

92. The time period of the electron in the ground state of hydrogen atom is two times the time period of the electron in the first excited state of a certain hydrogen like atom (Atomic number Z). The value of Z is

(a) 2 (b) 3
(c) 4 (d) None of these

93. An X-ray tube is operating at 150 kV and 10 mA. If only 1% of the electric power supplied is converted into X-rays, the rate at which the target is heated in calorie per second is

(a) 3.55 (b) 35.5 (c) 355 (d) 3550

94. A H-atom moving with speed v makes a head on collision with a H-atom at rest. Both atoms are in ground state. The minimum value of velocity v for which one of the atom may excite is

(a) 6.25×10^4 m/s (b) 8×10^4 m/s
(c) 7.25×10^4 m/s (d) 13.6×10^4 m/s

Note : $m_H = 1.67 \times 10^{-27}$ kg

95. The ratio of speed of the electron in the first Bohr orbit of hydrogen and the speed of light is equal to (where e, h and c have their usual meanings)

(a) $\frac{2\pi hc}{e^2}$ (b) $\frac{e^2 c}{2\pi h}$ (c) $\frac{e^2 h}{2\pi c}$ (d) $\frac{e^2}{2\varepsilon_0 hc}$

96. In a hydrogen atom, the binding energy of the electron in the ground state is E_1. Then, the frequency of revolution of the electron in the nth orbit is

(a) $\frac{2E_1}{n^3 h}$ (b) $\frac{2E_1 n^3}{h}$ (c) $\sqrt{\frac{2mE_1}{n^3 h}}$ (d) $\frac{E_1 n^2}{h}$

97. The acceleration of electron in the first orbit of hydrogen atom is

(a) $\frac{4\pi^2 m}{h^3}$ (b) $\frac{h^2}{4\pi^2 mr}$ (c) $\frac{h^2}{4\pi^2 m^2 r^3}$ (d) $\frac{m^2 h^2}{4\pi^2 r^3}$

98. An α-particle accelerated through V volts is fired towards a nucleus. Its distance of closest approach is r. If a proton accelerated through the same potential is fired towards the same nucleus, the distance of closest approach of proton will be

(a) r (b) 2r (c) $\frac{r}{2}$ (d) $\frac{r}{4}$

99. In an experiment on photoelectric effect, light of wavelength 400 nm is incident on a cesium plate at the rate of 5.0 W. The potential of the collector plate is made sufficiently positive with respect to the emitter so that the current reaches its saturation value. Assuming that on the average one out of every 10^6 photons is able to eject a photoelectron, the photocurrent in the circuit is

(a) 0.4 μA (b) 0.8 μA (c) 1.2 μA (d) 1.6 μA

100. If momentum of an electron is changed by Δp, then the de-Broglie wavelength associated with it changes by 0.50%. The initial momentum of the electron will be

(a) $\frac{\Delta p}{200}$ (b) $\frac{\Delta p}{199}$ (c) $199\,\Delta p$ (d) $400\,\Delta p$

101. An electron from various excited states of hydrogen atom emit radiation to come to the ground state. Let λ_n, λ_g be the de-Broglie wavelength of the electron in the nth state and the ground state, respectively. Let Λ_n be the wavelength of the emitted photon in the transition from the nth state to the ground state. For large n, (A, B are constants) **(2018 Main)**

(a) $\Lambda_n^2 \approx \lambda$ (b) $\Lambda_n \approx A + \frac{B}{\lambda_n^2}$
(c) $\Lambda_n \approx A + B\lambda_n^2$ (d) $\Lambda_n^2 \approx A + B\lambda_n^2$

102. A photoelectric material having work-function ϕ_0 is illuminated with light of wavelength $\lambda \left(\lambda < \frac{hc}{\phi_0} \right)$. The fastest photoelectron has a de-Broglie wavelength λ_d. A change in wavelength of the incident light by $\Delta\lambda$ results in a change $\Delta\lambda_d$ in λ_d. Then, the ratio $\frac{\Delta\lambda_d}{\Delta\lambda}$ is proportional to **(2017 Adv.)**

(a) $\frac{\lambda_d^2}{\lambda^2}$ (b) $\frac{\lambda_d}{\lambda}$ (c) $\frac{\lambda_d^3}{\lambda}$ (d) $\frac{\lambda_d^3}{\lambda^2}$

Multiple Correct Options

103. In Bohr model of the hydrogen atom, let R, v and E represent the radius of the orbit, speed of the electron and the total energy of the electron respectively. Which of the following quantities are directly proportional to the quantum number n?

(a) vR (b) RE (c) $\frac{v}{E}$ (d) $\frac{R}{E}$

104. The magnitude of angular momentum, orbital radius and time period of revolution of an electron in a hydrogen atom corresponding to the quantum number n are L, r and T respectively. Which of the following statement(s) is/are correct?

(a) $\frac{rL}{T}$ is independent of n (b) $\frac{L}{T} \propto \frac{1}{n^2}$
(c) $\frac{T}{r} \propto n$ (d) $Lr \propto \frac{1}{n^3}$

105. In which of the following cases the heavier of the two particles has a smaller de-Broglie wavelength? When the two particles :
(a) move with the same speed
(b) move with the same linear momentum
(c) move with the same kinetic energy
(d) have the same change of potential energy in a conservative field

106. Hydrogen atom absorbs radiations of wavelength λ_0 and consequently emit radiations of 6 different wavelengths, of which two wavelengths are longer than λ_0. Choose the correct alternative(s).
(a) The final excited state of the atoms is $n=4$
(b) The initial state of the atoms is $n=2$
(c) The initial state of the atoms is $n=3$
(d) There are three transitions belonging to Lyman series

107. In coolidge tube, if f and λ represent the frequency and wavelength of K_α-line for a metal of atomic number Z, then identify the statement which represents a straight line
(a) $\sqrt{f}$ versus Z
(b) $\dfrac{1}{\sqrt{\lambda}}$ versus Z
(c) f versus Z
(d) λ versus Z

108. For photo-electric effect with incident photon wavelength λ, the stopping potential is V_0. Identify the correct variation(s) of V_0 with λ and $\dfrac{1}{\lambda}$. **(2015 Adv.)**

(a) 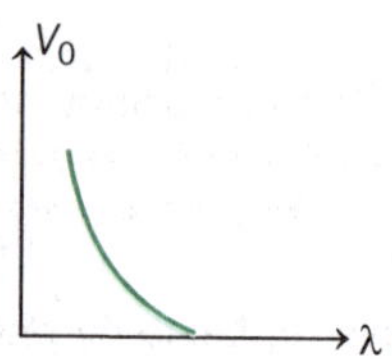

(b) 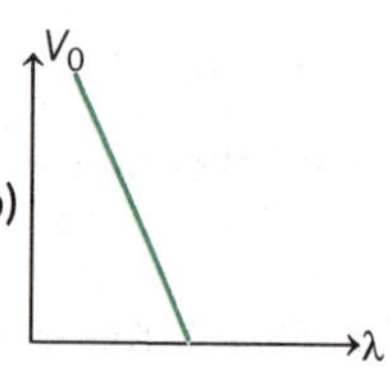

(c) 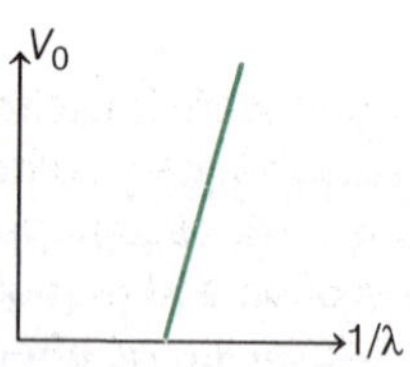

(d) 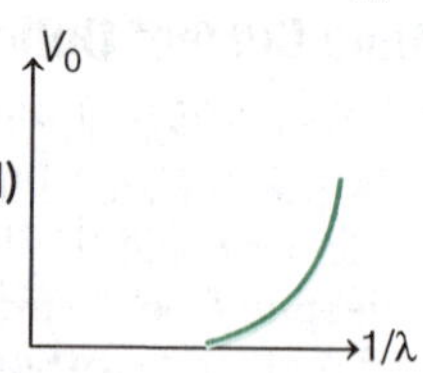

109. When photons of energy 4.25 eV strike the surface of a metal A, the ejected photoelectrons have maximum kinetic energy T_A expressed in eV and de-Broglie wavelength λ_A. The maximum kinetic energy of photoelectrons liberated from another metal B by photons of energy 4.70 eV is $T_B=(T_A-1.50 \text{ eV})$. If the de-Broglie wavelength of these photoelectrons is $\lambda_B=2\lambda_A$, then **(1994 JEE)**
(a) the work function of A is 2.25 eV
(b) the work function of B is 4.20 eV
(c) $T_A=2.00$ eV
(d) $T_B=2.75$ eV

110. The potential difference applied to an X-ray tube is increased. As a result, in the emitted radiation **(1988 JEE)**
(a) the intensity increases
(b) the minimum wavelength increases
(c) the intensity remains unchanged
(d) the minimum wavelength decreases

Passage Based Questions

Passage 1 (Q. No. 111 to 113)

When a surface is irradiated with light of wavelength 4950 Å, a photocurrent appears which vanishes if a retarding potential greater than 0.6 volt is applied across the phototube. When a second source of light is used, it is found that the critical retarding potential is changed to 1.1 volt.

111. The work-function of the emitting surface is
(a) 2.2 eV (b) 1.5 eV (c) 1.9 eV (d) 1.1 eV

112. The wavelength of the second source is
(a) 6150 Å (b) 5150 Å (c) 4125 Å (d) 4500 Å

113. If the photoelectrons (after emission from the source) are subjected to a magnetic field of 10 tesla, the two retarding potentials would
(a) uniformly increase (b) uniformly decrease
(c) remain the same (d) None of these

Passage 2 (Q. No. 114 to 116)

In a mixture of H and He^+ gas (He^+ is singly ionized He atom), H atoms and He^+ ions are excited to their respective first excited states. Subsequently, H atoms transfer their total excitation energy to He^+ ions (by collisions). Assume that the Bohr model of atom is exactly valid. **(2008 JEE)**

114. The quantum number n of the state finally populated in He^+ ions is
(a) 2 (b) 3 (c) 4 (d) 5

115. The wavelength of light emitted in the visible region by He^+ ions after collisions with H atoms is
(a) 6.5×10^{-7} m (b) 5.6×10^{-7} m
(c) 4.8×10^{-7} m (d) 4.0×10^{-7} m

116. The ratio of the kinetic energy of the $n=2$ electron for the H atom to that of He^+ ion is
(a) 1/4 (b) 1/2 (c) 1 (d) 2

Match the Columns

117. Match the following two columns for hydrogen spectrum.

	Column I		Column II
(a)	Lyman series	(p)	infrared region
(b)	Balmer series	(q)	visible region
(c)	Paschen series	(r)	ultraviolet region
(d)	Brackett series	(s)	X-rays

118. Ionization energy from first excited state of hydrogen atom is E. Match the following two columns for He^+ atom.

	Column I		Column II
(a)	Ionization energy from ground state	(p)	4 E
(b)	Electrostatic potential energy in first excited state.	(q)	– 16 E
(c)	Kinetic energy of electron in ground state.	(r)	– 8 E
(d)	Ionization energy from first excited state.	(s)	16 E

119. Maximum kinetic energy *versus* frequency of incident light and stopping potential *versus* frequency of incident light graphs are shown in figure. Match the following two columns.

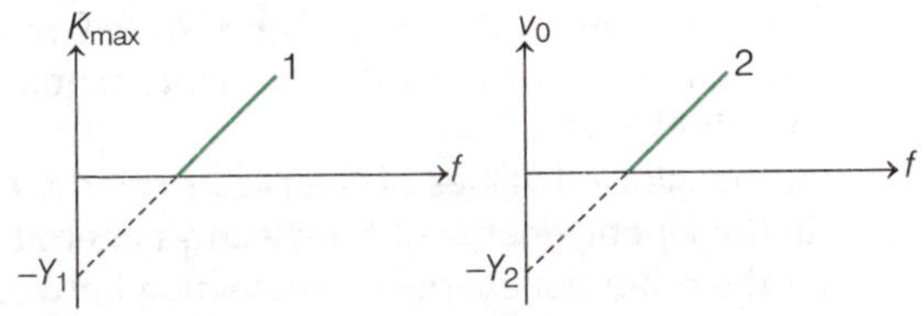

	Column I		Column II
(a)	Slope of line-1	(p)	h/e
(b)	Slope of line-2	(q)	h
(c)	Y_1	(r)	W
(d)	Y_2	(s)	W/e

Here, h = Planck constant, $e = 1.6 \times 10^{-19}$ C and W = work-function.

120. For hydrogen and hydrogen like atoms, match the following two columns.

	Column I		Column II
(a)	Time period	(p)	Proportional to n/Z
(b)	Angular momentum	(q)	Proportional to n^2/Z
(c)	Speed	(r)	Proportional to n^3/Z^2
(d)	Radius	(s)	None of these

121. In hydrogen atom wavelength of second line of Balmer series is λ. Match the following two columns corresponding to the wavelength.

	Column I		Column II
(a)	First line of Balmer series	(p)	$(27/20)\ \lambda$
(b)	Third line of Balmer series	(q)	$(\lambda/4)$
(c)	First line of Lyman series	(r)	$(25/12)\ \lambda$
(d)	Second line of Lyman series	(s)	None of these

122. Match the following (Give most appropriate one matching)

	Column I		Column II
(a)	Characteristic X-ray	(p)	Inverse process of photoelectric effect
(b)	X-ray production	(q)	Potential difference
(c)	Cut off wavelength	(r)	Moseley's law
(d)	Continuous X-ray	(s)	None of these

123. In a photoelectric effect experiment. If f is the frequency of radiations incident on the metal surface and I is the intensity of the incident radiations, then match the following columns.

	Column I		Column II
(a)	If f is increased keeping I and work-function constant	(p)	Stopping potential increases
(b)	If distance between cathode and anode is increased	(q)	Saturation current increases
(c)	If I is increased keeping f and work-function constant	(r)	Maximum kinetic energy of photoelectron increases
(d)	Work-function is decreased keeping f and I constant	(s)	Stopping potential remains same

Subjective Questions

124. The wavelength for $n = 3$ to $n = 2$ transition of the hydrogen atom is 656.3 nm. What are the wavelengths for this same transition in (a) positronium, which consists of an electron and a positron (b) singly ionized helium (**Note:** A positron is a positively charged electron).

125. (a) Find the frequencies of revolution of electrons in $n = 1$ and $n = 2$ Bohr orbits.

(b) What is the frequency of the photon emitted when an electron in an $n = 2$ orbit drops to an $n = 1$ hydrogen orbit?

(c) An electron typically spends about 10^{-8} s in an excited state before it drops to a lower state by emitting a photon. How many revolutions does an electron in an $n = 2$ Bohr hydrogen orbit make in 1.00×10^{-8} s?

126. (a) A gas of hydrogen atoms in their ground state is bombarded by electrons with kinetic energy 12.5 eV. What emitted wavelengths would you expect to see?

(b) What if the electrons were replaced by photons of same energy?

127. The hydrogen atom in its ground state is excited by means of monochromatic radiation. Its resulting spectrum has six different lines. These radiations are incident on a metal plate. It is observed that only two of them are responsible for photoelectric effect. If the ratio of maximum kinetic energy of photoelectrons in the two cases is 5 then find the work-function of the metal.

128. Electrons in hydrogen like atoms ($Z = 3$) make transitions from the fifth to the fourth orbit and from the fourth to the third orbit. The resulting radiations are incident normally on a metal plate and eject photoelectrons. The stopping potential for the photoelectrons ejected by the shorter wavelength is 3.95 volts. Calculate the work-function of the metal and the stopping potential for the photoelectrons ejected by the longer wavelength.

129. An electron and a proton are separated by a large distance and the electron approaches the proton with a kinetic energy of 2 eV. If the electron is captured by the proton to form a hydrogen atom in the ground state, what wavelength photon would be given off?

130. Hydrogen gas in the atomic state is excited to an energy level such that the electrostatic potential energy of H-atom becomes -1.7 eV. Now, a photoelectric plate having work-function $W = 2.3$ eV is exposed to the emission spectra of this gas. Assuming all the transitions to be possible, find the minimum de-Broglie wavelength of the ejected photoelectrons.

131. A gas of hydrogen like atoms can absorb radiation of 68 eV. Consequently, the atom emits radiations of only three different wavelengths. All the wavelengths are equal or smaller than that of the absorbed photon.

(a) Determine the initial state of the gas atoms.

(b) Identify the gas atoms.

(c) Find the minimum wavelength of the emitted radiations.

(d) Find the ionization energy and the respective wavelength for the gas atoms.

132. A photon with energy of 4.9 eV ejects photoelectrons from tungsten. When the ejected electron enters a constant magnetic field of strength $B = 2.5$ mT at an angle of 60° with the field direction, the maximum pitch of the helix described by the electron is found to be 2.7 mm. Find the work-function of the metal in electron-volt. Given that specific charge of electron is 1.76×10^{11} C/kg.

133. For a certain hypothetical one-electron atom, the wavelength (in Å) for the spectral lines for transitions originating at $n = p$ and terminating at $n = 1$ are given by

$$\lambda = \frac{1500p^2}{p^2 - 1}, \quad \text{where} \quad p = 2, 3, 4$$

(a) Find the wavelength of the least energetic and the most energetic photons in this series.

(b) Construct an energy level diagram for this element showing the energies of the lowest three levels.

(c) What is the ionization potential of this element?

134. A photocell is operating in saturation mode with a photocurrent 4.8 mA when a monochromatic radiation of wavelength 3000 Å and power of 0.388 W is incident. When another monochromatic radiation of wavelength 1650 Å and power 5 mW is incident, it is observed that maximum velocity of photoelectron increases to two times. Assuming efficiency of photoelectron generation per incident photon to be same for both the cases, calculate

(a) the threshold wavelength for the cell

(b) the efficiency of photoelectron generation per incident photon

(c) the saturation current in second case

135. The negative muon has a charge equal to that of an electron but a mass that is 207 times as great. Consider hydrogen like atom consisting of a proton and a muon.

(a) What is the reduced mass of the atom?

(b) What is the ground-level energy (in eV)?

(c) What is the wavelength of the radiation emitted in the transition from the $n = 2$ level to the $n = 1$ level?

136. Assume a hypothetical hydrogen atom in which the potential energy between electron and proton at separation r is given by $U = [k \ln r - (k/2)]$, where k is a constant. For such a hypothetical hydrogen atom, calculate the radius of nth Bohr orbit and energy levels.

137. An electron is orbiting in a circular orbit of radius r under the influence of a constant magnetic field of strength B. Assuming that Bohr postulate regarding the quantisation of angular momentum holds good for this electron, find

(a) the allowed values of the radius r of the orbit.

(b) the kinetic energy of the electron in orbit

(c) the potential energy of interaction between the magnetic moment of the orbital current due to the electron moving in its orbit and the magnetic field B.

(d) the total energy of the allowed energy levels.

(e) the total magnetic flux due to the magnetic field B passing through the nth orbit.

(Assume that the charge on the electron is $-e$ and the mass of the electron is m).

138. A mixture of hydrogen atoms (in their ground state) and hydrogen like ions (in their first excited state) are being excited by electrons which have been accelerated by same potential difference V volts. After excitation when they come directly into ground state, the wavelengths of emitted light are found in the ratio 5 : 1. Then, find

(a) the minimum value of V for which both the atoms get excited after collision with electrons.

(b) atomic number of other ion.

(c) the energy of emitted light.

139. When a surface is irradiated with light of $\lambda = 4950$ Å, a photocurrent appears which vanishes if a retarding potential 0.6 V is applied. When a different source of light is used, it is found that critical retarding potential is changed to 1.1 volt. Find the work-function of emitting surface and wavelength of second source. If photoelectrons after emission from surface are subjected to a magnetic field of 10 tesla, what changes will be observed in the above two retarding potentials?

140. In an experiment on photoelectric effect light of wavelength 400 nm is incident on a metal plate at the rate of 5 W. The potential of the collector plate is made sufficiently positive with respect to emitter so that the current reaches the saturation value. Assuming that on the average one out of every 10^6 photons is able to eject a photoelectron, find the photocurrent in the circuit.

141. A light beam of wavelength 400 nm is incident on a metal of work-function 2.2 eV. A particular electron absorbs a photon and makes 2 collisions before coming out of the metal
(a) Assuming that 10% of existing energy is lost to the metal in each collision find the final kinetic energy of this electron as it comes out of the metal.
(b) Under the same assumptions find the maximum number of collisions, the electron should suffer before it becomes unable to come out of the metal.

142. A gas of identical hydrogen-like atoms has some atoms in the lowest (ground) energy level A and some atoms in a particular upper (excited) energy level B and there are no atoms in any other energy level. The atoms of the gas make the transition to a higher energy level by absorbing monochromatic light of photon energy 2.7eV. Subsequently, the atoms emit radiation of only six different energy photons. Some of the emitted photons have an energy of 2.7 eV, some have more energy and some less than 2.7 eV. **(1989 JEE)**
(a) Find the principal quantum number of the initially excited level B.
(b) Find the ionization energy for the gas atoms.
(c) Find the maximum and the minimum energies of the emitted photons.

143. A doubly ionised lithium atom is hydrogen-like with atomic number 3. **(1985 JEE)**
(a) Find the wavelength of the radiation required to excite the electron in Li^{2+} from the first to the third Bohr orbit. (Ionisation energy of the hydrogen atom equals 13.6 eV.)
(b) How many spectral lines are observed in the emission spectrum of the above excited system?

144. The ionization energy of a hydrogen like Bohr atom is 4 rydberg. **(1984 JEE)**
(a) What is the wavelength of the radiation emitted when the electron jumps from the first excited state to the ground state?
(b) What is the radius of the first orbit for this atom?

145. Hydrogen atom in its ground state is excited by means of monochromatic radiation of wavelength 975° Å. How many different lines are possible in the resulting spectrum? Calculate the longest wavelength amongst them. You may assume the ionization energy for hydrogen atom as 13.6 eV. **(1982 JEE)**

146. A single electron orbits around a stationary nucleus of charge $+Ze$. Where Z is a constant and e is the magnitude of the electronic charge. It requires 47.2 eV to excite the electron from the second Bohr orbit to the third Bohr orbit. **(1981 JEE)**
Find
(a) the value of Z.
(b) the energy required to excite the electron from the third to the fourth Bohr orbit.
(c) the wavelength of the electromagnetic radiation required to remove the electron from the first Bohr orbit to infinity.
(d) the kinetic energy, potential energy and the angular momentum of the electron in the first Bohr orbit.
(e) the radius of the first Bohr orbit.
(The ionization energy of hydrogen atom $=13.6$ eV, Bohr radius $=5.3\times10^{-11}$m, velocity of light $=3\times10^{8}$m/s. Planck's constant $=6.6\times10^{-34}$ J-s).

147. Assume that the de-Broglie wave associated with an electron can form a standing wave between the atoms arranged in a one dimensional array with nodes at each of the atomic sites. It is found that one such standing wave is formed if the distance d between the atoms of the array is 2Å. A similar standing wave is again formed if d is increased to 2.5 Å but not for any intermediate value of d. Find the energy of the electron in eV and the least value of d for which the standing wave of the type described above can form. **(1997 JEE)**

148. In a photoelectric experiment set-up, photons of energy 5 eV falls on the cathode having work function 3 eV. (a) If the saturation current is $i_A = 4\mu A$ for intensity 10^{-5} W/m^2, then plot a graph between anode potential and current. (b) Also, draw a graph for intensity of incident radiation 2×10^{-5}W/m^2. **(2003 JEE)**

149. In a photoelectric effect set-up a point of light of power 3.2×10^{-3} W emits monoenergetic photons of energy 5.0 eV. The source is located at a distance of 0.8 m from the centre of a stationafry metallic sphere of work function 3.0 eV and of radius 8.0×10^{-3}m. The efficiency of photoelectrons emission is one for every 10^6 incident photons. Assume that the sphere is isolated and initially neutral and that photoelectrons are instantly swept away after emission. **(1995 JEE)**
(a) Calculate the number of photoelectrons emitted per second.
(b) Find the ratio of the wavelength of incident light to the de-Broglie wavelength of the fastest photoelectrons emitted.
(c) It is observed that the photoelectrons emission stops at a certain time t after the light source is switched on why?
(d) Evaluate the time t.

150. A monochromatic point source S radiating wavelength 6000 Å, with power 2 W, an aperture A of diameter 0.1 m and a large screen SC are placed as shown in figure. A photoemissive detector D of surface area 0.5 cm^2 is placed at the centre of the screen. The efficiency of the detector for the photoelectron generation per incident photon is 0.9. **(1991 JEE)**

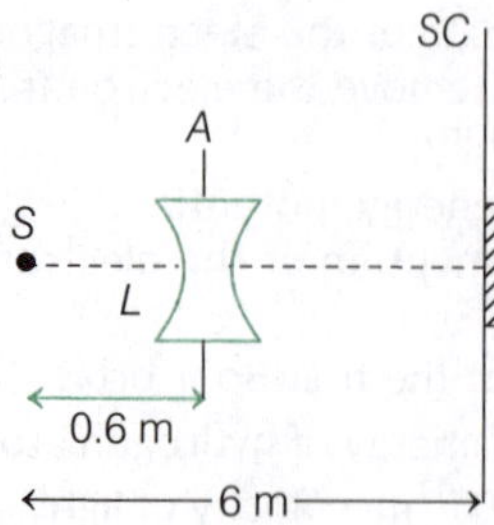

(a) Calculate the photon flux at (per unit area per unit time) the centre of the screen and the photocurrent in the detector.

(b) If the concave lens L of focal length 0.6 m is inserted in the aperture as shown, find the new values of photon flux and photocurrent. Assume a uniform average transmission of 80% from the lens.

(c) If the work function of the photoemissive surface is 1 eV, calculate the values of the stopping potential in the two cases (without and with the lens in the aperture).

151. Electrons in hydrogen-like atom ($Z = 3$) make transitions from the fifth to the fourth orbit and from the fourth to the third orbit. The resulting radiations are incident normally on a metal plate and eject photoelectrons. The stopping potential for the photoelectrons ejected by the shorter wavelength is 3.95 V. Calculate the work function of the metal, and the stopping potential for the photoelectrons ejected by the longer wavelength (Rydberg's constant $= 1.094 \times 10^7 m^{-1}$) **(1990 JEE)**

152. Calculate the Rydberg constant R if He^+ ions are known to have the wavelength difference between the first (of the longest wavelength) lines of the Balmer and Lyman series equal to $\Delta\lambda = 133.7$ nm. **(Irodov 6.34)**

153. Find the wavelength of the first line of the He^+ ion spectral series whose interval between the extreme lines is $\Delta\omega = 5.18 \times 10^{15}\ s^{-1}$. **(Irodov 6.36)**

154. A stationary hydrogen atom emits a photon corresponding to the first line of the Lyman series. What velocity does the atom acquire? **(Irodov 6.41)**

155. A stationary He^+ ion emitted a photon corresponding to the first line of the Lyman series. That photon liberated a photoelectron from a stationary hydrogen atom in the ground state. Find the velocity of the photoelectron. **(Irodov 6.43)**

Integer Type Questions

156. A hydrogen-like atom has atomic number Z. Photons emitted in the electronic transitions from level $n = 4$ to level $n = 3$ in these atoms are used to perform photoelectric effect experiment on a target metal. The maximum kinetic energy of the photoelectrons generated is 1.95 eV. If the photoelectric threshold wavelength for the target metal is 310 nm, the value of Z is ....

[Given : $hc = 1240$ eV-nm and $Rhc = 13.6$ eV, where R is the Rydberg constant, h is the Planck's constant and c is the speed of light in vacuum] **(2023 Adv.)**

157. In a photoemission experiment, the maximum kinetic energies of photoelectrons from metals P, Q and R are E_P, E_Q and E_R, respectively, and they are related by $E_P = 2E_Q = 2E_R$. In this experiment, the same source of monochromatic light is used for metals P and Q while a different source of monochromatic light is used for the metal R. The work functions for metals P, Q and R are 4.0 eV, 4.5 eV and 5.5 eV, respectively. The energy of the incident photon used for metal R, in eV, is .... **(2021 Adv.)**

158. In a photoelectric experiment, a parallel beam of monochromatic light with power of 200 W is incident on a perfectly absorbing cathode of work function 6.25 eV. The frequency of light is just above the threshold frequency, so that the photoelectrons are emitted with negligible kinetic energy.

Assume that the photoelectron emission efficiency is 100%. A potential difference of 500 V is applied between the cathode and the anode. All the emitted electrons are incident normally on the anode and are absorbed. The anode experiences a force $F = n \times 10^{-4}$ N due to the impact of the electrons. The value of n is .... (Take mass of the electron, $m_e = 9 \times 10^{-31}$ kg and eV $= 1.6 \times 10^{-19}$ J) **(2018 Adv.)**

Answers

Level 1

1. (a) **2.** (b) **3.** (c) **4.** (a) **5.** (b) **6.** (c) **7.** (a) **8.** (a) **9.** (d) **10.** (a)
11. (d) **12.** (b) **13.** (a) **14.** (a) **15.** (c) **16.** (b) **17.** (d) **18.** (d) **19.** (c) **20.** (a)
21. (c) **22.** (b) **23.** (a) **24.** (c) **25.** (a) **26.** (b) **27.** (b) **28.** (d) **29.** (b) **30.** (d)
31. (c) **32.** (a) **33.** (c) **34.** (a) **35.** (c) **36.** (b) **37.** (d) **38.** (d) **39.** (b) **40.** (d)
41. (d) **42.** (d) **43.** (a) **44.** (d) **45.** (d) **46.** (b) **47.** (c) **48.** (c) **49.** (a) **50.** (b)
51. (d) **52.** (b) **53.** (a) **54.** (d) **55.** (b) **56.** (a) **57.** (b) **58.** (b) **59.** (a) **60.** (a)
61. (a) 2.47×10^{-19} J = 1.54 eV (b) 804 nm, infrared **62.** (a) 5.0×10^{14} Hz (b) 2.3×10^{20} photons/s
63. (a) 5.92×10^{20} Hz (b) 5.06×10^{-13} m **64.** (a) $K_2 = 4K_1$ (b) $E_2 = 2E_1$ **65.** (a) 2.52×10^{19} (b) 3.33×10^{-8} N
66. 10^{-8} N **67.** (a) 2.27 eV (b) 2.75×10^{17} (c) 9% **68.** (a) – 5.08 eV (b) – 5.63 eV **69.** 1.9 V
70. 1.81 eV, 9.0×10^5 ms, 3.0×10^5 m/s
71. 0.148 m **72.** 1.2 V **73.** (24) **74.** $\frac{h}{mc}$ **75.** (35) **76.** (27) **77.** (136) **78.** (3) **79.** (5)
80. (286) **81.** (15) **82.** (3) **83.** (6) **84.** (2) **85.** (2)

Level 2

86. (b) **87.** (b) **88.** (c) **89.** (b) **90.** (d) **91.** (a) **92.** (c) **93.** (c) **94.** (a)
95. (d) **96.** (a) **97.** (c) **98.** (a) **99.** (d) **100.** (c) **101.** (b) **102.** (d) **103.** (a,c) **104.** (a,b,c)
105. (a,c) **106.** (a,b,d) **107.** (a,b) **108.** (a,c) **109.** (a,b,c) **110.** (a,d)
111. (c) **112.** (c) **113.** (c) **114.** (c) **115.** (c) **116.** (a)
117. (a → r; b → q; c → p; d → p) **118.** (a → s; b → r; c → s; d → p) **119.** (a → q ; b → p ; c → r ; d → s)
120. (a → r; b → s; c → s; d → q) **121.** (a → p; b → s; c → q; d → s) **122.** (a → r; b → p; c → q; d → q)
123. (a → p,r; b → s; c → q,s; d → p,r) **124.** (a) 1.31 μm (b) 164 nm
125. (a) 6.58×10^{15} Hz, 0.823×10^{15} Hz (b) 2.46×10^{15} Hz (c) 8.23×10^6 revolutions
126. (a) 102 nm, 122 nm, 651 nm (b) No lines
127. $W = 11.925$ eV **128.** 2 eV, 0.754 V **129.** 793.3 Å **130.** 3.8 Å
131. (a) $n_i = 2$ (b) $Z = 6$ (c) 28.43 Å (d) 489.6 eV, 25.3 Å **132.** 4.5 eV
133. (a) 2000 Å, 1500 Å (b) $E_1 = -8.25$ eV, $E_2 = -2.05$ eV and $E_3 = -0.95$ eV (c) 8.25 V
134. (a) 4125 Å (b) 5.1% (c) 34 μA
135. (a) 1.69×10^{-28} kg (b) – 2.53 keV (c) 0.653 nm **136.** $r_n = \frac{nh}{2\pi\sqrt{mk}}$, $E_n = k \ln\left\{\frac{nh}{2\pi\sqrt{mk}}\right\}$
137. (a) $r_n = \sqrt{\frac{nh}{2\pi Be}}$ (b) $K = \frac{nhBe}{4\pi m}$ (c) $U = \frac{nheB}{4\pi m}$ (d) $E = \frac{nheB}{2\pi m}$ (e) $\frac{nh}{2e}$
138. (a) 10.2 volt (b) $Z = 2$ (c) 10.2 eV and 51 eV **139.** 1.9 eV, 4125 Å, No change is observed
140. 1.6 μA **141.** (a) 0.31 eV (b) 4 **142.** (a) 2 (b) 14.4 eV (c) 13.5 eV, 0.7 eV **143.** (a) 113.74 Å (b) 3
144. (a) 300 Å (b) 0.2645 Å **145.** (6, 1.875 μm)
146. (a) 5 (b) 16.53 eV (c) 36.4 Å (d) 340 eV, – 680 eV, 1.05×10^{-34} kg-m²/s (e) 1.06×10^{-11} m **147.** 150.8 eV, 0.5 Å
148. See the hints **159.** (a) 10^5/s (b) 285.1 (d) 111 s
150. (a) 2.87×10^{13} $s^{-1}m^{-2}$, 2.07×10^{-10} A (b) 2.06×10^{13} $s^{-1}m^{-2}$, 1.48×10^{-10} A (c) 1.06 eV **151.** (2 eV, 0.74 V) **152.** $R = 1.09 \times 10^7$ m^{-1}
153. $\lambda = 0.47$ μm **154.** $v = 3.25$ m/s **155.** $v = 3.1 \times 10^6$ m/s **156.** (3) **157.** (6) **158.** (24)

See hints on pages 326-348.

Hints & SOLUTIONS

Module 1.

1. $\because \quad \lambda = \frac{h}{\sqrt{2qVm}} \Rightarrow V = \frac{h^2}{2qm\lambda^2}$

2. $\lambda = \frac{h}{\sqrt{2qVm}} \propto \frac{1}{\sqrt{qVm}}$

$$\therefore \quad \frac{\lambda_\alpha}{\lambda_p} = \frac{\sqrt{q_p V_p m_p}}{\sqrt{q_\alpha V_\alpha m_\alpha}} = \sqrt{\frac{1 \times 100 \times 1}{2 \times 800 \times 4}} = \frac{1}{8}$$

$$\therefore \quad \lambda_\alpha = \frac{\lambda_p}{8} = \frac{\lambda_0}{8}$$

3. $\lambda = \frac{h}{\sqrt{2Em}}$

where, $\lambda = \text{constant}$

$\therefore \quad Em = \text{constant}$

or $\quad E \propto \frac{1}{m}$

4. As, $\lambda = \frac{h}{\sqrt{2qVm}}$

$$\Rightarrow \quad \lambda \propto \frac{1}{\sqrt{m}}$$

$$\frac{\lambda_1}{\lambda_2} = \sqrt{\frac{m_2}{m_1}}$$

So, $\quad \frac{\lambda_1}{\lambda_2} = \sqrt{\frac{M}{m}}$

$$\Rightarrow \quad \lambda_2 = \lambda_1 \sqrt{\left(\frac{m}{M}\right)} = \lambda \sqrt{\frac{m}{M}}$$

5. Momentum of an energetic particle is given by

$$p = \sqrt{2KEm}$$

$$\lambda = \frac{h}{p} \Rightarrow \frac{\lambda_p}{\lambda_e} = \frac{p_e}{p_p} = \sqrt{\frac{2Km_e}{2Km_p}}$$

$$= \sqrt{\frac{m_e}{m_p}} = \sqrt{\frac{1}{1849}} = \frac{1}{43}$$

6. de-Broglie wavelength is given by

$$\lambda = \frac{h}{mv} = \frac{h}{\sqrt{2mq\Delta v}}$$

According to the question,

$$\frac{\lambda_\alpha}{\lambda_p} = \sqrt{\frac{m_p v_p q_p}{m_\alpha v_\alpha q_\alpha}}$$

$$\Rightarrow \quad \frac{\lambda_\alpha}{\lambda_p} = \sqrt{\frac{1 \times 2 \times 1}{4 \times 4 \times 2}} = \frac{1}{4}$$

$$\Rightarrow \quad \lambda_p : \lambda_\alpha = 4:1$$

7. de-Broglie wavelength of electron in terms of kinetic energy K,

$$\lambda = \frac{h}{\sqrt{2mK}} \Rightarrow \lambda \propto \frac{1}{\sqrt{K}} \Rightarrow \frac{\lambda_1}{\lambda_2} = \sqrt{\frac{K_2}{K_1}}$$

If $K_2 = \frac{E}{4}$ and $K_1 = E$ (Given in question)

$$\therefore \quad \frac{\lambda_1}{\lambda_2} = \sqrt{\frac{E/4}{E}} = \left(\frac{1}{4}\right)^{1/2} = \frac{1}{2}$$

or $\quad \lambda_2 = 2\lambda_1 = 2\lambda$

8. For a gas molecule at absolute temperature T, $v_{rms} \propto \sqrt{T}$

Hence, momentum of gas molecule,

$$p \propto \sqrt{T}$$

$$\Rightarrow \quad \frac{p_2}{p_1} = \sqrt{\frac{T_2}{T_1}} = \sqrt{\frac{600}{300}}$$

$$\Rightarrow \quad p_2 = \sqrt{2}p_1 \text{ or } \frac{p_1}{p_2} = \frac{1}{\sqrt{2}}$$

So ratio of de-Broglie wavelength is

$$\frac{\lambda_2}{\lambda_1} = \frac{\frac{h}{p_2}}{\frac{h}{p_1}} = \frac{p_1}{p_2} = \frac{1}{\sqrt{2}} \Rightarrow \lambda_2 = \frac{\lambda_1}{\sqrt{2}}$$

9. Given de-Broglie wavelength of proton and electron have same value;

$$\lambda_p = \lambda_e$$

$$\frac{h}{p_p} = \frac{h}{p_e} \quad \{p = \text{momentum}, h = \text{Planck's constant}\}$$

$$\Rightarrow \quad p_p = p_e$$

$$\therefore \quad \text{Ratio } \frac{p_p}{p_e} = 1:1$$

10. de-Broglie wavelength,

$$\lambda = \frac{h}{p} = \frac{h}{\sqrt{2mK}} \Rightarrow K = \frac{p^2}{2m}$$

Also, in given case, kinetic energy K is constant, so

$$\lambda \propto \frac{1}{\sqrt{m}}$$

As, $\quad m_\alpha > m_p > m_e \Rightarrow \lambda_\alpha < \lambda_p < \lambda_e$

11. de-Broglie wavelength (λ) is related with potential difference as

$$\lambda = \frac{h}{\sqrt{2mqV}} \Rightarrow \frac{\lambda_1}{\lambda_2} = \sqrt{\frac{V_2}{V_1}} \quad \text{...(i)}$$

Here, $\lambda_1 = \lambda$, $\lambda_2 = \lambda_1 + 50\%$ of λ_1

$$= \lambda_1 + \frac{\lambda_1}{2} = \frac{3\lambda}{2}$$

$\therefore$ From Eq. (i), we have

$$\frac{V_2}{V_1} = \left(\frac{\lambda_1}{\lambda_2}\right)^2 = \left(\frac{\lambda}{\frac{3\lambda}{2}}\right)^2 = \left(\frac{2}{3}\right)^2 = \frac{4}{9}$$

$$\Rightarrow \quad \frac{V_1}{V_2} = \frac{9}{4}$$

12. de-Broglie wavelength of a charged particle accelerated by a potential V,

$$\lambda = \frac{h}{p} = \frac{h}{\sqrt{2mqV}}$$

$$\frac{\lambda_\alpha}{\lambda_\beta} = \sqrt{\frac{m_p}{m_\alpha} \cdot \frac{q_p}{q_\alpha}} = \sqrt{\frac{m_p}{4m_p} \cdot \frac{q_p}{2q_p}}$$

$$= \frac{1}{\sqrt{8}} = \frac{1}{\sqrt{m}} \quad \text{(given)}$$

$$\therefore \quad m = 8$$

13. de-Broglie wavelength of a moving particle with kinetic energy KE is given as

$$\lambda = \frac{h}{\sqrt{2m\text{KE}}} \text{ or KE} = \frac{h^2}{2m\lambda^2}$$

For same wavelength, $KE \propto \frac{1}{m}$

$\because$ Mass of α-particle $= 4$ (mass of proton)

$$\frac{\text{KE}_p}{\text{KE}_\alpha} = \frac{m_\alpha}{m_p} = \frac{4m_p}{m_p} = \frac{4}{1}$$

14. Let m be the mass of nuclei B and C.

So, the given situation can be shown in the figure below

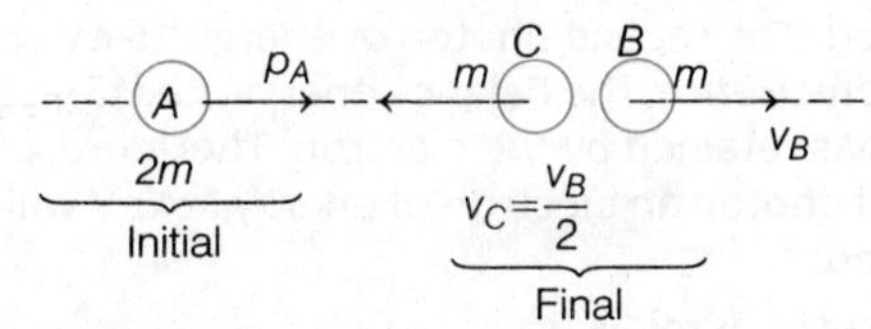

Now, according to the conservation of linear momentum,

Initial momentum = Final momentum

$$\Rightarrow \quad p_A = p_B + p_C$$

$$\text{or} \quad 2mv_A = mv_B + mv_C$$

$$2mv_A = mv_B - \frac{mv_B}{2}$$

$$\Rightarrow \quad 2v_A = \frac{1}{2}v_B \Rightarrow v_B = 4v_A \quad \text{...(i)}$$

$$\text{and} \quad v_C = \frac{v_B}{2} = 2v_A \quad \text{...(ii)}$$

So, momentum of B and C respectively, can now be given as

$$p_B = m_B v_B = m4v_A = 2(2mv_A) \quad \text{[using Eq. (i)]}$$

$$\text{or} \quad p_B = 2p_A \quad \text{...(iii)}$$

$$\text{and} \quad p_C = m_C v_C = m2v_A \quad \text{[using Eq. (ii)]}$$

$$\text{or} \quad p_C = p_A \quad \text{...(iv)}$$

From the relation of de-Broglie wavelength, i.e. $\lambda = \frac{h}{p}$

where, p is momentum and h is Planck's constant.

So, for A, $\lambda_A = \frac{h}{p_A}$ or $p_A = \frac{h}{\lambda_A}$ ...(v)

From Eq. (v) and Eq. (iii), λ_B can be written as

$$\lambda_B = \frac{h}{2 \times \frac{h}{\lambda_A}} = \frac{\lambda_A}{2}$$

Similarly, for C, $\lambda_C = \frac{h}{p_C} = \frac{h}{p_A}$ [using Eq. (iv)]

Similarly, from Eq. (v), λ_C can be written as

$$\lambda_C = \frac{h}{\frac{h}{\lambda_A}} = \lambda_A$$

15. Kinetic energy in magnetic field remains unchanged while in electric field it will increase. Further,

$$\lambda \propto \frac{1}{\sqrt{K}}$$

16. $E = \frac{hc}{\lambda}, P = \frac{h}{\lambda}$

17. Number of photons emitted per second,

$$N_1 = \frac{\text{Power of source}}{\text{Energy of one photon}} = \frac{P}{(hc/\lambda)} = \frac{P\lambda}{hc}$$

At a distance r, these photons are falling on an area $4\pi r^2$.

$\therefore$ Number of photons incident per unit area per unit time,

$$N_2 = \frac{N_1}{4\pi r^2} = \frac{P\lambda}{(4\pi r^2)hc}$$

18. $\lambda = \frac{h}{\sqrt{2qVm}} \Rightarrow \lambda \propto \frac{1}{\sqrt{qm}}$

$$\frac{\lambda_p}{\lambda_d} = \sqrt{\frac{(qm)_d}{(qm)_p}} = \sqrt{\frac{1 \times 2}{1 \times 1}} = \sqrt{2}$$

19. $\lambda = \frac{h}{\sqrt{2Km}}$

$$\Rightarrow \quad \lambda \propto \frac{1}{\sqrt{m}}$$

$$\frac{\lambda_d}{\lambda_\alpha} = \sqrt{\frac{m_\alpha}{m_d}} = \sqrt{\frac{4}{2}} = \sqrt{2}$$

20. $\lambda = \frac{h}{mv}$

(a) $\lambda = \frac{6.63 \times 10^{-34}}{(46 \times 10^{-3})(30)}$

$$= 4.8 \times 10^{-34} \text{ m}$$

(b) $\lambda = \frac{6.63 \times 10^{-34}}{9.31 \times 10^{-31} \times 10^7}$

$$= 7.12 \times 10^{-11} \text{ m}$$

21. (a) $\lambda = \frac{h}{p} \Rightarrow p = \frac{h}{\lambda}$

(b) $\lambda (\text{in Å}) = \sqrt{\frac{150}{\text{KE (in eV)}}}$

22. $v_{rms} = \sqrt{\frac{3RT}{M}} = v$ (say)

and $\lambda = \frac{h}{mv} = \frac{h}{m}\sqrt{\frac{M}{3RT}}$

Substituting the values, we get

$$\lambda = \frac{6.63 \times 10^{-34}}{(2/6.02 \times 10^{23}) \times 10^{-3}} \sqrt{\frac{2 \times 10^{-3}}{3(8.31)(20+273)}}$$

$$= 1.04 \times 10^{-4}\ \text{m} = 1.04\ \text{Å}$$

Module 2.

Introductory Exercise

1. The expressions of kinetic energy, potential energy and total energy are

$$K_n = \frac{me^4}{8\varepsilon_0^2 n^2 h^2} \Rightarrow K_n \propto \frac{1}{n^2}$$

$$U_n = \frac{-me^4}{4\varepsilon_0^2 n^2 h^2} \Rightarrow U_n \propto -\frac{1}{n^2}$$

and $$E_n = \frac{-me^4}{8\varepsilon_0^2 n^2 h^2} \Rightarrow E_n \propto -\frac{1}{n^2}$$

In the transition from some excited state to ground state, the value of n decreases, therefore kinetic energy increases, but potential and total energy decrease.

2.

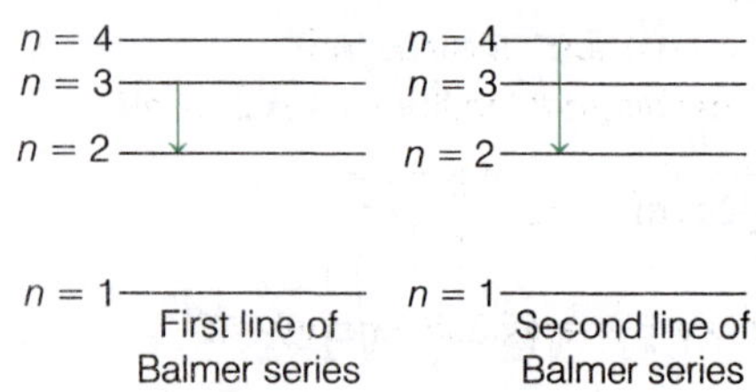

For hydrogen or hydrogen type atoms,

$$\frac{1}{\lambda} = RZ^2\left(\frac{1}{n_f^2} - \frac{1}{n_i^2}\right)$$

In the transition from $n_i \longrightarrow n_f$,

$$\therefore \quad \lambda \propto \frac{1}{Z^2\left(\frac{1}{n_f^2} - \frac{1}{n_i^2}\right)}$$

$$\therefore \quad \frac{\lambda_2}{\lambda_1} = \frac{Z_1^2\left(\frac{1}{n_f^2} - \frac{1}{n_i^2}\right)_1}{Z_2^2\left(\frac{1}{n_f^2} - \frac{1}{n_i^2}\right)_2}$$

$$\lambda_2 = \frac{\lambda_1 Z_1^2\left(\frac{1}{n_f^2} - \frac{1}{n_i^2}\right)_1}{Z_2^2\left(\frac{1}{n_f^2} - \frac{1}{n_i^2}\right)_2}$$

Substituting the values, we have

$$= \frac{(6561\ \text{Å})(1)^2\left(\frac{1}{2^2} - \frac{1}{3^2}\right)}{(2)^2\left(\frac{1}{2^2} - \frac{1}{4^2}\right)} = 1215\ \text{Å}$$

$\therefore$ Correct option is (a).

3. The series in U-V region is Lyman series. Largest wavelength corresponds to minimum energy which occurs in transition from $n=2$ to $n=1$.

$$\therefore \quad 122 = \frac{\frac{1}{R}}{\left(\frac{1}{1^2} - \frac{1}{2^2}\right)} \quad \text{...(i)}$$

The smallest wavelength in the infrared region corresponds to maximum energy of Paschen series.

$$\therefore \quad \lambda = \frac{\frac{1}{R}}{\left(\frac{1}{3^2} - \frac{1}{\infty}\right)} \quad \text{...(ii)}$$

Solving Eqs. (i) and (ii), we get

$$\lambda = 823.5\ \text{nm}$$

$\therefore$ Correct option is (b).

4. The first photon will excite the hydrogen atom (in ground state) to first excited state (as $E_2 - E_1 = 10.2$ eV). Hence, during de-excitation a photon of 10.2 eV will be released. The second photon of energy 15 eV can ionise the atom. Hence, the balance energy, i.e.$(15 - 13.6)$ eV $= 1.4$ eVis retained by the electron. Therefore, by the second photon an electron of energy 1.4 eV will be released.

$\therefore$ Correct answer is (c).

5. In second excited state $n = 3$,

So, $l_H = l_{Li} = 3\left(\frac{h}{2\pi}\right)$

while $E \propto Z^2$

and $Z_H = 1, Z_{Li} = 3$

So, $|E_{Li}| = 9|E_H|$ or $|E_H| < |E_{Li}|$

6. Energy of infrared radiation is less than the energy of ultraviolet radiation. In options (a), (b) and (c), energy released will be more, while in option (d) only, energy released will be less.

7. For hydrogen and hydrogen like atoms,

$$E_n = -13.6\frac{(Z^2)}{(n^2)}\ \text{eV}$$

Therefore, ground state energy of doubly ionized lithium atom ($Z=3, n=1$) will be

$$E_1 = (-13.6)\frac{(3)^2}{(1)^2} = -122.4 \text{ eV}$$

$\therefore$ Ionization energy of an electron in ground state of doubly ionized lithium atom will be 122.4 eV.

8. Shortest wavelength will correspond to maximum energy. As value of atomic number (Z) increases, the magnitude of energy in different energy states gets increased. Value of Z is maximum for doubly ionised lithium atom ($Z=3$) among the given elements. Hence, wavelength corresponding to this will be least.

$\therefore$ Correct option is (d).

9. Longest wavelength means minimum energy.

$$(\Delta E)_{min} = E_3 - E_2 = -\frac{13.6}{9} + \frac{13.6}{4} = 1.9 \text{ eV}$$

$$\lambda \text{ (in Å)} = \frac{12375}{1.9} = 6513 \text{ or } \lambda \approx 651 \text{ nm}$$

10. $Z=3$ for doubly ionized atom $E \propto Z^2$

Ionization energy of hydrogen atom is 13.6 eV.

$\therefore$ Ionisation energy of this atom

$$= (3)^2(13.6) = 122.4 \text{ eV}$$

11. $E_n = \frac{-13.6}{(n)^2} = -1.51$

$\Rightarrow$ $n = 3$

Now, $L_n = n\left(\frac{h}{2\pi}\right)$

12. $5E - E = hf \Rightarrow E = \frac{hf}{4}$ ...(i)

Between 5E and 4E

$$5E - 4E = hf_1$$

$\therefore$ $f_1 = \frac{E}{h} = \frac{f}{4}$ [from Eq. (i)]

Between 4E and E

$$4E - E = hf_2$$

$\therefore$ $f_2 = \frac{3E}{h} = 3\left(\frac{f}{4}\right) = \frac{3}{4}f$

Exercise

1. Kinetic energy of an electron in nth orbit of hydrogen atom is $K = \frac{me^4}{8\varepsilon_0^2 h^2 n^2}$ and total energy of electron in nth orbit is

$$E = -\frac{me^4}{8\varepsilon_0^2 h^2 n^2}, \frac{K}{E} = -1 \text{ or } K = -E$$

2. When an electron jumps from lower orbit to higher orbit, it absorbs energy. If f be the frequency of absorbed photon, then

$$hf = E_2 - E_1$$

where, E_2 is energy of higher state and E_1, is energy of lower state.

$\Rightarrow$ $f = (E_2 - E_1)/h$

So, only statement II is correct.

3. $v \propto \frac{1}{n}$, $r \propto n^2$, $E \propto \frac{1}{n^2}$

4. $(2\pi r_2) = 2\lambda_2$

$$(2\pi r_3) = 3\lambda_3$$

$\therefore$ $\frac{\lambda_2}{\lambda_3} = \frac{3r_2}{2r_3}$ ...(i)

Now, $r \propto n^2$

$\therefore$ $\frac{r_2}{r_3} = \left(\frac{2}{3}\right)^2$

Substituting in Eq. (i), we get

$$\frac{\lambda_2}{\lambda_3} = \frac{2}{3}$$

5. $v_1^H = 2.19 \times 10^6 \text{ m/s} \approx \frac{c}{137}$

6. $E \propto \frac{Z^2}{n^2}$

$\therefore$ $\frac{(-13.2)\times(Z)^2}{(2)^2} = -13.6$

$\therefore$ $Z = 2$

7. $U_1 = -27.2$ eV

U_1 is assumed zero. Therefore, it is increased by 27.2 eV at all points.

$E_\infty = 0$ under normal conditions.

Hence, in charged conditions it is 27.2 eV.

8. $r_n \propto \frac{n^2}{Z}$ or $r_n \propto \frac{1}{Z}$

9. Frequency $\propto$ energy and energy $\propto Z^2$

10. $E \propto \frac{Z^2}{n^2}$

$\therefore$ $\frac{Z^2}{n^2} = 1$ or $n = Z = 3$

11. In Bohr's atom (H-atom), radius of nth orbit is given by

$$R = \frac{Kn^2}{Z}$$

Let R' = radius of 4th orbit and

R = radius of 3rd orbit then,

$$\frac{R}{R'} = \frac{\frac{K(3)^2}{Z}}{\frac{K(4)^2}{Z}}$$

$$\frac{R}{R'} = \frac{9}{16} \Rightarrow R' = \frac{16}{9}R$$

12. For He^+

$$E = -13.6\frac{Z^2}{n^2} = -13.6 \times \frac{4}{4}$$
$$= -13.6 \text{ eV}$$

13. Given, $U = \frac{1}{2} m\omega^2 r^2$

Using Bohr's postulate :
Angular momentum,

$$L = mvr = \frac{nh}{2\pi} \text{ or } mr^2\omega^2 = \frac{nh}{2\pi}$$

where, n is number of orbit.

$$r^2 \propto n \Rightarrow r \propto \sqrt{n}$$

14. Bohr's orbit is orbit of ground state of atom.
So, in first orbit angular momentum

$$L = \frac{h}{2\pi}$$

In second orbit angular momentum

$$L' = \frac{2h}{2\pi}$$

Hence, change in angular momentum is

$$\Delta L = L' - L = \frac{2h}{2\pi} - \frac{h}{2\pi} = \frac{h}{2\pi} \text{ or } L$$

15. We know that, $E = \frac{hc}{\lambda}$

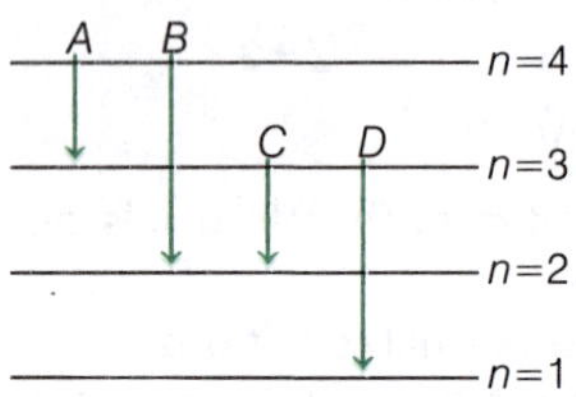

$$\Rightarrow \quad \lambda = \frac{hc}{E}$$

For λ_{min}, E must be maximum and E is maximum for (D).
Hence, option (a) is correct.

16. Given, energy of the electron beam
$= 12.5$ eV

According to Bohr's postulate, an electron makes jump to higher energy orbital if it absorbs a photon of energy equal to different between the energies of an excited state and the ground state. Assuming that collided electron takes energy equal to 10.2 eV or 12.09 eV from incoming electron beam. The maximum excited state is $n = 3$. So number of spectral lines is $\frac{3(3-1)}{2} = 3$.

17. The energy of an electron in nth orbit is given as

$$E_n = -Rhc\frac{Z^2}{n^2}$$

Electron is making an transition from 4th energy state to 2nd energy state, then energy released

$$\Delta E = E_4 - E_2$$
$$= -Rhc\frac{Z^2}{4^2} - \left(-Rhc\frac{Z^2}{2^2}\right)$$
$$\Rightarrow \quad \Delta E = Rhc\left(\frac{1}{2^2} - \frac{1}{4^2}\right)Z^2$$

For hydrogen like atom, $Z = 4$

$$\Delta E = 13.6\left(\frac{1}{4} - \frac{1}{16}\right) \times (4)^2$$
$$= 13.6 \times \left(\frac{3}{16}\right) \times (4)^2$$
$$\Rightarrow \quad \Delta E = 40.8 \text{ eV}$$

Alternate Solution

When an electron of a hydrogen like atom, jumps from the energy state n_2 to energy state n_1, then released energy,

$$\Delta E = E_2 - E_1 = \frac{-13.6\,Z^2}{n_2^2} - \left[\frac{-13.6\,Z^2}{n_1^2}\right]$$
$$= 13.6\,Z^2\left[\frac{1}{n_1^2} - \frac{1}{n_2^2}\right] = 13.6 \times 4^2\left[\frac{1}{2^2} - \frac{1}{4^2}\right]$$

[Here, $Z = 4$, $n_1 = 2$, $n_2 = 4$]

$$= 40.8 \text{eV}$$

18. Given, wavelength of photon,

$\lambda = 124.1 \text{ nm} = 1.24 \times 10^{-7}$ m

$h = 6.62 \times 10^{-34}$ J-s

$\therefore$ Energy of photon,

$$E = \frac{hc}{\lambda} = \frac{6.62 \times 10^{-34} \times 3 \times 10^8}{1.24 \times 10^{-7}}$$
$$= 1.6 \times 10^{-18} \text{ J} = \frac{1.6 \times 10^{-18}}{1.6 \times 10^{-19}} \text{ eV}$$
$$= 10 \text{ eV}$$

Energy of photon in transition D,

$$E' = 0 - (-10) = 10 \text{ eV}$$

19. (a) $E_1 = -13.6$ eV

$$\therefore \quad KE = |E_1| = 13.6 \text{ eV}$$
$$\lambda_1 \text{ (in Å)} = \sqrt{\frac{150}{KE \text{ (in eV)}}} \text{ for an electron}$$
$$= \sqrt{\frac{150}{13.6}} = 3.32 \text{ Å}$$
$$2\pi r_1 = 2\pi(0.529 \text{ Å})$$
$$\approx 3.32 \text{ Å}$$

(b) $E_4 = \frac{E_1}{(4)^2} = \frac{-13.6}{(4)^2} = -0.85$ eV

$$\lambda_4 = \sqrt{\frac{150}{0.85}} \text{ as } KE = |E_4| = 0.85 \text{ eV}$$
$$\approx 13.3 \text{ Å}$$
$$2\pi r_4 = 2\pi(n)^2 r_1 \quad (\text{as } r \propto n^2)$$
$$= 53.15 \text{ Å} \approx 4\lambda_4$$

20. $E_n = E_1 = \frac{12375}{1023}$

or $\frac{-13.6}{(n)^2} + 13.6 = 12.1$

Solving this equation, we get $n = 3$

$\therefore$ Total possible emission lines $= \frac{n(n-1)}{2} = 3$

Longest wavelength means, minimum energy, which is corresponding to $n = 3$ to $n = Z$

$$\therefore \quad \lambda_{max} = \frac{12375}{E_3 - E_2}$$

Here, $E_3 - E_2 = -\frac{13.6}{(3)^2} + \frac{13.6}{(4)^2} = 1.9 \text{ eV}$

$$\therefore \quad \lambda_{max} = \frac{12375}{1.9} = 6513 \text{ Å}$$

21. In hydrogen atom,

$$\Delta E_1 = E_3 - E_1 = 12.1 \text{ eV}$$

$$E \propto Z^2$$

$\therefore$ For $Z = 3$,

$$\Delta E_2 = (3)^2 \Delta E_1 = (3)^2 (12.1) = 108.9 \text{ Å}$$

$$\therefore \quad \lambda = \frac{12375}{108.9} \approx 113 \text{ Å}$$

22. $E_n - E_1 = \Delta E_1 + \Delta E_2$

$$\therefore \quad \left[-\frac{13.6}{n^2} + 13.6\right](Z)^2 = \frac{12375}{1085} + \frac{12375}{304}$$

Putting $Z = 2$ for He^+, we get

$$n = 5$$

23. (a) Ionization energy $= 15.6$ eV

$\therefore$ Ionization potential $= 15.6$ V

(b) $E_\infty - E_2 = 5.3$ eV

$$\therefore \quad \lambda = \frac{12375}{5.3} = 2335 \text{ Å}$$

(c) $E_3 - E_1 = 12.52$ eV

$\therefore$ Excitation potential is 12.52 V.

(d) $E_3 - E_1 = 12.52$ eV

$$\therefore \quad \lambda = \frac{12375}{12.52} \text{ Å} = 988.41 \text{ Å}$$

$$\therefore \text{Wave number} = \frac{1}{\lambda} = \frac{1}{988.41 \times 10^{-10}} \text{ m}^{-1}$$

$$= 1.01 \times 10^7 \text{ m}^{-1}$$

24. Given,

Initial state $n_i = 3$, final state $n_f = 2$

$$\Delta E = 13.6\left[\frac{1}{n_f^2} - \frac{1}{n_i^2}\right] \quad \text{...(i)}$$

$$= 13.6\left[\frac{1}{4} - \frac{1}{9}\right] = 1.9 \text{ eV}$$

$$\Delta E = \frac{hc}{\lambda}$$

$$\Rightarrow \quad \lambda = \frac{hc}{\Delta E} \quad \text{...(ii)}$$

$$p_i = p_f \quad \text{(momentum conservation)}$$

$$0 = -mv + \frac{h}{\lambda'}$$

$$\Rightarrow \quad v = \frac{h}{m\lambda'} \quad \text{...(iii)}$$

Change in kinetic energy,

$$\Delta E = \frac{h^2}{2m\lambda'^2} + \frac{hc}{\lambda'}$$

$$\lambda'^2 \Delta E - hc\lambda' - \frac{h^2}{2m} = 0$$

Using quadratic equation solution.

$$\lambda' = \frac{hc \pm hc\sqrt{1 + \frac{2\Delta E}{mc^2}}}{2\Delta E} \quad \text{...(iv)}$$

$$\frac{\lambda'}{\lambda} = \frac{1 + \left(1 + \frac{2\Delta E}{mc^2}\right)^{1/2}}{2}$$

Using binomial expansion,

$$\frac{\lambda'}{\lambda} = \frac{1 + 1 + \frac{\Delta E}{mc^2}}{2} = 1 + \frac{\Delta E}{2mc^2}$$

Error in wavelength

$$= \frac{\lambda' - \lambda}{\lambda} = \frac{\Delta E}{2mc^2}$$

$$= \frac{1.9 \times 1.6 \times 10^{-19}}{2 \times 1.67 \times 10^{-27} \times 9 \times 10^{16}} = 10^{-9}$$

Percentage change $= 10^{-9} \times 100\% = 10^{-7}$

Correct answer $= 7$

Alternate Solution

H-atom falls from $n = 3$ to $n = 2$,

energy of emitted photon,

$$E = (-1.5) - (-3.4) \text{ eV}$$

$$= 1.9 \text{ eV}$$

Momentum of emitted photon,

$$p = \frac{E}{c} = \frac{1.9 \times 1.6 \times 10^{-19}}{3 \times 10^8}$$

$$= 10^{-27} \text{ N-s}$$

To conserve momentum, H-atom must have,

$$p = 10^{-27} \text{ N-s}$$

$$\text{KE of atom, KE} = \frac{p^2}{2m} = \frac{(10^{-27})^2}{2 \times 1.6 \times 10^{-27}}$$

$$= 3.13 \times 10^{-28}$$

Percentage loss in energy of photon

$$= \frac{\text{loss in energy}}{\text{initial energy}} \times 100\%$$

$$= \frac{3.13 \times 10^{-28}}{1.9 \times 1.6 \times 10^{-19}} \simeq 10^{-7}$$

25. Given, lowest wavelength of Lyman series $=917$ Å

For lowest wavelength of Lyman series

$$\frac{1}{\lambda}=RZ^2\left(\frac{1}{1^2}-\frac{1}{\infty^2}\right)=RZ^2$$

For lowest wavelength of Balmer series,

$$\frac{1}{\lambda'}=RZ^2\left(\frac{1}{2^2}-\frac{1}{\infty^2}\right)=\frac{RZ^2}{4}$$

$$\Rightarrow \quad \lambda'=\frac{4}{RZ^2}=4\times 917=3668 \text{ Å}$$

26. Wavelength of emitted radiation is

$$\frac{1}{\lambda}=R\left(\frac{1}{n_1^2}-\frac{1}{n_2^2}\right)$$

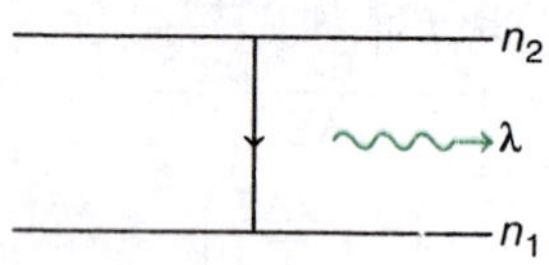

For H_α line, $n_2=3$, $n_1=2$

For H_β line, $n_2=4$, $n_1=2$

So, $$\frac{1}{\lambda_\alpha}=R\left(\frac{1}{4}-\frac{1}{9}\right)=\frac{5R}{36}$$

and $$\frac{1}{\lambda_\beta}=R\left(\frac{1}{4}-\frac{1}{16}\right)=\frac{12}{64}R$$

So, ratio $$\frac{\lambda_\alpha}{\lambda_\beta}=\frac{27}{20}=\frac{x}{20}$$

Therefore, $x=27$

27. We know that radius of nth orbit of H-atom is given as,

$$r_n=r_0\times\frac{n^2}{Z}$$

For 2nd orbit of He^+,

$$Z=2, n=2$$

$$\therefore \quad r_1=r_0\cdot\frac{2^2}{2}=2r_0$$

$$\Rightarrow \quad r_1=2r_0 \quad \text{...(i)}$$

Similarly, for fourth orbit Be^{3-}

$$Z=4, x=4$$

$$\therefore \quad r_2=r_0\times\frac{4^2}{4}=4r_0$$

$$\therefore \quad \frac{r_1}{r_2}=\frac{2r_0}{4r_0}=\frac{1}{2}$$

$$\Rightarrow \quad \frac{r_2}{r_1}=\frac{2}{1}=\frac{x}{1} \quad \text{[Given]}$$

$$\therefore \quad x=2$$

28. We know that,

$$r_n=\frac{0.51n^2}{Z}\text{ Å}$$

For Li^{++}, $Z=3$

$$r_5=0.51\times\frac{25}{3}\times 10^{-10}\text{ m}$$
$$=17\times 25\times 10^{-12}\text{ m}$$
$$=425\times 10^{-12}\text{ m}$$

29. Using, $E=\frac{Ke^2}{2r} \Rightarrow r=\frac{Ke^2}{2E}$

Given, $E=12.8\text{ eV}=12.8\times e\text{J}$

$$r=\frac{9\times 10^9\times e^2}{2\times 12.8e}$$
$$=\frac{9\times 10^9\times 1.6\times 16^{-19}}{2\times 12.8}$$
$$=\frac{9\times 10^{-10}}{2\times\frac{12.8}{1.6}}=\frac{9\times 10^{-10}}{\frac{25.6}{1.6}}$$
$$=\frac{9\times 10^{-10}}{16}=\frac{9}{x}\times 10^{-10}\text{m}$$

$$x=16$$

30. According to given situation,

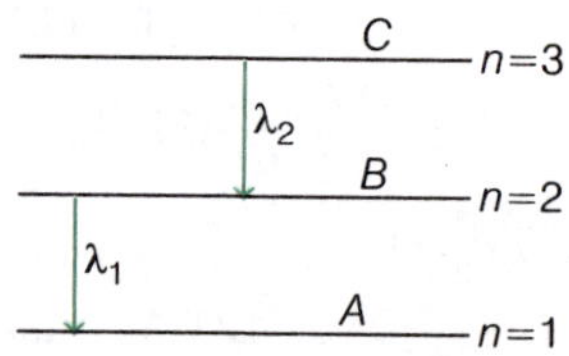

$$E_B-E_A=\frac{hc}{\lambda_1}$$

$$\Rightarrow \quad \frac{-13.6}{2^2}-\frac{(-13.6)}{1^2}=\frac{hc}{\lambda_1}$$

$$\Rightarrow \quad 10.2=\frac{hc}{\lambda_1} \Rightarrow \frac{hc}{\lambda_1}=10.2 \quad \text{...(i)}$$

Similarly, $E_C-E_B=\frac{hc}{\lambda_2}$

$$\Rightarrow \quad \frac{-13.6}{3^2}-\left(-\frac{13.6}{2^2}\right)=\frac{hc}{\lambda_2}$$

$$\Rightarrow \quad 13.6\left(\frac{1}{4}-\frac{1}{9}\right)=\frac{hc}{\lambda_2}$$

$$\Rightarrow \quad 13.6\times\frac{5}{36}=\frac{hc}{\lambda_2} \Rightarrow 1.89=\frac{hc}{\lambda_2}$$

$$\Rightarrow \quad \frac{hc}{\lambda_2}=1.89 \quad \text{...(ii)}$$

On dividing Eq. (ii) by Eq. (i), we get

$$\frac{\frac{hc}{\lambda_1}}{\frac{hc}{\lambda_2}}=\frac{10.2}{1.89} \Rightarrow \frac{\lambda_2}{\lambda_1}=5.6$$

$$\Rightarrow \quad \frac{\lambda_1}{\lambda_2}=\frac{1}{5.6}=\frac{7}{4\times 9.8}=\frac{7}{4n} \quad \text{[Given]}$$

$$\therefore \quad n=9.8$$

31. Energy of photon, $E = 12.75$ eV

Let, the electron makes transition from ground states ($n = 1$) to $(n-1)$th excited state (or nth shell), then we can write.

$$E = 13.6\left(\frac{1}{1^2} - \frac{1}{n^2}\right) \times Z^2 \text{ (in eV)}$$

For hydrogen atom, $Z = 1$,

$$E = 13.6\left(\frac{1}{1} - \frac{1}{n^2}\right)$$

$$12.75 = 13.6\left(1 - \frac{1}{n^2}\right)$$

$$\Rightarrow \quad n = 4$$

Angular momentum,

$$L = \frac{nh}{2\pi} = 4 \times \frac{4.14 \times 10^{-15}}{2\pi} \text{ eV-s}$$

$$\Rightarrow \quad L = \frac{828}{\pi} \times 10^{-17} \text{ eV-s}$$

Module 3.

Introductory Exercise

1. K_α transition takes place from $n_1 = 2$ to $n_2 = 1$

$$\therefore \quad \frac{1}{\lambda} = R(Z-b)^2\left[\frac{1}{(1)^2} - \frac{1}{(2)^2}\right]$$

For K-series, $b = 1$

$$\therefore \quad \frac{1}{\lambda} \propto (Z-1)^2$$

$$\Rightarrow \quad \frac{\lambda_{Cu}}{\lambda_{Mo}} = \frac{(Z_{Mo}-1)^2}{(Z_{Cu}-1)^2} = \frac{(42-1)^2}{(29-1)^2}$$

$$= \frac{41 \times 41}{28 \times 28} = \frac{1681}{784} = 2.144$$

2. Cut off wavelength depends on the applied voltage not on the atomic number of the target. Characteristic wavelengths depend on the atomic number of target.

3. $\frac{1}{\lambda} \propto (Z-1)^2$

$$\therefore \quad \frac{\lambda_1}{\lambda_2} = \left(\frac{Z_2-1}{Z_1-1}\right)^2$$

$$\text{or} \quad \frac{1}{4} = \left(\frac{Z_2-1}{11-1}\right)^2$$

Solving this, we get $Z_2 = 6$

$\therefore$ Correct answer is (a).

4. Wavelength λ_k is independent of the accelerating voltage (V), while the minimum wavelength λ_c is inversely proportional to V. Therefore, as V is increased, λ_k remains unchanged whereas λ_c decreases or $\lambda_k - \lambda_c$ will increase.

5. The continuous X-ray spectrum is shown in figure.

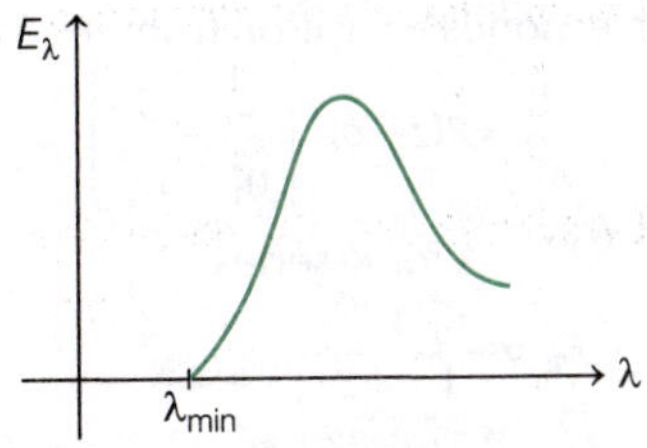

All wavelengths $> \lambda_{min}$ are found, where

$$\lambda_{min} = \frac{12375}{V \text{ (in volt)}} \text{ Å}$$

Here, V is the applied voltage.

6. $\Delta E = h\nu = Rhc\,(Z-b)^2\left(\frac{1}{n_1^2} - \frac{1}{n_2^2}\right)$

For K-series, $b = 1$

$$\therefore \quad \nu = Rc\,(Z-1)^2\left(\frac{1}{n_1^2} - \frac{1}{n_2^2}\right)$$

Substituting the values,

$$4.2 \times 10^{18} = (1.1 \times 10^7)(3 \times 10^8)(Z-1)^2\left(\frac{1}{1} - \frac{1}{4}\right)$$

$$\therefore \quad (Z-1)^2 = 1697$$

$$\text{or} \quad Z - 1 \approx 41$$

$$\text{or} \quad Z = 42$$

Exercise

1. $\lambda_{min}(\text{in Å}) = \dfrac{12375}{V \text{ (in volts)}}$

$$\lambda_{min} = \frac{12375}{20 \times 10^3} = 0.62 \text{ Å}$$

2. For K_α transition should be from $n = 2$ to $n = 1$

$$\frac{1}{\lambda_{K_\alpha}} = R(Z-1)^2\left(\frac{1}{1^2} - \frac{1}{2^2}\right)$$

$$= \frac{3}{4}R(Z-1)^2$$

$$\therefore \quad (Z-1) = \frac{2}{\sqrt{3R\lambda_{K_\alpha}}}$$

Here, R = Rydberg's constant

$= 1.097 \times 10^7$ m^{-1} and

$\lambda_{K_\alpha} = 0.76$ Å

$= 0.76 \times 10^{-10}$ m (Given)

Substituting the values, we have

or $Z = 41$

3. X-rays are electromagnetic waves and electromagnetic waves travel with the speed of light i.e. 3.0×10^8 m/s.

4. K_α corresponds to transition from $n=2$ to $n=1$ and K_β corresponds transition from $n=3$ to $n=1$

$$\frac{1}{\lambda_K}=R(z-b)^2\left[\frac{1}{n_1^2}-\frac{1}{n_2^2}\right]$$

$b=1$ for K-series

$$\lambda_K \propto \frac{1}{\frac{1}{n_1^2}-\frac{1}{n_2^2}}$$

Since, $E_{31}>E_{21}$ and $E \propto \frac{1}{\lambda}$

$$\therefore \quad \lambda_{K_\beta}<\lambda_{K_\alpha} \text{ or } \lambda_{K_\beta}=\lambda_{K_\alpha}\left[\frac{\frac{1}{1^2}-\frac{1}{2^2}}{\frac{1}{1^2}-\frac{1}{3^2}}\right]$$

$$=0.32\left(\frac{3/4}{8/9}\right)=0.27\text{ Å}$$

5. Cut-off wavelength is given by

$$\lambda_{min}=\left\{\frac{12375}{V(\text{in volts})}\right\}(\text{in Å})$$

with increase in applied voltage V, speed of electrons striking the anode is increased or cut-off wavelength of the emitted X-rays decreases.

Further, with increase in number of electrons striking the anode more number of photons of X-rays will be emitted. Therefore, intensity of X-rays will increase.

6. Ionisation energy

$$E_1 \propto\left[\frac{1}{1^2}-\frac{1}{\infty}\right] \quad \text{...(i)}$$

and $E_1=40\text{ keV}$ ($\because$ Binding energy)

Minimum energy to produce X-rays in the transition for $n=2$ to $n=1$ is

$$E_2 \propto\left[\frac{1}{1^2}-\frac{1}{2^2}\right] \quad \text{...(ii)}$$

Dividing Eq. (ii) by Eq. (i),

$$E_2=\frac{3}{4}E_1=30\text{ keV}$$

Therefore minimum voltage required is 30 keV or 30×10^3 V and the energy of characteristic radiation will be, 30 keV or 30×10^3 eV.

7. Cut-off wavelength depends on the accelerating voltage, not the characteristic wavelengths. Further, approximately 2% kinetic energy of the electrons is utilised in producing X-rays. Rest 98% is lost in heat. Therefore, both Assertion and Reason are true but Reason is not the correct explanation of Assertion.

8. Theory based question.

9. Energy of X-ray >13.6 eV

10. $K_{max}=18\times 10^3\text{ eV}=\frac{1}{2}mv_{max}^2$

$$\therefore \quad v_{max}=\sqrt{\frac{2\times 18\times 10^3\times 1.6\times 10^{-19}}{9.1\times 10^{-31}}}$$

$$=8\times 10^7\text{ m/s}$$

11. $\lambda_{min}\text{ (in Å)}=\frac{12375}{V\text{ (in volts)}}$

For $\lambda_{min}=1\text{ Å}$

$V=12375\text{ V}\approx 12.4\text{ kV}$

12. $P=\frac{h}{\lambda}$

13. $\lambda_{min}\propto\frac{1}{V}\propto V^{-1}$

% change in $\lambda_{min}=(-1)$ (% change in V) for small % changes

14. Energy, $E=eV=h\nu_{max}=\frac{hc}{\lambda_{min}}$

$$\therefore \quad \lambda_{min}=\frac{hc}{eV}$$

15. Since, atomic number is same,

$$\lambda_1=\lambda_2=\lambda_3 \quad \text{or} \quad \lambda_2=\sqrt{\lambda_1\lambda_3}$$

16. Here a depends on the transition states n_1 and n_2 and b depends upon the series.

17.

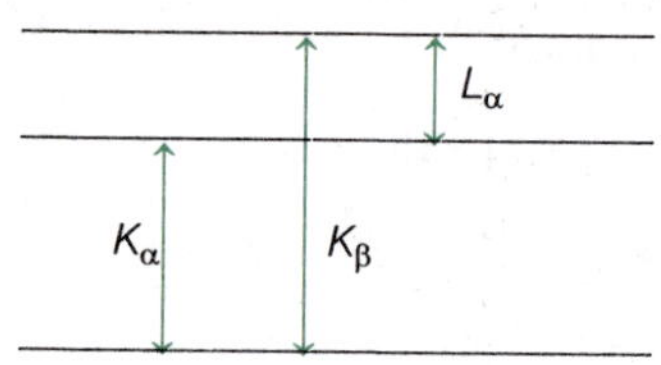

$$E_{L_\alpha}=E_{K_\beta}-E_{K_\alpha}$$

$$\therefore \quad \frac{hc}{\lambda_{L_\alpha}}=\frac{hc}{\lambda_{K_\beta}}-\frac{hc}{\lambda_{K_\alpha}}$$

or

$$\lambda_{L_\alpha}=\frac{\lambda_{K_\alpha}\lambda_{K_\beta}}{\lambda_{K_\alpha}-\lambda_{K_\beta}}$$

$$=\frac{0.71\times 0.63}{0.71-0.63}=5.59\text{ nm}$$

18. $\lambda_{K_\alpha}=0.71\text{ nm}=7.1\text{ Å}$

$$E_2-E_1=\frac{12375}{7.1}=1743\text{ eV}$$

$$\therefore \quad E_1=E_2-1743$$

$$=-2870-1743$$

$$=-4613\text{ eV}$$

$$\lambda_{K_\beta}=0.63\text{ nm}=6.3\text{ Å}$$

$$E_3-E_1=\frac{12375}{6.3}=1964\text{ eV}$$

$$\therefore \quad E_3=E_1+1964$$

$$=-4613+1964$$

$$=-2649\text{ eV}$$

19. $\Delta E_1 = 50\%$ of 50 keV = 25 keV

$$\therefore \quad \lambda_1 = \frac{12375}{25 \times 10^3} = 0.495 \text{ Å}$$
$$= 49.5 \text{ pm}$$
$$\Delta E_2 = 50\% \text{ of } 25 \text{ keV}$$
$$= 12.5 \text{ keV}$$
$$\therefore \quad \lambda_2 = \frac{12375}{12.5 \times 10^3} = 0.99 \text{ Å}$$
$$= 99 \text{ pm}$$

20. 26 pm = 0.26 Å

Now, $0.26 = \frac{12375}{V} - \frac{12375}{1.5\,V}$

Solving this equation, we get, $v = 15865$ volt

21. (a) $P = Vi = (40 \times 10^3)(10 \times 10^{-3})$
$$= 400 \text{ W}$$

1% of 400 W is 4 W.

(b) Heat generated = 400 W − 4 W
$$= 396 \text{ W} = 396 \text{ J/s}$$

Module 4.

Introductory Exercise

1. Energy corresponding to 248 nm wavelength
$$= \frac{1240}{248} \text{ eV} = 5 \text{ eV}$$
Energy corresponding to 310 nm wavelength
$$= \frac{1240}{310} \text{ eV} = 4 \text{ eV}$$
$$\frac{KE_1}{KE_2} = \frac{u_1^2}{u_2^2} = \frac{4}{1} = \frac{5 \text{ eV} - W}{4 \text{ eV} - W}$$
$$\Rightarrow \quad 16 - 4W = 5 - W$$
$$\Rightarrow \quad 11 = 3W$$
$$\Rightarrow \quad W = \frac{11}{3} = 3.67 \text{ eV}$$
$$\simeq 3.7 \text{ eV}$$

2. Saturation current is proportional to intensity while stopping potential increases with increase in frequency.
Hence, $f_a = f_b$ while $I_a < I_b$
Therefore, the correct option is (a).

3. $$\lambda (\text{in Å}) = \frac{12375}{W \text{ (eV)}} = \frac{12375}{4.0} \text{ Å} \approx 3093 \text{ Å}$$
or $\lambda \approx 309.3$ nm
or ≈ 310 nm

4. Stopping potential is the negative potential applied to stop the electrons having maximum kinetic energy. Therefore, stopping potential will be 4 V.

5. Theory based question.

6. $K_{min} = 0$
and
$$K_{max} = E - W$$
$$= \frac{12375}{2000} - 3.0$$
$$\approx 3.19 \text{eV}$$

7. $K_{max} = E - W = hf - hf_0$
$$= h(f - f_0)$$
$$\therefore \quad K_{max} \propto (f - f_0)$$

8. $K_{max} = E - W$
$$1.2 = E - W \quad \text{...(i)}$$
$$4.2 = 1.5\,E - W \quad \text{...(ii)}$$
Solving these equations, we get
$$W = 4.8 \text{ eV} = hf_0$$
$$\therefore \quad f_0 = \frac{4.8 \times 1.6 \times 10^{-19}}{6.63 \times 10^{-34}}$$
$$= 1.16 \times 10^{15} \text{ Hz}$$

Exercise

1. $K_{max} = h\nu - W$
Therefore, K_{max} is linearly dependent on frequency of incident radiation.

2. Kinetic energy of photoelectrons depends upon the frequency of incident radiation.

3. Maximum energy of photoelectrons increases with increase in frequency of incident light. So, if intensity is increased by increasing frequency of incident light, maximum energy will increase. If intensity is increased merely by increasing number of photons incident per second, maximum energy of photoelectrons will not change. So, question is incomplete because it is not told how the intensity is increased ?

4. No solution.

5. Already emitted electrons will repel the new electrons.

6. In case of wave it is possible.

7. Intensity = energy incident per unit area per unit time or $I = n(hf)$.
Here, n = number of photons incident per unit area per unit time.
f = frequency of incident photons. Hence, $I \propto nf$.
Hence, intensity can be increased either by increasing n or f. But saturation current only depends on n ($I_s \propto n$).
By increasing n and decreasing f, we can increase the saturation current even without increasing the intensity.

8. If power of light source is increased, then frequency of light source increases. Thus, stopping potential is increased also. Hence, statement I is incorrect.
For a given metal, the maximum kinetic energy of the photoelectron depends on the wavelength (or frequency) of the incident radiation.

9. Statement I is correct (true) but Statement II is false.
Among Microwaves, infrared rays and ultraviolet rays, Ultraviolet rays are the most effective for the emission of electron from metallic surface.
Option (d) is correct.
Explanation UV rays have maximum frequency hence are most effective for emission of electrons from the metallic surface.

$$KE_{max} = hf - hf_0$$

Thus, $KE_{max} \propto f$

10. $E = \dfrac{12375}{3000} = 4.125 \text{ eV}$

Since, $E < W$ no photoelectric effect will be observed.

11. $K_{max} = E - W = 2 \text{ eV} = 3.2 \times 10^{-19} \text{ J}$

12. $eV_0 = \dfrac{hc}{\lambda_1} - Wz$ ...(i)

Similarly, $e(2V_0) = \dfrac{hc}{\lambda_2} - W$ ...(ii)

Subtracting Eq. (i) from Eq. (ii), we get

$$eV_0 = \frac{hc(\lambda_1 - \lambda_2)}{\lambda_1 \lambda_2}$$

$$\therefore \quad V_0 = \frac{hc(\lambda_1 - \lambda_2)}{e\lambda_1\lambda_2}$$

$$= \frac{(6.63 \times 10^{-34})(3 \times 10^8)(110)}{1.6 \times 10^{-19} \times 330 \times 220 \times 10^{-9}}$$

$$= \frac{15}{8} \text{ V}$$

13. $\because \quad E = \dfrac{hc}{\lambda} - W$ ...(i)

$4E = \dfrac{hc}{\lambda/3} - W$ ...(ii)

Solving these equations, we get

$$W = \frac{hc}{3\lambda}$$

14. $e(5V_0) = \dfrac{hc}{\lambda} - W$ ...(i)

$eV_0 = \dfrac{hc}{3\lambda} - W$ ...(ii)

Solving these equations, we get

$$W = \frac{hc}{6\lambda}$$

15. $eV_0 = 2h\nu_0 - h\nu_0$

$\therefore \quad h\nu_0 = eV_0$

In second condition,

$$eV = 3h\nu_0 - h\nu_0$$
$$= 2h\nu_0 = 2eV_0$$

or $V = 2V_0$

16. $\dfrac{1}{2}mv_1^2 = h\nu_1 - W$

$\dfrac{1}{2}mv_2^2 = h\nu_2 - W$

From these two equations, we can see that

$$v_1^2 - v_2^2 = \frac{2h}{m}(\nu_1 - \nu_2)$$

17. $K_1 = hf - W$

$\Rightarrow \quad K_2 = 2hf - 2W$

$\therefore \quad \dfrac{K_1}{K_2} = \dfrac{1}{2}$

18.

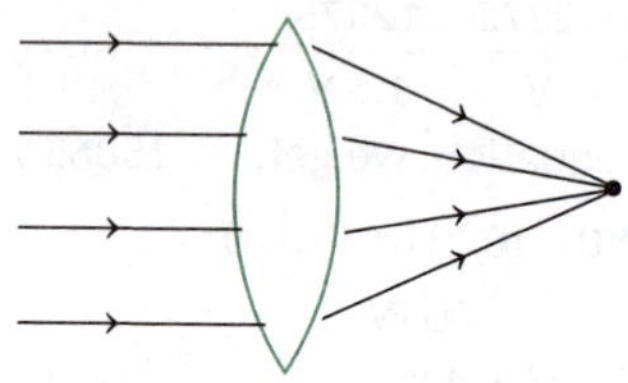

Intensity of image formed by lens does not depends on focal length of lens.
It only depends on diameter of lens.
As intensity remains same in both cases, so there is no change in photo current.

19. Given lights are of same wavelength, so the stopping potential will remain same.
Since $I_2 > I_1$ (Intensity), this signifies that saturation current corresponding to I_2 will be greater than that corresponding to I_1.

20. Given, $\phi_A = 9 \text{ eV}$, $\phi_B = 4.5 \text{ eV}$

Threshold wavelength of metal surface, A

$$\lambda_A = \frac{1242}{\phi_A} \text{ nm} = \frac{1242}{9} \text{ nm}$$

Similarly, $\lambda_B = \dfrac{1242}{4.5}$

$$\lambda_B - \lambda_A = \frac{1240}{4.5} - \frac{1240}{9} = 275.55 - 137.77$$
$$= 137.78 \simeq 138 \text{ nm}$$

Alternate solution

Given, $\phi_A = 9 \text{ eV}, \phi_B = 4.5 \text{ eV}$

We know, $E = \dfrac{hc}{\lambda} - \phi_0$ or for $E = 0$

$$\therefore \phi_0 = \frac{hc}{\lambda} \Rightarrow \lambda = \frac{hc}{\phi} \Rightarrow \lambda_A = \frac{hc}{\phi}, \lambda_B = \frac{hc}{\phi_B}$$

$$\lambda_B - \lambda_A = \frac{hc}{\phi_B} - \frac{hc}{\phi_A} = hc\left\{\frac{1}{4.5} - \frac{1}{9}\right\}$$
$$= 1242\left\{\frac{1}{9}\right\} = 138 \text{ nm}$$

$\Rightarrow \quad \Delta\lambda = 138 \text{ nm}$

21. Given, $E = KE + \phi_0$

Now, $$\frac{hc}{\lambda} = eV_0 + \phi_0 \quad \text{... (i)}$$

and $$\frac{hc}{2\lambda} = \frac{eV_0}{4} + \phi_0 \quad \text{...(ii)}$$

Eq. (ii) $\times$ 4

$$\frac{hc}{2\lambda} \times 4 = \left(\frac{eV_0}{4} + \phi_0\right) \times 4$$

$$\frac{2hc}{\lambda} = eV_0 + 4\phi_0$$

Putting value of $eV_0 = \frac{hc}{\lambda} - \phi_0$

$$\frac{2hc}{\lambda} = \frac{hc}{\lambda} - \phi + 4\phi_0$$

$$\frac{2hc}{\lambda} - \frac{hc}{\lambda} = 3\phi_0$$

$$\frac{hc}{\lambda} = 3\phi_0 \Rightarrow \frac{hc}{\lambda} = \frac{3hc}{\lambda_0} \left[\phi = \frac{hc}{\lambda_0}\right]$$

$$\frac{1}{\lambda} = \frac{3}{\lambda_0} \Rightarrow \lambda_0 = 3\lambda$$

22. Using $KE_{max} = eV_s = hf - \phi_0$

Where, ϕ_0 = work function

V_s = Stopping potential

f = frequency

$$V_s = \frac{h}{e} f - \frac{\phi_0}{e}$$

This equation is similar to

$$y = mx + c$$

where, $m = \frac{h}{e}$ and $c = -\frac{\phi_0}{c}$

Therefore, the slope m will be same for all graphs and will be independent of ϕ_0.

23. From Einstein's photoelectric equation, we have, $eV_0 = h\nu - \phi$

$$\Rightarrow \quad 0 = h\nu - \phi$$

$$\Rightarrow \quad \phi = h\nu = 6.6 \times 10^{-34} \times 5 \times 10^{14}$$

$$= 33 \times 10^{-20} \text{ J}$$

$$= \frac{33 \times 10^{-20}}{1.6 \times 10^{-19}} \text{ eV} = 2.07 \text{ eV}$$

24. Using the photoelectric equation

$$hf = hf_0 + eV_0$$

$$\Rightarrow \quad hf = hf_0 + \frac{1}{2} mv_{max}^2$$

In case (i) $f = 2f_0$, $v_{max} = v_1$

$$h(2f_0) = hf_0 + \frac{1}{2} mv_1^2$$

$$\frac{1}{2} mv_1^2 = hf_0 \quad \text{...(i)}$$

In case (ii) $f = 5f_0$

$$h(5f_0) = hf_0 + \frac{1}{2} mv_2^2$$

$$\Rightarrow \quad \frac{1}{2} mv_2^2 = 4hf_0 \quad \text{...(ii)}$$

On dividing Eq. (i) and Eq. (ii), we get

$$\left(\frac{v_1}{v_2}\right)^2 = \frac{1}{4} \text{ or } \frac{v_1}{v_2} = \frac{1}{2}$$

25. Energy corresponding to incident radiation,

$$E = \frac{hc}{\lambda} = \frac{1240}{\lambda \text{(in nm)}} = \frac{1240}{350}$$

$$E = 3.54 \text{ eV}$$

Work function for metal-A,

$$\phi_A = 4.8 \text{ eV}$$

and for metal-B, $\phi_B = 2.2$ eV

If energy of incident radiation is greater than work function of metal then photoelectron will emit. For metal-B, $E > \phi_B$ and for metal-A, $E < \phi_A$.

So, metal-A will not emit photoelectron but metal-B will emit.

26. Number of photons incident per second

$$= \frac{\text{Power}}{\text{Energy of one photon}} = \frac{P}{(hc/\lambda)} = \frac{P\lambda}{hc}$$

Number of electrons emitted per second

$$= 0.1\% \text{ of}$$

$$\frac{P\lambda}{hc} = \frac{P\lambda}{1000\,hc}$$

$\therefore$ Current = Charge (on photoelectrons per second)

$$= \frac{P\lambda e}{1000\,hc}$$

$$= \frac{(1.5 \times 10^{-3})(400 \times 10^{-9})(1.6 \times 10^{-19})}{(1000)(6.63 \times 10^{-34})(3 \times 10^{8})}$$

$$= 0.48 \times 10^{-6} \text{ A} = 0.48 \text{ μA}$$

27. Stopping potential = 10.4 V

$\therefore$ $K_{max} = 10.4$ eV

$$E = W + K_{max} = 1.7 + 10.4 = 12.1 \text{ eV}$$

$$\lambda = \frac{12375}{12.1} = 1022 \text{ Å}$$

12.1 eV is the energy gap between $n = 3$ and $n = 1$ in hydrogen atom.

28. $$E = hf = \frac{(6.63 \times 10^{-34})(1.5 \times 10^{15})}{1.6 \times 10^{-19}} \text{ eV} = 6.21 \text{ eV}$$

$$K_{max} = E - W = 6.21 - 3.7 = 2.51 \text{ eV}$$

29. $\lambda_0 = 5000$ Å

$$W = \frac{12375}{5000} = 2.475 \text{ eV}$$

Stopping potential is 3V. Therefore, $K_{max} = 3$ eV

$$E = W + K_{max} = 5.475 \text{ eV}$$

$$\lambda = \frac{12375}{5.475} = 2260 \text{ Å}$$

30. (a) $f_0 = f_A = 10 \times 10^{14}\ \text{Hz} = 10^{15}\ \text{Hz}$

(b) $W = |K_{max}|_c = 4\ \text{eV}$

(c) $W = hf_0 \Rightarrow h = \dfrac{W}{f_0}$

31. Energy of incident photons,

$$E_i = 10.6\ \text{eV}$$
$$= 10.6 \times 1.6 \times 10^{-19}\ \text{J}$$
$$= 16.96 \times 10^{-19}\ \text{J}$$

Energy incident per unit area per unit time (intensity) $= 2\ \text{J}$

$\therefore$ Number of photons incident on unit area in unit time

$$= \frac{2}{16.96 \times 10^{-19}} = 1.18 \times 10^{18}$$

Therefore, number of photons incident per unit time on given area $(1.0 \times 10^{-4}\ \text{m}^2)$

$$= (1.18 \times 10^{18})(1.0 \times 10^{-4}) = 1.18 \times 10^{14}$$

But only 0.53% of incident photons emit photoelectrons

$\therefore$ Number of photoelectrons emitted per second (n)

$$n = \left(\frac{0.53}{100}\right)(1.18 \times 10^{14})$$
$$n = 6.25 \times 10^{11}$$
$$K_{min} = 0$$

and $K_{max} = E_i - \text{work function}$

$$= (10.6 - 5.6)\ \text{eV}$$
$$= 5.0\ \text{eV}$$

$\therefore$ $K_{max} = 5.0\ \text{eV}$ and $K_{min} = 0$

32. When 800 Å wavelength falls on hydrogen atom (in ground state) 13.6 eV energy is used in liberating the electron. The rest goes to kinetic energy of electron. Hence, $K = E - 13.6$ (in eV)

or $$(1.8 \times 1.6 \times 10^{-19}) = \frac{hc}{800 \times 10^{-10}} - 13.6 \times 1.6 \times 10^{-19} \quad \text{...(i)}$$

Similarly, for the second wavelength :

$$(4.0 \times 1.6 \times 10^{-19}) = \frac{hc}{700 \times 10^{-10}} - 13.6 \times 1.6 \times 10^{-19} \quad \text{...(ii)}$$

Solving these two equations, we get

$$h \approx 6.6 \times 10^{-34}\ \text{J-s}$$

33. Einstein's photoelectric equation

$$eV_0 = hf - W$$

$\therefore$ $$V_0 = \left(\frac{h}{e}\right)f - \frac{W}{e}$$

V_0 *versus* f graph is a straight line with slope $= \dfrac{h}{e} = a$ universal constant. Therefore, the ratio of two slopes should be 1.

Unit Exercise (Cumulative)

Level 1

1. Theory based question.

2. $q\mathbf{E} + q(\mathbf{v} \times \mathbf{B}) = 0$

$\Rightarrow$ $\mathbf{E} = -(\mathbf{v} \times \mathbf{B})$

or $\mathbf{B} \times \mathbf{v}$

E, **B** and **v** are mutually perpendicular.

3. $n_f = 6$

Total emission lines $= \dfrac{n_f(n_f - 1)}{2} = 15$

4. $E_2 - E_1 = 40.8\ \text{eV}$

$\therefore$ $$\frac{E_1}{(2)^2} - E_1 = 40.8\ \text{eV}$$

or $$-\frac{3}{4}E_1 = 40.8\ \text{eV}$$

or $$E_1 = -54.4\ \text{eV}$$
$$|E_1| = 54.4\ \text{eV}$$

5. Longest wavelength of Lyman series means, minimum energy corresponding $n = 2$ to $n = 1$.

$\therefore$ $$(E_2 - E_1)_H = (E_n - E_2)_{He^+}$$

$\therefore$ $$\frac{-13.6}{(2)^2} + \frac{13.6}{(1)^2} = \frac{-13.6(Z)^2}{n^2} + \frac{13.6(Z)^2}{(2)^2}$$

Putting $Z = 2$, we get $n = 4$.

6. $m_e v_e = \dfrac{h}{\lambda}$

$\therefore$ $$v_e = \frac{h}{\lambda m_e}$$
$$= \frac{6.63 \times 10^{-34}}{(5200 \times 10^{-10}) \times 9.1 \times 10^{-31}}$$
$$\approx 1400\ \text{m/s}$$

7. In hydrogen atom, $E_2 - E_1 = 10.2\ \text{eV}$

Since, $5\ \text{eV} < 10.2\ \text{eV}$

The electron cannot excite the hydrogen atom. The collision must be therefore elastic.

8. $\Delta E \approx \dfrac{12375}{1085} \approx 11.4\ \text{eV}$

Third Balmer line is corresponding to the transition,

$$n = 5 \text{ to } n = 2$$
$$E_5 - E_2 \approx 11.4$$

$\therefore$ $$\frac{E_1}{(5)^2} - \frac{E_1}{(2)^2} \approx 11.4$$

$$E_1 \approx -54.28\ \text{eV}$$

$\therefore$ $$|E_1| \approx 54.28\ \text{eV}$$

9. $E_4 - E_3 = 32.4$

$$\therefore \quad \frac{-13.6(Z)^2}{(4)^2} + \frac{13.6(Z)^2}{(3)^2} = 32.4$$

Solving, we get

$$Z = 7$$

10. $\sqrt{f} \propto (Z-b)\sqrt{\left(\frac{1}{n_1^2} - \frac{1}{n_2}\right)^2}$

$$\therefore \quad \text{Slope} \propto \sqrt{\frac{1}{n_1^2} - \frac{1}{n_2^2}}$$

$$\therefore \quad \frac{\text{Slope}_1}{\text{Slope}_2} = \frac{\sqrt{1-1/9}}{\sqrt{1-\frac{1}{4}}} = \sqrt{\frac{32}{27}}$$

For K_β, $n_1 = 1, n_2 = 3$
For K_α, $n_1 = 1, n_2 = 2$

11. $E_n \propto \frac{1}{n^2}$ and $L_n \propto n$

12.

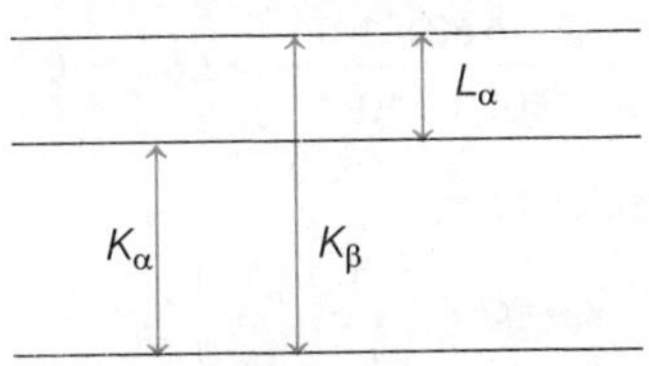

$$E_{K_\beta} = E_{K_\alpha} + E_{L_\alpha}$$

$$\therefore \quad h\gamma_2 = h\gamma_1 + h\gamma_3$$

$$\therefore \quad \gamma_2 = \gamma_1 + \gamma_3$$

13. According to Bohr first postulate,

$$mvr = \frac{nh}{2\pi}$$

$$\therefore \quad 2\pi r = n\left(\frac{h}{mv}\right) = n\lambda$$

For $n=1$, $\lambda = 2\pi r$

14. $E \propto m$ and $r \propto \frac{1}{m}$

i.e. Energy will become two times and radius will become half.

15. Wave number is reciprocal of wavelength,

$$\therefore \quad \frac{1}{\lambda} = R\left[\frac{1}{n_1^2} - \frac{1}{n_2^2}\right]$$

$$= R\left[\frac{1}{2^2} - \frac{1}{4^2}\right] = R\left[\frac{1}{4} - \frac{1}{16}\right] = \frac{3R}{16}$$

16. For $n=3$ to $n=2$ transition,

$$\frac{1}{\lambda_1} = R\left[\frac{1}{2^2} - \frac{1}{3^2}\right] = \frac{5R}{36}$$

For $n=4$ to $n=2$ transition,

$$\frac{1}{\lambda_2} = R\left[\frac{1}{2^2} - \frac{1}{4^2}\right] = \frac{3R}{16}$$

$$\therefore \quad \frac{\lambda_2}{\lambda_1} = \frac{20}{27}$$

$$\therefore \quad \lambda_2 = \frac{20}{27}\lambda_1 = \frac{20}{27}\lambda_0$$

17. $a = \omega^2 r$

$$\omega = \frac{v}{r}, v \propto \frac{1}{n} \text{ and } r \propto n^2$$

$$\therefore \quad \omega \propto \frac{1}{n^3} \text{ and } r \propto n^2$$

$$a \propto \frac{1}{n^4}$$

$$\frac{a_M}{a_L} = \left(\frac{2}{3}\right)^4 = \frac{16}{81}$$

18. $P = \frac{E}{c}$

$$F = \left(\frac{dP}{dt}\right) = \frac{dE/dt}{c}$$

70% means 14 watt is absorbed ($\Delta P = P_i$) and 30% means 6 watt is reflected ($\Delta P = 2P_i$)

$$\therefore \quad F = \frac{14}{3\times 10^8} + \frac{2(6)}{3\times 10^8} = 8.67\times 10^{-8}\text{ N}$$

19. $\text{KE} = \frac{1}{4\pi\varepsilon_0}\frac{(2e)(92e)}{r_{min}}$

$$\therefore \quad r_{min} = \frac{(184e^2)(1/4\pi\varepsilon_0)}{\text{KE}}$$

$$= \frac{184\times(1.6\times 10^{-19})^2(9\times 10^9)}{5\times 1.6\times 10^{-13}}$$

$$= 5.3\times 10^{-14}\text{ m} = 5.3\times 10^{-12}\text{ cm}$$

20. $\frac{1}{\lambda} \propto Z^2$ or $\lambda \propto \frac{1}{Z^2}$

$$\lambda_1 : \lambda_2 : \lambda_3 : \lambda_4 = \frac{1}{(1)^2} : \frac{1}{(1)^2} : \frac{1}{(2)^2} : \frac{1}{(3)^2}$$

$$= 36 : 36 : 9 : 4$$

21. Speed of an electron in n^{th} Bohr's orbit is given as,

$$v_n \propto \frac{1}{n}$$

$$\Rightarrow \quad \frac{v_7}{v_3} = \frac{3}{7} \quad \Rightarrow \quad \frac{3.6\times 10^6}{v_3} = \frac{3}{7}$$

$$\Rightarrow \quad v_3 = \frac{7}{3}\times 3.6\times 10^6$$

$$\Rightarrow \quad v_3 = 8.4\times 10^6\text{ ms}^{-1}$$

22. Energy released during transition from $n=4$ to $n=1$

$$\Delta E = \frac{-13.6}{4^2} - \left(-\frac{13.6}{1^2}\right) = 13.6 - \frac{13.6}{4^2}$$

$$= 13.6\left(1 - \frac{1}{16}\right) = 12.75\text{ eV}$$

$$= 12.75\times 1.6\times 10^{-19}\text{ J}$$

Since, $\Delta E = \dfrac{hc}{\lambda}$

$$\Rightarrow \quad \lambda = \frac{hc}{\Delta E} = \frac{6.63\times 10^{-34}\times 3\times 10^{8}}{12.75\times 1.6\times 10^{-19}}\text{ m}$$

$$= 0.975\times 10^{-7}\text{ m}$$

$$= 97.5\text{ nm}$$

23. From Bohr's atomic model,
Energy associated with n level is

$$E_n = \frac{-13.6}{n^2}\text{ eV}$$

$$\Rightarrow \quad \frac{E_2 - E_1}{E_\infty - E_1} = \frac{13.6\left(1-\frac{1}{4}\right)}{13.6} = \frac{3}{4}$$

24. $\text{KE} = |E| = 3.4\text{ eV}$

$$\lambda\text{ (in Å)} = \sqrt{\frac{150}{\text{KE (in eV)}}}$$

$$= \sqrt{\frac{150}{3.4}} = 6.6\text{ Å}$$

25. By Bohr's quantisation rule,

$$L_n = \frac{nh}{2\pi}$$

$$\Rightarrow \quad mvr = \frac{nh}{2\pi}$$

$$\Rightarrow \quad mv = \frac{nh}{2\pi r} \Rightarrow p = \frac{nh}{2\pi r}$$

26. For hydrogen atom $n = 1$, energy in terms of Rydberg constant is given by,

$$E = \frac{-RchZ^2}{n^2} \Rightarrow E_1 = \frac{-Rch}{(1)^2}(1)$$

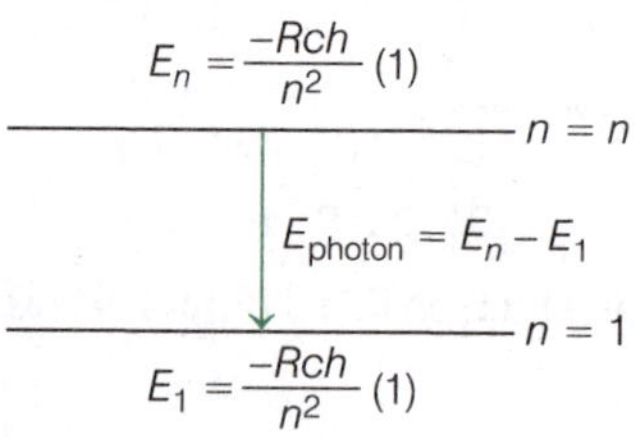

$$\Rightarrow \quad \frac{-Rch}{(n)^2} + \frac{Rch}{1} = \frac{hc}{\lambda}$$

$$\Rightarrow \quad \frac{-R}{n^2} + R = \frac{1}{\lambda} \Rightarrow R - \frac{1}{\lambda} = \frac{R}{n^2}$$

$$\Rightarrow \quad \frac{\lambda R - 1}{\lambda} = \frac{R}{n^2}$$

$$n^2 = \frac{\lambda R}{\lambda R - 1} \Rightarrow n = \sqrt{\frac{\lambda R}{\lambda R - 1}}$$

27. Change in energy,

$$\Delta E - E_f - E_i \left[\frac{-13.6}{n_f^2} = \frac{-13.6}{n_i^2}\right] Z^2\text{ eV}$$

$$\Rightarrow \quad 12.09 = E_f - (-13.6)$$

$$\Rightarrow \quad E_f = -1.51\text{ eV} \Rightarrow \frac{-13.6}{n^2} = -1.51$$

$$\Rightarrow \quad n^2 = 9 \Rightarrow n = 3$$

So, $\quad \Delta L = L_f - L_i$

$$= \frac{h}{2\pi}(3-1) = \frac{2h}{2\pi}$$

$$= \frac{h}{\pi} = \frac{6.63\times 10^{-34}}{3.14}$$

$$= 2.11\times 10^{-34}\text{ J-s}$$

28. According to Bohr's postulate on radius and velocity of H-like atom speed of e^- in nth orbit is given by

$$v_n = \frac{2.18\times 10^6}{n}\times Z$$

$$\therefore \quad v_n \propto Z$$

$$\frac{(v_3)\text{He}^+}{(v_3)_\text{H}} = \frac{Z_{\text{He}^+}}{Z_\text{H}} = \frac{2}{1}$$

29. $\Delta p = 2\left(\dfrac{h}{\lambda}\right) = \dfrac{2\times 6.63\times 10^{-34}}{5030\times 10^{-10}} = 2.63\times 10^{-27}\text{ kg-m/s}$

30. Using Moseley Law,

$$v_0 = cRZ^2\left(\frac{1}{n_1^2} - \frac{1}{n_2^2}\right)$$

$$v_1 = cRZ^2\left(\frac{1}{1^2} - \frac{1}{3^2}\right) \quad \text{...(i)}$$

Put $\quad v_1 = 2.92\times 10^{15}\text{ Hz}$ (Given)

$$v_2 = cRZ^2\left(\frac{1}{1^2} - \frac{1}{2^2}\right) \quad \text{...(ii)}$$

Dividing Eq. (ii) by Eq. (i), we get

$$v_2 = 2.46\times 10^{15}$$

31. The wavelength of spectral line of the third member of Lyman series is given by

$$\frac{1}{\lambda} = R\left[\frac{1}{n_f^2} - \frac{1}{n_i^2}\right]$$

$$n_f = 1 \Rightarrow n_i = 4$$

$$\frac{1}{\lambda_1} = R\left[\frac{1}{9} - \frac{1}{16}\right]$$

$$\Rightarrow \quad \lambda_1 = \frac{16}{15R}$$

The wavelength of spectral line of the first member of Paschen series is given by

$$\frac{1}{\lambda_2} = R\left[\frac{1}{9} - \frac{1}{16}\right]$$

$$\Rightarrow \quad \lambda_2 = \frac{144}{7R} \quad \text{...(ii)}$$

Dividing Eq. (ii) by Eq. (i) we get

$$\frac{\lambda_1}{\lambda_2} = \frac{16}{15R}\times\frac{7R}{144} = \frac{7}{135}$$

32. In transition from $n=4$ to $n=3$, we have

$$\frac{1}{\lambda_1}=R\left(\frac{1}{3^2}-\frac{1}{4^2}\right)=R\left(\frac{7}{9\times 16}\right) \quad \text{...(i)}$$

In transition from $n=3$ to $n=2$, we have

$$\frac{1}{\lambda_2}=R\left(\frac{1}{2^2}-\frac{1}{3^2}\right)=R\left(\frac{5}{9\times 4}\right) \quad \text{...(ii)}$$

So, from Eqs. (i) and (ii), the ratio of $\frac{\lambda_1}{\lambda_2}$ is

$$\frac{\lambda_1}{\lambda_2}=\frac{\left(\frac{9\times 16}{7R}\right)}{\left(\frac{9\times 4}{5R}\right)}=\frac{20}{7}$$

33. As, for conservative fields

$$\mathbf{F}=-\left(\frac{d\mathbf{U}}{dr}\right)$$

$\therefore$ Magnitude of force on particle is

$$\Rightarrow \quad F=\frac{dU}{dr}=\frac{d}{dr}\left(\frac{1}{2}kr^2\right)$$

$$\Rightarrow \quad F=kr$$

This force is acting like centripetal force.

$$\therefore \quad \frac{mv^2}{r}=kr \quad \text{...(i)}$$

Multiply m on both side

So, for n^{th} orbit,

$$\Rightarrow \quad m^2v_n^2=mkr_n^2$$

$$\Rightarrow \quad \frac{n^2h^2}{4\pi^2r^2}=mkr_n^2 \quad \left[\because v_n=\frac{nh}{2\pi mr}\right]$$

Therefore, $r_n^4 \propto n^2$

$$\Rightarrow \quad r_n^2 \propto n$$

So, $\quad r_n \propto \sqrt{n}$

Energy of particle is

$$E_n=\text{PE}+\text{KE}$$

$$=\frac{1}{2}kr_n^2+\frac{1}{2}mv_n^2$$

$$=\frac{1}{2}kr_n^2+\frac{1}{2}kr_n^2 \quad \text{[using Eq. (i)]}$$

$$=kr_n^2$$

So, energy, $E_n \propto r_n^2$

$$\Rightarrow \quad E_n \propto n$$

34. Lyman series ends at $n=1$

$\therefore$ Series limit frequency of the Lyman series is given by,

$$\nu_L=RcZ^2\left(\frac{1}{1^2}-\frac{1}{\infty^2}\right)$$

$$\Rightarrow \quad \nu_L=RcZ^2$$

Pfund series ends at $n=5$.

$\therefore$ Series limit frequency of the Pfund series,

$$\nu_P=RcZ^2\left(\frac{1}{5^2}-\frac{1}{\infty^2}\right)=\frac{RcZ^2}{25}$$

or $\quad \nu_P=\frac{\nu_L}{25}$

35. We have, $\quad \lambda=\frac{hc}{\Delta E}, \lambda_1=2E-E,$

$$\lambda_2=\frac{4}{3}E-E$$

$$\therefore \quad \frac{\lambda_1}{\lambda_2}=\frac{hc/\Delta E_1}{hc/\Delta E_2}=\frac{\Delta E_2}{\Delta E_1}$$

$$=\frac{\left(\frac{4}{3}E-E\right)}{2E-E}=\frac{1}{3}$$

36. $r_3=(3)^2\cdot r_1=9x$

Now, $\quad 3\lambda_3=(2\pi r_3)=18\pi x$

$\therefore \quad \lambda_3=6\pi x$

37. Change in energy of electron when transitioning from one state to another is,

$$\Delta E=h\nu$$

$$E_n=\frac{-13.6}{n^2}\text{ eV}$$

$$\nu=\frac{\Delta E}{h}=k\left[\frac{1}{(n-1)^2}-\frac{1}{n^2}\right]$$

$$=\frac{k(2n)}{n^2(n-1)^2}\approx\frac{2k}{n^3}\propto\frac{1}{n^3}$$

38. We know that,

$$(r_m)=\left(\frac{m^2}{Z}\right)(0.53\text{ Å})$$

Here 0.53 Å, is Bohr's radius,

$$=(n\times 0.53)\text{ Å}$$

$$\therefore \quad \frac{m^2}{Z}=n$$

$$m=5 \text{ for } {}_{100}\text{Fm}^{257}$$

(the outermost shell) and $Z=100$

$$\therefore \quad n=\frac{(5)^2}{100}=\frac{1}{4}$$

39. $\frac{M}{L}=\frac{q}{2m}=\frac{e}{2m}$

$$\therefore \quad M=\left(\frac{e}{2m}\right)L$$

$$=\left(\frac{e}{2m}\right)\left(\frac{nh}{2\pi}\right)=\left(\frac{neh}{4\pi m}\right)$$

40. According to question, 24.6 eV (ϕ) is required to remove one of the electrons from a neutral He atom

For helium ion, $Z=2$ and for first orbit $n=1$

$$\therefore \quad E=\frac{-13.6\times z^2}{n^2}=\frac{-13.6}{(1)^2}\times 2^2=-54.4\text{ eV}$$

$\therefore$ Energy required to remove this

$$e^- = +54.4 \text{ eV } E_r = E + \phi$$

$\therefore$ Total energy required

$$= 54.4 + 24.6 = 79 \text{ eV}$$

41. By Bohr's IInd postulate, for revolving electron,

Angular momentum $= mvr_n = \dfrac{nh}{2\pi}$

$\Rightarrow$ Momentum of electron,

$$p = mv = \frac{nh}{2\pi r_n}$$

de-Broglie wavelength associated with electron is

$$\lambda_n = \frac{h}{p} = \frac{2\pi r_n}{n}$$

Given, $n = 3$, $r_n = 4.65$ Å

$$\therefore \quad \lambda_n = \frac{(2 \times \pi \times 4.65)}{3}$$

$$\approx 9.7 \text{ Å}$$

42. $\lambda_\alpha - \lambda'_m = 3(\lambda_\alpha - \lambda_m)$

$$\therefore \quad \frac{12375}{10.2\,(Z-1)^2} - \frac{12375}{20 \times 10^3} = 3\left[\frac{12375}{10.2(Z-1)^2} - \frac{12375}{10 \times 10^3}\right]$$

Solving we get $Z = 29$

43. For elastic collision, momentum is conserved

$$p_{\text{before collision}} = p_{\text{after collision}}.$$

$$mv = mv_A + \frac{m}{2} v_B$$

$$2v = 2v_A + v_B \quad \dots \text{(i)}$$

Now, coefficient of restitution,

$$e = \frac{v_B - v_A}{u_A - u_B}$$

Here, $u_B = 0$ and for elastic collision $e = 1$

$$\therefore \quad 1 = \frac{v_B - v_A}{v}$$

$$\Rightarrow \quad v = v_B - v_A \quad \dots \text{(ii)}$$

From Eq. (i) and Eq. (ii)

$$v_A = \frac{v}{3} \text{ and } v_B = \frac{4v}{3}$$

Hence,
$$\frac{\lambda_A}{\lambda_B} = \frac{\left(\dfrac{h}{mv_A}\right)}{\dfrac{h}{\dfrac{m}{2} \cdot v_B}} = \frac{v_B}{2v_A} = \frac{4/3}{2/3}$$

$$= 2$$

44. For dust particles it will be most difficult to experimentally verify de-Broglie wavelength as it has mass greater than the electron proton or an α-particle.

45. Energy in joule (E) = charge $\times$ potential difference in volt

$E_{\text{electron}} = q_e V$ and $E_{\text{proton}} = q_p 4V$

de-Broglie wavelength is given by

$$\lambda = \frac{h}{p} = \frac{h}{\sqrt{2mE}} \Rightarrow \lambda_e = \frac{h}{\sqrt{2m_e eV}}$$

and $$\lambda_p = \frac{h}{\sqrt{2m_p e 4V}} \; (\because q_e = q_p = e)$$

$$\therefore \quad \frac{\lambda_e}{\lambda_p} = \frac{\dfrac{h}{\sqrt{2m_e eV}}}{\dfrac{h}{\sqrt{2m_p e\, 4V}}} = \sqrt{\frac{2m_p e 4V}{2m_e eV}} = 2\sqrt{\frac{m_p}{m_e}}$$

46. $\lambda_{ph} = \lambda_e$

$$\therefore \quad \frac{h}{P_{ph}} = \frac{h}{p_e}$$

$$\therefore \quad P_{ph} = p_e$$

$$\therefore \quad \frac{E_{ph}}{c} = \frac{2E_e}{v}$$

$$\therefore \quad \frac{E_e}{E_{ph}} = \frac{v}{2c}$$

47. $\dfrac{mv^2}{a_0} = \dfrac{1}{4\pi\varepsilon_0} \dfrac{(e)(e)}{a_0^2} \Rightarrow v = \dfrac{e}{\sqrt{4\pi\varepsilon_0 m a_0}}$

48. $I = 0.2 I_0 = I_0 e^{-\alpha x}$

$$\Rightarrow \quad \left(\frac{1}{5}\right) = e^{-\alpha x}$$

$$\Rightarrow \quad \ln 5 = \alpha x \text{ or } x = \frac{\ln 5}{\alpha}$$

49. Photoelectric effect cannot be explained by wave theory of light.

Maximum kinetic energy of photoelectrons depends on frequency of incident radiation.

Stopping potential depends on incident frequency and work function.

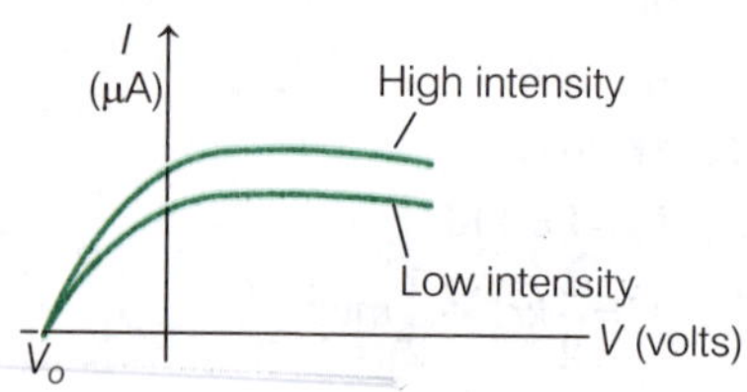

As intensity increases, saturation value of photocurrent increases.

Stopping potential,

$$V_0 = \frac{h\nu}{e} - \frac{\phi_0}{e} = \frac{1}{e}(h\nu - \phi_0)$$

Thus, stopping potential depends both on work function and frequency of incident radiation.

50. By Einstein's photoelectric equation,

$$E = \frac{hc}{\lambda} - \phi \quad \text{...(i)}$$

and $$2E = \frac{hc}{\lambda'} - \phi \quad \text{...(ii)}$$

(For double the energy)

Subtracting Eq. (i) from Eq. (ii), we get

$$E = hc\left(\frac{1}{\lambda'} - \frac{1}{\lambda}\right)$$

$$\Rightarrow \quad \lambda' = \frac{hc\lambda}{E\lambda + hc}$$

51. According to question

$$E = E_0 [\sin \omega_1 t + \sin \omega_2 t]$$

For maximum KE, we will take higher frequency i.e.,

$$\left(f = \frac{9 \times 10^{15}}{2\pi} \text{Hz}\right) \qquad \left(\because f = \frac{\omega}{2\pi}\right)$$

$$(\text{KE})_{max} = hf - \phi$$

$$= \left(\frac{4.14 \times 10^{-15} \times 9 \times 10^{15}}{2\pi} - 2.50\right) \text{eV}$$

$$= 5.93 - 2.50$$

$$= 3.43 \text{ eV}$$

nearest is 3.42 eV

52. Using Einstein's photoelectric equation.

$$(\text{KE})_{max} = \frac{hc}{\lambda} - \frac{hc}{\lambda_0}$$

where, λ_0 = cut off wavelength.

So, $\quad K_1 = \frac{hc}{\lambda_1} - \frac{hc}{\lambda_0}$

$$\Rightarrow \quad 3K_1 = \frac{3hc}{\lambda_1} - \frac{3hc}{\lambda_0}$$

$$\Rightarrow \quad 3K_1 = \frac{hc}{\lambda_2} - \frac{3hc}{\lambda_0} \qquad \text{...(ii)}$$

Similarly, $\quad K_2 = \frac{hc}{\lambda_2} - \frac{hc}{\lambda_0}$ ...(ii)

Substracting Eq. (ii) from Eq. (i), we get

$$3K_1 - K_2 = \frac{-2hc}{\lambda_0}$$

$$\Rightarrow \quad K_2 - 3K_1 = \frac{2hc}{\lambda_0}$$

$$\Rightarrow \quad K_2 - 3K_1 = 2\phi$$

$$\Rightarrow \quad K_2 > 3K_1$$

$$\Rightarrow \quad K_1 < \frac{K_2}{3}$$

53. $\frac{hc}{\lambda} = \phi + 6 \qquad (\phi = \text{work function})$ ...(i)

For wavelength $\lambda = 4$ Å

$$\frac{hc}{4\lambda} = \phi + 0.6 \qquad \text{...(ii)}$$

Subtracting Eq. (i) from Eq. (ii),

$$\frac{3hc}{4\lambda} = 5.4 \text{ eV}$$

$$= \frac{hc}{\lambda} = \frac{4 \times 4.5 \text{ eV}}{3}$$

Put in Eq. (i)

$$\therefore \quad \phi = 1.2 \text{ eV}$$

$$\Rightarrow \quad \lambda = \frac{3}{4} \times \frac{6.63 \times 10^{-24} \times 3 \times 10^8}{5.4 \times 1.6 \times 10^{-19}}$$

$$= 1.72 \times 10^{-7} \text{ m}$$

54. Einstein's photoelectronic equation is given by

$$(\text{KE})_{max} = \frac{hc}{\lambda} - \phi$$

$$= \frac{hc}{500} - \phi \qquad \text{...(i)}$$

Now, $3(\text{KE})_{max} = \frac{hc}{200} - \phi$ ...(ii)

For $\quad \lambda = 200$ nm

Divide Eq. (ii) by Eq. (i)

$$\frac{3}{1} = \frac{\frac{hc}{200} - \phi}{\frac{hc}{500} - \phi}$$

Put the value of $hc = 1237.5$

and solving, we get work function

$$\phi = 0.61 \text{ eV}$$

55. From graph, threshold frequency,

$$\nu_0 = 4 \times 10^{14} \text{ Hz (where, } V_0 = 0)$$

$\therefore$ Work function, $W = h\nu_0$

$$\Rightarrow \quad W = 6.63 \times 10^{-34} \times 4 \times 10^{14} \text{ J}$$

$$\Rightarrow \quad W = \frac{6.63 \times 4 \times 10^{-20}}{1.6 \times 10^{-19}} \text{ eV}$$

$$= 1.657 \text{ eV}$$

$$\approx 1.66 \text{ eV}$$

56. $K_{max} = E - W = \frac{hc}{\lambda} - W$

Here, W = work function

For wavelength, $\lambda = \frac{3\lambda}{4}$

For wavelength

Similarly $K'_{max} = \frac{hc}{(3\lambda/4)} - W$

$$= \frac{4}{3}\frac{hc}{\lambda} - W = \frac{4}{3}\left[\frac{hc}{\lambda} - W\right] + \frac{W}{3}$$

$$= \frac{4}{3}K_{max} + \frac{W}{3}$$

$$\Rightarrow \quad K'_{max} > \frac{4}{3}K_{max}$$

or $\quad v' > \left(\sqrt{\frac{4}{3}}\right) v$

57. We know that, $\frac{hc}{\lambda}-\phi=eV_0$

For $\lambda=0.4\,\mu m=0.3\times10^{-6}$ m and $V_0=1$ V

$$\frac{hc}{0.3\times10^{-6}}-\phi=2e \quad \text{...(i)}$$

Similarly, for $\lambda=0.4\,\mu m$

$=0.4\times10^{-6}$ m

$$\frac{hc}{0.4\times10^{-6}}-\phi=1e \quad \text{...(ii)}$$

Subtracting Eq. (ii) from Eq. (i)

$$hc\left(\frac{1}{0.3}-\frac{1}{0.4}\right)10^6=e$$

$$\Rightarrow \quad hc\left(\frac{0.1}{0.12}\times10^6\right)=e$$

$$\Rightarrow \quad h=0.64\times10^{-33}$$

$$=6.4\times10^{-34}\text{ J-s}$$

58. Given, $B=3\times10^{-4}$ T, $r=0.1$ m

Radius of circular path in uniform magnetic field is given by,

$$r=\frac{\sqrt{2Km}}{Bq} \quad (K=\text{kinetic energy})$$

$$\therefore \quad r_{max}=\frac{\sqrt{2K_{max}\,m}}{Bq}$$

$$\text{or} \quad K_{max}=\frac{B^2q^2r_{max}}{2m} \quad \text{...(i)}$$

Further, $K_{max}=E-W$ ...(ii)

[where, W is work function]

Here, $E=E_3-E_2$

In eV,

$$E_3=\frac{-13.6}{(3)^2}=-1.51\text{ eV}$$

and

$$E_2=\frac{-13.6}{(2)^2}=-3.4\text{ eV}$$

Solving all these equations we can find the work function, which comes out to be 1.1 eV.

59. $E_1=\frac{1240}{550}=2.25$ eV,

$E_2=\frac{1240}{450}=2.75$ eV $\quad \left(\because E=\frac{1240}{\lambda}\text{ eV}\right)$

$E_3=\frac{1240}{350}=3.54$ eV

E_1 cannot emit photoelectrons from q and r plates. E_2 can not emit photoelectrons from r.

Further, work function of p is least and it can emit photoelectrons from all three wavelengths. Hence magnitude of its stopping potential and saturation current both will be maximum. Hence, option (a) represent correct graph.

60. Since, the voltage across the X-ray tube is constant, the cut-off wavelength will remain constant. Wavelength of K_α line will be

$$\frac{1}{\lambda}=R_e(Z-b)^2\left(\frac{1}{n_1^2}-\frac{1}{n_2^2}\right)$$

If $\lambda_0=$ cut-off wavelength, then

$$\frac{1}{2\lambda_0}=R_e(46-1)^2\left(\frac{1}{1^2}-\frac{1}{2^2}\right) \quad \text{... (i)}$$

For material (2)

$$\frac{1}{r'\lambda_0}=R_e(41-1)^2\left(\frac{1}{1^2}-\frac{1}{2^2}\right) \quad \text{... (ii)}$$

Eqs. (i)/(ii) gives,

$$\frac{r'}{2}=\frac{(45)^2}{(40)^2}=\frac{81}{64}=1.27$$

$$r'=1.27\times2=2.54$$

$\therefore$ The correct answer is (a).

61. (a) $p=\frac{E}{c} \Rightarrow E=pc$

(b) $\lambda=\frac{12375}{E\text{ (in eV)}}=\frac{12375}{1.54}=8035$ Å

≈ 804 nm

So, this wavelength lies in infrared region.

62. (a) $f=\frac{c}{\lambda}$

(b) $\because$ Number of photons emitted per second

$$N_1=\frac{\text{Power of source}}{\text{Energy of one photon}}=\frac{P}{hc/\lambda}$$

$$N_1=\frac{P\lambda}{hc}=\frac{(75)(600\times10^{-9})}{(6.63\times10^{-34})(3\times10^8)}$$

$$\approx 2.3\times10^{20}\text{ photons/s}$$

63. (a) $E=hf \Rightarrow f=\frac{E}{h}$

(b) $\lambda=\frac{c}{f}$

64. (a) $K=\frac{p^2}{2m}$ or $K\propto p^2$

If momentum is doubled, kinetic energy becomes four times.

(b) $p=\frac{E}{c}$ or $E\propto p$ (for a photon)

If p is doubled, E will also become two times.

65. (a) Number of photons incident per second

$=$ number of photons absorbed per second

$$=\frac{\text{Power}}{\text{Energy of one photon}}$$

$$N=\frac{P}{hc/\lambda}=\frac{P\lambda}{hc}$$

(b) Force = Rate of change of momentum = (Number of photons absorbed per second) × (momentum of one photon)

$$=\left(\frac{P\lambda}{hc}\right)\left(\frac{h}{\lambda}\right)=\frac{P}{c} \qquad (\because P = \text{power})$$

66. Force = Rate of change of momentum

$$=2[N]\left[\frac{h}{\lambda}\right]\cdot\cos 60°$$

N = number of photons striking per second

$\frac{h}{\lambda}$ = momentum of one photon.

67. (a) $E = hf = (6.6\times10^{-34})(5.5\times10^{14})$

$$=36.3\times10^{-20}\ \text{J}$$

$$=2.27\ \text{eV}$$ **Ans.**

(b) Number of photons leaving the source per second,

$$n=\frac{P}{E}=\frac{0.1}{36.3\times10^{-20}}$$

$$=2.75\times10^{17}$$ **Ans.**

(c) Number of photons falling on cathode per second,

$$n_1=\frac{0.15}{100}\times2.75\times10^{17}$$

$$=4.125\times10^{14}$$

Number of photoelectrons emitting per second,

$$n_2=\frac{6\times10^{-6}}{1.6\times10^{-19}}=3.75\times10^{13}$$

$$\therefore \quad \%=\frac{n_2}{n_1}\times100$$

$$=\frac{3.75\times10^{13}}{4.125\times10^{14}}\times100$$

$$=9\%$$ **Ans.**

68. (a) Energy of photon $=\frac{12375}{8600}\text{ eV}=1.44\text{ eV}$

$\therefore$ Internal energy after absorption

$$=-6.52+1.44=-5.08\text{ eV}$$

(b) Energy of emitted photon $=\frac{12375}{4200}=2.946\text{ eV}$

Internal energy after emission $=-2.68-2.946$

$$=-5.626\text{ eV}$$

69. K_{max} (in eV) $=E-W$

$$=\frac{12375}{2000}-4.3$$

$$=1.9\text{ eV}$$

Therefore, stopping potential is 1.9 V.

70. $E_1=\frac{12357}{3000}=4.125\text{ eV}$

$$E_2=\frac{12357}{6000}=2.0625\text{ eV}$$

Maximum speed ratio is 3 : 1. Therefore, maximum kinetic ratio is 9 : 1.

Now, $9K_{max}=4.125-W$ ...(i)

$K_{max}=2.0625-W$ ...(ii)

Solving these two equations, we get

$W\approx1.81$ eV and $K_{max}=0.26$ eV

Putting $K_{max}=\frac{1}{2}mv_{max}^2$ we can find v_{max}. Here, m is the mass of electron.

71. $E=\frac{12375}{1800}=6.875\text{ eV}$

K_{max} or $K=E-W=4.875$ eV

$$r=\frac{\sqrt{2Km}}{Bq}$$

$$=\frac{\sqrt{2\times4.875\times1.6\times10^{-19}\times9.1\times10^{-31}}}{5\times10^{-5}\times1.6\times10^{-19}}$$

$$=0.148\text{ m}$$

72. $f=\frac{\omega}{2\pi}=\frac{(1.57\times10^7)\,c}{2\pi}$

$$E=\frac{hf}{1.6\times10^{-19}}\text{ eV}$$

$$=\frac{(6.63\times10^{-34})(1.57\times10^7)(3\times10^8)}{1.6\times10^{-19}\times2\times\pi}\text{ eV}$$

$$=3.1\text{ eV}$$

$K_{max}=E-W=1.2$ eV

$\therefore$ Stopping potential is 1.2 V.

73. nth line of Lyman series means transition from $(n+1)^{th}$ state to first state.

$$\frac{1}{\lambda}=RZ^2\left[1-\frac{1}{(n+1)^2}\right] \quad ...(i)$$

de-Broglie wavelength in $(n+1)^{th}$ orbit:

$$\lambda=\frac{h}{mv}=\frac{hr}{mvr}=\frac{hr}{(n+1)\frac{h}{2\pi}}=\frac{(2\pi)(hr)}{(n+1)h}=\frac{2\pi r}{(n+1)}$$

or

$$\frac{1}{\lambda}=\frac{(n+1)}{2\pi r} \quad ...(ii)$$

Equating Eqs. (i) and (ii), we get

$$\left(\frac{n+1}{2\pi r}\right)=RZ^2\left[\frac{n(n+2)}{(n+1)^2}\right] \quad ...(iii)$$

Now, as $r\propto\frac{n^2}{Z}$

$$\therefore \quad r=\frac{(n+1)^2}{11}r_o$$

Substituting in Eq. (iii), we get

$$\frac{11}{2\pi r_o}=\frac{R(11)^2(n)(n+2)}{(n+1)}$$

or $(n+1)=(1.09\times10^7)(11)(2\pi)\times(0.529\times10^{-10})(n^2+2n)$

Solving this equation,

We get, $n=24$

74. $E = mc^2 = \dfrac{hc}{\lambda}$

$\therefore \quad \lambda = \dfrac{h}{mc}$

and dimensions of λ is same as the dimension of length.

75. According to first condition,

$$\frac{hc}{\lambda_0} = \frac{-13.6}{3^2} - \left(\frac{-13.6}{2^2}\right)$$

$$\Rightarrow \quad \frac{hc}{\lambda_0} = \frac{13.6 \times 5}{36} \quad \text{... (i)}$$

According to second condition,

$$\frac{hc}{\lambda'} = \frac{-13.6}{4^2} - \left(\frac{-13.6}{3^2}\right)$$

$$= \frac{13.6}{9} - \frac{13.6}{16}$$

$$\frac{hc}{\lambda'} = \frac{13.6 \times 7}{16 \times 9} \quad \text{...(ii)}$$

On dividing Eq. (i) by Eq. (ii), we get

$$\frac{\frac{hc}{\lambda_0}}{hc/\lambda'} = \frac{13.6 \times 5}{36} \times \frac{16 \times 9}{13.6 \times 7}$$

$$\Rightarrow \quad \frac{\lambda'}{\lambda_0} = \frac{4}{7} = \frac{20}{35}$$

$$\Rightarrow \quad \lambda' = \frac{20}{35}\lambda_0 = \frac{20}{x}\lambda_0 \quad \text{[Given]}$$

$$\therefore \quad x = 35$$

76. For hydrogen atom, when electron makes an transition from nth level to ground state, then wavelength of emitted photon is given as

$$\frac{1}{\lambda} = R\left(\frac{1}{1^2} - \frac{1}{n^2}\right)$$

For transition-1,

$$\frac{1}{\lambda_1} = R\left(\frac{1}{1^2} - \frac{1}{3^2}\right)$$

$$\Rightarrow \quad \frac{1}{\lambda_1} = R\left(1 - \frac{1}{9}\right) = \frac{8R}{9}$$

$$\text{or} \quad \lambda_1 = \frac{9}{8R} \quad \text{...(i)}$$

For transition-2,

$$\frac{1}{\lambda_2} = R\left(\frac{1}{1^2} - \frac{1}{2^2}\right)$$

$$\Rightarrow \quad \frac{1}{\lambda_2} = R\left(1 - \frac{1}{4}\right) = \frac{3}{4}R$$

$$\Rightarrow \quad \lambda_2 = \frac{4}{3R} \quad \text{...(ii)}$$

On dividing Eq. (i) and Eq. (ii), we get

$$\frac{\lambda_1}{\lambda_2} = \frac{27}{32} = \frac{x}{32} \quad \text{[Given]}$$

$$\therefore \quad x = 27$$

77. Binding energy of an electron is negative of total energy in that state.

$$\text{BE} = -\text{Total energy}$$

$$= -\left(-13.6\frac{Z^2}{n^2}\right) = 13.6\frac{Z^2}{n^2}\ \text{eV}$$

For Li^{++}, $Z = 3$, $n = 2 + 1 = 3$

$$\text{BE} = 13.6\frac{(3)^2}{(3)^2} = 13.6\ \text{eV}$$

$$= 136 \times 10^{-1}\text{eV}$$

On comparing, $x = 136$

78. Impact parameter b is given by

$$b = \frac{Ze^2 \cdot \cot(\theta/2)}{4\pi\varepsilon_0 \cdot (\text{KE}_\alpha)} \quad \text{or} \quad b \propto \cot\frac{\theta}{2}$$

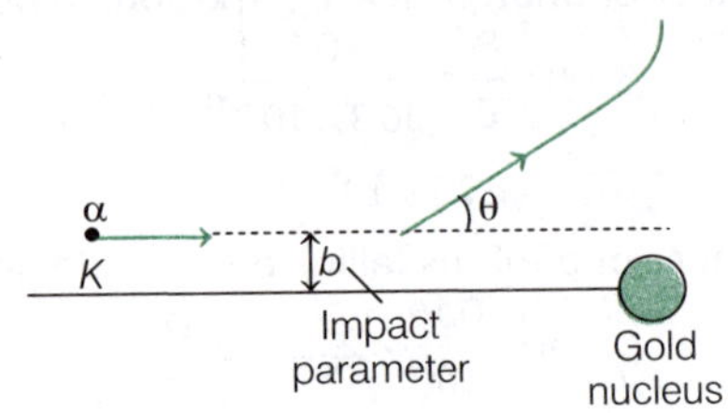

With given values, we have

$$\therefore \quad \frac{\sqrt{d_1}}{\sqrt{d_2}} = \frac{\cot(60°/2)}{\cot(90°/2)} = \frac{\cot 30°}{\cot 45°}$$

$$\text{or} \quad \frac{\sqrt{d_1}}{\sqrt{d_2}} = \frac{\sqrt{3}}{1} \Rightarrow d_1 = 3d_2$$

Hence, value of x is 3.

79. For first line of Lyman

$$\frac{1}{\lambda} = R\left(1 - \frac{1}{4}\right) = R\left(\frac{3}{4}\right)$$

$$\Rightarrow \quad \lambda = \frac{4}{3R} \quad \text{...(i)}$$

3rd line (Paschen)

$$\frac{1}{\lambda_3} = R\left(\frac{1}{3^2} - \frac{1}{6^2}\right) = \frac{R}{9} \times \frac{3}{4}$$

2nd line (Balmer)

$$\frac{1}{\lambda_2} = R\left(\frac{1}{2^2} - \frac{1}{4^2}\right) = \frac{R}{4} \times \frac{3}{4}$$

$$\text{Thus.} \quad a\lambda = \lambda_3 - \lambda_2 = \frac{12}{R} - \frac{16}{3R} = \frac{20}{3R}$$

Putting in Eq, (i), we get

$$a\left(\frac{4}{3R}\right) = \frac{20}{3R} \Rightarrow a = 5$$

80. As, $E_n = \dfrac{(\text{PE})_n}{2} = -\dfrac{1.08}{2} = -0.544$

$$E = \frac{-13.6}{n^2} Z^2\ \text{eV}$$

$$Z = 1$$

So, ΔE,

$$E_f - E_i = -0.544 - \left(-\frac{13.6}{2^2}\right)$$
$$= 3.4 - 0.544 \approx 2.86 \text{ eV}$$
$$= 286 \times 10^{-2} \text{ eV}$$

81. Wavelength is given by

$$\frac{1}{\lambda} = Rz^2\left(\frac{1}{n_1^2} - \frac{1}{n_2^2}\right) \quad \text{...(i)}$$

where, λ = wavelength of light emitted,
R = Rydberg's constant,
Z = atomic number,
n_1 = principal quantum number of lower energy level
and n_2 = principal quantum number of higher energy level.

Therefore, for 1st spectral line of Balmer series, $n_1 = 2$ and

$$n_2 = 3; \frac{1}{\lambda_1} = Rz^2\left(\frac{1}{2^2} - \frac{1}{3^2}\right)$$
$$\Rightarrow \quad \frac{1}{\lambda_1} = Rz^2\left(\frac{5}{36}\right) \quad \text{...(ii)}$$

Similarly, for 3rd spectral line, $n_1 = 2$ and $n_2 = 5$

$$\frac{1}{\lambda_3} = Rz^2\left(\frac{1}{2^2} - \frac{1}{5^2}\right)$$
$$\Rightarrow \quad \frac{1}{\lambda_3} = Rz^2\left(\frac{21}{100}\right) \quad \text{...(iii)}$$

Now, dividing Eq. (iii) by Eq. (ii), we get

$$\frac{\frac{1}{\lambda_3}}{\frac{1}{\lambda_1}} = \frac{Rz^2\left(\frac{21}{100}\right)}{Rz^2\left(\frac{5}{36}\right)}$$
$$\Rightarrow \quad \frac{\lambda_1}{\lambda_3} = \frac{21}{100} \times \frac{36}{5}$$
$$\Rightarrow \quad \frac{\lambda_1}{\lambda_3} = 1.512 = 15.12 \times 10^{-1}$$

Comparing with the given value in the question i.e. $x \times 10^{-1}$, the value of $x = 15$.

82. As we know that,

$$\Delta E = 13.6Z^2\left[\frac{1}{n_f^2} - \frac{1}{n_i^2}\right]$$
$$\Delta E_{2-1} = 13.6 \times Z^2\left[1 - \frac{1}{4}\right] = 13.6 \times Z^2\left[\frac{3}{4}\right]$$
$$\Delta E_{3-2} = 13.6 \times Z^2\left[\frac{1}{4} - \frac{1}{9}\right]$$
$$= 13.6 \times Z^2\left[\frac{5}{36}\right]$$
$$\therefore \quad \Delta E_2 = \Delta E_{3-2} + 74.8 \text{ eV}$$
$$13.6 \times Z^2\left[\frac{3}{4}\right] = 13.6 \times Z^2\left[\frac{5}{36}\right] + 74.8$$
$$13.6 \times Z^2\left[\frac{3}{4} - \frac{5}{36}\right] = 74.8 \Rightarrow Z^2 = 9$$
$$\therefore \quad Z = 3$$

83. Energy of incident light (in eV)

$$E = \frac{12375}{\lambda} \text{ eV}$$
$$E = \frac{12375}{970} = 12.7 \text{ eV} \quad [\lambda = 970 \text{ nm}]$$

After excitation, let the electron jumps to nth state, then

$$\frac{-13.6}{n^2} = -13.6 + 12.7$$

Solving this equation, we get

$$n = 4$$

$\therefore$ Total number of lines in emission spectrum,

$$= \frac{n(n-1)}{2} = \frac{4(4-1)}{2} = 6$$

84. Kinetic energy of ejected electron
= Energy of incident photon − energy required to ionize the electron from nth orbit (all in eV)

$$\therefore \quad 10.4 = \frac{1242}{90} - |E_n|$$
$$= \frac{1242}{90} - \frac{13.6}{n^2} \quad \left(\text{as } E_n \propto \frac{1}{n^2} \text{ and } E_1 = -13.6 \text{ eV}\right)$$

Solving this equation, we get

$$n = 2$$

85. According to Bohr's 2nd postulate

$$\text{Angular momentum} = n\left(\frac{h}{2\pi}\right) = 3\left(\frac{h}{2\pi}\right)$$
$$\therefore \quad n = 3$$
$$r_n \propto \frac{n^2}{Z} \Rightarrow r_3 = \frac{(3)^2}{3}(a_0) = 3a_0$$

Now, $$mv_3r_3 = 3\left(\frac{h}{2\pi}\right)$$
$$\therefore \quad mv_3(3a_0) = 3\left(\frac{h}{2\pi}\right)$$
or $$\frac{h}{mv_3} = 2\pi a_0 \text{ or } \frac{h}{P_3} = 2\pi a_0 \quad (\because P = mv)$$
or $$\lambda_3 = 2\pi a_0 \quad \left(\lambda = \frac{h}{P}\right)$$

$\therefore$ Answer is 2.

86. $$\frac{mv^2}{r} = \frac{GMm}{r^2} \quad \text{...(i)}$$
$$mvr = \frac{h}{2\pi} \quad (\text{for } n = 1) \quad \text{...(ii)}$$

Solving these two equations, we can find v and r. Then,

$$E = \frac{1}{2}mv^2 - \frac{GMM}{r}$$

87. $\dfrac{M}{L}=\dfrac{q}{2m}=\text{constant}$

$$M \propto L$$

and $L=\dfrac{nh}{2\pi}$ or $L \propto n$

$\therefore$ $M \propto n$

88. $i=qf=q\left(\dfrac{v}{2\pi r}\right)$

or $i \propto \dfrac{v}{r} \propto \dfrac{(1/n)}{(n)^2}$

or $i \propto \dfrac{1}{n^3}$

$$\frac{i_1}{i_2}=\left(\frac{n_2}{n_1}\right)^3=(2)^3=8$$

89. $A=\pi r^2$

$$A \propto r^2$$

or $A \propto n^4$ (as $r \propto n^2$)

$\therefore$ $\dfrac{A_n}{A_1}=(n)^4$

$$\ln\left(\frac{A_n}{A_1}\right)=4\ln(n)$$

Therefore, $\ln\left(\dfrac{A_n}{A_1}\right)$ *versus* $\ln n$ graph is a straight line of slope 4.

90. $B=\dfrac{\mu_0 i}{2\pi}$ or $B \propto \dfrac{i}{r}$

$$i \propto \frac{1}{n^3}$$

and $r \propto n^2$

$\therefore$ $B=\dfrac{1}{n^5}$

$\therefore$ $\dfrac{B_1}{B_2}=\left(\dfrac{n_2}{n_1}\right)^5=(2)^5=32$

91. $\dfrac{1}{\lambda}=R\left(1-\dfrac{1}{4}\right)=\dfrac{3R}{4}$

$\therefore$ $p=\dfrac{h}{\lambda}=\dfrac{3Rh}{4}=\text{momentum of photon}$

From conservation of linear momentum,

Momentum of photon = Momentum of hydrogen atom

$\therefore$ $\dfrac{3Rh}{4}=Mv$

$\Rightarrow$ $v=\dfrac{3Rh}{4M}$

92. $T=\dfrac{2\pi r}{v}$ or $T \propto \dfrac{r}{v}$

or $T \propto \dfrac{(n^2/Z)}{(Z/n)}$

$\therefore$ $T \propto \dfrac{n^3}{Z^2}$

$$\left(\frac{T_1}{T_2}\right)=\left(\frac{n_1}{n_2}\right)^3=\left(\frac{Z_2}{Z_1}\right)^2$$

$$2=\left(\frac{1}{2}\right)^3\left(\frac{Z}{1}\right)^2$$

$\therefore$ $Z=4$

93. $P=Vi=150\times 10^3\times 10\times 10^{-3}=1500\text{ W}$

$$99\%\text{ of }P=1500\times\frac{99}{100}\text{ J/s}=1485\text{ J/s}$$

$$=\frac{1485}{4.18}\text{ cal/s}$$

$$\approx 355\text{ cal/s}$$

$$=2.63\times 10^{-27}\text{ kg-m/s}$$

94. Minimum 10.2 eV energy is required to excite a hydrogen atom. In perfectly inelastic collision, maximum energy is lost.

$\therefore$ $\dfrac{1}{2}mv^2=\dfrac{1}{2}(2m)\left(\dfrac{v}{2}\right)^2$

$$=10.2\times 1.6\times 10^{-19}$$

$$\frac{1}{4}mv^2=1.632\times 10^{-18}$$

$\therefore$ $v=\sqrt{\dfrac{1.632\times 4\times 10^{-18}}{1.67\times 10^{-27}}}$

$$=6.25\times 10^4\text{ m/s}$$

95. Speed of electron in first orbit of hydrogen atom is given by

$$v=\frac{e^2}{2\varepsilon_0 h}$$

$\therefore$ $\dfrac{v}{c}=\dfrac{e^2}{2\varepsilon_0 hc}$

96. $E_1=\dfrac{me^4}{8\varepsilon_0^2 h^2}$

$$f_n=\frac{v_n}{2\pi r_n}=\frac{(e^2/2\varepsilon_0 nh)}{(2\pi)\varepsilon_0 n^2h^2/\pi me^2}$$

$$=\frac{me^4}{4\varepsilon_0^2 n^3h^3}=\frac{8E_1\varepsilon_0^2h^2}{4\varepsilon_0^2 n^3h^3}$$

$$=\frac{2E_1}{n^3h}$$

97. $mvr=\dfrac{h}{2\pi}$ (in first orbit)

$\therefore$ $v=\dfrac{h}{2\pi mr}$

$$a=\frac{v^2}{r}=\frac{h^2}{4\pi^2m^2r^3}$$

98. Decrease in kinetic energy = increase in potential energy

$\therefore \quad qV = \frac{1}{4\pi\varepsilon_0} \cdot \frac{Q \cdot q}{r}$

$\therefore \quad r = \frac{Q}{(4\pi\varepsilon_0) V}$

i.e. r is independent of q.

99. Number of photons emitted per second,

$$n_1 = \frac{\text{Power}}{\text{energy of one photon}}$$

$$= \frac{P}{hc/\lambda} = \frac{P\lambda}{hc}$$

Number of electrons emitted per second,

$$n_2 = \frac{n_1}{10^6} = \frac{P\lambda}{10^6 hc}$$

Current in μA,

$$i = (n_2 e) \times 10^6 = \frac{p\lambda e}{hc}$$

$$= \frac{5 \times 400 \times 10^{-9} \times 1.6 \times 10^{-19}}{6.6 \times 10^{-34} \times 3 \times 10^8}$$

$$= 1.6 \,\mu\text{A}$$

100. As, $\lambda = \frac{h}{p}$

$\Rightarrow \quad \lambda - \Delta\lambda = \frac{h}{p + \Delta p}$

$\Rightarrow \quad \frac{199\lambda}{200} = \frac{h}{p + \Delta p}$

$\Rightarrow \quad p + \Delta p = \frac{200}{199} p$

$\Rightarrow \quad p = 199 \,\Delta p$

101. According to Bohr's theory

$$2\pi r = n\lambda_n$$

$$\lambda_n = \frac{2\pi r}{n} = \frac{2\pi r_0 n^2}{n} = 2\pi r_0 n \quad \text{...(i)}$$

$$\frac{1}{\Lambda_n} = R\left\{\frac{1}{1^2} - \frac{1}{n^2}\right\}$$

$\Rightarrow \quad \Lambda_n = \frac{1}{R}\left\{1 + \frac{1}{n^2 - 1}\right\}$

$$\Lambda_n = \frac{1}{R}\left\{1 + \frac{1}{n^2}\right\} \quad (n >> 1) \quad \text{...(ii)}$$

From Eqs. (i) and (ii),

$$\Lambda_n = \frac{1}{R}\left\{1 + \frac{4\pi^2 r_0^2}{\lambda_n^2}\right\} = A + \frac{B}{\lambda_n^2}$$

102. According to photoelectric effect equation

$$KE_{max} = \frac{hc}{\lambda} - \phi_0$$

$\Rightarrow \quad \frac{p^2}{2m} = \frac{hc}{\lambda} - \phi_0 \qquad [KE = p^2/2m]$

$\Rightarrow \quad \frac{(h/\lambda_d)^2}{2m} = \frac{hc}{\lambda} - \phi_0 \qquad [p = h/\lambda]$

Assuming small changes, differentiating both sides,

$$\frac{h^2}{2m}\left(-\frac{2d\lambda_d}{\lambda_d^3}\right) = -\frac{hc}{\lambda^2} d\lambda$$

$\Rightarrow \quad \frac{d\lambda_d}{d\lambda} \propto \frac{\lambda_d^3}{\lambda^2}$

103. $R \propto n^2, v \propto \frac{1}{n}$ and $E \propto \frac{1}{n^2}$

104. $L \propto n, r \propto n^2$ and $T = \frac{2\pi r}{v}$

or $\quad T \propto \frac{r}{v} \propto \frac{n^2}{(1/n)}$ or $T \propto n^3$

105. $\lambda = \frac{h}{p} = \frac{h}{mv} = \frac{h}{\sqrt{2Km}}$

$\lambda \propto \frac{1}{m} \qquad$ (if v is same)

$\lambda \propto \frac{1}{\sqrt{m}} \qquad$ (if K is same)

If change in potential energy is same, then change in kinetic energy is also same. But, this does not mean that kinetic energy is same.

106. $\frac{n_f(n_f - 1)}{2} = 6$

$\Rightarrow \quad n_f = 4$

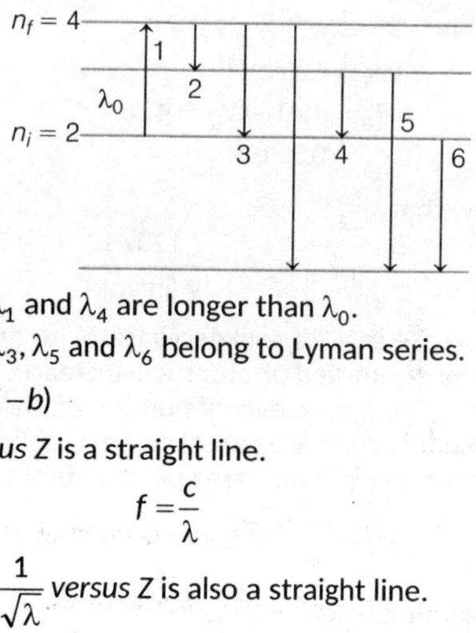

λ_1 and λ_4 are longer than λ_0.

λ_3, λ_5 and λ_6 belong to Lyman series.

107. $\sqrt{f} \propto (Z - b) \qquad$ ...(i)

If f *versus* Z is a straight line.

$$f = \frac{c}{\lambda}$$

Hence, $\frac{1}{\sqrt{\lambda}}$ *versus* Z is also a straight line.

108. $eV_0 = \frac{hc}{\lambda} - W$

$$V_0 = \left(\frac{hc}{e}\right)\left(\frac{1}{\lambda}\right) - \frac{W}{e}$$

V_0 *versus* $\frac{1}{\lambda}$ graph is in the form

$$y = mx - c$$

Therefore option (c) is correct.

Clearly, V_0 *versus* λ graph is not a straight line but V_0 decreases with increase in λ and V_0 becomes zero when $\frac{hc}{\lambda}=W$.

i.e. $\lambda=\lambda_0$ (Threshold wavelength)

$\therefore$ Option (a) is also correct.

109. From Einstein photo-electric equation

$$K_{max}=E-W$$

Therefore, $T_A=4.25-W_A$ ...(i)

$$T_B=(T_A-1.50)=4.70-W_B \quad ...(ii)$$

From Eqs. (i) and (ii),

$$W_B-W_A=1.95 \text{ eV} \quad ...(iii)$$

de-Broglie wavelength is given by

$$\lambda=\frac{h}{\sqrt{2Km}}$$

or $$\lambda\propto\frac{1}{\sqrt{K}}$$

K = KE of electron

$$\therefore \quad \frac{\lambda_B}{\lambda_A}=\sqrt{\frac{K_A}{K_B}}$$

or $$2=\sqrt{\frac{T_A}{T_A-1.5}}$$

$$\Rightarrow \quad T_A=2 \text{ eV}$$

From Eq. (i) $W_A=4.25-T_A=2.25$ eV

From Eq. (iii) $W_B=W_A+1.95$ eV

$$=(2.25+1.95) \text{ eV}$$

$$\Rightarrow \quad W_B=4.20 \text{ eV}$$

$$\Rightarrow \quad T_B=4.70-W_B=4.70-4.20$$

$$=0.50 \text{ eV}$$

110. We know that,

$$\lambda_m \text{ (in Å)}=\frac{12375}{V \text{ (in volt)}}$$

With increase in V, λ_m will decrease. With decrease in λ_m energy of emitted photons will increase. Hence, intensity will increase even if number of photons emitted per second are constant. Because intensity is basically energy per unit area per unit time.

111. $E_1=\frac{12375}{4950}=2.5$ eV

K_1 = maximum kinetic energy = 0.6 eV

$$W=E_1-K_2=1.9 \text{ eV}$$

112. $K_2=1.1$ eV

$$E_2=W+K_2=3.0 \text{ eV}$$

$$\therefore \quad \lambda_2=\frac{12375}{3.0}=4125 \text{ Å}$$

113. Magnetic field cannot change the kinetic energy of charged particle.

114. $E=-\frac{13.6}{n^2}$ eV for $n=1,2$

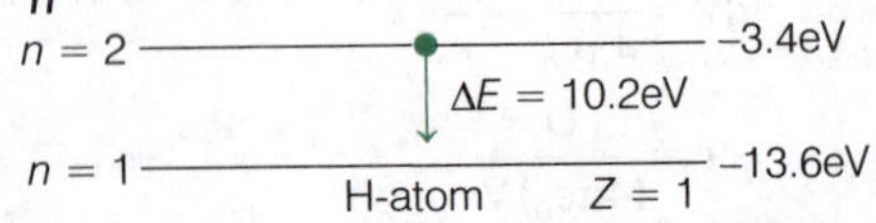

Energy given by H-atom in transition from $n=2$ to $n=1$ is equal to energy taken by He^+ atom in transition from $n=2$ to $n=4$.

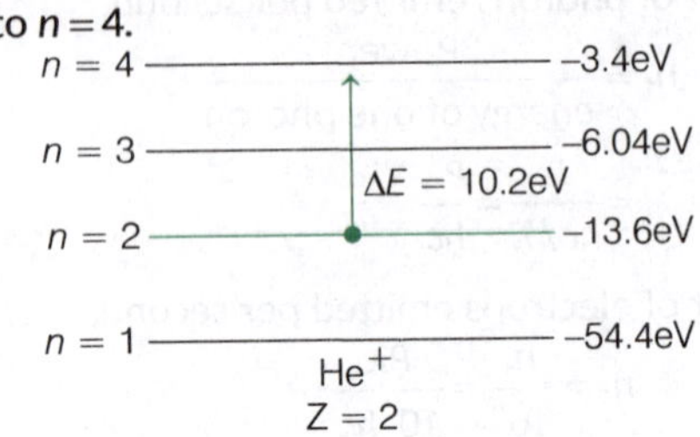

115. Visible light lies in the range, $\lambda_1=4000$ Å to $\lambda_2=7000$ Å. Energy of photons corresponding to these wavelengths (in eV) would be

$$E=\frac{12375}{\lambda} \text{ eV}$$

$$E_1=\frac{12375}{4000}=3.09 \text{ eV} \Rightarrow E_2=\frac{12375}{7000}=1.77. \text{ eV}$$

From energy level diagram of He^+ atom, we can see that in transition from $n=4$ to $n=3$, energy of photon released will lie between E_1 and E_2.

$$\Delta E_{43}=-3.4-(-6.04)=2.64 \text{ eV}$$

Wavelength of photon corresponding to this energy,

$$\lambda=\frac{12375}{2.64} \text{ Å}=4687.5 \text{ Å}=4.68\times10^{-7} \text{ m}$$

$$\simeq 4.8\times10^{-7} \text{ m}$$

116. (a) Kinetic energy, $K\propto Z^2$

$$\therefore \quad \frac{K_H}{K_{He^+}}=\left(\frac{1}{2}\right)^2=\frac{1}{4}$$

117. Theory based question.

118. For He^+, $Z=2$

$$E\propto\frac{Z^2}{n^2}$$

$E_2=-3.4$ eV

$E_1=-13.6$ eV

H - atom

Ionisation energy from first, excited state of H-atom

$$=|E_2|=3.4 \text{ eV}=E \quad \text{(given)}$$

(a) $|E_1|=(13.6 \text{ eV})(2)^2=16(3.4 \text{ eV})=16E$

(b) $U_2=2E_2=2(-13.6)\frac{(2)^2}{(2)^2}=-8(3.4 \text{ eV})=-8E$

(c) $K_1=|E_1|=16E$

(d) $|E_2|=(13.6)\frac{(2)^2}{(2)^2}=4(3.4 \text{ eV})=4E$

119. $K_{max} = hf - W$

$\therefore$ K_{max} *versus* f graph is a straight line of slope h and intercept $-W$.

$$eV_0 = hf = W$$

$$\therefore \quad V_0 = \left(\frac{h}{e}\right)f - \frac{W}{e}$$

$\therefore V_0$ *versus* f graph is again a straight line of slope $\frac{h}{e}$ and intercept $\frac{W}{e}$.

120. $T = \frac{2\pi r}{v}$

or $$T \propto \frac{r}{v} \propto \frac{n^2/Z}{Z/n}$$

$$\therefore \quad T \propto \frac{n^3}{Z^2}$$

$$L = \frac{nh}{2\pi} \quad \text{or} \quad L \propto n$$

$$v \propto \frac{Z}{n}$$

and $$r \propto \frac{n^2}{Z}$$

121. $\frac{1}{\lambda} \propto \left(\frac{1}{n_1^2} - \frac{1}{n_2^2}\right)$

or $$\frac{\lambda_2}{\lambda_1} = \frac{(1/n_1^2 - 1/n_2^2)_i}{(1/n_1^2 - 1/n_2^2)_f}$$

or $$\lambda_2 = \frac{(1/4 - 1/16)\lambda}{(1/n_1^2 - 1/n_2^2)_f}$$

$$= \left(\frac{3}{16}\lambda\right)\left[\frac{1}{(1/n_1^2 - 1/n_2^2)_f}\right]$$

(a) For first line of Balmer series,

$$n_1 = 2, n_2 = 3 \quad \therefore \quad \lambda_2 = \left(\frac{27}{20}\right)\lambda$$

(b) For third line of Balmer series,

$$n_1 = 2, n_2 = 5 \quad \therefore \quad \lambda_2 = \left(\frac{25}{28}\right)\lambda$$

(c) For first line of Lyman series,

$$n_1 = 1, n_2 = 2 \quad \therefore \quad \lambda_2 = \frac{\lambda}{4}$$

(d) For second line of Lyman series,

$$n_1 = 2, n_2 = 3 \quad \therefore \quad \lambda_2 = \left(\frac{27}{128}\right)\lambda$$

122. Theory based question.

123. Stopping potential increases with increase in maximum kinetic energy of photoelectrons of frequency of incident light.

With increase in distance between cathode and anode, f remains unchanged.

$$K_{max} = hf - W = eV_0$$

If W is decreased, K_{max} and V_0 both will increase.

124. (a) Reduced mass of positronium and electron is $\frac{m}{2}$, where, m = mass of electron

$$E \propto m$$

$$\therefore \quad \lambda \propto \frac{1}{m}$$

m has become half, so λ will become two times or 1312 nm or 1.31 μm.

(b) $E \propto Z^2$

$$\therefore \quad \lambda \propto \frac{1}{Z^2}$$

For singly ionized helium atom $Z = 2$

$$\therefore \quad \lambda \text{ is } \frac{1}{4}\text{th} \quad \text{or} \quad 164 \text{ nm}$$

125. (a) $f = \frac{v}{2\pi r}$

$$f_1 = \frac{(2.2 \times 10^6)}{(2\pi)(0.529 \times 10^{-10})}$$

$$\approx 6.58 \times 10^{15} \text{ Hz}$$

$$v \propto \frac{1}{n} \quad \text{and} \quad r \propto n^2$$

$$f \propto \frac{v}{r} \Rightarrow f \propto \frac{1}{n^3}$$

$$\therefore \quad f_2 = \frac{f_1}{8}$$

(b) $\Delta E = E_2 - E_1 = 10.2 \text{ eV} = hf$

$$\therefore \quad f = \frac{10.2 \times 1.6 \times 10^{-19}}{6.6 \times 10^{-34}} \approx 2.46 \times 10^{15} \text{Hz}$$

(c) In option (a), we have found that

$$f_2 = 0.823 \times 10^{15} \text{ Hz}$$

$$T_2 = \frac{1}{f_2}$$

$$N = \frac{t}{T_2} = tf_2 = (10^{-8})(0.823 \times 10^{15})$$

$$= 8.23 \times 10^6 \text{ revolutions}$$

126. (a) $E_n - E_1 = 12.5$

$$\therefore \quad -\frac{13.6}{n^2} + 13.6 = 12.5$$

Solving we get, $n = 3.51$

Hence, electron jumps to $n = 3$. So, possible lines are between $n = 3$ to $n = 2$, $n = 3$ to $n = 1$ and between $n = 2$ to $n = 1$.

For $n = 3$ to $n = 2$,

$$\Delta E = E_3 - E_2 = -\frac{13.6}{9} + \frac{13.6}{4} = 1.9 \text{ eV}$$

$\therefore \quad \lambda = \frac{12375}{1.9} \text{ Å} = 6513 \text{ Å}$

$\approx 651 \text{ nm}$

Similarly, other wavelengths can also be obtained.

(b) $n = 3.51$ (in option-*a*)

A photon always transfers its energy completely. So, it cannot excite the ground state electrons to $n = 3$ (like and electrons excited it in part-a).

127. $\frac{K_1}{K_2} = 5$

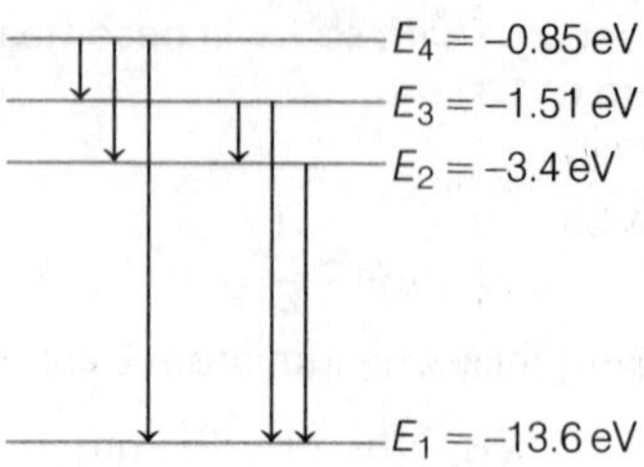

$$\therefore \quad \frac{\Delta E_1 - W}{\Delta E_2 - W} = 5 \qquad \text{...(i)}$$

Here, $\Delta E_1 = E_4 - E_1 = 12.75$ eV

and $\Delta E_2 = E_3 - E_1 = 12.09$ eV

Substituting in Eq. (i) and solving, we get

$W = 11.925$ eV **Ans.**

128. For shorter wavelength

$$\Delta E = E_4 - E_3 = \frac{(-13.6)(3)^2}{(4)^2} - \left[\frac{(-13.6)(3)^2}{(3)^2}\right]$$

$= 5.95$ eV

$W = E - K_{max} = (5.95 - 3.95)$ eV $= 2$ eV

For longer wavelength

$$\Delta E = E_5 - E_4 = \frac{(-13.6)(3)^2}{(5)^2} - \left[\frac{(-13.6)(3)^2}{(4)^2}\right]$$

$= 2.754$ eV

$\therefore K_{max} = E - W = 0.754$ eV

or stopping potential is 0.754 V. **Ans.**

129. Energy of electron in ground state of hydrogen atom is -13.6 eV. Earlier it had a kinetic energy of 2 eV. Therefore, energy of photon released during formation of hydrogen atom,

$\Delta E = 2 - (-13.6) = 15.6$ eV

$$\therefore \quad \lambda = \frac{12375}{\Delta E} = \frac{12375}{15.6}$$

$= 793.3$ Å **Ans.**

130. $U = -1.7$ eV

$$\therefore \quad E = \frac{U}{2} = -0.85 \text{ eV} = \frac{-13.6}{n^2}$$

$\therefore \quad n = 4$

Ejected photoelectron will have minimum de-Broglie wavelength corresponding to transition from $n = 4$ to $n = 1$.

$\Delta E = E_4 - E_1 = -0.85 - (-13.6)$

$= 12.75$ eV

$K_{max} = \Delta E - W = 10.45$ eV

$$\therefore \quad \lambda = \sqrt{\frac{150}{10.45}} \text{ Å} \qquad \text{(for an electron)}$$

$= 3.8$ Å **Ans.**

131. (a) $\frac{n(n-1)}{2} = 3$

$\therefore \quad n = 3$

i.e. after excitation atom jumps to second excited state. Hence, $n_f = 3$. So, n_i can be 1 or 2.

If $n_i = 1$, then energy emitted is either equal to or less than the energy absorbed. Hence, the emitted wavelength is either equal to or greater than the absorbed wavelength. Hence, $n_i \neq 1$.

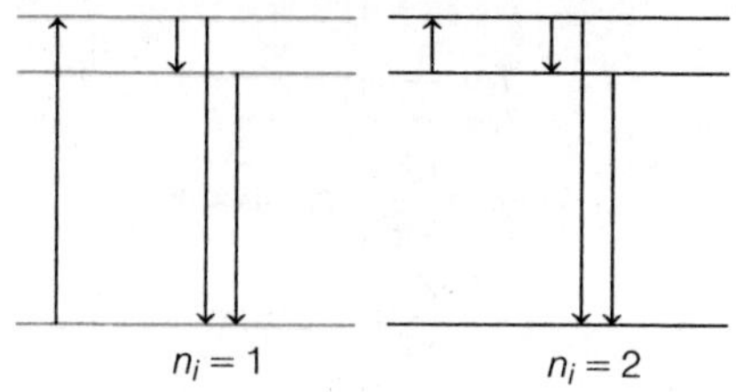

If $n_i = 2$, then $E_e \geq E_a$.

Hence, $\lambda_e \leq \lambda_b$

$\therefore \quad n_i = 2$ **Ans.**

(b) $E_3 - E_2 = 68$ eV

$$\therefore \quad (13.6)(Z^2)\left(\frac{1}{4} - \frac{1}{9}\right) = 68$$

$\therefore \quad Z = 6$ **Ans.**

(c) $$\lambda_{min} = \frac{12375}{E_3 - E_1}$$

$$= \frac{12375}{(13.6)(6)^2\left(1 - \frac{1}{9}\right)} = 28.43 \text{ Å}$$ **Ans.**

(d) Ionization energy $= (13.6)(6)^2 = 489.6$ eV **Ans.**

$$\lambda = \frac{12375}{489.6} = 25.3 \text{ Å}$$ **Ans.**

132. Pitch of helical path, $p = (v \cos \theta) T = \frac{vT}{2}$ (as $\theta = 60°$)

$$T = \frac{2\pi m}{Bq} = \frac{2\pi}{B\alpha} \qquad \left(\alpha = \frac{q}{m}\right)$$

$$\therefore \quad p = \frac{\pi v}{B\alpha}$$

or $$v = \frac{B\alpha p}{\pi} \qquad \text{...(i)}$$

$$KE = \frac{1}{2}mv^2 = E - W$$

$$\therefore \quad W = E - \frac{1}{2}mv^2 \qquad \text{...(ii)}$$

Substituting value of v from Eq. (i) in Eq. (ii), we get

$$W = 4.9 - \frac{1}{2} \times \frac{9.1\times10^{-31}\times(2.5\times10^{-3})^2\,(1.76\times10^{11})^2}{\dfrac{(2.7\times10^{-3})^2}{\pi^2\times1.6\times10^{-19}}}$$

$= (4.9 - 0.4)\ \text{eV} = 4.5\ \text{eV}$ **Ans.**

133. (a) $\lambda = 1500\left(\dfrac{1}{1-1/p^2}\right)$

λ_{max} corresponds to least energetic photon with $p = 2$.

$\therefore \quad \lambda_{max} = 1500\left(\dfrac{1}{1-1/4}\right) = 2000\ Å$ **Ans.**

λ_{min} corresponds to most energetic photon with $p = \infty$

$\therefore \quad \lambda_{min} = 1500\ Å$ **Ans.**

(b) $\lambda_{\infty-1} = 1500\ Å$

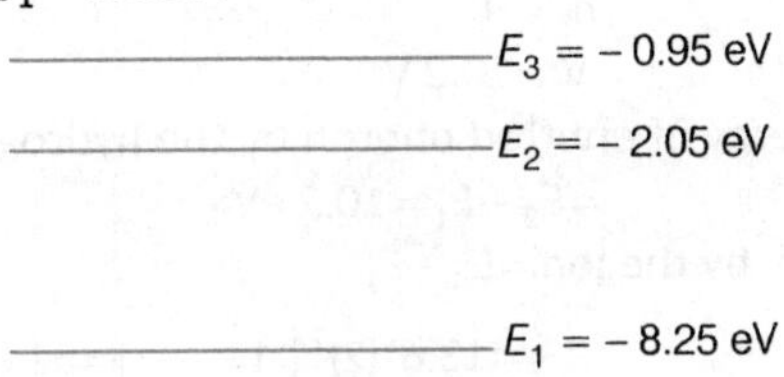

$\therefore \quad E_\infty - E_1 = \dfrac{12375}{1500}\ \text{eV} = 8.25\ \text{eV}$

$\therefore \quad E_1 = -8.25\ \text{eV}$ (as $E_\infty = 0$)

$\lambda_{2-1} = 2000\ Å$

$\therefore \quad E_2 - E_1 = \dfrac{12375}{2000}\ \text{eV} = 6.2\ \text{eV}$

$\therefore \quad E_2 = -2.05\ \text{eV}$

Similarly, $\quad \lambda_{31} = 1500\left(\dfrac{1}{1-1/9}\right)$

$= 1687.5\ Å$

$\therefore \quad E_3 - E_1 = \dfrac{12375}{1687.5}\ \text{eV}$

$= 7.32\ \text{eV}$

$\therefore \quad E_3 = -0.95\ \text{eV}$

(c) Ionization potential $= 8.25$ V **Ans.**

134. (a) $K_1 = \dfrac{12375}{3000} - W$ ...(i)

$K_2 = \dfrac{12375}{1650} - W$ ...(ii)

$v_2 = 2v_1 \quad \therefore \quad K_2 = 4K_1$ ...(iii)

Solving these equations, we get

$W = 3\ \text{eV}$

$\therefore$ Threshold wavelength,

$\lambda_0 = \dfrac{12375}{3} = 4125\ Å$ **Ans.**

(b) Energy of photon in first case,

$= \dfrac{12375}{3000} = 4.125\ \text{eV}$

or $\quad E_1 = 6.6\times10^{-19}\ \text{J}$

Rate of incident photons

$= \dfrac{P_1}{E_1} = \dfrac{0.388}{6.6\times10^{-19}}$

$= 5.88\times10^{17}$ per second

Number of electrons ejected

$= \dfrac{4.8\times10^{-3}}{1.6\times10^{-19}}$ per second

$= 3.0\times10^{16}$ per second

$\therefore$ Efficiency of photoelectrons generation

$= \dfrac{3.0\times10^{16}}{5.88\times10^{17}}\times100$

$= 5.1\%$ **Ans.**

(c) $E_2 = \dfrac{12375}{1650} = 7.5\ \text{eV}$

$= 12\times10^{-19}\ \text{J}$

Therefore, number of photons incident per second

$n_2 = \dfrac{P_2}{E_2} = \dfrac{5.0\times10^{-3}}{12\times10^{-19}}$

$= 4.17\times10^{15}$ per second

Number of electrons emitted per second ($\eta = 5.1\%$)

$= \dfrac{5.1}{100}\times4.17\times10^{15}$

$= 2.13\times10^{14}$ per second

$\therefore$ Saturation current in second case

$i = (2.13\times10^{14})(1.6\times10^{-19})$ A

$= 3.4\times10^{-5}$ A

$= 34\ \mu\text{A}$ **Ans.**

135. (a) Reduced mass

$\mu = \dfrac{m_1m_2}{m_1+m_2}$

$= \dfrac{(1837m_e)(207m_e)}{1837m_e + 207m_e}$

$= 186m_e$

$= 186\times9.1\times10^{-31}$

$= 1.69\times10^{-28}$ kg **Ans.**

(b) $E_n \propto m$

Here, reduced mass is 186 times mass of electron. Hence, ground state energy will also be 186 times that of hydrogen atom.

$\therefore \quad E_1 = 186(-13.6)\ \text{eV}$

$= -2529.6\ \text{eV} \approx -2.53\ \text{keV}$ **Ans.**

(c) $E_2 = 186\,(-3.4)\ \text{eV} = -632.4\ \text{eV}$

$\therefore \quad \Delta E_{21} = 1897.2\ \text{eV}$

$\therefore \quad \lambda_{21} = \dfrac{12375}{\Delta E_{21}}\ Å$

$= \dfrac{12375}{1897.2}\ Å$

$= 6.53\ Å \approx 0.653\ \text{nm}$ **Ans.**

136. Force of interaction between electron and proton is

$$F = -\frac{dU}{dr} = \frac{-k}{r}$$

Force is negative. It means there is an attraction between the particles and they are bound to each other. This force provides the necessary centripetal force for the electron.

$$\therefore \quad \frac{mv^2}{r} = \frac{k}{r} \quad ...(i)$$

According to Bohr's assumption,

$$mvr = n\frac{h}{2\pi} \quad ...(ii)$$

Solving Eqs. (i) and (ii), we get

$$r = \frac{nh}{2\pi\sqrt{mk}} \text{ and } v = \sqrt{\frac{k}{m}}$$

$$\therefore \quad E = U + \frac{1}{2}mv^2 = k\ln r - \frac{k}{2} + \frac{k}{2} = k\ln r$$

Thus, $r_n = \frac{nh}{2\pi\sqrt{mk}}$

and $E_n = k\ln\left\{\frac{nh}{2\pi\sqrt{mk}}\right\}$ **Ans.**

137. (a) $$r = \frac{mv}{Be} \quad ...(i)$$

$$mvr = \frac{nh}{2\pi} \quad ...(ii)$$

Solving these two equations, we get

$$r = \sqrt{\frac{nh}{2\pi Be}}$$

and $$v = \sqrt{\frac{nhBe}{2\pi m^2}}$$

(b) $K = \frac{1}{2}mv^2 = \frac{nhBe}{4\pi m}$ **Ans.**

(c) $M = iA = \left(\frac{e}{T}\right)(\pi r^2)$

$$= \frac{e}{\left(\frac{2\pi r}{v}\right)}(\pi r^2) = \frac{evr}{2}$$

$$= \frac{e}{2}\sqrt{\frac{nh}{2\pi Be}}\sqrt{\frac{nhBe}{2\pi m^2}}$$

$$= \frac{nhe}{4\pi m}$$

$$U = -MB\cos 180°$$

$$= \frac{nheB}{4\pi m}$$

Note *Angle between* **M** *and* **B** *will be 180°. Think why?*

(d) $E = U + K = \frac{nheB}{2\pi m}$

(e) $|\phi| = B\pi r^2 = \frac{nh}{2e}$

138. (a) and (b) When hydrogen atom is excited, then

$$eV = E_0\left(\frac{1}{1} - \frac{1}{n^2}\right) \quad ...(i)$$

When ion is excited,

$$eV = E_0 Z^2\left[\frac{1}{2^2} - \frac{1}{n_1^2}\right] \quad ...(ii)$$

Wavelength of emitted light,

$$\frac{hc}{\lambda_1} = E_0\left(\frac{1}{1} - \frac{1}{n^2}\right) \quad ...(iii)$$

$$\frac{hc}{\lambda_2} = E_0 Z^2\left(\frac{1}{1} - \frac{1}{n_1^2}\right) \quad ...(iv)$$

Further it is given that

$$\frac{\lambda_1}{\lambda_2} = \frac{5}{1} \quad ...(v)$$

Solving the above equations, we get

$$Z = 2,$$
$$n = 2,$$
$$n_1 = 4$$

and $V = 10.2$ V **Ans.**

(c) Energy of emitted photon by the hydrogen atom

$$= E_2 - E_1 = 10.2 \text{ eV}$$ **Ans.**

and by the ion $= E_4 - E_1$

$$= (13.6)(2)^2\left(1 - \frac{1}{16}\right) = 51 \text{ eV}$$ **Ans.**

139. $0.6 = \frac{12375}{4950} - W \quad ...(i)$

$$1.1 = \frac{12375}{\lambda} - W \quad ...(ii)$$

Solving above two equations, we get

$$W = 1.9 \text{ eV}$$

and $\lambda = 4125$ Å **Ans.**

140. $E = \frac{12375}{4000} = 3.1$ eV

Number of photoelectrons emitted per second,

$$n = \left(\frac{1}{10^6}\right)\left(\frac{5}{3.1 \times 1.6 \times 10^{-19}}\right)$$

$$= 1.0 \times 10^{13} \text{ per second}$$

$$\therefore \quad i = ne$$

$$= 1.0 \times 10^{13} \times 1.6 \times 10^{-19}$$

$$= 1.6 \times 10^{-6} \text{ A}$$

$$= 1.6\ \mu\text{A}$$ **Ans.**

141. (a) $E = \frac{12375}{4000} = 3.1$ eV

Energy of electron after first collision

$E_1 = 90\%$ of $E = 2.79$ eV (as 10% is lost)

Energy of electron after second collision

$E_2 = 90\%$ of $E_1 = 2.51$ eV

KE of this electron after emitting from the metal surface

$$= (2.51 - 2.2) \text{ eV} = 0.31 \text{ eV}$$ **Ans.**

(b) Energy after third collision,

$E_3 = 90\%$ of $E_2 = 2.26$ eV

Similarly, $E_4 = 90\%$ of $E_3 = 2.03$ eV
So, after four collisions it becomes unable for the electrons to come out of the metal.

142. (a) In emission spectrum total six lines are obtained. Hence, after excitation if n_f be the final principal quantum number then,

$$\frac{n_f(n_f - 1)}{2} = 6 \quad \text{or} \quad n_f = 4$$

i.e. after excitation atom goes to 4th energy state. Hence, n_i can be either 1, 2 or 3.

$$\Delta E = -13.6\left[\frac{1}{n_f^2} - \frac{1}{n_i^2}\right]$$

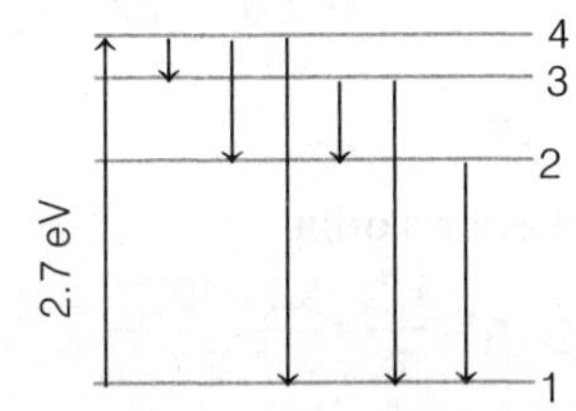

$n_i = 1$

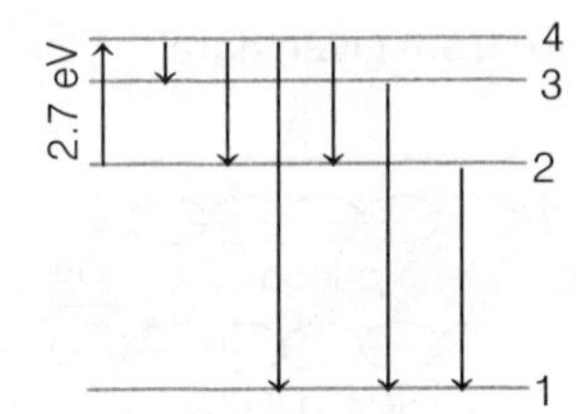

$n_i = 2$

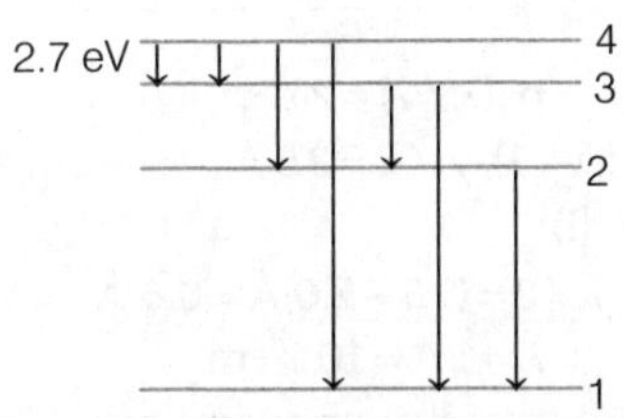

$n_i = 3$

Absorption and emission spectrum corresponding to $n_i = 1, n_i = 2$ and $n_i = 3$ are shown in figure.
For $n_i = 1$, energy of emitted photons ≤ 2.7 eV
For $n_i = 2$, energy of emitted photons $= 2.7$ eV and
For $n_i = 3$, energy of emitted photons ≥ 2.7 eV.
As per the given condition $n_i = 2$.

(b) $$E_4 - E_2 = 2.7 \text{ eV}$$

or $$\frac{E_1}{16} - \frac{E_1}{4} = 2.7$$

or $$-\frac{3}{16}E_1 = 2.7$$

$$E_1 = -14.4 \text{ eV}$$

Therefore, ionization energy for the gas atoms is $|E_1|$ or 14.4 eV.

(c) Maximum energy of the emitted photons is corresponding to transition from $n = 4$ to $n = 1$.

$$\therefore \quad E_{max} = E_4 - E_1$$

$$= \frac{E_1}{16} - E_1 = \frac{-15E_1}{16}$$

$$= \left(-\frac{15}{16}\right)(-14.4)$$

$$= 13.5 \text{ eV}$$

Similarly, minimum energy of the emitted photons is corresponding to transition from $n = 4$ to $n = 3$.

$$\therefore \quad E_{min} = E_4 - E_3$$

$$= \frac{E_1}{16} - \frac{E_1}{9} = -\frac{7E_1}{16 \times 9}$$

$$= \frac{7 \times 14.4}{16 \times 9} = 0.7 \text{ eV}$$

143. Given, $Z = 3, E_n \propto \frac{Z^2}{n^2}$

(a) To excite the atom from $n = 1$ to $n = 3$, energy of photon required is

$$E = -\frac{13.6}{n^2}(Z^2) \text{ eV}$$

$$\Delta E = E_3 - E_1 = \frac{(-13.6)(3)^2}{(3)^2} - \left[\frac{(-13.6)(3)^2}{(1)^2}\right]$$

$$= 108.8 \text{ eV}$$

Corresponding wavelength will be,

$$\lambda(\text{in Å}) = \frac{12375}{\Delta E(\text{in eV})}$$

$$= \frac{12375}{108.8}$$

$$= 113.74 \text{ Å}$$

(b) From n^{th} orbit total number of emission lines can be $\frac{n(n-1)}{2}$.

$\therefore$ Number of emission lines

$$= \frac{3(3-1)}{2} = 3$$

144. 1 Rydberg $= 2.2 \times 10^{-18}$ J $= Rhc$

Ionisation energy is given as 4 Rydberg

$$= 8.8 \times 10^{-18} \text{ J}$$

$$= \frac{8.8 \times 10^{-18}}{1.6 \times 10^{-19}} = 55 \text{ eV}$$

$\therefore$ Energy in first orbit $E_1 = -55$ eV

Energy of radiation emitted when electron jumps from first excited state ($n = 2$) to ground state (n=1)

$$E_{21} = \frac{E_1}{(2)^2} - E_1 = -\frac{3}{4}E_1 = 41.25 \text{ eV}$$

$\therefore$ Wavelength of photon emitted in this transition would be

$$\lambda = \frac{12375}{41.25} = 300 \text{ Å}$$

(b) Let Z be the atomic number of given element. Then

$$E_1 = (-13.6)(Z^2)$$

or $\quad -55 = (-13.6)(Z^2)$

or $\quad Z \approx 2$

Now, as $\quad r \propto \dfrac{1}{Z}$

Radius of first orbit of this atom,

$$r_1 = \frac{r_{H_1}}{Z} = \frac{0.529}{2} \text{ Å} = 0.2645 \text{ Å}$$

145. Energy corresponding to given wavelength

$$E \text{ (in eV)} = \frac{12375}{\lambda (\text{in Å})} = \frac{12375}{975}$$

$$= 12.69 \text{ eV}$$

Now, let the electron excites to n^{th} energy state. Then,

$$E_n - E_1 = 12.69$$

or $\quad \dfrac{(-13.6)}{(n^2)} - (-13.6) = 12.69$

$\therefore \quad n \approx 4$

i.e. electron excites to 4th energy state. Total number of lines in emission spectrum would be

$$\frac{n(n-1)}{2} = \frac{4 \times 3}{2} = 6$$

Longest wavelength will correspond to the minimum energy and minimum energy is released in transition from $n = 4$ to $n = 3$.

$$E_{4-3} = E_4 - E_3$$

$$= \frac{-13.6}{(4^2)} - \left[\frac{-13.6}{(3)^2}\right]$$

$$= 0.66 \text{ eV}$$

$\therefore$ Longest wavelength will be,

$$\lambda_{max} = \frac{12375}{E \text{ (in eV)}} = \frac{12375}{0.66} \text{ Å}$$

$$= 1.875 \times 10^{-6} \text{ m} = 1.875 \text{ μm}$$

146. (a) Given, $E_3 - E_2 = 47.2$ eV

Since $\quad E_n \propto \dfrac{Z^2}{n^2} \quad$ (for hydrogen like atoms)

or $\quad (-13.6)\left(\dfrac{Z^2}{9}\right) - \left[(-13.6)\left(\dfrac{Z^2}{4}\right)\right] = 47.2$

Solving this equation, we get

$$Z = 5$$

(b) Energy required to excite the electron from 3rd to 4th orbit :

$$E_{3-4} = E_4 - E_3$$

$$= (-13.6)\left(\frac{25}{16}\right) - \left[(-13.6)\left(\frac{25}{9}\right)\right]$$

$$= 16.53 \text{ eV}$$

(c) Energy required to remove the electron from first orbit to infinity (or the ionisation energy) will be

$$E = (13.6)(5)^2$$

$$= 340 \text{ eV}$$

The corresponding wavelength would be,

$$\lambda = \frac{hc}{E} = \frac{6.6 \times 10^{-34} \times 3 \times 10^8}{340 \times 1.6 \times 10^{-19}}$$

$$= 0.0364 \times 10^{-7} \text{ m}$$

$$= 36.4 \text{ Å}$$

(d) In first orbit, total energy $= -340$ eV

kinetic energy $= +340$ eV

Potential energy $= -2 \times 340$ eV

$= -680$ eV and

Angular momentum $= \dfrac{h}{2\pi}$

$$= \frac{6.6 \times 10^{-34}}{2\pi} \qquad [\because n = 1]$$

$$= 1.05 \times 10^{-34} \text{ kg - m}^2/\text{s}$$

(e) Also, $r_n \propto \dfrac{n^2}{Z}$

Radius of first Bohr's orbit

$$r_1 = \frac{r_1^H}{Z} = \frac{5.3 \times 10^{-11}}{5}$$

$$= 1.06 \times 10^{-11} \text{ m}$$

147. Draw the figure from given data

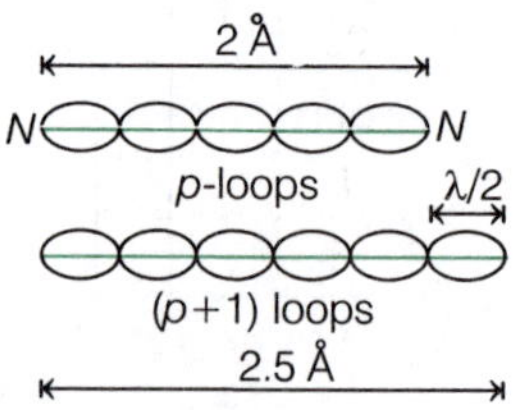

$$p \cdot (\lambda/2) = 2 \text{ Å} \qquad \text{...(i)}$$

$$(p+1) \cdot \lambda/2 = 2.5 \text{ Å} \qquad \text{...(ii)}$$

Eq. (ii) – Eq. (i)

$\therefore \quad \lambda/2 = (2.5 - 2.0) \text{Å} = 0.5 \text{ Å}$

or $\quad \lambda = 1 \text{ Å} = 10^{-10}$ m.

(a) de-Broglie wavelength is given by

$$\lambda = \frac{h}{p} = \frac{h}{\sqrt{2Km}}$$

Here, K = kinetic energy of electron

$\therefore \quad K = \dfrac{h^2}{2m\lambda^2}$

$$= \frac{(6.63 \times 10^{-34})^2}{2(9.1 \times 10^{-31})(10^{-10})^2}$$

$$= 2.415 \times 10^{-17} \text{ J}$$

$$= \left(\frac{2.415 \times 10^{-17}}{1.6 \times 10^{-19}}\right) \text{eV}$$

$\therefore \quad K = 150.8$ eV

(b) The least value of d will be, when only one loop is formed.

$\therefore \quad d_{min} = \lambda/2$ or $d_{min} = 0.5$ Å

148. Maximum kinetic energy of the photoelectrons would be

$$K_{max} = E - W$$
$$= (5-3)\ eV = 2\ eV$$

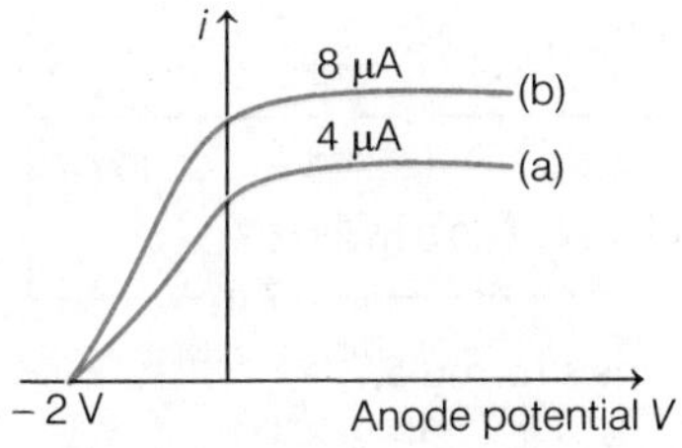

Therefore, the stopping potential is 2 V. Saturation current depends on the intensity of light incident. When the intensity is doubled the saturation current will also become two fold. The corresponding graphs are shown in above figure.

149. (a) Energy of emitted photons

$$E_1 = 5.0\ eV = 5.0 \times 1.6 \times 10^{-19}\ J$$
$$= 8.0 \times 10^{-19}\ J$$

Power of the point source is 3.2×10^{-3} W or

3.2×10^{-3} J/s.

Therefore, energy emitted per second,

$$E_2 = 3.2 \times 10^{-3}\ J$$

Hence, number of photons emitted per second

$$n_1 = \frac{E_2}{E_1} \text{ or } n_1 = \frac{3.2 \times 10^{-3}}{8.0 \times 10^{-19}}$$

$$\Rightarrow \quad n_1 = 4.0 \times 10^{15} \text{ photon/s}$$

Number of photons incident on unit area at a distance of 0.8 m from the source S will be

$$n_2 = \frac{n_1}{4\pi (0.8)^2} = \frac{4.0 \times 10^{15}}{4\pi (0.64)}$$
$$\approx 5 \times 10^{14} \text{photon/ s -m}^2$$

The area of metallic sphere over which photons will fall is

$$A = \pi r^2 = \pi (8 \times 10^{-3})^2\ m^2$$
$$\approx 2.01 \times 10^{-4}\ m^2$$

Therefore, number of photons incident on the sphere per second are

$$n_3 = n_2 A = (5.0 \times 10^{14} \times 2.01 \times 10^{-4})$$
$$\approx 10^{11}/s$$

One photoelectron is emitted for every 10^6 photons, hence number of photoelectrons emitted per second.

$$n = \frac{n_3}{10^6} = \frac{10^{11}}{10^6} = 10^5/s \text{ or } n = 10^5/s$$

(b) Maximum kinetic energy of photoelectrons

$$K_{max} = \text{Energy of incident photons} - \text{work function}$$
$$= (5.0 - 3.0)\ eV = 2.0\ eV$$
$$= 2.0 \times 1.6 \times 10^{-19}\ J$$
$$K_{max} = 3.2 \times 10^{-19}\ J$$

The de-Broglie wavelength of these photoelectrons will be

$$\lambda_1 = \frac{h}{p} = \frac{h}{\sqrt{2K_{max} m}}$$

Here, h = Planck's constant and
m = mass of electron

$$\lambda_1 = \frac{6.63 \times 10^{-34}}{\sqrt{2 \times 3.2 \times 10^{-19} \times 9.1 \times 10^{-31}}}$$
$$= 8.68 \times 10^{-10} = 8.68\ Å$$

Wavelength of incident light λ_2 (in Å)

$$= \frac{12375}{E_1 (\text{in eV})}$$

or $$\lambda_2 = \frac{12375}{5} = 2475\ Å$$

Therefore, the desired ratio is

$$\frac{\lambda_2}{\lambda_1} = \frac{2475}{8.68} = 285.1$$

(c) As soon as electrons are emitted from the metal sphere, it gets positively charged and acquires positive potential. The positive potential gradually increases as more and more photoelectrons are emitted from its surface. Emission of photoelectrons is stopped when its potential is equal to the stopping potential required for fastest moving electrons. Because this positive potential/charge will attract the electrons.

(d) As discussed in part (c), emission of photoelectrons is stopped when potential on the metal sphere is equal to the stopping potential of fastest moving electrons.
Since, $K_{max} = 2.0$ eV
Therefore, stopping potential
$V_0 = 2$ V. Let q be the charge required for the potential on the sphere to be equal to stopping potential or 2 V. Then

$$2 = \frac{1}{4\pi \varepsilon_0} \cdot \frac{q}{r}$$
$$= (9.0 \times 10^9) \frac{q}{8.0 \times 10^{-3}}$$
$$\therefore \quad q = 1.78 \times 10^{-12}\ C$$

Photoelectrons emitted per second $= 10^5$ [Part (a)]

or charge emitted per second

$$= (1.6 \times 10^{-19}) \times 10^5\ C$$
$$= 1.6 \times 10^{-14}\ C$$

Therefore, time required to acquire the charge q will be

$$t = \frac{q}{1.6 \times 10^{-14}}\ s$$
$$= \frac{1.78 \times 10^{-12}}{1.6 \times 10^{-14}}\ s$$

or $$t \approx 111\ s$$

150. (a) Energy of one photon,

$$E = \frac{hc}{\lambda} = \frac{(6.6 \times 10^{-34})(3.0 \times 10^{8})}{6000 \times 10^{-10}}$$

$$= 3.3 \times 10^{-19} \text{ J}$$

Power of the source is 2 W or 2 J/s. Therefore, number of photons emitting per second,

$$n_1 = \frac{2}{3.3 \times 10^{-19}} = 6.06 \times 10^{18}/\text{s}$$

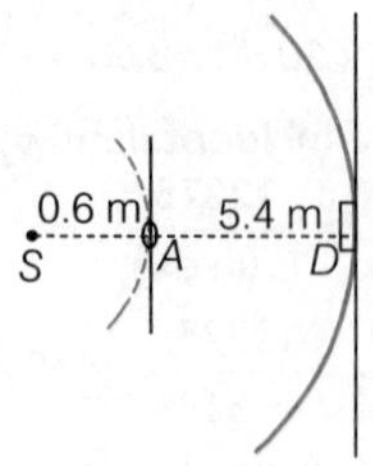

At distance 0.6 m, number of photons incident per unit area per unit time :

$$n_2 = \frac{n_1}{4\pi(0.6)^2} = 1.34 \times 10^{18}/\text{m}^2/\text{s}$$

Area of aperture is,

$$S_1 = \frac{\pi}{4} d^2 = \frac{\pi}{4}(0.1)^2$$

$$= 7.85 \times 10^{-3} \text{ m}^2$$

∴ Total number of photons incident per unit time on the aperture,

$$n_3 = n_2 S_1 = (1.34 \times 10^{18})(7.85 \times 10^{-3})/\text{s}$$

$$= 1.052 \times 10^{16}/\text{s}$$

The aperture will become new source of light. Now, these photons are further distributed in all directions. Hence, at the location of detector, photons incident per unit area per unit time

$$n_4 = \frac{n_3}{4\pi(6 - 0.6)^2} = \frac{1.052 \times 10^{16}}{4\pi(5.4)^2}$$

$$= 2.87 \times 10^{13} \text{ s}^{-1}\text{m}^{-2}$$

This is the photon flux at the centre of the screen. Area of detector is 0.5 cm^2 or 0.5×10^{-4} m^2.

Therefore, total number of photons incident on the detector per unit time

$$n_5 = (0.5 \times 10^{-4})(2.87 \times 10^{13})$$

$$= 1.435 \times 10^9 \text{ s}^{-1}$$

The efficiency of photoelectron generation is 0.9. Hence, total photoelectrons generated per unit time

$$n_6 = 0.9 n_5$$

$$= 1.2915 \times 10^9 \text{ s}^{-1}$$

or, photocurrent in the detector

$$i = (e) n_6 = (1.6 \times 10^{-19})(1.2915 \times 10^9)$$

$$= 2.07 \times 10^{-10} \text{ A}$$

(b) Using the lens formula :

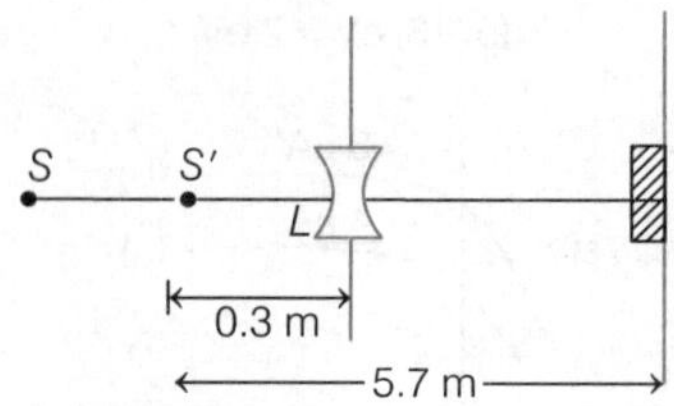

Using lens's formula,

$$\frac{1}{v} - \frac{1}{-0.6} = \frac{1}{-0.6}$$

or $\quad v = -0.3 \text{ m} \qquad (f = 0.6 \text{ m})$

i.e. image of source (say S', is formed at 0.3 m) from the lens.

Total number of photons incident per unit time on the lens are still n_3 or 1.052×10^{16}/s. 80% of it transmits to second medium. Therefore, at a distance of 5.7 m from S' number of photons incident per unit area per unit time will be

$$n_7 = \frac{(80/100)(1.052 \times 10^{16})}{(4\pi)(5.7)^2}$$

$$= 2.06 \times 10^{13} \text{ s}^{-1}\text{m}^{-2}$$

This is the photon flux at the detector

New, value of photocurrent is

$$i' = (2.06 \times 10^{13})(0.5 \times 10^{-4})(0.9)(1.6 \times 10^{-19})$$

$$= 1.48 \times 10^{-10} \text{ A}$$

(c) Energy of incident photons (in both the cases) :

$$E = \frac{12375 \text{ eV-Å}}{6000 \text{ Å}} = 2.06 \text{ eV}$$

Work function $W = 1.0$ eV

∴ Maximum kinetic energy of photoelectrons in both cases,

$$K_{max} = E - W = 1.06 \text{ eV}$$

or the stopping potential will be 1.06 V.

151. The stopping potential for shorter wavelength is 3.95 V i.e. maximum kinetic energy of photoelectrons corresponding to shorter wavelength will be 3.95 eV. Further energy of incident photons corresponding to shorter wavelength will be in transition from $n = 4$ to $n = 3$.

$$E_{4-3} = E_4 - E_3 = \frac{-(13.6)(3)^2}{(4)^2} - \left[\frac{-(13.6)(3)^2}{(3)^2}\right]$$

$$= 5.95 \text{ eV}$$

Now, from the equation,

$$K_{max} = E - W$$

we have $W = E - K_{max}$

$$= E_{4-3} - K_{max}$$

$$= (5.95 - 3.95) \text{ eV}$$

$$= 2 \text{ eV}$$

Longer wavelength will correspond to transition from $n=5$ to $n=4$. From the relation,

$$\frac{1}{\lambda}=RZ^2\left(\frac{1}{n_f^2}-\frac{1}{n_i^2}\right)$$

The longer wavelength,

$$\frac{1}{\lambda}=(1.094\times 10^7)(3)^3\left(\frac{1}{16}-\frac{1}{25}\right)$$

or $\lambda=4.514\times 10^{-7}\text{ m}=4514\text{ Å}$

Energy corresponding to this wavelength,

$$E=\frac{12375\text{ eV-Å}}{4514\text{ Å}}=2.74\text{ eV}$$

∴ Maximum kinetic energy of photo-electrons

$$K_{max}=E-W=(2.74-2)\text{ eV}=0.74\text{ eV}$$

or the stopping potential is 0.74 V.

152. $\frac{1}{\lambda}=RZ^2\left(\frac{1}{n_1^2}-\frac{1}{n_2^2}\right)$

or $$\lambda=\frac{(n_1n_2)^2}{RZ^2(n_2^2-n_1^2)} \qquad (Z=2)$$

Longest wavelength of Balmer series ($n_1=2$ and $n_2=3$) is,

$$\lambda_1=\frac{(2\times 3)^2}{R(2)^2(3^2-2^2)}=\frac{9}{5R}$$

Similarly longest wavelength of Lyman series, ($n_1=1$ and $n_2=2$) is,

$$\lambda_2=\frac{(1\times 2)^2}{R(2)^2(2^2-1^2)}=\frac{1}{3R}$$

Given $\lambda_1-\lambda_2=133.7\text{ nm}$

Substituting the values, we can find the value of R.

153. $\frac{1}{\lambda}=RZ^2\left(\frac{1}{n_1^2}-\frac{1}{n_2^2}\right)$

Now, $$f=\frac{c}{\lambda}=RcZ^2\left(\frac{1}{n_1^2}-\frac{1}{n_2^2}\right)$$

$$\omega=2\pi f=2\pi RcZ^2\left(\frac{1}{n_1^2}-\frac{1}{n_2^2}\right)$$

$$\omega_1=2\pi RcZ^2\left(\frac{1}{n_1^2}-\frac{1}{\infty}\right)$$

$$\omega_2=2\pi RcZ^2\left[\frac{1}{n_1^2}-\frac{1}{(n_1+1)^2}\right]$$

∴ $$\Delta\omega=\omega_1-\omega_2=\frac{2\pi RcZ^2}{(n_1+1)^2}$$

Substituting the values, we can first find n_1 and then using the relation,

$$\frac{1}{\lambda}=RZ^2\left[\frac{1}{n_1^2}-\frac{1}{(n_1+1)^2}\right]$$

We can also find the asked wavelength.

154.

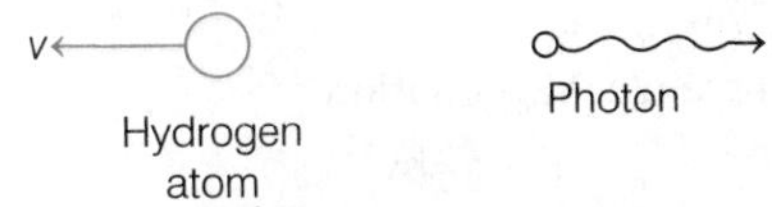

(a) Energy gap between first excited state and ground state of hydrogen atom is 10.2 eV.

(b) From energy conservation,

$10.2\times 1.6\times 10^{-19}$ J = kinetic energy of recoiling hydrogen atom + energy of emitted photon

∴ $$10.2\times 1.6\times 10^{-19}=\frac{1}{2}mv^2+E \qquad \text{...(i)}$$

Here m is mass of hydrogen atom and E is energy of photon.

(c) From momentum conservation,

$$\Sigma p_i=\Sigma p_f$$

∴ $$0=mv-\frac{E}{c}$$

or $$mv=\frac{E}{c} \qquad \text{...(ii)}$$

We have two unknowns v and E.

Solving these two equations we can find v and E both and v comes out to be,

$$v=3.25\text{ m/s}$$

155. Energy of photon corresponding to first line of Lyman series for He^+ ion, ($n=2$ to $n=1$),

$$E_1=(\Delta E_{21})_H Z^2 \qquad (\text{as } E\propto Z^2)$$

$$=(10.2\text{ eV})(2)^2 \qquad (Z=2 \text{ for } He^+ \text{ ion})$$

$$=40.8\text{ eV}$$

Energy required to liberate the single electron of hydrogen atom in ground state is,

$$E_2=\text{ionization energy}$$
$$=13.6\text{ eV}$$

Therefore, kinetic energy of emitted electron,

$$K=E_1-E_2=27.2\text{ eV}$$
$$=27.2\times 1.6\times 10^{-19}\text{ J}$$

Putting this kinetic energy equal to $\frac{1}{2}mv^2$, we can find speed v of electron. Here m is mass of electron. After calculations v comes out to be,

$$v=3.1\times 10^6\text{ m/s}$$

156. $AE=E_4-E_3$

$$h\nu=13.6Z^2\left(\frac{1}{9}-\frac{1}{16}\right)=13.6\times\frac{7}{9\times 16}(Z^2)$$

$$KE_{max}=h\nu-\phi$$

$$1.95=h\nu-\frac{1240}{310}$$

$$h\nu=1.95+4$$

⇒ $$5.95=13.6\times\frac{7}{9\times 16}(Z^2)$$

$$Z^2=9 \Rightarrow Z=3$$

157. For P and Q

Using Einstein's P.E. equation

$$E-\phi=h\nu$$

$\Rightarrow$ $E_1-4=E_P$

$\Rightarrow$ $E_1-4.5=E_Q$

Since, $E_P=2E_Q$

$\therefore$ $E_1-4=2(E_1-4.5)$

$\Rightarrow$ $E_1=5$ eV

Thus, $E_P=1$ eV,

$\therefore$ $E_Q=E_R=0.5$ eV

For $E_2-5.5=0.5$

$\Rightarrow$ $E_2=6$ eV

158. We know that,

$\therefore$ Power $=nhf$

(where, $n=$ number of photons incident per second)

Since, KE $=0$, $hf=$ work-function W

$$200=nW=n[6.25\times1.6\times10^{-19}]$$

$$\Rightarrow \quad n=\frac{200}{1.6\times10^{-19}\times6.25}$$

As photon is just above threshold frequency KE_{max} is zero and they are accelerated by potential difference of 500 V.

$$\therefore \quad KE_f=q\Delta V$$

$$\frac{P^2}{2m}=q\Delta V$$

$$\Rightarrow \quad P=\sqrt{2\,mq\,\Delta V}$$

Since, efficiency is 100%, number of electrons emitted per second = number of photons incident per second. As, photon is completely absorbed, force exerted

$$=n(mV)=nP$$

$$=n\sqrt{2mq\Delta V}$$

$$=\frac{200}{6.25\times1.6\times10^{-19}}\times\sqrt{2\,(9\times10^{-31})\times1.6\times10^{-19}\times500}$$

$$=24$$

UNIT-12

MODERN PHYSICS - 2

Learning Modules

1. Radioactivity
2. Nuclear Physics

MODULE 1

Radioactivity

Nuclear Stability and Radioactivity

Among about 1500 known nuclides, less than 260 are stable. The others are unstable that decay to form other nuclides by emitting α and β-particles and γ-electromagnetic waves. This process is called radioactivity. It was discovered in 1896 by Henry Becquerel.

Whilst the chemical properties of an atom are governed entirely by the number of protons in the nucleus (i.e. the proton number Z), the stability of an atom appears to depend on both the number of protons and the number of neutrons. For light nuclei, the greatest stability is achieved when the numbers of protons and neutrons are approximately equal ($N \approx Z$).

For heavier nuclei, instability caused by electrostatic repulsion between the protons is minimized when there are more neutrons than protons.

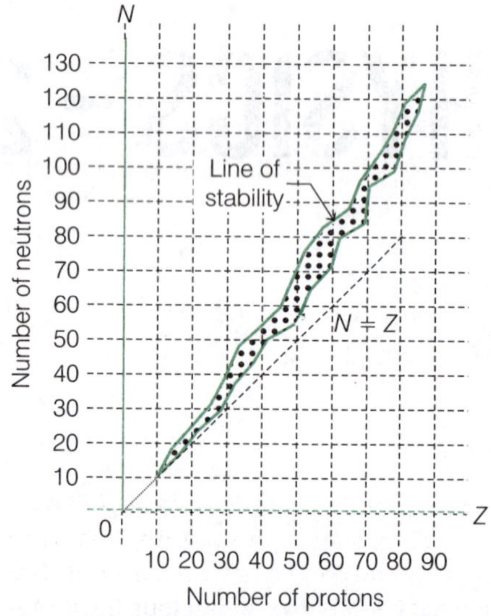

The stable nuclides plotted on a graph of neutron number, N, *versus* proton number, Z. Note that for heavier nuclides, N is larger relative to Z. The stable nuclides group along a curve called the line of stability.

Figure shows a plot of N *versus* Z for the stable nuclei. For mass numbers upto about $A = 40$, we see that $N \approx Z$.

$_{40}$Ca is the heaviest stable nucleus for which $N = Z$. For larger values of Z, the (short range) nuclear force is unable to hold the nucleus together against the (long range) electrical repulsion of the protons unless the number of neutrons exceeds the number of protons. At Bi ($Z = 83$, $A = 209$), the neutron excess is $N - Z = 43$. There are no stable nuclides with $Z > 83$.

The nuclide $^{209}_{83}$Bi is the heaviest stable nucleus.

Atoms are radioactive if their nuclei are unstable and spontaneously (and randomly) emit α and β particles and or γ radiations. When naturally occurring nuclei are unstable, we call the phenomena **natural radioactivity.** Other nuclei can be transformed into radioactive nuclei by various means, typically involving irradiation by neutrons, this is called **artificial radioactivity.**

A radioactive nucleus is called a **parent nucleus,** the nucleus resulting from its decay by particle emission is called **daughter nucleus.** For unstable nuclides and radioactivity, the following points can be made.

(i) Disintegrations tend to produce new nuclides near the stability line and continue until a stable nuclide is formed.

(ii) Radioactivity is a nuclear property, i.e. α, β and γ emission take place from the nucleus.

(iii) Nuclear processes involve huge amount of energy so the particle emission rate is independent of temperature and pressure. The rate depends solely on the concentration of the number of atoms of the radioactive substance.

(iv) A radioactive substance is either an α-emitter or a β-emitter, γ-rays emit with both.

Alpha Decay

An alpha particle is a helium nucleus. Thus, a nucleus emitting an alpha particle loses two protons and two neutrons. Therefore, the atomic number Z decreases by 2, the mass number A decreases by 4 and the neutron number N decreases by 2. The decay can be written as

$$^{A}_{Z}X = ^{A-4}_{Z-2}Y + ^{4}_{2}He$$

where, X is the parent nucleus and Y the daughter nucleus. As examples U^{238} and Ra^{226} are both alpha emitters and decay according to

$$^{238}_{92}U \longrightarrow ^{234}_{90}Th + ^{4}_{2}He$$

$$^{226}_{88}Ra \longrightarrow ^{222}_{86}Rn + ^{4}_{2}He$$

If the original nucleus has a mass number A that is 4 times an integer, the daughter nucleus and all those in the chain will also have mass numbers equal to 4 times an integer. (Because in α-decay A decreases by 4 and in β-decay it remains the same).

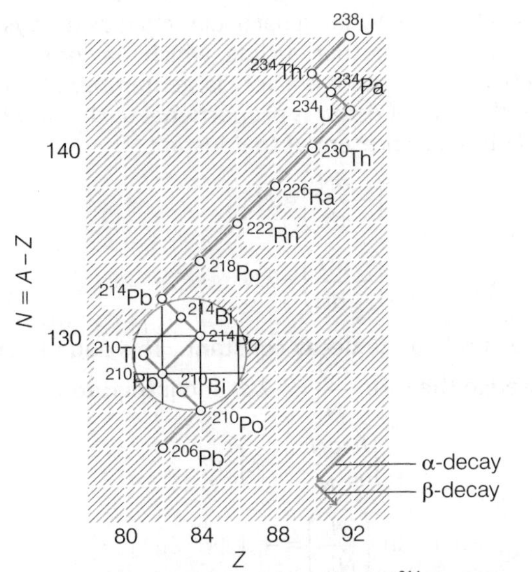

The uranium decay series($A = 4n + 2$). The decay of $^{214}_{83}Bi$ may proceed either by alpha emission and then beta emission or in the reverse order.

Similarly, if the mass number of the original nucleus is $4n + 1$, where n is an integer, all the nuclei in the decay chain will have mass numbers given by $4n + 1$ with n decreasing by 1 in each α-decay. We can see therefore, that there are four possible α-decay chains, depending on whether A equals $4n$, $4n + 1$, $4n + 2$ or $4n + 3$, where n is an integer.

Series $4n + 1$ is now not found. Because its longest lived member (other than the stable end product Bi^{209}) is Np^{237} which has a half-life of only 2×10^6 years. Because this is much less than the age of the earth, this series has disappeared.

Figure shows the uranium ($4n + 2$) series. The series branches at Bi^{214}, which decays either by α-decay or β-decay to Po^{214}. The branches meet at the lead isotope Pb^{210}.

Table 1. lists the four radioactive series.

Table 1. Four Radioactive Series

Mass numbers	Series	Parent	Half-life, Years	Stable product
$4n$	Thorium	$^{232}_{90}Th$	1.39×10^{10}	$^{208}_{82}Pb$
$4n + 1$	Neptunium	$^{237}_{93}Np$	2.25×10^6	$^{209}_{83}Bi$
$4n + 2$	Uranium	$^{238}_{92}U$	4.47×10^9	$^{206}_{82}Pb$
$4n + 3$	Actinium	$^{235}_{92}U$	7.07×10^8	$^{207}_{82}Pb$

Beta Decay

Beta decay can involve the emission of either electrons or positrons. A positron is a form of antimatter which has a charge equal to $+e$ and mass equal to that of an electron.

The electrons or positrons emitted in β-decay do not exist inside the nucleus. They are only created at the time of emission, just as photons are created when an atom makes a transition from a higher to a lower energy state.

In β^- decay a neutron in the nucleus is transformed into a proton, an electron and an antineutrino.

$$n \longrightarrow p + e^- + \bar{\nu}$$

To conserve energy and momentum in the process, the emission of an antineutrino ($\bar{\nu}$) (alongwith proton and electron) was first suggested by W. Pauli in 1930, but it was first observed experimentally in 1957.

Thus, a parent nucleus with atomic number Z and mass number A decays by β^- emission into a daughter with atomic number $Z + 1$ and the same mass number A.

$$^A_ZX \xrightarrow{\beta^-} {}^{A}_{Z+1}Y$$

β^- decay occurs in nuclei that have too many neutrons. An example of β^- decay is the decay of carbon-14 into nitrogen,

$$^{14}_{6}C \longrightarrow {}^{14}_{7}N + e^- + \bar{\nu}$$

In β^+ decay, a proton changes into a neutron with the emission of a positron (and a neutrino)

$$p \longrightarrow n + e^+ + \nu$$

Positron (e^+) emission from a nucleus decreases the atomic number Z by 1 while keeping the same mass number A.

$$^A_ZX \xrightarrow{\beta^+} {}^{A}_{Z-1}Y$$

B^+ decay occurs in nuclei that have too few neutrons. A typical β^+ decay is

$$^{13}_{7}N \longrightarrow {}^{13}_{6}C + e^+ + \nu$$

Gamma Decay

Very often a nucleus that undergoes radioactive decay (α or β-decay) is left in an excited energy state (analogous to the excited states of the orbiting electrons, except that the energy levels associated with the nucleus have much larger energy differences than those involved with the atomic electrons). The typical half-life of an excited nuclear state is 10^{-10} s. The excited nucleus (X^*) then undergoes to a lower energy state by emitting a high energy photon, called the γ-ray photon. The following sequence of events represents a typical situation in which γ-decay occurs.

$$^{12}_{5}B \longrightarrow {}^{12}_{6}C^* + e^- + \bar{\nu}$$

$$^{12}_{6}C^* \longrightarrow {}^{12}_{6}C + \gamma$$

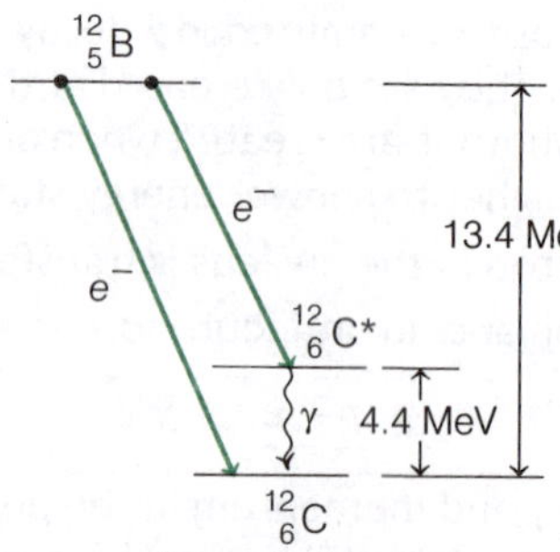

Gamma decay

Figure shows decay of B^{12} nucleus. It can either decay directly to the ground state of C^{12} by emitting a 13.4 MeV electron or undergo β-decay to an excited state of $^{12}_{6}C^*$ followed by γ-decay to the ground state. The later process results in the emission of a 9.0 MeV electron and a 4.4 MeV photon.

Note *(i) In both α and β-decay, the Z value of a nucleus changes and the nucleus of one element becomes the nucleus of a different element. In γ-decay, the element does not change, the nucleus merely goes from an excited state to a less excited state.*

(ii) Unless mentioned, β-decay means β^- decay.

Important POINTS

- After emission of one alpha particle and two β^- decays isotopes are produced. This is because after the emission of one alpha particle, atomic number decreases by 2. Further, after the emission of two β^- decays atomic number increases by 2. So, finally atomic number remains unchanged.
- From beta emission mass number does not change. Therefore, isobars will be produced.

Example 1 Mass number of a nucleus *X* is *A* and atomic number is *Z*. Find mass number and atomic number of the new nucleus (say *Y*) after the emission of *m*-alpha particles and *n*-beta particles.

Sol. By the emission of one alpha particle, atomic number decreases by 2 and by the emission of one beta particle atomic number increases by 1. Therefore, the atomic number of nucleus *Y* is $Z' = Z - 2m + n$

Further, by the emission of one alpha particle mass number decreases by 4 and by the emission of beta particle, mass number does not change. Therefore, the mass number of *Y* is

$$A' = A - 4m$$

Radioactive Decay Law

Radioactive decay is a random process. Each decay is an independent event and one cannot tell when a particular nucleus will decay. When a particular nucleus decays, it is transformed into another nuclide, which may or may not be radioactive. When there is a very large number of nuclei in a sample, the rate of decay is proportional to the number of nuclei, *N*, that are present at that instant.

$$\therefore \quad \left(-\frac{dN}{dt}\right) \propto N$$

$$\text{or} \quad \left(-\frac{dN}{dt}\right) = \lambda N$$

where, λ is called the **decay constant.** This equation may be expressed in the form $\frac{dN}{N} = -\lambda dt$ and integrated,

$$\int_{N_0}^{N} \frac{dN}{N} = -\lambda \int_0^t dt$$

$$\text{or} \quad \ln\left(\frac{N}{N_0}\right) = -\lambda t$$

where, N_0 is the initial number of parent nuclei at $t = 0$. The number that survives at time *t* is therefore,

$$\boxed{N = N_0 e^{-\lambda t}} \quad \text{...(i)}$$

This function is plotted in figure.

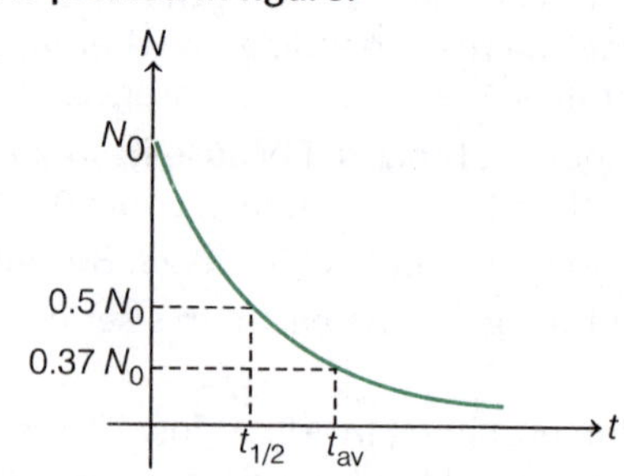

Half-life The time required for the number of parent nuclei to fall to 50% is called half-life $t_{1/2}$ and may be related to λ as follows.

$$0.5\,N_0 = N_0 e^{-\lambda t_{1/2}}$$

We have $\quad \lambda t_{1/2} = \ln(2) = 0.693$

$$\therefore \quad \boxed{t_{1/2} = \frac{\ln(2)}{\lambda} = \frac{0.693}{\lambda}} \quad \text{...(ii)}$$

Mean life The average or mean life t_{av} is the reciprocal of the decay constant.

$$\boxed{t_{av} = \frac{1}{\lambda}} \quad \text{...(iii)}$$

The mean life is analogous to the time constant in the exponential decrease in the charge on a capacitor in an *C-R* circuit. After a time equal to the mean life time, the number of radioactive nuclei decreases to $\frac{1}{e}$ times or approximately 37% of their original values.

Activity of a Radioactive Substance

The decay rate R of a radioactive substance is the number of decays per second. And as we have seen above

$$-\frac{dN}{dt} \propto N$$

or $$-\frac{dN}{dt} = \lambda N$$

Thus, $$R = -\frac{dN}{dt}$$

or $$R \propto N$$

or $$R = \lambda N$$

or $$R = \lambda N_0 e^{-\lambda t}$$

or $$\boxed{R = R_0 e^{-\lambda t}} \quad \text{...(iv)}$$

where, $R_0 = \lambda N_0$ is the activity of the radioactive substance at time $t = 0$. The activity *versus* time graph is also shown in the figure.

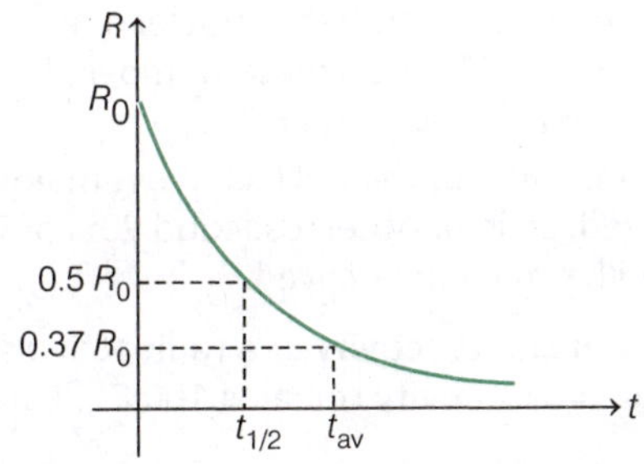

Thus, the number of nuclei and hence the activity of the radioactive substance also decreases exponentially with time.

Units of activity The SI unit for the decay rate is the Becquerel (Bq), but the curie (Ci) and rutherford (rd) are often used in practice.

$$\boxed{1\text{ Bq} = 1\text{ decays/s},\ 1\text{ Ci} = 3.7 \times 10^{10}\text{ Bq and } 1\text{ rd} = 10^6\text{ Bq}}$$

Important POINTS

- After n half-lives,

  (a) number of nuclei left $= N_0 \left(\frac{1}{2}\right)^n$

  (b) fraction of nuclei left $= \left(\frac{1}{2}\right)^n$ and

  (c) percentage of nuclei left $= 100 \left(\frac{1}{2}\right)^n$

- Number of nuclei decayed after time t,

  $$= N_0 - N = N_0 - N_0 e^{-\lambda t} = N_0 (1 - e^{-\lambda t})$$

  The corresponding graph is as shown in figure.

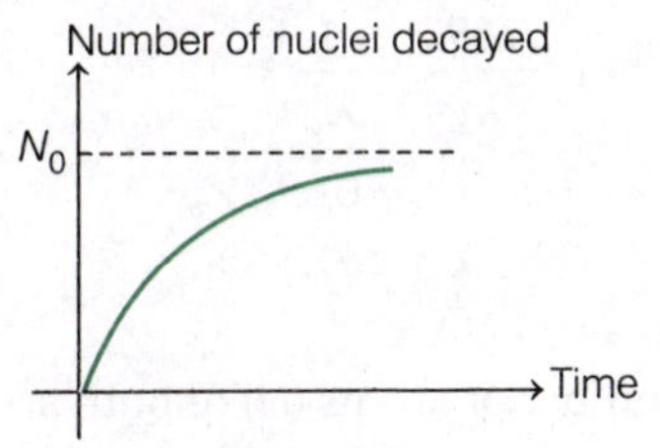

- Probability of a nucleus for survival upto time t,

  $$P\text{ (survival)} = \frac{N}{N_0} = \frac{N_0 e^{-\lambda t}}{N_0} = e^{-\lambda t}$$

  The corresponding graph is shown in figure.

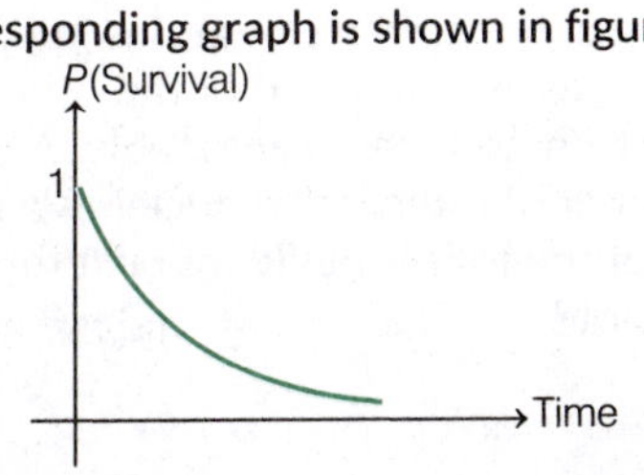

- Probability of a nucleus to disintegrate in time t is,

  $P\text{ (disintegration)} = 1 - P\text{ (survival)} = 1 - e^{-\lambda t}$

  The corresponding graph is as shown in figure.

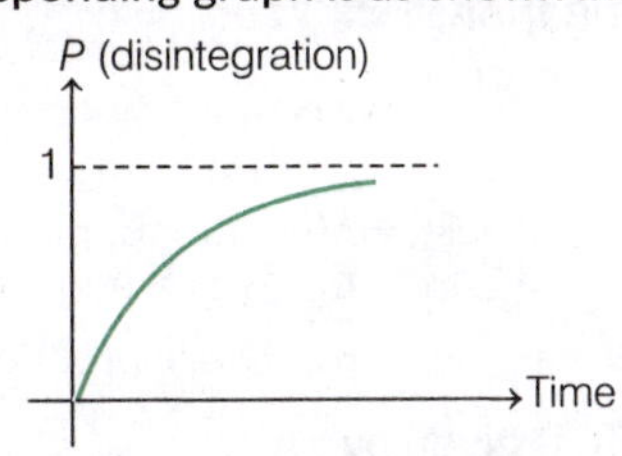

- Half-life and mean life are related to each other by the relation,

  $$\boxed{\begin{aligned} t_{1/2} &= 0.693\, t_{av} \\ \text{or} \quad t_{av} &= 1.44 t_{1/2} \end{aligned}}$$

- As we have discussed above, number of nuclei decayed in time t are $N_0 (1 - e^{-\lambda t})$. This expression involves power of e.

  So, to avoid power of e we can use

  $$\boxed{\Delta N = \lambda N \Delta t}$$

  where, ΔN are the number of nuclei decayed in time Δt at the instant when total number of nuclei are N. But, this can be applied only when $\Delta t << t_{1/2}$.

  Proof $$-\frac{dN}{dt} = \lambda N$$

  $\Rightarrow$ $$-dN = \lambda N dt$$

  or $$\Delta N = \lambda N \Delta t$$

- In same interval of time, equal percentage (or fraction) of nuclei are decayed (or left undecayed).

Example 2 At time $t=0$, number of nuclei of a radioactive substance are 100. At $t=1$ s these numbers become 90. Find the number of nuclei at $t=2$ s.

Sol. In 1 second, 90% of the nuclei have remained undecayed, so in another 1 second 90% of 90, i.e. 81 nuclei will remain undecayed.

Example 3 At time $t=0$, activity of a radioactive substance is 1600 Bq, at $t=8$ s activity remains 100 Bq. Find the activity at $t=2$ s.

Sol. $R=R_0\left(\frac{1}{2}\right)^n$

Here, n is the number of half-lives.

Given, $$R=\frac{R_0}{16} \qquad \left(\text{as } 100\text{ Bq}=\frac{1600\text{ Bq}}{16}\right)$$

$$\therefore \quad \frac{R_0}{16}=R_0\left(\frac{1}{2}\right)^n \quad \text{or} \quad n=4$$

Four half-lives are equivalent to 8 s. Hence, 2 s is equal to one half-life. So, in one half-life activity will remain half of 1600 Bq, i.e. 800 Bq.

Example 4 From a radioactive substance, n_1 nuclei decay per second at an instant when total number of nuclei are n_2. Find half-life of the radioactive substance.

Sol. Using the equation,

$$-\frac{dN}{dt}=\lambda N$$

We have, $$n_1=\lambda n_2$$

$$\therefore \quad \lambda=\frac{n_1}{n_2}$$

Now, half-life is given by

$$t_{1/2}=\frac{\ln 2}{\lambda}=\frac{\ln 2}{(n_1/n_2)}$$

$$=\left(\frac{n_2}{n_1}\right)\ln 2 \qquad \textbf{Ans.}$$

Example 5 Half-life of a radioactive substance is T. At time t_1 activity of a radioactive substance is R_1 and at time t_2 it is R_2. Find the number of nuclei decayed in this interval of time.

Sol. Half-life is given by

$$t_{1/2}=\frac{\ln 2}{\lambda}$$

$$\therefore \quad \lambda=\frac{\ln 2}{t_{1/2}}=\frac{\ln 2}{T}$$

Activity $R=\lambda N$

$$\therefore \quad N=\frac{R}{\lambda}=\frac{RT}{\ln 2}$$

When activity is R_1, numbers of nuclei are

$$N_1=\frac{R_1 T}{\ln 2}$$

Similarly, $$N_2=\frac{R_2 T}{\ln 2}$$

$$\therefore \text{ Numbers decayed}=N_1-N_2=\frac{(R_1-R_2)T}{\ln 2} \qquad \textbf{Ans.}$$

Example 6 Two radioactive materials X_1 and X_2 have decay constants 10λ and λ, respectively. If initially they have the same number of nuclei, then the ratio of the number of nuclei of X_1 to that of X_2 will be $1/e$ after a time **(2000 JEE)**

(a) $1/10\lambda$ (b) $1/11\lambda$ (c) $11/10\lambda$ (d) $1/9\lambda$

Sol. $$\frac{N_{X_1}(t)}{N_{X_2}(t)}=\frac{1}{e}$$

or $$\frac{N_0 e^{-10\lambda t}}{N_0 e^{-\lambda t}}=\frac{1}{e}$$

(Initially, both have same number of nuclei say N_0)

or $$e^{-9\lambda t}=e^{-1} \quad \text{or} \quad e=e^{9\lambda t}$$

or $$9\lambda t=1 \quad \text{or} \quad t=\frac{1}{9\lambda}$$

$\therefore$ The correct option is (d).

Example 7 The half-life period of a radioactive element x is same as the mean life time of another radioactive element y. Initially, both of them have the same number of atoms. Then, **(1999 JEE)**

(a) x and y have the same decay rate initially
(b) x and y decay at the same rate always
(c) y will decay at a faster rate than x
(d) x will decay at a faster rate than y

Sol. $(t_{1/2})_x=(t_{\text{mean}})_y$

or $$\frac{0.693}{\lambda_x}=\frac{1}{\lambda_y}$$

$$\therefore \quad \lambda_x=0.693\,\lambda_y$$

$$\lambda_x<\lambda_y$$

Rate of decay $=\lambda N$

Initially, number of atoms (N) of both are equal but since $\lambda_y>\lambda_x$, therefore, y will decay at a faster rate than x.

$\therefore$ The correct option is (c).

Example 8 A radioactive sample consists of two distinct species having equal number of atoms initially. The mean life of one species is τ and that of the other is 5τ. The decay products in both cases are stable. A plot is made of the total number of radioactive nuclei as a function of time. Which of the following figure best represents the form of this plot? **(2001 JEE)**

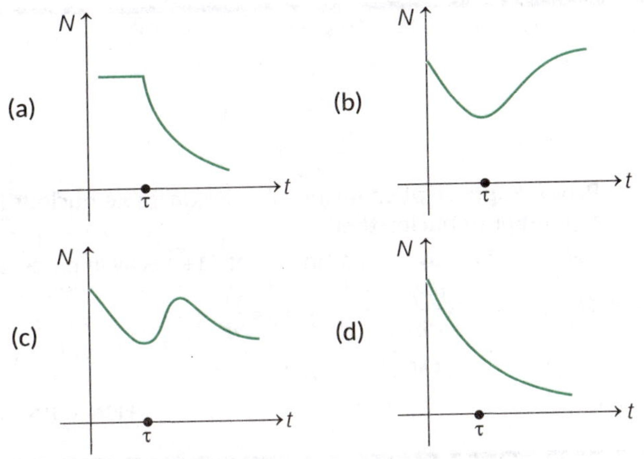

Sol. The total number of atoms can neither remain constant (as in option a) nor can ever increase (as in options b and c). They will continuously decrease with time. Therefore, (d) is the appropriate option.

INTRODUCTORY Exercise

1. The decay constant of a radioactive sample is λ. The half-life and mean life of the sample are respectively given by **(1989 JEE)**
   (a) $1/\lambda$ and $(\ln 2)/\lambda$ (b) $(\ln 2)/\lambda$ and $1/\lambda$
   (c) $\lambda(\ln 2)$ and $1/\lambda$ (d) $\lambda/(\ln 2)$ and $1/\lambda$
2. Consider α-particles, β-particles and γ-rays each having an energy of 0.5 MeV. In increasing order of penetrating powers, the radiations are **(1994 JEE)**
   (a) α, β, γ (b) α, γ, β
   (c) β, γ, α (d) γ, β, α
3. Which of the following is a correct statement? **(1999 JEE)**
   (a) Beta rays are same as cathode rays
   (b) Gamma rays are high energy neutrons
   (c) Alpha particles are singly ionized helium atoms
   (d) Protons and neutrons have exactly the same mass
4. During a negative beta decay, **(1987 JEE)**
   (a) an atomic electron is ejected
   (b) an electron which is already present within the nucleus is ejected
   (c) a neutron in the nucleus decays emitting an electron
   (d) a part of the binding energy of the nucleus is converted into an electron
5. A freshly prepared radioactive source of half-life 2 h emits radiation of intensity which is 64 times the permissible safe level. The minimum time after which it would be possible to work safely with this source is **(1988 JEE)**
   (a) 6 h (b) 12 h
   (c) 24 h (d) 128 h
6. A radioactive sample S_1 having an activity of 5 μCi has twice the number of nuclei as another sample S_2 which has an activity of 10 μCi. The half-lives of S_1 and S_2 can be **(2008 JEE)**
   (a) 20 yr and 5 yr, respectively
   (b) 20 yr and 10 yr, respectively
   (c) 10 yr each
   (d) 5 yr each
7. Half-life of a radioactive substance A is 4 days. The probability that a nucleus will decay in two half-lives is **(2006 JEE)**
   (a) $\frac{1}{4}$ (b) $\frac{3}{4}$ (c) $\frac{1}{2}$ (d) 1
8. After 280 days, the activity of a radioactive sample is 6000 dps. The activity reduces to 3000 dps after another 140 days. The initial activity of the sample in dps is **(2004 JEE)**
   (a) 6000 (b) 9000 (c) 3000 (d) 24000
9. The half-life of ^{215}At is 100 μs. The time taken for the activity of a sample of ^{215}At to decay to $\frac{1}{16}$th of its initial value is **(2002 JEE)**
   (a) 400 μs (b) 63 μs (c) 40 μs (d) 300 μs
10. The half-life of the radioactive radon is 3.8 days. The time, at the end of which 1/20 th of the radon sample will remain undecayed, is (given $\log_{10} e = 0.4343$) **(1981 JEE)**
    (a) 3.8 days (b) 16.5 days (c) 33 days (d) 76 days
11. Activity of a radioactive substance decreases from 8000 Bq to 1000 Bq in 9 days. What is the half-life and average life of the radioactive substance?
12. A radioactive substance has a half-life of 64.8 h. A sample containing this isotope has an initial activity ($t = 0$) of 40 μCi. Calculate the number of nuclei that decay in the time interval between $t_1 = 10.0$ h and $t_2 = 12.0$ h.
13. A freshly prepared sample of a certain radioactive isotope has an activity of 10 mCi. After 4.0 h its activity is 8.00 mCi.
    (a) Find the decay constant and half-life
    (b) How many atoms of the isotope were contained in the freshly prepared sample?
    (c) What is the sample's activity 30.0 h after it is prepared?
14. A radioactive substance contains 10^{15} atoms and has an activity of 6.0×10^{11} Bq. What is its half-life?
15. Two radioactive elements X and Y have half-life periods of 50 minutes and 100 minutes, respectively. Initially, both of them contain equal number of atoms. Find the ratio of atoms left N_X/N_Y after 200 minutes.

Answers

1. (b)	**2.** (a)	**3.** (a)	**4.** (c)
5. (b)	**6.** (a)	**7.** (b)	**8.** (d)
9. (a)	**10.** (b)	**11.** 3 days, 4.32 days	

12. 9.36×10^9 nuclei

13. (a) 1.55×10^{-5}/s, 12.4 h (b) 2.39×10^{13} atoms (c) 1.87 mCi

14. 1.16×10^3 s **15.** $\frac{1}{4}$

See hints on pages 382-383.

Important POINTS

- If an unstable nucleus decays by two different processes and decay constants in two processes are λ_1 and λ_2, then effective value of λ is

$$\boxed{\lambda = \lambda_1 + \lambda_2}$$

Now, the above equation can also be written as

$$\frac{\ln 2}{T} = \frac{\ln 2}{T_1} + \frac{\ln 2}{T_2} \qquad (T = \text{half-life})$$

or $$\frac{1}{T} = \frac{1}{T_1} + \frac{1}{T_2}$$

$\Rightarrow$ $$T = \frac{T_1 T_2}{T_1 + T_2}$$

Proof Suppose at some instant, the unstable nucleus has N number of nuclei, then

net rate of decay = decay in process 1+ decay in process 2

or $$-\frac{dN}{dt} = \left(-\frac{dN}{dt}\right)_1 + \left(-\frac{dN}{dt}\right)_2$$

$\therefore$ $$\lambda N = \lambda_1 N + \lambda_2 N$$

or $$\lambda = \lambda_1 + \lambda_2$$

Hence Proved.

Successive Disintegration

Suppose a parent radioactive nucleus A (decay constant $= \lambda_a$) has number of atoms N_0 at time $t = 0$. After disintegration it converts into a nucleus B which is further radioactive. Suppose decay constant of B is λ_b. Initially ($t = 0$), number of atoms of B are zero. We are interested in finding N_b, the number of atoms of B at time t.

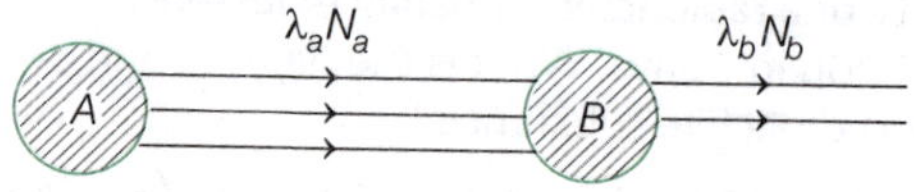

	A	B
At $t = 0$	N_0	0
At $t = t$	$N_a = N_0 e^{-\lambda_a t}$	$N_b = ?$

At time t, net rate of formation of B = rate of disintegration of A – rate of disintegration of B

$\therefore$ $$\frac{dN_b}{dt} = \lambda_a N_a - \lambda_b N_b$$

or $$\frac{dN_b}{dt} = \lambda_a N_0 e^{-\lambda_a t} - \lambda_b N_b \qquad (\text{as } N_a = N_0 e^{-\lambda_a t})$$

or $dN_b + \lambda_b N_b dt = \lambda_a N_0 e^{-\lambda_a t}$

Multiplying this equation by $e^{\lambda_b t}$, we have

$$e^{\lambda_b t} dN_b + e^{\lambda_b t} \lambda_b N_b \, dt = \lambda_a N_0 e^{(\lambda_b - \lambda_a) t}$$

$\therefore$ $$d\{N_b e^{\lambda_b t}\} = \lambda_a N_0 e^{(\lambda_b - \lambda_a) t} dt$$

Integrating both sides, we get

$$N_b e^{\lambda_b t} = \left(\frac{\lambda_a}{\lambda_b - \lambda_a}\right) N_0 e^{(\lambda_b - \lambda_a) t} + C \qquad \text{...(i)}$$

where, C is the constant of integration, which can be found as under.

At time, $t = 0$, $N_b = 0$

$\therefore$ $$C = -\left(\frac{\lambda_a}{\lambda_b - \lambda_a}\right) N_0$$

Substituting this value in Eq. (i), we have

$$\boxed{N_b = \frac{N_0 \lambda_a}{\lambda_b - \lambda_a} (e^{-\lambda_a t} - e^{-\lambda_b t})} \qquad \text{...(ii)}$$

Now, the following conclusions may be drawn from the above discussion.

1. From Eq. (ii) we can see that $N_b = 0$ at time $t = 0$ (it was given) and at $t = \infty$, N_b is again zero (because B is also radioactive).
2. N_a will continuously decrease with time while N_b will first increase (until $\lambda_a N_a > \lambda_b N_b$), reaches to a maximum value (when $\lambda_a N_a = \lambda_b N_b$) and then decreases (when $\lambda_b N_b > \lambda_a N_a$). The two graphs for N_a and N_b with time are as shown below.

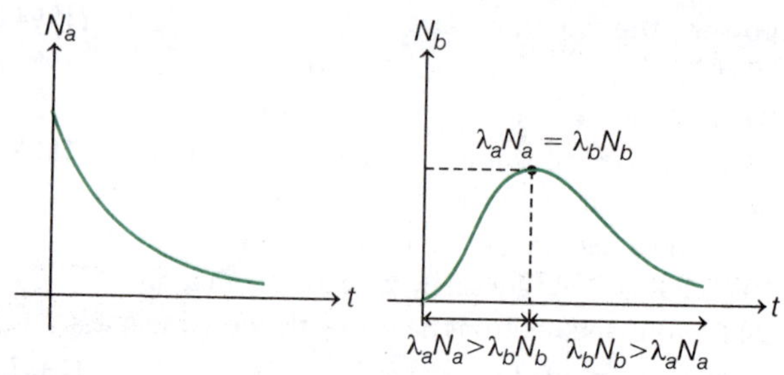

Example 9 A radio nuclide X is produced at constant rate α. At time $t = 0$, number of nuclei of X are zero. Find

(a) the maximum number of nuclei of X.

(b) the number of nuclei at time t.

Decay constant of X is λ.

Sol. (a) Let N be the number of nuclei of X at time t.

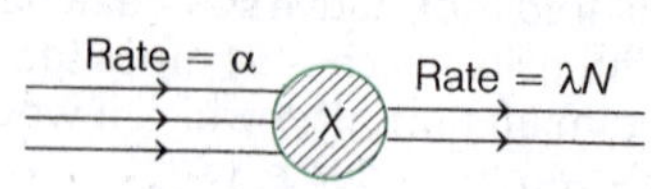

Rate of formation of $X = R_1 = \alpha$ (given)

Rate of disintegration $= R_2 = \lambda N$

R_1 is constant while R_2 is increasing (as $R_2 \propto N$). Initially $R_1 > R_2$ because N (and therefore R_2) is increasing with time. So, numbers are increasing.

Number of nuclei of X will increase until both the rates will become equal. Therefore,

$$\alpha = \lambda N_{max}$$

$$\therefore \quad N_{max} = \frac{\alpha}{\lambda}$$ **Ans.**

(b) Net rate of formation of X at time t is

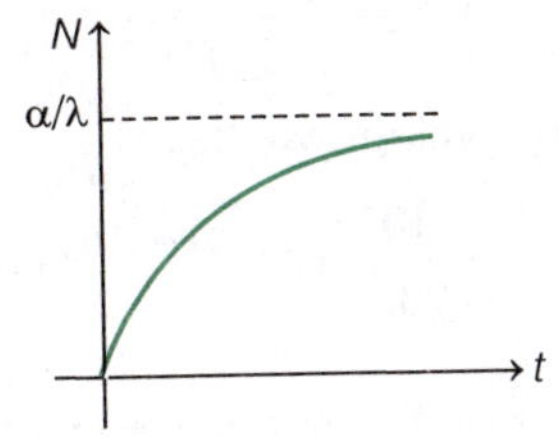

$$\frac{dN}{dt} = \alpha - \lambda N$$

$$\therefore \quad \frac{dN}{\alpha - \lambda N} = dt$$

Integrating with proper limits, we have

$$\int_0^N \frac{dN}{\alpha - \lambda N} = \int_0^t dt$$

or $$N = \frac{\alpha}{\lambda}(1 - e^{-\lambda t})$$ **Ans.**

This expression shows that number of nuclei of X are increasing exponentially from 0 to $\frac{\alpha}{\lambda}$.

Example 10 In the above problem if each decay produces E_0 energy, then find

(a) power produced at time t

(b) total energy produced upto time t

Sol. (a) $\because \quad N = \frac{\alpha}{\lambda}(1 - e^{-\lambda t})$

At time t, number of decays per second

$$= \lambda N = \alpha(1 - e^{-\lambda t})$$

Each decay produces E_0 energy. Therefore, energy produced per second or power.

= (number of decays per second) (energy produced in each decay)

$$= (\lambda N) E_0$$

$$= \alpha E_0 (1 - e^{-\lambda t})$$

or $$P = \alpha E_0 (1 - e^{-\lambda t})$$ **Ans.**

(b) Power is a function of time. Therefore, total energy produced upto time t can be obtained by integrating this power or

$$E_{Total} = \int_0^t P dt$$

Alternate Method

Energy is produced only in decay. Up to time t total αt nuclei are produced at constant rate α and N nuclei are left. So, total number of nuclei decayed.

$$N_d = \alpha t - N = \alpha t - \frac{\alpha}{\lambda}(1 - e^{-\lambda t})$$

$$= \alpha\left[t - \frac{1}{\lambda}(1 - e^{-\lambda t})\right]$$

Each decay produces E_0 energy. Therefore, total energy produced up to time t,

$$E_{Total} = N_d E_0$$

$$= \alpha E_0\left[t - \frac{1}{\lambda}(1 - e^{-\lambda t})\right]$$ **Ans.**

Miscellaneous Examples

Ex. 1 At a given instant, there are 25% undecayed radioactive nuclei in a sample. After 10 s the number of undecayed nuclei reduces to 12.5%. Calculate **(1996 JEE)**

(a) mean life of the nuclei,

(b) the time in which the number of undecayed nuclei reduce to 6.25% of some initial numbers.

Sol. (a) In 10 s, number of nuclei has been reduced to half (25% to 12.5%).

Therefore, its half-life is

$$t_{1/2} = 10 \text{ s}$$

Relation between half-life and mean life is

$$t_{mean} = \frac{t_{1/2}}{\ln 2} = \frac{10}{0.693} \text{ s}$$

$$t_{mean} = 14.43 \text{ s}$$ **Ans.**

(b) From initial 100% to reduction till 6.25%, it takes four half-lives.

$$100\% \xrightarrow{t_{1/2}} 50\% \xrightarrow{t_{1/2}} 25\% \xrightarrow{t_{1/2}} 12.5\% \xrightarrow{t_{1/2}} 6.25\%$$

$$\therefore \quad t = 4t_{1/2} = 4(10)\text{ s} = 40 \text{ s}$$

$$t = 40 \text{ s}$$ **Ans.**

Ex. 2 A radioactive element decays by β-emission. A detector records n beta particles in 2 s and in next 2 s it records 0.75 n beta particles. Find mean life correct to nearest whole number. Given ln $|2| = 0.6931$, ln $|3| = 1.0986$. **(2003 JEE)**

Sol. Let n_0 be the number of radioactive nuclei at time $t = 0$.

Number of nuclei decayed in time t are given by $n_0(1 - e^{-\lambda t})$, which is also equal to the number of beta particles emitted during the same interval of time. For the given condition,

$$n = n_0(1 - e^{-2\lambda}) \quad \text{...(i)}$$

$$(n + 0.75n) = n_0(1 - e^{-4\lambda}) \quad \text{...(ii)}$$

Dividing Eq. (ii) by Eq. (i), we get

$$1.75 = \frac{1-e^{-4\lambda}}{1-e^{-2\lambda}}$$

or $\quad 1.75 - 1.75\,e^{-2\lambda} = 1 - e^{-4\lambda}$

$\therefore \quad 1.75\,e^{-2\lambda} - e^{-4\lambda} = \frac{3}{4}$ ...(iii)

Let us take $e^{-2\lambda} = x$

Then, the above equation is

$$x^2 - 1.75x + 0.75 = 0$$

or $\quad x = \frac{1.75 \pm \sqrt{(1.75)^2 - (4)(0.75)}}{2}$

or $\quad x = 1 \text{ and } \frac{3}{4}$

$\therefore \quad e^{-2\lambda} = 1$

or $\quad e^{-2\lambda} = \frac{3}{4}$

but $e^{-2\lambda} = 1$ is not acceptable because this means $\lambda = 0$.

Hence, $\quad e^{-2\lambda} = \frac{3}{4}$

or $\quad -2\lambda \ln(e) = \ln(3) - \ln(4) = \ln(3) - 2\ln(2)$

$\therefore \quad \lambda = \ln(2) - \frac{1}{2}\ln(3)$

Substituting the given values,

$$\lambda = 0.6931 - \frac{1}{2} \times (1.0986)$$

$$= 0.14395\ \text{s}^{-1}$$

$\therefore$ Mean life, $t_{mean} = \frac{1}{\lambda} = 6.947$ s

$\therefore$ The correct answer is 7. **Ans.**

Ex. 3 A small quantity of solution containing Na^{24} radio nuclide (half-life = 15 h) of activity 1.0 microcurie is injected into the blood of a person. A sample of the blood of volume 1 cm^3 taken after 5h shows an activity of 296 disintegrations per minute. Determine the total volume of the blood in the body of the person. Assume that the radioactive solution mixes uniformly in the blood of the person. **(1994 JEE)**

(1 curie $= 3.7 \times 10^{10}$ disintegrations per second)

Sol. $\because \quad \lambda$ = Disintegration constant

$$\frac{0.693}{t_{1/2}} = \frac{0.693}{15}\,\text{h}^{-1} = 0.0462\,\text{h}^{-1}$$

Let R_0 = initial activity = 1 microcurie $= 3.7 \times 10^4$ disintegrations per second

r = Activity in 1 cm^3 of blood at $t = 5$h

$= \frac{296}{60}$ disintegration per second

= 4.93 disintegration per second, and

R = Activity of whole blood at time $t = 5$h

Total volume of blood should be

$$V\ (\text{in cm}^3) = \frac{\text{Activity in whole blood}}{\text{Activity in 1 cm}^3 \text{ of blood}}$$

$$\therefore \quad V = \frac{R}{r} = \frac{R_0 e^{-\lambda t}}{r}$$

Substituting the values, we have

$$V = \left(\frac{3.7 \times 10^4}{4.93}\right) e^{-(0.0462)(5)}\ \text{cm}^3$$

$$V = 5.95 \times 10^3\ \text{cm}^3$$

or $\quad V = 5.95$ L **Ans.**

Ex. 4 A radioactive nucleus X decays to a nucleus Y with a decay constant $\lambda_X = 0.1\ s^{-1}$. Y further decays to a stable nucleus Z with a decay constant $\lambda_Y = 1/30\,s^{-1}$. Initially, there are only X nuclei and their number is $N_0 = 10^{20}$.

Set up the rate equations for the populations of X, Y and Z. The population of Y nucleus as a function of time is given by $N_Y(t) = \{N_0 \lambda_X / (\lambda_X - \lambda_Y)\}\,[\exp(-\lambda_Y t) - \exp(-\lambda_X t)]$.

Find the time at which N_Y is maximum and determine the populations X and Z at that instant. **(2001 JEE)**

Sol. (a) Let at time $t = t$, number of nuclei of Y and Z are N_Y and N_Z. Then,

Rate equations of the populations of X, Y and Z are

$$\left(\frac{dN_X}{dt}\right) = -\lambda_X N_X \quad \text{...(i)}$$

$$\left(\frac{dN_Y}{dt}\right) = \lambda_X N_X - \lambda_Y N_Y \quad \text{...(ii)}$$

and $\quad \left(\frac{dN_Z}{dt}\right) = \lambda_Y N_Y$ ...(iii)

(b) Given, $N_Y(t) = \frac{N_0 \lambda_X}{\lambda_X - \lambda_Y}[e^{-\lambda_Y t} - e^{-\lambda_X t}]$

For N_Y to be maximum $\frac{dN_Y(t)}{dt} = 0$

i.e $\quad \lambda_X N_X = \lambda_Y N_Y$ ...(iv)

[from Eq. (ii)]

or $\quad \lambda_X (N_0 e^{-\lambda_X t}) = \lambda_Y \frac{N_0 \lambda_X}{\lambda_X - \lambda_Y}[e^{-\lambda_Y t} - e^{-\lambda_X t}]$

or $\quad \frac{\lambda_X - \lambda_Y}{\lambda_Y} = \frac{e^{-\lambda_Y t}}{e^{-\lambda_X t}} - 1$

$$\frac{\lambda_X}{\lambda_Y} = e^{(\lambda_X - \lambda_Y)t}$$

or $\quad (\lambda_X - \lambda_Y)\,t\ln(e) = \ln\left(\frac{\lambda_X}{\lambda_Y}\right)$

or $$t=\frac{1}{\lambda_X-\lambda_Y}\ln\left(\frac{\lambda_X}{\lambda_Y}\right)$$

Substituting the values of λ_X and λ_Y, we have

$$t=\frac{1}{(0.1-1/30)}\ln\left(\frac{0.1}{1/30}\right)=15\ln(3)$$

or $t=16.48\text{ s}$ **Ans.**

(c) The population of X at this moment,

$$N_X=N_0\,e^{-\lambda_X t}=(10^{20})\,e^{-(0.1)(16.48)}$$

$$N_X=1.92\times10^{19}$$

$$N_Y=\frac{N_X\,\lambda_X}{\lambda_Y} \quad \text{[From Eq. (iv)]}$$

$$=(1.92\times10^{19})\frac{(0.1}{(1/30)}$$

$$=5.76\times10^{19}$$

$$N_Z=N_0-N_X-N_Y$$

$$=10^{20}-1.92\times10^{19}-5.76\times10^{19}$$

or $N_Z=2.32\times10^{19}$

Ex. 5 The mean lives of an unstable nucleus in two different decay processes are 1620 yr and 405 yr, respectively. Find out the time during which three-fourth of a sample will decay.

Sol. Let at some instant of time t, number of nuclei are N. Then,

$$\left(\frac{-dN}{dt}\right)_{net}=\left(\frac{-dN}{dt}\right)_1+\left(\frac{-dN}{dt}\right)_2$$

If the effective decay constant is λ, then

$$\lambda N=\lambda_1 N+\lambda_2 N$$

or $$\lambda=\lambda_1+\lambda_2=\frac{1}{1620}+\frac{1}{405}=\frac{1}{324}\text{ year}^{-1}$$

Now, $$\frac{N_0}{4}=N_0\,e^{-\lambda t}$$

$\therefore$ $$-\lambda t=\ln\left(\frac{1}{4}\right)=-1.386$$

or $$\left(\frac{1}{324}\right)t=1.386$$

$\therefore$ $t=449\text{ yr}$ **Ans.**

Ex. 6 In the chemical analysis of a rock the mass ratio of two radioactive isotopes is found to be 100 : 1. The mean lives of the two isotopes are 4×10^9 years and 2×10^9 years, respectively. If it is assumed that at the time of formation the atoms of both the isotopes were in equal proportional, calculate the age of the rock. Ratio of the atomic weights of the two isotopes is 1.02 : 1 .

Sol. At the time of observation $(t=t)$,

$$\frac{m_1}{m_2}=\frac{100}{1} \quad \text{(given)}$$

Further it is given that $\frac{A_1}{A_2}=\frac{1.02}{1}$

Number of atoms, $N=\frac{m}{A}$

$\therefore$ $$\frac{N_1}{N_2}=\frac{m_1}{m_2}\times\frac{A_2}{A_1}=\frac{100}{1.02} \quad \text{...(i)}$$

Let N_0 be the number of atoms of both the isotopes at the time of formation, then

$$\frac{N_1}{N_2}=\frac{N_0\,e^{-\lambda_1 t}}{N_0\,e^{-\lambda_2 t}}=e^{(\lambda_2-\lambda_1)t} \quad \text{...(ii)}$$

From Eqs. (i) and (ii), we have

$$e^{(\lambda_2-\lambda_1)t}=\frac{100}{1.02}$$

or $$(\lambda_2-\lambda_1)t=\ln 100-\ln 1.02$$

$\therefore$ $$t=\frac{\ln 100-\ln 1.02}{\left(\frac{1}{2\times10^9}-\frac{1}{4\times10^9}\right)}$$

Substituting the values, we have

$t=1.834\times10^{10}\text{ yr}$ **Ans.**

Ex. 7 A ^{118}Cd radio nuclide goes through the transformation chain.

$$^{118}\text{Cd}\xrightarrow[30\text{ min}]{}{}^{118}\text{In}\xrightarrow[45\text{ min}]{}{}^{118}\text{Sn (stable)}$$

The half-lives are written below the respective arrows. At time $t=0$ only Cd was present. Find the fraction of nuclei transformed into stable over 60 minutes.

Sol. At time $t=t$, $N_1=N_0\,e^{-\lambda_1 t}$ and

$$N_2=\frac{N_0\lambda_1}{\lambda_2-\lambda_1}(e^{-\lambda_1 t}-e^{-\lambda_2 t})$$

$\therefore$ $$N_3=N_0-N_1-N_2$$

$$=N_0\left[1-e^{-\lambda_1 t}-\frac{\lambda_1}{\lambda_2-\lambda_1}(e^{-\lambda_1 t}-e^{-\lambda_2 t})\right]$$

$\therefore$ $$\frac{N_3}{N_0}=1-e^{-\lambda_1 t}-\frac{\lambda_1}{\lambda_2-\lambda_1}(e^{-\lambda_1 t}-e^{-\lambda_2 t})$$

$$\lambda_1=\frac{0.693}{30}=0.0231\text{ min}^{-1}$$

$$\lambda_2=\frac{0.693}{45}=0.0154\text{ min}^{-1}$$

and $t=60\text{ min}$

$\therefore$ $$\frac{N_3}{N_0}=1-e^{-0.0231\times60}-\frac{0.0231}{0.0154-0.0231}(e^{-0.0231\times60}-e^{-0.0154\times60})$$

$$=1-0.25+3(0.25-0.4)$$

$$=0.31$$ **Ans.**

Ex. 8 Natural uranium is a mixture of three isotopes $^{234}_{92}U$, $^{235}_{92}U$ and $^{238}_{92}U$ with mass percentage 0.01%, 0.71%% and 99.28% respectively. The half-life of three isotopes are 2.5×10^5 yr, 7.1×10^8 yr and 4.5×10^9 yr respectively. Determine the share of radioactivity of each isotope into the total activity of the natural uranium.

Sol. Let R_1, R_2 and R_3 be the activities of U^{234}, U^{235} and U^{238} respectively.

Total activity, $R = R_1 + R_2 + R_3$

Share of U^{234}, $\dfrac{R_1}{R} = \dfrac{\lambda_1 N_1}{\lambda_1 N_1 + \lambda_2 N_2 + \lambda_3 N_3}$

Let m be the total mass of natural uranium.

Then, $m_1 = \dfrac{0.01}{100} m$, $m_2 = \dfrac{0.71}{100} m$ and $m_3 = \dfrac{99.28}{100} m$

Now, $N_1 = \dfrac{m_1}{M_1}$, $N_2 = \dfrac{m_2}{M_2}$ and $N_3 = \dfrac{m_3}{M_3}$

where M_1, M_2 and M_3 are atomic weights.

$$\therefore \quad \frac{R_1}{R} = \frac{\left(\frac{m_1}{M_1}\right)\frac{1}{T_1}}{\frac{m_1}{M_1}\cdot\frac{1}{T_1} + \frac{m_2}{M_2}\cdot\frac{1}{T_2} + \frac{m_3}{M_3}\cdot\frac{1}{T_3}}$$

$$= \frac{\frac{(0.01/100)}{234} \times \frac{1}{2.5 \times 10^5 \text{ years}}}{\left(\frac{0.01/100}{234}\right)\left(\frac{1}{2.5 \times 10^5}\right) + \left(\frac{0.71/100}{235}\right)\left(\frac{1}{7.1 \times 10^8}\right) + \left(\frac{99.28/100}{238}\right)\left(\frac{1}{4.5 \times 10^9}\right)}$$

$$= 0.648 \approx 64.8\ \%$$

Similarly, share of $U^{235} = 0.016\%$

and of $U^{238} = 35.184\ \%$ **Ans.**

Ex. 9 Uranium ores on the earth at the present time typically have a composition consisting of 99.3% of the isotope $_{92}U^{238}$ and 0.7% of the isotope $_{92}U^{235}$. The half-lives of these isotopes are 4.47×10^9 yr and 7.04×10^8 yr, respectively. If these isotopes were equally abundant when the earth was formed, estimate the age of the earth.

Sol. Let N_0 be number of atoms of each isotope at the time of formation of the earth ($t = 0$) and N_1 and N_2 the number of atoms at present time ($t = t$). Then,

$$N_1 = N_0 e^{-\lambda_1 t} \quad \text{...(i)}$$

and

$$N_2 = N_0 e^{-\lambda_2 t} \quad \text{...(ii)}$$

$$\therefore \quad \frac{N_1}{N_2} = e^{(\lambda_2 - \lambda_1)t} \quad \text{...(iii)}$$

Further it is given that

$$\frac{N_1}{N_2} = \frac{99.3}{0.7} \quad \text{...(iv)}$$

Equating Eqs. (iii) and (iv) and taking log on both sides, we have

$$(\lambda_2 - \lambda_1)t = \ln\left(\frac{99.3}{0.7}\right)$$

$$\therefore \quad t = \left(\frac{1}{\lambda_2 - \lambda_1}\right)\ln\left(\frac{99.3}{0.7}\right)$$

Substituting the values, we have

$$t = \frac{1}{\frac{0.693}{7.04 \times 10^8} - \frac{0.693}{4.47 \times 10^9}}\ln\left(\frac{99.3}{0.7}\right)$$

or $= 5.97 \times 10^9$ yr **Ans.**

MODULE 1 Exercise

Fill in the Blank

1. The radioactive decay rate of a radioactive element is found to be 10^3 disintegration/second at a certain time. If the half-life of the element is one second, the decay rate after one second is .... and after three seconds is .... **(1983 JEE)**

Assertion and Reason

See directions on page 11.

2. **Assertion :** Rate of radioactivity cannot be increased or decreased by increasing or decreasing pressure or temperature.
   Reason : Rate depends on the number of nuclei present in the radioactive sample.
3. **Assertion :** Only those nuclei which are heavier than lead are radioactive.
   Reason : Nuclei of elements heavier than lead are unstable.
4. **Assertion :** γ-rays are produced by the transition of a nucleus from some higher energy state to some lower energy state.
   Reason : Electromagnetic waves are always produced by the transition process.

Single Correct Option

5. The half-life of a radioactive substance is 20 min. The approximate time interval $(t_1 - t_2)$ between the time t_1 when 2/3 of it has decayed and time t_2 when 1/3 of it had decayed is
   (a) 7 min (b) 14 min (c) 20 min (d) 28 min
6. What are the respective number of α and β-particles emitted in the following radioactive decay?
   $$^{200}_{90}X \to ^{168}_{80}Y$$
   (a) 6 and 8 (b) 6 and 6 (c) 8 and 8 (d) 8 and 6
7. $\frac{7}{8}$th of the active nuclei present in a radioactive sample has decayed in 8 s. The half-life of the sample is
   (a) 2 s (b) 1 s (c) 7 s (d) $\frac{8}{3}$ s
8. A sample of radioactive substance loses half of its activity in 4 days. The time in which its activity is reduced to 5% is
   (a) 12 days (b) 8.3 days
   (c) 17.3 days (d) None of these
9. In a radioactive sample, the fraction of initial number of radioactive nuclei, which remains undecayed after n mean lives is
   (a) $\frac{1}{e^n}$ (b) e^n (c) $1-\frac{1}{e^n}$ (d) $\left(\frac{1}{e-1}\right)^n$
10. A radioactive element is disintegrating having half-life 6.93 s. The fractional change in number of nuclei of the radioactive element during 10 s is
    (a) 0.37 (b) 0.63
    (c) 0.25 (d) 0.50
11. The activity of a radioactive sample goes down to about 6% in a time of 2 hour. The half-life of the sample in minute is about
    (a) 30 (b) 15
    (c) 60 (d) 120
12. What is the probability of a radioactive nucleus to survive one mean life?
    (a) $\frac{1}{e}$ (b) $\frac{1}{e+1}$ (c) $1-\frac{1}{e}$ (d) $\frac{1}{e}-1$
13. In which sequence, the radioactive radiations are emitted in the following nuclear reactions?
    $$_ZX^A \to {}_{Z+1}Y^A \to {}_{Z-1}K^{A-4} \to {}_{Z-1}K^{A-4}$$
    (a) β, α and γ (b) α, β and γ
    (c) β, γ and α (d) γ, α and β
14. A radioactive substance A disintegrates into a radioactive substance B. Let n_A and n_B denote the number of nuclei of A and B surviving against radioactive decay at any moment and λ_A and λ_B be the respective disintegration constants. The rate of change in number of nuclei of the substance B is given by
    (a) $\frac{dn_B}{dt} = \lambda_A n_A - \lambda_B n_B$ (b) $\frac{dn_B}{dt} = -\lambda_A n_A + \lambda_B n_B$
    (c) $\frac{dn_B}{dt} = -\lambda_A n_A - \lambda_B n_B$ (d) $\frac{dn_B}{dt} = \lambda_A n_A + \lambda_B n_B$
15. A radioactive sample has N_0 active atoms at $t = 0$. If the rate of disintegration at any time is R and the number of atoms is N, then the ratio R/N varies with time as

(a)
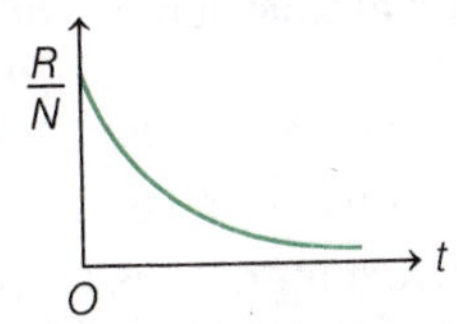

(b)
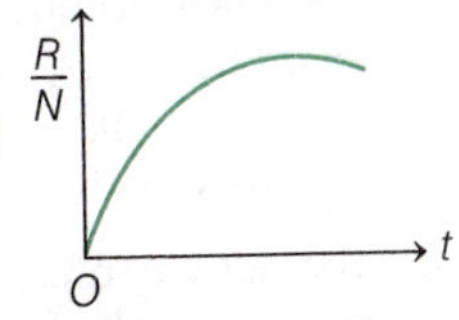

(c)
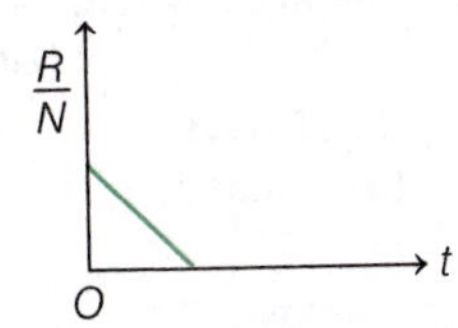

(d)
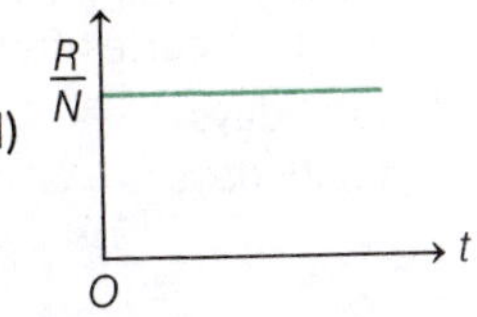

16. A radioactive nucleus is being produced at a constant rate α per second. Its decay constant is λ. If N_0 are the number of nuclei at time $t = 0$, then maximum number of nuclei possible are

(a) $\frac{\alpha}{\lambda}$ (b) $N_0 + \frac{\alpha}{\lambda}$

(c) N_0 (d) $\frac{\lambda}{\alpha} + N_0$

17. A radioactive material is reduced to 1 : 8 of its original amount in 3 days. If 8×10^{-3} kg of the material is left after 5 days the initial amount of the material is **(2023 Main)**

(a) 256 g (b) 32 g

(c) 64 g (d) 40 g

18. The half-life of a radioactive nucleus is 5 years. The fraction of the original sample that would decay in 15 years is **(2023 Main)**

(a) $\frac{1}{4}$ (b) $\frac{7}{8}$

(c) $\frac{1}{8}$ (d) $\frac{3}{4}$

19. Two radioactive elements A and B initially have same number of atoms. The half life of A is same as the average life of B. If λ_A and λ_B are decay constants of A and B respectively, then choose the correct relation from the given options. **(2023 Main)**

(a) $\lambda_A = 2\lambda_B$ (b) $\lambda_A \ln 2 = \lambda_B$

(c) $\lambda_A = \lambda_B$ (d) $\lambda_A = \lambda_B \ln 2$

20. Substance A has atomic mass number 16 and half-life of 1 day. Another substance B has atomic mass number 32 and half-life of $1/2$ day.

If both A and B simultaneously start undergo radioactivity at the same time with initial mass 320 g each, how many total atoms of A and B combined would be left after 2 days. **(2023 Main)**

(a) 1.69×10^{24} (b) 6.76×10^{24}

(c) 3.38×10^{24} (d) 6.76×10^{23}

21. Consider the following radioactive decays process

$$^{218}_{84}A \xrightarrow{\alpha} A_1 \xrightarrow{\beta^-} A_2 \xrightarrow{\gamma} A_3 \xrightarrow{\alpha} A_4 \xrightarrow{\beta^+} A_5 \xrightarrow{\gamma} A_6$$

The mass number and the atomic number of A_6 are given by **(2023 Main)**

(a) 211 and 80 (b) 210 and 80

(c) 210 and 82 (d) 210 and 84

22. The activity of a radioactive material is 6.4×10^{-4} curie. Its half life is 5 days. The activity will become 5×10^{-6} curie after **(2022 Main)**

(a) 7 days (b) 15 days

(c) 25 days (d) 35 days

23. The disintegration rate of a certain radioactive sample at any instant is 4250 disintegrations per minute. 10 minutes later, the rate becomes 2250 disintegrations per minute. The approximate decay constant is [Take, $\log_{10} 1.88 = 0.274$] **(2022 Main)**

(a) 0.02 min^{-1}

(b) 2.7 min^{-1}

(c) 0.063 min^{-1}

(d) 6.3 min^{-1}

24. The half-life of a radioactive substance is 5 years. After x years a given sample of the radioactive substance gets reduced to 6.25% of its initial value of x is .... **(2022 Main)**

(a) 20 (b) 40

(c) 10 (d) 5

25. A radioactive nucleus can decay by two different processes. Half life for the first process is 3.0 hours while it is 4.5 hours for the second process. The effective half-life of the nucleus will be **(2022 Main)**

(a) 3.75 hours

(b) 0.56 hours

(c) 0.26 hours

(d) 1.80 hours

26. A heavy nucleus Q of half-life 20 min undergoes α-decay with probability of 60% and β-decay with probability of 40%. Initially, the number of Q nuclei is 1000. The number of α-decays of Q in the first one hour is **(2021 Adv.)**

(a) 50 (b) 75

(c) 350 (d) 525

Subjective Questions

27. The disintegration rate of a certain radioactive sample at any instant is 4750 disintegrations per minute. Five minutes later the rate becomes 2700 per minute. Calculate

(a) decay constant and

(b) half-life of the sample

28. Obtain the amount of ^{60}Co necessary to provide a radioactive source of 8.0 Ci strength. The half-life of ^{60}Co is 5.3 years?

29. The half-life of $^{238}_{92}U$ against alpha decay is 4.5×10^9 year. How much disintegration per second occurs in 1 g of $^{238}_{92}U$?

30. What is the probability that a radioactive atom having a mean life of 10 days decays during the fifth day?

31. The half-lives of radioisotopes P^{32} and P^{33} are 14 days and 25 days respectively. These radio isotopes are mixed in the ratio of 4 : 1 of their atoms. If the initial activity of the mixed sample is 3.0 mCi, find the activity of the mixed isotopes after 60 years.

Integer Type Questions

32. A radioactive element $^{242}_{92}X$ emits two α-particles, one electron and two positrons. The product nucleus is represented by $^{234}_{P}Y$. The value of P is .... **(2023 Main)**

33. In a radioactive decay process, the activity is defined as $A = -\frac{dN}{dt}$, where $N(t)$ is the number of radioactive nuclei at time t. Two radioactive sources, S_1 and S_2 have same activity at time $t = 0$. At a later time, the activities of S_1 and S_2 are A_1 and A_2, respectively. When S_1 and S_2 have just completed their 3rd and 7th half-lives, respectively, the ratio A_1 / A_2 is ...... **(2023 Adv.)**

34. In a radioactive decay chain reaction, $^{230}_{90}$Th nucleus decays into $^{214}_{84}$Po nucleus. The ratio of the number of α to number of β^{-1} particles emitted in this process is .... **(2022 Adv.)**

35. Two radioactive materials A and B have decay constants 25λ and 16λ respectively. If initially they have the same number of nuclei, then the ratio of the number of nuclei of B to that of A will be "e" after a time $\frac{1}{a\lambda}$. The value of a is .... **(2022 Main)**

36. A radioactive sample has an average life of 30 ms and is decaying. A capacitor of capacitance 200 μF is first charged and later connected with resistor R. If the ratio of charge on capacitor to the activity of radioactive sample is fixed with respect to time then the value of R should be ....Ω. **(2021 Main)**

Answers

1. (500, 125)		**2.** (b)	**3.** (d)	**4.** (c)	**5.** (c)	**6.** (d)	**7.** (d)	**8.** (c)	**9.** (a)
10. (b)	**11.** (a)	**12.** (a)	**13.** (a)	**14.** (a)	**15.** (d)	**16.** (a)	**17.** (a)	**18.** (b)	**19.** (d)
20. (c)	**21.** (b)	**22.** (d)	**23.** (c)	**24.** (a)	**25.** (d)	**26.** (d)	**27.** (a) 0.113 min^{-1} (b) 6.132 min		
28. 7.11×10^{-3}g		**29.** 1.23×10^4 dps		**30.** 0.39	**31.** 0.205 mCi		**32.** (87)	**33.** (16)	
34. (2)	**35.** (9)	**36.** (150)							

See hints on pages 383-386.

MODULE 2

Nuclear Physics

Equivalence of Mass and Energy

In 1905, while developing his special theory of relativity, Einstein made the suggestion that energy and mass are equivalent. He predicted that if the energy of a body changes by an amount E, its mass changes by an amount m given by the equation,

$$\boxed{E = mc^2}$$

where, c is the speed of light. In nuclear physics, mass is measured in **unified atomic mass units (u)**, 1 u being one-twelfth of the mass of carbon-12 atom and equals 1.66×10^{-27} kg. It can readily be shown using $E = mc^2$ that, 1 u mass has energy 931.5 MeV.

Thus, $\boxed{1\text{ u} = 931.5\text{ MeV}/c^2}$

Example 1 Find the increase in mass of water when 1.0 kg of water absorbs 4.2×10^3 J of energy to produce a temperature rise of 1 K.

Sol. $m = \dfrac{E}{c^2} = \dfrac{4.2 \times 10^3}{(3.0 \times 10^8)^2}$ kg

$= 4.7 \times 10^{-14}$ kg **Ans.**

Binding Energy and Nuclear Stability

The existence of a stable nucleus means that the nucleons (protons and neutrons) are in a bound state. Since, the protons in a nucleus experience strong electrical repulsion, there must exist a stronger attractive force that holds the nucleus together.

The **nuclear force** is a short range interaction that extends only to about 2 fm. (In contrast, the electromagnetic interaction is a long-range interaction). An important feature of the nuclear force is that it is essentially the same for all nucleons, independent of charge.

The **binding energy** (E_b) of a nucleus is the energy required to completely separate the nucleons. The origin of the binding energy may be understood with the help of mass-energy relation, $\Delta E = \Delta mc^2$, where Δm is the difference between the total mass of the separated nucleons and the mass of the stable nucleus. The mass of the stable nucleus is less than the sum of the mass of its nucleons. The binding energy of a nuclide $_ZX^A$ is thus,

$$\boxed{E_b = [Zm_p + (A - Z)\, m_N - m_X]\, c^2} \quad ...(i)$$

where, m_p = mass of proton, m_N = mass of neutron and m_X = mass of nucleus

Note *(i) $\Delta m = [Zm_p + (A - Z)\, m_N - m_X]$ is called the mass defect. This much mass is lost during the formation of a nucleus. Energy $\Delta E = (\Delta m)\, c^2$ is liberated during the making of the nucleus. This is the energy due to which nucleons are bound together. So, to break the nucleus in its constituent nucleons this much energy has to be given to the nucleus.*

*(ii) **Stability**: Although nuclides with Z values upto $Z = 92$ (uranium) occur naturally, not all of these are stable. The nuclide $^{209}_{83}Bi$ is the heaviest stable nucleus. Even though uranium is not stable, however, its long lived isotope ^{238}U, has a half-life of some 4 billion year.*

Binding energy per nucleon If the binding energy of a nucleus is divided by its mass number, the binding energy per nucleon is obtained. A plot of binding energy per nucleon E_b/A as a function of mass number A for various stable nuclei is shown in figure.

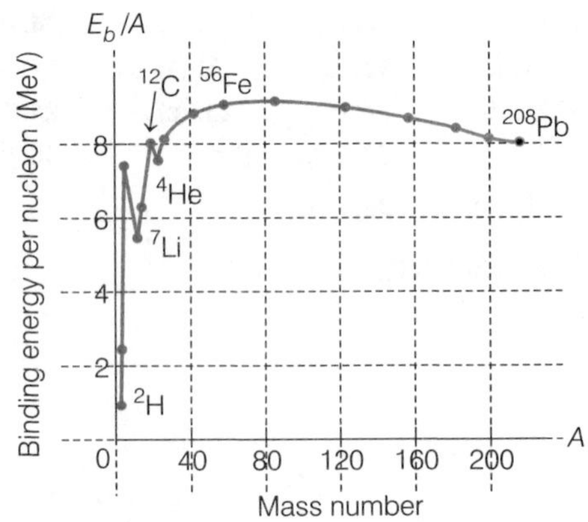

The binding energy per nucleon, E_b/A, as a function of the mass number A

Note *That it is the binding energy per nucleon which is more important for stability of a nucleus rather than the total binding energy.*

Following conclusions can be drawn from the above graph.

1. The greater the binding energy per nucleon the more stable is the nucleus. The curve reaches a maximum of about 8.75 MeV in the vicinity of $^{56}_{26}Fe$ and then gradually falls to 7.6 MeV for $^{238}_{92}U$.
2. In a nuclear reaction energy is released if total binding energy is increasing. Let us take an example.

   Suppose a nucleus X, which has total binding energy of 100 MeV converts into some another nucleus Y which has total binding energy 120 MeV. Then, in this process 20 MeV energy will be released. This is because 100 MeV energy has already been released during the formation of X while in case of Y it is 120 MeV. So, the remaining 20 MeV will be released now.

Energy is released if ΣE_b is increasing

3. ΣE_b in a nuclear process is increased if binding energy per nucleon of the daughter products gets increased. Let us take an example. Consider a nucleus X ($A_X = 100$) breaks into lighter nuclei Y ($A_Y = 60$) and Z($A_Z = 40$).

$$X \to Y + Z$$

Binding energy per nucleon of these three are say, 7 MeV, 7.5 MeV and 8.0 MeV. Then, total binding energy of X is $100 \times 7 = 700$ MeV and that of $Y + Z$ is $(60 \times 7.5) + (40 \times 8.0) = 770$ MeV. So, in this process 70 MeV energy will be released.

4. Binding energy per nucleon is increased if two or more lighter nuclei combine to form a heavier nucleus. This process is called **nuclear fusion.**

In **nuclear fission** a heavy nucleus splits into two or more lighter nuclei of almost equal mass.

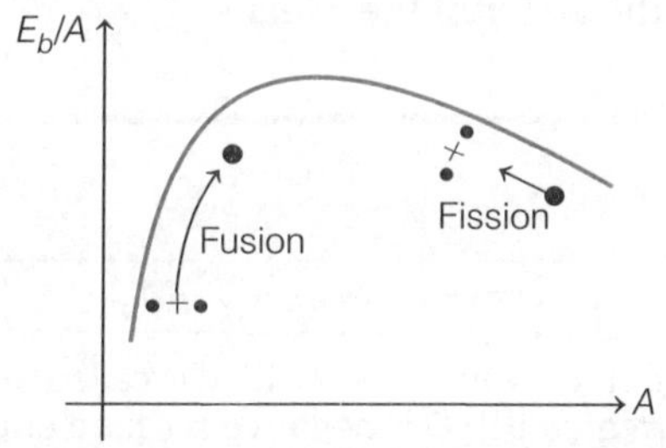

In both the processes E_b/A is increasing. Thus, energy will be released.

Nuclear Fission (Divide and Conquer)

As we saw in the above article nuclear fission occurs when a heavy nucleus such as ^{235}U, splits into two lighter nuclei. In nuclear fission, the combined mass of the daughter nuclei is less than the mass of the parent nucleus. The difference is called the mass defect. Fission is initiated when a heavy nucleus captures a thermal neutron (slow neutrons). Multiplying the mass defect by c^2 gives the numerical value of the released energy. Energy is released because the binding energy per nucleon of the daughter nuclei is about 1 MeV greater than that of the parent nucleus.

The fission of ^{235}U by thermal neutrons can be represented by the equation,

$$^1_0n + ^{235}_{92}U \longrightarrow ^{236}_{92}U^* \longrightarrow X + Y + \text{neutrons}$$

where, $^{236}U^*$ is an intermediate excited state that lasts only for 10^{-12} s before breaking into nuclei X and Y, which are called fission fragments. In any fission equation there are many combinations of X and Y that satisfy the requirements of conservation of energy and charge with uranium, for example, there are about 90 daughter nuclei that can be formed. Fission also results in the production of several neutrons, typically two or three. On the average, about 2.5 neutrons are released per event.

A typical fission reaction for uranium is

$$^1_0n + ^{235}_{92}U \longrightarrow ^{141}_{56}Ba + ^{92}_{36}Kr + 3^1_0n$$

About 200 MeV is released in the above process. The fission energy appears mostly as kinetic energy of the fission fragments (e.g. barium and krypton nuclei) which fly apart at great speed. The kinetic energy of the fission neutrons also makes a slight contribution. In addition one or both of the large fragments are highly radioactive and small amount of energy takes the form of beta and gamma radiation.

Chain Reaction Shortly after nuclear fission was discovered, it was realized that, the fission neutrons can cause further fission of ^{235}U and a chain reaction can be maintained.

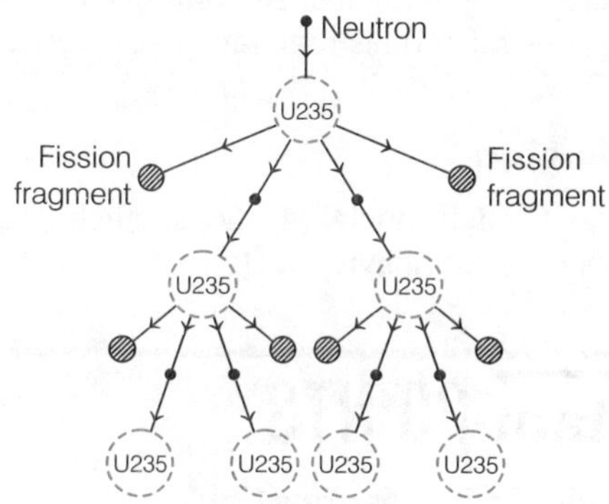

A chain reaction

In practice only a proportion of the fission neutrons is available for new fissions since, some are lost by escaping from the surface of the uranium before colliding with another nucleus. The ratio of neutrons escaping to those causing fission decreases as the size of the piece of uranium-235 increases and there is a **critical size** (about the size of a cricket ball) which must be attained before a chain reaction can start.

In the **'atomic bomb'** an increasing uncontrolled chain reaction occurs in a very short time when two pieces of uranium-235 are rapidly brought together to form a mass greater than the critical size.

Nuclear Reactors In a nuclear reactor the chain reaction is steady and controlled so that on average only one neutron from each fission produces another fission. The reaction rate is adjusted by inserting neutron absorbing rods of boron steel into the uranium 235.

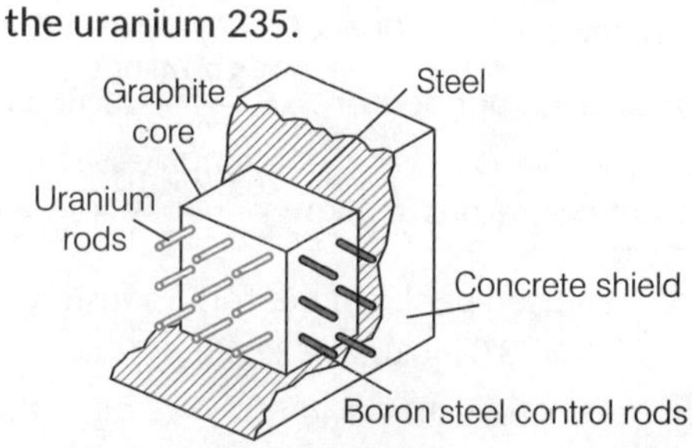

Nuclear reactor

Graphite core is used as a **moderator** to slow down the neutrons. Natural uranium contains over 99% of ^{238}U and less than 1% of ^{235}U. The former captures the medium speed fission neutrons without fissioning. It fissions with very fast neutrons. On the other hand ^{235}U (and plutonium-239) fissions with slow neutrons and the job of moderator is to slow down the fission neutrons very quickly so that most of them escape by capturing from ^{238}U and they can cause the fission of ^{235}U.

A bombarding particle gives up most energy when it has an elastic collision with a particle of similar mass. For neutrons, hydrogen atoms would be most effective but they absorb the neutrons. Deuterium (in heavy water) and carbon (as graphite) are most suitable as moderator.

To control the power level **control rods** are used. These rods are made of materials such as cadmium, that are very efficient in absorbing neutrons. The first nuclear reactor was built by Enrico Fermi and his team at the University of Chicago in 1942.

Nuclear Fusion

Binding energy for light nuclei ($A < 20$) is much smaller than the binding energy for heavier nuclei.

This suggests a process that is the reverse of fission.

When two light nuclei combine to form a heavier nucleus, the process is called nuclear fusion. The union of light nuclei into heavier nuclei also lead to a mass defect and as a result liberation of energy. Such a reaction has been achieved in **'hydrogen bomb'** and it is believed to be the principal source of the sun's energy.

A reaction with heavy hydrogen or deuterium which yields 3.3 MeV per fusion is

$$\boxed{{}_1^2H + {}_1^2H \rightarrow {}_2^3He + {}_0^1n}$$

By comparison with the 200 MeV per fission of ^{235}U this seems small, but per unit mass of material it is not. Fusion of two deuterium nuclei, i.e. deuterons, will only occur if they overcome their mutual electrostatic repulsion.

This may happen, if they collide at very high speed when, for example, they are raised to a very high temperature ($10^8 - 10^9$ K). So much high temperature is obtained by using an atomic (fission) bomb to trigger off fusion.

If a controlled fusion reaction can be achieved, an almost unlimited supply of energy will become available from deuterium in the water of the oceans.

Important POINTS

- ***Q*-value of a nuclear reaction**

  Consider a nuclear reaction in which a target nucleus *X* is bombarded by a particle *'a'* resulting in a daughter nucleus *Y* and a particle *b*.

  $$\boxed{a + X \rightarrow Y + b}$$

  Sometimes this reaction is written as $X(a, b)Y$

  The reaction energy *Q* associated with a nuclear reaction is defined as the total energy released as a result of the reaction. Thus,

  $$\boxed{Q = (M_a + M_X - M_Y - M_b)\,c^2}$$

  A reaction for which *Q* is positive is called **exothermic.** A reaction for which *Q* is negative is called **endothermic.**

  In an exothermic reaction, the total mass of parent nuclei is greater than that of the daughter nuclei and the *Q*-value is positive.

  If the total mass of the parent nuclei is less than that of the daughter nuclei, energy is required for reaction to take place and the reaction is said to be endothermic.

Example 2 In the fusion reaction ${}_1^2H + {}_1^2H \longrightarrow {}_2^3He + {}_0^1n$, the masses of deuteron, helium and neutron expressed in amu are 2.015, 3.017 and 1.009 respectively. If 1 kg of deuterium undergoes complete fusion, find the amount of total energy released. 1 amu $\equiv 931.5\ \text{MeV}/c^2$.

Sol. $\Delta m = 2\,(2.015) - (3.017 + 1.009) = 0.004$ amu

$\therefore$ Energy released $= (0.004 \times 931.5)$ MeV $= 3.726$ MeV

Energy released per deuteron $= \dfrac{3.726}{2} = 1.863$ MeV

Number of deuterons in 1 kg $= \dfrac{6.02 \times 10^{26}}{2} = 3.01 \times 10^{26}$

$\therefore$ Energy released per kg of deuterium fusion

$= (3.01 \times 10^{26} \times 1.863)$

$= 5.6 \times 10^{26}$ MeV

$\approx 9.0 \times 10^{13}$ J **Ans.**

Example 3 A nucleus with mass number 220 initially at rest emits an α-particle. If the *Q*-value of the reaction is 5.5 MeV, calculate the kinetic energy of the α-particle. **(2003 JEE)**

(a) 4.4 MeV (b) 5.4 MeV

(c) 5.6 MeV (d) 6.5 MeV

Sol. Given that $K_1 + K_2 = 5.5$ MeV ...(i)

From conservation of linear momentum,

$$p_1 = p_2$$

or $\sqrt{2K_1\,(216m)} = \sqrt{2K_2\,(4m)}$

as $p = \sqrt{2Km}$

$\therefore$ $K_2 = 54\,K_1$ ...(ii)

Solving Eqs. (i) and (ii), we get

$K_2 =$ KE of α-particle $= 5.4$ MeV

$\therefore$ The correct option is (b).

Example 4 Binding energy per nucleon *versus* mass number curve for nuclei is shown in figure. W, X, Y and Z are four nuclei indicated on the curve. The process that would release energy is **(1999 JEE)**

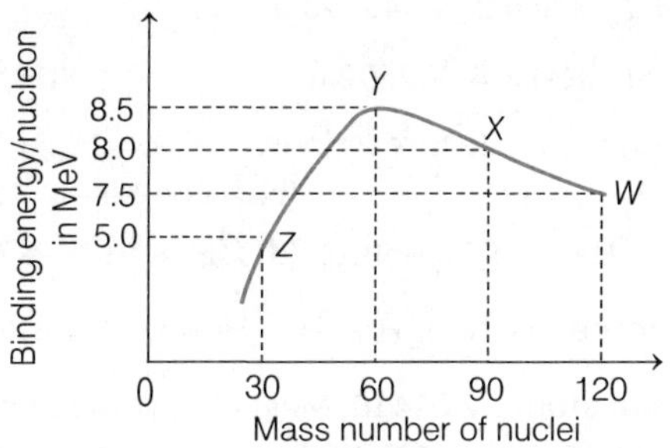

(a) $Y \to 2Z$ (b) $W \to X + Z$
(c) $W \to 2Y$ (d) $X \to Y + Z$

Sol. Energy is released in a process when total binding energy of the nucleus (= binding energy per nucleon × number of nucleons) is increased or we can say, when total binding energy of products is more than the reactants. By calculation we can see that only in option (c), this happens. Given, $W \to 2Y$

Binding energy of reactants $= 120 \times 7.5 = 900$ MeV

and binding energy of products $= 2\,(60 \times 8.5)$

$= 1020$ MeV > 900 MeV

$\therefore$ The correct option is (c).

Example 5 A star initially has 10^{40} deuterons. It produces energy *via* the processes ${}_1H^2 + {}_1H^2 \to {}_1H^3 + p$ and ${}_1H^2 + {}_1H^3 \to {}_2He^4 + n$. If the average power radiated by the star is 10^{16} W, the deuteron supply of the star is exhausted in a time of the order of **(1993 JEE)**

(a) 10^6 s (b) 10^8 s (c) 10^{12} s (d) 10^{16} s

The masses of the nuclei are as follows

$M(H^2) = 2.014$ amu; $M(n) = 1.008$ amu,

$M(p) = 1.007$ amu; $M(He^4) = 4.001$ amu

Given :

$$1 \text{ amu} = 931 \frac{\text{MeV}}{c^2}$$

Sol. The given reactions are

$${}_1H^2 + {}_1H^2 \longrightarrow {}_1H^3 + p$$

$${}_1H^2 + {}_1H^3 \longrightarrow {}_2He^4 + n$$

$$\Rightarrow \quad 3\,{}_1H^2 \longrightarrow {}_2He^4 + n + p$$

Mass defect,

$$\Delta m = (3 \times 2.014 - 4.001 - 1.007 - 1.008) \text{ amu}$$
$$= 0.026 \text{ amu}$$

Energy released $= 0.026 \times 931$ MeV

$= 0.026 \times 931 \times 1.6 \times 10^{-13}$ J

$= 3.87 \times 10^{-12}$ J

This is the energy produced by the consumption of three deuteron atoms.

$\therefore$ Total energy released by 10^{40} deuterons

$$= \frac{10^{40}}{3} \times 3.87 \times 10^{-12} \text{ J}$$
$$= 1.29 \times 10^{28} \text{ J}$$

The average power radiated is $P = 10^{16}$ W or 10^{16} J/s.

Therefore, total time to exhaust all deuterons of the star will be

$$t = \frac{1.29 \times 10^{28}}{10^{16}}$$
$$= 1.29 \times 10^{12} \text{ s} \approx 10^{12} \text{ s}$$

$\therefore$ The correct option is (c).

Example 6 Assume that the nuclear binding energy per nucleon (B/A) *versus* mass number (A) is as shown in the figure. Use this plot to choose the correct choice(s) given below. **(2008 JEE)**

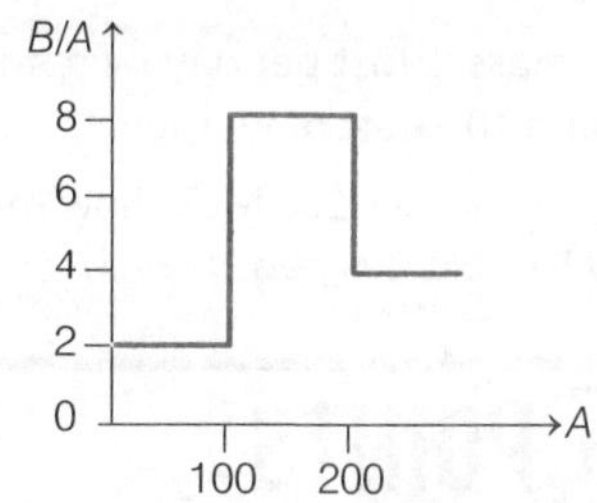

(a) Fusion of two nuclei with mass numbers lying in the range of $1 < A < 50$ will release energy.

(b) Fusion of two nuclei with mass numbers lying in the range of $51 < A < 100$ will release energy.

(c) Fission of a nucleus lying in the mass range of $100 < A < 200$ will release energy when broken into two equal fragments.

(d) Fission of a nucleus lying in the mass range of $200 < A < 260$ will release energy when broken into two equal fragments.

Sol. In fusion, two or more lighter nuclei combine to make a comparatively heavier nucleus. In fission, a heavy nucleus breaks into two or more lighter nuclei.

Further, energy will be released in a nuclear process if total binding energy increases.

$\therefore$ The correct options are (b) and (d).

INTRODUCTORY Exercise

1. If a star can convert all the He nuclei completely into oxygen nuclei. The energy released per oxygen nuclei is (Mass of the helium nucleus is 4.0026 amu and mass of oxygen nucleus is 15.9994 amu) **(2005 JEE)**
   (a) 7.6 MeV (b) 56.12 MeV (c) 10.24 MeV (d) 23.4 MeV
2. Fast neutrons can easily be slowed down by **(1994 JEE)**
   (a) the use of lead shielding
   (b) passing them through heavy water
   (c) elastic collisions with heavy nuclei
   (d) applying a strong electric field
3. During a nuclear fusion reaction, **(1987 JEE)**
   (a) a heavy nucleus breaks into two fragments by itself
   (b) a light nucleus bombarded by thermal neutrons breaks up
   (c) a heavy nucleus bombarded by thermal neutrons breaks up
   (d) two light nuclei combine to give a heavier nucleus and possibly other products
4. The equation $4\,{}_1^1\text{H} \longrightarrow {}_2^4\text{He}^{2+} + 2e^- + 26\,\text{MeV}$ represents **(1983 JEE)**
   (a) β-decay
   (b) γ-decay
   (c) fusion
   (d) fission
5. (a) How much mass is lost per day by a nuclear reactor operated at a 10^9 watt power level?
   (b) If each fission releases 200 MeV, how many fissions occur per second to yield this power level?
6. Find energy released in the alpha decay,
   $${}_{92}^{238}\text{U} \longrightarrow {}_{90}^{234}\text{Th} + {}_2^4\text{He}$$
   Given, $M({}_{92}^{238}\text{U}) = 238.050784$ u
   $M({}_{90}^{234}\text{Th}) = 234.043593$ u
   $M({}_2^4\text{He}) = 4.002602$ u
7. Complete the nuclear reactions.
   (a) ${}_3^6\text{Li} + ? \longrightarrow {}_4^7\text{Be} + {}_0^1n$ (b) ${}_{17}^{35}\text{Cl} + ? \longrightarrow {}_{16}^{32}\text{S} + {}_2^4\text{He}$
   (c) ${}_4^9\text{Be} + {}_2^4\text{He} \longrightarrow 3({}_2^4\text{He}) + ?$ (d) ${}_{35}^{79}\text{Br} + {}_1^2\text{H} \longrightarrow ? + 2({}_0^1n)$
8. Consider the reaction ${}_1^2\text{H} + {}_1^2\text{H} = {}_2^4\text{He} + Q$. Mass of the deuterium atom = 2.0141u. Mass of helium atom = 4.0024 u. This is a nuclear .... reaction in which the energy Q released is .... MeV. **(1996 JEE)**
9. The binding energies per nucleon for deuteron (${}_1\text{H}^2$) and helium (${}_2\text{He}^4$) are 1.11 MeV and 7.0 MeV respectively. The energy released when two deuterons fuse to form a helium nucleus (${}_2\text{He}^4$) is .... **(1988 JEE)**

Answers

1. (c) 2. (b) 3. (d) 4. (c)
5. (a) 9.6×10^{-4} kg (b) 3.125×10^{19} 6. 4.27 MeV
7. (a) ${}_1^2\text{H}$ (b) ${}_1^1\text{H}$ (c) ${}_0^1n$ (d) ${}_{36}^{79}\text{Kr}$
8. Fusion, 24 9. 23.6 MeV

See hints on page 386.

Important POINTS

1. **Classification of nuclei** The nuclei have been divided in isotopes, isobars and isotones on the basis of number of protons (atomic number) or the total number of nucleons (mass number) or neutrons.

Isotopes The elements having the same number of protons but different number of neutrons are called isotopes. In other words, isotopes have same value of atomic number (Z) but different values of mass number (A). Almost every element has isotopes. Because of the same atomic number isotopes of an element have the same place in the periodic table. The isotopes of some elements are given below.

Element	Its isotopes	Number of protons	Number of neutrons
Hydrogen	${}_1\text{H}^1$	1	0
	${}_1\text{H}^2$	1	1
	${}_1\text{H}^3$	1	2
Oxygen	${}_8\text{O}^{16}$	8	8
	${}_8\text{O}^{17}$	8	9
	${}_8\text{O}^{18}$	8	10

Element	Its isotopes	Number of protons	Number of neutrons
Chlorine	${}_{17}\text{Cl}^{35}$	17	18
	${}_{17}\text{Cl}^{37}$	17	20
Uranium	${}_{92}\text{U}^{235}$	92	143
	${}_{92}\text{U}^{238}$	92	146

In nature, the isotopes of chlorine (${}_{17}\text{Cl}^{35}$ and ${}_{17}\text{Cl}^{37}$) are found in the ratio 75.4% and 24.6%. Therefore, its atomic mass is found to be

$$M = (35 \times 0.754) + (37 \times 0.246) = 35.5$$

Note *Since, the isotopes have the same atomic number, they have the same chemical properties. Their physical properties are different as they have different mass numbers. Two isotopes, thus cannot be separated by chemical method, but they can be separated from the physical methods.*

Isobars The elements having the same mass number (A) but different atomic number (Z) are called isobars. They have different places in periodic table. Their chemical (as well as physical) properties are different.

${}_1\text{H}^3$ and ${}_2\text{He}^3$, ${}_8\text{O}^{17}$ and ${}_9\text{F}^{17}$ are examples of isobars.

Isotones Elements having the equal number of neutrons $(A - Z)$ are called isotones.

$_3Li^7$ and $_4Be^8$, $_1H^3$ and $_2He^4$ are examples of isotones.

2. **Nuclear forces** In nucleus the positively charged protons and the uncharged neutrons are held together in an extremely small space ($\approx 10^{-15}$ m) in spite of the strong electrostatic repulsion between the protons. Obviously, there are some strong attractive forces operating within the nucleus between the nucleons. The nuclear forces are non-electric and non gravitational forces. These forces are extremely short-range forces. They become operative only when the distance between two nucleons is a small multiple of 10^{-15} m. Nuclear forces between protons and protons between neutrons and neutrons and between protons and neutrons are all essentially the same in magnitude. Thus, we can say that nuclear forces are charge independent.

Yukawa's meson theory of nuclear forces A Japanese scientist Yukawa in 1935 suggested that the nuclear forces are 'exchange forces'. Which are produced by the exchange of new particles called π-mesons between nucleons. These particles were later on actually discovered in cosmic radiation. There are three types of π-mesons, π^+, π^- and π^0. There is a continuous exchange of π-mesons between protons and neutrons due to which they continue to be converted into one another. When a π^+- meson jumps from a proton to a neutron, the proton is converted into a neutron and the neutron is converted into a proton.

$$p - \pi^+ \longrightarrow n$$

and $$n + \pi^+ \longrightarrow p$$

Conversely, when a π^-- meson jumps from a neutron to a proton, then neutron is converted into a proton and the proton is converted into a neutron. Thus,

$$n - \pi^- \longrightarrow p$$

and $$p + \pi^- \longrightarrow n$$

The exchange of π^+ and π^-- mesons between protons and neutrons is responsible for the origin of nuclear forces between them. Similarly, nuclear forces between two protons and between two neutrons are generated by a continuous exchange of π^0-mesons between them. Thus, the basis of nuclear forces is the exchange of mesons and hence these are called 'exchange forces'.

3. **Size and shape of the nucleus** The Rutherford scattering experiment established that mass of an atom is concentrated within a small positively charged region at the centre which is called the nucleus of the atom. The nuclear radius is given by

$$\boxed{R = R_0 A^{1/3}}$$

Here, A is the mass number of the particular nucleus and $R_0 = 1.3$ fm (fermi) $= 1.3 \times 10^{-15}$ m. This means that the nucleus radius is of the order of 10^{-15} m.

4. **Nuclear density** Let us consider the nucleus of an atom having the mass number A.

Mass of nucleus $\approx A \times 1.67 \times 10^{-27}$ kg

Volume of the nucleus $= \frac{4}{3}\pi R^3$

$$= \frac{4}{3}\pi (R_0 A^{1/3})^3 = \frac{4}{3}\pi R_0^3 A$$

$\therefore$ Density of the nucleus, $\rho = \frac{\text{mass}}{\text{volume}}$

or $$\rho = \frac{A \times 1.67 \times 10^{-27}}{\frac{4}{3} \times \pi \times (1.3 \times 10^{-15})^3 \times A}$$

$$= 1.8 \times 10^{17} \text{ kg/m}^3$$

Thus, density of a nucleus is independent of the mass number A and of the order of 10^{17} kg/ m^3.

5. **Magic numbers** We know that the electrons in an atom are grouped in 'shells' and 'sub-shells'. Atoms with 2, 10, 18, 36, 54 and 86 electrons have all of their shells completely filled. Such atoms are unusually stable and chemically inert. A similar situation exists with nuclei also. Nuclei having 2, 8, 20, 28, 50, 82 and 126 nucleons of the same kind (either protons or neutrons) are more stable than nuclei of neighbouring mass numbers. These numbers are called as 'magic numbers'.

6. **Fundamental particles** The particles which are not constituted by any other particles are called fundamental particles. A brief discussion of important fundamental particles is as follows.

(i) **Electron** It was discovered in 1897 by Thomson. Its charge is $-e$ and mass is 9.1×10^{-31} kg. Its symbol is e^- (or $_{-1}\beta^0$).

(ii) **Proton** It was discovered in 1919 by Rutherford in artificial nuclear disintegration. It has a positive charge $+e$ and its mass is 1836 times (1.673×10^{-27} kg) the mass of electron. In free state, the proton is a stable particle. Its symbol is p^+. It is also written as $_1H^1$.

(iii) **Neutron** It was discovered in 1932 by Chadwick. Electrically, it is a neutral particle. Its mass is 1839 times (1.675×10^{-27} kg) the mass of electron. In free state the neutron is unstable (mean life ≈ 17 minutes) but it constitutes a stable nucleus with the proton. Its symbol is n or $_0n^1$.

(iv) **Positron** It was discovered by Anderson in 1932. It is the antiparticle of electron, i.e. its charge is $+e$ and its mass is equal to that of the mass of electron. Its symbol is e^+ (or $_{+1}\beta^0$).

(v) **Antiproton** It is the antiparticle of proton. It was discovered in 1955. Its charge is $-e$ and its mass is equal to that of the mass of proton. Its symbol is p^-.

(vi) **Antineutron** It was discovered in 1956. It has no charge and its mass is equal to the mass of neutron. The only difference between neutron and antineutron is that if they spin in the same direction, their magnetic momenta will be in opposite directions. The symbol for antineutron is $\bar{n}$.

(vii) **Neutrino and antineutrino** The existence of these particles was predicted in 1930 by Pauli while explaining the emission of β-particles from radioactive nuclei, but these particles were actually observed experimentally in 1956. Their rest mass and charge are both zero but they have energy and momentum. These are mutually antiparticles of each other. They have the symbol ν and $\bar{\nu}$.

(viii) **Pi-mesons** The existence of pi-mesons was predicted by Yukawa in 1935, but they were actually discovered in 1947 in cosmic rays. Nuclear forces are explained by the exchange of pi-mesons between the nucleons. pi-mesons are of three types, positive π-mesons (π^+), negative pi-mesons (π^-) and neutral π-mesons (π^0). Charge on $\pi^{\pm}$ is $\pm e$. Whereas mass of $\pi^{\pm}$ is 274 times the mass of electron. π^0 has mass nearly 264 times the electronic mass.

(ix) **Mu-Mesons** These were discovered in 1936 by Anderson and Neddermeyer. These are found in abundance in the cosmic rays at the ground level. There are two types of mu-mesons. Positive mu-meson (μ^+) and negative mu-meson (μ^-). There is no neutral mu-meson. Both the mu-mesons have the same rest mass 207 times the rest mass of the electron.

(x) **Photon** These are bundles of electromagnetic energy and travel with the speed of light. Energy and momentum of a photon of frequency ν are $h\nu$ and $\frac{h\nu}{c}$, respectively.

Antiparticles For every fundamental particle there exists an identical fundamental particle just opposite in some property. For example electron and positron are identical in all respects, except that charges on them are opposite. The following table shows various particles and their antiparticles. Some particles are their own antiparticles. For example π^0 and photons.

Name of particle	Symbol	Antiparticle	Mass in comparison to mass of electron	Average life (in seconds) for the unstable particles
Electron	e^-	e^{+1}	1	stable
Proton	p^+	p^-	1836	stable
Neutron	n	$\bar{n}$	1839	1010
Neutrino	ν	$\bar{\nu}$	0	stable
Pi-Mesons	π^+	π^-	274	2.6×10^{-8}
	π^0	π^0	264	0.9×10^{-16}
Mu-Mesons	μ^-	μ^+	207	2.2×10^{-6}
Photon	γ	γ	0	Stable

Miscellaneous Examples

Ex. 1 In a nuclear reactor ^{235}U undergoes fission liberating 200 MeV of energy. The reactor has a 10% efficiency and produces 1000 MW power. If the reactor is to function for 10 yr, find the total mass of uranium required. **(2001 JEE)**

Sol. The reactor produces 1000 MW power or 10^9 J/s. The reactor is to function for 10 yr. Therefore, total energy which the reactor will supply in 10 yr is

$$E = (\text{power})\ (\text{time})$$
$$= (10^9 \text{ J/s})\ (10 \times 365 \times 24 \times 3600 \text{ s})$$
$$= 3.1536 \times 10^{17} \text{ J}$$

But since the efficiency of the reactor is only 10%, therefore actual energy needed is 10 times of it or 3.1536×10^{18} J. One uranium atom liberates 200 MeV of energy or $200 \times 1.6 \times 10^{-13}$ J or 3.2×10^{-11} J of energy.

So, number of uranium atoms needed are

$$\frac{3.1536 \times 10^{18}}{3.2 \times 10^{-11}} = 0.9855 \times 10^{29}$$

or number of kg-moles of uranium needed are

$$n = \frac{0.9855 \times 10^{29}}{6.02 \times 10^{26}} = 163.7$$

Hence, total mass of uranium required is

$$m = (n)M = (163.7)\ (235) \text{ kg}$$

or $\quad m \approx 38470$ kg

or $\quad m = 3.847 \times 10^4$ kg

Ex. 2 The element curium $^{248}_{96}$Cm has a mean life of 10^{13} s. Its primary decay modes are spontaneous fission and α-decay, the former with a probability of 8% and the later with a probability of 92%. Each fission releases 200 MeV of energy. The masses involved in decay are as follows **(1997 JEE)**

$^{248}_{96}$Cm = 248.072220 u, $^{244}_{94}$Pu = 244.064100 u and $^4_2$He = 4.002603 u. Calculate the power output from a sample of 10^{20} Cm atoms. ($1 \text{ u} = 931 \text{ MeV}/c^2$)

Sol. The reaction involved in α-decay is

$$^{248}_{96}\text{Cm} \rightarrow {}^{244}_{94}\text{Pu} + {}^4_2\text{He}$$

Mass defect, Δm = mass of $^{248}_{96}$Cm − mass of $^{244}_{94}$Pu − mass of $^4_2$He

$$= (248.072220 - 244.064100 - 4.002603)\text{u} = 0.005517 \text{ u}$$

Therefore, energy released in α-decay will be

$$E_\alpha = (0.005517 \times 931) \text{MeV} = 5.136 \text{ MeV}$$

Similarly, $E_{fission} = 200$ MeV (given)

Mean life is given as $t_{mean} = 10^{13}\text{ s} = 1/\lambda$

$\therefore$ Disintegration constant $\lambda = 10^{-13}\text{ s}^{-1}$

Rate of decay at the moment when number of nuclei are 10^{20}

$$= \lambda N = (10^{-13})(10^{20})$$
$$= 10^7 \text{ disintegration per second}$$

Of these, 8% are in fission and 92% are in α-decay.

Therefore, energy released per second

$$= (0.08 \times 10^7 \times 200 + 0.92 \times 10^7 \times 5.136)\text{ MeV}$$
$$= 2.074 \times 10^8 \text{ MeV}$$

$\therefore$ Power output (in watt) = energy released per second (J/s)

$$= (2.074 \times 10^8)(1.6 \times 10^{-13})$$
$$= 3.32 \times 10^{-5}\text{ Js}^{-1}$$

$\therefore$ Power output $= 3.32 \times 10^{-5}$ W

Ex. 3 A nucleus X, initially at rest, undergoes alpha-decay according to the equation. **(1991 JEE)**

$${}^{A}_{92}X \rightarrow {}^{228}_{Z}Y + \alpha$$

(a) Find the values of A and Z in the above process.

(b) The alpha particle produced in the above process is found to move in a circular track of radius 0.11 m in a uniform magnetic field of 3T. Find the energy (in MeV) released during the process and the binding energy of the parent nucleus X.

Given that $m(Y) = 228.03$ u, $m({}^1_0 n) = 1.009$ u

$m({}^4_2\text{He}) = 4.003$ u, $m({}^1_1\text{H}) = 1.008$ u

$$1\text{u} = 931.48\ \frac{\text{MeV}}{c^2}$$

Sol. (a) $A - 4 = 228$

$\therefore \quad A = 232$

$92 - 2 = Z \quad \text{or} \quad Z = 90$

(b) From the relation,

$$r = \frac{\sqrt{2Km}}{Bq} \Rightarrow K_\alpha = \frac{r^2B^2q^2}{2m}$$
$$= \frac{(0.11)^2(3)^2\ (2 \times 1.6 \times 10^{-19})^2}{2 \times 4.003 \times 1.67 \times 10^{-27} \times 1.6 \times 10^{-13}}\text{ MeV}$$
$$= 5.21 \text{ MeV}$$

From the conservation of momentum,

$$p_Y = p_\alpha$$

or $\sqrt{2K_Ym_Y} = \sqrt{2K_\alpha m_\alpha}$

$$\therefore \quad K_Y = \left(\frac{m_\alpha}{m_Y}\right)K_\alpha = \frac{4.003}{228.033} \times 5.21$$
$$= 0.09 \text{ MeV}$$

$\therefore$ Total energy released $= K_\alpha + K_Y = 5.3$ MeV

Total binding energy of daughter products

$= [92 \times (\text{mass of proton}) + (232 - 92)(\text{mass of neutron}) - (m_Y) - (m_\alpha)] \times 931.48$ MeV

$= [(92 \times 1.008) + (140)(1.009) - 228.03 - 4.003]\ 931.48$ MeV

$= 1828.5$ MeV

$\therefore$ Binding energy of parent nucleus

= binding energy of daughter products − energy released

$= (1828.5 - 5.3)$ MeV

$= 1823.2$ MeV

Ex. 4 It is proposed to use the nuclear fusion reaction, ${}^2_1\text{H} + {}^2_1\text{H} \rightarrow {}^4_2\text{He}$ in a nuclear reactor 200 MW rating. If the energy from the above reaction is used with a 25 per cent efficiency in the reactor, how many grams of deuterium fuel will be needed per day? (The masses of ${}^2_1\text{H}$ and ${}^4_2\text{He}$ are 2.0141 atomic mass units and 4.0026 atomic mass units respectively.) Take $1\text{u} = 931.48\ \frac{\text{MeV}}{c^2}$ **(1990 JEE)**

Sol. Mass defect in the given nuclear reaction,

$$\Delta m = 2(\text{mass of deuterium}) - (\text{mass of helium})$$
$$= 2\,(2.0141) - (4.0026) = 0.0256$$

Therefore, energy released

$$\Delta E = (\Delta m)(931.48)\text{ MeV} = 23.85 \text{ MeV}$$
$$= 23.85 \times 1.6 \times 10^{-13}\text{ J} = 3.82 \times 10^{-12}\text{ J}$$

Efficiency is only 25%, therefore,

$$25\% \text{ of } \Delta E = \left(\frac{25}{100}\right)(3.82 \times 10^{-12})\text{ J}$$
$$= 9.55 \times 10^{-13}\text{ J}$$

i.e. by the fusion of two deuterium nuclei, 9.55×10^{-13} J energy is available to the nuclear reactor.

Total energy required in one day to run the reactor with a given power of 200 MW,

$$E_{Total} = 200 \times 10^6 \times 24 \times 3600 = 1.728 \times 10^{13}\text{ J}$$

$\therefore$ Total number of deuterium nuclei required for this purpose,

$$n = \frac{E_{Total}}{\Delta E/2} = \frac{2 \times 1.728 \times 10^{13}}{9.55 \times 10^{-13}}$$
$$= 0.362 \times 10^{26}$$

$\therefore$ Mass of deuterium required = (Number of g-moles of deuterium required) × 2 g

$$= \left(\frac{0.362 \times 10^{26}}{6.02 \times 10^{23}}\right) \times 2 = 120.26 \text{ g}$$

Ex. 5 Neon-23 decays in the following way,

$${}^{23}_{10}\text{Ne} \longrightarrow {}^{23}_{11}\text{Na} + {}^{0}_{-1}e + \bar{\nu}$$

Find the minimum and maximum kinetic energy that the beta particle (${}^{0}_{-1}e$) can have. The atomic masses of ^{23}Ne and ^{23}Na are 22.9945 u and 22.9898 u, respectively.

Sol. Here, atomic masses are given (not the nuclear masses), but still we can use them for calculating the mass defect because mass of electrons get cancelled both sides. Thus,

Mass defect $\Delta m = (22.9945 - 22.9898) = 0.0047$ u

$\therefore \quad Q = (0.0047 \text{ u})(931.5 \text{ MeV/u}) = 4.4 \text{ MeV}$

Hence, the energy of beta particles can range from 0 to 4.4 MeV. **Ans.**

Ex. 6 A proton is bombarded on a stationary lithium nucleus. As a result of the collision, two α-particles are produced. If the direction of motion of the α-particles with the initial direction of motion makes an angle $\cos^{-1}(1/4)$, find the kinetic energy of the striking proton. Given, binding energies per nucleon of Li^7 and He^4 are 5.60 and 7.06 MeV, respectively.
(Assume mass of proton $\approx$ mass of neutron).

Sol. Q-value of the reaction is

$$Q = (2 \times 4 \times 7.06 - 7 \times 5.6) \text{ MeV} = 17.28 \text{ MeV}$$

Note *Single proton doesn't have any binding energy.*

Applying conservation of energy for collision,

$$K_p + Q = 2K_\alpha \quad \text{...(i)}$$

(Here, K_p and K_α are the kinetic energies of proton and α-particle respectively)

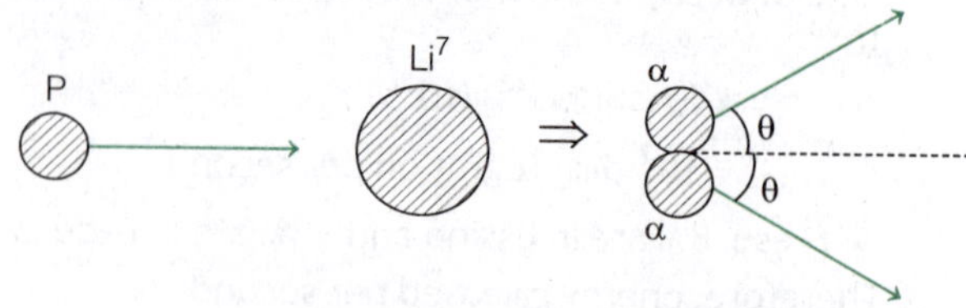

From conservation of linear momentum,

$$\sqrt{2m_pK_p} = 2\sqrt{2m_\alpha K_\alpha}\cos\theta \quad \text{...(ii)}$$

$$\therefore \quad K_p = 16K_\alpha\cos^2\theta$$

$$= (16K_\alpha)\left(\frac{1}{4}\right)^2 \quad (\text{as } m_\alpha = 4m_p)$$

$$\therefore \quad K_\alpha = K_p \quad \text{...(iii)}$$

Solving Eqs. (i) and (iii) with $Q = 17.28$ MeV

We get

$$K_p = 17.28 \text{ MeV}$$ **Ans.**

MODULE 2 Exercise

Assertion and Reason

See directions on page 11.

1. Assertion : If we compare the stability of two nuclei, then that nucleus is more stable whose total binding energy is more.

Reason : More the mass defect during formation of a nucleus more will be the binding energy.

2. Assertion : In a nuclear process energy is released if total binding energy of daughter nuclei is more than the total binding energy of parent nuclei.

Reason : If energy is released then total mass of daughter nuclei is less than the total mass of parent nuclei.

3. Assertion : 1 amu is equal to 931.48 MeV.

Reason : 1 amu is equal to $\frac{1}{12}$ th the mass of C^{12} atom.

4. Assertion : The nuclear density of nuclides ${}^{10}_{5}B$, ${}^{6}_{3}Li$, ${}^{56}_{26}Fe$, ${}^{20}_{10}Ne$ and ${}^{209}_{83}Bi$ can be arranged as $\rho^N_{Bi} > \rho^N_{Fe} > \rho^N_{Ne} > \rho^N_B > \rho^N_{Li}$ **(2023 Main)**

Reason : The radius R of nucleus is related to its mass number A as $R = R_0A^{1/3}$, where R_0 is a constant.

Single Correct Option

5. For uranium nucleus how does its mass vary with volume? **(2003 JEE)**

(a) $m \propto V$ (b) $m \propto 1/V$
(c) $m \propto \sqrt{V}$ (d) $m \propto V^2$

6. In the nucleus of helium if F_1 is the nuclear force between two protons, F_2 is the force between two neutrons and F_3 is the force between a proton and a neutron. Then,

(a) $F_1 = F_2 = F_3$ (b) $F_1 > F_2 > F_3$
(c) $F_2 > F_3 > F_1$ (d) $F_2 = F_3 > F_1$

7. The binding energies of the nuclei A and B are E_A and E_B, respectively. Three atoms of the element B fuse to give one atom of element A and an energy Q is released. Then, E_A, E_B and Q are related as

(a) $E_A - 3E_B = Q$ (b) $3E_B - E_A = Q$
(c) $E_A + 3E_B = Q$ (d) $E_B + 3E_A = Q$

8. The sun radiates energy in all directions. The average radiations received on the earth's surface from the sun is 1.4 kW/m^2. The average earth-sun distance is 1.5×10^{11} m. The mass lost by the sun per day is (1 day = 86400 s)

(a) 4.4×10^9 kg (b) 7.6×10^{14} kg
(c) 3.8×10^{12} kg (d) 3.8×10^{14} kg

9. In the reaction ${}_1^2H + {}_1^3H \rightarrow {}_2^4He + {}^1n_0$, if the binding energies of ${}_1^2H$, ${}_1^3H$ and ${}_2^4He$ are respectively a, b and c (in MeV), then the energy (in MeV) released in this reaction is
(a) $c+a-b$ (b) $c-a-b$ (c) $a+b+c$ (d) $a+b-c$

10. A nuclear reaction along with the masses of the particles taking part in it is as follows

A	+	B	$\rightarrow$	C	+	D	+ Q MeV
1.002 amu		1.004 amu		1.001 amu		1.003 amu	

The energy Q liberated in the reaction is
(a) 1.234 MeV (b) 0.931 MeV
(c) 0.465 MeV (d) 1.863 MeV

11. Which of the following nuclear fragments corresponding to nuclear fission between neutron $({}_0^1n)$ and uranium isotope $({}_{92}^{235}U)$ is correct? **(2024 Main)**
(a) ${}_{56}^{144}Ba + {}_{36}^{89}Kr + 4{}_0^1n$ (b) ${}_{56}^{140}Xe + {}_{38}^{94}Sr + 3{}_0^1n$
(c) ${}_{51}^{153}Sb + {}_{41}^{99}Nb + 3{}_0^1n$ (d) ${}_{56}^{144}Ba + {}_{36}^{89}Kr + 3{}_0^1n$

12. The ratio of the density of oxygen nucleus $({}_8^{16}O)$ and helium nucleus $({}_2^4He)$ is **(2023 Main)**
(a) 8 : 1 (b) 2 : 1 (c) 1 : 1 (d) 4 : 1

13. The mass of proton, neutron and helium nucleus are respectively 1.0073 u, 1.0087 u and 4.0015 u. The binding energy of helium nucleus is **(2023 Main)**
(a) 14.2 MeV (b) 28.4 MeV (c) 7.1 MeV (d) 56.8 MeV

14. ${}_{92}^{238}A \longrightarrow {}_{90}^{234}B + {}_2^4D + Q$
In the given nuclear reaction, the approximate amount of energy released will be
[Given, mass of ${}_{92}^{238}A = 238.05079 \times 931.5$ MeV/c^2,
mass of ${}_{92}^{234}B = 234.04363 \times 931.5$ MeV/c^2,
mass of ${}_2^4D = 4.00260 \times 931.5$ MeV/c^2] **(2023 Main)**
(a) 3.82 MeV (b) 5.9 MeV (c) 2.12 MeV (d) 4.25 MeV

15. Nucleus A is having mass number 220 and its binding energy per nucleon is 5.6 MeV. Its splits in two fragments B and C of mass numbers 105 and 115. The binding energy of nucleons in B and C is 6.4 MeV per nucleon. The energy Q released per fission will be : **(2022 Main)**
(a) 0.8 MeV (b) 275 MeV (c) 220 MeV (d) 176 MeV

16. Find the binding energy per nucleon for ${}_{50}^{120}Sn$. Mass of proton $m_p = 1.00783$ U, mass of neutron $m_n = 1.00867$ U and mass of tin nucleus $m_{Sn} = 119.902199$ U. [Take 1 U = 931 MeV] **(2020 Main)**
(a) 7.5 MeV (b) 9.0 MeV (c) 8.0 MeV (d) 8.5 MeV

17. An unstable heavy nucleus at rest breaks into two nuclei which move away with velocities in the ratio of 8 : 27. The ratio of the radii of the nuclei (assumed to be spherical) is **(2018 Main)**
(a) 8 : 27 (b) 2 : 3 (c) 3 : 2 (d) 4 : 9

Subjective Questions

18. Complete the following reactions.
(a) ${}_{88}^{226}Ra \rightarrow \alpha +$ (b) ${}_8^{19}O \rightarrow {}_9^{19}F +$
(c) ${}_{13}^{25}Al \rightarrow {}_{12}^{25}Mg +$

19. 8 protons and 8 neutrons are separately at rest. How much energy will be released if we form ${}_8^{16}O$ nucleus?
Given : Mass of ${}_8^{16}O$ atom = 15.994915 u
Mass of neutron = 1.008665 u
Mass of hydrogen atom = 1.007825 u

20. Assuming the splitting of U^{235} nucleus liberates 200 MeV energy, find
(a) the energy liberated in the fission of 1 kg of U^{235} and
(b) the mass of the coal with calorific value of 30 kJ/g which is equivalent to 1 kg of U^{235}.

21. ${}_{83}^{212}Bi$ decays as per following equation.
$${}_{83}^{212}Bi \rightarrow {}_{81}^{208}Tl + {}_2^4He$$
The kinetic energy of α-particle emitted is 6.802 MeV. Calculate the kinetic energy of Tl recoil atoms.

22. In a neutron induced fission of ${}_{92}U^{235}$ nucleus, usable energy of 185 MeV is released. If ${}_{92}U^{235}$ reactor is continuously operating it at a power level of 100 MW power, how long will it take for 1 kg of uranium to be consumed in this reactor?

Integer Type Questions

23. A nucleus disintegrates into two nuclear parts, in such a way that ratio of their nuclear sizes is $1 : 2^{1/3}$. Their respective speed have a ratio of n : 1. The value of n is .... **(2023 Main)**

24. A nucleus with mass number 242 and binding energy per nucleon as 7.6 MeV breaks into two fragments each with mass number 121. If each fragment nucleus has binding energy per nucleon as 8.1 MeV, the total gain in binding energy is .... MeV. **(2023 Main)**

25. Nucleus A having $Z = 17$ and equal number of protons and neutrons has 1.2 MeV binding energy per nucleon. Another nucleus B of $Z = 12$ has total 26 nucleons and 1.8 MeV binding energy per nucleons. The difference of binding energy of B and A will be .... MeV. **(2023 Main)**

Answers

1. (d)	2. (b)	3. (d)	4. (d)	5. (a)
6. (a)	7. (a)	8. (d)	9. (b)	10. (d)
11. (d)	12. (c)	13. (b)	14. (d)	15. (d)
16. (d)	17. (c)	18. (a) ${}_{86}Rn^{222}$ (b) $\bar{e} + \bar{\nu}$ (c) $e^+ + \nu$		
19. 127.2 MeV		20. (a) 8.19×10^{13} J (b) 2.7×10^6 kg		
21. 0.1308 MeV		22. 8.78 day	23. (2)	24. (121)
25. (6)				

See hints on pages 386-388.

Unit Exercise (Cumulative)

Level 1

Single Correct Option

1. If an atom of ${}^{235}_{92}U$, after absorbing a slow neutron, undergoes fission to form an atom of ${}^{138}_{54}Xe$ and an atom of ${}^{94}_{38}Sr$, the other particles produced are

(a) one proton and two neutrons
(b) three neutrons
(c) two neutrons
(d) one proton and one neutron

2. Nucleus A is converted into C through the following reactions,

$$A \to B + \alpha$$
$$B \to C + 2\beta$$

then,

(a) A and B are isotopes (b) A and C are isobars
(c) A and B are isobars (d) A and C are isotopes

3. A gamma ray photon creates an electron-positron pair. If the rest mass energy of an electron is 0.5 MeV and the total kinetic energy of the electron-positron pair is 0.78 MeV, then the energy of the gamma ray photon must be

(a) 0.78 MeV (b) 1.78 MeV
(c) 1.28 MeV (d) 0.25 MeV

4. An atom of mass number 15 and atomic number 7 captures an α-particle and then emits a proton. The mass number and atomic number of the resulting product will respectively be

(a) 14 and 2 (b) 15 and 3
(c) 16 and 4 (d) 18 and 8

5. The half-lives of a radioactive sample are 30 years and 60 years for two decay processes. If the sample decays by both the processes simultaneously. The time after which, only one-fourth of the sample will remain is

(a) 10 years (b) 20 years
(c) 40 years (d) 60 years

6. The activity of a radioactive sample falls from $700\ s^{-1}$ to $500\ s^{-1}$ in 30 minutes. Its half-life is close to **(2020 Main)**

(a) 72 min
(b) 62 min
(c) 66 min
(d) 52 min

7. Consider the nuclear fission reaction $W \to X + Y$. What is the Q-value (energy released) of the reaction?

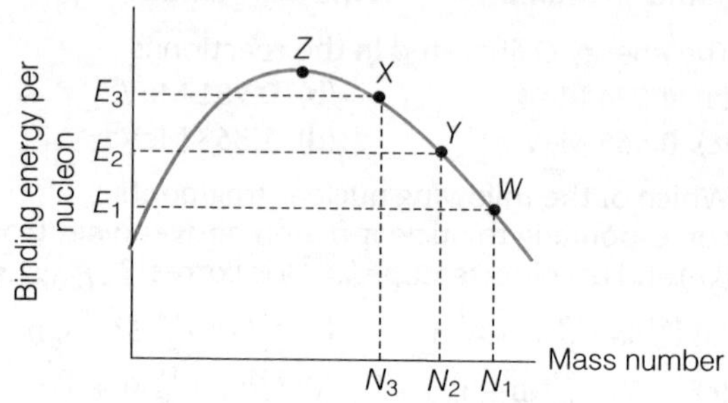

(a) $E_1N_1 - (E_2N_2 + E_3N_3)$ (b) $(E_2N_2 + E_3N_3 - E_1N_1)$
(c) $E_2N_2 + E_1N_1 - E_3N_3$ (d) $E_1N_1 + E_3N_3 - E_2N_2$

8. The energy released by the fission of a single uranium nucleus is 200 MeV. The number of fissions of uranium nucleus per second required to produce 16 MW of power is
(Assume efficiency of the reactor is 50%)

(a) 2×10^6 (b) 2.5×10^6
(c) 5×10^6 (d) None of these

9. A radioactive isotope is being produced at a constant rate A. The isotope has a half-life T. Initially, there are no nuclei, after a time $t >> T$, the number of nuclei becomes constant. The value of this constant is

(a) AT (b) $\frac{A}{T}\ln 2$ (c) $AT\ln 2$ (d) $\frac{AT}{\ln 2}$

10. Two radioactive substances A and B have decay constants 5λ and λ, respectively. At $t = 0$, a sample has the same number of the two nuclei. The time taken for the ratio of the number of nuclei to become $\left(\frac{1}{e}\right)^2$ will be **(2019 Main)**

(a) $2/\lambda$ (b) $1/2\lambda$ (c) $1/4\lambda$ (d) $1/\lambda$

11. A nucleus X initially at rest, undergoes alpha decay according to the equation

$${}^{232}_{Z}X \to {}^{A}_{90}Y + \alpha$$

What fraction of the total energy released in the decay will be the kinetic energy of the alpha particle?

(a) $\frac{90}{92}$ (b) $\frac{228}{232}$
(c) $\sqrt{\frac{228}{232}}$ (d) $\frac{1}{2}$

12. A radioactive nucleus A with a half-life T, decays into a nucleus B. At $t=0$, there is no nucleus B. After sometime t, the ratio of the number of B to that of A is 0.3. Then, t is given by **(2017 Main)**

(a) $t = T\frac{\log 1.3}{\log 2}$ (b) $t = T\log 1.3$

(c) $t = \frac{T}{\log 1.3}$ (d) $t = \frac{T\log 2}{2\log 1.3}$

13. A radioactive nucleus of mass M emits a photon of frequency ν and the nucleus recoils. The recoil energy will be

(a) $h^2\nu^2/2Mc^2$ (b) zero

(c) $h\nu$ (d) $Mc^2 - h\nu$

14. A particular nucleus in a large population of identical radioactive nuclei did survive 5 half-lives of that isotope. Then, the probability that this surviving nucleus will survive the next half-life, is

(a) $\frac{1}{32}$ (b) $\frac{1}{5}$

(c) $\frac{1}{2}$ (d) $\frac{1}{10}$

15. A radioactive nuclei with decay constant 0.5/s is being produced at a constant rate of 100 nuclei/s. If at $t=0$ there were no nuclei, the time when there are 50 nuclei is **(2014 Main)**

(a) 1 s (b) $2\ln\left(\frac{4}{3}\right)$s (c) ln 2s (d) $\ln\left(\frac{4}{3}\right)$s

16. Which of the following processes represent a γ-decay? **(2002 JEE)**

(a) ${}^AX_Z + \gamma \rightarrow {}^AX_{Z-1} + a + b$

(b) ${}^AX_Z + {}^1n_0 \rightarrow {}^{A-3}X_{Z-2} + c$

(c) ${}^AX_Z \rightarrow {}^AX_Z + f$

(d) ${}^AX_Z + e_{-1} \rightarrow {}^AX_{A-1} + g$

17. The half-life of ^{131}I is 8 days. Given a sample of ^{131}I at time $t=0$, we can assert that **(1998 JEE)**

(a) no nucleus will decay before $t=4$ days

(b) no nucleus will decay before $t=8$ days

(c) all nuclei will decay before $t=16$ days

(d) a given nucleus may decay at any time after $t=0$

18. Masses of two isobars ${}_{29}Cu^{64}$ and ${}_{30}Zn^{64}$ are 63.9298 u and 63.9292 u respectively. It can be concluded from these data that **(1997 JEE)**

(a) both the isobars are stable

(b) Zn^{64} is radioactive, decaying to Cu^{64} through β-decay

(c) Cu^{64} is radioactive, decaying to Zn^{64} through γ-decay

(d) Cu^{64} is radioactive, decaying to Zn^{64} through β-decay

19. During a nuclear fusion reaction **(1987 JEE)**

(a) a heavy nucleus breaks into two fragments by itself

(b) a light nucleus bombarded by thermal neutrons breaks up

(c) a heavy nucleus bombarded by thermal neutrons breaks up

(d) two light nuclei combine to give a heavier nucleus and possibly other products

20. The equation; $4\,{}^1_1H \longrightarrow {}^4_2He^{2+} + 2e^- + 26$ MeV represents **(1983 JEE)**

(a) β-decay (b) γ-decay

(c) fusion (d) fission

Multiple Correct Options

21. In a radioactive decay chain, ${}^{232}_{90}$Th nucleus decays to ${}^{212}_{82}$Pb nucleus. Let N_α and N_β be the number of α and β-particles respectively, emitted in this decay process. Which of the following statements is (are) true? **(2018 Adv.)**

(a) $N_\alpha = 5$ (b) $N_\alpha = 6$

(c) $N_\beta = 2$ (d) $N_\beta = 4$

22. The mass number of a nucleus is **(1986 JEE)**

(a) always less than its atomic number.

(b) always more than its atomic number.

(c) sometimes equal to its atomic number.

(d) sometimes more than and sometimes equal to its atomic number.

23. From the following equations pick out the possible nuclear fusion reactions **(1984 JEE)**

(a) ${}_6C^{13} + {}_1H^1 \longrightarrow {}_6C^{14} + 4.3$ MeV

(b) ${}_6C^{12} + {}_1H^1 \longrightarrow {}_7N^{13} + 2$ MeV

(c) ${}_7N^{14} + {}_1H^1 \longrightarrow {}_8O^{15} + 7.3$ MeV

(d) ${}_{922}U^{235} + {}_0n^1 \longrightarrow {}_{54}Xe^{140} + 36\,Sr^{94} + {}_0n^1 + {}_0n^1 + \gamma + 200$MeV

Match the Columns

24. List-I shows different radioactive decay processes and List-II provides possible emitted particles. Match each entry in List-I with an appropriate entry from List-II, and choose the correct option. **(2023 Adv.)**

	List-I		List-II
P.	${}^{238}_{92}U \rightarrow {}^{234}_{91}Pa$	1.	One α-particle and one β^+-particle
Q.	${}^{214}_{82}Pb \rightarrow {}^{210}_{82}Pb$	2.	Three β^--particles and one α-particle
R.	${}^{210}_{81}Tl \rightarrow {}^{206}_{82}Pb$	3.	Two β^--particles and one α-particle
S.	${}^{228}_{91}Pa \rightarrow {}^{224}_{88}Ra$	4.	One α-particle and one β^--particle

	P	Q	R	S		P	Q	R	S
(a)	4	3	2	1	(b)	4	1	2	5
(c)	5	3	1	4	(d)	5	1	3	2

25. Match the nuclear processes given in Column I with the appropriate option(s) in Column II. **(2015 Adv.)**

	Column I		Column II
(a)	Nuclear fusion	p.	absorption of thermal neutrons by $^{235}_{92}U$
(b)	Fission in a nuclear reactor	q.	$^{60}_{27}Co$ nucleus
(c)	β-decay	r.	Energy production in stars via hydrogen conversion to helium
		t.	Neutrino emission

26. Match Column I of the nuclear process with Column II containing parent nucleus and one of the end products of each process and then select the correct answer using the codes given below the lists. **(2013 Adv.)**

	Column I		Column II
P.	Alpha decay	1.	$^{15}_{8}O \longrightarrow ^{15}_{7}N + ...$
Q.	β^+ decay	2.	$^{238}_{92}U \rightarrow ^{234}_{90}Th + ...$
R.	Fission	3.	$^{185}_{83}Bi \rightarrow ^{184}_{82}Pb + ...$
S.	Proton emission	4.	$^{239}_{94}Pu \rightarrow ^{140}_{57}La + ...$

Codes

	P	Q	R	S		P	Q	R	S
(a)	4	2	1	3	(b)	1	3	2	4
(c)	2	1	4	3	(d)	4	3	2	1

27. Some laws/processes are given in Column I. Match these with the physical phenomena given in Column II. **(2006 JEE)**

	Column I		Column II
(a)	Nuclear fusion	(p)	Converts some matter into energy
(b)	Nuclear fission	(q)	Generally possible for nuclei with low atomic number
(c)	β-decay	(r)	Generally possible for nuclei with higher atomic number
(d)	Exothermic nuclear reaction	(s)	Generally possible for weak nuclear forces

Subjective Questions

28. There is a stream of neutrons with a kinetic energy of 0.0327 eV. If the half-life of neutrons is 700 s, what fraction of neutrons will decay before they travel a distance of 10 m? **(1986 JEE)**

29. How many beta-particles are emitted during one hour by 1.0 μg of Na^{24} radionuclide whose half-life is 15 hours? **(Irodov 6.216)**

30. To investigate the beta-decay of Mg^{23} radionuclide, a counter was activated at the moment $t = 0$. It registered N_1 beta-particles by a moment $t_1 = 2.0$ s, and by a moment $t_2 = 3t_1$ the number of registered beta-particles was 2.66 times greater. Find the mean life time of the given nuclei. **(Irodov 6.217)**

31. A stationary $\dot{P}o^{210}$ nucleus emits an alpha-particle with kinetic energy $K_\alpha = 5.77$ MeV. Find the recoil velocity of a daughter nucleus. What fraction of the total energy liberated in this decay is accounted for by the recoil energy of the daughter nucleus? **(Irodov 6.234)**

32. Assuming that the splitting of a U^{235} nucleus liberates the energy of 200 MeV, find:
(a) the energy liberated in the fission of one kilogram of U^{235} isotope, and the mass of coal with calorific value of 30 kJ/g which is equivalent to that for one kg of U^{235}
(b) the mass of U^{235} isotope split during the explosion of the atomic bomb with 30 kt trotyl equivalent if the calorific value of trotyl is 4.1 kJ/g. **(Irodov 6.261)**

33. What amount of heat is liberated during the formation of one gram of He^4 from deuterium H^2? What mass of coal with calorific value of 30 kJ/g is thermally equivalent to the magnitude obtained? **(Irodov 6.262)**

Integer Type Questions

34. The energy released per fission of nucleus of ^{240}X is 200 MeV. The energy released, if all the atoms in 120 g of pure ^{240}X undergo fission is ...... $\times 10^{25}$ MeV. (Given, $N_A = 6 \times 10^{23}$) **(2023 Main)**

35. Two lighter nuclei combine to form a comparatively heavier nucleus by the relation given below
$$^2_1X + ^2_1X = ^4_2Y$$
The binding energies per nucleon for ^2_1X and ^4_2Y are 1.1 MeV and 7.6 MeV, respectively. The energy released in the process is .... MeV. **(2022 Main)**

36. The minimum kinetic energy needed by an alpha particle to cause the nuclear reaction $^{16}_{7}N + ^4_2He \longrightarrow ^1_1H + ^{19}_{8}O$ in a laboratory frame is n (in MeV). Assume that $^{16}_{7}N$ is at rest in the laboratory frame. The masses of $^{16}_{7}N$, ^4_2He, ^1_1H and $^{19}_{8}O$ can be taken to be 16.006 u, 4.003 u, 1.008 u and 19.003 u respectively, where 1 u = 930 MeVc^{-2}. The value of n is .... **(2022 Adv.)**

37. From the given data, the amount of energy required to break the nucleus of aluminium $^{27}_{13}Al$ is $x \times 10^{-3}$ J.
Mass of neutron = 1.00866 u
Mass of proton = 1.00726 u
Mass of aluminium nucleus = 27.18846 u
(Assume 1 u corresponds to x joule of energy)
(Round off to the nearest integer) **(2021 Main)**

Level 2

Single Correct Option

38. The count rate observed from a radioactive source at t second was N_0 and at $4t$ second it was $\frac{N_0}{16}$. The count rate observed at $\left(\frac{11}{2}\right)t$ second will be

(a) $\frac{N_0}{128}$ (b) $\frac{N_0}{64}$
(c) $\frac{N_0}{32}$ (d) None of these

39. A radioactive element A of decay constant λ_A decays into another radioactive element B of decay constant λ_B. Initially, the number of active nuclei of A was N_0 and B was absent in the sample. The maximum number of active nuclei of B is found at $t = 2\frac{\ln 2}{\lambda_A}$. The maximum number of active nuclei of B is

(a) $\frac{N_0}{4}$ (b) $\frac{\lambda_A}{\lambda_B}N_0 e^{-\lambda_B t}$
(c) $\frac{\lambda_A}{\lambda_B}\frac{N_0}{4}$ (d) None of these

40. A bone containing 200 g carbon-14 has a β-decay rate of 375 decay/min. Calculate the time that has elapsed since the death of the living one. Given the rate of decay for the living organism is equal to 15 decay per min per gram of carbon and half-life of carbon-14 is 5730 years.

(a) 27190 years (b) 1190 years
(c) 17190 years (d) None of these

41. Two identical samples (same material and same amount) P and Q of a radioactive substance having mean life T are observed to have activities A_P and A_Q respectively at the time of observation. If P is older than Q, then the difference in their age is

(a) $T\ln\left(\frac{A_P}{A_Q}\right)$ (b) $T\ln\left(\frac{A_Q}{A_P}\right)$
(c) $T\left(\frac{A_P}{A_Q}\right)$ (d) $T\left(\frac{A_Q}{A_P}\right)$

42. Two radioactive samples of different elements (half-lives t_1 and t_2 respectively) have same number of nuclei at $t = 0$. The time after which their activities are same is

(a) $\frac{t_1t_2}{0.693(t_2-t_1)}\ln\frac{t_2}{t_1}$ (b) $\frac{t_1t_2}{0.693}\ln\frac{t_2}{t_1}$
(c) $\frac{t_1t_2}{0.693(t_1+t_2)}\ln\frac{t_2}{t_1}$ (d) None of these

43. A radioactive material of half-life T was kept in a nuclear reactor at two different instants. The quantity kept second time was twice of that kept first time. If now their present activities are A_1 and A_2 respectively, then their age difference equals

(a) $\frac{T}{\ln 2}\ln\frac{2A_1}{A_2}$ (b) $T\ln\frac{A_1}{A_2}$
(c) $\frac{T}{\ln 2}\ln\frac{A_2}{2A_1}$ (d) $T\ln\frac{A_2}{2A_1}$

44. The activity of a sample of radioactive material is A_1 at time t_1 and A_2 at time $t_2 (t_2 > t_1)$. Its mean life is T. Then:

(a) $A_1t_1 = A_2t_2$ (b) $\frac{A_1 - A_2}{t_2 - t_1} = \text{constant}$
(c) $A_2 = A_1 e^{\left(\frac{t_1 - t_2}{T}\right)}$ (d) $A_2 = A_1 e^{\left(\frac{t_1}{t_2 T}\right)}$

45. Two radioactive nuclei A and B have disintegration constants λ_A and λ_B and initially N_A and N_B number of nuclei of them are taken, then the time after which their undecayed nuclei are same is

(a) $\frac{\lambda_A\lambda_B}{(\lambda_A - \lambda_B)}\ln\left(\frac{N_B}{N_A}\right)$ (b) $\frac{1}{(\lambda_A + \lambda_B)}\ln\left(\frac{N_B}{N_A}\right)$
(c) $\frac{1}{(\lambda_B - \lambda_A)}\ln\left(\frac{N_B}{N_A}\right)$ (d) $\frac{1}{(\lambda_A - \lambda_B)}\ln\left(\frac{N_B}{N_A}\right)$

46. For a radioactive sample at given instant, number of active nuclei is N_0 and its decay constant is λ, then the **incorrect** relation is

(a) $N_0\lambda$ = activity at given instant
(b) λ = decay probability per unit time of a nucleus
(c) after the next $\frac{1}{\lambda}$ time interval active nuclei in the sample will be $\frac{N_0}{e}$
(d) The half-life of the sample $= \frac{\ln 2}{\lambda}$

47. The half-life of radium is 1620 yr and its atomic weight is 226 kg/k-mol. The number of atoms that will decay from its 1 g sample per second will be (Avogadro number $N = 6.023 \times 10^{23}$ atom/mol)

(a) 3.61×10^{10} (b) 3.6×10^{12}
(c) 3.11×10^{15} (d) 31.1×10^{15}

48. A fission reaction is given by ${}^{236}_{92}U \rightarrow {}^{140}_{54}Xe + {}^{94}_{38}Sr + x + y$, where x and y are two particles. Considering ${}^{236}_{92}U$ to be at rest, the kinetic energies of the products are denoted by K_{Xe}, K_{Sr}, K_x (2 MeV) and K_y(2 MeV), respectively. Let the binding energies per nucleon of ${}^{236}_{92}U$, ${}^{140}_{54}Xe$ and ${}^{94}_{38}Sr$ be 7.5 MeV, 8.5 MeV and 8.5 MeV, respectively. Considering different conservation laws, the correct options is : **(2015 Adv.)**

(a) $x = n, y = n, K_{Sr} = 129$ MeV, $K_{Xe} = 86$ MeV
(b) $x = p, y = e^-, K_{Sr} = 129$ MeV, $K_{Xe} = 86$ MeV
(c) $x = p, y = n, K_{Sr} = 129$ MeV, $K_{Xe} = 86$ MeV
(d) $x = n, y = n, K_{Sr} = 86$ MeV, $K_{Xe} = 129$ MeV

49. In the options given below, let E denote the rest mass energy of a nucleus and n a neutron. The correct option is **(2007 JEE)**
(a) $E({}^{236}_{92}U) > E({}^{137}_{53}I) + E({}^{97}_{39}Y) + 2E(n)$
(b) $E({}^{236}_{92}U) < E({}^{137}_{53}I) + E({}^{97}_{39}Y) + 2E(n)$
(c) $E({}^{236}_{92}U) < E({}^{140}_{56}Ba) + E({}^{94}_{36}Kr) + 2E(n)$
(d) $E({}^{235}_{92}U) < E({}^{140}_{56}Ba) + E({}^{94}_{36}Kr) + E(n)$

Multiple Correct Options

50. At $t = 0$, number of radioactive nuclei of a radioactive substance are x and its radioactivity is y. Half-life of radioactive substance is T. Then,
(a) $\frac{x}{y}$ is constant throughout
(b) $\frac{x}{y} > T$
(c) value of xy remains half after one half-life
(d) value of xy remains one fourth after one half-life

51. Choose the correct options.
(a) Isotopes have same number of atomic number
(b) Isobars have same atomic weight
(c) Isotones have same number of neutrons
(d) In isotopes number of electrons are same

52. Choose the correct options.
(a) By gamma radiations atomic number is not changed
(b) By gamma radiations mass number is not changed
(c) By the emission of one α and two β particles isotopes are produced
(d) By the emission of one α and four β particles isobars are produced

53. Two radioactive substances have half-lives T and $2T$. Initially, they have equal number of nuclei. After time $t = 4T$, the ratio of their number of nuclei is x and the ratio of their activity is y. Then,
(a) $x = 1/8$
(b) $x = 1/4$
(c) $y = 1/2$
(d) $y = 1/4$

54. Regarding the nuclear forces, choose the correct options.
(a) They are short range forces
(b) They are charge independent forces
(c) They are not electromagnetic forces
(d) They are exchange forces

55. Regarding a nucleus choose the correct options.
(a) Density of a nucleus is directly proportional to mass number A
(b) Density of all the nuclei is almost constant of the order of 10^{17} kg/m^3
(c) Nucleus radius is of the order of 10^{-15}m
(d) Nucleus radius $\propto A$

56. Assume that the nuclear binding energy per nucleon (B/A) *versus* mass number (A) is as shown in the figure. Consider a nucleus of $A = 110$. Fission of this nucleus results into 2 fragments.

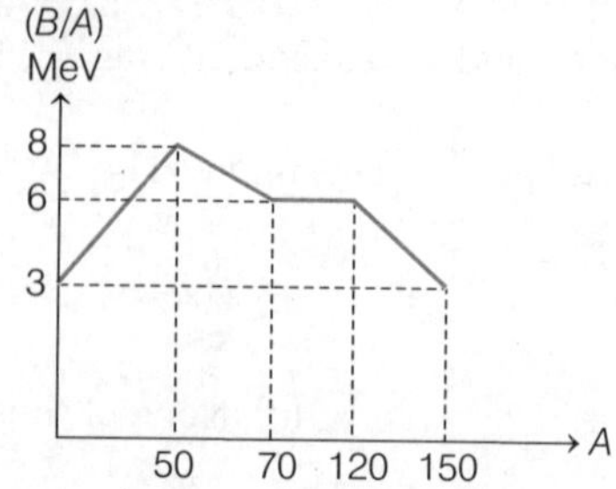

Which of the following could possibly be the mass number of the resulting nuclei to release energy in fission?
(a) 55 and 55 (b) 60 and 50
(c) 100 and 10 (d) 90 and 20

57. Let m_p be the mass of proton, m_n the mass of neutron. M_1 the mass of ${}^{20}_{10}Ne$ nucleus and M_2 the mass of ${}^{40}_{20}Ca$ nucleus. Then **(1998 JEE)**
(a) $M_2 = 2M_1$ (b) $M_2 > 2M_1$
(c) $M_2 < 2M_1$ (d) $M_1 < 10(m_n + m_p)$

Passage Based Questions

Passage 1 (Q. No. 58 to 60)

The atomic masses of the hydrogen isotopes are

Hydrogen $m({}_1H^1) = 1.007825$ *amu*

Deuterium $m({}_1H^2) = 2.014102$ *amu*

Tritium $m({}_1H^3) = 3.016049$ *amu*

58. The energy released in the reaction, ${}_1H^2 + {}_1H^2 \rightarrow {}_1H^3 + {}_1H^1$ is nearly
(a) 1 MeV (b) 2 MeV (c) 4 MeV (d) 8 MeV

59. The number of fusion reactions required to generate 1 kWh is nearly
(a) 10^8 (b) 10^{18}
(c) 10^{28} (d) 10^{38}

60. The mass of deuterium, ${}_1H^2$ that would be needed to generate 1 kWh energy is :
(a) 3.7 kg (b) 3.7 g
(c) 3.7×10^{-5} kg (d) 3.7×10^{-8} kg

Passage 2 (Q. No 61 to 62)

A parent nucleus of mass $M + \Delta m$ *is at rest and decays into two daughter nuclei of equal mass* $\frac{M}{2}$ *each. Speed of light is* c.

61. The binding energy per nucleon for the parent nucleus is E_1 and that for the daughter nuclei is E_2. Then,
(a) $E_2 = 2E_1$ (b) $E_1 > E_2$
(c) $E_2 > E_1$ (d) $E_1 = 2E_2$

62. The speed of daughter nuclei is

(a) $c\dfrac{\Delta m}{M+\Delta m}$ (b) $c\sqrt{\dfrac{2\Delta m}{M}}$

(c) $c\sqrt{\dfrac{\Delta m}{M}}$ (d) $c\sqrt{\dfrac{\Delta m}{M+\Delta m}}$

Match the Columns

63. At $t = 0$, x nuclei of a radioactive substance emit y nuclei per second. Match the following two columns.

	Column I		Column II
(a)	Decay constant λ	(p)	(ln 2) (x/y)
(b)	Half-life	(q)	x/y
(c)	Activity after time $t = \frac{1}{\lambda}$	(r)	y/e
(d)	Number of nuclei after time $t = \frac{1}{\lambda}$	(s)	None of these

64. Corresponding to the graph shown in figure, match the following two columns.

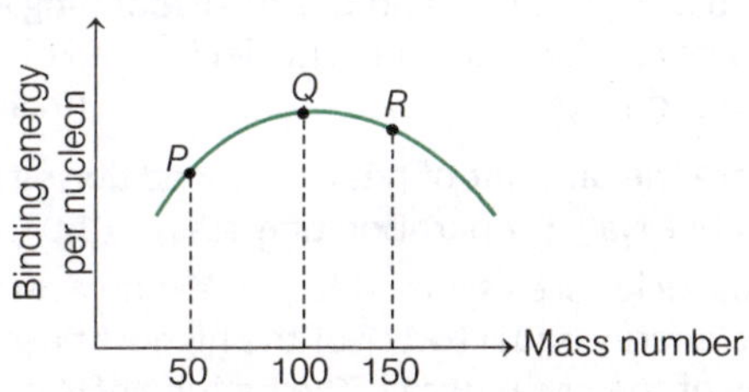

	Column I		Column II
(a)	$P+P=Q$	(p)	energy is released
(b)	$P+P+P=R$	(q)	energy is absorbed
(c)	$P+R=2Q$	(r)	No energy transfer will take place
(d)	$P+Q=R$	(s)	data insufficient

65. In the following chain,

$$A \rightarrow B \rightarrow C$$

A and B are radioactive, while C is stable. Initially, we have only A and B nuclei. There is no nucleus of C. As the time passes, match the two columns.

	Column I		Column II
(a)	Nuclei of $(A + B)$	(p)	will increase continuously
(b)	Nuclei of B	(q)	will decrease continuously
(c)	Nuclei of $(C + B)$	(r)	will first increase then decrease
(d)	Nuclei of $(A + C)$	(s)	data insufficient

66. Match the following two columns.

	Column I		Column II
(a)	The energy of air molecules at room temperature	(p)	0.02 eV
(b)	Binding energy of heavy nuclei per nucleon	(q)	2 eV
(c)	X-ray photon energy	(r)	10 keV
(d)	Photon energy of visible light	(s)	7 MeV

Subjective Questions

67. A F^{32} radio nuclide with half-life $T = 14.3$ hours is produced in a reactor at a constant rate $q = 2\times 10^9$ nuclei per second. How soon after the beginning of production of that radio nuclide will its activity be equal to $R = 10^9$ disintegration per second?

68. Consider a radioactive disintegration according to the equation $A \rightarrow B \rightarrow C$. Decay constant of A and B is same and equal to λ. Number of nuclei of A, B and C are N_0, 0, 0 respectively at $t = 0$. Find
(a) number of nuclei of B as function of time t.
(b) time t at which the activity of B is maximum and the value of maximum activity of B.

69. A solution contains a mixture of two isotopes A (half-life $= 10$ days) and B (half-life $= 5$ days). Total activity of the mixture is 10^{10} disintegration per second at time $t = 0$. The activity reduces to 20% in 20 days. Find (a) the initial activities of A and B, (b) the ratio of initial number of their nuclei.

70. A radio nuclide with disintegration constant λ is produced in a reactor at a constant rate α nuclei per second. During each decay energy E_0 is released. 20% of this energy is utilized in increasing the temperature of water. Find the increase in temperature of m mass of water in time t. Specific heat of water is s. Assume that there is no loss of energy through water surface.

71. A stable nuclei C is formed from two radioactive nuclei A and B with decay constant of λ_1 and λ_2 respectively. Initially, the number of nuclei of A is N_0 and that of B is zero. Nuclei B are produced at a constant rate of P. Find the number of the nuclei of C after time t.

72. Polonium ($^{210}_{84}Po$) emits ^4_2He particles and is converted into lead ($^{206}_{82}Pb$). This reaction is used for producing electric power in a space mission. Po^{210} has half-life of 138.6 days. Assuming an efficiency of 10% for the thermoelectric machine, how much ^{210}Po is required to produce 1.2×10^7 J of electric energy per day at the end of 693 days. Also find the initial activity of the material.

Given : Masses of nuclei $^{210}Po = 209.98264$ amu, $^{206}Pb = 205.97440$ amu, $^4_2He = 4.00260$ amu, 1 amu $= 931$ MeV/c^2 and Avogadro's number $= 6\times 10^{23}$/mol.

73. A radio nuclide consists of two isotopes. One of the isotopes decays by α-emission and other by β-emission with half-lives $T_1 = 405$ s and $T_2 = 1620$ s, respectively. At $t = 0$, probabilities of getting α and β-particles from the radio nuclide are equal. Calculate their respective probabilities at $t = 1620$ s. If at $t = 0$, total number of nuclei in the radio nuclide are N_0. Calculate the time t when total number of nuclei remained undecayed becomes equal to $N_0/2$.
$\log_{10}2 = 0.3010$, $\log_{10}5.94 = 0.7742$ and $x^4 + 4x - 2.5 = 0$, $x = 0.594$

74. Find the amount of heat generated by 1 mg of Po^{210} preparation during the mean life period of these nuclei if the emitted alpha particles are known to possess kinetic energy 5.3 MeV and practically all daughter nuclei are formed directly in the ground state.

75. In an agricultural experiment, a solution containing 1 mole of a radioactive material ($T_{1/2} = 14.3$ days) was injected into the roots of a plant. The plant was allowed 70 h to settle down and then activity was measured in its fruit. If the activity measured was 1 μCi, what percentage of activity is transmitted from the root to the fruit in steady state?

76. A rock is 1.5×10^9 yr old. The rock contains ^{238}U which disintegrates to form ^{206}Pb. Assume that there was no ^{206}Pb in the rock initially and it is the only stable product formed by the decay. Calculate the ratio of number of nuclei of ^{238}U to that of ^{206}Pb in the rock. Half-life of ^{238}U is 4.5×10^9 yr. ($2^{1/3} = 1.259$) **(2004 JEE)**

77. Nuclei of a radioactive element A are being produced at a constant rate α. The element has a decay constant λ. At time $t = 0$, there are N_0 nuclei of the element. **(1998 JEE)**
(a) Calculate the number N of nuclei of A at time t.
(b) If $\alpha = 2N_0\lambda$, calculate the number of nuclei of A after one half-life of A and also the limiting value of N as $t \to \infty$.

78. At a given instant there are 25% undecayed radioactive nuclei in a sample. After 10 s the number of undecayed nuclei reduces to 12.5%. Calculate
(a) mean life of the nuclei, **(1996 JEE)**
(b) the time in which the number of undecayed nuclei will further reduce to 6.25% of the reduced number.

79. In a nuclear reactor ^{235}U undergoes fission liberating 200 MeV of energy. The reactor has a 10% efficiency and produces 1000 MW power. If the reactor is to function for 10 yr, find the total mass of uranium required. **(2001 JEE)**

80. A nucleus at rest undergoes a decay emitting an α-particle of de-Broglie wavelength, $\lambda = 5.76 \times 10^{-15}$ m. If the mass of the daughter nucleus is 223.610 amu and that of the α-particle is 4.002 amu. Determine the total kinetic energy in the final state. Hence obtain the mass of the parent nucleus in amu.
(1 amu $= 931.470$ MeV/c^2) **(2001 JEE)**

81. It is proposed to use the nuclear fusion reaction;
$$^2_1H + ^2_1H \rightarrow ^4_2He$$
in a nuclear reactor of 200 MW rating. If the energy from the above reaction is used with a 25 per cent efficiency in the reactor, how many grams of deuterium fuel will be needed per day? (The masses of ^2_1H and ^4_2H are 2.0141 atomic mass units and 4.0026 atomic mass units respectively).

82. Knowing the decay constant λ of a nucleus, find:
(a) the probability of decay of a particular nucleus during the time from 0 to t
(b) the mean lifetime τ of the nucleus. **(Irodov 6.214)**

83. The mean path length of alpha-particles in air under standard conditions is defined by the formula $R = 0.98 \times 10^{-27} v_0^3$ cm, where v_0 (cm/s) is the initial velocity of an alpha-particle. Using this formula, find for an alpha-particle with initial kinetic energy 7.0 MeV:
(a) its mean path length
(b) the average number of ion pairs formed by the given alpha-particle over the whole path R as well as over its first half, assuming the ion pair formation energy to be equal to 34 eV. **(Irodov 6.237)**

84. Taking the values of atomic masses from the tables, find the maximum kinetic energy of beta-particles emitted by Be^{10} nuclei and the corresponding kinetic energy of recoiling daughter nuclei formed directly in the ground state. **(Irodov 6.239)**

85. Evaluate the amount of heat produced during a day by a β^--active Na^{24} preparation of mass $m = 1.0$ mg. The beta-particles are assumed to possess an average kinetic energy equal to 1/3 of the highest possible energy of the given decay. The half-life of Na^{24} is $T = 15$ hours. **(Irodov 6.240)**

86. An alpha-particle with kinetic energy $K_\alpha = 7.0$ MeV is scattered elastically by an initially stationary Li^6 nucleus. Find the kinetic energy of the recoil nucleus if the angle of divergence of the two particles is $\theta = 60°$. **(Irodov 6.249)**

87. A neutron collides elastically with an initially stationary deuteron. Find the fraction of the kinetic energy lost by the neutron **(Irodov 6.250)**
(a) in a head-on collision
(b) in scattering at right angles.

Integer Type Questions

88. For a radioactive material, its activity A and rate of change of its activity R are defined as $A = -\dfrac{dN}{dt}$ and $R = -\dfrac{dA}{dt}$, where $N(t)$ is the number of nuclei at time t. Two radioactive sources P (mean life τ) and Q (mean life 2τ) have the same activity at $t = 0$. Their rate of change of activities at $t = 2\tau$ are R_P and R_Q, respectively. If $\dfrac{R_P}{R_Q} = \dfrac{n}{e}$, then the value of n is **(2015 Adv.)**

89. A nuclear power plant supplying electrical power to a village uses a radioactive material of half life T years as the fuel. The amount of fuel at the beginning is such that the total power requirement of the village is 12.5% of the electrical power available from the plant at that time. If the plant is able to meet the total power needs of the village for a maximum period of nT years, then the value of n is **(2015 Adv.)**

90. A freshly prepared sample of a radioisotope of half-life 1386 s has activity 10^3 disintegrations per second. Given that $\ln 2 = 0.693$, the fraction of the initial number of nuclei (expressed in nearest integer percentage) that will decay in the first 80 s after preparation of the sample is **(2013 Adv.)**

91. The activity of a freshly prepared radioactive sample is 10^{10} disintegrations per second, whose mean life is 10^{-9} s. The mass of an atom of this radioisotope is 10^{-25} kg. The mass (in mg) of the radioactive sample is **(2011 JEE)**

Answers

Level 1

1. (b) **2.** (d) **3.** (b) **4.** (d) **5.** (c) **6.** (b) **7.** (b) **8.** (d) **9.** (d) **10.** (b)
11. (b) **12.** (a) **13.** (a) **14.** (c) **15.** (b) **16.** (c) **17.** (d) **18.** (d) **19.** (d) **20.** (c)
21. (a,c) **22.** (c,d) **23.** (b,c) **24.** (a) **25.** ($a \to r$; $b \to p,s$; $c \to p,q,r,t$; $d \to p,q,r,t$) **26.** (c)
27. ($a \to p,q$; $b \to p,r$; $c \to p,s$; $d \to p,q,r$) **28.** (3.96×10^{-6}) **29.** 1.2×10^{15} **30.** $\tau \approx 16$ s
31. $v = 3.4 \times 10^5$ m/s, 0.020 **32.** (a) 8.2×10^{10} kJ, $m = 27 \times 10^6$ kg (b) $m \approx 1.5$ kg
33. (a) $E_2 = 5.74 \times 10^8$ kJ (b) $m \approx 2 \times 10^4$ kg **34.** (6) **35.** (26) **36.** (2.325) **37.** (27.16)

Level 2

38. (b) **39.** (c) **40.** (c) **41.** (b) **42.** (a) **43.** (c) **44.** (c) **45.** (c) **46.** (b) **47.** (a)
48. (a) **49.** (a) **50.** (a,b,d) **51.** (a,b,c,d) **52.** (a,b,c) **53.** (b,c) **54.** (a,b,c,d) **55.** (b,c) **56.** (a,b) **57.** (c,d)
58. (c) **59.** (b) **60.** (d) **61.** (c) **62.** (b) **63.** ($a \to s$; $b \to p$; $c \to r$; $d \to s$)
64. ($a \to p$; $b \to p$; $c \to p$; $d \to s$) **65.** ($a \to q$; $b \to s$; $c \to p$; $d \to s$) **66.** ($a \to p$; $b \to s$; $c \to r$; $d \to q$) **67.** 14.3 h
68. (a) $N_B = \lambda N_0 (te^{-\lambda t})$ (b) $t = \frac{1}{\lambda}$, $R_{max} = \frac{\lambda N_0}{e}$ **69.** (a) 0.73×10^{10} dps, 0.27×10^{10} dps (b) 5.4
70. $\frac{0.2 E_0 \left[\alpha t - \frac{\alpha}{\lambda}(1 - e^{-\lambda t})\right]}{ms}$ **71.** $N_c = N_0 (1 - e^{-\lambda_1 t}) + P\left(t + \frac{e^{-\lambda_2 t} - 1}{\lambda_2}\right)$
72. 10 g, 4.57×10^{21} disintegrations/day **73.** $\frac{1}{9}, \frac{8}{9}$, 1215 s **74.** 1.55×10^6 J **75.** 1.26×10^{-11} %
76. (3.861) **77.** (a) $N = \frac{1}{\lambda}[\alpha - (\alpha - \lambda N_0) e^{-\lambda t}]$ (b) $N = \frac{3}{2} N_0$, $N = 2N_0$ **78.** (14.43s, 40 s)
79. (3.847×10^4 kg) **80.** (6.25 MeV, 227.6 amu) **81.** (120.26 g) **82.** (a) $P = 1 - e^{-\lambda t}$ (b) Average life $= \frac{1}{\lambda}$
83. (a) 6.1 cm (b) 21×10^5 and 0.77×10^5 respectively **84.** 0.56 MeV and 47.5 eV **85.** 5 MJ **86.** 6.0 MeV
87. (a) 0.89 (b) 2/3 **88.** (2) **89.** (3) **90.** (4) **91.** (1)

See hints on pages 388-399.

Hints & SOLUTIONS

Module 1.

Introductory Exercise

1. Formula based question.
2. Penetrating power is maximum for γ-rays, then of β-particles and then α-particles because basically it depends on the velocity. However, ionization power is in reverse order.
3. Both the beta rays and the cathode rays are made up of electrons. So, only option (a) is correct.
   (b) Gamma rays are electromagnetic waves.
   (c) Alpha particles are doubly ionized helium atoms and
   (d) Protons and neutrons have approximately the same mass.
   Therefore, (b), (c) and (d) are wrong options.
4. Following nuclear reaction takes place
   $${}_0n^1 \longrightarrow {}_1H^1 + {}_{-1}e^0 + \bar{\nu}$$
   $\bar{\nu}$ is antineutrino.
5. From $R = R_0\left(\frac{1}{2}\right)^n$
   we have, $1 = 64\left(\frac{1}{2}\right)^n$
   or $n = 6$ = number of half-lives
   $\therefore$ $t = n \times t_{t_{1/2}} = 6 \times 2 = 12$ h
6. Activity of $S_1 = \frac{1}{2}$ (activity of S_2)
   or $\lambda_1 N_1 = \frac{1}{2}(\lambda_2 N_2)$ or $\frac{\lambda_1}{\lambda_2} = \frac{N_2}{2N_1}$
   or $\frac{T_1}{T_2} = \frac{2N_1}{N_2}$ $\left(T = \text{half - life} = \frac{\ln 2}{\lambda}\right)$
   Given, $N_1 = 2N_2$
   $\therefore$ $\frac{T_1}{T_2} = 4$
   $\therefore$ Correct option is (a).
7. After two half-lives $\frac{1}{4}$th fraction of nuclei will remain un-decayed. Or, $\frac{3}{4}$th fraction will decay. Hence, the probability that a nucleus decays in two half-lives is $\frac{3}{4}$.
8. Activity reduces from 6000 dps to 3000 dps in 140 days. It implies that half-life of the radioactive sample is 140 days. In 280 days (or two half-lives) activity will remain $\frac{1}{4}$th of the initial activity. Hence, the initial activity of the sample is
   $$4 \times 6000 \text{ dps} = 24000 \text{ dps}$$
   Therefore, the correct option is (d).
9. $R = R_0\left(\frac{1}{2}\right)^n$ ...(i)
   Here, R = activity of radioactive substance after n half-lives $= \frac{R_0}{16}$ (given)
   Substituting in Eq. (i), we get $n = 4$
   $\therefore$ $t = (n)\, t_{1/2} = (4)(100\,\mu s) = 400\,\mu s$
10. Using $N = N_0 e^{-\lambda t}$
    where, $\lambda = \frac{\ln 2}{t_{1/2}} = \frac{\ln 2}{3.8}$
    $\therefore$ $\frac{N_0}{20} = N_0 e^{-\frac{\ln 2}{3.8}t}$
    Solving this equation with the help of given data we find
    $t = 16.5$ days
    $\therefore$ Correct option is (b).
11. $1000 = \left(\frac{1}{2}\right)^n 8000$
    $\therefore$ $n = 3$ = number of half-lives
    These half-lives are equivalent to 9 days. Hence, one half-life is 3 days.
    $t_{av} = 1.44\, t_{1/2} = 1.44 \times 3 = 4.32$ days
12. $R_0 = \lambda N_0 \Rightarrow N_0 = \frac{R_0}{\lambda}$
    where, $\lambda = \frac{\ln 2}{t_{1/2}}$
    $N = N_0 e^{-\lambda t}$
    Find $N_1 = N_0 e^{-\lambda t_1}$
    and $N_2 = N_0 e^{-\lambda t_2}$
    $\therefore$ Number of nuclei decayed in given
    time $= N_1 - N_2$
13. (a) $R = R_0 e^{-\lambda t}$
    $R_0 = 10$ mCi
    $R = 8$ mCi
    $t = 4.0$ h
    Find λ.
    (b) $R_0 = \lambda N_0$. Find $N_0 = \frac{R_0}{\lambda}$
    (c) Find $R = R_0 e^{-\lambda t}$
14. $R_0 = \lambda N_0$
    $$6.0 \times 10^{11} = \lambda(10^{15})$$
    $\therefore$ $\lambda = 6.0 \times 10^{-4}$ s

$$t_{1/2} = \frac{\ln 2}{\lambda} = \frac{0.693}{6.0 \times 10^{-4}} = 1.16 \times 10^3 \text{ s}$$

15. In 200 minute time,

n_1 = number of half-lives of X

$$= \frac{200}{50} = 4$$

n_2 = number of half-lives of Y

$$= \frac{200}{100} = 2$$

$$\frac{N_X}{N_Y} = \frac{N_0(1/2)^4}{N_0(1/2)^2} = \frac{1}{4}$$

Exercise

1. At $t = 1$ s, $n = 1$

$$\therefore \quad R = 10^3\left(\frac{1}{2}\right) = 500 \text{ disintegration/s}$$

At $t = 3$ s, $n = 3$

$$R = 10^3\left(\frac{1}{2}\right)^3 = 125 \text{ disintegration/s}$$

2. Huge amount of energy is involved in any nuclear process, which cannot be increased or decreased by pressure or temperature.

3. Some lighter nuclei are also radioactive.

4. In moving from lower energy state to higher energy state electromagnetic waves are absorbed.

5. $\frac{2}{3}N_0 = N_0\, e^{-\lambda t_2}$

$$\therefore \quad \lambda t_2 = \ln\left(\frac{3}{2}\right)$$

$$\left(\frac{\ln 2}{20}\right) t_2 = \ln(1.5) = 0.4 \quad \text{or} \quad t_2 = 11.7 \text{ min}$$

Similarly, $\frac{1}{3}N_0 = N_0 e^{-\lambda t_1}$

$$\therefore \quad \lambda t_1 = \ln 3$$

$$\therefore \quad \frac{\ln 2}{20} t_1 = \ln 3 = 1.1$$

$$\Rightarrow \quad t_1 = 31.7 \text{ min}$$

$$\therefore \quad t_1 - t_2 \approx 20 \text{ min}$$

6. Let $n-\alpha$ particles and $m-\beta$ particles are emitted. Then,

$$90 - 2n + m = 80 \quad \text{...(i)}$$

$$200 - 4n = 168 \quad \text{...(ii)}$$

Solving Eqs. (i) and (ii), we get

$$n = 8 \quad \text{and} \quad m = 6$$

7. Number of nuclei left $= \frac{1}{8}$th

Now, $$\frac{1}{8} = \left(\frac{1}{2}\right)^n$$

$\therefore$ n = number of half-lives

$$= 3$$

3 half-lives = 8 s

$$\therefore \quad 1 \text{ half-life} = \frac{8}{3} \text{ s}$$

8. $\lambda = \frac{\ln 2}{t_{1/2}} = \frac{\ln 2}{4} \text{ day}^{-1}$

Now, apply $R = R_0 e^{-\lambda t} \Rightarrow 5 = 100 e^{-\lambda t}$

Substituting value of λ, we can find t.

9. $$\frac{N}{N_0} = e^{-\lambda t} = e^{-\lambda\left(\frac{n}{\lambda}\right)} = \frac{1}{e^n}$$

10. $\lambda = \frac{\ln 2}{t_{1/2}} = \frac{0.693}{6.93} = \frac{1}{10} \sec^{-1}$

$$N = N_0 e^{-\lambda t}$$

$$\therefore \quad \frac{N}{N_0} = e^{-\lambda t} = e^{-\left(\frac{1}{10}\right)(10)} = e^{-1} \approx 0.63$$

11. Activity of atoms is 6.25% after four half-lives.

$\therefore$ Four half-lives $\approx 2 \text{ h} = 120$ min

$\therefore$ One half-life is 30 min.

12. Probability of survival,

$$P = \frac{\text{Number of nuclei left}}{\text{Initial number of nuclei}} = \frac{N_0 e^{-\lambda t}}{N_0}$$

At t = one mean life $= \frac{1}{\lambda}$

$$P = e^{-1} = \frac{1}{e}$$

13. From the emission of one β-particle, atomic number increases by 1and the mass number remains unchanged. So, the new values are $Z+1$ and A.

From the emission of one α-particle, atomic number decreases by 2 and the mass number by 4. Therefore, the values are $Z-1$ and $A-4$.

Finally from the emission of one γ-ray, values of A and Z remain unchanged. Hence, the final values are $Z-1$ and $A-4$.

14. 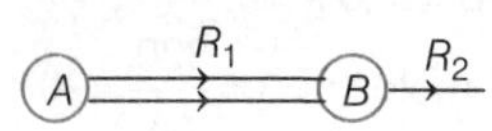

$$+\frac{dn_B}{dt} = R_1 - R_2 = \lambda_a N_a - \lambda_b N_b$$

15. $$R = \lambda N$$

$$\therefore \quad \frac{R}{N} = \lambda = \text{constant}$$

So, graph between $\frac{R}{N}$ and t will be a straight line parallel to the time axis.

16. Numbers are maximum, when

rate of production = rate of disintegration

$$\therefore \quad \alpha = \lambda N \Rightarrow N = \frac{\alpha}{\lambda}$$

17. Decay scheme for given radioactive material is

$$X \xrightarrow{T_{1/2}} \frac{X}{2} \xrightarrow{T_{1/2}} \frac{X}{4} \xrightarrow{T_{1/2}} \frac{X}{8}$$
$$\longleftarrow 3 \text{ days} \longrightarrow$$

So, half-life of material is 1 day.

Hence, amount left after 5 days is

$$X \xrightarrow{1\text{day}} \frac{X}{2} \xrightarrow{1\text{day}} \frac{X}{4} \xrightarrow{1\text{day}} \frac{X}{8} \xrightarrow{1\text{day}} \frac{X}{16} \xrightarrow{1\text{day}} \frac{X}{32}$$

$\therefore$ Amount left after 5 days is $\dfrac{X}{32} = 8 \times 10^{-3}$ kg (given)

So, $X =$ initial amount
$= 8 \times 32 \times 10^{-3}$ kg
$= 256 \times 10^{-3}$ kg $= 256$ g

18. Number of half lives, $n = \dfrac{t}{T_{1/2}} = \dfrac{15}{5} = 3$

We know that

$$N = N_0\left(\frac{1}{2}\right)^n \Rightarrow \frac{N}{N_0} = \left(\frac{1}{2}\right)^3$$

$$\Rightarrow \frac{N}{N_0} = \frac{1}{8} \Rightarrow N = \frac{N_0}{8}$$

$\therefore$ The fraction of original sample that would decay in 15 yr

$$= N_0 - N = N_0 - \frac{N_0}{8} = \frac{7N_0}{8}$$

19. Given, A B T-half life
$t = 0$ N_0 N_0 $\tau \rightarrow$ average life

$$T_A = \tau_B$$

Now,
$$\frac{\ln(2)}{\lambda_A} = \frac{1}{\lambda_B}$$
$$\lambda_A = \lambda_B \ln 2$$

20. Mass number of $A = 16$

Mass number of $B = 32$

Initial mass of $A =$ Initial mass of $B = 320$ g

So, Number of moles of $A = \dfrac{320}{16} = 20$

Number of moles of $B = \dfrac{320}{32} = 10$

Initial number of atoms of A present in sample $= 20 N_A$

Initial number of atoms of B present in sample $= 10 N_A$

Now, half-life of A is 1 day and half-life of B is $\dfrac{1}{2}$ day.

Following is decay scheme;

For A, $20N_A \xrightarrow[1 \text{ day}]{} 10N_A \xrightarrow[1 \text{ day}]{} 5N_A$

For B, $10N_A \xrightarrow[1/2 \text{ day}]{} 5N_A \xrightarrow[1/2 \text{ day}]{}$
$2.5N_A \xrightarrow[1/2 \text{ day}]{} 1.25\, N_A \longrightarrow 0.625\, N_A$

Total number of A and B left after 2 days.

$= 5N_A + 0.625N_A = 5.625N_A$
$= 5.625 \times 6.022 \times 10^{23}$
$= 33.8 \times 10^{23} = 3.38 \times 10^{24}$

21. In alpha ($^4_2$He) decay, mass number decreases by 4 units and charge number decreases by 2 units.

In β^- decay, mass number remains same but charge number increases by 1.

In β^+ decay, mass number remains same but charge number decreases by 1.

In γ-decay, there is no change in mass number or charge number.

$$^{218}_{84}A \xrightarrow{\alpha} {}^{214}_{82}A_1 \xrightarrow{\beta^-}$$
$$^{214}_{83}A_2 \xrightarrow{\gamma} {}^{214}_{83}A_3 \xrightarrow{\alpha}$$
$$^{210}_{81}Au \xrightarrow{\beta^+} {}^{210}_{80}A_5 \xrightarrow{\gamma} {}^{210}_{80}A_6$$

22. Given, Initial activity of radioactive material,

$$A_0 = 6.4 \times 10^{-4} \text{ curie}$$

Half life, $T_{1/2} = 5$ days

New activity, $A = A_0 e^{-\lambda t}$

$\Rightarrow$ $5 \times 10^{-6} = 6.4 \times 10^{-4} e^{-\lambda t}$ [$A = 5 \times 10^{-6}$ curie given]

$\Rightarrow$ $\dfrac{5}{6.4} \times 10^{-2} = e^{-\lambda t}$

$\Rightarrow$ $7.8 \times 10^{-3} = e^{-\lambda t}$

$\log(7.8 \times 10^{-3}) = -\lambda t$

$\Rightarrow$ $\log(7.8 \times 10^{-3}) = -\dfrac{\ln 2}{5} t$ $\left(\because T_{1/2} = \dfrac{\ln 2}{\lambda}\right)$

$\Rightarrow$ $t = \dfrac{5 \times 4.853}{0.693} = 35$ days

23. We have $R = R_0 e^{-\lambda t}$

$$4250 = R_0 e^{-\lambda t} \quad \text{...(i)}$$

At time $(t + 10)$, $R' = R_0 e^{-\lambda(t+10)}$

$$2250 = R_0 e^{-\lambda(t+10)} \quad \text{...(ii)}$$

Dividing Eq. (i) by Eq. (ii), we have

$$\frac{4250}{2250} = \frac{e^{-\lambda t}}{e^{-\lambda(t+10)}} \Rightarrow 1.88 = e^{10\lambda}$$

$\Rightarrow$ $\ln 1.88 = 10\lambda \Rightarrow \lambda = \dfrac{\ln 1.88}{10}$
$= 0.063 \text{ min}^{-1}$

24. Given, $T_{1/2} = 5$ years

Initial sample $= N_0$

Final $= 6.25\ N_0 = \dfrac{1}{16} N_0$

Then $\dfrac{N}{N_0} = \dfrac{1}{16} = \left(\dfrac{1}{2}\right)^4$

Compare with $\dfrac{N}{N_0} = \left(\dfrac{1}{2}\right)^n$

$n =$ number of half-life $= 4$

So, total time $x = 4$ half-life

$$x = 4 \times 5 \text{ years} = 20 \text{ years}$$

25. Decay constant is given by

$$\lambda = \frac{\ln 2}{t_{1/2}} \Rightarrow \lambda_{eq} = \lambda_1 + \lambda_2$$

$$\frac{\ln 2}{(t_{1/2})_{eq}} = \frac{\ln 2}{(t_{1/2})} + \frac{\ln 2}{(t_{1/2})_2}$$

$$\Rightarrow (t_{1/2})_{eq} = \frac{(t_{1/2})_1 (t_{1/2})_2}{(t_{1/2})_1 + (t_{1/2})_2}$$

$$= \frac{3 \times 4.5}{3 + 4.5} = \frac{3 \times 4.5}{7.5} = \frac{9}{5} \text{ h} = 1.8 \text{ h}$$

26. Given, out of 1000 nuclei of Q, 60% may go α-decay

$\Rightarrow$ 600 nuclei may have α-decay

$$\lambda = \frac{\ln 2}{t_{1/2}} = \frac{\ln 2}{20}$$

$$t = 1 \text{ h} = 60 \text{ min}$$

Using, radioactivity equation

$$N = N_0 e^{-\lambda t} = 600 \times e^{-\frac{\ln 2}{20} \times 60}$$

$$N = 75$$

$\Rightarrow$ 75 nuclei are left after one hour

So, number of nuclei decayed to α-particle

$$= 600 - 75 = 525$$

27. (a) $R = R_0 e^{-\lambda t}$

$R = 2700$ per minute, $R_0 = 4750$ per minute

$t = 5$ min

Find λ.

(b) $t_{1/2} = \dfrac{\ln 2}{\lambda}$

28. $\because \quad R = \lambda N$

$$\therefore \quad N = \frac{R}{\lambda} = \frac{R}{(\ln 2)/t_{1/2}} = \frac{R t_{1/2}}{\ln 2}$$

$$= \frac{(8 \times 3.7 \times 10^{10})(5.3)(365)(24)(3600)}{0.693} = 7.14 \times 10^{19}$$

$$m = \frac{7.14 \times 10^{9}}{6.02 \times 10^{23}} \times 60 \text{ g} = 7.11 \times 10^{-3} \text{ g}$$

29. $R = \lambda N = \left(\dfrac{\ln 2}{t_{1/2}}\right) N$

$$= \frac{0.693}{4.5 \times 10^9 \times 365 \times 24 \times 3600}\left(\frac{1}{238}\right) \quad (6.02 \times 10^{23})$$

$$= 1.23 \times 10^4 \text{ dps}$$

30. $\dfrac{1}{\lambda} = 10$ days

$$\therefore \quad \lambda = 0.1 \text{ day}^{-1}$$

Probability of decay

$$= \frac{\text{Number of atoms decayed}}{\text{Initial number of atoms}}$$

$$= \frac{N_0(1 - e^{-\lambda t})}{N_0} = 1 - e^{-\lambda t}$$

$$= 1 - e^{-0.1 \times 5} = 0.39$$

31. $\lambda_1 = \dfrac{\ln 2}{T_1}$ (T = half-life)

$$\lambda_2 = \frac{\ln 2}{T_2}$$

$R_{01} + R_{02} = 8$ mCi (given)

$\therefore \quad \lambda_1(4N_0) + \lambda_2(N_0) = 8$ mCi

From here we can find number

after $t = 60$ yr

$$R = R_1 + R_2 = (4\lambda_1 N_0)e^{-\lambda_1 t} + (\lambda_2 N_0)e^{-\lambda_2 t}$$

32. Given decay is

$${}^{242}_{92}X \longrightarrow 2\,{}^{4}_{2}\text{He} + \beta^- + 2\beta^+ + {}^{234}_{P}Y$$

$$\Rightarrow \quad {}^{242}_{92}X \longrightarrow 2\,{}^{4}_{2}\text{He} + {}^{0}_{-1}e + 2\,{}^{0}_{+1}e + {}^{234}_{P}Y$$

Conservation of charge number gives

$$92 = 4 - 1 + 2 + P \Rightarrow P = 87$$

33. n^{th} half life $= \dfrac{A_0}{23}$ for S_1

n^{th} half-life $= \dfrac{A_0}{2^7}$ for S_2

$$\frac{A_1}{A_2} = \frac{\frac{A_0}{2^3}}{\frac{A_0}{2^7}} = 2^4 = 16$$

34. ${}^{230}_{90}\text{Th} \longrightarrow {}^{214}_{84}\text{Po} + n\,{}^{4}_{2}\text{He} + m\,{}^{0}_{-1}e$

$\Rightarrow \quad A = 230 = 214 + 4n$

and $\quad Z = 90 = 84 + 2n - m$

$\Rightarrow \quad 16 = 4n$ and $6 = 2n - m$

$\Rightarrow \quad n = 4 \Rightarrow 6 = 8 - m \quad [\because n = 4]$

$\Rightarrow \quad m = 2$

So, $\quad \dfrac{n}{m} = \dfrac{4}{2} = 2$

Hence, the ratio is 2.

35. Radioactive material N_A have decay constant, $\lambda_1 = 25\lambda$

Radioactive material N_B have decay constant, $\lambda_2 = 16\lambda$,

$N = N_0 e^{-\lambda t}$

Ratio of activities of A and B materials,

$$\Rightarrow \quad \frac{N_B}{N_A} = \frac{e^{-\lambda_2 t}}{e^{-\lambda_1 t}} = e^{-\lambda_2 t} \cdot e^{\lambda_1 t}$$

$$e^1 = e^{(\lambda_1 - \lambda_2)t}$$

$$\Rightarrow \quad (\lambda_1 - \lambda_2)t = 1$$

$$\Rightarrow \quad t = \frac{1}{\lambda_1 - \lambda_2} = \frac{1}{25\lambda - 16\lambda} = \frac{1}{9\lambda}$$

Compare with $\dfrac{1}{a\lambda}$, so $a = 9$

36. The ratio of charge on capacitor q to the activity of radioactive sample is fixed and can be calculated as

$$\frac{q}{N} = \frac{Q_0 e^{-t/RC}}{N_0 e^{-\lambda t}} = \frac{Q_0}{N_0} e^{t\left(\lambda - \frac{1}{RC}\right)}$$

So, $\lambda = \frac{1}{RC}$

$$R = \frac{1}{\lambda C} = \frac{T_m}{c} = \frac{30 \times 10^{-3}}{200 \times 10^{-6}} = 150\,\Omega \quad [T_m = \text{average life}]$$

Module 2.

Introductory Exercise

1. $4(_2He^4) = {_8O^{16}}$

Mass defect, $\Delta m = \{4(4.0026) - 15.9994\} = 0.011$ amu

$\therefore$ Energy released per oxygen nuclei

$= (0.011)(931.48)$ MeV $= 10.24$ MeV

$\therefore$ Correct answer is (c).

2. Heavy water is used as moderators in nuclear reactors to slow down the neutrons.

4. During fusion process two or more lighter nuclei combine to form a heavy nucleus.

Hence, the correct option is (c).

5. (a) $m(c)^2 = P \times t$

$$\therefore \quad m = \frac{P \times t}{c^2} = \frac{(10^9)(24)(3600)}{(3 \times 10^8)^2} = 9.6 \times 10^{-4} \text{ kg}$$

(b) Number of fissions required per second

$$= \frac{\text{Energy required per second}}{\text{Energy released in one fission}}$$

$$= \frac{10^9}{200 \times 10^6 \times 1.6 \times 10^{-19}} = 3.125 \times 10^{19}$$

6. Mass defect $\Sigma m_i - \Sigma m_f = \Delta m$

$= (238.050784) - (234.043593 + 4.002602)$

$= 4.589 \times 10^{-3}$ u

Energy released $= \Delta m \times 931.48$ MeV $= 4.27$ MeV

7. Theory based question.

8. $Q = (\Delta m$ in atomic mass unit$) \times 931.4$ MeV

$= (2 \times \text{mass of } {_1H^2} - \text{mass of } {_2He^4}) \times 931.4$ MeV

$= (2 \times 2.0141 - 4.0024) \times 931.4$ MeV

$Q \approx 24$ MeV

9. $2\,{_1H^2} \longrightarrow {_2He^4}$

Binding energy of two deuterons,

$E_1 = 2[2 \times 1.1] = 4.4$ MeV

Binding energy of helium nucleus,

$E_2 = 4(7.0) = 28.0$ MeV

$\therefore$ Energy released $\Delta E = E_2 - E_1$

$= (28 - 4.4)$ MeV $= 23.6$ MeV

Exercise

1. Total binding energy per nucleon is more important for stability.

3. $(1\,\text{amu})(c^2) = 931.48$ MeV

4. Nuclear density is independent of mass number, hence A is incorrect. The radius R of nucleus is related to its mass number A as $R = R_0 A^{1/3}$

Where, R_0 is constant.

5. Nuclear density is constant hence,

mass $\propto$ volume or $m \propto V$

6. Nuclear force,

$F_{PP} = F_{NN} = F_{PN}$

7. 3 atoms of $B \longrightarrow$ one atom of A

$\therefore \quad Q = E_A - 3E_B$

8. Intensity, $I = 1.4 \times 10^3 \frac{\text{watt}}{\text{m}^2}$

Area, $A = 4\pi R^2 = 4\pi(1.5 \times 10^{11})^2 = 2.83 \times 10^{23}$ m^2

$\therefore$ Power radiated $= IA = 3.96 \times 10^{26}$ watt

Total energy radiated in 1 day,

$E = (3.96 \times 10^{26} \times 86400)$ J $= 3.42 \times 10^{31}$ J

$\therefore$ Mass lost per day,

$$m = \frac{E}{c^2} = \frac{3.42 \times 10^{31}}{(3 \times 10^8)^2} = 3.8 \times 10^{14} \text{ kg}$$

9. During fusion, BE of daughter nucleus is always greater than the total energy of the parent nuclei so energy released

$= c - (a + b) = c - a - b$

10. $Q = (1.002 + 1.004 - 1.001 - 1.003)(931.5)$ MeV

$= 1.863$ MeV

11. The complete nuclear fission reaction of U^{235} is,

$${^1_0n} + {^{235}_{92}U} \rightarrow {^{144}_{56}Ba} + {^{89}_{36}Kr} + 3\,{^1_0n}$$

Here, atomic and mass number are balanced. Hence option (d) is correct.

12. Nuclear density $= \frac{34}{4\pi R_0^3}$

We know that, nuclear density is independent of mass number or size of nucleus. Thus,

$\therefore \quad \rho_{O_2} : \rho_{He} = 1 : 1$

13. Binding energy $= \Delta mc^2$

$= [Zm_p + (A - Z)m_n - m_{He}]c^2$

$= [Zm_p + (A - Z)m_n - m_{He}] \times 931.5$ MeV

$= (2 \times 1.0073 + (4 - 2) \times 1.0087 - 4.00154) \times 931.5$

Binding energy $= 28.4$ MeV

14. In the given nuclear reaction, mass defect,

$\Delta m = [m({^{238}_{92}A}) - m({^{234}_{90}B}) - m({^4_2D})]$

$= 238.05079 - 234.04363 - 4.00260$

$=0.004564$ amu

$\therefore$ Amount of energy released

$$\Delta Q = \Delta m \times 931.5 \text{ MeV}$$
$$= 0.004564 \times 931.5 = 4.25 \text{ MeV}$$

15. $A^{220} \longrightarrow B^{105} + C^{115}$

$$= (105 \times 6.4) + (115 \times 6.4) - 220 \times 5.6 = 176 \text{ MeV}$$

16. Mass defect,

$$\Delta m = (50m_p + 70m_n) - (m_{s_n})$$
$$= (50 \times 1.00783 + 70 \times 1.008) - (119.902199)$$
$$= 1.096$$

Binding energy $= (\Delta m)c^2 = (\Delta m) \times 931$

$$= 1020.56$$

$$\frac{\text{Binding energy}}{\text{Nucleon}} = \frac{1020.5631}{120} = 8.5 \text{ MeV}$$

17. Let heavy nucleus breaks into two light nuclei of mass m_1 and m_2 and move away with velocities v_1 and v_2 respectively.

According to question, $\frac{v_1}{v_2} = \frac{8}{27}$

$$P_{\text{initial}} = P_{\text{final}}$$
$$P_{\text{int}} = 0 = m_1v_1 - m_2v_2$$

(opposite velocity) $m_1v_1 = m_2v_2$

$$\Rightarrow \quad \frac{m_1}{m_2} = \frac{v_2}{v_1} = \frac{27}{8} = \frac{\rho \times \frac{4}{3}\pi R_1^3}{\rho \times \frac{4}{3}\pi R_2^3} \left(\because \text{Density } \rho = \frac{\text{Mass}}{\text{Volume}}\right)$$

$$\Rightarrow \quad \left(\frac{R_1}{R_2}\right) = \left(\frac{27}{8}\right)^{\frac{1}{3}} = \left(\frac{3}{2}\right)^{3 \times \frac{1}{3}}$$

$$\therefore \quad \frac{R_1}{R_2} = \frac{3}{2}$$

18. Theory based question.

19. Energy released = binding energy

$$= \Delta m \times 931.5 \text{ MeV}$$
$$= (8 \times 1.007825 + 8 \times 1.008665 - 15.9994915) \times 931.5$$
$$= 127.62 \text{ MeV}$$

20. (a) Number of nuclei in 1 kg of U^{235},

$$N = \left(\frac{1}{235}\right)(6.02 \times 10^{26})$$

$\therefore$ Total energy released

$$= (N \times 200) \text{ MeV}$$
$$= \left(\frac{1}{235}\right)(6.02 \times 10^{26})(200)(1.6 \times 10^{-13})$$
$$= 8.19 \times 10^{13} \text{ J}$$

(b) $$m = \frac{8.19 \times 10^{13}}{30 \times 10^3} \text{ g}$$
$$= 2.73 \times 10^9 \text{ g}$$
$$= 2.73 \times 10^6 \text{ kg}$$

21. From momentum of conservation,

$$p_1 = p_2$$
$$\therefore \quad \sqrt{2K_1m_1} = \sqrt{2K_2m_2}$$
$$\therefore \quad K_2 = \frac{K_1m_1}{m_2} = \frac{(6.802)(4)}{208}$$
$$= 0.1308 \text{ MeV}$$

22. Number of nuclei in 1 kg of uranium,

$$N = \left(\frac{1}{235}\right)(6.02 \times 10^{26})$$

Now, $\left(\frac{1}{235}\right)(6.02 \times 10^{26})(185 \times 1.6 \times 10^{-13})$

$$= (100 \times 10^6)t$$
$$\therefore \quad t = 7.58 \times 10^5 \text{ s}$$
$$= \frac{7.58 \times 10^5}{60 \times 60 \times 24} \text{ day}$$
$$= 8.78 \text{ days}$$

23. Nuclear sizes are in the ratio

$$r_1 : r_2 = 1 : 2^{1/3} \Rightarrow \frac{r_1}{r_2} = \frac{1}{2^{1/3}} \quad \text{...(i)}$$

Since, linear momentum of the system must be conserved, so

$$m_1v_1 - m_2v_2 = 0 \quad \text{[initial momentum = 0]}$$

$$\Rightarrow \quad \frac{m_1}{m_2} = \frac{v_2}{v_1} \Rightarrow \frac{\rho \cdot \frac{4}{3}\pi r_1^3}{\rho \cdot \frac{4}{3}\pi r_2^3} = \frac{v_2}{v_1}$$

$$\Rightarrow \quad \left(\frac{r_1}{r_2}\right)^3 = \frac{v_2}{v_1}$$

$$\Rightarrow \quad \left(\frac{1}{2^{1/3}}\right)^3 = \frac{v_2}{v_1} \quad \text{[From Eq. (i)]}$$

$$\Rightarrow \quad \frac{1}{2} = \frac{v_2}{v_1} \Rightarrow \frac{v_1}{v_2} = \frac{2}{1}$$

$$\Rightarrow \quad v_1 : v_2 = 2 : 1 = n : 1 \quad \text{[Given]}$$

$$\therefore \quad n = 2$$

24.

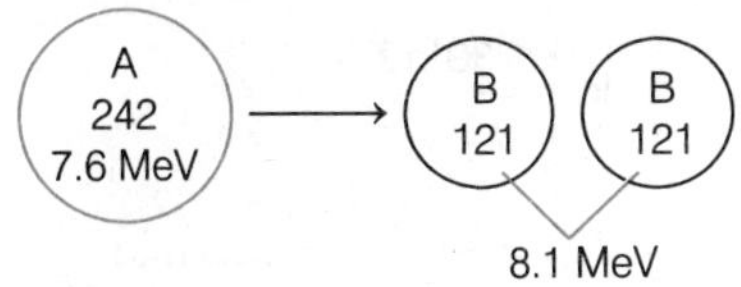

Total initial BE $= 242 \times 7.6$

$$= 1839.2 \text{ MeV}$$

Total final BE $= 121 \times 2 \times 8.1 = 1960.2$

Gain in BE $= 1960.2 - 1839.2 = 121$ MeV

25. For nucleus A,

Number of proton, $Z = 17$ and number of neutrons, $N = 17$

(Given $Z = N$) $A = Z + N = 17 + 17 = 34$

Binding energy per nucleon

$$=\frac{BE}{A}=1.2 \text{ MeV}$$

$$(BE)_A = 1.2\times A = 1.2\times 34 = 40.8 \text{ MeV}$$

For nucleus B,

Number of protons, $Z=12$,

Number of nucleons, $A=26$

$$\frac{BE}{A}=1.8 \text{ MeV}$$

$$(BE)_B = 1.8\times A = 1.8\times 26 = 46.8 \text{ MeV}$$

Therefore, difference in binding energy of B and A is

$$\Delta BE = BE_B - BE_A$$

$$\Rightarrow \quad \Delta BE = 46.8 - 40.8$$

$$\Rightarrow \quad \Delta BE = 6 \text{ MeV}$$

Unit Exercise (Cumulative)

Level 1

2. By emitting one α-particle, atomic number decreases by 2. By emitting two β-particles, atomic number increases by 2. Hence,

$$Z_A = Z_C$$

or A and C are isotopes.

3. $E=(0.5+0.5+0.78)\text{ MeV} = 1.78 \text{ MeV}$

4. ${}_7X^{15} + \alpha\text{-particle} \longrightarrow {}_9Y^{19} - {}_1H^1 \longrightarrow {}_8Z^{18}$

5. $\lambda = \lambda_1 + \lambda_2$

$$\therefore \quad \frac{\ln 2}{T}=\frac{\ln 2}{T_1}+\frac{\ln 2}{T_1} \qquad (T = \text{Half-life})$$

$$\text{or} \quad T=\frac{T_1T_2}{T_1+T_2}=20 \text{ y}$$

$\frac{1}{4}$th sample remains after 2 half-lives or 40 y.

6. Activity, $A = A_0e^{-\lambda t}$

$$A = A_0e^{-t\ln 2/T_{1/2}} \qquad \left(\because \lambda=\frac{\ln_2}{T_{1/2}}\right)$$

$$\Rightarrow \quad 500 = 700\, e^{-t\ln 2/T_{1/2}}$$

$$\Rightarrow \quad \ln\frac{7}{5}=\frac{30\ln 2}{T_{1/2}} \qquad (\because t = 30 \text{ min})$$

$$\Rightarrow \quad T_{1/2}=30\frac{\ln 2}{\ln 1.4}=61.8 \text{ min}$$

$$(\because \ln 2 = 0.693 \text{ and } \ln 1.4 = 0.336)$$

$$\Rightarrow \quad T_{1/2}\approx 62 \text{ min}$$

7. Q-value = Final binding energy

Initial binding energy

$$= E_2N_2 + E_3N_3 - E_1N_1$$

8. It means we are getting only 100 MeV of energy by the fission of one uranium nucleus.

Number of nuclei per second

$$=\frac{\text{Energy required per second}}{\text{Energy obtained by one fission}}=\frac{16\times 10^6}{100\times 1.6\times 10^{-13}}$$

$$=10^{18}$$

9. When the rate production = rate of disintegration, number of nuclei or maximum.

$$\therefore \quad \lambda N = A \quad \text{or} \quad \frac{\ln 2}{T}N = A$$

$$\text{or} \quad N=\frac{AT}{\ln 2}=\text{maximum}$$

10. Number of active nuclei remained after time t in a sample of radioactive substance is given by

$$N = N_0e^{-\lambda t}$$

where, N_0 = initial number of nuclei at $t=0$ and λ = decay constant.

Here, at $t=0$,

Number of nuclei in sample A and B are equal, i.e. initially

$$N_{0_A} = N_{0_B} = N_0$$

Also, $\quad \lambda_A = 5\lambda$ and $\lambda_B = \lambda$

So, after time t, number of active nuclei of A and B are

$$N_A = N_0e^{-5\lambda t} \text{ and } N_B = N_0e^{-\lambda t}$$

If $\frac{N_A}{N_B}=\frac{1}{e^2}$, then

$$\frac{N_A}{N_B}=\frac{N_0e^{-5\lambda t}}{N_0e^{-\lambda t}}=\frac{1}{e^2} \Rightarrow e^{(\lambda-5\lambda)t}=e^{-2}$$

Comparing the power of e on both sides, we get

$$4\lambda t = 2 \Rightarrow t=\frac{1}{2\lambda}$$

11. $A = 232 - 4 = 228$

From conservation of momentum,

$$p_\alpha = p_\gamma = \sqrt{2K_\alpha m_\alpha}=\sqrt{2K_\gamma m_\gamma}$$

$$\text{or} \quad \frac{K_\alpha}{K_\gamma}=\frac{m_\gamma}{m_\alpha}=\frac{228}{4}$$

$$\therefore \quad K_\alpha = \left(\frac{228}{228+4}\right)K_{\text{Total}} = \left(\frac{228}{232}\right)K_{\text{Total}}$$

12. Given, $\frac{N_B}{N_A}=0.3 \Rightarrow N_B = 0.3N_A$

Afte time t, $\quad N_0 = N_A + N_B = 1.3N_A$

Initial numbers of A,

After time t

$$N_A = N_0e^{-\lambda t} \quad \therefore \quad N_A = 1.3N_Ae^{-\lambda t}$$

$$\Rightarrow \quad \frac{1}{1.3}=e^{-\lambda t} \Rightarrow \log 1.3 = \lambda t$$

$$\Rightarrow \quad \log 1.3 = \frac{\log 2}{T}\cdot t$$

$$\therefore \quad t=\frac{T\cdot \log(1.3)}{\log 2}$$

13. Momentum of a photon,

$$p=\frac{h\nu}{c}$$

Hence, recoil energy $E=\frac{p^2}{2M}$

$$\therefore \quad E=\frac{\left(\frac{h\nu}{c}\right)^2}{2M} \quad \text{or} \quad E=\frac{h^2\nu^2}{2Mc^2}$$

14. In next half-life further 50% nuclei will remain undecayed. So, probability of survival upto next half time is $\frac{1}{2}$.

15. N be the number of nuclei at time t then,

$$\frac{dN}{dt}=100-\lambda N$$

$$\int_0^N \frac{dN}{(100-\lambda N)}=\int_0^t dt$$

$$=-\frac{1}{\lambda}[\log(100-\lambda N)]_0^N=t$$

$$\log(100-\lambda N)-\log 100=-\lambda t$$

$$e^{-\lambda t}=1-\frac{\lambda N}{100}$$

$$N=(1-e^{-\lambda t})\frac{100}{\lambda} \quad \text{... (i)}$$

as $N=50$, $\lambda=0.5$ /s. Put it in Eq. (i)

$$t=2\ln\left(\frac{4}{3}\right)\text{s}$$

16. During γ-decay, atomic number (Z) and mass number (A) do not change. So, the correct option is (c) because in all other options either Z, A or both is/are changing.

17. Number of nuclei decreases exponentially by equation

$$N=N_0 e^{-\lambda t}$$

and rate of decay $\left(-\frac{dN}{dt}\right)=\lambda N$

Therefore, decay process lasts upto $t=\infty$. Therefore, a given nucleus may decay at any time after $t=0$.

18. In beta decay, atomic number increases by 1 whereas the mass number remains the same.

Therefore, following equation can be possible

$$^{64}_{29}\text{Cu} \longrightarrow {}^{64}_{30}\text{Zn}+{}_{-1}e^0$$

Hence, Cu^{64} is radioactive, decaying to $^{64}_{30}\text{Zn}$ through β-decay.

19. During a nuclear fusion reaction, two light nuclei combine to give a heavier nucleus and possibly other product.

$$^2_1\text{H}+{}^2_1\text{H}\longrightarrow {}^3_2\text{He}+{}^1_0n$$

20. During fusion two or more light nuclei combine to form a stable nuclei and releases energy

$$4\,{}^1_1\text{H}\longrightarrow {}^4_2\text{He}^{2+}+2e^-+26\text{ MeV}$$

21. $^{232}_{90}\text{Th}$ is converting into $^{212}_{82}\text{Pb}$.

Change in mass number $(A)=20$

$\therefore$ Number of α-particle emitted $=\frac{20}{4}=5$

Due to 5 α-particles, Z will change by 10 units.

Since, given change is 8, therefore number of β-particles emitted is 2.

22. In case of ${}_1\text{H}^1$, mass number and atomic number are equal and in case of ${}_1\text{H}^2$, mass number is greater than its atomic number.

23. In fusion reaction, two or more light nuclei combines to form a comparatively heavier stable nucleus.

$$_6\text{C}^{12}+{}_1\text{H}^1\longrightarrow {}_7\text{N}^{13}+2\text{ MeV}$$

$$_7\text{N}^{14}+{}_1\text{H}^1\longrightarrow {}_8\text{O}^{15}+7.3\text{ MeV}$$

Hence, options (b) and (c) satisfies the condition.

24. In α-decays, mass number is decreased by 4 unit and atomic number is decreased by 2 units. In β^- decays, mass number remains unchanged but atomic number is increased by 1 unit. In β^+ decay, mass number remains unchanged but atomic number is decreased by 1 unit.

P - one α-particle and one β^- particle

Q - one α-particle and two β^- particle

Thus, using this, we find option (a) as correct one.

25. A–r

Nuclear fusion–Energy production in star via hydrogen conversion to helium.

b–(p, s)

Fission in a nuclear reactor –

Absorption of thermal neutrons by $^{235}_{92}\text{U}$

Heavy water is used to slow down fast moving neutron in reactor.

c–p, q, r, t

β-decay is observed in all above reactions.

d–p, q, r, t

γ-emission are high energy radiation released from nuclear reaction.

All above reaction produce γ-rays.

26. (P) In α-decay mass number decreases by 4 and atomic number decreases by 2.

$$^{238}_{92}\text{U}\longrightarrow {}^{234}_{90}\text{Th}+{}^4_2\text{He}$$

(Q) In β^+ decay, mass number remain same atomic number decreases by 1.

$$^{15}_{8}\text{O}\longrightarrow {}^{15}_{7}\text{N}+\beta^+$$

(R) Fission–When a heavy nuclei breaks into two or more stable nuclei.

$$^{239}_{94}\text{Pu}\longrightarrow {}^{140}_{57}\text{La}+\cdots\cdots$$

(S) Proton emission–Both mass number and atomic number decreases by 1.

$$^{185}_{83}\text{Bi}\longrightarrow {}^{184}_{82}\text{Pb}+\text{P}$$

27. a-(p, q)

Nuclear fusion When two light nuclei combine to form heavy stable nucleus.

Convert matter into energy. Generally possible with low atomic number.

b-(p, r)

Nuclear fission When a heavy nucleus break into two or more light nuclei.

Convert matter into energy. Generally, possible with higher atomic number.

c-(p, s)

β-decay Mass number remain same atomic number increase by 1.

(p, s) satisfy the conditions.

d-(p, q, r)

Exothermic nuclear reaction are those in which heat is a byproduct.

Option p, q, r all show exothermic nuclear reaction.

28. Speed of neutrons $=\sqrt{\dfrac{2K}{m}}$ $\qquad\left(\text{From } K=\dfrac{1}{2}mv^2\right)$

or $\quad v=\sqrt{\dfrac{2\times 0.0327\times 1.6\times 10^{-19}}{1.675\times 10^{-27}}}$ $\qquad [K = \text{eV}]$

$$\approx 2.5\times 10^3 \text{ m/s}$$

Time taken by the neutrons to travel a distance of 10 m :

$$t=\frac{d}{v}=\frac{10}{2.5\times 10^3}=4.0\times 10^{-3}\text{ s}$$

Number of neutrons decayed after time t

$$N=N_0(1-e^{-\lambda t})$$

$t_{1/2}$ of neutron $=700$ s

∴ Fraction of neutrons that will decay in this time interval

$$=\frac{N}{N_0}=(1-e^{-\lambda t})=1-e^{-\frac{\ln(2)}{700}\times 4.0\times 10^{-3}}$$

$$=3.96\times 10^{-6}$$

29. Initial number of nuclei in 1.0 μg of Na^{24},

$$N_0=\frac{1\times 10^{-6}}{24}\times 6.02\times 10^{23}=2.5\times 10^{16}\text{ Nuclei}$$

Therefore number of β-particles emitted during the time interval from 0 to t :

= number of nuclei decayed

$$=N_0(1-e^{-\lambda t}) \quad\text{or}\quad N_0-N_0\left(\frac{1}{2}\right)^n$$

Here, $t=1$ h

$$\lambda=\frac{\ln 2}{t_{1/2}}=\frac{0.693}{15}\text{h}^{-1}$$

and $\quad n=$ number of half-lives

$$=\frac{1}{15}$$

Substituting the values, we can get the answer.

30. Number of β-particles emitted or registered by the counter

= number of nuclei decayed

$$=N_0(1-e^{-\lambda t})$$

Now, as per given condition,

$$N_1=N_0(1-e^{-\lambda t_1}) \qquad \text{...(i)}$$

and $\quad 2.66N_1=N_0(1-e^{-3\lambda t_1}) \qquad$ ...(ii)

Dividing equation (ii) by equation (i) and then substituting the value of t_1 we can find value of λ and then the mean life is,

$$\tau=\frac{1}{\lambda}$$

31. $m_1=$ mass of Po nucleus

$m_2=$ mass of daughter nucleus Pb^{206}

$m_3=$ mass of α-particle He^4

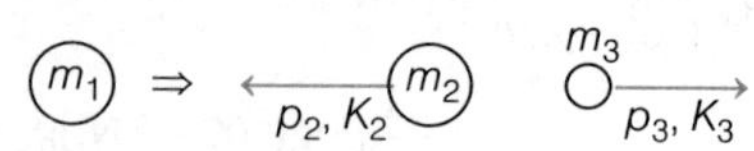

From linear momentum conservation, we have

$$\Sigma p_i=\Sigma p_f$$

⇒ $\quad 0=p_3-p_2$

or $\quad p_2=p_3$

∴ $\quad \sqrt{2K_2m_2}=\sqrt{2K_3m_3}$ or $\dfrac{K_2}{K_3}=\dfrac{m_3}{m_2}$

∴ $\quad K_2=\dfrac{m_3}{m_2}(K_3)=\dfrac{4}{206}(5.77)$

$$\approx 0.112\text{ MeV}$$

From kinetic energy we can also find the velocity.

Fraction of energy retained by daughter nucleus

$$=\frac{K_2}{K_2+K_3}=\frac{0.112}{5.77+0.112}=0.020$$

32. (a) (i) Number of nuclei in 1 kg of U^{235},

$$N=\frac{1000}{235}\times 6.02\times 10^{23}$$

∴ Energy released by 1 kg of U^{235},

$$E=N\times 200\text{ MeV}$$

$$=8.2\times 10^{10}\text{ kJ}$$

$$1\text{ MeV}=1.6\times 10^{-13}\text{ J}$$

$$=1.6\times 10^{-16}\text{ kJ}$$

Substituting the proper values, we get the answer.

(ii) Required mass of coal,

$$m=\frac{8.2\times 10^{10}\text{ kJ}}{30\text{ kJ/g}}$$

$$=2.7\times 10^9\text{ g}$$

$$m=2.7\times 10^6\text{ kg}$$

(b) Let mass of U^{235} required is m gm. Then number of nuclei,

$$N = \frac{m}{235} \times 6.02 \times 10^{23} \quad \text{...(i)}$$

∴ Energy released,

$$E_1 = N \times 200 \text{ MeV}$$
$$= N \times 200 \times 1.6 \times 10^{-16} \text{ kJ} \quad \text{...(ii)}$$

Energy obtained from 30 kt trotyl,

$$E_2 = (30 \times 10^3 \times 1000 \times 10^3)(4.1) \text{ kJ} \quad \text{...(iii)}$$

Equating E_1 and E_2 with value of N from equation (i), we get

$$m = 1.49 \times 10^3 \text{ g} \quad \text{or} \quad m \approx 1.5 \text{ kg}$$

33. (a) $H^2 + H^2 \longrightarrow He^4$

Energy released in the formation of 1 nucleus of He^4,

$$E_1 = (2m_{H^2} - m_{He^4})\, 931.48 \text{ MeV}$$

Here masses are represented in amu and

$$1 \text{ MeV} = 1.6 \times 10^{-16} \text{ kJ}$$

Number of nuclei in 1 g of He^4,

$$N = \frac{1}{4} \times 6.02 \times 10^{23}$$

∴Energy released during the formation of 1g of He^4,

$$E_2 = NE_1$$

Substituting the proper values, we get

$$E_2 = 5.74 \times 10^8 \text{ kJ}$$

(b) Mass of coal required,

$$m = \frac{5.74 \times 10^8 \text{ kJ}}{30 \text{ kJ/g}} = 1.9 \times 10^7 \text{ g}$$

$$m \approx 2 \times 10^4 \text{ kg}$$

34. Molar mass of given nucleus $(^{240}X) = 240$ g

So, in 240 g number of nucleus present

$$= N_A = 6 \times 10^{23} \quad \text{(as given in question)}$$

∴ In 120 g, number of nucleus present

$$= N_A/2 = 3 \times 10^{23}$$

1 nucleus gives 200 MeV of energy in fission.

So, total energy obtained by fission of 120 g of ^{240}X will be

$$3 \times 10^{23} \times 200 = 6 \times 10^{25} \approx 6 \times 10^{25} \text{ MeV}$$

35. Binding energy per nucleon for ^2_1X, $BE_1 = 1.1$ MeV and for ^4_2Y, $BE_2 = 7.6$ MeV

The given nuclear reaction,

$$^2_1X + ^2_1X = ^4_2Y$$

Total no. of nucleons in the reactant, $n_1 = 2 + 2 = 4$

Total no. of nucleons in the product, $n_2 = 4$

∴ The total energy released = Change in binding energy

$$= n_2 \times BE_2 - n_1 \times BE_1$$
$$= 4 \times 7.6 - 4 \times 1.1$$
$$= 30.4 - 4.4 = 26 \text{ MeV}$$

36. Given, $^{16}_7N + ^4_2He \longrightarrow ^1_1H + ^{19}_8O$

$$E = \Delta mc^2 \,(m_N + m_{He} - m_H - m_O) \times c^2$$
$$= (16.006 + 4.003 - 1.008 - 19.003) \times 930$$
$$= -1.86 \text{ MeV}$$

or, 1.86 MeV energy is absorbed in the process.

For minimum kinetic energy needed, loss in kinetic energy should be maximum.

or, the daughter nuclei should move with same velocity.

Thus, $\Sigma p_i = \Sigma p_f$

or $$4v - (1 + 19)v' \text{ or } v' = \frac{1}{5}v$$

Loss in kinetic energy,

$$\frac{1}{2}(4)v^2 - \frac{1}{2}(1 + 19)\,v'^2 = 1.86 \text{ MeV} \quad \text{...(i)}$$

Here, $\frac{1}{2}(4)(v^2)$ = minimum kinetic energy of α-particle $= K$ (say)

Substituting $v' = \frac{v}{5}$ in Eq. (i), we get

$$\frac{4}{5}(K) = 1.86 \text{ MeV}$$

∴ $$K = 2.325 \text{ MeV} \Rightarrow n = 2.325$$

37. Given, Mass of neutron $m_n = 1.00866$ u

Mass of proton, $m_p = 1.00726$ u

Mass of aluminium nucleus, $m_{Al} = 27.18846$ u

As we know that,

Binding energy (BE) $= \Delta mc^2$

Mass defect $(\Delta m) = Zm_p + (A - Z)m_n - m$

where, Z is atomic number or number of proton and $A - Z$ is number of neutron.

∴ $$\Delta m = 13 \times 1.00726 + 14 \times 1.00866 - 27.18846$$
$$= 13.09438 + 14.12124 - 27.18846$$
$$= 0.02716 \text{ J}$$

Now, $\quad BE = 27.16 \times 10^{-3}$ J

Level 2

38. $\frac{N_0}{16} = N_0\left(\frac{1}{2}\right)^n \Rightarrow n = 4$

So, $3t$ times is equivalent to four half-lives. Hence, one half-life is equal to $\frac{3t}{4}$.

The given time $\frac{11}{2}t - t = \frac{9}{2}t$ is equivalent to 6 half-lives.

∴ $$N = N_0\left(\frac{1}{2}\right)^6 = \frac{N_0}{64}$$

39. N_B are maximum when

$$\lambda_B N_B = \lambda_A N_A$$

∴ $$N_B = \frac{\lambda_A}{\lambda_B} \cdot N_A$$

The given time is equivalent to two half-lives of A.

Hence, $N_A = \frac{N_0}{4}$

$\therefore \quad N_B = \frac{\lambda_A}{\lambda_B}\left(\frac{N_0}{4}\right)$

40. $R_0 = 15 \times 200 = 3000$ decay/min from 200 g carbon.

Using $R = R_0\left(\frac{1}{2}\right)^n$

$\therefore \quad 375 = 3000\left(\frac{1}{2}\right)^n$

$\therefore \quad n =$ number of half-lives $= 3$

$\therefore \quad t = 5730 \times 3 = 17190$ y

41. $A_P = A_0 e^{-\lambda t_1}$

$$A_Q = A_0 e^{-\lambda t_2}$$

$$\lambda t_1 = \ln(A_0/A_P)$$

$$\therefore \quad t_1 = \frac{1}{\lambda}\ln(A_0/A_P) = T\ln(A_0/A_P)$$

Similarly, $t_2 = T\ln(A_0/A_Q)$

$$\therefore \quad t_1 - t_2 = T\ln\left(\frac{A_Q}{A_P}\right)$$

42. $R_1 = R_2$

$$R_{01}e^{-\lambda_1 t} = R_{02}e^{-\lambda t}$$

$$\therefore \quad \lambda_1 N_0 e^{-\lambda_1 t} = \lambda_2 N_0 e^{-\lambda_2 t} \quad \text{...(i)}$$

$$\lambda_1 = \frac{\ln 2}{t_1} = \frac{0.693}{t_1}$$

$$\lambda_2 = \frac{0.693}{t_2}$$

Substituting these values in Eq. (i), we can get the t.

43. Activity $A \propto$ Number of atoms

$$A_1 = A_0 e^{-\lambda t_1}$$

$$\therefore \quad t_1 = \frac{1}{\lambda}\ln\left(\frac{A_0}{A_1}\right) = \frac{T}{\ln 2}\ln\frac{A_0}{A_1}$$

$$A_2 = 2A_0 e^{-\lambda t_2}$$

$$t_2 = \frac{T}{\ln 2}\ln\left(\frac{2A_0}{A_2}\right)$$

$$t_1 - t_2 = \frac{T}{\ln 2}\left(\frac{A_0}{A_1} \times \frac{A_2}{2A_0}\right) = \frac{T}{\ln 2}\ln\left(\frac{A_2}{2A_1}\right)$$

44. $A_1 = A_0 e^{-\lambda t_1} = A_0\, e^{-\frac{t_1}{T}}$

$$A_2 = A_0 e^{-\frac{t_2}{T}}$$

$$\therefore \quad \frac{A_2}{A_1} = e^{\left(\frac{t_1 - t_2}{T}\right)}$$

$$A_2 = A_1 e^{\left(\frac{t_1 - t_2}{T}\right)}$$

45. $N_A e^{-\lambda_A t} = N_B e^{-\lambda_B t}$

$$\therefore \quad e^{(\lambda_B - \lambda_A)t} = \frac{N_B}{N_A}$$

$$\therefore \quad t = \frac{1}{\lambda_B - \lambda_A}\ln\left(\frac{N_B}{N_A}\right)$$

46. (a) Activity $-\frac{dN}{dt} = \lambda N_0$

(b) Decay probability $= \frac{N_0(1 - e^{-\lambda t})}{N_0} = 1 - e^{-\lambda t}$

This probability in unit time will be $1 - e^{-\lambda}$.

(c) $N = N_0 e^{-\lambda t}$

At $t = \frac{1}{\lambda}$, $N = \frac{N_0}{e}$

(d) $t_{\frac{1}{2}} = \frac{\ln 2}{\lambda}$

47. $\because \left(-\frac{dN}{dt}\right) = \lambda N$ ...(i)

$$\lambda = \frac{0.693}{T_{1/2}} = \frac{0.693}{1620 \times 365 \times 24 \times 60 \times 60} \quad \text{...(ii)}$$

and $N = \frac{6.023 \times 10^{23}}{226}$ ...(iii)

$$\therefore \quad \left(-\frac{dN}{dt}\right) = \frac{0.693 \times 6.023 \times 10^{23}}{1620 \times 365 \times 24 \times 60 \times 60 \times 226}$$

$$= 3.61 \times 10^{10}$$

48. ${}^{236}_{92}U \rightarrow {}^{140}_{54}Xe + {}^{94}_{38}Sr + x + y$

By conservation of charge and mass number.

$$x = y = n$$

$$x = {}^{1}_{0}n = y$$

BE per nucleon of U = 7.5 MeV

BE per nucleon of Xe, Sr = 8.5 MeV

Q = Net KE gain in the process.

$$= K_{Xe} + K_{Sr} + K_x + K_y \quad [K_x = K_y = 2 \text{ MeV}]$$

$$= K_{Xe} + K_{Sr} + 4 = Q \quad \text{...(i)}$$

As number of nucleon is conserved,

Q = Difference of BE of nuclei

$$140 \times 8.5 + 94 \times 8.5 - 236 \times 7.5 = 219 \text{ MeV} \quad \text{...(ii)}$$

From Eqs. (i) and (ii),

$$K_{Xe} + K_{Sr} = 219 - 4 = 215 \text{ MeV}$$

Xe and Sr have same momentum.

Hence lighter body has greater kinetic energy.

$$K_{Sr} = 129 \text{ MeV and } K_{Xe} = 86 \text{ MeV}$$

49. Rest mass of parent nucleus should be greater than the rest mass of daughter nuclei. Therefore, option (a) will be correct.

50. $y = \lambda x = \frac{\ln 2}{T} \cdot x$

$$\frac{x}{y} = \frac{1}{\lambda} = \text{constant}$$

$$\frac{x}{y} = \frac{T}{\ln 2} \text{ or } \frac{x}{y} > T \qquad (\text{as } \ln 2 = 0.693)$$

Further, $xy = x(\lambda x) = \lambda x^2$

After one half-life, x remains half.

Hence, x^2 remains $\frac{1}{4}$th.

51. Theory based question.

52. By the emission of an α-particle, atomic number decreases by 2 and by the emission of two particles atomic number increases by 2. Hence, net atomic number remains unchanged.

53. At $t = 4T$

Number of half-lives of first $n_1 = 4$ and number of half-lives of second $n_2 = 2$

$$\frac{N_1}{N_2} = x = \frac{N_0 (1/2)^4}{N_0 (1/2)^2} = \frac{1}{4}$$

$$y = \frac{R_1}{R_2} = \frac{\lambda_1 N_0 (1/2)^4}{\lambda_2 N_0 (1/2)^2}$$

$$= \frac{\lambda_1}{4\lambda_2} = \frac{T_2}{4T_1} = \frac{2T}{4T} = \frac{1}{2}$$

55. $R = R_0 A^{1/3}$ or $R \propto A^{1/3}$

56. To release energy in a nuclear process, binding energy per nucleon should increase.

57. Due to mass defect (which is finally responsible for the binding energy of the nucleus), mass of a nucleus is always less than the sum of masses of its constituent particles.

$^{20}_{10}Ne$ is made up of 10 protons plus 10 neutrons.

Therefore, mass of $^{20}_{10}Ne$ nucleus, $M_1 < 10(m_p + m_n)$

Up to iron, binding energy per nucleon normally increases with increase in mass number. For calcium

$$\frac{\text{BE}}{\text{nucleon}} = \frac{[20(m_p + m_n) - M_2]c^2}{40} > \frac{10[m_P + m_N - M_1]c^2}{20}$$

Solving this equation, we get

$$M_1 > \frac{M_2}{2} \text{ or } 2M_1 > M_2 \text{ or } M_2 < 2M_1$$

58. Energy released $= (\Delta m)(931.48)$ MeV

$$= [2 \times 2.01102 - 3.0160 - 1.007825] \times 931.5$$

$$= 4.03 \text{ MeV} \approx 4 \text{ MeV}$$

59. Let N number of fusion reactions are required, then

$$N \times 4 \times 1.6 \times 10^{-13} = 10^3 \times 3600$$

$$N = 5.625 \times 10^{18}$$

60. In one fusion reaction two ^2_1H nuclei are used. Hence, total number of ^2_1H nuclei are $2N$.

or 1.125×10^{19} Mass in kg $= \left(\frac{1.125 \times 10^{19}}{6.02 \times 10^{26}}\right)(2)$ kg

$$= 3.7 \times 10^{-8} \text{kg}$$

61. After decay, the daughter nuclei will be more stable, hence binding energy per nucleon will be more than that of their parent nucleus.

62. By conservation of momentum,

$$0 = \frac{M}{2}v_1 - \frac{M}{2}v_2$$

$$v_1 = v_2 \qquad \text{...(i)}$$

$$\Rightarrow \quad \Delta mc^2 = \frac{1}{2}\cdot\frac{M}{2}v_1^2 + \frac{1}{2}\cdot\frac{M}{2}\cdot v_2^2 \qquad \text{...(ii)}$$

$$\Rightarrow \quad \Delta mc^2 = \frac{M}{2}v_1^2$$

$$\Rightarrow \quad \frac{2\Delta mc^2}{M} = v_1^2$$

$$\Rightarrow \quad v_1 = c\sqrt{\frac{2\Delta m}{M}}$$

63. $\left(-\frac{dN}{dt}\right) = \lambda N$

$$\therefore \quad y = \lambda x \text{ or } \lambda = \frac{y}{x}$$

$$t_{1/2} = \frac{\ln 2}{\lambda} = (\ln 2)(x/y)$$

$$R = R_0 e^{-\lambda t}$$

$$= ye^{-\lambda(1/\lambda)} = y/e$$

$$R = \frac{y}{e} = \lambda N$$

$$\therefore \quad N = \frac{y}{e\lambda} = \frac{y}{e(y/x)} = \frac{x}{e}$$

64. Energy is released when daughter nuclei lie towards peak of this graph, so that binding energy per nucleon or total binding energy in the nuclear process increases.

65. A will continuously decrease, but C will increase. $(A + B)$ will continuously decrease as C is formed only from A and B.

$$(C + B) = \text{Total} - A$$

A is continuously decreasing. Hence, $(C + B)$ will continuously increase.

66. (a) E is of the order of kT, where k = Boltzmann constant and $T \approx 300$ K

(c) λ to X-rays is of the order of 1Å – 100 Å

$$E = \left[\frac{12375}{\lambda (\text{in Å})}\right] \text{in eV} = \left[\frac{12.375}{\lambda}\right] \text{in keV}$$

where, λ is in Å.

(d) λ is of the order of 4000 Å – 7000 Å

Now, $E \text{ (in eV)} = \frac{12375}{\lambda (\text{in Å})}$

67. $N=\dfrac{R}{\lambda}=\dfrac{10^9}{\dfrac{0.693}{14.3\times 3600}}=7.43\times 10^{13}$

Now, $\dfrac{dN}{dt}=q-\lambda N$ or $\displaystyle\int_0^N \frac{dN}{q-\lambda N}=\int_0^t dt$

$\therefore \quad N=\dfrac{q}{\lambda}(1-e^{-\lambda t})$

Substituting the values,

$$7.43\times 10^{13}=\frac{2\times 10^9}{\dfrac{0.693}{14.3\times 3600}}[1-e^{-(0.693/14.3\times 3600)t}]$$

Solving this equation we get,

$$t=14.3\,\text{h} \qquad \textbf{Ans.}$$

68. (a)

	A	B	C
At $t=0$	N_0	0	0
At t	N_1	N_2	N_3

Here, $N_1=N_0e^{-\lambda t}$ ...(i)

$$\frac{dN_2}{dt}=\lambda(N_1-N_2)$$

or $\dfrac{dN_2}{dt}=\lambda N_0e^{-\lambda t}-\lambda N_2$

or $dN_2+\lambda N_2dt=\lambda N_0e^{-\lambda t}$

$\therefore \quad e^{\lambda t}dN_2+\lambda N_2e^{\lambda t}dt=\lambda N_0dt$

or $d(N_2e^{\lambda t})=\lambda N_0dt$

$\therefore \quad N_2e^{\lambda t}=\lambda N_0t+C$

At $t=0$, $N_2=0$,

$\therefore \quad C=0$

$\therefore \quad N_2=\lambda N_0(te^{-\lambda t})$

(b) Activity of B is

$$R_2=\lambda N_2=\lambda^2N_0(te^{-\lambda t})$$

For maximum activity, $\dfrac{dR_2}{dt}=0$

$\therefore \quad t=\dfrac{1}{\lambda}$ **Ans.**

$\therefore \quad R_{max}=\dfrac{\lambda N_0}{e}$ **Ans.**

69. (a) Let R_{A_0} and R_{B_0} be the initial activities of A and Then,

$$R_{A_0}+R_{B_0}=10^{10}\text{ dps} \qquad \text{...(i)}$$

Activity of A after time $t=20$ days (two half-lives of A) is

$$R_A=\left(\frac{1}{2}\right)^2R_{A_0}=0.25\,R_{A_0}$$

Similarly, activity of B after $t=20$ days (four half-lives of B) is

$$R_B=\left(\frac{1}{2}\right)^4R_{B_0}=0.0625\,R_{B_0}$$

Now, it is given that $R_A+R_B=20\%$ of 10^{10}

or $0.25R_{A_0}+0.0625R_{B_0}=0.2\times 10^{10}$ dps ...(ii)

Solving Eqs. (i) and (ii), we get

$$R_{A_0}=0.73\times 10^{10}\text{ dps}$$

and $R_{B_0}=0.27\times 10^{10}$ dps

(b) $\dfrac{R_{A_0}}{R_{B_0}}=\dfrac{\lambda_AN_{A_0}}{\lambda_BN_{B_0}}=\dfrac{(t_{1/2})_B}{(t_{1/2})_A}\cdot\dfrac{N_{A_0}}{N_{B_0}}$

$\therefore \quad \dfrac{N_{A_0}}{N_{B_0}}=\left(\dfrac{R_{A_0}}{R_{B_0}}\right)\dfrac{(t_{1/2})_A}{(t_{1/2})_B}=\left(\dfrac{0.73}{0.27}\right)\left(\dfrac{10}{5}\right)$

$=5.4$

70. Let N be the number of radio nuclei at any time t. Then, net rate of formation of nuclei at time t is

$$\frac{dN}{dt}=\alpha-\lambda N$$

or $\displaystyle\int_0^N\frac{dN}{\alpha-\lambda N}=\int_0^t dt$

or $N=\dfrac{\alpha}{\lambda}(1-e^{-\lambda t})$

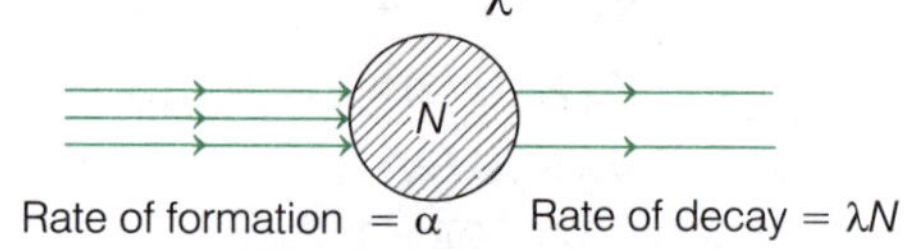

Number of nuclei formed in time $t=\alpha t$

and number of nuclei left after time

$$t=\frac{\alpha}{\lambda}(1-e^{-\lambda t})$$

Therefore, number of nuclei disintegrated in time

$$t=\alpha t-\frac{\alpha}{\lambda}(1-e^{-\lambda t})$$

$\therefore$ Energy released till time,

$$t=E_0\left[\alpha t-\frac{\alpha}{\lambda}(1-e^{-\lambda t})\right]$$

But only 20% of it is used in raising the temperature of water.

So, $0.2E_0\left[\alpha t-\dfrac{\alpha}{\lambda}(1-e^{-\lambda t})\right]=Q$

where, $Q=ms\Delta\theta$

$\therefore \Delta\theta=$ increase in temperature of water $=\dfrac{Q}{ms}$

$$\therefore \Delta\theta=\frac{0.2\,E_0\left[at-\dfrac{a}{\lambda}(1-e^{-\lambda t})\right]}{ms}$$

71. We have for B $\dfrac{dN_B}{dt}=P-\lambda_2N_B$

$\Rightarrow \displaystyle\int_0^{N_B}\frac{dN_B}{P-\lambda_2N_B}=\int_0^t dt$

$\Rightarrow \ln\left(\dfrac{P-\lambda_2N_B}{P}\right)=-\lambda_2t$

$\Rightarrow N_B=\dfrac{P(1-e^{-\lambda_2t})}{\lambda_2}$

The number of nuclei of A after time t is

$$N_A = N_0 e^{-\lambda_1 t}$$

Thus, $$\frac{dN_c}{dt} = \lambda_1 N_A + \lambda_2 N_B$$

$$\Rightarrow \quad \frac{dN_c}{dt} = \lambda_1 N_0 e^{-\lambda_1 t} + P(1 - e^{-\lambda_2 t})$$

$$\Rightarrow \quad N_c = N_0(1 - e^{-\lambda_1 t}) + P\left(t + \frac{e^{-\lambda_2 t} - 1}{\lambda_2}\right)$$

72. $^{210}_{84}\text{Po} \longrightarrow {}^{206}_{82}\text{Pb} + {}^{4}_{2}\text{He}$

$$\Delta m = 0.00564 \text{ amu}$$

Energy liberated per reaction $= (\Delta m) 931$ MeV

$$= 8.4 \times 10^{-13} \text{ J}$$

Electrical energy produced $= 8.4 \times 10^{-14}$ J

Let m g of ^{210}Po is required to produce the desired energy.

$$N = \frac{m}{210} \times 6 \times 10^{23}$$

$$\lambda = \frac{0.693}{t_{1/2}} = 0.005 \text{ per day}$$

$$\left(-\frac{dN}{dt}\right) = \lambda N = \frac{(0.005)(6 \times 10^{23} \text{ m})}{210} \text{ per day}$$

$\therefore$ Electrical energy produced per day

$$= \frac{(0.005)(6 \times 10^{23} \text{ m})}{210} \times 8.4 \times 10^{-14} \text{ J}$$

This is equal to 1.2×10^7 J (given)

$\therefore$ $m = 10$ g **Ans.**

Activity at the end of 693 days is

$$R = \frac{0.005 \times 6 \times 10^{23} \times 10}{210} = \frac{10^{21}}{7} \text{ per day}$$

$$= R_0 \left(\frac{1}{2}\right)^n$$

Here, n = number of half-lives $= \frac{693}{138.6} = 5$

$$\therefore \quad R_0 = R(2)^5 = 32 \times \frac{10^{21}}{7}$$

$$= 4.57 \times 10^{21} \text{ per day}$$ **Ans.**

73. (i) At $t = 0$, probabilities of getting α and β particles are same. This implies that initial activity of both is equal. Say it is R_0.

Activity after $t = 1620$ s,

$$R_1 = R_0 \left(\frac{1}{2}\right)^{1620/405} = \frac{R_0}{16}$$

and $$R_2 = R_0 \left(\frac{1}{2}\right)^{1620/1620} = \frac{R_0}{2}$$

Total activity, $R = R_1 + R_2 = \frac{9}{16} R_0$

Probability of getting α-particles,

$$= \frac{R_1}{R} = \frac{1}{9}$$

and probability of getting β-particles

$$= \frac{R_2}{R} = \frac{8}{9}$$ **Ans.**

(ii) $R_{01} = R_{02}$

$$\therefore \quad \frac{N_{01}}{T_1} = \frac{N_{02}}{T_2}$$

$$\therefore \quad \frac{N_{01}}{N_{02}} = \frac{1}{4}$$

Let N_0 be the total number of nuclei at $t = 0$.

Then, $$N_{01} = \frac{N_0}{5}$$

and $$N_{02} = \frac{4N_0}{5}$$

Given that $$N_1 + N_2 = \frac{N_0}{2}$$

or $$\frac{N_0}{5}\left(\frac{1}{2}\right)^{t/405} + \frac{4N_0}{5}\left(\frac{1}{2}\right)^{t/1620} = \frac{N_0}{2}$$

Let $$\left(\frac{1}{2}\right)^{t/1620} = x$$

Then, above equation becomes

$$x^4 + 4x - 2.5 = 0$$

$$\therefore \quad x = 0.594$$

or $$\left(\frac{1}{2}\right)^{t/1620} = 0.594$$

Solving, it we get $t = 1215$ s **Ans.**

74. $N = \frac{10^{-3}}{210} \times 6.02 \times 10^{23} = 2.87 \times 10^{18}$

During one mean life period 63.8% nuclei are decayed. Hence, energy released

$$E = 0.638 \times 2.87 \times 10^{18} \times 5.3 \times 1.6 \times 10^{-13} \text{ J}$$

$$= 1.55 \times 10^6 \text{ J}$$ **Ans.**

75. $R_0 = \lambda N = \frac{0.693}{14.3 \times 3600 \times 24} \times 6.02 \times 10^{23}$ per sec

$$= 3.37 \times 10^{17} \text{ per sec}$$

After 70 hours activity,

$$R = R_0 e^{-\lambda t} = (3.37 \times 10^{17}) e^{-(0.693/14.3 \times 24)(70)}$$

$$= 2.92 \times 10^{17} \text{ per sec}$$

In fruits activity was observed 1 μCi or 3.7×10^4 per sec. Therefore, percentage of activity transmitted from root to the fruit.

$$= \frac{3.7 \times 10^4}{2.92 \times 10^{17}} \times 100 = 1.26 \times 10^{-11} \%$$ **Ans.**

76. Let N_0 be the initial number of nuclei of ^{238}U.

After time t, $N_U = N_0 \left(\frac{1}{2}\right)^n$

Here n = number of half-lives

$$N = \frac{t}{t_{1/2}} = \frac{1.5 \times 10^9}{4.5 \times 10^9} = \frac{1}{3}$$

$$N_U = N_0 \left(\frac{1}{2}\right)^{\frac{1}{3}} \text{ and } N_{Pb} = N_0 - N_U$$

$$= N_0 \left[1 - \left(\frac{1}{2}\right)^{1/3}\right]$$

$$\therefore \quad \frac{N_U}{N_{Pb}} = \frac{\left(\frac{1}{2}\right)^{1/3}}{1 - \left(\frac{1}{2}\right)^{3}} = 3.861$$

77. (a) Let at time t, number of radioactive nuclei are N.

Net rate of formation of nuclei of A

$$\frac{dN}{dt} = \alpha - \lambda N \text{ or } \frac{dN}{\alpha - \lambda N} = dt$$

or $$\int_{N_0}^{N} \frac{dN}{\alpha - \lambda N} = \int_0^t dt$$

Solving this equation, we get

$$N = \frac{1}{\lambda}[\alpha - (\alpha - \lambda N_0)e^{-\lambda t}] \quad \text{...(i)}$$

(b)(i) Substituting $\alpha = 2\lambda N_0$ and $t = t_{1/2} = \frac{\ln(2)}{\lambda}$ in Eq. (i) we get,

$$N = \frac{3}{2} N_0$$

(ii) Substituting $\alpha = 2\lambda N_0$ and $t \to \infty$ in Eq. (i), we get

$$N = \frac{\alpha}{\lambda} = 2N_0 \text{ or } N = 2N_0$$

78. (a) In 10 s, number of nuclei has been reduced to half (25% to 12.5%).

Therefore, its half-life is $t_{1/2} = 10$ s

Relation between half-life and mean life is

$$t_{mean} = \frac{t_{1/2}}{\ln(2)} = \frac{10}{0.693} \text{ s}$$

$$t_{mean} = 14.43 \text{ s}$$

(b) From initial 100% to reduction till 6.25%, it takes four half lives.

$$100\% \xrightarrow{t_{1/2}} 50\% \xrightarrow{t_{1/2}} 25\% \xrightarrow{t_{1/2}} 12.5\% \xrightarrow{t_{1/2}} 6.25\%$$

$$\therefore \quad t = 4t_{1/2} = 4(10) \text{ s} = 40 \text{ s}$$

79. The reactor produces 1000 MW power or 10^9 J/s. The reactor is to function for 10 yr. Therefore, total energy which the reactor will supply in 10 yr is

$$E = (\text{power}) (\text{time})$$
$$= (10^9 \text{ J/s}) (10 \times 365 \times 24 \times 3600 \text{ s})$$
$$= 3.1536 \times 10^{17} \text{ J}$$

Since the efficiency of the reactor is only 10%, therefore actual energy needed is 10 times of it or 3.1536×10^{18} J. One uranium atom liberates 200 MeV of energy or $200 \times 1.6 \times 10^{-13}$ J or 3.2×10^{-11} J of energy. So, number of uranium atoms needed are

$$\frac{3.1536 \times 10^{18}}{3.2 \times 10^{-11}} = 0.9855 \times 10^{29}$$

or number of kg-moles of uranium needed are

$$n = \frac{0.9855 \times 10^{29}}{6.02 \times 10^{26}} = 163.7$$

Hence, total mass of uranium required is

$$m = (n)M = (163.7)(235) \text{ kg}$$

or $m \approx 38470$ kg

or $m = 3.847 \times 10^4$ kg

80. $\therefore$ Momentum of α-particle would be

$$p = \frac{h}{\lambda} = \frac{6.63 \times 10^{-34}}{5.76 \times 10^{-15}} \text{ kg-m/s}$$

or $p = 1.151 \times 10^{-19}$ kg-m/s

From law of conservation of linear momentum, this should also be equal to the linear momentum of the daughter nucleus (in opposite direction).

Let K_1 and K_2 be the kinetic energies of α-particle and daughter nucleus. Then total kinetic energy in the final state is

$$K = K_1 + K_2 = \frac{p^2}{2m} + \frac{p^2}{2M} = \frac{p^2}{2}\left(\frac{1}{m} + \frac{1}{M}\right)$$

$$K = \frac{p^2}{2}\left(\frac{M+m}{Mm}\right)$$

$$1 \text{ amu} = 1.67 \times 10^{-27} \text{ kg}$$

Substituting the values, we get

$$K = 10^{-12} \text{ J} \Rightarrow K = \frac{10^{-12}}{1.6 \times 10^{-13}}$$

$$= 6.25 \text{ MeV or } K = 6.25 \text{ MeV.}$$

$$\text{Mass defect, } \Delta m = \frac{6.25}{931.470} = 0.0067 \text{ amu}$$

Therefore, mass of parent nucleus = mass of α-particle + mass of daughter nucleus + mass defect (Δm)

$$= (4.002 + 223.610 + 0.0067) \text{ amu}$$
$$= 227.62 \text{ amu}$$

Hence, mass of parent nucleus is 227.62 amu.

81. Mass defect in the given nuclear reaction :

$$\Delta m = 2(\text{mass of deuterium}) - (\text{mass of helium})$$
$$= 2(2.0141) - (4.0026) = 0.0256 \text{ amu}$$

Therefore, energy released

$$\Delta E = (\Delta m)(931.48) \text{ MeV}$$
$$= 23.85 \text{ MeV} = 23.85 \times 1.6 \times 10^{-13} \text{ J}$$
$$= 3.82 \times 10^{-12} \text{ J}$$

Efficiency is only 25%, therefore,

$$25\% \text{ of } \Delta E = \left(\frac{25}{100}\right)(3.82 \times 10^{-12}) \text{ J}$$

$$= 9.55 \times 10^{-13}\,\text{J}$$

i.e. by the fusion of two deuterium nuclei, 9.55×10^{-13} J energy is available to the nuclear reactor.

Total energy required in one day to run the reactor with a given power of 200 MW :

$$E_{\text{Total}} = 200 \times 10^6 \times 24 \times 3600$$
$$= 1.728 \times 10^{13}\,\text{J}$$

$\therefore$ Total number of deuterium nuclei required for this purpose

$$n = \frac{E_{\text{Total}}}{\Delta E/2} = \frac{2 \times 1.728 \times 10^{13}}{9.55 \times 10^{-13}}$$
$$= 0.362 \times 10^{26}$$

$\therefore$ Mass of deuterium required

= (Number of g-moles of deuterium required) × 2 g

$$= \left(\frac{0.362 \times 10^{26}}{6.02 \times 10^{23}}\right) \times 2 = 120.26\,\text{g}$$

82. (a) Probability of decay during the time from 0 to t,

$$P = \frac{\text{Number decayed}}{\text{Initial numbers}} = \frac{N_0(1 - e^{-\lambda t})}{N_0}$$

or $\quad P = 1 - e^{-\lambda t}$

(b) **Average life or Mean life** Suppose N_1 nuclei survive upto time t_1, N_2 nuclei upto time t_2 and so on. Then,

$$\text{Average life} = \frac{\text{Total life of all nuclei}}{\text{Initial number of nuclei}}$$
$$= \frac{N_1 t_1 + N_2 t_2 + \dots}{N_0} = \frac{\Sigma(Nt)}{N_0}$$

Now suppose at time t, number of nuclei are N. Then,

$$-\frac{dN}{dt} = \lambda N \quad \text{or} \quad |dN| = \lambda N dt$$
$$= \lambda (N_0 e^{-\lambda t})\, dt$$

So, $|dN|$ nuclei decayed in time interval from t to $(t + dt)$. or we can say $|dN|$ nuclei survived upto time t.

So, using the above concept,

$$\text{Average life} = \frac{\int_0^\infty t|dN|}{N_0} = \frac{\int_0^\infty (\lambda N_0 e^{-\lambda t}) t\, dt}{N_0}$$

After completing this integration, we get

$$\text{Average life} = \frac{1}{\lambda}$$

83. (a) Kinetic energy of α-particle is given. So, we can find speed v_0 of the α-particle.

Then by putting this value of v_0 in the given expression of R we can find value of R.

(b) (i) Total number of ion pairs formed,

$$N_1 = \frac{\text{energy of } \alpha\text{-particle}}{\text{energy of formation of one pair}}$$

(ii) In part (a) we have obtained total mean path length R.

From the given formula of R find v_0 corresponding to $\frac{R}{2}$, then kinetic energy corresponding to this v_0.

So, it is also the kinetic energy at $\frac{R}{2}$. Energy lost,

$$\Delta E = \text{Initial kinetic energy} - \text{kinetic energy at } \frac{R}{2}$$

$$\therefore \quad N_2 = \frac{\Delta E}{\text{energy of formation of one pair}}$$

84. The given reaction is,

$$\text{Be}^{10} \longrightarrow \text{B}^{10} + e^- + \bar{\nu}$$

$K_1 = 0$	K_2	K_3
$p_1 = 0$	p_2	p_3
m_1	m_2	m_3

For maximum kinetic energy of β-particle, energy of antineutrino should be zero. Momentum and energy conservation give the following equations,

$$p_2 = p_3 \quad \text{or} \quad \sqrt{2K_2 m_2} = \sqrt{2K_3 m_3}$$

or $$\frac{K_2}{K_3} = \frac{m_3}{m_2} \qquad \text{...(i)}$$

$$(m_1 - m_2 - m_3)c^2 = K_2 + K_3 \qquad \text{...(ii)}$$

Solving these two equations with proper values, we can find K_2 and K_3.

85. Using the concept of previous problem we can find highest (or maximum) kinetic energy K_3 of electrons or β-particles.

Now, according to problem, average kinetic energy of electron,

$$K = \frac{K_3}{3}$$

Number of nuclei in 1 mg of Na^{24}.

$$N_0 = \frac{10^{-3}}{24} \times 6.02 \times 10^{23}$$

Numbers decayed in time t,

$$N_d = N_0(1 - e^{\lambda t})$$

Here, $\quad \lambda = \frac{\ln 2}{T}$ and $t = 1$ day

So, total heat produced, $H = K \times N_d$

Substituting the proper values, we can get the answer.

86.

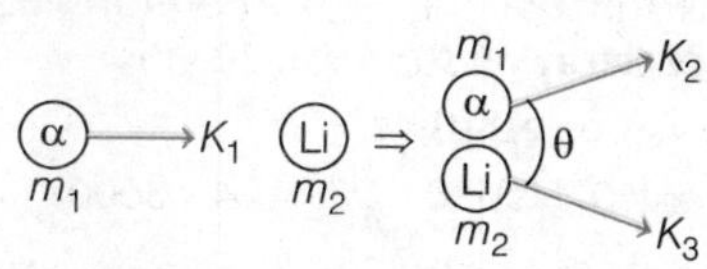

$$\theta = 60°$$
$$K_1 = K_\alpha = 7\,\text{MeV}$$
$$\Sigma p_i = \Sigma p_f$$

or $\sqrt{2m_1K_1}=\sqrt{p_2^2+p_3^2+2p_2p_3\cos\theta}$

$\therefore$ $\sqrt{2m_1K_1}=\sqrt{2m_1K_2+2m_2K_3+2\sqrt{m_1K_2m_2K_3}\cos\theta}$

and $\Sigma K_i=\Sigma K_f$ or $K_1=K_2+K_3$

Solving these equations with proper values we can get the answer.

87. (a)

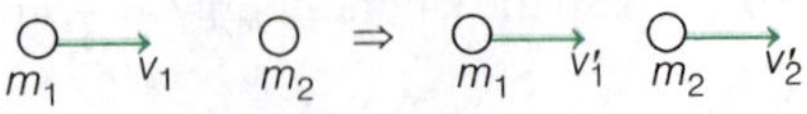

m_1 = mass of neutron

m_2 = mass of deuteron $\approx 2m_1$

In head-on elastic collision,

$$v_1'=\left(\frac{m_1-m_2}{m_1+m_2}\right)v_1+\left(\frac{2m_2}{m_1+m_2}\right)v_2$$

Putting $v_2=0$ and $m_2=2m_1$, we get

$$v_1'=-\frac{v_1}{3}$$

Speed remains $\frac{1}{3}$rd, so kinetic energy will remain $\frac{1}{9}$th. So fraction of energy lost will be $\left(1-\frac{1}{9}\right)$ or $\frac{8}{9}$ or 0.89.

(b)

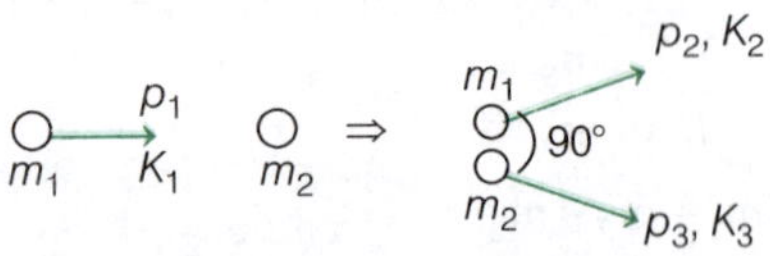

From momentum conservation,

$$p_1^2=p_2^2+p_3^2$$

Here $p_1=\sqrt{2K_1m_1}$

$p_2=\sqrt{2K_2m_1}$

and $p_3=\sqrt{2K_3m_2}$

Further, $K_1=K_2+K_3$

From the above equations, we can determine K_2 in terms of K_1. Then fractional loss $=\frac{K_1-K_2}{K_1}$.

88. $N=N_0e^{-\lambda t}$

Given, $A=-\frac{dN}{dt}$ and $R=-\frac{dA}{dt}$

$$R=\frac{d}{dt}\left(\frac{dN}{dt}\right)=\frac{d^2N}{dt^2}$$

$$\Rightarrow\quad R=\frac{d^2}{dt^2}[N_0e^{-\lambda t}]=\lambda A_0e^{-\lambda t} \quad \text{... (i)}$$

for P Rate of decay

$$R_P=\lambda_p' A_0e^{-\lambda_p t} \quad \text{... (ii)}$$

and for Q $\quad R_Q=\lambda_QA_0e^{-\lambda_Q t} \quad$ ... (iii)

for P $\quad \lambda=\frac{1}{\tau}$

for Q $\quad \lambda=\frac{1}{2\tau}$

and $\quad t=2\tau$

Put this in Eqs. (iii) and (ii).

Then divide Eqs. (ii) by (iii)

$$\frac{R_P}{R_Q}=\frac{(A_0/\tau)_e-(2\tau/\tau)}{(A_0/2\tau)e^{-(2\tau/2\tau)}}=\frac{2}{e}$$

$$\frac{2}{e}=\frac{n}{e} \qquad (\because n=2)$$

89. Let initial power available from the plant is P_0. After time $t=nT$ or n half lives, this will become $\left(\frac{1}{2}\right)^nP_0$. Now, it is given that, $\left(\frac{1}{2}\right)^nP_0=12.5\%$ of $P_0=(0.125)P_0$

Solving this equation, we get

$$n=3$$

90. Number of nuclei decayed in time t,

$$N_d=N_0(1-e^{-\lambda t})$$

$\therefore$ % decayed $=\left(\frac{N_d}{N_0}\right)\times 100$

$$=(1-e^{-\lambda t})\times 100 \quad \text{...(i)}$$

$$e^x\approx 1+x \text{ if } |x|<<1$$

$\therefore$ % decayed

$$=[1-(1-\lambda t)]\times 100$$

$$=(\lambda t)(100)$$

Here, $\lambda=\frac{0.693}{1386}=5\times 10^{-4}\text{ s}^{-1}$ $\quad [T_{1/2}=1386\text{ s}]$

$\therefore$ % decayed $\approx(\lambda t)\times 100$

$$=(5\times 10^{-4})(80)(100)=4$$

91. Activity $\left(-\frac{dN}{dt}\right)=\lambda N=\left(\frac{1}{t_{mean}}\right)\times N$

$$\therefore\quad N=\left(-\frac{dN}{dt}\right)\times t_{mean}$$

= Total number of atoms

Mass of one atom is 10^{-25} kg $=m$ (say)

$\therefore$ Total mass of radioactive substance

= (number of atoms) $\times$ (mass of one atom)

$$=\left(-\frac{dN}{dt}\right)(t_{mean})(m)$$

Substituting the values, we get

Total mass of radioactive substance = 1 mg

$\therefore$ Answer is 1.

UNIT-13

SEMICONDUCTORS

Learning Modules

1. Semiconductors
2. Junction Diodes
3. Transistors
4. Logic Gates

MODULE 1

Semiconductors

Introduction

In all electronic devices controlled flow of electrons is required. Semiconductors are the devices which allow controlled flow of electrons. Their conductivity lies between conductors and insulators.

Before 1948, such devices were mostly vacuum tubes. In a vacuum tube there were two electrodes *viz*, anode and cathode. In these devices the electrons can flow only in one direction, from cathode to anode. This is the reason, why such devices are generally referred to as valves.

These vacuum tubes were replaced by semiconductor devices because vacuum tubes are bulky, consume high power, operate at high voltages and have limited life and low reliability.

In vacuum tubes the mobile electrons were obtained from heating the cathode and they were made to flow in an evacuated space or vacuum. Otherwise the moving electrons may lose their energy on collision with the air molecules in their path.

In semiconductors there is no such requirement as the charge carriers are within the solid itself.

Conductors, Semiconductors and Insulators

On the basis of electrical conductivity solids can be classified as : (i) conductors (ii) semiconductors and (iii) insulators. Conductivity of Silicon (a semiconductor) is about 10^{11} times smaller than that of copper (a conductor) and is about 10^{13} times larger than that of fused quartz (an insulator).

The order of electrical conductivity (σ) and resistivity $\left(\rho = \frac{1}{\sigma}\right)$ of metals (or conductors), semiconductors and insulators are given below in tabular form.

Table 1.

S.No	Types of solid	$\rho\,(\Omega\text{-m})$	$\sigma\,(\Omega^{-1}\text{-m}^{-1})$
1.	Metals	$10^{-2} - 10^{-8}$	$10^{2} - 10^{8}$
2.	Semiconductors	$10^{-5} - 10^{6}$	$10^{5} - 10^{-6}$
3.	Insulators	$10^{11} - 10^{19}$	$10^{-11} - 10^{-19}$

Energy Bands in Solids

Let us consider the case of Si crystal containing N-atoms. For Si, the outer most orbit is the third orbit ($n = 3$). The number of electrons in the outermost orbit is 4. Hence the total number of outermost electrons in the crystal is 4N.

Region A

The electron energy will be same if all the atoms are separated from each other by a large distance (or they are in gaseous state)

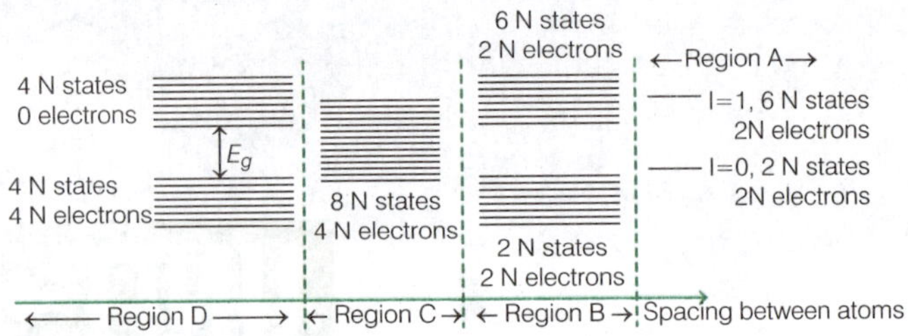

Region B

Suppose these atoms start coming nearer to each other to form a solid. The energies of these electrons in the outermost orbit may change due to the interaction between the electrons of different atoms. The 6N states for $l = 1$ which originally had identical energies in the isolated atoms now form an energy band. Similarly, the 2N states for $l = 0$, form an another band, separated from the first one by an energy gap.

Region C

If distance between different atoms is further decreased then two energy bands merge with each other.

Region D

Finally if the distance between the atoms further decreases, the energy bands again split apart and are separated by an energy gap E_g. The lower band which is completely filled is called the valence band (VB) and the upper band which is completely empty is called the conduction band (CB).

Now, electrical conductivity of conductors, insulators and semiconductors can be explained by these energy bands.

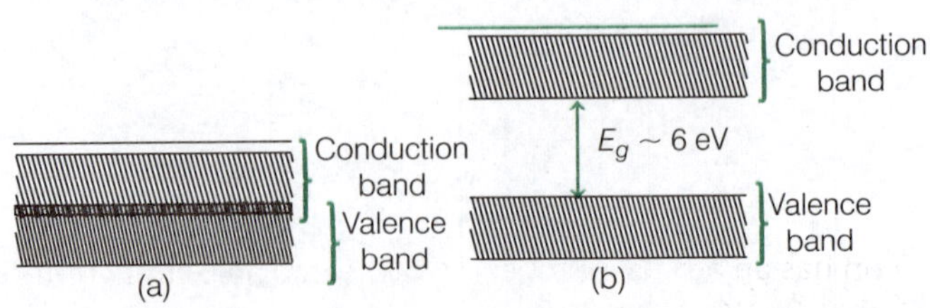

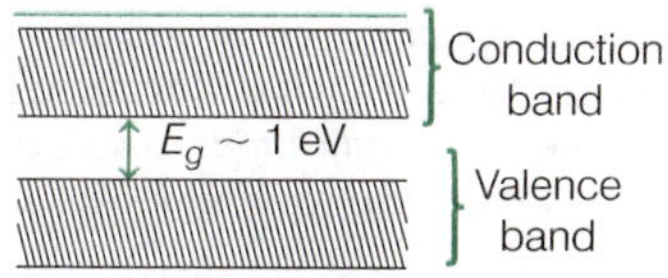

(c)

Energy band diagram for a (a) metal, (b) insulator and (c) semiconductor.

Conductors In conductors, conduction band overlaps with completely filled valence band.

Insulators The conduction band is separated from the valence band by a wide energy gap (e.g. 6 eV for diamond). But at any non-zero temperature, some electrons can be excited to the conduction band.

Semiconductors It is similar to that of an insulator but with a comparatively small energy gap. At absolute zero temperature, the conduction band of semiconductors is totally empty, and all the electrons are in the valence band.

The absence of electrons in the conduction band at absolute zero does not allow current to flow under the influence of an electric field. Therefore, they are insulators at low temperatures.

However at room temperatures some valence electrons acquire thermal energy greater than the energy gap E_g and move to the conduction band where they are free to move under the influence of even a small electric field. Thus, a semiconductor originally an insulator at low temperatures becomes slightly conducting at room temperature. Unlike conductors the resistance of semiconductors decreases with increasing temperature.

Example 1 What is the energy band gap of :
(i) silicon and (ii) germanium?

Sol. The energy band gap of silicon is 1.1 eV and of germanium is about 0.7 eV.

Example 2 In a good conductor, what is the energy gap between the conduction band and the valence band.

Sol. In a good conductor, conduction band overlaps with the valence band. Therefore, the energy gap between them is zero.

Intrinsic and Extrinsic Semiconductors

As discussed above, in semiconductors the conduction band and the valence band are separated by a relatively small energy gap. For silicon, this gap is 1.1 eV and for germanium it is 0.7 eV.

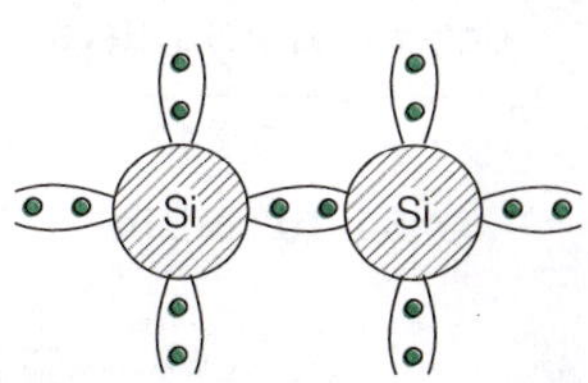

Silicon has an atomic number 14 and electronic configuration $1s^2, 1s^2, 2p^6, 3s^2, 3p^2$.

The chemistry of silicon tells us that it has a valency 4. Each silicon atom makes covalent bonds with the four neighbouring silicon atoms. On the basis of bonds the atoms make with their neighbouring atoms, semiconductors are divided in two groups.

Intrinsic Semiconductors A pure (free from impurity) semiconductor which has a valency 4 is called an intrinsic semiconductor. Pure germanium, silicon or carbon in their natural state are intrinsic semiconductors. As discussed above, each atom makes four covalent bonds with their neighbouring atoms. At temperature close to zero, all valence electrons are tightly bound and so no free electrons are available to conduct electricity through the crystal. At room temperature, however a few of the covalent bonds are broken due to thermal agitation and thus some of the valence electrons become free. Thus, we can say that a valence electrons is shifted to conduction band leaving a **hole** (vacancy of electron) in valence band. Thus, in intrinsic semiconductors,

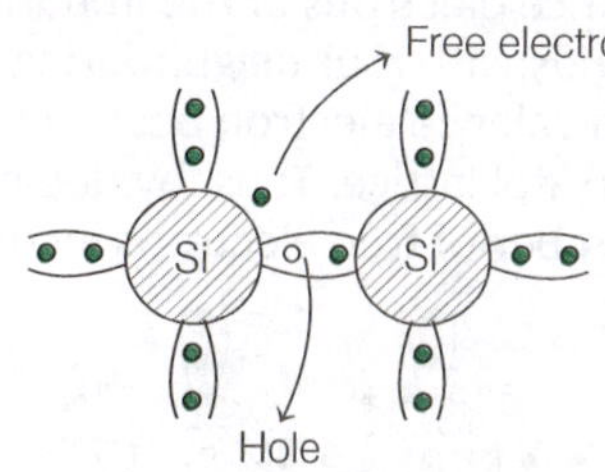

Number of holes = Number of free electrons or $n_h = n_e$

Extrinsic Semiconductors The conductivity of an intrinsic semiconductor is very poor (unless the temperature is very high). At ordinary temperature, only one covalent bond breaks in 10^9 atoms of Ge. Conductivity of an intrinsic (pure) semiconductor is significantly increased, if some pentavalent or trivalent impurity is mixed with it. Such impure semiconductors are called extrinsic or doped semiconductors.

Extrinsic semiconductors are again of two types (i) *p*-type and (ii) *n*-type.

(i) ***p*-type semiconductors** When a trivalent (e.g. boron, aluminium, gallium or indium) is added to a germanium or silicon crystal it replaces one of the germanium or silicon atom. Its three valence electrons form covalent bonds with neighbouring three Ge (or Si) atoms while the fourth valence electron of Ge (or Si) is not able to form the bond. Thus, there remains a hole (an empty space) on one side of the impurity atom.

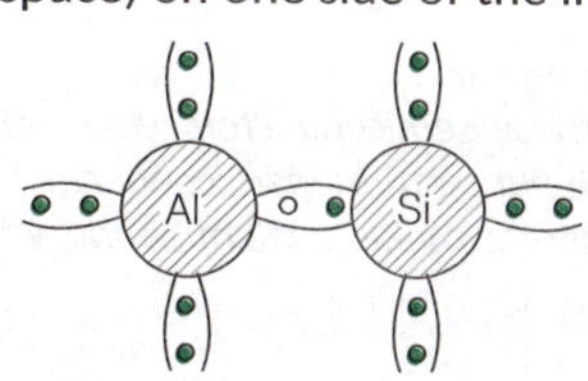

The trivalent impurity atoms are called **acceptor atoms** because they create holes which accept electrons.

Following points are worthnoting regarding *p*-type semiconductors.

(a) Holes are the majority charge carriers and electrons are minority charge carriers in case of *p*-type semiconductors or number of holes are much greater than the number of electrons.

$$\boxed{n_h >> n_e}$$

(b) *p*-type semiconductor is electrically neutral.

(c) *p*-type semiconductor can be shown as

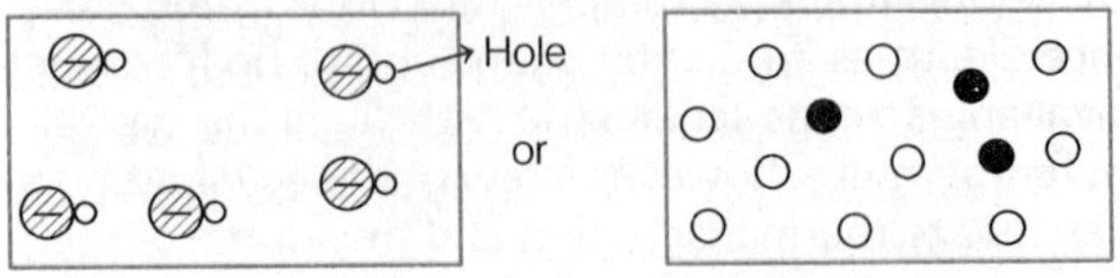

(ii) **n-type semiconductors** When a pentavalent impurity atom (antimony, phosphorus or arsenic is added to a Ge (or Si) crystal it replaces a Ge (or Si) atom. Four of the five valence electrons of the impurity atom form covalent bonds with four neighbouring Ge (or Si) atoms and the fifth valence electron becomes free to move inside the crystal lattice. Thus, by doping pentavalent impurity number of free electrons increases.

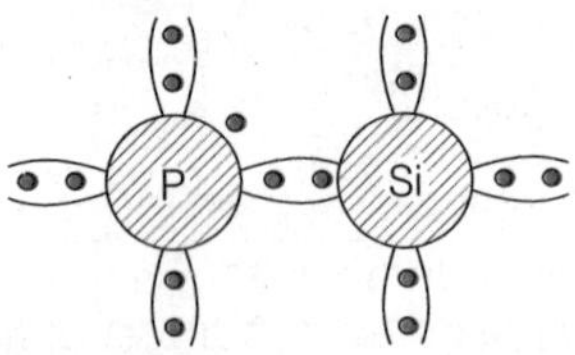

The impurity (pentavalent) atoms are called **donor atoms** because they donate conduction electrons inside the crystal. Following points are worthnoting regarding *n*-type semiconductors,

(a) Electrons are the majority charge carriers and holes are minority or number of electrons are much greater than the number of holes

$$\boxed{n_e >> n_h}$$

(b) *n*-type semiconductor is also electrically neutral.

(c) *n*-type semiconductor can be shown as

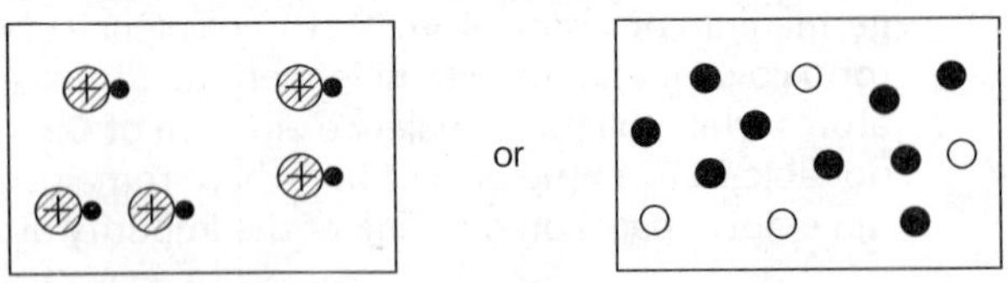

Note *In n-type extrinsic semiconductors when pentavalent impurity is mixed with pure intrinsic semiconductors and four electrons of impurity atoms make covalent bands with the pure semiconductors then fifth electron gets annoyed with other four electrons and its energy gap is reduced to 0.01- 0.05 eV. Now this fifth electron easily jumps to conduction band. Or, in common language we can say that it becomes a free electron.*

Example 3 C, Si and Ge have same lattice structure. Why is C insulator while Si and Ge intrinsic semiconductors?

Sol. The energy gap between conduction band and valence band is least for Ge, followed by Si and highest for C. Hence, number of free electrons are negligible for C. This is why carbon is insulator.

Example 4 In an *n*-type silicon, which of the following statements is true?

(a) Electrons are majority carriers and trivalent atoms are the dopants.

(b) Electrons are minority carriers and pentavalent atoms are the dopants.

(c) Holes are minority carriers and pentavalent atoms are the dopants.

(d) Holes are majority carriers and trivalent atoms are the dopants.

Sol. (c) Holes are minority charge carriers and pentavalent atoms are the dopants in an *n*-type silicon.

Example 5 Which of the statements given in above example is true for *p*-type semiconductors?

Sol. (d) Holes are majority carriers and trivalent atoms are the dopants in an *p*-type semiconductors.

Note *The electron and hole concentration in a semiconductor in thermal equilibrium is given by :*

$$\boxed{n_e n_h = n_i^2}$$

Here n_i is called intrinsic carrier concentration.

Example 6 Suppose a pure Si crystal has 5×10^{28} atoms /m^3. It is doped by 1 ppm (parts per million) concentration of pentavalent As. Calculate hole concentration. Given that $n_i = 1.5 \times 10^{16} \text{m}^{-3}$.

Sol. 1 ppm means $1e^-$ in 10^6 atoms.

Note that thermally generated electrons are negligibly small as compated to those produced by doping.

$$\therefore \quad n_e \approx \frac{5 \times 10^{28}}{10^6} \qquad \text{(Given 1 ppm)}$$

$$= 5 \times 10^{22}$$

Further, $n_e n_h = n_i^2$

$$\therefore \quad n_h = \frac{n_i^2}{n_e} = \frac{(1.5 \times 10^{16})^2}{5 \times 10^{22}}$$

$$\approx 4.5 \times 10^9 \text{ per m}^3$$

Ans.

Electrical Conduction through Semiconductors

When a battery is connected across a semiconductor (whether intrinsic or extrinsic) a potential difference is developed across its ends. Due to the potential difference, an electric field is produced inside the semiconductor. A current (although very small) starts flowing through the semiconductor. This current may be due to the motion of (i) free electrons and (ii) holes. Electrons move in opposite direction of electric field while holes move in the same direction.

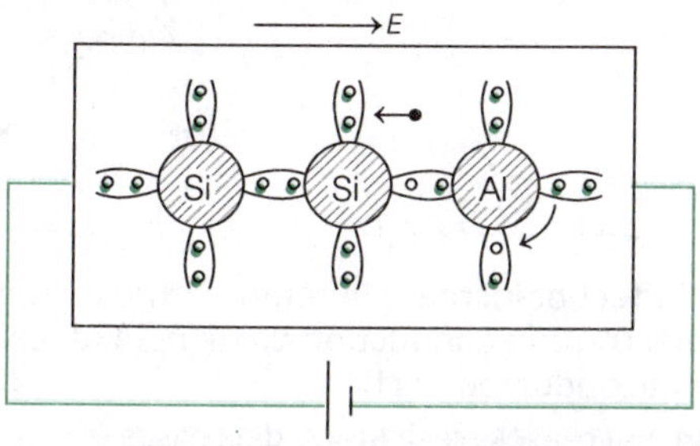

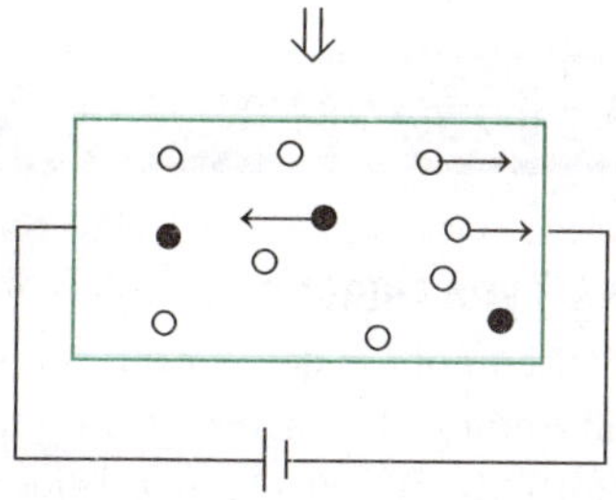

The motion of holes towards right (in the figure) take place because electrons from right hand side come to fill this hole, creating a new hole in their own position. Thus, we can say that holes are moving from left to right. Thus, current in a semiconductor can be written as,

$$i = i_e + i_h$$

But it should be noted that mobility of holes is less than the mobility of electrons.

Miscellaneous Examples

Ex. 1 Sn, C, Si and Ge are all group XIV elements. Yet, Sn is a conductor, C is an insulator while Si and Ge are semiconductors. Why ?

Sol. It all depends on energy gap between valence band and conduction band.

The energy gap for Sn is 0 eV, for C is 5.4 eV, for Si is 1.1 eV and for Ge is 0.7 eV.

Ex. 2 What is the range of energy gap (E_g) in insulators, semiconductors and conductors?

Sol. For insulators $E_g > 3$ eV, for semiconductors,

$E_g = 0.2$ eV to 3eV while for conductors (or metals) $E_g = 0$.

Ex. 3 *n*-type extrinsic semiconductor is negatively charged, while p-type extrinsic semiconductor is positively charged. Is this statement true or false?

Sol. False. Intrinsic as well as extrinsic semiconductors are electrically neutral.

Ex. 4 What is resistance of an intrinsic semiconductor at 0K?

Sol. At 0K number of holes (or number of free electrons) in an intrinsic semiconductor become zero. Therefore, resistance of an intrinsic semiconductor becomes infinite at 0 K.

Ex. 5 A piece of copper and the other of germanium are cooled from the room temperature to 80 K. What will happen to their resistance?

Sol. Copper is conductor and germanium is semiconductor. With decrease in temperature resistance of a conductor decreases and that of semiconductor increases. Therefore resistance of copper will decrease and that of germanium will increase.

MODULE 1 Exercise

Statement Type Questions

(a) Statement I is correct but Statement II is incorrect
(b) Statement I is incorrect but Statement II is correct
(c) Both Statement I and Statement II are incorrect
(d) Both Statement I and Statement II are correct

1. **Statement I :** When a Si sample is doped with Boron, it becomes *p*-type and when doped by Arsenic it becomes *n*-type semiconductor such that *p*-type has excess holes and *n*-type has excess electrons.
Statement II : When such *p*-type and *n*-type semiconductors are fused to make a junction, a current will automatically flow which can be detected with an externally connected ammeter. **(2023 Main)**

2. **Statement I :** By doping silicon semiconductor with pentavalent material, the electrons density increases.
Statement II : The *n*-type semiconductor has net negative charge. **(2021 Main)**

Single Correct Option

3. The conductivity of a semiconductor increases with increase in temperature because
(a) only number density of free current carriers increases
(b) relaxation time increases
(c) both number density of carriers and relaxation time decreases but effect of decrease in relaxation time is much less than increase in number density.
(d) number density of current carriers increases, relaxation time decreases but effect of decrease in relaxation time is much less than increase in number density

4. Hole is
(a) an anti-particle of electron
(b) a vacancy created when an electron leaves a covalent bond
(c) absence of free electrons
(d) an artificially created particle

5. The resistivity (ρ) of semiconductor varies with temperature. Which of the following curve represents the correct behaviour? **(2023 Main)**

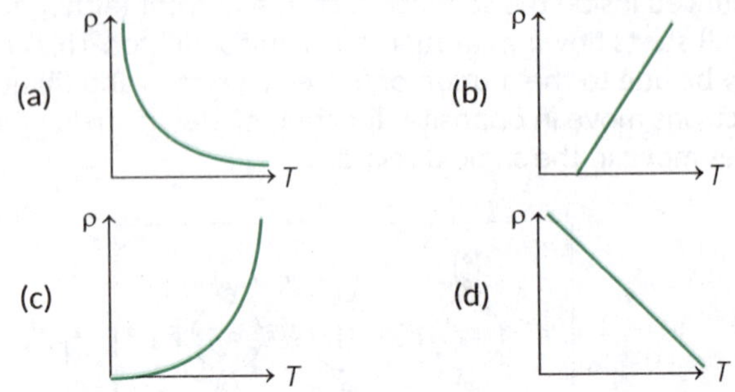

6. The effect of increase in temperature on the number of electrons in conduction band (n_e) and resistance of a semiconductor will be as **(2023 Main)**
(a) n_e increases, resistance decreases
(b) Both n_e and resistance decrease
(c) n_e decreases. resistance increases
(d) Both n_e and resistance increase

7. The electrical conductivity of a semiconductor increases when electromagnetic radiation of wavelength shorter than 2480 nm is incident on it. The band gap (in eV) for the semiconductor is **(1997 JEE)**
(a) 0.9 (b) 0.7 (c) 0.5 (d) 1.1

Multiple Correct Options

8. Holes are charge carriers in **(1997 JEE)**
(a) intrinsic semiconductors
(b) ionic solids
(c) *p*-type semiconductors
(d) metals

9. The impurity atoms with which pure silicon should be doped to make a *p*-type semiconductor are those of **(1988 JEE)**
(a) phosphorus (b) boron
(c) antimony (d) aluminium

Answers

1. (a)	**2.** (a)	**3.** (d)	**4.** (b)	**5.** (a)
6. (a)	**7.** (c)	**8.** (a,c)	**9.** (b,d)	

See hints on page 434.

MODULE 2

Junction Diodes

In *n*-type semiconductors, free electrons are the majority charge carriers whereas in *p*-type semiconductors, holes are the majority charge carriers. When the *n*-type semiconductor is joined with the *p*-type semiconductor, a *p-n* junction is formed. This *p-n* junction, which is formed when the *p*-type and *n*-type semiconductors are joined, is called as *p-n* junction diode.

A *p-n* junction diode is one of the simplest semiconductor devices which has the electrical characteristic of passing current through itself in one direction only. If the diode is forward biased, it allows the electric current flow. On the other hand, if the diode is reverse biased, it blocks the electric current flow.

The basic symbol of *p-n* junction diode under forward bias and reverse bias is shown in the below figure

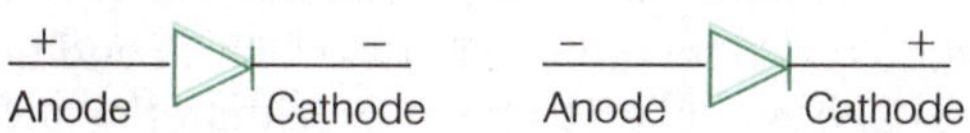

Forward biased Reverse biased

However, unlike a resistor, a diode does not behave linearly with respect to the applied voltage. Instead it has an exponential current-voltage (*I-V*) relationship.

Depletion Region and Potential Barrier

In an *n*-type semiconductor, the concentration of electrons is more compared to the concentration of holes. Similarly, in a *p*-type semiconductor, the concentration of holes is more than the concentration of electrons.

During the formation of the *p-n* junction, due to the concentration difference across *p* and *n* sides, holes diffuse from *p* side to *n* side, and electrons diffuse from the *n*-side to the *p*-side.

When an electron diffuses from *n* to *p*, it leaves behind a positive charge on the *n*-side. This positive charge is immobile as it is bonded to the surrounding atoms.

As the electrons continue to diffuse from *n* to *p*, a layer of positive charge on the *n*-side of the junction is developed.

When a hole diffuses from *p* side to *n* side due to the concentration difference, it leaves behind a negative charge which is immobile. As the holes continue to diffuse, a layer of negative charge (or negative space-charge region) on the *p*-side of the junction is developed. This space-charge region on either side of the junction together is known as the **depletion region.**

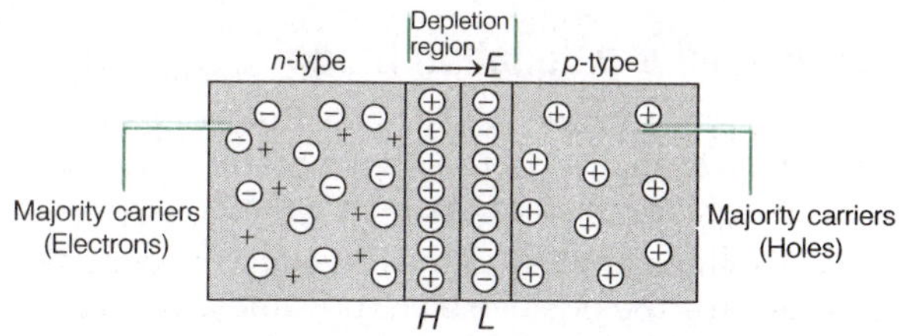

Depletion region in a *p-n* junction

The thickness of the depletion region is very small and is of the order of one-tenth of a micrometer. Due to the positive space-charge region on the *n*-side of the junction and negative space charge region on the *p*-side of the junction, an electric field directed from positive charge to negative charge develops.

Due to this electric field further diffusion of electrons (from *n* side to *p* side) and holes (from *p* side to *n* side) stops. Because we can see that force on electrons and holes due to this electric field is in opposite direction of their diffusion. Electric field is also associated with a potential difference. The potential difference developed by this electric field is called **potential barrier.** Value of this potential barrier is 0.3 V in case of Ge and 0.7 V in case of Si diode.

Diffusion Current and Drift Current

Because of concentration difference, holes try to diffuse from the *p*-side to the *n*-side at the *p-n* junction. This diffusion give rise to a current from *p*-side to *n*-side called **diffusion current** (I_{df}).

Because of thermal collisions, electron-hole pair are created at every part of a diode.

However, if an electron-hole pair is created in the depletion region, the electron is pushed by the electric field towards the *n*-side and the hole towards the *p*-side. This gives rise to a current from *n*-side to *p*-side called the **drift current** (I_{dr}).

Thus,

$I_{df} \longrightarrow$ from *p*-side to *n*-side

$I_{dr} \longrightarrow$ from *n*-side to *p*-side

When diode is unbiased $I_{df} = I_{dr}$ or $I_{net} = 0$.

Biasing of a *p-n* Junction Diode

There are three possible "biasing" conditions for the standard junction diode and these are :

- **Zero Bias or Unbiased** No external voltage potential is applied to the *p-n* junction diode.

- **Reverse Biased** The voltage potential is connected negative (–ve) to the *p*-type material and positive (+ve) to the *n*-type material across the diode which has the effect of increasing the depletion layer.
- **Forward Biased** The voltage potential is connected positive, (+ve) to the *p*-type material and negative, (–ve) to the *n*-type material across the diode which has the effect of decreasing the depletion layer.

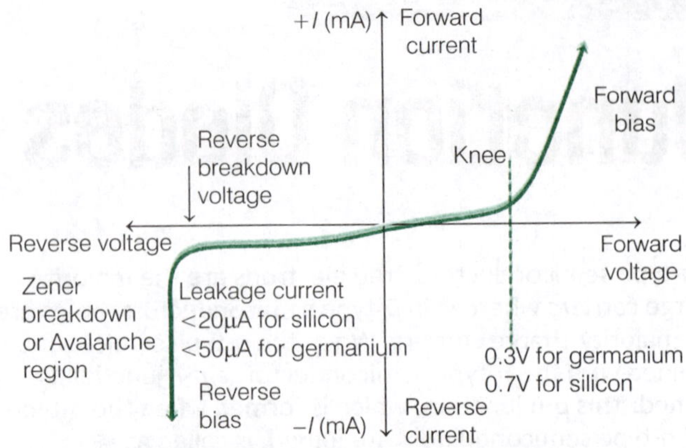

I-V characteristic graph of *p-n* junction diode

Reverse Biased *p-n* Junction Diode

When a diode is connected in a Reverse Bias condition, a positive voltage is applied to the *n*-type material and a negative voltage is applied to the *p*-type material.

The positive voltage applied to the *n*-type material attracts electrons towards the positive electrode and away from the junction, while the holes in the *p*-type end are also attracted away from the junction towards the negative electrode.

The net result is that the depletion layer grows wider due to a lack of electrons and holes and presents a high resistance path (almost an insulator) and a high potential barrier is created across the junction thus preventing current from flowing through the semiconductor material.

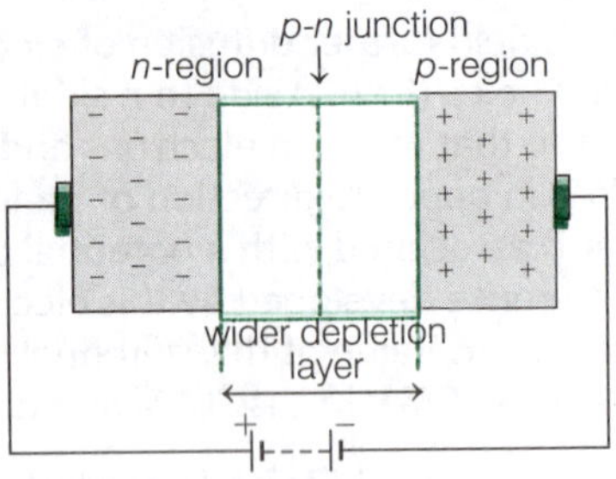

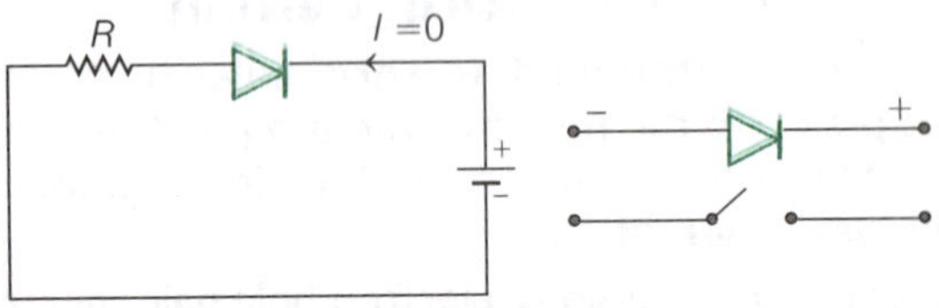

Reverse biasing voltage

This condition represents a high resistance value to the *p-n* junction and practically zero current flows through the junction diode. However, a very small **reverse leakage current** does flow through the junction (due to minority charge carriers both sides) which can normally be measured in micro-amperes.

If the reverse bias voltage applied to the diode is increased to a sufficiently high enough value, it will cause the diode's *p-n* junction to overheat and fail due to the avalanche effect around the junction. This may cause the diode to become shorted (or like a conductor) and will result in the flow of very high current. This is also called **avalanche breakdown**.

Forward Biased *p-n* Junction Diode

When a diode is connected in a **Forward bias** condition, a negative voltage is applied to the *n*-type material and a positive voltage is applied to the *p*-type material.

If this external voltage becomes greater than the value of the potential barrier, approximately 0.7 V for Silicon and 0.3 V for Germanium, the potential barriers opposition will be overcome and current will start to flow.

This is because the negative voltage pushes or repels electrons of *n*-side towards the junction giving them the energy to cross over and combine with the holes of *p*-side being pushed in the opposite direction towards the junction by the positive voltage.

This results in a characteristics curve of almost zero current flowing up to the voltage of potential barrier called the **knee point** and then a high current flows through the diode with little increase in the external voltage as shown in figure.

The application of a forward biasing voltage on the junction diode results in the depletion layer becoming very thin and narrow which represents a low resistance path through the junction thereby allowing high currents to flow.

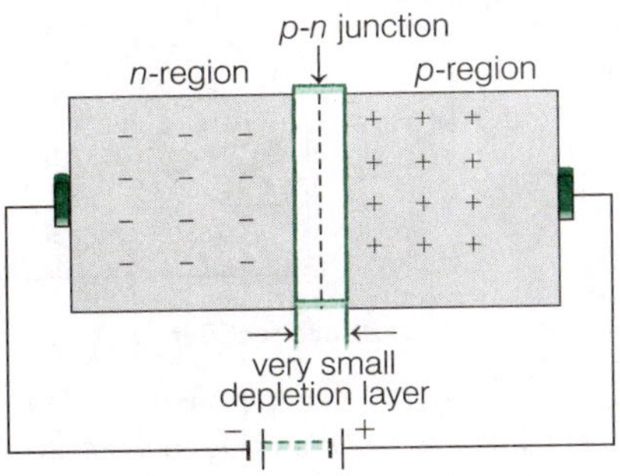

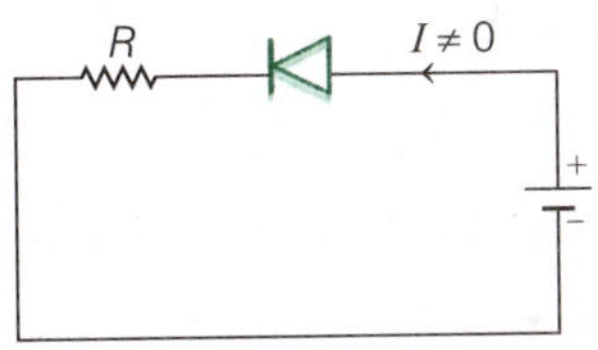

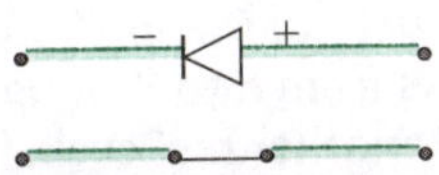
Forward biasing voltage

Example 1 Can we take one slab of *p*-type semiconductor and physically join it to another *n*-type semiconductor to get *p*-*n* junction?

Sol. No. Any slab will have some roughness. Hence continuous contact at the atomic level will not be possible. For the charge carriers, the junction will behave as a discontinuity.

Example 2 Find current passing through $2\,\Omega$ and $4\,\Omega$ resistance in the circuit shown in figure.

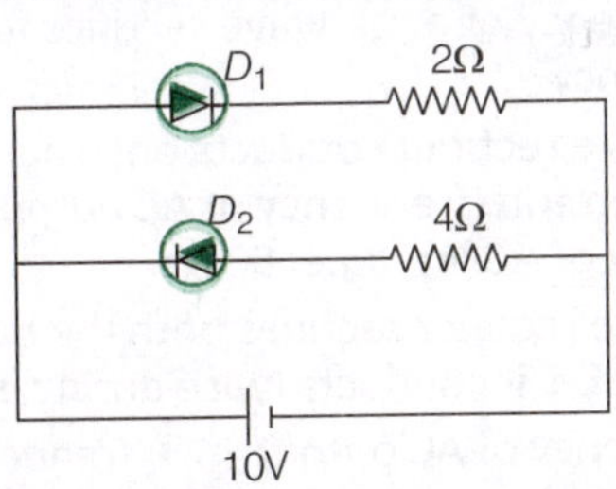

Sol. In the given circuit diode D_1 is forward biased and D_2 reverse biased. Hence, D_1 will conduct but D_2 not. Therefore, current through $4\,\Omega$ resistance will be zero while through $2\,\Omega$ resistance will be, $\frac{10}{2} = 5$ A.

Note *In forward biased condition, resistance of a diode may be assumed to be zero. In reverse biased it may be assumed infinite.*

Example 3 Ge and Si diodes start conducting at 0.3 V and 0.7 V respectively. In the following figure, if Ge diode connection are reversed, the value of V_0 changes by: (assume that the Ge diode has large breakdown voltage)

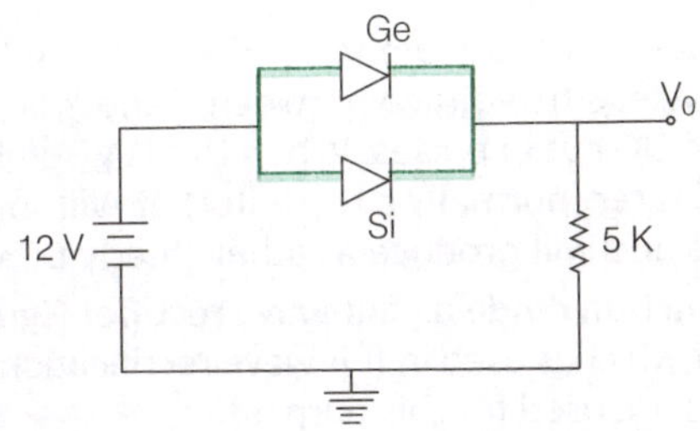

(a) 0.8 V (b) 0.6 V (c) 0.2 V (d) 0.4 V

Sol. Initially current will flow across Ge diode (because $0.3\text{ V} < 0.7\text{ V}$) and 0.3 V will drop across Ge diode. So,

$$V_0 = 12 - 0.3 = 11.7\text{ V}$$

When Ge diode is reverse biased current will flow across Si diode. In this case 0.7 V will drop across Si diode. Thus,

$$V_0' = 12 - 0.7 = 11.3\text{ V}$$

$$\therefore \quad |\Delta V_0| = 11.7 - 11.3 = 0.4\text{ V}$$

$\therefore$ The correct option is (d).

Junction Diode as a Rectifier

A rectifier is a device which converts an alternating current (or voltage) into a direct (or unidirectional) current (or voltage). A *p*-*n* junction diode can work as an excellent rectifier. It offers a low resistance for the current to flow when it is forward biased, but a very high resistance when reverse biased. Thus, it allows current through it only in one direction and acts as a rectifier. The junction diode can be used either as an half-wave rectifier or as a full-wave rectifier.

(i) ***p*-*n* junction diode as half-wave rectifier** A simple rectifier circuit called the half-wave rectifier, using only one diode is shown in figure.

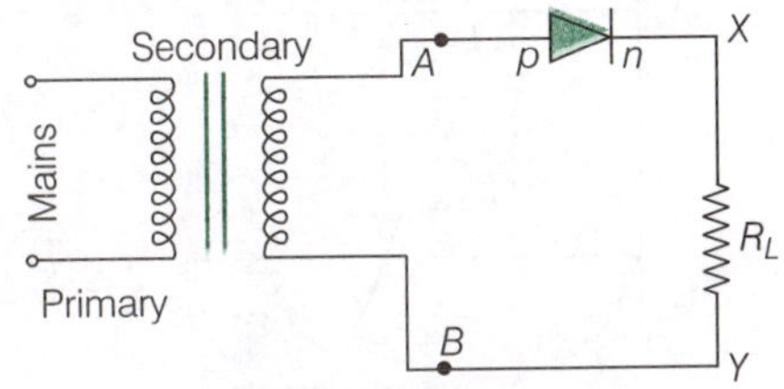

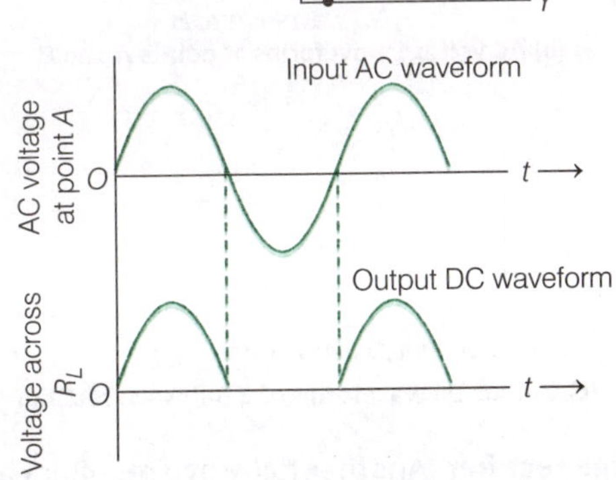

When the voltage at *A* is positive, the diode is forward biased and it conducts and when the voltage at *A* is negative, the diode is reverse biased and does not conduct. Since, the diode conducts only in the positive half cycles, the voltage between X and Y or across R_L will be DC but in pulses. When this is given to a circuit called filter (normally a capacitor), it will smoothen the pulses and will produce a rather steady DC voltage.

(ii) ***p-n* junction diode as full-wave rectifier** Figure shows a circuit which is used in full-wave rectification. Two diodes are used for this purpose.

The secondary coil of the transformer is wound in two parts and the junction is called a Centre-Tap (point C). During one-half cycle (when $V_A > V_B$) or ($V_A > V_C > V_B$) D_1 is forward biased and D_2 is reverse biased. Therefore, D_1 conducts but D_2 does not, current flows from X to Y through load resistance R_L along the path AD_1XYCA. During another half cycle (when $V_B > V_A$) or ($V_B > V_C > V_A$) D_2 is forward biased and D_1 reverse biased. Therefore, D_2 conducts and D_1 does not. In this half cycle also current through R_L flows from X to Y along the path BD_2XYCB. Thus, current through R_L in both the half cycles is in one direction, i.e. from X to Y.

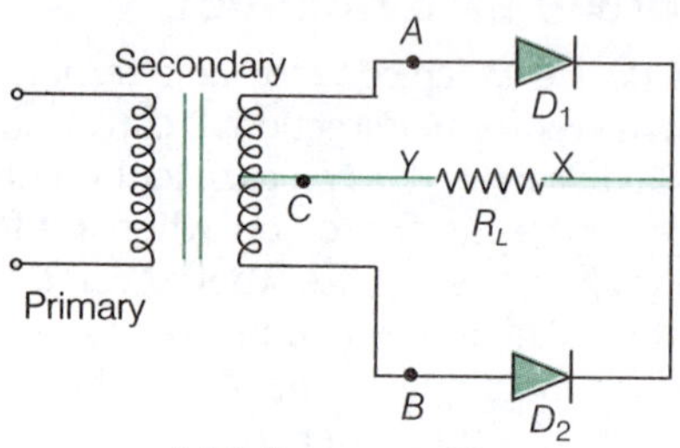

(a) Full-wave rectifier

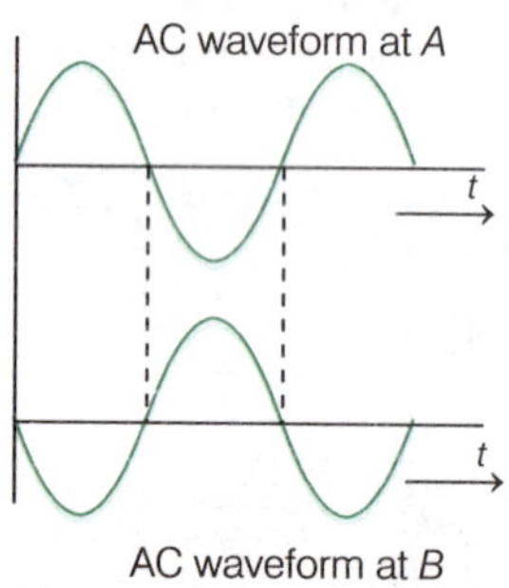

(b) AC voltage waveforms at points A and B

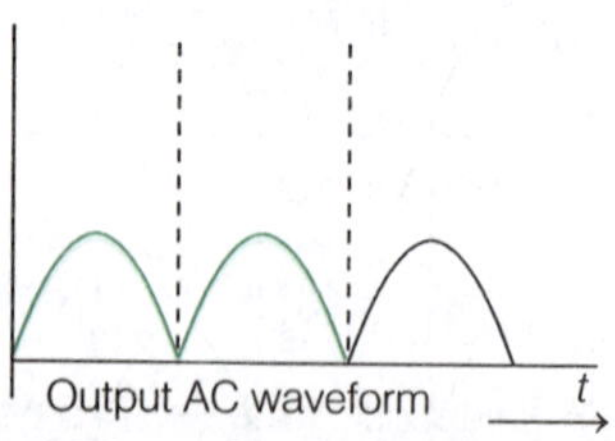

(c) Output DC waveforms of a full-wave rectifier

Bridge rectifier Another full-wave rectifier called the bridge rectifier which uses four diodes is shown in figure.

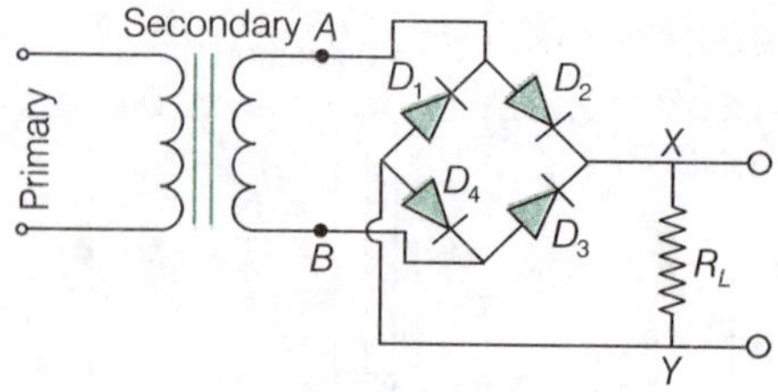

(a) Bridge rectifier

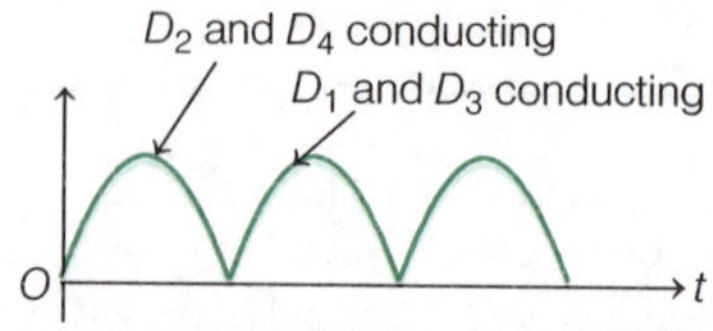

(b) output waveforms for a bridge rectifier

For one-half cycle (when $V_B > V_A$) diodes D_1 and D_3 are forward biased and D_2 and D_4 are reverse biased. So, D_1 and D_3 conduct but D_2 and D_4 don't. Current through R_L flows from X to Y along the path BD_3XYD_1AB. In another half cycle (when $V_A > V_B$) D_2 and D_4 are forward biased and D_1 and D_3 are reverse biased. So, in this half cycle D_2 and D_4 conduct but D_1 and D_3 do not. Current again flows from X to Y through R_L along the path AD_2XYD_4BA. Thus, we see that current through R_L always flows in one direction from X to Y.

Note *Even after rectification ripples are present in the output which can be removed upto great extent by a filter circuit. A filter circuit consists of a capacitor.*

Example 4 In half-wave rectification, what is the output frequency, if the input frequency is 50 Hz? What is the output frequency of a full-wave rectifier for the same input frequency?

Sol. A half-wave rectifier conducts once during one half cycle. Therefore frequency of AC output is also the frequency of AC input i.e. 50 Hz.

A full-wave rectifier rectifies both the half cycles of the AC output i.e. it conducts twice during a cycle.

So, Frequency of AC output $= 2 \times$ frequency of AC input

$= 2 \times 50 = 100$ Hz **Ans.**

Example 5 In the figure, the input is across the terminals A and C and the output is across B and D. Then the output is

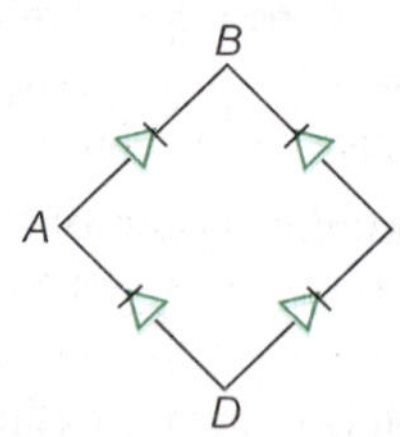

(a) zero
(b) same as the input
(c) full-wave rectified
(d) half-wave rectified

Sol. (c) During the half cycle when $V_M > V_N, D_1$ and D_3 are forward biased. Hence, the path of current is *MABPQDCNM*.

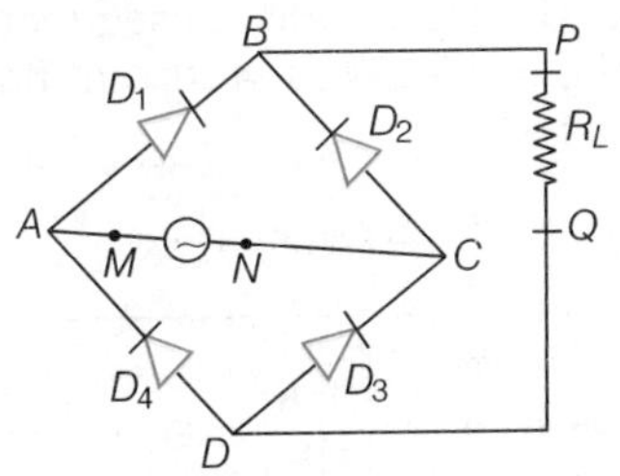

In the second half cycle, when $V_N > V_M, D_2$ and D_4 are forward biased while D_1 and D_3 are reverse biased. Hence, the path of current is *NCBPQDAMN*.

Therefore, in both half cycles current flows from P to Q from load resistance R_L. Or, it is a full-wave rectifier.

Applications of *p-n* Junction Diodes

Zener Diode

The Zener diode behaves like a voltage regulator. The function of a voltage regulator is to provide a constant output voltage to a load connected in parallel with Zener diode.

The Zener diode (also known as breakdown diode) is a standard *p*-*n* junction diode which is used in reverse biased condition. Symbol of Zener diode, *I*-*V* characteristic of Zener diode and the circuit with Zener diode are shown below.

Symbol

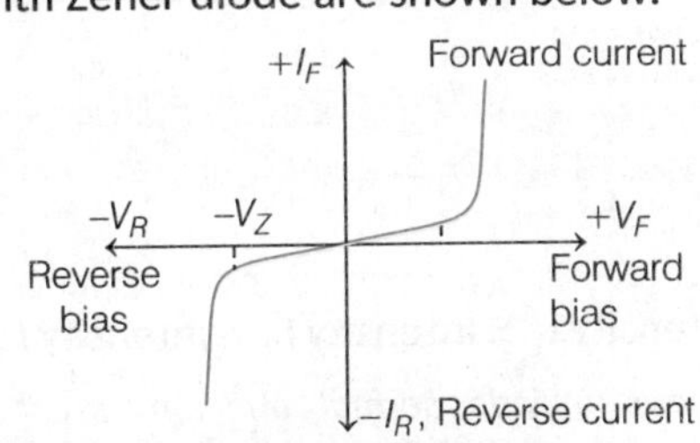

***I-V* characteristics**

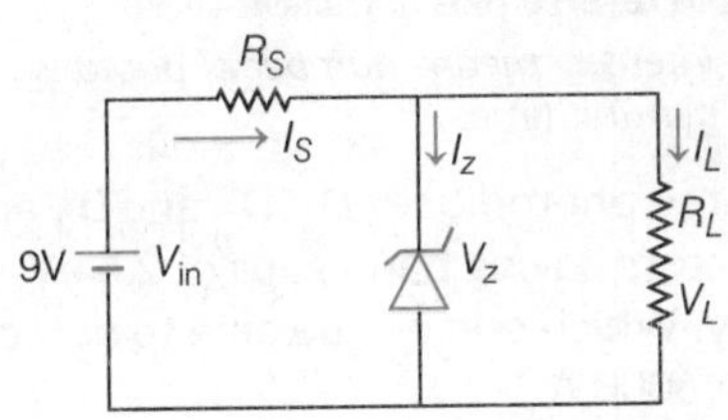

Zener diode as voltage regulator

In the circuit we can see that *p*-side of the Zener diode is connected with negative terminal of the input voltage V_{in}.

Here $-V_z$ in the figure is breakdown voltage in reverse biased condition. Negative sign is only for reverse biasing otherwise it has no relation with the magnitude of voltage.

When voltage across Zener diode is less than breakdown voltage it behaves like a normal diode which does not allow current (or allows very small current due to minority charge carriers) in reverse bias condition.

When input voltage V_{in} increases, then voltage across Zener diode also increases and after a certain value it crosses V_z and current through Zener diode suddenly increases because after that voltage covalent bonds in Zener diode are broken and it becomes highly conducting and its resistance suddenly decreases.

Under this condition voltage across the load resistance R_L is stabilised according to the following equation.

$$V_L \text{ or } V_Z = V_{in} - I_S R_S \quad \text{...(i)}$$

When V_{in} increases and V_Z in reverse biased crosses reverse breakdown voltage, Zener diode, which is a semiconductor device becomes conducting. So its resistance decreases. When parallel resistance in a circuit decreases, then net resistance of the circuit also decreases. So main current I_S increases.

From equation (i), we can see that I_S is also increasing when V_{in} is increasing. So, V_L or V_Z remains almost constant.

Note *Normal diodes are normally damaged after breakdown voltage. But Zener diodes are so made that they come to their natural form once the applied voltage is again less than the breakdown voltage.*

Example 6 For the circuit shown below, the current through the Zener diode is :

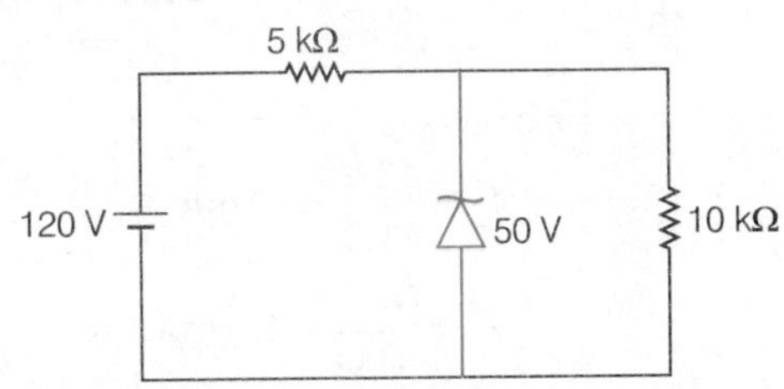

(a) 9 mA (b) 5 mA (c) Zero (d) 14 mA

Sol. $V_{10k\Omega} = 50\text{V}$

$$\therefore \quad I_{10\,k\Omega} = \frac{50\text{V}}{10\,k\Omega} = 5\text{ mA}$$

$$V_{5\,k\Omega} = (120 - 50)\text{ V} = 70\text{ V}$$

$$\therefore \quad I_{5\,k\Omega} = \frac{70\text{ V}}{5\,k\Omega} = 14\text{ mA}$$

Hence, current through zener diode,

$$I_Z = I_{5\,k\Omega} - I_{10\,k\Omega} = 9\text{ mA}$$

$\therefore$ The correct option is (a).

Example 7 The figure represents a voltage regulator circuit using a Zener diode. The breakdown voltage of the Zener diode is 6 V and the load resistance is $R_L = 4\,k\Omega$. The series resistance of the circuit is $R = 1\,k\Omega$. If the battery voltage V_B varies from 8 V to 16 V, what are the minimum and maximum values of the current through Zener diode?

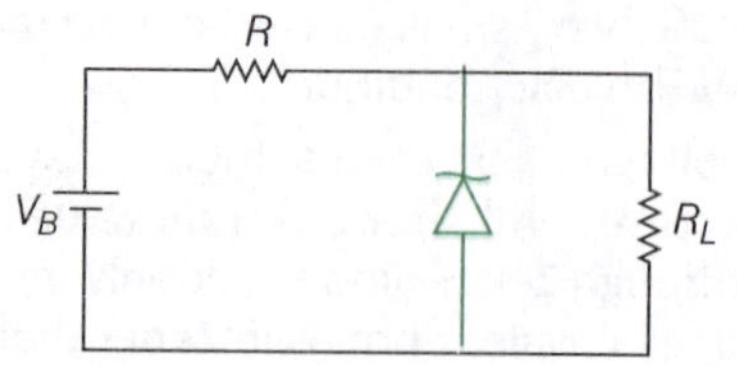

(a) 0.5 mA, 0.6 mA (b) 1 mA, 8.5 mA
(c) 1.5 mA, 8.5 mA (d) 0.5 mA, 8.5 mA

Sol. Minimum Current

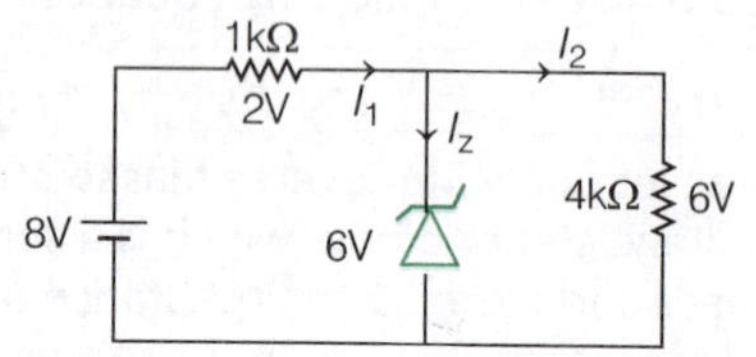

$$I_1 = \frac{2V}{1\,k\Omega} = 2\,mA$$

$$I_2 = \frac{6\,V}{4\,k\Omega} = 1.5\,mA$$

$\therefore$ $$I_z = I_1 - I_2 = 0.5\,mA$$

Maximum current

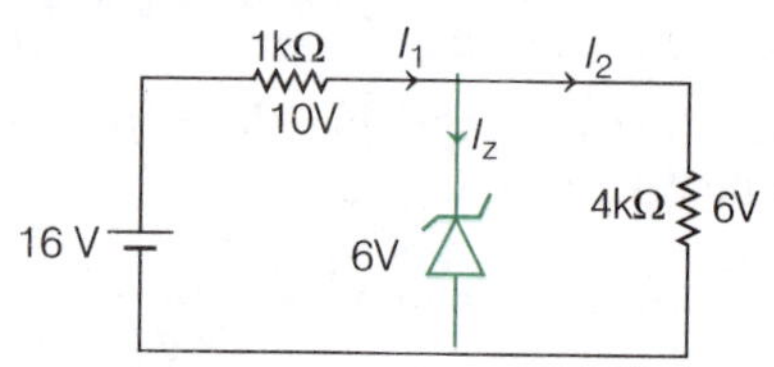

$$I_1 = \frac{10\,V}{1\,k\Omega} = 10\,mA$$

$$I_2 = \frac{6\,V}{4\,k\Omega} = 1.5\,mA$$

$\therefore$ $$I_z = I_1 - I_2 = 8.5\,mA$$

$\therefore$ The correct option is (d).

Photodiode

A photodiode is a *p-n* junction diode that consumes light energy to produce an electric current. They are also called a photo-detector, a light detector, or a photo-sensor. Photodiodes are designed to work in reverse bias condition.

Symbol of Photodiode

The following image shows the symbol of the photodiode.

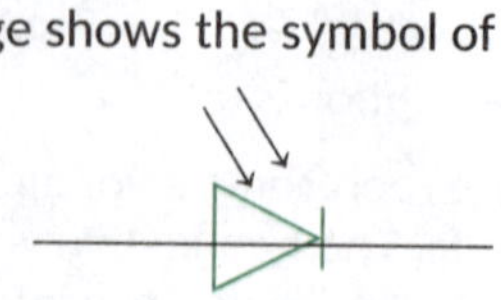

Photodiode Working

A photodiode is subjected to photons in the form of light. If the energy of the falling photons (*hf*) is greater than the energy gap (E_g) of the semiconductor material, electron-hole pairs are created near the depletion region of the diode. Due to the electric field the electron-hole pairs created are separated from each other before recombining . The direction of the electric field in the diode forces the electrons to move towards the *n*-side and consequently the holes move towards the *p*-side. Thus, a current flow is observed in the circuit.

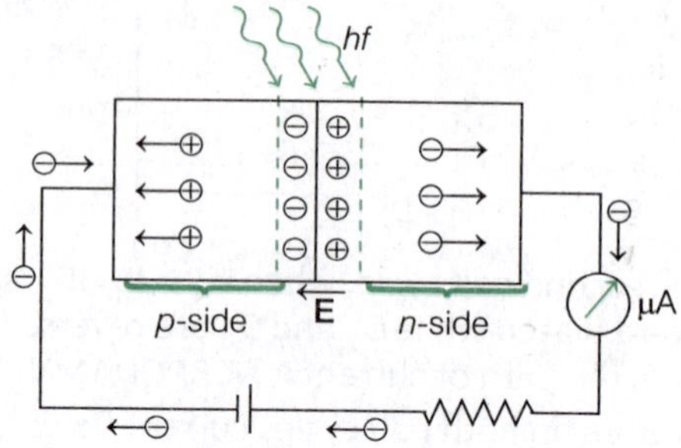

The magnitude of current depends directly upon the intensity of the incident light.

Since photodiodes generate current flow directly depending upon the light intensity received, they can be used as photo detectors to detect optical signals.

The *V-I* characteristics for reverse biased photodiode is given below.

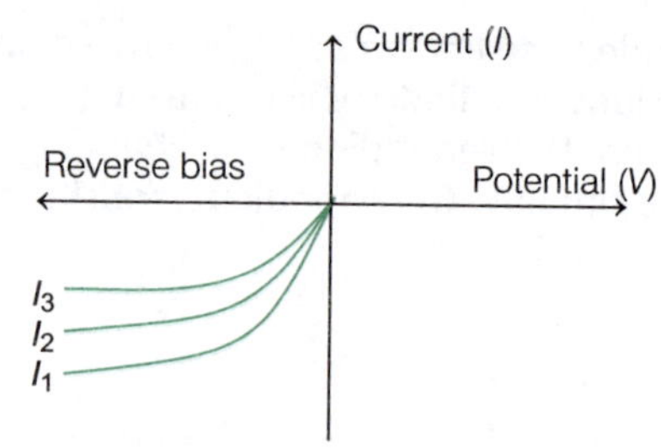

Intensity I_1 > Intensity I_2 > Intensity I_3

Note (i) *Under normal condition current through diode is zero in reverse bias condition. But in case of photodiodes current flows in reverse bias condition.*

(ii) *Here intensity means number of photons incident per unit area per unit time.*

Example 8 Three photodiodes D_1, D_2 and D_3 are made of semiconductors having band gaps of 2.5 eV, 2 eV and 3 eV, respectively. Which one will be able to detect light of wavelength 6000 Å ?

Sol. Energy of incident light

$$E\,(\text{in eV}) = \frac{12375}{\lambda\,(\text{in Å})}$$

$\Rightarrow$ $$E = \frac{12375}{6000}\,\text{eV}$$

or $$E = 2.06\,\text{eV}$$

For the incident radiation to be detected by the photodiode, energy of incident radiation should be greater than the band gap. This is true only for D_2. Therefore only D_2 will detect this radiation.

Light Emitting Diode

Light-emitting diode (LED) is a widely used standard source of light in electrical equipment. It has a wide range of applications ranging from your mobile phone to large advertising billboards. They mostly find applications in devices that show the time and display different types of data.

A light-emitting diode (LED) is a semiconductor device that emits light when an electric current flows through it. When current passes through an LED, the electrons recombine with holes, emitting light in this process. LEDs allow the current to flow in the **forward direction** and blocks the current in the reverse direction.

Light-emitting diodes are heavily doped *p-n* junction diodes. Based on the semiconductor material used and the amount of doping, an LED will emit a coloured light at a particular spectral wavelength when forward biased.

The LED symbol is the standard symbol for a diode, with the addition of two small arrows denoting the emission of light.

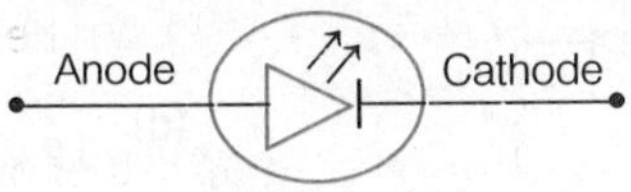

LED symbol

The figure below shows a simple LED circuit.

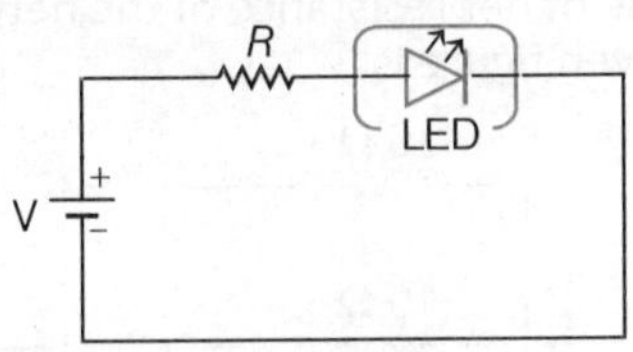

LED circuit

How does an LED work?

When the diode is forward biased, then the electrons and holes are moving fast across the junction and they are combined constantly. Electrons move from the *n*-side to the *p*-side and it combines with the holes, then it disappears. Hence, it makes a complete stable atom having low energy. The energy gap is released in the form of photon or light.

Note *When a normal p-n junction diode is forward biased, the same phenomenon takes place. But the effect is insignificant because they are not highly doped unlike LEDs.*

Working Principle of LED

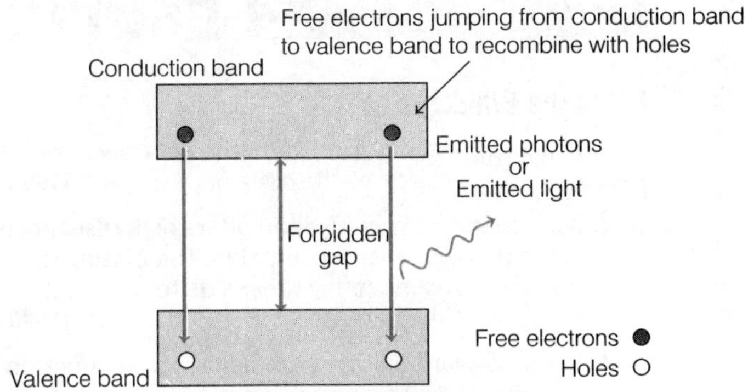

Process of light emission in LED

The energy is released in the form of photons on recombination.

The colour of an LED is determined by the material used in the semiconducting element (or the energy gap).

Solar Cells

A solar cell consists of a layer of *p*-type silicon placed next to a layer of *n*-type silicon.

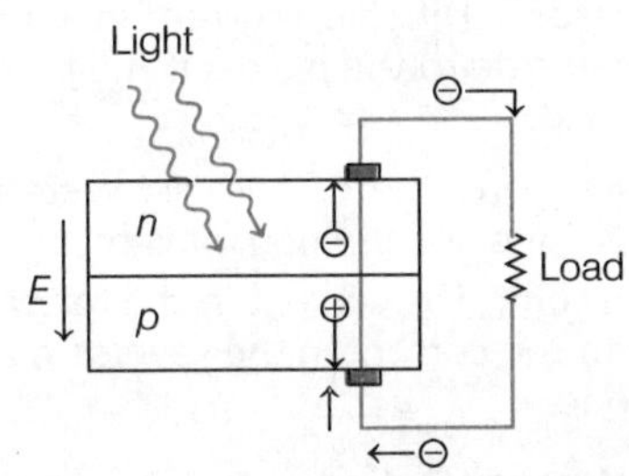

When sunlight strikes a solar cell, electrons in the silicon are ejected, which results in the formation of holes. If this happens in the electric field (or depletion zone), the field will move electrons to the *n*-type layer and holes to the *p*-type layer. As the concentration of electrons becomes higher on *n*-side and concentration of holes becomes more in *p*-side of the junction, the *p-n* junction will behave like a small battery cell. If we connect a small load across the junction, there will be a tiny current flowing through it.

Note *You can see that principle is very similar to the principle of photodiodes.*

MODULE 2 Exercise

Fill in the Blanks

1. In a .... biased *p-n* junction, the net flow of holes is from the *n* region to the *p* region. **(1993 JEE)**

2. .... biasing of *p-n* junction offers high resistance to current flow across the junction. The biasing is obtained by connecting the *p*-side to the .... terminal of the battery. **(1990 JEE)**

3. In the forward bias arrangement of a *p-n* junction rectifier, the *p* end is connected to the .... terminal of the battery and the direction of the current is from .... to ...... in the rectifier. **(1988 JEE)**

Assertion and Reason

See directions on page 11.

4. **Assertion :** Diffusion current in a *p-n* junction is greater than the drift current in magnitude if the junction is forward biased.

   Reason : Diffusion current in a *p-n* junction is from the *n*-side to the *p*-side, if the junction is forward biased. **(2023 Main)**

5. **Assertion :** Photodiodes are preferably operated in reverse bias condition for light intensity measurement.

   Reason : The current in the forward bias is more than the current in the reverse bias for a *p-n* junction diode. **(2023 Main)**

Single Correct Option

6. In an unbiased *p-n* junction, holes diffuse from the *p*-region to *n*-region because
   (a) free electrons in the *n*-region attract them
   (b) they move across the junction by the potential difference
   (c) hole concentration in *p*-region is more as compared to *n*-region
   (d) All of the above

7. When a forward bias is applied to a *p - n* junction. It
   (a) raises the potential barrier
   (b) reduces the majority carrier current to zero
   (c) lowers the potential barrier
   (d) All of the above

8. In figure, assuming the diodes to be ideal,

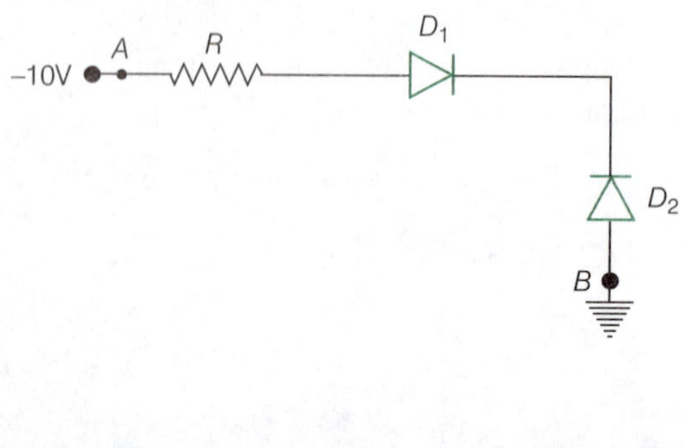

   (a) D_1 is forward biased and D_2 is reverse biased and hence current flows from *A* to *B*.
   (b) D_2 is forward biased and D_1 is reverse biased and hence no current flows from *B* to *A* and *vice-versa*.
   (c) D_1 and D_2 are both forward biased and hence current flows from *A* to *B*.
   (d) D_1 and D_2 are both reverse biased and hence no current flows from *A* to *B* and *vice-versa*.

9. Which of the following circuits is reverse-biased? **(2024 Main)**

   (a) 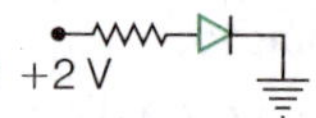

   (b) 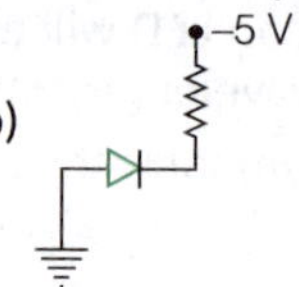

   (c) 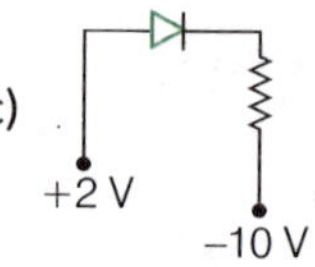

   (d) 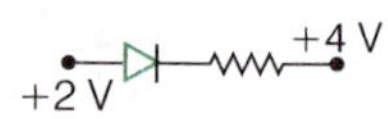

10. The value of net resistance of the network as shown in the given figure is **(2024 Main)**

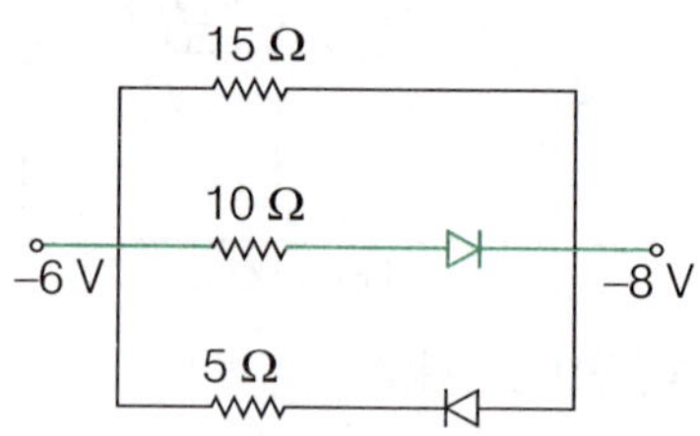

   (a) 6Ω (b) $\left(\frac{15}{4}\right)\Omega$ (c) $\left(\frac{5}{2}\right)\Omega$ (d) $\left(\frac{30}{11}\right)\Omega$

11. Which of the following statements is **not true** ? **(1997 JEE)**
   (a) The resistance of intrinsic semiconductors decreases with increase of temperature.
   (b) Doping pure Si with trivalent impurities give *p*-type semiconductors.
   (c) The majority carriers in *n*-type semiconductors are holes.
   (d) A *p-n* junction can act as a semiconductor diode.

12. The reading of the ammeter for a silicon diode in the given circuit is **(2018 Main)**

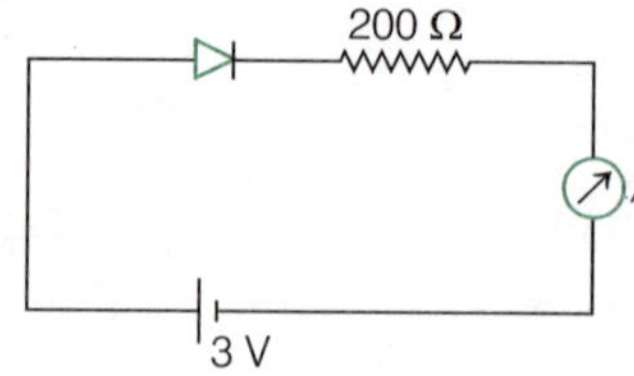

(a) 13.5 mA (b) 0
(c) 15 mA (d) 11.5 mA

13. A Zener diode of power rating 1.6 W is to be used as voltage regulator. If the Zener diode has a breakdown of 8 V and it has to regulate voltage fluctuating between 3 V and 10 V. The value of resistance R_S for safe operation of diode will be **(2023 Main)**

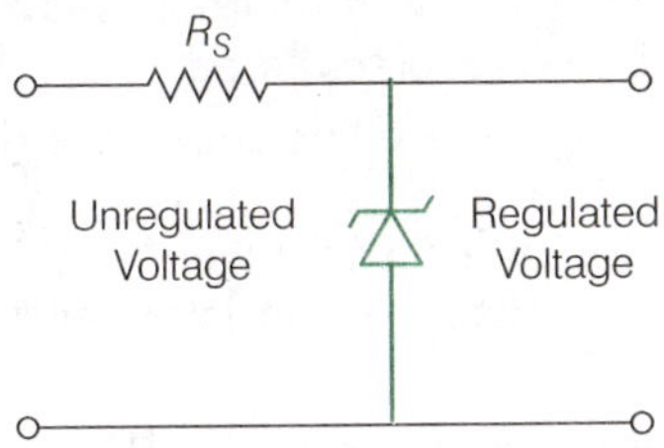

(a) 13.3Ω (b) 10Ω
(c) 13Ω (d) 12Ω

14. Choose the correct statement about zener diode. **(2023 Main)**
(a) It works as a voltage regulator in reverse bias and behaves like simple *p-n* junction diode in forward bias.
(b) It works as a voltage regulator only in forward bias.
(c) It works as a voltage regulator in forward bias and behaves like simple *p-n* junction diode in reverse bias.
(d) It works as a voltage regulator in both forward and reverse bias.

15. Zener breakdown occur in a *p-n* junction having *p* and *n* both **(2021 Main)**
(a) lightly doped and have wide depletion layer
(b) heavily doped and have narrow depletion layer
(c) lightly doped and have narrow depletion layer
(d) heavily doped and have wide depletion layer

16. Figure shows a DC voltage regulator circuit, with a Zener diode of breakdown voltage = 6 V. If the unregulated input voltage varies between 10 V to 16 V, then what is the maximum Zener current? **(2019 Main)**

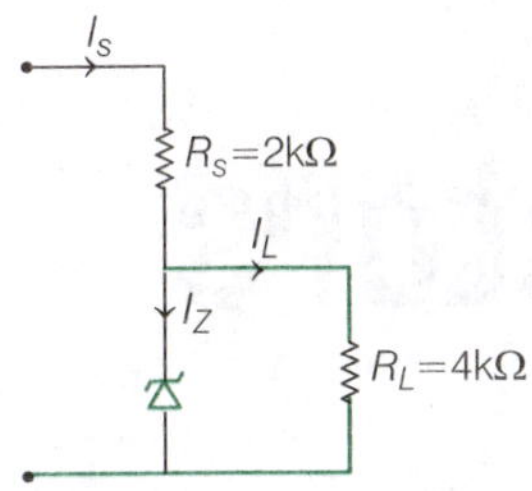

(a) 2.5 mA (b) 1.5 mA
(c) 7.5 mA (d) 3.5 mA

17. Which one of the following statement is **not correct** in the case of light emitting diodes?
A. It is a heavily doped *p-n* junction.
B. It emits light only when it is forward biased.
C. It emits light only when it is reverse biased.
D. The energy of the light emitted is equal to or slightly less than the energy gap of the semiconductor used. **(2023 Main)**

(a) B (b) C
(c) A (d) C and D

Subjective Questions

18. A *p* -*n* photodiode is fabricated from a semiconductor with band-gap of 2.8 eV. Can it detect a wavelength of 6000 nm?

19. Each diode shown in figure has a resistance of 25Ω in forward bias condition and infinite resistance in reverse bias. What will be the values of the current I_1, I_2, I_3 and I_4?

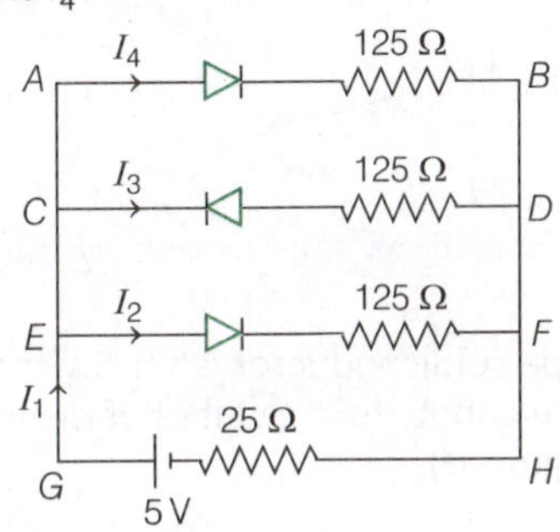

Answers

1. reverse	**2.** Reverse, negative	**3.** positive, *p*-side, *n*-side	**4.** (c)	**5.** (b)	**6.** (c)	**7.** (c)	**8.** (b)
9. (d)	**10.** (a)	**11.** (c)	**12.** (d)	**13.** (b)	**14.** (a)	**15.** (b)	**16.** (d)
17. (b)	**18.** (No)						

19. $I_1 = 0.05A$, $I_2 = 0.025A$, $I_3 = 0$, $I_4 = 0.025A$

See hints on pages 434-436.

MODULE 3

Transistors

A junction transistor is formed by sandwiching a thin wafer of one type of semiconductor between two layers of another type. The *n-p-n* transistor has a *p*-type wafer between two *n*-type layers. Similarly, the *p-n-p* transistor has a *n*-type wafer between two *p*-type layers.

p-n-p Transistor

Figure shows a *p-n-p* transistor, in which a thin layer of *n*-type semiconductor is sandwiched between two *p*-type semiconductors. The middle layer (called the base) is very thin (of the order of 1 μm) as compared to the widths of the two layers at the sides. Base is very lightly doped. One of the side layer (called emitter) is heavily doped and the other side layer (called collector) is moderately doped.
figure (c) shows the symbol of *p-n-p* transistor.

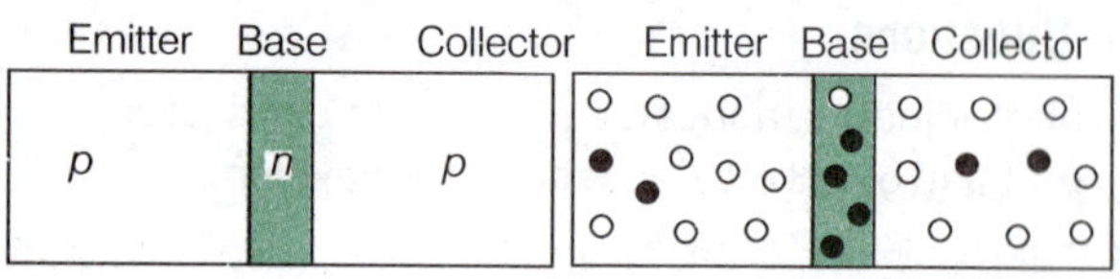

(a) (b)

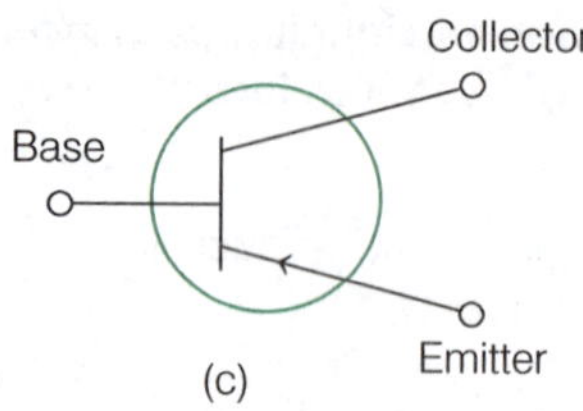

(c)

n-p-n Transistor

In *n-p-n* transistor, *p*-type semiconductor is sandwiched between two *n*-type semiconductors. Symbol of *n-p-n* transistor is shown in figure (f).

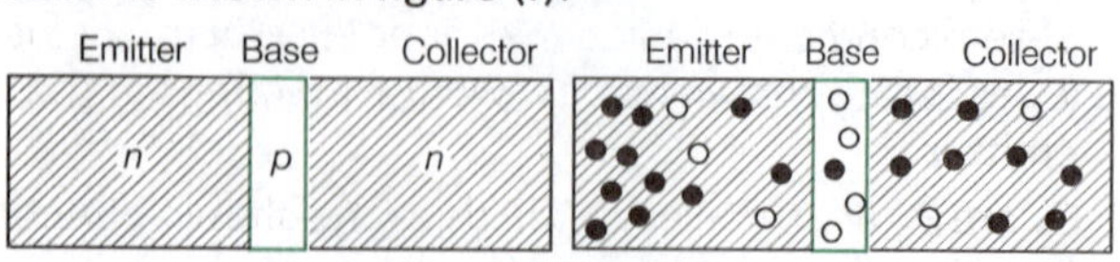

(d) (e)

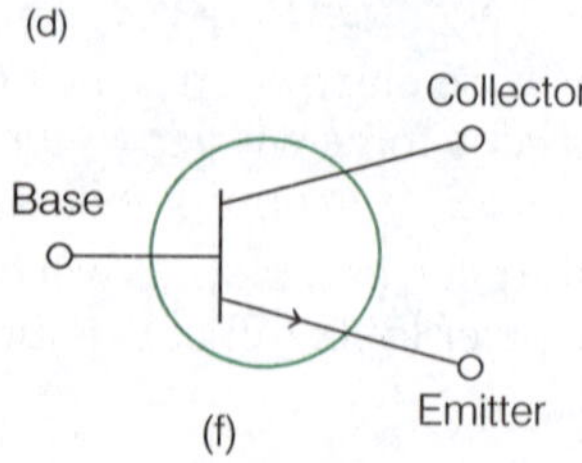

(f)

A transistor is basically a three-terminal device. Terminals come out from the emitter, base and the collector for external connections. In normal operation of a transistor, the emitter-base junction is always forward biased and collector-base junction is reverse biased.

The arrow on the emitter-base line shows the direction of current between emitter and base. In an *n-p-n* transistor for example, the direction of electric current at this junction is from the base to the emitter. A transistor can be operated in three different modes.

(i) Common emitter (or grounded-emitter)

(ii) Common collector (or grounded-collector) and

(iii) Common base (or grounded-base)

In common emitter mode, emitter is kept at zero potential. Similarly in common collector mode collector is at zero potential and so on.

Working of a *p-n-p* Transistor

Let us consider the working of a *p-n-p* transistor in common base mode. In emitter (*p*-type) holes are in majority. Since, emitter-base is forward biased, holes move towards base. Few of them combine with electrons in the base and rest go to the collector. Since, base-collector is reverse biased, holes coming from base move toward the terminal of collector. They combine with equal number of electrons entering from collector terminal.

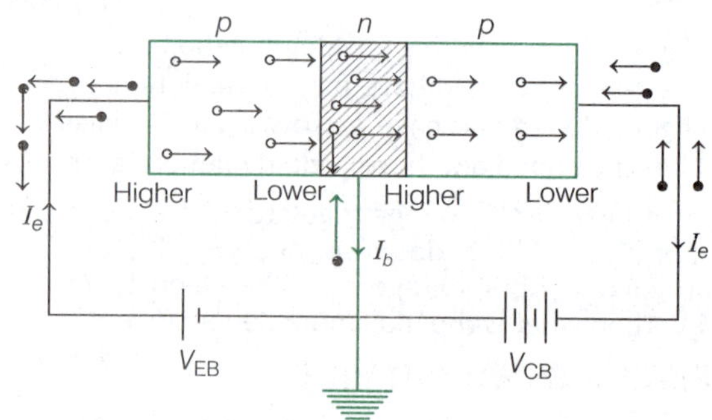

Let us take an example with some numerical values.

Suppose 5 holes enter from emitter to base. This deficiency of 5 holes in emitter is compensated when 5 electrons emit from emitter and give rise to I_e.

One out of five holes which reach the base combine with one electron entering from base (the equivalent current is I_b). Rest four holes enter the collector and move towards its terminal. On the other hand, 5 electrons which leave the emitter (as I_e) come to the base, emitter and collector junction.

One electron of it goes to base and rest four to collector. These four electrons give rise to I_c (the collector current) and combine with the four holes coming from the base, and thus circuit is complete. From the figure, we can see that,

$$I_e = I_c + I_b$$

***Note** that I_b is only about 2% of I_e, or roughly around 2% of holes coming from emitter to base combine with the electrons. Rest 98% move to collector.*

Working of *n-p-n* Transistor

A common base circuit of an *n-p-n* transistor is shown in figure. Majority charge carriers in the emitter (*n*-type) are electrons. Since, emitter-base circuit is forward biased. The electrons rush from emitter to base. Few of them leave the base terminal (comprising I_b) and rest move to collector. These electrons finally leave the collector terminal (give rise to I_c). Electrons coming from base and from collector meet at junction O and they jointly move to emitter, which gives rise to I_e.

Thus, here also we can see that :

$$I_e = I_b + I_c$$

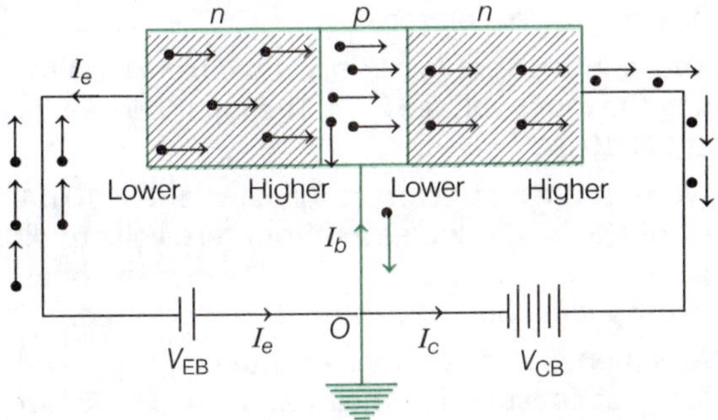

***Note** (i) Although the working principle of p-n-p and n-p-n transistors are similar but the current carriers in p-n-p transistors are mainly holes whereas in n-p-n transistors the current carriers are mainly electrons. Mobility of electrons are however more than the mobility of holes, therefore n-p-n transistors are used in high frequency and computer circuits where the carriers are required to respond very quickly to signals.*

(ii) Later on V_{EB} or V_{BE} is also written as V_{BB} and V_{CB} as V_{CC}.

Transistors as an Amplifier

A transistor can be used for amplifying a weak signal.

When a transistor is to be operated as amplifier, three different basic circuit connections are possible. These are :

(i) common emitter, (ii) common base and

(iii) common collector.

Whichever circuit configuration, the emitter-base junction is always forward biased, while the collector-base junction is always reverse biased.

Common Emitter Amplifier Using an *n-p-n* Transistor

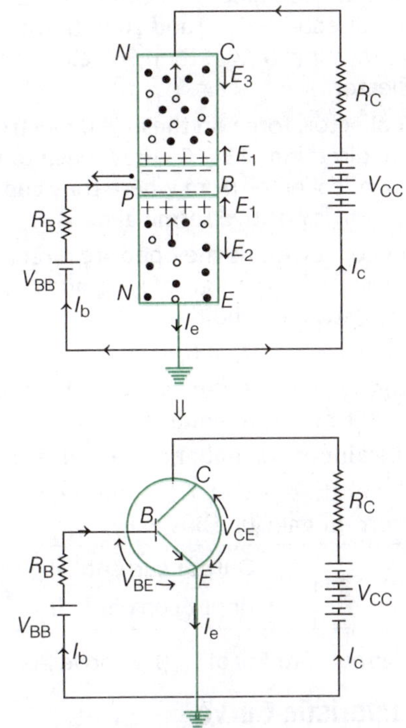

(i) $E \rightarrow$ emitter, $B \rightarrow$ base and $C \rightarrow$ collector.

(ii) Emitter is common and earthed. So, here potential may be assumed zero or, $V_E = 0$

(iii) Let us suppose that V_{BB} (shown in figure) is 1V and V_{CC} is 10V. Then :

$$V_B = 1\text{ V and } V_C = 10\text{ V}$$

(iv) Emitter is *n*-type semiconductor and $V_E = 0$. Base is *p*-type semiconductor and $V_B = 1$ V.

$\therefore$ $V_E < V_B$ or $V_{n\text{-type}} < V_{p\text{-type}}$. So, emitter-base is forward biased.

(v) Collector is *n*-type semiconductor and $V_C = 10$ V.

Thus, $V_C > V_B$ or $V_{n\text{-type}} > V_{p\text{-type}}$. So, base-collector is reverse biased.

(vi) Two potential barriers (0.7 V if we take Si-semiconductor) and corresponding electric fields (E_1 each) are shown across two *p-n* junctions in the emitter.

(vii) E_2 are E_3 are the electric fields in the shown directions because, $V_B > V_E$ and then $V_C > V_B$.

(viii) Emitter is *n*-type, so electrons are majority charge carriers. Due to E_2 a force will act on them towards base. Force due to E_1 is in opposite direction.

Therefore to start current, first we will have to break the potential barrier (of 0.7 V) at *E*-*B* junction.

That's why we have taken $V_{BB} = 1$ V (> 0.7 V). Now let us assume that 1000 electrons enter from E to B (in the opposite direction of E_2) and 20 of them move towards positive terminal of V_{BB}, then 980 electrons will enter the collector.

In the collector, force on these 980 electrons are in opposite direction of E_3. So they reach to the other terminal of collector from where they come out and move towards positive terminal of V_{CC}.

(ix) Direction of current is the opposite direction of motion of electrons. So directions of I_e, I_b and I_c are as shown in figure, with the condition,

$$I_e = I_b + I_c$$

(x) V_{BE} in the second diagram is called the input voltage and V_{CE} as the output voltage.

(xi) I_b is called input current and I_c as the output current. The ratio of these two I_c/I_b or sometimes $\Delta I_c/\Delta I_b$ is called current gain (β). Thus,

$$\text{Current gain } \beta = \frac{\text{Output current}}{\text{Input current}} = \frac{I_c}{I_b} \text{ or } \frac{\Delta I_c}{\Delta I_b}$$

As I_b is about 1 to 5% of I_e, β is above 20 to 100.

Input Characteristic Curve

Graph between input current I_b and input voltage V_{BE} (V_{CE} = constant) is called input characteristic curve.

The graph is as shown below.

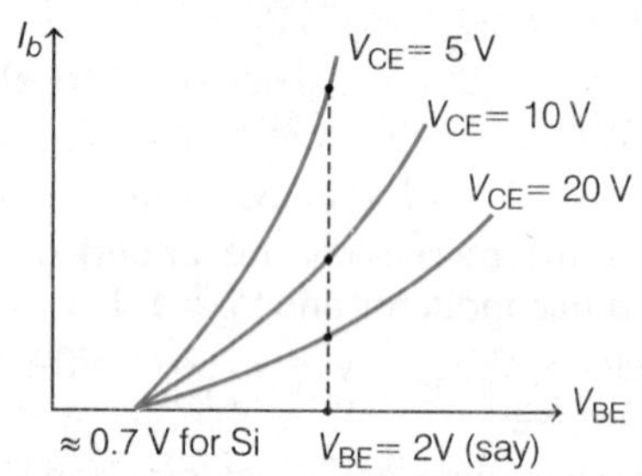

Until V_{BE} is 0.7V (for Si) I_b is zero. After that I_b increases as V_{BE} increases. If we fix V_{BE} at 2V (say) then I_b at $V_{CE} = 20$ V is less than $V_{CE} = 10$ V. The reason is : we had assumed that 1000 electrons enter from emitter to base and 20 of them come out from base. Only 980 are attracted towards collector.

If V_{CE} is increased then more electrons will be attracted towards collector. So, less number of electrons will come out from the base. So, I_b will decrease. In the graph we have shown the same thing.

Input Resistance

The ratio of change in input voltage ΔV_{BE} and change in input current ΔI_b of constant value of output voltage V_{CE} is called input resistance R_{in} : Thus,

$$R_{in} = \left(\frac{\Delta V_{BE}}{\Delta I_b}\right)_{V_{CE} = \text{constant}}$$

Output Characteristic Curve

In common emitter configuration, the curve drawn between output current I_C and output voltage V_{CE} at a constant base current I_B is called output characteristic curve. The characteristic curve for the typical n-p-n transistor in common emitter configuration is shown in the figure below.

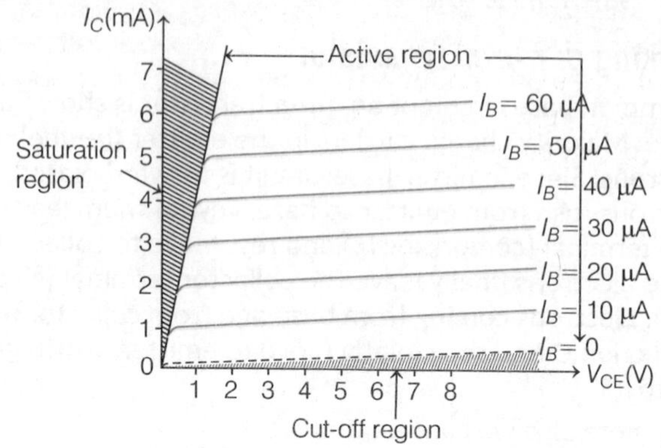

When the base current or input current $I_B = 0\ \mu$A, the transistor operates in the cut-off region. In this region, both junctions are reverse biased.

Next, the input current (I_B) is increased from 0 μA to 10 μA by adjusting the input voltage (V_{BE}). The input current (I_B) is kept constant at 10 μA.

After we kept the input current (I_B) constant at 10 μA, the output voltage (V_{CE}) is increased from zero volts to different voltage levels. For each voltage level of output voltage (V_{CE}), the corresponding output current (I_C) is recorded.

A curve is then drawn between output current I_C and output voltage V_{CE} at constant input current I_B (10 μA). This region is known as the active region of a transistor. In this region, emitter-base junction is forward biased and the collector-base junction is reverse biased.

This steps are repeated for higher fixed values of input current I_B (i.e. 20 μA, 30 μA, 40 μA and so on).

When output voltage V_{CE} is reduced to a small value (0.2 V), the collector-base junction becomes forward biased.

As we know that the emitter-base junction is already forward biased. Therefore, when both the junctions are forward biased, the transistor operates in the saturation region. In this region, a small increase in output voltage V_{CE} will rapidly increase the output current I_C.

Important Points in Output Characteristic Curve

(i) In saturation region both E-B and B-C are forward biased.

In active region E-B is forward biased and B-C is reversed biased

In cutoff region both are reverse biased.

(ii) Transistor can be used as an amplifier in active region.

(iii) In saturation region, transistor acts like ON stage of a switch and in the cutoff region it acts like the OFF stage of a switch.

(iv) **Output resistance**

$$r_0 = \left(\frac{\Delta V_{CE}}{\Delta I_C}\right)_{I_b = \text{constant}}$$

Emitter as an Amplifier

Since, the base-emitter circuit is forward biased, input resistance is low. Similarly, collector-emitter circuit is reverse biased, therefore output resistance is high. The weak input AC signal is superimposed on V_{BB} and the amplified output signal is obtained across the collector-emitter circuit.

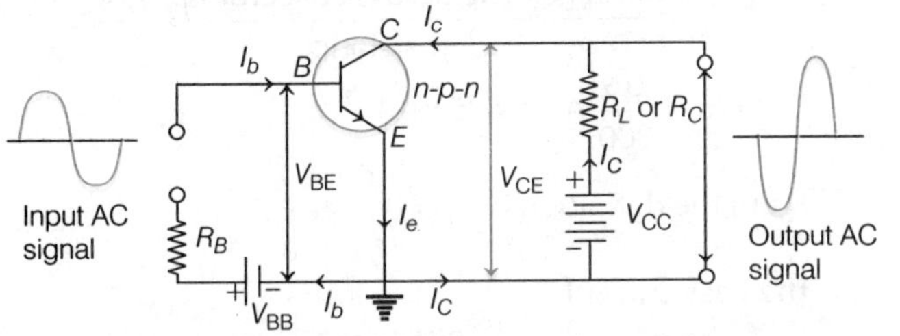

In the figure we can see that,

$$V_{CE} = V_{CC} - I_c R_L$$

When the input AC voltage signal is applied across the base-emitter circuit, it fluctuates V_{BB} and hence the emitter and base currents.

This in turn changes the collector current I_c. Consequently V_{CE} varies in accordance with the above equation. This variation in V_{CE} appears as an amplified output.

Current Gain, Voltage Gain and Power Gain

(i) **Current gain** Also called ac current gain (β_{ac}), is defined as the ratio of the collector current to the base current at constant collector to emitter voltage.

$$\beta_{ac} \text{ or simply } \beta = \left(\frac{\Delta I_c}{\Delta I_b}\right) \quad (V_{CE} = \text{constant})$$

(ii) **Voltage gain** It is defined as the ratio of the change in the output voltage to the change in the input voltage. It is denoted by A_V. Thus,

$$A_V = \frac{\Delta I_c \times R_{out}}{\Delta I_b \times R_{in}}$$

or

$$A_V = \beta\left(\frac{R_{out}}{R_{in}}\right)$$

(iii) **Power gain** It is defined as the ratio of change in output power to the change in the input power. Since,

$$P = VI$$

Therefore, power gain = current gain × voltage gain

or

$$\text{Power gain} = \beta^2\left(\frac{R_{out}}{R_{in}}\right)$$

Transconductance (g_m) There is one more term called transconductance (g_m) in common-emitter mode. It is defined as the ratio of the change in the collector current to the change in the base to emitter voltage at constant collector to emitter voltage. Thus,

$$g_m = \left(\frac{\Delta I_c}{\Delta V_{BE}}\right) \quad (V_{CE} = \text{constant})$$

The unit of g_m is Ω^{-1} or siemen (S). By simple calculation we can prove that,

$$g_m = \frac{\beta}{R_{in}}$$

Note (i) *By superimposing an input AC signal over V_{BB} (or in input signal), the net value of V_{BE} or input voltage fluctuates. Due to which all other values like I_e, I_c, I_b and output voltage also fluctuates.*

Let us take an example :

Suppose constant value of V_{BB} is 1V and input AC signal varies between 0.2 V and – 0.2 V. Then net value of V_{BE} will fluctuate between (1 + 0.2) V, or 1.2 V and (1 – 0.2) V or 0.8 V.

(ii) *The output voltage signal is 180° out of phase with the input voltage.*

This is because : when net value of V_{BE} increases, I_b and I_c also increase. So, from the equation

$$V_{CE} = V_{CC} - I_C R_L$$

output voltage V_{CE} decrease. Thus, input voltage is increasing and output voltage is decreasing. So, it implies that there is a phase difference of 180° between input voltage and output voltage.

Common Base Amplifier Using a *p-n-p* Transistor

In common base amplifier, the input signal is applied across the emitter and the base, while the amplified output signal is taken across the collector and the base. This circuit provides a very low input resistance, a very high output resistance and a current gain of just less than 1. Still it provides a good voltage and power amplification. There is no phase difference between input and output signals.

The common base amplifier circuit using a *p-n-p* transistor is shown in figure. The emitter base input circuit is forward biased by a low voltage battery V_{BB}. The collector base output circuit is reversed biased by means of a high voltage battery V_{CC}. Since, the input circuit is forward biased, resistance of input circuit is small. Similarly, output circuit is reverse biased, hence resistance of output circuit is high.

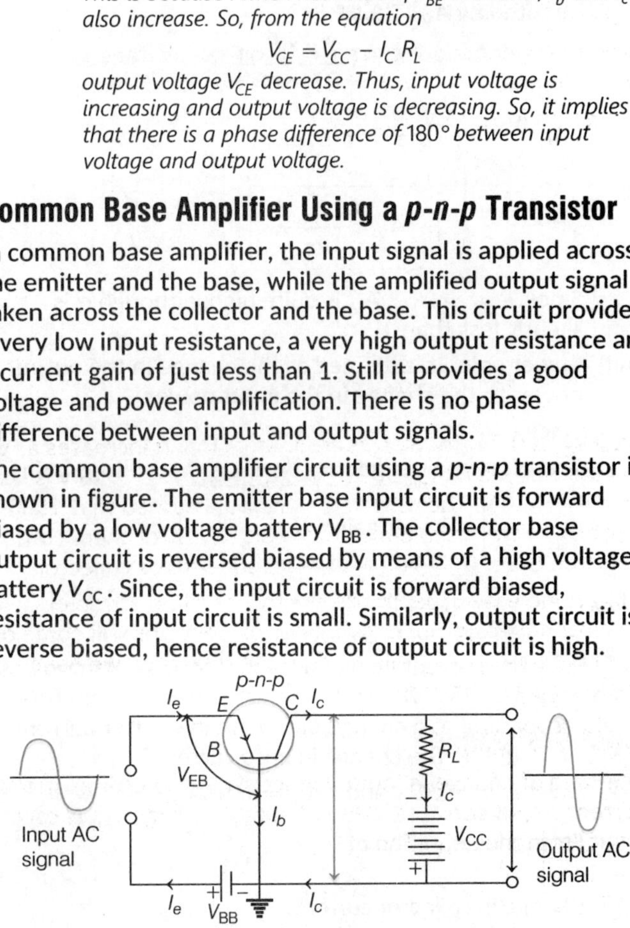

The weak input AC voltage signal is superimposed on V_{BB} and the amplified output signal is obtained across collector-base circuit. In the figure we can see that,

$$V_{CB} = V_{CC} - I_c R_L$$

The input AC voltage signal changes net value of V_{EB}. Due to fluctuations in V_{EB}, the emitter current I_e also fluctuates which in turn fluctuates I_c. In accordance with the above equation there are fluctuations in V_{CB}.

If V_{EB} increases then I_b increases but I_c decreases ($I_c = I_e - I_b$). So, V_{CB} also increase. Therefore input and output are in same phase.

Current gain, Voltage gain and Power gain

(i) **Current gain** Also called AC current gain (α_{ac}), is defined as the ratio of the change in the collector current to the change in the emitter current at constant collector-base voltage.

Thus, α_{ac} or simply $\boxed{\alpha = \dfrac{\Delta I_c}{\Delta I_e}}$ (V_{CB} = constant)

As stated earlier also, α is slightly less than 1.

(ii) **Voltage gain** It is defined as the ratio of change in the output voltage to the change in the input voltage. It is denoted by A_V. Thus,

$$A_V = \frac{\Delta I_c \times R_{out}}{\Delta I_e \times R_{in}}$$

but $\dfrac{\Delta I_c}{\Delta I_e} = \alpha$, the current gain.

$$\therefore \quad \boxed{A_V = \frac{a R_{out}}{R_{in}}}$$

Since, $R_{out} >> R_{in}$, A_V is quite high, although α is slightly less than 1.

(iii) **Power gain** It is defined as the change in the output power to the change in the input power.

Since $P = VI$

Therefore, power gain = current gain × voltage gain

or $\boxed{\text{Power gain} = \alpha^2 \cdot \dfrac{R_{out}}{R_{in}}}$

Note $\boxed{\beta = \dfrac{\alpha}{1-\alpha}}$

Example 1 The current gain of a transistor in a common base arrangement in 0.98. Find the change in collector current corresponding to a change of 5.0 mA in emitter current. What would be the change in base current?

Sol. Given, $\alpha = 0.98$ and $\Delta I_e = 5.0\,\text{mA}$

From the definition of, $\alpha = \dfrac{\Delta I_c}{\Delta I_e}$

Change in collector current,

$$\Delta I_c = (\alpha)(\Delta I_e) = (0.98)(5.0)\,\text{m}$$
$$= 4.9\,\text{mA}$$

Further, change in base current,

$$\Delta I_b = \Delta I_e - \Delta I_c = 0.1\,\text{mA}$$ **Ans.**

Example 2 A transistor is connected in common emitter configuration. The collector supply is 8 V and the voltage drop across a resistor of 800 Ω in the collector circuit is 0.5 V. If the current gain factor (α) is 0.96, find the base current.

Sol. $\beta = \dfrac{\alpha}{1-\alpha} = \dfrac{0.96}{1-0.96} = 24$

The collector current is,

$$I_c = \frac{\text{voltage drop across collector resistor}}{\text{resistance}}$$
$$= \frac{0.5}{800}\,\text{A} = 0.625 \times 10^{-3}\,\text{A}$$

From the definition of $\beta = \dfrac{I_c}{I_b}$

the base current

$$I_b = \frac{I_c}{\beta} = \frac{0.625 \times 10^{-3}}{24}\,\text{A}$$
$$= 26\,\mu\text{A}$$ **Ans.**

Example 3 In a common emitter amplifier, the load resistance of the output circuit is 500 times the resistance of the input circuit. If $\alpha = 0.98$, then find the voltage gain and power gain.

Sol. Given $\alpha = 0.98$ and $\dfrac{R_{out}}{R_{in}} = 500$

$$\Rightarrow \quad \beta = \frac{\alpha}{1-\alpha} = \frac{0.98}{1-0.98} = 49$$

(i) Voltage gain $= (\beta)\dfrac{R_{out}}{R_{in}} = (49)(500) = 24500$

(ii) Power gain $= (\beta^2)\dfrac{R_{out}}{R_{in}} = (49)^2(500) = 1200500$

Example 4 A change of 8.0 mA in the emitter current brings a change of 7.9 mA in the collector current. How much change in the base current is required to have the same change 7.9 mA in the collector current? Find the values of α and β.

Sol. We know that,

$$I_e = I_b + I_c$$
$$\therefore \quad \Delta I_e = \Delta I_b + \Delta I_c \quad \text{or} \quad \Delta I_b = \Delta I_e - \Delta I_c$$

Substituting the given values of the question,

We have $\Delta I_b = (8.0 - 7.9)\,\text{mA} = 0.1\,\text{mA}$

Hence, a change of 0.1 mA in the base current is required to have a change of 7.9 mA in the collector current.

Further, $\alpha = \dfrac{I_c}{I_e}$ or $\dfrac{\Delta I_c}{\Delta I_e} = \dfrac{7.9}{8.0} = 0.99$ **Ans.**

$\beta = \dfrac{I_c}{I_b}$ or $\dfrac{\Delta I_c}{\Delta I_b} = \dfrac{7.9}{0.1} = 79$ **Ans.**

Example 5 A transistor is used in common-emitter mode in an amplifier circuit. When a signal of 20 mV is added to the base-emitter voltage, the base current changes by 20 μA and the collector current changes by 2 mA. The load resistance is 5 kΩ. Calculate (a) the current gain β (b) the input resistance R_{in} (c) the transconductance and (d) the voltage gain.

Sol. (a) **Current gain β**

$$\beta = \frac{\Delta I_c}{\Delta I_b}$$

Substituting the given values, we have

$$\beta = \frac{2 \times 10^{-3}}{20 \times 10^{-6}} = 100 \qquad \textbf{Ans.}$$

(b) **Input Resistance R_{in}**

$$R_{in} = \frac{\Delta V_{BE}}{\Delta I_b} = \frac{20 \times 10^{-3}}{20 \times 10^{-6}} = 10^3\ \Omega$$

$$= 1\ \text{k}\Omega \qquad \textbf{Ans.}$$

(c) **Transconductance g_m**

$$g_m = \frac{\Delta I_c}{\Delta V_{BE}} = \frac{2 \times 10^{-3}}{20 \times 10^{-3}}$$

$$= 0.1\ \text{mho} \qquad \textbf{Ans.}$$

(d) **Voltage Gain A_V**

$$A_V = \beta \left(\frac{R_{out}}{R_{in}} \right)$$

Substituting the values we have,

$$A_V = (100) \left(\frac{5 \times 10^3}{1 \times 10^3} \right)$$

$$= 500 \qquad \textbf{Ans.}$$

Example 6 An *n-p-n* transistor is connected in common-emitter configuration in which collector supply is 8V and the voltage drop across the load resistance of 800 Ω connected in the collector circuit is 0.8 V. If current amplification factor is 25, determine collector-emitter voltage and base current. If the internal resistance of the transistor is 200 Ω, calculate the voltage gain and the power gain.

Sol. The corresponding circuit is shown in figure.

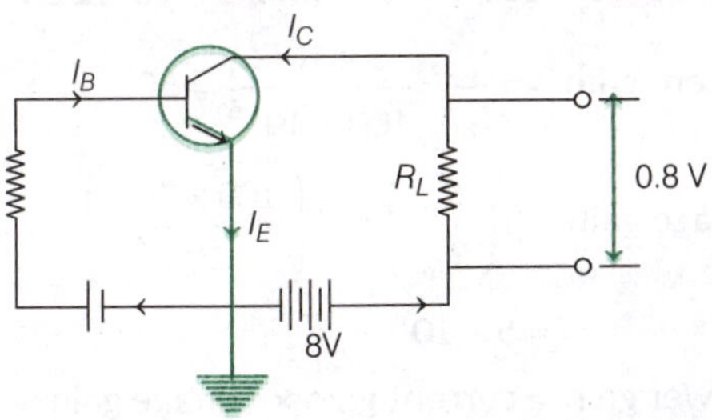

Voltage across R_L:

$$= I_c R_L = 0.8\ \text{V} \quad \text{(given)}$$

$$\therefore \quad I_c = \frac{0.8}{R_L} = \frac{0.8}{800}\ \text{A} = 1\ \text{mA}$$

Further it is given that,

$$\beta = 25 = \frac{I_c}{I_b}$$

$$\therefore \quad I_b = \frac{I_c}{25} = 40\ \mu\text{A} \qquad \textbf{Ans.}$$

Collector-Emitter Voltage (V_{CE})

$$V_{CE} = (8 - 0.8)\ \text{V} = 7.2\ \text{V} \qquad \textbf{Ans.}$$

Voltage gain (A_V)

Voltage gain, $A_V = \beta \left(\frac{R_{out}}{R_{in}} \right)$

or $$A_V = 25 \left(\frac{800}{200} \right) = 100 \qquad \textbf{Ans.}$$

Power gain

$$\text{Power gain} = \beta^2 \left(\frac{R_{out}}{R_{in}} \right)$$

$$= (25)^2 \left(\frac{800}{200} \right) = 2500 \qquad \textbf{Ans.}$$

Example 7 An *n-p-n* transistor in a common-emitter mode is used as a simple voltage amplifier with a collector current of 4 mA. The positive terminal of a 8 V battery is connected to the collector through a load resistance R_L and to the base through a resistance R_B. The collector-emitter voltage $V_{CE} = 4$ V, the base-emitter voltage $V_{BE} = 0.6$ V and the current amplification factor $\beta = 100$. Calculate the values of R_L and R_B.

Sol. Given, $I_c = 4$ mA

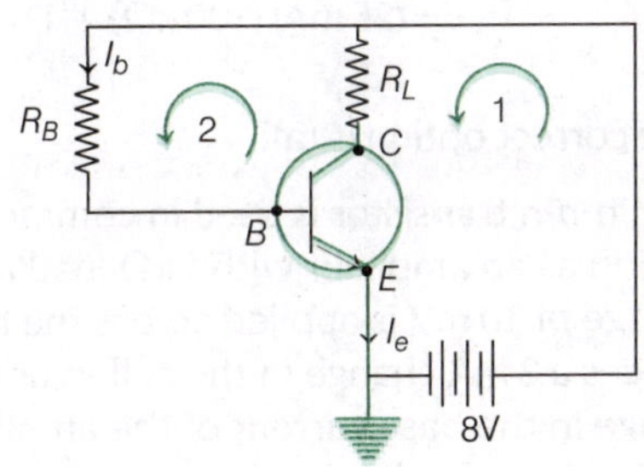

Applying potential equation in loop 1, we have

$$V_{CE} = 8 - I_c R_L$$

$$\therefore \quad R_L = \frac{8 - V_{CE}}{I_c} = \frac{8 - 4}{4 \times 10^{-3}}$$

$$= 1000\ \Omega = 1\ \text{k}\Omega \qquad \textbf{Ans.}$$

Further, $\beta = \frac{I_c}{I_b}$

$$\therefore \quad I_b = \frac{I_c}{\beta} = \frac{4 \times 10^{-3}}{100}\ \text{A} = 40\ \mu\text{A}$$

Now, $$V_{BE} = 8 - I_b R_B$$

$$\therefore \quad R_B = \frac{8 - V_{BE}}{I_b} = \frac{8 - 0.6}{40 \times 10^{-6}}$$

$$= 1.85 \times 10^5\ \Omega \quad \textbf{Ans.}$$

Example 8 In the figure, given that V_{BB} supply can vary from 0 to 5.0 V, $V_{CC} = 5$ V, $\beta_{dc} = 200$, $R_B = 100$ kΩ, $R_C = 1$ kΩ an $V_{BE} = 1.0$ V. The minimum base current and the input voltage V_{BB} at which the transistor will go to saturation, will be respectively :

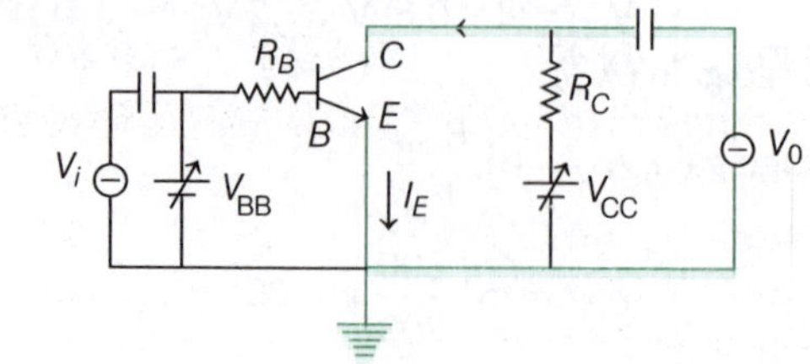

(a) 25 μA and 3.5 V (b) 20 μA and 3.5 V
(c) 25 μA and 2.8 V (d) 20 μA and 2.8 V

Sol. At saturation, $V_{CE} = 0$

$$\therefore \quad V_{CE} = V_{CC} - I_C R_C = 0$$

$$\therefore \quad I_C = \frac{V_{CC}}{R_C} = \frac{5}{10^3} = 5 \times 10^{-3}\ \text{A}$$

Now $\beta_{dc} = \dfrac{I_c}{I_b}$

$$\therefore \quad I_b = \frac{I_c}{\beta_{dc}} = \frac{5 \times 10^{-3}}{200}$$

$$= 25\ \mu\text{A} \quad \textbf{Ans.}$$

Further, $V_{BB} = I_b R_B + V_{BE}$

$$= (25\ \text{mA})\,(100\ \text{k}\Omega) + 1$$

$$= 3.5\ \text{V} \quad \textbf{Ans.}$$

∴ The correct option is (a).

Example 9 An *n-p-n* transistor is used in common emitter configuration as an amplifier with 1 kΩ load resistance. Signal voltage of 10 mV is applied across the base-emitter. This produces a 3 mA change in the collector current and 15 μA change in the base current of the amplifier. The input resistance and voltage gain are

(a) 0.67 kΩ, 300 (b) 0.67 kΩ, 200
(c) 0.33 kΩ, 1.5 (d) 0.33 kΩ, 300

Sol. Input resistance

$$R_{in} = \frac{\Delta V_i}{\Delta I_i} = \frac{\Delta V_{BE}}{\Delta I_b} = \frac{10 \times 10^{-3}}{15 \times 10^{-6}} = \frac{2}{3} \times 10^3$$

$$= 0.67\ \text{k}\Omega \quad \textbf{Ans.}$$

$$\text{Current gain } \beta = \frac{\Delta I_o}{\Delta I_i} = \frac{\Delta I_c}{\Delta I_b}$$

$$= \frac{3 \times 10^{-3}}{15 \times 10^{-6}} = 200$$

$$\text{Now voltage gain} = \frac{\text{(Output resistance)}\ (\beta)}{\text{(Input resistance)}}$$

$$= \left(\frac{10^3}{\frac{2}{3} \times 10^3}\right)(200) = 300 \quad \textbf{Ans.}$$

∴ The correct option is (a).

Example 10 An *n-p-n* transistor operates as a common emitter amplifier, with a power gain of 60 dB. The input circuit resistance is 100 Ω and the output load resistance is 10 kΩ. The common emitter current gain β is:

(a) 6×10^2 (b) 10^2 (c) 60 (d) 10^4

Sol. $60 = 10 \log_{10}\left(\dfrac{P}{P_0}\right)$

$$\therefore \quad \frac{P}{P_0} = 10^6 = \text{power gain}$$

$$= \beta^2 \left(\frac{R_o}{R_{in}}\right)$$

$$\therefore \quad \beta = \sqrt{10^6 \left(\frac{R_{in}}{R_o}\right)}$$

$$= \sqrt{\frac{(10^6)\,(100)}{(10^4)}} = 10^2 \quad \textbf{Ans.}$$

∴ The correct option is (b).

Example 11 The transfer characteristic curve of a transistor, having input and output resistance 100 Ω and 100 kΩ respectively, is shown in the figure. The voltage and power gain, are respectively :

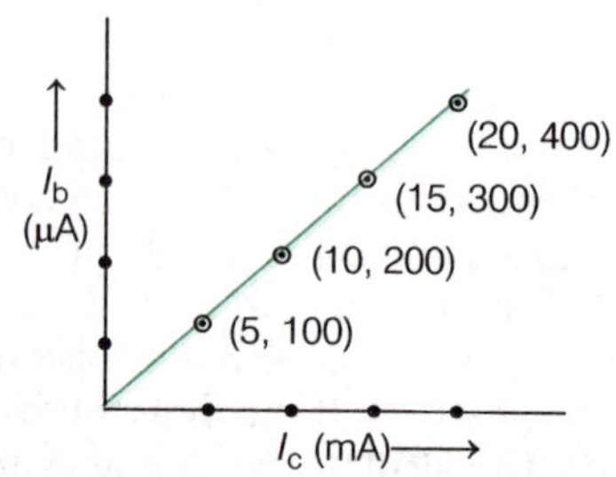

(a) $5 \times 10^4, 2.5 \times 10^6$ (b) $5 \times 10^4, 5 \times 10^6$
(c) $5 \times 10^4, 5 \times 10^5$ (d) $2.5 \times 10^4, 2.5 \times 10^6$

Sol. Current gain $\beta = \dfrac{I_c}{I_b} = \dfrac{5 \times 10^{-3}}{100 \times 10^{-6}} = 50$

$$\text{Voltage gain} = \beta\left(\frac{R_o}{R_{in}}\right) = 50\left(\frac{100 \times 10^3}{100}\right)$$

$$= 5 \times 10^4 \quad \textbf{Ans.}$$

Power gain = current gain × voltage gain

$$= (50)\,(5 \times 10^4) = 2.5 \times 10^6 \quad \textbf{Ans.}$$

∴ The correct option is (a).

MODULE 3 Exercise

Statement Type Questions

(a) Statement I is incorrect but Statement II is correct
(b) Both Statement I and Statement II are incorrect
(c) Both Statement I and Statement II are correct
(d) Statement I is correct but Statement II is incorrect

1. Given below are two statements :

Statement I : In a typical transistor, all three regions emitter, base and collector have same doping level.

Statement II : In a transistor, collector is the thickest and base is the thinnest segment. **(2023 Main)**

2. Given below are two statements:

Statement I : *p-n* junction diodes can be used to function as transistor, simply by connecting two diodes, back to back, which acts as the base terminal.

Statement II : In the study of transistor, the amplification factor β indicates ratio of the collector current to the base current. **(2021 Main)**

Single Correct Option

3. For a given transistor amplifier circuit in CE configuration $V_{CC} = 1\,V$, $R_C = 1\,k\Omega$, $R_b = 100\,k\Omega$ and $\beta = 100$. Value of base current I_b is **(2023 Main)**

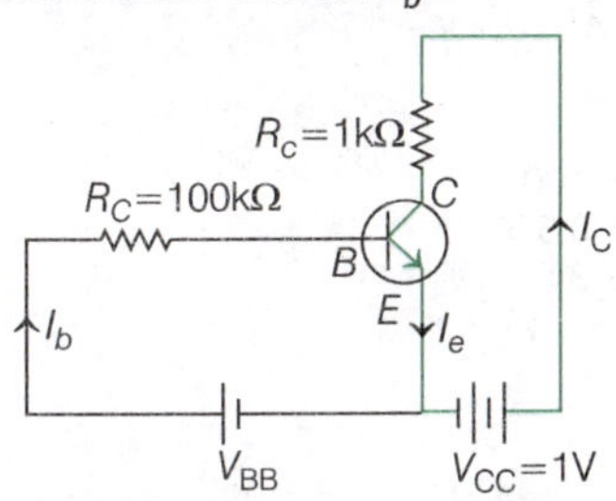

(a) $I_b = 0.1\,\mu A$ (b) $I_b = 10\,\mu A$
(c) $I_b = 100\,\mu A$ (d) $I_b = 1.0\,\mu A$

4. In an *n-p-n* common emitter (CE) transistor the collector current changes from 5 mA to 16 mA for the change in base current from 100 μA and 200 μA, respectively. The current gain of transistor is .... **(2023 Main)**

(a) 0.9 (b) 210 (c) 110 (d) 9

5. An *n-p-n* transistor with current gain $\beta = 100$ in common emitter configuration is shown in figure. The output voltage of the amplifier will be **(2022 Main)**

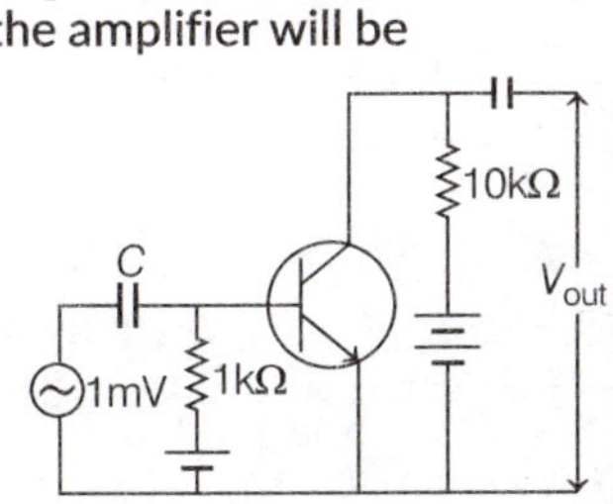

(a) 0.1 V (b) 1.0 V (c) 10 V (d) 100 V

6. For a constant collector emitter voltage of 8 V, the collector current of a transistor reached to the value of 6 mA from 4 mA, whereas base current changed from 20 μA to 25 μA value. If transistor is in active state, small signal current gain (current application factor) will be : **(2022 Main)**

(a) 240 (b) 400 (c) 0.0025 (d) 200

7. For a transistor to act as a switch, it must be operated in

(a) Active region
(b) Saturation state only
(c) Cut-off state only
(d) Saturation and cut-off state

8. For a transistor in CE mode be used as an amplifier, it must be operated in **(2021 Main)**

(a) both cut-off and saturation region
(b) saturation region only
(c) cut-off region only
(d) the active region only

9. A common emitter amplifier circuit, built using an *n-p-n* transistor, is shown in the figure. Its DC current gain is 250, $R_C = 1\,k\Omega$ and $V_{CC} = 10\,V$. What is the minimum base current for V_{CE} to reach saturation? **(2019 Main)**

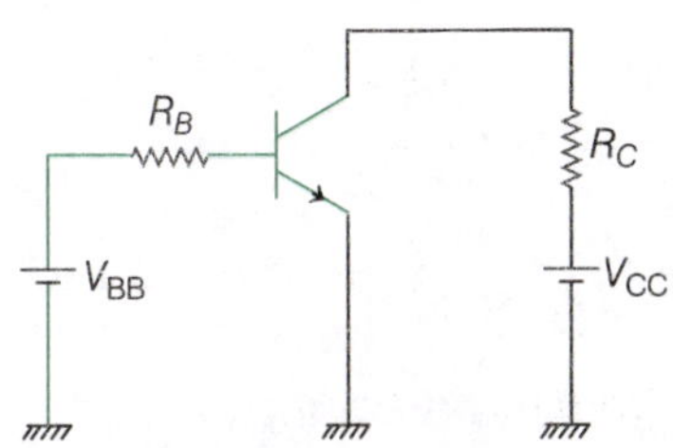

(a) 40 μA (b) 10 μA
(c) 100 μA (d) 7 μA

Multiple Correct Options

10. In an *n-p-n* transistor circuit, the collector current is 10 mA. If 95 per cent of the electrons emitted reach the collector, which of the following statements are true?

(a) The emitter current will be 8 mA.
(b) The emitter current will be 10.53 mA.
(c) The base current will be 0.53 mA.
(d) The base current will be 2 mA.

Subjective Questions

11. Consider an amplifier circuit using a transistor. The output power is several times greater than the input power. Where does the extra power come from?

12. A transistor has three impurity regions, emitter, base and collector. Arrange them in order of increasing doping levels.

13. In the circuit shown in figure when the input voltage of the base resistance is 10 V. Find the values of I_B, I_C and β.

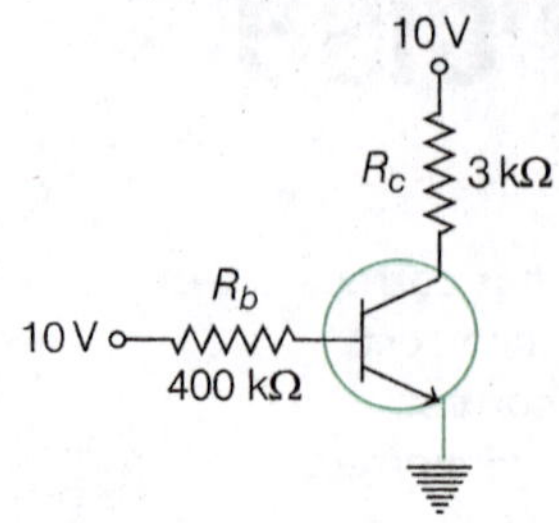

14. For the transistor circuit shown in figure, evaluate V_E, R_B and R_E. Given $I_C = 1$ mA, $V_{CE} = 3$ V, $V_{BE} = 0.5$ V, $V_{CC} = 12$ V and $\beta = 100$.

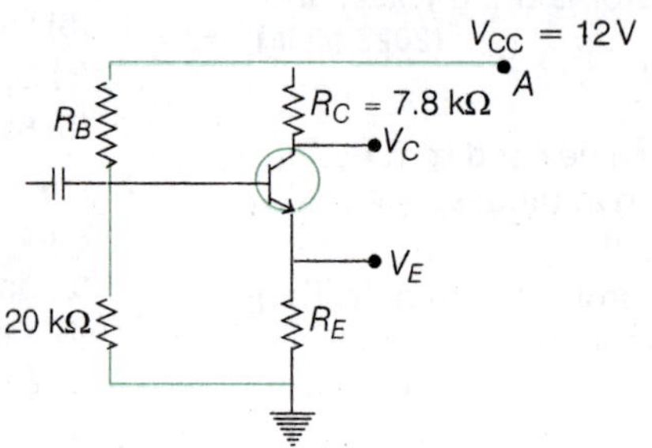

15. In the circuit shown in figure, find the value of R_C.

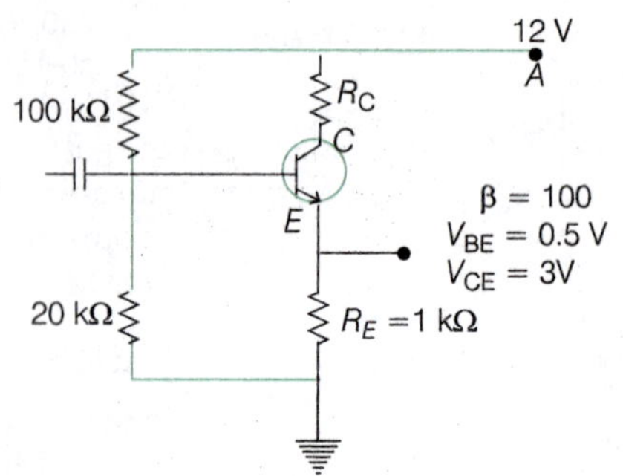

Answers

1. (a) 2. (a) 3. (b) 4. (c) 5. (b) 6. (b) 7. (d) 8. (d) 9. (a) 10. (b,c)
11. From the *dc* source 12. base < collector < emitter
13. $I_B = 25\,\mu$A, $I_C = 3.33$ mA, $\beta = 133$ 14. $V_E = 1.2$ V, $R_B = 108$ kΩ, $R_E = 1.2$ kΩ 15. 0.56 kΩ

See hints on pages 436-438.

MODULE 4

Logic Gates

Binary System

There are a number of questions which have only two answers Yes or No. A statement can be either True or False. A switch can be either ON or OFF. These values may be represented by two symbols 0 and 1. In a number system, in which we have only two digits is called a binary system. (decimal system for example has ten digits).

In binary system usually we write 1 for positive response (e.g. when a switch is ON) and 0 for negative (when switch is OFF).

Truth Table

To understand the concept of truth table let us take an example. A bulb is connected to an AC source *via* two switches S_1 and S_2.

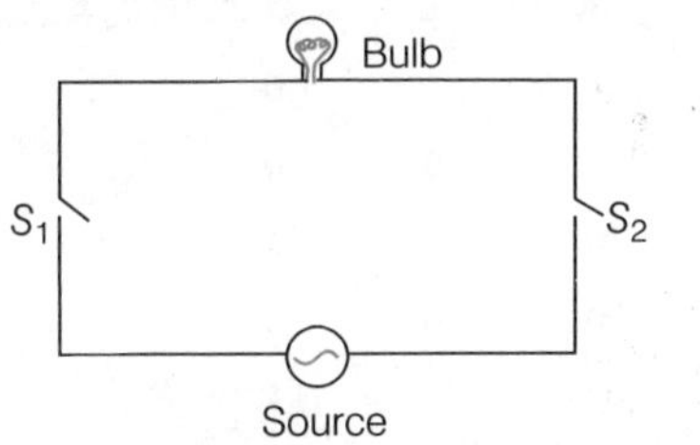

In binary system, we will write 0, if the switch (or bulb) is off and write 1 if it is on. Further let us write

A for state of switch S_1

B for state of switch S_2

and *C* for state of the bulb.

Now, let us make a table (called truth table) which is self explanatory.

Table 1.

Switch S_1	Switch S_2	Bulb	*A*	*B*	*C*
Off	On	Off	0	1	0
On	Off	Off	1	0	0
Off	Off	Off	0	0	0
On	On	On	1	1	1

Example 1 Make a truth table corresponding to the circuit shown in figure.

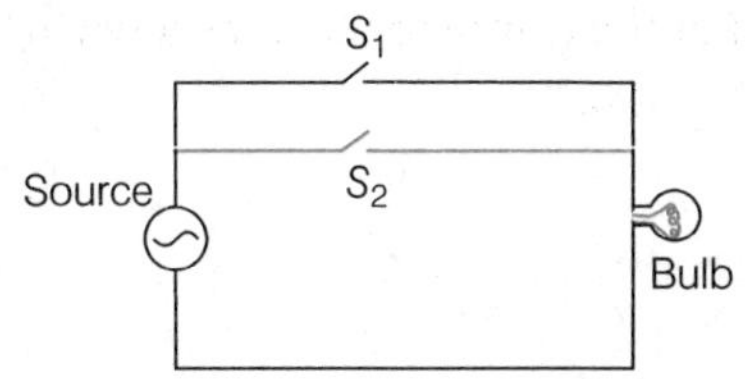

Sol.

Table 2.

Switch S_1	Switch S_2	Bulb	*A*	*B*	*C*
On	Off	On	1	0	1
Off	On	On	0	1	1
Off	Off	Off	0	0	0
On	On	On	1	1	1

Logic Gates

Logic gates are important building blocks in digital electronics. These are circuits with one or more inputs and one output. The basic gates are OR, AND, NOT, NAND, NOR and XOR.

OR Gate

The boolean expression of OR gate is $Y = A + B$, read as *Y* equals *A* 'OR' *B*.

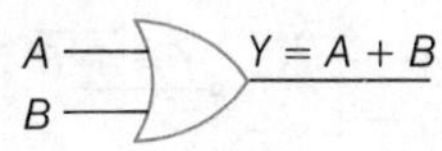

The truth table of a two-input OR basic gate is given as :

Table 3.

A	*B*	*Y*
0	0	0
0	1	1
1	0	1
1	1	1

AND Gate

The boolean expression of AND gate is $Y = A \cdot B$

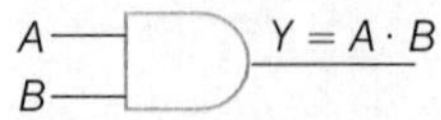

The truth table of a two-input AND basic gate is given as ;

Table 4.

A	B	Y
0	0	0
0	1	0
1	0	0
1	1	1

NOT Gate

The boolean expression is $Y = \overline{A}$, read as *Y* equals NOT *A*.

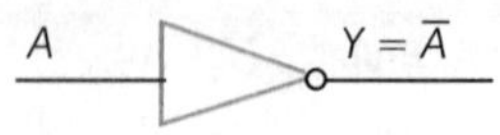

The truth table of NOT gate is as follows;

Table 5.

A	Y
0	1
1	0

The three gates (OR, AND and NOT), when connected in various combinations, give us basic logic gates such as NAND and NOR gates, which are the universal building blocks of digital circuits.

NAND Gate

The basic logic gate is combination of AND and NOT gate.

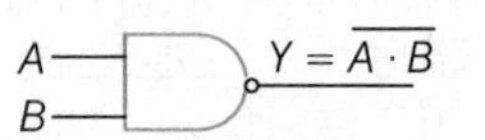

The boolean expression of NAND gate is $Y = \overline{A \cdot B}$

The truth table of a NAND gate is given as ;

Table 6.

A	B	$A \cdot B$	$Y = \overline{A \cdot B}$
0	0	0	1
0	1	0	1
1	0	0	1
1	1	1	0

NOR Gate

The gate is the combination of OR and NOT gate.

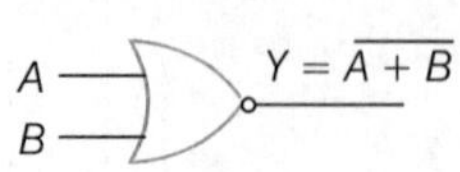

The boolean expression of NOR gate is $Y = \overline{A + B}$

The truth table of a NOR gate is as follows ;

Table 7.

A	B	$A + B$	$Y = \overline{A + B}$
0	0	0	1
0	1	1	0
1	0	1	0
1	1	1	0

Exclusive-OR gate (XOR gate)

The boolean expression of the XOR gate is $Y = A \cdot \overline{B} + B \cdot \overline{A}$

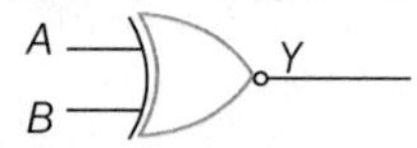

or the truth table of an XOR gate is;

Table 8.

A	B	$\overline{A}$	$\overline{B}$	$A \cdot \overline{B}$	$B \cdot \overline{A}$	$Y = A \cdot \overline{B} + B \cdot \overline{A}$
0	0	1	1	0	0	0
0	1	1	0	0	1	1
1	0	0	1	1	0	1
1	1	0	0	0	0	0

Summary

Table 9.

S.No	Name of Gate	Symbol	Boolean Expression
1	OR	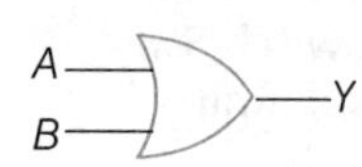	$Y = A + B$
2	AND	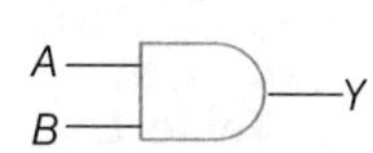	$Y = A \cdot B$
3	NOT	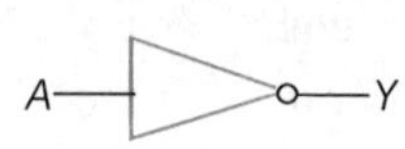	$Y = \overline{A}$
4	NAND	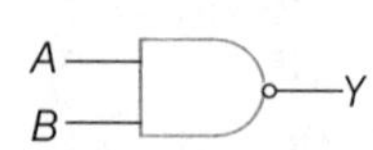	$Y = \overline{A \cdot B}$
5	NOR	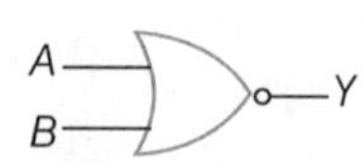	$Y = \overline{A + B}$
6	XOR	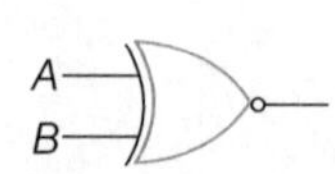	$Y = A \cdot \overline{B} + B \cdot \overline{A}$

Note In digital electronics only two voltage levels are present. Conventionally these are 5 V and 0 V, referred to as 1 and 0. They are also referred as high and low.

Example 2 Using two diodes make construction of an OR gate.

Sol. Figure shows construction of an OR gate using two diodes.

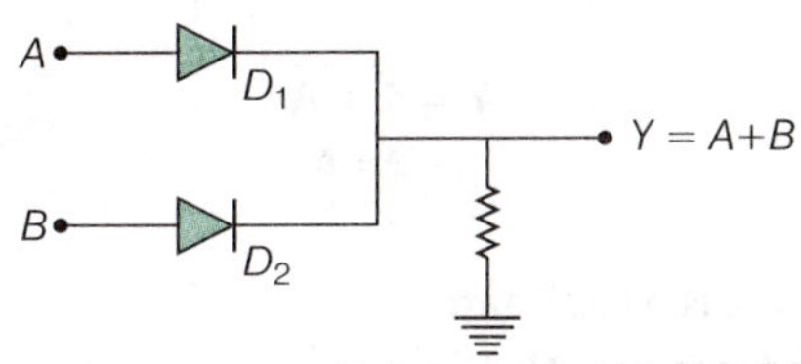

When either of point A or B (or both) has potential $+5V$, diodes D_1 or D_2 (or both) are forward biased and potential at Y is same as the common potential at A and B which is 5V.

Thus, $Y = 1$ when either of A or B is 1. Or, both A and B are 1.

Example 3 Using two diodes make construction of AND gate.

Sol. Figure shows construction for an AND gate using two diodes D_1 and D_2.

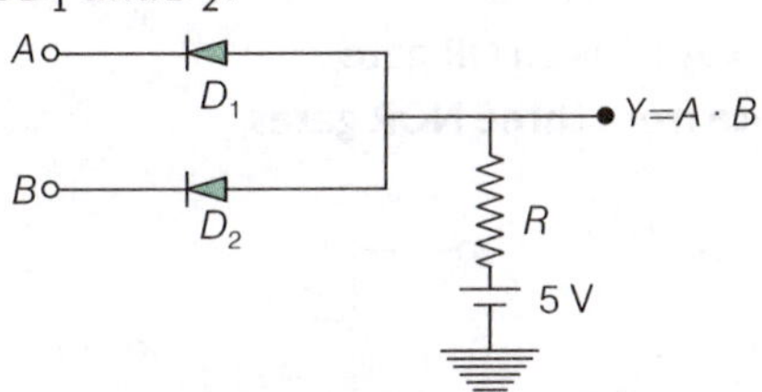

When potentials at A and B both are zero, then both the diodes are forward biased and offer no resistance. The potential at Y in this position is equal to the potential at A or B i.e. 0. Thus $Y = 0$, when both A and B are zero. Now suppose potential at A is zero but at B is 5V, then D_1 is forward biased. In this situation potential at Y is also zero.

Thus, $Y = 0$ when $A = 0$. Similarly, we can see that $Y = 0$ when $B = 0$. Lastly when potentials at both A and B are 5V, so that both the diodes are unbiased and there will be no current through R and the potential at Y will be equal to 5V. Thus, $Y = 1$ when A and B both are 1.

Note A NOT gate cannot be constructed with diodes. Transistor is used for realisation of a NOT gate, but at this stage students do not require it.

Example 4 Make the output waveform (Y) of the OR gate for the following inputs A and B.

Table 10.

Time	A	B
For $t < t_1$	0	0
From t_1 to t_2	1	0
From t_2 to t_3	1	1
From t_3 to t_4	0	1
From t_4 to t_5	0	0
From t_5 to t_6	1	0
For $t > t_6$	0	1

Sol. Output value Y corresponding to OR gate is given in the following table.

Table 11.

Time	A	B	Y = A + B
For $t < t_1$	0	0	0
From t_1 to t_2	1	0	1
From t_2 to t_3	1	1	1
From t_3 to t_4	0	1	1
From t_4 to t_5	0	0	0
From t_5 to t_6	1	0	1
For $t > t_6$	0	1	1

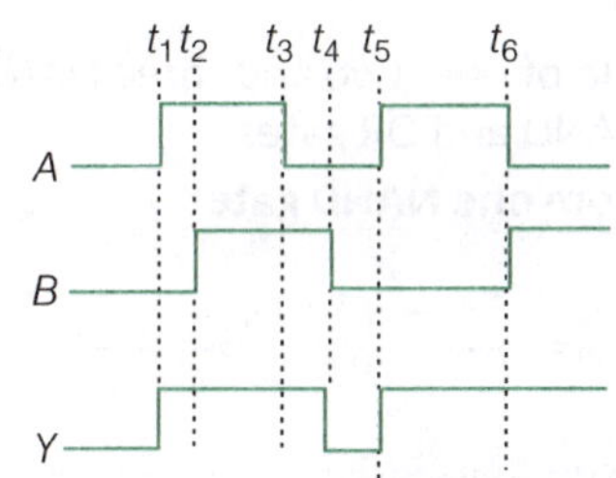

Therefore, the waveform Y will be as shown in the figure.

Example 5 Take A and B inputs similar to that in above example. Sketch the output waveform obtained from AND gate.

Sol. Output value, Y corresponding to AND gate is given in the following table.

Table 12.

Time	A	B	Y = A · B
For $t < t_1$	0	0	0
From t_1 to t_2	1	0	0
From t_2 to t_3	1	1	1
From t_3 to t_4	0	1	0
From t_4 to t_5	0	0	0
From t_5 to t_6	1	0	0
For $t > t_6$	0	1	0

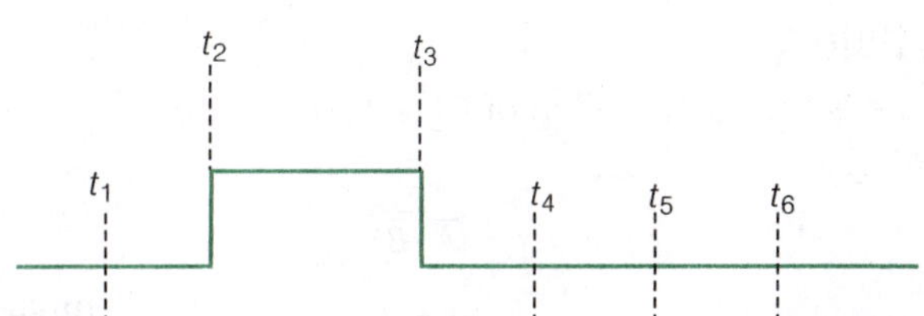

Based on the above table, the output waveform Y for AND gate can be drawn as in figure.

Rules of Boolean Algebra and Demorgan's Theorem

Following are given some Boolean algebra rules :

(i) $A+0=A$ (Rule - 1)

(ii) $A+A=A$ (Rule - 2)

(iii) $A\cdot A=A$ (Rule - 3)

(iv) $A\cdot\overline{A}=0$ (Rule - 4)

(v) $\overline{\overline{A}}=A$ (Rule - 5)

Demorgan's theorem has following two equations.

(i) $\overline{A\cdot B}=\overline{A}+\overline{B}$ (Rule - 6)

(ii) $\overline{A+B}=\overline{A}\cdot\overline{B}$ (Rule - 7)

Now with the help of these seven rules let us try to solve some complex problems of logic gates.

Example 6 Prove that NAND and NOR gates are universal gates. Because with the help of these two gates we can make NOT, AND and OR gates.

Sol. **NAND Gate**

With the help of one, two and three NAND gates we can make NOT, AND and OR gates.

NOT gate from one NAND gate

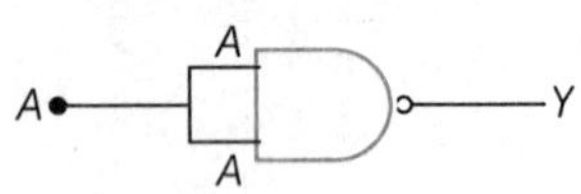

$$Y=\overline{A\cdot A}$$
$$=\overline{A}+\overline{A} \quad \text{(Rule - 6)}$$
$$=\overline{A} \quad \text{(Rule - 2)}$$

So, $Y=\overline{A}$ is a NOT gate.

AND gate from two NAND gate

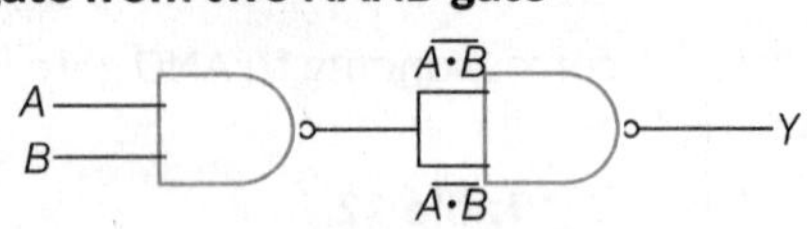

$$Y=\overline{(\overline{A\cdot B})\cdot(\overline{A\cdot B})}$$
$$=\overline{\overline{A\cdot B}}+\overline{\overline{A\cdot B}} \quad \text{(Rule - 6)}$$
$$=\overline{\overline{A\cdot B}} \quad \text{(Rule - 2)}$$
$$=A\cdot B \quad \text{(Rule - 5)}$$

Hence, $Y=A\cdot B$ is a NAND gate.

OR gate from three NAND gates

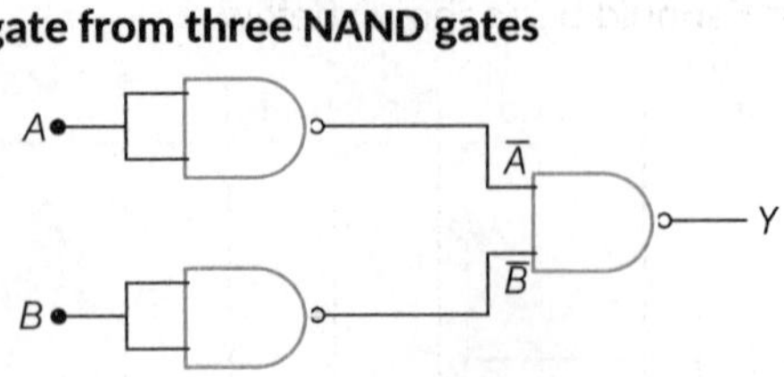

$$Y=\overline{(\overline{A}\cdot\overline{B})}$$
$$=\overline{\overline{A}}+\overline{\overline{B}} \quad \text{(Rule - 6)}$$
$$=A+B \quad \text{(Rule - 5)}$$

Thus, $Y=A+B$ is an OR gate.

NOR gate

NOT gate from one NOR gates

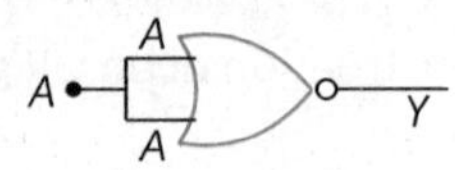

$$Y=\overline{A+A}$$
$$=\overline{A}\cdot\overline{A} \quad \text{(Rule - 7)}$$
$$=\overline{A} \quad \text{(Rule - 3)}$$

Thus, $Y=\overline{A}$ is a NOT gate.

OR gate from two NOR gates

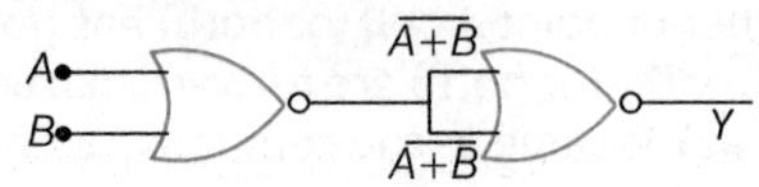

$$Y=\overline{(\overline{A+B})+(\overline{A+B})}$$
$$=\overline{\overline{(A+B)}}\cdot\overline{\overline{(A+B)}} \quad \text{(Rule - 7)}$$
$$=\overline{\overline{A+B}} \quad \text{(Rule - 3)}$$
$$=A+B \quad \text{(Rule - 5)}$$

Thus, $Y=A+B$ is an OR gate

AND gate from three NOR gates

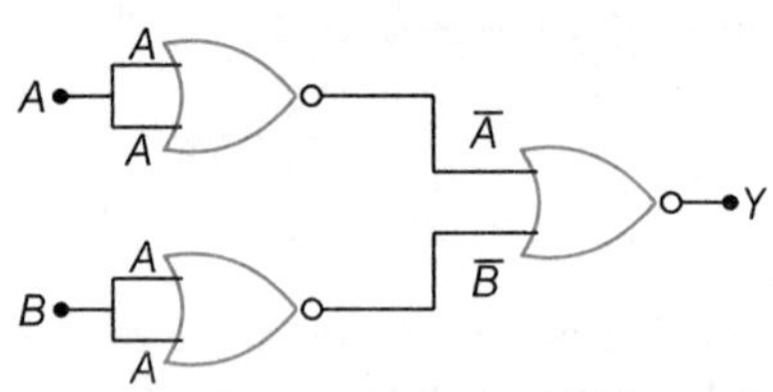

$$Y=\overline{(\overline{A}+\overline{B})}$$
$$=\overline{\overline{A}}\cdot\overline{\overline{B}} \quad \text{(Rule - 7)}$$
$$=A\cdot B \quad \text{(Rule - 5)}$$

Therefore, $Y=A\cdot B$ is an AND gate.

Example 7 The following configuration of gates is equivalent to:

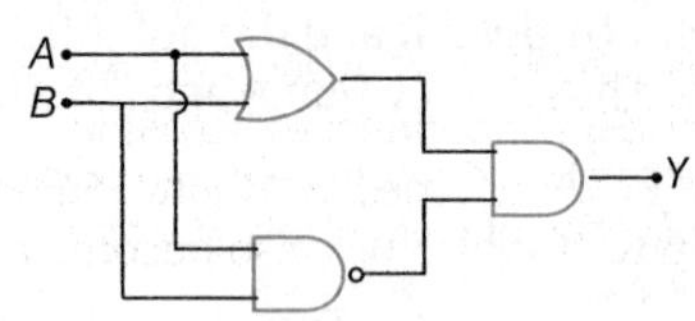

(a) NAND (b) OR

(c) XOR (d) NOR

Sol.

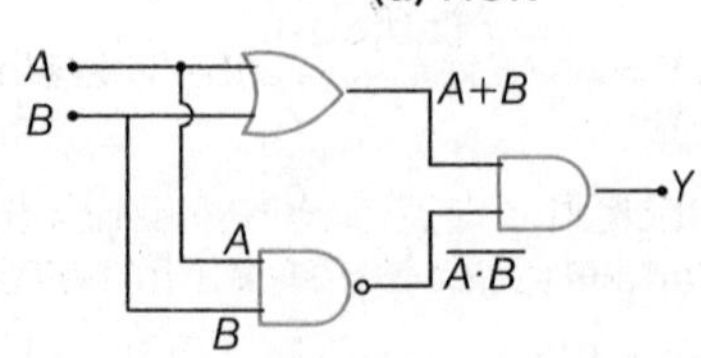

$$Y=(A+B)\cdot(\overline{A\cdot B})$$

$$= (A+B)\cdot(\overline{A}+\overline{B}) \quad \text{(Rule - 6)}$$
$$= A\cdot\overline{A} + A\cdot\overline{B} + B\cdot\overline{A} + B\cdot\overline{B}$$
$$= 0 + A\cdot\overline{B} + B\cdot\overline{A} + 0 \quad \text{(Rule - 4)}$$
$$= A\cdot\overline{B} + B\cdot\overline{A}$$

Now, $Y = A\cdot\overline{B} + B\cdot\overline{A}$ is a XOR gate. Therefore the correct option is (c).

Example 8 The circuit shown here is logically equivalent to:

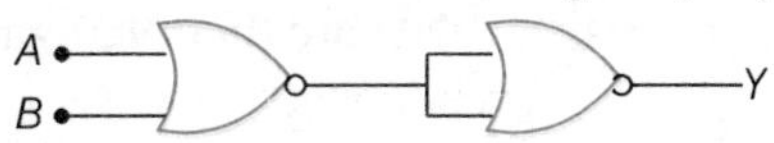

(a) OR gate (b) AND gate (c) NOT gate (d) NAND gate

Sol. $X = \overline{A+B}$

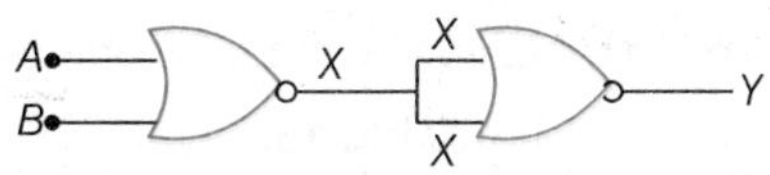

Now X and X inputs are connected to one NOR gate and in figure, we have seen that it becomes a NOT gate.

Thus,

$$Y = \overline{X} = \overline{\overline{A+B}}$$
$$= A + B \quad \text{(Rule - 5)}$$

Thus, $Y = A + B$ is an OR gate or the correct option is (a).

Example 9 The combination of the gates shown here will produce :

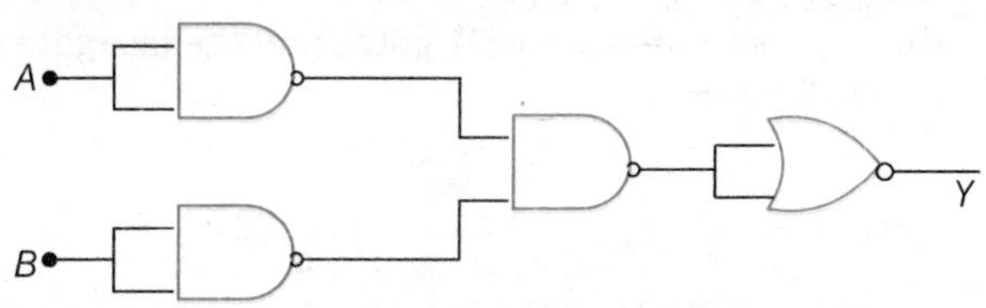

(a) OR gate (b) AND gate (c) NOR gate (d) NAND gate

Sol.

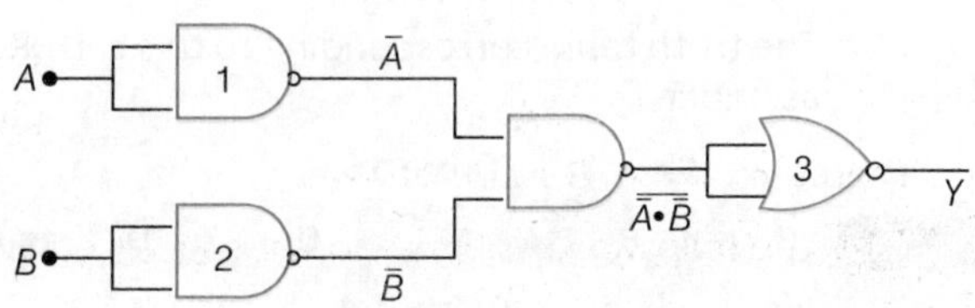

In the figure 1 and 2 are NAND gates and same inputs A and A or B and B are connected across it. So, we have read earlier that it will become a NOT gate. Same logic can be applied to gate-3, which will also become a NOT gate.

Thus, $Y = \overline{\overline{\overline{A}\cdot\overline{B}}}$

$$= \overline{A}\cdot\overline{B} \quad \text{(Rule - 5)}$$
$$= \overline{A+B} \quad \text{(Rule - 7)}$$

Therefore, $Y = \overline{A+B}$ is a NOR gate. Therefore the correct option is (c).

Example 10 The logic circuit shown below has the input waveforms A and B as shown. Pick out the correct output waveform.

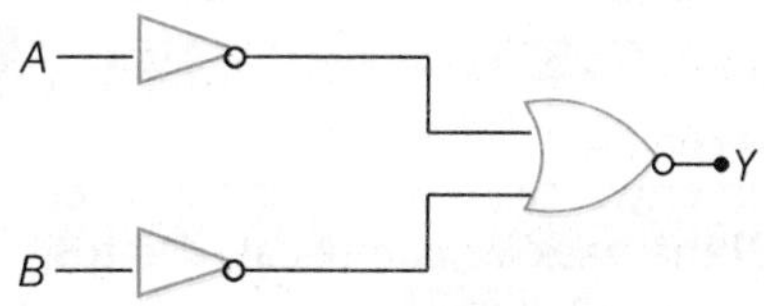

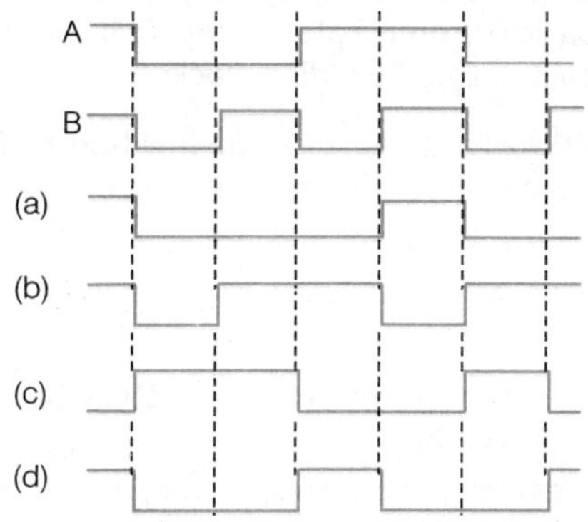

Sol.

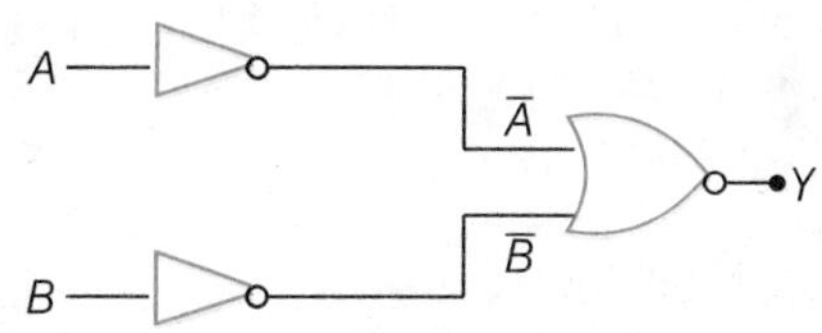

$$Y = \overline{\overline{A}+\overline{B}}$$
$$= \overline{\overline{A}}\cdot\overline{\overline{B}} \quad \text{(Rule - 7)}$$
$$= A\cdot B \quad \text{(Rule - 5)}$$

Thus, $Y = A\cdot B$ is an AND gate. Now the values of given inputs A and B and corresponding to them $Y = A\cdot B$ are given below in tabular form.

Table 13.

Region	A	B	$Y = A\cdot B$
I	1	1	1
II	0	0	0
III	0	1	0
IV	1	0	0
V	1	1	1
VI	0	0	0
VII	0	1	0

Now corresponding to last column of the above table output Y should be as shown below.

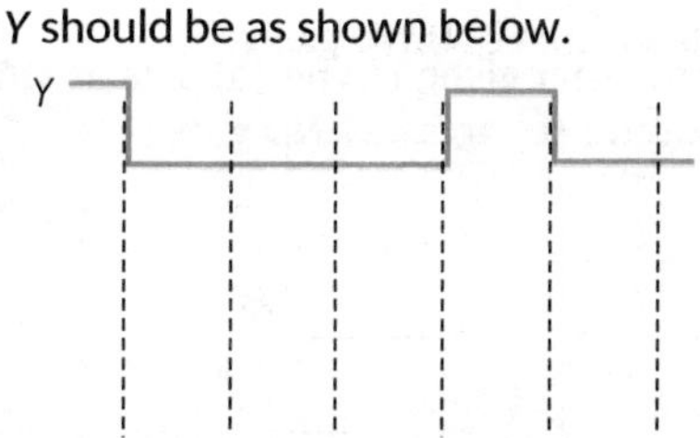

Therefore the correct option is (a).

Miscellaneous Examples

Ex. 1 Name two gates which can be used repeatedly to produce all the basic or complicated gates.

Sol. NAND and NOR gates can be used repeatedly to produce all the basic or complicated gates. This is why these gates are called digital building blocks.

Ex. 2 Construct the truth table for the function X of A and B represented by figure shown here.

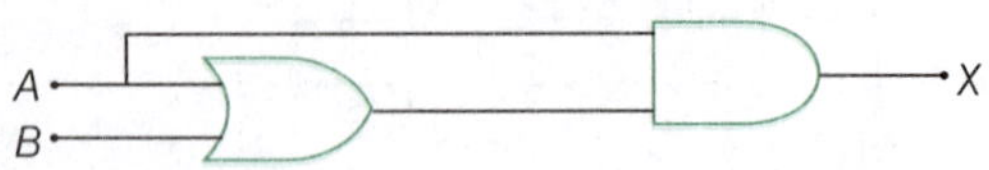

Sol. The output X in terms of the input A and B can be written as, $X = A \cdot (A + B)$

Let us make the truth table corresponding to this function.

Table 14.

A	B	A+ B	$X = A \cdot (A + B)$
0	0	0	0
0	1	1	0
1	0	1	1
1	1	1	1

Ex. 3 Let $X = (A) \cdot (\overline{B \cdot C})$. Evaluate X for

(a) $A = 1, B = 0, C = 1$ (b) $A = B = C = 1$ and

(c) $A = B = C = 0$

Sol. (a) When $A = 1, B = 0$ and $C = 1$

$$B \cdot C = 0$$

$\therefore$ $$\overline{B \cdot C} = 1$$

or $$(A) \cdot (\overline{B \cdot C}) = 1$$ **Ans.**

(b) When $$A = B = C = 1$$

Then, $$B \cdot C = 1$$

or $$\overline{B \cdot C} = 0$$

$\therefore$ $$(A) \cdot (\overline{B \cdot C}) = 0$$ **Ans.**

(c) When $$A = B = C = 0$$

Then, $$B \cdot C = 0$$

$\therefore$ $$\overline{B \cdot C} = 1$$

or $$(A) \cdot (\overline{B \cdot C}) = 0$$ **Ans.**

Ex. 4 Show that given circuit (a) acts as OR gate while the given circuit (b) acts as AND gate.

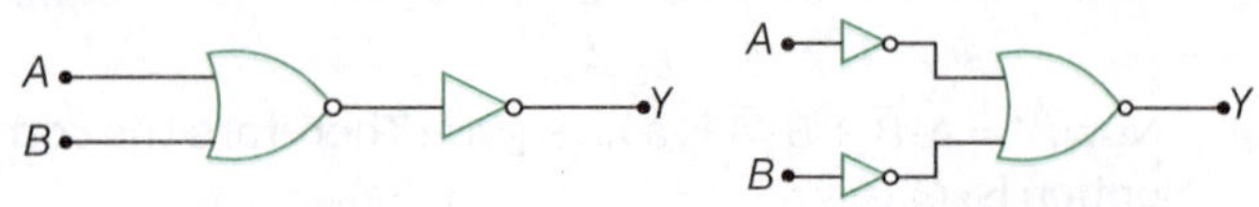

(a) (b)

Sol. (a) The first gate is NOR gate then NOT gate

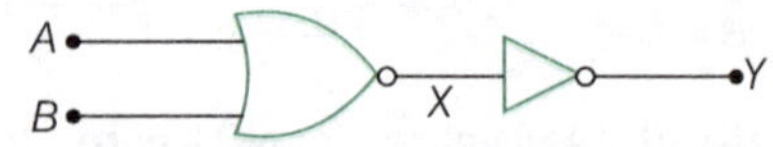

Thus, $X = \overline{A + B}$ and $Y = \overline{X}$

The truth table can be made as below.

Table 15.

A	B	A + B	$X = \overline{A + B}$	$Y = \overline{X}$
1	0	1	0	1
0	1	1	0	1
1	1	1	0	1
0	0	0	1	0

The last column of Y is similar to third column of $A + B$ which is the truth table corresponding to OR gate.

(b) First two gates are NOT gates and the last gate is NOR gate.

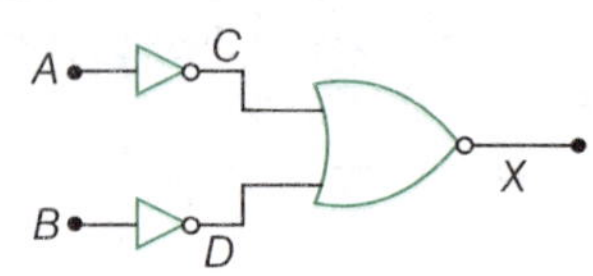

Thus, $C = \overline{A}$ and $D = \overline{B}$

$$X = \overline{C + D}$$

The truth table corresponding to this can be made as under.

Table 16.

A	B	$A \cdot B$	$C = \overline{A}$	$D = \overline{B}$	$C + D$	$X = \overline{C + D}$
1	0	0	0	1	1	0
0	1	0	1	0	1	0
1	1	1	0	0	0	1
0	0	0	1	1	1	0

The last column of X is similar to third column of $A \cdot B$, which is the truth table corresponding to AND gate.

MODULE 4 Exercise

Single Correct Option

1. Name the logic gate equivalent to the diagram attached **(2023 Main)**

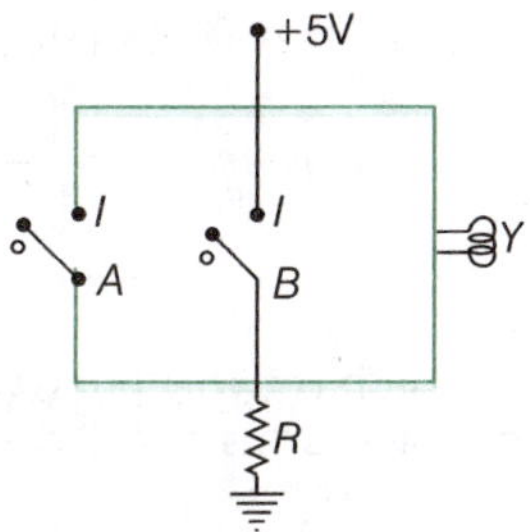

(a) OR (b) NAND (c) NOR (d) AND

2. The logic operations performed by the given digital circuit is equivalent to **(2023 Main)**

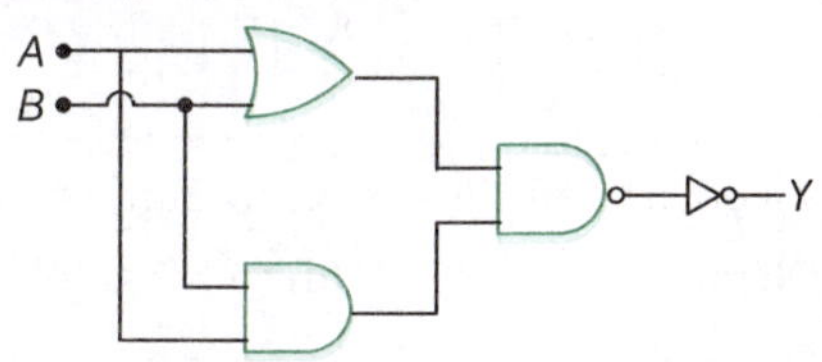

(a) NAND (b) OR (c) NOR (d) AND

3. For the following circuit and given inputs A and B, choose the correct option for output Y. **(2023 Main)**

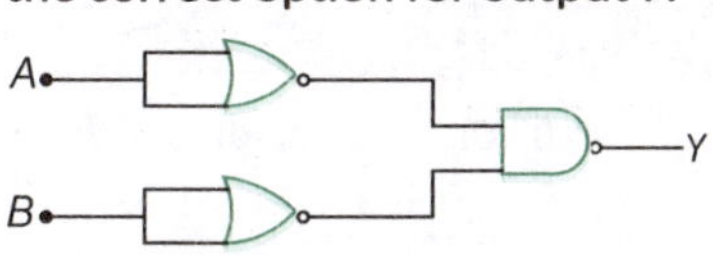

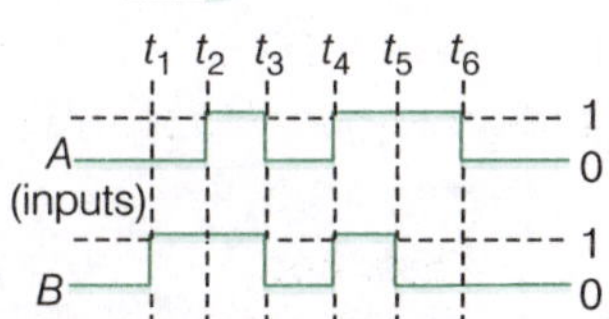

(a)

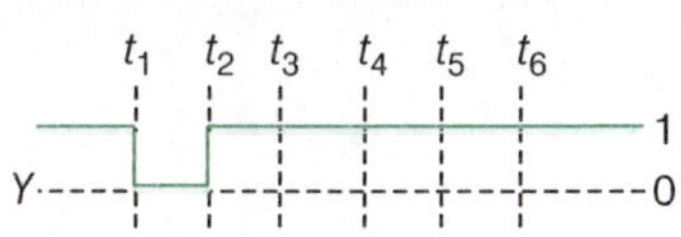

(b)

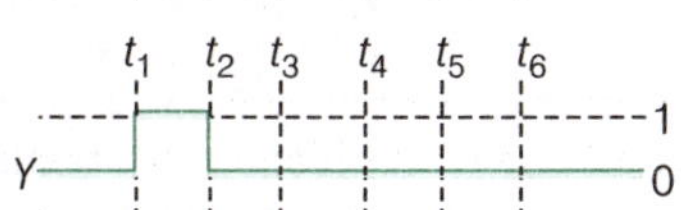

(c)

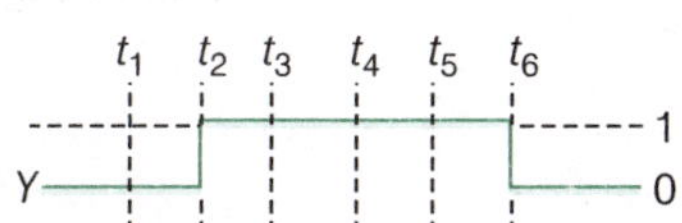

(d)

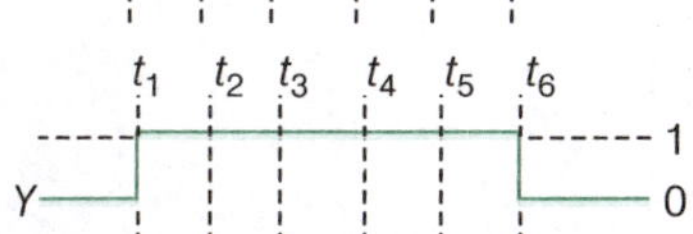

4. The output from a NAND gate having inputs A and B given below will be, **(2023 Main)**

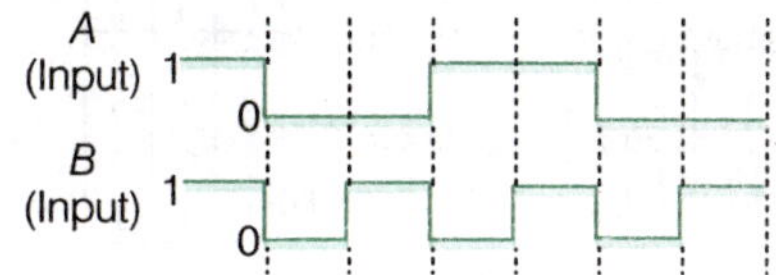

(a)

(b)

(c)

(d)

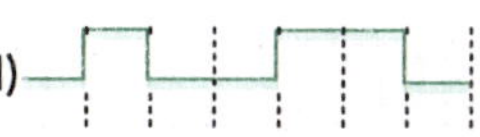

5. The logic gate equivalent of the given circuit diagram is **(2023 Main)**

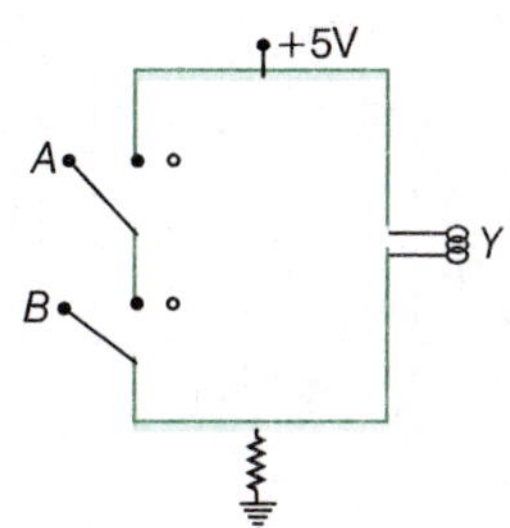

(a) NAND (b) AND
(c) NOR (d) OR

6. For the given logic gates combination, the correct truth table will be **(2023 Main)**

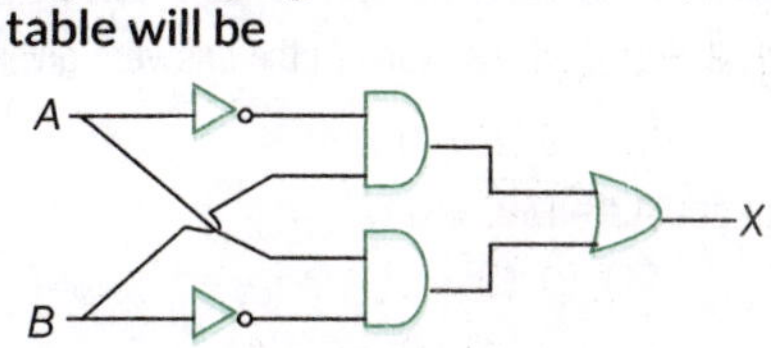

(a)

A	B	X
0	0	1
0	1	0
1	0	1
1	1	0

(b)

A	B	X
0	0	1
0	1	0
1	0	0
1	1	0

(c)

A	B	X
0	0	0
0	1	1
1	0	1
1	1	1

(d)

A	B	X
0	0	0
0	1	1
1	0	1
1	1	0

7. The output Y for the inputs A and B of circuit is given by : **(2023 Main)**

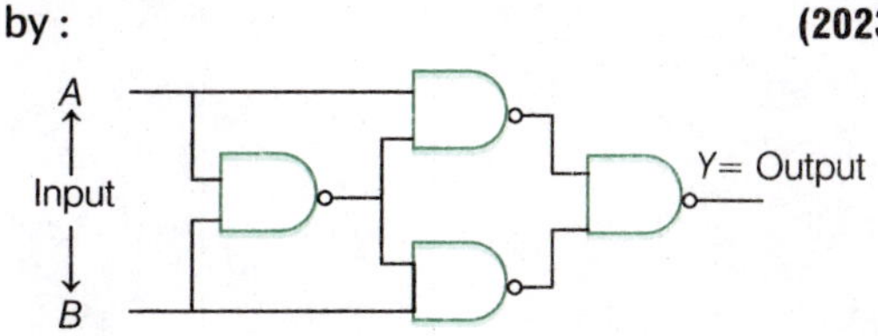

Truth table of the shown circuit is

(a)

A	B	Y
0	0	0
0	1	1
1	0	1
1	1	0

(b)

A	B	Y
0	0	1
0	1	1
1	0	1
1	1	0

(c)

A	B	Y
0	0	0
0	1	1
1	0	1
1	1	1

(d)

A	B	Y
0	0	1
0	1	0
1	0	0
1	1	1

8. The output waveform of the given logical circuit for the following inputs *A* and *B* as shown below, is **(2023 Main)**

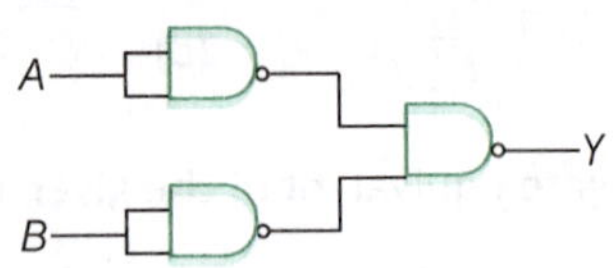

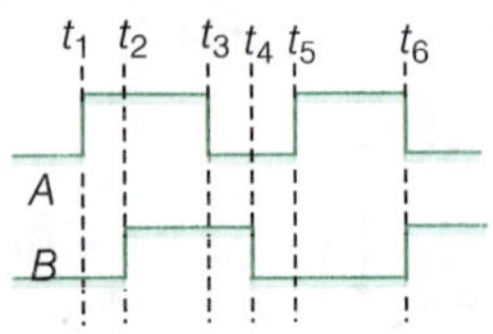

Inputs

(a) 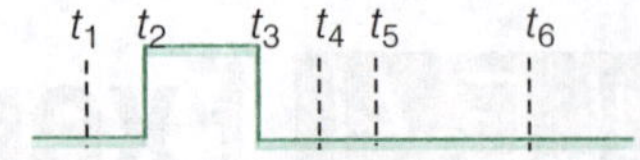

(b) 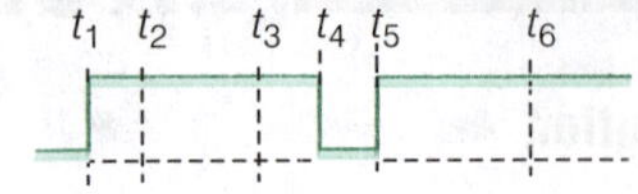

(c) 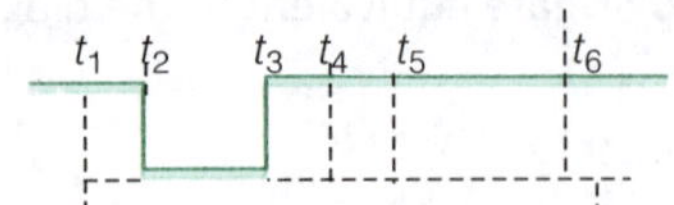

(d) 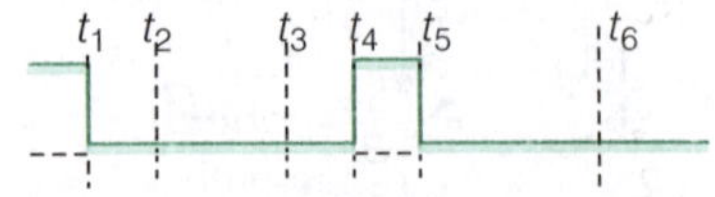

9. A logic gate circuit has two inputs *A* and *B* and output *Y*. The voltage waveforms of *A*, *B* and *Y* are shown below

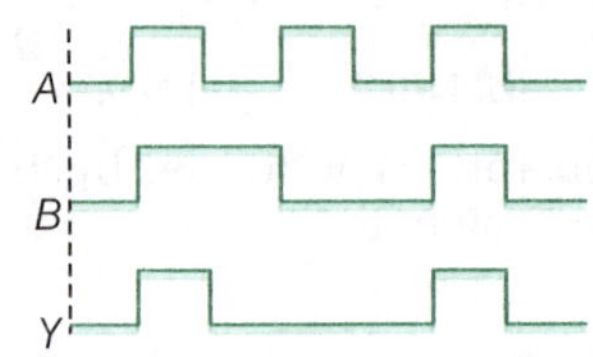

The logic gate circuit is **(2022 Main)**

(a) AND gate (b) OR gate
(c) NOR gate (d) NAND gate

Answers

1. (c)	**2.** (d)	**3.** None of the answers given was correct	**4.** (a)	**5.** (a)	**6.** (d)	**7.** (a)
8. (b)	**9.** (a)					

See hints on pages 438-439.

Unit Exercise (Cumulative)

Single Correct Option

1. The *V-I* characteristics of a *p-n* junction diode in forward bias is shown in the figure. The ratio of dynamics resistance, corresponding to forward bias voltages of 2V and 4V respectively, is **(2022 Main)**

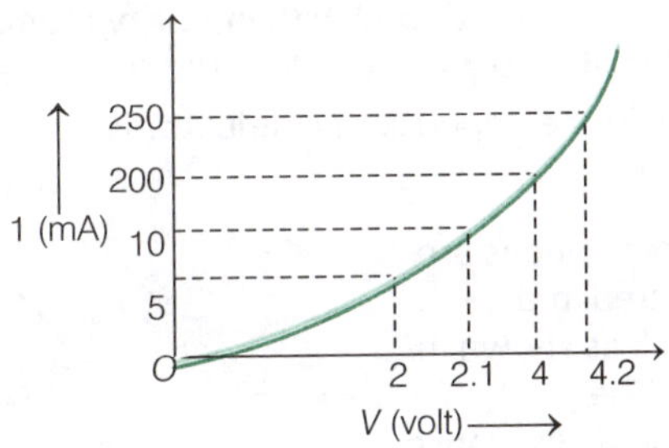

(a) 1 : 2 (b) 5 : 1
(c) 1 : 40 (d) 20 : 1

2. When a diode is forward biased, it has a voltage drop of 0.5 V. The safe limit of current through the diode is 10 mA. If a battery of emf 1.5 V is used in the circuit, the value of minimum resistance to be connected in series with the diode, so that the current does not exceed the safe limit is **(2020 Main)**

(a) 300 Ω
(b) 50 Ω
(c) 100 Ω
(d) 200 Ω

3. Two identical *p-n* junctions may be connected in series with a battery in three ways . The potential drops across the two *p-n* junctions are equal in **(1989 JEE)**

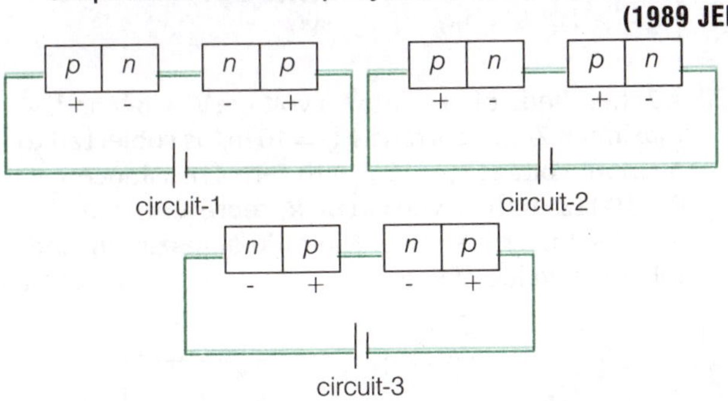

(a) circuit-1 and circuit-2 (b) circuit-2 and circuit-3
(c) circuit-3 and circuit-1 (d) circuit-1 only

4. Identify the solar cell characteristics from the following options. **(2022 Main)**

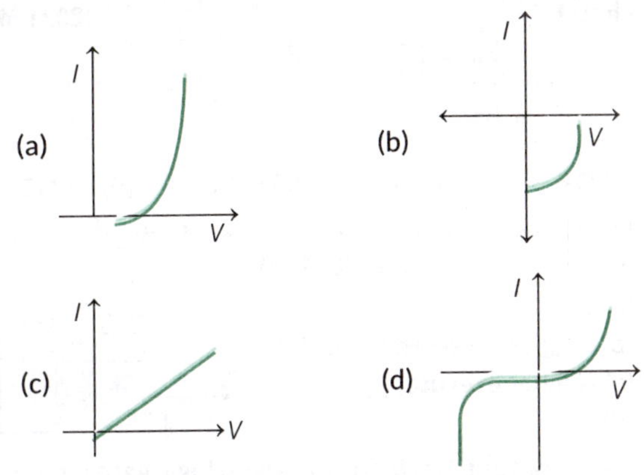

5. In a common emitter amplifier circuit using an *n-p-n* transistor, the phase difference between the input and the output voltages will be **(2017 Main)**

(a) 90° (b) 135° (c) 180° (d) 45°

6. Identify the logic operation performed by the given circuit **(2022 Main)**

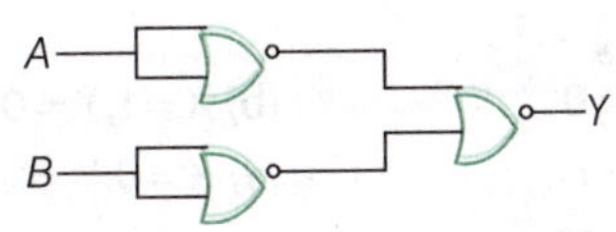

(a) AND gate (b) OR gate
(c) NOR gate (d) NAND gate

7. Identify the correct logic gate for the following output *Y* of two inputs *A* and *B*. **(2022 Main)**

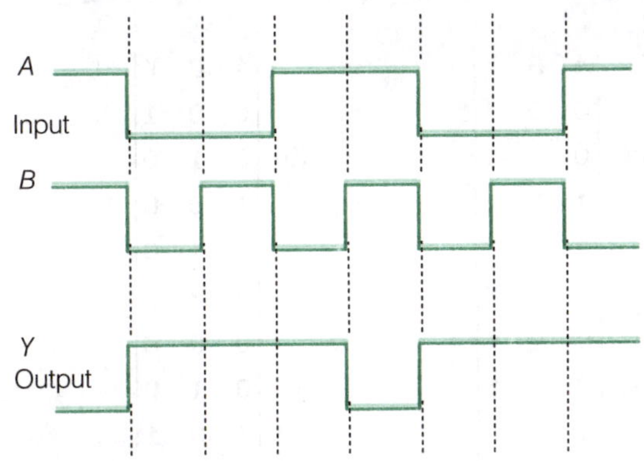

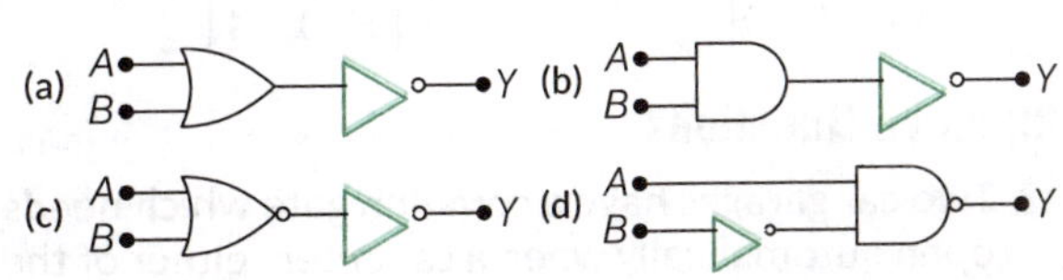

8. In the following logic circuit the sequence of the inputs A, B are (0, 0), (0, 1), (1, 0) and (1, 1). The output Y for this sequence will be **(2021 Main)**

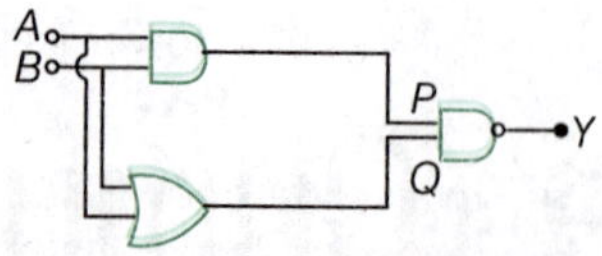

(a) 1, 0, 1, 0 (b) 0, 1, 0, 1 (c) 1, 1, 1, 0 (d) 0, 0, 1, 1

9. Identify the logic operation carried out by the given circuit. **(2021 Main)**

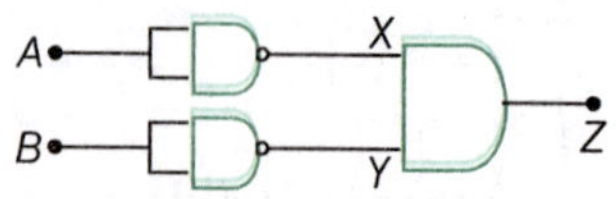

(a) OR (b) AND (c) NOR (d) NAND

10. In the given circuit, value of Y is **(2020 Main)**

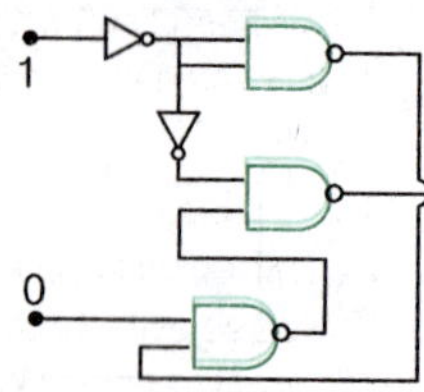

(a) 0
(b) toggles between 0 and 1
(c) will not execute
(d) 1

11. To get output 1 at R, for the given logic gate circuit, the input values must be **(2019 Main)**

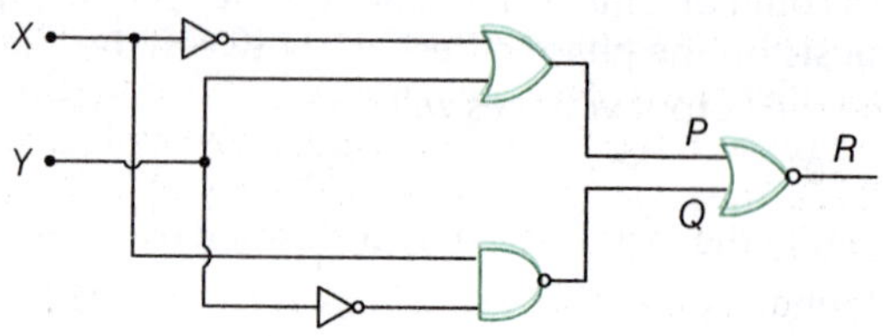

(a) $X = 0, Y = 0$ (b) $X = 1, Y = 0$
(c) $X = 1, Y = 1$ (d) $X = 0, Y = 1$

12. The truth table for the circuit given in the figure is **(2019 Main)**

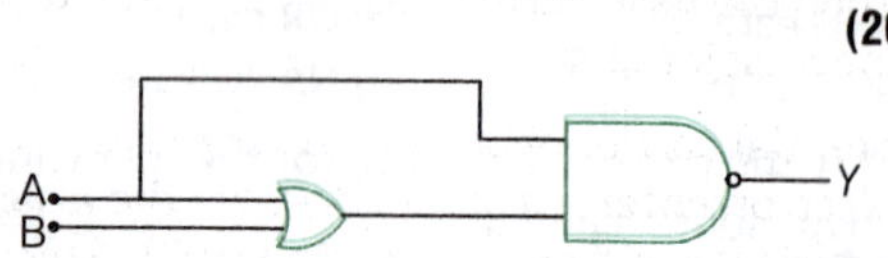

(a)

A	B	Y
0	0	1
0	1	1
1	0	1
1	1	1

(b)

A	B	Y
0	0	1
0	1	0
1	0	0
1	1	0

(c)

A	B	Y
0	0	1
0	1	1
1	0	0
1	1	0

(d)

A	B	Y
0	0	0
0	1	0
1	0	1
1	1	1

Subjective Questions

13. Two car garages have a common gate which needs to open automatically when a car enters either of the garages or cars enter both. Devise a circuit that resembles this situation using diodes for this situation.

14. Two amplifiers are connected one after the other in series (cascaded). The first amplifier has a voltage gain of 10 and the second has a voltage gain of 20. If the input signal is 0.01 V, calculate the output AC signal.

15. How would you set up a circuit to obtain NOT gate using a transistor?

Integer Type Questions

16. In a semiconductor, the number density of intrinsic charge carriers at 27°C is 1.5×10^{16} /m^3. If the semiconductor is doped with impurity atom, the hole density increases to 4.5×10^{22} /m^3. The electron density in the doped semiconductor is .... $\times 10^9$/m^3. **(2021 Main)**

17. Two ideal diodes are connected in the network as shown in figure. The equivalent resistance between A and B is ......Ω **(2022 Main)**

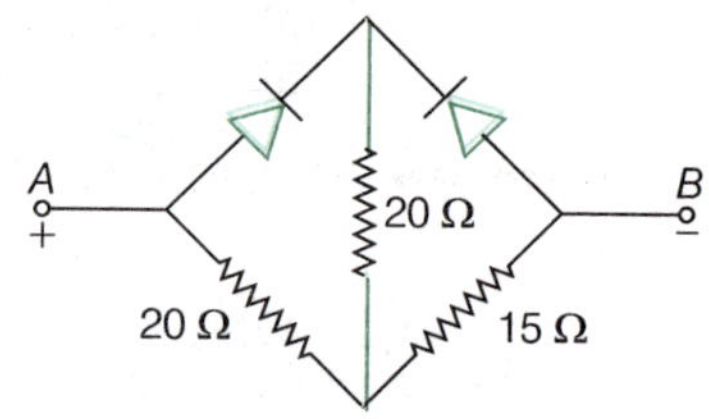

18. If the potential barrier across a p-n junction is 0.6 V. Then the electric field intensity, in the depletion region having the width of 6×10^{-6} m, will be .... $\times 10^5$ N/C. **(2022 Main)**

19. The cut-off voltage of the diodes (shown in figure) in forward bias is 0.6 V. The current through the resister of 40Ω is .... mA. **(2022 Mainl)**

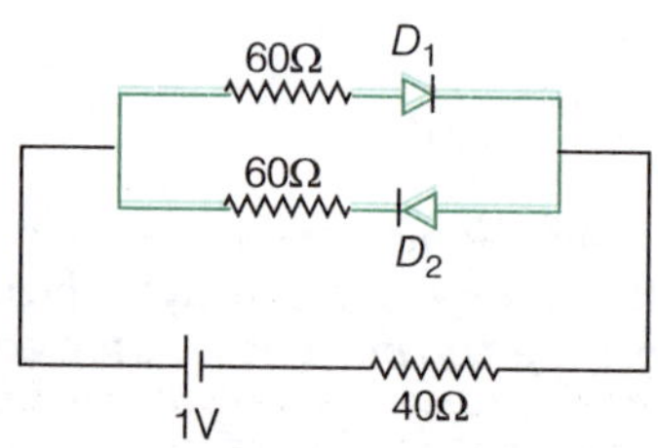

20. A Zener diode of breakdown voltage $V_Z = 8$ V and maximum Zener current, $I_{ZM} = 10$ mA is subjected to an input voltage $V_i = 10$ V with series resistance, $R = 100 \Omega$. In the given circuit R_L represents the variable load resistance. The ratio of maximum and minimum value of R_L is .... **(2022 Main)**

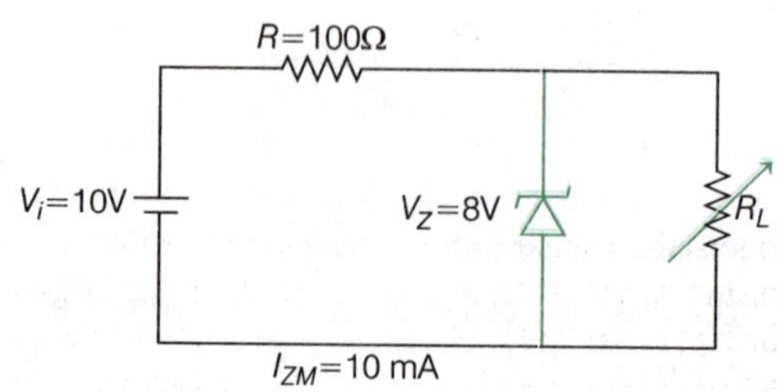

21. A 8 V Zener diode along with a series resistance R is connected across a 20 V supply (as shown in the figure). If the maximum Zener current is 25 mA, then the minimum value of R will be ....Ω. **(2022 Main)**

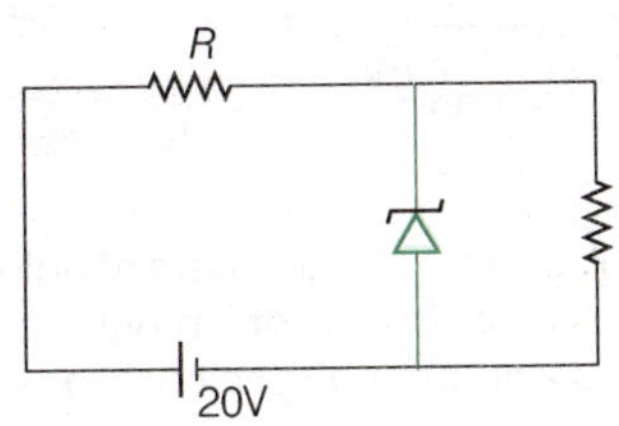

22. In the circuit shown below, maximum Zener diode current will be .... mA. **(2022 Main)**

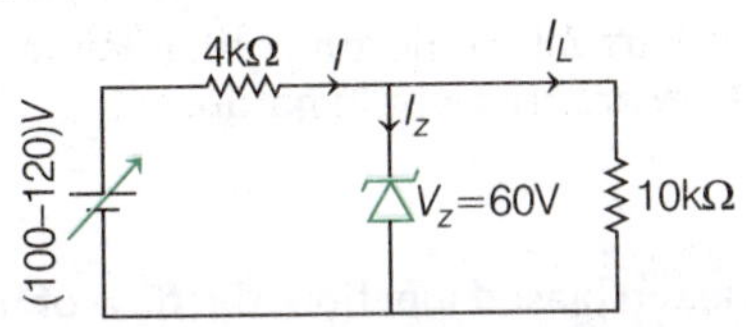

23. In the given circuit the value of current I_L will be .... mA. **(2022 Main)**

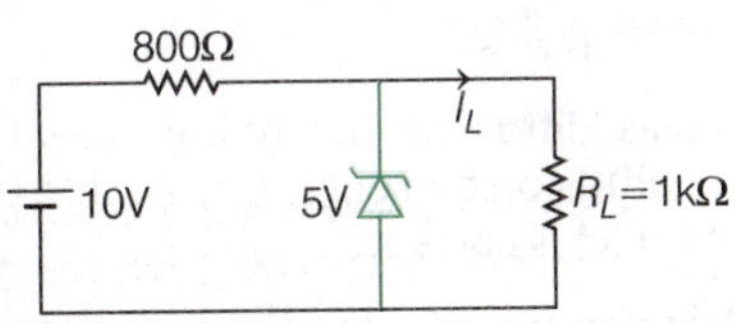

24. In connection with the circuit drawn below, the value of current flowing through 2 kΩ resistor is .... $\times 10^{-4}$ A. **(2021 Main)**

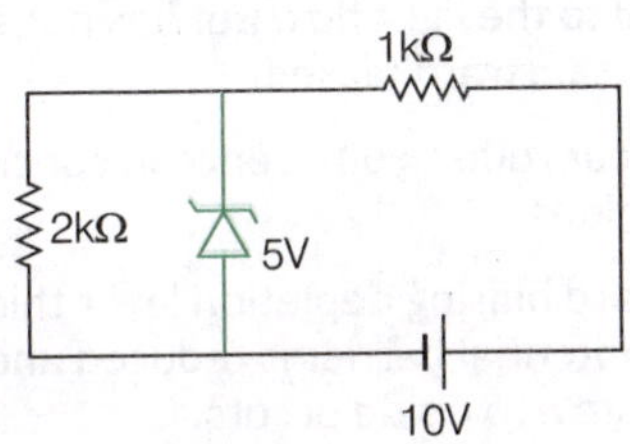

25. From the given graph of a transistor in CE configuration. The value of power gain of this configuration is 10^x, for $R_B = 10\ k\Omega$, and $R_C = 1\ k\Omega$. The value of x is .... **(2023 Main)**

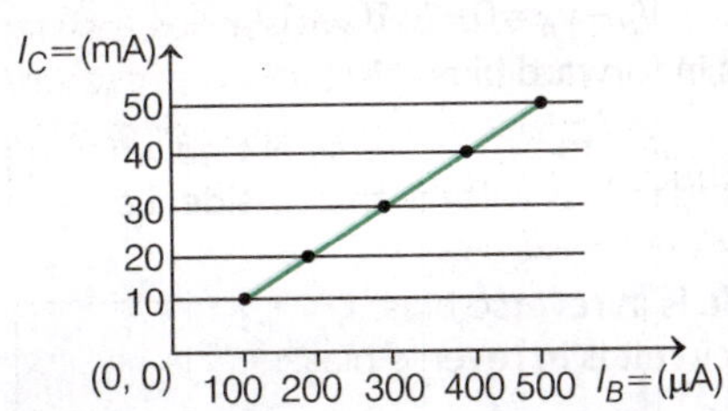

26. A transistor is used in an amplifier circuit in common emitter mode. If the base current changes by 100 μA, it brings a change of 10 mA in collector current. If the load resistance is 2 kΩ and input resistance is 1 kΩ, the value of power gain is $x \times 10^4$. The value of x is .... **(2022 Main)**

27. In an experiment of CE configuration of *n-p-n* transistor, the transfer characteristics are observed as given in figure.

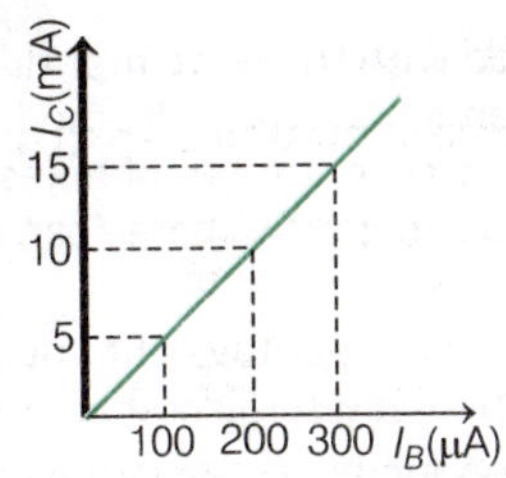

If the input resistance is 200 Ω and output resistance is 60 Ω the voltage gain in this experiment will be .... **(2022 Main)**

28. A transistor is used in common emitter mode in an amplifier circuit. When a signal of 10 mV is added to the base emitter voltage, the base current changes by 10 μA and the collector current changes by 1.5 mA. The load resistance is 5 kΩ. The voltage gain of the transistor will be .... **(2022 Main)**

29. An *n-p-n* transistor operates as a common emitter amplifier with a power gain of 10^6. The input circuit resistance is 100 Ω and the output load resistance is 10 kΩ. The common emitter current gain β will be ....
(Rounded off to the nearest integer) **(2021 Main)**

30. A transistor is connected in common emitter circuit configuration, the collector supply voltage is 10 V and the voltage drop across a resistor of 1000 Ω in the collector circuit is 0.6 V. If the current gain factor (β) is 24, then the base current is .... μA. (Round off to the nearest integer) **(2021 Main)**

31. A potential barrier of 0.4 V exists across a *p-n* junction. An electron enters the junction from the *n*-side with a speed of $6.0 \times 10^5\ ms^{-1}$. The speed with which electron enters the *p* side will be $\frac{x}{3} \times 10^5\ ms^{-1}$. The value of x is ....
(Given mass of electron $= 9 \times 10^{-31}$ kg, charge on electron $= 1.6 \times 10^{-19}$ C) **(2022 Main)**

Answers

1. (b)	**2.** (c)	**3.** (b)	**4.** (b)	**5.** (c)
6. (a)	**7.** (b)	**8.** (c)	**9.** (c)	**10.** (a)
11. (b)	**12.** (c)	**13.** OR gate	**14.** (2V)	
15. See the hints	**16.** (5)	**17.** (25)	**18.** (1)	
19. (4)	**20.** (2)	**21.** (480)	**22.** (9)	**23.** (5)
24. (25)	**25.** (3)	**26.** (2)	**27.** (15)	**28.** (750)
29. (100)	**30.** (25)	**31.** (14)		

See hints on pages 439-442.

Hints & SOLUTIONS

Module 1.

1. When Si is doped with trivalent impurities like boron, then a *p*-type semiconductor is formed. In *p*-type semiconductor, excess number of holes are found because holes are majority charge carrier in *p*-type semiconductor.

   When Si is doped with pentavalent impurities (like arsenic), then an *n*-type semiconductor is formed.

   In *n*-type semiconductor, excess number of electrons are found because these are majority charge carrier. Thus, statement I is correct.

   When *p*-type semiconductor and *n*-type semiconductor are fused to make a junction, a potential barrier is produced across the junction which stops the flow of current.

   Thus, no current is detected by externally connected ammeter

   Hence, statement II is incorrect.

2. Intrinsic semiconductor and impurity both are electrically neutral.

3. With increase in temperature, number of electrons reaching conduction band increases but, mean relation time decreases. Effect of decrease in relation time is much less than that of increase in number density of charge carriers.

4. Hole is a vacancy created by an electron moving from valance band to conduction band.

5. A semiconductor starts conducting more as the temperature increases. It means resistance decreases with increase in temperature. So, if temperature increases its resistivity decreases.

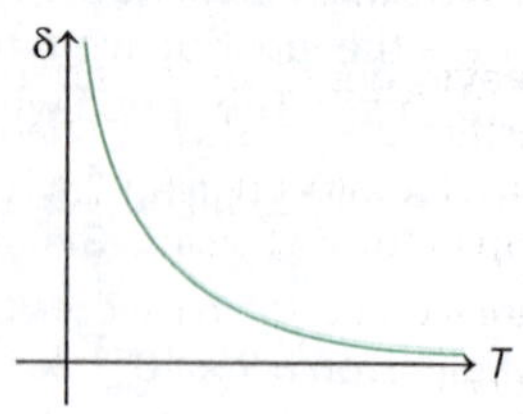

   Also, $$\rho = \frac{m}{ne^2\tau}$$

   as temperature increases, τ decreases but n increases and n is dominant over τ, thus reducing overall resistivity of the semiconductor.

6. As temperature increases, more electrons are excited to conduction band and hence conductivity increases, therefore resistance decreases.

7. $\lambda_{min} = 2480 \text{ nm} = 24800 \text{ Å}$

   $$\text{Energy (in eV)} = \frac{12375}{\lambda(\text{in Å})}$$

   $$E = \frac{12375}{24800} \text{ eV}$$

   $$E \approx 0.5 \text{ eV}$$

8. In intrinsic semiconductors, numbers of holes = number of free electrons while in case of a *p*-type semiconductor, number of holes > number of free electrons.

   Hence, options (a) and (c) are correct.

9. To make a *p*-type semiconductor, a trivalent impurity should be added to pure tetravalent compound.

   As silicon is tetravalent, Boron or Aluminium needs to be added as they are trivalent in nature.

Module 2.

1. In a reverse *p*-*n* biased junction, the flow of holes is from the *n*-region to *p*-region.

2. Reverse, Negative

3. Positive, *p*-side, *n*-side.

4. In forward bias, diffusion current is greater than drift current and diffusion current is from *n* side to *p* side. Hence, option (c) is correct.

5. The photodiodes are used in reverse bias condition because the change in reverse current through the photodiode due to change in light flux can be measured easily as the reverse saturation current is directly proportional to the light flux. But it is not so when photodiode is forward biased.

6. Diffusion occurs due to difference in concentrations in different regions.

7. Due to forward biasing depletion layer thickness decreases, potential barrier is reduced and diffusion of electrons from *n* to *p* side occurs.

8. For diode D_1,

   $$V_p - V_n = -10 - 0 = -10 \text{ V}$$

   So, D_1 is in reverse bias.

   For diode D_2,

   $$V_p - V_n = 0 - (-10) = 10 \text{ V}$$

   So, D_2 is in forward bias.

9. A diode is said to be in reverse biased when *p*-side is connected to less voltage than *n*-side. i.e.

   $V_p - V_n = 2 - 4 = -2(-\text{ve})$

   So, diode is in reverse bias.

   Hence, circuit is in reverse bias.

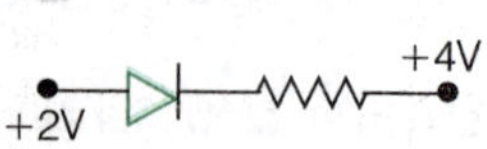

10. Diode 2 is connected in reverse bias, so no current will flow.

Diode 1 is forward bias. Now drawing the simplified circuit

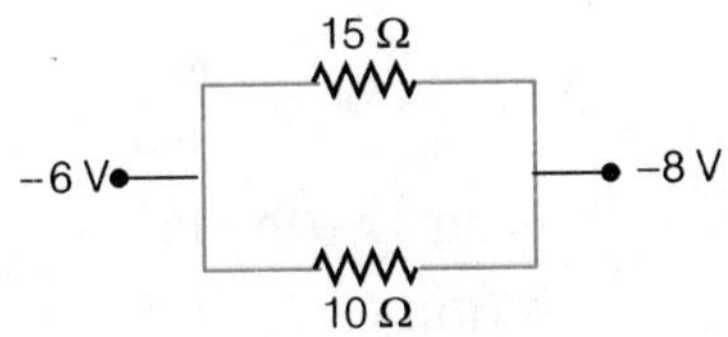

15 Ω and 10 Ω are in parallel connection.

$$R_{eq} = \frac{R_1 R_2}{R_1 + R_2}$$

$$= \frac{15 \times 10}{15 + 10} = 6\,\Omega$$

Hence, option (a) is correct.

11. In *n*-type semiconductors, electrons are the majority charge carriers.

12. For silicon diode, potential barrier is 0.7 V. Therefore, the given circuit is as shown in figure.

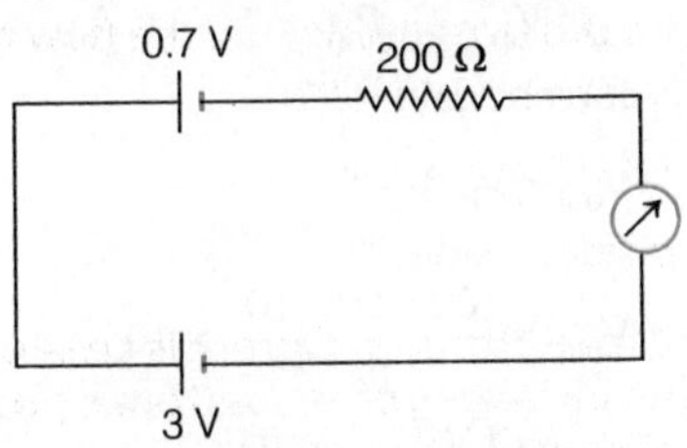

$$I = \frac{\text{net emf}}{\text{net resistance}} = \frac{3 - 0.7}{200}\,\text{A}$$

$$= 11.5\ \text{mA}$$

13.

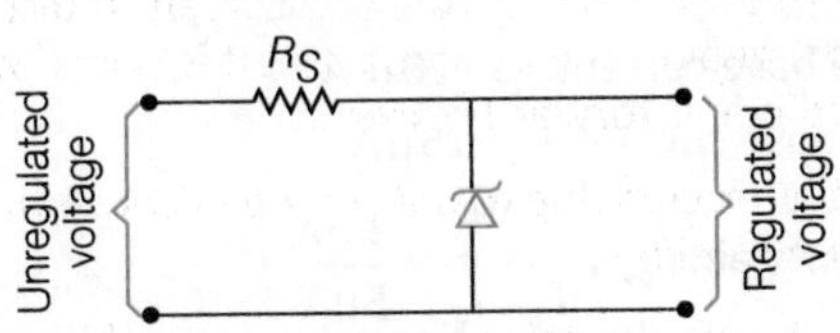

Power rating of Zener diode = 1.6 W

Maximum voltage across Zener diode = 8 V

Using $P = VI$; for Zener diode,

$$I = \frac{P}{V} = \frac{1.6}{8} = 0.2\ \text{A}$$

Hence, for safe operation 2V (excess voltage of 10 V) potential drop must occur in series resistor R_S.

For R_S, $V = 2\,\text{V}, I = 0.2\,\text{A}$

Using $V = IR$,

$$R = \frac{2}{0.2} = 10\,\Omega$$

14. Zener diode is a reverse biased heavily doped *p*-*n* junction diode. It is operated in breakdown region. Zener diode is designed to operate in the reverse breakdown voltage continuously without being damaged.

15. As Zener diode is heavily doped *p*-*n* junction diode, so it has narrow depletion layer and hence breakdown occur at junction.

16. In given voltage regulator, circuit breakdown of Zener occurs at 6 V.

After breakdown, voltage across load resistance ($R_L = 4\text{k}\Omega$) is, $V = V_Z = 6\text{V}$

∴ Load current after breakdown,

$$I_L = \frac{V_Z}{R_L} = \frac{6}{4000} = 1.5 \times 10^{-3}\ \text{A}$$

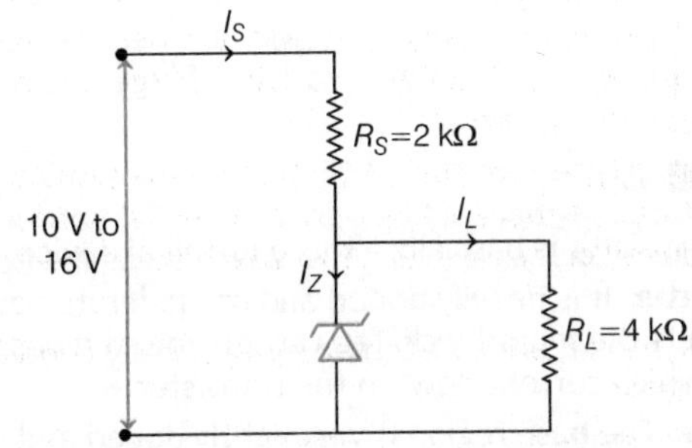

When unregulated supply is of 16 V, potential drop occurring across series resistance ($R_S = 2\ \text{k}\Omega$) is;

$$V_S = V - V_Z = 16 - 6 = 10\ \text{V}$$

So, current across series resistance is

$$I_S = \frac{V_S}{R_S} = \frac{10}{2 \times 10^3}$$

$$= 5 \times 10^{-3}\ \text{A}$$

So, current across Zener diode is

$$I_Z = I_S - I_L$$

$$= 5 \times 10^{-3} - 1.5 \times 10^{-3}$$

$$= 3.5 \times 10^{-3}\ \text{A}$$

$$= 3.5\ \text{mA}$$

17. An LED is a heavily doped *p*-*n* junction. When an electron transits from conduction band to valence band in forward bias, it emits energy which is nearly equal to the energy gap in form of visible radiation.

So, an LED cannot be used in reverse bias.

18. We use, $E_g = \frac{hc}{\lambda}$

$$\Rightarrow \quad E_g = \frac{1240\ \text{eV}\cdot\text{nm}}{600\,\text{nm}}$$

$$\approx 2\ \text{eV}$$

So, photon energy is less than that required (2.8 eV). So, detector is not able to detect this wavelength.

19. Current flows only in branches *AB* and *EF* as diode of *CD* branch is in reverse bias. ($\therefore I_3 = 0$)

So, given circuit is equivalent to

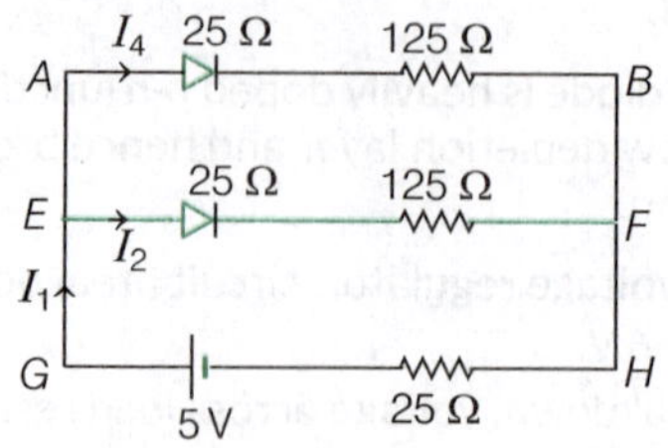

Current through cell is

$$i_1 = \frac{V}{R_{Total}} = \frac{5}{100} = 0.05 \text{ A}$$

Also by symmetry,

$$I_2 = I_4 = \frac{0.05}{2} = 0.025 \text{ A}$$

Module 3.

1. A transistor is basically a three terminal device.

Emitter It is heavily doped and of moderate size as it injects the majority charge carriers into the base region by which current flows in the transistor.

Base The base region is very lightly doped and thin. Most of the charge carriers emitted pass through it to the collector.

Collector The doping level of collector lies between the doping levels of emitter and base. The size of the collector region is larger than the other two regions because it collects the charge carriers from the base.

2. Transistor is a device used as switch or amplifier.

It is made by sandwiching three semiconductors, i.e. *p-n-p* or *n-p-n*.

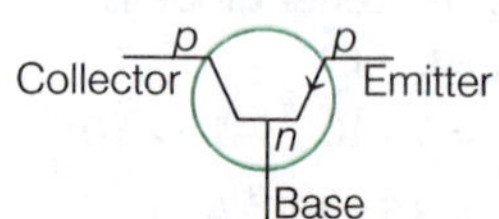

p-n-p-transistor

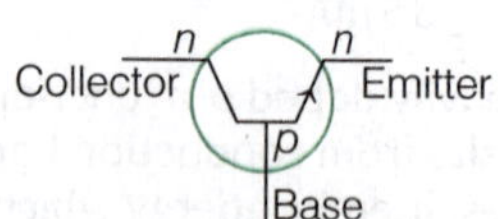

n-p-n-transistor

Hence, Statement I is false, because we cannot make transistor from diode.

As we know that, amplification factor (β) is the ratio of collector current to base current.

$$\therefore \qquad \beta = \frac{I_C}{I_B}$$

Hence, Statement II is true.

Therefore, option (a) is correct.

3. Given, $V_{CC} = 1\text{ V}$

$$\therefore \qquad I_C R_C = 1\text{ V} \qquad (\because V_{CC} = I_C R_C)$$

$$\Rightarrow \qquad I_C = \frac{1\text{V}}{10^3 \Omega} = 10^{-3}\text{A}$$

Now, $\beta = \text{Current amplification} = \frac{I_C}{I_B}$

$$\Rightarrow \qquad 100 = \frac{10^{-3}}{I_B} \text{ or } I_B = \frac{10^{-3}}{100}$$

$$= 10^{-5} \text{ A} = 10 \times 10^{-6} \text{ A}$$

$$= 10\,\mu\text{A}$$

4. Given, change in collector current $(\Delta I_C) = (16 - 5)$ mA $= 11$ mA

Change in base current

$$(\Delta I_B) = (200 - 100)\,\mu\text{A}$$
$$= 100\,\mu\text{A}$$

Current given of transistor is given by

$$\beta = \frac{\Delta I_C}{\Delta I_B} = \frac{11 \text{ mA}}{100\,\mu\text{A}} = 110$$

5. Voltage gain is given as

$$\frac{V_{out}}{V_{in}} = \beta \frac{R_{out}}{R_{in}}$$

where β is current gain

$$\Rightarrow \qquad V_{out} = V_{in} \beta \frac{R_{out}}{R_{in}} \qquad [\beta = 100 \text{ given}]$$

$$\Rightarrow \qquad V_{out} = \frac{100 \times 10 \times 10^3}{10^3} \times 10^{-3}$$

$$= 1 \text{ V}$$

6. Collector emitter voltage, $V_{CE} = 2$ V

Initial collector current, $I_C = 4$ mA

Final collector current, $I_C' = 6$ mA

Initial base current, $I_B = 20\,\mu$ A

Final base current, $I_B' = 25\,\mu$A

$$\text{Current gain } \beta_{av} = \frac{I_C' - I_C}{I_B' - I_B} = \frac{2\text{mA}}{5\mu\text{A}}$$

$$\Rightarrow \qquad \beta_{av} = \frac{2}{5} \times 10^3 = \frac{2000}{5} = 400$$

Hence current amplification factor is 400.

7. In cut-off and saturation region, transistor act as a switch.

8. In cut-off and saturation region transmitter acts as switch and in active region act as amplifier.

9. For a common emitter *n-p-n* transistor, DC current gain is

$$\beta_{DC} = \frac{I_C}{I_B}$$

At saturation state, V_{CE} becomes zero.

$$\therefore \qquad V_{CC} - I_C R_C = 0$$

$$I_C \approx \frac{V_{CC}}{R_C} = \frac{10}{1000} = 10^{-2} \text{ A}$$

Hence, saturation base current,

$$I_B = \frac{I_C}{\beta_{DC}} = \frac{10^{-2}}{250} = 40\,\mu A$$

10. In an n-p-n transistor,

$$I_E = I_B + I_C$$

$$\text{As } I_C = \frac{95}{100} I_E \Rightarrow I_E = \frac{100}{95} \times I_C$$

$$= \frac{100}{95} \times 10\,\text{mA} = 10.53\,\text{mA}$$

So, $I_B = 0.53$ mA

11. The extra power required for amplified output is obtained from the DC source.

12. The order of increasing doping levels is
base < collector < emitter.

13. Given circuit is equivalent to

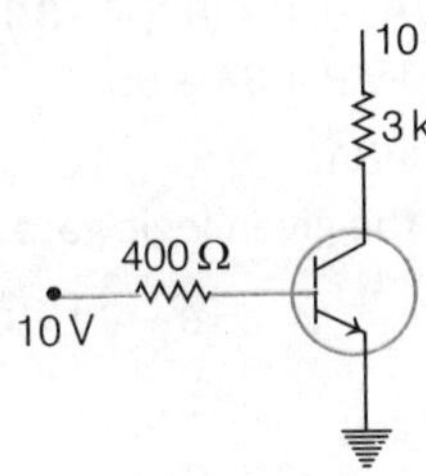

In base emitter loop,

$$V_B = I_B R_B$$

$$\Rightarrow \quad I_B = \frac{V_B}{R_B} = \frac{10}{400 \times 10^3}$$

$$= 25 \times 10^{-6}\,\text{A}$$

$$= 25\,\mu\text{A}$$

In emitter-collector loop,

$$V_C = I_C R_C$$

$$\Rightarrow \quad I_C = \frac{10}{3 \times 10^3} = 3.33\,\text{mA}$$

$$\text{and} \quad \beta_{DC} = \frac{I_C}{I_B} = \frac{3.33\,\text{mA}}{25\,\mu\text{A}}$$

$$= 133$$

14. Consider the figure given here to solve this problem

$$I_C = I_E \quad \text{[As base current is very small]}$$

$$R_C = 7.8\,\text{k}\Omega$$

From the figure, $I_C(R_C + R_E) + V_{CE} = 12$

$$(R_E + R_C) \times 1 \times 10^{-3} + 3 = 12$$

$$R_E + R_C = 9 \times 10^3 = 9\,\text{k}\Omega$$

$$R_E = 9 - 7.8 = 1.2\,\text{k}\Omega$$

$$V_E = I_E \times R_E$$

$$= 1 \times 10^{-3} \times 1.2 \times 10^3 = 1.2\,\text{V}$$

Voltage, $V_B = V_E + V_{BE} = 1.2 + 0.5 = 1.7$ V

$$\text{Current,} \quad I = \frac{V_B}{20 \times 10^3} = \frac{1.7}{20 \times 10^3}$$

$$= 0.085\,\text{mA}$$

$$\text{Resistance, } R_B = \frac{12 - 1.7}{\frac{I_C}{\beta} + 0.085} = \frac{10.3}{0.01 + 0.085}$$

[Given, $\beta = 100$]

$$= 108\,\text{k}\Omega$$

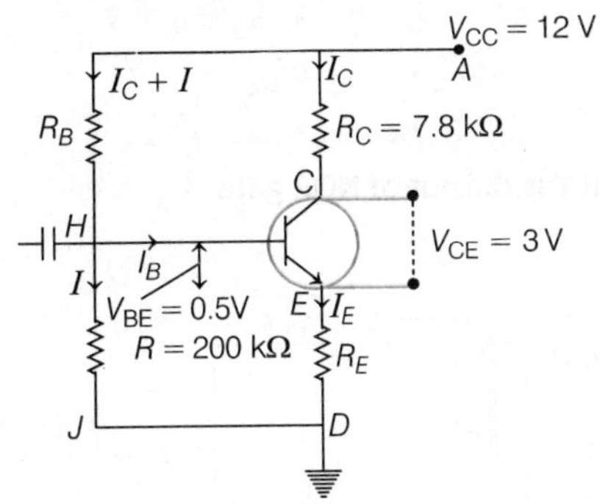

15. Consider the figure to solve this question,

$$I_E = I_C + I_B \text{ and } I_C = \beta I_B \quad \text{...(i)}$$

$$I_C R_C + V_{CE} + I_E R_E = V_{CC} \quad \text{...(ii)}$$

$$R I_B + V_{BE} + I_E R_E = V_{CC} \quad \text{...(iii)}$$

$$I_E = I_C = \beta I_B$$

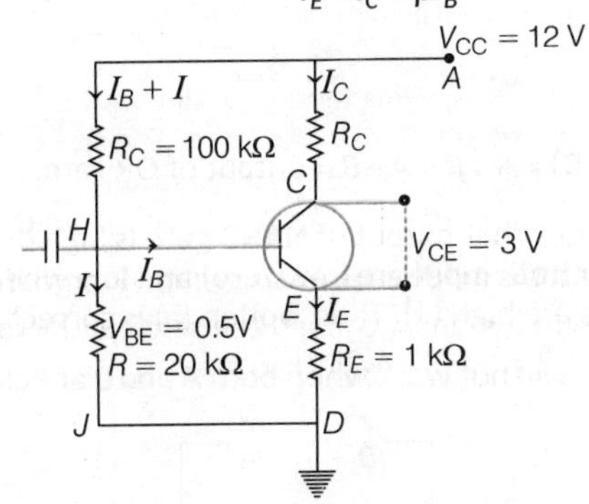

From Eq. (iii),

$$(R + \beta R_E) I_B = V_{CC} - V_{BE}$$

$$\Rightarrow \quad I_B = \frac{V_{CC} - V_{BE}}{R + \beta R_E} = \frac{12 - 0.5}{80 + 1.2 \times 100}$$

$$= \frac{11.5}{200}\,\text{mA}$$

From Eq. (ii),

$$(R_C + R_E) = \frac{V_{CE} - V_{BE}}{I_C}$$

$$= \frac{V_{CC} - V_{CE}}{\beta I_B} \quad (\because I_C = \beta I_B)$$

$$(R_C + R_E) = \frac{2}{11.5}(12 - 3)\,\text{k}\Omega$$

$$= 1.56\,\text{k}\Omega$$

$$R_C + R_E = 1.56$$

$$R_C = 1.56 - 1$$

$$= 0.56\,\text{k}\Omega$$

Module 4.

1. Truth table for the given logic gate is

A	B	Y
0	0	1
0	1	0
1	0	0
1	1	0

Output Y is output of NOR gate.

2. Given,

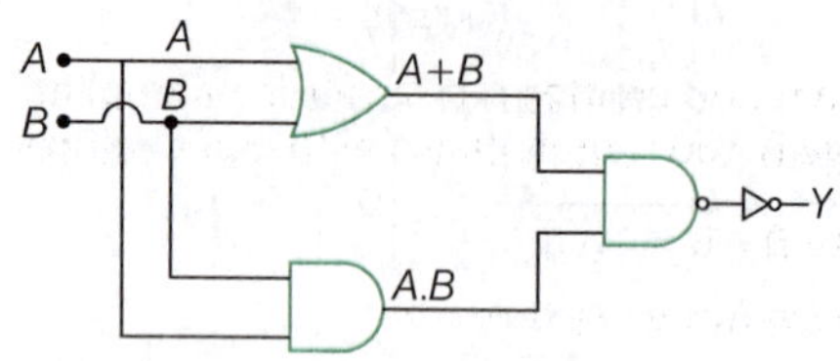

$$Y=(A+B)(AB)=(A+B)(AB)$$
$$=AAB+BAB=AB+ABB$$
$$=AB=\text{output of AND gate}$$

3.

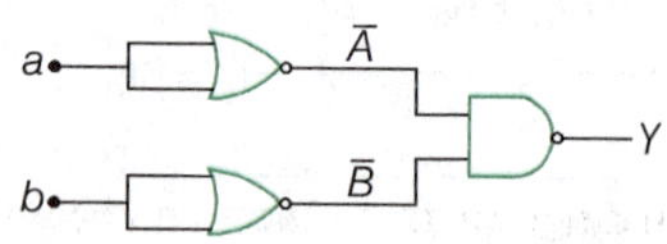

$Y=\overline{(\bar{A}\cdot\bar{B})}=\bar{\bar{A}}+\bar{\bar{B}}=A+B=$ output of OR gate.

4. We know that output of NAND gate is high only when one or both input are low (zero) and low when both inputs are high (1). Thus, option (a) is correct.

5. Circuit will not work when both A and B are closed.

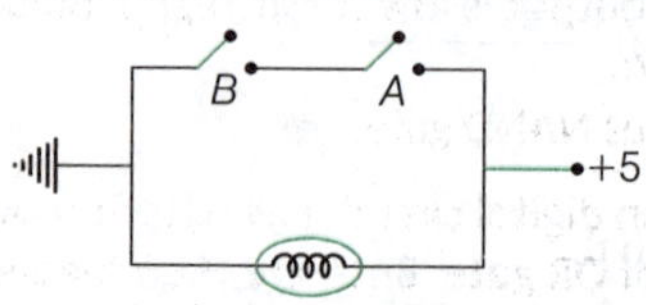

So above circuit is logic equivalent of NOT + AND = NAND

6.

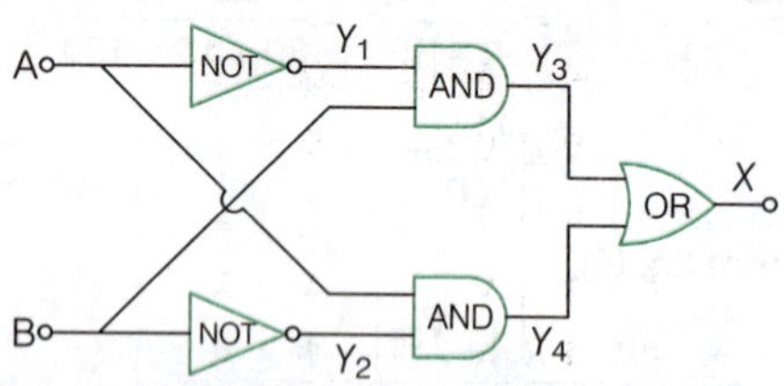

Truth table of above gate is

A	B	Y_1	Y_2	Y_3	Y_4	X
0	0	1	1	0	0	0
1	0	0	1	0	1	1
0	1	1	0	1	0	1
1	1	0	0	0	0	0

7. The logic circuit diagram is given as

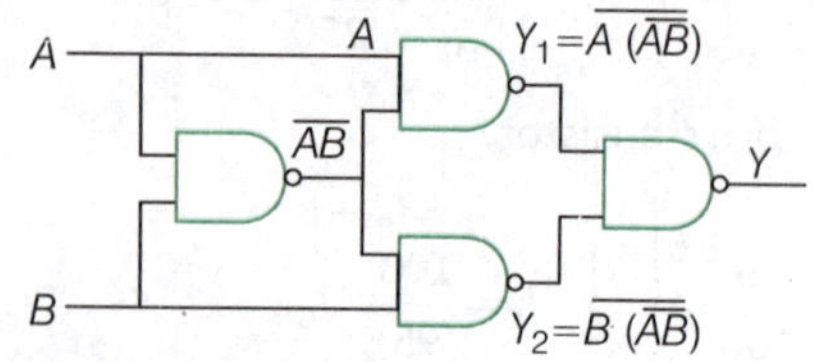

Output is given by, $Y=\overline{\overline{Y_1}\cdot\overline{Y_2}}$ ...(i)

where, $Y_1=\overline{A(\overline{AB})}=\bar{A}+\overline{\overline{AB}}=\bar{A}+AB$

Similarly, $Y_2=\bar{B}+AB$

$\therefore$ From Eq. (i), we get

$$Y=\overline{(\bar{A}+AB)(\bar{B}+AB)}$$
$$=\overline{(\bar{A}+AB)}+\overline{(\bar{B}+AB)}$$
$$=(\bar{\bar{A}}\cdot\overline{AB})+(\bar{\bar{B}}\cdot\overline{AB})$$
$$=(A\cdot(\bar{A}+\bar{B}))+(B\cdot(\bar{A}+\bar{B}))$$
$$=A\bar{A}+A\bar{B}+B\bar{A}+B\bar{B}$$
$$=A\bar{B}+B\bar{A}$$

$\therefore$ Truth table for the given logic gate is

A	B	$\bar{A}$	$\bar{B}$	$Y=A\bar{B}+B\bar{A}$
0	0	1	1	0
0	1	1	0	1
1	0	0	1	1
1	1	0	0	0

8.

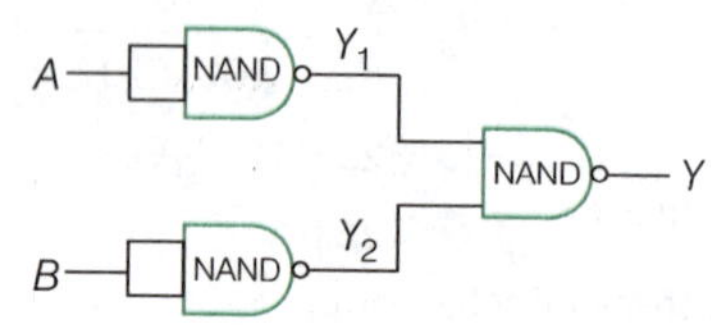

Truth table for given combination of gate is

A	B	Y_1	Y_2	$Y=\overline{Y_1\cdot Y_2}$
0	0	1	1	0
1	0	0	1	1
0	1	1	0	1
1	1	0	0	1

So, this logical circuit is of OR gate.

Now, input and corresponding output waveforms are as shown,

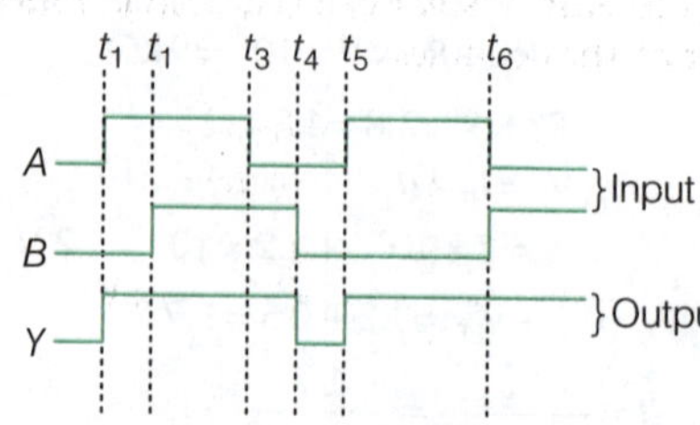

9.

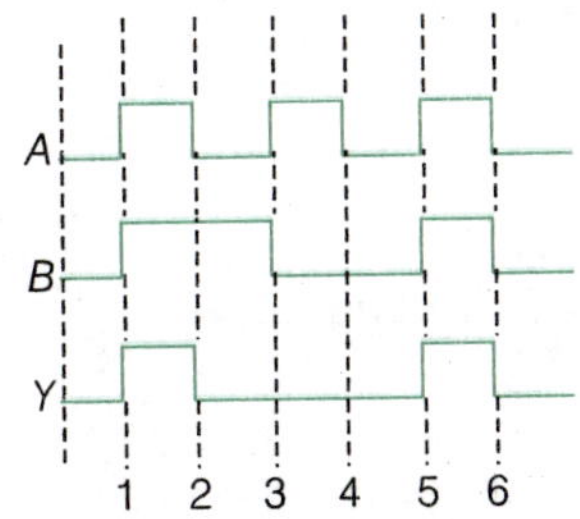

When

	$A=0,$	$B=0$	$\Rightarrow Y=0$
2.	$A=1,$	$B=1$	$\Rightarrow Y=1$
3.	$A=0,$	$B=1$	$\Rightarrow Y=0$
4.	$A=1,$	$B=0$	$\Rightarrow Y=0$

So, this must be AND gate.

Unit Exercise (Cumulative)

1. The slope of *V-I* graph give *R*

$$R=\frac{\Delta V}{\Delta i}$$

$$\frac{R_1}{R_2}=\frac{\Delta V_1}{\Delta i_1}\times\frac{\Delta i_2}{\Delta V_2}=\frac{2.1-2}{10-5}\times\frac{250-200}{4.2-4}$$

$$=\frac{0.1}{5}\times\frac{50}{0.2}=\frac{5}{1}$$

2. Given circuit according to question is

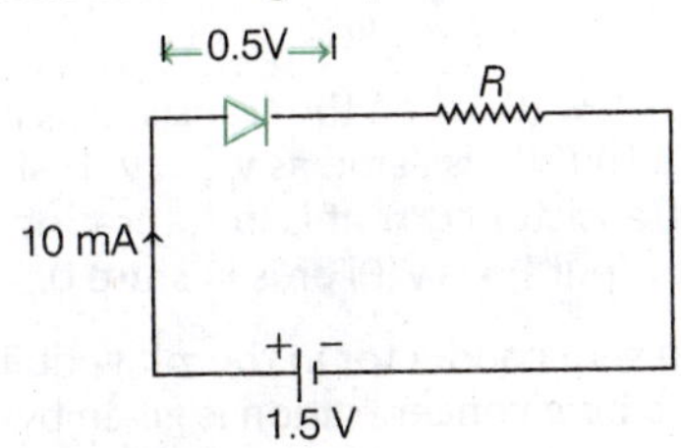

$$V_{diode}=0.5\text{ volt}=V_{internal}$$

$$V_R=E-V_{iinternal}$$

$$V_R=1.5-0.5=1\text{ volt}$$

$$iR=V_R$$

$$R=\frac{1}{i}=\frac{1}{10^{-2}}=100\,\Omega$$

3. In circuit 2 both the diodes are forward biased and in circuit 3 both the diodes are reverse biased.
Hence, circuit 2 and 3 have same potential.

4. *V-I* characteristic of solar cell is drawn in fourth quadrant as shown below

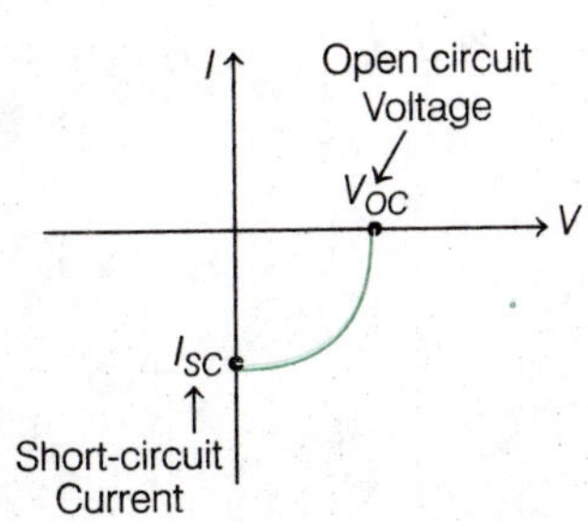

5.

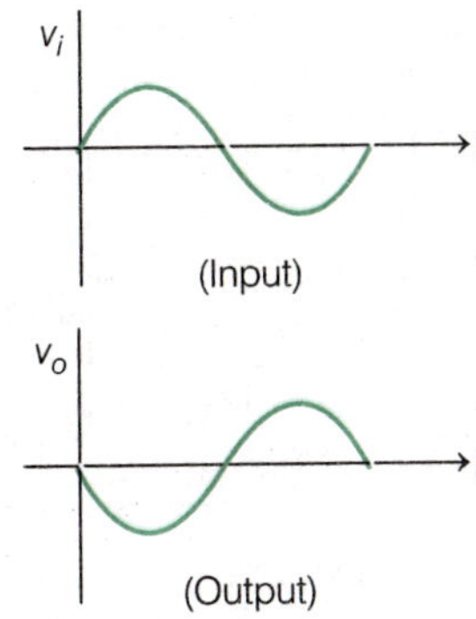

In a common emitter *n-p-n* transistor amplifier, output voltage is 180° out of phase with input voltage.

6. $\overline{\overline{A+A}+\overline{B+B}}=\overline{\overline{A}+\overline{B}}$

Using De-morgan's theorem

$$=\overline{\overline{A}}\cdot\overline{\overline{B}}=A\cdot B$$

$\Rightarrow$ AND Gate

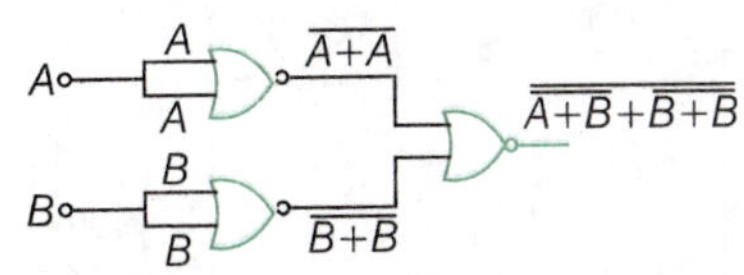

7. From given diagram, truth table can be written as

A	B	Output
1	1	0
0	0	1
0	1	1
1	0	1

Since, the output is low for all high inputs and high if any input is low.
This gives us NAND gate.

8. In the given digital circuit, *P* is output of AND gate, and *Q* is output of OR gate. Both are then feeded to input of NAND gate. For different values of *A* and *B* output *y* is as follows

A	B	P	Q	Y
0	0	0	0	1
0	1	0	1	1
1	0	0	1	1
1	1	1	1	0

Output $Y=\overline{(A\cdot B)\cdot A+B)}$ matches with option (c).

9. For different values of *A* and *B* input, obtain output *Z* where *X* and *Y* are output of NAND gate and also acts as input of AND gate.

A	B	X	Y	Z
1	1	0	0	0
1	0	0	1	0
0	1	1	0	0
0	0	1	1	1

Therefore, the given circuit represents NOR gate.

10.

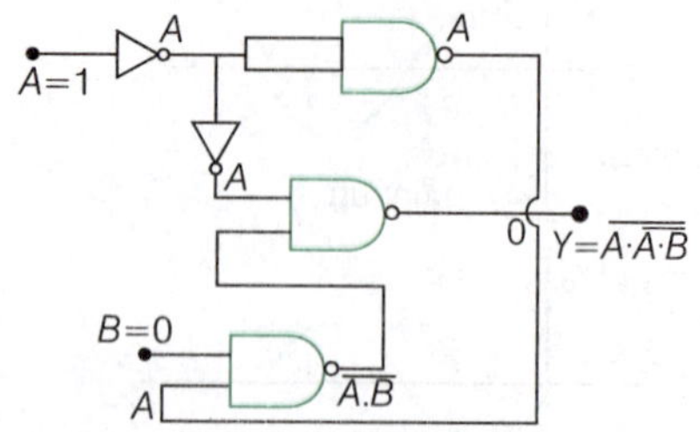

Using De-morgan's theorem,

$$Y=\overline{\overline{AB}\cdot A}+\overline{\overline{AB}}+\overline{A}=AB+\overline{A}$$

For $A=1, B=0$

$$Y=(1)\times 0+0$$

$\Rightarrow$ $Y=0+0=0$

11. The given circuit can be drawn as shown in the figure given below

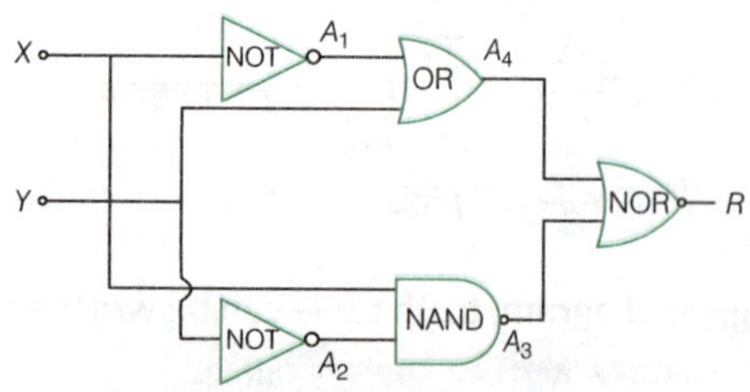

Truth table for this given logic gate is

Given inputs in the options		A_1	A_2	A_3	A_4	R
X	Y					
0	0	1	1	1	1	0
1	0	0	1	0	0	1
1	1	0	0	1	1	0
0	1	1	0	1	1	0

So to get output $R=1$, inputs must be $X=1$ and $Y=0$.

12. Given circuit is

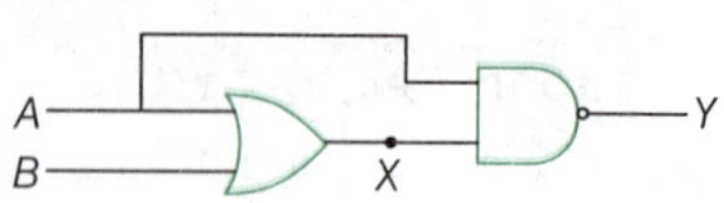

Let the intermediate state X of OR gate is shown in figure.

Clearly, $Y=\overline{AX}$ ...(i)

Here, $X=A+B$ ...(ii)

$\therefore$ $Y=\overline{A(A+B)}=\overline{AA+AB}$

$=\overline{A+AB}$ $(\because AA=A)$

$=\overline{A(1+B)}$

$\Rightarrow$ $Y=\overline{A}$ $(\because 1+B=1)$

So, truth table shown in option (c) is correct.

13. An "OR" gate may be made to operate motor relays for garage gates.

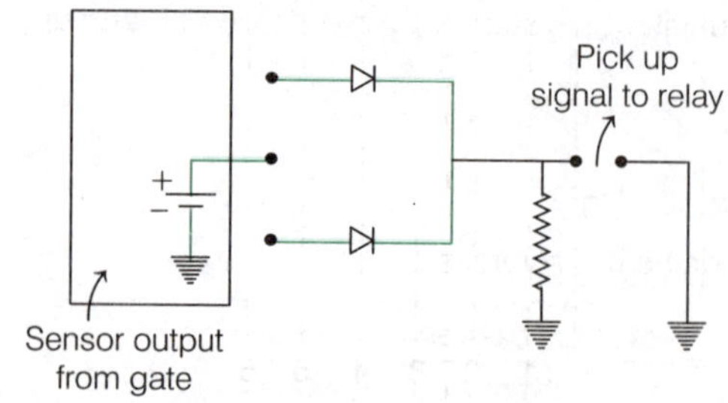

14. Such combination is called "Cascade" combination.

$$A_{V(\text{net})}=A_{V_1}\times A_{V_2}$$

$$=10\times 20=200$$

$\therefore$ $V_0=$ output voltage

$$=A_{V(\text{net})}\times V_i=200\times 0.01$$

$$=2\text{ V}$$

15. A NOT gate can be formed by proper biasing of a transistor as shown.

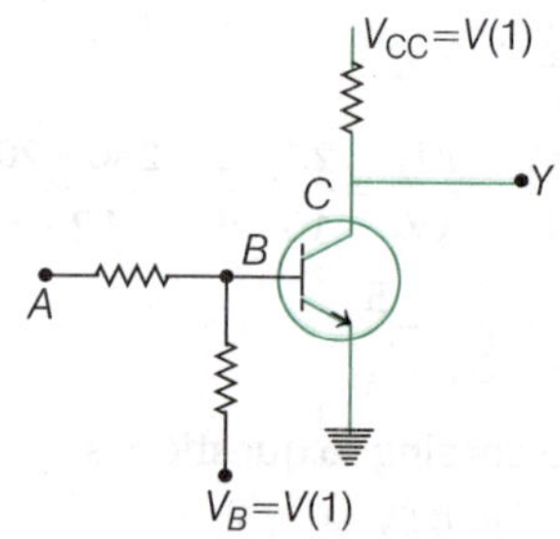

If input (A) is low (0), then the transistor is in cut off stage and output (Y) is same as $V_{CC}=V(1)$. If input (A) is high, then transistor current is in saturation and the net voltage at output (Y) is $V(0)$ or is in state 0.

16. For a doped semiconductor in thermal equilibrium, the electron and hole concentration is given by

$$n_e n_h=n_i^2$$

$\Rightarrow$ $$n_e=\frac{n_i^2}{n_h}=\frac{(1.5\times 10^{16})^2}{4.5\times 10^{22}}$$

$$=\frac{1.5\times 1.5\times 10^{32}}{4.5\times 10^{22}}=5\times 10^9\text{ m}^{-3}$$

17. Given circuit is redrawn as

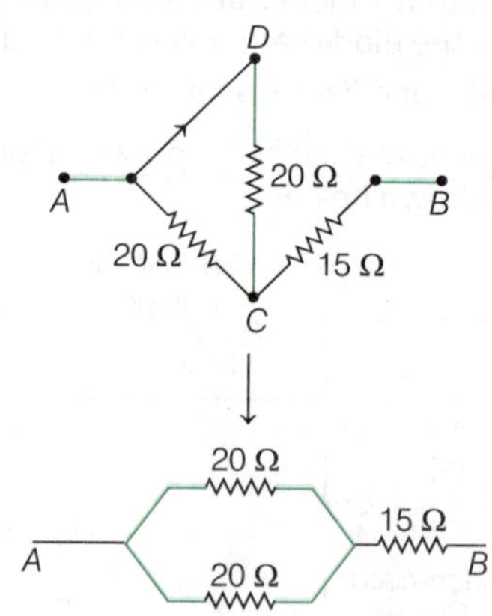

$\therefore$ Equivalent resistance between points A and B,

$$R_{AB} = \frac{20 \times 20}{20 + 20} + 15$$
$$= 10 + 15 = 25\Omega$$

18. Electric field is given as, $E = \frac{V}{d}$

$$= \frac{\text{Potential barrier across junction}}{\text{Width of depletion layer}}$$

$[V = 0.6\text{ V},\ d = 6 \times 10^{-6}\text{ m, given}]$

$$= \frac{0.6\text{ V}}{6 \times 10^{-6}\text{ m}} = 1 \times 10^5\text{ V/m}$$
$$= 1 \times 10^5\text{ N/C}$$

19. As D_1 is forward bias and D_2 is reverse bias

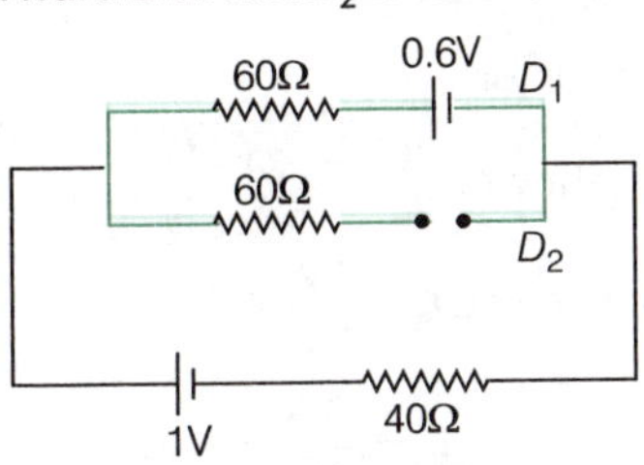

So, D_2 will be open circuited and D_1 will be replaced by 0.6 V battery.

$$R_{eq} = 60 + 40 = 100\Omega$$
$$V_{net} = 1 - 0.6 = 0.4\text{ V}$$

So, $$i = \frac{V_{net}}{R_{eq}} = \frac{0.4}{100}\text{ A}$$
$$= 4\text{ mA}$$

20. When diode is non conductive, current through load resistance R_L,

$$i_L = \frac{V}{R_L + R} \quad \text{or} \quad i_L = \frac{10}{100 + R_L}$$

So, potential drop across R_L,

$$V_L = i_L . R_L = \frac{10}{100 + R_L} \times R_L$$

This potential drop when reaches 8 V, then breakdown occurs, so minimum R_L is given by

$$\frac{10}{100 + R_L} \times R_L = 8$$
$$\Rightarrow \quad R_{L(min)} = 400\ \Omega$$

At maximum value of load resistance current through Zener diode,

$$I_Z = 10\text{ mA}$$

So, by Kirchhoff's current rule,

$$I_R = I_{R_L} + I_Z$$
$$\Rightarrow \quad \frac{2}{100} = \frac{8}{R_2} + 10 \times 10^{-3}$$

($\because$ only 2V potential drop occurs 100Ω resistance)

$$\Rightarrow \quad R_{L(max)} = 800\ \Omega$$

Hence, $$\frac{R_{L(max)}}{R_{L(min)}} = 2$$

21. Given,

Zener current, $I = 25$ mA

$$= 25 \times 10^{-3}\text{ A},\ V_z = 8\text{ V}$$

Apply KVL in loop $ABEF$

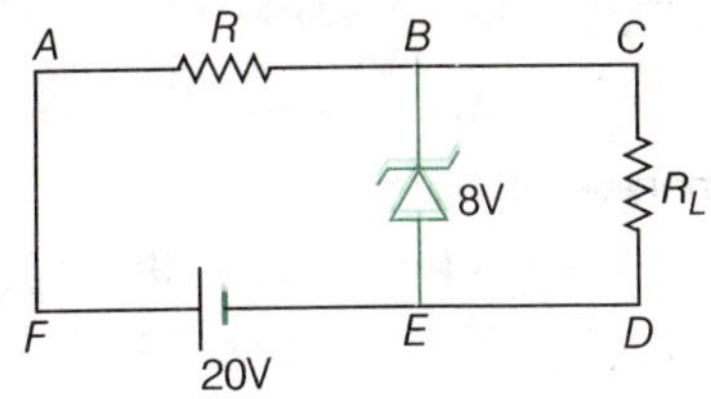

$$\varepsilon - IR - V_Z = 0\ ;\ 20 - IR - 8 = 0$$
$$IR = 12 \Rightarrow 25 \times 10^{-3} R = 12$$
$$\Rightarrow \quad R = \frac{12}{25 \times 10^{-3}} = 480\Omega$$

22. Maximum potential across 4 kΩ resistance is

$$= 120 - 60 = 60\text{ V}$$

Current through 4 kΩ resistance,

$$I_1 = \frac{60}{4000} = 0.015\text{ A}$$

The current through 10 kΩ will be

$$I_2 = \frac{60}{10000} = 0.006$$

Hence, maximum current through Zener diode is

$$I_Z = I_1 - I_2 = 0.009\text{ A} = 9\text{ mA}$$

23. $V_{\text{Zener diode}} = 10 \times \frac{1}{1 + 0.8}$

$$= \frac{10}{1.8} = 5.56\text{ V} > V_z$$

So, Zener diode will act as a constant voltage regulator and voltage across it will be equal to $V_z = 5$ V.

$$\therefore \quad I_L = \frac{V_Z}{R_L} = \frac{5\text{ V}}{1\text{k}\Omega} = 5\text{ mA}$$

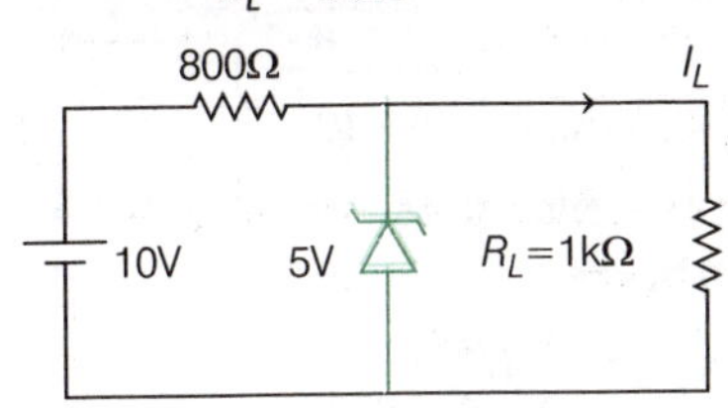

24. Current through 2 kΩ resistance is

$$I = \frac{V}{R}$$
$$I = \frac{5}{2 \times 10^3}$$
$$= 2.5 \times 10^{-3}\text{ A}$$
$$\Rightarrow \quad I = 25 \times 10^{-4}\text{ A}$$

25.

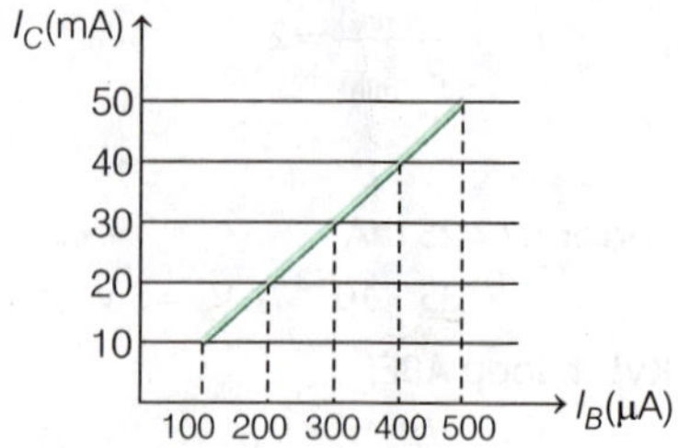

$\because$ Current gain, $\beta = \dfrac{\Delta I_C}{\Delta I_B}$

$$= \frac{10\,\text{mA}}{100\,\mu\text{A}} = \frac{10 \times 10^{-3}}{100 \times 10^{-6}} = 100$$

$\because$ Power gain $= \beta^2 \dfrac{R_C}{R_B} = (100)^2 \times \dfrac{1}{10}$

$$= 10^3 = 10^x \quad \text{(Given)}$$

$\therefore$ $x = 3$

26. Power gain $=$ (current gain)$^2 \times \dfrac{R_0}{R_1}$

where $R_0 =$ load resistance

$R_i =$ input resistance

Put the value in above equation

$$= \left(\frac{\Delta I_C}{\Delta I_B}\right)^2 \times \frac{R_0}{R_i} = \left(\frac{10 \times 10^{-3}}{100 \times 10^{-6}}\right)^2 \times \frac{2}{1}$$

$$= \left(\frac{10^{-2}}{10^{-4}}\right)^2 \times 2 = 2 \times 10^4$$

27. Voltage gain of CE transistor is given by

$$A_v = \left(\frac{R_0}{R_{in}}\right)\left(\frac{I_c}{I_B}\right) = \left(\frac{60}{200}\right)\left(\frac{5 \times 10^{-3}}{100 \times 10^{-6}}\right)$$

Where I_c, I_b are current in base and collector.

$\therefore$ $A_v = \dfrac{3}{10} \times \dfrac{10^3}{20} = 15$

28. Voltage gain is given by

$$A_v = \left(\frac{R_0}{R_i}\right) \cdot \frac{\Delta I_C}{\Delta I_B} = \left(\frac{5 \times 10^3}{\dfrac{10 \times 10^{-3}}{10 \times 10^{-6}}}\right) \times \left(\frac{1.5 \times 10^{-3}}{10 \times 10^{-6}}\right)$$

$$= \left(\frac{5 \times 10^4 \times 10^{-6}}{10^{-2}}\right) \times 150$$

$$= 5 \times 150 = 750$$

29. Power gain $= \dfrac{R_{out}}{R_{in}}$ (Current gain)^2

Given, power gain $= 10^6$,

$$R_{out} = 10^4\,\Omega, R_{in} = 100\,\Omega$$

$\Rightarrow$ $10^6 = \dfrac{10 \times 10^3}{100} \times \beta^2$

$\Rightarrow$ $\beta^2 = 10^4$

$\therefore$ Current gain, $\beta = 100$

30. Given, resistance across collector, $R_C = 1000\,\Omega$

Voltage drop across collector resistance, $\Delta V = 0.6$

Current gain factor, $\beta = 24$

$\because$ We know that,

Current gain factor,

$$\beta = \frac{I_C}{I_B} \Rightarrow 24 = \frac{I_C}{I_B} \quad \text{...(i)}$$

$\because$ Collector current, $I_C = \dfrac{\Delta V}{R_C}$

$\Rightarrow$ $I_C = \dfrac{0.6}{1000} = 6 \times 10^{-4}$ ...(ii)

From Eqs. (i) and (ii), we get

$\Rightarrow$ $24 = \dfrac{6 \times 10^{-4}}{I_B}$

$\Rightarrow$ $I_B = \dfrac{6 \times 10^{-4}}{24}$

$\Rightarrow$ $I_B = 25\,\mu\text{A}$

31. Potential barrier will reduce electron's kinetic energy by $qV_{barrier}$

So, $K_f - K_i = qV_{barrier}$

Put all the value in above equation

$\Rightarrow$ $\dfrac{1}{2} \times 9.1 \times 10^{-31} \times (36 \times 10^{10} - V_i^2)$

$$= 1.6 \times 10^{-19} \times 0.4$$

$\Rightarrow$ $(36 \times 10^{10} - V_i^{2}) = 1.40 \times 10^{11}$

$\Rightarrow$ $2.2 \times 10^{11} = V_i^2$

$\Rightarrow$ $V_i = 4.67 \times 10^5$ m/s

$\Rightarrow$ $V_i = \dfrac{14}{3} \times 10^5$ m/s

$\therefore$ $x = 14$